P9-EDR-136

Managerial
Cost Accounting

The Willard J. Graham Series in Accounting

Consulting Editor   **Robert N. Anthony**   Harvard University

Managerial Cost Accounting

Gordon Shillinglaw
Professor of Accounting
Graduate School of Business
Columbia University

Fifth Edition

1982

RICHARD D. IRWIN, INC.
Homewood, Illinois   60430

The first three editions of this book were published under the title
Cost Accounting: Analysis and Control.

© RICHARD D. IRWIN, INC., 1961, 1967, 1972, 1977, and 1982

ISBN 0-256-02597-5

Library of Congress Catalog Card No. 81–82453

Printed in the United States of America

3 4 5 6 7 8 9 0 D 9 8 7 6 5 4

To Carl L. Nelson
A valued colleague and good friend

Preface

Mastery of cost accounting techniques unaccompanied by an understanding of what they are designed to achieve is no mastery at all. This book builds the techniques of cost accounting on a description of the needs of its users, with an emphasis on the underlying conceptual framework connecting need and technique. The coverage is comprehensive, but the emphasis is managerial. Our main interest is in what managers want or need to know and how best to provide this information.

Most students facing this material for the first time will have completed a one- or two-semester course in financial accounting. The only prerequisite, however, is an understanding of the basic structure of financial accounting; detailed familiarity with generally accepted financial accounting principles is unnecessary. It is taken for granted that the reader knows what an income statement is and is generally familiar with the historical cost basis of asset and expense measurement.

Outline

Cost accounting contributes both to managerial accounting and to accounting for external financial reporting. Part 1, consisting of the first 13 chapters, describes the basic structure of cost accounting and the financial and managerial accounting setting in which it takes place. Chapter 1 describes the underlying managerial processes, Chapter 2 introduces a basic system of cost accumulation, and Chapter 3 relates data collected in this way to the process of external financial reporting. Chapters 4, 5, and 8 are concerned with the use of cost accounting data in managerial planning and decision making, while Chapters 6 and 7 provide additional information on the cost accumulation structure. Chapters 9 through 12 focus for the most part on cost accounting's contribution to internal control reporting, and Chapter 13 shows how the accountants bridge the gaps between internal control reports and published financial statements.

Part 2 extends the discussion of cost accounting for planning purposes. It does this first by examining methods of costing not covered in Part 1; second by describing a number of decision models which require cost accounting data; and third by introducing several analytical techniques that though not part of cost accounting proper are essential to the cost accountant's training. Appendix A provides tables of present value factors to be used in conjunction with time-affected decision problems, particularly those discussed in Chapter 18.

The final chapter in Part 2 relates cost accounting to situations in which outside agencies—customers or charitable funding bodies—reimburse the organization for the costs it has incurred in carrying out activities they have commissioned or which they wish to support.

Part 3 describes and analyzes accounting systems for financial control reporting, ranging from systems designed to help first-line factory managers control their costs to those used by the top management of multiproduct, decentralized corporations to evaluate the profitability of divisional activities and the performance of the division managers.

Study suggestions

Each chapter is designed to help the student understand the concepts and apply them to practical problems. No accounting book reads like a detective story, however, not even this one. Understanding comes only with some effort. Many students find it useful to make their own calculations as they read the text, verifying the numbers in the illustrations and tracing the relationships among the exhibits as they are introduced.

The instructor is likely to assign one or more problems as preparation for each class session. These may be all the practice many students will need. Others will find it useful to work the independent study problems, using the captions on these problems to choose those most relevant to the topics to be covered in class. These problems should also be useful in reviewing the materials before scheduled examinations. Solutions for the independent study problems are provided in Appendix B.

The fifth edition

The structure of this edition is basically the same as that of the fourth edition. Reimbursement costing has been elevated from an appendix to full-chapter status, but this is the only new chapter. Although a good part of this new chapter is devoted to discussion of the standards issued by the Cost Accounting Standards Board, the coverage has been expanded to provide a broader institutional and conceptual framework than the fourth edition appendix supplied.

Discussion of the impact of uncertainty on managerial decisions and the treatment of cost variances in external financial reporting has been moved into Part 1 in this edition. Coverage of profit-volume charts is now integrated in Chapter 5 with the review of other techniques for incorporating adjustments for uncertainty in managerial decision making.

Aside from these structural changes and extensive rewriting designed to make the text clearer and easier to read, the most significant change in this edition is in the coverage of interdepartmental cost allocations. The discussion of the conceptual foundations of these allocations in the fourth edition turned out to be less than adequate. As a result, Chapter 7 has been expanded and enriched to provide thorough, conceptually sound coverage of this important topic. The use of allocations in control reporting has been integrated with the discussion of flexible budgeting in Chapter 10, where it should have been all along.

This edition is longer than the fourth edition, mainly because a large number of new problems and exercises have been added. Most of these new problems and exercises are designed to help students develop computational skills; in general, they have clear-cut numerical answers, tied to the problem-solving methods described in the chapters to which they are attached. The number of issue-centered problems which require the exercise of judgment hasn't been reduced. I tend to emphasize these in my own courses because they expose the thought processes that underlie the choice of cost accounting system. These issue-centered problems do require more effort on the students' part, however.

The strength of the book remains in its conceptual orientation, its emphasis on managerial relevance rather than procedural detail, and in its special coverage of important topics that often receive less attention elsewhere—behavioral aspects of responsibility accounting systems, divisional performance measurement, transfer pricing, and reimbursement costing are the most important of these; each has its own chapter.

Acknowledgments

I owe much to many for their help and encouragement as this book has gone through five editions. It is difficult to single out some without slighting others, but I'll always be indebted to Myron J. Gordon, Carl L. Nelson, and the late Willard J. Graham for the enormous contributions they made to the success of the first four editions, and to Frank P. Smith for getting me started on the right track.

Several users of the fourth edition took the time and trouble to let me know what they liked and what they didn't like. In particular, I'd like to thank Joseph Cheung, whose well-chosen comments on the coverage of interdepartmental cost allocations led me to revise that coverage extensively; Charles W. Bastable and Harvey Babiak, whose meticulous reading of the text revealed flaws in the fourth edition; also Arne Riise, and Angelos Tsaklanganos. William Baber offered useful suggestions on the mathematical notation in the appendix to Chapter 9. Jan Bell commented on the behavioral chapter, and Da-Hsien Bao helped me make corrections in the introductory chapter on decision analysis. Wayne Campbell and L. J. Brooks made particularly useful comments on the fourth edition from a Canadian perspective.

None of these friendly critics is responsible for defects that may survive in this edition, of course. I can only hope that I have been able to take advantage of the help that has been offered me.

Harvey Babiak, Lawrence Benninger, John C. Burton, Eric Flamholtz, Michael Ginzberg, Michael Jensen, Philip Meyers, Carl L. Nelson, David Solomons, and Russell Taussig have been most generous in letting me use or modify problems or cases they have written. I am also grateful to the IMEDE

Management Development Institute in Lausanne, Switzerland, for permission to use cases I wrote while serving on the IMEDE faculty. Charles Summer was my coauthor on the AB Thorsten (D) case, appearing at the end of Chapter 26, and I acknowledge his contribution most gratefully. I also thank the Institute of Management Accounting, the American Institute of Certified Public Accountants, and the Society of Management Accountants of Canada for letting me use or adapt materials from their professional examinations. These materials are identified by the letters *CMA, CPA,* or *SMAC;* the word *adapted* is used to identify any of these materials which were modified to make them fit more neatly into the chapter structure.

Mindy Lazarus was cheerfully efficient in helping me prepare parts of the manuscript for editing, while Kathleen Andrews, Krishna Kumar, Carol McNair, and B. N. Srinidhi did a heroic job of checking the problems and looking for errors in the text. I've long since bowed to the impossibility of finding and correcting all typographical errors in manuscript or text, but I'm confident we've kept these to a minimum in this edition.

Gordon Shillinglaw

Contents

PART ONE
THE BASIC STRUCTURE

1. Planning, control, and cost accounting 3

   Managerial planning: *Strategic planning. Long-range periodic planning. Project and situation planning. Short-range periodic planning. The activity: Focus of planning. Cost accounting for managerial planning.* Managerial control: *Yes/no controls. Steering controls. Scorecard controls. Accounting's contribution to control processes.* Financial, tax, and reimbursement accounting: *Financial accounting. Tax accounting. Reimbursement accounting.* Organizing the accounting function. Cost accounting practitioners. Cost accounting in perspective.

   Case 1–1:   Derek Steele, Grocer, 19

2. The costing structure and job order costing 21

   The three major dimensions of cost: *Classification by organization segment. Classification by object of expenditure. Classification by activity. Size of the costing entity.* Costing individual activities: Job order costing: *Direct materials costs. Direct labor costs. Factory overhead costs. The completed cost sheet. Overhead rates based on normal volume.* Cost classification problems: *Costs incurred for similar purposes. Separate accruals: Employee benefits. Overtime premiums. Rejected units. Rework labor. Scrap recovery.*

   Case 2–1:   Tipografia Stanca, S.p.A., 48

3. Job cost flows and financial statements 52

   Purchase and use of materials. Labor costs. Other factory overhead costs. Overhead cost absorption. Job completions and sales. Summary of the cost flows. Disposing of under- or overabsorbed factory overhead. Manufacturing cost statement.

4. Decision concepts and cost behavior 72

   Basic principles underlying resource-allocation decisions: *Using net cash flows to measure results. Identifying incremental cash flows. Turning averages into differentials. Sunk costs. Opportunity cost.* Short-term cost-volume relationships: *Variable costs. Fixed costs: Responsive activities. Fixed costs: Programmed activities. Semivariable costs. Marginal cost.* Impact of cost variability on short-term resource-allocation decisions: *Evaluat-*

ing special orders: Opportunities to use idle capacity. Using materials from inventory. Capacity rationing decisions. Product emphasis decisions.

5. **Profit-volume charts, payoff tables, and decision trees** **111**

Profit sensitivity analysis using profit charts: *The basic cost-volume-profit chart. The break-even point and the margin of safety. Income tax effects. Cash flow and funds flow diagrams. Minimum profit level: Fixed charge coverage. The customary volume range. Profit responsiveness. Product profit charting in multiproduct businesses. Multiproduct profit functions. Dynamic effects.* Payoff tables and expected value: *Outcomes and payoffs. Probabilities. Expected value. Decision rules. Utility.* Decision tree analysis. Probability-adjusted profit charts.

6. **Variable costing** **150**

The basis for variable costing: *A job costing illustration. Handling nonlinear cost relationships.* Effect of variable costing on reported income: *Condition 1: Production equals sales at normal volume. Condition 2: Production exceeds sales. Condition 3: Production equals sales at subnormal volume. Condition 4: Sales exceed production. End-of-period adjustments.* Preliminary appraisal of variable costing: *Providing data for managerial decision making. Measuring income. The concept of attributable cost.*

7. **Incorporating service costs in predetermined overhead rates** **175**

Cost reassignment methods: *Apportionment. Interdepartmental allocation. One-step allocations. Cross allocations. Sequential allocation. Preliminary distributions of centrally-tabulated costs.* Full-cost overhead rates: Sequential allocation: *Choosing allocation denominators for full costing. An allocation illustration: Basic data. The first allocation: Building services costs. The second allocation: Clerical costs. The third allocation: Management costs. The final allocation: Factory management costs. Allocation summary: Departmental overhead rates.* Allocations for predetermined overhead rates in variable costing: *Allocating stepped costs of service centers. Identifying the variability of service usage.* Allocations under attributable costing.

Appendix: Cross allocation procedures, 196

8. **Budgetary planning** **209**

Background for budgeting. The statement of objectives. The marketing plan: *Estimating product cost. Estimating contribution margin. Estimating branch sales and expenses. Consolidating the branch office proposals. Testing the tentative marketing plan for feasibility. Assembling the final marketing proposal.* The production plan and manufacturing cost budget: *Estimating direct materials requirements. Estimating direct labor requirements. Estimating factory overhead costs. Summarizing manufacturing costs. Preparing physical resource plans and production schedules.* The profit plan: *Allocating manufacturing costs. Assembling the tentative profit plan.* The financial budget: *The capital budget. The cash budget.* Budget review, revision and approval: *Reviewing the operating budget. Reviewing the financial budget. Budget review: An iterative process.* Seasonal patterns. The purposes of budgeting. Program budgeting and zero-base budgeting.

Case 8–1:   The Clearville Store (preparing a budget proposal), 245
Case 8–2:   Cycle World, Inc. (revising budget proposals), 248
Case 8–3:   Verlies & Winst, N.V. (testing for feasibility and profitability), 251

9. Standard costs: Controlling direct labor and materials   255

Performance standards for direct labor and materials: *Historical performance standards. Standard costs.* Variances from standard cost: The basic concept: *Calculating usage variances. Measuring price variances. Reconciling the variances.* Usage variances for scorecard reports: *Measuring input costs. Measuring output. Calculating the usage variances. The need for dollar variances.* Standard costing on the basic plan: *Recording materials purchases. Isolating the usage variance. Isolating the labor rate variance. Reconciling the variances. Characteristics of the basic plan.* Standard cost files: *Standard materials prices. Standard labor rates. Standard materials quantities. Standard labor quantities. Standard product costs.*

Appendix: Variance notation, 278
Case 9–1: Frozen Meals, Inc., 293

10. Flexible budgets: Controlling supportive overhead costs   300

Reporting cost performance: Flexible budgets and spending variances: *The flexible budget. Departmental overhead spending variances. Price and usage components of the overhead spending variance. Reporting noncontrollable costs. Reports for higher management. Transitory influences on the spending variances.* Developing the flexible budgets: *Estimating cost-volume relationships. Deciding how to measure volume. Behavioral problems in flexible budgeting.* Interdepartmental allocations for control reporting: *Purposes of periodic allocations. Developing the flexible budget for allocations. Determining monthly charges for service and support. Under-/overdistribution of service and support costs. Use of the two-part tariff in monthly applications.*

Case 10–1: Rigazio Enterprises (flexible budgeting), 329

11. Analysis of factory overhead cost variances   333

The origins of the total overhead cost variance: *Identifying the total overhead cost variance.* Analyzing the overhead variance: The two-variance approach: *The spending variance. The volume variance. Interpreting the volume variance. Reconciling the variances.* Overhead variance analysis: A three-variance approach: *The spending variance. The labor efficiency variance. The volume variance. Reconciling the variances.* Variance analysis without standard costing: *The total overhead cost variance. The spending variance. The volume variance. Reconciliation of the overhead variances.*

12. Profit contribution reporting: Controlling marketing costs   361

The marketing function. Profit contribution reporting: *The case for profit contribution reporting. Reporting attributable profit. Reporting controllable profit.* Profit reporting standards. A reporting system: *Base level profit reports. Reporting to the general sales manager. Reporting to the product manager.* Profit reports in analyses of marketing operations: *Marketing response functions. Time lags.* Profit contribution reporting under full costing: *Single-segment operation. Multisegment operations.*

Case 12–1: The Federal Company, 390

13. Cost variances in external reporting   394

Classifying variances for annual reporting: *Taking all variances to income. Assigning all variances to the balance sheet. Approximating average historical cost. Current practice in the United States.* Reconciling standard costs with the financial statements: *Newly adopted standards. Prorated variances. LIFO inventory adjustment. Prorating materials cost variances. Adjusting for changes in standard costs.*

PART TWO
FURTHER TOPICS IN ACTIVITY COSTING AND DECISIONS

14. Process costing 413

Feasibility of process costing. Calculating product cost: *Identifying the production centers. Measuring costs. Measuring output. Calculating unit cost. Calculating product cost: The final step.* Integrating process costing into financial statements: *Why special calculations are needed for financial accounting purposes. First-in, first-out method. Moving average method. Recording costs in process costing.* Using process costing information in control reporting: *Historical costing. Standard costing. Flexible budgets.* Shrinkage, accretion, and spoilage: *Adjusting the number of units in process. Accounting for the costs of spoilage.* Variable costing in process production: *Process costing for wholly variable costs. Variable costing with semivariable costs.*

15. Costing joint products 450

Recognizing joint products and joint costs. Joint costs in decision making: *Joint products as a group. Individual joint products. Separable costs and joint production decisions.* Costing co-products for financial reporting: *Physical unit basis of allocation. Net realization basis of allocation. Uniform percentage contribution basis of allocation. Relative sale value at split-off point method. Relevance of the unit cost figures.* The costing of by-products: *Defining by-products. Illustration of by-product costing. Extending the by-product method to main products.* Joint costs of variable-yield processes: *Measurement difficulties.*

Case 15–1:   The Williamson Chocolate Co., Ltd., 473

16. Costing marketing and service activities 476

Functional cost analysis: *Reasons for functional cost analysis. Approaches to functional cost analysis. Time recording. Engineering techniques. Control of functional activities.* Segment cost analysis: *Stage 1. Identifying marketing segments. Stage 2. Identifying segment-traceable costs. Stage 3. Assigning the costs of responsive functions. Stage 4. Nontraceable, attributable programmed costs.* Product-line analysis: *Traceable costs. Product-related service costs. Customer-related service costs. Nontraceable programmed costs. Consistency with incremental approach.* Cost analysis by size of order: *Basic method. The quantity discount problem. Exclusion of manufacturing cost differentials.* Applications in service businesses: *Commercial banking. Intercity trucking.*

Case 16–1:   Robson, Ltd. (profitability of small orders), 510

17. Short-run optimization models. 513

Rationing capacity: A trial-and-error solution: *Estimating the relationships. The first trial solution. The second trial solution. The optimal solution.* Rationing capacity by linear programming: *Constructing the program. Graphic solution. Developing shadow prices. Sensitivity analysis. Accounting data required. Solutions by the simplex method.* Inventory decision models: *The economic order quantity. Safety stocks and reorder points. Data requirements.*

18. **Capital expenditure decisions** 548

Decisions based on net present value: *Future value. Present value. The meaning of the discount rate. The argument for net present value. Calculating net present value: The procedure. The internal rate of return. The compounding interval. Other measures of the acceptability of proposals.* Estimating the cash flows. Initial outlays: *Outlays for plant and equipment. Existing facilities used. Working capital. Displaced facilities. Tax effects of the initial outlay.* Estimating cash flows: Secondary outlays. Estimating operating cash flows: *Translating income into cash flow. Adjusting for income taxes. Aftertax operating cash flows.* End-of-life residual value: *Pretax residual values. Taxes on the residual values.* Evaluating the proposal: *Calculating present value. Verifying the benchmark. Adjusting for uncertainty.* The impact of inflation. Economic life. Multiple alternatives. Some recurring questions: *Unamortized costs. Depreciation on new facilities. Allocations and cost absorption. The treatment of interest.*

Appendix: The cost of capital, 579
Case 18–1:   Sovad, S.A. (expansion proposal), 592

19. **Costs for pricing decisions** 596

Pricing strategies: *Choosing an initial pricing strategy. Changing from skimming to penetration pricing.* A short-run economic pricing model: *The basic model. Estimating price-volume relationships. Limitations of the model.* Cost-based pricing formulas: *Reasons for cost-based formula pricing. The structure of the cost base. The markup percentage. Departures from formula-based prices.* Price differentiation: *The benefits of price differentiation. Bases for price differentiation. Limitations on price differentiation.*

Case 19–1:   Sanders Company (contract bidding), 626
Case 19–2:   Clovis, S.A. (price differentiation), 628

20. **Statistical cost estimation** 631

Nonmathematical methods: *Judgment method. Graphic method. High-low points method.* The least squares method: Simple linear regression: *Preparing the data. Calculating the regression equation. Tests of reliability. Technical assumptions. Evaluating the equation.* Other least squares regressions: *Multiple regression analysis. Nonlinear regression. Lagged regression.* Learning curve analysis: *Nature of the learning curve. Learning curve applications. Locating the learning curve.*

21. **Reimbursement costing: Cost accounting standards** 664

Basic criteria for reimbursement costing: *Inclusiveness: The full-costing criterion. Causality: The primary implementation criterion. Traceability: Presumptive evidence of causality. Variability: A secondary criterion. Capacity provided: Another secondary criterion. Beneficiality: A criterion of last resort.* Standards issued by the Cost Accounting Standards Board: *Constraining standards. Standards for assigning costs to periods. Standards for assigning costs to cost objectives.*

PART THREE
FURTHER TOPICS IN PERIODIC PLANNING AND CONTROL

22. **Behavioral aspects of responsibility accounting** 691

Behavioral factors in system design: *Other elements as motivating forces. Participation. Reasonably attainable standards. Management by exception. The controllability criterion.*

Harmonization of conflicting goals. Behavioral problems in system administration: *Insensitivity of the budgeting staff. Irresponsibility of operating managers.*

23. **Classification and analysis of variances from standard cost** 713

Usage variances in standard costing on the comprehensive plan: *Characteristics of the comprehensive plan. Comprehensive plan reporting to management. Recording the causes of quantity variances. Factorywide Work-in-Process accounts. Cost and benefits of the comprehensive plan.* Statistical approaches to variance investigation: *Statistical control limits. An investigation decision model.* Analytical examination of cost variances: *Materials yield component of labor usage variance. Labor or equipment substitution variances. Labor mix variances. Materials mix and yield variances. Seasonal variations in the overhead volume variance.*

Appendix: Calculation of control limits, 732

24. **Project control** 746

Project approval: *Approval criteria. Review of proposals.* Detailed scheduling: *Network diagrams. Float diagrams. Resource commitment tables and charts. Uncertainty and PERT time estimates.* Progress review: *Project reporting. Departmental performance review.*

Case 24–1: Space Constructors, Inc. (B) (project reporting), 774

25. **Divisional profit reporting** 777

The organizational setting: *Profit centers. Investment centers. Administered centers. Why companies decentralize. Service centers. Quasi-profit centers and pseudo-profit centers.* Evaluating profit performance: *Operations evaluation. Economic evaluation. Managerial evaluation.* Choosing the measure of profit performance: *Profit contribution. Net income. Return on investment (ROI).* Residual income. Income measurement problems: *Common costs. Interest expense. Revenue interdependence. Depreciation. Income taxes. Adjusting for changing resource prices.* Investment measurement problems: *Defining the investment base. Allocating centrally administered assets. Allocating centrally administered liabilities. Accumulated depreciation. Adjusting investment figures for changes in resource prices.* Achieving long-term goals: *Multiple performance criteria. Centrally administered constraints and guidelines.*

Case 25–1: Dundee Products, Inc., 812

26. **Interdivisional transfer pricing** 816

Purposes of transfer prices. Criteria for transfer pricing: *Divisional resource allocation decisions. Evaluating managerial performance. Economic evaluation of the division's activities. Fiscal management.* Managerially oriented transfer pricing between profit centers: *Dictated prices based on full cost. Dictated prices based on marginal cost. Dictated prices based on market price quotations. Market-based negotiated prices.* Pricing transfers when negotiation is inappropriate: *Variable cost plus retainer. Market in/cost out. Mathematically programmed prices.*

Case 26–1: The Wolsey Corporation (freedom to buy outside), 844
Case 26–2: Hoppit Chemical Company (programmed prices), 846
Case 26–3: AB Thorsten (D) (transfers to foreign subsidiary), 847

27. **Profit analysis.** 854

Sales volume, price, and spending variances: *Sales volume variance. Selling price variance. Input price and spending variance. Variance summary. Effect of the analytical sequence.* Sales mix variance: *Composite index of volume.* Profit variance analysis in manufacturing companies: *Sales volume variance. Sales mix variance. Selling price variances. Production cost variances. Impact of production volume on income. Profit variance analysis: Variable costing basis.* Limitations of the analysis. Profit ratio and trend analysis.

APPENDIX A: Compound interest tables for present value calculations, 887

APPENDIX B: Solutions to independent study problems, 893

INDEX 939

part 1

The basic structure

1

Planning, control, and cost accounting

cost objectives

Cost accounting deals with the means used by an organization to reach individual cost objectives. A cost objective is a purposeful use of resources, and cost is the amount of resources that have been or must be sacrificed to achieve some objective. Manufacturing a product is an objective, operating an office is an objective, filling an order is an objective. Each of these has a cost.

Putting these pieces together, we can see that cost accounting is the process of measuring, estimating, reporting, and analyzing individual organizations' costs of reaching specific objectives, together with the entire body of concepts, methods, procedures, and record-keeping systems necessary to do this.

Cost accounting doesn't exist for its own sake; we have it because someone needs the information it can provide. The purpose of this chapter is to explain in a general way how cost accounting contributes to four major processes:

1. Managerial planning and control.
2. Preparation of financial statements for distribution to outsiders.
3. Preparation of business income tax returns.
4. Determination of the reimbursable amounts under cost-based contracts or similar pricing or funding arrangements.

We'll also see how responsibility for cost accounting fits into the organization structure.

Managerial planning

Much of cost accounting is designed to help management plan for the future. Managerial planning is the process of deciding how to use the resources available to the organization. It takes four forms:

1. Strategic planning.
2. Long-range periodic planning.
3. Project and situation planning.
4. Short-range periodic planning.

Strategic planning

Strategic planning establishes the basic direction and shape top management wants the organization to take. It is an attempt to answer questions such as, What does our organization have that others don't have? What are its goals? How much risk should it expose itself to? What kinds of business should it be in? (For the nonprofit organization, what role should it play in society?)

These are all questions for top management, and top managers need to weigh very carefully the alternatives before them. Strategic planning doesn't take place on any regular schedule, only when management feels that fundamental changes may have taken place.

fundamental ▷

Long-range periodic planning

If strategic planning sets the course to be steered, long-range planning establishes in a preliminary way the resources that this course will require and what it is expected to accomplish, year by year. What kinds of facilities will be required and when should they be built? How much cash will be available to finance these facilities?

Long-range planning is a periodic activity, usually carried out once a year. It produces a forecast, a statement of intentions, not a firm commitment. The long-range plan typically extends three, five, or even ten years into the future.

intentions

Project and situation planning

Project and situation planning consists of decisions to use parts of the organization's resources in specified ways. Examples are decisions to borrow money, build a new factory, price a new product, start a research project, start an advertising campaign, or hire more people. Each of these decisions requires a choice among competing alternatives; each deals with a unique problem or opportunity.

The relationships of this form of planning to the two we have just discussed are indicated by the direction of the two arrows at the left in Exhibit 1–1.

Exhibit 1–1 Managerial planning processes

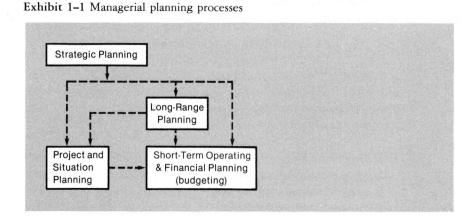

Strategic plans and long-range plans establish the framework; project and situation decisions translate it into action. Unlike strategic and long-range planning, each project or situation decision is a commitment to use some of the organization's resources in a specified way. Unless the decision is reversed fairly promptly, it leads to actions, not just predictions. This means that individual project and situation decisions affecting more than the current period should be consistent with the decisions implicit in the long-range plans; if not, one or the other should be changed.

Short-range periodic planning

Short-range periodic planning—*budgeting,* for short—completes the planning cycle illustrated in Exhibit 1–1.[1] It is the process by which management decides how the organization's resources will be used during a specific time period, and predicts the results of those decisions. The operating and financial plan, or *budget,* shows what resources the organization has decided to use, where it plans to get them, where and how it plans to use them, and what it expects to accomplish during this specific period. Typically, it is the first year of the long-range plan.

Budgeting takes place periodically, usually once a year. It pulls together all the project and situation decisions that have already been made, makes a preliminary forecast of those to be made and implemented during the coming period, and produces an integrated plan for the period. Many of the decisions embodied in the plan can still be changed as the period goes on and more information is available, but inclusion in the budget is the next thing to a firm commitment.

The approved budget serves two main purposes. First, it acts as a reminder of what has been decided. Managers need to keep their part of the plan in front of them as they go along, just as builders have to consult the architects' drawings from time to time. Second, it serves as a benchmark with which future performance can be compared. We'll have more to say about this in the section on control.

We should emphasize that all of these types of planning are decision processes, although the term decision making is often applied only to project or situation planning. Choosing a marketing program for a new product in March is really no different from deciding in November what the whole company's marketing plan for the next year will look like. The only reason for a separate category is that the budgeting process is too cumbersome, too tied to the calendar. Price decisions and plant expansions are too important to be held up until it is time to prepare the annual operating plan as a whole.

The activity: Focus of planning

The planning mechanism focuses on individual activities and groups of activities because management's resource-allocation decisions are keyed to the activities

---

[1] The term *budgeting* is sometimes used to describe a process almost devoid of decision content. The advantages of seeing budget preparation as a decision process are enormous, as we shall explain when we return to this topic in Chapter 8.

that resources are or might be committed to. An *activity* is an action or set of actions requiring the use of resources in an effort to achieve an objective or group of related objectives. Performing a research project is an activity; manufacturing and marketing a product is an activity; billing customers is an activity. By controlling the activity structure, management is able to control the flows of resources.

This is not always obvious. Some decisions seem to focus on organization units, as in decisions to open new branch offices or to close existing ones. On closer analysis, however, it becomes clear that the decision focus is not the organization unit itself but the activities it encompasses or the means of carrying them out. The branch's activity is the servicing of a given group of customers and prospects. The managerial question is how best to carry out this activity, or whether it is worth carrying out at all. The organization structure affects and is affected by these decisions, but it's the activity that matters.

Cost accounting for managerial planning

Accounting makes its contribution to managerial planning through *managerial accounting,* the process of measuring, analyzing, estimating, and reporting to management on the costs, benefits, and current status of individual activities and segments of the organization. Cost accounting makes a major contribution to the planning aspects of managerial accounting by providing data on the costs of individual activities or groups of related activities. In fact, cost accounting for planning purposes must be so integrated with other aspects of managerial accounting that we see no reason to try to separate the two. For our purposes we must view cost accounting as including *all* of managerial accounting.

Managerial control

The second role of managerial accounting is to help management control the organization. No matter how carefully a plan is conceived or how faithfully it is carried out, many things can happen to cause it to go astray or make it obsolete. Control consists of management's efforts to prevent undesirable departures from planned actions, to keep track of what is happening, to interpret this information, and to take action in response to it.[2]

Our interest in control focuses on the kinds of control information management might be able to use profitably. These fall into three categories:

1. Yes/no controls.
2. Steering controls.
3. Scorecard controls.[3]

---

[2] Many definitions of control are broader than this. Planning, for example, may be the most important way of influencing or controlling the organization's destiny because it determines how much money is spent and what it is spent for. For a definition that incorporates planning in the control process, see Robert N. Anthony, *Planning and Control Systems* (Boston: Harvard Graduate School of Business Administration, Division of Research, 1965).

[3] This classification is derived from an interesting book by William H. Newman, *Constructive Control* (Englewood Cliffs, N.J.: Prentice-Hall 1975). Newman uses the term *post-action controls* where we use scorecard controls, but the meaning is the same.

The relationships among these are diagrammed in Exhibit 1–2, but a few words about each are necessary.

Exhibit 1–2 Types of controls

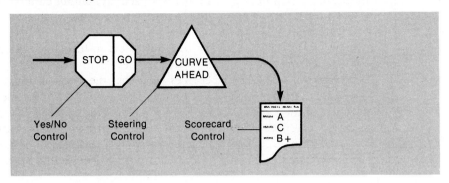

Yes/no controls

rules

Yes/no controls are rules that must be consulted before certain kinds of actions are taken. These rules list the conditions that must be met if the manager is to proceed. A good example is the "open to buy" allowance for department store buyers. These allowances are reduced when the buyers place orders and are ordinarily increased as merchandise is sold. By looking at the current figures, the buyers know whether they are free to buy the quantities they have in mind.

defensive

Yes/no controls are generally defensive controls. They come into play before money is spent rather than afterward. They make it relatively safe for higher management to delegate authority because they reduce the size of the mistakes lower managers can make. Every organization has to have some of them, but bureaucratic paralysis sets in when there are too many. They stifle initiative by reducing the manager's freedom. To do something when the rule says no, managers must ask for permission and take the risk that events will prove them right. Many managers won't willingly expose themselves to this kind of risk.

Steering controls

signals

Steering controls provide signals. These signals are intended either to reassure management that its present course is satisfactory or to indicate the need for some kind of action. The producers of a Broadway play, for example, are likely to receive daily reports from the box office, perhaps containing information like that in Exhibit 1–3.

To use this as a steering control, the producers would need to know whether attendance at this level was enough to cover daily operating costs. They would also need to know what level of advance sales was necessary to keep the show running. At the first sign of trouble, the producers should consider their alternatives: spend more on advertising, sell half-price tickets to students,

Exhibit 1–3

```
┌─────────────────────────────────────────┐
│                                           │
│       DAILY BOX OFFICE REPORT             │
│                                           │
│              Date: April 13, 19x1         │
│                               No. of      │
│                               Seats       │
│      Attendance:                          │
│          Matinee ...............    423   │
│          Evening ...............    494   │
│      Advance sales:                       │
│          Today's sales ...........  212   │
│          Cumulative bookings .....  4,462 │
│                                           │
│      Today's cash receipts ....... $7,591 │
│                                           │
└─────────────────────────────────────────┘
```

ask the cast to accept salary cuts, or prepare to close the show as soon as revenues go below the break-even level.

The best steering controls are forecasts of what will happen if management continues to follow its present script, compared with some measure of what management wants to achieve. Few steering controls fit this specification, simply because adequate data are not available. Instead, steering control signals generally spotlight differences between actual results and planned results.

Active responses to steering control signals are of two kinds. A *corrective response* leaves the objective alone but tries to change the methods being used to reach it. An *adaptive response* is an action by management to restate its objectives and develop new plans for achieving them.

Management's decision to make a corrective response assumes three things: the original plan is still all right, the cause of the poor performance is inside the organization, and the manager can do something about it. An adaptive response, on the other hand, presumes that the cause is outside. Either the forecast was wrong or the world has changed. Since the manager doesn't have the power to change outside conditions, the only course of action is to see how best to adapt to the emerging situation. This means a new decision, or *replanning*.

Scorecard controls

Top management can't control everything directly. It must delegate part of its authority to executives and supervisors at lower levels in the organization. Each of these is then responsible for using resources effectively and efficiently. (*Effectiveness* means getting the job done as it was supposed to be done; *efficiency* means maintaining a satisfactory relationship between costs and benefits.)

Managers are seldom able to remain intimately familiar with the operations they have delegated to their subordinates. Instead, they rely on scorecard controls to keep them informed on progress toward the organization's goals. Scorecard controls are summary reports on the performance of various activities or organization segments and of the managers responsible for them. Our theatrical producers, for example, might get a report containing the information in Exhibit 1–4.

Management uses scorecard reports of this kind for three reasons:

managerial evaluation

1. To evaluate the effectiveness and efficiency of individual managers and groups in the organization (*managerial evaluation*).

motivation

2. To reinforce the managers' *motivation* to work toward the goals behind the agreed-upon plan.

3. To identify activities that seem to be either particularly good or particularly bad uses of the organization's resources so that top management can con-

economic evaluation

   sider putting additional resources in or taking some out (*economic evaluation*).

Exhibit 1–4

OPERATIONS REPORT		
	Month: April 19x1	
	Actual	**Budget**
Revenues...........	$204,300	$220,000
Expenses	192,400	190,000
Income	$ 11,900	$ 30,000
Cash on hand	$ 38,000	$ 55,000

The theatrical producers, for example, hope the theater manager's motivation to control costs and expand ticket sales will be reinforced by knowing that one of these reports will be issued each month. They use the report itself to summarize the manager's success in controlling costs and to judge the profitability of the current production. Are the results encouraging enough to take this play on the road? Should pricing or promotional methods be reconsidered? Finally, the theater manager uses the report to judge whether the control efforts made in the past month have been effective. If not, something else should be tried.

Scorecard controls bear very much the same relationships to planning as steering controls. These relationships are diagrammed in Exhibit 1–5. Planning produces a plan. This becomes a set of instructions to be executed. The results of these actions are then compared with the plan in a series of reports. These are interpreted to determine what kind of response is appropriate. A corrective response requires a change in the way the plan is carried out, while an adaptive response requires replanning. Each of these leads back to an earlier phase of the process and the loop is completed.

scorecard & steering controls; control by feedback response

Both scorecard controls and steering controls use data on what has happened. Both use a kind of information known as *feedback,* and both can be referred to as *control by feedback response.* The main differences are that steering controls typically come earlier and more often, and the response, if any, comes sooner. The similarity becomes even more pronounced once we realize that scorecard

Exhibit 1–5 Planning and control loops

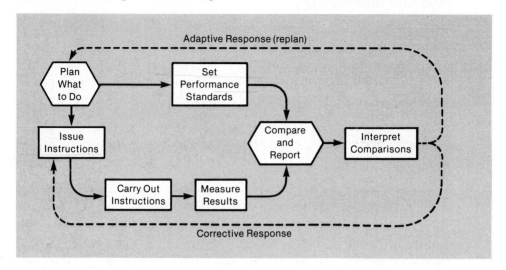

reports on segments and activities at lower levels serve as signals (steering controls) for top management action.

One final point should be recognized. Control is not achieved by issuing feedback reports. Control is accomplished by management. All the reports in the world won't control anything or anyone unless they trigger some sort of action.

Accounting's contribution to control processes

Accounting information is vital to the control process. It makes its contribution mainly by measuring and reporting on various aspects of the performance of individual *responsibility centers* and their managers. A responsibility center is an organization segment headed by a single person, answerable to higher authority, and obligated to perform certain tasks.[4]

The authority/responsibility patterns in an organization are usually drawn in the shape of a pyramid, as in Exhibit 1–6. Each segment in this chart represents an executive, and each of these executives is responsible for the use of the resources in that segment. He or she is also responsible for the use of resources by the executives in the segments farther down in the pyramid. The president is responsible for the whole organization. The vice president of segment A is responsible for that segment, including the activities of the people in sections A1, A2, and A3. The manager of section A1 is responsible only for what goes on in that small area.

Accountants participate in the control process, either by designing reporting

---

[4] Responsibility for an organization segment's work may be shared by two or more persons. If the sharing is complete, they will act as a single person on all matters. In the more usual case, they divide the tasks of managing the segment between them. This effectively creates two responsibility centers within the segment.

Exhibit 1–6 Organization chart

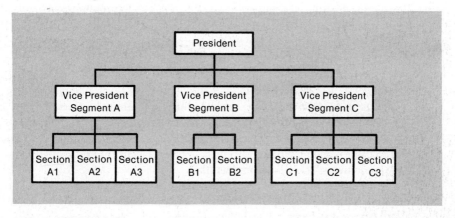

systems, by measuring and reporting actual results, or by interpreting control reports and providing advice. These activities are the second side of managerial accounting, complementing the accountants' activities in the planning process. Strictly speaking, the control side of cost accounting is only one part of managerial accounting, making its contribution to control reporting by specifying, providing, and interpreting the cost information that is included in the managerial accounting system. To do full justice to the cost accounting aspects of control, however, we shall have to describe *all* of the control side of managerial accounting. For this reason, we find it appropriate to treat all of managerial accounting as if it were part of cost accounting.

Financial, tax, and reimbursement accounting

Cost accounting serves many masters. One of these is managerial accounting, as we have just seen. Cost accounting also contributes to financial accounting, tax accounting, and that diverse set of activities we refer as reimbursement accounting. A few words about each of these are necessary to round out this introductory description.

Financial accounting

Every organization must submit financial statements to people who do not take part in the day-by-day administration of the organization's activities. The business corporation submits reports to its shareholders, to lenders, and in some instances to public supervisory bodies such as the U.S. Securities and Exchange Commission. The symphony orchestra or charitable foundation submits reports to its board of trustees and to governmental bodies such as state corporations offices.

These financial statements are the concern of financial accounting. Cost accounting serves financial accounting by distinguishing between costs that are to be charged against current revenues and those to be assigned to the company-produced goods that are still in inventory at the end of the period for which the financial statements are prepared. In the United States, it also provides the cost classifications necessary to enable large business organizations to report separately the results of individual company segments ("lines of business"), as required by the accounting profession, the Securities and Exchange Commission, and other government agencies.

Financial accounting is more restrictive than managerial accounting. For managerial accounting, management is free to decide how costs are to be measured; for financial accounting the measurement criteria come from outside. We shall see in Chapter 6, for example, that for some managerial purposes the cost accountant may exclude some manufacturing costs from estimates of the costs of manufactured products. For financial accounting, all elements of manufacturing costs must be included.

Measurement criteria for financial accounting are governed by *generally accepted accounting principles.* These are based on centuries of accounting practice and are now largely embedded in formal pronouncements of various professional accounting committees and boards. The current rule-making body in the United States is the Financial Accounting Standards Board, with members chosen from the public accounting profession, industry, the universities, government, and the investment community.

Tax accounting

In some countries, inventory figures for financial accounting must be the same as those used for tax purposes; in others, different figures are permitted. When differences are allowed, as in the United States, tax rules and regulations are likely to be more detailed than financial accounting guidelines.

The cost accountants' roles in tax accounting are exactly the same as in financial accounting. They must look to the rules and regulations for guidance. These establish the limits the cost figures must fall between. Because tax accounting is so specialized and is constantly changing, we shall not attempt to deal with it in any way.

Reimbursement accounting

Cost accounting plays a role in a fourth kind of accounting activity in some organizations. We refer to this kind of activity as *reimbursement accounting* or *reimbursement costing,* although the activity is somewhat broader than this title implies. Reimbursement accounting is the process by which costs are estimated or assigned to individual products, services, activities, or programs for outsiders to use in calculating the prices to be paid or, in some not-for-profit organizations, amounts to be contributed to the organizations in the form of gifts or grants.

Cost-reimbursement contracts are fairly common, particularly in commercial dealings between governmental agencies and firms in the private sector. When the two parties to the contract are both outside the government, the contract itself must spell out how cost is to be measured. The less specific the contract, the more likely the two parties will be arguing the definition of cost in court before they are finished. The cost accountants' work in contract accounting is known as *contract costing.*

Although some steps toward uniformity have been taken, U.S. government departments and agencies use a number of different sets of standards to govern accounting measurements in connection with contracts in which the contract price is based, at least in part, on cost data submitted to the government. One set of standards is embodied in the Armed Services Defense Acquisition Regulations, incorporating the standards promulgated by the Cost Accounting Standards Board (CASB). The CASB's standards are summarized in Chapter 21.

Formal reimbursement agreements made by not-for-profit organizations are also likely to incorporate fairly specific accounting standards. Hospital cost reimbursement agreements tend to fall in this category. Reimbursement costing is also used in less formal arrangements, however, such as in appeals by performing arts organizations for financial support. Accounting standards in these situations are likely to be equally informal.

Organizing the accounting function

The chief accounting officer, who usually has the title of *controller,* has responsibility for all accounting functions. The controller generally reports to the president or to a financial vice president.

Despite the title, the controller doesn't control anything outside the controller's department. He or she has a staff relationship with executives in other parts of the organization, with authority to give advice and provide help but with no direct power of enforcement. Even so, the controller is often an active and influential member of top management, gaining influence and power gradually by doing the job well and winning the respect of others in the organization.

In small organizations the functions of controllership are likely to be highly centralized. As the organization grows, first clerical employees and then members of the controller's staff are likely to be moved out of the controller's office to other locations within the organization. As the organization continues to grow, these satellite departments grow, too. Their function becomes less and less one of collecting data for processing in the home office. Instead, the outlying staff spends more and more of its time providing managerial accounting services to local management.

The cycle is complete when these people are transferred from the central controller's payroll to report directly to local management. In a large manufacturing corporation, for example, each operating division is likely to have its own divisional controller, reporting directly to the division manager. Within the divisions each factory is likely to have a plant controller, reporting to the plant manager.

This decentralization of the controller's organization is desirable in that it identifies the role of the controller's staff as service to management. It creates some problems, however. First, it raises the possibility that each division will go its own way in accounting matters, making it difficult for the central account-

Exhibit 1–7 Positions of divisional and plant controllers

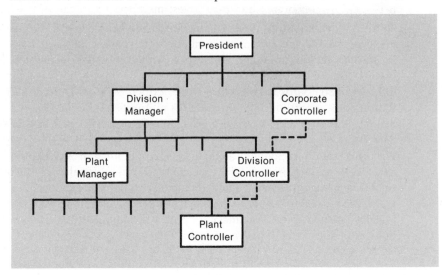

ing staff to report to top management or outside investors. The usual solution to this is to have the corporate controller maintain a "dotted line" relationship with the divisional and plant controllers, providing control over the technical aspects of their work. (See Exhibit 1–7.)

Second, the divisional and plant controllers are likely to see their road to advancement along the dotted lines—that is, to other positions in controllership rather than to other kinds of managerial positions. This may lead them to sacrifice the interests of local management when conflicts arise between service to local management and the demands of the corporate controller.[5]

Cost accounting practitioners

People acquire the skills necessary to become cost accountants in a number of different ways. Some start in minor clerical positions and move up through the ranks with little formal education at the college or university level. Others enter cost accounting after receiving bachelor's or master's degrees in business administration or accounting.

Although job titles such as cost accountant or cost analyst abound, the practice of cost accounting is so closely interwoven with other aspects of managerial accounting that the major practitioners' associations no longer recognize cost accountants as a separate group. The most influential practitioner-based membership organizations in the United States are the National Association of Accountants (NAA) and the Financial Executives Institute (FEI). The NAA

[5] This danger was exposed and explored in a book as valid today as when it was written. Herbert A. Simon, George Kozmetsky, Harold Guetzkow, and Gordon Tyndall, *Centralization vs. Decentralization in Organizing the Controller's Department* (New York: Controllership Foundation, 1954).

has a very broad membership base, ranging from technical-level accounting personnel to corporate chief executives; membership in the FEI, with a few exceptions, is limited to corporate controllers, treasurers, and other high-level financial officers.

Similar organizations are found in other western industrial nations. Canada, for example, has the Society of Management Accountants of Canada (La Société des Comptables en Management du Canada). In Britain the major membership organization is the Institute of Cost and Management Accountants.

Practitioners in Canada, Great Britain, and a number of other countries have long had professional certification programs. In Canada, for example, a practitioner can become a Registered Industrial Accountant (RIA) by completing an educational and examination program designed and administered by the Society of Management Accountants of Canada.

The United States now has a comparable designation, the Certificate in Management Accounting (CMA). This certificate is granted to those who meet the experience, educational, and examination requirements of the Institute of Management Accounting, an offshoot of the National Association of Accountants. Unlike its Canadian counterpart, the IMA doesn't prescribe a specific program of studies or design specific courses. It does prepare and administer the qualifying examinations, however, and enforces the continuing education requirements it has prescribed.

Individuals can serve in senior positions in managerial accounting and financial management even if they lack formal professional certification. The main requirement is to perform the functions to management's satisfaction. Certification is important in some companies, however, and is more likely to be a requirement for advancement in Canadian or British businesses, where the certification programs are many decades old, than in the United States, where they are relatively new.

Cost accounting in perspective

We sometimes get too close to our own systems to see their faults and their limitations. With this in mind, let us end this introductory chapter with four simple observations:

1. The managerial accountant is not management's only source of data for planning and control.   Accounting has always focused on quantities that can be expressed in monetary terms, in dollars. Management needs other kinds of information, expressed in units of time, weight, volume, or presence. It may even call for qualitative statements of conditions or results, such as "good" or "likely to succeed." As a result, most organizations have a lot of physical data, plus a good deal of information on what is happening outside the organization. This could be made part of managerial accounting, but in most cases it is not.

2. Accounting procedures often suffer from a confusion of purposes.   Figures that are necessary for reimbursement costing or for tax or financial accounting may be misleading if management tries to use them for planning or control. To cite just one example, sales are usually recorded in the accounts when goods are shipped or services are performed for clients or customers. This is done for financial accounting and for tax accounting. To the sales force, however, the sale takes place when the customer places an order. The accountant's easiest course of action is to use the figures on shipments for all purposes. This may be very misleading to management, at least in some periods.

3. Accounting systems often measure resources at prices that have no relevance to current managerial decisions. The data recorded in the accounts should be regarded solely as a point of departure, as a set of indicators rather than as gospel truth.

4. All data-gathering and classification schemes are subject to the law of diminishing productivity. Beyond some point successive increments of data have progressively smaller managerial payoffs. Ideally, the amount of data provided should be determined from the application of a cost-benefit model, comparing the value of information with its cost. Although formal efforts to apply such models are scarce, they are always implicit in the system. Every system represents a set of decisions as to how much and what kinds of information will be productive.

Summary

Cost accounting is the process of measuring, estimating, reporting, and interpreting individual organizations' costs of reaching specific objectives, together with the underlying body of concepts, methods, procedures, and record-keeping systems. It serves managerial accounting, financial accounting, tax accounting, and reimbursement accounting, but the emphasis in this book will be on cost accounting's contribution to managerial accounting.

Managerial accounting contributes to the two interrelated managerial processes of planning and control. Planning is the process of deciding how to use the organization's resources. To serve management's planning needs, the managerial accountant focuses on the individual activities the organization is engaged in. Control, on the other hand, consists of observing, interpreting, and reporting what is going on and taking action in response to this information. It consists of yes/no controls, steering controls, and scorecard controls. It is exercised through the organization's responsibility structure. Managerial accounting contributes to this process by providing steering control and scorecard information to the responsible managers.

Managerial accounting and cost accounting are among the responsibilities of the chief accounting officer or controller. In large organizations each major subdivision is likely to have its own controller. This emphasizes the importance of the controller's role as adviser and servant of management.

Independent study problems (solutions in Appendix B)

1. **Focus of planning decisions.** Marquard Associates is a small but growing consulting firm with a head office in New York and branch offices in Chicago and Atlanta. One of the partners in the firm is in charge of the Atlanta office and three others operate out of Chicago; all other partners are based in New York.

The Atlanta office hasn't shared in the growth of the firm in the past two years and the partners are considering closing that office, moving the professional staff either to Chicago or New York. Is this an exception to the dictum in this chapter that decisions focus on activities rather than on organization units? To answer this question you must analyze the decision to see how it would affect the firm's operations.

Required:

What kinds of data would be relevant to management's decision on the question of closing the Atlanta branch?

2. **Content of managerial accounting; role of the controller.** Marquard Associates (see problem 1) has a bookkeeper whose duties are to prepare invoices, payrolls, and other documents and to record all transactions in appropriate journals and ledgers. The firm's annual financial statements are prepared by a public accounting firm, which supervises the annual closing of the books.

The managing partner has decided these arrangements are no longer adequate; no managerially oriented accounting information is available. The partners are now considering whether to hire a full-time controller to take charge of the accounting function and expand the system to provide managerially oriented accounting information.

Required:

What kinds of information not required for external financial reporting would you expect the new controller to begin to assemble? How would these data be used?

3. **Scorecard and steering control information.** Prairie Airways, Inc., provides scheduled passenger airline service connecting Chicago with 14 other airports in the Midwest. It operates 18 flights each weekday and 10 flights each Saturday and Sunday. Each flight either originates or terminates in Chicago; some are nonstop but most take two or more stops on the way to or from Chicago.

Prairie Airways has a small staff of ground personnel at each airport it serves. Routine maintenance of its aircraft is performed on contract in Chicago by a major airline.

Required:

What kinds of steering control and scorecard control information do you think Prairie's management should have?

Exercises and problems

4. **Planning and control loops.** You have just been elected president of a local group which raises funds and sponsors a variety of recreational and educational activities for young people in your community. To what extent do the planning and control loops in Exhibit 1–5 apply to your organization? Be specific as to who in the organization would do what at each of the points in this diagram.

5. **Role of the controller.** "I don't care what you say. You're only the controller. You may not like my proposal, but you don't make the decisions. The president and the executive committee have the say on this one and there's nothing you can do about it."

A division manager made the foregoing statement in response to the controller's analysis of a divisional proposal. The controller's conclusion was that the estimates used to justify the proposal were flawed and the benefits therefore were too meager to cover the costs of the proposal.

Required:

What is the role of the controller in situations like this? Is the division manager right?

6. **Different purposes of cost accounting.** A company manufactures and sells 100,000 shovels a year. Some shovels are short and flat, others are rounded and have long handles. The company has 14 different kinds of shovels in all, and its annual operating costs are:

Manufacturing (including such items as the cost of steel and lumber, depreciation on equipment, and the plant manager's salary)	$150,000
Selling (including sales commissions and showroom rentals) . . .	50,000
Administration (including the costs of an outside bookkeeping service and the president's salary)	30,000
Total	$230,000

Required:

Use this information to illustrate the statement in the chapter that cost accounting must develop different sets of cost figures for different purposes. For example, which costs in the three categories in the table above might management find useful in deciding whether one shovel model should be dropped from the line, or in setting a desired price on another model, or in evaluating the plant manager's success in controlling costs, or in measuring inventories of shovels for public financial reporting? What problems do you think you would encounter in developing these figures? *Numerical answers are not expected.*

7. **Planning.** You are considering enrolling next term in a course in managerial economics. By itself, this is a project planning decision. Prepare a short report to relate this to your strategic educational plan, your long-range educational plan, and your short-range educational plan.

8. **Steering and scorecard controls.** The manager of a chain of motion-picture theaters relies on written reports to keep informed about the operations of the individual theaters. Films are booked for a week at a time, with an unlimited renewal option. Runs of six to eight weeks are not uncommon, but many films are replaced at the end of one week. The film shown at one theater may also be shown at one or more others in the chain, but a separate booking decision is made at each theater each week.

Each theater has a manager, responsible for maintaining and operating the theater. Employees are hired by the local manager, but salaries must be approved by the chain manager. The chain manager selects the films to be shown, makes all the booking decisions, and hires the theater managers.

Required:
  a. What reports is the chain manager likely to find useful? Indicate how each of these reports would be used and whether you regard it as a steering control or as a scorecard control.
  b. What would you report to the individual theater managers, and how frequently would you report it? Indicate how the manager would use this information and whether it would be steering control or scorecard control information.
  c. To what extent should the theater managers be held responsible for income from sale of refreshments? How would you evaluate their performance?

9. **Steering and scorecard controls.** You own a two-year-old automobile. You have been satisfied with its performance and it is still in good condition. There is no bus service or other form of public transportation where you live. You need to use an automobile to get to work; a car pool is impossible because none of your neighbors works where you do.

You ordinarily have the car serviced and repaired at a garage near your office, delivering it in the morning on your way to work and picking it up on your way home. Occasionally a neighbor can deliver you to a bus stop if your car is out of service, but he has to go several miles out of his way to do this, and you ask his help as seldom as you can.

A friend has offered, without charge, to prepare control reports you think would be useful to you as owner of the car, and to keep any records necessary to provide data for these reports.

Required:

   a. Prepare a short statement indicating the purpose(s) you would like the reports to serve.

   b. What reports would you like to receive, what would they contain, and how often would you like to receive them?

   c. Identify each report as either a steering control or a scorecard control. Indicate how you would use it and how your friend would get the data necessary to prepare it.

Case 1–1. Derek Steele, Grocer*

"Well, I seem to manage, somehow," Derek Steele said, "But I'll have to think about it a bit before I can tell you just how I do it."

Mr. Steele was the proprietor of a small grocery store in Panbridge, England. He sold several hundred different items of packaged goods, bread, wines, and household supplies, as well as a line of fresh dairy produce—milk, cheese, butter, etc. Mr. Steele's son-in-law, a recent graduate in management studies, had asked him how he planned and controlled the inventories of the items that he offered for sale in his store.

Mr. Steele decided to make a few notes about the process. Bread and dairy produce, he noted, were delivered daily. Except for unusual items ordered for specific customers, he never placed an order for these items. Instead, he told the delivery man each day what he thought he would need until the next day's delivery. Any unsold bread could be returned the next day to the delivery man, but at a reduced price. Milk could be kept in the store for two days, and Mr. Steele was always careful to sell any milk left over from the previous day before placing the current day's delivery in the display case. Butter, cheese, and similar items could be kept a good deal longer, and Mr. Steele ordinarily ordered several days' requirements at a time.

Most other items were ordered either by telephone or from wholesalers' or manufacturers' representatives who called at the store. Three or four of these representatives would stop at Mr. Steele's store in a typical day. For some items ordered in this way, delivery was made the following day; for others, the delay was longer, sometimes as long as two weeks.

Mr. Steele knew that he could obtain lower purchase prices on some items if he would buy larger quantities in each order. To do this, however, he would have to order much farther ahead of the desired delivery date, and he would also have to prepare additional storage space behind his store. When his son-in-law asked him how much he could save by making purchases in larger quantities, Mr. Steele had to reply that he didn't know, but he was happy doing business as he was.

Most of Mr. Steele's customers bought only a few items at a time, things that they had forgotten during their last visit to the chain store or things that would not justify a trip to the chain store on the high street. Mr. Steele's prices were a little higher than chain store prices, but he did not feel that he would get any more business of this sort if he reduced his prices to the chain store level.

"I don't know how you'd describe my system," he said, "but I watch my shelves fairly closely. When I see that I'm running low on an item, I order it. If I buy something

---

* Copyright 1968 by l'Institut pour l'Etude des Méthodes de Direction de l'Entreprise (IMEDE), Lausanne, Switzerland. Reproduced by permission.

and it doesn't sell well, I notice that too, and the next time the salesman asks me to order it I tell him no. If he comes in with something new, I try to decide whether my customers will like it and how much shelf space it will take. Some things come in several sizes and colors, and I might have to push several items aside to make room for one new one. That new line of toilet soap, for example, comes in three sizes and each size comes in three colors. I had to drop one brand of laundry detergent to make room for all that variety, but my customers like the soap and I think I made the right choice.

"Actually, my biggest problem comes from the daily deliveries. If I order too little, my stock is exhausted before the end of the afternoon. Overordering is not as serious a mistake, because I can adjust the next day's order on everything but bread.

"Most of this I do myself. My clerk is a pleasant young fellow, but he's not very bright. He can follow instructions, but I have to make it quite clear what he is expected to do."

a. Describe the planning portion of the process used by Mr. Steele to plan and control his inventories. What kinds of data might he find useful at this point? Where might he expect to find these data?

b. Describe the feedback portion of the process. What kinds of data would be useful and where would they come from?

c. To what extent is Mr. Steele's planning and control system a decision-making process? How much of the work could Mr. Steele safely delegate to his clerk?

2 The costing structure and job order costing

Cost accounting systems classify operating costs in many ways. The purpose of this chapter is to identify the principal ways in which a relatively simple manufacturing company would be likely to classify its operating costs.

The three major dimensions of cost

The cost accountants' first task is to decide how the operating costs of individual periods are to be classified. The three most important ways to classify operating costs are:

1. By organization segment.
2. By object of expenditure.
3. By activity.

Classification by organization segment

The first dimension of the cost accounting structure parallels the organization chart. Exhibit 2–1 shows the main elements of the organization structure of the Apex Company, a small manufacturer of electrical components. Each block in this diagram represents a responsibility center. The four-digit number in the block is the organizational account number.

In making their initial assignments of costs to responsibility centers, the accountants use the *traceability* criterion—that is, they assign each cost to the lowest responsibility center it is traceable to. A cost is traceable to a center if it is incurred entirely to support one or more of the activities of that center or the activities of the centers below it in the organization chart. The salary of the machine shop manager, for example, is traceable all the way down to the machine shop department, while the factory manager's salary is traceable only to his office, one level higher up.[1] In accounting language, the factory manager's salary is a *direct cost* of the factory, but an *indirect cost* of the first-

---

[1] In practice, the salaries of executives and department heads are recorded separately to keep the figures confidential. Wherever they are recorded, however, they are usually coded by responsibility center.

Exhibit 2–1
APEX COMPANY Partial organization chart and organizational account codes

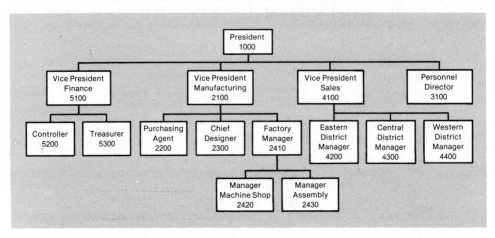

level responsibility centers. Any cost that is traceable to a cost objective is a direct cost of that cost objective.

We should point out that the organization structure sometimes doesn't subdivide costs finely enough to satisfy management's needs for data. A factory department, for example, may have both mechanized and manual operations. The costs of the mechanized operations are likely to be so different from those of the manual operations that management will expect the accountant to be able to keep them separate.

One answer to this problem is to subdivide some responsibility centers into subunits known as *cost centers.* A cost center is either a whole responsibility center or part of one for which the accountant wishes to collect separate cost data.

The fourth digit in Apex's organizational account code is used to identify cost centers within departments. For example, the account code 2420 is a summary account for the machine shop as a whole. The fourth digit is a zero, indicating that this account applies to an entire department. The accountants may wish, however, to identify a number of cost centers within this department. They might use the code 2421 to identify the accounts in which the department head's office costs are accumulated, the code 2422 for costs associated with the department's drill presses, and so on. We have omitted the cost-center classification from Exhibit 2–1 to keep the diagram simple. In fact, we have taken the diagram down to the departmental level in one segment only—the factory. This is all we need to demonstrate this structure.

Classification by object of expenditure

Management's decisions affect many variables, such as the volume and location of production. Many of these decisions affect cost. Knowing the relationships between costs and the factors that determine costs therefore should help management make decisions. This knowledge should also be helpful in cost control. The manager can control cost only by acting on the determinants of cost.

This suggests that accounting data should be collected in ways that make it easier to identify the relationships between costs and their determinants. In other words, the costs in any one class should be *homogeneous*—they should all show the same pattern of response to the various determinants of cost. For example, if the costs of lubricating oil vary with the number of machine-hours and the costs of cleaning supplies vary with the number of labor hours, putting them in the same account would be likely to obscure the underlying relationships.

Dividing departments into cost centers is one way of getting more homogeneous data, as we saw just a moment ago. Another way is to classify a cost center's costs into their "natural elements," such as salaries, supplies, electric power, and so on. This is often referred to as classification by *object of expenditure*. (Supplies are the *object* obtained by the *expenditure* of funds.) If the organizational classification shows *where* the cost was incurred, the object of expenditure classification shows *what* resources were used.

Exhibit 2–2 shows the coding system used in the Apex Company's factory. The object-of-expenditure account titles and code numbers are shown at the left; the full two-dimensional account codes are shown in the three columns at the right. When a cost is incurred, it must be classified both by cost center and by object of expenditure. If John Jones works a full eight hours repairing

Exhibit 2–2
APEX COMPANY Chart of factory cost accounts

	Department:	2410 Factory Manager	2420 Machine Shop	2430 Assembly
	Element			
01	Direct materials	2410.01	2420.01	2430.01
02	Direct labor	2410.02	2420.02	2430.02
11	Supervision	2410.11	2420.11	2430.11
12	Labor—travel time	2410.12	2420.12	2430.12
13	Labor—idle time	2410.13	2420.13	2430.13
14	Labor—clerical	2410.14	2420.14	2430.14
15	Labor—maintenance	2410.15	2420.15	2430.15
21	Overtime premium	2410.21	2420.21	2430.21
22	Vacation and holiday pay	2410.22	2420.22	2430.22
23	Payroll taxes	2410.23	2420.23	2430.23
24	Pensions	2410.24	2420.24	2430.24
31	Travel allowances	2410.31	2420.31	2430.31
51	Tools	2410.51	2420.51	2430.51
52	Supplies	2410.52	2420.52	2430.52
53	Equipment rental	2410.53	2420.53	2430.53
54	Depreciation	2410.54	2420.54	2430.54
61	Insurance	2410.61	2420.61	2430.61
71	Other	2410.71	2420.71	2430.71

equipment in the machine shop at an hourly rate of $12, the account 2420.15 (Machine Shop Labor—Maintenance) will be charged with $12 \times 8 = \$96$.

Classification by activity

The third dimension of the cost accounting structure is the activity classification. Activities, or the results of activities, are the reasons why the organization incurs costs. If the first two dimensions of the costing structure are the where and what dimensions, activity costing is the *why* dimension.

Each activity or group of activities for which costs are measured or estimated is a *costing entity.* For our present purposes, we can identify four kinds of costing entities:

1. *Order-getting activities:* designed to induce customers to buy or place orders for goods or services.
2. *Direct-production activities:* undertaken to produce specific finished goods or services for delivery to outsiders or for future use (e.g., component parts produced for inventory or factory equipment manufactured in the company's own factory for its own future use).
3. *Order-filling activities:* undertaken primarily to insure that goods and services are delivered to the specific customers who have ordered them and to insure that these goods and services will be paid for.
4. *Service and support activities:* undertaken to provide internal support to two or more order-getting, direct-production, or order-filling activities.

Accounting systems sometimes provide for the identification of the costs of individual order-getting, order-filling, service, and support activities. Our concern in this chapter, however, is with the methods used to measure the costs of direct-production activities or, more precisely, with the specific goods or services each of them yields—that is, each costing entity will be one or more units of product or service produced for delivery or for future use. To simplify our terminology, we'll use the term *product costing* to refer to the process of measuring the costs of these costing entities.

Size of the costing entity

Product costing can be extremely detailed, with each production order or even each iteration of a task treated as a costing entity. Often, however, neither management nor any outside party needs much detail. When this is the case, the costing entities may be very large indeed. A factory, for example, may classify its products in several groups, each group serving as a costing entity. Or, a symphony orchestra may classify and accumulate costs for entire *programs* rather than for individual concerts. (A program is a group of activities combined in some purposeful structure during a substantial period of time to achieve a single objective or group of related objectives. One of the programs of a symphony orchestra, for example, may be all performances in the winter series, or all summer pops concerts, taken as a group.)

The reason for choosing large costing entities is to reduce the cost of record-keeping. If all of the organization's activities were lumped together in a single costing entity, for example, we wouldn't have to examine transactions to see what activities they related to, and the employees therefore would have no need to keep records showing how long they worked on each activity. With two costing entities, the accountants would have more work to do, but their efforts could still be minimal. If they had to cope with 100 or more costing entities at the same time, however, they would need 100 or more locations (computer storage segments, for example) to store the detailed data, they would need clerical personnel to enter and retrieve data in these locations, and they would need to spend more time insuring that the system was working properly. In general, the more costing entities the organization wants to identify, the more it will have to spend to keep track of its costs.

The clerical savings from using large costing entities don't come free of charge, of course. To get these savings, management has to give up cost information on the individual activities, products, or services that have been lumped together in a costing entity. How can management get detailed cost information if the main costing procedures don't provide it? Three avenues are open:

1. Identify some measurable characteristic that is common to each of the components in the costing entity (e.g., the time required or weight of each), and distribute the total cost of the costing entity in proportion to the individual components' shares of this characteristic.
2. Use detailed estimates prepared in advance on the basis of historical data or special studies or both.
3. Collect detailed data for a sample of the components in the costing entity and assume that the costs of the whole were incurred in the same proportions as the costs of the sample.

Which avenue management decides to take will depend on how much accuracy management is willing to pay for and on how many data are already available. The first alternative is likely to be relatively cheap but subject to a great deal of dispute; the third alternative is likely to be more accurate but costly and time consuming.

Costing individual activities: Job order costing

The method used to assign costs to end-product activities depends in the first place on how the organization gets its work done. *Job order costing* is the appropriate method when individual cost centers are likely to work on the production of several different products or services in any given time period. The costing entity in job order costing is the individual *job*—that is, a project, contract, or batch of products that is clearly distinguishable from other projects, contracts, or batches while processing is taking place.

The Apex Company has a job order costing system in its factory. In the next few pages we'll see how Apex identifies the three groups of costs it assigns to individual job orders:

1. Direct materials.
2. Direct labor.
3. Factory overhead.

Direct materials costs

Production in the Apex Company's factory begins when someone in authority issues a *production order* or *job order,* calling for the manufacture of a specified quantity of one of the company's products or component parts. The production order contains detailed instructions, specifying the materials required, the operations to be performed, and the production centers to be used. (A *production center* in a job shop is a cost center which works directly on individual job orders.)

Issuance of materials. For many jobs, production begins when the workers receive some or all of the *direct materials* that will be needed for that job. Direct materials are all raw materials and component parts that can be traced readily to individual job orders. When direct materials are *issued*—that is, transferred from a storeroom for use on a job order—the manager receiving them ordinarily must initial a form known as a *materials requisition.* Exhibit 2–3, for example, is a requisition for direct materials. It shows the number and description of the item, the quantity issued, the cost center it is to be used in, and the job number. Unit price and total cost figures are entered later, in the office.

Exhibit 2–3 Materials requisition

APEX COMPANY MATERIALS REQUISITION			
		# 17426 Date: 5/3/x1	
Item	Quantity	Price	Total
Shell No. 14	2,100		
Cost Center: 2421 Job No.: 1234 Acct. No.: _____		Rec'd by: *F. Smith*	

Apex's factory personnel requisitioned three different kinds of direct materials for use on job order 1234 during May, with quantities and costs as follows:

Date	Item	Quantity	Price	Amount
5/3	Shell No. 14	2,100	$1.32	$2,772
5/5	Handle No. 142	2,000	0.41	820
5/10	Paint	2	6.00	12

Return of materials. As it turned out, the factory didn't need all the shells that were issued for this job. When the first crucial operations were completed, 50 shells had been damaged and discarded, but another 50 shells had not been used at all. A production supervisor returned these to the storeroom, where the storeroom clerk recorded the quantity returned on a *returned materials card*, identical in format to a materials requisition form.

Summary of materials costs. These transactions were all posted to a record known as a *job cost sheet*, designed to accumulate all the costs assigned to a specific job. Exhibit 2–4 shows a simplified job cost sheet for job order 1234, with the direct materials transactions entered in the section at the upper left. Similar information is recorded on the storeroom inventory records for Shell No. 14, Handle No. 142, and paint.

Exhibit 2–4 Job cost sheet

APEX COMPANY
JOB COST SHEET

Description: Canister No. 278   Job Order No.: 1234
Date Ordered: 5/1/x1   Date Completed: 5/12/x1
Quantity Ordered: 2,000   Quantity Completed: 2,000

Date	Item	Quantity	Price	Amount	Cost Summary
		Materials Cost			
5/3	Shell No. 14	2,100	$1.32	$2,772	Materials . . . .
5/4	Shell No. 14	(50)	1.32	(66)	Labor . . . .
5/5	Handle No. 142	2,000	0.41	820	Overhead . . . .
5/10	Paint	2	6.00	12	Total . . . .
	Total			$3,538	Unit cost . . . .

Date	Cost Center	Hours	Rate	Amount	Hours	Overhead Rate	Amount
		Labor Cost				**Overhead Cost**	
	Total						

Direct labor costs

Direct labor costs are the costs of the time workers spend on specific job orders. To identify these costs, some companies have employees fill in labor time tickets like the one in Exhibit 2–5. Each of these tickets identifies the worker, the cost center, the job, the time the worker started on this job, and the completion time. Employees in service organizations, rather than fill in individual time tickets, are likely to keep some form of running diary of how they spend their time. These diaries are processed by clerical personnel, perhaps at the end of each week or at the end of each month.

Exhibit 2–5 Labor time ticket

```
APEX COMPANY
TIME TICKET              # 22663

Name T. Jones                      Date 5/4/x1
Employee No. 204-46-4765
Pay grade    6
Cost center   2421
Job No.    1234        Start    10:10
Acct. No.              Finish   11:40
                       Elapsed    90 min.
```

At the Apex Company's factory, the direct labor time tickets were processed daily and posted to the job cost sheets. The direct labor costs of job order 1234 were as follows:

Date	Hours	Rate	Amount	Cost Center
5/4	6	$14	$ 84	2421
5/6	10	10	100	2422
5/10	14	7	98	2431
5/11	4	8	32	2431

Factory overhead costs

Up to now, job order costing has been straightforward. The traceability criterion has worked quite well. It has enabled us to identify the *prime costs*—that is, direct materials and direct labor—and enter these on the job cost sheets. A problem has been lurking in the background, however. What do we do with the costs that can't be traced readily to individual job orders—that is, the *indirect costs* of the jobs, otherwise known as *common costs* or *factory overhead costs?* These costs are necessary to the production of the various job orders, and for the moment at least we shall assume this means they are part of the cost of these jobs.

Types of factory overhead costs. Factory costs fall in the overhead category for two reasons. Some are classified as overhead because the cost and effort required to trace them to individual jobs is prohibitive—e.g., the costs of the glue and upholstery nails used in making furniture. Most overhead costs, however, are classified as overhead because the accountants cannot trace them to individual jobs, no matter how hard they try. The costs of floor cleaning compounds and lubricating oil usually fall in this second category. The machines need to be oiled once in a while and the accountant has no way of saying how much oil is used on one job and how much on another.

The first two major categories of overhead costs are indirect materials and indirect labor. *Indirect materials* are any materials the accountants can't trace readily to specific jobs. Issues of indirect materials are recorded on materials requisition forms. A requisition for indirect materials is identical to one for direct materials except that it shows an object-of-expenditure overhead cost account number in the lower left-hand corner instead of a job order number.

Indirect labor is any labor time that can't be traced readily to specific jobs. Indirect labor time, like direct labor time, is recorded initially on labor time tickets or on labor time sheets or diaries. A time ticket for indirect labor in the Apex Company's factory shows the object-of-expenditure account number in the lower left-hand corner (see Exhibit 2–5) instead of a job order number. Several indirect labor accounts may be used if management wishes to separate the costs of various subcategories of indirect labor time. Apex, for example, recognizes five categories of indirect labor cost—supervision, travel time, idle time, clerical, and maintenance.

Factory overhead also includes costs such as depreciation on equipment, electricity, telephone service, and so on. These are recorded in separate object-of-expenditure accounts as they occur.

Assigning overhead costs to individual jobs.   Since overhead costs can't be traced readily to individual job orders, if we wish to assign them to jobs we have to use a formula of some sort. The usual formula includes two elements—an overhead rate[2] and a measure of the size of the job:

$$
\boxed{\begin{array}{c}\text{Overhead}\\ \text{rate}\end{array}} \quad \times \quad \boxed{\begin{array}{c}\text{Size}\\ \text{of job}\end{array}} \quad = \quad \boxed{\begin{array}{c}\text{Overhead cost}\\ \text{assigned to job}\end{array}}
$$

An overhead rate measures the average amount of overhead that is provided to support a unit of operating volume. It is calculated as follows:

$$
\text{Overhead rate} = \frac{\text{Overhead costs}}{\text{Operating volume}}
$$

For example, the Apex Company might measure volume by the number of direct labor hours. If overhead cost is $76,000 a month and volume is 9,500 direct labor hours, then an overhead rate based on direct labor hours would be:

$$
\frac{\$76,000}{9,500} = \$8 \text{ per direct labor hour}
$$

---

[2] Overhead rates are also known as *burden rates.* Because this latter term seems to imply that overhead costs are unproductive, it is gradually going out of fashion.

If this rate were used, then a job using 100 direct labor hours would be assigned $100 \times \$8 = \$800$ in factory overhead costs.

Measuring operating volume. If the overhead rate is to be usable, the volume denominator must be a measurable characteristic of individual jobs. For example, if we have a rate based on direct labor hours, we must know how many direct labor hours are used on each job if we are to use the rate to assign overhead costs to individual jobs.

The most obvious job characteristic is the number of units of product or service it yields—that is, the size of the job can be measured by its *output.* The output of the Apex Company's job 1234, for instance, was 2,000 units of Cannister No. 278. Unfortunately, we can't use output units to measure operating volume in a typical job order production operation. The reason is that the number of units of output doesn't necessarily measure the job's share of the factors that cause overhead costs to be incurred. We must remember that the overhead rate is supposed to indicate the amount of overhead that has been provided to support an average unit of operating volume. Different product units are likely to require different amounts of support. A product requiring ten minutes of machine time needs less support than one that stays on the same machine for five hours. The volume figures that overhead rates are based on should reflect these differences.

The result is that overhead rates are almost always based on some measure of production *input,* such as direct labor hours, direct labor cost, machine-hours, or pounds of direct materials processed. Other things being equal, the choice should fall on the measure that most closely corresponds to the factors requiring overhead support. If most of the overhead cost consists of equipment depreciation and maintenance, then a machine-hour rate probably best meets this test. Only if the preferred measure would be relatively expensive to collect should an inferior measure be used. In practice, overhead rates are often based on direct labor hours or direct labor cost simply because these figures are readily available.

Predetermined overhead rates. Overhead rates can be calculated each month, after all the overhead costs have been counted and operating volume has been measured. This is often inconvenient, however—the accountant can't assign overhead costs to jobs as the work is done, but must wait until all overhead costs are known.

After-the-fact overhead rates also produce inconsistent cost figures. Average overhead costs are likely to fluctuate from month to month and the amount of overhead charged to a particular job will depend on when the work is done. The salary of the manager of a soft drink bottling plant, for example, is likely to be just as high in the winter, when volume is low, as in the peak bottling season. Other things being equal, average cost will be higher when volume is low and lower when volume is high (see Exhibit 2–6).

One way to avoid these problems is to use a predetermined overhead rate, the *estimated* average overhead cost, and stick to it for a period of time, usually a year. When this is done, entries to the job cost sheets can be made just as soon as the work is finished. Furthermore, job cost will not be affected by

Exhibit 2–6 Relationship between volume and average cost

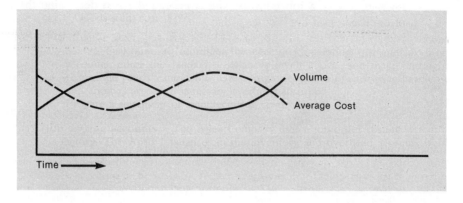

fluctuations in average overhead costs arising from causes entirely unrelated to the job order itself.

The use of predetermined rates introduces a complexity into the system, in that the total amount of factory overhead cost in any period is very unlikely to equal the total of the amounts assigned to individual job orders in that period (Overhead rate × Total activity on all jobs). The difference between these two totals is the amount of *over- or underabsorbed overhead.* We'll look at over- or underabsorbed overhead more closely in Chapter 3.

Cost center overhead rates.   Overhead costs are more important in some production centers than in others. Recognizing this, cost accountants often use a separate rate for each production center or for each of several groups of production centers. The purpose is to get a more accurate measure of the amount of costs attributable to individual jobs.

Each grouping of costs for which an overhead rate has been developed is known as an *overhead center* or *burden center.* Although each of Apex's two production departments has more than one cost center, differences in overhead relationships within departments are relatively small. For this reason the company treats each department as a single overhead center for product costing purposes. It uses a machine-hour rate for work done in the machine shop, and a labor-hour rate for assembly work. The calculation of these rates is summarized in Exhibit 2–7.

Exhibit 2–7
APEX COMPANY Departmental overhead rates

		Machine Shop	Assembly
1.	Normal volume	10,000 machine-hours	4,000 direct labor hours
2.	Estimated overhead cost at normal volume	$60,000	$12,000
3.	Overhead rate [(2)/(1)]	$6/machine-hour	$3/direct labor hour

Factory overhead component of job order cost. The final step in measuring the cost of a job is to use the overhead rates to determine the amount of overhead cost applicable to that job. To do this for job order 1234, Apex had to record the amount of work the job required in each overhead center. Combining these work figures (machine-hours and labor-hours) with the rates given in Exhibit 2–7, the company's accountants made the following calculations:

Date	Cost Center	Hours	Overhead Rate	Overhead Assigned
5/4	2421	9 machine-hours	$6	$ 54
5/6	2422	12 machine-hours	6	72
5/10	2431	14 direct labor hours	3	42
5/11	2431	4 direct labor hours	3	12
Total				$180

For example, the first line shows that job 1234 used nine machine-hours in cost center 2421. This is one of two cost centers in the machine shop. The overhead rate for the machine shop, from Exhibit 2–7, is $6 a machine-hour. This first set of operations therefore required the accountant to charge $9 \times \$6 = \$54$ of overhead costs against job 1234.

The completed cost sheet

Exhibit 2–8 shows the fully completed job cost sheet for job 1234. The cost figures for direct materials and direct labor are on the left-hand side of the form; the amounts of factory overhead costs assigned to this job are shown in the box at the lower right. Once all three sets of figures were entered, the accountants filled in the box at the upper right, summarizing all of the costs that had been assigned to the job. This shows that the total cost of job 1234 was $4,032. Since the output of this job was 2,000 finished castings (recorded on the right-hand side of the heading of the job cost sheet), the average cost was $4,032/2,000 = $2.016 a unit. The principal steps in the procedure leading to this result are summarized in Exhibit 2–9.

Overhead rates based on normal volume

The overhead rates we have used in this illustration are predetermined rates, developed before actual overhead costs and activity levels are known. In developing these rates, we had to choose between rates reflecting the conditions expected in the coming year or rates representing the estimated average overhead cost in a "normal" or typical period:

$$\text{Overhead rate} = \frac{\text{Estimated overhead costs in a normal month}}{\text{Total volume in a normal month}}$$

Our vote is for overhead rates based on normal cost experience, rather than expected cost experience in a particular year. As we said earlier, the overhead rate is supposed to indicate the average amount of overhead necessary

Exhibit 2–8 Job cost sheet

APEX COMPANY
JOB COST SHEET

Description: Canister No. 278   Job Order No.: 1234
Date Ordered: 5/1/x1   Date Completed: 5/12/x1
Quantity Ordered: 2,000   Quantity Completed: 2,000

	Materials Cost				Cost Summary	
Date	Item	Quantity	Price	Amount		
5/3	Shell No. 14	2,100	$1.32	$2,772	Materials	$3,538
5/4	Shell No. 14	(50)	1.32	(66)	Labor	314
5/5	Handle No. 142	2,000	0.41	820	Overhead	180
5/10	Paint	2	6.00	12	Total	$4,032
	Total			$3,538	Unit cost	$2.016

		Labor Cost			Overhead Cost		
Date	Cost Center	Hours	Rate	Amount	Hours*	Overhead Rate	Amount
5/4	2421	6	$14	$ 84	9 MH	$6	$ 54
5/6	2422	10	10	100	12 MH	6	72
5/10	2431	14	7	98	14 DLH	3	42
5/11	2431	4	8	32	4 DLH	3	12
	Total			$314			$180

* MH = machine-hours; DLH = direct labor hours.

Exhibit 2–9 Steps in costing a factory job order

1. Develop an overhead rate or rates.
2. Identify the job.
3. Set up a job cost sheet.
4. Identify the costs of direct labor and direct materials and enter them on the job cost sheet.
5. Multiply each overhead rate by the number of activity units used on the job—direct labor hours, pounds of materials, etc.—and enter the totals on the job cost sheet.
6. Add the costs on the job cost sheet.
7. If unit cost is desired, divide the job cost sheet total by the number of good units in the job lot.

to support a unit of operating volume. This average amount includes the cost of a normal amount of idleness. In designing its plants, management knows that the facilities will be partly idle some of the time because market conditions don't remain constant. Total designed capacity therefore is usually greater than the average expected rate of operation. This fact is built into the definition

normal volume

of *normal volume,* defined as the designed capacity of the facilities less an allowance for the average amount of idleness management expected when it set up the facilities in the first place. Fluctuations in the amount of idle time affect average cost, but these changes in average cost don't reflect changes in the amount of necessary support costs.

Cost classification problems

Some factory costs are classified as overhead even though they are or appear to be traceable to individual job orders:

1. Costs too small in the aggregate to justify the clerical effort that would be required to trace them to jobs.
2. Costs with purposes similar to other costs that are classified as overhead.
3. Costs which are identifiable only by means of two or more separate accruals (e.g., employee compensation).
4. Costs that hit unevenly from job to job but are a function of the process rather than of the individual job.

We have already discussed the first of these; the remainder of this chapter will be devoted to a discussion of costs in the other three categories.

Costs incurred for similar purposes

traceability

A cost may be traceable to a particular job while other costs incurred for the same object-of-expenditure and for similar purposes are not traceable to individual jobs. Classifying a cost of this sort as a direct cost would lead to double counting because the overhead rate already includes a provision for this cost.

Costs of this kind are most likely to be encountered when inputs other than direct labor and direct materials can be classified as direct costs of individual jobs. For example, some jobs require work to be performed on customers' premises. The costs of employees' travel to and from the customers' places of business can be classified as direct costs of specific jobs if the travel is always engaged in exclusively for a single customer. Suppose, however, an employee visits five or six customers during the course of a day. Both the travel time and the costs of transportation, food, and lodging are common costs of all the jobs they support. As common costs, they must be classified as overhead and assigned to jobs by some averaging procedure. If the averaging procedure is to include them in the overhead rate applicable to all jobs, then classifying single-customer travel time and cost as a direct cost would constitute double counting.

Two solutions are available. The simpler approach is to classify all of these costs as overhead, even though some of them are traceable to individual jobs. A more accurate but more expensive solution is to distribute the common costs only to the jobs they support. In our example, the regular overhead rate would include no provision for travel to customers' premises; travel costs would be traced to customers if possible or spread by formula among the specific jobs served by specific travel activities.

The key phrase in this discussion is "incurred for similar purposes." A company classifies factory labor time as direct labor if it is for the purpose of performing operations on specific jobs; the labor time of the same employees used for other purposes is classified as overhead. Similarly, travel costs for on-site work can be classified as direct costs while travel costs for other purposes are classified as overhead. The problem is to design record-keeping procedures that will clearly and effectively make these classifications.

Separate accruals: Employee benefits

The employees' wage rates always understate the amounts the company pays for their services. The reason is that the wage rates don't include the costs of fringe benefits, including paid vacations, paid holidays, company-sponsored recreation and education programs, medical insurance, unemployment benefits, and so forth. Exhibit 2–10 shows the contrast between the wage rate and the full cost of labor time.

Exhibit 2–10 Wage rate versus hourly labor cost

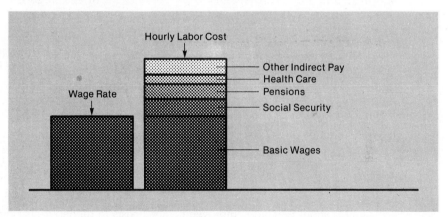

The costs of fringe benefits are often classified as overhead costs because this is a convenient way to handle them. In concept, however, the costs of these benefits are part of the hourly labor cost. If the labor time is traceable to a job, then the fringe benefits attributable to that time should be included in the rate used to record direct labor on the job cost sheet. This kind of comprehensive labor rate is referred to as a *charging rate*.

Classifying the costs of employee benefits as overhead costs may affect the amounts of cost assigned to individual jobs. For example, suppose the employee benefit ratio is 30 percent of the wage rate, and employees work 2,000 hours on two jobs, as follows:

	Direct Labor Hours	Direct Labor Wage Rate	Direct Labor Cost
Job 1	1,200	$10	$12,000
Job 2	800	8	6,400
Total	2,000		$18,400

If the costs of employee benefits are assigned to job orders as part of the direct labor charging rate, they will be distributed to the two jobs in the following amounts:

Job 1	$12,000 × 30% = $3,600
Job 2	6,400 × 30% = 1,920
Total	$5,520

If these costs are classified as overhead, however, and if the overhead rate is based on direct labor hours, the benefits cost component of the overhead rate will be $5,520/2,000 = $2.76 a direct labor hour. The distribution of benefits costs between the two jobs will be as follows:

Job 1	1,200 × $2.76 = $3,312
Job 2	800 × $2.76 = 2,208
Total	$5,520

The effect is to shift $288 from job 1, which used labor with a larger average wage rate, to job 2. Since the costs of employee benefits are related more closely to dollar wages than to labor hours, classifying them as overhead under these circumstances will understate the cost of job 1 by $288 and overstate the cost of job 2 by a similar amount.

This problem could be avoided, of course, by using direct labor cost as the denominator of the overhead rate fraction. If most of the other overhead costs are more closely related to variables such as the number of direct labor hours or the weight of the direct materials processed, however, one of those variables is likely to be used as the denominator of the overhead rate. If the average wage rate of the workers varies substantially from job to job, the accountants should include employee benefits costs in the labor charging rate.

Overtime premiums

Employees in certain categories who work nights, weekends and holidays, or more than a specified number of hours a week are paid wage premiums in addition to their regular wages. Overtime premium, for example, is the amount added to the basic hourly wage rate for hours worked in excess of some specified number each day or each week. If the basic or straight-time wage rate is $10 an hour and the overtime rate is $15, the overtime premium is $5 for each overtime hour.

Overtime premiums are assignable to individual jobs only if they were *caused* by work on *specific* jobs. This is true only if (1) the employees work full-time on a specific job, both on regular time and on overtime, and (2) employees can't be transferred freely to or from other duties. In all other situations overtime premiums are correctly regarded as overhead.

Many people don't agree that traceability should be defined this narrowly. Overtime, for example, is often added to meet a specific customer's rush order. Why shouldn't the overtime premiums be charged to this order? The answer is that overtime results from a *total* demand on the production facilities in excess of regular-time capacity. *All* production shares equally in the responsibility for the overtime. Whenever workers can be transferred from job to job, overtime premiums are just as much the result of sticking to the original production schedule on the first jobs scheduled as they are to speeding up the rush order.

Except in the rare cases in which overtime premiums are fully caused by specific jobs in the manner we described earlier, therefore, the best solution is to charge overtime *hours* to jobs or to indirect labor at the same charging rate used to charge them for regular time hours, at regular time ("straight-time") rates. The overtime premiums are classified as overhead costs and are provided for in the overhead rates.

Rejected units

The number of good units emerging from a job order is often smaller than the number placed in production. The question is whether any costs should be removed from the job cost sheet before the unit cost is calculated. If no costs are removed, then all costs incurred on the lost or defective units will be spread over the good units in the lot. Unit cost is calculated by dividing total job cost by the number of good units.

For example, the costs assigned to job 1234 amounted to $4,032. The production order called for production of 2,000 units, but suppose only 1,920 units passed inspection tests—the remainder were damaged in production and discarded. Unit cost is:

$$\frac{\text{Total job cost}}{\text{Total good production}} = \frac{\$4,032}{1,920 \text{ units}} = \$2.10 \text{ a unit}$$

If all 2,000 units had passed inspection, average cost would have been only $4,032/2,000 = $2.016, the figure we saw in Exhibit 2–8. Defective production therefore added $2.10 − $2.016 = $0.084 to the unit cost of this job.

This treatment is based on either of two assumptions: (1) the reject percentage is small; or (2) the rejection rate depends on the characteristics of individual jobs rather than on the characteristics of the production process itself. If the rejection rate is process related, however, then the rejection rate on any particular job will depend on how good the process happens to be when that particular job is processed. In other words, the process, not the job, is the cause of the defects.

In such cases, the cost of the job should only include the cost of a normal number of lost units. To achieve that, the accountants should (1) include in the overhead rate a provision for the costs of a normal percentage of rejects, and (2) remove the costs actually incurred on defective units from the cost sheet and reclassify them as overhead. The amount removed would usually be the average materials cost plus an average allowance for labor.

Rework labor

Defective units are not always destroyed or sold as second-quality items. The defects are often worth correcting. The labor costs of these corrective efforts are referred to as *rework labor.*

The distinction we made for the rejection rate applies to rework labor as well. Rework labor time should be classified as direct labor if it is job related and as overhead if it is process related. In practice, rework labor is generally assumed to be process related. Amounts that are readily measurable are generally classified as overhead.

Scrap recovery

Units or materials that are disposed of as scrap often have market values. The market value of scrap is almost never big enough to justify the effort to trace it to individual jobs, however. Instead, the net market value of scrap recovered is typically credited to overhead. The result is to overstate the cost of direct materials and understate average overhead, but the inaccuracy in product cost is likely to be immaterial.

Summary

To provide data that management will find helpful in planning and controlling the organization's operations, the accountant classifies operating costs on three separate bases: by organization segment or cost center, by object of expenditure, and by activity.

In assigning costs to individual activities, the accountant's basic objective is to identify the costs caused by those activities. Other things being equal, a cost that is traceable to an activity is generally assumed to be caused by that activity. In job order costing, for example, the accountant identifies as direct labor and direct materials all labor and materials costs that can be traced economically to individual jobs.

The traceability test must be applied carefully. Overtime premiums, for example, are generally attributable to the total volume of operations, not to the jobs that happen to be produced in the overtime hours. Rework labor, too, may be the result of characteristics of the process rather than the result of the characteristics of the individual job orders that have required the rework effort.

Nontraceable (overhead) costs are assigned to jobs by multiplying cost averages, known as overhead rates, by some measure of the size of the job, such as the number of direct labors hours used on the job. The object is to assign to each job the amount of overhead cost that was provided to support the amount of activity the job represented. For this purpose, most overhead rates are based on estimates made at the beginning of the year, and a separate overhead rate is used for each production cost center or group of related production centers.

Independent study problems (solutions in Appendix B)

1. **Cost classification systems.** The Montague Company was originally established to distribute a new type of waterproof, heat-resistant glue to shoe manufacturers. The glue was produced under contract by a large chemical company, and product sales were made by a field sales force of four sales representatives who contacted shoe manufacturers directly. These representatives were all chemical engineers and had the responsibility of training their customers' personnel in the proper method of applying the glue. The revenues and expenses of the company have been recorded in a fairly simple set of accounts:

Sales	Office Supplies
Sales Returns and Allowances	Rent
Cost of Goods Sold	Printing and Postage
Sales Salaries	Telephone and Telegraph
Sales Commissions	Retirement Expense
Travel Expenses	Insurance Expense
Office Salaries	Miscellaneous Expenses

The president of the company has just decided to expand operations in two ways: first by taking on the distribution of a line of shoe findings (miscellaneous small items used in shoe manufacture), and second by marketing the company's glue to furniture manufacturers. Two new representatives are to be added to the shoe trade sales force. The furniture trade sales force will consist initially of three new salespeople to be hired for that purpose. The president, who heretofore has also acted as sales manager and controller, has decided to promote the company's senior sales representative to the position of sales manager. The present office manager will become controller and office manager, with a new assistant to be hired.

Required:

What changes, if any, should the company make in its cost classification system? Why would these changes be desirable?

2. **Job cost and overhead variance.** Chailly, Inc., uses a job order costing system in its factory with a predetermined overhead rate based on direct labor hours at normal volume. Job No. 423 was started on March 3 and was finished on March 28. You are given the following additional information:

	Job No. 423	All Jobs (in March)	Annual Budget at Normal Volume
Direct labor hours	60	10,000	100,000
Direct labor cost	$400	$ 60,000	$ 350,000
Direct materials cost	800	150,000	1,300,000
Budgeted factory overhead cost			900,000

Required:

a. Calculate the overhead rate the company used in March.
b. Calculate the cost of job No. 423.

3. **Classifying labor costs.** J. Jones worked 45 hours last week, 9 hours a day for five days. His wage rate was $8 an hour, with time-and-a-half for overtime hours in excess of 40 hours a week. Mr. Jones spent all of his time last week

on job M227, except for three hours on Wednesday morning on equipment maintenance and the final hour on Friday on job M246.

Mr. Jones is one of several production workers who could have worked on job M227. Some of these earned overtime last week; others did not. A total of 50 overtime hours were recorded last week. Management authorized the overtime to avoid the necessity of hiring and training another worker to handle a seasonal peak load in the factory.

Required:

How much of Mr. Jones's wages last week should have been assigned to job M227 as part of the normal product costing routine?

Exercises and problems

4. **Job costs.** A factory uses a job order costing system. A careless bookkeeper has lost the file of job order cost sheets covering the work done last week, but the underlying documents are still available. You have the following data:

   1. The factory had no work in process at the beginning of the week.
   2. A predetermined overhead rate was used, based on direct labor hours at a volume of 1,500 direct labor hours a month. At this volume overhead costs were expected to total $7,500 a month.
   3. Requisitions and time tickets showed the following usage of direct labor and direct materials last week:

Job Order	Direct Materials	Direct Labor Hours
498	$1,500	116
506	960	16
507	415	18
508	345	42
509	652	24
511	308	10
512	835	30
Total	$5,015	256

   4. The labor rate for direct labor was $8 an hour.
   5. Indirect labor last week cost $740; other overhead costs amounted to $868.
   6. Work on jobs 498, 506, and 509 was completed during the week; the completed units were transferred to the finished goods inventory.

   Required:
   a. Calculate the overhead rate the factory used in product costing last week.
   b. Prepare a summary table that will show the amount of each cost element and of all costs in total assigned to each job last week.
   c. Calculate the cost of the work in process at the end of last week.

5. **Labor charging rate.** The work week of employees in the foundry department of the ABC Company ranges between 42 and 50 hours, with all hours in excess of 40 per week being paid at a rate of one and one half times the basic hourly wage rate of $7.20 an hour. On the average, each worker works 45 hours a week.

   Required:
   a. What is the foundry labor cost per hour that should be included in product unit cost for public financial reporting? How much of this should be shown as direct labor? Explain your answer.

b. Management is trying to decide whether certain products are profitable enough to continue manufacturing. From this point of view, what is the foundry labor cost of a product that requires ten hours of foundry labor? Explain.

6. **Overtime premiums; nonmanufacturing.**   The firm of Rundell Associates does a number of kinds of drafting, lettering, and commercial artwork for outside clients. A system of requisitions and time sheets is used to accumulate the costs of materials and personal services consumed on individual job orders.

Although a few jobs are accepted on a flat-fee basis, most jobs are priced to customers on a cost-plus-time basis. On these jobs, the customer's bill includes four elements:

Cost of materials used.

Personal service fees (at predetermined hourly rates, including markup over hourly cost).

Overtime premiums paid for work on specific jobs.

Miscellaneous out-of-pocket costs incurred on specific jobs.

Materials costs on some jobs are substantial, and occasionally a customer will complain of being charged for too many spoiled materials. In general, however, materials costs amount to less than 10 percent of the gross amount of the customer invoice.

Customers complain frequently about the size of the personal service fee, but this appears to be part of a bargaining strategy to impress on Rundell Associates the need to watch costs carefully on subsequent orders. Complaints about the overtime premiums are considerably stronger and often lead to downward revision of the invoices. During recent months these downward revisions have been large enough to cut the firm's net profit in half and the managing partners are worried.

Required:

Indicate any changes that you would make in the company's cost accounting and billing procedures, giving reasons for your changes. If you wish to leave the present system unchanged, indicate briefly why you think no improvement is called for.

7. **Terminology: Direct versus indirect cost.**   Harrow, Inc., has a single factory, with 12 departments, each one a cost center. One of these is the factory manager's office; all others perform work on specific job orders.

Production is on a job order basis. The factory manufactures 20 regular catalog products and a large number of specialty items to meet customers' individual needs. The regular products fall into three different product lines; specialty items are regarded as a separate product line. About 30 percent of the direct labor costs are expended on the specialty line, which brings in about 40 percent of the total revenue.

Customers are solicited and served through six branch offices, with between 5 and 12 sales representatives operating out of each branch. Each sales representative handles all of the company's products. Each branch has a full-time manager who calls on a few major customers and supervises the sales representatives in that branch. The branch managers all report to the marketing vice president.

Required:

Indicate whether each of the following costs is a direct cost of a job order, a direct cost of a product line, a direct cost of a division (marketing or manufacturing), or a direct cost of a first-level cost center (factory production department or sales branch). The cost may be direct in all, some, or none of these categories:

a. Lubricating oil for factory machinery.
b. Materials used on a specific job order.
c. The factory manager's salary.
d. The president's secretary's salary.

    e. Gasoline for sales representatives' cars.
    f. Sales commissions (3 percent of net sales).
    g. Overtime premium for worker in factory production department.
    h. Rent on San Francisco branch office.
    i. Salary of factory department head.
    j. National advertising for product X.

8. **Unit cost; Spoilage.** Job order X150 was placed in production in December 19x1. During December, materials costing $800 were issued for use on this job, and 60 direct labor hours were expended at an average rate of $8.80 an hour. The overhead rate in 19x1 was $1 a direct labor *dollar.*

The company's new fiscal year began on January 1, 19x2. Job order X150 was finished in January with the additional expenditure of 90 direct labor hours at an average wage of $9.20 an hour, and additional direct materials amounting to $250 were issued for use in this job. The overhead rate in 19x2 was set at $9 a direct labor *hour.*

The job consisted of 500 product units, but 20 of these units were spoiled at the very end of processing and were discarded as trash. The remaining 480 units were placed in the finished goods stockroom on Janurary 28, 19x2. The next day 100 of these units were sold and shipped to customers.

Required:

    a. List the alternative ways of reflecting spoilage costs in the accounts and identify the one you prefer, giving the reasons for your preference.
    b. Calculate the cost of job X150, element by element and in total. Your calculation should be consistent with the method of accounting for spoilage you selected in answer to *a.*

9. **Rework labor.** Carson, Inc. manufactures a number of products. Past records indicate that about 5 percent of the units will be defective and will have to be reworked. This is true of all products. Rework labor time averages 8 percent of the amount of productive direct labor (productive time excludes rework time).

Job No. 563 consisted of 200 sole plates, of which 20 were defective and had to be reworked. Productive direct labor on this job amounted to $500, and rework labor to correct the defects cost an additional $65.

Required:

Would you charge the cost of rework labor cost to the job order cost sheet in this case? If not, how would you record it? Give your reasons.

10. **Overhead rate: Estimated versus normal volume.** The Bolt Company's factory has had a great deal of idle capacity for the past year and this situation seems likely to persist this year. Management has asked you for an accurate estimate of the cost of job No. 222, which has just been completed. A customer has offered to place an order for delivery of a batch of this product each month for the next two years; management would like to quote a price that would cover the full cost of this product and leave a margin for profit. You have the following data:

1. Estimated factory overhead cost at normal volume (10,000 machine-hours a month), $30,000.
2. Estimated factory overhead cost at estimated actual volume for this year (8,000 machine-hours a month), $28,000.
3. Job No. 222 required the use of 1,000 machine-hours.

Required:

    a. Calculate the amount of overhead the company would charge to job No. 222 if it used a predetermined overhead rate based on normal volume.

  b. Calculate the amount of overhead the company would charge to job No. 222 if it used a predetermined overhead rate based on estimated volume for the current year.

  c. Which of these two cost figures would you regard as a more accurate response to management's request? State the reasons for your preference.

11. **Direct versus indirect costs; double counting.**   Management wants product cost to be an accurate estimate of the full cost of manufacturing each product, neither undercounting nor overcounting any one cost element. Each of the following paragraphs describes a cost that is clearly traceable to a specific job order.

  a. Company A classifies the costs of general purpose tooling as factory overhead. The company has just bought special tooling at a cost of $8,700 for use solely on job T791.

  b. The costs of the labor time spent moving materials, parts, and partly finished work from work station to work station in company B's factory are classified as overhead costs because the amount of time spent handling these materials for individual jobs is too difficult to identify. An employee with a labor rate of $6 an hour worked full time for four weeks (160 hours) moving materials and partly finished work in connection with job X769.

  c. Factory employees in company C do little traveling. Their traveling is confined to occasional visits to customers' premises to get a better understanding of how certain products are used, visits to equipment manufacturers for instruction in the use of equipment, and occasional installation work on customers' premises. Time spent on travel and all costs incurred by employees for transportation, food, and lodging are classified as overhead. Company C is now working on an unusual special order, doing most of the work on the customer's premises. Paid travel time and the costs of employees' transportation, food, and lodging are substantial, amounting to about 40 percent of the cost of the time spent working on the job.

Required:

In each case you are to decide (1) whether to classify the cost as a direct cost of the job or as overhead cost, and (2) whether any compensating changes should be made in the overhead rates or in the classification of other costs. You should also explain why your recommended treatment meets management's costing specifications.

12. **Departmental overhead rates.**   The Robertson Company has been using a single plantwide overhead rate in its factory. The rate has been a predetermined rate per direct labor hour, based on production volume in a normal year.

  The company's controller has proposed switching to departmental overhead rates. These rates, too, would be predetermined rates per direct labor hour, based on production volume in a normal year. To help you evaluate this proposal, you have collected the following information:

  1. The factory manufactures only three products (A, B, C) and the factory is organized into three departments which perform all the production operations on these three products.

  2. Direct labor hours required for each unit of product are:

Product	X	Y	Z	Total
A	2	1	1	4
B	0	2	3	5
C	2	3	2	7

3. Products produced and sold in a normal year: A, 40,000 units; B, 40,000 units; and C, 10,000 units.
4. Overhead costs incurred in a normal year: department X, $440,000; department Y, $330,000; and department Z, $90,000.
5. Production last year: A, 20,000 units; B, 50,000 units; and C, 10,000 units.

Required:

a. Calculate the effects of switching from a plantwide rate to departmental overhead rates on the unit cost of each product.
b. State the arguments for and against making this change.

13. **Cost classification systems.** The Ace Maintenance Company provides routine equipment maintenance service and performs equipment repairs for a large number of industrial users in the New York metropolitan area. The company will service or repair almost any factory equipment and has built a reputation for prompt, efficient service.

Ace Maintenance was founded 10 years ago by Paul Mace, a highly gifted salesman and administrator. Mr. Mace is still president of the company, doing most of the direct selling himself. His vice president, Don Wynant, is responsible for hiring all service personnel and for the day-to-day operation of the service end of the business.

The company's operating cost accounts for a typical month show the following balances:

	Executive Office	Accounting	Operations
Salaries and wages	$10,000	$3,000	$26,000
Overtime premiums	—	—	1,100
Materials and supplies	500	450	1,000
Repair parts	—	—	14,000
Utilities	1,200	—	—
Payroll taxes	300	120	1,200
Pension plan	700	150	1,300
Travel	100	—	2,100
Advertising	200	—	—
Insurance	800	—	—
Taxes...................	900	—	—
Rent	2,500	—	—
Miscellaneous	400	30	600
Total	$17,600	$3,750	$47,300

A large industrial service company has offered to buy Mr. Mace's interest in the business. Mr. Mace would retire and his place would be taken by a president and a salaried sales manager.

Required:

a. The company's chart of accounts has three departmental codes (one each for the executive office, accounting, and operations) and the 13 object-of-expenditure classifications listed in the table above. In what ways, if any, will the chart of accounts have to be changed to meet the needs of the new owners and the new manager? Give reasons for your suggestions.
b. What problems would you be likely to encounter in trying to carry out your suggestions?

14. **Cost classification.**   The Harrell School is a nonprofit educational institution. It has both day students and boarding students enrolled in a college preparatory high school program.

The school also conducts an evening program for older children and young adults who have dropped out of high school but are now working to earn their high school diplomas on a part-time basis.

The school also sponsors various noncredit adult education courses in a variety of subjects ranging from foreign languages to home repair techniques.

Athletic fields, a dormitory, and a classroom and office building are all located on the school's campus, far from the downtown area of a medium-sized city. The dormitory contains kitchen and dining facilities, as well as rooms for the boarding students. Boarding students take all of their meals in the dining room, seven days a week; day students may either bring their lunch or eat in the dining room with the boarding students upon payment of a weekly fee. No dining service is provided to the students and faculty of the evening programs.

The school's administrative staff consists of a headmaster (who also teaches one course in the day program), an admissions director, a director of the evening programs, a guidance counselor, an administrative assistant, a bookkeeper, and two secretaries.

The dormitory staff consists of a director, a dietitian, a head cook, two "residents," and a number of people who do the cooking, serving, and cleaning. Three people take care of the buildings and grounds on a full-time basis, bringing in part-time help as needed for special or evening work.

The school has a full-time faculty for the day program. The evening programs are staffed on a part-time basis, with fees negotiated separately for each course. The buildings and grounds staff are paid extra for evening work.

A small endowment fund is invested in long-term securities. The income from these investments supplements the revenues from tuition and fees and the annual gifts from foundations, alumni, and friends of the school.

Textbooks are provided free to students in the evening high school program. Students in the day program and in the adult education courses buy their books from the school. All book sales are handled by the administrative assistant.

Required:

a. Draw an organization chart for the Harrell School.
b. Outline a cost classification system for this school, with organizational, object-of-expenditure, and activity dimensions to the extent you deem appropriate. You need not prepare a full list of accounts, but you should indicate how extensive each of the classifications should be. (You may assume that an adequate revenue classification scheme can be developed to go with your cost classifications.)
c. What problems, if any, would you expect to encounter in classifying costs in the ways you suggest?

15. **Overhead rate, nonmanufacturing firm.**   Franklin Associates is a management consulting firm. Each consulting engagement is covered by a contract. The contract price is negotiated in advance, sometimes as a fixed fee, sometimes as professional staff time plus traceable expenses. The billing rates for the various members of the professional staff are always fixed in advance and are expected, in the aggregate, to cover nontraceable (indirect) costs and provide a margin of profit.

The company uses a job costing system to measure the costs of each contract. All costs not directly traceable to specific contracts are recorded as indirect costs; a single predetermined overhead rate is used to assign indirect costs to contracts, based on the number of *professional staff hours.*

Budgeted time and costs for the year and actual time and costs for February were as follows:

	Annual Budget		February	
	Hours	Cost	Hours	Cost
Direct costs:				
Professional staff	25,000	$300,000	1800	$25,000
Secretarial staff	6,000	36,000	550	3,300
Art work and printing		7,000		800
Copying		2,000		200
Travel		35,000		2,700
Total		380,000		32,000
Indirect costs:				
Professional staff	5,000	60,000	600	7,400
Secretarial staff	12,000	72,000	800	3,300
Art work and printing		3,000		300
Copying		1,000		100
Travel		8,000		400
Other		56,000		4,700
Total		200,000		16,200

Required:

a. Prepare a predetermined hourly rate for indirect costs.
b. The following direct cost data were recorded during February for one of the company's contracts. How much cost was assigned to this contract during February?

Professional staff (70 hours)	$910
Secretarial staff (10 hours)	65
Art work and printing	60
Copying	10
Travel	280

c. How much indirect cost was assigned to all contracts, in total, in February?
d. An observer has objected that the company's practice of classifying some secretarial costs as direct costs and some as indirect costs could lead to double counting on some contracts. Under what circumstances would the company's practice lead to double counting? What assumption as to the nature of secretarial work justifies the company's practice?
e. Would this contract have been more profitable or less profitable if the overhead rate had been based on the company's actual cost experience in February?

16. **Interpreting job cost data.** Jerry Blaine is a contractor specializing in small house remodeling jobs. Most of his employees are free-lance specialists who work for other contractors as well, so that the size of his payroll rises and falls with fluctuations in the amount of work to be done. Higher wage rates are paid to the more highly skilled workers, but the average wage rate in the construction industry in Mr. Blaine's area is about $10 an hour.

Mr. Blaine recently installed a job order costing system and now has the following labor cost data:

Job Number	Estimated Labor Hours	Estimated Labor Cost	Actual Labor Hours	Actual Labor Cost
T12	700	$7,000	680	$ 7,500
T15	300	3,000	330	3,600
T16	800	8,000	750	8,200
T18	100	1,000	90	1,000
T19	900	9,000	980	11,700
T20	400	4,000	500	5,600
T21	500	5,000	450	4,700

During the period covered by these figures, Mr. Blaine submitted bids on 18 jobs. Other contractors underbid him on 11 of these; he was the low bidder on the 7 jobs shown above. Mr. Blaine's profit margin was considerably lower than that of most of his competitors during this period.

Required:

a. What advice can you give Mr. Blaine on the basis of these figures? Do they help explain his low profit margin? Is there anything he can do about it?
b. What further data would you probably find in the job cost sheets or supporting documents that would throw further light on these questions?
c. Would charging overhead costs to individual job orders provide Mr. Blaine with useful information?

17. **Job cost sheet: Identifying direct costs.**   The Gentry Company uses job order costing in its factory, with departmental predetermined overhead rates based on direct labor hours at normal volume. The overhead rates for the factory's two production departments were based on the following estimates of average monthly overhead costs at normal volume:

	Department A	Department B
Supervision	$ 5,000	$ 4,500
Rework labor	4,000	1,500
Other indirect labor	8,000	10,000
Overtime premium	500	400
Supplies	1,000	2,000
Scrap recovery	—	(900)
Other	1,500	7,500
Total overhead cost	20,000	$25,000
Normal volume (direct labor hours)	10,000	5,000

One of the jobs in the factory during June was job No. 422, calling for the manufacture of 100 Flister Blidgets. The following partial list of the factory's transactions during the month of June includes all of the transactions that were related directly to job No. 422 and some transactions that were not related directly to that job. (The number at the left of each item is the day of the month on which the transaction was recorded.)

1 The storeroom issued 200 pounds of material X at 75 cents a pound to department A for use on job No. 422.
4 The storeroom issued 50 pounds of material Z at $3.20 a pound to department A for use on job No. 422.
5 The labor expended on job No. 422 during the week amounted to 76 hours in department A at $8 an hour; 6 of these hours were classified as overtime. Employees earn 150 percent of their straight-time wage rates for each overtime hour.

8 The storeroom issued lubricants and cleaning compounds to department A, $100.
11 Department A returned 10 pounds of material Z to the storeroom because the quality was not up to the specifications required by job No. 422.
11 The storeroom issued 25 pounds of material Z at $3.30 a pound to department A for use on job No. 422.
12 The labor expended on job No. 422 during the week amounted to 33 hours in department A at $8 an hour and 10 hours in department B at $7 an hour. None of the hours expended on job No. 422 was classified as overtime, but the employee in department B who worked on job No. 422 recorded a total of 50 hours during the week, including 10 hours classified as overtime.
15 Department B discovered defects in five Flister Blidgets, which were then sent back to department A for reworking.
16 The storeroom issued 20 pounds of material P to department B at $2 a pound for use on job No. 422.
17 Department B damaged five pounds of material P originally issued for job No. 422, and transferred them to the scrap bin.
19 The labor expended on job No. 422 during the week amounted to 3 hours in department A (reworking defective units) at $8 an hour, and 30 hours in department B at $7 an hour. No overtime hours were recorded in either department this week.
19 Department B finished job No. 422 and transferred 100 finished Flister Blidgets to the shipping department.
30 A laborer collected the month's scrap from department B, 1,000 pounds with a scrap value of 40 cents a pound. The total weight of the materials and semifinished products processed by department B in June amounted to 50,000 pounds.

Required:

a. Prepare a list of the costs that should be assigned to job No. 422. Provide a brief explanation of your treatment of each item.
b. Calculate the unit costs of materials, labor, and overhead for job No. 422. How are these unit cost figures likely to be used?

Case 2–1. Tipografia Stanca, S.p.A.*

Mr. Giulio Cattani, founder and president of Tipografia Stanca, S.p.A., was worried. The company was doing more business than ever before—sales were at an annual rate of about $625,000 a year—but net income had decreased slightly during recent months and the ratio of income to sales had dropped sharply. Mr. Cattani wondered what had gone wrong and what he could do about it. He called in his chief (and only) accountant, Mr. Gaetano Pareto, and asked him to find out what was happening.

Tipografia Stanca was an Italian corporation located in Milan and doing a general printing business on a customer order basis. Mr. Cattani set the price to be charged for each job. When possible, he waited until the work was done and then quoted a price equal to 140 percent of the cost of the paper stock used, plus $12.50 for each labor hour. Straight-time wage rates in the past, adjusted for recent wage rate increases, had averaged about $4 an hour, and this formula seemed to provide an adequate margin to cover overhead costs and provide a good profit.

Most of Tipografia Stanca's work was done on the basis of predetermined contract prices. In bidding on these jobs, Mr. Cattani applied his standard pricing formula to

* Copyright 1968 by l'Institut pour l'Etude des Méthodes de Direction de l'Entreprise (IMEDE), Lausanne, Switzerland, revised and updated in 1976. Published by permission. The figures have been restated in dollars for convenience.

his own estimates of the amount of labor and paper stock the job would require. He prided himself on his ability to make these estimates, but he sometimes quoted a price that was higher or lower than the formula price, depending on his judgment of the market situation.

Stanca's production procedures were fairly simple. When a customer's order was received, it was assigned a production order number and a production order was issued. The material to be printed, known as the customer's copy, was given to a copy editor who indicated on the copy the sizes and styles of type that should be used. The editor sometimes made changes in the copy, usually after telephoning the customer to discuss the changes.

Once the customer's material had been copy-edited, it was sent to the composing room, where it was set in type. A proof copy was printed by hand and returned to the copy editor, who checked the printed copy against the original. Any errors in the proof were indicated in the margin and the marked proof was sent to the customer for approval. At this point the customer might decide to make changes in the copy, and these changes, as well as corrections of typesetting errors, were made as soon as the corrected proof was returned to the composing room.

In some cases a second proof was sent to the customer for his approval, but at Tipografia Stanca most orders were sent to the pressroom as soon as the customer's corrections had been made and the second proof had been approved by the copy editor.

At this point, the order was ready for production on one of the presses in the pressroom. Printing instructions were contained in the production order which specified the particular press to be used; the number of copies to be printed; the color, size, style, weight, and finish of the stock or paper to be used; and similar details. Copies were then printed, bound, and packaged for delivery to the customer.

An order could take as little as one day in the copy-editing and composing-room stages or as long as several weeks. Printing, binding, and packaging seldom took more than two days except on very large production runs of multipage booklets.

For many years the shop had had enough work to keep it busy steadily throughout the year, without serious seasonal slack. As a result, Tipografia Stanca's before-tax profit had fluctuated between 13 and 15 percent of net sales. The interim profit report for the first half of 1968 therefore came as a great shock to Mr. Cattani. Although volume was slightly greater than in the first half of 1967, profit was down to 8.8 percent of sales, an all-time low. The comparison, with all figures expressed as percentages of net sales, was as follows:

	1968	1967
Net sales	100.0%	100.0%
Production costs	77.6	72.3
Selling and administrative costs	13.6	13.9
Profit	8.8	13.8

Mr. Pareto knew that the company's problem must be either low prices or excessive costs. Unfortunately, the cost data already available told him little about the cost-price relationship for individual jobs. Tipografia Stanca's operating costs were classified routinely into 20 categories, such as salaries, pressroom wages, production materials, depreciation, and so forth. Individual job cost sheets were not used and the cost of goods in process was estimated only once a year, at the end of the fiscal year.

Detailed data were available on only two kinds of items: paper stock issued and labor time. When stock was issued, a requisition form was filled out, showing the kind of stock issued, the quantity, the unit cost, and the production order number. Similar details were reported when unused stock was returned to the stockroom.

As for labor, each employee directly engaged in working on production orders filled in a time sheet each day, on which he recorded the time he started on a given task, the time he finished it or moved on to other work, and (in the case of time spent directly on a specific production order) the order number. His department number and pay grade were recorded on the time sheet by the payroll clerk.

Mr. Pareto's first step was to establish some overall cost relationships. Employees, for example, fell into three different pay grades, with the following regular hourly wage rates:

Grade	Rate
1	$6
2	4
3	3

These rates applied to a regular work week of 44 hours a week. For work in excess of this number of hours, employees were paid an overtime premium of 50 percent of their hourly wage. Overtime premiums were negligible when the work load was light, but in a normal year they averaged about 5 percent of the total amount of hourly wages computed at the regular hourly wage rate. In a normal year this was approximately 20 cents a direct labor hour.

In addition to their wages, the employees also received various kinds of benefits, including vacation pay, health insurance, and old-age pensions. The cost of these benefits to Tipografia Stanca amounted to about 70 percent of direct labor cost, measured at regular straight-time hourly rates. The overtime premiums didn't affect the amount of fringe benefits paid or accrued.

Mr. Pareto estimated that all other shop overhead costs—that is, all copy department, composing room and pressroom costs other than direct materials, direct labor, overtime premiums, and employee benefits on direct labor payrolls—would average $2 a direct labor hour in a normal year.

Table 1 Partial list of materials requisitions (for the week of October 5–9)

Req. No.	Job No.	Amount*
4058	A-467	$150
R162	A-469	(10)
4059	A-467	30
4060	A-442	3
R163	A-455	(5)
R164	A-472	(4)
4060	A-467	18
R165	A-465	(6)
4062	A-467	48
4063	A-471	160
4064	A-473	132
4065	A-458	11
R166	A-467	(16)
4066	A-481	88

* Amounts in parentheses are returned materials.

Armed with these estimates of general relationships, Mr. Pareto then proceeded to determine the costs of several recent production orders. One of these was order A–467. This was received for copy editing on Monday, October 5 and delivered to the customer on Friday, October 9. Mr. Cattani had quoted a price of $900 on this job in advance, on the basis of an estimate of $240 for paper stock costs and 45 direct labor hours. All requisitions and time records relating to order A–467 are included in the lists in Tables 1 and 2. (To save space, some of the details shown on the requisitions and time tickets have been omitted from these tables.)

Table 2 Partial summary of labor time sheets (for the week of October 5–9)

Employee No.	Pay Grade	Dept.	Job No.*	Hours
14	2	Copy	A-463	6.6
14	2	Copy	A-467	1.4
15	1	Copy	A-467	3.3
15	1	Copy	—	2.7
15	1	Copy	A-467	8.8
18	3	Press	A-467	4.0
18	3	Press	A-472	4.6
22	1	Composing	A-455	3.8
22	1	Composing	A-467	8.4†
22	1	Composing	—	1.5
23	2	Press	A-458	3.4
23	2	Press	A-467	4.7
23	2	Press	—	1.1
23	2	Press	A-459	2.5†
24	2	Copy	A-470	7.4
28	1	Press	A-467	7.0
28	1	Press	A-458	1.0
31	3	Press	—	8.0
33	1	Composing	A-471	7.6
33	1	Composing	A-472	4.2
40	2	Press	A-469	3.6
40	2	Press	A-467	4.9
40	2	Press	—	0.2
43	1	Press	A-467	3.5
43	1	Press	A-481	5.8

* A dash indicates time spent on general work in the department and not on any one job.

† Employee No. 22 worked six hours of overtime during the week, none of them on job A-467, while employee No. 23 worked eight hours of overtime, including four hours spent on job A-467.

a. Develop a costing rate or rates for labor costs, to be used to charge a job cost sheet or factory overhead account for an hour of labor time. You must decide whether to use a single rate for all pay grades or a separate rate for each. You must also decide whether to include various kinds of fringe benefit costs in the labor costing rates or to regard these as overhead. Also develop an overhead rate for use in charging shop overhead costs to individual job orders.

b. Prepare a job order cost sheet for production order A–467, and enter the costs that would be assigned to this order, using the costing rates you developed in the answer to (*a*) above.

c. What conclusions might Mr. Pareto have reached on the basis of his analysis of this order? What suggestions would you make to Mr. Cattani?

b. What could be the advantages of developing product unit costs routinely for every job? Do you think that these advantages would be great enough to persuade Mr. Cattani to hire an additional clerk for this purpose at an annual cost of about $10,000?

3 Job cost flows and financial statements

Job order costing is used in the first instance to develop data management can use in evaluating the profitability of individual products and product lines and in estimating product costs in the future. The same data can be used to distinguish the costs of the company's inventories, reported on the company's balance sheets (asset costs), from the costs that will be deducted from revenues on the income statement for the current period (expenses).

To understand how job cost data can serve this second purpose and to see how the use of predetermined overhead rates affects this process, we need to look at the so-called *cost accounting cycle,* tracing the flow of factory costs through a set of ledger accounts. For this purpose we have divided the cycle into four stages:

1. Purchase and use of materials.
2. Use of labor services.
3. Overhead cost absorption.
4. Job completions and product sales.

To make the picture as clear as possible, we shall study the transactions of a simple factory which uses only a single, factory-wide overhead rate.

Purchase and use of materials

Materials costs enter the factory accounts with the purchase of materials. For example, the company bought materials during May at a cost of $30,000 and placed them in the factory storeroom. Payment for these materials was to be made within 30 days. In summary form, the entry to record these purchases was:

(1)

Materials Inventory	30,000	
Accounts Payable		30,000

That is, the purchases increased both the assets and the liabilities by $30,000.

The Materials Inventory account is a *control account.* This means that the balance in this account is supposed to equal the sum of the balances in a set

subsidiary ledger

of subsidiary accounts, one for each kind of materials in the inventory. The file of subsidiary accounts is known as a *subsidiary ledger*. For each purchase, an entry is made in one or more subsidiary accounts. A summary entry in the control account is made periodically to record the total of the amounts entered in the subsidiary ledger during the period. Entry (1) is one of these summary entries.

The storeroom clerk issued materials costing $22,675 to factory departments during the month. Of this sum, $22,145 represented the cost of materials issued specifically for individual jobs, to be charged as direct material on those jobs. The remaining $530 was the cost of supplies for general use in the factory, not easily traceable to any specific job. In other words, it was a factory overhead cost. The following entry summarizes these transactions:

(2)

Work-in-Process Inventory	22,145	
Indirect Materials	530	
Materials Inventory		22,675

This entry records the transfer of materials cost from one asset category (Materials Inventory) to another (Work-in-Process Inventory) and to an overhead cost category (Indirect Materials). These cost flows are diagrammed in Exhibit 3–1.

Exhibit 3–1 Flow of materials costs

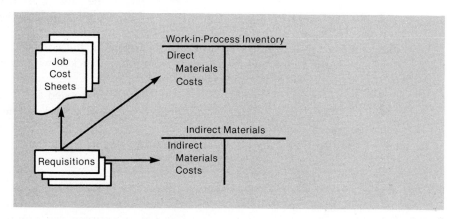

The file of job cost sheets is a type of subsidiary ledger, Work-in-Process Inventory being the control account.

In practice, each cost center has its own object-of-expenditure indirect materials cost accounts. To keep the illustration simple, we are representing these by a single, factorywide account.

Labor costs

Payroll accounting has two sides: the first dealing with the *liability-payment* aspects of the transactions and the second having to do with the identification of the cost with various segments of activity, usually referred to as the *distribution* of labor cost.

Payroll accrual. The liability-payment aspects of payroll accounting are not part of cost accounting, and only the briefest summary is necessary here. Wage and salary liabilities are accrued on the basis of information from two sources: personnel records and attendance or production records. For each employee, a master personnel record is maintained, showing his or her employment history with the company, job classification, title, current rate of pay, and authorized deductions for hospitalization insurance, pension plans, savings plans, union dues, and so forth.

The attendance record is usually provided by an in-and-out clock card from which it is possible to compute the total elapsed time the employee has been on duty. Elapsed time is classified between regular time and overtime.

For salaried employees, the payroll liability is ordinarily taken directly from the master personnel record. For hourly employees, wage liability is computed by multiplying the rate shown on the personnel record by the number of hours worked, as shown on the clock card. If a shift differential is paid for workers on second and third shifts, the basic rate is adjusted to provide for this differential. Overtime hours are paid for at the overtime rate applicable to the particular employee and shift.

Labor cost distribution. Labor cost distributions in job order production are usually based on the individual time tickets described earlier. Because these time tickets are prepared as work is performed, the company has the option of distributing wage costs directly from the time tickets without waiting for reconciliation with the attendance records.[1]

The factory payrolls for May in our sample company totaled $19,330. This amount included $14,225 for the portion of production workers' time that could be traced to individual jobs (the direct labor), and $5,105 for various types of indirect labor. A summary entry to record these payrolls is:

(3)

direct labor

Work-in-Process Inventory	14,225	
Indirect Labor	5,105	
Payrolls Payable*		19,330

* This liability, or most of it, was extinguished almost immediately by the payment of cash. When and how liabilities are liquidated has no bearing on cost accounting, however, and payment transactions therefore can be ignored in this illustration.

The direct labor costs were also entered on the individual job cost sheets. These cost flows are diagrammed in Exhibit 3–2. Not surprisingly, it looks just like Exhibit 3–1—only the names of the source documents and the title of the overhead account are different.

[1] Payroll accrual and cost distribution can be performed simultaneously if the payroll period and cost reporting period coincide. The procedure described here is useful if cost reports are needed more frequently or if different clerical personnel process the payrolls and distribute the costs.

Exhibit 3–2 Flow of labor costs

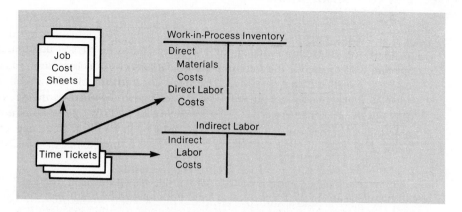

Actually, each cost center may have several object-of-expenditure accounts for indirect labor. Some of these, bearing titles such as Waiting for Materials, Waiting for Repairs, and Rework Labor, are used to accumulate the costs of various kinds of nonproductive time, otherwise known as *downtime.* Use of a separate account is justified whenever a particular kind of event is likely to happen often enough and with a large enough effect to require routine feedback information. For example, if machine breakdowns are frequent, a separate account is likely to be useful, but if machine breakdowns are likely to cause ten hours of idle time a year in a ten-employee cost center, management probably doesn't need precise data on breakdown time.

Other factory overhead costs

Our sample factory had overhead costs in addition to the costs of indirect materials and indirect labor. Some of these, such as electric power and telephone charges, represented services purchased and used during the month. These totaled $4,655. Others represented amortizations of the costs of plant and equipment ($1,220) and factory property insurance ($550) purchased in previous months and years.

Entries were made in detailed cost center object-of-expenditure accounts, but once again we shall use a single account to represent them all:

(4)

Other Factory Overhead		6,425
Accumulated Depreciation	1,220	
Prepaid Insurance	550	
Accounts Payable	4,655	

We've used three accounts to accumulate overhead costs in this illustration. Sometimes these accounts are so numerous that a single control account may be used to represent them all in the principal ledger. When this is done, the detailed accounts will be kept in a subsidiary ledger or file; the balance in the control account should always equal the sum of the balances in the various detailed accounts.

Overhead cost absorption

Direct labor and direct materials costs go directly into the job cost sheets and simultaneously to the Work-in-Process account. Accountants can't do this with factory overhead costs, though, because they can't trace these costs to specific jobs. Instead, they accumulate the actual costs in overhead accounts and use overhead rates to charge overhead costs to the job cost sheets. The total of these charges to the job cost sheets is also assigned to the Work-in-Process Inventory account by a process known as *overhead absorption.* The total amount of factory overhead assigned to jobs in any period is known as the amount of *overhead absorbed:*

Overhead absorbed

> **Total overhead absorbed = Overhead rate × Total production volume**

During May our sample factory recorded 1,500 direct labor hours. It used a single plantwide overhead rate of $7 a direct labor hour. This means that $7 × 1,500 = $10,500 was entered in the various job cost sheets. The entry to record this total in the ledger was:

(5)

Work-in-Process Inventory	10,500	
Factory Overhead Absorbed		10,500

The Factory Overhead Absorbed account is a contra account to the set of factory overhead cost accounts. Whereas they accumulate the costs, this one accumulates the amounts that are soaked up by the production that actually took place. If there is no production, there is nothing to absorb the costs. These relationships are diagrammed in Exhibit 3–3.

Exhibit 3–3 Relationship of factory overhead absorbed to factory overhead cost

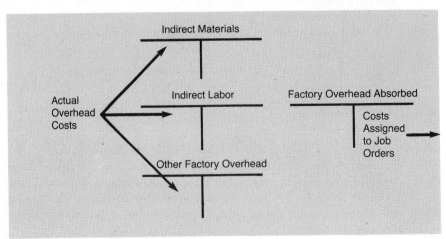

Job completions and sales

Two more steps remain in the cost accounting cycle. The first is the completion of job orders; the second is the sale of finished products.

Completion of a job is the signal for removing the job cost sheet from the in-process file. It also triggers an entry to record the transfer of costs from the work-in-process to the finished goods category. Our sample factory had no work in process at the beginning of May. It worked on four jobs during the month. The job cost sheets for these four jobs are represented in Exhibit 3–4. (The costs on these job cost sheets add up to the amounts charged to the Work-in-Process Inventory account in entries [2], [3], and [4].)

Exhibit 3–4 The job cost file

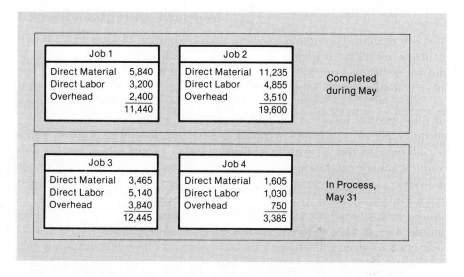

Job 1		
Direct Material	5,840	Completed during May
Direct Labor	3,200	
Overhead	2,400	
	11,440	

Job 2		
Direct Material	11,235	
Direct Labor	4,855	
Overhead	3,510	
	19,600	

Job 3		
Direct Material	3,465	In Process, May 31
Direct Labor	5,140	
Overhead	3,840	
	12,445	

Job 4		
Direct Material	1,605	
Direct Labor	1,030	
Overhead	750	
	3,385	

Jobs 1 and 2 were completed during May, and were transferred to the finished goods warehouse. An entry was made to transfer the costs accumulated on these two jobs from one asset account to another:

(6)

Finished Goods Inventory	31,040	
Work-in-Process Inventory		31,040

In other factories some job orders are for the manufacture of parts or subassemblies, and these are returned to factory stockrooms rather than to finished goods inventory locations. The costs of these jobs would be transferred to a Materials Inventory account rather than to Finished Goods Inventory.

The final step in the cost accounting cycle is the recognition that some costs have become *expenses*. An expense is any cost that is deducted from revenues on the income statement.[2] In this case the cost to be classified as expense is the cost of the goods sold during the period.

[2] The term *manufacturing expense* is often used in practice to refer to factory overhead costs. To avoid confusion, we shall use the term *expense* only to describe deductions from revenues.

Job costs are reclassified as expenses when the revenues from the sale of finished products are recognized. Job 1, for example, was for 1,100 water pumps. All of these were sold during May, and the full cost of $11,440 was transferred from the Finished Goods Inventory account to the Cost of Goods Sold account. Job 2 consisted of 500 oil burners. With total job cost of $19,600, the unit cost was $39.20. The sales force sold 425 oil burners during the month, for a cost of goods sold of 425 × $39.20 = $16,660. The total cost of goods sold therefore was $11,440 + $16,660 = $28,100. The transfers of costs were summarized in the following entry:

(7)

Cost of Goods Sold	28,100	
Finished Goods Inventory		28,100

This established the transfer of costs from the asset category to their new status as expenses.

The goods sold during this period brought in revenues of $42,000, all from credit sales. The summary entry to record these sales was as follows:

(8)

Accounts Receivable	42,000	
Sales Revenues		42,000

Summary of the cost flows

The complete cycle is summarized in Exhibit 3–5. Costs enter the factory accounts at the left of the diagram. Some are stored temporarily in inventory,

Exhibit 3–5 Cost flows for income determination in manufacturing

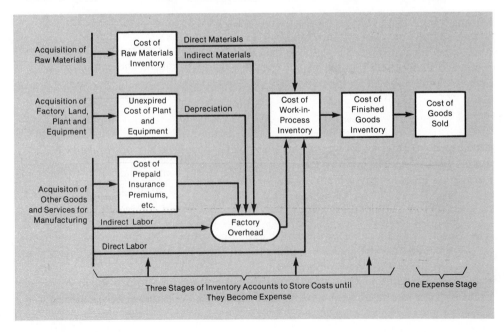

fixed asset, or prepayment accounts which appear on the company's balance sheet. Others (direct labor) go directly to Work-in-Process, while others go temporarily into Factory Overhead accounts. As materials are issued and work is performed, costs move out of the accounts at the left and into work-in-process, either directly or by way of the Factory Overhead accounts. Factory overhead is charged to work-in-process by means of predetermined overhead rates.

As jobs are completed, the costs are transferred from Work-in-Process Inventory to the Finished Goods Inventory account. They are still shown on the balance sheet because they are still the costs of assets. Finally, as the revenues from particular goods are recognized, the costs leave the balance sheet and go to the income statement under the heading "Cost of goods sold." Some costs, in other words, go through three kinds of balance sheet accounts before being recognized as expense.

Disposing of under- or overabsorbed factory overhead

The completion of the cost accounting cycle leaves one loose end, the $1,560 difference between the actual overhead costs for the period and the amount absorbed by production. This difference is called the *overhead cost variance*, as shown in Exhibit 3–6. If the overhead costs have exceeded the amount absorbed, as in this case, overhead is said to be *underabsorbed* and the variance is referred to as *unfavorable*. Whenever the amount absorbed is greater than the amount of cost charged to the overhead accounts, on the other hand, overhead is said to be *overabsorbed* and the variance is *favorable*.

Exhibit 3–6 The overhead cost variance

Actual Overhead	
Indirect materials	$ 530
Indirect labor	5,105
Other overhead	6,425
	$12,060

Overhead Absorbed by Production	
1,500 direct labor hours × $7	$10,500

Overhead Variance	
$12,060 − $10,500 =	$1,560

How should these variances be reflected in the company's financial statements? Three alternatives are possible:

1. To transfer the entire overhead variance to the income statement.
2. To leave the entire amount on the balance sheet, as a deferred charge or credit to the operations of future periods.
3. To divide the variance between inventory and cost of goods sold in some way that will make these figures approximate average historical cost.

We shall return in Chapter 23 to face the conceptual issues underlying the choice among these three solutions. For the moment we must be content to note that variances of U.S. corporations are likely to be taken to the income statement in their entirety unless they are material in amount. In such cases they will be split between the income statement and the balance sheet.

Manufacturing cost statement

The cost flows in our example, together with information on inventory balances, can be summarized in a table like the statement of manufacturing costs in Exhibit 3–7.

Exhibit 3–7
ANY COMPANY Statement of manufacturing costs for the month ended May 31, 19x1

Direct materials:			
Materials and supplies inventory, May 1			$52,485
Purchases			30,000
Cost of materials and supplies available			82,485
Less: Supplies used		$ 530	
Materials and supplies inventory, May 31		59,810	60,340
Direct materials used			22,145
Direct labor			14,225
Factory overhead:			
Indirect labor		5,105	
Supplies		530	
Depreciation		1,220	
Insurance		550	
Other overhead		4,655	
Total overhead		12,060	
Less: Overhead unabsorbed		1,560	
Overhead applied to production			10,500
Total product cost			46,870
Add: Work in process, May 1			—
			46,870
Less: Work in process, May 31			15,830
Cost of goods finished			$31,040

This statement is too cluttered to be suitable for managerial reporting, but it does show how all the figures fit together. The upper part shows the costs of operating the factory ($22,145 in direct materials, $14,225 in direct labor, and $12,060 in factory overhead). These differ from the amounts charged to jobs by the amount of the unabsorbed overhead, $1,560 in this case. The cost of goods finished is equal to the amount charged to jobs, plus or minus the change in the work-in-process inventory. Because this factory had no work in process on May 1, the cost of goods finished was equal to total product cost less the costs of the jobs still in process at the end of the month (jobs 3 and 4).

This statement can be converted into a statement of the cost of goods sold by adding or subtracting the change in the finished goods inventory.

Summary

Management uses job cost data in evaluating the profitability of its present activities and in preparing estimates of the costs of future jobs. These data are also used to divide production costs between the income statement and balance sheet for external financial reporting. The costs of purchased materials are classified first as the costs of materials inventories. When direct materials are issued, the costs of these materials are reclassified as the costs of the work in process, along with the costs of direct labor and the amount of overhead absorbed by application of the overhead rates. As jobs are finished, the costs that have been assigned to them are reclassified as the costs of the finished goods inventory. All three of these inventories are part of the company's assets. When the goods are sold, however, the costs that have been assigned to them are reclassified as expenses (cost of goods sold) and reported on the income statement.

The total amount of factory overhead assigned to individual job orders in a period (The overhead rate × Total production volume in the period) is known as the amount of absorbed factory overhead. The difference between this amount and the total of the actual factory overhead costs during the period is the over- or underabsorbed overhead or factory overhead cost variance. In most cases this amount is added to or subtracted from the cost of goods sold on the income statement for the period.

Independent study problems (solutions in Appendix B)

1. **Unit cost and journal entries.** The Basic Foundry prepares metal castings for specific orders, using a job order costing system. The costs of lost or damaged units in a job order are spread over the good units manufactured in that job. Factory overhead is charged to jobs at a predetermined rate of $4 a direct labor hour. The following information about job No. 103 is available:

   1. Direct materials issued: 21,000 pounds at 66 cents a pound.
   2. Direct labor used: 2,000 hours at $6.68 an hour.
   3. Unused direct materials returned to storeroom for future use: 800 pounds.
   4. Castings started, 10,000; castings completed, 9,800.

   Required:
   a. Calculate unit cost of production to the nearest cent.
   b. Prepare journal entries to record these transactions.

2. **Manufacturing cost flows.** The Ace Appliance Company had the following inventories on October 1:

Material and supplies	$12,650
Work in process	8,320
Finished goods	11,100

   The following transactions took place during the month:

   1. Purchased material and supplies on account at a cost of $4,500.
   2. Issued direct material, $6,320; indirect material (supplies), $930.

3. Accrued payrolls: direct labor, $3,300; indirect labor, $1,880; selling and administrative salaries, $2,600.
4. Purchased and used miscellaneous services from outside vendors:
   Classified as manufacturing overhead costs, $2,700.
   Classified as selling and administrative expenses, $1,835.
5. Applied manufacturing overhead at 150 percent of direct labor cost.
6. Completed jobs during the month: factory cost of these jobs, $12,650.
7. Earned sales revenue from goods sold on account, $19,350.
8. Counted the ending inventory of finished goods, $9,250.

Required:

a. Record the opening balances in inventory accounts, and record the above transactions, using the following T-accounts in addition to the three inventory accounts: Accounts Payable, Accrued Payroll, Cost of Goods Sold, Accounts Receivable, Sales Revenues, Indirect Materials, Indirect Labor, Other Factory Overhead, Factory Overhead Absorbed, Selling and Administrative Salaries, Other Selling and Administrative Expenses.
b. Calculate the closing balances in the three inventory accounts and the amount of overhead over- or underabsorbed.
c. Prepare an income statement for the month, with a supporting schedule of the cost of goods manufactured and sold. (Overhead over- or underabsorbed is to be included in the cost of goods sold.)

Exercises and problems

3. **Overhead rate and absorption.** A company uses a job order costing system with a predetermined overhead rate based on normal volume. Overhead costs are budgeted at $10,000 a month plus $2 for each direct labor hour. Normal volume is 10,000 direct labor hours. Actual volume for August was 9,000 direct labor hours, and actual overhead cost totaled $28,700. Job No. 423 was started on August 6 and completed on August 20, with the expenditure of 40 direct labor hours.

Required:

a. How much overhead was charged to Job No. 423?
b. How much overhead was charged to all jobs during August?
c. What was the total factory overhead variance for August?

4. **Job costing accounts.** The Simmons Company's factory uses a job costing system. Inventories at the beginning and end of 19x1 were:

	January 1	December 31
Materials	$50,000	$43,000
Work in process	12,000	16,000
Finished goods	63,000	61,000

Transactions during the year were:
1. Purchases of materials on account for direct and indirect use, $169,000.
2. Unusable materials returned to suppliers for credit, $2,000.
3. Direct labor, various job orders, $80,000.
4. Indirect labor, $7,000.
5. Indirect materials issued from materials inventories, $6,000.
6. Factory heat, power and light costs accrued, $7,000.
7. Factory depreciation, $13,000.
8. Miscellaneous factory costs accrued, $1,000.
9. Factory overhead absorbed, $32,000.

10. Direct materials issued from materials inventories, $???.
11. Goods finished: cost, $???.
12. Goods sold: cost, $???.

Required:

a. Set up T-accounts to represent the necessary operating cost and inventory accounts, enter the January 1 balances given above, and make entries to record the year's transactions. Use a single account for factory overhead costs and another account for factory overhead absorbed.
b. Prepare a statement of manufacturing costs.

5. **Job costing accounts.**   The Apex Company uses a job order costing system in its factory. The April 1 balances in the inventory and overhead accounts were:

Raw material $35,000
Work in process 8,000
Finished goods 26,000
Overhead underabsorbed to date 3,000

1. Raw materials costing $23,000 were purchased on account in April.
2. Raw materials costing $31,000 were put into process in April.
3. Factory labor costs were accrued in April: direct labor, $14,000; indirect labor, $8,000.
4. Bills were received for the costs of electric power used in the factory in April, $2,500.
5. Factory depreciation for April amounted to $500.
6. Factory supplies costing $2,000 were purchased on account during April and were used in the factory during that month.
7. Other manufacturing costs were incurred in April, giving rise to accounts payable of $5,000.
8. Selling and administrative salaries amounting to $6,000 were accrued in April.
9. Other selling and administrative costs were incurred in April, giving rise to accounts payable of $3,000.
10. The overhead rate in effect in April was 140 percent of direct labor cost.
11. At the close of operations on April 30, the production orders still in process, all of which had been started during April, had been charged with the following direct costs: direct materials, $4,000; direct labor, $1,500.
12. The cost of the finished goods inventory on April 30 totaled $18,000.

Required:

a. Using a single Factory Overhead account to accumulate all factory overhead costs, a Factory Overhead Absorbed account, and other appropriate account titles, prepare journal entries to record the information given above, including a final entry to close the Factory Overhead and Factory Overhead Absorbed accounts into the Overhead Underabsorbed to Date account at the end of the month.
b. List the balances in the inventory accounts and the amount of the over- or underabsorbed overhead as of April 30.

6. **Overhead absorption.**   Burger Company uses a job order costing system in its factory, with departmental predetermined overhead rates based on normal volume. The factory has two production departments, machining and assembly. The overhead rate used for product costing in the machining department is based on machine-hours; the overhead rate in assembly is based on direct labor hours. You have the following information:

1. At normal volume, the company would expect the following annual totals:

	Machining	Assembly
Factory overhead cost	$240,000	$180,000
Direct labor hours	48,000	120,000
Machine-hours	120,000	—

2. Actual factory overhead cost in May amounted to $23,000 in machining and $14,000 in assembly. Actual volume in each department was exactly $\frac{1}{12}$ the normal annual volume.

3. Job No. 816, yielding 1,500 product units, was started and completed in May. The job cost sheet for this job showed the following:

	Machining	Assembly
Direct materials, from storeroom	$2,500	$1,200
Direct labor cost	4,800	700
Direct labor hours	400	100
Machine-hours	800	—

Required:

a. Calculate the predetermined overhead rate for each department.

b. Calculate the amount of overhead over- or underabsorbed in each department in May.

c. Calculate the total cost of job No. 816 and the average cost per unit of finished product.

7. **Estimated versus normal volume.** The Burger Company's factory controller (see problem 6) has estimated that volume in each department next year will be only 80 percent of normal, while factory overhead cost will be 90 percent of normal.

Required:

a. Assuming that the overhead rates are the rates you calculated in problem 6, calculate the amount of overhead cost to be over- or underabsorbed in each department next year.

b. Recalculate the overhead rates for next year, based on estimated costs and estimated volume for next year.

c. If the rates you calculated in answer to (b) are used next year, and if overhead costs and volume are at their estimated levels, over- or underabsorbed overhead will be avoided. Does this establish conclusively that these rates should be used instead of rates based on normal volume? State your reasoning on this question.

8. **Fill in the blanks.** The Dowbar Company manufactures candlesticks on a job-order basis, using a plantwide predetermined overhead rate based on normal volume. You have the following data for three recent years:

	19x1	19x2	19x3
Normal direct labor hours	8,000	8,500	?
Actual direct labor hours	?	9,000	8,000
Overhead rate per direct labor hour.....................	$?	$?	$ 3.20
Overhead absorbed	30,000	27,900	?
Actual overhead	29,000	?	27,000
Overhead over (under) absorbed	?	(600)	?
Overhead cost at normal direct labor hours ..	24,000	?	28,800

Required:

Make the necessary calculations and supply the figures missing from this table.

9. **Distributing manufacturing costs.** The Eagleby Company uses a job order costing system with a predetermined factorywide overhead rate based on normal volume. The overhead rate in 19x1 was $2.50 a direct labor hour. Over(under)absorbed overhead is included in full each month as a component of the cost of goods sold.

On May 1 and May 31, 19x1, the company had the following inventories:

	May 1	May 31
Raw materials	$20,000	$17,000
Work in process	13,000	15,000
Finished goods	32,000	32,500

You have the following information about the factory's transactions during the month of May, 19x1:

1. Raw materials purchased: $8,000.
2. Direct labor used: 5,000 hours, $45,000.
3. Factory overhead cost: $14,000.
4. Indirect materials used: None.

Required:

a. Calculate the cost of direct materials used during May.
b. Prepare a schedule showing (1) the costs to be accounted for during May and (2) the amounts of these costs to be assigned to each inventory category and to the cost of goods sold.
c. How much of the cost of goods sold represented over(under)absorbed overhead?

10. **Calculating inventory costs: proposed allocation of overhead variance.** On November 30, a fire destroyed the plant and factory offices of the Swadburg Company. The following data survived the fire:

1. From the balance sheet at November 1 you find the beginning inventories: materials, $5,000; work in process, $15,000; finished goods, $27,500.
2. The factory overhead rate in use during November was $0.80 per dollar of direct material cost.
3. Total sales for the month amounted to $60,000. The gross profit margin constituted 25 percent of selling price.
4. Purchases of materials during November amounted to $30,000.
5. The payroll records show wages accrued during November as $25,000, of which $3,000 was for indirect labor.
6. The charges to factory overhead accounts totaled $18,000. Of this, $2,000 was for indirect materials and $3,000 was for indirect labor.
7. The cost of goods completed during November was $52,000.
8. Underabsorbed overhead amounted to $400. This amount was not deducted in the computation of the gross profit margin [item (3) above].

Required:

a. Calculate the amount of cost that had been assigned to the inventories of raw materials, work in process, and finished goods that were on hand at the time of the fire on November 30.
b. The Swadburg Company's management has claimed that a portion of the underabsorbed overhead should be assigned to the inventory, thereby increasing the amount due from the insurance company. The insurance company has denied this claim and you have been called upon to arbitrate the dispute. What answer would you give? What arguments would you advance to support it?

11. **Effects of errors on overhead variances.** The Daly Dayworks uses a job order costing system in its factory with departmental predetermined overhead rates.

The overhead rates for the three departments and the amounts of overhead over- or underabsorbed were as follows in 19x1:

	Overhead Rate	Over(under) Absorbed
Department A	$3 per direct labor hour	$(7,200)
Department B	150% of direct labor cost	4,500
Department C	$2 per machine-hour	(3,100)

A key employee in the factory office retired in September, 19x1. Replacement personnel made numerous mistakes during the next three months as they learned the company's system. The key employee was coaxed back from retirement for a few weeks to help correct the errors before the books were closed and the financial statements were prepared for 19x1.

Required:

Indicate the effects that correction of each of the following errors would have on over- or underabsorbed overhead and on the ending inventory balance:

a. Twenty direct labor hours at $10 an hour spent on job No. 722 in department A were incorrectly classified as indirect labor. The output of job No. 722 was sold before the end of 19x1.

b. Thirty indirect labor hours at $7 an hour in department B were incorrectly classified as direct labor on job No. 818. Job No. 818 was still in process on December 31, 19x1.

c. The bookkeeper failed to record 50 machine hours in department C on job No. 537. Half the output of this job was sold in 19x1; the other half was still in finished goods inventory at the end of 19x1.

d. Sixty direct labor hours in department B at $12 an hour were charged to job No. 881, but were incorrectly recorded as hours spent in department A. The output of job No. 881 was sold in 19x1.

12. **Factory ledger; journal entries.** You have the following information relating to the operations of the factory of Dreyfus, Inc., in the week beginning March 5:

1. The opening inventory of finished goods on that date consisted of 4,000 units of product from job No. 497, completed in the preceding week.

2. Requisitions and time tickets showed the following usage of direct labor and direct materials during the week:

Job No.	Direct Materials	Direct Labor Hours
498	$1,500	116
506	960	16
507	415	18
508	345	42
509	652	24
511	308	10
512	835	30
Total	$5,015	256

3. The wage rate for direct labor was $8 an hour.

4. Indirect labor during the week cost $740; other overhead costs amounted to $868.

5. A predetermined overhead rate was used, based on direct labor hours at a volume of 1,500 direct labor hours a month. At this volume overhead costs were expected to total $7,500 a month.

6. Work on jobs 498, 506, and 509 was completed during the week; the completed units were transferred to the finished goods inventory room at the factory.
7. The factory shipped the following finished goods to customers during the week: 2,000 units from job No. 497, and all of the output of jobs Nos. 498 and 506.

Dreyfus uses a factory ledger consisting of the following accounts only:

Account	Opening Balance, March 5
Materials inventory	$13,612 Dr.
Work in process inventory	—
Finished goods inventory	8,220 Dr.
Factory overhead	14,873 Dr.
Factory overhead absorbed	15,305 Cr.
Home office ledger............	21,400 Cr.

The Home Office Ledger account can be regarded as the equity account in the factory ledger representing the home office's investment in factory inventories and operating costs. It is credited when materials and other services are received from suppliers (the home office pays all vendor invoices), it is credited for the total amount of factory payrolls (the home office pays all salaries and wages earned in the factory), it is debited when finished goods are shipped to customers or to other locations within the Dreyfus organization, and it is either debited or credited with the amount of the overhead variance at the end of each year.

Entries to record the receipt of materials, for example, take the following form:

    Materials Inventory   xxx
        Home Office Ledger   xxx

If these materials come from outside vendors, the home office makes an entry in its own books, with the following effects on accounts in the home office general ledger:

    Factory Ledger   xxx
        Accounts Payable   xxx

The balance in the Factory Ledger account shows how much the home office has invested in factory inventories and operating costs and has not yet recovered from the factory. At all times the balance in the Factory Ledger account should be identical but opposite in sign to the balance in the Home Office Ledger account in the factory ledger.

Required:
a. Calculate the overhead rate the factory used in product costing during the week of March 5.
b. Establish T-accounts representing the six factory ledger accounts listed above, and enter the beginning-of-week balances. Using these accounts only, enter the effects of all of the week's factory transactions and calculate the end-of-week balances.
c. Calculate the amount of overhead over- or underabsorbed during the week.
d. Why does Dreyfus use a factory ledger rather than keep the factory inventory and factory overhead accounts in the home office general ledger? In practice, is it likely that a single account would be used in a factory ledger to accumulate all factory overhead costs?

13. **System evaluation; disposal of overhead cost variances.** Hudson Company uses job order costing in its factory, with departmental predetermined overhead rates based on direct labor hours at normal volume.

Earlier this year, Hudson entered into a contract with a customer under which it agreed to supply the customer 2,000 units of product each month for six months at factory cost plus 20 percent. As part of this contract, Hudson agreed to allow the customer to review the cost records on which the monthly billings were based.

After three months of satisfactory performance, Hudson and the customer amended the contract to increase the rate of delivery to 3,000 units a month for the remaining three months of the contract. The fourth month's shipment was delivered, and Hudson billed the customer $19,476, calculated as follows:

Cost of job No. M223 (3,000 units):

Direct materials	$ 3,380
Direct labor	6,760
Factory overhead:	
Forming department	1,450
Finishing department	4,640
Total job cost	16,230
20% margin	3,246
Invoice price	$19,476

The average price per unit had been close to $6.10 in each of the first three months. The customer was dismayed to see the price increase instead of decrease when the size of the order went up. You have been called in and assigned the task of reviewing Hudson's costing procedures. You have discovered the following:

1. Direct materials costs are recorded on job cost sheets from requisitions showing actual quantities issued multiplied by the average costs of the items in inventory.
2. Direct labor costs are recorded on job cost sheets on the basis of labor time tickets showing the job number, the actual time spent, and a labor rate per hour, covering the employee's straight-time wage rate plus a 30 percent allowance for payroll taxes and fringe benefits. You have found that 30 percent closely approximates the company's actual costs of payroll taxes and fringe benefits on factory payrolls.
3. Factory overhead is charged to job orders on the basis of the following predetermined rates, based on normal volume:

	Forming Department	Finishing Department
Overhead rate per direct labor hour	$30,000/5,000 = $6	$60,000/6,000 = $10
Direct labor on job No. M223	200 hours	400 hours

4. The factory overhead costs are adjusted to include the average overhead variances for the month. This adjustment was negligible in the first three months of the contract. The adjustment for the fourth month was calculated as follows:

	Forming Department	Finishing Department
(1) Average overhead cost per direct labor hour	$29,000/4,000 = $7.25	$58,000/5,000 = $11.60
(2) Predetermined rate	6.00	10.00
(3) Supplementary rate [(1) − (2)]	$1.25	$1.60
(4) Direct labor hours, job No. M223	200	400
(5) Adjustment [(4) × (3)]	$250	$640

Required:

a. Perform the necessary calculations to verify the contract price. The straight-time wage rate was $8 an hour in forming and $9 an hour in finishing.
b. Indicate the extent to which you agree or disagree with the methods Hudson used to assign costs to this contract and state the reasons for your agreements and disagreements. Should the customer dispute the bill?

14. **Job order costing; service organization.**   Sarfaty Associates is a small architectural firm. It has two departments, design and drafting. All work in both departments is on a job order basis. Departmental overhead costs are assigned to job orders on the basis of departmental predetermined overhead rates. The following costs are classified as direct costs of job orders:

1. Professional staff time devoted to specific job orders.
2. Secretarial time devoted to specific job orders.
3. Costs of employees' transportation, food, and lodging in connection with travel related to specific job orders.
4. Costs of printing, copying, and art work done by suppliers in connection with specific job orders.

Time spent by professional and secretarial staff on work not directly related to specific job orders, together with all other travel, printing, copying, art work, and all other costs, are classified as departmental overhead. Variances in overhead costs are reported to the principals in the firm, but are not reassigned to individual job orders.

Professional and secretarial staff time is charged to contracts and to overhead accounts at hourly rates set at 130 percent of each individual's annual salary divided by 1,680 hours, the presumed annual working time exclusive of overtime. The 30 percent factor is to provide for pensions, insurance, and payroll taxes. You have the following data on time and costs:

	Annual Budget		October, Actual		Job TP444, Actual	
	Design	Drafting	Design	Drafting	Design	Drafting
Professional staff hours:						
Direct	18,900	15,120	1,500	1,280	130	240
Indirect	6,300	1,680	650	100	xxx	xxx
Direct costs of job orders:						
Professional staff	$378,000	$151,200	$30,600	$13,440	$2,652	$2,520
Secretarial	18,000	3,100	1,300	350	180	30
Travel	65,000	25,500	4,200	2,150	568	—
Printing, etc.	15,000	21,500	800	2,320	135	465
Total	476,000	201,300	36,900	18,260	3,535	3,015
Overhead costs:						
Professional staff						
salaries	126,000	16,800	13,260	1,050		
Secretarial salaries	66,000	25,000	5,820	1,990		
Travel	25,000	3,000	3,300	320		
Other	47,600	23,240	4,950	2,460		
Total	264,600	68,040	27,330	5,820		

Required:

a. Prepare departmental predetermined overhead rates based on professional staff time.
b. Calculate the amount of cost assigned to job TP444.

    c. Calculate the total amount of overhead over- or underabsorbed in each department in October.

    d. Professionals often work overtime hours without overtime pay. What impact would this practice have on the accuracy of Sarfaty's job costing system? Should Sarfaty change its system in any way? Why?

15. **Job costing transactions.** The Farquar Corporation uses job order costing in its factory. The inventory accounts showed the following balances on February 1:

Materials and Supplies $40,000
Jobs in Process 57,000
Finished Goods 73,000

    The job cost file showed the following details at that time:

	Materials	Labor	Overhead	Total
No. D1762	$ 600	$ 1,900	$ 2,850	$ 5,350
No. D1783	2,900	3,200	4,800	10,900
No. E0004	4,000	1,400	2,100	7,500
No. E0010	6,500	1,000	1,500	9,000
No. E0011	14,000	2,000	3,000	19,000
No. E0013	4,000	500	750	5,250
Total	$32,000	$10,000	$15,000	$57,000

The following transactions were recorded during February:

1. Materials and supplies purchased on account and received in the factory storeroom, $62,000.
2. Materials and supplies issued by the storeroom to factory departments for current use:

Job No. E0004 .... $ 500
Job No. E0010 1,000
Job No. E0013 2,500
Job No. E0015 8,000
Job No. E0016 11,000
Job No. E0017 6,000
Job No. E0018 9,000
Indirect materials, department M 4,800
Indirect materials, department P 500
Indirect materials, department A 2,200
    Total $45,500

3. Labor performed in factory departments:

Job No.	Department	Cost
D1762	A	$ 200
D1783	M	300
D1783	P	400
E0004	M	7,200
E0010	P	3,400
E0010	A	5,300
E0011	M	12,000
E0013	M	3,100
E0013	P	1,400
E0013	A	3,300
E0015	A	3,600
E0016	P	2,500
E0016	M	6,500
E0017	A	3,800
E0017	M	8,800
E0017	P	2,400
E0018	M	3,000
Indirect	M	19,900
Indirect	P	3,100
Indirect	A	8,500
Total		$98,700

4. Other overhead costs charged to the factory and credited to salaries payable, accounts payable, or accumulated depreciation, as appropriate:

	Department M	Department P	Department A
Supervision	$11,000	$3,200	$ 8,300
Maintenance	6,500	1,900	400
Heat, light, and power	2,400	700	1,500
Payroll taxes and pensions ...	12,400	2,600	5,300
Depreciation	7,800	800	900
Miscellaneous	600	400	200
Total	$40,700	$9,600	$16,600

5. Predetermined departmental overhead rates, expressed as percentages of direct labor cost, were as follows: department M, 150 percent; department P, 140 percent; department A, 180 percent.
6. Jobs completed and transferred to finished goods: Nos. D1762, D1783, E0004, E0010, E0013, E0017.
7. Cost of finished goods sold, $138,000.

Required:

a. Enter the February 1 balances in individual job cost sheets and record the month's transactions on these sheets.
b. Enter the February 1 balances in the inventory accounts and record the month's transactions. A single account may be used for each department's overhead costs.
c. Compute the amount of the under- or overabsorbed overhead in each department.
d. Prepare a statement of the cost of goods manufactured and sold. The under/overabsorbed is not to be included in the cost of goods sold.

4 Decision concepts and cost behavior

Management's decisions determine how the organization's resources are to be used. The cost figures supplied to management for this purpose must be estimates of the effects of those decisions on the costs that will prevail during the period affected by the decisions—that is, future costs. A major question therefore must be how cost figures assembled by the methods we described in Chapter 2 must be modified if they are to provide useful estimates of these decision-oriented cost figures. The purpose of this chapter is to answer this question in a preliminary way. The chapter has three parts:

1. An explanation of a basic set of analytical principles underlying resource-allocation decisions.
2. A review of the ways costs are likely to vary in response to variations in the rate at which the organization's facilities are used.
3. Analysis of the relevance of information on cost variability to a set of illustrative resource-allocation decisions.

Basic principles underlying resource-allocation decisions

A decision is always a choice among the alternative courses of action available to the decision maker. Since management can only affect the differences between alternatives, it follows that decision analysis should focus on these differences. We call this precept the *differential principle* or *incremental principle.* Our first task is to decide how to measure the increments (differences between alternatives).

Using net cash flows to measure results

Each alternative can be described by the costs it will entail, the benefits management expects it to yield, and the degree of certainty management attaches to these estimates. In a business organization, both costs and benefits are measured by the cash flows associated with the alternative being considered—that is, costs are measured by cash outlays or disbursements, and benefits are measured by cash receipts.

The reason for this emphasis on cash flows is that in most circumstances cash is the only resource management can use to get productive goods and services or to reward the shareholders and pay creditors. Noncash resource outflows, such as depreciation on existing equipment, reduce the income figure for financial reporting, but they don't reduce management's current purchasing power. Noncash resource inflows, on the other hand, add to reported income but not to management's current ability to pay the company's bills.

Many decisions can be based on their effects on the cash flows of a single period of time. Ignoring questions of risk and uncertainty for the moment, in these situations management will choose the alternative which promises the greatest excess of cash receipts over cash outlays in the relevant time period. We refer to this difference as the _net cash flow_ in that time period.

The distinction between net income and net cash flow is diagrammed in Exhibit 4–1. To make the diagram possible, we have assumed that total revenue exceeds cash receipts, total expense exceeds total cash outlay, and net income exceeds net cash flow. Other combinations are possible, but more difficult to diagram.

Exhibit 4–1 Cash flows versus other resource flows

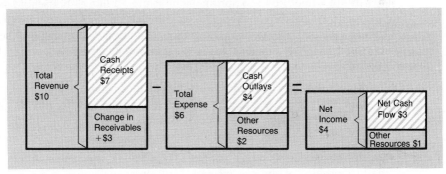

Identifying incremental cash flows

One way to state the results of each possible course of action is to estimate for each the net cash flow _for the company as a whole_ or for a major company segment. These net cash flow estimates then can be compared with each other to identify the most profitable alternative.

This approach is cumbersome for decisions which affect only a small part of the company's or segment's business. For these decisions it is generally preferable to measure the anticipated effects of each alternative as the _difference between the results expected under that alternative and the results expected from some other alternative_.

This idea is illustrated in Exhibit 4–2. The block at the left represents the net cash flow resulting from one alternative; the block in the center identifies the net cash flow associated with another alternative management has chosen as the reference point. The difference between the net cash flows of these two alternatives in this time period is known as the _differential cash flow, incremental cash flow,_ or _incremental profit._

Since we want to compare the alternatives with each other, each of them

Exhibit 4–2 Cash flow attributable to a proposed action

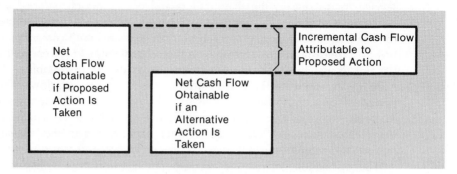

should be compared with the same alternative—that is, with a *common* reference point. We prefer to use the *benchmark alternative* for this purpose—the action management will take if none of the proposals being considered is approved.

For example, Anne England, president of the Peerless Spring Company, was evaluating a proposal to add a newly designed window catch to the company's product line. Peerless Spring manufactured a line of household and industrial hardware products. It had a strong distribution organization, but intensified competition had cut into its sales volume, leaving the company with substantial idle capacity. Ms. England was deciding which of the following actions to take:

1. Reject the offer; continue with the existing product line.
2. Use the company's regular sales organization to offer the new product to Peerless Spring's present customers.
3. Set up a new sales force to market the new product.

She designated the first of these as the benchmark alternative. In other words, the profitability of the second and third alternatives was to be measured by the *differences* between the results ensuing from these actions and the results under the alternative of continuing the existing operations.

Ms. England's next step was to estimate what each of the other two alternatives would *add* to the cash flows from present operations. After a good deal of study, she and her staff came up with the following estimates of the differential cash flows:

	Use Regular Sales Force	Add Special Salespeople
Additional sales volume (units)	300,000	400,000
Additional cash received from customers	$450,000	$600,000
Additional cash payments:		
Factory costs	300,000	360,000
Selling costs	70,000	180,000
Royalties	30,000	40,000
Total	400,000	580,000
Net differential cash flow	$ 50,000	$ 20,000

(margin note: benchmark alternative)

To repeat, these figures measure <u>differences between the stated alternatives and the benchmark.</u>

On this basis Ms. England concluded that adding the new window catch would be a profitable thing to do and that she would be better off to market it through the regular sales organization than to add a specialized sales force. The steps she followed in reaching this conclusion are summarized in Exhibit 4–3.

Exhibit 4–3 Steps in profit-based decision analysis, ignoring uncertainty

1. Define the problem or opportunity to be examined.
2. Identify the actions that might be taken—these are known as the *alternatives.*
3. Select a *benchmark alternative* to serve as a point of reference for the others.
4. For each alternative estimate the *difference* in anticipated *net cash flows* between this alternative and the benchmark alternative.
5. Identify the alternative with the greatest anticipated differential net cash inflow (or lowest differential net cash outflow.)

Compare each alternative to benchmark to find differential cash flow

Notice that we have not said how much money Peerless Spring was making or losing on its existing operations. That was irrelevant. Our only concern was whether the company could improve its profit performance by taking on the new product. This was the inevitable result of Ms. England's decision to use a benchmark alternative. <u>A benchmark alternative, *by definition,* is a course of action management is willing to take if it can find nothing better to do.</u> The question of what to do with the existing operations was decided when management agreed to use continued operations as the benchmark alternative. If management is now unhappy with this alternative, it should reopen the issue and see whether other possible alternatives would be better.

Turning averages into differentials

The message in Exhibit 4–2 can be summarized succinctly: the general rule in resource-allocation analysis is to examine, for each time period affected by the decision, <u>differences in *total* cash flows</u>:

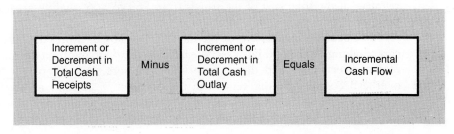

In some cases, total cash receipts will be unaffected by the decision to be made; incremental cash flow then will be measured by the difference in the total cash outlay each period that will result from choosing one alternative instead of the other. This difference is usually referred to as *differential cost or incremental cost.*

Differential costs are likely to be very different from the costs emerging from costing systems of the kind we described in Chapter 2. For example, Peerless Spring is now operating its factory 3,000 direct labor hours a week, far less than the plant's capacity. Another company is having difficulty fulfilling a large government contract and has asked Peerless Spring to assemble 400 door panels a week for the next six months at a price of $65 each.

The factory accountants have prepared the following estimates of manufacturing costs for the door panels:

	Unit Cost	Total Cost (400 panels)
Direct materials	$30	$12,000
Direct labor (3 hours per panel at $8 an hour)	24	9,600
Factory overhead ($5 per direct labor hour)	15	6,000
Total factory cost	$69	$27,600

The $5 hourly overhead figure is the overhead rate in Peerless's assembly department, where the work will be done.

Knowing that some factory overhead costs would not increase if the door panel contract were taken on, Ms. England asked the accountants to prepare a new cost estimate, reflecting average cost at the new production volume. They came up with the following figures:

	Anticipated Volume	Anticipated Volume +400 Panels
Number of direct labor hours	3,000	4,200
Total factory overhead	$15,000	$16,800
Average factory overhead per direct labor hour	$ 5	$ 4
Average factory overhead per panel	$15	$12

The addition of panel assembly to the present work load thus would reduce average overhead cost per hour from $5 to $4, a reduction of $1 an hour and $3 for each panel. Using this new rate, the accountants reduced their estimate of the total cost of the panels from $69 to $66, slightly greater than the $65 Peerless was offered for doing the work.

This calculation is also wrong. Neither $69 nor $66 measures the differential cost of taking on the new business. We have no reason to question the relevance of the direct labor and direct materials costs here, but differential factory overhead cost is very different from the average. It amounts to $1,800, or $4.50 a panel, as shown in Exhibit 4–4. The total differential cost thus comes to $23,400, calculated as follows:

	Total	Per Panel
Direct materials	$12,000	$30.00
Direct labor	9,600	24.00
Factory overhead	1,800	4.50
Total differential cost	$23,400	$58.50

This shows that the company can take on this business and add $65 − $58.50 = $6.50 to its profits for each panel it assembles. The differential profit from 400 panels therefore will amount to $2,600 a month.

Exhibit 4–4 Differential factory overhead costs of door panel production

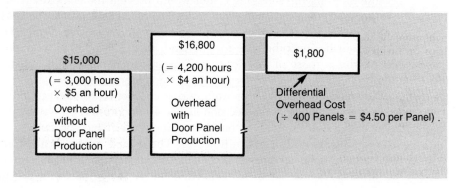

Sunk costs

A term frequently used in decision analysis is *sunk cost*. Although some people use the term differently, we prefer to define sunk cost as <u>any cost that will be unaffected by the decision to be made. For any given decision, all costs can be divided into two classes—sunk costs and differential costs.</u>

The amounts paid in the past to buy a plot of land are sunk costs. Nothing management can do now can change that amount. The same is true of costs that have already been incurred to develop a new product that management is now considering placing on the market. Even <u>the plant manager's salary is a sunk cost</u> in an analysis of whether to take on another order. In other words, the term is used to identify costs that are <u>irrelevant to a particular decision.</u> "These costs are sunk, and we don't need to consider them."

Opportunity cost

Proposals sometimes call for the <u>use of resources the company already controls. No cash outlay has to be made</u> to obtain them. <u>They have a differential cost, however, measured by the net cash inflow that will be lost if they are diverted</u> from their best alternative use. This differential cost is known as the *opportunity cost* of these resources. It is the value of an opportunity forgone. It belongs in the analysis because *an action that eliminates a cash inflow is exactly equivalent to an action that requires a cash outflow.* The effect on the company's cash position is identical.

For example, a variety chain paid $500,000 ten years ago for a plot of land as a site for a shopping center. Uncertainty as to state highway relocation plans forced management to postpone the project, and the land has lain idle ever since. The route of the new highway has now been established, and the company is again considering the possibility of using the land as a shopping center site.

The original purchase price of the land is a sunk cost, irrelevant to the decision. The shopping center proposal must be charged for the land, however, because building the shopping center would prevent the company from using it to generate cash in other ways. If we find that the land can be sold for a net price of $800,000, after deducting all commissions, fees, and taxes, and if the chain has no other use for the land, then $800,000 is its opportunity cost for the purpose of this decision. This amount should be included among the cash outflows required by the shopping center proposal.

We wouldn't need the opportunity cost concept if we always listed all the alternatives available to the decision maker. In the illustration we could simply have labeled one alternative "build shopping center" and another "sell land." We can't always do this easily, however. The owned resources to be incorporated into a particular project are often a small part of the total project, and several such resources may be involved. A full set of alternatives would include one for each possible combination of resource uses, and the number could get so large as to be unwieldy. The better procedure ordinarily is to calculate an opportunity cost for each resource.

Short-term cost-volume relationships

Many resource-allocation decisions focus on management's efforts to use existing capacity profitably. Increasing or decreasing the amount of capacity takes time, and in the meantime management must try to do its best with what it has. Anyone wishing to estimate incremental costs in these circumstances needs to understand how operating costs are likely to respond to variations in operating volume—that is, variations in the degree to which the organization's available capacity is used.

We'll begin by assuming that all costs can be divided into two categories, fixed and variable. With this behind us, we'll move on to two related concepts: semivariable cost and marginal cost.

Variable costs

All organizations engage in *responsive activities*—that is, activities imposed on a responsibility center by activities outside it. Manufacturing is a responsive activity, meeting demands arising out of marketing activities. Preparing payrolls is a responsive activity, meeting demands arising out of all the firm's activities.

Some costs of responsive activities go up or down almost automatically in response to small changes in operating volume. Operating volume, or *level of activity,* is the rate at which resources are used (pounds of material per hour) or at which goods or services are produced (meals served per week). Any cost that must be increased if the firm is to achieve a small increase in ✷ the level of activity is a *variable cost.*

One possible pattern of variability is illustrated in Exhibit 4–5. The lines in both charts in this exhibit represent a cost that changes in direct proportion to changes in volume. A good example is a royalty or commission payment calculated by multiplying the number of units sold by a constant amount per unit. As the diagram in the left-hand portion of Exhibit 4–5 shows, this amounts to zero when volume is zero and rises in a straight line as volume increases. The average variable cost per unit remains constant, as the right-hand chart shows.

Exhibit 4–5 Proportionately variable costs

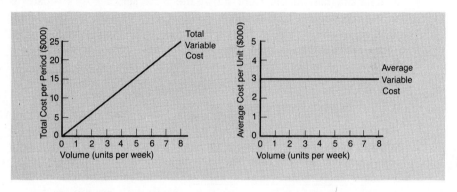

Another possible pattern of variation is reflected in the following figures:

Volume	Total Variable Cost
1	$ 5.00
2	9.00
3	12.00
4	15.00
5	18.00
6	21.00
7	24.50
8	29.20
9	36.00
10	46.00

The variable cost of producing the first unit is $5. The second unit adds $4 to the total, and the third, fourth, fifth, and sixth add $3 each. Total variable cost starts up more sharply again with the seventh unit, which adds $3.50 to the total. The eighth unit adds another $4.70, and so on.

This pattern is illustrated in Exhibit 4–6. The total cost rises sharply as volume moves up in the lower portion of the volume range, then rises more gradually as volume achieves normal operating levels, and finally rises sharply again as operations begin to approach the limits of existing capacity.

Exhibit 4–6 Progressively variable costs

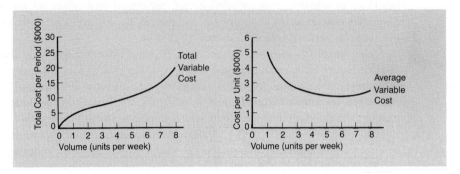

The diagram at the right shows the same set of cost estimates expressed as averages instead of as totals. Average cost is high at low volumes while total cost is rising sharply. Average cost falls as the increase in total cost becomes more gradual. Finally, after total variable cost begins to rise more steeply as volume approaches capacity, average variable cost begins to rise.

Fixed costs: Responsive activities

Costs that do not change as a necessary result of small changes in volume are known as *fixed costs*. Some of these are the fixed costs of responsive activities, also known as *capacity costs*. They are the costs of the resources used to provide or maintain current operating capacity. As we said at the beginning, capacity is likely to remain relatively constant during the planning period. This means that average capacity cost per unit will decline as the use of capacity increases. A cost that amounts to $4,200 a week, no matter what the operating volume, will average $2,100 a unit if volume is two units a week or $420 a unit if volume is 10 units.

This is illustrated in Exhibit 4–7. With total fixed costs of $4,200 a week, average fixed cost falls from $4,200 at a weekly volume of one unit to $525 at a volume of eight units a week. In other words, average fixed cost usually falls as volume increases within capacity limits. Average variable cost, as we

Exhibit 4–7 Fixed costs

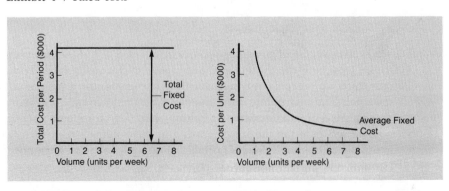

have already seen, is likely to remain constant or increase. This means that
average total cost—fixed costs plus variable costs—will fall as long as average
variable cost remains constant or as long as the reduction in average fixed
cost exceeds any increase in average variable cost.

Some capacity costs are likely to be constant over the entire output range;
others are apt to vary in steps, similar to the diagram in Exhibit 4–8. For
example, one departmental supervisor may be adequate for single-shift operation, but operation of a second shift will require a second supervisor.

Exhibit 4–8 Step-variable capacity costs

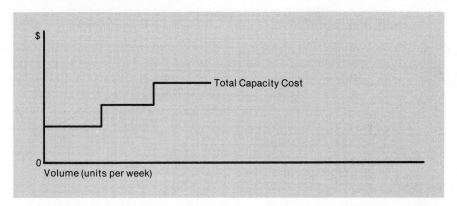

Step-variable capacity costs are classified by economists as variable costs.
Executives and accountants classify them as fixed if the steps are wide, as in
Exhibit 4–8. The basic block of fixed costs provides the capacity to operate
at volumes up to the limit of the first step. When fixed costs move up to the
next level, they provide more capacity, enough to support operating volumes
up to the limit of the next step. To get still more capacity, a third batch of
fixed costs must be incurred.

Some steps are narrower than these because the fixed costs are more divisible
than in this diagram. The salary costs of a billing department with 15 billing
clerks, for example, are divisible into at least 15 steps. If costs are this divisible,
they may be averaged out for most analytical purposes and treated as part of
the variable costs.

Fixed costs: Programmed activities

Every organization has a second group of fixed costs, fundamentally different
from the first. These are the costs of *programmed activities,* undertaken at management's initiative to meet objectives other than meeting demands for service
imposed on the organization from the outside. Research and development
are programmed activities; so is sales promotion; so are methods improvement
studies.

Programmed activities determine the organization's scope and direction.
Some of them are *innovative,* designed to enable the organization to change

Fixed Costs
A. Responsive   B. Programmed
  1. Capacity Costs   1) Innovative
                          2) promotional

promotional the way it operates—by developing new products, acquiring other firms, improving operating methods, and so forth. Others are *promotional,* intended to stimulate demands for the organization's goods and services—most selling activities fall in this category.

Programmed activities are very different from responsive activities. <u>Responsive activities are more or less imposed on the organization by the success of its programmed activities.</u> The costs of responsive activities must adapt to changes in volume if the organization is to meet its commitments; <u>the costs of programmed activities need not go up if responsive activities expand.</u>

Semivariable costs

both fixed + variable components

Some costs don't fit neatly into either the fixed cost or the variable cost category. We shall refer to these as <u>semivariable costs.</u> Many patterns of variability are possible. Three of these are illustrated in Exhibit 4-9. The first chart might represent the cost of equipment maintenance. The amount varies with the rate at which the equipment is used, but some maintenance is necessary even if the equipment is not used at all. This kind of cost has both fixed and variable components.

Exhibit 4-9 Semivariable costs

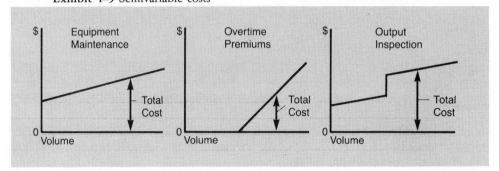

The second chart is a picture of the costs of overtime work. Overtime premiums are likely to be very small for large parts of the possible operating range. <u>They begin when the operating rate starts to approach capacity and rise sharply from then on.</u>

The third chart is a diagram of the costs of inspecting the output of an assembly line that can be run either one shift or two shifts a day. Each shift has a salaried inspector and a variable number of assistants who are paid according to the number of hours they work. As the factory moves to a second shift, the fixed component of cost (the inspectors' salaries) jumps up. Like the costs in the first chart, this cost element includes both fixed and variable components.

Marginal cost

Accountants are interested not only in total costs but also in the change in cost as volume moves from one level to another. <u>The increase in total cost</u>

that results from increasing the volume of activity by one unit per period is known as the *marginal cost*.

If there are no steps either in the fixed costs or in the semivariable costs, then marginal cost will be measured by the change in total variable cost. If total variable cost moves along a straight line, so that average variable cost is constant, each additional unit will have the same variable cost as the one before. In other words, marginal cost will be constant and equal to average variable cost. This is diagrammed in Exhibit 4–10. If the slope of the total cost line is flat, the marginal cost will be small. If the total cost line is steep, marginal cost will be high.

Exhibit 4–10 Constant marginal cost

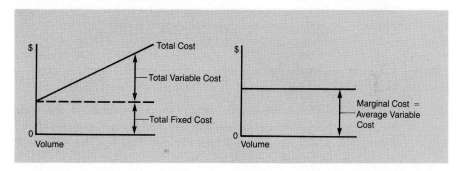

Marginal costs will not trace a straight line if fixed costs move up in steps or if average variable cost changes with volume. Exhibit 4–11 shows two possibilities. In the chart at the left, marginal cost remains constant for most of the output range, then begins to rise at volume X as volume begins to approach existing capacity limits. A diagram of total costs would show total costs sloping upward to the right in a straight line until volume X, then sloping upward more and more sharply as volume moved up beyond that point.

The chart at the right represents a factory that can run either one, two, or three shifts. Marginal cost remains constant through most of the output range of single-shift operations, begins to rise at volume X, and continues

Exhibit 4–11 Rising marginal cost

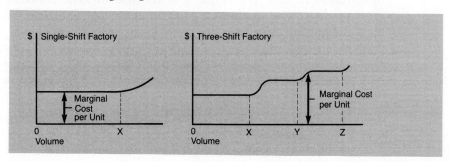

to rise until it gets high enough to make a second shift more economical. Marginal cost is higher for second-shift operations than for the first shift, but it remains steady until volume Y is reached, when it begins another upward climb. And so on. Each of the three shifts follows the same cost pattern. A total cost curve here would rise gradually in a straight line at first, then rise more steeply through the second shift and more steeply still for third-shift operations.

The concept of marginal cost has no meaning in connection with programmed costs unless they are truly contingent on sales revenues. Marginal costs measure the effects of increasing volume; most programmed costs don't change as a direct result of changes in volume. Marginal cost therefore consists of increments in the costs of responsive activities, together with any increments in the volume-contingent costs of programmed activities. The only programmed costs that are truly contingent on volume are sales commissions.

Impact of cost variability on short-term resource-allocation decisions

The anticipated response of operating costs to variations in operating volume has an impact on most resource-allocation decisions. It is particularly relevant to decisions which determine how a business will use the capacity it already has. To see how information on cost variability can affect these decisions, let's close this chapter by looking at four short-term decision situations:

1. Evaluating special opportunities to use temporarily idle capacity.
2. Using materials from inventory.
3. Rationing scarce capacity.
4. Deciding which products to emphasize.

In these analyses we'll assume that all cash flows are known with certainty. The implications of uncertainty will be examined in Chapter 5.

Evaluating special orders: Opportunities to use idle capacity

Business organizations have to provide capacity before they know how much of that capacity will be used in any short period. We shouldn't be surprised to find, therefore, that more capacity is available in some periods than the organization is able to use in its regular business with its regular customers.

In these circumstances, management is likely to seek opportunities to use some of its idle capacity. The question is whether these additional opportunities seem likely to bring in enough incremental revenues to cover their incremental costs. Our problem is to find out how these incremental revenues and incremental costs should be identified. We'll look at three cases:

Case 1: The decision affects only direct revenues and variable manufacturing costs.

Case 2:   The decision affects direct revenues and both fixed and variable costs.

Case 3:   The decision has indirect price effects.

Case 1.   Accepting a small order.   In some situations opportunities may arise to accept small orders for special work that won't affect the company's revenues from its regular, ongoing business. In a case of this sort, incremental cash receipts ordinarily can be measured by the revenues generated by the order itself; incremental cash outlays can be measured by the costs of factory direct labor, direct materials, and the variable portion of factory overhead.

For example, suppose management is considering a possible order for 100 units of hydrogenated widgets to be manufactured in department 82. The first step is to list all the overhead costs in that department in a normal month, and classify them by their estimated variability:

Supervision	$2,700—all fixed
Indirect labor	3,000—all variable
Supplies	500—all variable
Power	800—all variable
Depreciation	400—all fixed
Other	600—half variable
Total	$8,000

The second step is to estimate the average rate of variability. In this case, normal volume is 2,000 direct labor hours a month, and the average is calculated as follows:

Indirect labor	$3,000
Supplies	500
Power	800
Other	300
Total variable	$4,600

Average variable overhead = $4,600/2,000 = $2.30 an hour.

The final step is to estimate the direct inputs and add the overhead component. Each widget requires $8 of direct materials and 0.3 direct labor hour at a wage rate of $8 an hour. For 100 widgets, the estimated incremental costs are as follows:

Direct materials	$ 800
Direct labor: 30 hours at $8	240
Variable overhead: 30 hours at $2.30	69
Total differential cost	$1,109

The average differential cost therefore is $11.09 a unit. If the estimates prove to be correct, any price higher than $11.09 will be profitable.

The same result can be achieved indirectly, by subtracting the fixed cost portion of the overhead rate from estimates based on full cost. In this case the full overhead rate is $8,000/2,000 = $4 a direct labor hour. We've already established that variable costs account for $2.30 of this; the remaining $1.70 is an estimate of average fixed overhead cost. Incremental overhead cost can be estimated as follows:

Full overhead cost: 30 hours @ $4	$120
Less: Fixed cost component: 30 hours @ $1.70	51
Incremental factory overhead cost	$ 69

Case 2: Accepting a large special order. We were able to ignore the fixed costs in our analysis of the special order in Case 1 because the order was relatively small. Suppose, however, the customer is interested in placing an order for 1,000 hydrogenated widgets a month for six months, rather than a single order for 100 units. Department 82 has enough equipment to handle this larger order and additional workers are available in the local labor force. Management estimates that direct materials and direct labor costs will continue to be $8 and $2.40 a unit, and variable overhead costs will continue to average $2.30 a direct labor hour.

Fixed overhead costs will be affected, however, because a second supervisor/inspector will have to be added to the department's work force at a monthly salary of $1,800. The incremental analysis therefore shows the following:

Direct materials: 1,000 units @ $8	$ 8,000
Direct labor: 300 hours @ $8	2,400
Variable overhead: 300 hours @ $2.30	690
Fixed overhead: additional supervision	1,800
Total incremental cost	$12,890

In other words, the incremental cost of accepting this order averages $12.89 a unit; the contract price will have to exceed that amount for the company to make a profit on the job.

Case 3: Indirect price effects. Accepting a special order at a lower than usual price/cost relationship may lead to reductions in the prices obtainable from the company's other business. Suppose, for example, that the buyer of hydrogenated widgets has offered a price of $15 a unit for delivery of 1,000 widgets a month for six months (as in Case 2). Word of this arrangement is likely to reach at least some other customers, and management estimates it will have to make price concessions amounting to $3,000 a month to these other customers. The incremental cash receipts therefore are:

Direct contract price: 1,000 × $15	$15,000
Less: Indirect price effects	3,000
Incremental cash receipts	$12,000

Since we saw in Case 2 that incremental cost is expected to total $12,890, management should not accept this additional business unless it seems likely to be the forerunner of a substantial volume of new business with this customer at profitable prices.

Special order analysis: Cautionary notes

1. Some of the variable costs may not be differential costs—for example, the order may use materials that otherwise would merely deteriorate, or it may provide work for employees who otherwise would remain on the payroll with nothing to do. We'll return to this point in the next subsection.
2. If many of these decisions are made in any given period, management must consider their cumulative effect—for example, accepting 10 orders like this one may require hiring an additional supervisor.
3. The special order may affect the rate at which the variable cost elements vary.
4. Calculating differential cost does not mean that price should be set at or near this level—the cost figure merely gives management one element in the pricing equation, and many other factors must be considered.

Using materials from inventory

Until now we have assumed that the incremental costs of direct materials can be approximated by finding out how much would be charged to the job in the normal record-keeping routine. This may be wrong, for any of three reasons.

First, routine charges to jobs may be based on the historical inventory records, which show the prices paid for the materials at some time in the past. If the company will buy new materials to keep its inventories at constant levels, then incremental cost should be measured by the *replacement costs* of the materials rather than by their historical costs. The reason is simple. If the materials are used, purchases will be made and cash payments equal to replacement costs will follow; if the materials are not used, no purchases will be necessary and the cash flow will be zero. Replacement cost in this situation is clearly the correct measure of the incremental cash flow for materials.

The second reason for ignoring the routine accounting figures for materials costs is that the company may have no other use for these materials if they aren't used for the special order. They may be obsolete or highly perishable or no longer compatible with the company's product line. In such cases the incremental cost is equal to the current resale or salvage value of the materials, not their replacement cost or their historical cost. This conclusion once again can be demonstrated by comparing the alternatives:

If Management Decides to	Cash Flows for Materials Will Equal	And Incremental Cash Flow Will Equal
Accept the special order ...	Zero	Proceeds from resale or salvage
Reject the special order	Proceeds from resale or salvage	

This calculation is another application of the opportunity cost concept we introduced earlier.

The third possible situation is that the materials will be the <u>semiprocessed output of previous processing operations in the company's factories</u>. The costs assigned to these materials will include the costs of processing labor and manufacturing overhead as well as the costs of materials purchased from outside vendors. Incremental cost may be smaller than the total of these costs.

For example, Stillwell Products Company is interested in placing an order with Dalton Electronics for 500 units of a new product that has been designed by Stillwell's engineers. The 500 units will be used by Stillwell's sales force to test the product's commercial appeal. If the test proves favorable, Stillwell will ask several competing manufacturers to bid on a long-term contract to supply the product on a mass-production basis.

Stillwell has offered Dalton a price of $40 a unit for manufacturing the test models. Dalton's marketing people want to accept this order because filling the special order would give them the experience necessary to prepare a realistic bid on the long-term contract. Unit costs for the follow-on contract would be a good deal lower than for this special order, which they expect to average as follows:

Direct materials	$26
Direct labor	12
Factory overhead	24
Total	$62

The staff estimates that at normal volume 25 percent of the factory overhead costs are variable—that is, one fourth of the overhead rate represents variable costs and three fourths is fixed. Their estimates of variable costs therefore show the following:

Direct materials	$26
Direct labor	12
Variable factory overhead	6
Total differential cost	$44

This still leaves them with a differential cost estimate $4 greater than the $40 limit.

What the specialty products people have overlooked in this case is that the materials for this order are fabricated parts that would be produced in Dalton's own factories. The $26 in materials costs therefore includes some of these factories' fixed overhead costs. The transmutation of fixed overhead costs into direct materials costs is illustrated schematically in Exhibit 4–12.

To dig out the differential costs of these materials, the staff has gone back and pulled the fixed component out of each of the overhead rates reflected in the $26 figure. This analysis has shown that $5 of fixed factory overhead is included in the $26 materials cost figure. Excluding this amount brings the estimate of differential cost down to $39, just $1 less than the price offered. If the estimates are correct, Dalton can fill the order without reducing its overall profit.

Exhibit 4–12 The fixed overhead component of the costs of some materials

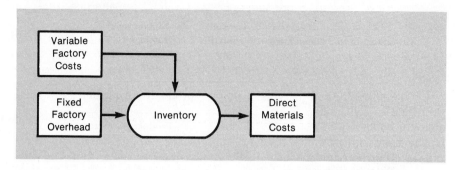

Capacity rationing decisions

The third capacity utilization decision we have chosen to illustrate at this point is the capacity rationing decision. Capacity rationing is called for when the company lacks enough of one or more elements of input—such as machine time, labor time, or materials quantities—to supply all the output it could sell at profitable prices.

contribution margin

In its simplest form, the analysis of a capacity rationing problem calls for a new measure of product profitability known as *contribution margin.* Contribution margin is the spread between the net price of a unit of a product or service and the average variable cost of producing and distributing a unit of that product or service. It may be expressed as a rate per unit or as a percentage of the selling price. This rate or percentage is known as the *contribution margin ratio;* it is used to approximate the profit effects of changes in sales volume.

contrib. margin ratio

When only one resource is scarce and the variable costs of each product vary proportionally with variations in product volume, the analysis of a capacity rationing problem is a four-step process:

1. Calculate the contribution margin per unit for each of the products or services that can be produced using the scarce resource.
2. Calculate the amount of the scarce resource a unit of each product or service requires.
3. Calculate the contribution margin per scarce resource unit for each product or service—that is, divide the results of step 1 by the results of step 2.
4. Array the products or services in descending order of contribution margin per unit and allocate the available capacity by starting from the top of the list, working down until all capacity has been assigned.

For example, suppose labor time in department X is the scarce resource. Several departments, including department X, perform production operations on two of the company's products, A and B. The company could sell 800 units of product A and 1,600 units of product B, if it had the capacity. Unfortunately, department X has only 400 hours of direct labor available for these two products, enough to produce either of them but not both:

Contrib. margin provides an amount to offset fixed costs ⇒ contributes to gross +'s.

Product	Units per Direct Labor Hour	Maximum Demand (units)	Hours Needed for Maximum Demand
A	2	800	400
B	4	1,600	400

The contribution margins of the two products are as follows:

	Product A	Product B
Variable unit costs:		
Direct materials	$1.50	$1.25
Direct labor, department X	4.00	2.00
Variable overhead, department X	1.00	0.50
Variable costs, other departments	2.00	3.75
Total variable cost	8.50	7.50
Unit price	9.25	8.00
Contribution margin per unit	0.75	0.50
Direct labor hours per unit	0.50	0.25
Contribution margin per direct labor hour	$1.50	$2.00

This calculation shows that the company will maximize its contribution margin if it uses the available direct labor hours to produce product B instead of product A. We can verify this by calculating the total contribution margin available from each product:

Product	Contribution Margin per Unit	Number of Units	Total Contribution Margin
A	$0.75	800	$600
B	0.50	1,600	800

Notice that in this case two of the determinants of contribution margin are really sunk costs. No matter which product is manufactured, department X will use all 400 available direct labor hours. Its total direct labor cost therefore will amount to $400 \times \$8 = \$3,200$ under either alternative. This being the case, we can ignore direct labor costs in choosing the product to produce. Furthermore, since variable overhead costs in department X vary with the number of direct labor hours, they too will be the same in total no matter which product is produced. This means we can ignore variable overhead costs, too. It does no harm to leave the direct labor and variable overhead costs in the analysis, however, because they will cancel themselves out in the comparison of alternatives.

Product emphasis decisions

A major use of contribution margin ratios is in product emphasis decisions—that is, decisions affecting the *product mix*, the relative proportions in which

the various products are sold. To study this question, let's assume the company
has three products with the following contribution margin ratios:

	Product A	Product B	Product C
Selling price per unit	$20	$10	$ 5
Variable costs per unit	15	6	2
Contribution margin per unit	$ 5	$ 4	$ 3
Contribution margin ratio	25%	40%	60%

The contribution margin ratio shows how profit would respond if volume
were to increase or decrease by small amounts, other factors remaining unchanged. Before we recommend actions to management based on these ratios,
however, we need to consider three other influences:

1. Effort/result ratios are unequal.
2. Management must change the total amount spent on sales promotion if
   it wishes to change the product mix favorably.
3. Sales of some products are interdependent.

Differences in effort/result ratios.   One way to influence the product
mix is to shift advertising or the time of salespeople from one product to
another. Shifts of this sort should not be based solely on product-to-product
differences in contribution margin, however. Some products are harder to
sell than others, and the response to the increased effort on these may be
too small to offset the effects of lost sales of other products.

For example, if salespeople can sell $2 worth of product B in the time it
would take them to sell $1 worth of product C, they should stick to product
B. $2 of B yields a contribution margin of $2 × 40 percent = 80 cents,
while $1 of C yields only 60 cents.

Changes in marketing expenditures.   The second way to shift the product
mix is to change the amounts spent to promote individual products. Analyzing
the profitability of these changes is a five-step process:

1. Estimate the fixed costs required by each proposal and the proposed net
   selling price for each product (gross price less discounts, allowances, and
   uncollectible amounts).
2. Using variable costing data and the proposed net selling prices, calculate
   the estimated contribution margin per unit for each product.
3. For each proposal, estimate the sales of each product.
4. Multiply the estimated unit contribution margins by the estimated sales
   and subtract the estimated fixed costs.
5. Evaluate the risks each proposal will entail and choose the proposal that
   offers the risk-profit combination that management finds most acceptable.

For example, management has prepared the following estimates for two
different marketing proposals:

	Contribution Margin per Unit	Proposal X		Proposal Y	
		Units Sold	Contribution Margin	Units Sold	Contribution Margin
Product A	$5	90,000	$450,000	66,000	$ 330,000
Product B	4	90,000	360,000	132,000	528,000
Product C	3	60,000	180,000	132,000	396,000
Total contribution margin			990,000		1,254,000
Total fixed cost			627,000		927,000
Income before taxes ..			$363,000		$ 327,000

In the absence of strong contradictory information, this analysis clearly points to proposal X as the preferred choice.

Product complementarity and substitutability. One contradictory factor in the situation we just discussed might be that proposal Y is significantly riskier than proposal X. Risk management is a topic of its own, however, and we'll postpone taking a look at it until Chapter 5. The only factor we'll examine here is the likelihood that increased sales of one product may either increase or decrease sales of one or more others. A product's contribution margin ratio therefore may understate or overstate the effects of changes in product volume.

For example, the contribution margin for proposal X at the anticipated product mix is as follows:

	Product A	Product B	Product C	Total
Units sold	90,000	90,000	60,000	
Sales revenues	$1,800,000	$900,000	$300,000	$3,000,000
Variable costs	1,350,000	540,000	120,000	2,010,000
Contribution margin	$ 450,000	$360,000	$180,000	$ 990,000
Contribution margin percent of sales ...	25%	40%	60%	33%

The company expects to have $627,000 in fixed costs, leaving income before taxes of $363,000.

Not satisfied with this probable result, management is considering spending an extra $20,000 a month on its efforts to sell product C. Management is convinced that this would increase sales of product C to 70,000 units a month, 10,000 more than the rate currently anticipated. If this forecast is correct, product C's contribution margin would be:

	New Proposal	Increase over Present Proposal
Sales revenues	$350,000	$50,000
Variable costs (40 percent of sales)	140,000	20,000
Contribution margin	$210,000	$30,000

In other words, management believes that spending the extra $20,000 would add $30,000 to the contribution margin, a net benefit of $10,000.

Management knows, however, that some of the company's customers see products B and C as possible substitutes for each other. Product B sells for $10, double the price of product C. Some customers are willing to pay this price, while others find the $10 price too high and buy product C. If the additional promotional effort succeeds in increasing sales of product C, sales of product B are likely to fall.

substitution effects

In fact, management estimates that 10 percent of any added sales of product C would be a direct result of customers shifting away from product B. These shifts are known as *substitution effects.* In this case an additional 10,000 units of product C would divert 1,000 buyers away from product B. At a $10 price, these lost sales would add up to $10,000 a month. With a 40 percent contribution margin ratio, $4,000 in contribution margin would be lost. This amount must be subtracted in any calculation of the profit to be derived from the increased effort to be devoted to product C, as follows:

Added contribution margin from product C ...	$30,000
Lost contribution margin from product B	(4,000)
Increased promotional expenditures	(20,000)
Differential profit	$ 6,000

We are not quite finished with our illustration. Management knows that many people buy product A only because they use product C. Every sale of a unit of product C adds a tenth of a unit to the sales of product A, without any increase in the fixed selling costs of product A. In other words, products A and C are *complementary* products, not substitutes. (Razors and blades, cameras and film, and pens and refills are familiar examples.)

complementary effects

Since the proposal would increase sales of product C by 10,000 units a month, product A's sales should go up by one tenth of that, or 1,000 units. At a selling price of $20 a unit and a 25 percent contribution margin, this would bring in $20,000 in revenues and $5,000 in contribution margin. The final estimates can be put together easily:

Added contribution margin from product C ...	$30,000
Added contribution margin from product A ...	5,000
Lost contribution margin from product B	(4,000)
Increased promotional expenditures	(20,000)
Net differential profit	$11,000

These figures show that, risk differences apart, management will improve the company's cash flows by accepting the proposal to increase marketing expenditures on product C.

Summary

Decisions should always be based on estimates of differences among the alternatives available. Only differential or incremental profits are relevant to decisions: sunk costs should be ignored, and opportunity costs must not be overlooked. Furthermore, the profit differences among alternatives should be measured in terms of the effects of the decisions on the flows of cash into and out of the organization.

One major determinant of cost is operating volume, the rate at which the organization uses its resources. Variable costs respond to variations in operating volume within the limits of existing capacity; fixed costs either generate volume or maintain the organization's capacity to do business, and do not respond to variations in operating volume.

Although fixed costs may not change if the decision affects only a small portion of the volume range, some fixed costs may be incremental if the decision has a major effect on volume. Since fixed costs are assigned to products by means of averages, these averages must be adjusted to make them relevant to decisions in which the average doesn't conform to the increment. In any case, decisions should be based on differences in totals; average costs are likely to be poor approximations to decision-generated differences in total costs.

Contribution margin is a measure of product profitability that is often useful in short-term resource-allocation decisions, particularly as a means of estimating the impact of volume changes that result from changes in varibles such as product emphasis or the level of marketing effort. It also is useful in the kind of profit-volume analysis we'll study in Chapter 5.

Independent study problems (solutions in Appendix B)

1. **Cost-volume relationships.** From the following estimates of total cost at different volumes, compute (a) average total cost, (b) average fixed cost, (c) average variable cost, and (d) marginal cost for each volume of activity. (Note: For this problem assume that fixed cost is the same at all volumes.)

Volume (units)	Cost
0	$10
1	11
2	12
3	13
4	14
5	15
6	16
7	17
8	18
9	20
10	23

2. **Using average costs in decisions.** The manager of a department in a social welfare agency has proposed the inauguration of a new social service, requiring the addition of 15 social workers to his department's payroll. The costs of other departments in the agency would not be affected by the addition of this new service, except as noted below.

The director of the agency agrees that the social service would fill an important need and that providing it would be consistent with the agency's charter. She can make $200,000 available to finance this service by discontinuing one of the services now being provided by one of the agency's other departments, but will do so only if the new service can be provided for $200,000 or less.

The department head has developed the following figures:

	If Service Is	
	Provided	Not Provided
Total number of social workers in department	25	10
Average cost of department's operations	$14,000	$15,500

Required:

Calculate differential cost. Should the proposal be approved?

3. **Opportunity cost.** Nancy Smith bought 100 shares in Hydrophonics Ltd., on January 15, 19x1, paying $15 a share. She bought an additional 100 shares on March 18, 19x4, paying $20 a share. The market price of this stock fell rapidly in 19x5, reaching a low point of $6 a share. Early in 19x6 the market price had recovered to $8 a share. At that point General Enterprises, Inc., offered to buy all shares tendered to it at a price of $10 a share.

   Required:

   What cost figure should Ms. Smith use in evaluating this offer?

4. **Product emphasis decision.** Cartright, Inc., manufactures two products, A and B, in its only factory. Product A has a contribution margin of $3 a unit; product B has a contribution margin of $5 a unit. Fixed manufacturing costs amount to $60,000 a month, and none of this amount is traceable specifically to either product. Selling and administrative costs amount to $20,000 a month.

   Cartright is now selling 20,000 units of product A and 10,000 units of product B each month. Marketing management is considering two alternatives to its present pattern of operations:

		Expected Monthly Results
Alternative		
Increase emphasis on product A	Sales of A	24,000 units
	Sales of B	9,000 units
	Selling and administrative costs	$18,000
Increase emphasis on product B	Sales of A	15,000 units
	Sales of B	14,000 units
	Selling and administrative costs	$24,000

Required:

Should either of these alternatives be selected, or should Cartright continue on its present course?

5. **Make or buy decision.** The purchasing agent of Planette, Inc. has just recommended that the company purchase its requirements of three machine parts that are used in repairing some of the machines in Planette's factory. These parts are now being manufactured in the company's own repair shop.

   The purchasing agent has collected the following data to support the recommendation:

Part No.	Estimated Monthly Requirements	Purchase Price per Unit	Manufacturing Cost per Unit			
			Labor	Materials	Overhead	Total
104	120 units	$4.00	$2.00	$1.80	$1.51	$ 5.31
173	200 units	7.00	3.90	2.30	2.94	9.14
221	50 units	8.00	4.80	2.20	3.62	10.62

The factory engineer opposes the purchasing agent's proposal, pointing out that direct labor and direct materials costs are less than the purchase price for each part.

As controller of the company, you have the following additional information:

1. Full-cost overhead rates are used in each factory department, including the repair shop. These are predetermined rates, based on anticipated overhead costs at normal production volume.

2. Production volume in the repair shop is measured by the amount of direct labor cost in that department. Normal volume is $13,000 direct labor cost. If the repair shop continues to manufacture these three parts, its monthly operating volume is expected to average $11,500 in direct labor costs during the coming year.

3. If the parts are purchased, all of the direct labor of manufacturing them can be saved—that is, the total direct labor payroll will be reduced by this amount.

4. The repair shop's operating costs other than direct labor and direct materials are as follows:

	Direct Labor Cost per Month		
	$10,000	$11,500	$13,000
Overhead:			
Supervision	$ 1,200	$ 1,200	$ 1,200
Indirect labor	2,000	2,300	2,600
Indirect materials	500	575	650
Service charges	3,500	3,575	3,650
Depreciation	800	800	800
Other fixed charges	900	900	900
Total overhead	$ 8,900	$ 9,350	$ 9,800
Overhead/direct labor	$ 0.890	$ 0.813	$ 0.754

5. None of the present equipment in the shop will be retired if the proposal is accepted because the shop must always be in readiness to perform emergency work. Similarly, the size of the inventory will not be affected by this decision.

6. If the proposal is accepted, purchasing and handling costs will be increased by $100 a month for each part the company decides to buy.

Required:

Prepare a recommendation on this proposal, giving figures to support your conclusions.

Exercises and problems

6. **Marginal cost.** The line in each of the following diagrams shows how total cost for one cost element varies with volume. For each of these, indicate whether marginal cost increases with volume, decreases, remains constant, or behaves in some other way:

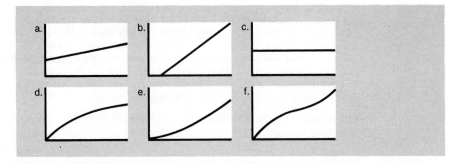

7. **Average variable cost.**   For each of the diagrams in problem 6, indicate whether average variable cost increases, decreases, remains constant, or follows some other pattern as volume increases.

8. **Cost-volume relationship.**   From the following estimates of hourly cost at different hourly volumes, compute (*a*) average total cost, (*b*) average fixed cost, (*c*) average variable cost, and (*d*) marginal cost for each volume of activity. (Note: For this problem assume that fixed cost is the same at all volumes.)

Units	Cost
0	$100
1	200
2	250
3	290
4	330
5	370
6	410
7	450
8	500
9	570
10	670

9. **Variations in fixed costs.**   The following letter was received from a cost accounting student:

> Dear Sir:
>
>   In your book you say that fixed costs may be affected by changes in the volume of activity. I have had three economics instructors, all of whom have their doctoral degrees, tell me that this definition is incorrect. They argue that if a cost is fixed it does not change. Would you please explain to me this difference of opinion?
>
> Sincerely,

Required:
How would you answer this letter?

10. **Incremental analysis; multiple choice.**   In each of the following, select the choice that best answers the question:

1. Light Company has 2,000 obsolete light fixtures that are carried in inventory at a manufacturing cost of $30,000. If the fixtures are reworked for $10,000, they can be sold for $18,000. Alternatively, the fixtures can be sold for $3,000 to a jobber located in a distant city. In a decision model used to analyze the reworking proposal, the opportunity cost should be entered as:

(*a*) zero,   (*b*) $3,000,   (*c*) $10,000,   (*d*) $13,000,   (*e*) $30,000.

2. Woody Company, which manufactures sneakers, has enough idle capacity to accept a special order of 20,000 pairs of sneakers at $6 a pair. The normal selling price is $10 a pair. Variable manufacturing costs are $4.50 a pair, and fixed manufacturing costs are $1.50 a pair. Woody will incur no incremental selling expenses as a result of the special order, nor will total fixed manufacturing costs be affected. The effect on income before taxes if the special order can be accepted without affecting normal sales will be:

(a) zero, (b) $30,000 increase, (c) $90,000 increase, (d) $120,000 increase.

3. Argus Company, a manufacturer of lamps, budgeted sales of 400,000 lamps at $20 a unit for the year 19x0. Variable manufacturing costs were budgeted at $8 a unit, and fixed manufacturing costs were budgeted at $5 a unit. A special offer to buy 40,000 lamps for $11.50 each was received by Argus in April 19x0. Argus had enough plant capacity to manufacture the additional quantity of lamps; the production would have to be done by the regular work force on an overtime basis, however, at an estimated additional cost of $1.50 per lamp. Argus would incur no incremental selling expenses as a result of the special order. What would be the effect on income before taxes if the special order could be accepted without affecting normal sales?

(a) $60,000 decrease, (b) $80,000 increase, (c) $120,000 decrease, (d) $140,000 increase.

4. Cardinal Company needs 20,000 units of a certain part to use in its production cycle. The following information is available:

Cost to Cardinal to make the part:	
Direct materials	$ 4
Direct labor	16
Variable overhead	8
Fixed overhead applied	10
Total	$38
Cost to Cardinal if it buys	
the part from the Oriole Comapny	$36

If Cardinal buys the part from Oriole instead of making it, Cardinal will not be able to use the released facilities in another manufacturing activity. Sixty percent of the fixed overhead applied will continue if Cardinal buys the part from Oriole. In deciding whether to make or buy the part, the total relevant costs to make the part are:

(a) $560,000, (b) $640,000, (c) $720,000, (d) $760,000.

5. Motor Company manufactures 10,000 units of part M-1 for use in its production annually. The following costs are reported:

Direct materials	$ 20,000
Direct labor	55,000
Variable overhead	45,000
Fixed overhead	70,000
Total	$190,000

Valve Company has offered to sell Motor 10,000 units of part M-1 for $18 a unit. If Motor accepts the offer, some of the facilities presently used to manufacture part M-1 can be rented to a third party at an annual rental of $15,000. Additionally, $4 a unit of the fixed overhead will be eliminated. Should Motor accept Valve's offer, and why?

a. No, because it would be $5,000 cheaper to make the part.
b. Yes, because it would be $10,000 cheaper to buy the part.
c. No, because it would be $15,000 cheaper to make the part.
d. Yes, because it would be $25,000 cheaper to buy the part.

(AICPA, adapted)

11. **Incremental and sunk costs.**   Last year Mogul Movies, Inc., paid $300,000 for the screen rights to a novel, *Virtue Is Its Own Reward*. The film was made earlier this year at a cost of $1 million. This figure includes $100,000 for depreciation on studio facilities and $250,000 for costumes and rental charges on equipment used during filming. This latter amount has not yet been paid, but arrangements have been made to pay it later this year.

   The author of *Virtue Is Its Own Reward* has just been arrested and has pleaded guilty to a charge of plagiarism. The novel actually was written by two other people. The real authors will allow the film to be released if Mogul Movies will pay them $500,000 in cash. Costs of insuring, advertising, and delivering the films to the theaters will amount to $50,000 if the film is released.

   Top management at Mogul Movies estimates that if the film is released in its present form, Mogul's share of the theater receipts will be $700,000, spread out over the next 10 months.

   Required:
   a. Classify each of the costs described in this problem as either relevant or irrelevant to the decision to release the film.
   b. Should the film be released? Show your calculations.

12. **Incremental and sunk costs.**   An oil company has paid a foreign government $12 million for the rights to explore for oil. If oil is found, the agreement calls for the oil company to pay the government $24 for every barrel produced.

   The company has spent $9 million on the drilling operation and has just struck oil. Management estimates that it will be able to recover 10 million barrels of oil from this field. This oil can be sold for $30 a barrel and it will cost $3 a barrel to get it out of the ground.

   Yesterday the government imposed an additional fee of $1.80 a barrel, to pay for insurance against damages caused by oil spills that might take place in the future.

   Required:
   Should the company begin producing oil? Prepare an analysis to support your recommendation.

13. **Opportunity cost; special order.**   As a result of an expansion program, Pasabache Industries has excess capacity which is expected to be absorbed by the domestic market in a few years. Twenty-five thousand excess machine-hours are available for the next year.

   It has received inquiries from two firms located abroad. One offers to buy 2 million units of product A at 3.8 cents a unit; the second offers to buy 3 million units of product B at 5 cents a unit. Management has made the following estimates:

	Product A	Product B
Unit costs:		
Variable costs	$0.029	$0.042
Fixed costs	0.009	0.012
Total costs	$0.038	$0.054
Machine-hours per thousand units	6	8

   Required:
   One of the two orders will be accepted. Which should it be? Why?

14. **Incremental cost: Special order.** The overhead rate of a factory is $3 a machine-hour, based on estimated costs at a normal operating volume of 10,000 machine-hours a month. Operating volume is now running at a rate of 9,000 machine-hours a month and overhead costs at this volume total $28,800, an average of $3.20 an hour. No change in cost or volume is in sight unless management accepts the order described in the next paragraph.

A customer has offered to buy all of its requirements of a machined part for the next year. This order would add 1,000 machine-hours a month to the factory's volume. The price received would exceed the cost of direct labor and direct materials by $2,900 a month.

Required:

Would you use $3.20, $3, or some other cost per hour to estimate overhead cost for the purpose of deciding whether to accept this order? Give your reasons. Would you accept the order?

15. **Average costs; minimum price.** A factory's costs can be estimated accurately from the following schedule of average cost per hour:

Hours	Cost
4,000	$6.25
4,500	6.11
5,000	6.00
5,500	5.91

The company has a chance to bid on a new job that would add 500 hours a month for two months to the factory's volume. Efficient workers for this job can be obtained without difficulty or loss of efficiency. The job would have no effect on nonfactory costs.

Without this job, the factory would operate at a monthly volume of 4,000 hours. When built, the plant was expected to operate 5,000 hours a month, on the average.

Required:

What is the minimum price the company could afford to quote for this job without being worse off?

16. **Make or buy.** The Blade Division of Dana Company produces hardened steel blades. One third of the Blade Division's output (10,000 blades) is sold to the Lawn Products Division of Dana; the remainder is sold to outside customers. The Blade Division's estimated sales and cost data for the coming year are as follows:

	Lawn Products	Outsiders
Sales revenues	$15,000	$40,000
Variable cost of goods sold	(10,000)	(20,000)
Fixed cost of goods sold	(3,000)	(6,000)
Gross margin	$ 2,000	$14,000

The Lawn Products Division now has an opportunity to buy 10,000 blades of identical quality from an outside supplier on a continuing basis at a delivered cost of $1.25. The Blade Division cannot sell any additional products to outside customers, and average fixed cost in the Blade Division will increase from its present 30 cents to a new level of 40 cents a blade if Lawn Products buys its blades from the outside supplier.

Required:

By how much will Dana Company's income before tax increase or decrease if Lawn Products buys the blades from the outside supplier?

(AICPA, adapted)

17. **Make or buy; maximum price.** Golden, Inc., manufactures Part 10541 in one of its factories, along with many other products. This part is used in the manufacture of one of Golden's most highly profitable products. The company has been manufacturing 5,000 units of Part 10541 each month, and at this level of production, the manufacturing cost per unit is as follows:

Direct materials	$ 2
Direct labor	8
Variable factory overhead	4
Fixed factory overhead applied	6
Total	$20

None of the fixed factory overhead costs is specifically traceable to the manufacture of Part 10541.

Brown Company has offered to sell Golden 5,000 units of Part 10541 each month if a suitable price can be negotiated. If Golden buys Part 10541 from Brown, Golden will be able to use the idled manufacturing capacity to manufacture an additional 10,000 units of product RAC. These additional units of RAC would increase RAC's total contribution margin by $14,000 a month with no increase in fixed selling and administrative costs associated with RAC. Golden's total fixed manufacturing overhead would decrease by $2,000 a month if the company were to buy Part 10541 from Brown and manufacture product RAC instead. Golden has no other manufacturing capacity available to expand its production of RAC.

Required:

a. Prepare an estimate of the maximum unit price Golden could afford to pay Brown for Part 10541. Show and label your calculations clearly.
b. Indicate, with figures, the extent to which the concept of opportunity cost is relevant to this decision.

(AICPA, adapted)

18. **Relevant benchmark; adding a product.** The Downtown Business Institute has two classrooms for which it pays monthly rentals of $800 each. These classrooms are adequate for the three courses the institute now offers its students. These three courses make the following monthly profits:

Course	Profit
Bookkeeping	$1,600
Typing	1,300
Shorthand	960

These profit figures are the differences between revenues and the costs directly associated with each course; no deductions for classroom rentals or top management expenses have been made.

Management is thinking of offering a course in computer programming. This could be done in the existing classroom, but only if one of the three current courses were to be discontinued. Additional classroom space is available in the institute's present building, however, and management is trying to decide whether to rent this space and offer the new course.

The additional space can be rented for $1,100 a month. The expected monthly profit from the new programming course is as follows:

Tuition and fees		$6,000
Expenses:		
Teaching salaries	$2,400	
Equipment rental	400	
Telephone charges	300	
Books and supplies	600	
Other	200	
Total expenses		3,900
Profit		$2,100

Required:

What should the institute do? Cite figures to support your conclusions.

19. **Differential cost; marginal cost.** A manufacturing plant operates with a single shift five days a week. It can produce up to 8,000 units of output a week without the use of overtime or extra-shift operation. Fixed costs for single-shift operation amount to $30,000 a week. Average variable cost is a constant $10 a unit at all output rates up to 8,000 units a week. The plant's output can be increased to 12,000 units a week by going on overtime or adding Saturday operations or both. This entails no increase in fixed costs, but the variable cost is $12 a unit for any output in excess of 8,000 units a week up to the 12,000-unit capacity.

The plant also operates a second shift if sales volume warrants, and if second-shift operation is more efficient than overtime or Saturday operation. The maximum capacity of the second shift is 7,000 units a week. The variable cost on the second shift is $10.50 a unit, and operation of a second shift entails additional fixed costs of $4,500 a week.

Required:

a. At what operating volume does it become economical to operate a second shift? (Assume that the product cannot be inventoried in any substantial quantities.)

b. Prepare a schedule of marginal cost for output rates ranging from 5,000 units a week to 17,000 units a week, in 1,000-unit intervals, assuming that any overtime or Saturday operations are performed by the first shift.

20. **Bidding on a special order.** The Argus Company has just received an invitation to quote a price for installing the electrical wiring in a new building. Mr. Jason Argus, the company's president, estimates that this job would require 250 labor hours *each month for two months.* Total materials cost of the job would be $850.

Mr. Argus says that the work force is flexible enough to let him operate at any volume between 2,000 and 2,500 labor hours a month. Volumes in excess of 2,500 labor hours are completely beyond the company's current capacity, because trained personnel are not available and the present work force will not add further to their overtime hours.

Mr. Argus estimates that the company's average operating costs, excluding materials cost, ought to be as follows:

Total Monthly Volume (labor hours)	Average Cost per Labor Hour
2,000	$7.92
2,250	7.70
2,500	7.90

Mr. Argus also tells you that all of his other work is priced at $10 a labor hour, plus materials costs.

Required:

Assuming that these estimates are correct, calculate the minimum price the company could charge for this job without losing money on it if, without this job, the company would have enough other work to operate at a volume of:

a.   2,000 labor hours a month.
b.   2,250 labor hours a month.
c.   2,500 labor hours a month.

21. **Rationing limited capacity.**   Overhead costs in department Z vary with the quantity of materials processed in the department. The following formula is used to derive estimates of overhead cost:

Department Z overhead cost = $10,000 per month + $1 per pound of materials.

The overhead rate used for product costing is 50 percent of direct labor cost.

The department manufactures several products and is now operating at its full physical capacity of 12,500 pounds of materials each month. The marketing manager has suggested that production of product A be discontinued, to make room for production and sale of a new product, product B. Either product would be processed completely in department Z. The following estimates of monthly costs and revenues have been presented to management:

	Product A	Product B
Materials quantity required	2,500 lbs.	2,500 lbs.
Revenues from sales	$32,000	$28,000
Production costs:		
Direct materials	4,600	5,000
Direct labor	13,000	9,000
Overhead (50 percent of direct labor)	6,500	4,500
Total production costs	24,100	18,500
Profit margin	$ 7,900	$ 9,500

The manufacture of product B would require additional quality control inspection. This would increase fixed factory overhead costs by $900 a month. Adequate quantities of direct labor and direct materials could be obtained for either product; the total size of the labor force can be increased or decreased without penalty.

Selling and administrative expenses will be unaffected by the choice between these two products.

Required:

Which of these two products should be manufactured? Present figures to support your conclusion.

22. **Make or buy; using idle space.**   Datamine Corporation manufactures a line of minicomputers which are built with subassemblies supplied by electronic equipment manufacturers. The company builds none of these subassemblies at the present time, but the production, engineering, and accounting departments have gathered the following data to help management decide whether to set up a new production department to manufacture one of the most critical subassemblies:

1.   Number of units required—50,000 a year.
2.   Direct materials cost—$19 a unit.
3.   Direct labor cost, four hours @ $12.50—$50 a unit.
4.   Vacant space is available in the factory building to set up this production department; this space is not suitable for rental to outsiders.
5.   Salaried supervisory staff needed for the new department:

Department manager	$3,500 a month
Two manager assistants	1,500 a month (each)
Chief production engineer	2,000 a month
Three line supervisors	1,500 a month (each)

6. All necessary production equipment can be leased for a total monthly payment of $32,000 a month.
7. The current purchase price of the subassembly is $100 a unit.
8. Depreciation on existing equipment in Datamine's factory is $100,000 a year.
9. Variable factory overhead is currently applied at a rate of $5 a direct labor hour; this rate would not change with the addition of the new department.
10. The company now pays $15,000 a month to lease its production building. The new department would take up 20 percent of the usable space in that building.

Required:

a. Should Datamine Corporation continue to purchase the subassembly or set up the production department and manufacture it? Show all supporting calculations.

b. What other factors would be considered before a final decision was made?

(SMAC, adapted)

23. **Using materials on hand.** Jones Company has 2,000 yards of a plastic material on hand; 1,000 yards were purchased last month for $2 a yard and 1,000 yards were purchased later for $2.20 a yard. This material deteriorates in storage and the present inventories will become worthless if the company doesn't use or sell them during the next six weeks.

Some of the inventory of the plastic material could be used to make product A. Each unit of product A would require one yard of the material plus $3 in other incremental costs. A maximum of 500 units of product A could be sold at a price of $5.25 a unit.

The company is also thinking of manufacturing product B. Each unit of B would require one yard of the material plus $4 in other incremental costs.

The Jones Company could sell any quantity of the plastic material, without further processing, for $1.80 a yard. It could also buy additional quantities of this material for $2.40 a yard.

a. A customer has offered to buy 1,500 units of product B in the next six weeks if the price is right and if Jones agrees to sell no product B to anyone else during that period. What unit cost would you compare with the offer price in evaluating the desirability of accepting this order?

b. How would your answer to (*a*) differ if the offer was for 2,000 units, with each unit to bear the same price? 2,500 units?

c. How would your answers to (*a*) and (*b*) differ if the customer were willing to pay a different price for each successive batch of 500 units to be delivered in the next six weeks? In other words, calculate a unit cost for the first 1,500 units, a separate unit cost for the next 500 units, and another separate unit cost for the final 500 units.

d. Suppose the customer in (*a*) has offered to buy 2,000 units at a price of $6 a unit. The customer will not accept any units unless Jones supplies the full 2,000 units ordered. Should Jones accept this order and produce and sell 500 units of product A as well?

(From a problem by Alfred Oxenfeldt)

24. **Using available capacity.** In March of last year, Alicia Cranshaw was trying to decide what to do. Ms. Cranshaw was the owner-president of Cranshaw Packaging Services, Inc., a small firm located in Bethlehem, Pennsylvania. The Cranshaw

firm advised its clients with ideas about how to package their products, worked with clients' personnel to keep packaging equipment operating efficiently and even supplied people and equipment from time to time to do small specialty packaging jobs that clients were not equipped to do themselves.

Ms. Cranshaw's immediate concern was whether to take a job for one of the packaging machines, the AX-40. This machine had been developed by Ms. Cranshaw and one of her engineers several years earlier to provide the company with capacity to wrap regularly packed products in special gift wrappings. It had proved so successful that it was always fully booked during the months of August through mid-November, as clients prepared for the annual holiday trade. It often remained partly idle during the rest of the year, however, because few local companies needed special packaging work in the off season.

Ms. Cranshaw had worked untiringly to find more off-season jobs for the AX-40, but her efforts had been only partly successful. Now two local manufacturers who had never before been Cranshaw clients had expressed an interest in using the machine during the spring months, but only at prices lower than Cranshaw Packaging usually charged. One of these, Maurer Products, Inc., offered to pay $30,000 for the use of the equipment for a period of 35 days. The work would be done by Cranshaw employees in the Cranshaw shop. The other prospect, Franklin Packing Company, wished to use the equipment in its own plant, with its own employees. The contract would be for a 60-day period, including shipping and installation time. Franklin Packing would pay $10,000 plus all costs of transportation and installation, including transport insurance.

No other potential users were in sight, and Ms. Cranshaw thought that if she took on one of these jobs she might make some money and gain a steady customer to boot. Before going ahead, however, she asked Robert Underwood, her assistant, to work up the costs for the two proposals. Mr. Underwood returned with the following figures:

	Maurer	Franklin
Days required	35	60
Proposed contract price	$30,000	$10,000
Estimated costs:		
Labor	17,500	100
Supplies	2,000	—
Maintenance	500	750
_F.O.H._ — Depreciation ($20/day)	700	1,200
SUNK — Amortization of development costs ($100/day)	3,500	6,000
_V.O.H_ — Power	2,100	—
_F.O.H._ — Insurance	100	250
_V.O.H_ — Administrative expenses (5 percent of sales)	1,500	500
Total costs	27,900	8,800
Profit margin	$ 2,100	$ 1,200

The maintenance cost figures in this table represent the estimated out-of-pocket cost of overhauling and adjusting the machine at the end of the contract. The insurance figures represent the cost of fire, theft, and vandalism insurance. The insurance company charged a higher premium for any day the machine was not on the Cranshaw company's property.

Mr. Underwood reminded Ms. Cranshaw that the costs of developing and building the AX-40 had not yet been completely amortized. For this reason, this machine would remain fairly costly to operate for about two more years.

Required:

Only one of these two proposals could be accepted because both customers wanted to use the machine at about the same time. What would you have recommended?

25. **Special order.** George Jackson operates a small machine shop. He manufactures one standard product which he sells in competition with many other similar businesses and he also manufactures products to customer order. His accountant has prepared the following summary from the annual income statement:

	Custom Sales	Standard Sales	Total
Sales revenues	$50,000	$25,000	$75,000
Expenses:			
Material	10,000	8,000	18,000
Labor	20,000	9,000	29,000
F Depreciation	6,300	3,600	9,900
✓ Power	700	400	1,100
F Rent	6,000	1,000	7,000
✓ Heat and light	600	100	700
½ Miscellaneous	400	900	1,300
Total expenses	44,000	23,000	67,000
Income before taxes	$ 6,000	$ 2,000	$ 8,000

The depreciation charges are for machines used in the respective product lines. The power charge is apportioned on estimates of the amounts of power consumed by each line. The rent is for the building space which has been leased for 10 years at $7,000 a year. The rent, heat, and light are apportioned to the product lines based on the amount of floor space occupied. All other costs are directly traceable to the specific product lines.

Power costs for each product line tend to vary with the amount of materials processed for that line. Miscellaneous expenses are half fixed for each product line; the variable portion varies with the labor cost in the line.

A valued customer of custom products has asked Mr. Jackson if he would manufacture 5,000 special units for him. Mr. Jackson is working at capacity and would have to give up some other business in order to take this business. He can't renege on custom orders already agreed to but he could reduce the output of his standard product by about one half for one year while producing the specially requested custom product.

The customer is willing to pay $7 for each custom unit. The material cost would be about $2 a unit and the labor would be $3.60 a unit. Mr. Jackson would have to spend $2,000 for a special device which would be discarded when the job was done.

Required:

a. Calculate and present the following:
   (1) The incremental cost of producing the special units, ignoring the impact of this production on other production.
   (2) The opportunity cost of taking the order.
b. Should Mr. Jackson take the order? Explain your answer.

(CMA, adapted)

26. **Incremental cost from full-cost data; long-term versus short-term** Arden Corporation manufactures a plastic compound known as TFC-2. Its entire output of this compound, about 1 million pounds a year, has been used in the production of several of the company's finished products; none has been sold to outside customers.

Arden uses 100,000 pounds of TFC-2 a year in the manufacture of flanges. Ten pounds of TFC-2 are used for each box of flanges manufactured. You have the following estimates of manufacturing costs for the company's *total* volumes of TFC-2 and flanges:

	TFC-2	Flanges
Annual volume (units)	1 million pounds	10,000 boxes
Cost per unit:		
Direct materials...............	$0.80	$ 4*
Direct labor	1.60	10
Variable overhead	1.20	6
Fixed overhead	1.00	8
Total	$4.60	$28* + 10(4.60)

* Plus 10 pounds of TFC-2 per box.

Henley Corporation has just developed a substitute for TFC-2, known as antrex, and has offered to sell 100,000 pounds of this product to Arden for use in the manufacture of flanges during the coming year. The price would be $4.10 a pound. Antrex has one advantage over TFC-2: it can be used directly in the manufacture of flanges without further processing in the flanges plant. Management estimates this would reduce the direct labor cost of manufacturing flanges by $2 a box, or 20 percent of the total direct labor cost in the flanges factory.

The manager of the flanges factory has asked management to approve the purchase of 100,000 pounds of antrex from Henley, on the basis of the following cost comparison:

Purchase price of antrex: 10 × $4.10	$41.00
Less: Reduction in processing time	
($2 + 20 percent of overhead)	4.80
Net cost of antrex	36.20
Cost of TFC-2: 10 × $4.60	46.00
Net saving per box	$ 9.80

The manager of the TFC-2 plant has objected, saying the TFC-2 plant's fixed costs would go on anyway; therefore, the net cost of antrex to Arden would be $36.20 + 10 × $1 = $46.20.

Total fixed costs in the flanges plant wouldn't change if antrex were to be substituted for TFC-2. Variable overhead costs in each factory vary in proportion to changes in direct labor costs.

Required:

a. Should Arden buy antrex? Summarize the figures on which your answer is based and show how you calculated them.

b. Calculate the maximum price Arden could afford to pay Henley for an order of 100,000 pounds of antrex.

c. Suppose Arden was considering discontinuing the manufacture of TFC-2 entirely, using antrex obtained from Henley in all products now based on TFC-2. Antrex has the same advantages over TFC-2 in all these products that it has in the manufacture of flanges. Would the maximum purchase price of antrex probably be greater, less, or equal to the maximum purchase price you calculated in your answer to (b)? Explain.

27. **Special order; adjusting average cost.** More than two years ago, a large railway system decided to change its system of track control signals. This decision led to an abrupt decline in the sales volume of one of Valley Manufacturing Company's largest industrial customers, and this reduced the sales volume of several Valley Manufacturing products. Since that time, Valley Manufacturing has been unable

to keep its factory operating at normal volume, despite a vigorous sales promotion program.

Yesterday morning, Bob Pettifogg, the company's sales manager, handed Tom Pruitt, the marketing vice president, a customer order for 12,000 foot wrinklers, to be made and delivered within the next six months. To get this order, Mr. Pettifogg had quoted a price less than the standard catalog price, which meant that Mr. Pruitt's approval was necessary.

Although the factory would have to put a number of workers on overtime for the next six months to meet the required delivery schedule, Mr. Pettifogg is convinced that the order should be accepted. "First," he said, "all of the work would be done in department 27, which we can't seem to keep busy no matter how hard we try. If we don't take this order, we'll be running only 7,000 machine-hours a month in that department, against a normal monthly volume of 10,000 machine-hours. This order will bring in 1,000 machine-hours of work each month for six months, and that's a big difference. Some of our people are now on a short workweek, and this order will let us put them back on the full-time payroll and give them some overtime pay, too.

"Second, while I'll admit that the margin is slim, the price I have quoted is greater than our cost, even after allowing for the abnormal amount of overtime. The price is $2.50 a unit and the cost is $2.40. That gives us a margin of about 4 percent of sales. That isn't much, but it's better than nothing."

Mr. Pettifogg then handed Mr. Pruitt the following cost and profit summary to back up his recommendation:

Cost per unit:
Direct materials	$0.57
Direct labor (0.2 hour × $7)	1.40
Factory overhead:	
Normal (0.5 mach.-hr. × $0.80)	0.40
Overtime premium adjustment	0.03
Total cost per unit	2.40
Selling price	2.50
Profit margin per unit	$0.10

"The provision for factory overhead," Mr. Pettifogg continued, "is based on the department's normal overhead rate of 80 cents for each machine-hour used, plus an allowance for extra overtime premiums that would have to be paid to get this job out on time. Normal overheads are shown in this second table, together with a monthly overhead cost forecast for the next six months at a monthly volume of 7,000 machine-hours:

	Forecast at 7,000 Hours	Normal at 10,000 Hours
Indirect labor	$3,100	$4,000
Overtime premium	...	800
Supplies	840	1,200
Depreciation	1,100	1,100
Other	750	900
Total	$5,790	$8,000
Average per machine-hour	$0.827	$0.80

"The cost accountant tells me that except for the overtime premium adjustment, we can get a reasonably good estimate of overhead cost at any volume between 7,000 and 10,000 machine-hours per month by interpolating between the figures given in this table."

"I understand the normal overhead charge," Mr. Pruitt replied, "but what is this overtime premium adjustment? I thought they didn't have enough to keep busy down there and yet they're charging us for extra overtime."

Mr. Pettifogg was ready for this question. "It's true that they have plenty of idle capacity," he said, "but it's idle machine time, not idle labor. They could increase the size of the work force by hiring people, but they won't do that unless they can see good prospects for keeping them busy for a lot longer than six months. They figure that it would be cheaper to go on overtime than to train new workers, use them, and let them go six months from now.

"This means that we have to adjust the overhead rate to allow for the unusual amount of overtime. I made the overtime premium adjustment myself, on the basis of estimates prepared by the factory scheduling department. These show that overtime premiums for department 27 as a whole would probably average 14 cents a machine-hour until this order was finished. The overhead rate already includes 8 cents for overtime premiums, so I added another 6 cents an hour, or 3 cents a unit, to allow for this factor."

Acceptance of this order would have no effect on total selling and administrative expenses, but the average ratio of selling and administrative expense to total sales would be reduced by about one fifth of one percent.

Required:

Mr. Pruitt sees no reason why acceptance of this order would lead to reductions in the prices the company would be able to get in the future for this or other products; his sole concern is whether the quoted price is a profitable one. What would you tell him?

28. **Dropping a product: Interdependencies.** The Upson Company manufactures four products in a single factory. Factory volume is considerably lower than normal, and as a result some of the fixed factory overhead costs are not assigned to any product. Instead, they are listed on the income statement as "underabsorbed overhead."

Sales, cost, and expense data for the four products are shown in the accompanying table:

	Product A	Product B	Product C	Product D	Total
Sales	$2,000,000	$2,500,000	$1,000,000	$500,000	$6,000,000
Cost of goods sold:					
Materials	300,000	400,000	200,000	40,000	940,000
Labor	500,000	600,000	400,000	100,000	1,600,000
Overhead	600,000	800,000	500,000	100,000	2,000,000
Total cost of goods sold	1,400,000	1,800,000	1,100,000	240,000	4,540,000
Gross margin	600,000	700,000	(100,000)	260,000	1,460,000
Selling and administrative expenses (15% of sales)	300,000	375,000	150,000	75,000	900,000
Unadjusted income	$ 300,000	$ 325,000	$ (250,000)	$185,000	560,000
Underabsorbed overhead ..					300,000
Income before taxes ..					$ 260,000

The overhead component of the cost of goods sold is based on predetermined factory overhead rates. Factory overhead is approximately 40 percent variable at the normal operating volumes on which the predetermined overhead rates are based. Variable selling and administrative expenses amount to approximately 5 percent of sales.

The substantial losses reported for product C have led management to consider discontinuing its manufacture, but the company's controller has opposed any such action, saying that company profits would be even lower without product C than with it.

Required:

a. Prepare a report that would support the controller's position and provide a better indicator of the relative profitability of each of the company's products.

b. The president of the company agrees with your figures but says that as soon as practical product C should be dropped. "In the long run," he says, "we cannot afford to retain any product that does not cover its costs." At what time would you consider it "practical" to drop product C? What information would you find useful in making such a decision?

c. Is it conceivable that even in the long run it might be profitable to keep product C in the line? Under what conditions?

d. A copy of the report you prepared in answer to (*a*) is brought to the attention of the manager of the market research department, who calls you in and tells you that you have overlooked the following relevant facts:

(1) Fifty percent of the sales of product C are for applications in which product D can also be used. If product C were not available, sales of product D could be increased by $400,000 a year without any substantial change in fixed selling expenses.

(2) Twenty percent of the sales of product C are sold in conjunction with product A. These customers would not be able to substitute product D and would seek other sources of supply of product A. It is estimated that sales of product A would decline by 10 percent if product C were withdrawn from the company's line.

(3) The company's controller has also estimated that a complete abandonment of product C would permit a reduction of fixed factory, selling, and administrative costs in the amount of $100,000 a year. If product C were kept in the line only as a service to product A customers, receiving no direct selling effort or advertising, the reduction in fixed costs would amount to only $40,000 a year.

In view of this additional information, prepare a report indicating whether sale of product C should be continued, or discontinued entirely, or continued only as a service to the small group of product A customers whose business would be lost if product C were not available.

5 Profit-volume charts, payoff tables, and decision trees

All the analytical methods we have dealt with so far have been deterministic—that is, they have reflected the assumption that all estimates are perfect. Deterministic methods are very reassuring. With perfect knowledge, the optimal decision is clearly signaled.

Unfortunately, very few decisions are made with perfect or even near-perfect knowledge of the consequences. We lack the space to cover uncertainty analysis in any detail, but we can examine three of the devices management can use:

1. Profit-volume charts.
2. Payoff tables and expected values.
3. Decision trees.

Profit sensitivity analysis using profit charts

One of the oldest devices for uncertainty analysis is the profit chart, used to portray the sensitivity of profit to variations in operating volume. We'll study how profit charts are constructed and examine the assumptions on which they are built, first for a single product and then for the products of a multiproduct business.

The basic cost-volume-profit chart

The basic cost-volume-profit chart is a diagram showing the amount of revenue, cost, and profit to be expected at various sales volumes. For example, a company sells a single product at a price of $10 a unit. Fixed costs are $240,000 a year and variable costs are a flat $6 a unit. The cost-volume relationship is represented by the "Total Cost" line in Exhibit 5–1. At zero volume total cost is $240,000—i.e., no variable costs. At 10,000 units total cost is $240,000 + 10,000 × $6 = $300,000. And so on.

At a price of $10 a unit, total revenues will be zero if sales are zero, $100,000 if 10,000 units are sold, and so on. This is shown by the "Total Revenue" line. The vertical distance between the two lines at any volume is the anticipated profit or loss at that volume. If sales amount to only 10,000 units, then a loss of $300,000 − $100,000 = $200,000 is predicted.

Exhibit 5–1 Cost-volume-profit chart

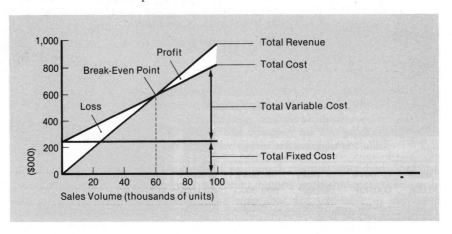

Our terminology here is slightly fuzzy. *Revenue* is an income statement term, but is used here on the assumption that in a normal period net revenues and cash receipts from customers will be identical. We don't use two other income statement terms, however—*expense* and *income*. Expenses are costs deducted from revenues on the income statement; income is the difference between revenues and expenses. These terms are not used here because we don't know whether the operating cost of any given period will equal the amount reported as expense. To cite just one example, the costs in these charts typically reflect estimates of the current purchase prices of raw materials used in production. The actual cost of goods sold, however, may include some materials prices from the preceding year (as under FIFO) or even from years far in the past (as under LIFO, in some circumstances). In general, the differences will not be great. We shall use the terms cost and profit in profit charting because everyone else uses them.

The break-even point and the margin of safety

Profit charts are devices management can use to harness its judgment about the uncertainties and risks in many of its decisions. These judgments center on the location of the break-even point and the size of the margin of safety.

The break-even point is the operating volume at which total revenue equals total cost. It shows up in Exhibit 5–1 as a sales volume of 60,000 units, the point at which the revenue and cost lines cross. At lower volumes the company loses money; at higher volumes it makes a profit. In fact, the break-even point is so prominent that these charts are sometimes called *break-even charts*.

The break-even point can be calculated arithmetically if the cost and revenue lines are straight lines. The formula is:

$$\text{Break-even volume} = \frac{\text{Total fixed costs}}{\text{Contribution margin per unit}}$$

In this case fixed costs amount to $240,000 and the contribution margin (the difference between selling price and variable cost) is $4 a unit. The break-even volume therefore is $240,000/$4 = 60,000 units.

This makes sense. If the company sells one unit, it covers $4 of the fixed costs. If two units are sold, $8 of the fixed costs are covered. By dividing $4 into the total fixed cost we can find out how many units have to be sold to cover all of the fixed costs.

The break-even point itself enters the decision process in expressions such as, "we'll need at least 60,000 units to break even," or "the break-even volume represents a 40 percent market share." The break-even point is also used to calculate the *margin of safety,* the gap between the forecasted volume and the break-even volume. Exhibit 5–2, for example, is the same chart as Exhibit 5–1 with forecasted sales of 70,000 units drawn in. With a break-even volume of 60,000 units, the margin of safety is 10,000 units, or one seventh of the forecasted sales.

Exhibit 5–2 The margin of safety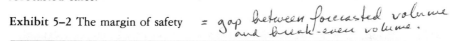

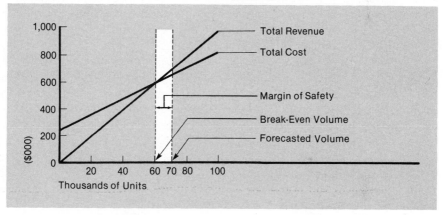

The margin of safety is a measure of risk. A firm that has a high margin of safety is less vulnerable to unexpected changes in demand. Therefore, a decision that will narrow the margin of safety is presumed to be riskier than one that will not. Its significance depends on the size of the forecasting error, however. A low margin of safety is not very risky if the forecasting error is small; a large margin of safety may be highly risky if the forecasting error is also large. In other words, the margin of safety is an aid to judgment, not a substitute for it.

Income tax effects

The simple cost-volume-profit chart in Exhibit 5–2 ignores income tax effects. Tax effects should be included, because the spread between the cost and revenue lines is intended to represent the amount of resources current operations make available for other purposes, such as dividends, debt retirement, and capital growth.

Taxes are usually introduced into the chart on a proportional basis—that is, the tax rate is assumed to be identical at all volume levels and taxable income or loss is equal to the spread between the cost and revenue lines. In algebraic terms, this gives us the following profit equation:

Profit = (1 − Tax rate) (Total pretax contribution margin − Total fixed cost)

Exhibit 5–3 is a cost-volume-profit chart reflecting this proportionality assumption, using a 40 percent tax rate. This diagram reflects an assumption that tax carry-forwards or other forms of tax offset are available when taxable losses are created. This assumption explains why the loss portrayed in the zone to the left of the break-even volume is reduced by an amount proportional to the tax rate.

Exhibit 5–3 Aftertax cost-volume-profit chart

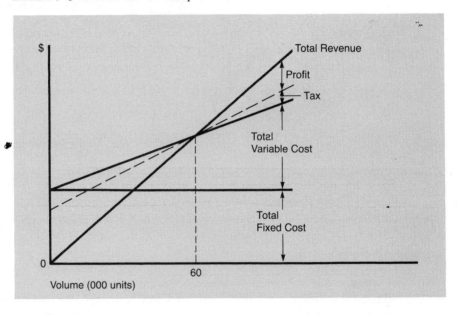

Notice that the interjection of the tax factor hasn't affected the location of the break-even point, which remains at 60,000 units. The proportionality assumption locates the aftertax zero-profit point at the same volume as the pretax zero-volume profit—that is, the volume at which pretax contribution equals total fixed costs (and taxable income is zero).

Taxes can affect the location of the break-even point as well as the size of the profit spread, but only if the proportionality assumption is dropped. Special tax credits, for example, differential tax rates on different portions of the income stream, and other nonproportional elements of the tax structure will lead to a profit chart of greater complexity than the one in Exhibit 5–3.

Cash flow and funds flow diagrams

Most profit charts represent variations in total revenues and total costs with variations in operating volume. Cost-volume-profit diagrams can be drawn, however, to represent total receipts and total disbursements in the current period, or total inflows and outflows of funds. These diagrams will differ from the more conventional charts in at least three ways:

1. Depreciation and amortization charges will not be included among the fixed costs.
2. Tax flows will not be proportional to the spread between pretax receipts and outlays because (*a*) this spread will not measure income taxable in the current period; and (*b*) deferred taxes will not be included in the cash outlays.
3. The relationships between revenues and receipts and between expenses and outlays are likely to vary with volume.

Use of the more conventional cost-volume-profit diagrams is likely to be appropriate when management wishes to portray a normal or continuing set of relationships; cash flow or funds flow diagrams should be used when management's concern is focused on the cash flows or funds flows of the immediate period.

Minimum profit level: Fixed charge coverage

Business firms are not in business to break even. For this reason, the basic cost-volume-profit charts are often drawn to include a specific dividend requirement or a specific minimum profit objective as an additional *fixed charge*. A fixed charge is any specified amount that must be deducted from contribution margin in the calculation of a specified measure of profit. The fixed charge may include a dividend requirement, a sinking fund obligation, or even an amount management regards as necessary to finance a given level of capital expenditures.

Exhibit 5–4 is an example of a chart containing a fixed charge component. It differs from Exhibit 5–3 in two ways. First, a new line is drawn above and parallel to the total cost line. The distance of this line above the total cost line represents the size of the dividend requirement. Second, the total cost line includes income taxes as a cost. The reason is that funds are not available for dividends or other non-tax-deductible expenditures until taxes have been provided for.

Exhibit 5–4 shows not one but two break-even points. The first of these, at 60,000 units, is the same one we calculated earlier. It shows the zero-profit level, and at this level none of the $60,000 dividend requirement has been met. The second break-even point, at 85,000 units, is the volume at which profit after tax is just equal to the $60,000 dividend requirement. The spread between the total revenue and total-cost-plus-dividend-requirement lines measures the extent to which earnings either fall short of meeting the dividend requirement (the "earnings gap") or provide earnings for reinvestment.

Exhibit 5–4 Profit chart with fixed dividend requirement

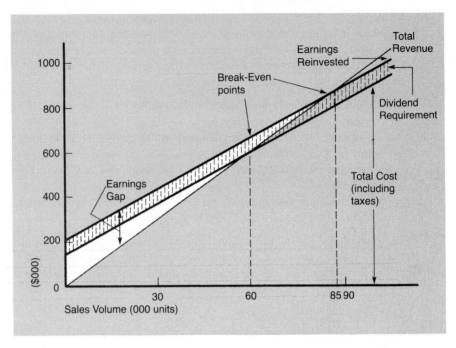

The inclusion of income taxes has an important impact on this analysis, because the interjection of a non-tax-deductible fixed charge has a greater effect on the break-even point than a similar increase in tax-deductible fixed costs. For example, remember that with fixed costs of $240,000 and a pretax contribution margin of $4 a unit, the break-even volume was 60,000 units. Suppose now that fixed costs increase by $60,000, while the contribution margin remains at $4 a unit. The tax rate is 40 percent. The break-even volume therefore goes up to 75,000 units:

$$\text{Break-even volume} = \frac{(1 - 0.4)(\$240,000 + \$60,000)}{(1 - 0.4) \times \$4} = 75,000 \text{ units}$$

If we keep the fixed costs at $240,000, however, and insert a $60,000 dividend requirement, the break-even volume becomes 85,000 units:

$$\text{Break-even volume} = \frac{(1 - 0.4) \times \$240,000 + \$60,000}{(1 - 0.4) \times \$4} = 85,000 \text{ units}$$

Another way of looking at this is to recognize that at a tax rate of 40 percent, $60,000 in tax-deductible costs is equivalent to only $36,000 of aftertax charges. With an aftertax contribution margin of $(1 - 0.4) \times \$4 = \$2.40$, the extra $36,000 adds 15,000 units to the break-even volume. If the $60,000 isn't tax deductible, however, the increase in the break-even volume is

$60,000/$2.40 = 25,000 units, bringing it up to the 85,000-unit level shown in Exhibit 5–4.

The customary volume range

Costs and revenues in the profit charts we have been looking at so far have been drawn as straight lines because the charts assume that marketing costs and selling prices will not change during the period the charts relate to, and that the costs of responsive activities will vary in a linear pattern.

The assumption that marketing costs and selling prices are fixed is not unreasonable. They are embodied in the marketing strategy management has adopted, and this strategy typically establishes the selling prices and the market-ing outlays to be made during the period covered by the chart. If the strategy works well, volume will be high and so will profit. If the marketing efforts are ineffective, volume will be low and so will profit.

Profit-volume patterns are likely to include at least some nonlinearities, but accountants generally assume that they lie in the portions of the volume range the company seldom operates in. The usual profit charts describe cost and profit behavior within this customary operating range, not outside it. Within this portion of the range, the lines are likely to be fairly straight, as in the center section of Exhibit 5–5. The apparent inconsistency arises because we extend these lines to the left and to the right, also as straight lines. We do this to focus attention on the amount of fixed cost and the rate of variability within the customary range. To be accurate, the portions of the chart outside the customary volume limits should be erased, perhaps to be replaced by the extensions labeled "True Curves" in the exhibit.

Exhibit 5–5 Cost-profit behavior beyond the customary volume range

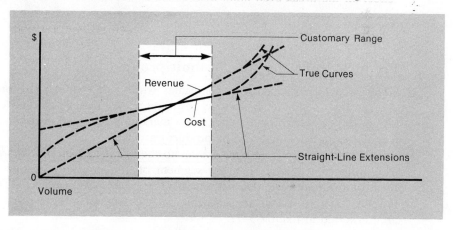

In other words, we use straight lines because management wants the chart to show the effects on profit of variations in the *effectiveness* of marketing effort, not the effects of changes in the *amount* of effort expended. Cost variations or price changes designed to produce volume variations do not appear in the chart.

Profit responsiveness

Calculation of break-even points and the margin of safety emphasizes the negative side of profit-volume analysis. A more neutral approach is to emphasize the contribution margin itself, reflecting the sensitivity of profit to variations in volume. If the contribution margin ratio is high, profit should respond very sharply to volume changes; if the contribution margin ratio is low, large volume shifts will be necessary to make significant changes in profit.

We can emphasize this element in profit-volume analysis by redrawing the profit chart as in Exhibit 5–6. Vertical distances in the shaded area represent total fixed cost (or fixed cost plus fixed charges, if the analysis includes the latter), while total contribution margin is represented by the height of the wedge-shaped area at each volume. A wide-angled wedge shows a high profit responsiveness; a narrow wedge represents a relatively unresponsive situation. High responsiveness heightens the impact of a shortfall in volume, but it also increases the reward from a favorable volume response.

Exhibit 5–6 Contribution margin chart

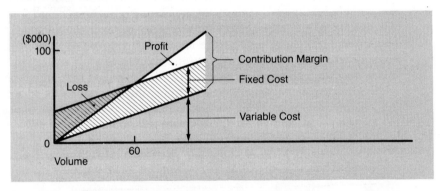

Product profit charting in multiproduct businesses

Some fixed overhead costs in companies which sell two or more products are traceable to individual products or groups of products. Product advertising falls in this category, for example; other marketing costs and even some fixed manufacturing costs may also be product-traceable.

Product-traceable fixed costs enter into the calculation of *profit contribution.* The profit contribution from any segment of the company's business is the total contribution margin of that segment (revenues minus variable expenses), less the fixed costs that are traceable to that segment. These relationships are illustrated in Exhibit 5–7.

Profit contribution figures are usually stated as monthly totals. They show how much each segment of the firm's business (product, territory, and so forth) contributes to the common kitty to help pay for the general costs of administering the company and serving its customers. These costs are necessary to support operations, but they are not traceable to individual segments.

Product profit charts reflecting the profit contribution concept are relatively

Exhibit 5–7 Derivation of the profit contribution of a business segment

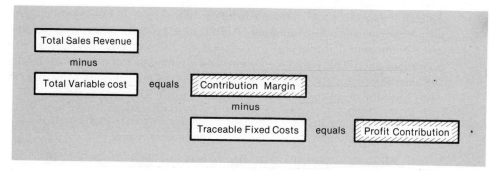

simple. The break-even volume is the point at which the product's contribution margin just equals the total of the traceable fixed costs. All organizations also have common fixed costs, however—that is, costs incurred to support two or more segments simultaneously. If some of these costs are assigned to a specific product, a second break-even point can be calculated, the volume at which the product's total contribution margin just covers both the fixed costs traceable to the product and its assigned share of the common fixed costs as well.

These two break-even points are diagrammed in Exhibit 5–8. The size of the spread between the break-even volumes depends on the amount of fixed

Exhibit 5–8 Profit chart for an individual product in a multiproduct firm

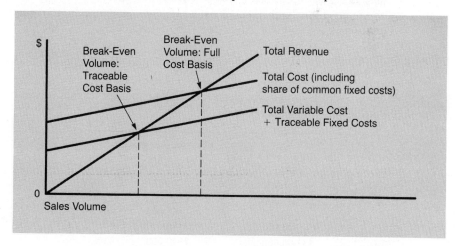

cost assigned to the product and the size of the contribution margin per unit of volume. The first break-even point, at which profit contribution is zero, has a clearer meaning than the other, but the sum of these volumes for all products combined is bound to fall short of the overall volume necessary for the company as a whole to break even.

Multiproduct profit functions

Diagramming the profit function is more difficult for the multiproduct firm as a whole than for the individual product. One problem is that total volume can't be measured in physical units—units of different products vary in size and importance. This means we have to find a synthetic unit of volume, usually the amount of sales revenue. If volume is measured in sales dollars, the overall contribution margin ratio can be derived from the following formula:

$$\text{Overall contribution margin ratio} = \frac{\text{Total sales revenue} - \text{Total variable cost}}{\text{Total sales revenue}}$$

If the relationships are all linear, the break-even volume can be calculated from the following formula:

$$\text{Break-even volume} = \frac{\text{Total fixed cost}}{\text{Overall contribution margin per revenue dollar}}$$

vs cm/unit

The second problem is that the contribution margin ratio is likely to vary from product to product. The overall contribution margin ratio therefore depends on the product mix, the relative proportions in which the various products are sold. This means that variations in product mix affect both the location of the break-even point and the sensitivity of profit to variations in volume.

For example, a company has three products with the following sales volumes and contribution margins:

	Product A	Product B	Product C	Total
Selling price per unit	$20	$10	$5	
Variable costs per unit	15	6	2	
Contribution margin per unit	$ 5	$ 4	$3	
Volume:				
Units sold.....................	90,000	90,000	60,000	
Sales revenues	$1,800,000	$900,000	$300,000	$3,000,000

At the present product mix, the average contribution margin in this company is 33 percent of sales revenues:

		Contribution Margin		
Product	Sales Revenues	Per Unit	Total	Percent of Revenues
A	$1,800,000	$5	$450,000	25%
B	900,000	4	360,000	40
C	300,000	3	180,000	60
Total	$3,000,000		$990,000	33%

The company's fixed costs amount to $627,000; the break-even volume therefore is $627,000/0.33 = $1.9 million.

The picture would be very different if the mix could be shifted to a 40–40–20 basis, leaving total revenues unchanged. The contribution margins would be:

Product	Sales Revenues	Contribution Margin
A	$1,200,000	$ 300,000
B	1,200,000	480,000
C	600,000	360,000
Total	$3,000,000	$1,140,000

The average contribution margin would be $1,140,000/$3,000,000 = 38 percent, and the break-even point would drop substantially, to $627,000/ 0.38 = $1,650,000.

These two product-mix assumptions are illustrated in Exhibit 5–9. The contribution margin spread is wider in chart B than in chart A, the break-even point is farther to the left, and the margin of safety is greater. At a $3 million sales volume, profit is $363,000 in chart A and $513,000 in chart B, a 41 percent increase.

The profit spread in each of the charts in Exhibit 5–9 shows what will happen to profit if volume changes with no change in mix and no change in fixed costs. The differences between the profit spreads in the two charts show how profit will be affected if mix changes on its own, with no change in

Exhibit 5–9 Effect of product mix on profit margins

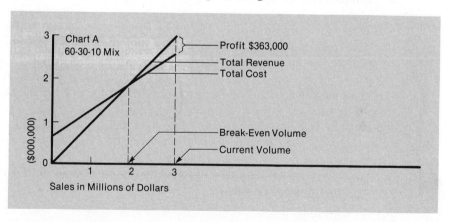

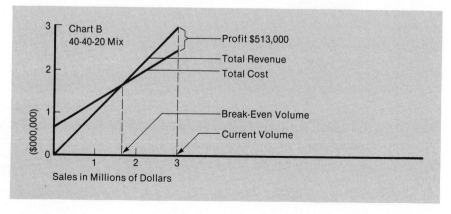

marketing effort. Taken individually and together, they illustrate another form of profit sensitivity analysis.

Dynamic effects

Profit graphs are static devices, designed to illustrate the profit normally associated with steady operation at various operating volumes, assuming no changes in the contribution margin ratios (also known as the P/V ratios), product mix, or total fixed cost. Costs are not likely to follow the cost line on the profit chart all the time, for various reasons. Three situations are worth noting:

1. A rapid movement from one volume level to another.
2. A temporary shift in the level of activity.
3. A persistent shift in product demand.

Transitional effects. When volume moves rapidly from one level to another, the costs of responsive activities may respond either faster or more slowly than the chart indicates. A volume expansion may be sustained for a while without moving up to a new step in certain semivariable costs such as supervision. At the same time, variable costs may rise even more sharply than the chart indicates as the firm has to buy materials on rush orders or has to use untrained personnel.

Temporary volume shifts. Management may choose to support an excessive cost structure for a short period if volume has declined and the decline seems likely to be temporary. Layoffs of personnel are expensive and the company may be better off to pay standby salaries for a while than to pay severance wages and train new workers when volume picks up again. By the same token, if volume increases temporarily, the company may find it more economical to resort to abnormal overtime, subcontracting, or other costly practices than to add to its permanent staff. Again, actual costs will depart from the levels indicated on the chart. The dashed line in Exhibit 5–10 may be a more accurate picture of the movement of costs as volume moves temporarily away fom a stable base.

Exhibit 5–10 Profit response to temporary shifts in demand

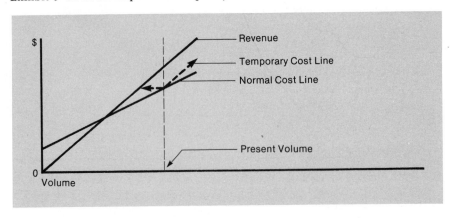

Persistent shifts in demand. The usual profit charts reflect a specific economic climate, a specific management attitude. If the climate changes, management's attitudes will change, too. Cost behavior is likely to be affected.

For example, as volume moves down toward or even below the break-even point, management's attitudes toward activities it has thought of as essential are likely to change. Discretionary activities such as window washing and even some responsive activities may feel the hot breath of the cost cutter. For this reason, the actual zero-profit volume is likely to be a good deal lower than the break-even volume on the chart.

By the same token, if demand has shifted upward, fixed costs are likely to inch up, a movement sometimes referred to as *creep*. Cost control seems less urgent, and fringe activities seem more attractive because "after all, the company can afford it."

Payoff tables and expected value

Forecasts of cash flows are uncertain for two reasons. First, cash flows will be affected by the conditions prevailing in the future (*events or states of nature*), and these conditions can't be known with certainty. Second, cash flows are affected by many factors other than the state of nature, and these relationships are uncertain.

One way of summarizing the decision maker's uncertainties from the first of these sources is to construct a payoff table. In this section we shall use the payoff table to illustrate several important concepts:

1. Outcomes and payoffs.
2. Probabilities.
3. Expected values.
4. Decision rules.

Outcomes and payoffs

Decision making is the process of selecting from a number of possible managerial actions. As we have already seen, it requires estimates of the results likely to be achieved by each of these actions. The payoff table is simply a means of displaying the results to be expected under each possible combination of managerial action and state of nature.

Results can be stated either by describing what will happen or by listing the net benefits to be derived. A description of a result is known technically as an *outcome;* the net benefit is known as the *payoff*. (Net benefit is the difference between total benefit and total cost.) Since decisions focus on costs and benefits, the payoff table focuses on payoffs.

The first step in drawing a payoff table is to identify as many managerial actions as management is willing to examine. These are listed at the left of the table. A manager deciding whether to introduce a new product, for example, might list two possible actions:

1. Add the product to the line carried by the regular sales force.
2. Set up a specialized sales force to promote the new product.

The second step is to list as many <u>states of nature as</u> might influence the decision. These are listed across the top of the table. Sales of our illustrative new product, for example, may depend mainly on the availability of a government subsidy to potential buyers, the subject of a bill now being debated in Congress. The manager might identify three possible states of nature:

1. The bill is rejected in its entirety.
2. The bill is passed in its present form.
3. The bill is passed with an amendment doubling the size of the subsidy.

The result so far is a two-dimensional table with six empty boxes or cells:

State of Nature / Managerial Action	No Bill	Present Bill	Amended Bill
Regular sales force			
Specialized sales force			

Each of these cells represents a unique combination of actions and states of nature. With two possible actions and three possible states of nature, we have $2 \times 3 = 6$ cells. <u>The figure to be placed in each cell is the anticipated payoff</u> for that action/state of nature combination.

The third step, therefore, is to <u>estimate</u> these payoffs. The introduction of a specialized sales force would increase the fixed costs of the company's operations. The purpose would be to increase the total sales potential. If successful, the specialized sales force would produce a high net cash inflow; if unsuccessful, the high fixed costs would lead to a high cash outflow. Using the regular sales force would produce less leverage, a smaller possible loss, and a smaller possible gain.

The result is the <u>set of differential cash flows (the difference between the anticipated cash flow with the new product and the anticipated cash flow without it)</u> in Exhibit 5–11. The figure in each cell shows what the payoff will be under the action shown if the state of nature listed at the head of the column turns out to be the real one. Thus if management chooses to set up a specialized

Exhibit 5–11 Table of actions, states of nature, and payoffs

State of Nature / Managerial Action	No Bill	Present Bill	Amended Bill
Regular sales force	−$250	+$500	+$1,200
Specialized sales force	−$400	+$200	+$2,000

sales force, only to find that Congress has defeated the bill, the payoff is a $400 cash outflow.

Probabilities

This payoff table would be a useful way of demonstrating the sensitivity of the payoff to variations in the state of nature. It ignores one crucial element, however—the likelihood that each of the states of nature will occur. This is important information. If the manager is convinced the bill will pass in its present form, the table points to using the regular sales force to market the new product. This will produce a larger cash flow than either alternative. If the bill is likely to be defeated, however, the new product should not be introduced at all.

The likelihood that an event will occur is known as its *probability,* expressed as a percentage or as a decimal with a value between 0.0 and 1.0. A probability of 0.3, for example, means that this event will occur 3 times out of 10. The total of the probabilities for all the possible events or states of nature is 1.0. For example, a weather forecaster is likely to say that the probability of rain tomorrow is 20 percent (= 0.2). This means:

Event	Probability
Rain	0.2
No rain	0.8
Total	1.0

Some probability figures are known as *objective probabilities* because they can be established by logical reasoning, by analysis of historical data, or by experimentation. The probabilities in coin-tossing exercises and dice games are objective probabilities. We know, for example, that a tossed coin can come down either head up or tail up. Logically, we have no reason to assume the coin will come up heads either more or less often than it comes up tails. The probability of each outcome is 0.5, established by logical reasoning. We can test this empirically, if we wish, by tossing a coin or coins a number of times and recording the results. If the coins are unbiased, the likelihood of their coming up heads half the time is greater than the likelihood of any other percentage.

The probabilities applicable to managerial decisions are likely to differ from these. They are more likely to represent managerial judgment than historical or experimental averages. These *subjective probabilities* are based on the managers' past experience, combined with information about the current state of the market and current happenings. Sometimes they reflect forecasts of various key variables made by others.

The issue is not whether such probabilities will be used. The only issue is whether they will be stated explicitly. Any managerial decision reflects, either explicitly or implicitly, management's judgment of the likelihood of different states of nature. The manager may decide to set up a specialized sales force, for example, on the grounds that this will yield a greater cash flow than marketing the product through the regular sales force. If so, this decision reflects a judgment that the amended bill has a very high probability of passage.

Expected value

Once we have drawn a payoff table, we realize that we don't know which alternative will maximize cash flow. In our example, we have three different ways of maximizing cash flow, depending on the circumstances (see Exhibit 5–12).

Exhibit 5–12 Table of optimal actions

State of Nature	Cash Flow Maximizing Action
The bill is defeated	Keep the new product off the market.
The bill is passed	Market the new product through the regular sales force.
The amended bill is passed	Set up a specialized sales force to market the new product.

Before examining some of the possible ways to resolve this dilemma, we must introduce one more concept, _expected value._ The expected value of a managerial action is the average payoff, determined by weighting each possible payoff by its associated probability. For example, suppose our manager assigned probabilities of 0.2, 0.5, and 0.3 to the three states of nature. The expected value of using the regular sales force is:

	(1)	(2)	(3)
			Weighted Payoff
State of Nature	Payoff	Probability	(1) × (2)
No bill	−$ 200	0.2	−$ 40
Present bill	+ 500	0.5	+ 250
Amended bill	+ 1,200	0.3	+ 360
Expected value			+$570

Performing the same calculations for the specialized sales force alternative, we get an expected value of $620:

No bill:	−$ 400 × 0.2		−$ 80
Present bill:	+ 200 × 0.5		+ 100
Amended bill:	+ 2,000 × 0.3		+ 600
Expected value			+$620

These figures have been inserted in the completed payoff table shown in Exhibit 5–13.

expected value = possible payoff × probability

Exhibit 5–13 Payoff table with expected value

State of nature / Action	Probability			
	0.2	0.5	0.3	
	No Bill	Present Bill	Amended Bill	Expected Value
Regular sales force	− $250	+ $500	+ $1,200	+ $570
Specialized sales force	− $400	+ $200	+ $2,000	+ $620

Decision rules

Expected value is calculated because it is the basis for the decision rule, *maximize the expected value* of the future cash flows. (A decision rule is a set of instructions for choosing a managerial action consistent with management's objectives.) If the probabilities are estimated correctly, and if management makes many decisions of this sort, management is likely to maximize its cash flows by consistently taking actions with the greatest expected values. If our manager had 100 identical decisions, for example, and chose in each case to set up a specialized sales force (the alternative with the greater expected value), the result would be as follows:

State of Nature	Number of Times the State of Nature Occurred	Cash Flow Each Time	Total Cash Flow
No bill	20	−$ 400	−$ 8,000
Present bill	50	+ 200	+ 10,000
Amended bill	30	+ 2,000	+ 60,000
Total cash flow			+$62,000

This of course is just the calculation of expected value with the probabilities multiplied by 100.

Maximizing expected value is one possible decision rule, but not the only one. Here are three other possibilities:

1. Minimize the possible loss. Management could minimize the possible loss by not introducing the product at all. Each of the other alternatives would lead to a worse result in the worst state of nature (no bill). This is probably the most pessimistic decision rule of all—always assume the worst.

2. Maximize the possible gain. To do this, management should set up the specialized sales force because in no other way does it have a chance of gaining a $2,000 cash inflow. This is the inveterate optimist's decision rule—always assume the best.

3. Maximize the most likely gain. This means ignoring the extremes, going with the state of nature management thinks most likely to occur. In the present case, it leads to the use of the regular sales force because management expects

the bill to pass (Probability $= 0.5$) and in this state of nature the regular sales force brings in the greatest cash flows.

Maximizing the most likely gain is the decision rule implicit in the deterministic analyses we discussed in Chapter 4. If we applied it to our present illustration, we would (1) forecast the differential cash outlays required by each marketing plan; (2) forecast the differential cash receipts from each plan; and (3) subtract the first set of forecasts from the second. The figures might be as follows:

	Most Likely Cash Outlay	Most Likely Cash Receipts	Most Likely Net Cash Flow
Regular sales force	$ 800	$1,300	+$500
Specialized sales force	2,300	2,500	+ 200

Each of these six figures is single-valued. It implies that choosing the marketing plan determines the outcome, with no uncertainty.

Two conditions must be present if maximizing the most likely gain is to lead to the same decisions as a decision rule calling for the maximization of expected value: (1) the possible payoffs must be distributed symmetrically around the most likely value; and (2) the probabilities of the various states of nature must be distributed symmetrically around the probability of the most likely state of nature.

Suppose our marketing manager made the following estimates:

	0.2 No Bill	0.6 Present Bill	0.2 Amended Bill	Expected Value
Regular sales force	−$250	+$500	+$1,250	+$500
Specialized sales force	− 400	+ 200	+ 800	+ 200

Notice what we had to do to make the payoffs from the specialized sales force symmetrical. We had to reduce the optimistic payoff from $2,000 to $800. Given our original estimates, maximizing the most likely payoff would be a very poor decision rule, on the average; only when the payoffs and probabilities are symmetrically distributed does it make sense.

Utility

Maximizing the expected value of the cash flows is a sensible decision rule as long as the decision maker regards each dollar of anticipated gain or loss as equal in utility. For example, if the company has 250 other products, generating $100,000 in cash flows, the manager is likely to regard a possible gain of $2,000 as five times as important as a $400 loss. Suppose the new product is only the second, however, and the first now generates only $100 in cash flows. In this situation a $2,000 gain is likely to be enticing but a $400 loss would be a disaster. The gain means more meat on the table; the loss means the table will be repossessed.

This asymmetrical attitude toward possible gains and losses is an illustration of a phenomenon known as a *nonlinear utility function*. Exhibit 5–14 shows

uliveu
utility fx

one of these functions. This depicts a common assumption in economic theory, that the more money consumers have, the less they will value a single dollar. The $20 necessary to buy a theater ticket has much less value to rich people than to the poor. The reason is that buying a ticket might force a wealthy person to eat a $30 meal instead of a $40 meal after the theater; a poor person might have to forgo more essential purchases.

utility =
value on
money

The value people place on money is impossible to measure except in special situations. Economists have a name for it, however—they call it *utility.* A utility function is linear if doubling the amount of money will double the amount of utility, or value placed on the money. A linear utility function in Exhibit 5–14, for example, would be a horizontal straight line. Each dollar would have the same value, no matter how many dollars the owner had.

Exhibit 5–14 Nonlinear utility function

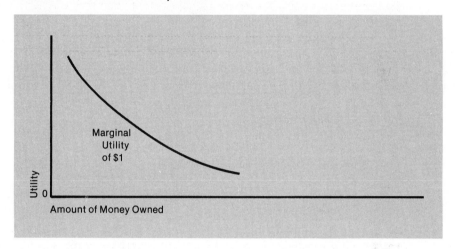

In large organizations the utility function ordinarily can be assumed to be linear for most of the decision situations the managers find themselves in. They may not make 100 identical decisions, but they do make 100 decisions with roughly similar potential impacts. Using the expected-value rule consistently over a period of time should lead to a greater cash flow than could be reached with some other decision rule. In such cases it doesn't even matter whether the utility function is linear because the manager's decisions can be evaluated as a group, not one by one. The mistakes will be more than covered by the brilliant successes.

Decision Tree Analysis

Payoff tables deal with one level of probability only. The payoff associated with a given outcome is often uncertain in itself, however. It may depend on a second set of states of nature or on a second level of decisions.

Dealing with these complexities is far from simple. In general, only the computer offers any hope of a successful analysis. The structure of the problem can be demonstrated fairly easily, however, by drawing a decision tree, a diagram of the relationships among decisions, states of nature, and outcomes or payoffs.

Our earlier payoff table, for example, has been redrawn as a decision tree in Exhibit 5–15. The three alternative actions are shown as three separate *decision branches* spreading out from the single *decision point.* Each of these branches is branched in its turn at what we call an *event node.* The smaller branches spreading out from the event nodes are known as *event branches* and each ends in a payoff.

Exhibit 5–15 Decision tree with one decision point

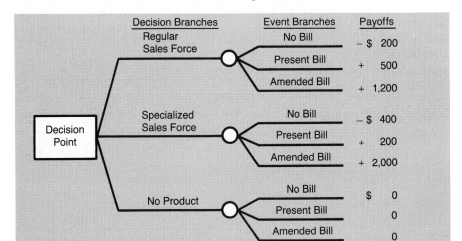

To get a better picture of a decision tree, we have to use a slightly more complicated example. Suppose management is considering whether to continue a research project now in progress. If it does, the project may fail or it may succeed. If it succeeds, in the sense that it yields a new product that is capable of satisfying consumers' needs, management will have to decide either to produce and sell the product or to hold it off the market. If it decides to sell, competitors may enter, or they may not.

These possibilities are diagrammed in Exhibit 5–16. The squares again identify decision points; the circles are event nodes. Each final event node leads to two branches (events) labeled "competitor enters" or "competitor stays out." Each has a separate and distinct payoff.

The payoffs are shown at the right, one at the end of each branch of the tree. They are based on the following estimates:

1. Continuing the project will cost $400 that could be avoided by canceling the project now.
2. If the company decides not to commercialize the product but a competitor enters the market, the competitor will take some of the company's present

Exhibit 5–16 Decision tree with two decision points

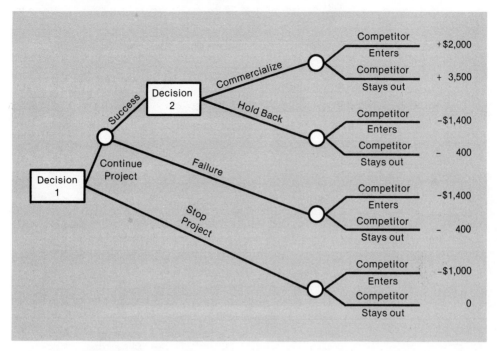

business away. This lost business is now generating a $1,000 net cash inflow.

3. If the research is successful, the company decides to commercialize the product, and competitors stay out, the new product will generate cash flows of $3,500 over and above the cost of the project itself; if a competitor also enters the market, the net payoff will be only $2,000.

Several characteristics of the decision tree can be identified from this diagram:

1. Each decision point leads to two or more decision branches.
2. Each decision branch ends in an event node.
3. Each event node leads to two or more event branches.
4. Each event branch ends in (a) a decision point, (b) an event node, or (c) a payoff.
5. The tree is fully grown when all the end branches have led to payoffs.

Although the decision tree now has all its branches, it still has no leaves, in the form of probability estimates. We could use the tree without these, as a way of laying out the range of possible consequences, but this array can be difficult to understand once it gets beyond eight or ten final branches. In the more general case, the main purpose of the tree is to collect the probability figures in a form suitable for a computerized solution.

What we have to do is estimate the probabilities at each event node. A set of these probabilities has been inserted in Exhibit 5–17. Once this has

Exhibit 5–17 Decision tree with probabilities and expected values

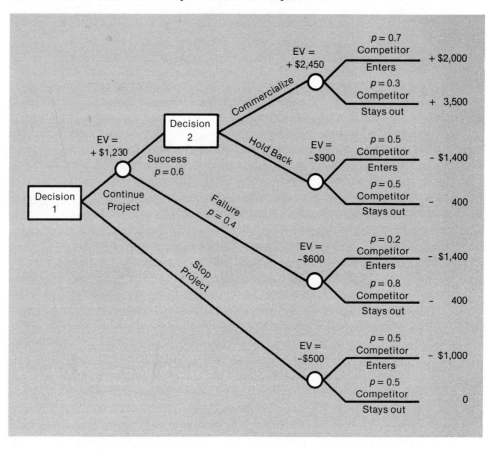

been done, the expected values of each decision branch can be calculated by working backward.

The expected value of the decision to commercialize, for example, is calculated as follows:

State of Nature	Payoff	Probability	Contribution to Expected Value
Competitor enters	+$2,000	0.7	+$1,400
Competitor stays out	+ 3,500	0.3	+ 1,050
Expected value			+$2,450

This expected value figure has been entered in Exhibit 5–17 just above the last event node in the top branch. Similar calculations were made to derive the expected values of each of the other event nodes at the right. Comparison of the first two of these shows that, once the project has succeeded, commercializing the product is a much better alternative (expected value = $2,450) than holding it off the market (expected value = −$900).

We need to go through the same procedure again to calculate the expected value of the first event node in the upper branch—that is, the expected value of the decision to continue the project. We can ignore the rejected limb on this upper branch because we won't take this route if the project is successful. The expected value of continuing the project, therefore, is calculated by treating the expected values of the next event nodes as payoffs:

State of Nature	Derived Payoff	Probability	Contribution to Expected Value
Success	+$2,450	0.6	+$1,470
Failure	− 600	0.4	− 240
Expected value			+$1,230

This is far better than the −$500 expected payoff from killing the project now. The project should be continued.

Notice that the only decision to be made now is the decision to go ahead with the project. The company is in no way committed to commercialize the product if the project is successful. We need to forecast that future decision, however, to make our present decision. If we forecast that we won't commercialize the new product even if we are successful in developing it, this forecast will reflect itself in an unfavorable expected value of the decision to continue.

Probability-adjusted profit charts

The presence of uncertainty can be recognized in many ways other than in payoff tables or decision trees. One such possibility is to graft probability estimates onto profit charts. The diagram in Exhibit 5–18, for example, shows both a profit-volume line and a bell-shaped probability curve. To avoid unnecessary clutter, the profit-volume relationship is represented by a single profit line instead of by the intersecting revenue and expense lines we used in earlier profit charts. The area under the bell-shaped curve between any two volumes represents management's estimate of the probability that the actual volume will fall in this portion of the range. Thus the unshaded area under the curve

Exhibit 5–18 Profit chart with probability distribution

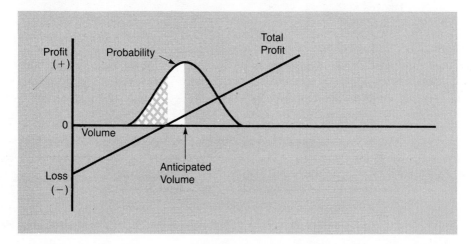

represents the total probability that profit will be positive but less than the planned amount. The hatched area under the curve at the left shows the probability of reporting a loss; the shaded area under the curve at the right shows the probability of exceeding planned profit.

The information conveyed by the two lines in Exhibit 5–18 can be consolidated in a single line which matches the profitability at any volume with the probability of getting there. For example, suppose a set of probability-rated forecasts shows the following:

Weekly Volume (units)	Profit (loss)	Probability
4,000	$(20,000)	0.05
5,000	(10,000)	0.1
6,000	0	0.2
7,000	10,000	0.3
8,000	20,000	0.2
9,000	30,000	0.1
10,000	40,000	0.05

We could show this information in a single curve tracing the probability of each profit/volume combination. We find it easier to use a *cumulative* curve, however, as in Exhibit 5–19. Since the chance of a loss greater than $20,000 is zero, the probability that the profit level will be no worse than this is 100 percent. The probability of doing as well as or better than a $10,000 loss is only a little less than this, 0.95, so the curve dips slightly as it makes this first move to the right. The probability of breaking even or better is 0.85, the sum of the probabilities assigned to volumes of 6,000 units or more. The probability of reaching or exceeding the planned profit of $10,000 is 0.65.

Management's main concern will be with the height of the line in the

Exhibit 5–19 Cumulative profit probabilities

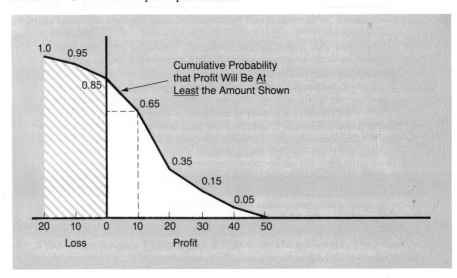

vicinity of the planned profit and with its slope in that zone. A steep slope indicates sharply decreasing probabilities of doing better, high probability of doing worse. A flat curve, on the other hand, shows that the probability of doing slightly better or worse is almost as good as the probability of reaching the objective. The combination of a low cumulative profitability level and a steep slope indicates the attainment of the planned profit is very doubtful.

steep slope — high prob. of doing worse

Summary

Uncertainty surrounds all managerial decisions. Cash flows are uncertain because:

1. The values of important independent variables (e.g., the spendable income of the company's customers) are uncertain.
2. The relationship between the independent variable and the dependent variable (e.g., product sales) is uncertain.

One device to help management allow for uncertainty is the profit-volume chart or break-even chart. These charts show how rapidly profit is likely to rise or fall if the market for the company's products or services is better or poorer than anticipated. The charts can help management decide whether the anticipated payoff is acceptable, in view of their sensitivity to variations in uncertain quantities.

These uncertainties become much more visible if they are displayed in payoff tables or decision trees. Decision trees can encompass whole series of uncertainties; payoff tables can deal with only one at a time.

Displays of the range of possible values can be strengthened if probabilities can be assigned to different possible states of nature. These probabilities can be used to combine the estimates into expected values, in which the various possible payoffs are weighted according to their likelihood of occurrence. The decision maker can use maximization of the expected value as the decision rule if it can be assumed that the utility of the payoffs is proportional to their amount.

Independent study problems (solutions in Appendix B)

1. **Profit-volume charts; break-even points; risk.**   The Cranby Company manufactures and sells a single product. You have the following data:

Fixed costs	$32,000 a month
Variable costs	$3 a unit
Selling price	$5 a unit
Anticipated sales	20,000 units a month

   Required:
   a. Construct a profit-volume chart, measuring volume in physical units.
   b. Calculate the break-even point (in units), the margin of safety, and the anticipated income before taxes at the anticipated sales volume.
   c. The company is considering increasing the selling price to $5.50. At this price it expects to sell 18,000 units.
      (1) Recalculate the break-even point (in units), the margin of safety, and the anticipated income before taxes.

(2) Redraw the profit-volume chart, showing both the old and the new profit spreads.
(3) How many units would have to be sold at the new price to increase income before taxes by 10 percent over its current level?
(4) How, if at all, would acceptance of this proposal affect the riskiness of Cranby's business?

d. The sales manager has offered a counterproposal. The price would be reduced to $4.60, and an additional $4,000 a month would be spent on advertising.
(1) Recalculate the break-even point, in units per month.
(2) How many units would have to be sold at the new price to increase income before taxes by 10 percent over its current level?
(3) How, if at all, would acceptance of this proposal affect the riskiness of Cranby's business?

2. **Aftertax profit chart; income targets.** The Gruber Company manufactures and sells a single product. The effective income tax rate is 40 percent of taxable income. The amounts shown on the tax return are the same as those shown in the income statement. Unlike the company in the illustration in the text of this chapter, however, Gruber will not receive a tax credit or refund if it reports a loss. Management's aftertax income target is $6,300 a month. You have the following additional information:

Selling price . . . . $8 a unit
Variable costs . . . . 5 a unit
Fixed costs . . . . 33,000 a month

Required:
a. Construct an aftertax profit-volume chart, measuring volume in physical units.
b. At what unit volume will Gruber meet its income target?
c. At what quarterly unit volume will Gruber's net income just equal its quarterly dividend of $10,800?

3. **Effect of product mix.** The Carillo Company sells two products, A and B, with contribution margin ratios of 40 and 30 percent and selling prices of $5 and $2.50 a unit. Fixed costs amount to $72,000 a month. Monthly sales average 30,000 units of product A and 40,000 units of product B.

Required:
a. Assuming that three units of product A are sold for every four units of product B, calculate the dollar sales volume necessary to break even. Calculate the margin of safety in sales dollars.
b. As part of its cost accounting routine, Carillo Company assigns $36,000 in fixed costs to each product each month. Calculate the break-even dollar sales volume for each product. Explain why the total of these two figures differs from the break-even volume you calculated in your answer to (a).
c. Carillo Company is considering spending an additional $9,700 a month on advertising, giving more emphasis to product A and less emphasis to product B. If its analysis is correct, sales of product A will increase to 40,000 units a month, but sales of product B will fall to 32,000 units a month. Recalculate the break-even sales volume, in dollars, at this new product mix. Would the company be riskier or less risky than it is now? Should the proposal to spend the additional $9,700 a month be accepted?

4. **Payoff table, expected value, and decision rules.** A company is trying to decide how much to produce. Unsold units must be destroyed. Each unit costs $2 and sells for $3. The probabilities of various sales volumes are:

Units Sold	Probability
10	0.1
11	0.2
12	0.3
13	0.2
14	0.15
15	0.05

Required:

a. Set up a payoff table.
b. What level of production would maximize the expected value of the payoffs?
c. How much should be produced if the company decides to maximize the possible gain? Minimize the possible loss?

5. **Decision tree analysis.**   Loreen Green commutes to work in a large city. She can take a No. 33 bus to the end of the No. 1 subway line and take that subway to her office. Alternatively, she can take the train to the city and then take either a No. 66 bus or a No. 5 subway to the office.

   The first of these is slightly more expensive than the second, but it is also slightly more comfortable. These two factors balance out, and Ms. Green will choose the combination that seems most likely to minimize her travel time. If everything is on time, the train-bus combination is the fastest, but the train is sometimes late and so is the No. 66 bus.

   She has made the following estimates of commuting time (probability figures are given in parentheses):

   1. If she takes the bus to the end of the subway line:
      a.   40 minutes if everything is on time (0.5).
      b.   55 minutes if either bus or subway is late (0.3).
      c.   70 minutes if both bus and subway are late (0.2).
   2. If she takes the train but the train is late; and if she then takes the No. 66 bus:
      a.   50 minutes if the bus is on time (0.7).
      b.   65 minutes if the bus is late (0.3).
   3. If she takes the train but the train is late; and if she takes the No. 5 subway from the train station:
      a.   55 minutes if the subway is on time (0.8).
      b.   60 minutes if the subway is late (0.2).
   4. If she takes the train and the train is on time; and if she then takes the No. 66 bus:
      a.   35 minutes if the bus is on time (0.7).
      b.   50 minutes if the bus is late (0.3).
   5. If she takes the train and the train is on time; and if she takes the No. 5 subway from the train station:
      a.   40 minutes if the subway is on time (0.8).
      b.   45 minutes if the subway is late (0.2).
   6. The probability of the train being on time is 0.7.

Required:

a. Draw a decision tree and enter the payoffs and probabilities.
b. Calculate the expected values. How should Ms. Green travel to work?
c. If the work day starts at 9 A.M. and Ms. Green's boss is willing to allow her to be late as often as 10 percent of the days without penalty, at what time should she leave home each day? You may assume that transportation is always available.

Exercises and problems

6. **Price change; break-even point.** A company is considering a proposal to change its marketing strategy. The new strategy would enable the company to reduce its fixed costs, but would require a substantial price reduction. The following data are available:

	Present	Proposed
Selling price	$ 15.00	$13.50
Monthly sales (units)	10,000	13,000
Variable cost per unit........	$ 9.00	$ 9.00
Fixed costs per month	$41,000	$35,000

Required:

a. Would the change in strategy be profitable? Show your calculations.
b. What is the crossover volume (the minimum unit sales volume necessary to make the new strategy as profitable as the present strategy)?
c. What would be effect of the proposed price change on the break-even point in units and in sales dollars? How might knowledge of the effect on the break-even point affect the pricing decision?

7. **Profit-volume diagram.** Dave's Garage has five mechanics on its payroll. They are paid $8 an hour and ordinarily work between 30 and 40 hours each week. The garage charges its customers $18 an hour for repair work. Parts are priced at cost plus 25 percent. Parts sales average 20 percent of the amounts billed customers for labor time. Fixed overhead amounts to $1,000 a week and variable overhead averages $2 an hour.

The mechanics are now working 175 repair labor hours each week.

Required:

a. Calculate the break-even volume in repair labor hours, the margin of safety, and the current profit margin.
b. Draw a profit-volume diagram.

8. **Break-even: Salaried employees.** Each of the mechanics in Dave's Garage (see problem 7) has just been put on a salary of $300 a week. This entitles Dave to 40 hours of labor time each week if enough customers can be found.

Required:

a. How does the change affect the fixed and variable costs of Dave's Garage? How does it affect total cost per week at the current operating volume?
b. Redraw the profit-volume diagram to reflect the new situation and recalculate the break-even volume.

9. **Exercises in break-even analysis; single product.**

1. Oxford Company has sales of $3,000,000, variable costs of $1,800,000, and fixed costs of $800,000 for product Brum. What would be the amount of sales dollars at the break-even point?

   a. $2,000,000, b. $2,400,000, c. $2,600,000, d. $2,760,000.

2. The Seahawk Company is planning to sell 200,000 units of product B. The fixed costs are $400,000 and the variable costs are 60 percent of the selling price. To realize income before taxes of $100,000, the selling price per unit would have to be

   a. $3.75, b. $4.17, c. $5.00, d. $6.25

3. Bert Company has projected cost of goods sold of $2,000,000, including fixed costs of $400,000. Variable costs of goods sold are expected to be ¨5 percent of net sales. What are the projected net sales?

   a. $2,133,333, b. $2,400,000, c. $2,666,667, d. $3,200,000.

4. Day Company is a medium-sized manufacturer of lamps. During 19x9 a new line called Twilight was made available to Day's customers. The break-even point for sales of Twilight is $400,000 with a contribution margin of 40 percent. Assuming that the income before taxes for the Twilight line for 19x9 amounted to $200,000, total sales for 19x9 amounted to:

   a. $600,000, b. $840,000, c. $900,000, d. $950,000.

(AICPA)

10. **Exercises in break-even analysis; multiple products.**

   1. The Insulation Corporation sells two products, D and W. Insulation sells these products at a rate of two units of D to three units of W. The contribution margin is $4 per unit for D and $2 per unit for W. Insulation Corporation has fixed costs of $420,000. How many units of both products combined would be sold at the break-even point?

      a. 140,000, b. 150,000, c. 168,000, d. 180,000.

   2. Thomas Company sells products X, Y, and Z. Thomas sells three units of X for each unit of Z, and two units of Y for each unit of X. The contribution margins are $1 per unit of X, $1.50 per unit of Y, and $3 per unit of Z. Fixed costs are $600,000. How many units of X would Thomas sell at the overall break-even point?

      a. 40,000, b. 120,000, c. 360,000, d. 400,000.

   3. The Ship Company is planning to produce two products, Alt and Tude. Ship is planning to sell 100,000 units of Alt at $4 a unit and 200,000 units of Tude at $3 a unit. Variable costs are 70 percent of sales for Alt and 80 percent of sales for Tude. To realize a total income before taxes of $160,000, what must total fixed costs be?

      a. $80,000, b. $90,000, c. $240,000, d. $600,000.

   4. The Ship Company (exercise 3) wishes to calculate the break-even volume for each product line. Product Alt has fixed costs averaging 45 cents a unit at planned volume. Product Tude has fixed costs averaging 18 cents a unit at planned volume. The total of the individual break-even volumes for the two products is

      a. 97,500 units, b. 101,250 units, c. $81,000, d. $337,500.

(AICPA; Exercise 4 added)

11. **Expected value exercise.** Duguid Company is considering a proposal to introduce a new product, XPL. An outside marketing consultant has prepared the following payoff probability distribution describing the relative likelihood of monthly sales volume levels and related income (loss) for XPL:

Monthly Sales Volume	Probability	Income (loss)
3,000	0.10	$(35,000)
6,000	0.20	5,000
9,000	0.40	30,000
12,000	0.20	50,000
15,000	0.10	70,000

Required:

How much will the expected value of the added monthly income before taxes be if Duguid decides to market XPL?

(AICPA)

12. **Payoff table; bidding on a special order.** Yvette Barclay, the sales manager of Franglais Company, has been asked to submit a price quotation for 100,000 units of a product used by a customer. The out-of-pocket cost of filling the order, if it can be obtained, is $90,000. Three possible prices are being considered: $1, $1.25, and $1.50.

Ms. Barclay is not certain how busy competitors' factories are, but in the light of their bids on recent jobs she thinks that the chance of their operating at a rate as high as 80 percent of capacity or higher is only 20 percent. Similarly, she believes that the probability that competitors are operating at 60 percent of capacity or less is 30 percent.

She estimates that if competitors' operating rates are 80 percent or higher, she can secure the order at any bid up to and including $1.50. If competitors are operating between 61 and 79 percent of capacity, a price of $1.25 or less will secure the bid, but if competitors' operating rates are 60 percent or less it will take a bid of $1 to land the order.

Required:

a. Prepare a payoff table to reflect these data.
b. Assuming that the decision rule is to maximize the expected value of the monetary return, which bid should be submitted?

13. **Decision tree.** Draw a decision tree to display the data in problem 12. In a situation as simple as this, would you prefer the decision tree or the payoff table? What are the advantages of each?

14. **Probability-adjusted profit charts.** You have the following probability-adjusted profit charts for two different companies:

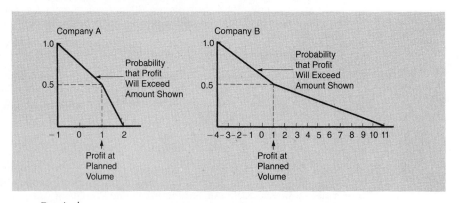

Required:

How do these two situations differ? Which situation would you prefer to be in? Explain.

15. **Dividend coverage.** The Argus Company sells products with an average pretax contribution margin of 40 percent of sales. Its sales volume is $2 million and its fixed costs amount to $500,000. The income tax rate is 50 percent and dividends of $80,000 are paid.

Required:

a. Calculate net income (net income is always an after-tax figure).
b. Calculate the volume at which net income equals the dividend.

    c. Calculate the volume at which net income is twice the dividend.

    d. The prices of the variable inputs are expected to increase by 5 percent next year. Fixed costs will also increase by 5 percent. Selling prices will remain the same. Management will maintain the dividend at its present level if net income is $126,000 next year. What volume will have to be achieved to provide this income?

16. **Payoff table; expected value.** Vendo, Inc., has been operating the concession stands at the university football stadium. The university has had successful football teams for many years; as a result the stadium is always full. The university is located in an area which suffers no rain during the football season. From time to time, Vendo has found itself very short of hot dogs and at other times it has had many left. A review of the records of sales of the past five seasons revealed the following frequency of hot dogs sold.

	Total Games
10,000 hot dogs	5
20,000 hot dogs	10
30,000 hot dogs	20
40,000 hot dogs	15
Total	50

    Hot dogs sell for 50 cents each and cost Vendo 30 cents each. Unsold hot dogs are given to a local orphanage without charge. Hot dogs are paid for with the proceeds of the day's sales.

Required:

    a. Assuming that only the four quantities listed were ever sold and that the occurrences were random events, prepare a payoff table (ignore income taxes) to represent the four possible strategies of ordering 10,000; 20,000; 30,000; or 40,000 hot dogs.

    b. Using the expected-value decision rule determine the best strategy.

                                            (CMA, adapted)

17. **Break-even analysis, multiple products; sensitivity analysis.** Forsyth Company has two products, A and B, with contribution margin ratios of 60 percent and 20 percent, respectively. Product A has traceable fixed costs of $900,000 and an annual sales volume of $2,400,000; product B has traceable fixed costs of $700,000 and sales of $3 million. Common fixed costs amount to $200,000. Management fears that the next recession may reduce sales of both products by as much as 10 percent.

Required:

    a. Calculate the break-even volume, in sales dollars, at the present mix.

    b. Calculate the volume of each product's sales at which it has a zero profit contribution. Comment on the factors affecting the relationship between the total of these amounts and your answer to *(a)*.

    c. Calculate the consequences of a 10 percent overall volume decline. Would the company operate at a loss? Would either product operate at a loss?

    d. Which product's sales decline would have more serious consequences from the viewpoint of the Forsyth Company as a whole? Explain.

    e. Further analysis indicates that management could maintain sales volume of one product in a recession by shifting the company's selling efforts and spending an additional $100,000 a year; sales of the other product then would fall 20 percent from the present level. Should the money be spent and, if so, on which product? (You should assume that both products would continue to be sold, even if losses would be reported; the objective is to maximize income before taxes or minimize the loss.)

18. **Decision tree; expected value.** John Smith holds 100 shares of a company which is currently being traded at $45 a share. He faces two alternatives:

1. Sell the shares immediately.
2. Wait until September 1, then decide whether to sell or hold the shares on the basis of the market on that date, and on the company's future prospects.

For personal reasons he must sell the shares by December 31 at the latest.

Mr. Smith feels there is a 60 percent chance that the market will rise before September 1, and a 40 percent chance that it will decline. If it rises, the price will be $48. If it declines, the price will be $38. If the market rises before September 1, he estimates there is a 70 percent chance the market will continue to rise until the end of the year to a price of $50, and a 30 percent chance of a decline to a year-end price of $42. If the market declines before September 1, Mr. Smith believes there is a 60 percent chance that it will continue to fall to a price of $32 by year-end, and a 40 percent chance that it will recover to $45.

Required:

a. Draw a decision tree to show the above relationships, including the probabilities.
b. Assuming Mr. Smith wishes to maximize the expected value of the proceeds from the sale of his shares, what should he do now? (Ignore dividends, income taxes, and interest costs.)
c. How would you justify a decision other than the decision you recommended in answer to *(b)*?

(SMAC, adapted)

19. **Decision tree: Product development.** The Premier Company has already spent $1.1 million to develop a new product. Laboratory tests have been completed satisfactorily, and the next step is to set up and operate an experimental production line on a small scale to test the feasibility of manufacturing the product in commercial quantities. The cost of this experimental production will be $200,000.

The knowledgeable managers agree that the following outcomes of the production experiment are likely:

1. There is a 0.1 probability that the test will show that the product should be dropped.
2. There is a 0.7 probability that the test will show that the product can be manufactured in a standard plant costing $2 million.
3. There is a 0.2 probability that the test will show that the product can be manufactured only in a complex plant costing $4 million.

Once the plant has been built, the product faces an uncertain market:

1. There is a 0.2 probability that substantial sales will be made to chain stores. If this happens, the present value of the operating cash inflows will be $5 million.
2. There is a 0.8 probability that the market will be limited to independent retailers and institutional customers. If this happens, the present value of the operating inflows will be $3.5 million.

Required:

a. Draw a decision tree and enter the probabilities and payoffs.
b. Calculate the expected value of each managerial action. Should the experimental production line be set up?

(Prepared by Alexander A. Robichek)

20. **Decision tree: product development.** You are general manager of the Technical Products Corporation. Your chief designer is 90 percent certain of developing a new gas measuring instrument if you will allocate $100,000. He's a skilled designer but also an optimist, in your judgment, so you set these probabilities:

0.7   that he will develop the instrument for $100,000.

0.3   that he will spend the $100,000 without success and then come back saying, "I need $100,000 more."

0.4   that, if not successful at first and if given the additional $100,000 (total $200,000), he will be successful.

0.6   that, if not successful at first and if given the additional $100,000 (total $200,000), he will be unsuccessful.

You consult next with your sales manager about expected sales of the instrument and you both agree that if the design of the instrument is successful you can expect the following:

1.   A one-third probability that manufacture and sale of the gas measuring instrument will break even, but with no contribution to repay development costs and provide a profit.

2.   A two-thirds probability that the contribution to development costs and profit will be $300,000.

Required:

a.   Draw the decision tree.

b.   Calculate the expected values. Should the $100,000 be allocated?

(Prepared by Alexander A. Robichek)

21.   **Payoff table; expected value.** Jackston, Inc., manufactures and distributes a line of toys. The company neglected to keep its dollhouse line current for several years. As a result, sales decreased to about 10,000 units a year from a previous high of 50,000 units. The dollhouses have now been redesigned and are considered by company executives to be competitive with its competitors' models. The company plans to redesign the dollhouse each year to allow it to retain its reestablished competitive position.

Joan Blocke, the sales manager, is not sure how many units can be sold next year, but she is willing to place probabilities on her estimates. Ms. Blocke's estimates of the number of units which can be sold during the next year and the related probabilities are as follows:

Estimated Sales in Units	Probability
20,000	0.10
30,000	0.40
40,000	0.30
50,000	0.20

The units are to be sold at a price of $20 each.

The inability to estimate sales more precisely is a problem for Jackston. The number of units of this product is small enough to schedule the entire year's sales in one production run. If the demand is greater than the number of units manufactured, sales will be lost. If demand is less than supply, however, the extra units cannot be carried over to the next year; instead, Jackston gives them to various charitable organizations. The production and distribution cost estimates are as follows:

	Units Manufactured			
	20,000	30,000	40,000	50,000
Variable costs	$180,000	$270,000	$360,000	$450,000
Fixed costs	140,000	140,000	160,000	160,000
Total costs	$320,000	$410,000	$520,000	$610,000

Required:

a. Prepare a payoff table for the different sizes of production runs required to meet the four sales estimates prepared by Ms. Blocke.

b. If Jackston, Inc., relies solely on the expected monetary value approach to make decisions, what size of production run should be selected?

(CMA adapted)

22. **Variations in product mix.** The Mossback Company manufactures and sells five products. All products are sold and serviced by a single sales force; none has its own product manager or marketing staff. The company's manufacturing facilities are also general-purpose facilities, and all products require operations in every department of the factory. The company has five products, for which you have the following data (all dollar figures are averages per unit):

	Prod. A	Prod. B	Prod. C	Prod. D	Prod. E
Annual/sales (units)	200,000	1,000,000	500,000	400,000	800,000
Discounts and allowances ..	$0.05	$0.03	$0.12	$0.16	$0.10
Variable costs	1.42	0.84	2.81	3.12	5.22
Fixed costs	0.84	0.46	1.95	2.42	1.46
Unit price	2.50	1.50	3.95	5.70	8.00

None of the fixed costs is traceable to a specific product. These costs are assigned to products on the basis of various predetermined overhead rates; the amounts assigned to any one product depend on its relative use of various portions of the company's facilities. No overhead costs remain unassigned at the rates and volumes shown in the table.

Required:

a. Calculate the break-even volume for each product, in dollars of gross sales, reflecting the fixed costs the company plans to assign to that product.

b. Calculate the break-even volume for the company as a whole, in dollars of gross sales, at the present product mix. Why does this differ from the sum of the break-even volumes you calculated in answer to *(a)?*

c. Given your knowledge of the nature of the fixed costs in this company, how reliable are the estimates of break-even volume you derived in *(a)* and *(b)?* Explain.

d. Prepare a forecast of the company's income before taxes if the company's selling efforts produce the following product sales instead of those shown in the earlier table, all other factors remaining unchanged:

Product	Unit Sales
A	150,000
B	800,000
C	400,000
D	500,000
E	1,000,000

e. If fixed selling expenses had to be increased by $400,000 a year to effect the shift in product mix described in part *(d),* would you recommend taking this action?

23. **Make or buy decision: expected value; break-even volume.** The Unimat Company manufactures a unique thermostat which yields dramatic cost savings from effective climatic control of large buildings. The efficiency of the thermostat is dependent upon the quality of a specialized thermocouple. These thermocouples are purchased from Cosmic Company for $15 each.

For the last two years, an average of 10 percent of the thermocouples purchased from Cosmic have not met Unimat's quality standards. Unimat has had to buy additional thermocouple units to replace the defective units because the rejection rate of the units is within the range agreed upon in the contract with Cosmic.

Unimat is considering a proposal to manufacture the thermocouples. The company has the facilities and equipment to produce and assemble the components. The engineering department has designed a manufacturing system which will produce the thermocouples with a defective rate of 4 percent of the number of units produced. The following schedule presents the engineers' estimates of the probabilities that different levels of variable manufacturing cost per thermocouple will be incurred under this system:

Estimated Variable Manufacturing Cost per Good Thermocouple Unit	Probability of Occurrence
$10	0.1
12	0.3
14	0.4
16	0.2

The variable manufacturing cost per unit includes a cost adjustment for the defective units at the 4 percent rejection rate. Additional annual fixed costs incurred by Unimat if it manufactures the thermocouple will amount to $32,500. Unimat will need 18,000 good thermocouple units to meet its annual thermostat production requirements.

Required:

a. Prepare an expected value analysis to determine whether Unimat Company should manufacture the thermocouples.

b. A recession could reduce Unimat's need for thermocouples; exceptionally favorable business conditions would increase its needs beyond 18,000 units. Either Cosmic Company or Unimat's proposed manufacturing operation could supply enough units at the projected cost levels to meet any conceivable demand in the near future. Calculate the smallest volume (measured by the number of good thermocouple units required) at which Unimat would find it profitable to manufacture its own thermocouple. Explain how you would use this information in deciding whether to make or buy the units.

(CMA, adapted)

24. **Probability-adjusted profit charts.** The Stafford Company makes a cleaning fluid which it sells to wholesalers at a price of $2 a gallon. Following guidelines established by higher management, Polly Ortner, the marketing vice president, submitted a marketing plan which she estimated would produce sales revenues with the following probabilities:

Volume Range (million gallons)	Probability
11–12	0.05
10–11	0.10
9–10	0.30
8– 9	0.25
7– 8	0.15
6– 7	0.10
5– 6	0.05

Management has made the following estimates of operating costs at various volumes:

Volume (million gallons)	Cost ($ millions)
12	$20.7
11	19.2
10	17.8
9	16.5
8	15.3
7	14.1
6	12.9
5	11.7

Estimates of cost at volumes between the levels shown in this table can be derived by linear interpolation.

Not satisfied with the original proposal, Ms. Ortner has developed an entirely different marketing plan to present to higher management as an alternative to the first. It would increase spending on order-getting activities by $500,000, but Ms. Ortner expects it would increase sales volume substantially. The new probability distribution is as follows:

Volume Range (million gallons)	Probability
11–12	0.10
10–11	0.20
9–10	0.30
8– 9	0.25
7– 8	0.10
6– 7	0.05
5– 6	—

Required:

a. Calculate the expected value of each proposal. (*Suggestion:* In calculating profitability of sales in any volume range, use the mid-range volume—e.g., use a volume of 11.5-million gallons in calculating the profitability of sales in the 11- to 12-million gallon range.)

b. Prepare a probability-adjusted profit chart for each plan, using cumulative probabilities.

c. Given your answers to (a) and (b), which proposal would you recommend? Prepare a brief statement of the reasoning underlying your recommendation.

25. **Break-even analysis: nontraceable fixed costs; response to changes in volume and mix.** Schmelzer Nostrums, Inc., manufactures several highly perishable items, all of which are subject to marked seasonal fluctuations in demand. On the basis of sales forecasts furnished by the sales department, raw materials price forecasts supplied by the purchasing department, and cost data prepared by various operating personnel, the controller has prepared the following project operating statement:

		Cost Breakdown	
	Total	Fixed	Variable
Gross sales	$6,000,000		
Sales discounts and allowances	192,000		
Net sales	5,808,000		
Expenses:			
Manufacturing cost of goods sold*	3,750,000	$ 294,000	$3,456,000
Administration	420,000	342,000	78,000
Marketing and selling	438,000	384,000	54,000
Total expense	4,608,000	$1,020,000	$3,588,000
Income before taxes	$1,200,000		

*Year-end inventories are small and unlikely to change significantly.

The company has four products. The accounting system provides for a full distribution of the fixed costs not traceable to any specific product. Sales discounts and allowances are fully traceable to individual products. Your analysis has produced the following table:

			Fixed Costs			Income/(loss) before Income Taxes
Product	Gross Sales	Discounts and Allowances	Product-Traceable	All Other	Variable Costs	
A	$2,000,000	$ 60,000	$105,000	$195,000	$1,100,000	$ 540,000
B	2,500,000	100,000	184,000	266,000	1,500,000	450,000
C	1,000,000	20,000	56,000	172,000	780,000	(28,000)
D	500,000	12,000	5,000	37,000	208,000	238,000
Total	$6,000,000	$192,000	$350,000	$670,000	$3,588,000	$1,200,000

Required:

a. Calculate the volume of gross sales at which each product would cover its traceable fixed costs. Also calculate the volume at which it would cover all of the costs assigned to the product. Which of these two sets of figures is more meaningful? Why?

b. Calculate the volume of gross sales at which the company would break even if it retained its present product mix.

c. Management is concerned that a recession would impair its ability to pay the annual cash dividend of $500,000. Cash flow and net income are virtually identical, after allowing for normal equipment replacement expenditures. The income tax rate is 40 percent. Calculate the effect on net income of a 10 percent reduction in volume.

d. If management reorganizes its sales force and redistributes its marketing effort as proposed by the marketing vice president, the expected effect will be to increase total fixed cost by $200,000 and to produce the following sales mix:

Product	Gross Sales
A	$2,300,000
B	2,100,000
C	700,000
D	900,000
Total	$6,000,000

Would this proposal improve the company's profit performance? Would it increase the degree of risk? Show your calculations and explain.

26. **Uncertain estimates; sensitivity analysis.** Samuel Telford is a promoter. He invests capital for short periods in new ventures in the expectation of selling out at a profit after the ventures have been fully financed. Through a privately owned corporation, Plexco, Inc., he also markets a constantly changing line of gadgets, games, novelty gifts, and office accessories. Few of these products remain on the market for more than a few months. "My products have very short life cycles," he said recently. "Once in a while I get one that catches on, like the felt-tip pen, but when that happens I look for a buyer and sell out. I'd rather get my money back and move on to something new."

Plexco has a small sales force for products that are marketed through retail outlets. Most production is either subcontracted or turned out on temporary production lines, although the company does have a small-scale manufacturing facility of its own.

Mr. Telford recently considered marketing a new wall decoration for use in executive offices, reception rooms, and so on. This product would be sold entirely by mail. A direct-mail company would charge $20,000 to print and mail a descriptive brochure to a list of about 100,000 selected executives. Plexco's previous experience with mailings of this kind indicated a likely response percentage of about 3 percent—that is, about 3,000 units would be sold as a result of the mailing.

The wall decorations would be sold at a price of $20 each. A small assembly line would be set up for a one-month production run. The project was expected to produce a net cash inflow of $6,000, reflecting the following incremental costs and revenues:

	Unit Amount	Total
Sales	$20	$60,000
Costs:		
Materials	8	24,000
Labor (¼ hour per unit)...................	2	6,000
Manufacturing overhead	—	4,000
Mailing...............................	—	20,000
Total cost	xx	54,000
Incremental cash flow	xx	$ 6,000

All of the incremental manufacturing overhead costs would be fixed costs.

Mr. Telford was not wholly convinced. "I can't argue with your estimates of materials costs, wage rates, and overhead costs," he said, "but the labor time figure and response percentage could be way off. The supervisor says the workers can turn out a unit in 10 minutes if everything goes right, but if we get hit with a slowdown as we did last year, average time could even go up to half an hour."

Required:

a. Errors in forecasting the response percentage are seldom greater than 33.33 percent of the forecasted percentage, labor time may be off by the amounts indicated above, but forecasting errors in the other profit determinants are generally 10 percent or less. For which of the parameters is the decision sensitive to forecasting errors of these magnitudes?

b. How large would the forecasting error have to be to make the decision sensitive to errors in forecasting the response percentage, materials cost, or labor time?

c. The possible response percentages range from about 0.5 percent to a little more than 5 percent. Prepare a table showing the incremental profit or loss for response rates of 0.5, 1.5, 2.5, 3.5, 4.5, and 5.5 percent.

d. The probabilities of the various response rates are approximately as follows:

Percent Response		
Range	Average	Probability
0.51–1.5	1.0	0.10
1.51–2.5	2.0	0.25
2.51–3.5	3.0	0.50
3.51–4.5	4.0	0.10
4.51 or more	5.0	0.05

Add a column to the table you prepared in answer to (c), showing the cumulative probabilities of response rates and incremental profits less than the amounts indicated in the first two columns.

e. Plot profit or loss and cumulative probability on a sheet of graph paper, draw a smooth line through the plotted points, and use this line to estimate the probability that introducing the new product will be profitable.

6 Variable costing

The factory job costing system we described in Chapter 2 is known as a *full costing* or *absorption costing* system, in which each job absorbs a share of each of the costs of operating the factory cost centers working on that job. Product costs assembled on this basis don't give us the kinds of information on cost variability we discussed in Chapters 4 and 5. The purpose of this chapter is to examine an alternative basis for product costing which does give this information, known as *variable costing*. In the first part of the chapter we'll see which operating costs are included in product cost in a variable costing system; in the final section we'll see how the use of variable costing might affect reported income.

The basis for variable costing

In a variable costing system, product cost includes only those factory costs that vary in response to short-run changes in the rate of production—that is, the variable costs. An Exhibit 6–1 shows, direct materials, direct labor, and the variable portion of factory overhead are product costs in a variable costing

Exhibit 6–1 Product costs under variable costing

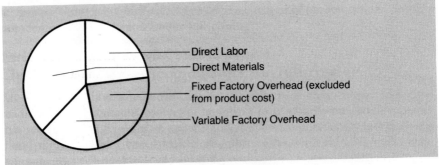

Direct Labor

Direct Materials

Fixed Factory Overhead (excluded from product cost)

Variable Factory Overhead

FOH NOT prod. cost

system. Fixed manufacturing overheads are not assigned to individual end-product activities—they are not classified as product costs.[1]

A job costing illustration

Variable costing is not an alternative to job costing. It is simply another way of measuring the costs of individual jobs. For example, suppose departmental volume is measured in machine-hours and departmental overhead costs are expected to vary as follows:

	Fixed per Month	Variable per Machine-Hour
Supervision	$1,800	—
Indirect labor	—	$0.15
Indirect materials	—	0.10
Maintenance	200	0.11
Power	—	0.04
Total	$2,000	$0.40

In this case the variable costing overhead rate would be 40 cents a machine hour. In variable costing, a job order requiring 10 machine hours in this department would be charged $4.00 (10 hours × $0.40) for variable overhead, and no charge would be made for any portion of the $2,000 in fixed costs. In full costing, the overhead rate would include a provision for fixed costs.

full costing: rate include provision for fixed costs

Two points should be noticed in this illustration. First, overhead costs were assigned to the job by means of an overhead rate. Variable overhead is no easier to trace to individual jobs than fixed overhead. The only way to assign overhead costs to job orders is to use overhead rates.

VOH rates

Second, variable costing can be used even if some cost elements contain both fixed and variable components. Since the overhead rate is predetermined, all the accountants have to do is estimate the *rate* of variability. They don't have to record the fixed and variable components separately. In this case they are able to include 11 cents in the overhead rate to provide for variable maintenance costs, even though they probably have no way of labeling most maintenance expenditures as either fixed or variable when they are made. (Of two drops of oil placed on a bearing, which one is the variable drop and which one is fixed? The question is unanswerable and the accountant wisely doesn't try.)

Handling nonlinear cost relationships

Cost variation is not always well-described by straight lines, as we saw in Chapter 4. Two such situations are illustrated in Exhibit 6–2. The cost steps in the upper chart are not all the same size, but they are relatively small and close together. In other words, fairly small changes in volume will lead to

[1] These systems are also known as *direct costing* systems. We find this term misleading because the term *direct* refers to the traceability of a cost, not to its variability. Variable overhead costs are not traceable to individual job orders.

Exhibit 6–2 Step functions and variable costing rates

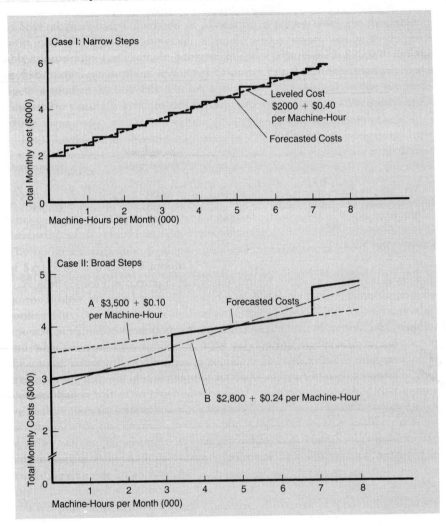

Case I: Narrow Steps

Total Monthly cost ($000)

Leveled Cost
$2000 + $0.40
per Machine-Hour

Forecasted Costs

Machine-Hours per Month (000)

Case II: Broad Steps

Total Monthly Costs ($000)

A $3,500 + $0.10
per Machine-Hour

Forecasted Costs

B $2,800 + $0.24 per Machine-Hour

Machine-Hours per Month (000)

slope of "leveled" cost line = avg. rate of variability

changes in the amount of this cost. Since this is what the variable costing figures are supposed to show, the average rate of change should be included in the variable costing overhead rate. The slope of the "leveled cost" line measures the average rate of variability (40 cents a machine-hour).

The situation represented in the lower half of Exhibit 6–2 is not as clear-cut. For fairly large ranges of volume variation, the rate of cost variability is represented by the slope of line A, 10 cents a machine-hour. If the entire volume span from zero to capacity is included, however, the leveled cost line would be the one labeled B and the rate of cost variability would be more than twice as high, 24 cents a machine-hour instead of 10 cents.

We would use line A in this situation, for two reasons. First, estimates of average variable cost are typically applied to decisions leading to fairly small differences in operating volume; averaging in the steps in fixed costs would overstate the effects of these decisions on the company's cash flows. For a better information base, the steps should be presented separately.

Second, since the company is normally operating in the central portion of its volume range, it does have $3,500 in fixed costs most of the time. Line A emphasizes that. Line B, in contrast, implies that the company has only $2,800 in fixed costs, even though the solid line shows that management is forecasting no less than $3,000 in fixed costs at any volume.

We may generalize from this illustration. *When variable costing is used, the overhead rate should represent the average rate of cost variation within the customary volume range.* The point at which a straight line reflecting this rate intersects the vertical scale at zero volume is of no analytical significance. Fixed costs should be identified separately and explicitly.

y- intercept insignificant — fixed costs considered separately.

Effect of variable costing on reported income

The objective of variable costing is to provide product unit costs for use by management. It is not designed to provide data for public financial reporting and in fact has been specifically rejected for this purpose by the accounting profession in most countries. It may be used for internal financial reporting, however, and some accountants still advocate it for external reporting. For these reasons we need to see how the use of variable costing affects reported income. We'll study four different conditions:

*u. costing
 internal
 reports*

1. Production equals sales at normal volume.
2. Production exceeds sales.
3. Production equals sales at subnormal volume.
4. Sales exceed production.

To avoid unnecessary complications, we'll assume that our illustrative company has no inventory of finished products at the beginning of our illustration. We'll also assume that all under- and overabsorbed factory overhead cost balances are added to or subtracted from the cost of goods sold on the income statement. Neither assumption is essential to the argument, but they allow us to use a much simpler set of illustrations.

Condition 1: Production equals sales at normal volume

To illustrate the income effects of variable costing, let's suppose a company manufactures only one product. Its costs at a normal volume of 50,000 units are as follows:

	Total	Per Unit
Variable factory costs	$37,500	$0.75
Fixed factory costs	12,500	0.25
Total	$50,000	$1.00

154

The fixed costs are totally fixed, without steps, and the variable costs are proportional to volume—that is, the factory cost total can always be determined from the following formula:

Total factory cost = $12,500 + $0.75 × Units manufactured

In period 1, both sales and production were at the normal volume of 50,000 units. Under variable costing, all fixed factory overhead costs are treated as period costs; they are taken directly to the income statement as expenses of the current period, without passing through product inventory accounts. Thus the income statement for period 1 would show the following manufacturing costs:

*FOH costs →
expenses on
inc. state
—do NOT pass
thru inv. acct.*

Variable cost of goods sold (50,000 × $0.75)	$37,500
Fixed factory costs	12,500
Total costs shown as expense	$50,000

Under absorption costing, the cost of goods sold is determined by multiplying sales volume by the full unit cost at normal volume. In this case, during period 1:

sales volume

Cost of goods sold = 50,000 × $1 = $50,000

The amount of cost absorbed by production is determined by multiplying production volume by full unit cost at normal volume, in this case $1. At this rate the production volume of 50,000 units would have just absorbed the $50,000 in factory cost that was normal at this volume.

prod'n volume

In other words, $50,000 of manufacturing costs would appear on the income statement under either system.

Condition 2: Production exceeds sales

In period 2, production rose to 55,000 units, but sales fell to 47,000 units. The remaining 8,000 units were in the finished goods inventory at the end of the period:

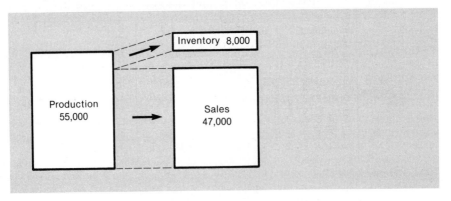

Again, production costs were at the levels anticipated for the actual volume of production:

$$\text{Total factory costs} = \$12,500 + 55,000 \times \$0.75 = \$53,750$$

Under variable costing, total expense for a sales volume of 47,000 units would be:

Variable cost of goods sold (47,000 × $0.75)	$35,250
Fixed factory costs	12,500
Total expense	$47,750

Under absorption costing, $55,000 would be assigned to the 55,000 units produced in period 2, $47,000 going to the cost of goods sold and $8,000 to the inventory. The story wouldn't end there, however. Fixed factory costs would be overabsorbed by $1,250:

Absorbed fixed costs (55,000 × $0.25) $13,750
Actual fixed costs 12,500
Overabsorbed fixed costs ....$ 1,250

If all of this were to be reported on the current income statement, the absorption costing company would report a net expense of $45,750:

Cost of goods sold (47,000 × $1) $47,000
Less: Overabsorbed factory cost 1,250
Total expense $45,750

This is $2,000 less than the total expense under variable costing.[2]

Explaining the expense difference. The $2,000 difference between the two expense figures for period 2 lies entirely in the amount of fixed cost assigned to the end-of-period inventory. Whereas variable costing would have charged the entire $12,500 as period 2 expense, absorption costing would have assigned $2,000 of this to the 8,000-unit addition to inventories (at the 25-cent burden rate), leaving only $10,500 for the income statement:

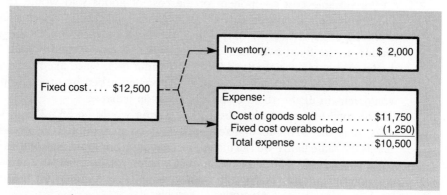

[2] If the $1,250 is regarded as "material" in amount, part of it will be subtracted from the cost of goods sold and part from the cost of the ending inventory. Assuming a zero opening inventory, the fixed costs assigned to the units sold will be 47/55 of $12,500, or $10,680. This is $1,820 less than the $12,500 fixed cost reported as expense under variable costing. In other words, regardless of whether the variance is split in this way or taken in its entirety to current income, variable costing and full costing figures are likely to differ.

The effect on income. The absorption effect is even more striking in relation to the amount of income reported. Suppose the product sells for $1.20 a unit and the firm has no selling and administrative expenses. The income statements in the first two periods would show the following:

	Absorption Costing		Variable Costing	
	Period 1	Period 2	Period 1	Period 2
Sales revenues	$60,000	$56,400	$60,000	$56,400
Expenses	50,000	45,750	50,000	47,750
Income before taxes	$10,000	$10,650	$10,000	$ 8,650

Despite the 3,000-unit decrease in sales, under absorption costing the company would report a $650 *increase* in reported income. Under variable costing, the 3,000-unit reduction in sales would be reported as a $1,350 reduction in income. This latter figure can also be calculated by multiplying 3,000 units by the product's 45-cent contribution margin ($1.20 selling price minus $0.75 variable cost).

Condition 3: Production equals sales at subnormal volume

We have already seen that the two costing methods produce the same income result when both production and sales are at normal volume. Let's see whether that will continue to hold true if production and sales are both less than normal volume. This happened in period 3, when production dropped to 47,000 units and sales remained at that level. Expenses under variable costing would be as follows:

Variable cost of goods sold (47,000 × $0.75) .. $35,250
Fixed factory costs 12,500
　　Total expense $47,750

The variable cost component of the cost of goods sold would remain at $35,250 under absorption costing. At a 25-cent absorption rate for the fixed overhead costs, however, only $11,750 would be recorded in the normal routine as the fixed overhead component of the cost of goods sold. This is shown in the upper right-hand block of Exhibit 6–3. Since fixed costs actually amounted to $12,500, and only $11,750 was absorbed by production, $750 would remain unabsorbed, to be treated as an expense.

The total expense under absorption costing would be $35,250 in variable costs, plus the $12,500 in fixed costs derived in Exhibit 6–3, or $47,750. This is the same figure we calculated for variable costing. Income before income taxes would be $8,650, no matter which costing method was used in period 3:

	Absorption Costing	Variable Costing
Sales revenues	$56,400	$56,400
Expenses	47,750	47,750
Income before taxes	$ 8,650	$ 8,650

Exhibit 6–3 Distribution of fixed factory overhead under absorption costing, period 3

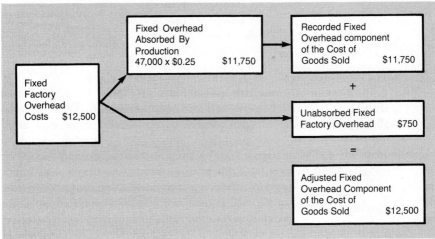

Although the two methods yield the same income figure in period 3, they show the *change* from period 2 very differently. Under variable costing, income would stay the same in period 3 as in period 2 because sales volume stayed the same. Under absorption costing, income would drop by $2,000, from $10,650 to $8,650.

The reason for this apparent inconsistency is that management did not have 8,000 units of extra unsold production in period 3 to absorb a share of fixed overhead, as it had had in period 2. So, even though sales stabilized at 47,000 units in period 3 and management took prudent action to prevent a further unwanted increase in inventory, absorption costing would give a signal to investors that the company's earnings position had deteriorated in period 3.

Condition 4: Sales exceed production

The cycle was completed in period 4, when production was cut to 44,000 units while sales went up to 52,000, completely eliminating the inventory of finished units. Total expense under variable costing would be:

Variable cost of goods sold (52,000 × $0.75) ...$39,000
Fixed costs 12,500
    Total expense $51,500

Total expense under absorption costing would be:

Cost of goods sold (52,000 × $1) $52,000
Unabsorbed fixed overhead (50,000 − 44,000
    = 6,000 × $0.25) 1,500
    Total expense $53,500

The income statement would show the following:

	Absorption Costing	Variable Costing
Sales revenues	$62,400	$62,400
Expenses	53,500	51,500
Income before taxes	$ 8,900	$10,900

In other words, variable costing income would be $2,000 greater than absorption costing income in period 4 because absorption costing would charge all of period 4's fixed costs against current revenues as well as $2,000 of the fixed costs of prior periods. Variable costing income would be $2,250 greater than in periods 2 and 3, while absorption costing income would go up only $250 from the period 3 level.

End-of-period adjustments

If a company uses variable costing in deriving the data for income statements for internal reporting to management, it must make adjustments periodically to include portions of fixed factory overhead costs in the inventory and cost of goods sold figures used for external financial reporting. A suitable entry in period 2, when 8,000 units were added to inventory, would be as follows:

| Fixed Overhead Costs in Inventory . . . . | 2,000 | |
| Inventory Adjustment to Income . . . . | | 2,000 |

The debit in this entry (representing 8,000 units at 25 cents each) would establish an asset balance; the Inventory Adjustment to Income account would be a contra account to the Cost of Goods Sold account, and crediting this account therefore would have the effect of decreasing the reported cost of goods sold and increasing reported income.

A reverse entry would be required in period 4, when the inventory was reduced to zero:

| Inventory Adjustment to Income . . . . | 2,000 | |
| Fixed Overhead Costs in Inventory . . . . | | 2,000 |

The debit to Inventory Adjustment to Income in that period would have the effect of increasing the cost of goods sold and decreasing reported income.

To keep management informed of the income figures that will be reported to shareholders and others outside the management, the accountants are likely to report the inventory adjustment at the bottom of the income statement they present to management. For example, for period 2 they might report the following:

Sales revenues		$56,400
Less: Variable cost of goods sold	$35,250	
Fixed overhead costs	12,500	47,750
Income for managerial purposes		8,650
Add: Fixed costs transferred to inventory for external reporting		2,000
Income for external reporting		$10,650

In practice, of course, inventories seldom fall to zero and overhead rates change from period to period. This means that a debit balance would always remain in the Fixed Overhead Costs in Inventory account, and amounts could ✳— be transferred either to or from this account even if inventory quantities didn't change, if the overhead rate changed and some method other than LIFO was used to account for inventory costs. The principle remains the same, however— management should be kept informed of any difference between internal and external reporting to avoid embarrassing surprises when the external financial statements are issued.

Preliminary appraisal of variable costing

A full evaluation of variable costing requires more background than we have been able to provide in the first five chapters. Even so, we can make a few general observations on the role variable costing can play in managerial decision analysis and in income measurement.

Providing data for managerial decision making

The main advantage of variable costing is that it provides a more flexible data base than full costing. The product cost figures it generates approximate the incremental costs that are relevant to short-run utilization-of-capacity deci- ✳ sions, unclouded by the application of fixed factory overheads. Furthermore, *Short* by keeping fixed costs out of the product cost totals, variable costing highlights *run* what we might call the lumpiness of fixed costs, forcing attention on the deci- *decisions* sions that create fixed costs.

In other words, variable costing forces the accountants to emphasize that fixed costs arise as totals for a period of time, not as gradual responses to ✳ changes in the level of activity. The fixed costs then can be classified into those that are traceable to the business segments management is studying and those that provide general capacity and support for all segments combined.

Measuring income

The income comparisons we made in the preceding section are the basis for the argument that variable costing should be used for income reporting, at least for management's use. This argument stems from the proposition that revenues are the source of the firm's operating income. Other things being ✳ equal, when revenues go up, income should go up; and when revenues fall, income should fall.

Our income illustrations in the preceding section showed that these relation- ✳ ships don't necessarily hold when absorption (full) costing is used. The income figures for the four periods covered by that illustration are plotted in Exhibit 6–4. The solid line, tracing the movements in income on a variable costing basis, moves in sympathy with movements in sales volume; the dashed line, reflecting absorption costing income, does not.

Exhibit 6–4 Effect on income of choice between absorption costing and variable costing

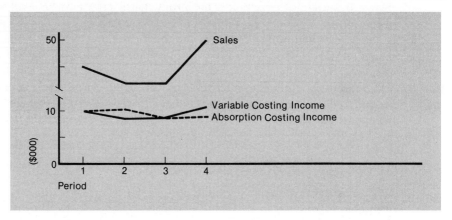

Absorption costing income can be influenced significantly by the level of production, and management's decisions on the rate of production can smooth or accentuate period-to-period income fluctuations that are caused by changes in the level of sales revenues.[3] This is why absorption costing income in our example was almost constant despite large fluctuations in revenues. The potential amount of smoothing varies inversely with the rate of inventory turnover and with the length of the reporting period. In other words, monthly financial statements are more vulnerable to this effect than annual statements; statements of companies with slow-moving inventories are more vulnerable than those of high-turnover firms.

This argument should be judged on the basis of the ability of variable costing financial statements to improve investor decisions. Lacking such evidence, the accounting profession continues to subscribe to full costing for public financial reporting. Since all factory costs are necessary to production, it is a generally accepted accounting principle that every factory overhead cost should be reflected in one overhead rate or another for inclusion in product cost.

The concept of attributable cost

Although stating segment costs as a set of fixed amounts plus a rate or rates to cover the variable costs has the advantages we just discussed, variable costing doesn't answer all analytical questions. No product, for example, should stay in the line on a continuing basis unless the revenues it brings in are adequate to cover all of the costs that could be saved or phased out if it were withdrawn

---

[3] This problem disappears if revenue is recognized at the time of production, which is consistent with generally accepted accounting principles under certain circumstances. In most cases, however, accountants lack the assurances necessary to allow them to recognize revenues at the time of production. See Gordon Shillinglaw, Myron J. Gordon and Joshua Ronen, *Accounting: A Management Approach,* 6th ed. (Homewood, Ill.: Richard D. Irwin, 1979), chap. 8.

from the market. By the same reasoning, a company introducing a new product needs to know how much cost the product will cause, on the average, at a volume appropriate to the capacity of the facilities it requires. At least some of these costs will be fixed costs in the short run.

It would be a mistake, however, to respond to this argument by jumping from variable costing all the way to full costing. Cost estimates for the purposes described in the preceding paragraph should reflect the concept of *attributable cost* rather than either variable cost or full cost. The attributable cost of any activity is the amount of cost that could be eliminated, in time, if that activity were discontinued and capacity were to be reduced accordingly.

Two factors lead attributable cost to differ from full cost. The first of these is cost *indivisibility*. A cost is indivisible if it represents the minimum set of resources necessary to provide a large percentage of total capacity. Indivisibility arises because some capacity-providing resources are available in large aggregates only. In one company's maintenance shop, for example, a reduction of 90 percent in the work load would not have permitted the disposal of a single piece of equipment. Each piece had to be available to do its own specialized work whenever an emergency arose. The cost of keeping those machines in working order therefore was an indivisible fixed cost, not attributable to any single activity requiring maintenance support.

Indivisibilities permit the expansion of capacity with a less than proportional increase in total fixed cost; contraction of capacity will produce a less than proportional decrease in total fixed cost. In other words, the fixed cost component of long-run marginal cost is smaller than average fixed cost at the current capacity level. (Long-run marginal cost is the increase in total cost accompanying the provision and use of one additional unit of capacity.)

If the fixed costs are indivisible, therefore, average fixed cost will overstate the incremental cost accompanying a change in capacity—the more indivisible the fixed cost, the farther the increment will be from the average. For example, if average fixed cost amounts to $10 and none of the fixed costs is divisible, then incremental average fixed cost will be zero, not $10. If 90 percent of the fixed costs are proportionately divisible, however, average fixed cost will only overstate the increment by $1.

The second factor that leads incremental cost away from average full cost is that changes in capacity change not only the total but the structure of the fixed costs as well. Average fixed cost will decline as capacity increases, at least up to a point, not only because the indivisible cost elements are spread over larger and larger volumes but also because larger volumes permit the company to use more efficient technology.

This kind of cost reduction is the result of *economies of scale.* The availability of economies of scale means that although *total* cost will increase as capacity increases, *average* cost will fall if the additional capacity is utilized. Some economies of scale reduce average variable costs per unit; others reduce average fixed cost.

Given indivisibilities and economies of scale, an overhead rate reflecting the concept of attributable cost will be smaller than an overhead rate reflecting the full cost concept. It will exclude indivisible fixed costs; it will include divisible fixed costs at less than their current average level if economies of scale are still available.

For example, assume that a department with a normal operating volume of 10,000 machine hours has the following budgeted overhead costs at normal volume:

	Total Overhead Cost per Month	Normal Overhead Cost per Machine-Hour
Variable overhead costs	$3,000	$0.30
Divisible fixed overhead costs	2,000	0.20
Indivisible fixed overhead costs	1,000	0.10

A full cost overhead rate would be 60 cents a machine hour, while a rate based on attributable cost would be 50 cents (or less, to allow for economies of scale). A rate for the variable overhead costs would be only 30 cents.

Since overhead rates based on attributable costing are likely to be smaller than full-cost rates, fewer overhead costs will be absorbed at any given volume than would be absorbed by full-cost rates. Using the rates we developed in the preceding paragraph, for example, the total amount absorbed at a volume of 9,000 machine hours would be $900 less than under full costing:

Absorbed by full cost overhead rate: 9,000 × $0.60 . . . . $5,400
Absorbed by attributable-cost overhead rate: 9,000 × $0.50 . .   4,500
   Difference in amount absorbed: 9,000 × $0.10 . . . . $ 900

If actual overhead costs amount to, say, $5,500, then the amount unabsorbed will be $1,000 instead of a mere $100.

The decrease in cost absorption need not disturb us. We must remember that the purpose of the overhead rate is to measure the overhead cost component of product cost, not to absorb overhead. If product costs are to be used to estimate the impact of managerial decisions which have a long time horizon, however, any cost estimate that goes beyond attributable cost is overstated.

The main weakness of attributable costing is that it requires the exercise of judgment. Calculating a full cost overhead rate is essentially an arithmetic process—put all the costs in the pot and divide by volume. If we want attributable-cost rates, however, we have to study each component of overhead cost and decide how much to include. This isn't easy, and the results are always open to question.

Even so, we are convinced that revelance to management is a stronger criterion than mathematical precision. Attributable cost figures are designed for management's use, not for outsiders, and management can always question the basis on which analytical judgments have been made. Full costing appears to have arisen originally in response to management's demands for estimates of the amounts of cost resulting from the provision and use of capacity to produce individual products, and this is what attributable cost is intended to measure.

Summary

Unit costs based on full absorption of factory overhead costs are used to measure inventories for external financial reporting. Full costs are difficult to use in differential cost analysis, however. For this reason, factory product costs are often calculated on a variable costing basis—that is, unit cost is defined as the average variable cost of production. Fixed factory overhead costs are not included.

Variable costing facilitates the calculation of contribution margin and the construction of profit charts. An additional advantage is that variable costing emphasizes the lumpiness of fixed costs. Fixed costs that are traceable to an individual business segment can be deducted from that segment's contribution margin to determine its profit contribution. Fixed costs that aren't traceable to any business segment remain a general charge against the profit contributions of all the segments, taken together.

Although variable costing is essentially a method of assigning costs to products rather than a device for absorbing overhead costs for income measurement purposes, it also has some income measurement advantages. Variations in fixed cost absorption arising from variations in the level of production unmatched by variations in sales volume do not affect reported income. Accordingly, variable costing may be used for internal income measurement even though it can't be used for external financial reporting. When it is used in this way, it must be accompanied by adjustments designed to assign an appropriate portion of fixed overhead costs to inventory for external reporting.

Variable costing data don't meet every managerial need for product cost information. Management often needs estimates of the amount of cost that is incurred to provide and use the amount of capacity required by individual products or product lines. We call these estimates of attributable cost and regard them as superior to full cost for these managerial purposes.

Independent study problems (solutions in Appendix B)

1. **Product cost under variable costing.**   A company manufactures many products. Each product passes through two production departments, which have the following overhead cost structures:

	Department A	Department B
Normal monthly volume	5,000 direct labor hours	10,000 pounds of material
Monthly fixed overhead costs at normal volume	$10,000	$40,000
Monthly variable overhead costs at normal volume	15,000	20,000

Two of the job orders that went through the factory last month had the following results:

	Job 1 (Product X)		Job 2 (Product Y)	
	Quantity	Cost	Quantity	Cost
Direct inputs:				
Direct materials (pounds)	480	$2,400	1,500	$4,800
Direct labor:				
Department A (hours)......	180	1,620	100	900
Department B (hours)......	60	420	40	280
Output (units)	600		1,000	

Required:

a. Calculate the unit cost of each of these jobs on a full costing basis.
b. Recalculate unit costs on a variable costing basis.
c. Why are the relative variable costs of these two products so different from their relative full costs?

2. **Variable costing income statements.** Sales and income of the Feaster Manufacturing Company for the first two quarters of the year were:

	First	Second
Sales	$300,000	$450,000
Income before taxes	55,000	57,000

The directors are concerned that a 50 percent increase in sales has resulted in only a small increase in operating income. The chief cost accountant explains that unabsorbed overhead was charged to second-quarter operations. The income statements reflect the following data:

	First Quarter	Second Quarter
Sales—units	20,000	30,000
Production—units	30,000	24,000
Ending inventory—units	10,000	4,000
Selling price per unit	$ 15	$ 15
Variable manufacturing cost per unit	5	5
Fixed manufacturing overhead costs	180,000	180,000
Fixed overhead per unit (overhead rate)	6	6
Selling and administrative expenses	25,000	27,000

The company uses a first-in, first-out (FIFO) method for costing inventory. All underabsorbed or overabsorbed manufacturing costs are closed out to Cost of Goods Sold at the close of each quarter.

Required:

a. Prepare income statements for the two periods, using the method now employed by the Feaster Manufacturing Company. Calculate the cost of each quarter's ending inventory.
b. Prepare similar statements using the variable costing method.
c. What would second-quarter income before taxes have been under each method if production in that period had been 30,000 units?

Exercises and problems

3. **Income on a variable costing basis.** Indiana Corporation began its operations on January 1, 19x9, and produced a single product selling for $9 a unit. Indiana

used an actual (historical) costing system under which each unit produced during a year was costed at the average actual cost of production in that year. There were 100,000 units produced and 90,000 units sold in 19x9. The company had no work-in-process inventory on December 31, 19x9. Manufacturing costs and selling and administrative expenses for 19x9 were as follows:

	Fixed Costs	Variable Costs
Direct materials	—	$1.75 per unit produced
Direct labor	—	1.25 per unit produced
Factory overhead	$100,000	0.50 per unit produced
Selling and administrative	70,000	0.60 per unit sold

Required:

a.   Calculate Indiana's income before taxes for 19x9 on a variable costing basis.
b.   Calculate Indiana's income before taxes for 19x9 on a full costing basis.
c.   How would your answers to (a) and (b) differ if Indiana's production for 19x9 had been 110,000 units and sales had been 90,000?

(AICPA, adapted)

4.   **Variable costing income statement.**   Grobeck Company manufactures and sells a single product. The company uses variable costing to facilitate the calculation of unit contribution margin and the construction of profit-volume charts. You have the following data:

1.   Selling price: $10 a unit.
2.   Direct materials: $3 a unit.
3.   Direct labor: one-fourth hour per unit at a wage rate of $10 an hour.
4.   Variable factory overhead: $2 a direct labor hour.
5.   Fixed factory overhead: $200,000.
6.   Variable selling and administrative expenses: 10 cents a unit.
7.   Fixed selling and administrative expenses: $150,000.
8.   Normal production volume: 100,000 units.
9.   Production volume this year: 90,000 units.
10.   Sales volume this year: 85,000 units.
11.   Inventories at the beginning of this year: none.

Required:

a.   Calculate the cost of the inventory on hand at the end of this year, based on the variable costing approach.
b.   Prepare an income statement for Grobeck for this year, based on variable costing and using the contribution margin format.
c.   Income is reported externally on a full costing basis, with factory overhead applied to products by means of a predetermined rate reflecting normal production volume. Over- or underabsorbed overhead is written off each year as an adjustment to the cost of goods sold. Calculate the amount of income before income taxes to be reported externally.

5.   **Product cost under variable costing.**   A company used a job order costing system with a factory wide predetermined overhead rate based on estimated costs at a normal volume of operations. Factory overhead costs were classified into three categories:

1.   Fixed: unaffected by month-to-month changes in production volume.
2.   Semivariable: affected by changes in volume, but less than proportionally.
3.   Variable: proportional to volume.

Factory volume was measured by the number of direct labor hours. You are given the cost and volume expected during a normal month and actual data for the month of May:

	Normal	May
Factory overhead costs:		
Fixed..........................	$ 50,000	$49,500
Semivariable	30,000	29,000
Variable	20,000	19,000
Total	$100,000	$97,500
Factory volume (direct labor hours)	50,000	45,000

Costs in the semivariable category were expected to vary at a rate of 50 cents a direct labor hour.

Required:

a. Prepare a predetermined overhead rate based on the variable costing concept.
b. Using the predetermined overhead rate you developed in answer to (*a*), calculate unit cost for a job lot of 1,000 units requiring a total of $1,000 in direct materials and 500 direct labor hours at an average wage rate of $8 an hour.
c. How much factory overhead cost was charged to all jobs combined during May if the overhead rate was predetermined and product cost was based on variable costing? State the meaning of the difference between actual factory overhead in May and the total amount charged to jobs during the month.

6. **Overhead rate under variable costing.** Variations in overhead costs in department X can be predicted from the following formula:

$3,600 a month + $1.60 a direct labor hour for the first 3,000 direct labor hours in any month + $2 a direct labor hour for each direct labor hour in excess of 3,000 hours in the month.

Volume in department X is almost never less than 3,000 direct labor hours in any month; normal volume is 4,000 direct labor hours a month.

Required:

a. Calculate a variable costing overhead rate for department X on the assumption that the objective of the rate is to absorb all variable overhead costs at normal volume.
b. Calculate a variable costing overhead rate for department X on the assumption that the objective of the rate is to help the accountants provide product cost data that will help management make short-term, utilization-of-capacity decisions.
c. The rate you calculated in answer to (*b*) is the only rate used in product costing in this department. Calculate the amount of the department's overhead cost that is not assigned to products if the department operates at normal volume. Is the amount you have calculated consistent with the frequently repeated statement that under variable costing all of the variable costs and none of the fixed costs is assigned to products (absorbed)?
d. Would you recommend that the company's variable costing system use the rate you calculated in answer to (*a*) or the rate you calculated in your answer to (*b*)? State the reason for your choice.

7. **Variable costing; adjustment to financial reporting basis.** Sterling Company used a predetermined overhead rate of $1 a machine hour both in 19x4 and in 19x5, based on variable costing. It used full costing for public financial reporting, however, with a predetermined overhead rate of $2.50 a machine hour in each year. Overhead costs included in inventories for external financial reporting totaled $50,000 on January 1, 19x5, and $75,000 on December 31, 19x5. Inventories were reported at FIFO cost, and under- or overabsorbed factory overhead cost

was closed out to the income statement at the end of each year. Sales took place at a steady rate throughout the year.

Sterling recorded a total of 96,000 machine hours in 19x5, at the rate of 8,000 hours a month. Actual overhead costs amounted to $270,000, incurred at a steady rate of $22,500 a month. The company's published income statement for 19x5, reflecting all adjustments, showed income before income taxes of $90,000.

Required:

a. Calculate Sterling's 19x5 income before income taxes on a variable costing basis.
b. Sterling used an account titled Fixed Costs in Inventories. Calculate the balance in this account on January 1, 19x5, and its correct balance at the close of business on December 31, 19x5. What amount should Sterling have entered in this account *each month* to reconcile income calculated on a variable costing basis with income calculated on a public reporting basis?

8. **Variable costing: Cost of materials used.**   Banford Company sells 14,000 units of product X each month at a price of $6 a unit with total fixed selling and administrative expense of $10,000. The company has two factories: factory 1 and factory 2. Product X is manufactured in factory 1. Costs in factory 1 for an output of 14,000 units of product X are:

Materials	$35,000
Labor	14,000
Variable overhead	12,600
Fixed overhead	8,400
Total	$70,000

The raw materials cost in this table is the amount charged to factory 1 for product A, which is manufactured in factory 2. Each unit of product X requires two units of product A as a raw material.

Factory 2 sells part of its output to factory 1 and part to outside customers. Its normal monthly volume is 50,000 units of product A, and the cost of producing this volume are:

Materials	$10,000
Labor	5,000
Variable overhead	2,500
Fixed overhead	45,000
Total	$62,500

Factory 1 uses variable costing; factory 2 follows the full costing concept in product costing. Personnel in one factory have no access to the other factory's cost records.

Required:

a. You are the factory controller for factory 1. Compute the variable unit cost of product X as you would see it in your factory. Is the product profitable? What is its break-even volume?
b. How would your answer to (a) have differed if *both* factories had used variable costing?

9. **Effect of production on income before tax.**   Early in December, 19x1, Dastard Company estimated that its income before income taxes would be lower than in the preceding year unless something could be done in December to generate additional income. The company's sales dollar at normal volume (which exceeded the company's volume in 19x1) was broken down as follows:

Direct materials	$0.10
Direct labor	0.25
Factory overhead	0.50
Selling and administrative expenses	0.10
Income before income taxes	0.05
Total	$1.00

70 percent of the factory overhead at normal volume was fixed; the remainder was proportionally variable with production volume. Ninety percent of the selling and administrative expense at normal volume was fixed; the remainder was proportionally variable with sales volume. Inventory was measured on a full-cost, FIFO basis, using a predetermined factory overhead rate. The predetermined overhead rate used in 19x1 was equal to the rate used in 19x0. Factory overhead over- or underabsorbed was written off on the income statement in its entirety each year.

Management considered taking either or both of the two following actions before the end of 19x1:

1. Increase production by an amount that had a sales value of $1 million. Adequate warehouse space was available to store these additional products; production would create no unusual problems.
2. Increase 19x1 sales by $1 million by persuading a customer to accept delivery in December 19x1 rather than in January 19x2. The merchandise to be shipped was already in the company's warehouse and was not needed for other customers.

Required:

a. Calcualte the effect *each* of these actions, taken separately, would have had on the company's income before income taxes in 19x1.
b. Calculate the effect each of these actions would have had on income before income taxes if the company had been using variable costing.
c. To what extent would these calculations support or refute an argument that variable costing should be classified as an acceptable method of determining the cost of goods sold for external financial reporting? As a method of determining the cost of the ending inventory?

(Adapted from a problem by Carl L. Nelson)

10. **Overhead rates under variable costing; attributable costing.** The management of the Leininger Company has decided to use variable costing for cost estimating purposes. Full cost figures will be entered on the job order cost sheets and in the financial accounts. The estimated overhead costs of factory department 77 at a normal volume of 4,000 direct labor hours a month are as follows:

Supervision	$ 4,000
Indirect labor	6,000
Fringe benefits	8,400
Supplies	1,200
Power	1,000
Depreciation	800
Miscellaneous	600
Total	$22,000

You have the following additional information:

1. Supervision costs remain at $4,000 a month for any volume between 3,000 and 5,000 direct labor hours. If volume drops below 3,000 hours, supervision can be cut to $2,800; if volume exceeds 5,000 hours, supervision costs will go up to $5,000 a month.

2. One third of indirect labor costs at normal volume are fixed; two thirds are proportional to the number of direct labor hours.
3. Fringe benefits amount to 20 percent of labor cost, including direct labor, supervision, and indirect labor. Direct labor wage rates average $8 an hour.
4. Supplies and power costs should be proportional to the number of direct labor hours.
5. Depreciation and miscellaneous overhead costs are entirely fixed. Depreciation charges relate to the equipment used in the department. The department has 22 machines of four different machine types. About one third of the miscellaneous overhead costs consist of charges for machine maintenance; most of the remainder consists of a fixed licensing fee for the process used in department 77.
6. The volume of activity ordinarily fluctuates between 3,200 and 4,600 direct labor hours.

Required:

a. Calculate predetermined overhead rates for this department, both for variable costing and for full costing.
b. How much of department 77's costs should be included in the fixed cost in inventory category for external financial reporting if the year-end inventory includes products which have used 2,000 hours of direct labor in this department?
c. Derive an overhead rate based on the attributable costing concept. Identify the judgmental decisions you had to make and explain the assumptions underlying the choices you made.

11. **Variable costing: New product decision.**   Tortilla Flatware, Inc., manufactures a single product in its only factory. Variable manufacturing cost is $9 a unit, fixed manufacturing costs average $3.40 a unit, and selling and administrative expenses average $1.93 a unit at the present volume of 83,000 units a month. The product has a selling price of $17 a unit and generates income before taxes of $2.67 a unit.

Tortilla is considering marketing a new deluxe model, priced at $22. Management is convinced it could capture its proportionate share of the market for a product in this price bracket, about 20,000 units a month. Most of these would be sold to customers who would otherwise buy competitors' products; sales of Tortilla's regular model would be reduced by only 3,000 units a month, to 80,000 units a month.

Adequate physical capacity is available to manufacture the new model, but an additional assembly line would have to be put in operation, with additional supervisors, inspectors, and other personnel. Selling and administrative costs would also go up.

Tortilla measures product cost on a variable costing basis, using a supplemental rate to calculate the amount of fixed overhead cost to be assigned to inventories for external financial reporting. Addition of the new model would lead the company to recalculate its supplemental rate. A new average would also be calculated for selling and administrative costs. Using these new rates, the company's accountants have prepared the following revised unit cost and profit estimates for the two products:

	Regular	Deluxe
Unit cost:		
Direct materials	$ 3.00	$10.00
Direct labor	4.50	6.00
Variable factory overhead	1.50	2.00
Total variable cost	9.00	18.00
Fixed factory overhead	3.00	4.00
Selling and administrative costs	1.80	1.80
Total unit cost	13.80	23.80
Selling price	17.00	22.00
Profit (loss) per unit	$ 3.20	$(1.80)

Required:

a. Should the new model be introduced if management accepts the estimates summarized above? Show your calculations.

b. To what extent, if at all, did the company's variable costing system make this analysis easier? Did the supplemental overhead rates help?

c. Would the company's present model be more profitable or less profitable if the new model were introduced than it is now? Does the use of variable costing make it easier to demonstrate this?

12. **Costs of transferred materials.** A company has three multiproduct factories for which the following data are available:

	Factory 1	Factory 2	Factory 3
Normal monthly volume	50,000	30,000	100,000 lbs.
	labor hours	machine hours	of product
Expected overhead costs at normal volume:			
Variable	$75,000	$30,000	$20,000
Fixed	25,000	90,000	80,000

All three factories use predetermined, full-cost overhead rates for product unit costing:

Factory 1 makes product X, with the following input requirements per unit: materials—two and a half pounds of material A from factory 3, two units of material B from factory 2, one unit of material C from an outside vendor at $5; direct labor—three hours at $8 an hour.

Direct labor and materials costs in factory 3 average 70 cents a pound. A unit of material B has a direct labor and direct materials cost in factory 2 of $2 a unit and requires one and a half hours of machine time in factory 2.

The manager of factory 1 is also in charge of a small sales force which has the responsibility of bringing in orders to keep the factory busy. Business has been very slack lately throughout the industry. Being anxious to secure additional business, the manager of factory 1 has authorized the sales force to quote prices only slightly higher than the costs of the factory's labor, materials, and variable overhead. The factory's products are of recognizably competitive quality, but the low-price quotations haven't been low enough to get the orders. The manager has no reason to suspect that the factory is any less efficient than those of competing companies.

Required:

a. Compute the unit cost of product X following the full costing principle.

b. Compute the unit cost of product X following the variable costing principle.

c. Why does the manager of factory 1 find it difficult to estimate the variable cost of product X? How far off is the estimate? What are the consequences of the manager's failure to measure variable costs accurately?

13. **Effect of costing method on reported income.**   The Dowd Company operates one small factory in which it manufactures a single product for sale to customers in the chemical and plastics industries. The company's costing system is based on the full costing concept. The following results were reported for the years 19x1 and 19x2:

	19x1	19x2
Sales—units	25,000	37,500
Beginning inventory—units	5,000	15,000
Ending inventory—units	15,000	7,500
Production—units	35,000	30,000
Fixed factory overhead costs	$280,000	$290,000
Selling and administrative expenses . . .	30,000	36,000

Although materials prices and wage rates increased during these years, the company was able to offset these increases to a large extent by a vigorous program of cost reduction. Accordingly, variable cost remained unchanged at $7 a unit during these two years. The selling price of the product also remained constant, at $20 a unit. Factory fixed costs were assigned to products in both years on the basis of an overhead rate of $8 a unit.

All underabsorbed or overabsorbed factory costs were taken to the income statement for the year in which they arose.

Required:

a. Calculate income before taxes each year by (1) full costing and (2) variable costing.

b. The Dowd Company uses variable costing for internal purposes and full costing for external reporting. Calculate the amount of fixed cost in inventory at the beginning and end of each year. How do these amounts relate to the income differences you identified in answer to (a)?

c. Now assume that production in 19x2 amounted to 37,500 units at a total fixed factory overhead cost of $290,000; sales also totaled 37,500 units in 19x2. Calculate the company's income before taxes for 19x2 under (1) full costing, and (2) variable costing. To what extent does the volume of production affect reported income? Should it have this effect?

14. **Income measurement.**   Bicent Company uses the following projected unit costs for the one product it manufactures:

Direct material (all variable)	$30.00
Direct labor (all variable)	19.00
Manufacturing overhead:	
Variable cost	6.00
Fixed cost (based on 10,000 units a month)	5.00
Selling, general and administrative:	
Variable cost	1.40
Fixed cost (based on 10,000 units a month)	5.40

The projected selling price is $80 a unit. The fixed costs remain fixed within the normal range of 4,000 to 16,000 units of production and sales.

Management has also projected the following physical unit data for next month:

Beginning inventory	2,000
Production	9,000
Available	11,000
Sales	7,500
Ending inventory	3,500

The unit cost of the beginning inventory was based on cost figures identical to those listed at the beginning of this problem.

Required:

a. Prepare a projected statement of income before taxes on a variable costing basis.

b. Calculate the effect on income before taxes of using full costing instead of variable costing for inventory measurement. The entire over(under)absorbed overhead should be treated as an adjustment to the cost of goods sold.

(AICPA, adapted)

15. **Product cost: Variable costing and attributable costing.** A factory has four production departments. Predetermined overhead rates are calculated on both variable costing and full costing bases, as follows:

Department	Variable Cost	Full Cost
A	$3 per direct labor hr.	$4 per direct labor hr.
B	$3 per machine hr.	$9 per machine hr.
C	$2 per direct labor hr.	$3 per direct labor hr.
D	$1 per pound of direct materials	$2 per pound of direct materials

A special study group has established that some fixed overhead costs are highly indivisible and unlikely to change even with substantial changes in departmental capacity. The estimated amounts in this category, together with the normal volume figures used in determining the overhead rates, are as follows:

Department	Indivisible Fixed Costs per Month	Normal Volume per Month
A	$2,000	5,000 direct labor hours
B	9,000	6,000 machine-hours
C	1,000	8,000 direct labor hours
D	4,000	10,000 pounds of direct materials

In scheduling three representative jobs last month, management prepared the following estimates:

	Job 1	Job 2	Job 3
Department A—direct labor hours	90	20	50
Department B—machine-hours	10	50	30
Department C—direct labor hours	50	40	80
Department D—direct materials pounds	100	75	45

Required:

a. Calculate the amount of overhead to be included in the cost of each job, under variable costing and under full costing.

b. Calculate the amount of overhead to be charged to each job if management wishes to reflect the concept of attributable cost. Why is this concept unlikely to be reflected in the predetemined overhead rates used routinely for product costing in this company or in others like it?

c. Management uses estimates of manufacturing cost in preparing bids on possible customer orders. Assuming that the full costing figures would be calculated anyway for financial reporting purposes, would calculating variable costs give management additional useful information for preparing its bids?

16. **Costing method: Product profitability.** The Bertles Company manufactures a number of products. You have the following data for three of these:

	Dugran	Lorgran	Pilgran
Price	$3.80	$6.00	$7.50
Manufacturing cost per unit:			
Direct materials	$1.50	$1.75	$3.00
Direct labor	0.50	0.50	0.75
Overhead	1.00	1.00	1.50
Total	$3.00	$3.25	$5.25
Traceable marketing costs........	$75,000	$775,000	$150,000
Units sold	100,000	250,000	50,000

All three products are manufactured with other products in a large factory. A predetermined factorywide overhead rate of 200 percent of direct labor cost is used to assign overhead costs to products on a full costing basis. Overhead costs in this factory at a direct labor cost of $500,000 a year are as follows:

Supervision	$ 130,000
Indirect labor	120,000
Pensions and payroll taxes	150,000
Indirect materials	180,000
Power.......................	70,000
Heat and light	60,000 ⎤
Depreciation	50,000 ⎟ *Fixed*
Taxes and insurance	160,000 ⎦
Miscellaneous	80,000 — 1/2 var
Total	$1,000,000

You have the following additional information:

1. Products other than Dugran, Lorgran, and Pilgran now use $200,000 a year in direct labor cost.
2. Factory supervision costs will be $25,000 less if total direct labor cost falls below $300,000 a year.
3. Indirect labor, indirect materials, and power costs are proportionately variable with direct labor cost.
4. Pensions and payroll taxes are calculated at 20 percent of total labor cost.
5. Heat and light, depreciation, and taxes and insurance are wholly fixed.
6. Half of the miscellaneous overhead costs at normal volume are variable.
7. Marketing and administrative costs other than those directly traceable to individual product lines amount to $300,000 a year. A share of these costs is assigned to each product in the company's line on the basis of its share of total company sales at normal volume. Dugran's share is $30,000, Lorgran's is $120,000, and Pilgran's is $24,000. The total of these costs would be the same even if none of these three products was marketed.
8. The traceable marketing costs of Pilgran include $50,000 a year to amortize the costs incurred to develop this product initially. This cost will be completely amortized three years from now.
9. The company sells its products for cash on delivery and therefore has no receivables. Its inventories are financed entirely by its trade creditors—that is, inventories equal trade accounts payable.

Required:

a. Calculate a predetermined factory overhead rate on a variable costing basis, using direct labor cost as the denominator.

b. Assume the factory will continue to manufacture all of its other products, no matter what decisions it makes about the three products described here; the only doubtful products are Dugran, Lorgran, and Pilgran. Calculate the total factory direct labor cost under the assumption that, of these three products, the factory will:

    (1) Continue to manufacture all three products.
    (2) Manufacture only Dugran and Lorgran.
    (3) Manufacture only Dugran and Pilgran.
    (4) Manufacture only Lorgran and Pilgran.

c. Calculate the amount of income or loss the company's present full-costing methods attribute to each product. Ignore income taxes.

d. Calculate the incremental profit or loss that appears likely to result from (1) discontinuing the manufacture and sale of Dugran, (2) discontinuing the manufacture and sale of Lorgran, and (3) discontinuing the manufacture and sale of Pilgran, each considered independently. Which, if any, of these products should be discontinued if the decisions are based on these estimates of incremental profit or loss?

e. Calculate the total amount of under- or overabsorbed factory overhead under each of the four assumptions listed in (*b*). To what extent can this information be used to explain the differences between your answers to (*c*) and (*d*)? What other factors contributed to these differences?

f. Would variable costing contribute to a better understanding of the profitability of individual products in this company? What additional information on product cost should management have that variable costing does not provide? Would full costing provide that additional information?

7 Incorporating service costs in predetermined overhead rates

Some cost centers do not engage directly in end-product activities. These cost centers are either *service centers,* providing services to other cost centers, or *support centers,* providing either facilities or administrative support and direction to two or more cost centers. Exhibit 7–1 shows a simplified version of a typical situation, with products flowing through two production centers while the service and support centers serve the two production centers and each other, doing no work on the products themselves.

Exhibit 7–1 Product flows versus service and support flows

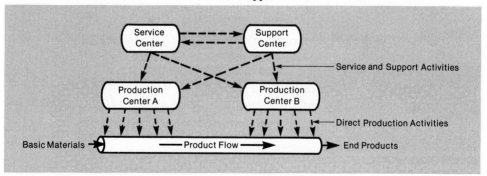

Costs of service and support centers may be redistributed to other cost centers or to individual products, for any or all of four reasons:

1. To include service and support center costs in product costs for external financial reporting.
2. To produce estimates of costs for managerial decision making.
3. To emphasize the responsibility of department heads to control the use of other departments' services.
4. To provide the cost data necessary to obtain reimbursement for work done under cost-based contracts or, in not-for-profit organizations, to obtain financial support from outside benefactors.

The first two of these generally call for reassignments of estimated costs, prepared before the costs are actually incurred; the third and fourth reasons may require both before-the-fact and after-the-fact cost reassignments. The purpose of this chapter is to see how the estimated costs of service and support centers in factories can be included in the predetermined overhead rates used to assign factors overhead costs to individual jobs or products for inventory costing or managerial decision making. We'll study cost reassignments for control and reimbursement purposes in Chapter 10 and Chapter 21.

Cost reassignment methods

Predetermined overhead rates reflect budgeted costs at specified operating volumes. The budget for every cost center begins with the costs that can be traced clearly to that cost center. The costs that are traceable to individual production centers therefore can be included directly in their overhead rates; the question is how to include the costs that are traceable to service and support centers in overhead rates for product costing purposes. The answer can take either of two forms:

1. Apportionment.
2. Interdepartmental allocation.

Apportionment

The apportionment method is to assemble service and support costs in one or more pools and then reassign the costs in each pool to individual jobs or products without intervening distributions to other cost centers or pools. This process is diagrammed in Exhibit 7–2.

Apportionment is carried out by means of apportionment rates, one for each pool. An apportionment rate is the ratio of the total of the costs in a

Exhibit 7–2 The apportionment process

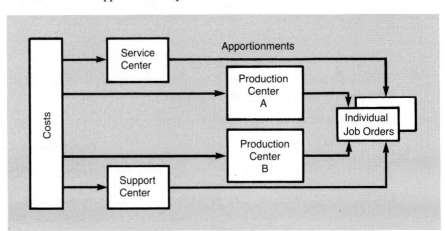

pool to the total of some product-identifiable quantity, such as total direct labor hours; a pool consists of the direct costs of one or more service and support centers. To use apportionment to distribute the costs in a pool, the accountant multiplies the apportionment rate by each product's share of the quantity serving as the denominator of the rate.

For example, suppose a factory has two production centers, one support center, and one service center, as in Exhibits 7–1 and 7–2. The support center has budgeted direct costs of $4,000 a month; the service center budgets direct costs of $3,000 a month. Management has decided to combine these costs in a single pool and assign them to products by direct apportionment, based on direct labor hours. Normal volume in production center A is 5,000 direct labor hours a month; normal volume in production center B is 2,000 direct labor hours.

A plantwide direct apportionment rate in this case would be ($4,000 + $3,000)/7,000 = $1 a direct labor hour. A product needing 10 direct labor hours would be charged $10 for service and support overhead, no matter which production center the work was performed in.

Interdepartmental allocation

Use of the apportionment method implies that the apportionment rate is a reasonable representation of the causal relationship existing between the product-identifiable quantity and the total of the costs in the pool. Service and support centers serve other cost centers, not products, however, and some cost centers need much more service or support than others. This means that an hour spent in one production center may have a greater impact on service and support center costs than an hour's work in another production center. For example, a direct labor hour in a machining department ordinarily will be supported by much more maintenance cost than a direct labor hour in assembly, where the ratio of equipment to people is much smaller.

The cost reassignment method that attempts to reflect departmental relationships is known as *interdepartmental cost allocation* (or *allocation,* for short). Interdepartmental cost allocation is a process by which service and support center costs are distributed to other cost centers. If allocations are used in product costing, the overhead rate for each production center will include a provision for that center's proportionate share of the costs of service and support centers.

Terminology reminder

A cost that is traceable to a product, activity, or organization segment is a *direct cost* of that product, activity, or organization segment. A cost traceable to a service or support center is a direct cost of that center. The costs of service or support centers that are reassigned to other cost centers are *indirect costs* of those other centers.

One-step allocations

If the accountants wish to use allocations to redistribute the costs of service and support centers, they have several allocation methods to choose among. The simplest of these is one-step allocation. In a one-step allocation procedure, the direct costs of a service or support center are allocated to production centers only. None of these costs is assigned to other service or support centers.

For example, suppose the support center in our illustration provides 20 percent of its support to the service center, 30 percent to production center A, and 50 percent to production center B. In a one-step allocation, the only relevant percentages are those for the two production centers—that is, the 80 percent of the total support that goes to these two centers. Three eighths (30 percent divided by 80 percent) of this portion of support goes to production center A; the other five eighths goes to production center B. Using these percentages, the $4,000 budgeted direct costs of the support center would be divided as follows:

	Percent of Total Support	Percent of Support Provided to Production Centers	Allocation of Support Center Costs
Production center A	30%	30%/80% = 37.5%	$1,500
Production center B	50	50%/80% = 62.5	2,500
Total	80%	100.0%	$4,000

The same procedure would be applied to the service center. Suppose the service center normally provides 10 percent of its services to the support center, 45 percent to production center A, and 45 percent to production center B. The budgeted direct cost of the service center is $3,000. A one-step allocation would be as follows:

	Percent of Total Service	Percent of Service Provided to Production Centers	Allocation of Service Center Costs
Production center A	45%	45%/90% = 50%	$1,500
Production center B	45	45%/90% = 50	1,500
Total	90%	100%	$3,000

In other words, production center A would get $1,500 of the support center's budgeted costs and $1,500 of the service center's budget, a total of $3,000, to be spread over its 5,000 budgeted labor hours, an average of 60 cents an hour, Production center B would get $2,500 + $1,500 = $4,000 of these costs, to be spread over its budgeted 2,000 direct labor hours, an average of $2 an hour. Two products, each needing 10 direct labor hours, therefore would be assigned very different amounts of service and support center costs if the one-step allocation method were used:

	Service and Support Cost per Hour	Product X		Product Y	
		Direct Labor Hours	Service and Support Costs	Direct Labor Hours	Service and Support Costs
Production center A........	$0.60	9	$5.40	1	$ 0.60
Production center B........	2.00	1	2.00	9	18.00
Total			$7.40		$18.60

Cross allocations

The main defect of the one-step method is that it ignores relationships between service and support centers. A second method, cross allocation, recognizes these relationships. Cross allocation is a procedure in which *each* service or support center receives a pro rata share of the costs of *all other* service and support centers which provide it with service or support. The allocations are determined simultaneously, as the solution to a set of simultaneous equations.

The cross-allocation method is illustrated in Exhibit 7–3. Each service or support center receives costs from the other. Each of these charges covers both the direct costs of the center and the allocations it receives from the other.

Exhibit 7–3 Cross allocation of service center costs

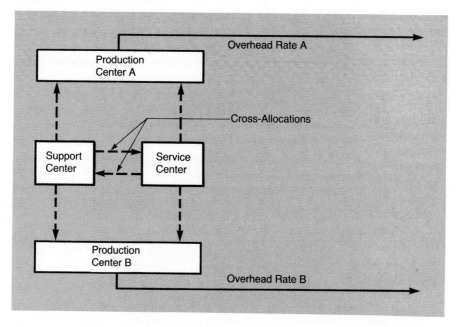

To apply this method to our simple example, we need to state the relationships in algebraic terms:

Cost of support center = $4,000 + 10% of the cost of service center
Cost of service center = $3,000 + 20% of the cost of support center

Solving these two equations simultaneously, we get the following:

$$\text{Cost of support center} = \$4,387.75$$
$$\text{Cost of service center} = \$3,877.55$$

Applying the production centers' service and support ratios to these figures we get the following allocations:

	Production Center A	Production Center B
Support center's costs	30% × $4,387.75 = $1,316.32	50% × $4,387.75 = $2,193.88
Service center's costs	45% × $3,877.55 = 1,744.90	45% × $3,877.55 = 1,744.90
Total allocated	$3,061.22	$3,938.78

The sum of the allocations remains the same, $7,000.

Sequential allocation

In many organizations, cross allocation seems so mysterious or so complicated that management is reluctant to use it. A third allocation method, sequential allocation, recognizes some of the relationships between individual service and support centers, but seems simpler and more understandable.

In sequential allocation, the costs of service and support centers are allocated one cost center at a time. A service or support center's costs are allocated both to other service and support centers and to production centers. Once a center's costs have been allocated, however, it ceases to figure in subsequent steps in the procedure. When the final service or support center's costs have been allocated, all service and support costs have been reassigned to the production centers.

This method is illustrated in Exhibit 7–4. In this diagram the support center's costs are allocated first, to the service center and to the two production centers. Allocation of the service center's costs, including its allocated share of the support center's costs, completes the process. All costs are now in position to be included in the production centers' overhead rates for use in product costing.

Putting this in numerical terms, we can allocate the support center's $4,000 budgeted direct costs as follows, using the support percentages we mentioned earlier:

	Service Center	Production Center A	Production Center B
Percent of total support..................	20%	30%	50%
Cost allocation (Percent × $4,000)	$800	$1,200	$2,000

The next step is to allocate the costs of the service center. These allocations go only to the production centers because the sequential method ignores relationships with service or support centers that have already had their costs

Exhibit 7–4 Sequential cost allocation

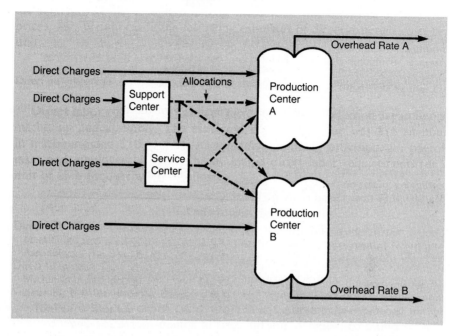

allocated. The total cost of the service center is now $3,800, the sum of its direct costs and its share of the support center's costs. Because the two production centers use equal amounts of service, each gets half of the service center's costs, or $1,900.

The two sets of allocations can be summarized as follows:

	Support Center	Service Center	Production Center A	Production Center B
Direct support and service costs	$4,000	$3,000	—	—
Allocations:				
Support center's costs	(4,000)	800	$1,200	$2,000
Service center's costs		(3,800)	1,900	1,900
Total			$3,100	$3,900

Sequential allocations are inaccurate because they ignore some of the relationships between service and support centers. To keep the inaccuracy to a minimum, the accountants try to start the allocations with the service or support center which receives the least service or support from the other centers. Applying this criterion to our simple illustration, we allocated the support center's costs first because it provided more support to the service center than it received.

In summary, the three allocation methods produce the following allocations in this simple case:

	Costs Allocated	
	Production Center A	Production Center B
One-step	$3,000.00	$4,000.00
Cross	3,061.22	3,938.78
Sequential	3,100.00	3,900.00

When the differences are this small, any of the three methods is likely to be acceptable.

Preliminary distributions of centrally-tabulated costs

Some overhead costs are accumulated initially on a factorywide or even companywide basis even though they relate fairly clearly to the operations of specific cost centers. Equipment depreciation, purchased power, and certain kinds of insurance are examples that come to mind.

Whenever the causal link between these costs and individual cost centers are clear, accuracy requires that they be distributed among the cost centers *before* the costs of the service and support centers are either apportioned or allocated. Remember that these are distributions of individual object-of-expenditure cost *elements,* not the costs of administrative *cost centers* containing many different cost elements. The latter must be handled either by apportionment or by allocation. (Distributions of centrally-tabulated cost elements is so common that apportionments and allocations are often referred to as *redistributions.*)

We won't dwell on this point, except to say that these preliminary distributions should be made only when the causal relationships seem very clear. Costs properly distributed by the application of this criterion are virtually indistinguishable from the direct costs of the cost centers to which the distributions are made. Other centrally tabulated costs should be regarded as the costs of head office service and support centers, to be apportioned or allocated by the methods we described earlier.

Full-cost overhead rates: Sequential allocation

A slightly more complex illustration than the one we have been using will help us understand some of the subtleties of the allocation process. In this section we'll use sequential allocations to derive a set of predetermined production center overhead rates under full costing.

Choosing allocation denominators for full costing

All allocations should measure casual relationships if they can be identified readily. The accountants' problem, therefore, is to identify measurable factors that seem to be the causes of service and support center costs. Having found these, the accountant can calculate allocation rates with these factors in the denominators. Three kinds of causal factors can be distinguished:

1.   Usage.
2.   Activity.
3.   Capacity.

Usage denominators.   Probably the most obvious indicator of causation is the amount of service other cost centers use. In other words, costs are incurred because services are used.

Two kinds of usage measures may be identified. One of these is the number of units of *service inputs* that can be identified with the cost centers being served. One example is the number of hours the workers of a maintenance department spend doing maintenance work in other departments.

The second kind of usage measure is the number of units of *service output* that can be identified with the cost centers being served. A good example is the number of pounds of steam a factory's steam plant supplies to other departments in the factory.

The charging rates underlying usage charges can be limited to the variable costs of providing the services, with the fixed costs allocated on different bases. If the fixed costs of providing service tend to increase or decrease, in time, roughly in proportion to changes in the quantity of service provided, however, they can be included with the variable costs in the usage-based charging rate for full cost allocation.

Activity denominators.   If no reliable usage index is available, an activity index may be a good denominator of the ratio used for cost allocation. An activity index is a measure of the volume of activity *in the cost centers served or supported* by the costs being allocated. For example, the number of labor hours in other departments may be used to allocate the costs of a factory personnel department. The notion is that the costs being allocated are caused by, and vary with, the amount of activity in other departments.

The fixed costs of the service or support center should be allocated on an activity basis if it appears that they will vary, in time, with the same index of activity as the short-term variable costs. Most personnel department costs, for example, are likely to be fixed in the short run, but are also likely to increase or decrease from year to year as the number of employees increases or decreases. If the available data reveal the presence of this kind of long-term variability, the full-cost allocation should be by activity charge.

Capacity denominators.   The costs of some support centers are entirely fixed in the short run and vary in the long run not with the activity of the cost centers they support but with the amount of support capacity they provide. In such cases, the appropriate allocation denominator is a measure of the support center's capacity that can also be identified with the cost centers being supported. Building ownership and operation costs are often allocated in proportion to floor space occupied, reflecting this concept.

Capacity is a peak-load concept. That is, the support center is equipped and staffed at levels adequate to enable it to support a given maximum amount of activity. The costs of providing this capacity should be divided among the cost centers in proportion to their shares of the total need for support when the support center is operating at its peak load.

Several peak-based methods of allocating capacity costs are available. In most industrial situations, however, a simple peak-proportional method is probably appropriate. For example, suppose a support center with $20,000 a month in fixed costs can support any level of activity in the departments it serves up to a total of 50,000 labor hours a month. If the activity in the supported departments actually reaches this level, it is expected to be distributed as follows:

Department	Number of Labor Hours
A	5,000
B	15,000
C	30,000
Total	50,000

The budgeted allocation to department A therefore should be 5,000/50,000 of $20,000, or $2,000 a month.

A cost center's percentage of the amount of support center capacity it requires is often referred to as the amount of *benefit* it receives from the support center. The term benefit is a misnomer in this context. The accountants don't know how valuable the support is—that is, the amount of benefit it provides—and what's more, they don't care. Cost accounting is a process of measuring the causal relationships between activities and costs—that is, the cost of an activity is the amount of cost that the activity causes or makes necessary. When we say that a cost center benefits from the activity of another cost center, we really mean that the cost center wouldn't be able to conduct its operations as efficiently or as effectively without the support the other center provides. In other words, the support is *necessary* to the cost center's operations. The only question is how much of the support and therefore how much of its cost is attributable to each of the cost centers being supported.

Two-part allocations. Fixed costs are the costs of providing capacity; variable costs arise because capacity is used. If the factors determining the amount of capacity differ from those determining the amount of use of capacity, we may wish to use separate allocation rates for these two groups of costs. This is known as a *two-part tariff* or *dual rate* system.

For example, the capacity of a maintenance department may be geared to the maximum demand for maintenance service, while the actual usage of maintenance service varies with the number of machine hours used in production departments. If so, the budgeted fixed costs of maintenance may be allocated in proportion to relative maintenance usage at peak demand, while the budgeted variable costs are allocated in proportion to budgeted actual usage.

Our decision to use a two-part tariff instead of a single allocation rate doesn't depend on whether we wish to develop overhead rates based on variable costing. The question is whether a dual rate represents the causal relationships more accurately than a single rate. Taking this even farther, we can develop different rates for different portions of the fixed costs or different elements of variable cost—one based on total labor hours in other departments, for example, and the other based on consumption of materials and supplies in those departments, because different causal factors are at work on different cost elements.

Allocating residual costs.   Sometimes neither usage nor capacity occupancy can be measured, nor can a clear relationship to activity be identified. If the production center rates are to reflect the full cost of factory operations, some basis must be found for distributing costs of these kinds, which we'll refer to as *residual costs.*

Residual costs are usually distributed by either apportionment ratios or activity-based allocation ratios. The main alternatives are a single input index (such as the number of direct labor hours), a total cost input index (the sum of the direct and indirect costs assigned to products by other means), or some form of *value-added* index (total cost input less the costs of selected inputs such as the costs of direct materials and subcontracted services).

Remember that the available data don't show a clear-cut statistical relationship between these costs and any of these three measures of the volume of activity; if such a relationship could be found, we'd classify the allocation as an activity-based causal relationship. We may try to choose an activity denominator in another way, however, by examining the functions performed in the centers in which the costs take place. If the functions cover a broad range, from dealing with suppliers of materials to participating in collective bargaining, then a total cost input base is probably preferable, at least on conceptual grounds. If little time is devoted to materials-related problems, then a value-added or labor input base probably should be used.

The use of this kind of activity index produces allocations that represent only in a very approximate way the cost effects of causative factors in the cost centers being served. For this reason, they should be used only as a last resort, after efforts to find better causal evidence have failed or have been deemed too costly to pursue. As long as management or the external reporting standards require full cost overhead rates, however, the accountants must use these indexes if the underlying cost relationships can't be identified more clearly.

An allocation illustration: Basic data

Summit, Inc., is a small manufacturer of metal products. It uses full-cost, predetermined overhead rates, mainly to comply with the tenet of generally accepted accounting principles that the costs of inventories of manufactured products should include an appropriate share of all elements of manufacturing overhead cost. Summit's controller also uses cost estimates based on these rates to establish pricing and profit targets for individual products.

Production in Summit's factory takes place in three production centers—machining, welding, and assembly. The factory also has four service or support

Exhibit 7-5
SUMMIT COMPANY Factory costs and statistics in a normal month

	Building Services	Clerical	Maintenance	Factory Management	Machining	Welding	Assembly	Total
Statistics:								
Floor space (square feet)	500	2,000	4,000	3,000	22,000	5,000	14,000	50,500
Employee hours	900	1,100	1,300	1,200	4,000	1,500	12,000	22,000
Maintenance hours	40	10	—	—	700	200	100	1,050
Direct labor hours	—	—	—	—	3,500	1,300	11,000	15,800
Machine hours	—	—	—	—	8,300	—	—	8,300
Costs:								
Direct materials	$ —	$ —	$ —	$ —	$24,000	$ 1,000	$100,000	$125,000
Direct labor	—	—	—	—	39,900	14,100	70,000	124,000
Identified overhead:								
Labor	7,000	9,000	14,000	20,000	8,000	2,000	10,000	70,000
Other	13,000	6,200	4,360	5,340	16,200	2,900	5,500	53,500
Total identified overhead	$20,000	$15,200	$18,360	$25,340	$24,200	$ 4,900	$ 15,500	$123,500

centers—building services, clerical, maintenance, and factory management. For brevity, we'll refer to each of these as a service center.

Summit's products vary widely in the relative amounts of work required in the factory's three production centers. Since the importance of overhead costs also depends on where the work is done, Summit uses three separate overhead rates in product costing, one rate for each production center.

In preparing the overhead rates for next year, Summit's controller has collected the estimates tabulated in Exhibit 7–5. All of these estimates are the amounts that will be budgeted in an average month in a year in which the factory is operating at normal volume. The "identified overhead" figures in the lower half of the exhibit consist of all costs other than product-direct labor and materials. They include distributions of centrally-tabulated costs, in this case mainly equipment depreciation. To simplify our terminology in the remainder of this section, we'll refer to all of these as *traceable overheads*.

Summit's controller uses a sequential allocation procedure to place the estimated normal costs of the factory's service centers in position to be incorporated in the production centers' overhead rates. The building services center receives much less service or support from the other service centers than it provides to them. For this reason its costs are allocated first, followed by those for clerical services, maintenance, and factory management.

The first allocation: Building services costs

Some building services costs are the costs of building ownership, such as depreciation, property taxes, and insurance. Others are the costs of maintaining and protecting the factory building. All of them are incurred to provide operating capacity to enable the other departments to operate. It seems reasonable, therefore, to allocate the estimated normal costs of building services in proportion to the amount of capacity (floor space) they occupy.

> ### Terminology
>
> A *charging rate* is a dollar amount per unit to be multiplied by a number of physical, temporal, or monetary units such as square feet, hours, or payroll dollars, to determine the amount of cost to assign to a given class of cost objectives.

From Exhibit 7–5 we find that the normal costs readily identifiable with building services are expected to average $20,000 a month. The factory contains 50,500 square feet of usable floor space, but 500 square feet of this is used by building services personnel themselves, leaving 50,000 square feet for the other six cost centers. The average monthly cost of building services therefore is $20,000/50,000 = 40 cents a square foot. We can use this figure as the charging rate for including building services costs in the estimated normal costs of the other six cost centers. The allocations are as follows:

	Clerical	Mainte-nance	Factory Manage-ment	Machining	Welding	Assembly	Total
No. of sq. feet	2,000	4,000	3,000	22,000	5,000	14,000	50,000
Building services costs allocated ($0.40 × no. of sq. feet)	$800	$1,600	$1,200	$8,800	$2,000	$5,600	$20,000

Each of these allocations is a *capacity charge,* defined as a fee to cover one cost center's share of the costs of providing service or support capacity in some other cost center. To use capacity charges, we have to find a way of measuring the relative amounts of the service center's capacity each cost center requires. Floor space is a good measure of capacity required if each square foot of space is equally responsible for building service costs. If some portions of the space are more costly to build or to operate than others, then the measure should be modified to reflect these differences.

The second allocation: Clerical costs

The costs of the cost center for clerical services are the next to be distributed because this cost center receives less service from maintenance and factory management than it provides to them. Clerical workers in the factory process the payrolls, keep track of inventories and production orders, and perform other routine bookkeeping, clerical, and secretarial duties. Little of their time relates clearly to the operations of specific factory departments, so usage doesn't provide a usable basis for cost allocations in this case.

The amount of clerical capacity required isn't a useful basis for cost allocation either, even though clerical costs are almost entirely fixed costs in short periods. Even if we define capacity as the amount of available clerical time, we don't know how much of that capacity is provided to meet the needs of each of the other cost centers. It turns out, however, that the size of the clerical work force tends to be adjusted upward or downward as budgeted production volume changes. Summit's management has discovered that clerical costs tend to rise and fall with changes in the amount of labor time in the rest of the factory. This information is enough to convince the accountants to use total employee hours in the remaining five cost centers as the denominator of the allocation ratio for clerical costs.

Referring back to the figures in Exhibit 7–5, we can calculate the sum of the employee hours in maintenance, factory management, machining, welding, and assembly, a total of 20,000 hours. The budgeted costs of clerical services are $16,000, calculated as follows:

Costs traceable to the clerical cost center ...	$15,200
Building services costs allocated to the clerical cost center	800
Total	$16,000

The average budgeted clerical cost therefore is $16,000/20,000 = 80 cents per employee hour in the remaining five cost centers. The allocations based on this ratio are as follows:

	Mainte-nance	Factory Management	Machining	Welding	Assembly	Total
Number of employee hours.......	1,300	1,200	4,000	1,500	12,000	20,000
Clerical costs allocated ($0.80 x Number of employee hours)......	$1,040	$ 960	$3,200	$1,200	$ 9,600	$16,000

These allocations are based on *activity charges,* in which the denominator of the allocation ratio is a measure of the total volume of activity in the cost centers to which the allocations are made. Activity charges should be used when the amount of service provided is difficult to measure, but the costs of the service center correlate with the total activity of the cost centers receiving its services.

The third allocation: Maintenance costs

It isn't clear that the maintenance center receives less service or support from factory management than it provides to factory management. A straightforward, causally related basis for allocation—the number of maintenance hours—is available for maintenance costs, however, whereas the amount of factory management services required by the maintenance cost center is much less clear. Since our approach is to reflect causation insofar as we can, we'll allocate the maintenance center's costs next.

Once again our full-cost methodology requires us to allocate not only the budgeted costs traceable to the maintenance center but its share of building services and clerical costs as well:

Costs traceable to the maintenance center	$18,360
Building services costs allocated to maintenance	1,600
Clerical costs allocated to maintenance	1,040
Total	$21,000

Again referring back to Exhibit 7–5, we find that maintenance provides 1,000 hours of service to the three production centers. The service it provides to building services and clerical operations is ignored, because the sequential method has already disposed of the costs of those cost centers. The average full cost of the services to the production centers is $21,000/1,000 = $21 an hour, and the allocations are:

	Factory Management	Machining	Welding	Assembly	Total
Number of maintenance hours.......	—	700	200	100	1,000
Maintenance cost allocated (Number of maintenance hours × $21)	—	$14,700	$4,200	$2,100	$21,000

These allocations are *usage charges,* in which the denominator of the allocation ratio is a measure of the volume of activity in the service center in which the costs originate, in this case the maintenance center. If the service center isn't homogeneous, separate charging rates can be used for the different services or the different service inputs the center provides.

The usage measure in this illustration, incidentally, is a measure of service *inputs,* the number of hours spent by maintenance personnel. We might also use output measures, such as the number of tasks performed, if we can identify them. Repairing a faucet is a task; replacing a drill head is a task. In budgeting, however, the number of tasks ordinarily will be related back to the amount of input required to complete those tasks, so the input and output measures are likely to be equivalent.

The final allocation: Factory management costs

The fourth service center is factory management, and under the sequential method only the three production centers are still available to receive its costs. Neither usage of factory management services nor the amount of factory management capacity required can be measured for individual production centers. The allocation of factory management costs therefore must be based on some measure of production center activity.

Summit's management has tried and failed to find a measure of factory activity that is demonstrably superior to the others. Few factory management activities relate to the purchase or handling of materials, however, so management has decided to use total cost less direct materials cost as the denominator of the factory management allocation ratio. Excluding direct materials costs, the budgeted costs of the three production centers after the first three allocations are as follows:

	Machining	Welding	Assembly	Total
Direct labor	$39,900	$14,100	$ 70,000	$124,000
Traceable overhead	24,200	4,900	15,500	44,600
Allocations:				
Building services	8,800	2,000	5,600	16,400
Clerical	3,200	1,200	9,600	14,000
Maintenance	14,700	4,200	2,100	21,000
Total	$90,800	$26,400	$102,800	$220,000

Budgeted factory management costs amount to $27,500, calculated as follows:

Costs traceable to factory management	$25,340
Allocation of building services costs	1,200
Allocation of clerical costs	960
Total factory management cost	$27,500

The full-cost allocation ratio for factory management costs therefore is $27,-500/$220,000 = $0.125 for each dollar of costs other than direct materials. Allocations based on this ratio are:

	Machining	Welding	Assembly	Total
Total costs other than direct materials	$90,800	$26,400	$102,800	$220,000
Allocation of factory management costs (cost base × 0.125)	11,350	3,300	12,850	27,500

This final allocation is more subjective and less reliable than the others, because the causal relationship it purports to represent is less clear. For this reason, an effort should be made to reduce the amount of costs in pools such as this. Examination of the cost elements may reveal, for example, that the costs of telephone usage are assigned in their entirety to factory management, whereas the statistical basis for distributions of telephone charges based on equipment location and usage is readily available. The accuracy of the cost allocations can be improved by pulling this cost element out of the factory management category and distributing it before the allocation process begins.

Allocation summary: Departmental overhead rates

The objective of Summit's factory cost allocation exercise is to place the budgeted costs of its factory service centers in a position to be included in the predetermined overhead rates of the three production centers. The overhead rate in the machining department is to be calculated with the number of machine-hours as the denominator, because most of the costs in the department, including its large share of maintenance costs, are more closely attributable to machine usage than to labor time. The overhead rates in welding and in assembly are to be based on direct labor hours, however, because most of the overhead costs in these production centers are related more to labor time than to other volume measures.

The entire process of distributing overhead and developing overhead rates is summarized in Exhibit 7–6. The sloping structure of the upper half of this table illustrates why the sequential method is often referred to as the *stepdown* method. As each service center's costs are distributed, the accountant moves down a stairstep to the next service center, leaving preceding service centers behind.

At the end of the allocation process, all of the factory's budgeted overhead costs at normal volume are assembled in the cost budgets and overhead rates of the three production centers. In other words, the sum of the overhead costs on the "total overhead" line of Exhibit 7–6 ($62,250 + $15,600 + $45,650) is the same as the total overhead cost in Exhibit 7–5, $123,500.

Allocations for predetermined overhead rates in variable costing

Companies which use variable costing to measure product cost will need to apportion or allocate some of the costs of service and support centers if the

Exhibit 7-6
SUMMIT COMPANY Allocation of budgeted factory overhead costs at normal volume

	Building Services	Clerical	Maintenance	Management	Machining	Welding	Assembly
Traceable overhead (Exhibit 7–5)	$20,000	$15,200	$18,360	$25,340	$24,200	$4,900	$15,500
Allocations:							
Building services ($0.40 × square feet)	(20,000)	800	1,600	1,200	8,800	2,000	5,600
Clerical ($0.80 × employee hours)		(16,000)	1,040	960	3,200	1,200	$ 9,600
Maintenance ($21 × maintenance hours)			(21,000)	—	14,700	4,200	2,100
Factory management (12.5% × cost base)				(27,500)	11,350	3,300	12,850
Total overhead					$62,250	$15,600	$45,650
Number of machine hours (Exhibit 7–5)					8,300		
Number of direct labor hours (Exhibit 7–5)						1,300	11,000
Overhead rate per hour					$7.50	$12.00	$4.15

rate of cost variability is significant. Allocations in variable costing systems can be made either by usage charges or by activity charges; capacity charges are inappropriate in variable costing because capacity costs are fixed costs. Only two problems are unique to variable costing:

1. Allocating stepped costs of service centers.
2. Identifying the variability of service usage.

Allocating stepped costs of service centers

Some service center costs are lumpy—that is, they vary with volume, but in steps. In fact, they may even appear to be fixed in any given short period. As overall volume moves up or down by a substantial amount, however, service center costs also move up or down. This pattern is reflected in the stepped line in Exhibit 7–7, describing the budgeted costs of Summit's clerical cost center. In this case the steps are regular enough and close enough together to justify drawing the straight line in Exhibit 7–7 to approximate the cost relationship. (Volume, we should recall, is measured by the number of employee hours in the factory.) The rate of change in clerical cost according to this line of relationship is 60 cents an employee hour; only the amount of cost at zero volume, $4,000, is treated as fixed.

Exhibit 7–7 Budgeted clerical services costs

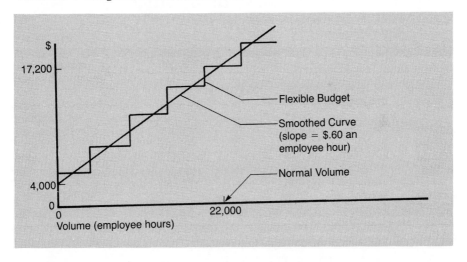

Suppose we find that the variable component of indirect labor usage in the assembly department amounts to 5/100 of an indirect labor hour for each direct labor hour in assembly. The clerical cost component of the assembly department's variable costing overhead rate therefore is as follows:

	Amount per Direct Labor Hour in Assembly
Amount supporting a direct labor hour	$0.60
Amount supporting the variable portion of indirect labor: 5/100 × $0.60	0.03
Clerical cost component of variable costing overhead rate	$0.63

Identifying the variability of service usage

Product cost in a variable costing system measures the responsiveness of factory cost to changes in production volume. This means that a cost which varies with the amount of service used should not be included in the overhead rates if the amount of service used is fixed.

For example, the budgeted costs of the maintenance center in Summit's factory amount to $21,000 at normal volume, according to the calculations we made in the preceding section. Suppose we find that the variable portions of these costs amount to the figures shown in the following table:

	Fixed	Variable	Total
Labor	$1,925	$12,075	$14,000
Other traceable costs ...	2,260	2,100	4,360
Building services	1,600	—	1,600
Clerical	410	630	1,040
Total	$6,195	$14,805	$21,000

The variable components of the maintenance center's costs are expected to vary proportionally with the number of maintenance hours. The rate of variability in the normal volume range therefore can be calculated by dividing total variable cost at normal volume by the normal number of maintenance hours:

$$\text{Rate of variation} = \frac{\$14,805}{1,050} = \$14.10 \text{ a maintenance hour}$$

Now suppose we find that the machining department's budgeted usage of maintenance services is as follows:

$$\text{Maintenance hours} = 385 \text{ a month} + \frac{1}{20} \times \text{number of machine-hours}$$

The 385 hours a month are to provide routine maintenance; they are part of the machining department's fixed costs. The department's variable overhead rate includes only the variable cost of $\frac{1}{20}$ of a maintenance hour for each machine hour in the machining department. At $14.10 a maintenance hour, the maintenance cost component of the machining department's variable costing overhead rate is $\frac{1}{20} \times \$14.10 = \$0.705$ per machine hour.

Allocations under attributable costing

The product costs emerging from full-costing systems are often interpreted as the costs that result from decisions to keep individual products in the line on a long-term, continuing basis. We argued in Chapter 6 that if management wants product cost data of this sort, it should replace full costing with a system we have referred to as *attributable costing*.

Terminology reminder

The *attributable cost* of any activity is the cost that could be eliminated, in time, if that activity were discontinued and capacity were to be reduced accordingly. It includes short-run variable cost together with the activity's proportionate share of those capacity costs that are divisible enough so that increases or decreases in normal volume will be accompanied, in time, by proportional increases or decreases in capacity costs.

Allocations and apportionments in an attributable-costing system differ from those in full costing in that they exclude costs for which reasonably clear long-term causal relationships to costing objectives are lacking. In practice, only those service center costs that are highly indivisible are likely to be treated as nonattributable. The plant manager's salary, depreciation on repair equipment that is available only in large-capacity units, and certain kinds of license or franchise fees are examples of indivisible fixed costs.

In attributable costing, the costs of service centers that are assigned to individual products are those that will respond, in time, to major changes in product volume. A service center cost may be divisible, and therefore may be attributed to the various cost centers the service center serves. If the use of this service by a particular production center is indivisible, however, its costs cannot be classified as attributable to the products produced by that production center.

The appropriate criterion underlying the attribution of the fixed costs of service centers to products is the capacity-required criterion—that is, how much service capacity is provided to support each product? Products don't occupy physical capacity, however, and the index used to measure capacity requirements can be used only in the allocation of fixed costs from the service center to other cost centers. The fixed costs of service centers enter product cost, in attributable costing as in full costing, through the overhead rates of the production centers; the denominators of these rates are measures of activity.

Application of the attributability concept requires the use of judgment, and the results will not be precise. The purpose of attributable cost is to bring product cost closer to the concept full cost is often assumed to represent, long-run marginal cost. To the extent the accountants succeed in achieving this goal, product costs will be able to serve more satisfactorily in long-run, product continuation and expansion decisions.

Summary

When an organization uses predetermined departmental rates to assign overhead costs to individual products or job orders, it must devise procedures to include in overhead rates the overhead costs that are not directly traceable to the production centers for which overhead rates are to be developed.

Some centrally-tabulated cost elements, such as equipment depreciation and certain utilities costs, can be distributed to individual cost centers on the basis of data which clearly identify the causal relationships. After these distributions have been made, the accountants may choose to assemble the budgeted costs of service centers in a small number of pools and develop an apportionment ratio for each pool on the basis of a denominator which is a measurable characteristic of each product or production order. These apportionment ratios then can be used to assign service center costs to individual products and production orders. The production center overhead rates then will be limited to the overhead costs traceable to individual production centers.

Apportionment ratios should be used whenever the costs of service centers are sensitive to characteristics of the products but insensitive to variations in the relative utilization of the various production centers. If the production center mix has a significant impact on service center costs, however, these costs should be allocated to the cost centers they serve or support, thereby allowing them to be included in the overhead rates of the production centers themselves.

Allocations may be effected by one-step, sequential, or cross-allocation methods, and they may be based on the amount of anticipated usage, activity, or capacity required. Cross allocation is generally regarded as the most accurate, because it most fully reflects the interdependencies among the various services.

The same range of choices is available for apportionments or allocations reflecting variable costing or attributable costing, except that capacity charges are inappropriate in variable costing systems.

Appendix to Chapter 7: Cross allocation procedures

Cross allocations are calculated by solving a set of equations simultaneously. In practice there will be so many equations that a computer must be used. The procedure is straightforward, however:

1. Set up a set of costing equations, each showing the resources used by one department, cost center, or overhead cost pool.
2. Solve the equations for the service and support cost centers to determine inclusive cost-center totals.
3. Substitute these values in the costing equations for the production centers to determine the amounts to be allocated to those centers.

For example, suppose we have a factory with four service and support centers (B, C, E, and M) and three production centers (A, F, and P). The costing equations are as follows:

$$B = \$\ 8{,}000 + 0.04E$$
$$C = \$\ 5{,}540 + 0.04B + 0.048E$$
$$E = \$10{,}320 + 0.06B$$
$$M = \$\ 8{,}040 + 0.06B + 0.0625C + 0.096E$$

$$A = \$ \ 6,580 + 0.3B + 0.5C + 0.384E + 0.1M$$
$$F = \$15,520 + 0.4B + 0.3125C + 0.336E + 0.75M$$
$$P = \$13,100 + 0.14B + 0.125C + 0.096E + 0.15M$$

The dollar figure in each equation is the cost traceable to that cost center; the sum of these figures, $67,100, is the total factory overhead cost. Each letter stands for the total cost of a specific cost center. The sum of the coefficients for any letter is 1.0, meaning that all of the costs of the cost center corresponding to that letter will be distributed.

By solving the four service center equations simultaneously, we redistribute these amounts as follows:

$$B = \$ \ 8,433$$
$$C = \quad 6,397$$
$$E = \quad 10,826$$
$$M = \quad 9,985$$

The total of these four figures is greater than the total of the direct costs of the four cost centers because each service center's costs also include a portion of the costs of one or more other service centers. The purpose of this stage of the calculation is to determine the cost of operating each cost center; the total of these figures has no significance and should be ignored.

Substituting these values in the equations for the production centers, we get the following cost distribution:

$$A = \$17,463$$
$$F = \quad 32,019$$
$$P = \quad 17,618$$
$$\text{Total} \quad \$67,100$$

This illustrates a fundamental characteristic of the cross-allocation method: *the total of the costs assigned to the production departments equals total factory cost.* No cost is added; none is overlooked.

Independent study problems (solutions in Appendix B)

1. **Allocations for product costing.** A factory has four direct production departments and three service departments. One of these service departments, department S, has costs of $2,000 a month plus 20 cents for each unit of department S service provided to other departments.

   Monthly service unit consumption and volume of production activity in the factory's four direct production departments are normally as follows:

Department	Service Units Used	Production Volume
1	1,000	10,000 direct labor hours
2	5,000	8,000 direct labor hours
3	8,000	20,000 machine hours
4	6,000	15,000 direct labor hours
Total	20,000	

Service consumption is wholly fixed in department 1 and proportionally variable with volume in the other three departments.

Each batch of 1,000 units of product A requires 10 direct labor hours in department 1, 20 direct labor hours in department 2, 100 machine-hours in department 3, and 5 direct labor hours in department 4. Overhead is charged to products on the basis of predetermined departmental overhead rates, including provisions for service department costs.

Required:

a. How much department S cost should be included in the cost of a batch of product A if costing is on a full costing basis?
b. How much department S cost should be included in the cost of a batch of product A if costing is on a variable costing basis?

2. **Cost distribution sheet.** A factory has two production departments (Able and Baker), and four service departments (building, office, storeroom, and maintenance). The company uses predetermined departmental overhead rates for product costing on a full costing basis.

To develop these overhead costing rates, the company allocates normal service department costs to the two production departments sequentially, using the following statistics for operations at normal volume:

	Direct Labor Hours	Total Labor Hours	Percent of Floor Space	Main- tenance Hours	Percent of Requi- sitions	Direct Overhead Costs
Building	—	500	—	—	—	$ 5,000
Office	—	600	15	10	—	6,370
Storeroom	—	300	10	—	—	2,260
Maintenance	—	500	5	—	5	6,000
Able	5,000	5,600	40	150	35	2,770
Baker	2,000	2,500	30	250	60	3,100
Total						$25,500

Required:

a. Prepare a cost distribution sheet and develop departmental fixed and variable overhead rates for Able and Baker, based on direct labor hours. You should distribute the service department costs in the following sequence and on the following bases:

Building .... Percent of floor space
Office .... Total labor hours
Storeroom .... Percent of requisitions
Maintenance .... Maintenance hours

b. Calculate full cost departmental overhead rates that would be used under direct apportionment, using direct labor hours as the absorption base for all overhead costs. Three rates should be developed, one for each production department and one for all service departments combined.

c. Calculate the amount of overhead assigned to the following two jobs, first using the allocated rates you developed in (a), then using the direct apportionment rates you developed in (b):

	Job 123	Job 321
Direct labor hours—Able	5	2
Direct labor hours—Baker ...	2	5

3. **Cross allocations.** The Tisket Tasket Casket Company, manufacturers of burial caskets and morticians' equipment, has three service departments and eight production departments. The company has decided to use predetermined rates as the basis for service department cost allocation. The budgeted direct departmental charges for the three service departments for the current year are as follows:

Department A .... $12,000 a month
Department B .... 18,000 a month
Department C .... 20,000 a month

The estimated numbers of service units budgeted for this year are as follows:

Department Providing Service	Budgeted Monthly Service Consumption by Departments				
	A	B	C	Production	Total
A	—	1,200	800	6,000	8,000
B	600	—	1,400	8,000	10,000
C	2,000	1,000	—	12,000	15,000

This table should be read as follows: service department A provides 1,200 units of service to service department B, 800 units of service to service department C, and 6,000 units of service to various production departments.

Required:

a. Compute, for each of the three service departments, a charging rate per service unit that covers only the costs directly traceable to that department (direct departmental charges). In other words, the charging rate will not include any provision for the costs of other service departments, nor will service departments becharged for their use of other service departments' services.

b. Compute charging rates by sequential allocation, taking the service departments in alphabetical order.

c. Compute charging rates which give full recognition to the interdependence of the three service departments, using cross-allocations. Three equations must be solved simultaneously, one for each service department. The equation for department A is:

$$\text{Charging rate } A = \frac{\$12,000 + 600 \times \text{Charging rate } B + 2,000 \times \text{Charging rate } C}{8,000 \text{ total service units consumed}}$$

Exercises and problems

4. **Allocations for full costing and variable costing.** Calnan Company's Elmira factory has seven production and four service departments. One of the service departments, department S, has the following monthly budget at its normal monthly volume of 1,400 service hours:

Service labor $14,700
Supervision 2,250
Supplies 420
Depreciation 2,475
Other costs 105
    Total $19,950

All of these except supervision and depreciation are proportionately variable with volume. Supervision cost is the department head's salary. Depreciation is the straight-line amortization of the cost of the equipment used in department S (seven identical service machines).

Raw materials for product X are processed in department 1 and then transferred to department 2 for finishing. Product X is only one of the many products these two production departments work on every month.

Normal monthly operating statistics for these two departments are as follows:

	Department 1	Department 2
Normal monthly operating volume	25,000 pounds of output	10,000 direct labor hours
Normal monthly consumption of department S services	300 service hours	200 service hours

Consumption of department S services in these two departments varies in direct proportion to changes in operating volume.

One unit of product X weighs 10 pounds and requires four direct labor hours in department 2.

Required:

a. How much department S cost should be included in the cost of a unit of product X on a full cost basis?

b. How much department S cost should be included in the cost of a unit of product X on a variable costing basis?

5. **Allocations: Peak costing.** Department S in Calnan Company's Elmira factory (problem 4) usually can perform its work in department 1 in off-peak hours. When department S is operating at its peak volume of 1,800 hours in any month, it will ordinarily be providing 100 service hours to department 1 and 400 service hours in department 2. Department 1's maximum usage of department S services is 400 service hours a month, while department 2's maximum usage is 500 service hours a month.

Required:

How will your answers to problem 4 change if the departmental overhead rates are to be based on peak usage? Show and explain your calculations.

6. **Attributable costing.** Suppose Calnan Company's management (problems 4 and 5) has asked that departmental overhead rates be based on attributable costing. (The costs attributable to a department are the costs that could be eliminated, in time, if the department were eliminated and its operations discontinued.)

Required:

a. How much of department S's budgeted costs appear to be attributable to the operations of department 1? Of department 2?

b. Using the allocations you developed in answer to (*a*), calculate the amount of department S's costs that would be included in departmental overhead rates for departments 1 and 2 (per pound or per direct labor hour) if these rates were to reflect the concept of attributable cost. Departmental overhead rates in departments 1 and 2 are calculated at normal volume in those departments. Use these rates to determine the amount of department S cost to be assigned to product X. What assumptions must be made to justify using these rates in an evaluation of the desirability of producing product X?

7. **Single service department: Fixed and variable service usage.** Department 3 is a production center in Calnan Company's Elmira factory (see problem 4). It uses a good deal of department S service. Under normal conditions, it will use 100 hours of service each month for routine work plus one service hour for every 100 direct labor hours in department 3.

Normal volume in department 3 is 10,000 direct labor hours a month, and a full-cost departmental overhead rate is computed on that basis.

Department 3 uses an outside company, Goodbody, Inc., to do some work that Calnan's own service departments are not equipped to do. Goodbody has now offered to expand its services by doing the work now done by department S in department 3. The price would be a flat fee of $2,100 a month. The decision on this proposal is to be made by the manager of the Elmira factory. Department S will continue to service the factory's other departments in any case.

Required:

a. How large is the department S component of department 3's predetermined full-cost overhead rate (per direct labor hour) if each hour of department S service used is charged to department 3 at department S's expected average full cost at normal volume?

b. How large would the department S component of department 3's overhead rate be if the rate (per direct labor hour) reflected the variable costing principle?

c. Analyze the Goodbody proposal and recommend a course of action, giving reasons for your recommendation. Did the company's allocation system help you reach this conclusion? Explain.

8. **Direct apportionment.** Calnan Company's management (see problem 4) may change from an allocation system to the direct apportionment method for assigning department S's costs to individual products. The Elmira factory completes 1,400 jobs in an average month, weighing a total of 84,000 pounds and requiring 28,000 direct labor hours.

Required:

a. Calculate a full-cost apportionment rate for department S's costs, using pounds of product as the denominator of the apportionment ratio.

b. If the rate you derived in answer to (a) were used, how much department S cost would be included in the cost of a unit of product X?

c. Management's decision to use the apportionment rate you calculated in answer to (a) reflects management's conclusions on at least two key questions. Identify the questions and state at least one good argument to support management's conclusion on each question.

9. **Allocations: Two determinants of support center costs.** Support center alpha provides necessary support to all production centers in omega factory. Although the work it does can't be identified with individual production centers, some of alpha's costs vary with the total number of direct labor hours in omega factory. Alpha's other costs provide its operating capacity; the level of these costs appears to be determined by the total number of production operations omega factory's production centers are expected to perform in a normal month.

Alpha's capacity costs amount to $20,000 a month, while its variable costs are expected to vary at the rate of 5 cents a direct labor hour.

In a normal month omega factory uses 20,000 direct labor hours and performs 10,000 production operations. Production center delta's share of these totals is 3,000 direct labor hours and 4,200 production operations. Delta's predetermined overhead rate for product costing has direct labor hours as its denominator.

Required:

How much of alpha's budgeted costs should be included in delta's overhead rate (per direct labor hour)? Explain your reasoning.

10. **Bases for allocation.** A factory has a number of departments, including the following:

1. The personnel department recruits prospective employees, organizes on-the-job training programs, conducts personal performance reviews, maintains the

personnel files, and carries out other personnel-related work. Ninety percent of the department's direct costs consist of salaries and fringe benefits. This department has ten employees.

2. The steam plant provides steam to heat the building and drive production equipment in several factory departments. Sixty percent of the department's direct costs are for fuel, another 20 percent is for depreciation and equipment maintenance. The department has eight employees.

3. The scheduling department prepares production schedules, coordinates materials flows, and keeps track of the progress of individual jobs. Ninety percent of its direct costs are salaries and fringe benefits of its five employees.

4. The building service department is responsible for keeping the factory building clean, attractive, and in good working condition. Eighty percent of the department's direct costs consist of salaries and fringe benefits. The department has nine employees.

5. The factory manager's office provides overall direction of factory operations, maintains liaison with marketing and head office personnel, handles community relations, analyzes issues as they arise, and performs other duties typical of the factory management function. All of its costs are fixed, 75 percent being the salaries of the factory manager and five other employees in this office.

Required:

For each of these departments, indicate whether allocations should reflect anticipated usage, the anticipated level of activity, or the occupancy of capacity. If a level-of-activity measure is appropriate, indicate whether it appears to reflect a reasonably clear causal relationship or serves to distribute residual costs.

11. **Single versus two-part allocation.** Service department gamma has costs of $32,000 in a normal month. The fixed portion of these costs amounts to 80 percent of the total. These fixed costs are incurred to give gamma the capacity to perform its support functions; gamma capacity is expanded or contracted in proportion to changes in the number of supervisory personnel in other departments.

No measure of the usage of gamma's services is available, but gamma's variable costs are expected to be proportional to the number of employee hours in other departments. You have the following additional information about two of the factory's eight production departments and the total of the departments gamma serves:

	Production Baker	Production Delta	Total, All Departments
Supervisory personnel	2	4	40
Employee hours	6,000	5,000	80,000

Required:

a. Calculate the amounts of gamma's budgeted costs to be allocated to baker and to delta using (1) a single allocation ratio for all of gamma's costs, based on the number of employee hours, and (2) separate rates for the fixed and variable portions of gamma's costs.

b. Using figures from this problem to illustrate your answer, state the case for using two rates instead of one to allocate costs of departments such as gamma.

c. Would the same arguments be valid if gamma's fixed costs were determined by the number of gamma service hours at normal volume and its variable costs were determined by the number of gamma service hours used? Explain any differences you can identify between these two situations.

12. **Cross allocations.** A factory has four departments, two production departments (A and B) and two service departments (C and D). Volume in each production department is measured in direct labor hours (DLH). Costs are shown in the following table:

		Traceable Variable Overhead Costs			
	Traceable Fixed				
	Overhead	Per	Per Unit	Units of C's	Units of D's
Department	Costs	DLH	of Service	Services Required	Services Required
A	$50,000	$2.00	—	0.010 per DLH	—
B	30,000	1.50	—	0.035 per DLH	0.0475 per DLH
C	19,350	—	$2.00	—	0.050 per unit of C's services
D	9,780	—	3.00	0.010 per unit of D's services	—

Each line in this table shows the inputs required by one department. The line for department A, for example, shows that the traceable fixed costs of this department are $50,000, direct variable overhead costs are $2 per direct labor hour, and 0.01 of a unit of service provided by department C is needed for each direct labor hour in department A.

Normal production volume is 29,000 direct labor hours in department A and 20,000 direct labor hours in department B.

Required:

a. Use cross allocation to calculate a full cost overhead rate for each production department.

b. Use cross allocation to calculate variable costing overhead rates for the two production departments.

13. **Direct apportionment; one-step allocation; sequential allocation.** Parker Manufacturing Company has two production departments (fabrication and assembly) and three service departments (administration, maintenance, and cafeteria). Each year Parker develops predetermined departmental overhead rates on a full costing basis for the fabrication and assembly departments. Costs and other data at normal volume are budgeted at the following levels:

	Fabrication	Assembly	Adminis- tration	Mainte- nance	Cafeteria
Direct labor costs	$3,840,000	$3,120,000			
Direct material costs	3,130,000	950,000	—		
Factory overhead costs	1,154,000	986,000	$300,000	$420,000	$500,000
Direct labor hours	240,000	520,000	—	—	—
Number of employees	140	240	12	8	20
Square footage occupied ..	90,000	60,000	10,000	4,000	6,000

Parker is now deciding whether to use direct apportionment or an allocation scheme to assign service department costs to individual job orders. If allocations are used, the appropriate denominator for the factory cafeteria is the number of employees in the other departments. Budgeted maintenance department costs would be allocated in proportion to square footage, while the costs of the administration department would be allocated to production centers in proportion to total cost input.

Required:

a. Allocate the service department costs by the one-step allocation method and calculate an overhead rate for each of the production departments, based on direct labor hours.

b. Allocate the service department costs by the sequential method, starting with the service department with the greatest costs, and calculate an overhead rate for each of the production departments, based on direct labor hours.

c. Develop an apportionment rate based on direct labor hours for the costs of the service departments, treated as a single overhead pool, and recalculate the overhead rates for the two production departments.

d. Using each of these three sets of rates in turn, calculate the total amount of overhead cost assignable to a job requiring 100 direct labor hours in fabrication and 50 direct labor hours in assembly. How different are the resulting cost figures? Is one of them clearly a more accurate measure of product cost than the others? Explain.

(AICPA, adapted)

14. **Comparing allocation methods.** A woodworking company has five departments, two of which are production departments (shaping and finishing) and three are service departments (power, accounting, and repair). Overhead costs traceable to each of these five departments have been determined to be:

Shaping	$80,000
Finishing	70,000
Power	18,000
Accounting	9,000
Repair	20,000

It has been determined that the work load of the service departments is distributed as follows:

	Power	Accounting	Repair
Shaping	25%	20%	60%
Finishing	35	40	15
Power	—	15	20
Accounting	10	—	5
Repair	30	25	—
Total	100%	100%	100%

Required:

a. Allocate service department costs directly to the production departments, ignoring the interrelationships between service departments.

b. Allocate service department costs sequentially, starting with the costs of the service department with the highest direct cost.

c. Allocate service department costs sequentially, distributing first the costs of the service department that receives the least service from other service departments.

d. Allocate service department costs on a basis that recognizes all interrelationships fully.

e. How crucial is the choice of allocation method in this case? Which method would you choose and why would you choose it?

(Carl L. Nelson)

15. **Relevance of allocations to order acceptance decision.** John Lebec has a small factory consisting of two production departments, a machinery maintenance department, a methods and scheduling department, and a small factory office.

The building is rented at a monthly rental that covers the cost of heat, light, building maintenance, etc.

Mr. Lebec is considering whether to accept an order for 100 units of product X at a reduced price for delivery six months from now. Adequate capacity will be available to handle this order, and fixed costs will be essentially the same whether the order is accepted or rejected. Each unit of product X requires one hour of department A labor, one hour of department B labor, three machine hours in department A, and half a machine hour in department B.

The overhead costs traceable to the two production departments, A and B, are as follows in a typical month:

	Production A	Production B
Fixed	$20,797	$ 5,710
Variable	12,943	5,445
Total	$33,740	$11,155

Variable direct overhead costs vary with machine hours in department A and with direct labor hours in department B. Indirect labor costs are fixed in both departments.

In a typical month, the costs of general factory overhead and of the service departments are as follows:

Plant manager's salary	$2,600
Rent	9,600
Direct department costs—service departments:	
Factory office	4,430
Methods and schedules	4,400
Maintenance	8,550

All of these costs are regarded as wholly fixed and indivisible except those of the factory office and the maintenance department. The factory office costs include the salaries of the factory accountant and the bookkeeper, depreciation on office equipment, and utilities ($3,990 a month), and forms, paper supplies, etc. ($440 in an average month—$90 fixed and $350 variable with total labor hours in the other departments).

Of the direct maintenance department costs, $3,600 represents the salary of the maintenance supervisor, depreciation on shop equipment, and other costs of providing maintenance capacity. The remaining $4,950 represents the wages of the maintenance staff and the costs of supplies required for a maintenance volume of 330 maintenance hours a month. This $4,950 is regarded as a variable cost in that, in periods of low maintenance requirements, maintenance employees are assigned to other productive work elsewhere in the factory. The number of maintenance hours in any department is expected to vary with the number of machine hours used in that department.

Physical statistics for a typical month are:

	Factory Office	Methods and Schedules	Main-tenance	Production Department A	Production Department B
Employees	2	2	3	18	27
Direct labor hours	—	—	—	3,000	4,500
Total labor hours	350	350	525	3,150	4,725
Machine hours	—	—	—	5,000	4,000
Maintenance hours	30	—	—	180	120
Floor space (sq. ft.)	900	300	1,200	6,400	3,200

The company uses full cost departmental overhead rates for inventory measurement and to identify products with profit rates above or below normal.

Required:

a. Derive a full cost overhead rate for each production department, first distributing the plant manager's salary and factory rent among the five departments, and then redistributing service department costs sequentially, in the sequence shown in the following table:

	Denominator of Allocation Ratio
Plant manager's salary	Employees
Rent	Floor space
Factory office	Total labor hours
Methods and schedules	Machine hours
Maintenance	Maintenance hours

A machine-hour overhead rate should be used in department A; the overhead rate for department B should be based on direct labor hours.

b. How much overhead cost should be assigned to each unit of product X for purposes of Mr. Lebec's present decision? You need not necessarily use the overhead rates from (*a*), but you should explain briefly your reasons either for using these rates without adjustment or for using different figures.

16. **Choosing an allocation procedure.** ABC Company's factory has three production centers, J, K, and L, and three service and support centers, S, T, and U. The appropriate denominators of the allocation rates are:

S: Number of "service S" hours used by other centers.
T: Number of employees in centers supported by T.
U: Number of square feet occupied by other centers.

The following budgeted cost and statistical data reflect budgeted conditions at the normal operating volume in each cost center:

	Service or Support Center			Production Center		
	S	T	U	J	K	L
Square feet occupied	500	2,000	300	3,000	5,000	1,000
Employees	10	15	10	15	40	60
Service S hours used......	—	100	30	1,000	300	70
Direct labor hours	—	—	—	2,200	5,800	9,000
Costs traceable to cost center but not to individual production orders (per month)	$30,600	$8,500	$16,500	$15,000	$10,000	$5,000

Required:

a. Using direct labor hours as the denominator in each case, calculate predetermined overhead rates for the three production centers, allocating service and support center costs sequentially in the following order: (1) S; (2) T; (3) U. Round allocated amounts to the nearest dollar; round each overhead rate to the nearest 10th of a cent.

b. Using direct labor hours as the denominator in each case, calculate predetermined overhead rates for the three production centers, allocating service and support center costs sequentially in the following order: (1) U; (2) T; (3) S.

c. Using direct labor hours as the denominator in each case, calculate predetermined overhead rates for the three production centers, allocating service and support center costs by the cross-allocation method.

d. Calculate predetermined overhead rates on the assumption that service and support center costs are to be apportioned to job orders on a direct labor base and are not to be allocated to the production centers.

e. Two jobs use the following number of direct labor hours:

Job A: 100 hours in J, 1,000 hours in K, 50 hours in L.
Job B: 1,000 hours in J, 100 hours in K, 50 hours in L.

Calculate the amount of overhead cost to be assigned to each of these jobs by each of the four sets of rates you calculated in answer to the other parts of this question.

f. If the company uses sequential allocation, should it use the sequence prescribed in (a) or the sequence prescribed in (b)? Would direct apportionment be a reasonable approximation if service costs are governed by characteristics of the departments in which service is performed?

17. **Cost distribution sheet; sequential allocations.** Premier Company's factory has four production departments and four service departments—office, buildings, maintenance, and logistics.

All accounting, personnel, and plant management functions are performed in the office department. The buildings department is responsible for heating, lighting, and maintaining the factory building and grounds. The maintenance department handles repairs of all equipment except office equipment, the latter being serviced on contract by an outside firm. The logistics department handles all incoming shipments of materials and parts and operates the stock room.

At normal volume, the factory overhead costs traceable to factory departments would be budgeted at the following levels:

Shaping	$ 29,584
Drilling	24,624
Finishing	109,012
Assembly	5,200
Office	73,040
Buildings	34,000
Maintenance	19,860
Logistics	8,680
Total	$304,000

Budgeted operating data at normal monthly volume are:

	Direct Labor Hours	Direct Labor Cost	Floor Space (square feet)	Employees	Maintenance Labor Hours	Number of Requisitions
Shaping	6,000	90,000	18,000	50	560	400
Drilling	5,000	60,000	16,000	40	610	600
Finishing	14,000	140,000	33,000	100	930	800
Assembly	9,000	72,000	20,000	60	500	500
Office	—	—	10,000	34	—	—
Buildings	—	—	1,000	11	20	10
Maintenance	—	—	1,000	17	—	40
Logistics	—	—	2,000	6	—	—
Total	34,000	$362,000	101,000	318	2,620	2,350

Required:

a. Prepare an overhead cost distribution sheet, allocating the full costs of service departments in the following sequence and on the following bases: (1) buildings—floor space; (2) office—number of employees; (c) maintenance—maintenance labor hours; and (4) logistics—number of requisitions.

b. Prepare a full cost overhead rate for each production department, using the number of direct labor hours as the denominator in each case. (Calculate departmental allocations to the nearest dollar and the overhead rates to the nearest cent.)

c. The company's new controller doesn't understand why office costs aren't classified as residual costs and distributed last, on the basis of total departmental cost other than direct materials. Prepare a cost distribution sheet reflecting this approach, with the other three service departments allocated in the sequence prescribed above. How large an impact on the departmental overhead rates would adoption of the controller's suggestion have?

d. You have been with the company for many years and are convinced that allocating office costs on the basis of the number of employees early in the sequence is better than treating them as residual costs. What conditions or relationships must be present if your position is correct?

8 Budgetary planning

Data emerging from product costing systems such as those we outlined in earlier chapters may be used in various one-of-a-kind decisions. They probably play their most important role in managerial decision making, however, as inputs to annual budgetary planning. The annual budget, built on the foundation of the organization's strategic plan, provides management with a coordinated framework in which to make its major resource utilization decisions. Our purpose in this chapter is to describe what the budget is, why it can be useful, and how it can be prepared. We'll do this by following the management of the Caldwell Company, a small manufacturer of cutting tools, as it developed its budget for the year 19x2.

Background for budgeting

The budget has two major parts, the operating budget and the financial budget. The *operating budget* lists the amounts and costs of the goods and services the organization plans to consume during the operating period, and the benefits it expects its activities to produce. The main components of Caldwell's operating budget are diagrammed in the left-hand side of Exhibit 8–1. Separate budget statements are prepared for the actions management plans to take, their costs, and the profit or income they will generate.

The *financial budget* shows the amounts of cash to be generated or consumed by operations, together with dividends, capital expenditures, new borrowing, and other sources and uses of cash during the budget period. The main components of Caldwell's financial budget are diagrammed in the right-hand side of Exhibit 8–1. The center of the financial plan is the cash budget, which links the operating plan, the capital expenditure budget, and the plan for external financing.

Exhibit 8–1 shows the structure of the budget, but says nothing about the process by which it is prepared. This process is too complex to portray in a simple diagram. For one thing, budgeting is a decision-making process, and the budget is the result of a great deal of analytical work, reflecting choices among alternative operating plans. Second, executives in various parts of the organization are likely to participate in the budgetary process, and they have

Exhibit 8–1 Budget components

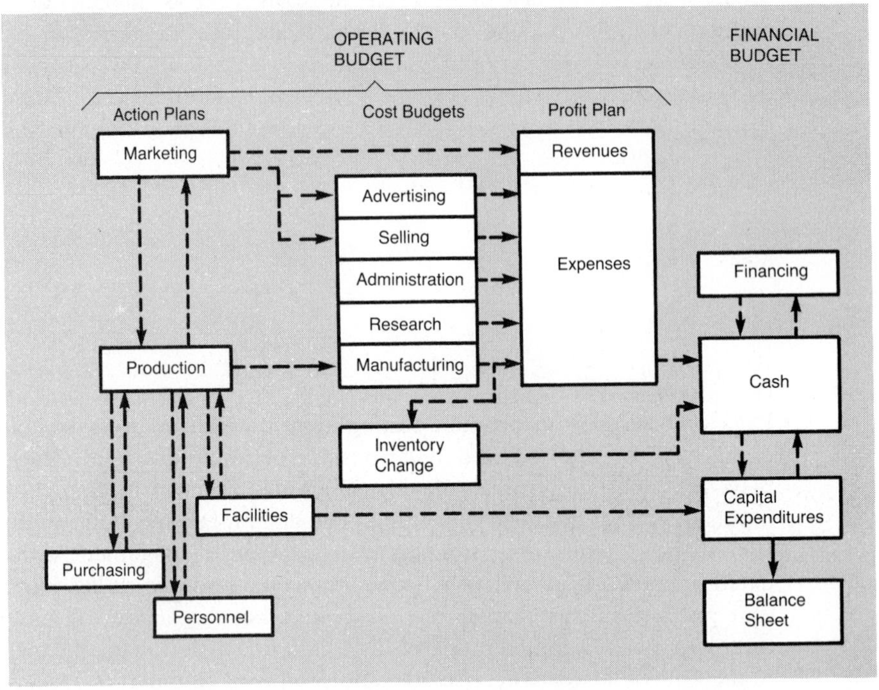

to coordinate their individual activities. Third, budgeting is an iterative process, in which initial decisions are subject to revision as the various parts of the budget are brought together and reviewed, and the revisions are subjected to the same kind of review and modification until management is satisfied with the plan.

We'll introduce some of these complexities as we proceed through our illustration. For convenience, we'll divide the process into six separate activities:

1. Set tentative operating objectives.
2. Prepare a marketing plan.
3. Develop a production plan and manufacturing cost budget.
4. Produce a tentative profit plan.
5. Assemble the financial budget.
6. Review the tentative plan as a whole and revise, as necessary.

Once we have completed our discussion of these activities, we'll close the chapter with an overall evaluation of the budgetary process, with suggestions for refinements management may wish to introduce.

The statement of objectives

Budgeting is a goal-directed process, built on an understanding of the organization's basic goals and its overall strategy. Goals and strategy in small organizations are often implicit and can be identified only by studying the decisions management makes. Other organizations devote a good deal of time and energy to deciding the relative importance of goals such as income, growth, risk, and industry position, and to developing strategies consistent with these goals.

The Caldwell Company has a simple structure, manufacturing only two products, the Craftmaster and the Handyman. Both products are made in the same factory and are sold by the same sales force, working out of company-owned branch offices. Some of the key organizational relationships are diagrammed in Exhibit 8–2.

Exhibit 8–2
CALDWELL COMPANY Partial organization chart

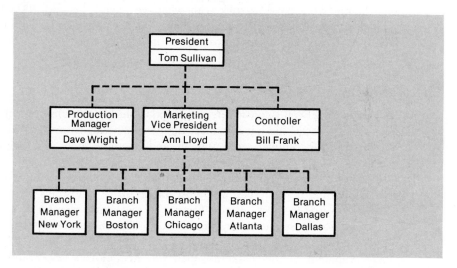

With such a simple organization, Caldwell has no need for an elaborate system of goal formation and strategy determination. Before beginning the budgeting process for 19x2, Tom Sullivan, Caldwell's president, reviewed the company's goals and basic strategy with the board of directors. The board affirmed an earlier decision that the company's basic goals were to achieve a modest rate of growth, low exposure to risk, and profit levels consistent with this low-risk posture. The board also supported Mr. Sullivan's recommendation that Caldwell's best strategy was to keep its product line narrow and to sell its products primarily in its traditional markets.[1]

Some organizations move directly into budget preparation once basic goals and strategies have been agreed upon. Mr. Sullivan decided to take one additional step, however. He wanted to set tentative targets for sales and net income before the division managers started making their plans. Early in Sep-

---

[1] For a discussion of the principles of goal formation and strategic planning, see a book such as Theodore A. Smith, *Dynamic Business Strategy: The Art of Planning for Success* (New York: McGraw-Hill, 1977); George A. Steiner, *Strategic Planning: What Every Manager Must Know* (New York: Free Press, 1979); or Donald L. Bates and David L. Eldredge, *Strategy and Policy: Analysis, Formulation, and Implementation* (Dubuque, I.: Wm. C. Brown, 1980).

tember 19x1, therefore, with the board meeting behind him, he assembled his three main subordinates in his office. Looking at the company's performance for the first eight months of the year and forecasts of economic activity prepared by the company's bankers, he suggested that 19x2 ought to be a good year. He asked his division managers to work toward a 15 percent increase in sales and a 25 percent increase in net income.

Ann Lloyd, the marketing vice president, and Dave Wright, the production manager, thought these targets were too high. They cited the narrow product line, old factory equipment, and intense foreign competition, particularly for the Handyman cutter. Mr. Sullivan said he was looking at merger possibilities, but none of these could be negotiated before the end of 19x2. "For the time being, we'll have to stick with what we have," he said. "Maybe you can't meet the objectives I have in mind, but I think they're within reach. Give it a try and see what you can come up with."

The marketing plan

Bill Frank, Caldwell's controller, was responsible for administering the budget—that is, it was his job to collect budget proposals from Ms. Lloyd, Mr. Wright, and Mr. Sullivan, review them, and assemble them in a coordinated package.

Mr. Frank's usual starting point was the development of the marketing plan. Marketing is the largest and most important of Caldwell's programmed activities, as it is in most business firms. The marketing plan for 19x2 would determine how busy the factory would be, how much warehouse space would be necessary, and how large the clerical staff would have to be.

Development of the marketing plan was Ms. Lloyd's responsibility. She took the following steps:

1. She obtained estimates of the average variable cost of making each product.
2. She estimated each product's contribution margin.
3. She had the branch managers estimate market share, sales, and branch expenses under at least two alternative marketing plans.
4. She reviewed and consolidated the estimates, revising them as appropriate, in consultation with the branch managers.
5. She tested the tentative plan for feasibility.
6. Working with the branch managers, she prepared a revised proposal, which she submitted to Mr. Frank.

Estimating product cost

Many marketing decisions call for estimates of the costs of individual products. Ms. Lloyd asked Mr. Wright for estimates of variable product costs for 19x2. Mr. Wright gave her separate figures on direct materials, direct labor, and variable factory overhead.

Direct materials costs. The specification sheets for each product listed the materials to be used. Combining these lists with estimates of materials prices, Mr. Wright made the following estimates of direct materials costs per unit:

	Craftmaster	Handyman
Direct materials costs	$6.90	$9.04

Direct labor costs. The Caldwell factory had two production departments, machining and assembly. The estimated direct labor rate was $16 an hour in machining and $10 an hour in assembly, including provisions for payroll taxes and employee benefits. The estimated direct labor requirements for a unit of each product were as follows:

	Craftmaster	Handyman
Direct labor hours:		
Machining	0.8	0.6
Assembly	1.0	0.9
Direct labor cost:		
Machining at $16 an hour	$12.80	$ 9.60
Assembly at $10 an hour	10.00	9.00
Total direct labor cost	$22.80	$18.60

Variable overhead costs. Mr. Wright's next move was to estimate variable overhead cost. To do this, he had to develop a variable overhead costing rate for each department. He worked with his department heads and with Mr. Frank to develop the cost estimates summarized in Exhibit 8–3.

Exhibit 8–3
CALDWELL COMPANY Estimated variable factory overhead costs for 19x2

	Machining	Assembly
Indirect labor	$138,000	$22,900
Maintenance	27,600	7,000
Supplies	46,000	45,800
Power	55,200	14,300
Miscellaneous	3,200	800
Total variable overhead	$270,000	$90,800
Direct labor hours	180,000	227,000
Variable overhead costing rate	$1.50/direct labor hour	$0.40/direct labor hour

Dividing estimated variable overhead costs by the estimated number of direct labor hours in each department yielded the variable overhead rates shown at the bottom of Exhibit 8–3. These were then multiplied by the estimated direct labor hours required to manufacture each product. The variable product cost calculation is summarized in Exhibit 8–4.

Exhibit 8–4
CALDWELL COMPANY Estimated variable product costs

	Craftmaster	Handyman
Direct materials	$ 6.90	$ 9.04
Direct labor:		
Machining at $16 per direct labor hour	12.80	9.60
Assembly at $10 per direct labor hour	10.00	9.00
Variable overhead:		
Machining at $1.50 per direct labor hour	1.20	0.90
Assembly at $0.40 per direct labor hour	0.40	0.36
Total	$31.30	$28.90

Estimating contribution margin

Ms. Lloyd's second step was to estimate the contribution margin provided by a unit of each product. To do this, she had to estimate the net amount the company would realize from each unit sold.

The Craftmaster units were priced at $54 each, to be competitive with comparable products of other manufacturers. The Handyman units sold for $35 each. Discounts and allowances were expected to average 5 percent of gross sales for Craftmasters and 6 percent of gross sales for Handyman units. Ms. Lloyd used these percentages to derive the following estimates of net revenue per unit:

	Craftmaster	Handyman
Gross price	$54.00	$35.00
Discounts and allowances	2.70	2.10
Net revenue	$51.30	$32.90

Putting these figures together with the estimates of variable factory cost, Ms. Lloyd got the following estimates of contribution margin per unit:

	Craftmaster	Handyman
Net revenue	$51.30	$32.90
Variable factory cost	31.30	28.90
Contribution margin	$20.00	$ 4.00

These figures were to help Ms. Lloyd decide how much to spend on marketing each product and how much to spend in each region.

Estimating branch sales and expenses

Ms. Lloyd next asked her branch managers to estimate sales and branch expenses on the assumption that the same marketing strategy would be used in 19x2 as in 19x1, the same selling prices, and the same sales force. She then asked them to do this again on the assumption that the price of the Handyman would be raised to $40. She reminded them that the Craftmaster was a much more profitable model and should be emphasized whenever possible. She also asked them to suggest ways headquarters could help them market the company's products more effectively.

The branch managers were very much opposed to the price increase on the Handyman model. Several competing models were already available at lower prices, and raising the Handyman price in their opinion would cut Handyman sales by more than half. On total branch expenditures of $760,000, including product-traceable marketing expenditures, they estimated the following sales volumes (in units):

	Craftmaster	Handyman
At a $35 Handyman price	105,000	110,000
At a $40 Handyman price	105,000	50,000

Caldwell's approach to sales forecasting was a *grass-roots approach,* with the line selling organization preparing its own sales forecasts. The company had two reasons for doing it this way. First, the salespeople knew more about their own customers than the central marketing staff could know. In other words, Ms. Lloyd believed that she got a better sales forecast by relying on the sales force. Second, by helping set their own budgets, the salespeople become more fully committed to them. This meant a stronger motivation and presumably better performance.

This is not to deny the value of central sales forecasting or market research in this or other situations. Even if the basic forecasts are made in the field, the market research staff can be of material assistance. It can conduct qualitative research to reveal market potentialities, environmental trends, and competitive activities. It can engage in quantitative research to estimate how much can be sold, by product and by territory or by other major categories of the company's business. These estimates can be checked against the field estimates to reveal any wide discrepancies which then can be traced further. Market research can also perform a service function to the field sales force, analyzing data supplied from the field and helping sales managers review sales forecasts made by individual salespeople.

We should emphasize that sales forecasting is not the same as sales budgeting. Forecasting is essentially a passive activity; budgeting is more active. Sales volume depends on the amount and kinds of marketing effort, and a separate forecast has to be made for each marketing program management wants to consider.

Consolidating the branch office proposals

When all the tentative branch office budgets were in her hands, Ms. Lloyd reviewed them with her staff. Although she discounted her branch managers' pessimism, and remained convinced that a price increase would increase cash flow slightly in the short run, she agreed to hold the Handyman price at $35.

One reason for this decision was that the Dallas branch was forecasting a 25 percent increase in unit sales of the Handyman. This was far greater than in any of the other branches and much larger than the growth rates in the Southwest would suggest. The branch manager explained that the Handyman units the sales force had placed in a local supermarket chain in August were selling very well and that prospects for the future were very promising. Ms. Lloyd was impressed, and suggested using the supermarket channel in other areas as well, with someone from headquarters to work closely with the branch sales forces on the supermarket accounts. The other branch managers were enthusiastic, and Ms. Lloyd tentatively agreed to move one of the more experienced salespeople into the head office to help in supermarket sales.

Ms. Lloyd also found that the manager in Atlanta was budgeting 1,000 fewer Craftmasters in 19x2 than in 19x1, even though this seemed to be a growing market. The manager explained that the sales force could not cover the growing suburban markets effectively without losing their old customers in the cities in the Atlanta region. To take care of this problem, Ms. Lloyd worked with the Atlanta branch manager to draw up a new plan calling for the hiring of an additional sales representative.

Testing the tentative marketing plan for feasibility

New sales forecasts were made on the basis of the revised plans, and the total came to 255,000 units. Ms. Lloyd checked with Dave Wright, the production manager, and found that no more than 240,000 units could be delivered in 19x2. The factory had enough capacity to make more, but the supplier of a patented ratchet that went into each unit had limited Caldwell to 20,000 ratchets a month for the next year while its own plant expansion program was under way.

This limitation is known as a *constraint,* defined as a limit to action set by law, policy, custom, or shortage. The presence of a shortage-based constraint requires management to allocate the resource that is in short supply among the activities that need it. To do this in a profit-oriented organization, management needs to estimate how much profit a unit of the scarce resource can contribute in each of its possible uses.

Contribution for this purpose is defined as the net revenue from the sale of a unit, less all the variable costs except the cost of the scarce resource itself. (Since the total amount of this resource will be used under any likely solution, its total cost will be the same under all of them and therefore can be ignored.) We saw earlier that the variable cost of a Craftmaster was $31.30, against $28.90 for a Handyman. Each of these figures included $1 to cover the cost of a ratchet. The contribution of each ratchet therefore was calculated as follows:

	Craftmaster	Handyman
Total variable cost	$31.30	$28.90
Less: ratchet costs	1.00	1.00
Other variable costs	$30.30	$27.90
Net revenue	51.30	32.90
Contribution of each rachet	$21.00	$ 5.00

The difference between these two contribution figures was so great that Ms. Lloyd cut 15,000 Handyman units out of the tentative sales plan to bring sales and production into balance. She decided to go ahead with the supermarket venture, however, because this would absorb 60,000 Handyman units in 19x2, even after the cutback, with a promise of substantial growth and profit in later years.

Assembling the final marketing proposal

Once the allocation decisions were made, Ms. Lloyd was able to prepare the tentative marketing budget shown in Exhibit 8–5. The profit contribution concept is reflected at two levels in this table:

Exhibit 8–5
CALDWELL COMPANY Proposed marketing budget

	Craftmaster	Handyman	Total
Units sold..........................	110,000	130,000	240,000
Gross sales	$5,940,000	$4,550,000	$10,490,000
Discounts and allowances	297,000	273,000	570,000
Net sales	5,643,000	4,277,000	9,920,000
Variable cost of goods sold	3,443,000	3,757,000	7,200,000
Contribution margin	2,200,000	520,000	2,720,000
Direct product marketing expenses	80,000	100,000	180,000
Product profit contribution	2,120,000	420,000	2,540,000
General marketing expenses:			
Branch offices.....................			620,000
Headquarters			140,000
Total general marketing			760,000
Marketing profit contribution			$ 1,780,000

1. The fixed costs traceable to each product have been subtracted from the product's contribution margin to get a profit contribution figure for that product.
2. The general expenses traceable to the marketing division but not to individual products have been subtracted to get the divisional profit contribution figure.

Notice all that happened after Ms. Lloyd got the first tentative proposals from the branches:

1. Pricing policy was reviewed.
2. One branch proposal was sent back for revision.
3. A strategic decision was made in the head office to make a major move affecting all branches.
4. The entire plan was found to be unfeasible due to production restrictions; the sales budgets were reduced.

This was not a sterile exercise in filling out forms. It was a highly dynamic, creative process.

The production plan and manufacturing cost budget

Once the tentative marketing plan was ready, Mr. Wright was able to put the production plan in shape. The top executives agreed that if the supermarket venture was successful, the Caldwell Company would want to go into 19x3 prepared to increase its deliveries of the Handyman model substantially. Additional ratchets were expected to be available by that time to support a substantial expansion in volume.

To prepare for this, Mr. Wright proposed to build an inventory of component parts for 10,000 Craftmaster and 10,000 Handyman units, fitting them into the machining department's schedule whenever convenient. They would be assembled in 19x3, when additional ratchets were expected to become available. Mr. Wright took six steps to get his budget proposal in shape:

1. He estimated direct materials requirements.
2. He estimated direct labor requirements.
3. He estimated factory overhead requirements.
4. He prepared a summary of the estimated manufacturing costs.
5. He prepared physical resource plans.
6. He prepared tentative production schedules, in detail, for the first three months of 19x2.

Estimating direct materials requirements

The first step was to multiply direct materials costs per unit by estimated production quantities. These calculations are summarized in Exhibit 8–6. Separate estimates were made for ratchet costs (based on total production of 240,000 finished units) and for other materials, enough to produce the 240,000 finished units and add 20,000 units to the inventory of partly processed tools.

Exhibit 8–6
CALDWELL COMPANY Direct materials cost budget

	Craftmaster	Handyman	Total
Units placed in production	120,000	140,000	
Units finished	110,000	130,000	
Direct materials costs per unit:			
Ratchet	$ 1.00	$ 1.00	
Other materials	5.90	8.04	
Total	6.90	9.04	
Total materials costs:			
Ratchets (units finished)	$110,000	$ 130,000	$ 240,000
Other materials (units placed in production)	708,000	1,125,600	1,833,600
Total	$818,000	$1,255,600	$2,073,600

Estimating direct labor requirements

Mr. Wright then used his estimates of the number of direct labor hours required for a unit of each product to calculate total direct labor hours. For example, we see in the first column of Exhibit 8–7 that each Craftmaster required 0.8 of an hour of labor time in the machining department. Since machining work was to be performed for 120,000 Craftmasters in 19x2, production would require 96,000 direct labor hours in 19x2. Multiplying the direct labor hour totals by the estimated direct labor rates then yielded the estimates of direct labor costs shown at the bottom of Exhibit 8–7.

Exhibit 8–7
CALDWELL COMPANY Direct labor budget

	Craftmaster	Handyman	Total
Direct labor hours per unit:			
Machining	0.8	0.6	
Assembly	1.0	0.9	
Production requirements (number of units):			
Machining	120,000	140,000	260,000
Assembly	110,000	130,000	240,000
Total direct labor hours:			
Machining	96,000	84,000	180,000
Assembly	110,000	117,000	227,000
Total direct labor cost:			
Machining at $16 per direct labor hour	$1,536,000	$1,344,000	$2,880,000
Assembly at $10 per direct labor hour	1,100,000	1,170,000	2,270,000
Total	$2,636,000	$2,514,000	$5,150,000

Estimating factory overhead costs

The Caldwell Company measured product costs on a variable costing basis. To estimate the variable overhead costs, Mr. Wright started with the tentative variable overhead rates he had given Ms. Lloyd earlier (Exhibit 8–3). He confirmed those earlier estimates and also worked with his department heads to estimate the amount of fixed factory overhead costs necessary to support the anticipated volume of production. The resulting estimates of factory overhead costs were as follows:

	Machining	Assembly	Factory Administration	Total
Variable overhead	$270,000	$ 90,800	—	$ 360,800
Fixed overhead	380,000	85,000	$375,000	840,000
Total overhead	$650,000	$175,800	$375,000	$1,200,800

Summarizing manufacturing costs

Mr. Wright summarized all of the factory cost data in the statement of budgeted manufacturing costs shown in Exhibit 8-8. This exhibit contains only one new bit of information, the provision for an increase in raw materials inventories,

Exhibit 8–8
CALDWELL COMPANY Budgeted manufacturing costs

Product costs:	
Direct materials:	
Inventory, January 1, 19x2	$ 255,400
Purchases	2,148,200
Total	2,403,600
Inventory, December 31, 19x2	330,000
Direct materials issued (Exhibit 8–6)	2,073,600
Direct labor (Exhibit 8–7)	5,150,000
Variable overhead	360,800
Total product cost	7,584,400
Fixed factory overhead costs	840,000
Total manufacturing cost	$8,424,400

necessary because production levels in 19x2 were to be considerably higher than in 19x1. The increase in the inventory of materials and purchased parts was calculated as follows:

Materials Inventory, January 1, 19x2	$255,400
Materials Inventory, December 31, 19x2	330,000
Increase in materials inventory	$ 74,600

Mr. Wright's budgeting job was relatively easy because the Caldwell Company had only two products. He could move directly from the tentative sales budget to a detailed list of production requirements, and from these to a list of physical input requirements. Other approaches are likely to be necessary if the product line is extremely broad. One company, for example, develops three separate tentative sales budgets, one for each of the following product groups:

1. Major catalog products, budgeted in both physical units and sales dollars.
2. Minor catalog products, budgeted in dollars only.
3. Custom products, also budgeted in dollars.

The input requirements for products in the second and third categories are based on group averages, which remain relatively stable. Estimates of materials and labor requirements for custom products, for example, are based on average historical relationships between the sales value of production and labor and materials inputs.

Preparing physical resource plans and production schedules

Caldwell's production plan was expressed in physical input requirements as well as in costs. The physical figures helped management prepare its personnel and purchases budgets, which we have omitted to reduce the amount of detail in our illustration. Physical budgets aren't the same as production or purchasing schedules, however. Schedules provide immediate instructions to first-line production personnel. Which products are to be manufactured in which departments by which personnel on which machines on what days?

Production schedules are seldom prepared more than a few months in advance, and are frequently revised from day to day as conditions change. The production plan, on the other hand, typically covers the entire year and is not revised. Its main purpose is to show how sales plans will be implemented, thereby giving production management a chance to evaluate alternative production methods and select the combination that seems to meet planned delivery requirements at minimum cost.

The profit plan

The profit plan is the focal point of the operating budget. In larger companies which are organized in divisions, each division management submits a proposed profit plan, incorporating the current revenues and expenses implicit in its marketing plan, production plan, and proposals to spend money for administrative support, engineering, and other operating purposes.

The Caldwell Company is too small to be divisionalized, and the controller has the responsibility of assembling the various components into a tentative profit plan. The president and the board then review this proposal in conjunction with the tentative financial budget.

Allocating manufacturing costs

Bill Frank, Caldwell's controller, had worked closely with Ms. Lloyd and Mr. Wright throughout the budgeting process and was thoroughly familiar with their figures. Before putting the tentative profit plan in finished form, however, he had to estimate how much of the manufacturing costs would be reported as the cost of goods sold and how much would be added to the cost of the inventories during the year.

Variable costs.   The company's internal accounting records were kept on a variable costing basis. Mr. Frank's first step was to estimate the increment in the variable cost of the inventories of work in process and finished goods expected to be on hand at the end of 19x2.

All factory inventories were measured on a last in, first out (LIFO) basis. This means that the 20,000-unit increase in semiprocessed products would be measured at the 19x2 costs of the machining operations, including all materials except the ratchets. These calculations are summarized in Exhibit 8–9.

The quantities of finished goods on hand were not expected to change in 19x2. These, too, were accounted for on a Lifo basis, and the reported cost of the ending inventory therefore was expected to be the same as the reported cost of the beginning inventory.

Fixed costs.   Variable costing is not an acceptable method of measuring inventory costs for external financial reporting, as we pointed out in Chapter 6. Since the work-in-process inventory was expected to increase in 19x2, the

Exhibit 8–9
CALDWELL COMPANY Variable cost of increment in work-in-process inventory

	Craftmaster	Handyman	Total
Unit costs (from Exhibit 8–4):			
Direct materials, except ratchets	$ 5.90	$ 8.04	
Machining direct labor	12.80	9.60	
Machining variable overhead	1.20	0.90	
Total variable unit cost	$ 19.90	$ 18.54	
Units added to inventory	10,000	10,000	
Variable costs of units added to inventory	$199,000	$185,400	$384,400

amount of fixed costs assigned to the work-in-process inventory would also have to go up.

Normal volume in the machining department was 200,000 direct labor hours. Budgeted fixed costs totaled $380,000 (from the table under "Estimating factory overhead costs," above). The supplemental overhead rate for 19x2 therefore was $380,000/200,000 = $1.90 per direct labor hour. The increment in the amount of fixed overhead costs assigned to the inventories was calculated as follows:

	Machining Hours per Unit	Units	Total Machining Hours	Total Fixed Overhead at $1.90
Craftmaster	0.8	10,000	8,000	$15,200
Handyman	0.6	10,000	6,000	11,400
Total			14,000	$26,600

Small though this amount was, Mr. Frank decided to reflect it in the budget for 19x2. He rounded the dollar figure to $27,000 and made the following calculations:

	Variable	Fixed
Total manufacturing costs (from Exhibit 8–8)	$7,584,400	$840,000
Less: Increases in work-in-process inventories	384,400	27,000
Expenses to be entered in tentative profit plan	$7,200,000	$813,000

Assembling the tentative profit plan

Once he had made these calculations, Mr. Frank prepared the tentative profit plan shown in Exhibit 8–10. The numbers in the upper part of this exhibit came from the tentative marketing plan (Exhibit 8–5). The fixed factory overhead figure came from the calculation at the end of the preceding paragraph.

Mr. Frank developed the figure for administration expenses by assembling the budget proposals from the head office administrative departments (includ-

Exhibit 8–10
CALDWELL COMPANY Tentative profit plan

	Craftmaster	Handyman	Total
Gross sales	$5,940,000	$4,550,000	$10,490,000
Discounts and allowances	297,000	273,000	570,000
Net sales	5,643,000	4,277,000	9,920,000
Variable cost of goods sold	3,443,000	3,757,000	7,200,000
Contribution margin	2,200,000	520,000	2,720,000
Direct product marketing expense	80,000	100,000	180,000
Profit contribution	2,120,000	420,000	2,540,000
General expenses:			
Fixed factory overhead			813,000
Marketing........................			600,000
Administration			320,000
Interest			80,000
Income taxes			289,000
Total general expense			2,102,000
Net income			$ 438,000

ing his own). The interest expense estimate he prepared on his own. He knew the interest expense would be affected by any decisions to borrow or repay loans in 19x2, but for the moment he estimated interest expense on the assumption that the debt schedule would remain unchanged. The income tax expense then could be estimated by applying the appropriate income tax rates to the estimates of income before income taxes.

The financial budget

The controller is likely to review the tentative profit plan as soon as it is assembled, and may return portions of it to their sponsors if these portions seem to be inconsistent, unfeasible, or unlikely to win top management's approval. This kind of review usually encompasses both the profit plan and the various components of the financial budget, however, and therefore we'll postpone our discussion of the review process until we have examined the financial budget itself.

The capital budget

While working on the operating plan, each of the company's executives also put together a set of proposals for the purchase or construction of plant and equipment. These were assembled by the controller into a proposed *capital budget.*

Capital budgeting is a complicated process. We'll discuss it in some depth in Chapter 18. At the Caldwell Company, Mr. Frank reviewed each proposal, sent some of them back to Mr. Wright or Ms. Lloyd for further information or analysis, and finally put together the tentative capital budget summarized in Exhibit 8–11. Mr. Frank included all these proposals because each of them

Exhibit 8–11
CALDWELL COMPANY Tentative capital budget.

	Payments to Be Made	
	19x2	19x3
Projects approved in 19x1,		
to be completed in 19x2	$ 70,000	—
New projects:		
Automatic assembly equipment	260,000	$ 40,000
Machinery department		
equipment replacements	240,000	—
Factory extension	600,000	200,000
Office equipment	50,000	—
Total	$1,220,000	$240,000

met the company's profitability tests on its own, but he didn't know yet whether all of them could be financed.

The cash budget

The final link in the chain is the cash budget. Not until this is put together can management decide whether the firm has enough cash to do everything that is being proposed. Cash budgeting is essentially a five-step process:

1. Estimate cash receipts from operations.
2. Estimate operating cash payments.
3. Estimate other cash receipts and disbursements.
4. Identify expenditure limits.
5. Ration scarce cash.

Mr. Frank and his staff were responsible for the first four steps; the fifth was the president's job.

   1. Estimate cash receipts from operations.   The company's main continuing source of cash is its collections from its customers. Collections may be either less or greater than revenues, but in a growing company collections usually lag behind the growth in revenues. Mr. Frank estimated that in this case the increase in budgeted sales would require a $112,000 increase in accounts receivable. This reduced anticipated receipts to $9,808,000:

Net sales (Exhibit 8–10)	$9,920,000
Less: Increase in receivables	112,000
Collections from customers	$9,808,000

   2. Estimate operating cash payments.   Increases in revenues usually require increases in inventories as well as increases in expenses. The first approximation to the amount of cash required to pay for operations therefore is the sum of expenses and inventory changes. Several things may interfere, however.

Depreciation charges, for example, do not represent current cash payments and these must be subtracted from the total. Similarly, any increases in accounts payable, wages payable, or taxes payable will reduce the amounts to be paid currently in cash. They, too, must be subtracted. Any decreases in these items of course must be added.

Exhibit 8–12 shows how Mr. Frank adjusted the expenses in the tentative profit plan to estimate cash disbursements. The figures in the left-hand column came from the tentative profit plan (Exhibit 8–10). The inventory changes listed in the second column reconcile the profit plan with the operating cost budgets for the year, shown in column (3). The portions of these flows not requiring current cash flows are listed in column (4). Adjusting for these gave Mr. Frank the cash flow estimates in the right-hand column.

Exhibit 8–12
CALDWELL COMPANY Cash disbursement worksheet

	(1) Operating Expense	(2) Change in Inventory	(3) Total Operating Cost	(4) Cash Flow Adjustment	(5) Cash Disbursement
Variable manufacturing cost	$7,200,000				
Increase in materials inventory		+$ 74,600			
Increase in work-in-process inventory		+ 384,400	$7,659,000		
Increase in accounts payable				−$ 21,000	$7,638,000
Fixed manufacturing cost	813,000				
Increase in work-in-process inventory		+ 27,000	840,000		
Depreciation				− 295,000	545,000
Marketing costs:					
Direct product marketing	180,000		180,000		180,000
General marketing	600,000		600,000		600,000
Administration	320,000		320,000		320,000
Interest	80,000		80,000		80,000
Income taxes	289,000		289,000		
Increase in taxes payable				− 40,000	249,000
Total	$9,482,000	+$486,000	$9,968,000	−$356,000	$9,612,000

The difference between the total cash disbursement shown at the foot of column (5) in Exhibit 8–12 and the estimated cash receipts (calculated in step 1 above) can be identified as the *net operating cash flow* for 19x2:

Collections from customers	$9,808,000
Payments to employees and suppliers	9,612,000
Cash generated by operations	$ 196,000

3. Estimate other cash receipts and disbursements. To complete the tentative cash budget, management must estimate the amounts to be received from such sources as planned borrowing, the sale of shares of stock, and the sale of long-term assets or plant and equipment. In this case, Mr. Frank anticipated no asset sales, no long-term borrowing or debt retirement, and no sales of stock. He included dividends in the tentative cash budget at the same amount as in 19x1, $200,000, along with the $1,220,000 current portion of the tentative capital budget (Exhibit 8–11).

4. Identify expenditure limits.   Caldwell's practice in the past had been to finance all its capital expenditures either from current operating funds or from long-term sources. Interest rates were expected to remain at very high levels throughout 19x2, however, and the stock market was depressed. Mr. Frank knew that the board of directors would go to the long-term financial markets only if the company's survival seemed to depend on it. Any financing in 19x2 would have to be from short-term sources.

Mr. Frank's discussions with the company's bankers and with Mr. Sullivan convinced him that the maximum amount the company either could obtain or was willing to obtain by short-term borrowing in 19x2 was $800,000, net of interest. This set a tentative expenditure limit of $996,000 for 19x2:

Cash from operations	$196,000
Maximum borrowing	800,000
Expenditure limit	$996,000

5. Ration scarce cash.   The tentative estimates of cash inflows and outflows are summarized in Exhibit 8–13. From this it is clear that Caldwell could not finance all the activities included in the tentative operating plan and capital budget. Cutbacks improving cash flows by at least $424,000 would have to be made unless the internal cash flow stream could be increased.

Exhibit 8–13
CALDWELL COMPANY Tentative cash flow forecast

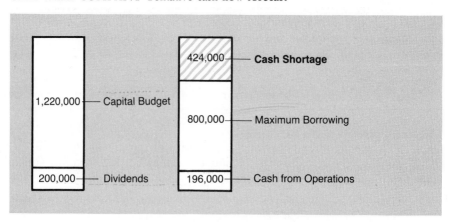

Budget review, revision and approval

Top management needs to review the tentative budget carefully, even if the company has all the cash the proposal would require. Is the profit plan appropriate, given the company's strategy, its resources, and the anticipated economic climate? Are the capital expenditure proposals as desirable as their sponsors claim? Is the proposed research and development program too timid or too ambitious? In the next few pages we'll see how the Caldwell Company wrestled with these questions and others like them.

Reviewing the operating budget

Sometimes top management has no quarrel with any specific component of the plan, but is unwilling to accept the overall result. Then managers in all departments have to review their proposals and come up with something better. Ideally, this would lead managers at lower levels to redouble their efforts to find ways to reduce costs or market their products more effectively.

In practice, a different result is more likely. Most operating budget proposals include many programmed activities that are not expected to provide substantial cash benefits in the immediate future. Research and community service activities are good examples. Budgets also include provisions for activities that are re- sponsive to service demands, but only after a delay. Preventive maintenance is an example—it can be deferred, although at a cost. To meet a current profit target, management may choose to cut down on activities like these, despite the unfavorable future consequences of doing this.

Returning to the Caldwell Company, we find that Mr. Frank knew the president would be very unhappy with a net income of only $438,000 and with the $420,000 profit contribution of the Handyman drill. The high cost of manufacturing the Handyman made this a marginal product at best, but it accounted for more than half the unit sales. Without it, the company would barely break even in 19x2.

Ms. Lloyd reminded Mr. Frank that the budgeted profit contribution from the Handyman drill was up substantially from the 19x1 level, thanks to the new supermarket venture. Mr. Wright maintained that the best way to reduce production costs would be to simplify the product. He saw no way of putting the redesigned product into production before the end of 19x2, but he did decide to prepare a proposal to buy automated assembly equipment that would be needed for the redesigned product.

Mr. Sullivan, Caldwell's president, agreed with this proposal. He was con- vinced that any reductions of operating expenditures would hurt the company in the future. In fact, he asked Ms. Lloyd and Mr. Wright to spend some time during the next six months evaluating the desirability of inaugurating a modest research program to identify and develop new products or product improvements that could be introduced in the future. He also decided to keep the proposed inventory buildup. Without it, he reasoned, a substantial and profitable market expansion in 19x3 would be impossible.

Reviewing the financial budget

Having reviewed the operating plan, Mr. Sullivan turned to the other elements in the financial budget. The cash flow gap had to be closed one way or another. Mr. Frank outlined five possibilities for Mr. Sullivan to consider:

1. Reduce the dividend.
2. Eliminate the increase in the inventory of semiprocessed products.
3. Defer the equipment replacements.
4. Defer the assembly automation project.
5. Defer the plant expansion.

The most obvious of these might seem to be the dividend. Mr. Sullivan knew, however, that the board of directors would take this route only as a last resort. Cutting the dividend would depress the price of the company's stock and make raising new funds in the future much more difficult.

Turning to the items in the capital budget, Mr. Sullivan decided to cut the machinery department's equipment replacement request by $10,000, a decision that might be reversed later in the year when specific expenditure proposals were submitted. In general, however, he accepted Mr. Wright's argument that meeting production cost and delivery targets in 19x2 would be impossible if the bulk of the replacements weren't made.

Mr. Sullivan was more severe with the office equipment budget. He pointed out that no specific information had been submitted to support the request, which was $20,000 greater than the average annual expenditure in the recent past. Mr. Frank said he planned to submit a specific proposal later in the year, but Mr. Sullivan told him that the cash flow in 19x2 couldn't support any major outlays. He approved a $30,000 budget, but suggested that some of this might remain unspent if Mr. Frank's major proposal called for a major change in the structure of office operations in 19x3.

These actions made only a slight dent in the estimated cash flow gap. Mr. Sullivan finally decided to close the gap by postponing the plant expansion and automation proposals until the company had more experience with the supermarket venture. He left the automation proposal and equivalent financing in the budget but ruled out any expenditure on the project until more data on supermarket sales were available toward the middle of the year.

These decisions closed the cash flow gap by bringing the cash flow estimates to the following levels:

Cash receipts:	
Collections from customers	$ 9,808,000
New borrowing (net of interest)	594,000
Total cash receipts	$10,402,000
Cash disbursements:	
Operating cash disbursements	$ 9,612,000
Dividends	200,000
Capital expenditures:	
Completion of existing projects	70,000
Machinery replacement	230,000
Office equipment	30,000
Automated assembly equipment	260,000
Total cash disbursements	$10,402,000

In other words, even if the automated assembly equipment project were undertaken later in the year, the company would have to take down only $594,000 of its estimated $800,000 borrowing capacity. If the assembly project were to be postponed even longer, only $334,000 of new borrowing would have to be negotiated.

Budget review: An iterative process

Exhibit 8–14 emphasizes the iterative nature of the budgeting process, in which budget proposals move haltingly, level by level, up through the organization. An additional loop could be built into the diagram in Exhibit 8–14 to show the controller questioning the desirability of a proposal and reviewing it with its sponsors. Furthermore, the "Managers Prepare Proposal" block itself could be replaced by a series of blocks and diamonds, representing the decision process at lower management levels. Budget proposals are prepared, submitted to the next management level, sent back for revision or further evidence, resubmitted, approved, and passed up to the next level, reviewed there and sent back down, revised again and resubmitted, and so on.

Exhibit 8–14 Responses to budget proposals

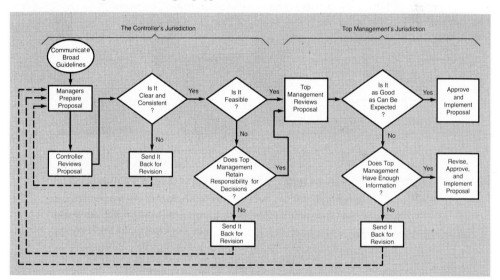

The process is not as inefficient as it may seem, however. In a well designed system, people talk to each other as they go along. It is ideas and suggestions, rather than formal documents, that are most likely to go up and down the chain of command. Furthermore, both top management and division management have staff assistants to handle analytical problems and keep the process moving.

Seasonal patterns

Annual totals may obscure significant seasonal patterns in profit or cash flow. The cash budget may be in surplus for the year as a whole, but deep in deficit for part of the year, as in Exhibit 8–15.

Exhibit 8–15 Seasonal imbalances in cash flows

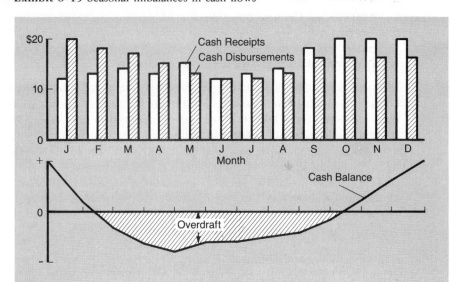

Management must forecast these seasonal patterns, so that it can adjust the timing of enough receipts and disbursements to keep the cash balance at an adequate level. It can borrow seasonally, shift the timing of discretionary expenditures such as purchases of equipment, or invest temporarily idle cash in short-term securities.

Monthly profit plans are also useful, mainly to serve as bases of comparison with actual performance as the year goes on. Important though these seasonal translations are, however, they raise no new conceptual problems that require further discussion here.

The purposes of budgeting

Even the sketchy description of budgetary planning in the last few pages should be enough to show that budgeting is a lot of work. Each division manager in a large company is expected to submit a proposed operating plan and capital expenditure budget well ahead of the end of the year. Putting these proposals together may take two or three months. Reviewing them, making necessary adjustments, and assembling them in a coordinated companywide plan takes another month or two.

No one does this for fun. It must have a good payoff if management is to go to all this trouble. Six potential advantages are worth noting:

1. To force managers to *analyze* the company's activities critically and creatively.
2. To direct some of management's attention from the present to the *future*.
3. To enable management to *anticipate* problems or opportunities in time to deal with them effectively.

4.   To reinforce the managers' *motivation* to work to achieve the company's goals and objectives.
5.   To give managers a continuing *reminder* of the actions they have decided on.
6.   To provide a *reference point* for control reporting.

Only one of these, the motivational aspect, calls for an additional comment at this time. Given the amount of work it requires, budgeting may not seem to be a very useful vehicle for motivating managers. Furthermore, the budget itself is not a motivating force. It is just a piece of paper. The motivation comes, if at all, from the process of producing the budget, not from the end product. Put another way, the objective is to use the process to *reinforce* the manager's motivation to work to achieve the company's goals. It is only one of several motivational elements and will work only if the others are also active.

Budgeting works in part because in working on the budget the managers are constantly reminded of the goals of their own sections of the organization. They are asked to judge each budgeting decision by its likely effect on progress toward these goals. Furthermore, by participating in preparing it, the managers are expected to make personal commitments to the successful execution of the plan. It becomes their plan, not something imposed on them from above. We'll have a good deal more to say about this in Chapter 22.

Program budgeting and zero-base budgeting

The budget typically follows the organization chart—that is, a budget is prepared for each responsibility center on the chart. The budgets for responsibility centers at higher organization levels summarize the budgets for the responsibility centers below them. This is called *organizational budgeting*.

Organizational budgeting is essential because it identifies the resources individual managers are expected to use and the objectives they are expected to achieve. This may not be enough, however. The budget for each responsibility center covers all of that center's activities. When the center is engaged in more than one activity, the part each is to play is not clear unless the budget is subdivided by activity. In a research department, for example, a separate budget is likely to be prepared for each research project and for departmental administrative activities.

Developing budgets for individual activities or for groups of related activities has two main advantages. First, it makes the plan itself a lot clearer. This makes it a better guide for the manager and a better basis for comparison with actual results. Second, it gives management a better foundation for decision making. The best way to review budget proposals is to calculate the costs and benefits of individual activities. Subdividing the budget by activity makes this feasible.

Program budgeting is the name for the process of building the activity dimension into the budget. In concept, it applies to any kind of activity, but in practice the term generally refers to the budgets for major groups of related activities, or programs. These may cut across organizational lines as shown in Exhibit 8–16. Each of the responsibility centers in this exhibit has two activities. Three of these activities are independent, while three are part of an integrated program. In a research organization, for example, these might all relate to a new product or customer service. In a book publishing company they might relate to a coordinated set of study materials. In such cases the main decision focus is on the larger program rather than on the individual activities within the responsibility centers.

Exhibit 8–16 Responsibilities, activities, and programs

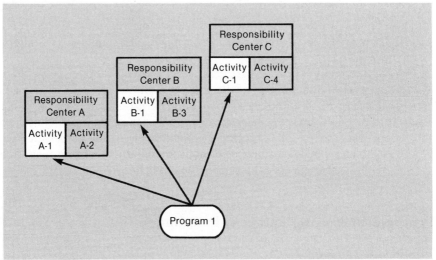

In reviewing budgetary proposals, management needs to compare their costs with the benefits they will yield. Unfortunately, the benefits of many activities can't be measured readily in monetary terms. Attempts to get around this difficulty were a central feature of a massive effort in the 1960s to introduce program planning and budgeting systems (PPBS) in governmental departments and agencies.[2] Government executives were asked to classify their budget requests by activity (program budgeting or program planning) and to estimate the benefits arising from each activity. In an effort to put costs and benefits on a comparable plane, efforts were made to measure benefits in dollars.

The main reason for seeking dollar measures of benefits is that having these would make it easier to compare budget requests from different agencies. Without these, requests can be ranked only on an ordinal scale—this proposal is better than that one, which is better than another, and so on.

Business firms have these same problems. Proposals to pay dividends are not directly comparable to proposals to sponsor employee recreation activities because benefits are not measured in comparable terms. These problems must be solved, and the solutions must reflect management's judgment. To help

[2] See David Novick, *Program Budgeting,* 2d ed. (New York: Holt, Rinehart & Winston, 1969).

management apply its judgment, some authorities suggest a systematized approach known as zero-base budgeting.[3] Zero-base budgeting has three main features:

1.   The activities of individual responsibility centers are divided into a series of incremental "packages."
2.   Each package is ranked ordinally.
3.   Managers at higher levels consolidate the proposals submitted by their subordinates, providing their own ordinal rankings.

For example, suppose a manager of a community relations department has submitted a proposed budget of $300,000. Under zero-base budgeting, this would be subdivided into packages, perhaps as follows:

	Packages	Amount	Rating
1.	Base package: department's manager and secretary, adult job training	$150,000	6
2.	Summer youth sports program	70,000	5
3.	Winter youth sports program	40,000	4
4.	College scholarships	20,000	3
5.	Educational television	20,000	3

The manager's superior must combine this set of proposals with those submitted by the other department heads. This isn't easy, because the ordinal scales used by the various managers aren't comparable. Should the community relations manager's 3 be given the same priority as a 3 from the personnel manager?

Easy or not, sooner or later these proposals must be merged. In the end, higher management will probably have to reject some spending proposals; to do this it will have to identify certain proposals as less desirable than others. By definition, the proposals management rejects are those management classifies as least desirable. Zero-base budgeting merely systematizes the process by which this classification is made.

Zero-base budgeting is not a panacea. Managers are reluctant to admit that all of their activities are not of the highest priority. They are also likely to define activity packages broadly enough to attach pet projects to the coattails of other, more easily justified activities. These tendencies are difficult to control. Furthermore, the process may seem so mechanistic that managers may come to regard it as a meaningless exercise.

The concepts it is based on are worth implementing, however. Few activities are indivisible, and managers should be encouraged to evaluate the incremental costs and benefits of each subactivity they are responsible for. The use of ordinal rankings is also to be encouraged, particularly for discretionary programmed activities such as support of philanthropic and cultural activities.

Ordinal rankings can also be used for certain kinds of responsive activities, those for which the technological relationships between volume and response is weak. For example, a company can probably hire employees without a hiring

---

[3] See Peter A. Pyhrr, "Zero-Base Budgeting," *Harvard Business Review*, November–December 1970, pp. 111–21.

manager. The more people it needs to hire, the more awkward it becomes not to have someone in charge of the logistics of the hiring function. The benefits of having a hiring manager, however, are difficult to estimate in dollars. A possible solution is to rank this proposal with others on an ordinal scale.

Summary

Budgeting is a form of decision making. It has many purposes—to force managers to consider alternatives, to reinforce their motivation to work toward the organization's goals, to identify emerging problems and opportunities, to coordinate the organization's activities, and to produce a set of documents that will guide managers and serve as a benchmark for later control reporting.

We have tried to convey a feeling for the complexity and dynamism of the budgeting process. Budget preparation starts at the top, with the formulation of broad statements of policy and the establishment of the basic framework. The next step is taken at the grass-roots level, as local managers work on their marketing plans, translate these into production plans, and back them up with proposals for capital investment. These plans are reviewed, revised, and consolidated as they move up the organizational ladder toward final top management approval. They all come together eventually in a series of profit plans and cash budgets that are both feasible and acceptable to top management.

As this would imply, budgeting is a responsibility of line management; the controller or budget director administers the system and provides useful advice and assistance. When finally completed, the budget becomes a managerial commitment and a benchmark against which future performance can be measured.

Independent study problem (solution in Appendix B)

1. **Profit planning and cash budgeting.** The Darnell Company is organized in three divisions, each with a division manager, a small office staff, and its own sales force. The various divisions sell different kinds of products and deal with different groups of customers.

   The company's budget director has received the following proposals and estimates for next year from the division managers:

	Division A	Division B	Division C
Divisional marketing costs amounting to	$ 150	$ 500	$ 300
Will produce revenues of	1,000	3,000	2,100
And cost of goods sold of	650	1,650	1,260
Administrative expenses to support these activities will total	150	300	200
Accounts receivable will increase by	10	200	50
Inventories will exceed this year's ending balance by	50	100	50
Accounts payable will increase by	15	50	80

The expenses of the company's central management are tentatively budgeted at $400 for the year, to be paid in cash. Cash purchases of equipment amounting to $130 and cash dividends of $350 are also proposed. Of the equipment purchases, $60 is to replace existing equipment and $70 is for expansion. The expansion proposals, which management has approved in principle, will have no effect on next year's income statement.

Depreciation is included in the administrative expense figures above as follows: central management, $10; division A, $5; division B, $15; division C, $20.

Required:

a. Prepare a tentative profit plan and cash budget for next year, on the assumption that all of these proposals are approved.

b. The company will start next year with a cash balance of $290 and an unused line of bank credit of $100. The minimum cash balance is 5 percent of sales. Is the tentative plan feasible?

Exercises and problems

2. **Cash budgeting; constraints.**   The management of Salisbury Products Company at the beginning of 19x1 anticipated (1) a decrease in sales as compared with 19x0 because of production time lost in converting to new products, and (2) a considerably smaller profit margin due to higher material and labor costs. You have the following forecasts:

Change in accounts receivable in 19x1	$ 50,000 decrease
Change in accounts payable in 19x1	10,000 decrease
Change in inventories in 19x1	15,000 decrease
Sales revenues ($200,000 less than in 19x0)	2,000,000
Additions to plant and equipment (gross)	150,000
Depreciation, 19x1	110,000
Income before taxes, 19x1	100,000
Income tax expense, 19x1 (payable in 19x2) ...	40,000
Dividend payments (at 19x0 rates)	45,000

The cash balance on January 1, 19x1 was $54,000, about $25,000 less than management felt was necessary to ensure prompt payment of bills and maintain the company's credit rating. The accrued tax liability on January 1, 19x1, arising from 19x0 taxable income, amounted to $93,000. The company had no bank loans outstanding.

Required:

a. Assuming that any balance sheet items not listed above would be unchanged, prepare a schedule of forecasted cash receipts and cash disbursements for 19x1 and determine the expected cash balance on December 31, 19x1.

b. What action would you expect management to take when it sees the cash flow estimates for the year?

3. **Cash budgeting exercises: Multiple choice.**   Make the calculations required in each of the following exercises.

1. Walsh, Inc., is preparing its cash budget for the month of November. The following information is available concerning its inventories:

Inventories at beginning of November	$180,000
Estimated cost of goods sold in November	900,000
Estimated inventories at end of November	160,000
Estimated payments in November for purchases prior to November ...	210,000
Estimated payments in November for purchases in November	80%

What are the estimated cash disbursements for inventories in November?

a. $720,000   b. $914,000   c. $930,000   d. $1,042,000

2. The Fresh Company is preparing its cash budget for the month of May. The following information is available concerning its accounts receivable:

Estimated credit sales in May	$200,000
Actual credit sales in April	150,000
Estimated collections in May:	
For credit sales in May	20%
For credit sales in April	70%
For credit sales prior to April	$ 12,000
Estimated write-offs in May for	
uncollectible accounts from credit sales	8,000
Estimated provision for bad debts in	
May for credit sales in May	7,000

What are the estimated cash receipts from accounts receivable collections in May?

a. $142,000   b. $149,000   c. $150,000   d. $157,000

3. Serven Corporation has estimated its activity for June, 19x1. Selected data from these estimates are as follows:

Gross sales revenue	$700,000
Gross margin (based on gross sales)	30%
Increase in trade accounts receivable	
during month (at invoice prices, before	
write-offs of uncollectible accounts)	$ 20,000
Change in accounts payable during month	0
Increase in inventory during month	10,000

Total selling, general and administrative expense (SG&A) is $71,000 a month plus 15 percent of gross sales.

Serven Corporation classifies deductions for uncollectible accounts as variable selling expenses instead of as a determinant of net sales. The variable SG&A figure cited in the preceding paragraph includes a deduction for uncollectible accounts amounting to 1 percent of gross sales.

Depreciation expense of $40,000 a month is included in fixed SG&A.

On the basis of the above data, what are the estimated cash disbursements for operations in June?

a. $619,000   b. $626,000   c. $629,000   d. $636,000

4. Davis Company has budgeted its activity for April. Selected data from estimated amounts are as follows:

Net income	$120,000
Increase in gross amount of trade accounts	
receivable during month	35,000
Uncollectible accounts written off during month	0
Decrease in accounts payable during month	25,000
Depreciation expense	65,000
Provision for income taxes during month	80,000
Income taxes paid during month	0
Provision for doubtful accounts receivable	
during month	45,000

On the basis of the above data, Davis has budgeted a cash increase for the month in the amount of

a. $90,000   b. $195,000   c. $250,000   d. $300,000

(AICPA, adapted)

4. **Profit planning; review criteria.**   Canyon, Inc. operates two stores that sell and install automobile seat covers and a few automotive supplies such as upholstery cleaner and auto washing compounds. The company's president has heard that budgetary planning is a good thing and has decided that a profit plan should be prepared for the coming year. The managers of the two stores have submitted the following tentative budgets:

	Downtown Store	Suburban Store
Sales revenue:		
Seat covers	$400,000	$720,000
Auto supplies	72,000	160,000
Total	472,000	880,000
Store expenses:		
Supervisory and clerical salaries	47,200	47,600
Installers' wages	40,800	80,000
Store clerks' wages	18,400	18,800
Rent	38,400	35,200
Utilities	6,000	8,400
Other	2,800	5,200
Total	$153,600	$195,200

During the coming year, the purchase cost of seat covers is expected to average 55 percent of selling prices, while the selling prices of auto supplies will be about twice their purchase cost. The president has prepared a tentative head office budget for the coming year:

Executive salaries	$100,000
Clerical salaries	48,000
Advertising	40,000
Rent	24,000
Office supplies	4,000
Utilities	4,800
Legal and consultants' fees	6,800
Other	2,000
Total	$229,600

Required:

a. Assemble these data into a tentative profit plan for the coming year. Use a profit contribution format.
b. What problems do you think the president and the store managers encountered in preparing their tentative sales and expense plans? What were their principal sources of information?
c. What criteria would you use in reviewing these proposals?
d. Prepare a revised profit plan, using additional data that your instructor will provide.

5. **Monthly budget schedules.**   The Grumball Company sells merchandise on credit. You have the following data:

1. Budgeted gross sales (at list prices) for the first quarter of the coming year are:

January	$260,000
February	243,000
March	293,000

2. Customers are required to pay for their purchases within 30 days, and the Grumball Company offers a 2 percent cash discount from list price if payment is made within 10 days.

3. Past experience indicates that customers' accounts are settled according to the following timetable:

Month of sale	65%
Next month	33
Third month	1

   The remaining 1 percent eventually prove uncollectible.

4. Accounts receivable on January 1 are expected to amount to $130,000. Of this amount, $105,000 will have arisen from December sales, $6,000 from November sales, and $19,000 from sales made prior to November. No accounts have been written off as uncollectible so far this year, but a number of the accounts now on the books are doubtful. Management sees no reason to change its estimate of the average rate of customer defaults.

5. Of the customer accounts settled in any month, 90 percent are settled within the discount period and the customers take the discount.

6. The cost of goods sold is budgeted at 60 percent of gross sales. Sales commissions amount to 3 percent of gross sales. Other operating expenses will amount to $60,000 a month, including $5,000 a month for depreciation. Sales commissions are paid the month following the month they are earned. Cash payments arising from other operating expenses are paid 70 percent immediately and the remainder in the following month.

7. Budgeted purchases of merchandise for the three months are $150,000, $175,000, and $160,000, respectively. Purchases are paid for 30 days after the date of purchase.

8. Accounts, sales commissions, and wages payable on January 1 are expected to be as follows:

Accounts payable for merchandise	$139,500
Sales commissions payable	9,000
Other accounts and wages payable	16,500

9. The capital budget calls for the purchase of equipment in February for $100,000. Payment is to be made in March, with $60,000 of this amount to be covered by new bank borrowing at that time.

10. A $50,000 cash dividend is to be paid in January.

11. Income taxes are accrued monthly at 40 percent of pretax income. The only tax payment to be made in this three-month period is a payment of $40,000 in January.

Required:

a. Prepare a schedule of revenues and expenses for each of the three months.

b. Prepare a schedule of cash flows for each of the three months, with a line for the cumulative effect on the cash balance.

6. **Budgeting discretionary expenditures.** Sportsgear, Inc., is a small, growing manufacturer of sporting goods. Its product line is relatively narrow, centering on skates, skis, and related equipment. It has national distribution, with outlets located in most of the main winter sports centers and nearby urban centers.

   After examining all the feasible alternatives, Sportsgear's management has decided on a set of marketing, production, and administrative plans for next year that meet feasibility and profitability tests. These call for a significant increase in marketing expenditures to maintain the present 20 percent annual growth rate in sales, bringing sales volume up to $5 million next year.

The budget director has given management the following summary of the anticipated operating cash flows implicit in these tentative plans for next year:

Maximum net cash flow .....   +$580,000
Expected net cash flow ......   + 400,000
Minimum net cash flow ......   + 180,000

You have the following additional information:

1. Some additional seasonal financing will be available for seasonal needs next year; otherwise, all expenditures must be financed from the company's cash flows.
2. The cash dividend to the company's shareholders has totaled $100,000 in each of the last three years. Earnings have increased each year, so the dividend payout percentage has been falling. Management would like to increase the cash dividend to $140,000 next year, to bring the payout ratio up to 40 percent.
3. The corporate relations department has proposed that the company engage in three new activities that have not yet been included in the budget for next year:

Summer street recreation program for children in Sportswear's
  headquarters city $100,000
Grant to the local public television station to support local telecasts
  in March and April of figure skating championships   80,000
Grant to support student scholarships at a graduate business
  school at which the company recruits actively   20,000

4. Capital expenditure proposals received from various departments:

New extruding machine to permit manufacture
  of components now purchased outside .... $ 70,000
Replacements for various factory machines   130,000
Replacements of office equipment   10,000

5. Depreciation for next year is expected to total $30,000 on buildings and $90,000 for equipment.
6. The proposed budget for replacement of factory machines consists of eight specific proposals adding up to $110,000 plus a requested appropriation of $20,000 to cover small requests factory management can't anticipate now. Six of the specific proposals carry internal rate of return estimates exceeding the company's capital expenditure hurdle rate; the other two are listed as urgent and nonpostponable.
7. The proposed budget for office equipment replacements consists of five specific proposals, one of which carries an internal rate of return estimate, and a $2,000 provision for minor items.
8. Management will meet next week to adopt the budget for next year, and needs to decide how many of the expenditures listed above are to be included in the budget. The budget director has time to talk to the various executives responsible for these proposals, and even to get further written justification for each, but no one will be able to gather any data not already presented in support of the individual proposals.

Required:

a.   What is the maximum total amount of discretionary expenditures you would recommend including in next year's budget? Why did you choose this amount?

b. Calculate the amount by which the discretionary proposals exceed the maximum amount you specified in your answer to (a).

c. Prepare a tentative list of the expenditures you would recommend, giving your reasons for recommending each of these instead of the proposals you do not recommend. (Note: there is no "right" answer to this question; the acceptability of your recommendation will depend on your ability to support it with reasoned arguments.)

7. **Reviewing an operating budget proposal.** Frank Thomas is reviewing the tentative operating budgets his department heads have just submitted. Mr. Thomas is the administrative vice president of a food-processing company, a job he has held for the last three years.

Mr. Thomas has found it difficult to deal intelligently with his subordinates' annual budget proposals. Last year was a good one for the company and he felt little pressure to come in with a low budget proposal. He made few changes in his subordinates' proposals, merely endorsing most of them and including them in the divisional budget proposal submitted to the budget director. The year before, the heat was on, and he cut many of the proposals back sharply. The most persuasive and persistent department heads were cut back less than the others, however, and this made Mr. Thomas uneasy.

A particularly difficult budget to deal with is the budget for the personnel department. Jean Carlisle, the personnel manager, has requested a 23 percent increase over the budget for this year. About a fifth of this increase is to pay higher salaries and cover increased prices of supplies and other cost elements; the rest is to pay the salaries and expenses of a new professional development office, including the first session of a proposed new in-house executive development seminar to be taught by outside consultants. Ms. Carlisle is convinced that the company's management development efforts have been uneven and uncoordinated, but neither she nor anyone on her staff has been able to find time to do the job right.

In addition to management development, the personnel department is responsible for a number of activities, mainly recruiting and hiring new employees; maintaining personnel records; administering an annual performance review program; maintaining records of the company's antidiscrimination program; maintaining a personal skills inventory and suggesting candidates for promotion; administering the company's employee benefits program; supervising the job rating and salary administration program; operating a grievance procedure; and supervising an on-the-job training program for office personnel. This year's budget and the proposal for next year are as follows:

	This Year	Proposed, Next Year
Employees	20	23
Salaries	$325,000	$382,000
Employee benefits	71,500	86,000
Consultants and contractors	2,900	41,100
Travel	17,800	18,500
Computer	23,700	24,500
Advertising	14,200	14,900
Rent	36,000	36,000
Heat, light, and power	5,300	6,100
Postage and supplies	8,900	12,800
Other	2,100	2,500
Total	$507,400	$624,400

Mr. Thomas and Ms. Carlisle have often discussed the need for a better approach to management development and he wants to support the proposal for a professional development office. All of the other departments in Mr. Thomas's division are proposing increased spending, however, ranging from a low of 10 percent to a high of 20 percent. Mr. Thomas knows that he will never be able to get the top management budget committee to approve a 15 percent increase in his division's budget, no matter how eloquent he is or how convincing his case. Therefore, if personnel gets 23 percent, some other departments in the division will probably get little or nothing.

Mr. Thomas has asked you to pull together the budget proposals from all of the administrative departments and present them in a format that will help him make reasoned budgeting decisions. You intend to meet separately with each department head and ask for more information. The department heads must file the additional information or revised budget proposals a week from today.

Required:

You are now gathering your papers for your scheduled meeting with Ms. Carlisle 30 minutes from now. What further information could you reasonably ask her (and the others) to provide by next week's deadline? How would Mr. Thomas use this information?

8. **Revising a proposed operating budget.** The PDQ Company manufactures a line of high-quality office furniture which it sells to dealers in the northeast. Its sales force is divided into two divisions, each headed by a division manager. The preliminary profit plan for next year shows the following (in thousands of dollars):

	Atlantic	New England	Total
Sales	$900	$1,200	$2,100
Expenses:			
Variable cost of goods sold	540	660	1,200
Sales commissions (5 percent of sales)	45	60	105
Fixed expenses:			
Manufacturing	108	132	240
Marketing	71	106	177
Administration	36	42	78
Head office	30	40	70
Total expenses	830	1,040	1,870
Income before taxes	70	160	230
Income taxes at 50 percent	35	80	115
Net income	$ 35	$ 80	$ 115

You have the following additional information on these figures:

1. All products are manufactured in a single factory and product costs are calculated on a variable costing basis.
2. Fixed factory overhead costs are divided between the divisions in proportion to the cost of goods sold.
3. Division marketing and administrative expenses are completely traceable to the individual divisions.
4. Head office expenses are divided between the divisions in proportion to sales.
5. The company's factory has ample capacity to increase production by 40 percent without increasing the variable costing rate.

Top management is not satisfied with this proposal. Although economic conditions next year are expected to be considerably better than this year, the proposed budget shows virtually no change from this year's budget.

Top management has told the manager of the Atlantic Division that the division's marketing expenses must be reduced by $4,000 and administrative expenses reduced by $6,000 unless the division can come up with a better proposal. These reductions would not affect sales next year but might make future marketing more difficult.

As a result of this prodding, the manager of the Atlantic Division has proposed that sales promotion in this region be increased materially by adding a merchandising manager and two more sales representatives to the staff and by additional advertising. The annual fixed cost of these additional efforts would amount to $80,000. Sales would increase 20 percent if this were done, with no change in selling prices and no change in the product mix. If this proposal is accepted, the order to cut $10,000 out of the current expense budget will be rescinded.

The manager of the New England Division believes that physical sales volume can be increased by 15 percent if prices are reduced selectively to large customers who are particularly sensitive to price. List prices would be unchanged, but the average price realized in the division would be about 5 percent less than in the initial budget proposal. The product mix would not be affected, and no additional marketing or administrative expenses would be necessary. In fact, the manager has agreed to reduce the proposed divisional marketing expenses by $4,000, whether the price reductions are approved or not.

Executives in the head office have agreed to reduce their proposed operating expenditures by 5 percent. The factory manager has convinced top management that no further reduction in factory fixed costs is possible.

Required:

a. Recast the original budget proposals in a profit contribution format.
b. Calculate the anticipated profit contribution for each division if its revised proposal is accepted. Which of these proposals would you endorse?
c. Prepare a revised profit plan, in a profit contribution format, reflecting your answer to (b).

9. **Revising proposed plan to meet objectives.** The Barr Food Manufacturing Company is a medium sized publicly held corporation, producing a variety of consumer food and specialty products. Current year data were prepared as shown below for the salad dressing product line using five months of actual expenses and a seven-month projection. These data were prepared for a preliminary 19x9 budget meeting between the Specialty Products Division president, marketing vice president, production vice president, and the controller. The current year projection was accepted as being accurate but it was agreed that the projected income was not at a satisfactory level.

Barr Food Manufacturing Company
Projected Income Statement
For the Year Ended December 31, 19x8
(five months actual; seven months projected)
($000)

Volume in gallons	5,000
Gross sales	$30,000
Freights, allowances, discounts	3,000
Net sales	27,000
Less manufacturing costs:	
Variable.....................	13,500
Depreciation	700
Other fixed	2,100
Total manufacturing costs......	16,300
Gross profit....................	10,700
Less expenses:	
Marketing	4,000
Brokerage	1,650
General and administrative	2,100
Research and development	500
Total expenses	8,250
Income before taxes	$ 2,450

David Barr, the division president stated he wanted, at a minimum, a 15 percent increase in gross sales dollars and not less than 10 percent before-tax profit for 19x9. He also stated that he would be responsible for a $200,000 reduction in the general and administrative expenses to help achieve the profit goal.

Both the vice president-marketing and the vice president-production felt that the president's objectives would be difficult to achieve. However they offered the following suggestions to reach the objectives:

1. Sales volume—The current share of the salad dressing market is 15 percent and the total salad dressing market is expected to grow 5 percent for 19x9. Barr's current market share can be maintained by a marketing expenditure of $4.2 million. The two vice presidents estimated that the market share could be increased by additional expenditures for advertising and sales promotion. For each additional expenditure of $525,000 the market share can be raised by 1 percentage point until the market share reaches 17 percent. To get further market penetration beyond that, an additional $875,000 must be spent for each percentage point until the market share reaches 20 percent. Any advertising and promotion expenditures beyond this level are not likely to increase the market share to more than 20 percent.
2. Selling price—The selling price will remain at $6 per gallon. The selling price is very closely related to the costs of the ingredients, which are not expected to change in 19x9 from the costs experienced in 19x8.
3. Variable manufacturing costs—Variable manufacturing costs are projected at 50 percent of the net sales dollar (gross sales less freight, allowances, and discounts).
4. Depreciation—A projected increase in equipment will increase depreciation by $25,000 over the 19x8 projection.
5. Other fixed manufacturing costs—An increase of $100,000 is planned for 19x9.

6. Freight, allowances and discounts—The current rate of 10 percent of gross sales dollars is expected to continue in 19x9.
7. Brokerage expense—A rate of 5 percent of gross sales dollars is projected for 19x9.
8. General and administrative expense—A $200,000 decrease in general and administrative expense from the 19x8 forecast is projected; this is consistent with the president's commitment.
9. Research and development expense—A 5 percent increase from the absolute dollars in the 19x8 forecast will be necessary to meet divisional research targets.

Required:

a. The controller must put together a preliminary profit plan from the estimates given. Can the president's objectives be achieved? If so, present the profit plan which best achieves them. If not, present the profit plan which most nearly meets the president's objectives.
b. What is the advantage of having the president establish objectives such as those presented here? How should these objectives be determined? Does this procedure create any problems management must be prepared to deal with? (CMA, adapted)

10. **Budgeting in nonprofit organization; contingency budget.** DeMars College has asked your help in developing its budget for the coming academic year. You are supplied with the following data for the current year for the lower (freshman–sophomore) and upper (junior–senior) divisions:

	Lower	Upper
Average number of students per class	25	20
Average salary of faculty member	$15,000	$18,000
Average number of credit hours carried each year by each student	33	30
Enrollment (including scholarship students)	2,500	1,800
Average faculty teaching load in credit hours a year	20	18

Lower-division enrollment in the coming year is expected to increase by 10 percent, while the upper division's enrollment is expected to remain at the current year's level. Faculty salaries will be increased by a standard 5 percent, and additional merit increases to be awarded to individual faculty members will be $90,750 for the lower division and $85,000 for the upper division. Additional faculty can be hired as needed, at individual salaries of $15,750 in the lower division and $18,900 in the upper division. A small number of part-time faculty are available at the same equivalent annual salaries.

The current budget is $410,000 for operation and maintenance of plant and equipment; this includes $290,000 for salaries and wages. Experience of the past three months suggests that the current budget is realistic, but that expected increases for the coming year are 5 percent in salaries and wages and $9,000 in other expenditures for operation and maintenance of plant and equipment.

Other budget proposals for the coming year are as follows:

Administrative and general	$440,000
Library	160,000
Health and recreation	75,000
Athletics	320,000
Insurance and retirement	365,000
Interest	48,000
Capital outlay	300,000

The college expects to award 25 tuition-free scholarships to lower division students and 15 to upper division students. Tuition is $46 per credit hour and no other fees are charged.

The college has a small unrestricted endowment which has been invested in securities which now have a market value of approximately $4 million. In addition, commercial bank account balances total $50,000, but this amount is necessary to support the college's normal operations.

Budgeted revenues for the coming year from sources other than tuition are as follows:

From endowment $450,000
From auxiliary services   235,000
From athletics   280,000

The college's only other source of funds is an annual support campaign undertaken during the spring. From past experience, DeMars' fund-raising committee expects that this campaign will bring in contributions of between $350,000 and $400,000.

Required:

a. Prepare a schedule calculating (1) the anticipated enrollment, (2) the total credit hours to be carried by students, and (3) the number of faculty members needed for each division.

b. Calculate tuition revenues and faculty salaries for each division and for the school as a whole. Combine these with estimates of other revenues, other expenses, and capital outlays to form a tentative budget proposal for the coming year. Indicate how much money will have to be raised during the annual support campaign to cover all expenditures if this budget proposal is approved.

c. In what ways should the structure of the available budget information be changed to facilitate periodic planning?

d. The college's president is concerned about the effect on the college's finances if enrollments fall below the budgeted levels after all staff appointments for next year have been made. Prepare an alternative budget on the basis of an assumed 6 percent reduction in enrollment below the budgeted level in each division. Assume contributions of $350,000 from the spring support campaign. The number of scholarships would not be reduced. In what ways would you use this additional information? What other analyses would you want to carry out? What action might Demars' administration take to allow for this contingency?

(AICPA, adapted)

Case 8–1: The Clearville Store (preparing a budget proposal)

"We're having a great year," Marty Ormond said, "and they're going to expect even more from us next year. Let's see what kind of budget proposal we can come up with."

Mr. Ormond is manager of Danton Company's Clearville store. He made the statement quoted above as he and his department heads started to prepare budget proposals for next year. He began by collecting the following estimates of the results for the current year:

Revenues:		
Men's department	$2,100,000	
Women's department	3,150,000	$5,250,000
Cost of merchandise sold:		
Men's department	1,400,000	
Women's department	1,800,000	3,200,000
Gross margin		2,050,000
Operating expense:		
Executive and office salaries:		
Men's department	80,000	
Women's department	90,000	
Executive offices	250,000	
Floor staff salaries and wages:		
Men's department	400,000	
Women's department	550,000	
Rent	200,000	
Utilities	100,000	
Depreciation	40,000	
Charitable contributions	50,000	
Supplies, maintenance, and other	105,000	1,865,000
Store income contribution		$ 185,000

"We took the head office's economic forecasts for next year, analyzed each of the markets we serve, and considered the changes our competitors have recently made," Mr. Ormond remarked. "That analysis tells us that our revenues should be up 10 percent in the men's department and 8 percent in the women's department. Physical volume will increase by less than that, though, because selling prices will be up about 5 percent in both departments. The unit cost of the goods we sell will also go up by about 5 percent. Those forecasts should be pretty accurate unless economic conditions change a lot.

"We should be able to handle that volume of business with our present personnel but we'll have to increase all salaries by about 9 percent if we want to keep our good people. The escalator clause in the lease on our building will increase the rent by $30,000 next year, but equipment rentals will hold steady. Utility rates are up sharply, too, and we'd better budget a 25 percent increase on that line.

"We get more and more appeals for funds every year, but I guess we can hold charitable contributions at this year's level for another year. That's too bad, because those contributions are good public relations. Depreciation will be down about $2,000 unless we buy some new equipment or store fixtures. Supplies, maintenance, and other expenses are half fixed and half variable with sales revenues. I guess both the fixed portion and the variable rate will be about 10 percent higher next year."

"Okay, I'll work up a profit forecast on the basis of those assumptions," said Melanie Stephens, the store's controller, "but the head office won't like it. Our competitors in Clearville have been growing faster than we have, and their operating expense ratios are lower than ours. The corporate controller told me last week we ought to be able to get our expense ratio down to 34 percent next year and even lower after that."[1]

"I suppose we can cut $10,000 out of our charities budget if we have to," Mr. Ormond replied. "We can't give up the Little League or cut back on the United Way and other local charities, but instead of matching our employees' contributions to other charities in full we could reduce our matching grants to 50 percent. That

---

[1] The operating expense ratio is calculated by dividing total sales revenue into the total of all store expense except the cost of merchandise sold.

would save about $8,000. And we could discontinue that $2,000 student exchange fellowship."

"But, Marty, we always get good newspaper coverage of the student exchange fellowship. I think that $2,000 is well spent. Besides, it's not enough of a cut to satisfy the head office. I'd rather work on the salaries—that's where the big money is. Why don't we tell John and Alice they'll have to reduce their floor staffs by 5 percent?"

John Hadden is the manager of the men's department; Alice Brown is the manager of the women's department in the store. John agreed with the 5 percent cut in his floor staff, but asked that it be deferred until midyear when one of his salesmen will reach retirement age. "I don't want to force him out that close to retirement," Mr. Hadden said. "He's been with us too long. I'm still not sure I can do without a replacement, but I'll give it a try. If I find we're losing customers because we can't serve them promptly, I'll want to reverse the cut next year."

Ms. Brown is opposed to any cut in the size of the floor staff in her department. "We can barely handle the load now," she said, "and with the increase in volume we're forecasting I really ought to ask for a small increase in the budget to cover the seasonal peaks. I have a better idea, though. I'd like to convert one end of the first floor to a clothing boutique. We've been losing a lot of trade to those new small shops farther up the avenue and I think we're missing the boat. They put in a boutique over in our Belltown branch last year and it's been a huge success. If they can do it in Belltown we can do it here."

"I don't know how you can do that, Alice," Ms. Stephens replied. "We don't have an inch of space to spare in the store. Besides, don't those boutiques call for a lot of fancy fixtures? Can we afford them?"

"I thought of suggesting that John give up some of his floor space," Ms. Brown replied, "but I'd rather not fight that one through now. I've figured out that we can make the space available by getting rid of the bath shop and the budget handbags. The notions can go upstairs, where the bath shop is now. The new construction and relocations would only cost about $40,000. We'd also have to add to our floor staff. The boutique people can't be part-time in other departments. That's too bad, because both the bath shop and the budget handbags are covered on a part-time basis by floor clerks in other departments and we couldn't save much by closing them down. Even so, the boutique would be a profitable move."

To support her proposal, Ms. Brown presented the following estimates of next years results:

	Proposed New Boutique	Departments to Be Displaced	
		Bath Shop	Budget Handbags
Sales revenues	$400,000	$140,000	$40,000
Cost of merchandise sold	220,000	70,000	28,000
Floor staff salaries	38,000	8,000	—
Income contribution	$142,000	$ 62,000	$12,000

After their meeting with Ms. Brown, Mr. Ormond asked Ms. Stephens to assemble a tentative budget based on the figures she had. He also asked her whether any changes in the administrative budget could be worked out. "I was going to come to that, Marty," she replied. "Dave Cowan wants to hire an assistant to help him out in the personnel department. He says he's spending too much time interviewing potential new employees. The assistant would cost $18,000 a year. I've told him he should rely on the rest of us to do the interviewing for our own departments, but he feels a trained interviewer can do a better job of judging everything but technical competence, and we're already doing that part of the job anyway. If he has an assistant, he'll be able to handle grievances and the employee evaluation program better. He thinks we're lucky we haven't had any lawsuits from unhappy employees; a better evaluation program would put us in a much stronger position on that score."

"But Mel," Mr. Ormond broke in, "I want the administrative budget cut, not increased. How about your own department? You have six people working for you. Is there any way you can get by with five?"

"Not unless we contract our payroll preparation and customer billing, and we haven't found anyone yet who can save us money on those jobs. I could save maybe $2,000 by sending one of our rented copying machines back to the manufacturer, but you know how annoyed people get when they have to wait to use the copier."

"I just thought of something else, Mel. How much of the $40,000 Alice wants for her boutique would go into our operating expenses?"

"From the figures she gave me, I'd say about $30,000 would have to go through the capital budget. The other $10,000 would fall under maintenance, which we include in the other fixed expenses. We'd also take 10 percent of the $30,000 as depreciation the first year. She didn't include either of those expenses in her estimates. Adding the boutique wouldn't do anything to our utilities bills, but store supplies and other variable expenses probably would run 2 percent of gross sales. I'll have to figure out how much of the variable expenses we'd save if we cut out the bath shop and the budget handbag line."

"Those expense increases are going to hurt," Mr. Ormond observed. "Okay, let's see what it all comes to. I'd like you to put together a tentative budget proposal that will give us $100,000 more income before taxes than we expect to report this year. If the boutique proposal looks good, we'll put in for the $30,000 as a capital budget request."

a. Prepare an income forecast on the basis of Mr. Ormond's initial assumptions about the results to be achieved next year if no changes are made in staff levels, product lines, or discretionary spending.

b. What criteria appear to have been established to guide or constrain Mr. Ormond as he assembles his budget proposal?

c. Prepare a budget proposal that you would urge Mr. Ormond to submit to the head office. List the choices you had to make and how you made them. Does this proposal satisfy all of the criteria you identified in answer to (*b*)? If not, explain why you would urge Mr. Ormond to submit it.

d. On the basis of this exercise, state how a forecast differs from a plan. What is the relationship between a plan and a budget?

e. What changes, if any, would you make in the Danton Company's procedures for developing budget proposals for individual stores? Why would these changes be desirable? Do you regard them as major changes?

Case 8–2: Cycle World, Inc. (revising budget proposals)

Dave Burke, president of Cycle World, Inc., has been working on next year's budget for the past several weeks. The company, a retailer of bicycles and motorcycles, has managed to pay dividends to its shareholders ever since it was incorporated 10 years ago. At that time it moved into its present quarters, a one-story, concrete block structure with a showroom in front and a parts storeroom and repair shop in the rear. Sales volume increased rapidly at first, but the growth rate has been very small for the past five years. Rising operating costs have kept net income at about the same level it reached five years ago. The cash flow from operations has been about equal to the sum of net income and depreciation.

This pattern seems likely to continue for the next few years, and Mr. Burke sees little chance of increasing the size of the cash dividend on the company's stock, now running at $12,000 a year, unless he can come up with some new money-making ideas. "If we just go on as we have been going," he said, "we'll make about $14,000 a year. That will cover the dividend, but without much to spare."

A tentative profit budget drawn up on this basis is summarized in Table 1. Three items need some explanation: (1) product warranty reimbursements; (2) salaries; and (3) depreciation. Product warranty reimbursements are the amounts recovered from the manufacturers to cover Cycle World's costs of repairing defective merchandise under the terms of the manufacturers' warranties to purchasers of their bicycles and motorcycles. The amount shown for salaries includes Mr. Burke's $30,000 a year, together with the salaries of a salesperson and a bookkeeper-typist. Depreciation covers the building, various pieces of repair equipment, a typewriter, and storage cabinets for the company's inventories of spare parts. (A zero income tax rate has been assumed to eliminate unnecessary complexity in the case.)

Mr. Burke has always viewed budget preparation as an occasion for reviewing operations and discussing the firm's financial position with his banker. He has not hesitated to make major decisions at other times, as he did when he added a line of light motorcycles shortly after the firm moved into its present location, but many of the innovations he has made have emerged from his annual wrestling match with the budget.

Table 1 Preliminary projection of net income from present operations

Revenues:			
Product sales			$150,000
Repair services			100,000
Less: Uncollectible accounts			(3,000)
Net revenues			247,000
Expenses:			
Cost of goods sold		$ 85,000	
Mechanics' wages		43,000	
Salaries		55,000	
Repair supplies		20,000	
Heat and light		5,500	
Advertising	$10,000		
Less: Reimbursements from Sussex Bicycles	5,000	5,000	
Depreciation		6,000	
Property taxes		9,000	
Interest		2,000	
Other		6,000	
Total expenses		236,500	
Less: Product warranty reimbursements		3,500	
Total expenses			233,000
Net income			$ 14,000

"Maybe I'd better see what would happen if I took on that Ivrea line of motor scooters," he continued. "I've never sold scooters before, but I've been servicing the Ivreas for years and I know they're a good product. Dom Bosco (Ivrea's regional manager) has been pushing me to take on an exclusive dealership for this area. He started working on me two years ago, and his terms have gotten better and better. Now he says it's time to fish or cut bait; they'll set up their own sales branch if we don't accept this final offer."

Taking on the Ivrea line would require Cycle World to invest $20,000 in an inventory of scooters and repair parts. Adequate space is available to carry these added inventories. Ivrea would finance one half of this requirement with a permanent credit line of $10,000 and with no interest charge, but Cycle World would have to finance the remainder from other sources. Cycle World would also have to hire an additional full-time mechanic, who would be trained at Ivrea's expense before being transferred to the Cycle World payroll.

Judging from data provided by Mr. Bosco, combined with his own experience in introducing new lines in the past, and with some help from the bank, Mr. Burke has drawn up the forecasts for the Ivrea line summarized in Table 2. All of these figures represent increments to the figures arising from Cycle World's present business. According to Mr. Burke, the figures given for the second year seem likely to be representative of what later years would bring.

Table 2 Projection of income from introduction of Ivrea motor scooters

	First Year	Second Year
Revenues:		
Product sales	$50,000	$75,000
Repair services	11,000	13,000
Less: Uncollectible accounts	(1,000)	(1,500)
Net revenues	60,000	86,500
Expenses:		
Cost of goods sold	33,000	49,500
Mechanics' wages	14,500	14,800
Repair supplies	1,000	2,100
Advertising	4,000	4,000
Other	500	750
Total	53,000	71,150
Less: Product warranty reimbursements	1,500	2,000
Total expenses	51,500	69,150
Incremental Income	$ 8,500	$17,350

If the Ivrea line is taken on, Mr. Burke expects net accounts receivable (after deducting the allowance for uncollectible amounts) to go up by $30,000 during the first year and by another $20,000 in the second.

While he was thinking about this proposition, Mr. Burke had a call from the Sussex Bicycle Company, one of Cycle World's major suppliers. Sussex has been reimbursing Cycle World for the full cost of local advertising of Sussex bicycles, up to a $5,000 annual limit. Sussex has now offered to pay half of the cost of local advertising, with a $2,500 limit on its contribution. "We could cut this advertising out completely," Mr. Burke said, "but I know it has brought in quite a few customers in the past. Sussex is a good name, and it brings people into the store. We're selling about $30,000 worth of Sussex bikes now, at a 45 percent gross margin. I'd hate to take a chance of losing any of that."

Whether he takes on the Ivrea line or cuts back on Sussex advertising, Mr. Burke has a number of other projects under consideration for next year. For one thing, his chief mechanic has put in a request for $2,000 to buy several pieces of shop equipment to replace equipment which no longer functions reliably. The annual depreciation expense will go up by $100 if the replacements are made. If the replacements are not made, depreciation charges will remain at $6,000 a year, but other shop expenses will exceed the amounts in Table 1 by about $300 next year, mainly in increased equipment maintenance costs. During the past five years replacement expenditures have ranged from $1,000 to $2,000, averaging about $1,800 a year.

Another possible expenditure is $3,200 to modernize the showroom with better lighting, a new front window, and new interior decoration. This would be accounted for as a current expense.

A third proposal is to spend $1,900 to renovate the lavatory. It is difficult to keep clean, one of the units is permanently out of service, and the mechanics have been grumbling that they'd rather use the facilities in the gasoline station across the street. This expenditure would also be treated as an expense.

Finally, Mr. Burke is considering a request from the local Chamber of Commerce for $3,000 for the Chamber's municipal improvement fund, to be used to attract more business to stores and shops in the downtown area. Mr. Burke is one of the Chamber's directors this year. Cycle World itself is not located in the downtown area, but Mr. Burke is convinced that a decaying business center would eventually affect business in the outlying districts as well.

Cycle World has little access to capital other than the amounts it can generate by its own operations. When the business was incorporated 10 years ago, Mr. Burke and eight other people bought shares of stock in the new corporation. "I'm related to most of them in one way or another," Mr. Burke commented. "None of them has any extra money to invest, and they wouldn't give it to me if they did. We've paid their dividends regularly, but they all expected more than we've been able to cough up so far. I still own a controlling interest, but I'd sure get a lot of flak if I got the board to cut the dividend next year.

"The picture on borrowed money is a little brighter. We've got all the bank loans we can get on the basis of our present operations. I play golf with the president of the bank and he's really laid it on the line. I showed him our projections on the Ivrea line, though, and he and his chief loan officer have agreed to a new $20,000 term loan at 16 percent interest if we go through with the deal. But that's it; they won't go any farther." This loan would be made at the beginning of the year.

a. Prepare estimates of the incremental income and incremental cash flows associated with the Ivrea line for each of the first three years. Based on these figures, should Cycle World accept the Ivrea offer if enough funds can be found to finance it?

b. Prepare tentative schedules of cash flows for each of the next three years and a tentative income statement for next year, assuming that the Ivrea line is taken on and that all the requested expenditures are made this year. By what amounts are the company's cash resources inadequate to finance all the requested expenditures? (Ignore income taxes.)

c. List the major actions Mr. Burke might take to close the gap between anticipated receipts and anticipated disbursements. Choose the set of actions you would recommend and prepare a revised cash budget and profit plan reflecting these recommendations. Attach a brief explanation of the reasons for your recommendations.

Case 8–3: Verlies & Winst, N.V.* (testing for feasibility and profitability)

During the first nine months of 1976, Verlies & Winst, N.V. operated its only factory two shifts a day plus a good deal of overtime work, and expected to continue at this production rate through the end of the year. At this rate, it was unable to meet the growing demand for its products, and inventories of finished products had been reduced during 1976 to amounts that the management felt were inadequate in view of the company's reputation for delivering its products promptly on the dates promised.

To correct this situation and to satisfy customers' demands, the company's executives in November 1976 decided to consider the desirability of moving to three-shift operations. To provide data useful for this decision, Mr. J. C. Verlies, the company's controller, was to prepare a profit plan and cash budget for 1977.

* Copyright 1967, 1977 by l'Institut pour l'Etude des Méthodes de Direction de l'Entreprise (IMEDE), Lausanne, Switzerland. Reprinted by permission. The monetary amounts have been restated as dollar amounts.

The Verlies & Winst product line consisted of two items of unusual design, both invented by the company's president, Mr. H. L. Winst. One product was a desk calendar holder of unusual design called "Dagmat"; the other was a desk-size device in which to list frequently called telephone numbers, sold under the name "Telemat."

In addition to Mr. Winst, the company's management consisted of Mr. Verlies and two product managers, one for each of the two products. Because the company was small, Mr. Winst performed the duties of general sales manager and production manager, in addition to his functions as president.

Using an economic forecast supplied by the company's bank, together with reports of dealer sales and inventories gathered by the company's sales force, the two product managers gave Mr. Verlies the tentative budgets for 1977 shown in Table 1.

Table 1 Product managers' budget proposals for the year 1977

	Dagmat	Telemat
1977 sales (in units)	400,000	300,000
Increase over 1976	+ 100,000	+ 90,000
Price per unit (both years)	$ 1.00	$ 3.00
1977 production costs per unit:		
Material cost.............................	$ 0.25	$ 0.55
Labor cost	$ 0.15	$ 0.45
Machine-hours required	0.10	0.30
1977 product promotion expense	$ 50,000	$ 60,000
Increase over 1976	+$ 12,500	+$ 18,000
Increase in finished goods inventories required if sales remain at 1976 levels (units)	5,000	4,500
Additional increase in assets because of increased sales over 1976:		
Accounts receivable	+$ 20,000	+$ 54,000
Materials inventories	+$ 2,500	+$ 4,950
Finished goods inventories (units)	+ 5,000	+ 3,500
Work in process inventories	Neglibible	Negligible
Increase in accounts payable accompanying increased sales	+$ 2,500	+$ 4,950

Mr. Winst's estimates of maximum production capacity and "general factory costs" (all factory costs except materials, labor, and depreciation) were:

	Production Capacity (machine-hours)	General Factory Costs at Capacity Operating Rates
Two-shift operations	91,450	$ 90,000
Three-shift operations	122,900	118,000

These estimates included allowances for labor overtime and also provided for a normal amount of time lost due to machine breakdowns and other kinds of work interruptions. Factory personnel for the third shift could be obtained without difficulty, and new people required almost no training.

The increases in sales promotion expenditures in excess of 1976 levels would consist mostly of increases in local newspaper advertising and point-of-sale promotional displays. The projected increases in sales could not be obtained without these increased expenditures. No increase in the size of the sales force was anticipated.

Other estimates and budget proposals that were submitted to Mr. Verlies were:

General sales and administrative expenses (except depreciation)	$210,000
Depreciation:	
Factory and factory equipment	50,000
Office and sales facilities	25,000
Interest on long-term debt (maturing in 1985)..................	50,000
Dividends on common stock	30,000
Research and development expenditures	100,000
Equipment replacement expenditures.........................	90,000
Plant expansion expenditures (these additional facilities would not	
be completed in 1977)	300,000
Interest to be paid in 1977 on short-term bank loans was at a rate of	
8 percent on the balance of the bank loans outstanding at the end	
of 1976.	
Income taxes were computed at a rate of 47 percent of taxable income	
and were due in the first six months of the year following.	
Minimum cash balance	140,000

Research and development expenditures are charged to expense as incurred. Depreciation for 1977 would not be affected by replacement expenditure decisions for 1977. Taxable income and reported income before taxes are identical in this company.

Mr. Verlies estimated that working capital balances would be as follows on January 1, 1977:

Cash		$160,000
Accounts receivable		186,000
Inventories.................................		33,350
Total current assets		379,350
Less current liabilities:		
Bank loan payable........................	$30,000	
Accounts and interest payable	19,050	
Income taxes payable	54,000	103,050
Working capital.............................		$276,300

Mr. Verlies was convinced that the company would be unable to obtain any new long-term capital during 1977. Cash had to be paid for all assets and services purchased except that trade credit (i.e., accounts payable) was available to finance increases in raw materials inventories. In addition, bank credit was available up to 50 percent of the sum of the face amount of accounts receivable and the total cost of all inventories. (Finished goods were costed at their materials and labor costs only, general factory costs being considered an expense). Bank credit was available in units of $10,000. For budgeting purposes, it was assumed that any amounts borrowed during the year would be borrowed on July 1, 1977. Interest on bank loans in force during 1977 would be paid in cash during January, 1978.

a. Did the company have adequate production capacity to service the tentative sales budget? What criteria would you use to allocate productive capacity between the two product lines whenever total capacity is inadequate to meet all demands?

b. Prepare a *factory cost* and *production volume* plan for 1977 that would have been technically feasible. Factory capacity should be assigned to the products in such a way as to maximize company profits, subject to the following restrictions: (1) the sales of each product are to be at least as large as they were the preceding year; and (2) inventories of finished goods must be built up to the minimum established for the level of sales anticipated in your *revised* sales plan for 1977.

c. Prepare a tentative cash budget for 1977, reflecting your factory cost and production volume plan and all the other estimates and budget proposals listed above. Is this budget feasible? In case of a shortage of cash, how should management decide which expenditures to cut back?

d. Prepare a profit plan for the year that is both technically and financially feasible, and which meets the restrictions listed under (*b*) above. Would this plan be accepted automatically, or would management be likely to subject it to further tests?

9 Standard costs: Controlling direct labor and materials

Much of the discussion in the last eight chapters has related to managerial *planning*—that is, deciding how to use the organization's resources. We now turn our attention to *control,* the process of keeping an organization's behavior consistent with its objectives.

Control may be viewed as an 11-step process, as summarized in Exhibit 9–1. Management exercises control at every level in the organization. In this chapter we'll look at the control process at the bottom of the management hierarchy. We'll see what kinds of data the accountant can generate to help management monitor direct materials and direct labor costs in the factory.

Exhibit 9–1 Steps in the control process

1. Decide what to control.
2. Decide what purposes the control information is expected to serve.
3. Identify or assign responsibility for control.
4. Decide what measurements will be useful.
5. Set performance standards.
6. Measure results.
7. Compare results with performance standards.
8. Report these comparisons to the responsible executives.
9. Interpret deviations of results from standards.
10. Take responsive action, wherever appropriate.
11. Review the effects of these responsive actions.

Performance standards for direct labor and materials

Good control information is comparative. The idea is to direct management's attention to conditions that are not what they ought to be. This idea is embodied in the management principle known as *management by exception,* which states that management should devote its scarce time only to operations in which results depart significantly from established performance standards. Operations in which results are close to the performance standard are presumed to be under control.

A performance standard is a statement of the level of results management regards as appropriate under a specified set of circumstances. It may be stated as a rate per period of time, as a ratio of input to output (or output to input), or as a ratio of one input to another. (An *input* is any material or service used in a process. An *output* is any useful result of a process. Output is also referred to as the amount of *work done.*) Whatever the form, the standard can be either of two types, and we must choose one or the other:

1. Historical standards.
2. Fabricated standards.

Historical performance standards

Many cost reporting systems use historical performance standards—that is, control information consists of comparisons of actual costs with those of previous periods. This lets management see how rapidly costs are rising or falling. The accountant can analyze these data to find out how much of the change in cost is due to changes in such factors as materials prices and wage rates.

Historical performance standards have one main shortcoming. Comparisons with the costs of prior periods don't show whether costs are higher or lower than they ought to be. Performance may be better than in the past but still very bad—or worse than in the past but still very good.

Standard costs

The shortcomings of historical performance standards have led many companies to seek alternatives. For factory direct materials and direct labor costs, the most suitable performance standards are provided by *standard costs.* A standard cost is management's estimate, prepared in advance, of the costs of the inputs that should be necessary to obtain a specific material, product, or service. It takes three forms:

1. *Standard price.* The price that management estimates should be necessary to obtain a unit of material or an hour or labor services of a specific grade or quality. The standard price of labor time is known as a *standard labor rate.* The standard price of a unit of materials is a *standard materials price.*
2. *Standard operations cost.* The quantities of the various inputs that management estimates should be necessary to perform each production operation within the factory's capability, multiplied by their standard prices.
3. *Standard product cost.* The quantities of the various inputs that management estimates should be necessary to manufacture one unit of a particular product in production lots of a specified size, multiplied by their standard prices.

Variances from standard cost: The basic concept

Differences between actual and standard direct labor and materials costs are *spending variances.* For example, the difference between the actual cost of direct

Exhibit 9–2 The labor spending variance and its primary components

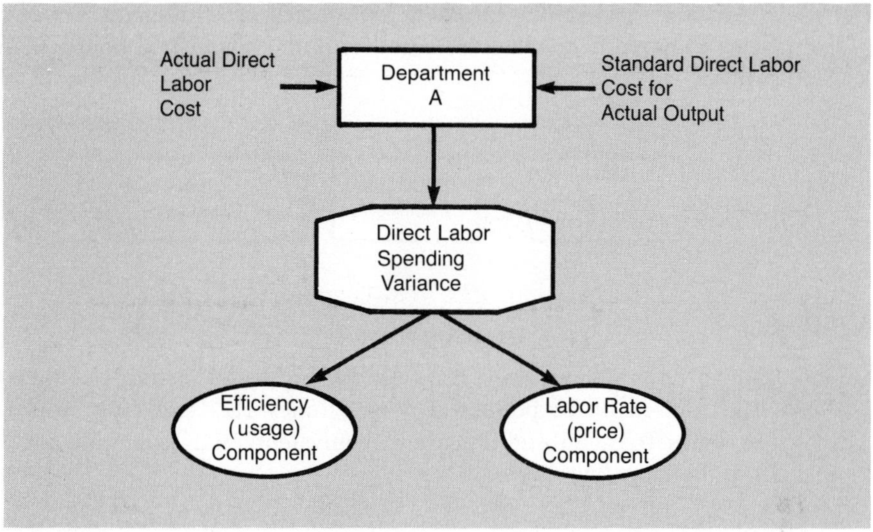

labor and the standard direct labor cost of the output it yields is the labor spending variance, shown in the center of Exhibit 9–2.

The accountants' main objective here is to identify the portion of the spending variance each manager is responsible for. They ordinarily begin by estimating how much of the variance is due to events which lead the company to use either more or fewer units of materials or labor than the standards for the work done call for (efficiency, usage, or quantity variances) and how much is due to events which affect the hourly labor rates of the company's employees or the prices it pays for materials (price or rate variances).

Calculating usage variances

Usage standards measure the level of physical *efficiency* the organization ought to be able to achieve—that is, they express standard relationships between the quantities of resources used and the quantities of the outputs derived from them. Differences between actual usage and standard usage—the usage variances—therefore reflect departures from standard efficiency. If the standards are appropriate under current conditions, the usage variances measure management's *effectiveness* in pursuing the goal of efficient operation. In the next few paragraphs we'll see how they can be measured, first in physical units and then in monetary terms.

Physical measures of usage variances.   Given enough data, we can always measure usage variances in physical units. For example, suppose that combining 1.2 pounds of material A with 0.3 hours of labor is expected to yield one unit of product Y. This relationship can be expressed in a formula:

$$\text{1.2 pounds A} + 0.3 \text{ labor hours} \rightarrow 1 \text{ unit Y}$$

Suppose further that on April 18, a batch of 10 units of Y was produced from 14 pounds of material A and required four labor hours. In schematic terms:

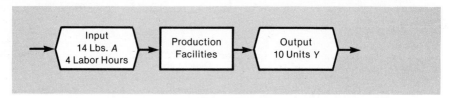

But 10 units of product Y can also be expressed in terms of their *standard input* content of 12 pounds of A (10 times 1.2) and three hours of labor (10 times 0.3). Substituting these equivalents and separating the materials from the labor, we have:

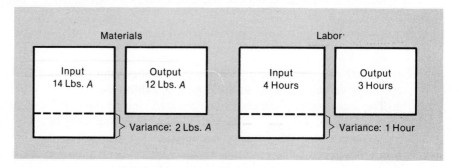

The usage variances are the differences between actual input quantities (14 pounds and 4 hours) and the standard input quantities for the work that has been done (12 pounds and 3 hours). In this example, the company used more materials (2 pounds) and more labor (1 hour) than the standards called for. These are called *unfavorable* variances. If the actual input quantities had been less than the standard usage for the actual output, we would refer to the differences as *favorable* variances.

Stating usage variances in dollars. Although usage variances represent physical quantities, they are usually measured in dollars. To get these dollar figures, the accountant multiplies the physical quantities by standard prices. If the standard labor rate is $8 an hour, the one-hour labor usage variance can be reported as an $8 variance, unfavorable.

Measuring price variances

Direct materials and direct labor spending variances also arise because actual purchase prices or actual wage rates differ from standard prices or wage rates.

Since the wage rate is the price of labor services, both of these can be referred to as price variances.

We generally calculate price variances by multiplying the actual input quantity by the difference between the actual input price and the standard input price. For example, our batch of product Y was produced by a factory employee who was paid $8.50 an hour to do the work. The standard wage rate was $8 an hour. The price variance for labor is called the *labor rate variance;* it amounted in this instance to 50 cents an hour for four hours, or $2 in total. Again, the variance is unfavorable, in that the company paid more than the standard allowed for.

Reconciling the variances

The method we used to subdivide the labor spending variance in our illustration is diagrammed in Exhibit 9–3. In this system the rate variance is determined by multiplying the actual labor input quantity by the difference between actual and standard wage rates; the usage variance is determined by multiplying the difference between actual and standard labor usage by the standard wage rate.

Exhibit 9–3 Subdividing the labor spending variance

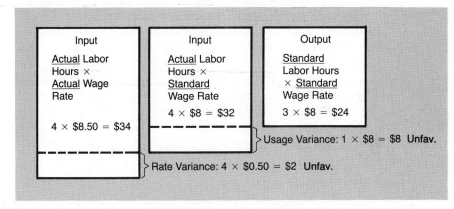

We could have subdivided the spending variance in other ways. For example, we could have measured the usage variance at the actual wage rate instead of at the standard wage rate:

$$\text{Labor usage variance} = (4 \text{ hours} - 3 \text{ hours}) \times \$8.50 = \$8.50$$

Measuring the usage variance in this way would have the advantage of giving management an up-to-date measure of the dollar effect of efficiency variations in the current period. It would have the disadvantage, however, of reducing the comparability of the usage variances in different periods. Last period, for example, the labor usage variance may have been $9.50; if we measure the usage variance each period at that period's actual prices, we won't know how much of the change from last period is due to changes in efficiency (usage) and how much is due to changes in wage rates.

Both components of the labor spending variance in our illustration were unfavorable—that is, they led to a cost that was higher than the standard cost of the work done. The following table should make it easy to distinguish between favorable and unfavorable variances:

	Unfavorable	Favorable
Usage variances	Actual input quantities greater than standard quantities required by work done	Actual input quantities smaller than standard quantities required by work done
Price (rate) variances	Actual input prices higher than standard prices	Actual input prices lower than standard prices

Usage variances for scorecard reports

In deciding which variances to report to a particular manager, we generally apply the *controllability criterion,* that managers should be assigned only those variances they are expected to control. The managers of production centers are expected to control usage variances; price variances are usually outside their jurisdiction and therefore are not reported to them.

The success of the production center manager's control efforts is not measured by how large a variance is recorded on any one job or operation. The real test is the center's overall efficiency during a period of time. To measure this, we must *cumulate* the production center's variances, to reflect the differences between the actual quantities of inputs used in the department and the department's output for a specified period, usually a week or a month.[1] To see how this might be done, let's look at one month's data for the forming department, a production center in the Galahad Company's factory.

Measuring input costs

The Galahad Company avoids reporting price variances to the managers of its production centers by measuring both input and output quantities at *standard* input prices. In 19x1 the company used a single standard labor rate of $8 an hour for all direct labor in the forming department. The department used only two kinds of direct materials during July, with standard prices of $7 and $2. The department was charged for the following direct labor and materials inputs in July, 19x1:

Material A: 4,800 pounds × $7 . . . . . . $33,600
Material B: 2,100 pounds × $2   4,200
    Total materials $37,800

Direct labor: 3,600 hours × $8 . . . . . . $28,800

---

[1] To simplify our terminology from here on, we shall refer to production centers as departments, reflecting an assumption that each department consists of one production center only. In practice, separate reports may be prepared for each production center in multicenter departments.

Measuring output

The output of any department during any period of time consists of the products is completes plus any increase (or minus any decrease) in the amount of work in process in the department during the period. These relationships are diagrammed in Exhibit 9–4. In this diagram the ending work in process is larger than the beginning work in process—therefore the *total* amount of work done (the output) is greater than the amount of work done on the jobs completed during the period. In calculating departmental efficiency, the department deserves to be given credit for producing increases in its work in process; these increases are part of the department's productive output. A decrease in departmental work in process, on the other hand, indicates that the number of units the department completed during the period overstates the amount of work the department actually accomplished.

Exhibit 9–4 Output, product completions, and work in process

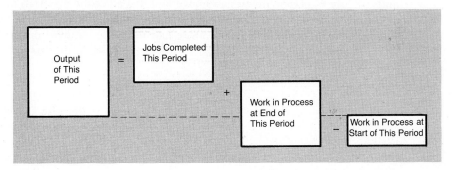

In standard costing calculations, all of the quantities in this diagram are measured by their standard costs—that is, the standard input quantities multiplied by their standard prices. The relationships among them can also be expressed in an equation:

Output = Standard cost of units completed
       + Standard cost of work in process at end of period
       − Standard cost of work in process at beginning of period

Galahad's forming department worked on only two products during July. It completed 900 units of product P and 2,000 units of product Q during the month and transferred them to the factory assembly department. The work in process consisted of 200 partly processed units of product P at the beginning of the month and 300 units of P on July 31. The standard forming department input quantities for these two products were:

1 pound of A + 0.5 hour of labor ⟶ 1 unit of P
2 pounds of A + 1 pound of B + 1.5 hours of labor ⟶ 1 unit of Q

Standard materials cost. The standard materials costs of the units completed during the month were as follows:

	Standard Materials Cost per Unit	Units Completed	Standard Materials Cost of Units Completed
Product P	1 × $7 = $ 7	900	$ 6,300
Product Q	2 × $7 = $14		
	1 × $2 = 2		
	$16	2,000	32,000
Total			$38,300

If the materials content of the work in process had been the same at the end of the month as at the beginning, the standard materials cost of the units completed would have been the standard materials cost of the month's output. Work in process increased, however, from 200 units of P on July 1 to 300 units on July 31. Upon investigation, we find that all of the materials necessary to complete these units had already been placed in production before the dates listed. A unit in process therefore had the same standard materials cost as a unit completed, and the standard costs of the work in process inventories were as follows:

	Number of Units of Product P	Standard Materials Cost per Unit	Standard Materials Cost of Work in Process
July 1	200	$7	$1,400
July 31	300	7	2,100
Increase in work in process			$ 700

The standard direct materials cost for the month therefore was as follows:

Standard materials cost of units completed	$38,300
Standard materials cost of increase in work in process	700
Total standard materials cost	$39,000

Standard labor cost. The calculation of standard labor cost is very similar to the calculation of standard materials cost. First we calculate the standard labor cost of the units completed during the month:

	Standard Labor Cost per Unit	Number of Units Completed	Standard Labor Cost of Units Completed
Product P	0.5 × $8 = $ 4	900	$ 3,600
Product Q	1.5 × $8 = 12	2,000	24,000
Total			$27,600

Upon investigation, we find that 40 percent of the labor operations had been performed in June on the units in process on July 1, and 60 percent of the work had been done on the units still in process on July 31. The standard costs of the work in process inventories therefore were as follows:

	Units of Product P	Standard Labor Cost per Unit	Standard Labor Cost of Work in Process
July 1	200	$4 × 40% = $1.60	$320
July 31	300	$4 × 60% = 2.40	720
Increase in work in process ..			$400

Calculating the usage variances

The standard direct materials cost and standard direct labor cost figures we just calculated are our measures of the forming department's _output_ for the month of July. When this information on ouput is combined with the input figures shown under the heading "Measuring input costs" above, calculating the usage variances is simple arithmetic: The $1,200 favorable materials usage

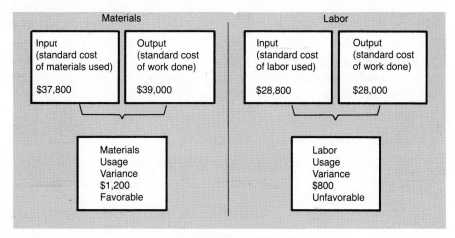

variance shows that the department used fewer materials than the standards called for. The $800 unfavorable labor usage variance means that the workers in the forming department turned out less production per hour than the standards prescribed.

The need for dollar variances

If production processes were all as simple as in this illustration, standard costing systems would be almost unnecessary. All usage variances could be stated in physical units, which often have a more direct meaning to the first-line supervisor. In the real world, however, each department is likely to use many different kinds of inputs, instead of just one, and to process many different products. The result is that statements of variances in physical terms become unwieldy, and some common denominator has to be found. The usual common denominator is the dollar (or franc or peso or pound or whatever monetary unit is in use).

This should not be thought of as a sacrifice of information, however. For one thing, the dollar totals are merely a convenient way of summarizing the underlying physical deviations from standard performance. Second, dollar variance information serves an important purpose in its own right, even when inputs and outputs are few in number. Expressing a variance in monetary terms gives management a measure of its relative importance, and a basis for deciding how much control effort is worthwhile.

Standard costing on the basic plan

An accounting system consists of a set of accounts, procedures, files, and reports, together with the concepts underlying them. When standard costs are included in this set, the system is said to be a *standard costing system*.

Standard costing systems differ from each other in many ways. Each one has its own distinguishing characteristics; each uses its own account structure to accumulate data. In this section we'll look at three aspects of a simple system we call a *basic plan* system:

1. Recording purchases of materials.
2. Using accounts to isolate usage variances.
3. Accounting for labor rate variances.

Recording materials purchases

The first characteristic of a basic plan system, and of some other types of systems as well, is that materials price variances are identified when the materials are purchased. The amounts entered in the materials inventory accounts are the actual quantities of goods received, multiplied by their standard purchase prices. Differences between the standard prices and the actual prices of the items bought are recorded in separate price variance accounts.

The Galahad Company, for example, uses one materials inventory account, entitled Materials and Parts, and one materials price variance account. During July, the company bought materials and parts from outside suppliers in a number of separate transactions. The total of the invoice prices was $35,000, less discounts of $1,500. The standard costs of these goods totaled $42,700, including provision for standard freight charges and discounts. Each invoice was recorded separately, of course, but we can summarize them all in a single entry:

(1a)

Materials and Parts	42,700	
Materials Price Variance		9,200
Accounts Payable		33,500

In other words, the asset was recorded at standard prices, the liability was recorded at net actual prices (after deducting the discounts allowable) and the difference was placed in the variance account.

The purchase price variance was not actually this large, however. The standard prices for the materials and parts included a provision for freight charges, but the actual purchase prices did not always cover freight charges. Separate freight charges on Galahad's July purchases amounted to $7,500. This amount was charged to the variance account because the amounts already charged to the inventory account contained a standard provision for these costs:

(1b)

Materials Price Variance 7,500
    Accounts Payable   7,500

Actual delivered cost, in other words, was $35,000 − $1,500 + $7,500 = $41,000. This was $1,700 less than the total standard cost of the materials purchased:

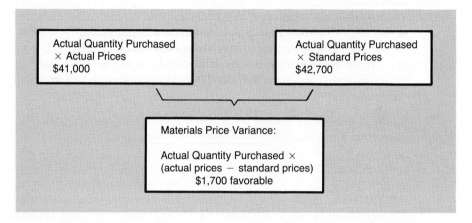

This same $1,700 variance appeared as a credit balance in the Materials Price Variance account after all the purchase-related transactions had been analyzed and recorded:

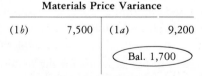

Materials Price Variance

(1b)	7,500	(1a)	9,200
		Bal. 1,700	

This conforms to a very simple pair of rules:

> **Favorable cost variances appear as credit balances.**
> **Unfavorable cost variances appear as debit balances.**

Calculating price variances at the time of purchase lets the accountant report them to management soon after they arise, not weeks or months later when the materials are finally used. It also permits savings in the cost of materials bookkeeping, in that all materials inventories are measured at standard prices which remain unchanged for a year or longer. Detailed inventory records can be maintained in physical units only; when dollar totals are desired, the physical quantities can be multiplied by standard prices.

Aggregate price variances, even when reported separately for each broad class of materials, ordinarily provide little information for the purchasing agent. Purchasing decisions center on the item, not on the class of materials, and the purchasing agents can identify the variances when they place orders. Total price variance information is useful mainly in cash and profit planning, and has few other applications.

Isolating the usage variance

A company's accountants can identify the departmental usage variances in a basic plan system by taking the following four steps:

1. Establish the departmental account structure.
2. Charge the input quantities the department uses to appropriate departmental accounts, measured at standard prices.
3. Credit completed output quantities to the accounts at standard costs.
4. Calculate and record the standard cost of end-of-period work-in-process inventories.

Step 1. Set up a separate account and enter the appropriate opening balance, if any, for each element of the work-in-process inventory; set up other accounts as necessary to record actual and standard input usage for each major cost element in each responsibility center. Many different combinations of accounts are feasible. To illustrate the process, we'll use a set that maximizes the visibility of the process, but we don't mean to imply that every basic plan uses the same account structure. To implement our approach, Galahad uses the following departmental accounts for direct materials and direct labor quantities:

Materials in Process—Forming
Direct Materials Used—Forming
Standard Direct Materials—Forming
Labor in Process—Forming
Direct Labor Used—Forming
Standard Direct Labor—Forming

Materials in Process—Assembly
Direct Materials Used—Assembly
Standard Direct Materials—Assembly
Labor in Process—Assembly
Direct Labor Used—Assembly
Standard Direct Labor—Assembly

Each department also has accounts for the materials and labor usage variances and a payroll cost summary account.

The forming department's work in process accounts had the following balances at the beginning of operations on July 1:

Materials in Process—Forming		Labor in Process—Forming	
Bal.	1,400	Bal.	320

These balances were the standard costs of the work that had already been done on the jobs that were in process at the start of operations on July 1, determined on the basis of a physical count taken at that time.

The other accounts had zero opening balances. In practice, they might be used to accumulate the effects of transactions for the entire year; we close them to zero balances at the end of each month to keep the illustration cleaner.

margin note: uncollability

Step 2.   Charge each responsibility center with the actual input quantities used, multiplied by standard input prices. This step is designed to implement the controllability criterion. For example, Galahad's forming department requisitioned several batches of materials during July. A clerk in the factory office multiplied each of these quantities by the standard price of that material. The resulting total, $37,800, was the standard cost of the materials actually used during the month. This amount was charged to the departmental usage account:

(2)

Direct Materials Used—Forming	37,800	
Materials and Parts		37,800

This entry identified the amounts for which the forming department was accountable and reduced the balance in the stockroom's inventory account. The records of individual materials inventory items were also updated at this time.

The Direct Materials Used account can be thought of as a temporary accumulation point for costs on their way to the Materials in Process account. At this point we know the actual quantity of materials used; we don't know the standard quantity. Accumulating direct materials costs in a separate account enables us to prepare a report comparing actual costs with standard costs without going back to the source documents. If we charged the Materials in Process account directly, we'd have to extract data on direct materials usage from some other source.

Labor costs in a basic plan system are charged to the departmental accounts in the same way—that is, these charges reflect the actual number of labor hours used, multiplied by standard wage rates. During July, the forming department was charged for 3,600 direct labor hours at $8 an hour, a total of $28,800. This amount was charged to the department's direct labor usage account:

(3)

Direct Labor Used—Forming	28,800	
Payroll Cost Summary—Forming		28,800

margin note: clearing acct

Payroll Cost Summary—Forming is a temporary account known as a clearing account, serving as a temporary proxy for a wages payable account. Its full purpose will become clear in a moment.

Step 3.   Credit each responsibility center with the standard cost of the products that have been finished and transferred out of the department. We calculated these standard costs earlier in this chapter:

	Number of Units Finished	Standard Materials Cost	Standard Labor Cost	Total
Product P	900	$ 6,300	$ 3,600	$ 9,900
Product Q	2,000	32,000	24,000	56,000
Total		$38,300	$27,600	$65,900

All of the units completed in July were transferred directly to the assembly department for use in production there. The entries recording these transfers are summarized in entry (4):

(4)

Direct Materials Used—Assembly	65,900	
Materials in Process—Forming		38,300
Labor in Process—Forming		27,600

The credit entries to the forming department accounts indicate that these goods are no longer in inventory in this department and the manager is no longer responsible for their costs. The charge to Direct Materials Used—Assembly records the assembly department manager's responsibility for controlling their use.[2]

Notice that the standard labor costs of the forming operation became part of the materials costs of the assembly department. The assembly department manager sees only the physical units, not the materials and labor from which they were made. The cost of forming labor is the responsibility of the forming department manager; all the assembly manager can do is control the number of units wasted in the assembly operation. When the department wastes a unit of product P, for example, it wastes both the materials and the labor that were used in the forming department to make that unit—the manager can't control one without controlling the other. For this reason, the entire standard cost of units received from forming is treated as a materials cost in the assembly department.

Step 4. Estimate the standard cost of the inventories in process at the end of the period and make any entries necessary to bring the work in process account balances to their correct levels. After the entries described in step 3 have been recorded, the balances in the work in process accounts are understated, because no entries have been made to record the standard cost of the work done during the period. Four figures appear in any basic plan work in process account, interrelated as follows:

$$\begin{matrix}\text{Standard} \\ \text{cost of} \\ \text{ending} \\ \text{inventory}\end{matrix} = \begin{matrix}\text{Standard} \\ \text{cost of} \\ \text{beginning} \\ \text{inventory}\end{matrix} + \begin{matrix}\text{Standard cost} \\ \text{of work done} \\ \text{during the} \\ \text{period}\end{matrix} - \begin{matrix}\text{Standard cost of} \\ \text{goods finished and} \\ \text{transferred out} \\ \text{during the period}\end{matrix}$$

Once the entries described in step 3 have been recorded and the standard cost of the ending inventory has been established, we know three of the elements in this equation. The fourth—standard cost of the work done—can be derived from the other three:

$$\begin{matrix}\text{Standard cost} \\ \text{of work done} \\ \text{during the} \\ \text{period}\end{matrix} = \begin{matrix}\text{Standard cost of} \\ \text{goods finished and} \\ \text{transferred out} \\ \text{during the period}\end{matrix} + \begin{matrix}\text{Standard} \\ \text{cost of} \\ \text{ending} \\ \text{inventory}\end{matrix} - \begin{matrix}\text{Standard} \\ \text{cost of} \\ \text{beginning} \\ \text{inventory}\end{matrix}$$

Galahad's forming department's work-in-process accounts showed the following after entry (4) was posted:

---

[2] The charge to the assembly department ordinarily includes a transfer of the forming department's standard overhead cost. We are ignoring this component to allow us to concentrate on direct labor and materials. (See Chapter 11 for a description of the treatment of standard overhead cost.)

Materials in Process—Forming		Labor in Process—Forming	
Bal. 1,400	(4) 38,300	Bal. 320	(4) 27,600
	Bal. 36,900		Bal. 27,280

Galahad counted the inventories in process at the end of July, revealing work in process in the forming department with a standard direct materials cost of $2,100 and a standard direct labor cost of $720. Since the materials-in-process account had a credit balance of $36,900, the only way to bring it back to its correct ending balance of $2,100 was to debit it by $39,000. This is the standard direct materials cost of the work done during July. The entry was:

(5)

Materials in Process—Forming	39,000	
Standard Direct Materials—Forming		39,000

(Remember that the standard cost of the work done in any period is the standard cost of the units finished, plus or minus the change in the standard cost of the work in process, in this case $38,300 + $2,100 − $1,400 = $39,000.)

A similar entry brings the labor-in-process account up to its correct end-of-month balance:

(6)

Labor in Process—Forming	28,000	
Standard Direct Labor—Forming		28,000

Once these entries were made, the departmental usage and standard cost accounts had the following balances:

Direct Materials Used—Forming		Standard Direct Materials—Forming	
(2) 37,800		(5) 39,000	

Direct Labor Used—Forming		Standard Direct Labor—Forming	
(3) 28,800		(6) 28,000	

The balances in the usage accounts measured actual input quantities used, multiplied by their standard prices; the balances in the standard cost accounts measured the standard input quantities for the month's output or work done, also measured at standard input prices. To prove a point, we can substitute these words for the dollar amounts in the two departmental materials accounts:

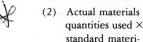

Direct Materials Used—Forming		Standard Direct Materials—Forming	
(2) Actual materials quantities used × standard materials prices		(5) Standard materials quantities of actual output × standard materials prices	

Since standard input prices were used in both accounts in each pair, the differences in their balances could only represent differences between standard and actual input quantities—that is, the usage variances. The materials accounts therefore were closed out by the following entry:

(7)

Standard Direct Materials—Forming	39,000	
Direct Materials Used—Forming		37,800
Materials Usage Variance—Forming		1,200

The credit to the variance account indicated that this variance was favorable in July.

The balances in the two labor accounts were closed out in a similar fashion, by the following entry:

(8)

Standard Direct Labor—Forming	28,000	
Labor Usage Variance—Forming	800	
Direct Labor Used—Forming		28,800

This time the usage variance account was debited, reflecting an unfavorable variance in this cost element.

Isolating the labor rate variance

By using standard wages rates, Galahad's accountants were able to process the labor time tickets as they came in. The labor rate variances could not be calculated, however, until the month's payrolls were prepared, establishing the actual labor cost for the month.

In practice, departmental payrolls will include overtime premiums and indirect labor time, both chargeable to overhead accounts. To keep this illustration simple, we'll ignore these components of the payroll. Actual direct labor wages in the forming department, measured at actual wage rates, totaled $29,500 in July: Of this, $5,500 was withheld for taxes and insurance premiums on the employees' behalf; the remaining $24,000 was payable directly to the employees. The entry to record this information was:

(9)

Payroll Cost Summary—Forming	29,500	
Wages Payable		24,000
Withholdings Payable		5,500

The two credit entries recorded the company's liabilities for these payrolls and need concern us no further. Our interest centers on the Payroll Cost Summary account. Remember that in entry (3) Galahad credited $28,800 to this account, representing 3,600 hours of direct labor at a standard wage rate of $8 an hour. Now we find that in entry (9) Galahad charged $29,500 to the Payroll Cost Summary account, representing the actual wages earned by employees for these 3,600 hours at straight-time wage rates (i.e., excluding overtime premiums). The account thus showed the following:

Payroll Cost Summary—Forming

(5) Actual labor hours × actual basic hourly wage rates 29,500	(3) Actual labor hours × standard hourly wage rates 28,800
Bal. 700	

Since the amounts on both sides of the account were based on the same number of labor hours (3,600), the $700 difference in the total could only be due to difference between actual and standard wage rates—that is, it was the labor rate variance. A credit balance would have shown up if actual wage rates had been lower than standard.

The procedure could end here, with the balance in the Payroll Cost Summary account interpreted as a rate variance for internal reporting purposes. Galahad's accountants liked to clear this account each month, however, and made the following entry at the end of July:

(10)

Labor Rate Variance—Forming 700
    Payroll Cost Summary—Forming   700

After this entry was posted, the payroll cost summary account had a zero balance, ready to receive payroll data for the month of August.

Reconciling the variances

With the calculation of the labor rate variance, the analysis of the direct labor spending variance is complete. For the forming department in July, we had the following figures:

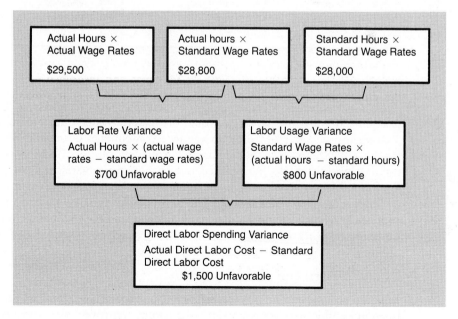

This tabulation illustrates a fundamental rule in variance analysis: *when a variance is to be subdivided into components, start with one of the two figures that bound the variance as a whole and change the determinants of that figure, one at a time, until the other figure bounding the variance is reached.* In this case we started with actual direct labor cost and changed the wage rate, leaving labor quantity unchanged. This gave us one component. We then changed the labor quantity, leaving the wage rate unchanged. This gave us a second component. Since the second change brought us to the other boundary of the total variance, the analysis was complete.

As the preceding diagram shows, the sum of standard direct labor cost and the two labor variances equals the actual direct labor cost for the period. For direct materials, however, the two variance components arise from two *independent* sets of transactions. The materials price variance relates to the actual quantity of materials *purchased;* the materials usage variance relates to the quantity of materials *issued.* The difference between these two quantity figures is an *inventory change,* not a variance:

Actual Quantity Purchased × Actual Prices	Actual Quantity Purchased × Standard Prices	Actual Quantity Issued × Standard Prices	Standard Quantity × Standard Prices
$41,000	$42,700	$37,800	$39,000

Materials Price Variance	Change in Materials Inventory	Materials Usage Variance
$1,700 Favorable	$4,900 Increase	$1,200 Favorable

Because materials inventories in the basic plan are measured at standard prices, we don't know the actual cost of the materials issued during the month. This means we can't add the two variance components in the way we could for the direct labor spending variance. Fortunately, this is of little importance for most purposes. As we pointed out earlier, price variances arise at the time of purchase, and management should be alerted to these at that time, not later when the materials are used. In preparing variance summaries, however, we'll refer to the sum of the materials price and materials usage variances as the *materials spending variance.*

Characteristics of the basic plan

Standard costing systems built on the basic plan have the six main characteristics listed in Exhibit 9–5. Items 4 and 5 are the most controversial. Usage variances

Exhibit 9–5 Characteristics of the basic plan

1. Materials price variances are identified and segregated when the materials are purchased; actual prices are not used in accounting for inventory costs.
2. Production centers are charged for the actual direct labor and materials quantities used, multiplied by standard materials prices and wage rates.
3. Production centers are credited for the standard costs of the units completed—i.e., standard direct labor and materials quantities, multiplied by standard materials prices and wage rates.
4. Labor and materials usage variances are identified at the end of the period, on the basis of a physical count of the work in process.
5. Labor and materials usage variances are identified as production center totals for the time period as a whole; they are not computed for individual job orders or individual operators.
6. Labor rate variances on production labor are determined by comparing gross payrolls at straight-time rates with the amounts charged the production centers for actual labor time at standard wage rates.

calculated in this way cannot be reported frequently or in great detail. This means that the first-line supervisors can use basic plan variance reports only as scorecard controls; they must supply their own steering control information by keeping a close watch on what is going on in their departments. If the first-line supervisors have to rely on the standard costing system to provide steering controls, a more elaborate system may be appropriate. We'll describe one such system in Chapter 23.

Successful application of the basic plan hinges on management's ability to measure work-in-process inventories quickly and cheaply. If the counting process is too difficult or too unreliable, the basic plan has to be rejected. Fortunately, in-process inventories in many processes can safely be assumed to be constant, so that output can be measured directly by the standard cost of the units completed during the period. In other cases, only a very few jobs are in process in any department at any time, and measurement is very simple. The simpler the solution to this measurement problem, the more frequently variance information can be reported. In some cases, daily reporting would be entirely feasible.

Standard cost files

The standard cost file is likely to contain five different kinds of data:

1. Standard materials prices.
2. Standard labor rates.
3. Standard materials quantities—the bill of materials.
4. Standard labor quantities—the operations flow sheet.
5. Standard product costs.

Standard materials prices

Standard materials prices should represent management's best estimates of the delivered costs of materials during the period covered by the standards. The standard for any particular item should include a provision for freight-in, variable handling costs, and expected discounts. For example, the standard price of a metal stamping might be determined as follows:

Purchase price, in 500-piece quantities	$6.00
Freight from supplier's plant	0.40
Receiving and stacking	0.20
Less: purchase discounts	(0.12)
Standard materials price	$6.48

Some companies treat freight-in, discounts, and variable handling costs in other ways, but they are inescapable components of materials price and should be accounted for as such unless the clerical costs are prohibitive.

Standard labor rates

Standard labor rates should include provisions for the costs of fringe benefits that vary with the size of the total payroll, along the lines we suggested in Chapter 2. For bookkeeping convenience, however, many companies limit the standard labor rate to the regular time wage rate, classifying fringe benefit costs as overhead costs.

Once this issue has been decided, management still has another choice to make: a single standard labor rate for the factory as a whole, a single rate for each department, or separate standard rates for each pay grade. Separate rates are the most accurate, but they are slightly more expensive to use. If different operations call for operators with very different degrees of skill and therefore very different labor rates, separate rate standards probably should be used. An hour of floor sweeping time simply cannot be equated with an hour of highly skilled machinists' time.

Standard materials quantities

Materials quantity standards start from product specifications as to size, shape, appearance, desired performance characteristics, and permissible tolerance limits. These are reflected in the bill of materials, which lists the quantity required of each of the various materials and parts that will go into the creation of the finished product. A sample bill of materials for a product known as a base plate is shown in Exhibit 9–6.

Notice that the standard allows for more than one anchor and brace for each base plate. Standards are expected to show what will happen when conditions are normal and costs are under control. Since some wastage of materials is inevitable in most processes, standard costs include allowances for normal wastage. In manufacturing these base plates for example, the company expects the factory to spoil or lose about 1 percent of the anchors issued and about 4 percent of the braces.

Exhibit 9–6 Bill of materials

STANDARD MATERIALS REQUIREMENTS

Item: Base Plate No. 423   Drawing No.: 9463
Standard Quantity: 1,000   Date: 11/14/–

Materials			Remarks
No.	Description	Required for Standard Lot	
176	Steel plate	4,200 lbs.	

Parts

Part No.	Description	Specs. per Unit	Required for Lot	Part No.	Description	Specs. per Unit	Required for Lot
201	Anchor	1	1,010				
217	Brace	2	2,080				

Standard labor quantities

Labor quantity standards also start from product specifications, which determine the factory operations necessary to manufacture the product. These operations are summarized on a flow sheet such as the one shown in Exhibit 9–7. This flow sheet specifies the operations to be performed and the labor quantities required for each. The column headed "Job Class" specifies the kind of employee who normally should be assigned to each operation. The form may also specify the equipment to be used and the amount of machine time required.

These labor time standards are usually slightly greater than the amount of time the operations themselves are expected to take. Workers cannot be expected to work at peak efficiency at all times. They take coffee breaks, attend to their personal needs, wait for someone to supply them with materials, or adjust their equipment. Since it is reasonable to expect that the amount of time spent in these ways should be proportional to the amount of productive

Exhibit 9–7 Operations flow sheet

STANDARD OPERATIONS LIST

Item: <u>Base Plate No. 423</u>   Drawing No.: <u>9463</u>
Standard Quantity: <u>1,000</u>   Date: <u>11/14/–</u>

Dept.	Operations No.	Operations Description	Job Class	Hours Allowed	Remarks
P	1731	Setup	1	2.0	
M	2146	Cut	2	5.5	
M	2172	Drill	2	21.0	
M	2175	Bevel	3	6.0	
M	2304	Polish	3	14.5	
A	2903	Press	5	2.5	
A	2905	Slip	5	2.5	

time, labor standards ordinarily include a provision for the normal amount of nonproductive time.

Labor time, like materials quantities, can't be predicted with pinpoint accuracy. Sometimes it will be less than standard; sometimes it will be greater. Management's task is to pick a point in this range that skilled operators should be expected to achieve, on the average.

One possible approach is to consult with engineers or other technical people. An experienced garment cutter, for example, usually can estimate quite accurately the number of men's suits that can be cut from a given quantity of cloth, because this job is so familiar. In other cases, industrial engineers can synthesize data from commercially available tables of time standards for individual work elements of specific operations (methods time measurement). Alternatively, a time study engineer can obtain data by observing a series of test runs (time studies and yield studies).

Observing test runs is relatively expensive and time consuming. As a result, controlled test runs are seldom undertaken except to meet other objectives, such as work standardization and methods improvement. When studies are made for these purposes, accurate quantity standards can be obtained as a by-product at little additional cost. When a company is first introducing standard costing, however, it may very well get an adequate set of initial standards by analyzing the quantity data in the historical cost records.

Standard product costs

Standard product costs are computed by entering the data from the bill of materials and the operations flow sheet, together with standard materials prices and wage rates, on a product standard cost sheet.

Data from the product standard cost sheets are used for many purposes. One of these is to measure departmental output for variance analysis, as we saw earlier. Another use is to measure inventories for financial reporting purposes; when variances are small, standard costs can be an acceptable approximation to historical cost. Still a third use is to help management estimate the consequences of its decisions on pricing, resource allocation, and manufacturing methods.

Standard manufacturing costs may not always be perfect for one or more of these uses, but they have the advantage of availability. Management can always question the assumptions on which the standard costs have been built; the figures in the standard cost file give management a head start on the analysis.

Summary

Control reports compare actual results with performance standards. For factory direct materials and direct labor costs, standard costs can be the performance standards. Differences between the standard costs of direct labor and materials and their actual costs are spending variances. The portion of a spending variance in direct labor or materials which is due to differences between actual and standard input quantities for the work done is referred to as a usage variance; the remainder is a price or rate variance, reflecting differences between actual and standard materials prices or wage rates.

The accountant uses standard costing systems to generate variance information for management. Standard costing systems differ from each other in many ways, but the most significant differences are in when and how variances are isolated. The simplest standard costing systems are basic plan systems, and the usage variances produced under these systems are in the form of departmental totals—the differences between the actual quantities of the inputs consumed in the department and the standard input equivalents of the department's actual output in each time period. When these physical quantities are multiplied by standard input prices, the result is the dollar usage variance that appears on the periodic performance report.

The basic plan is relatively inexpensive. It identifies the departments in which usage variances occur and provides management with a summary measure of cost control effectiveness in each department. It is appropriate when the department head relies on the standard costing system for scorecard control information only. Its main weakness is that it fails to provide detailed information from which management can identify the products, operators, machines, or operations in which the bulk of the variances occur. If management needs this information, a more expensive system may be justified. We shall examine one such system in Chapter 23.

Appendix to Chapter 9: Variance notation

The breakdown of a spending variance into price and usage components can be represented in mathematical notation. To start with, let's assume the department manufactures only one product, using only one type of labor. The standard labor cost of a unit of this product (c_s) is represented by the following relationship:

$$c_s = p_s q_s$$

in which

p_s = Standard wage rate per hour of labor
q_s = Standard number of labor hours required by one unit of product

If we represent the total standard labor cost of the output of any period by C_s and the number of units of output in that period by the symbol N_a, then

$$C_s = N_a p_s q_s$$

This expression for standard labor cost can be partitioned as follows:

$$C_s = p_s(N_a q_s)$$

The amount in parentheses ($N_a q_s$) is the standard labor quantity in the period—that is, the actual output (N_a) measured at standard input quantity per unit (q_s). If we use the symbol Q_s to represent the standard labor quantity, the expression for standard labor cost is

$$C_s = p_s Q_s$$

The purpose of calculating standard labor cost is to compare it with the actual labor cost of the same period (C_a) to get the labor spending variance (V_L). Actual labor cost can be represented by an expression identical in form to the expression for standard labor cost:

$$C_a = p_a(N_a q_a)$$

in which

p_a = Actual wage rate per hour of labor used during the specific period
q_a = Actual number of labor hours used to produce one unit of product during this period.

The expression in parentheses ($N_a q_a$) is the actual number of labor hours used during the period, which we can represent by Q_a. The actual labor cost in any period therefore can be written as

$$C_a = p_a Q_a$$

This is a useful way to write the expression because we always know the total number of labor hours; we may not know how many labor hours have been used on any one unit of any product.

Once we have identified actual and standard labor cost, we can calculate the labor spending variance:

$$V_L = C_a - C_s$$

This can also be written as

$$V_L = p_a(N_a q_a) - p_s(N_a q_s)$$

or as

$$V_L = p_a Q_a - p_s Q_s \qquad (1)$$

To use equation (1) to calculate the components of the spending variance, the accountant modifies it by adding *and* subtracting a new figure:

$$-p_s Q_a + p_s Q_a$$

Adding and subtracting the same figure produces a new equation which is exactly equivalent to equation (1):

$$V_L = p_a Q_a - p_s Q_a + p_s Q_a - p_s Q_s \qquad (2)$$

The next step is to group these elements:

$$V_L = (p_a Q_a - p_s Q_a) + (p_s Q_a - p_s Q_s) \qquad (3)$$

The difference between the two elements in the first parenthetical expression is the labor rate (price) variance (V_{LR}). It can be restated as follows:

$$V_{LR} = p_a Q_a - p_s Q_a = Q_a(p_a - p_s)$$

In other words, the rate variance is obtained by multiplying the actual labor quantity by the difference between actual and standard prices.

The elements in the second set of parentheses in equation (3) can also be factored, as follows:

$$V_{LU} = P_s Q_a - p_s Q_s = p_s(Q_a - Q_s)$$

This is the labor usage variance (V_{LU}), obtained by multiplying the *standard* price (wage rate) by the difference between actual and standard labor quantities used.

Equation (3) now can be restated in the form the accountants usually use:

$$V_L = V_{LR} + V_{LU}$$
$$V_L = Q_a(p_a - p_s) + p_s(Q_a - Q_s) \qquad (4)$$

A purist might object to this analysis, pointing out that some of the price variance can be attributed not only to price variations but to usage variations as well. The breakdown could take the following form:

A "pure" price variance: $Q_s(p_a - p_s)$
A joint price/usage variance: $(p_a - p_s)(Q_a - Q_s)$

These two variances, together with the usage variance we calculated earlier, are diagrammed in Exhibit 9–8, in which all variances are unfavorable.[3] The analysis is clearly valid, but its usefulness is doubtful. Management can respond to a usage variance by concentrating on the factors that determine physical efficiency (methods, morale, etc.). It can respond to a price variance by concentrating on the factors determining unit prices (choice of supplier, choice of materials, etc.). It has no unique response to the joint variance, however. Effective responses to the price and usage variances will take care of the joint variance automatically. For this reason we regard the joint variance as of academic interest only.

Exhibit 9–8 Three-way analysis of labor spending variance

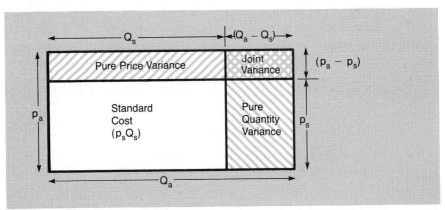

We can use the same notation to identify the materials variances. Again, let's assume that the department produces only one product which requires only one kind of material. If the materials price variance is separated at the time of purchase, we have two symbols to represent actual quantities:

Q_a' = Actual number of units purchased
Q_a = Actual number of units issued and used

The variances can be represented by the following symbols:

V_M = Materials spending variance
V_{MP} = Materials price variance
V_{MU} = Materials usage variance

The equation for the materials spending variance then can be written as follows:

$$V_M = Q_a'(p_a - p_s) + p_s(Q_a - Q_s) \qquad (5)$$

The increment in the inventory of unprocessed materials is $p_s(Q_a' - Q_a)$.

We have simplified this illustration by limiting ourselves to a single product,

---

[3] A similar diagram can be drawn with favorable variances; the area of the outer box in that case will represent standard costs, (p_sQ_s) while the unshaded area within the box is the actual cost (p_aQ_a).

a single kind of material, and a single type of labor. Extending the equations to cover aggregate variances in a multi-input, multiproduct setting is relatively simple, although the notation may look formidable. One way of writing the equation for the spending variance (V) is:

$$V = \sum_{i=1}^{n} Q_i^a(p_i^a - p_i^s) + \sum_{i=1}^{n} p_i^s(Q_i^a - Q_i^s) \qquad (6)$$

in which i stands for a particular kind of labor or materials input, and n identifies how many kinds of inputs are available for use.

The first term of this expression defines the aggregate price variance; the second term describes the usage variance. The expression is identical in form to equations (4) and (5); the only difference is that in equation (6) we are summing a number of inputs and the Q's represent the total input quantities used or required for all products, not just one:

$$Q_i^s = \sum_{j=1}^{m} N_j q_{ij}^s = \begin{array}{l}\text{The total standard quantity of input } i \text{ required to produce}\\ \text{the actual output } N_j \text{ of products 1 through } m\end{array}$$

$$Q_i^a = \begin{array}{l}\text{The total actual units of input } i \text{ used to produce the actual quantities}\\ \text{of products 1 through } m.\end{array}$$

Equation (6) can be modified as equation (5) was to handle the case in which the quantity purchased differs from the quantity used.

Independent study problems (solutions in Appendix B)

1. **Calculating standard cost of a product.** Egbert Company buys a powder, dissolves it in water, concentrates the solution by boiling, adds sugar, and then packages the final product in pint jars. In the initial mix, one pound of raw material added to 0.95 gallons of water yields one gallon of mix. In the boiling operation, a 25 percent reduction in volume takes place.

    Addition of one-half pound of sugar per gallon of concentrate completes the blending operation, and the mixture is allowed to cool. The addition of sugar and the cooling operation do not affect the total liquid volume. A loss of 2 percent of volume is expected during the filling operation due to spilling, evaporation, overfilling of some jars; and residue left in the blending kettles. Due to breakage and defective materials, 1,005 jars must be issued for every 1,000 jars filled.

    The powder costs 80 cents a pound, sugar has a standard price of 25 cents a pound, and jars cost $2.40 a dozen.

    Required:

    a. Diagram the flows of materials through this process.
    b. Calculate the standard quantity of powder and the standard quantity of sugar for a pint jar of finished product.
    c. Calculate the standard materials cost of a pint jar of the finished product.

2. **Calculating total standard cost for a period.** Product X has a standard direct labor cost of $40 a unit (five direct labor hours at $8 an hour). The company finished work on 10,000 units of product X last month. Its inventories of product X were as follows:

    Beginning of month: 4,000 units in process, with half of the necessary labor already applied.
    End of month: 1,000 units in process, with half of the necessary labor already applied.

Required:
Calculate the standard direct labor cost of the work performed on product X last month.

3. **Calculating materials variances.** A department produces two products, X and Y, for which you have the following information:

	Product X	Product Y
Standard materials cost per unit:		
Standard materials quantity (pounds)	10	5
Standard materials price (per pound)	$ 5	$ 5
Number of units started and completed in May	5,000	6,000

Inventories in process were negligible both at the beginning and at the end of May.

The materials used in these products are highly perishable and no inventories of unused materials are maintained. The department purchased and used 85,000 pounds of these materials in May; the purchase prices of these materials averaged $5.10 a pound.

Required:

a. Calculate the materials spending variance for the month of May and subdivide it into price and usage components in such a way as to facilitate the comparison of the usage variance with usage variances in other months.

b. Suppose the materials are not highly perishable, so that management can maintain an inventory of materials ready for use. The company bought 100,000 pounds of these materials in May at $5.10 a pound, and issued 85,000 pounds for immediate use. Recalculate the variances and explain why this set of variances differs from the set you calculated in answer to *(a)*.

4. **Calculating labor and materials variances.** Benedict Company operates a factory with two production departments: shaping and finishing. All materials are placed in the materials inventory when purchased; direct materials are issued from this inventory to the shaping department when they are needed in production. Shaping performs the initial operations on all products, then transfers them to finishing for further work. No direct materials are issued from materials inventory to the finishing department. You have the following information for the month of January:

1. Beginning work in process: none.
2. Beginning materials inventory (standard cost): $1,000.
3. Materials purchased on account: $320 (standard cost, $300).
4. Standard cost of direct materials issued: $500.
5. Direct labor used in shaping department: $760 ($720 at standard wage rates).
6. Standard cost of jobs completed by shaping department and transferred to finishing department (assume zero overhead): direct materials, $490; direct labor, $650.
7. Standard cost of ending work in process in shaping department: direct materials, $40; direct labor, $20.

Required:

a. Calculate the labor rate variance, the materials price variance, the labor usage variance, and the materials usage variance.

b. Recalculate the variances to reflect your discovery that the work in process in the shaping department on January 1 had a standard direct materials cost of $100 and a standard direct labor cost of $10.

5. **Basic plan cost flows.** Benedict Company (problem 4) uses a basic plan of standard costing, using an account structure similar to the one described in this chapter.

   Required:

   Set up T-accounts for the materials inventory, for the shaping department, and for any other accounts you find necessary. Enter the opening inventory account balances, record the month's transactions, and make any entries necessary to transfer all variances to appropriately titled variance accounts. The opening work-in-process balances are those specified in instruction 4(*b*).

Exercises and problems

6. **Labor usage variances: Month to month comparison.** Standard labor costs in the XYZ Company remained unchanged throughout the year. You have the following labor cost data for department 16:

	May	June
Actual direct labor hours....................	9,000	11,000
Actual direct labor wages	$72,900	$91,300
Standard direct labor rate per hour	$ 8.20	$ 8.20
Standard direct labor cost of production	$71,240	$88,600

   Required:

   Was the labor usage variance better or worse in June than in May? How much better or worse? Show and explain your calculations.

7. **Calculating and reporting labor variances.** Standard direct labor cost was $5 a unit for product A and $6 a unit for product B. The standard labor cost of work in process was $10,000 on September 1 and $5,000 on September 30. The standard wage rate was $8 an hour, and 7,500 direct labor hours were recorded during September. The direct labor payroll for September totaled $61,000, and 4,000 units of product A and 7,000 units of Product B were completed during the month.

   Required:

   a. Compute the standard direct labor cost of the month's output.
   b. Compute the direct labor usage variance, in dollars.
   c. Compute the direct labor rate variance.
   d. Management says, "All this talk about variances is accountants' talk. Can't you find some other way of giving us the same information you capture in the usage variance? And don't just give us the same variance figure with a new name." Comply with this request, using data for the month of September.

8. **Variance exercises: Multiple choice.** For each of the following, make the necessary calculations to answer the question.

   1. Matt Company uses a standard cost system. Information for raw materials for product RBI for the month of October is:

Standard unit price	$ 1.60
Actual purchase price per unit	1.55
Actual quantity purchased (units)	2,000
Actual quantity used (units)	1,900
Standard quantity allowed for actual production (units)	1,800

What is the materials purchase price variance?

a. $90 favorable, *b.* $90 unfavorable, *c.* $100 favorable, *d.* $100 unfavorable.

2. Information on Kennedy Company's direct material cost is as follows:

Standard unit price	$ 3.60
Actual quantity purchased (units)	1,600
Standard quantity allowed for actual production (units)	1,450
Materials purchase price variance (favorable)	$ 240

What was the actual purchase price per unit?

a. $3.06, *b.* $3.11, *c.* $3.45, *d.* $3.75.

3. Home Company manufactures tables with vinyl tops. The standard material cost for the vinyl used for each type R table is $7.80, based on six square feet of vinyl at a cost of $1.30 a square foot. A production run of 1,000 tables in January resulted in usage of 6,400 square feet of vinyl at a cost of $1.20 a square foot, a total cost of $7,680. The usage variance resulting from this production run was:

a. $120 favorable, *b.* $480 unfavorable, *c.* $520 unfavorable, *d.* $640 favorable.

4. Lion Company's direct labor costs for the month of January were as follows:

Actual direct labor hours	20,000
Standard direct labor hours	21,000
Direct labor rate variance (unfavorable)	$ 3,000
Total direct labor payroll	$126,000

What was Lion's direct labor efficiency (usage) variance?

a. $6,000 favorable, *b.* $6,150 favorable, *c.* $6,300 favorable, *d.* $6,450 favorable.

5. Sullivan Corporation's direct labor costs for the month of March were as follows:

Standard direct labor hours	42,000
Actual direct labor hours	40,000
Direct labor rate variance (favorable)	$ 8,400
Standard direct labor rate per hour	$ 6.30

What was Sullivan's total direct labor payroll for the month of March?

a. $243,600, *b.* $244,000, *c.* $260,000, *d.* $260,400.

6. Lab Corp. uses a standard cost system. Direct labor information for product CER for the month of October is as follows:

Standard rate	$ 6.00 an hour
Actual rate paid	6.10 an hour
Standard hours allowed for actual production	1,500 hours
Labor efficiency (usage) variance	$ 600 unfavorable

What are the actual hours worked?

a. 1,400, *b.* 1,402, *c.* 1,598, *d.* 1,600.

(AICPA)

9. **Sequential variance exercises.** Follow the instructions for each of the four exercises presented below:

Exercise A.   Usage Variances

Luceri, Inc., reports factory materials and labor usage variances to management monthly. It has two products, for which the following data are available:

	Materials Required per Unit	Labor Required per Unit	Units Pro- duced during March
Product A	4 lbs.	1.5 hrs.	1,000
Product B	5	4.0	2,000

Usage of materials and labor during March was as follows: materials, 13,000 pounds; labor, 10,000 hours.

Required:

a. Compute materials and labor usage variances for the month in terms of pounds of materials and labor hours. Indicate whether each variance is favorable or unfavorable.

b. The standard materials price is $5 a pound. The standard wage rate is $8 an hour. (1) Compute standard unit cost for each product in dollars. (2) Restate your usage variances (from *a*) in monetary terms.

Exercise B.   Variances, No Work in Process

A. B. See, Inc., uses a basic plan standard costing system. It had no inventory of materials on December 1 and no work in process either on December 1 or on December 31. The following information was collected for the month of December:

1. Materials:
    Standard price: $12 a pound.
    Purchased 10,000 pounds at a cost of $115,000.
    Used during December: 8,000 pounds.
2. Labor:
    Standard wage rate: $7.50 an hour.
    Used during December: 2,700 hours at a cost of $20,000.
3. Product output:
    Standard cost per unit of product:
      Materials: 3.9 pounds.
      Labor: 1.5 hours.
    Products manufactured during December: 1,900 units.

Required:

a. Compute labor and materials variances, in dollars, in whatever detail you think is appropriate.

b. Indicate to whom each of your variances should be reported.

Exercise C.   Variances, Work in Process

Herren, Inc., uses a standard cost system. The following information was collected for one department for the month of December:

1. Inventory of work in process, December 1 (at standard cost):
    Materials cost: $13,000.
    Labor cost: $8,000.
2. Used during month:
    Materials (at standard prices): $30,000.
    Labor:
      At actual wage rates, $15,000.
      At standard wage rates, $16,000.

3. Products finished and transferred out of the department during month (at standard cost):
   Materials cost: $31,200.
   Labor cost: $15,700.
4. Inventory of work in process, December 31 (at standard cost):
   Materials cost: $9,000.
   Labor cost: $9,000.

Required:

Compute labor and materials variances in whatever detail you think is appropriate.

Exercise D. Variances, Interdepartmental Transfers

Smythe, Ltd. has a factory with four production departments. Department Baker receives partly processed products from department Able, adds component materials to them, and then transfers them to department Charlie for further work. A standard cost system is in use. The following data are available for department Baker for the month of February:

1. Received from department Able during February:
   Product units received, 5,000.
   Unit cost in department Able:

	Standard	Actual
Materials	$1.00	$1.10
Labor	6.00	6.90

2. Received component materials from stock room during month, at standard prices, $2,100; standard cost of these materials, 40 cents per product unit.
3. Used 1,100 labor hours during February, $8,250 at standard wage rates; standard cost of department Baker labor was $1.80 per product unit.
4. Transferred to department Charlie during February, 4,800 product units.
5. Work in process inventories in department Baker were negligible both on February 1 and on February 28.
6. Damaged 200 product units in processing operations; these units were not usable and had no salvage value. About half of the processing labor operations had been performed on these units before they were damaged. All of the component materials had been applied prior to the damage.

Required:

a. Compute labor and materials usage variances for department Baker for the month of February.
b. Standard cost per product unit includes no allowances for losses of products during processing. How much of each of the variances computed in (*a*) was attributable to product losses? What do the remaining portions of the variances mean?

10. **Calculating departmental output.** Department T produces several products. You have the following statistics for the month of May:

	Standard Quantity per Unit			Units in Process	
Product	Materials (in pounds)	Labor (in hours)	Units Completed	May 1	May 31
A	4	2	1,000	100	200
B	2	5	300	80	100
C	6	1	2,000	300	200

Materials have a standard price of $3 a pound; the standard labor rate is $8 an hour. Units in process on any date already include all the materials required; half of the labor operations have been performed.

Required:

a. Calculate total standard labor cost and total standard materials cost for the month.

b. How would you get the data you would need to estimate the standard cost of the work in process on any date?

11. **Reporting materials variances.** Materials price variances are identified at the time of purchase. Materials inventories are costed at standard purchase prices.

Material X is the raw material for product A. Product A is the only output of department 1. The standard materials quantity is 0.38 pounds of material X for a gallon of product A. If the price of material X gets too high, the plant manager will convert the process so that product A can be manufactured from soybeans instead of from material X.

Material X has a standard purchase price of $8 a pound. The company purchased 3,000 pounds during January at a cost of $25,100. These materials were placed in warehouse W.

Department 1 used 4,000 pounds of material X during January. All of these came from warehouse H. They had been purchased six months earlier at a price of $7.50.

Department 1 produced 9,900 gallons of product A during the month of January.

Required:

a. Compute the materials price and materials usage variances for the month.

b. What managerially significant information on January operations would you report: (1) to the supervisor of department 1; (2) to the plant manager?

12. **Supplying missing information.** A basic plan standard costing system is in use in each of the Harrison Company's factories. You have the following data on direct materials and direct labor for three of these factories:

		Factory A	Factory B	Factory C
	Inventories, June 1, at standard cost:			
1.	Materials	$ 93,000	?	$163,000
2.	Materials in process	17,000	$ 9,500	21,000
3.	Labor in process	12,000	6,000	?
4.	Finished goods*	125,000	?	212,000
	Inventories, June 30, at standard cost:			
5.	Materials	?	128,000	139,000
6.	Materials in process	14,600	14,900	?
7.	Labor in process	9,200	?	3,500
8.	Finished goods*	?	104,000	229,000
	Totals for the month of June:			
9.	Materials purchased, at standard prices	?	72,000	51,000
10.	Materials purchased, at actual prices	38,400	?	49,800
11.	Materials issued, at standard prices	47,000	?	?
12.	Standard materials cost of jobs finished	?	46,200	80,400

		Factory A	Factory B	Factory C
	Inventories, June 1, at standard cost:			
13.	Standard materials cost of the work done	49,200	?	71,700
14.	Actual labor hours used ..	?	10,000 hours	7,000 hours
15.	Actual labor cost	$ 63,200	?	$ 65,100
16.	Standard wage rate	$ 8/hour	$7/hour	?
17.	Standard labor cost of the work done	$ 59,200	?	$ 60,500
18.	Standard labor cost of the jobs finished	?	69,000	66,000
19.	Standard labor and materials cost of the goods sold	131,600	107,200	?
20.	Materials price variance ..	2,400 U.	300 U.	?
21.	Labor rate variance	800 F.	1,300 U.	?
22.	Materials usage variance ..	?	4,400 U.	?
23.	Labor usage variance	?	1,000 F.	2,500 U.
24.	Total labor cost variance ..	4,000 U.	300 U.	?

* = Materials and labor costs only

Required:

Make the necessary calculations and fill in the blanks identified by question marks in this table.

13. **Recognizing materials price variances at time of use.** Product X is manufactured from material A in department 1. Material A has a standard price of $4 a gallon, delivered. The standard bill of materials for product X calls for 1.2 gallons of material A for every gallon of finished product.

This company keeps its materials inventory records on a FIFO historical cost basis. Its inventory of material A on August 1 amounted to 9,000 gallons of material A at a FIFO cost of $3.90 a gallon. The following transactions in material A and product X took place during August:

1. Purchased 8,000 gallons of material A at an invoice price of $3.80 a gallon, less a 2 percent discount for prompt payment.
2. Paid freight charges on this shipment, $2,560.
3. Issued 8,000 gallons of material A to department 1.
4. Produced 7,000 gallons of product X.

Required:

a. Assuming materials price variances are measured at the time of use, calculate the materials spending variance for August and subdivide it into price and usage components.
b. Calculate the materials price and usage variances the company would have identified if it had had no beginning inventory of material A.
c. Which of these two sets of variances is more consistent with the usual breakdown of the labor spending variance? Why? Which is likely to be more useful to management? Why?
d. How would your analyses in (a) and (b) have changed if the company had bought 10,000 gallons of material A in August, at a net delivered cost of $40,440?

14. **Usage variances: Actual versus standard rates.** The workers in Poitou Company's factory fit into several wage rate categories, depending on their individual

skills. Wages vary within each category on the basis of the worker's length of service.

Each worker is normally assigned to a particular department, but the union contract permits management to transfer workers temporarily to other departments as production requires. Transfers are only made, however, when the transferred worker has been officially rated as capable of performing the required work. Worker transfers are arranged by the scheduling department, not by the managers of the individual production departments.

The company calculates departmental labor usage variances each month at the actual average labor rate for that month. You have the following information for the fitting department, which has a standard labor rate of $10 an hour for all its operations:

	May	June	July
Actual direct labor hours	800	850	790
Actual direct labor cost	$8,400	$9,350	$7,742
Labor usage variance (unfavorable)	210	1,100	1,078
Standard direct labor cost			
of actual production	7,800	7,500	6,800

Management is not happy with cost performance in the fitting department, but is pleased that the direct labor cost situation got no worse in July.

Required:

a. Does management have reason to be pleased? Make any calculation necessary to document your position.

b. What is the probable justification for using actual wage rates to measure the usage variance? How strong is this argument?

c. If the usage variance is measured at actual rates, what is the meaning of the remainder of the labor spending variance this month? What advantage, if any, does management get by calculating this portion of the spending variance in this way?

15. **Physical unit comparisons.** Art Dangerfield had been department supervisor for 30 years. "All I want are a few key figures," he said. "The rest of the accounting figures are rubbish. I want to know my scrap percentage [pounds of scrap, divided by pounds of materials] and the materials yield [pounds of product divided by pounds of materials]. If scrap is less than 5 percent and the materials yield is better than 80 percent, I've got it made."

The department processes a number of different materials and a certain amount of waste is inherent in the process. Some materials are lost in the process itself; some take the form of recoverable scrap. Mr. Dangerfield retired last month and his longtime assistant, Dorothy Hellman, was promoted to take his place. The first report she saw contained the following statistics:

Scrap	3%
Materials yield	84%
Materials usage variance (% of standard)	10% unfavorable

"Art's formula doesn't seem to be working," she observed. "I'm well within his limits, but how did that usage variance get so big?" She asked the plant controller to look into the matter.

The controller analyzed the materials requisitions and production records and came up with the following figures:

	Standard Price (per pound)	Standard Usage (in pounds)	Quantity Used (in pounds)
Material A	$ 0.10	4,000	3,700
Material B	1.00	600	630
Material C	10.00	400	450
Total		5,000	4,780

The percentage statistics were correct: the output weighed 4,015 pounds, 84 percent of the weight of the materials used, and 143 pounds of scrap were recovered.

Required:

a. Analyze the controller's figures and provide an explanation for Ms. Hellman.
b. Does your analysis indicate that the standards should be changed? What other suggestions would you make?

16. **Basic plan accounts.** Using a basic plan of standard costing and carrying materials inventories at standard net delivered prices, record the following transactions in appropriate T-accounts. You should include an account for each variance you wish to identify separately.

Actual cost of materials purchased:

Gross invoice price	$50,000
Discounts received on purchases	800
Freight and delivery charges on materials purchased	2,300
Standard cost of materials purchased	51,000
Materials issued (at standard prices)	47,000

Direct labor:

At actual wage rates	30,000
At standard wage rates	28,000

Cost of goods finished (at standard):

Materials	40,000
Labor	26,000

Cost of goods in process, end of month (at standard):

Materials	5,200
Labor	5,100

There was no work in process at the beginning of the month. The materials inventory at the beginning of the month had a standard cost of $60,000.

17. **Measuring variances.** Department T makes two products, X and Y, with the following standard inputs:

Direct materials:	Product X	Product Y	Standard Price
A	1 pound	3 pounds	$5 a pound
B	2 pounds	—	3 a pound
C	—	1 pound	6 a pound
Direct labor	0.5 hour	0.7 hour	7 an hour

You have the following additional information:

1. A basic plan of standard costing is in use.
2. The standard costs of inventories on hand were:

	May 1	May 31
Materials	$47,340	$56,490
Materials in process—department T	2,370	1,920
Labor in process—department T	332	378

3. The following materials were purchased during May—A: 6,000 pounds, $31,300; B: 6,000 pounds, $19,800; C: none.
4. Materials issued to department T during May: A, 4,800 pounds; B, 3,050 pounds; C, 950 pounds.
5. No materials were issued to any other department.
6. Direct labor for the month was 1,650 hours, $11,500.
7. Products completed and transferred to finished goods inventory—X, 1,600 units; Y, 1,000 units.

Required:

a. Calculate the materials price variance, the labor rate variance, the materials usage variance, and the labor usage variance for department T.
b. Explain how the standard materials costs of the work in process could be lower on May 31 than on May 1, while the standard labor cost was greater at the end of the month than at the beginning.
c. How would your answer to (*a*) have differed if the May 31 materials inventory had been $56,000 instead of $56,490?
d. Why isn't this a good way to get steering control information for the manager of department T?

18. **Basic plan accounts.** The company in problem 17 uses a single account for materials inventories and separate accounts for materials in process and labor in process in each department.

Required:

a. Set up T-accounts representing these and any other accounts you find necessary. Enter the opening account balances from problem 17.
b. Record in these T-accounts your analyses of the month's transactions. Include an account for each variance.

19. **Basic plan accounts.** Eiseman, Inc., manufactures a line of children's sleds. It has a basic plan standard costing system in its factory. Materials price variances are separated at the time of purchase, and all materials inventories are costed at standard prices. The September 1 inventories of materials destined for use in the sled department had a total standard cost of $48,000.

Standard costs and production and inventory data for the four models manufactured in the sled department during September were:

Standard cost per unit:	Model 3	Model 5	Model 22	Model 30
Materials	$0.80	$1.20	$1.50	$ 2.00
Labor	2.00	4.00	6.00	10.00
Total	$2.80	$5.20	$7.50	$12.00
Units completed	5,000	10,000	4,000	2,000
Units in process, Sept. 1	None	1,000	100	200
Units in process, Sept. 30	None	800	300	None

Units in process on any given date are assumed to be 100 percent complete as to materials and 50 percent complete as to labor.

The following transactions relate to the sled department during the month of September:

1. Purchased materials on account (standard cost, $35,000), $35,400.
2. Issued direct materials, at standard cost, $24,500.
3. Accrued direct labor payrolls for the month, $91,800.
4. Direct labor hours (standard wage rate, $8 an hour), 11,900 hours.

Required:

a. Prepare a schedule or schedules showing the standard direct labor and materials costs of the inventories and of the goods completed during the month.

What were the standard direct materials and standard direct labor costs of the work done during the month?

b. Record the above information in appropriate T-accounts. Be sure to enter the opening balances. Include entries that will bring the inventory accounts to their correct ending balances. A separate account should be provided for each variance that you wish to identify.

20. **Variance analysis.** Ross Shirts, Inc., manufactures short- and long-sleeved men's shirts for large stores. Ross produces a single quality shirt in lots to each customer's order and attaches the store's label to each. The standard direct costs for a dozen long-sleeved shirts are:

Direct materials, 24 yards at $0.75 .... $18.00
Direct labor, 3 hours at $7.45 .... 22.35

During October Ross Shirts worked on three orders for long-sleeved shirts. Job cost records for the month disclose the following:

Lot	Units in Lot	Material Used	Hours Worked
30	1,000 dozen	24,100 yards	2,980
31	1,700 dozen	40,440 yards	5,130
32	1,200 dozen	28,825 yards	2,890

The following information is also available:

1. Ross purchased 95,000 yards of material during the month at a cost of $72,200. The materials price variance is recorded when goods are purchased and all inventories are carried at standard cost.
2. Direct labor incurred amounted to $82,500 during October.
3. There was no work in process at October 1. During October, lots 30 and 31 were completed. All material was issued for lot 32 and it was 80 percent completed as to labor on October 31.

Required:

a. Compute the materials price variance for October and indicate whether it was favorable or unfavorable.
b. Compute the total amount of each of the following variances and indicate in each case whether the variance was favorable or unfavorable: (1) materials usage variance in yards and dollars; (2) labor usage variance in hours and dollars; (3) labor rate variance in dollars.
c. Identify, for each production lot, the variances that resulted directly from the production of that lot. Would you expect this information to be available in a basic plan system? Explain how it would be derived.

(CPA, adapted)

21. **Departmental verses job order basis for variance accumulation.** The management of Ross Shirts, Inc. (see problem 20), relies on its standard costing system mainly to generate scorecard information. The company's new controller has pointed out that the company's system fails to generate variance information for individual departments.

Required:

a. What would the accountants have to do to obtain usage variance data by department? Would this be a formidable task if the factory had five production departments?
b. Suppose Ross Shirts' system were revised so that usage variance data were accumulated and reported by department rather than by job order. What would be gained and what would be lost if this were done? Should this change be made?

22. **Standard costing: Service organization.**   In an effort to control costs, Hilltop College has just established a "standard instructional cost per student" for each course in the college's catalog. A variance is then calculated each term for each course offered that term.

No standards have been developed for the costs of teaching materials and supplies, and the costs of these items are not assigned to individual courses.

The standard cost per student for Basket Weaving 476 is $90. In the spring term 30 students enrolled in this course. The actual cost assigned to the course that term was $5,500, representing one sixth of the annual salary and fringe benefits of the instructor, Professor J. B. Braithwaite, chairman pro tem of the basket weaving department, plus the cost of 100 hours spent by a graduate student writing multiple choice examination questions and grading student term papers.

The college's controller made the following analysis of the variance for this course:

Standard cost, actual enrollment: 30 × $90	$2,700	Enrollment variance = $1,800 unfavorable
Standard cost, planned enrollment: 50 × $90	4,500	Salary variance
Actual cost..........................	5,500	= $1,000 unfavorable
		Total variance = $2,800 unfavorable

The controller calculated that $800 of the salary variance arose because Professor Braithwaite's salary per course was $800 greater than the average salary of the members of the basket weaving faculty. The remainder arose because Professor Braithwaite used more graduate student time than was planned for this course.

Required:

a. How do the purposes of this system differ from the purposes of basic plan standard costing systems used in factory production departments? To what extent are they the same? In answering this, you should try to identify the actions management might take in response to information the system provides. Distinguish between the actions management might take in response to information contained in the standards themselves and actions it might take in response to variance information.

b. Does this system appear to be a good way to achieve the purposes you have identified in (*a*)? In answering this, try to identify any problems that might arise in implementing this system and indicate whether they can be solved without great difficulty.

Case 9–1: Frozen Meals, Inc.*

Frozen Meals, Inc., is a small but rapidly growing manufacturer of frozen tray dinners. The company processes and freezes the meals at a central plant and ships them to regional distribution centers where they are stored in refrigerated warehouses on a consignment basis. Sales are made principally to large wholesale grocery distributors, mostly in the western half of the United States. The company sold more than 4 million tray dinners last year and this year's total is likely to approach 6 million.

When the firm was first founded, top management was able to keep close tabs on the manufacturing operation. Elaborate cost control or even cost reporting systems did not seem necessary. The firm grew rapidly, however, and top management realized that it needed an accounting information system. Arthur Hesse, the company's president, saw the problem this way: "This is a low-margin business. Prices are generally set by competition and our profits are extremely vulnerable to small variations in unit costs.

---

* Adapted with permission from an article written by Patrick J. McCullagh, published by the National Association of Accountants. Revised, 1982.

This means that reliable and timely cost information is vital. This information must include accurate manufacturing costs for each menu.

We also need to know when our costs are getting out of line—even a penny or two on each meal can put a real dent in our profits. Even worse, our growth gives us an insatiable appetite for funds to finance our working capital requirements, and we can't afford mistakes that cut down our cash flow.''

To design and install the new accounting system, Mr. Hesse hired Margaret Bonomi, a business school graduate with five years of experience on the controller's staff of a large mail-order house. Ms. Bonomi was given the title of controller and was assigned responsibility for all accounting and clerical operations.

"I knew from the beginning," Ms. Bonomi said, "that I had to get the system going very quickly. Art Hesse no longer had the time to keep tabs on the factory on a daily basis. When he hired me, he also hired Ted Crawford as plant manager. The factory is Ted's baby. He expects the managers of the three production departments—preparation, assembly, and wrapping—to meet delivery schedules and keep costs under control. Ted does most of the production planning and helps the department heads out when problems arise, and this keeps him too busy to know everything that's going on all the time. He's been a great help to me in getting the system started. Fortunately, since we had no information system at all before I came, I could start fresh and really move. I hired an assistant and an accounting clerk and we had the new system working in about three months.''

Materials costs

Because materials costs bulk so large in the overall cost structure, Ms. Bonomi began by concentrating on developing cost standards and reporting procedures for materials costs. She found that the number of raw materials was relatively small, fewer than 100 kinds of items. She classified these into three major groups:

1. Entree items (meat, fish, etc.).
2. Vegetables.
3. Other ingredients and condiments.

She found that some items of raw materials are received daily, such as fresh meat, fresh vegetables, eggs, and butter. These are held for short periods under normal refrigeration before going into production. Other items, mainly vegetables, are received frozen and are stored in freezers until they are needed. Finally, nonperishable items such as flour, sugar, and salt are stored at normal temperature in an enclosed area in the factory.

The product unit for costing purposes is the *menu,* the company's term for its tray dinners. The company now has 10 different menus and will probably add more in the near future. Ms. Bonomi's first step in developing a system for reporting materials costs was to establish a standard quantity of each item used for each 1,000 meals. This information was developed by production personnel from the recipes used for each menu. These materials usage figures were recorded on a Cost Reference Sheet like the one in Exhibit 1. The physical quantities were then extended at standard prices supplied by the purchasing department to get total cost and cost per meal figures. These became the standard materials costs, different for each menu.

The Cost Reference Sheet also includes a section for packaging supplies. These fall into two categories: (1) aluminum trays and foil overwrap, and (2) cartons and labels. Since packaging is similar for each meal, the same standard cost is used for all menus.

The next step was to design a procedure for recording the purchase and use of materials and supplies. Because seasonal price fluctuations in this industry are the rule rather than the exception, Ms. Bonomi decided to extend all materials invoices at the standard unit prices developed by the purchasing department. Four inventory accounts are maintained in the general ledger—one each for fresh, frozen, and dry ingredi-

Exhibit 1

COST REFERENCE SHEET

Menu No.:   6   Date: 1/18
Meals produced: 1,000

		Quantity			Cost Analysis	
	Unit	Raw	Cooked	Unit Cost	Total Cost	Cost per Meal
Ingredient:						
Beef	Lb.	400	330	$2.96	$1,184.00	$1.18400
Potatoes	Lb.	230		0.14	32.20	0.03220
Lima beans	Lb.	150		0.52	78.00	0.07800
Butter	Lb.	11		1.75	19.25	0.01925
Etc.	—	—		—	—	—
						$ .xxxxx
Packaging supplies:						
Aluminum Trays		1,009 M		240.00	242.16	0.24216
Aluminum Overwrap		1,013 M		48.00	48.62	0.04862
Etc.		—		—	—	—
						$ .xxxxx
Direct labor:						
Preparation						0.28536
Assembly						
Line						0.14568
Wrapping						0.08560
Total						0.51664
Total						$ .xxxxx

ents and one for packaging supplies. The standard costs of the items purchased are entered in these four accounts whenever materials are received.

The general ledger accounts are backed up by a file of Material Record Cards, one for each item, as illustrated in Exhibit 2. When a shipment of materials is received, the physical quantity received is recorded in the column at the left of this card. Issues of materials to production departments are not recorded as they occur. Instead, a complete physical inventory is taken monthly to determine the quantity of each item on hand at the end of the month. This information is entered in the lower left-hand corner of the Material Record Cards (17,000 pounds of this item). Subtracting the ending inventory from the total material available for use (36,500 pounds) provides a measure of actual consumption for the month (19,500 pounds, in this case). This is entered at the right.

The final step is to calculate the standard consumption of each kind of materials. The daily production reports list the number of meals produced each day. These are summarized at the end of the month and the total quantities are entered on the Material Record Cards, as in the center columns of Exhibit 2. Standard consumption for the month is determined by multiplying the standard quantity figures in the upper half of the Material Record Card by the number of meals produced.

With this information, a usage variance can be calculated immediately for each kind of ingredient, measured in physical quantities only. Significant variances are identified by the controller's staff and reported to Mr. Crawford immediately. No attempt is made to classify these variances by menu, because actual usage is not recorded on

Exhibit 2

MATERIAL RECORD CARD				
Item: Lima beans	Grade: "A"	Unit (pound)		Standard Cost: $0.52
Standard consumption per 1,000 meals	Menu 1 ___ Menu 2 ___	Menu 3 200 Menu 4 ___		Menu 5 ___ Menu 6 150

Vendors: A. Grow Pak, Inc. B. Freeze Fresh Corp.

	Received		Production		Consumption		
Date	Vendor	Quantity	Menu	Meals	Standard	Actual	Variance
1/1	Inventory	6,500	3	62,000	12,400		
1/5	B	30,000	6	45,000	6,750		
1/31	Total	36,500			19,150	19,500	Plus 350 pounds
2/1	Inventory	17,000					

this basis. "We've found these variance figures very useful," Ms. Bonomi said. "The system has been in use for less than a year, but we've already made a number of improvements in processing methods after the variance reports have shown excessive consumption of some of the ingredients."

Labor costs

Unit cost standards have also been developed for direct and indirect labor costs. All direct labor employees are paid on an hourly basis. They are grouped into three wage categories:

Category A. $7.50 or less.
Category B. $7.55 to $8.50.
Category C. More than $8.50.

The standard direct labor costs of operations in the preparation department have been based on performance data collected by production personnel during a test period. An example of one of these test observations is shown in Exhibit 3. The manager of

Exhibit 3

DIRECT LABOR REPORT							
Department: Preparation					Date: 1/11		
Operation: Breading veal			Menu: 2		Meals prepared: 1,830		

Class of Labor	Number of Employees	Time From	Time To	Hours	Total Hours	Average Rate	Cost
A 2		8:00 A.M.	10:00 A.M.	2	4	$7	$28.00
B 3		8:00 A.M.	11:00 A.M.	3	9	8	72.00
C 2		10:00 A.M.	11:30 A.M.	1½	3	9	27.00
							127.00

Unit cost of operation per meal, $0.06940

the preparation department listed the preparation steps for each menu, noted the time taken for each step in each menu, and used these data to derive a set of standard time allowances. Ms. Bonomi's assistant extended these times at the average wage rate for workers in each wage category, thereby deriving a standard labor cost for each operation and a total standard labor cost for each menu.

A similar procedure was followed for the assembly and wrapping departments, except that a single standard direct labor cost was developed for all menus. All menus receive identical treatment during the operations performed in these two departments.

A standard is also used for indirect labor cost—the wages of all hourly workers other than those classified as direct labor. Indirect labor is not classified by department, however, and a single rate is used to cover all kinds of indirect labor. This rate is the estimated percentage of indirect labor to direct labor cost for the factory as a whole. Standard indirect labor cost for each menu is obtained by multiplying the standard direct labor cost by this estimated percentage.

At the beginning of each week production personnel supply the payroll clerk with a schedule showing the number of employees in each category assigned to each department for the week. One week's schedule, for example, showed the following:

Wage Category	Direct Labor Employees			
	Preparation	Assembly	Wrapping	Total
A	12	35	10	57
B	3	4	3	10
C	10	2	2	14
				81

Any midweek changes of assignment, which occur infrequently, are reported to the payroll clerk as they occur.

The payroll clerk then distributes the total direct labor payroll (including overtime premiums) to the departments in direct proportion to the number of employees. In the week described in the table above, for example, the assembly department was charged 35/57 of the total direct labor cost of all category A employees, 4/10 of the total direct labor cost of all category B employees, and so on.

Once the direct labor costs have been distributed in this way, they are compared with the standard direct labor cost of the work done in each department during the week. This information is reported to Mr. Crawford in a weekly labor cost report. This shows the net variance from standard direct labor cost for each department during the preceding week, together with the overall ratio of indirect to direct labor and the amount of the overtime premiums in the factory as a whole.

Factory overhead costs

Ms. Bonomi classified all factory costs other than direct materials, direct labor, and indirect labor as factory overhead costs. Because few of these are traceable to specific departments, the overhead costs are not departmentalized.

Using statistical techniques, Ms. Bonomi's assistant tried to find relationships between various overhead costs and the volume of production. Since he was able to find none, these costs are budgeted as fixed. Standard overhead costs have not yet been developed for the company's individual products.

Monthly control reports

Ms. Bonomi's assistant prepares a summary factory cost variance report at the end of each month. This report is based on a tally of the month's production. The number of each menu produced is multiplied by the standard cost per unit, using the form illustrated in Exhibit 4. The figures in the right-hand column are then cross-totaled for all menus to determine the total standard costs of meals completed during the month.

Exhibit 4

<table>
<tr><td colspan="4" align="center">STANDARD COST SUMMARY</td></tr>
<tr><td>Menu No.: _____</td><td></td><td colspan="2" align="right">Month: _____ 19__</td></tr>
<tr><td>Item</td><td>Standard Unit Cost</td><td>Total Units Produced</td><td>Total Standard Materials and Labor</td></tr>
<tr><td>1. Entree item . . . .</td><td>$0.xxxx</td><td></td><td>$</td></tr>
<tr><td>2. Vegetables . . . .</td><td>0.xxxx</td><td></td><td></td></tr>
<tr><td>3. Other ingredients . . . . .</td><td>0.xxxx</td><td></td><td></td></tr>
<tr><td>4. Trays and foil . . . .</td><td>0.xxxx</td><td></td><td></td></tr>
<tr><td>5. Packaging . . . .</td><td>0.xxxx</td><td></td><td></td></tr>
<tr><td>6. Direct labor . . . .</td><td>0.xxxx</td><td></td><td></td></tr>
<tr><td>7. Indirect labor . . . .</td><td>0.xxxx</td><td></td><td></td></tr>
<tr><td>Total . . . .</td><td>$0.xxxx</td><td></td><td>$</td></tr>
</table>

Before these totals are compared with actual costs for the month, the inventory of work in process is checked. Production personnel count the work in process at the close of business on the last working day of the month. This generally takes only a few minutes. A clerk extends these quantities at their standard cost. Actual costs and standard costs for the factory as a whole are then summarized in the Monthly Variance Summary illustrated in Exhibit 5. For factory overhead, the figure shown in the "standard" column is $1/12$ of the annual budget; for all other items it is the standard cost of meals completed, plus or minus the change in the standard cost of the work in process inventory.

Exhibit 5

<table>
<tr><td colspan="5" align="center">MONTHLY VARIANCE SUMMARY</td></tr>
<tr><td></td><td>Standard</td><td>Price Variance</td><td>Use Variance</td><td>Actual</td></tr>
<tr><td>Raw materials consumed . . . . . .</td><td>$ —</td><td>$ —</td><td>$ —</td><td>$ —</td></tr>
<tr><td>Packaging supplies . . . .</td><td>—</td><td>—</td><td>—</td><td>—</td></tr>
<tr><td>Direct labor . . . .</td><td>—</td><td></td><td>—</td><td>—</td></tr>
<tr><td>Indirect labor . . . .</td><td>—</td><td></td><td>—</td><td>—</td></tr>
<tr><td>Factory overhead . . . .</td><td>=</td><td></td><td></td><td>=</td></tr>
<tr><td>Cost of goods manufactured .</td><td>$ —</td><td></td><td></td><td>$ —</td></tr>
</table>

The first two lines on this report summarize the three categories of ingredients and two categories of packaging supplies tabulated in Exhibit 4. "We decided," Ms. Bonomi said, "that a report with too many figures would only make it more difficult for management to focus on the essentials. We can always bring these five items in as supplementary information if we need to. We can also show labor usage variances by department, but this extra detail goes only to factory management; top management wants only the broad picture, with an explanation of what is being done to correct unfavorable usage variances. We calculate the cost of goods sold each month by multiplying the number of cases sold by the standard cost per case. This means that we can put the monthly operating statement in management's hands three working days after the end of the month. The only variances we calculate weekly are the labor cost variances I described earlier; the others come out only once a month. Top management never sees the weekly labor cost reports."

Ms. Bonomi makes no effort to reconcile the monthly variance summaries with the variance information on the Materials Record Cards and on the weekly labor summaries. "The procedure we use gets the monthly variance summary out faster than if we tried to work from the detailed records. Besides, our method makes sure that the amounts shown in the inventory accounts represent the amounts actually on hand. If we've overlooked anything in the bookkeeping routine, we can pick it up here.

"We're still working on the system, but we think it has achieved its primary purpose—supplying timely information essential to profitable expansion and doing it at minimum cost and during a vital phase of growth."

Cost bookkeeping

The cost bookkeeping procedures at Frozen Meals, Inc., are designed to minimize the number of bookkeeping entries in the inventory accounts. Six inventory accounts are maintained; four for materials and supplies (as described earlier), one for work in process, and one for finished goods.

The standard costs of the materials and supplies are charged to the materials and supplies inventory control accounts at the time of purchase. These accounts are credited once a month for the standard materials and supplies costs of meals produced, on the basis of the data in the standard cost summaries (Exhibit 4); the accompanying debits are to the work in process account.

Actual labor costs are charged to direct and indirect labor cost control accounts as payrolls are accrued. Standard labor costs, again taken from the standard cost summaries, are credited to these accounts and charged to work in process.

Overhead costs are accumulated in a set of overhead cost accounts. The balances in these accounts are closed into the work-in-process account at the end of each month.

As soon as the clerk calculates the standard cost of the work in process at the end of the month, an entry is made to transfer to the finished goods account the amount necessary to reduce the balance in the work-in-process account to standard cost. Finished goods inventories are also counted and a transfer to cost of goods sold is made to bring the balance in the finished goods account down to the standard cost of the meals on hand at the end of the month.

Variances in the materials and labor cost control accounts are also transferred to the cost of goods sold account at the end of the month. The balances in all inventory accounts therefore represent the standard costs of the inventories on hand at the end of the month.

a. What were management's objectives? To what extent did these call for scorecard information and to what extent did they require steering control information?

b. What specifications and constraints did Ms. Bonomi have to observe as she approached her task?

c. How well did the new system meet management's objectives? How well did it meet the specifications and satisfy the constraints?

d. What future changes or system refinements should Ms. Bonomi consider, now that the system is in operation? Why would these be desirable? Would they be costly to implement?

10 Flexible budgets: Controlling supportive overhead costs

Companies which use standard costing in their factories usually develop standard overhead costs for their products just as they develop standard direct materials and direct labor costs. The standard overhead cost of a product is determined by multiplying some measurable characteristic of the product (e.g., the number of standard direct labor hours it requires) by an overhead rate representing the ratio of total overhead cost to the total of this characteristic for all products combined.

To illustrate, suppose a company has chosen to base the overhead rate on the number of standard direct labor hours. The total overhead cost is expected to be $50,000 in a period in which operating volume is 10,000 standard direct labor hours. These figures are used in the left-hand side of Exhibit 10–1 to derive the predetermined overhead rate, $5 a standard direct labor hour at normal volume. The standard direct labor time for product X is 2 hours a unit, and this is combined with the overhead rate in the center of

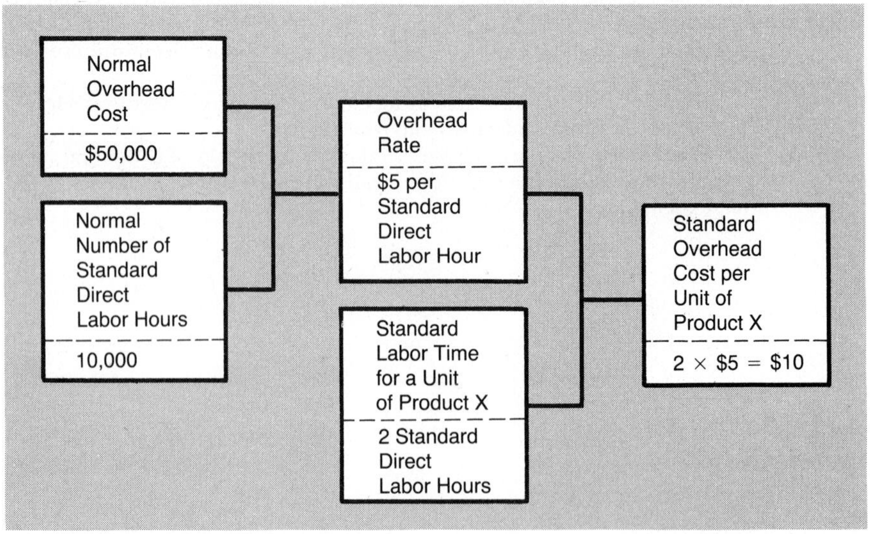

Exhibit 10–1 Calculating the standard overhead cost of product X

the diagram to derive the standard overhead cost of a unit of product X, $10.

Standard overhead cost can't be used as a standard for factory cost control because overhead costs include elements that don't vary in strict proportion to changes in production volume. For example, the horizontal line in Exhibit 10-2 shows that fixed costs are expected to amount to $20,000 a month regardless of volume. At a normal volume of 10,000 standard direct labor hours, fixed costs will average $2 an hour. If the department performs work calling for only 8,000 standard direct labor hours, total standard fixed overhead cost is only 8,000 × $2 = $16,000, the height of point P in Exhibit 10-2. The department's fixed overhead will exceed the standard fixed overhead cost for the month by $4,000, even if management does exactly what it is expected to do.

Exhibit 10-2 Standard fixed overhead cost: A poor cost control standard

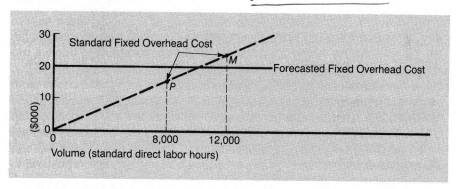

Standard overhead cost provides just as poor a control standard at high volumes. At a volume of 12,000 standard direct labor hours, for example, total standard overhead cost will include 12,000 × $2 = $24,000 for fixed costs, point M in Exhibit 10-2. This is $4,000 more than the manager ought to be spending.

The purpose of this chapter is to see how the accountant gets around this problem, thereby providing useful reports on the control of factory overhead costs and the overhead costs of other responsive activities. We'll refer to all of these as *supportive overhead costs.* Our discussion falls under three main headings:

1. Reporting cost performance for responsive overheads.
2. Developing the control standards.
3. Integrating interdepartmental allocations into the reporting structure.

Reporting cost performance: Flexible budgets and spending variances

Cost control standards for the overhead costs of responsive activities are provided by flexible budgets. In this section we'll see what flexible budgets are, how they can be integrated into control reports, and how to interpret variances between actual costs and flexible budget standards.

The flexible budget

The flexible budget consists either of a cost-volume formula (such as $20,000 + $3 × Standard direct labor hours) or a set of fixed budgets, one for each of a number of alternative production volumes in a given responsibility center. The first two columns of Exhibit 10–3 show the flexible budget for the drills department of a small metal products factory. Departmental volume in any month is measured by the number of standard direct labor hours required by that month's production.

Exhibit 10–3 Monthly overhead cost budget, drills department

Cost Element	Budgeted Monthly Fixed Cost	Budgeted Variable Cost per Standard Direct Labor Hour	Budgeted Cost at 4,000 Standard Direct Labor Hours
Supervision, at volume (standard direct labor hours) of:			
Less than 3,000	$2,600 ⎫		
3,000–4,499	3,400 ⎬	—	$ 3,400
4,500 or more	4,100 ⎭		
Materials handling labor	—	$0.12	480
Idle or lost time.....................	—	0.06	240
Other indirect labor	—	0.32	1,280
Overtime premium	—	*	—
Supplies	—	0.14	560
Power.............................	—	0.21	840
Maintenance.......................	1,200	0.20	2,000
Tools	—	0.10	400
Floor space	800	—	800
Equipment depreciation	600	—	600
Factory administration	1,400	—	1,400
Total	$7,400†	$1.15†	$12,000

* Ten cents for each standard direct labor hour in excess of 4,500 hours a month.
† Totals apply only to normal operating range of from 3,000 to 4,499 standard direct labor hours a month.

The budget in this illustration is presented as a set of formulas so that we can develop flexible budget allowances for any operating volume the department is likely to record. It can be drawn on a chart as a straight line from a volume of 3,000 standard direct labor hours to a volume of 4,500 standard direct labor hours. At that point both a jump in fixed costs and a 10-cent increase in the variable cost rate take place.

The budget formulas in the first two columns have been applied to the normal departmental volume of 4,000 standard direct labor hours to produce the budget allowances in the right-hand column. These figures are used both to calculate the predetermined overhead rate and to provide the control standard if volume in a particular month actually happens to be 4,000 standard direct labor hours. For any other volume a different set of figures has to be developed.

Departmental overhead spending variances

In control reporting for responsive overhead costs, the overhead costs charged to a responsibility center are compared to figures drawn from the flexible budget corresponding to the volume of activity actually achieved during the period covered by the report. The drills department's report for the month of May is reproduced in Exhibit 10–4. The left-hand column lists the costs assigned to the department during the month, determined mainly from documents such as requisitions, time tickets, and pay slips. The second column shows the comparable flexible budget standards, obtained by applying the budget formula in Exhibit 10–3 to the department's operating volume for the month, 3,600 standard direct labor hours. The supplies budget, for example, was calculated from the equation at the top of the next page:

Exhibit 10–4 Departmental overhead cost report, Drills department

DEPARTMENTAL OVERHEAD

Department: 10—Drills

Period: May 19xx
Volume: 3600 hours

Actual	Budget	(Over) Under		Actual	(Over) Under
			Controllable:		
			Materials		
$ 410	$ 432	$ 22	handling labor	$ 2,450	$ (218)
190	216	26	Idle or lost time	1,754	(638)
1,125	1,152	27	Other indirect labor	5,340	612
280	—	(280)	Overtime premium	1,545	(1,545)
2,080	1,920	(160)	Maintenance	5,027	(167)
530	504	(26)	Supplies	2,298	306
780	756	(24)	Power	3,620	100
610	360	(250)	Tools	1,955	91
6,005	5,340	(665)	Total controllable	23,989	(1,459)
			Noncontrollable:		
3,700	3,400	(300)	Supervision	17,600	(600)
800	800	—	Floor space	4,000	—
			Equipment		
625	600	(25)	depreciation	3,050	(50)
1,400	1,400	—	Factory administration	7,000	—
			Total departmental		
$12,530	$11,540	$(990)	overhead	$55,639	$(2,109)

(Header row spanning: **Current Month** covers Actual, Budget, (Over) Under; **Year to Date** covers Actual, (Over) Under)

Supplies budget for May = 3,600 × $0.14 = $504.

The third column then lists the differences between the figures in the first two columns. These are usually referred to as *overhead spending variances*. In this case the department spent $990 more in May than the flexible budget at 3,600 standard direct labor hours provided for.

The year-to-date columns at the right show the actual costs for the first five months of the year and the total spending variances for the same period. These figures provide a useful perspective on the current month's figures. The current variance in overtime premium, for example, was only slightly lower than the average for the previous four months, indicating a continuing situation that might need attention. The unfavorable variance in current maintenance costs, on the other hand, accounted for most of the cumulative variance in that item. The department head would probably look into this, but the manager at the next higher level would probably be undisturbed by a single month's departure from the norm.

Price and usage components of the overhead spending variance

The figures in the "actual" columns of Exhibit 10–4 are the amounts charged to the drills department during the month. Some of these are based on the standard prices of the resources used—indirect labor, for example, may be charged to the department at standard wage rates if the company has a standard costing system. Other resources are likely to be charged at the prices actually paid or accrued during the current period, because no standard prices have been developed for them. Telephone service, outside services, taxes, and so on are usually charged at actual input prices for this reason.

The term *actual* therefore should be interpreted as the amounts actually charged to the responsibility center rather than the actual costs to the company of the resources used in the department. For some items, at least part of the overhead spending variance may be an input price variance; for others, it will be a usage variance only.

For example, suppose the drills department uses only one kind of supplies. No standard price has been established. The department requisitioned and used 80 boxes of these supplies in May, for which it was charged $530, an average of $6.625 a box. The $504 flexible budget standard, however, embodied management's judgment *ex ante* that at a volume of 3,600 standard direct labor hours this department should have used only 72 boxes of supplies, at a budgeted price of $7 a box.

With this information we can make the analysis diagrammed in Exhibit 10–5. The first step is to restate the actual usage at the budgeted price: 80 boxes × $7 = $560. The $30 difference between this amount and the $530 charged the department was due to a favorable price break. The remainder of the spending variance in this item ($56, unfavorable) arose because the management used eight boxes of supplies more than the budget provided for.

Exhibit 10–5 Decomposition of spending variance into price and usage components

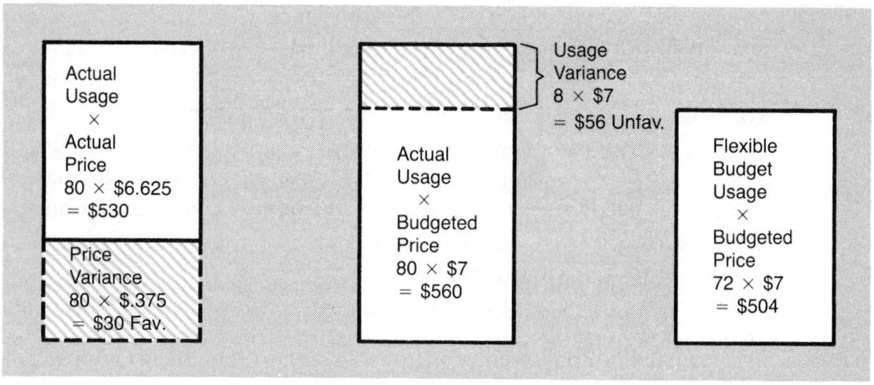

Reporting noncontrollable costs

Resource prices are almost always outside the user's control, at least at the first-line supervisory level. If standard prices haven't been established and price changes have been substantial, some effort should be made to estimate how much of the spending variance is due to price effects so that the user's success in controlling resource usage won't be obscured.

Some cost elements are even farther out of the user's control, in that both price and usage are determined elsewhere. One solution for these elements is to list them "below the line," as noncontrollable. Four cost elements were shown in this way on the drills department's report in Exhibit 10–4. Managers presumably should focus their attention on costs they can do something about, those appearing above the controllability line.

Another possible solution is to take the noncontrollable items out of the report entirely. This has several advantages:

1. It reduces the size of the report and heightens its visual impact.
2. It reduces the number of disputes about amounts charged to the department.
3. It keeps the manager's cost control efforts in perspective—when the noncontrollable variances grow large, they may make the controllable items look small by contrast, and the department head may conclude that control efforts are not very important.

Whether a cost should be classified as controllable is a matter of judgment. The amount of overtime premium, for example, depends in part on the size of the work force assigned to the department. The department head can affect the amount of the overtime premium, however, by dealing with the causes of delays as they arise, helping workers who are falling behind schedule, and so forth. Controllability means the ability of the manager to influence the cost, and this should be recognized even if responsibility is shared with others.

Reports for higher management

Monthly reports on departmental materials usage and labor usage variances generally serve the first-line manager as scorecard controls. They come too late and contain too little detail to be very useful as steering controls at that level. The monthly overhead report, in contrast, is much more likely to serve the department head as a steering control, mainly because spending variances are less visible when they occur. Recorded overhead costs fluctuate from day to day in ways that may have little to do with the day-to-day fluctuations in volume. It is not clear whether a cost is reasonable until after both total cost and total volume figures are available.

Scorecard and steering controls fuse into each other at the next managerial level. Higher level managers are not very interested in the details of departmental performance—they are concerned mainly with the total spending variance. This helps them decide where to direct their attention (steering control) and gives them a partial measure of the performance of the various department heads (scorecard control).

Following this reasoning, the reports issued to higher levels of management are likely to be more condensed than those issued to the department heads. It would not be unusual for each department to be represented by a single line on an overhead summary report for the factory as a whole. Copies of the more detailed departmental reports may be attached for information, but the section manager or plant manager should resist the temptation to get too far into these details. Only if the overall departmental spending variance is large and persists from month to month should higher management intervene.

The plant manager, like the department head, may get a condensed highlight report instead of a full listing of all the departments' results. Alternatively, or in addition, the plant manager may get a series of charts, perhaps like the one in Exhibit 10–6. If properly drawn, these can be used to identify the important areas quickly and with little effort.

Exhibit 10–6 Drills department, overhead cost performance chart

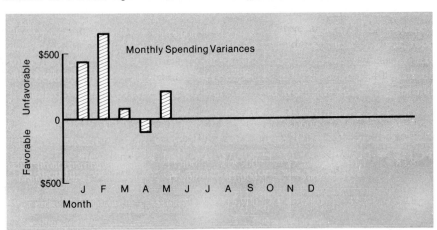

Transitory influences on the spending variances

The purpose of the flexible budget is to highlight *all* departures from efficient performance at the actual volume achieved. It may not show how much cost management is willing to incur in a particular period. Even discounting the possibility that the formula was wrong to start with, two other things may have occurred to throw it off:

1.   Volume may have changed so rapidly that overhead costs have not had time to settle down at amounts appropriate to the new level.
2.   Volume may have fallen temporarily and management has decided to reduce organizational stress by continuing to spend at the old level for a while.

For example, if volume moves down suddenly, as from Y to X in Exhibit 10–7, the cost standard on which the department head's performance should be judged may be at level A, not the height of the normal flexible budget line at the new volume. Similarly, if volume rises suddenly from Y to Z, the correct short-term standard may be level B (if rapid expansion leads to short-term cost penalties) or level C (if the existing overhead structure can support the new volume for a short period without breaking down).

Exhibit 10–7 Dynamic budget effects

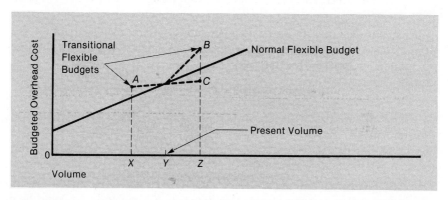

Spending variances may also arise because higher management has authorized the department to make off-budget expenditures. Exhibit 10–8 shows one way of allowing for these. In the second column we see that management authorized the department to incur up to $200 in overtime premiums this month, even though the flexible budget made no provision for overtime. The manager of the drills department also agreed to reductions of $60 and $70 in the budgets for other indirect labor and supplies, respectively. These changes gave the department a new set of rules to go by. As a result, the figures in the third column of Exhibit 10–8 are a better measure of cost performance than those in Exhibit 10–4.

To reduce clutter, only the three rightmost columns may be reported to the department head. The full schedule should be accessible, however, in case anyone wants to question how the adjusted budget figures were calculated.

Exhibit 10–8 Authorized budget changes

CURRENT OVERHEAD COST SUMMARY					
Department: 10—Drills				Period: May 19xx	
				Volume: 3600 hours	
	Original Budget	Authorized Changes	Adjusted Budget	Actual Cost	(Over)/Under Adj. Budget
Controllable:					
Materials handling labor .	$ 432	—	$ 432	$ 410	22
Idle or lost time	216	$(70)	146	190	(44)
Other indirect labor	1,152	(60)	1,092	1,125	(33)
Overtime premium	—	200	200	280	(80)
Maintenance	1,920	—	1,920	2,080	(160)
Supplies	504	—	504	530	(26)
Power	756	—	756	780	(24)
Tools	360		360	610	(250)
Total controllable	$5,340	$ 70	$5,410	$6,005	$(595)

Developing the flexible budgets

Before inaugurating a flexible budgeting system, management needs to decide how to develop the budget formulas. Three issues need to be discussed briefly here:

1. How to develop usable measures of cost-volume relationships.
2. How to measure volume.
3. How to persuade operating managers to accept flexible budget standards.

Estimating cost-volume relationships

In discussing cost behavior in Chapters 4 and 5, we made the simplifying assumption that the relationship between volume and cost could be described with perfect accuracy by drawing a single line on a cost-volume chart. Few relationships in the real world are this definite. In fact, the one illustrated in Exhibit 10–9, though far from perfect, is better than many. Each of the dots in this diagram represents the costs actually incurred during some period when costs were under control and volume was stable. To make the data comparable, costs observed in different periods have been divided by index numbers reflecting changes in purchase prices.

The line through the center of the diagram represents management's best effort to summarize the relationship traced by this past cost experience. This line has been drawn so that the actual observations cluster around it in a symmetrical pattern, with those below the line just balancing those above it.

Locating a set of flexible budget formulas that actually have these characteristics is not easy. One approach is to analyze historical data by a statistical tech-

Exhibit 10–9 Positioning the flexible budget

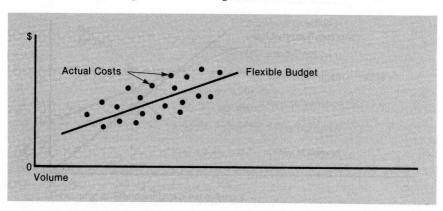

nique known as least squares regression analysis. We'll discuss this method in some detail in Chapter 20.

A much simpler approach is to go down the chart of accounts for each department, classifying each cost element as wholly fixed, wholly variable, or a mixture of both. This is known as the *judgment* method or *inspection of accounts* method. Having made this classification, the analyst estimates the monthly amount for each fixed cost element and the average unit cost for each proportionally variable element. The estimate of variable cost is often based on average historical cost per unit of activity adjusted for any changes in prices, wage rates, or other conditions that may have occurred or are expected to occur.

It may also be possible to budget step functions largely by the inspection of accounts method. For example, the number of supervisors required in a responsibility unit is likely to vary only with fairly substantial changes in volume. Without going to the trouble of detailed cost analysis, the department head should be able to specify the volume level at which additional supervisors will be required.

Deciding how to measure volume

The second technical problem is to select a measure or measures of the volume of activity in each department. Only three factors need enter into this decision:

1. How closely does the measure correlate with overhead cost?
2. Is the measure readily available?
3. Can the manager understand it?

Of these, the first is the most important. In fact, we'd like to go even farther, and find the factor that *causes* overhead costs to vary. Cause and effect are often difficult to prove, however, and we are generally willing to assume that the variable that correlates best with overhead cost is the variable that causes overhead cost to vary. If overhead costs are more likely to move up and down when direct labor hours change than when the amount of direct materials changes, then direct labor hours provides a better basis for evaluating the manager's ability to control these costs.

Management should use a measure of volume other than the one that correlates best only if collecting the preferred data would be too expensive or if the department head finds the preferred measure confusing and difficult to interpret.

In our illustration in this chapter, we are assuming that volume is best measured by the level of *output* (measured by the number of *standard* direct labor hours). In many situations, however, actual direct *inputs* are likely to represent the causal factors more closely than production output. Materials handling labor, for example, depends on the quantity of materials handled rather than on the yield from these materials. Even so, to avoid complicating this introductory explanation more than it needs to be, we'll drop the discussion of input-driven overhead costs now and pick it up again in the next chapter.

Some departments should use more than one index of volume because different costs vary with different input elements. This makes the system more expensive, of course, and may make it seem more complex than it really is. The additional cost is likely to be small, however, and if the relationships show up clearly, the extra indexes probably are worth using.

Behavioral problems in flexible budgeting

The best technical apparatus in the world won't produce a good flexible budgeting system if the reactions of the people affected by the system are not considered very carefully. In fact, the most difficult part of the job of installing a new system is to get the department heads to cooperate. Some may see flexible budgeting as an effort by top management to exert pressure down the line and make their lives more difficult. Others will see it simply as extra work, extra responsibility with no personal benefits, and no extra pay.

One part of the usual solution is to include both operating people and financial people in the groups responsible for getting the system going in the first place. In one company a team of supervisors, factory accountants, engineers, and headquarters staff people spent six months planning the first flexible budgeting cycle. The members of the team met frequently with the other first-line supervisors in the plant to identify and overcome technical problems and to explain the purposes of flexible budgeting. Even so, only slightly more than half of the first-line supervisors had made any real commitment to the program by the time the first budgeting cycle began. It wasn't until two years later that virtually all the supervisors and assistant supervisors were really convinced that flexible budgeting offered them more than it asked from them.

This presumes that the best way to introduce and operate a flexible budgeting system is to secure the active *participation* of the managers for whom the budgets will serve as performance standards. This is the common pattern for budgeting in the United States. The presumption is that participation leads the department heads to accept budgetary goals as their own, thereby increasing their motivation to try to reach them. The participation requirement, for example, would mean that the supervisors could override the conclusions of regression analyses of the costs if they could present logical arguments against them. A regression line may fit the data very well, but still may not describe the current situation because the data are biased or out of date.

The argument for participation is supported by the findings of a substantial body of empirical research. It raises a number of issues, however, that require a more complete discussion than we have room for here. We shall discuss these behavioral questions in Chapter 22.

Interdepartmental allocations for control reporting

Some of the resources used by a responsibility center are provided to it by the company's internal service and support centers rather than by the center's own employees or outside suppliers. When the responsibility center is charged for its use of these resources each period, its flexible budget must provide for them. In this section we'll see how the flexible budget for service and support inputs can be developed and used.

Terminology reminder

A *charging rate* is a dollar amount per unit, designed to be multiplied by a number of physical, temporal, or monetary units such as square feet, hours, or payroll dollars, to determine the amount of cost to assign to a given class of cost objectives.

Purposes of periodic allocations

Allocations can play a significant role in the determination of product costs, as we saw in Chapter 7. In most situations, however, this purpose is served by the allocation of budgeted costs in the determination of predetermined departmental overhead rates. *Ex post* allocations enter into product cost only in special contracting or cost reimbursement situations, or in the process production systems we'll describe in Chapter 14.

Aside from these situations, the main purpose of periodic interdepartmental cost allocations is to reinforce the department heads' motivation to control their usage of service center services. We must be careful, therefore, to make sure that increases in usage lead to increases in service charges, and vice versa.

A second possible purpose is to remind decision makers of the impact of their decisions on the organization's total operating costs. If a manager makes a decision that will add 1,000 hours to the direct labor budget, for example, the system should include some means of notifying the manager that this decision will increase service department costs, too.

We'll find this second possible purpose more convincing when we examine the kinds of data to be reported to higher management. The truth is that production people, whether at the departmental level or higher up, make few if any decisions that affect total production volume. As a result, monthly allocations are unlikely to have any significant impact on resource-allocation decisions.

Developing the flexible budget for allocations

The flexible budget standard for a cost allocated to a responsibility center has two components: a rate and a measure of usage, capacity occupied, or activity. Both of these components are based on information available when the budget is prepared.

The two sets of overlapping blocks at the left in the diagram in Exhibit 10–10 represent flexible budget schedules for four possible operating volumes in two different departments, drawn up at budget time. The cross-hatched block in the cluster at the upper left represents the flexible budget for a service department at a normal volume of operations. A charging rate is calculated from the costs in this block and the amount of service usage, service capacity required, or operating activity budgeted for all other departments combined.

For example, suppose the service department in Exhibit 10–10 is the maintenance department in our illustrative factory. Its budgeted costs amount to $32,000 at its normal volume of 2,000 service hours a month. A full-cost charging rate therefore is $32,000/2,000 = $16 a service hour.

The charging rate for a service department, based on its budgeted costs at its *normal* operating volume, enters into the flexible budgets of the other departments at *every* possible volume in those departments. The cluster of

Exhibit 10–10 Flexible budget allowances for allocated costs

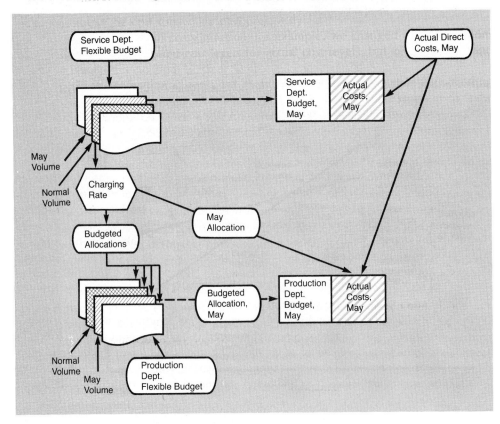

blocks in the lower left-hand corner of Exhibit 10–10 represents the flexible budgets of a production department, _prepared at budget time,_ before actual operating volume is known. The budgeted charging rate is combined with budgeted usage, capacity, or activity at _each_ of the production department's possible operating volumes. The cross-hatched block at the lower left represents the production department's normal volume; the diagonally shaded block represents its budget at the volume level which turned out to be the level actually achieved in May. The flexible budget standard for allocated costs in _both_ of these blocks comes from information available at budget time: actual data for May aren't known when the flexible budget is prepared.

Suppose the production department in Exhibit 10–10 is our illustrative drills department. This department's usage of maintenance department services is expected to be approximated by the following formula:

Hours used = 75 a month + 1/80 × standard direct labor hours.

If these hourly figures are multiplied by the maintenance department's budgeted charging rate of $16 an hour, we get the following flexible budget formula for the drills department's use of maintenance services:

Maintenance cost = $1,200 a month + $0.20 × standard direct labor hours.

This is the formula we included earlier in Exhibit 10–3.

With this formula we can develop budget allowances for any possible volume level in the drills department. For example:

Volume (Standard Direct Labor Hours)	Budgeted Allocation of Maintenance Costs
4,000	$1,200 + $0.20 × 4,000 = $2,000
3,600	1,200 + 0.20 × 3,600 = 1,920

These figures appear on the flexible budget schedules represented by the cross-hatched and diagonally shaded blocks in the lower left-hand portion of Exhibit 10–10.

Determining monthly charges for service and support

Once the drills department's flexible budget for May is determined, it must be compared with the amounts actually allocated to the department during the month, represented by the long diagonal arrow in the middle of the diagram. These amounts may be usage charges, capacity charges, or activity charges.

Usage charges.   Ideally, any differences between actual allocations to the drills department and its budgeted allocations should reflect the effects of the drills department's cost control efforts. The only allocations that provide control information are usage charges, determined by multiplying actual service usage by service department charging rates.

Two kinds of charging rates might be considered: (1) _predetermined_ rates, the charging rates that were used to establish the flexible budget allowances;

or (2) *actual average cost,* reflecting the service department's costs and volume for the current period. To choose between these, we need only recognize that department heads may be able to control the amounts of service they use, but they can't control the unit cost the service department incurs in providing that service.

For example, the workers in a machining department have nothing to do with the amount of fuel burned in the company's power plant to produce a given amount of power, but they may be able to help the power plant reduce its costs by reducing the amount of power they use. Variations in fuel efficiency are reflected in variations in the average cost of power; by predetermining the charging rate we can keep these variations out of the using department's spending variances.

Suppose in our illustration the maintenance department provides 130 hours of service to the drills department in May, at an average cost of $17 an hour. If we use the budgeted charging rate of $16, we get the following comparison in the drills department:

Actual Charge	Budgeted Charge at Actual Volume	Spending Variance
130 hours × $16 = $2,080	120 hours × $16 = $1,920	10 hours × $16 = $160 Unfav.

The spending variance represents the drills department's excessive usage of maintenance services (130 hours instead of 120), multiplied by the $16 budgeted rate.

If we use the actual average cost of $17, however, the amount of the charge would be 130 × $17 = $2,210, and the spending variance will be $2,210 − $1,920 = $290, unfavorable. The weakness of doing this should be apparent. The spending variance under this alternative would result both from a variance in the amount of service used ($160) and from a variance in the price charged for it ($130). This price variance may mean any or all of three things:

1. Maintenance department volume was down, increasing average fixed cost.
2. Maintenance department costs were not well controlled.
3. Wage rates or prices paid by the maintenance department went up.

Using a predetermined charging rate removes this price variance from the spending variance.

An even better system would be to use a predetermined unit price for each kind of maintenance job, so that variations in the efficiency of the maintenance force would be completely eliminated from the drills department report. Maintenance work is usually so varied, however, that this degree of predetermination is usually impossible to achieve. By predetermining the charging rate, at least we know that none of the variance results from variations in the price of an hour of maintenance service.

A maintenance department illustration has been used here because maintenance costs are usually allocated by usage charges. It is not always clear just how much responsibility production department managers have for the amount of maintenance work performed. Directly they may have none, with responsibility for both preventive maintenance and repairs lodged in the maintenance managers or managers. Even so, the operating manager often can do much to affect the amount of maintenance required, and this is therefore often regarded as an item to be controlled jointly by the maintenance and operating managers.

Capacity charges. Capacity charges have served their purpose once the overhead rates have been calculated. Individual department heads don't decide how much service or support capacity will be provided. Only higher management can change the amount of capacity provided; a change in the allocation therefore doesn't measure the effect of any action the department head may have taken.

Our preferred solution is to make no monthly allocations of the costs of providing capacity unless the users determine how much capacity is to be provided. If management insists on making allocations when the users have no such power, then capacity charges should be made at their budgeted amounts. If this is done for the floor space charge, the drills department will be charged $800 for its occupancy of floor space, just equal to its monthly budget (from Exhibit 10–3). The spending variance will be zero, as it should be when the department head has done nothing to cause or permit a variance to arise.

Activity charges. An activity charge is determined by multiplying a charging rate by some measure of the volume of activity of the departments to which costs are being allocated. Even if a service center's costs are affected by the demands placed on it by individual users, activity charges won't necessarily assign the costs of these demands to the users who occasion them. A department head who is conscientious in turning off unused lighting, for example, will still be charged a proportionate share of the power costs incurred by others who are less conscientious.

The only possible purpose in using monthly activity charges is to keep the users informed of the long-term effects of changes in their level of activity. As we have already said, however, department heads don't usually make the decisions which determine the level of activity. For this reason, our preferred solution once again is to make no monthly allocations at all, unless usage measurements can be found. If management insists, however, then we should use either a predetermined capacity charge or an activity charge with a predetermined rate. The result in either case will be a zero spending variance.

For example, if factory administrative costs were to be distributed by a predetermined activity charging rate of 35 cents a standard direct labor hour, the drills department would have to reclassify its charge for these costs as one of its variable costs, but the variance would still be zero:

Actual Allocation	Budgeted Allocation	Spending Variance
3,600 hours × $0.35 = $1,400	3,600 hours × $0.35 = $1,400	Zero

Preferred allocation methods for control reporting		
Service Characteristics	Allocation Method	Allocation Criterion
Usage measurable, service volume variable	Predetermined user charge	Service usage
Service or support volume fixed	No allocation or predetermined capacity charges	Percentage of service capacity needed
Service volume variable but not measurable	No allocation, predetermined capacity charges, or predetermined activity rates	Capacity or actual activity

Under-/overdistribution of service and support costs

If no allocations are made or if predetermined charging rates or predetermined charges are used, the costs of the service and support centers undoubtedly will differ each month from the amounts allocated. These differences are known as under- or overdistributions of service cost. For example, suppose the actual cost of operating the maintenance department in May amounts to $30,600 on a total volume of 1,800 maintenance hours, an average of $17 an hour. Using a predetermined charging rate of $16 an hour will lead to distributions of $1,800 \times \$16 = \$28,800$ of maintenance cost, leaving $1,800 undistributed.

Under- or overdistributions don't measure the cost control performance of the service or support center. Control performance in these centers is monitored in the same way as the control performance of production centers— that is, by comparing actual costs with flexible budget standards appropriate to current operating volume in the service or support center itself. These spending variances won't account for all of the amount that is under- or overdistributed, but we'll wait until Chapter 11 to account for the remainder.

Use of the two-part tariff in monthly applications

As long as the charging rate is predetermined, the variances in the user's periodic cost reports will reflect departures from the flexible usage standards. This is what we want the variances to mean, because in most cases the users can't control the average costs of the units of service they consume.

A second question is whether the charging rate should be based on average full cost or on some less inclusive figure, such as average variable cost or the average rate of short-term cost variability. Full-cost charging rates overstate the short-run variability of service costs; usage charges computed in this way may lead department heads to decide not to use services when in fact the company would be better off if they were used. Variable cost rates, on the other hand, may encourage the development of usage patterns that will persist into the future, requiring changes in the amount of service capacity provided. This additional capacity will be costly and this additional cost should be considered by the managers in their capacity-creating decisions.

One way to steer between these two perils is to use a two-part tariff—that is, charge each manager for actual service usage at a predetermined charging rate representing the average rate of short-term cost variability in the service department, plus the amount, determined at the beginning of the year, for the user's share of the budgeted capacity costs of the service department. The capacity charge would represent the user's proportionate share of total service usage at the time of peak load. This capacity charge wouldn't change during the year, but any manager who used the services heavily at peak periods would have to expect getting a bigger share of total capacity costs in the next year's budget.

For example, if maintenance costs vary at a rate of $10 a maintenance hour, production centers might be charged $10 instead of $16 an hour for maintenance services. Each production center would also be charged for its proportionate share of the fixed costs of operating the maintenance department, determined in advance.

The two-part tariff is justified mainly if the variable cost of providing the service is likely to be the only cost affected by usage decisions during the period covered by those decisions. If management can save a half hour of a $10 employee's time by using computer services with a variable cost of $3, the services should be used.

This reasoning has two defects: (1) some fixed costs will be affected even in the short run if service demand exceeds anticipated limits; and (2) usage patterns established in the short run are likely to affect the long-term need for capacity. By charging for service at a single rate reflecting average attributable cost, average full cost, or even an external market price, management can keep usage at levels that can be justified in long-run, cost-benefit comparisons.

Notice that these arguments for and against the two-part tariff in *ex post* cost allocation apply only if the amount of service provided can be measured. A case can also be made for using a two-part tariff if service can't be measured but costs vary in response to short-term fluctuations in the level of activity. The variable portion of the charge in that case would be an activity charge rather than a usage charge. Activity charges have no direct control purpose, however, and for this reason our general preference is for predetermined capacity charges if allocations are called for.

Summary

Control standards for the overhead costs of responsive activities take the form of departmental flexible budgets, consisting of a series of budget schedules for various volume levels within the normal operating range.

The differences between the costs charged to a responsibility center (which may include some resources at actual prices and some at standard prices) are known as overhead spending variances. These variances should be divided into controllable and noncontrollable categories; management may choose not to report the noncontrollable items at all, or to report them separately, "below the line."

Flexible budget standards also need to be prepared in each department for any service and support center costs to be allocated to it during the year. The only variances in these items the department heads should see on their performance reports are variances in controllable service usage. This calls for the use of predetermined charging rates or predetermined capacity charges.

Management may not expect the spending variances to be zero if volume is changing rapidly or if a recent volume change is expected to be temporary. The role of the flexible budget is simply to identify the variance; management's responsibility is to decide what action, if any, is called for.

Independent study problems (solutions in Appendix B)

1. **Components of the overhead spending variance.** A department's fixed overhead cost at normal volume is expected to be $12,000 a month. Other overhead costs, amounting to $8,000 a month at normal volume, are expected to vary with the amount of direct materials processed. The department is expected to use 10,000 pounds of direct materials a month to manufacture 2,500 units of product.

   The department used 9,000 pounds of direct materials during the month of August and manufactured 2,000 units of product. Fixed overhead costs in August amounted to $11,800; variable overhead costs totaled $9,900.

   Required:

   a. Calculate the overhead spending variance for the month.

   b. Fixed costs consist entirely of building and equipment rentals. Variable costs consist entirely of indirect labor. Wage rates have increased by 5 percent since the flexible budget was developed; rentals have increased by 2 percent. Use this information to subdivide the spending variance into input price and usage components.

   c. Instead of the situation described in (*b*), you find that half of the fixed costs consist of the wages of employees engaged in cleaning the equipment once an hour and performing similar tasks; the other half is equipment depreciation. Half of the variable costs consist of the royalty to be paid to the inventor of the equipment used in the department; the other half is the labor cost of moving materials into the department and moving finished work to the next department. Royalty payments are proportional to the number of pounds of materials processed. Which of these are controllable costs at the departmental level? Would your answer differ if the royalty payments were based on the number of units of product manufactured?

2. **Periodic performance reporting.** The Riptide Company uses full-cost overhead rates and departmental flexible budgets for cost reporting. The fiscal year is divided into 13 "months" of four weeks each. Department T has a normal production volume of 4,000 direct labor hours a month and the following flexible budget, valid for volumes between 3,000 and 4,500 direct labor hours a month:

	Fixed per Month	Variable per Direct Labor Hour
Nonproductive time, machine operators	—	$0.25
Other indirect labor........................	$2,000	0.50
Operating supplies	—	0.15
Depreciation...............................	2,000	—
Rent	700	—
Total	$4,700	$0.90

Actual costs and volumes in two successive months were as follows:

	Month 4	Month 5
Direct labor hours........	4,000	3,000
Nonproductive time	$ 800	$1,200
Other indirect labor	3,700	3,600
Operating supplies........	650	430
Depreciation	2,100	2,150
Rent	770	730

Required:

a. Calculate budget allowances and prepare a cost performance report for each of these months. This report should include each of the five overhead cost elements, arranged in any way you find appropriate.

b. Comment on the various items in these reports, indicating which items are likely to be of greatest significance in evaluating the cost control performance of the department supervisor.

c. Looking only at those items for which cost performance was poorer in month 5 than in month 4, what would be your reaction to the statement that the manager of this department had been lax in enforcing cost control during month 5? What remedial action would you suggest, if any?

3. **Flexible budget comparisons: Allocated overheads.** Service department S provides services to other departments of the company's manufacturing division. The amount of service provided depends on the needs of the other manufacturing departments, as determined by their respective managers.

The normal operating volume for department S is 10,000 service hours a month. Budgeted cost is $20,000 plus $2.50 per service hour. Actual department S cost for February was $42,000, at a volume of 8,000 service hours, including 1,100 service hours performed in production department M.

The normal operating volume for department M is 15,000 direct labor hours a month. At this volume, department M's budget allows for the consumption of 1,000 department S hours. During February, department M operated at a volume of 12,500 direct labor hours, and at this volume it had a budget standard of 900 department S hours.

The budgeted costs of department S are to be included in user departments' budgets on the basis of budgeted usage at normal volume, by means of a single full-cost charging rate.

Required:

a. How much should department M be charged for department S services for the month of February? State your reasons.

b. Compute the variance in the charge for department S services that would appear on department M's cost performance report for the month, using the allocation method you developed in (a). Give a one-sentence explanation of the meaning of this variance.

    c. Calculate department S's spending variance for the month and the amount of this department's under- or overdistributed overhead in February.

    d. Recalculate your answers to (*a*) and (*b*) on the assumption that a two-part tariff is in use for department S. Department M's budgeted share of usage at peak volume is the same percentage of the total as its share at normal volume.

Exercises and problems

4. **Overhead performance report.** The monthly flexible budget standards for the assembly department of the Boyce Furniture Company for various numbers of direct labor hours are shown in the following table:

	Direct Labor Hours				
	10,000	10,500	11,000	11,500	12,000
Supervision	$ 1,800	$ 1,800	$ 1,800	$ 1,800	$ 1,800
Indirect labor	7,000	7,350	7,700	8,050	8,400
Supplies	4,000	4,200	4,400	4,600	4,800
Power, fuel, and water	1,000	1,050	1,100	1,150	1,200
Depreciation	2,000	2,000	2,000	2,000	2,000
Space occupancy	3,000	3,000	3,000	3,000	3,000
General plant overhead ...	2,800	2,800	2,800	2,800	2,800
Total	$21,600	$22,200	$22,800	$23,400	$24,000

Actual charges to the department for the month of March were as follows:

Supervision	$ 1,900
Indirect labor	7,700
Supplies	4,020
Power, fuel, and water	930
Depreciation	1,950
Space occupancy	3,000
General plant overhead	3,000
Total	$22,500

The actual volume of production during March totaled 10,500 direct labor hours.

Required:

    a. How much of the budgeted overhead cost would you classify as fixed? What is the average budgeted variable cost per direct labor hour?

    b. Prepare a departmental overhead cost report for the month.

    c. Comment on the possible causes of each of the variances shown on the report.

5. **Validity of flexible budgeting.** Each factory department in the Balch Company has a monthly budget, agreed upon at the beginning of the year, and a set of flexible budget formulas, used for monthly performance reporting. The formulas for the finishing department are:

Supervision	$1,200 a month
Indirect labor	$800 a month + $1 per direct labor hour
Overtime premium	$0.50 for each direct labor hour in excess of 2,400 direct labor hours a month
Supplies	$0.40 a direct labor hour
Power	$200 a month + $0.15 a direct labor hour
Depreciation	$500 a month
Other overhead	$0.10 a direct labor hour

Normal volume in this department is 3,000 direct labor hours a month and planned volume for this year averages 2,700 hours a month. Volume in May was 2,500 direct labor hours. The actual costs for the month were as follows:

Supervision	$1,260
Indirect labor	3,340
Overtime premium	140
Supplies	860
Power	600
Depreciation	500
Other	300
Total	$7,000

Required:

a. Prepare a performance report for the month of May, using the flexible budget.
b. The company's president is not sure that flexible budgeting is a good idea because it may make department heads look good even though average cost keeps going up. The president prefers to compare average actual cost with average planned cost at planned volume. Prepare the figures for a report on this basis and draft a reply to the president's argument.

6. **Significance of spending variances.** Some indirect labor in the Balch Company (problem 5) is performed by regular bench operators who normally perform direct labor operations. Management is reluctant to lay these operators off for short periods of time. Instead, some of the indirect labor work, such as cleaning and adjusting machines, is deferred until the production schedule is light.

The manager of the finishing department thinks this should be built into the flexible budget, with larger flexible budget allowances when volume is low, and vice versa. This would eliminate erratic fluctuations in the indirect labor spending variances. The plant controller disagrees, arguing that production creates the need for indirect labor services, even though these services may not be performed when production takes place.

Required:

Prepare a brief report on this issue, stating your position and indicating how management should interpret and use the spending variances arising under the solution you are recommending.

7. **Choosing the measure of volume.** Overhead costs vary with the number of machine-hours used. Production output is measured by the number of standard machine-hours required by the goods manufactured. The overhead rate is $10 a machine-hour, of which $8 is fixed and $2 is proportionally variable. Normal volume is 800 machine-hours a month.

During October, production volume amounted to 1,000 standard machine-hours. The goods produced during the month actually required 1,100 machine-hours. Actual overhead cost amounted to $8,700.

Required:

a. Calculate the spending variance for the month.
b. Calculate the spending variance with the flexible budget based on standard machine-hours. Does this provide better or poorer cost control information than the spending variance you calculated in answer to (a)? Explain the reason(s) for your preference.

8. **Choosing the measure of volume.** The following data, adjusted for price changes, were recorded during 10 recent periods:

Period	Overhead Cost	Direct Labor Hours	Standard Direct Labor Hours	Machine-Hours
1	$2,010	3,000	3,100	5,000
2	2,270	3,500	3,400	5,100
3	2,050	3,100	3,000	5,400
4	2,100	3,200	3,300	4,800
5	2,200	3,400	3,500	5,200
6	2,300	3,600	3,700	6,000
7	2,420	3,800	3,900	5,700
8	2,390	3,700	3,600	5,300
9	2,140	3,300	3,200	5,500
10	2,460	3,900	3,800	5,600

Required:

a. Plot cost against each of the three measures of volume, one on each of three separate diagrams.

b. Which of these measures of volume would you select as the basis of a flexible budget formula? Explain your choice.

9. **Analysis of the spending variance.** A department's flexible budget is based on the following relationships:

	Fixed per Month	Variable per Direct Labor Hour
Supervision	$1,650	—
Indirect labor	800	$0.60
Vacation pay	197	0.54
Supplies	—	0.80
Power	—	0.40

Normal volume is 2,000 direct labor hours a month. Actual volume for the month of July amounted to 1,500 direct labor hours, and the following costs were charged to the department:

Supervision	$2,598
Indirect labor	1,750
Vacation pay	7,250
Supplies	1,310
Power	715

You have the following additional information, not reflected in the budget data above:

1. The budgeted wage rates for direct labor average $8.40 an hour. Wage rates for direct and indirect labor were increased 5 percent by a union contract negotiated in April. Supervisory salaries were also increased 5 percent at the same time.

2. Vacation pay was budgeted originally at 9 percent of supervisory pay and 6 percent of the cost of direct and indirect labor. Vacation pay is charged to departments as employees take their vacations.

3. Power costs were budgeted at a rate of 8 cents a kilowatt-hour; the rate in July was 9 cents.

4. Supplies costs were budgeted on the basis of prices prevailing at the beginning of the year. Inventory is costed on a FIFO basis. Actual purchase prices in July were 10 percent higher than the amounts at the beginning of the year. An eight-month inventory of supplies is maintained at all times.

5. The budget provides for a single supervisor in this department. The plant manager authorized the department head to borrow an additional half-time supervisor from another department to help with a special group of customer orders in July and August. The department was charged for the amount of time this supervisor spent in the department. All supervisors receive identical salaries.

Required:

a. Ignoring the five items of additional information provided above, calculate the flexible budget for all five cost elements at a volume of 1,500 direct labor hours and calculate the spending variances on this basis.

b. The accountants can use the additional information provided in this problem to (1) adjust the budget, (2) adjust actual charges to a basis consistent with the budget, or (3) adjust neither, but report the impact of the additional information on the spending variances. Which of these alternatives do you prefer? Why?

c. Prepare a report on this department's operations, analyzing the sources of the spending variances you calculated in answer to (a), insofar as you can identify these sources. Include in your report how much of the spending variances should be classified as currently controllable by the department head. How should the noncontrollable portions of the variances be reported?

10. **Selecting a basis for monthly allocations.** The budgeted costs of the power service department amount to $9,520 a month; of this amount $2,500 is considered to be a fixed cost. Costs during April amounted to $9,300.

Power consumption in this factory is measured by the number of horsepower hours. The monthly power requirements of the factory's four other departments, in horsepower hours, are as follows:

	Producing Departments		Service Departments	
	A	B	X	Y
Needed at capacity production	10,000	20,000	12,000	8,000
Budgeted	8,000	15,000	8,000	5,000
Used during April	8,000	13,000	7,000	6,000

What dollar amounts of power service department costs should be allocated to each of these four departments for the month of April?

(CPA, adapted)

11. **Allocations: Interpretation of variance.** The costs of a factory service department, such as maintenance, are frequently distributed to other departments by multiplying a "charging rate" by the number of units of service provided to each other department. The charging rate is computed so as to provide for a complete distribution of service department costs, using the following formula:

$$\frac{\text{Actual direct service dept. costs} + \text{Actual costs allocated to service dept.}}{\text{Total units of service provided to all other departments}}$$

The factory of Green, Inc., uses a system of this kind. The milling department in this factory has a budget allowance of 50 maintenance hours a month plus one maintenance hour for every 100 milling department machine-hours in excess of 8,000 hours a month.

During April, the milling department operated at a volume of 11,000 machine-hours and used 70 maintenance hours. The departmental overhead cost report for the month included the following line:

	Actual	Budget	Variance
Maintenance labor	$735	$720	$(15)

Required:

a. What conclusions can you draw from this unfavorable variance? How well did the milling department manager control maintenance costs this month? What other factors are likely to have contributed to the $15 variance?

b. What changes, if any, would you suggest in the company's interdepartmental cost allocation system? Give your reasons either for your suggested changes . or for your satisfaction with the present system.

12. **Allocations: Interpretation of variance.** Service department S provides services to a number of production departments. The cost budget for department S at a normal volume of 5,000 service hours per month, together with actual departmental charges for the month of March, is as follows (4,000 hours of service were provided to production departments during March):

	Budget at Normal Volume		March Actual
	Amount	Fixed or Variable	
Service labor	$15,000	V	$14,000
Supervision	2,000	F	2,000
Indirect labor	4,000	V	3,000
Supplies	1,000	V	1,100
Depreciation	5,500	F	5,600
Rent	2,500	F	2,900
Total	$30,000		$28,600

Depreciation charged each month is 1 percent of the original cost of equipment installed in the service department. The rental charge is based on the department's pro rata share, based on floor space occupied, of the costs charged to the building service department's accounts during the month.

Production department M uses department S services, and the supervisor in charge of department M is expected to control use of these services. Normal production volume in department M is 10,000 machine-hours. Department M's use of department S services is budgeted at one service hour for every 10 machine-hours.

Each production department is charged each month for the number of hours of department S services it uses. The number of hours used is multiplied by a single rate equal to the average total cost of operating department S. The rate is recalculated each month by dividing the total cost of department S in that month by the total number of hours of service provided to all departments during the month.

During March department M operated a total of 11,000 machine-hours and used 900 hours of department S service.

Required:

a. Express department M's cost budget for its use of department S services as a mathematical formula.

b. Compute department M's budget for department S service: (1) at normal volume, (2) at 11,000 machine-hours.

c. Compute the service charge to department M for March.

d. Calculate the spending variance for department M's use of department S services during March.

e. Analyze department M's March spending variance in department S charges, showing a breakdown between the variance due to factors over which department M had some control and the variance due to other causes.

13. **Impact of increasing allocations.** "I get overcharged by the graphics department every month, and I'm getting pretty tired of it," Patrick Denning said. Mr. Denning was the manager of his company's advertising department.

"I know we use a lot of graphics," he continued, "but the amount they charge me has gone up a lot faster than my usage. Besides, I know that most of the costs down there are fixed costs. It seems to me that incremental cost would be a better basis for the charge."

Janet MacKenzie, the controller, admitted that Mr. Denning's charges had gone up, but cited figures to show that the increases were justified. "We have worked out an hourly rate," she said, "and everyone is treated alike. The hourly cost has gone up every year as we have expanded the system and gotten more sophisticated equipment. We don't raise the rate within the year, though. The rate is based on the budget for the year and each department has a budgeted allocation. If they don't use more time, they don't get charged more.

"The annual rate covers all of the costs that have been budgeted for operating the department during the year. We divide this by the number of hours we expect to devote to productive work, and this gives us the rate. We don't attach any of the costs to idle time or to the time we use for training purposes within the department. These are necessary and we feel that everyone should bear a fair share of the total.

"Actually, Pat Denning has kept pretty well within his budget limits over the years. I don't know what he's complaining about. Besides, his department's jobs use more of the expensive equipment than the rest of our work put together. If anything, we should charge him more than we do now."

Required:

a. Why is Mr. Denning upset? Does he have reason to worry?

b. What should Ms. MacKenzie do in response to Mr. Denning's complaints?

14. **Incremental allocation rates.** The General Student Corporation of America purchased in December 19x4, a Comprox Sigma 1102 electronic data processing machine. The machine was bought primarily for department A, which began using about a third of its capacity.

After the machine was installed, four other departments (B, C, D, and E) decided they, too, would like to use it. They claimed, however, that they should pay for the direct costs of use only, and that the total overhead should be carried by department A. This arrangement would be fair, they claimed, because the purchase of the Sigma 1102 could be justified on the basis of its use in department A alone. Moreover, the opportunity cost of letting other departments use the machine would be nil,[1] because if the machine were not used it would just stand idle. Renting the machine to outsiders on a part-time basis was not considered appropriate.

The arrangement proposed by the four departments was put into force, to everyone's satisfaction. By January 19x5, the machine time was fully booked. At that point, a sixth department, F, also found ways to use the machine. The controller decided that machine time should be used where its benefits were the greatest. To accomplish this, a new system was devised, whereby each department would have to pay a share of the overhead, this cost being divided in proportion to the time used.

This new system reduced the hourly charges to department A, which then increased its usage to about half of the time available. Department B took one

---

[1] This assumption is made only to simplify the analysis of this problem. In general, this is a highly inaccurate characterization of this technology.

quarter of the machine time, but the other departments decided the system was too costly and took their work off the machine. The machine, therefore, remained idle one fourth of the time.

Criticize the two methods used to charge for machine time. Describe the method you would use, state what you would expect it to accomplish, and why you prefer it.

(Prepared by Michael Jensen)

15. **Performance report and variance analysis.** Overhead budgets for department 23 in the Broken Bend Manufacturing Company's main factory are prepared on the following basis:

| | Monthly Budget Allowance | |
	Fixed	Variable per Direct Labor Hour
Cost Element		
Indirect labor:		
Inspection	$ 800	$0.23
Helpers	1,200	1.00
Rework labor	—	0.30
Labor downtime	—	0.40
Other indirect labor	—	0.07
Total indirect labor	2,000	2.00
Supervision	2,000	—
Overtime premiums...........	—	0.60
Vacation and holiday pay	300	0.60
Payroll taxes.................	430	1.12
Pensions	200	0.50
Total labor	4,930	4.82
Supplies	—	0.50
Power......................	500	0.06
Other charges	1,830	—
Total overhead	$7,260	$5.38

During November, department 23 used 3,300 direct labor hours (DLH). Department 23 was charged for the following costs in November:

1. Labor time tickets, extended at actual wage rates:

Direct labor	$28,620
Inspection	1,610
Helpers	5,235
Rework labor	1,250
Labor downtime	845
Other indirect labor	315

2. Additional charges to department 23 from the factory payrolls for the month:

Supervision	$2,160
Overtime premiums	3,120

3. Supplies issued, $1,425.
4. Power consumed, $775.
5. Other charges, $1,850.

You have the following additional information:

1. All vacation pay, holiday pay, overtime premiums, payroll taxes, and pensions attributable to direct labor are classified as departmental overhead. These

costs are charged to the department monthly on the basis of the following percentages:

> Vacation and holiday pay: 9 percent of supervisory payrolls, 6 percent of all other departmental wages and salaries except overtime premiums.
>
> Payroll taxes: 10 percent of departmental wages and salaries, including amounts accrued for vacation and holiday pay.
>
> Pensions: 5 percent of departmental wages and salaries except overtime premiums and holiday and vacation pay.
>
> Overtime premiums: actual amounts earned.

2. The budgeted wage rate for direct labor was $8 an hour.
3. Normal volume is 3,000 direct labor hours a month.
4. A 7 percent increase in salaries and wage rates was negotiated after the flexible budget formulas were established: the fringe benefit formulas were left unchanged.
5. Inventories of materials and supplies are measured at standard prices.
6. Power rates increased 10 percent after the flexible budget formulas were drawn up.
7. All of the costs in the department's budget except "other charges" are classified as controllable by the department head.

Required:

a. Prepare a list of overhead cost elements and enter the amounts charged to department 23 in November.
b. Using the formulas quoted in the table at the beginning of the problem, calculate the flexible budget for the month, item by item, and use it to calculate the overhead spending variances.
c. Subdivide the spending variances into input price and usage components. Should the department head be concerned about the department's cost control performance during November?
d. What changes, if any, would you suggest in the basis on which costs are charged to the department or reported to management? State the reasons for your recommendations.

16. **Departmental reporting, including allocations.**   Alpha Company's factory has four production departments (shaping, drilling, finishing, and assembly) and four service departments (office, buildings, maintenance, and logistics).

All accounting, personnel, and plant management functions are performed in the office department. The buildings department is responsible for heating, lighting, and maintaining the factory building and grounds. The maintenance department handles repairs of all equipment except office equipment, the latter being serviced on contract by an outside firm. The logistics department handles all incoming shipments of materials and parts and operates the stock room.

Monthly cost reports are issued to the managers of each of the company's departments. These reports are to be used primarily in reviewing the effectiveness of cost control in each department. Production department managers are presumed to share responsibility with the maintenance department manager for the number of maintenance hours used.

Charges for service departments' services were made sequentially each month in 19x1, in the following sequence and using the following formulas:

1. Buildings . . . . $0.34 a square foot
2. Office . . . . $280 an employee
3. Maintenance . . . . $9.60 a maintenance hour
4. Logistics . . . . $4.80 a requisition

Alpha uses predetermined departmental overhead rates to assign factory overhead costs to individual job orders. The following rates per direct labor hour were used in 19x1:

Shaping	$ 9.50
Drilling	10.00
Finishing	11.50
Assembly	4.00

The flexible budgets of the finishing and maintenance departments were calculated from the following formulas in 19x1:

	Finishing	Maintenance
Budgeted direct overhead:		
Supervision	$2,200 + $1,800 for each 5,000 direct labor hours (or major portion thereof)	Fixed, $1,800
Other salaries	Fixed, $2,500	None
Indirect labor	$2.50 for each direct labor hour	$4.80 for each maintenance hour
Supplies	$0.70 for each direct labor hour	$150 + $0.65 for each maintenance hour
Depreciation—equipment	Fixed, $12,000	Fixed, $420
Other direct charges	$14,112 + $2 for each direct labor hour	$20 + $1.30 for each maintenance hour
Budgeted statistics:		
Employees	3 + 1 for each 150 direct labor hours (or major portion thereof) + 1 for each 5,000 direct labor hours (or major portion thereof)	1 for each 150 maintenance hours.
Floor space	Fixed	Fixed
Maintenance hours	230 + 5 for each 100 direct labor hours	None
Requisitions	5.71 for each 100 direct labor hours	None

Part-time employees are not used, and the flexible budget allowances reflect the notion that if more than half an employee is required, a fulltime employee will be hired.

The following operating and overhead cost data were recorded for the month of November:

	Direct Labor Hours	Direct Departmental Overhead	Employees	Maintenance Hours	Requisitions	Floor Space (square feet)
Shaping	6,500	$ 31,600	54	600	410	18,000
Drilling	5,500	25,720	42	650	650	16,000
Finishing	13,000	106,070	96	900	790	33,000
Assembly	7,500	4,950	50	550	400	20,000
Office	—	70,600	33	—	—	10,000
Buildings	—	38,400	11	—	—	1,000
Maintenance	—	21,000	18	—	—	1,000
Logistics	—	9,400	6	—	—	2,000
Total	32,500	$307,740	310	2,700	2,250	101,000

The direct departmental overhead costs of the finishing and maintenance departments were broken down further, as follows:

	Finishing	Maintenance
Supervision	$ 7,790	$ 1,860
Other salaries	2,550	—
Indirect labor	36,100	13,050
Supplies	8,230	1,760
Depreciation	12,000	420
Other direct charges	39,400	3,910
Total direct overhead	$106,070	$21,000

Required:

a. Set up a columnar table, with each department represented by a column and total direct departmental overhead for November listed on the first line. Complete the table by allocating service department costs sequentially as prescribed above. (Remember that in sequential allocation no allocation is made by a department to any department preceding it in the allocation sequence.)

b. Calculate the amount over- or underabsorbed in each production department and the amount over- or underdistributed in each service department. Enter these amounts at the bottom of your cost distribution sheet.

c. Prepare flexible budget allowances for November for the finishing and maintenance departments.

d. Prepare an overhead cost performance report for each of these two departments, including all allocated costs. You should assume that all direct overhead costs are controllable except supervision, other salaries, and equipment depreciation.

e. Speculate on possible reasons for the difference between the total spending variance for the maintenance department and the amount under- or overdistributed for this department in November.

Case 10–1: Rigazio Enterprises* (flexible budgeting)

Rigazio Enterprises manufactures a wide variety of metal products for industrial users in Italy and other European countries. Its head office is located in Milan and its mills in northern Italy provide about 80 percent of the company's production volume. The remaining 20 percent is produced in two factories—one in Lyon, France, and the other in Linz, Austria—both serving local markets exclusively through their own sales organizations.

Until 1964 the methods used by the Milan headquarters to review subsidiary operations were highly informal. The managing director of each subsidiary visited Milan twice a year, in October and in April, to review his subsidiary's performance and discuss his plans for the future. At other times the managing editor would call or visit Milan to report on current developments or to request funds for specified purposes. These latter requests were usually submitted as a group, however, as part of the October meeting in Milan. By and large, if sales showed an increase over those of the previous year and if local profit margins did not decline, the directors in Milan were satisfied and did nothing to interfere with the subsidiary manager's freedom to manage his business as he saw fit.

During 1963, the company found itself for the first time in 12 years with falling sales volume, excess production capacity, rising costs, and a shortage of funds to finance

---

* Copyright 1965 by l'Institut pour l'Etude des Méthodes de Direction de l'Entreprise (IMEDE), Lausanne, Switzerland. Published by permission. Monetary amounts have been restated in dollars for convenience.

new investments. In analyzing this situation, the Milan top management decided that one thing that was needed was a more detailed system of cost control in its mills, including flexible budgets for the overhead costs of each factory.

The Lyon mill was selected as a "pilot plant" for the development of the new system. Because the Lyon mill produced a wide variety of products in many production departments, it was not possible to prepare a single flexible budget for the entire mill. In fact, Mr. Spreafico, the company's controller, found that the work done in most of the production departments was so varied that useful cost-volume relationships could not even be developed on a departmental basis. He began, therefore, by dividing many of the departments into cost centers so that a valid single measure of work performed could be found for each one. Thus a department with both automatic and hand-fed cutting machines might be divided into two cost centers, each with a group of highly similar machines doing approximately the same kind of work.

The establishment of the cost centers did not change the responsibility pattern in the factory. Each department had a foreman who reported to one of two production supervisors; the latter were responsible directly to Mr. Forclas, the plant manager. Each foreman continued to be responsible for the operations of all the cost centers in his department. In some cases a cost center embraced an entire department, but most departments contained between two and five cost centers.

Once he had completed this task, Mr. Spreafico turned to the development of flexible budgets. For each cost center he selected the measure or measures of volume that seemed most closely related to cost (e.g., machine-hours) and decided what volume was normal for that cost center (e.g., 1,000 machine-hours per month). The budget allowance at the normal level of operations was to be used later as an element of standard product costs, but the budget allowance against which the foremen's performance was to be judged each month was to be the allowance for the volume actually achieved during that particular month.

Under the new system, a detailed report of overhead cost variances would be prepared in Lyon for the foreman in charge of a particular cost center and for his immediate superior, the production supervisor; a summary report, giving the total overhead variance for each cost center would be sent to the plant manager and to Mr. Duclos, the managing director of Rigazio France, S.A., in Lyon. The Milan top management would not receive copies of these reports but would receive a monthly profit and loss summary, with comments explaining major deviations from the subsidiary's planned profit for the period.

The preparation of the budget formulas had progressed far enough by mid-1964 to persuade Mr. Spreafico to try them out on the September cost data. A top management meeting was then scheduled in Milan to discuss the new system on the basis of the September reports. Mr. Duclos and Mr. Forclas flew to Milan to attend this meeting, accompanied by the controller of Rigazio France and a production supervisor responsible for some 30 cost centers in the Lyon factory.

Mr. Enrico Montevani, managing director of Rigazio Enterprises, opened the meeting by asking Mr. Spreafico to explain how the budget allowances were prepared. Mr. Spreafico began by saying that the new system was just in its trial stages and that many changes would undoubtedly be necessary before everyone was satisfied with it. "We started with the idea that the standard had to be adjusted each month to reflect the actual volume of production," he continued, "even though that might mean we would tell the factory they were doing all right when in fact we had large amounts of underabsorbed overhead. In that case the problem would be that we had failed to provide enough volume to keep the plant busy, and you can't blame the foremen for that. When you have fixed costs, you just can't use a single standard cost per hour or per ton or per unit, because that would be too high when we're operating near capacity and too low when we're underutilized. Our problem, then, was to find out how overhead cost varies with volume so that we could get more accurate budget allowances for overhead costs at different production volumes.

"To get answers to this question, we first made some preliminary estimates at headquarters, based on historical data in the accounting records both here and in Lyon. We used data on wage rates and purchase prices from the personnel and purchasing departments to adjust our data to current conditions. Whenever we could, we used a mathematical formula known as a 'least squares' formula to get an accurate measure of cost variability in relation to changing volume, but sometimes we just had to use our judgment and decide whether to classify a cost as fixed or variable. I might add that in picking our formulas we tried various measures of volume and generally took the one that seemed to match up most closely with cost. In some cost centers we actually used two different measures of volume, such as direct labor hours and product tonnage, and based some of our budget allowances on one and some on the other. These estimates were then discussed with Mr. Forclas and his people at Lyon, and the revised budget formulas were punched into tabulating cards for use in monthly report preparation.

"Although you have a complete set of the cost center reports, perhaps we might focus on the one for cost center 2122 [Table 1]. You can see that we have used two measures of volume in this cost center, direct labor hours and product tonnage. During September we were operating at less than standard volume, which meant that we had to reduce the budget allowance to $2,666, which averaged out at $115.91 a ton. Our actual costs were almost exactly 10 percent higher than this, giving us an overall unfavorable performance variance of $226, or $9.83 a ton.

Table 1 Overhead cost summary, cost center 2122, September

	Standard at Normal Volume (500 hours, 25 tons)	Budgeted at Actual Volume (430 hours, 23 tons)	Actual, Month of September	(Over) Under Budget
Supervision	$ 180	$ 180	$ 145	$ 35
Indirect labor	300	272	322	(50)
Waiting time	21	17	35	(18)
Hourly wage guarantee	14	13	6	7
Payroll taxes, etc.	321	282	301	(19)
Materials and supplies	30	26	28	(2)
Tools	150	129	128	1
Maintenance	320	307	375	(68)
Scrap loss	422	388	491	(103)
Allocated costs	1,052	1,052	1,061	(9)
Total	$ 2,810	$ 2,666	$ 2,892	$ (226)
Per ton	$112.40	$115.91	$125.74	$(9.83)

"I know that Mr. Duclos and Mr. Forclas will want to comment on this, but I'll be glad to answer any questions that any of you may have. Incidentally, I have brought along some extra copies of the formulas I used in figuring the September overhead allowances for cost center 2122, just in case you'd like to look them over." [See Table 2.]

a. Do you agree with Mr. Spreafico that $115.91 a ton (see Table 1) is a more meaningful standard for cost control than the "normal" cost of $112.40?

b. Comment on the variances in Table 1. Which of these are likely to be controllable by the foreman? What do you think the production supervisor should have done on the basis of this report?

c. What changes, if any, would you make in the format of this report or in the basis on which the budget allowances are computed?

d. In developing the budget allowances, did Mr. Spreafico make any mistakes that you think he could have avoided? Does his system contain any features that you particularly like?

Table 2 Flexible budget formula, cost center 2122

	Fixed Amount per Month	Variable Rate	Remarks
Supervision	$ 180	—	Percent of foreman's time spent in cost center
Indirect labor	100	$0.40/DLH*	—
Waiting time	—	0.04/DLH	Wages of direct labor workers for time spent waiting for work
Hourly wage guarantee	—	0.03/DLH	Supplement to wages of workers paid by the piece to give them guaranteed minimum hourly wage
Payroll taxes, etc.	41	0.56/DLH	Payroll taxes and allowances at 30% of total payroll, including direct labor payroll
Materials and supplies	—	0.06/DLH	—
Tools	—	0.30/DLH	—
Maintenance	160	6.40/ton	Actual maintenance hours used at predetermined rate per hour, plus maintenance materials used
Scrap loss	—	16.88/ton	Actual scrap multiplied by difference between materials cost and estimated scrap value per ton
Allocated costs	1,052	—	Actual cost per month, allocated on basis of floor space occupied

* Note: DLH = Direct labor hours.

11 Analysis of factory overhead cost variances

The overhead spending variances we discussed in Chapter 10 are only part of the total overhead cost variances many factory costing systems are able to identify. The purposes of this chapter are to explain how the total overhead cost variance arises and to study different methods the accountant is likely to use to subdivide it into two or more components. We'll try to answer three questions:

1. How the total overhead cost variance arises in a standard costing system.
2. How this variance can be subdivided into meaningful components.
3. What kind of overhead variance analysis is appropriate when standard costing is not used.

The origins of the total overhead cost variance

Absorbed overhead is the amount of factory overhead cost that is charged to products during a period of time. In our illustration of job order costing in Chapter 2, the amount of overhead cost absorbed was determined by multiplying the overhead costing rate by the number of direct *input* units (direct labor hours) actually used in that period. Under standard costing, the amount of overhead absorbed in any period is called *standard overhead cost* and is determined by the amount of *output* achieved during the period.

One way to calculate standard overhead cost is to count the number of equivalent units manufactured (units completed, plus or minus the change in work in process) and multiply this by the standard overhead cost per unit:

$$
\begin{array}{ccc}
\boxed{\begin{array}{c}\text{Standard}\\\text{overhead}\\\text{cost}\end{array}} & = & \boxed{\begin{array}{c}\text{Equivalent}\\\text{units of}\\\text{product}\\\text{produced}\end{array}} \quad \times \quad \boxed{\begin{array}{c}\text{Standard}\\\text{overhead}\\\text{cost per unit}\\\text{of product}\end{array}}
\end{array}
$$

This equation can also be stated in another form by replacing standard overhead cost per unit by its component parts:

$$
\boxed{\begin{array}{c}\text{Standard}\\\text{overhead}\\\text{cost per}\\\text{unit of}\\\text{product}\end{array}} = \boxed{\begin{array}{c}\text{Standard}\\\text{number of}\\\text{input units}\\\text{per unit of}\\\text{product}\end{array}} \times \boxed{\begin{array}{c}\text{Overhead}\\\text{rate per}\\\text{input unit}\end{array}}
$$

For example, suppose the overhead rate is the average overhead cost per standard direct labor hour. The amount of overhead charged to each unit of product therefore is determined by multiplying this overhead rate by the number of standard direct labor hours that product requires. The equation for total standard overhead cost in any period can be restated as follows:

$$
\boxed{\begin{array}{c}\text{Standard}\\\text{overhead}\\\text{cost}\end{array}} = \boxed{\begin{array}{c}\text{Equivalent}\\\text{units of}\\\text{product}\\\text{produced}\end{array}} \times \boxed{\begin{array}{c}\text{Standard}\\\text{number}\\\text{of direct}\\\text{labor hours}\\\text{per unit}\\\text{of product}\end{array}} \times \boxed{\begin{array}{c}\text{Overhead}\\\text{rate per}\\\text{standard}\\\text{direct}\\\text{labor hour}\end{array}}
$$

The standard overhead cost equation can be restated in still another way. By multiplying the equivalent number of units of product by the standard number of direct labor hours per unit, we can calculate the total number of standard direct labor hours in the period:

$$
\boxed{\begin{array}{c}\text{Standard}\\\text{direct}\\\text{labor hours}\end{array}} = \boxed{\begin{array}{c}\text{Equivalent}\\\text{units of}\\\text{product}\\\text{produced}\end{array}} \times \boxed{\begin{array}{c}\text{Standard}\\\text{number of}\\\text{direct labor}\\\text{hours per unit}\\\text{of product}\end{array}}
$$

The number of *standard* direct labor hours is a measure of *output* in which each unit of each product is weighted by the number of standard direct labor hours it requires. It depends only on the amount of production and is unaffected by variations in the number of actual direct labor hours. The equation for standard overhead cost can now be restated as follows:

$$
\boxed{\begin{array}{c}\text{Standard}\\\text{overhead}\\\text{cost}\end{array}} = \boxed{\begin{array}{c}\text{Standard}\\\text{direct}\\\text{labor hours}\end{array}} \times \boxed{\begin{array}{c}\text{Overhead rate}\\\text{per standard}\\\text{direct labor}\\\text{hour}\end{array}}
$$

To illustrate, suppose we find that the drills department of a small metal products factory uses standard direct labor hours as the basis for establishing the standard overhead cost of individual products. This department worked on two products in May, as follows:

	Product A	Product B	Total
Standard direct labor hours per unit	1	2	
Number of units completed	2,000	900	
Standard direct labor hours required by units completed ...	2,000	1,800	3,800
Standard direct labor hours required by work already done on units in process, May 31	200	300	500
	2,200	2,100	4,300
Standard direct labor hours required by work done in April on units in process, May 1	250	450	700
Total production (standard direct labor hours)	1,950	1,650	3,600

To get the standard overhead cost of this product, we have to multiply the number of standard direct labor hours by the standard overhead rate. The drills department's overhead budget can be represented by the following formula:

$$\text{Budgeted overhead} = \$7,400 + \$1.15 \times \text{Standard direct labor hours}$$

Normal volume was 4,000 standard direct labor hours and at this volume overhead cost was expected to amount to $7,400 + $1.15 × 4,000 = $12,000. The overhead rate incorporated in standard product costs therefore was $12,000/4,000 = $3 a standard direct labor hour.

We already know that production in May amounted to 3,600 standard direct labor hours. Standard overhead cost for the month therefore amounted to 3,600 × $3 = $10,800. We now can measure output in two different but equivalent ways:

	Jobs Completed		Ending Inventory		Beginning Inventory		Output
Standard direct labor hours	3,800	+	500	−	700	=	3,600
Standard overhead cost	$11,400	+	$1,500	−	$2,100	=	$10,800

Identifying the total overhead cost variance

The total overhead cost variance is the difference between actual overhead cost and the amount of absorbed overhead. If the actual overhead cost of the drills department in May amounted to $12,530, the total overhead variance was $1,730 and was unfavorable, as the diagram in Exhibit 11–1 shows.

This comparison doesn't appear out of thin air, of course. In fact, the main reason we identify the total overhead cost variance at all is that it emerges from the accounting system as a result of a decision to record standard overhead cost in the ledger accounts. We can begin to illustrate this by establishing

Exhibit 11–1 Derivation of total overhead cost variance

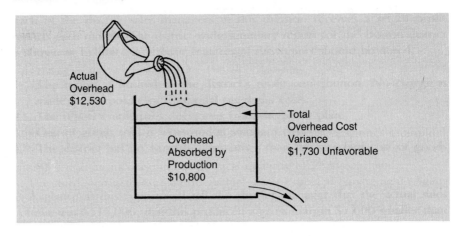

an overhead-in-process account for the drills department and entering the May 1 balance of $2,100 (700 standard direct labor hours × $3 an hour):

Overhead in Process—Drills

Bal. May 1 (at standard cost) 2,100	

Next, we can record the department's actual overhead cost for the month:

Overhead Summary—Drills

Actual overhead cost of the month's output 12,530	

The accompanying credit entries would be to such accounts as Accounts Payable, Wages Payable, Materials Inventory, and Accumulated Depreciation. The entry to the Overhead Summary account would be accompanied by debits to subsidiary accounts for supervision, indirect materials, and the other elements of departmental overhead that are itemized on the department's monthly performance report.

We also know from the table at the beginning of this illustration that the standard overhead cost of the units completed by the drills department in May amounted to $11,400 (3,800 standard direct labor hours × $3 an hour). These costs, along with the standard costs of the direct labor and materials in the completed work, would be transferred to a finished goods inventory account or to the work-in-process accounts of other departments to which the drills department sent its completed work. If the work went to the finished goods inventory, the standard overhead costs of these transfers would appear in our set of accounts as follows:

Overhead in Process—Drills			Finished Goods Inventory	
Bal. May 1	2,100	Standard overhead cost of the jobs completed 11,400 →	Bal. May 1	xxx
		→11,400		
		Bal. 9,300		

The Overhead in Process account now has a credit balance. The correct end-of-month balance in this account is $1,500 (500 standard direct labor hours × $3 an hour). To bring the account balance to its correct level, we need to debit it with the $10,800 standard overhead cost of the month's production:

Overhead in Process—Drills			
Bal. May 1	2,100	Completions	11,400
Standard overhead cost	10,800		
Bal. 1,500			

Since this entry is essentially an assignment of overhead costs to the inventory of work in process, we could make the accompanying credit to the Overhead Summary account. The balance in this account serves as a control total for the sum of the balances in the subsidiary overhead accounts, however. For this reason, it is useful to set up a separate account, called Overhead Absorbed or Standard Overhead. The complete entry therefore would be:

Overhead in Process—Drills	10,800	
Standard Overhead—Drills		10,800

This series of entries is summarized in Exhibit 11–2. Costs flow through the accounts from the upper left, following the arrows; the variance is the difference between the costs flowing in and the costs flowing out into inventory accounts. The total overhead variance emerges from these accounts as the difference between the debit balance in the Overhead Summary account and the credit balance in the Standard Overhead account.

To complete the series of entries and prepare the accounts for the next month's transactions, we could make one final entry closing out these two overhead accounts and transferring the variance to a separate account:

Overhead Variance—Drills	1,730	
Standard Overhead—Drills	10,800	
Overhead Summary—Drills		12,530

Exhibit 11–2 Overhead cost flows in standard costing

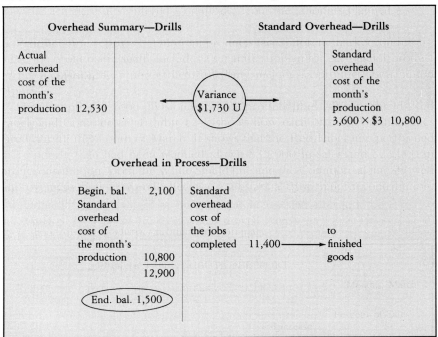

Analyzing the overhead variance: The two-variance approach

The main question we need to address is how the drills department's $1,730 total overhead cost variance arose. In this case, the total variance should be divided into two components, a spending variance and a volume variance.

The spending variance

The spending variance is the spread between actual overhead costs and the flexible budget for the actual volume of productive activity. The volume of activity in the drills department is measured by the department's output, represented by the number of standard direct labor hours. As we saw earlier, fixed overhead costs in this department were expected to amount to $7,400 a month; budgeted variable overhead costs were derived from the following formula:

$$\text{Total variable overhead cost} = \$1.15 \times \text{Standard direct labor hours}$$

Since volume in May was 3,600 standard direct labor hours, the flexible budget for the month of May was $7,400 + $1.15 × 3,600 = $11,540. The spending variance for the month therefore was as follows:

Actual overhead cost	$12,530
Budgeted overhead for actual volume	11,540
Spending variance	$ 990 unfavorable

This is the sum of the detailed spending variances we derived from this same set of facts in Exhibit 10–4 in Chapter 10.

The volume variance

The amount of fixed overhead absorbed in a full absorption costing system is proportional to volume. The overhead rate in this case included $1.85 to absorb fixed costs, calculated as follows:

$$\frac{\text{Total fixed cost}}{\text{Normal volume}} = \frac{\$7,400}{4,000 \text{ standard hours}} = \$1.85 \text{ a standard hour.}$$

If volume had reached 4,000 standard hours, then all the budgeted fixed costs would have been absorbed, as Exhibit 11–3 shows. Instead, actual volume was 400 standard direct labor hours less than normal. This means that the fixed costs that would have been absorbed by these 400 hours had no place to go, no product to absorb them. Low volume therefore accounted for 400 × $1.85 = $740 of the unabsorbed fixed overhead. We call this a *volume variance*. It arose because actual volume differed from the volume level on which the overhead rate was calculated.

Exhibit 11–3 The overhead volume variance

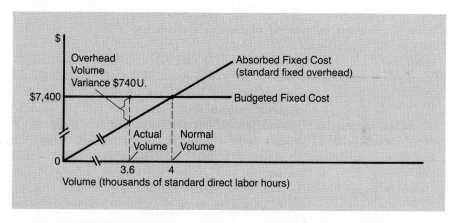

We don't need to break the overhead rate into fixed and variable components to calculate the volume variance. In fact, the correct way to calculate it is to compare the standard overhead cost for the period with the total of the flexible budget allowances for the actual volume of activity, as in the following table:

	Budgeted at 3,600 Standard Hours	Absorbed at 3,600 Standard Hours	Volume Variance
Variable overhead at $1.15	$ 4,140	$ 4,140	—
Fixed overhead	7,400	6,660	$(740)
Total	$11,540	$10,800	$(740)

Interpreting the volume variance

The overhead volume variance is the budgeted fixed cost of the number of hours of idle or overused capacity. The $740 volume variance in our illustration is the amount the company spent in May to provide production capacity the drills department didn't use. It doesn't mean that costs were $740 greater than expected because volume was lower than normal. It merely says that no production was available to absorb $740 of the costs that were expected to occur.

The volume variance can be favorable, because normal volume is usually less than maximum volume and actual volume is sometimes greater than normal. Under these circumstances, production volume will absorb more fixed costs than the company expects to incur.

The department heads don't establish their own production schedules. The volume of activity is determined outside the factory, on the basis of the number of customer orders in hand or anticipated. This being so, overhead volume variances aren't controllable by the department head or even by the plant manager. Therefore, they shouldn't be included in the departmental control reports. They should be reported to plant managers only to help them explain the total overhead variance to higher management.

Reconciling the variances

The decomposition of the overhead variance is summarized in Exhibit 11–4. This chart is an illustration of a fundamental rule in variance analysis: *the variances in any detailed list should always add up to the total variance being analyzed.*

Exhibit 11–4 Reconciliation of overhead cost variances: Two-variance method

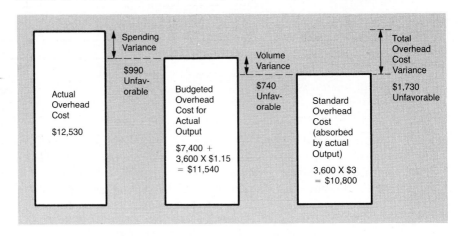

Exhibit 11–5 presents this same information in graphic form. This is like Exhibit 11–3 except that it includes the variable overhead costs as well as the fixed overheads. The amount of overhead absorbed at any volume is shown by the height of the straight line rising from the lower left-hand corner of the chart. The amount budgeted at a given volume is shown by the height

Exhibit 11–5 Diagram of overhead cost variances

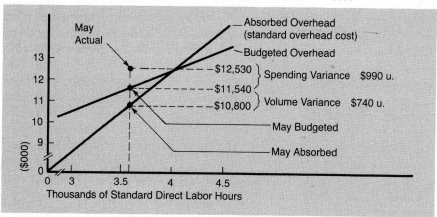

of the other line at that volume. Because some of the department's costs are fixed, the Budgeted Overhead line has a gentler slope than the Absorbed Overhead line. Variable overhead costs in this case are proportional to volume—$1.15 in budgeted variable overhead costs for each standard direct labor hour—and thus the flexible budget is shown as a straight line.

The amounts budgeted and absorbed at this month's volume of 3,600 standard hours are shown as large dots on these two lines. The actual amount spent is shown by another dot. By measuring the vertical distances between dots, we are able to identify the total variance and its two component parts.

Overhead volume variances at volumes in excess of normal volume represent overabsorption and are classified as favorable. Volume variances at volumes lower than normal, in the zone to the left of the intersection of the lines in the exhibit, represent underutilization and are referred to as unfavorable.

Notice that we could eliminate the volume variance simply by using an overhead rate based on actual volume rather than one based on normal volume. If we did this in this case, the overhead rate would be $11,540/3,600 = $3.2056, and the amount absorbed would be $11,540, just equal to the amount budgeted. We don't do this because *the purpose of the overhead rate is to assign overhead costs to products, not to absorb them.* A reduction in volume does not increase the cost of the products the factory produces; it merely increases the amount of cost that is unproductive. In other words, unabsorbed fixed cost is really the cost of the products the factory didn't produce; except in special reimbursement situations, it should not be assigned to the products the factory did produce.

Overhead variance analysis: A three-variance approach

So far we have assumed that overhead costs vary with (are caused by) the volume of output, represented in our illustration by total standard direct labor hours. In many cases, however, the need for overhead costs may be determined by direct *input* quantities, such as the number of direct labor hours actually used. In these cases the total overhead cost can be divided into three compo- nents instead of two: a spending variance, a volume variance, and an input efficiency variance.

The spending variance

If the need for overhead costs is determined by direct input quantities, the spending variance is the difference between the following two quantities:

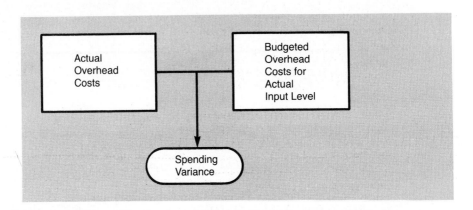

Suppose overhead costs in the drills department vary with actual direct labor hours, for example. The total overhead cost formula now reads as follows:

$$\text{Total overhead cost} = \$7,400 + \$1.15 \times \text{Actual direct labor hours}$$

The department's records show that the drills department actually used 3,700 direct labor hours during May. Budgeted overhead cost therefore was as fol- lows:

Fixed overhead	$ 7,400
Variable overhead: $1.15 × 3,700	4,255
Total budgeted overhead	$11,655

With the budget at this level, the overhead spending variance was $12,530 − $11,655 = $875 and was unfavorable, meaning that the department spent more than the budget allowed.

The labor efficiency variance

The spending variance we just calculated was $115 smaller than the spending variance we calculated under the two-variance method. The reason, of course, is that the flexible budget allowance for 3,700 hours is $115 greater than the allowance for 3,600 hours. This $115 is the *labor efficiency variance*, defined as the estimated effect of the direct labor usage variance on overhead cost. It arose because the production center used 100 direct labor hours more than the standards called for (3,700 hours instead of the standard 3,600). Labor inefficiency therefore added 100 × $1.15 = $115 to overhead costs. It shows

Exhibit 11–6 Labor efficiency variance

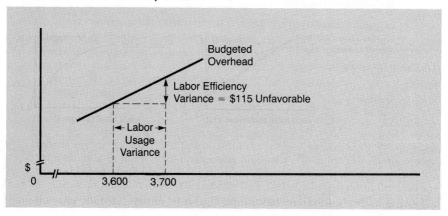

up in Exhibit 11–6 as the increase in the budget allowance as volume moves up from 3,600 to 3,700 direct labor hours.

The labor efficiency variance does not indicate how effectively the department has controlled overhead costs. Instead, it is another component of the direct labor usage variance. If the standard wage rate for direct labor in this production center was $8 an hour, for example, the full cost of an hour of lost time was $8 plus $1.15, or $9.15. In other words, the 100-hour labor usage variance could be reported as $915 instead of as $800.

In more general terms, the labor efficiency variance is an *input efficiency variance,* defined as the effect on overhead cost of variances in direct product inputs. If overhead costs vary with direct materials quantities, for example, the input efficiency variance is a materials efficiency variance.

The volume variance

The third component of the total overhead cost variance is the volume variance. As always, the volume variance is the effect on overhead cost absorption of the difference between actual volume and normal volume. Since normal volume in a standard costing system is defined in units of output (standard direct labor hours in this case), actual volume must be measured in these same units. In other words, the volume variance must be calculated in exactly the same way as in the two-variance method.

At the actual volume of 3,600 standard direct labor hours, 600 hours lower than the normal level, the volume variance was as follows:

Fixed cost absorbed at normal volume: 4,000 × $1.85 .... $7,400
Fixed cost absorbed at actual volume: 3,600 × $1.85 6,660
　Volume variance: 400 × $1.85 .... $ 740 unfavorable

The same figure can also be calculated as follows:

Budgeted at 3,600 standard direct labor hours $11,540
Absorbed at 3,600 standard direct labor hours 10,800
　Volume variance .... $ 740 unfavorable

Reconciling the variances

If overhead costs are expected to vary with production inputs, a three-variance analysis should be used. The three variances are diagrammed in Exhibit 11–7. As always, the sum of the three component variances adds up to the total overhead cost variance.

Exhibit 11–7 Reconciliation of variances: Three-variance method

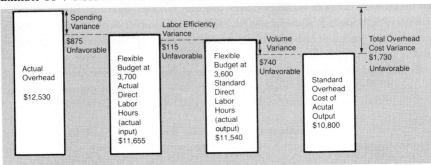

Notice how the component variances were calculated. Each component was measured by altering one of the underlying cost assumptions, recomputing cost on this basis, and then calculating the difference between this recomputed cost and the cost total calculated previously.

Starting with all costs at actual, for example, we changed one assumption, substituting budgeted cost levels for actual cost levels, but keeping input and

Exhibit 11–8 Three-variance analysis of overhead costs

output statistics unchanged. This allowed us to calculate the spending variance. Next we changed from actual input to standard input, leaving everything else unchanged. This gave us the labor efficiency variance. Finally, we moved from budgeted overhead to absorbed overhead, keeping standard input constant, and this led us to identify the volume variance.

This same progression from standard overhead cost to the actual amount spent is illustrated in Exhibit 11–8. Standard overhead cost is the point on the "absorbed" line at the 3,600-hour mark. The vertical distance between this point and the point on the budgeted line above is the volume variance. The labor efficiency variance is shown by the vertical distance traveled by a movement along the "budgeted" line from 3,600 to 3,700 hours. Finally, the spending variance is shown by the distance between the budget allowance for 3,700 hours and actual overhead cost for the month.

Whether the spending variance is $875 or $990 depends on the underlying pattern of cost variation. If overhead costs vary with labor inputs, then $875 is correct. If overhead depends on the rate of output, however, the answer is $990. *In other words, the size of the spending variance depends on the determinants of overhead cost and not on the method of analysis; in any given situation, only one method is appropriate.*

Variance analysis without standard costing

As we saw in Chapter 2, companies can and do use overhead rates to assign overhead costs to products even if they haven't developed standard costs and don't use standard costing systems. In this final section we'll see how our illustrative drills department would have analyzed its overhead costs if it hadn't had a standard costing system.

The total overhead cost variance

If a factory manufactures a variety of products but lacks standard cost figures, the amount of overhead absorption is likely to be based on actual direct inputs rather than on some measure of output. In the drills department, for example, absorbed overhead would have been determined by multiplying the overhead rate by the number of direct labor hours actually used during the month:

Absorbed overhead = $3 × 3,700 direct labor hours = $11,100.

The actual overhead cost is unaffected by the absorption method used, of course. The total overhead cost variance in May therefore would have been as follows:

Actual overhead	$12,530
Absorbed overhead	11,100
Total overhead cost variance	$ 1,430 unfavorable

The spending variance

The absence of standard costs makes it very difficult in a multiproduct production operation to use anything but an input index to measure volume for flexible budgeting purposes. The volume index is supposed to represent the factors causing costs to vary with volume, both for flexible budgeting and for product costing. This being the case, the drills department's flexible budget presumably would have been based on direct labor hours. The budget for May would have been:

Budgeted fixed overhead	$ 7,400
Budgeted variable overhead: $1.15 × 3,700	4,255
Total budgeted overhead	$11,655

The spending variance therefore would have been:

Actual overhead	$12,530
Budgeted overhead	11,655
Spending variance	$ 875 unfavorable

This of course is the same spending variance we calculated earlier in the three-variance analysis under standard costing. The reason is that the assumption is the same: Variable overhead cost is governed by the quantity of actual direct inputs, not by the volume of output.

The volume variance

We have already seen that the amount of overhead absorbed in this system depends on the number of actual direct labor inputs. The only reason absorbed overhead departs from the amount budgeted for that same number of direct inputs is that the number of these inputs differs from the number on which the overhead rate was based—in other words, the difference between budgeted and absorbed overhead is a volume variance.

The drills department's overhead rate included $1.85 to cover average fixed overhead, as we calculated earlier. Actual volume of 3,700 direct labor hours was 300 hours short of normal volume. The lack of volume therefore would have left 300 × $1.85 = $555 of the fixed costs unassigned.

This same figure can be developed by comparing the total amount absorbed with the total amount budgeted at 3,700 hours:

Budgeted overhead at 3,700 hours	$11,655
Absorbed overhead at 3,700 hours	11,100
Volume variance	$ 555 unfavorable

Reconciliation of the overhead variances

The volume variance differs from the volume variance under standard costing because the amount absorbed is calculated differently. Exhibit 11–9 shows how the two variance components would come together in an absorption system not based on standard costs. Once again we have changed one assumption at a time, first from actual to budgeted conditions, then from the budgeted cost to the absorbed cost. The result is to divide the variance into two components.

Exhibit 11–9 Two-variance analysis in the absence of standard costing

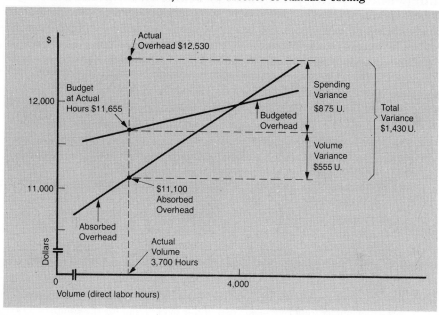

Summary

When the system used to assign factory overhead costs to products by means of predetermined overhead rates is integrated into the factory ledger, the account balances will include an amount known as the total overhead cost variance. This variance is the amount by which production has under- or overabsorbed factory overhead costs.

If a system of standard costs is in use, the total overhead cost variance can be subdivided into either two or three components, the choice depending on whether the level of overhead costs is determined primarily by the level of production output or by the amount of direct inputs. If overhead costs vary with output, the total variance should be subdivided into spending variance and volume variance components. If overhead costs vary with direct inputs, the total variance should be subdivided into spending variance, volume variance, and input efficiency variance components. If the governing input is direct labor, then the third component is called a labor efficiency variance.

The spending variance component in these systems is the same spending variance we discussed in Chapter 10. An unfavorable volume variance measures the fixed overhead cost of providing capacity which has remained idle; a favorable volume variance indicates the extent to which the actual use of capacity has exceeded normal levels. Finally, the labor efficiency variance shows the effect on budgeted overhead cost of variances in direct labor quantities.

If the factory doesn't use standard costing, the amount of overhead absorbed will be determined by the number of direct inputs. In this situation the total overhead cost variance can be subdivided only into spending variance and volume variance components.

Independent study problems (solutions in Appendix B)

1. **Overhead variances without standard costing.** Ajax Company uses predetermined departmental overhead rates in its factory but doesn't have a standard costing system. The factory's shaping department has an overhead cost budget of $10,000 a month plus $2.50 a direct labor hour. The department's overhead rate is $4.50 a direct labor hour. Actual overhead cost in May amounted to $19,900 on a departmental volume of 4,200 direct labor hours.

   Required:
   Calculate the total overhead variance for the month and subdivide it into its components.

2. **Overhead variance analysis: standard costing.** The flexible budget for a machining department is as follows:

Machine-Hours	Manufacturing Overhead Costs
8,000	$20,000
10,000	22,000
12,000	24,000
14,000	26,000

   The departmental overhead rate is $2 per standard machine-hour. Standard manufacturing overhead costs in this department for the company's two products are:

   Product A .... 1 machine-hour per unit = $2 per unit.
   Product B .... 1.5 machine-hours per unit = $3 per unit.

   During April the department produced 4,000 units of product A and 4,000 units of product B. A total of 9,500 machine-hours was recorded during April, and actual manufacturing overhead costs totaled $21,750.

   Required:
   a. Calculate and analyze the factory overhead cost variance.
   b. Reanalyze the variance on the assumption that factory overhead varies with standard machine-hours.

3. **Materials, labor, and overhead variances; use of accounts.** The Abel Company manufactures three products in two factory departments. It uses a full cost, basic plan factory standard costing system. You have the following data for department I:

	Product A	Product B	Product C
Standard unit cost:			
Department I materials.....................	$ 3	$ 6	$ 9
Department I labor (at $8 an hour)	16	24	20
Department I overhead (at $6 per direct			
labor hour)	12	18	15
Inventory and production (units):			
Department I work in process, March 1	—	100	200
Completed and transferred to department II,			
March	300	500	400
Department I work in process, March 31	200	100	—

   Work-in-process at both beginning and end of the month was complete as to materials and half-processed. Other data for the month were:

Materials inventories, March 1 (at standard prices) $11,400
Materials purchased ($5,400 at standard prices)   5,850
Materials issued to department I (at standard prices)   6,000
Actual direct labor payroll, department I (3,500 hours)   28,400
Actual overhead, department I   25,500

At normal volume and with actual direct labor time equal to standard direct labor time, variable overhead cost totals $8,000 a month and fixed overhead cost amounts to $16,000. It is assumed that variable overhead varies in direct proportion to variations in the number of direct labor hours used.

Required:

a. Enter these data, including the opening inventory balances, in appropriate T-accounts. Try to set up accounts that will help you identify the variances.
b. Prepare a list of variances for department I for the month of March. Be sure to label each variance clearly.

Exercises and problems

4. **Exercises in overhead variance analysis.**   Each of the following exercises covers a different aspect of standard costing for factory overhead.

Exercise A. Standard cost; accounts

Darlon, Inc., manufactures wire goods, using a basic plan standard costing system. Overhead costs in the coating department are assigned to products at $5 a standard coating hour. The company calculates the number of standard coating hours by multiplying the standard processing time for each unit for each stage in the coating process by the number of units processed in that stage. The coating process has five stages. Because each worker can process many products at the same time, the number of standard direct labor hours is only a fraction of the number of standard coating hours.

During December the department completed work on products with 12,500 standard coating hours, standard materials costs of $128,000, and standard coating direct labor cost of $9,500. These products were transferred immediately to the assembly department. The work in process in the coating department on December 1 had passed through three stages of the coating process; the work already done on these products amounted to 2,200 standard coating hours. The work in process at the end of the month had passed through four stages of the coating process, with work equivalent to 3,400 standard coating hours already preformed.

Required:

a. Calculate the standard overhead cost of the work done in December.
b. Prepare journal entries to record (1) overhead cost absorption, and (2) the standard cost of products transferred to assembly.

Exercise B. Two-variance analysis

The overhead costs in one department are budgeted on the basis of the following formula:

Overhead costs = $100,000 a month + $3 × Standard direct labor hours

Other data are: (1) normal volume, 50,000 standard direct labor hours; (2) actual overhead cost in June, $225,000; (3) actual direct labor hours in June, 40,000; and (4) standard direct labor hours in June, 39,000.

Required:

a. Calculate standard overhead cost for the month.
b. Calculate the total variance from standard overhead cost.
c. Use a two-variance analysis to separate the variance into component parts. Why is a two-variance analysis appropriate here instead of a three-variance analysis?

Exercise C. Three-variance analysis

The facts are the same as in Exercise B except that the overhead cost formula is as follows:

Overhead costs = $100,000 a month + $3 × Actual direct labor hours

Required:

a. Prepare a three-variance analysis of the total overhead variance.
b. What managerial use, if any, would be made of each of the variances you have calculated (i.e., who is being evaluated and in what connection)?

5. **Multiple choice.**

Exercise A.

Air, Inc., uses a standard cost system. Overhead cost information for the month of October is as follows:

Total actual overhead incurred	$12,600
Fixed overhead budgeted	$ 3,300
Total standard overhead rate per direct labor hour	$ 4
Standard variable overhead rate per direct labor hour	$ 3
Actual direct labor hours	3,600
Standard direct labor hours allowed for actual production	3,500

What is the overall (or net) overhead variance?

a. $600 favorable, b. $1,200 favorable; c. $1,400 favorable; d. $1,800 favorable.

Exercise B.

Alden Company has a standard costing and flexible budgeting system and uses a two-way analysis of overhead variances. Selected data for February are as follows:

Budgeted fixed factory overhead costs	$ 64,000
Actual factory overhead costs incurred	$230,000
Variable factory overhead rate per direct labor hour	$ 5
Standard direct labor hours for actual production	31,000
Actual direct labor hours	33,000

The overhead spending variance for February is:

a. $1,000 favorable; b. $1,000 unfavorable; c. $11,000 favorable; d. $11,000 unfavorable.

Exercise C.

If Alden Company (see exercise B) didn't have a standard costing system, but used a predetermined overhead rate based on a normal volume of 32,000 direct labor hours, its total overhead variance would be

a. $1,000 favorable; b. $6,000 unfavorable; c. $10,000 unfavorable; d. $13,000 unfavorable.

(CPA, adapted)

6. **Overhead variance analysis: standard costing.** Given the following data, calculate and analyze the overhead cost variance:

Actual factory overhead	$29,000
Standard overhead cost of goods finished..........	27,000
Standard overhead cost of goods in process:	
Beginning of month	5,000
End of month	7,700
Standard overhead cost	$ 3 per standard direct labor hour
Flexible budget	$15,000 + $1.50 per actual direct labor hour
Actual direct labor hours	9,500

7. **Overhead cost accounts.** Using the data from problem 6 and a set of accounts similar to those used in this chapter, enter the opening balances and record the month's transactions. Identify the account or accounts in which the overhead variance is to be found.

8. **Overhead variance analysis without standard costing.** Balch Company calculates product cost on a full costing basis. It uses predetermined departmental overhead rates based on normal volume. The flexible budget formulas for the finishing department last year were as follows:

Supervision	$1,200 a month
Indirect labor	$800 a month + $1 per direct labor hour
Overtime premium	$0.50 for each direct labor hour in excess of 2,400 direct labor hours a month
Supplies	$0.40 a direct labor hour
Power	$200 a month + $0.15 a direct labor hour
Depreciation	$500 a month
Other overhead	$0.10 a direct labor hour

Normal volume in the finishing department was 3,000 direct labor hours a month, but the profit plan last year called for a volume of only 2,700 direct labor hours a month. Volume in May last year was 2,500 direct labor hours. The actual overhead costs for the month were as follows:

Supervision	$1,260
Indirect labor	3,340
Overtime premium	140
Supplies	860
Power	600
Depreciation	500
Other	300
Total	$7,000

Required:

a. Calculate a predetermined overhead rate for the finishing department.

b. Calculate the total overhead variance for May, the total overhead spending variance, and the volume variance.

c. Was this volume variance larger or smaller than the amount reflected in the annual profit plan? To whom should this information be reported? Should management focus its attention on the volume variance itself, on the difference between this and the planned volume variance for the month, or on both of them?

d. It was suggested in this chapter that the volume variance can be calculated by multiplying average fixed cost by the difference between normal volume and actual volume. Test this suggestion here and explain your findings.

9. **Supplying missing figures: No standard costing.** Wilson Company's factory has three production departments. Standard costs are not used, but each department has a predetermined overhead rate and a flexible budget, based on actual direct labor hours. You have the following data:

		Dept. A	Dept. B	Dept. C
1.	Actual overhead, July	$20,000	$17,000	?
2.	Budgeted fixed cost per month	?	?	$5,000
3.	Budgeted variable overhead cost per direct labor hour	?	$3	$2
4.	Actual volume (direct labor hours), July	4,000	3,000	?
5.	Normal volume (direct labor hours)	5,000	?	?
6.	Predetermined overhead rate per direct labor hour at normal volume	?	?	$3
7.	Absorbed overhead, July	$19,600	?	?
8.	Budgeted overhead at actual volume, July	?	?	?
9.	Total overhead variance, July		2,000 U.	4,000 U.
10.	Overhead spending variance, July	500 F.	?	1,000 U.
11.	Overhead volume variance, July		1,000 F.	?

Required:

Make the necessary calculations and fill in the blanks identified by question marks in this table.

10. **Overhead variances: Nonlinear cost function.** Standard costs are not used in the Dandy Wagon Company's factory, but each department has a predetermined overhead rate based on normal volume. Volume in the axle department is measured by the number of axles manufactured. The budget formula for overhead costs in this department is as follows:

$6,000 a month + $2 an axle + $1 for each axle in excess of 2,000 in any month

You have the following additional information:

1. Normal volume is 2,500 axles a month.
2. Budgeted volume for the current year is 2,200 axles a month.
3. Actual overhead costs for April totaled $11,100.
4. The overhead volume variance for April was $160, unfavorable.

Required:

a. Prepare a diagram showing the amounts budgeted and absorbed at volumes ranging from 1,500 to 3,000 axles a month.
b. Calculate the operating volume for the month.
c. Calculate the overhead spending variance.
d. Enter operating volume, the volume variance and the spending variance on the diagram you prepared in answer to (*a*).
e. Should management be pleased with performance in this department during April? Explain your answer.

11. **Overhead variances: Supplying missing figures.** A factory has three departments. Standard overhead cost in each department is based on standard direct
labor hours. You have the following information related to overhead cost in
November:

	Dept. A	Dept. B	Dept. C
Budgeted fixed overhead	$100	$150	?
Budgeted variable overhead:			
Per actual direct labor hour	1	0	$ 1
Per standard direct labor hour	0	2	0
Normal output (standard direct labor			
hours).............................	50	50	100
Actual output (standard direct labor			
hours)	?	?	90
Overhead absorbed	$120	?	?
Actual overhead	145	$225	?
Actual direct labor hours	42	43	?
Overhead volume variance	?	$ 30 U.	$ 40 U.
Overhead spending variance	?	?	8 U.
Overhead labor efficiency variance	?	?	6 U.
Total overhead variance	?	?	?

Required:
Make the necessary calculations to supply the missing figures in the table.

(Prepared by Carl L. Nelson)

12. **Overhead variances: Two independent variables.** Bob Richards is the plant
manager. He has a number of departmental supervisors who are responsible
for labor and materials usage variances, but he alone is responsible for factory
overhead costs. Factory overhead cost is budgeted monthly on the basis of the
following formula:

Overhead = $50,000 + $2 per labor hour used + 20% of actual labor cost

Standard product costs are based on a standard labor rate of $5 an hour and
a standard overhead cost of $7 a labor hour.
Actual overhead cost in June was $84,500. The total standard cost of the
June output was $192,000, made up of the following:

Materials	$ 60,000
Labor	55,000
Overhead	77,000
Total	$192,000

Materials variances were negligible in June, but there was an unfavorable
labor usage variance of $2,000 and an unfavorable labor rate variance of $5,700,
the latter caused by a 10 percent wage increase due to a new labor union contract.

Required:
Mr. Richards has asked you to tell him whether his control efforts were effective.

13. **Overhead variances; itemized analysis.** The Schuyler Corporation uses a standard costing system in its factory. Statistical studies have shown that variation
in overhead costs in department X is more closely correlated with direct labor
input than with product output. The departmental overhead rate is $2 per direct
labor hour, and 15,000 direct labor hours were recorded during November.
Additional data are:

	Budget		
	Fixed per Month	Variable per Direct Labor Hour	Actual, November
Supervision	$ 5,600	—	$ 5,900
Indirect labor	500	$0.60	10,200
Supplies....................	—	0.25	3,400
Department S service	—	0.10	1,750
Building service	6,500	—	7,600
Total	$12,600	$0.95	$28,850

The standard overhead cost content of work in process was $8,000 on November 1 and $10,000 on November 30. The standard overhead cost content of the work completed and transferred out of the department during the month was $29,500. Production departments are charged for department S service at a rate of $5 per service hour. Production department managers have responsibility for controlling the amount of department S service used. Building service costs are allocated to production departments on the basis of floor space occupied. The actual costs of department S for November averaged $5.20 per service hour.

Required:

a. What is the normal volume of activity in department X?

b. Calculate total standard direct labor hours for November.

c. What was the effect on total departmental overhead cost of the variation from standard direct labor efficiency during November?

d. What was the total overhead variance for November?

e. What is the meaning of the spending variance in building service costs for department X?

f. Prepare a list of the overhead costs charged to department X in November, the flexible budget you would use in measuring the department's success in controlling overhead costs, and the resulting spending variances. Divide the list between the overhead items that were likely to be controllable by department X and the items that probably were not controllable at this level.

g. Prepare a summary table showing the various components of the total variance you calculated in (d). You need not break this down by object-of-expenditure account.

14. **Identifying controllability; reporting volume variances.** Production volume in department X of factory Alpha is measured by the number of direct labor hours. Normal volume is 10,000 direct labor hours a month (each "month" consists of four consecutive weeks), and the flexible budget allowances for this volume of activity are:

Supervision—fixed	$ 2,000
Indirect labor—variable	16,000
Supplies—variable	12,000
Maintenance—variable portion	2,000
Maintenance—fixed portion	2,000
Depreciation—fixed	10,000
Floor space charges—fixed	8,000

All variable cost elements are expected to vary in direct proportion to departmental direct labor hours.

The department used 11,250 direct labor hours during the month of March 2–March 29. The following costs were charged to the department during the month:

Supervision	$ 2,100
Indirect labor	19,000
Supplies	13,200
Maintenance	3,900
Overtime premiums	500
Depreciation	10,000
Floor space charges	8,500

The manager of factory Alpha receives a copy of each departmental overhead cost performance report each month, with the volume variance printed on a separate line at the bottom. The manufacturing vice president, with four factories to worry about, receives a one-page summary report each month. One line on this report shows the total volume variance for each of the four factories.

The controller explains that the volume variance figures on the plant manager's reports are intended to show how fully each department's capacity is being utilized. This information can be used in decisions on staffing the various departments and to some extent in decisions on work schedules for the factory. The volume variance figures on the manufacturing vice president's reports are intended to serve the same purposes at the factory level. They are also used to demonstrate to top management and to marketing management how much cost is unabsorbed or overabsorbed, to establish the relative need for additional volume.

Required:

a. Compute the month's flexible budget allowances and cost variances for each of these seven items. (Use the letters U and F to denote unfavorable and favorable variances.)

b. For each of the seven cost items listed above, indicate whether any variances are likely to be wholly or partly controllable by the department head. How might variances arise in the noncontrollable items?

c. Calculate an overhead rate based on normal volume and use this to measure the overhead volume variance for the month.

d. How likely are the volume variance figures in the plant manager's and marketing vice president's reports to serve their intended purposes? Try to suggest other ways of serving these purposes. Which would you prefer?

15. **Analyzing under- or overdistributed service department costs.** Zeta Company operates a factory with six production departments, three service departments, and a plant office. The costs of the service departments are charged to the production departments each month on the following bases:

Department	Amount Distributed Monthly	Basis of Distribution
A	Total budgeted cost	Fixed amount to each production department, determined in advance
B	Total actual cost	Ratio of actual service cost to the total number of direct labor hours in all production departments combined, multiplied by the actual number of direct labor hours used in each production department.
C	?	Fixed rate per service department hour, determined in advance, times actual service hours used by each production department

No service department costs are allocated to the plant office or to other service departments.

Each of the 10 departments has a flexible budget. The flexible budgets and other data for the three service departments for the month of July were as follows:

Department	Costs Charged to Department in July	Flexible Budget		Amount Distributed
		Fixed	Variable	
A	$10,800	$12,000	—	$12,000
B	22,000	7,000	$0.50 per direct labor hour	22,000 (at $0.88 per direct labor hour)
• C	19,100	5,000	$15 per service hour	18,000 (at $20 per service hour)

Required:

a. Calculate the amount under- or overdistributed in each of these three departments in July.

b. Calculate the flexible budget for each service department in July and calculate the spending variances.

c. For each department explain the difference, if any, between the amount you calculated in answer to (*a*) and the amount you calculated in answer to (*b*).

Review problems

The problems in this section are designed to integrate the materials covered in this chapter with those in previous chapters on standard costing, flexible budgeting, and cost allocation.

16. **Labor, materials, and overhead variances; T-accounts.** The Mooseheart Company uses a basic plan system of standard costing in its factory. The factory has only one processing department. Inventory balances, all priced at standard cost, were as follows on March 1:

Materials $1,500
Materials in process 600
Labor in process 200
Overhead in process 180

The following transactions occurred during March:

1. Materials received from vendors: actual price, $1,290; standard price, $1,200.
2. Materials issued (at standard prices): direct materials, $1,150; indirect materials, $100.
3. Summary of labor time tickets for the month (at standard wage rates): direct labor, $2,030; indirect labor, $340.
4. Actual payroll for the month, $2,450—includes overtime premium, $60, and apprentice pay, $25, to be charged to overhead; these two amounts are not included in the figures given in item (3).
5. Other overhead charges for the month, $1,300 (credit Accounts Payable).
6. Goods completed during March, and standard product costs:

Product	Units Completed	Standard Cost per Unit			
		Materials	Labor	Overhead	Total
X	100	$1.00	$2.00	$1.80	$4.80
Y	200	1.50	4.00	3.60	9.10
Z	300	3.00	2.50	2.25	7.75

7. The month's flexible budget allowances for factory overhead can be calculated from the following formula:

$$\text{Overhead costs} = \$1,000 + 0.4 \times \text{Standard direct labor cost}$$

8. Standard costs of work in process on March 31:

Materials in process $500
Labor in process 400
Overhead in process 360

Required:

a. Enter the opening inventory balances and record the month's transactions in approximately titled T-accounts.
b. Prepare a list of factory cost variances for the month, subdivided in any way you deem appropriate. Indicate for each variance whether it is favorable or unfavorable.

17. **Labor, materials, and overhead variances.** A company has two products, with the following standard costs and the following production for the month of March:

	Product A	Product B
Standard cost per unit:		
Materials	$ 1	$ 2
Labor	4	3
Overhead.....................................	8	6
Total	$13	$11
Units in process (all materials applied, but only half of labor operations performed and half of standard overhead absorbed):		
Beginning of month	1,000	3,000
End of month	2,000	3,000
Units completed during month	4,000	5,000

Factory overhead costs for the month were budgeted from the following formula:

$$\text{Overhead} = \$60,000 + 0.5 \text{ (actual direct labor hours} \times \text{Standard wage rates)}$$

The following costs were recorded during the month:

1. Materials purchased: standard cost, $20,000; actual cost, $21,200.
2. Direct materials issued (at standard prices): $17,000.
3. Direct labor payrolls, actual hours worked: at standard wage rates, $31,600; at actual wage rates, $34,000.
4. Miscellaneous overhead costs: $75,000.

Required:

a. Prepare a list of variances for the month. Indicate for each whether it was favorable or unfavorable. Show your calculations.
b. Compute the standard cost of work in process at the end of the month.

18. **Direct labor, materials, and overhead variances: Profit variability.** Milner Manufacturing Company uses a standard costing system. It manufactures one product. Standard unit manufacturing costs and budgeted average selling, general, and administrative expenses at normal volume are as follows:

Materials:	20 yards at $0.90 a yard	$18
Direct labor:	4 hours at $6 an hour	24
Total factory overhead:	Applied at five-sixths of direct labor (the ratio of variable costs to fixed costs is 3 to 1)	20
Variable selling, general, and administrative expenses		12
Fixed selling, general, and administrative expenses		7
Total unit cost		$81

Normal volume is 2,400 standard direct labor hours a month.
Actual activity for the month of October was as follows:

Materials purchased:	18,000 yards at $0.92 a yard	$16,560
Materials used:	9,500 yards	
Direct labor:	2,100 hours at $6.10 an hour	12,810
Total factory overhead:	. . . .	11,100
Units actually produced:	500	

Required:

a. Based on the standard costs and budget estimates, compute the inventoriable unit cost for internal reporting purposes under variable costing.

b. Based on the standard costs and budget estimates, a certain selling price and number of units sold will yield an operating profit of $5,200. Increasing this selling price by 4 percent will increase the operating profit to $6,800. Neither the costs nor the number of units sold will be affected by the price increase. Compute the selling price per unit and the number of units to yield an operating profit of $5,200.

c. Compute the variable factory overhead rate per standard direct labor hour and the total fixed factory overhead per month.

d. The company actually uses absorption costing for factory cost reporting. Prepare a schedule computing the following variances for the month of October, indicating for each whether it is favorable or unfavorable: (1) materials price variance; (2) materials usage variance; (3) labor rate variance; (4) labor usage variance; (5) overhead spending variance; and (6) overhead volume variance.

(CPA, adapted)

19. **Complete costing/reporting cycle: Departmental overhead rates, allocations, labor, materials, and overhead variances.** The King Supply Company's factory has four production departments and three service departments. A full cost, basic plan standard costing system is in use.

Budgeted overhead costs for the current year, at normal volume, together with other pertinent data, are as follows (DLH is direct labor hours):

Department	Floor Space	Employees	Dept. 23 Hours Used	Normal Volume per Month	Budgeted Direct Dept. Overhead
Production 11 ..	20%	80	600	10,000 DLH	$30,000
Production 12 ..	25	120	900	15,000 DLH	50,000
Production 13 ..	35	60	1,200	20,000 machine-hours	59,300
Production 14 ..	9	50	300	5,000 DLH	20,000
Service 21	—	6	—	—	10,000
Service 22	8	24	—	—	19,000
Service 23	3	20	—	3,000 hours	22,500

For the purpose of developing departmental predetermined overhead rates, budgeted service department costs are distributed in sequence as follows:

Department	Basis
Service 21	Floor space
Service 22	Number of employees
Service 23	Service 23 hours

Service department costs are distributed monthly on the following basis:

Service 21: To all departments: budgeted monthly cost of floor space occupied.
Service 22: To all departments except service 21: budgeted rate per employee × actual number of employees.
Service 23: To production departments: budgeted rate per department 23 hour × actual number of department 23 hours.

The following data relating to factory overhead costs were recorded during April:

Dept.	Volume of Activity	Employees	Dept. 23 Hours Used	Standard Overhead Cost Absorbed	Direct Dept. Overhead Cost
11	9,000 DLH	75	500	$38,000	$29,000
12	16,000 DLH	125	500	70,000	55,000
13	21,000 machine-hours	58	1,200	82,000	61,000
14	6,500 DLH	60	300	?	23,000
21	—	6	—	—	8,800
22	—	22	—	—	19,200
23	2,500 hours	16	—	—	19,000

You have the following additional information for production department 14 only (for the month of April):

1. Direct materials received from factory storeroom (at standard prices): $4,200.
2. Standard cost of work received from other departments (classified as direct materials costs in department 14): $214,800.
3. Direct labor payrolls ($39,000 at standard wage rates): $40,300.
4. Work in process April 1 (at standard cost): materials in process, $106,900; labor in process, $12,000; overhead in process (2,000 standard direct labor hours), __?__.
5. Work in process April 30 (at standard cost); materials in process, $87,200; labor in process, $4,800; overhead in process (800 standard direct labor hours), __?__.
6. Standard cost of goods finished: materials, $230,000; labor, $44,400; overhead (7,400 standard direct labor hours), __?__. All goods finished by department 14 are transferred immediately to the finished goods warehouse.
7. From the flexible budget:

	3,500 DLH	6,500 DLH
Direct departmental overhead	$17,000	$23,000
Number of employees	38	62
Department 23 hours used	250	350

Direct departmental overhead, number of employees, and department 23 hours used are expected to vary as the number of direct labor hours used varies within this range. The variations are expected to be in proportion to the variations in the number of direct labor hours, except that the number of employees must be a whole number. If a fraction of an employee is needed, a whole employee will be provided in the department.

Required:

a. Distribute budgeted service department costs and compute predetermined overhead rates for each of the four production departments for the current year. (Ignore all April data.)

b. Prepare an overhead cost distribution sheet for the month of April.

c. Compute the total overhead cost variance for the month for each of the four production departments and the total amount over- or underdistributed for each of the three service departments.

d. Prepare a complete variance summary for department 14.

d. Establish an appropriate set of T-accounts for department 14, together with any other accounts you find necessary. Enter the opening balances in the department 14 accounts and record the department's transactions for April. Be sure to include entries to transfer cost variances to appropriately titled variance accounts. You may use a single account for the departmental overhead variance (overhead under- or overabsorbed). The credits in entries recording costs transferred from other production departments should be to an account titled Interdepartmental Cost Transfers; the credits in entries recording costs transferred from service departments should be to accounts titled Costs Distributed, Department (department number); and the credits in entries recording other overhead costs in department 14 should be to Accounts Payable.

12 Profit contribution reporting: Controlling marketing costs

Accounting information on the effectiveness of the control of costs of responsive activities is usually provided by the usage variances we've been describing in the last few chapters. Cost variances can't measure management's effectiveness in spending on programmed activities, however. Because spending on these activities depends on management's estimates of the benefits they will provide, both the performance standard and the measure of actual results must reflect benefits as well as costs.

The benefits of marketing activities stem from the revenues they generate. Performance reporting for marketing therefore must reflect both revenues and costs—that is, control comparisons must be *profit* comparisons. Marketing costs, in other words, must be judged on their *effectiveness* in producing revenues. What matters is the spread between revenues and costs, not the cost/revenue ratio (a measure of *efficiency*).

For example, marketing expenses make up only 2 percent of total sales in the diagram at the top of Exhibit 12–1, as opposed to 10 percent in the lower diagram. Sales in the lower diagram are so much larger, however, that profit is substantially higher, even after allowing for the added marketing costs.

This is just another way of saying that minimizing costs is not what the marketing manager is expected to do. A favorable cost variance may even be worse than an unfavorable cost variance. Additional spending on programmed marketing activities is justified if it produces a greater amount of revenue, even if the cost/revenue ratio rises.

With this as background, our purpose in this chapter is to show how profit reports for programmed marketing activities can be developed to meet management's needs for information on the effectiveness of marketing expenditures. We'll examine five topics:

1. The marketing function.
2. The profit contribution concept.
3. Profit performance standards.
4. Profit reports for operations analysis.
5. Profit contribution reporting using full-cost data.

Exhibit 12–1 Ratios versus amounts as marketing standards

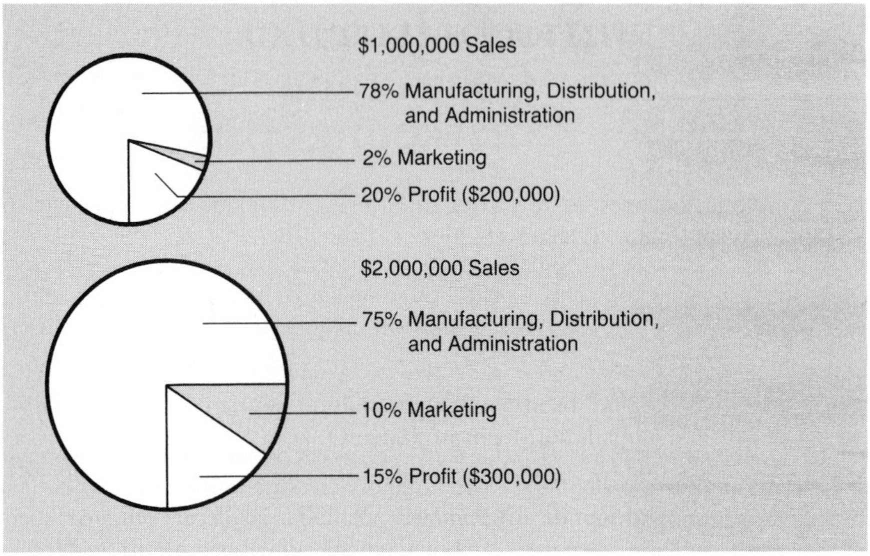

$1,000,000 Sales

78% Manufacturing, Distribution, and Administration

2% Marketing

20% Profit ($200,000)

$2,000,000 Sales

75% Manufacturing, Distribution, and Administration

10% Marketing

15% Profit ($300,000)

The marketing function

When we think of marketing, we usually think of activities designed to sell goods and services or to increase the effectiveness or efficiency of the selling effort. These are the *order-getting activities,* mainly market research, advertising, and direct selling. Order-getting costs differ from manufacturing costs in that they are volume-determining rather than volume-determined. To illustrate this, Exhibit 12–2 has all the arrows pointing from left to right. Order-getting activities produce customer orders; production activities are scaled to respond to the level of orders received.

Many marketing departments are responsible not only for volume-determining activities but also for the physical movement of products to the firm's

Exhibit 12–2 Volume-determining versus volume-determined activities

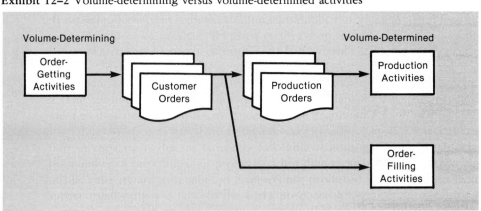

customers and for various clerical operations initiated by the filing of customer orders. These are sometimes referred to as order-filling activities. They include reviewing customers' credit-worthiness, warehousing, assembling goods to be shipped ("picking and packing"), preparing shipping documents, shipping, billing, maintaining the customer ledger, and collecting amounts due from customers.

Order-filling activities are responsive activities, necessary to service the volume of business generated by the order-getting activities. As such, they have the same general characteristics as manufacturing activities, except that their costs are likely to be more highly fixed in the short run.

Every marketing organization also has an administrative superstructure, designed to provide direction and logistical support to both order-getting and order-filling personnel. Some administrative personnel are located at marketing headquarters; others are at regional and branch locations. Most marketing administrative costs are pure capacity costs, determined by the volume of business the organization plans to generate and serve rather than by the actual volume of business generated.

Profit contribution reporting

Control reports in marketing are issued to the managers responsible for specific marketing segments. In deciding how to report profits to these managers, the accountant must try to reconcile two partially conflicting objectives. One is to identify all the costs and revenues *attributable* to a given set of marketing activities, to help management make decisions affecting these activities. The other is to identify the costs and revenues *controllable* by particular marketing managers to help them and their superiors evaluate their performance.

The usual solution doesn't do either of these things perfectly. It is to report profit contribution, the amount *traceable* to the specific marketing segment in question. Exhibit 12–3 illustrates the relationship between segment revenues and profit contribution. In the rest of this section we shall see how profit

Exhibit 12–3 Dividing the segment revenue dollar

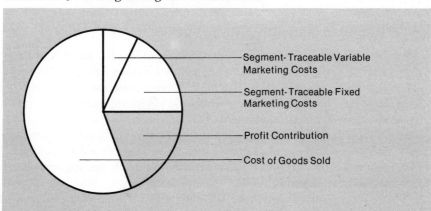

contribution reports can be used, how they relate to attributable profit, and how they can be tied into the controllability criterion.

The case for profit contribution reporting

The main advantage of the profit contribution approach is that it eliminates arbitrary, potentially misleading cost allocations. It gives marketing managers a clearer picture of the impact of their decisions on company profit than segment net income and doesn't saddle them with charges for things that don't concern them.

For example, suppose variations in branch sales don't affect the total amount of divisional and corporate administrative cost, but each branch is charged 20 percent of sales for divisional and corporate administrative services. The branch manager is comparing two possible ways of deploying the branch's sales force. One strategy will expand sales of product A, the other will sacrifice sales of A for sales of B. Product A has a higher price but a lower contribution margin per unit than product B. The manager makes the following comparison:

	First Strategy	Second Strategy
Sales	$1,000	$800
Cost of goods sold	650	480
Contribution margin	350	320
Branch expenses	80	80
Profit contribution	270	240
Allocated expenses...............	200	160
Income before taxes	$ 70	$ 80

The allocation makes the second strategy appear better, but the first strategy will produce a larger total profit contribution. Since total divisional and corporate administrative expenses are unaffected by variations in sales volume, they will be unaffected by the manager's decision in this case. This means that the decision should be based on the profit contribution figures, which point clearly to the first strategy.

Reporting attributable profit

This argument for profit contribution reporting has one major flaw. It is precisely relevant only when the segment's activities have no effect on fixed costs that aren't traceable to it. If some of these nontraceable fixed costs will change gradually in response to segment-based decisions, then profit contribution will overstate segment profitability.

This flaw can be corrected by reporting the segment's *attributable profit,* the excess of the segment's revenues over all expenses that could be eliminated, in time, if the company were to withdraw from the segment and reduce its capacity accordingly.

To get attributable profit, we must allocate some of the nontraceable costs. These allocations fall into the three classes we first identified in Chapter 7:

1. *Usage charges.*   For measurable services specifically used to support the segment's activities.
2. *Activity charges.*   For costs that, though nontraceable, are likely to vary with changes in the volume of activity in the segment.
3. *Capacity charges.*   For the amount of nontraceable fixed costs that could be eliminated if the company were to withdraw from the segment and reduce operating capacity accordingly.

Many companies try to approximate attributable profit by allocating *all* nontraceable costs to segments. To do this, they can't avoid making some allocations for which no clear cost-activity relationships can be found. Allocating the marketing vice president's salary among the various product lines, for example, is likely to be a job for a metaphysicist, not an accountant. If allocations of this kind are numerous, the measure of segment profit becomes meaningless.

Although we believe we have a clear conceptual basis for calculating attributable profit, we have some misgivings about suggesting that it be included in routine profit reports. The attributable portion of nontraceable fixed costs is difficult to estimate for routine profit reporting. Crude approximations may cast a cloud of doubt on the whole reporting system.

The simplest way to dispel this doubt is to eliminate all allocations except those effected by means of usage charges. Other nontraceable fixed costs would be allocated only as part of special profitability studies, aimed at specific managerial decisions. They would not be included in the routine periodic (monthly) segment financial reports. Alternatively, the company might estimate and allocate the attributable portions of nontraceable fixed costs, but only by means of predetermined charges, as described in the next section. This would satisfy the activity evaluation aspect of the control reports without introducing spurious variances into the evaluation of managerial performance.

Reporting controllable profit

The second flaw in using profit contribution to measure marketing performance is that it may not be fully consistent with the controllability criterion. Some costs may be fully traceable but not controllable at all. Some may be controllable but not fully traceable.

We have four ways of dealing with these problems:

1. *Exclude noncontrollable costs from the profit report.*   Management is likely to reject this because it would make the reports less useful in evaluating the segment's activities as a whole.
2. *Use predetermined charges.*   In other words, report all cost elements but report the noncontrollable elements at their budgeted amounts. This is a useful solution for any cost that is totally noncontrollable.
3. *Report the items, with variances, as noncontrollable.*   This is the usual solution. Higher management must be careful to remember, however, that variances "below the line" are noncontrollable.
4. *Use predetermined input prices.*   This should be adopted when input quantities are controllable but input prices are not. When the marketing manager

has no control over the prices of the merchandise sold, the cost of goods sold should be measured at budgeted prices. In a manufacturing company, this usually means standard costs.

Factory spending variances shouldn't be charged to marketing segments unless they clearly result from specific marketing activities. Some spending variances, of course, do arise because marketing managers mark orders for rush service or submit design changes after production operations have begun. Marketing managers should expect to be charged for these variances, but the charges should be calculated in advance whenever possible. If this is done, the marketing managers will know what they are getting into when they ask for special treatment. The cost then can be classified as controllable.

Profit reporting standards

Periodic responsibility reporting is designed to direct management's attention to activities and operations in which actual results depart significantly from standard performance. Although periodic profit reports can be used for several related purposes, we'll concentrate here on their use in the evaluation of marketing *management,* giving some attention to the evaluation of marketing *operations* later in the chapter.

The usual profit performance standard for managerial evaluation is the profit plan, presumably management's best estimate of the results the company can reasonably expect to achieve under anticipated conditions. Variances from the plan may reflect changes in conditions or forecasting errors, of course, but management can analyze the effects of these factors—the residual presumably reflects managerial performance.

The only serious alternative to the profit plan as a performance standard is actual profit performance in some previous period, usually the identical period of the preceding year. Probably the main reason for this is that the past is a known quantity, whereas planned results are always a guess. Comparing this year with last year therefore seems to give a more solid measure of progress than any comparison with the plan.

We have strong reasons for urging that historical comparisons be used mainly at the planning stage, not in control reporting. First, other interlocking activities are predicated on the activities and results embodied in the current plan. If results follow the plan, then no adjustments need be made in these other activities, no matter what the comparisons with last year or last month show.

The second argument against prior year comparison reporting is that last year's experience may be totally irrelevant under this year's conditions. For example, sales of new automobiles may be far smaller than in the preceding year because the economy is in a severe recession. Performance may be satisfactory, however, if the company's market share has increased, with sales exceeding planned levels.

As we have already seen, the profit plan is not a perfect benchmark for profit reporting, but it has two advantages. First, it reflects a set of interrelated decisions that management presumably has been implementing. Thus it means more than a set of past results which no one is using to guide his or her current actions. Second, it represents a managerial commitment, and management has the right to know how well that commitment is being met. Use of prior period comparisons diverts attention from these commitments and dilutes whatever motivational impact they may have.

A reporting system

Probably the best way to explain what we have been talking about and to raise one or two other issues is to see how one company's system works. Ormsby, Inc., a diversified manufacturer of plastic films and powders, chemicals, food products, and industrial textiles, has a typical reporting system for a company of its size. The company is organized in four major product divisions, as shown in the upper part of Exhibit 12–4. The division managers have extensive authority over the selection, design, manufacture, and marketing of their divisions' products.

The lower half of Exhibit 12–4 shows part of the internal structure of one of these divisions, the Food Division. We'll examine four aspects of this division's reporting system:

1. The reports issued to the district managers.
2. The reports prepared for the general sales manager.
3. The reports received by the division's product managers.
4. Possible improvements in the measurement system.

Exhibit 12–4
ORMSBY, INC. Division structure

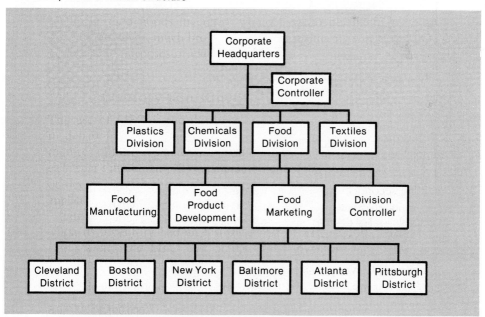

Base level profit reports

Each of the district sales managers in this division receives a set of profit reports each month. The district-wide summary report for the Boston district is shown in Exhibit 12–5. Four features of this report should be noted:

1. The report is limited to the district's profit contribution. No charge is made for corporate or divisional overhead costs.
2. The report emphasizes deviations from the profit plan.
3. Cost of goods sold is measured at standard cost.
4. The district has no variable costs other than the standard cost of goods sold.

A glance at this report will tell the district manager that the actual sales volume was $514,000, that this produced a gross margin $7,600 smaller than the profit plan called for, and that the district's profit contribution for the month was $8,000 short of its objective. It also shows that travel and entertainment costs departed substantially from their budgeted levels, but total operating expense was very close to budget. The usual columns for year-to-date comparisons have been omitted here because they are identical in form to the columns for the current month.

Exhibit 12–5 Food division—District profit contribution report

DISTRICT SALES AND EXPENSE SUMMARY			
District: Boston		Month:	March
	Actual	Budget	Increase (Decrease)
Net sales billed	$514,000	$500,000	$ 14,000
Standard cost of goods sold	301,600	280,000	21,600
Gross margin	212,400	220,000	(7,600)
District operating expenses:			
Branch salaries	2,800	2,800	—
Sales salaries	26,000	25,200	800
Travel	6,800	7,900	(1,100)
Entertainment	1,300	700	600
Local advertising	1,000	1,100	(100)
Storage and delivery	6,900	6,600	300
Branch office expense	1,400	1,700	(300)
Other	300	100	200
Total district operating expense	46,500	46,100	400
District profit contribution	$165,900	$173,900	$ (8,000)

Sales force performance reports.   District-wide totals fail to give the district manager any explanation of the structure of the main deviations from the profit plan. For this reason, the accountant might prepare another report like the one in Exhibit 12–6. This shows the items traceable to individual salespeople—sales, cost of goods sold, and sales salaries and direct expenses (travel and entertainment)—and identifies the deviation from planned profit performance for each sales representative.

Charging the sales representatives with the direct expenses of their own operations, as in this report, is a very useful feature. Stern, for example, sold $5,000 more than Edgar, but when all the costs traceable to these sales were deducted, Stern's profit contribution was $1,500 less than Edgar's. Edgar also exceeded the planned profit contribution, while Stern and six others fell short of theirs.

Notice that the budgeted profit contributions are not uniform. We can calculate the budgeted contributions by adding the actual profit contribution and the reported variance. Brown's budget, for example, was $11,500 + $4,900 = $16,400, while Cannon's budget was $9,500 + $1,900 = $11,400. Differences of this sort presumably reflect the differing characteristics of the individual sales territories and perhaps the differing experience levels of the

Exhibit 12–6 Food division—District sales report

SALES FORCE PERFORMANCE SUMMARY						
District: Boston					Month: March	
				Profit Contribution		
Sales Representatives	Net Sales Billed	Standard Cost of Goods Sold	Salary and Direct Expenses	Actual Amount	Over/ (Under) Budget	Percent of Sales
Brown	$ 40,000	$ 25,900	$ 2,600	$ 11,500	$(4,900)	28.8
Cannon	31,000	18,300	3,200	9,500	(1,900)	30.6
Edgar	63,000	34,500	4,300	24,200	1,200	38.4
Johnson	30,000	18,100	2,900	9,000	(2,400)	30.0
Kelly	54,000	31,100	4,200	18,700	(100)	34.6
Lusso	47,000	28,800	3,100	15,100	(200)	32.1
McGregor	76,000	42,200	3,800	30,000	3,900	39.5
Nelson	55,000	31,400	3,400	20,200	1,500	36.7
Stern	68,000	41,700	3,600	22,700	(800)	33.4
Williams	50,000	29,600	3,000	17,400	(4,200)	34.8
Total	514,000	301,600	34,100	178,300	(7,900)	34.7
General branch expenses				12,400	100	2.4
District profit contribution				$165,900	$(8,000)	32.3

various sales representatives as well. Management's next task is to find out why the actual results differed so radically from the amounts planned.

Product-line reports. Different products face different market conditions. Since the profit plan usually includes a separate subplan for each major product or product line, the report structure usually includes a product contribution report.

For example, the food division has three product lines—White Shield, Red Label, and Commercial. Exhibit 12–7 shows how each of these product lines fared during the month of March. It shows that the Red Label line performed more poorly than had been planned, down $35,000 in sales and $23,000 in profit contribution. Both the White Shield line and the Commercial line showed improvement, but the overall effect was a substantial drop in profit contribution.

Exhibit 12–7 Food division—District product line summary

PRODUCT CONTRIBUTION REPORT

District: Boston   Month: March

Product Line	Actual	Budget	Increase (Decrease)	Percent of Sales Actual	Budget
White Shield:					
Net sales	$225,000	$200,000	$ 25,000		
Standard cost of goods sold	108,100	94,000	14,100		
Other product expenses	1,000	1,100	(100)		
Profit contribution	115,900	105,000	11,000	51.5	52.5
Red Label:					
Net sales	145,000	180,000	(35,000)		
Standard cost of goods sold	96,000	108,000	(12,000)		
Profit contribution	49,000	72,000	(23,000)	33.8	40.0
Commercial:					
Net sales	144,000	120,000	24,000		
Standard cost of goods sold	97,500	78,000	19,500		
Profit contribution	46,500	42,000	4,500	32.3	35.0
All products:					
Net sales	514,000	500,000	14,000		
Standard cost of goods sold	301,600	280,000	21,600		
Other product expenses	1,000	1,100	(100)		
Product profit contribution	211,400	218,900	(7,500)	41.1	43.8
Other branch expenses	45,500	45,000	500		
District profit contribution	$165,900	$173,900	$ (8,000)	32.3	34.8

Even more disturbing is the decline in the ratio of profit contribution to sales. This ratio fell in all three lines, but the fall was most pronounced in the Red Label line. To determine how much of this was due to price erosion and how much was due to a deterioration in the quality of the product mix within each line, management would probably turn to the kind of variance analysis we'll describe in detail in Chapter 27.

Notice that in this exhibit a much smaller percentage of expenses is assigned to individual segments of the district's business than in the sales force report. Sales salaries and traveling expenses are traceable to individual salespeople, but not to individual product lines. The only product-traceable district costs are the costs of local advertising for the White Shield line, amounting only to $1,000.

Reporting to the general sales manager

The district managers in the Food Division all report to the division's general sales manager. Managers at this level are farther removed from the day-to-day operations of individual sales branches, and therefore are less likely to be aware of problems and opportunities as they emerge. As a result, they must rely heavily on accounting reports to direct their attention in the right directions. A scorecard report for a district manager becomes a steering control device for the general sales manager.

The general sales manager's needs might be met by preparing a set of district profit contribution reports, together with a short report on the costs of operating the central office. This would have two disadvantages. First, important figures might be lost in a welter of detail. Second, the general sales manager might be tempted to run individual branches by remote control, undermining the authority and motivation of the district managers.

The usual solution is to give the middle manager a more condensed set of reports. One such report is illustrated in Exhibit 12–8. Again the profit contribution format is used. Each district's results are summarized on a single line. Net sales, profit contribution, and the variance in profit contribution for each branch are taken directly from the District Sales and Expense Summary, illustrated for the Boston district in Exhibit 12–5.

General selling expenses for the marketing department as a whole and the costs of administering the general sales manager's office are grouped together in the lower half of the departmental report, but are not charged to individual districts. The bottom line in Exhibit 12–8 shows the amounts left to cover divisional and corporate overheads and to provide a profit for the company.

Reporting to the product manager

Marketing management often has a two-way organization structure. The sales force has a geographical structure, with branch managers, regional managers, and a headquarters sales manager. These managers have direct responsibility for building and maintaining the company's market position, getting customer

Exhibit 12-8 Food division—Marketing department profit summary

MARKETING DEPARTMENT
PROFIT PERFORMANCE SUMMARY
($000)

Month: <u>March</u>

| | Net Sales | Profit Contribution | | Contribution Margin: Ratio to Operating Expenses |
		Amount	Increase (Decrease)	
Boston	$ 514	$ 166	$ (8)	4.6
New York	946	409	25	5.9
Baltimore	472	150	(18)	3.7
Atlanta	348	109	15	3.6
Pittsburgh	588	197	3	4.1
Cleveland	627	210	(2)	4.6
Total	3,495	1,241	15	
Central marketing expense:				
Administration		40	(1)	
Marketing research		26	1	
Advertising		103	(10)	
Other		23	3	
Total		192	(7)	
Profit contribution		$1,049	$ 22	

Exhibit 12-9 Food division—Product managers

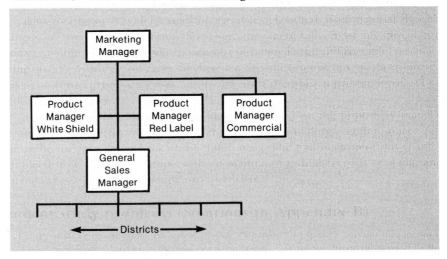

orders, and keeping informed on what customers and competitors are doing. So far, all of our discussion of Ormsby's reporting system has related to the needs of these managers.

This structure may be all the company needs, particularly if it sells only a few products and if the differences from region to region are more important than the differences between one product market and another. When the characteristics of individual products are extremely important, however, and the company can't afford to set up a separate sales force for each, management may appoint *product managers,* one for each major product or group of products handled by the common sales force. For example, Ormsby's Food Division has three product managers, working out of division headquarters, each responsible for one of the division's three product lines. Their position in the organization is diagrammed in Exhibit 12–9.

The reason for having product managers is to give the company's operations a program orientation, so that product design, manufacturing, and marketing will be seen as an integrated whole rather than as separate, independent activities. The product managers are expected to come up with marketing plans for their products, dealing with such matters as package design, distribution channels, advertising, pricing, and promotional tactics. They are also expected to do everything they can to see that the plan is carried out and that its goals are achieved.

Exhibit 12–10   Food division—Product manager's summary report

PRODUCT LINE SUMMARY
($000)

Product Line: White Shield   Month: March

	Sales		Local Product Expenses	Profit Contribution	
	Actual	Variance		Actual	Variance
Boston	$ 225	$ 25	$ 1	$116	$ 11
New York	568	86	4	292	44
Baltimore	126	(22)	—	60	(17)
Atlanta	162	58	1	81	29
Pittsburgh	264	63	2	135	30
Cleveland	274	79	2	142	29
Total	1,619	289	10	826	126
Product management expenses:					
Administration				12	—
Advertising				48	—
Total				60	—
Profit contribution				$766	$126

Product managers are in a very peculiar position to do all this. They have no direct authority over the sales force, but they are responsible for developing the market for the product or products under their wings. They have no authority over the production manager, but they have to see to it that their products come out of the factory on time, in the right quantities, and at the right quality. Anyone who can do all this well under these conditions is likely to go far.

Each product manager in the Ormsby food division gets monthly profit contribution reports like the one in Exhibit 12–10. White Shield sales were well ahead of plan everywhere but in Baltimore. The favorable profit variances were about half as big as the sales variances everywhere except in Cleveland. The product manager would probably concentrate on these two districts to see why performance was out of line.

Profit reports in analyses of marketing operations

Marketing planning is a highly judgmental process, but accounting data can be extremely helpful as marketing managers seek to review and restructure their operations.

Marketing response functions

The contribution margin ratio shows how segment profit will respond to changes in sales volume, other things being equal; profit contribution shows the effectiveness of past and present marketing efforts. These figures don't identify the underlying *marketing response functions,* however—the incremental relationships between marketing effort on the one hand and sales and profits on the other.

Ormsby's accountants make some effort to provide response function information. The ratios in the right-hand column of Exhibit 12–8 are intended to reflect the sensitivity of contribution margin to marketing effort in each district. For example, the contribution margin in New York was 5.9 times the operating expenses of the New York district. In other words, a dollar spent in New York brought in $5.90 of contribution margin, on the average, while a dollar in Baltimore produced only $3.70.

If the general sales manager were to interpret these figures literally, more money would be spent in Boston and New York and less in Baltimore and Atlanta. Unfortunately, the ratios in the table are averages, not increments. What the manager would really like to know is what would happen if the company spent a little more in New York, or what would happen if it spent less in Baltimore.

This information is difficult to generate because the marketing response functions are likely to be nonlinear. To get volume, the company has to find new customers or get its present customers to buy more. This costs money. The bigger the share of the market it already has, the harder it has to work to increase it. Each additional percentage point of market share will cost more

Exhibit 12–11   A simple marketing response function

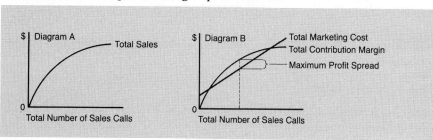

than the one before, either through additional marketing expenditures or through direct or indirect price reductions.

Diagram A in Exhibit 12–11, for example, shows one possible response function, reflecting a simple relationship between the number of calls made on potential customers and the total volume of sales. Sales increase as the number of calls is increased, but the sales increment gets smaller and smaller as customer offices get more and more saturated with visiting salespeople.

This information would be extremely valuable to management. By combining it with estimates of the contribution margin from sales and of the cost of increasing the number of calls, as in diagram B, management could determine the optimal number of calls to be made.

One way to get information on marketing response functions is to experiment. New consumer products, for example, are almost always launched in test markets before being placed in national distribution. Sales in these markets can be measured and the margins compared with the costs of marketing. Mail-order houses are even more ideally situated to identify response functions. Many of their sales can be traced back to specific mail lists and even to specific mailings or catalogs.

Even in these cases, however, most of the information reflects average relationships. It shows what a given set of marketing inputs have produced, not how many sales were obtained for each additional dollar of marketing effort.

Another possible approach is to relate the *change* in contribution margin from one period to another to the changes in marketing inputs. A comparison for the Boston district might show the following:

	Period 1	Period 2	Change
Contribution margin	$228	$273	+$45
Selling expenses	46	56	+ 10
Response ratio	5.0	4.9	4.5

These data must be interpreted very cautiously. Many conditions change from one period to another, and the change in contribution margin is the net result of all of these changes, not just one.

A final difficulty is that response functions are very complex. The effect of spending on samples depends not only on the total number of samples provided but also on the accompanying program for advertising the product and calling on customers. It also depends on the actions competitors take. A direct competitor who starts distributing reduced-price coupons will make Ormsby's sales less responsive to its own marketing efforts.

Time lags

Sales/expense and contribution margin/expense ratios may be misleading for another reason, too. Promotional effort is often made before the company recognizes the revenues it leads to. Sometimes this is due to a time lag between effort and results (orders); sometimes it is due to a time lag between results and accounting recognition of these results (revenues). These lags are illustrated in Exhibit 12–12.

Exhibit 12–12 Time lags between sales efforts and results

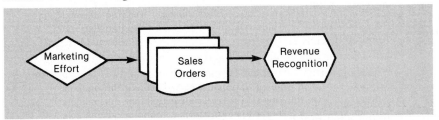

Most accounting systems are content to overlook these time lags, trusting in the good judgment of marketing executives and top management to make due mental allowances when reviewing reported results. Another possibility is to recognize revenues for internal reporting purposes on the basis of orders received, no matter what basis is used for external reporting. This would not solve the problem raised by the first kind of time lag, but it would adjust for the second.

The main obstacle to this solution is its cost. It requires entries in the factory ledger when the orders come in and another set of entries in the general ledger later on, when revenues are recognized. If the lag is short and stable, the extra cost probably isn't worthwhile.

Profit contribution reporting under full costing

Manufacturing companies using full cost to measure the cost of goods sold can use a hybrid form of profit contribution reporting in which the cost of goods sold is measured at standard full cost. When this is done, departures from normal production volume will create factory overhead volume variances, as described in Chapter 11. We'll deal with these first in a single-segment operation, in which the entire volume variance is unarguably traceable to the segment.

Single-segment operation

Suppose a company has only one product, product A, which has a standard manufacturing cost of $3 a unit ($2 in variable costs and $1 in fixed costs), with a normal volume of 1,000 units. Budgeted volume is equal to normal volume, but actual production and sales volume is only 800 units. The selling price is $4.50 a unit, and fixed marketing costs amount to $900. No spending variances have arisen. The segment's profit contribution is as follows:

	Variable Costing Basis		Full Costing Basis	
	Actual	Budget	Actual	Budget
Sales revenues	$3,600	$4,500	$3,600	$4,500
Product cost	1,600	2,000	2,400	3,000
Contribution margin	2,000	2,500	1,200	1,500
Traceable marketing costs	900	900	900	900
Fixed manufacturing costs	1,000	1,000	—	—
Overhead volume variance (200 units × $1)	—	—	200	—
Income before tax	100	600	100	600
Income variance	$(500)		$(500)	

The "Contribution margin" figure reported under full costing is a hybrid, in that some fixed costs are deducted from revenues to calculate it, but the variance in income before tax is $500, no matter which way we define product cost. The reason is that all the fixed costs get assigned to the income statement under either method, as long as production and sales volumes are identical and all cost variances are taken to the income statement as they arise. The only differences between budget and actual therefore will arise from spending variances or variations in selling price or volume.

In this case the entire income variance was due to the change in sales volume, which affected only the total revenue and the total variable cost. We can verify this by calculating the true contribution margin per unit ($4.50 − $2) and multiplying by the unit variance (1,000 − 800 = 200 units). The effect of the unit variance is a $500 reduction in income. Fixed costs don't enter into it.

Multisegment operations

The situation is different if two marketing segments share a common set of manufacturing facilities. In this situation, neither the fixed manufacturing overheads nor the volume variances can be traced to individual segments. Management has three alternatives:

1. Leave the volume variances unallocated.
2. Allocate the volume variances to segments in proportion to some characteristic of the individual segments.
3. Allocate the volume variances to segments so as to bring the variance in each segment's reported income to the level it would reach under variable costing.

Suppose the company has not only product A, but product B as well. Total fixed factory overhead is $2,500, allocated $1,000 to product A and $1,500 to product B at normal volume. Product B has a standard manufacturing cost of $8 a unit ($5 in variable costs and $3 in fixed costs), with a normal volume of 500 units. Suppose further that actual sales and production of product B are at the normal level (500 units), with a selling price of $12 and traceable fixed marketing costs of $1,100. Sales and expenses of product A are the same as in the preceding table. A profit contribution statement based on variable costing would show the following:

	Product A	Product B	Total
Sales revenue	$3,600	$6,000	$9,600
Product cost	1,600	2,500	4,100
Contribution margin	2,000	3,500	5,500
Traceable marketing costs	900	1,100	2,000
Profit contribution	1,100	2,400	3,500
Common fixed manufacturing costs			2,500
Income before tax			$1,000

A profit contribution statement in which the cost of goods sold is based on full cost would be somewhat different:

	Product A	Product B	Total
Sales revenue	$3,600	$6,000	$9,600
Product cost	2,400	4,000	6,400
Contribution margin	1,200	2,000	3,200
Traceable marketing costs	900	1,100	2,000
Profit contribution	300	900	1,200
Overhead volume variance (200 units of A × $1)			200
Income before tax			$1,000

Once again, the contribution market and profit contribution margin figures don't have quite the same meaning they have in a variable costing system, but the overall income figure are identical because production is equal to sales and the entire cost variance is taken to the income statement. Instead of the $500 gap we calculated earlier between the reported income for product A and its budgeted income of $600, however, we have only a $300 gap. "Contribution margin" on a full costing basis is only $4.50 − $3 = $1.50 a unit, or $300 in total. The other $200 is the overhead volume variance, due in this case entirely to low production of product A.

The first alternative in our list is to leave the volume variance undistributed. Since we already know that the income effect of product A's low volume is $500, we know this solution would be inaccurate. Its main advantage is that it doesn't produce an income variance in product B's segment.

Our second alternative is to distribute the overhead volume variance in proportion to some characteristic of the segment, such as absorption of fixed overhead at normal production volume. At normal volume product A absorbs $1,000/$2,500 = 40 percent of total fixed overhead; product B absorbs the other 60 percent. The allocation of the volume variance based on these percentages is $80 to product A and $120 to product B. This outcome is clearly undesirable because it imputes a $120 unfavorable volume variance to product B, which has in fact achieved its full normal volume. In many cases a segment could be assigned an unfavorable volume variance even though it actually experienced favorable variances in sales and production volumes, simply because other segments have fallen short of their goals.

The best way to allocate the volume variance is our third alternative, on the basis of the gap between normal and actual production, product by product. To do this, we need to break the standard product cost into fixed and variable components. Each segment then can be charged a predetermined lump sum for the amount of standard fixed cost accruing to it at normal volume (1,000 units × $1 for product A), plus the standard variable cost for the number of units actually sold (800 units × $2 for product A).

If this alternative is chosen, product A's statement will show the following (assuming that budgeted production and sales were at normal levels):

	Actual	Budget	Variance
Sales revenue	$3,600	$4,500	$(900)
Product cost:			
Variable	1,600	2,000	(400)
Fixed	1,000	1,000	—
Contribution margin	1,000	1,500	(500)
Traceable fixed marketing costs	900	900	—
Profit contribution	$ 100	$ 600	$(500)

This is another version of the two-part tariff we discussed earlier in connection with interdepartmental allocations. It differs from true profit contribution reporting only in that some common fixed costs are allocated to products, but it leads to the same variance calculation we get in variable costing.

Summary

Marketing costs can be divided into order-getting costs, order-filling costs, and administrative costs. Order-filling costs are responsive costs, much like manufacturing costs. Order-getting costs are programmed costs, controlled primarily by the profit-oriented decisions that set them up in the first place. Administrative costs are incurred to support the other two.

The main financial reports to marketing managers are likely to be profit contribution reports, identifying the amount of profit traceable to individual marketing segments. Profit contribution reports give marketing managers a picture of the effects of their marketing decisions unobscured by the frequently arbitrary cost allocations necessary to derive net income for individual segments.

Profit contribution reports may focus on individual responsibilities or individual product lines or programs. Most reporting systems are pyramidal, with marketing executives at successively higher levels receiving reports that are more and more condensed. Marketing managers may try to identify marketing response ratios from these reports in an attempt to direct marketing resources where they can be used most profitably.

Manufacturing companies which measure product costs on a full costing basis may use a hybrid form of profit contribution reporting in which fixed manufacturing overheads are included in product cost. To correct the inaccuracies inherent in this practice, any volume variances in factory overhead costs should be allocated to segments in such a way as to return the income variance to the level it would reach under variable costing.

Independent study problems (solutions in Appendix B)

1. **Segment reporting: Full cost basis.** Zodiac Advisory Services, Inc., provides both counselling and instructional services to individuals and organizations. It has both full-time and part-time professional staff at all levels; the part-time people provide enough flexibility in the work force to justify classifying professional salaries as variable costs.

   All marketing costs are fixed and are clearly traceable either to counselling services or to instructional services; administrative costs are fixed and are not traceable to individual service categories. Administrative costs are assigned to individual revenue segments by means of a predetermined rate of $3.60 per professional staff hour.

   You have the following information from Zodiak's operations last month:

	Actual		Budget	
	Counselling	Instruction	Counselling	Instruction
Revenues	$25,000	$15,000	$33,000	$12,000
Professional staff:				
Hours	600	475	800	450
Salaries	$10,400	$ 7,300	$13,200	$ 7,200
Marketing expenses	2,000	3,200	2,100	3,100
Administrative expenses ...	4,700		4,500	

   Required:

   a. Prepare a comparative income statement for each revenue segment and for the company as a whole, with variances, using a profit contribution format and the company's method of accounting for administrative expenses. Ignore income taxes.

   b. Calculate the volume variance in administrative expense and allocate it in such a way that each segment's profit variance measures as closely as possible the variance arising from that segment.

   c. Calculate the spending variance in administrative expense. A proposal has been made to allocate this amount to the segments in proportion to the budgeted allocations of administrative expenses. Calculate the amounts that would be allocated under this proposal and explain why you would favor it or oppose it.

2. **Converting to profit contribution reporting.** Talcott Company manufactures and sells two products. It has one factory, and all departments in the factory perform production operations on both products.

   A report summarizing the profit performance of each product is prepared each month. A similar set of reports is prepared for individual sales districts. The marketing vice president uses these reports to evaluate the performance of the branch managers and the two product managers and to monitor progress toward achievement of the goals of the current marketing plan.

The marketing manager is concerned with product A. Sales are up, but income is down, as the following income statement for last month shows:

	Actual	Budget	Over/(under) Budget
Net sales	$550	$500	$ 50
Expenses:			
Cost of goods sold (at standard)	385	350	35
Factory cost variances	22	4	18
Sales commissions	11	10	1
Delivery expenses	16	14	2
Product advertising	11	11	—
Sales salaries	10	8	2
Other marketing expenses	15	12	3
Administrative expenses	12	9	3
Total expenses	482	418	64
Income before income taxes	$ 68	$ 82	$(14)

You have the following additional information:

1. All of the company's operating expenses were distributed to one product or the other last month.
2. The budgeted amounts in the report were the amounts budgeted at the beginning of the year, not flexible budget allowances.
3. Approximately $290 of the budgeted standard cost of goods sold for product A was regarded as proportionally variable with volume; the remainder was an absorption of fixed factory costs.
4. Budgeted cost of goods sold for product A included $100 in standard factory overhead cost; the budgeted standard cost of goods sold for product B included $150 in standard factory overhead cost. None of the fixed factory overhead was traceable to individual products. Budgeted sales equalled budgeted production in both lines, and no volume variance in factory overhead costs was budgeted.
5. Manufacture of product A last month absorbed $110 in factory overhead cost, while manufacture of product B absorbed $90. The total factory overhead volume variance for the month was $30, unfavorable (both products combined).
6. The budget for product A included a provision for a $4 unfavorable spending variance in factory overhead costs, reflecting product A's share of a $10 one-time supplemental property tax on the factory building. Spending variances in the factory as a whole last month amounted to $10, none of them traceable specifically to either product.
7. Factory cost variances were assigned to the two products last month in proportion to their standard costs of goods sold.
8. Sales commissions and delivery expenses were regarded as proportionally variable with sales.
9. All product advertising costs were traceable to the individual products.
10. Sales salaries, other marketing expenses, and administrative expenses were allocated to products last month in proportion to sales volume.

Required:

a. Develop a profit contribution statement for product A for last month, based on variable costing and showing both actual and budgeted figures.
b. Management has seen your report and objects to your treatment of fixed factory overhead. You are instructed to rework your figures showing the cost of goods sold at standard full cost. All of the month's factory cost variances are to be allocated to individual products. Carry out these instructions and

set forth the arguments underlying your method of allocating factory spending variances and factory overhead volume variances.

c. Comment on product A's profit performance last month. Does the product need top management's attention?

Exercises and problems

3. **Preparing a profit contribution statement.** Company P is a manufacturing company with seven product lines. You have the following information for product line A:

Sales revenue	$1,000,000
Standard cost of goods sold	700,000
Marketing expenses	200,000
Administrative expenses	40,000
Income before taxes	$ 60,000

All the products in this product line are manufactured in factories which also manufacture products in other product lines, using the same personnel and the same facilities. Variable factory costs amount to 80 percent of total factory cost at normal volume. Standard factory overhead cost reflects operations at normal volume and the standard cost of goods sold is based on full costing, not variable costing.

Marketing expenses include sales commissions at a rate of 3 percent of sales revenue, and allocations of general company marketing expenses at a rate of 1 percent of sales revenue. All other marketing expenses are traceable to individual product lines. All marketing expenses except sales commissions are fixed.

Administrative expenses are entirely fixed. The amounts charged to product line A are product line A's share of general corporate administrative expenses, allocated to product lines at a rate of 4 percent of sales revenues.

Required:

Prepare a statement of contribution margin and profit contribution for product line A.

4. **Profit performance standard.** Each sales branch in Carson Company has a monthly sales and expense budget, prepared jointly by the branch manager and the regional sales manager at the beginning of the year. A summary financial report is prepared for each branch each month, showing variances from the original monthly budget. One of these reports showed the following (in thousands of dollars):

	Actual	Budget	Variance
Sales revenue	$1,100	$1,000	$100
Expenses:			
Cost of goods sold	650	600	(50)
Management salaries	40	40	—
Sales salaries	75	70	(5)
Advertising	25	20	(5)
Delivery	40	30	(10)
Rent	10	10	—
Total expense	840	770	
Profit contribution	$ 260	$ 230	$ 30

"It looks good to me," the marketing vice president said, "but I wonder whether it's as good as it should be at that volume. I wonder if we could apply flexible budgeting here."

All of the expenses shown on the report are traceable to the branch; the cost of goods sold figure is the total of the costs of the products actually sold by the branch during the period.

Required:

Prepare a response to the vice president's suggestion, illustrating your answer with figures from the branch sales report.

5. **Ratio performance standards.** "Marty, you've got to get your expense-to-sales ratio down," Clare David said. "Yours and Fran's are the highest in the company and we just can't support that kind of spending much longer. We'll okay your budget for this year, but let's see what you can do to turn things around by next year."

   Marty Johnson and Fran Wilkes were regional sales managers for Fabrications, Ltd.; Clare David was marketing vice president. You have the following information:

Budget:	Marty	Fran
Sales	$1,000,000	$1,500,000
Standard cost of goods sold	650,000	1,050,000
Regional marketing expenses	200,000	285,000
Actual:		
Sales	800,000	1,400,000
Standard cost of goods sold	530,000	980,000
Regional marketing expenses	140,000	252,000

Required:

a. Calculate the marketing expense-to-sales ratios.
b. Which manager appears to have done a better job of complying with the marketing vice president's directive? Was this a wise move?

6. **Preparing a segment performance report.** You have the following data on the operations of Trask Manufacturing Company's eastern sales region:

   1. Sales revenues: budgeted, $30,000; actual, $29,000.
   2. Standard cost of goods sold:
      a. Standard direct labor (500 standard direct labor hours) and standard direct materials cost: at budgeted volume, $9,000; at actual volume, $8,500.
      b. Standard variable factory overhead cost: at budgeted volume, $6,000; at actual volume, $5,400.
      c. Standard fixed factory overhead cost: at budgeted volume, $12,000; at actual volume, $10,800.
   3. Traceable fixed marketing costs: budgeted, $5,000; actual, $5,100.
   4. Total production volume (all products, all regions combined): budgeted, 10,000 standard direct labor hours; actual, 11,000 standard direct labor hours.
   5. Actual factory overhead costs: $31,000.
   6. The factory had no spending variances in direct labor or direct materials.
   7. A single factory serves all of the company's sales regions. Standard factory overhead cost is calculated at a normal volume of 10,000 standard direct labor hours, using the following flexible budget formula:

   $$\text{Factory overhead cost} = \$20,000 + \$1 \times \text{standard direct labor hours.}$$

Required:

Prepare a statement summarizing the profit performance of the eastern sales region for managerial evaluation purposes.

7. **Allocating factory spending variances.** Further information reveals that Trask Manufacturing Company (problem 6) did have spending variances in direct materi-

als and direct labor (all products), amounting to $850, unfavorable, and spending variances in factory overhead costs of $300, favorable. Production and sales volumes were identical this period. No spending variances were budgeted.

The spending variances in direct labor and direct materials were due to increases in resource prices; the spending variances in factory overhead reflected decreased use of inputs not specifically traceable to any product.

Required:

In what amounts, if any, would you modify your answer to problem 6 to reflect this additional information? Give the reasons for your position.

8. **Interpreting a profit contribution report.** The marketing vice president of a consumer goods company received the following summary report on the operations in the company's sales regions last month (in thousands of dollars):

	Sales		Profit Contribution	
	Amount	Over/(under) Budget	Amount	Over/(under) Budget
Atlanta	$ 680	$ 40	$182	$ 12
Boston	440	(20)	118	8
Chicago	420	(80)	92	(18)
Dallas	240	—	42	22
Denver	180	(60)	20	—
Los Angeles	580	(20)	132	12
New Orleans	280	(20)	36	(12)
New York	760	(40)	220	2
Pittsburgh	340	(60)	48	(32)
Seattle	260	(60)	50	(30)
Total	$4,180	$(320)	$940	$(36)

The marketing manager's own performance is judged on the division's success in reaching budgeted goals.

Required:

a. Calculate the profit contribution/sales ratio for each region.
b. How would you expect the marketing vice president to use this report? What significant facts does it reveal? Which regions seem to be the strongest? Which are the weakest?

9. **Attributable profit and controllable profit.** The following monthly profit contribution report was received by the manager of the Marston Company's Memphis branch:

	Actual		Budget		Variance
Sales		$205		$200	$ 5
Expenses:					
Cost of goods sold	$130		$125		(5)
Sales salaries	10		10		—
Other salaries	5		5		—
Travel	3		2		(1)
Advertising	9		6		(3)
Depreciation	2		2		—
Property taxes	5		3		(2)
Insurance	2		1		(1)
Utilities	1	167	1	155	—
Profit contribution		$ 38		$ 45	$(7)

You have the following additional information:

1. Salaries, insurance, and advertising expenditures are determined in the head office, not at the branch.
2. The branch office building was reassessed earlier in the year, resulting in a substantial increase in property taxes.
3. The head office investigates credit, prepares bills and payrolls, and collects the amounts due from customers. The cost of performing these activities for the Memphis branch and its customers is $6.

Required:

a. Using this information, distinguish among controllable profit, profit contribution, and attributable profit. Prepare a profit report reflecting the concept of controllable profit.
b. Comment on the performance of the Memphis branch. What seems to have happened?

10. **Performance standards.** Cable Company began operations several years ago to market a product of unique design. Two years ago it completed construction of a new factory with ample capacity to meet the company's needs for several years without further expansion. The product is basically standardized and marketing management doesn't interfere with production schedules once they have been established. You have the following information about the operations of Cable Company in the last two years:

1. Inventories and the cost of goods sold were measured at standard full factory cost; all factory cost variances were taken to the income statement as they arose.
2. Sales the year before last amounted to 100,000 units ($2,000,000), on marketing expenditures of $300,000, administrative expenses of $120,000, research and development expenditures of $50,000, and a $240,000 unfavorable factory overhead volume variance; income before income taxes amounted to $90,000.
3. Management's growth plan for last year called for sales of 140,000 units ($2,800,000) on marketing expenditures of $40,000, administrative expenses of $150,000, and research and development expenditures of $150,000.
4. Standard manufacturing costs last year were $12 a unit on a full cost basis. The factory cost budget was $600,000 + $9 a unit. An unfavorable factory overhead volume variance of $180,000 was budgeted last year.
5. Actual sales volume last year was 130,000 units ($2,600,000), on marketing costs of $398,000, administrative expenses of $155,000, and research and development expenditures of $85,000.
6. Factory spending variances last year amounted to $50,000, favorable; factory spending variances were negligible the year before last.
7. Factory production last year totaled 130,000 units; the production volume variance in factory overhead costs was $210,000, unfavorable.

Required:

a. Calculate income before income taxes for last year.
b. Evaluate marketing management's profit performance last year. Quantify your answer and explain your choice of an evaluation standard.
c. How, if at all, would your answer to (b) change if you found that production volume had amounted to 200,000 units last year, all other information remaining the same? Explain.

11. **Response functions.** Ramparts, Ltd., chose three test markets to try out different levels of marketing effort. The three markets were regarded as typical of the market as a whole and roughly comparable to each other. Spending was increased in markets B and C last month; spending in market A and in all other markets

was kept at the levels prevailing the month before last. You have the following data:

	Market A	Market B	Market C	All Other Markets
Marketing costs:				
Month before last	$ 40,000	$ 37,000	$ 50,000	$ 580,000
Last month	40,000	47,000	70,000	580,000
Sales revenues:				
Month before last	200,000	210,000	270,000	3,000,000
Last month	210,000	260,000	340,000	3,150,000

The company's products had an average contribution margin of 40 percent in each period. Sales revenues show no significant seasonal patterns. Carryover effects of marketing effort are minimal.

Required:

a. Calculate the profit contribution in each market last month and the month before.

b. Assuming these test markets are reasonably comparable and representative of the company's markets generally, estimate the responsiveness of income to variations in marketing expenditures. What recommendations would you make on the basis of this experiment? Explain your calculations and any assumptions you had to make.

12. **Allocating nontraceable costs and variances.** Andrews Company makes and sells only one product. The company has only one factory, but the marketing division is divided into two sales regions, each the responsibility of a regional sales manager. The product has a selling price of $10 a unit, a standard variable cost of $5 a unit, and a standard fixed factory overhead cost of $1 a unit. You have the following information for last year:

	Eastern Region	Western Region
Budget:		
Sales volume (units)	250,000	120,000
Traceable fixed marketing expenses	$375,000	$200,000
Allocations:		
Headquarters administrative and marketing		
expenses	225,000	108,000
Manufacturing cost variances	—	—
Actual:		
Sales volume (units)	300,000	100,000
Traceable fixed marketing expenses	$380,000	$198,000
Allocations:		
Headquarters administrative and marketing		
expenses*	252,000	84,000
Manufacturing cost variances (favorable)*	22,500Cr.	7,500Cr.

* Allocated as a percentage of sales.

Production volume was identical to sales volume during this period. The cost of goods sold in each region was measured at standard full manufacturing cost. Headquarters administrative and marketing expenses were entirely fixed and were not controllable by the regional managers. No factory spending variances were budgeted last year.

Required:

    a.   Calculate the variance in income before income taxes for each region, using the company's costing methods.

    b.   Do the income variances you calculated in answer to (*a*) provide a reasonable measure of the income-generating performance of the individual regional managers last year? Include in your answer a quantification of the effects of any measurement changes you would recommend, together with the reasons for your recommendations.

13. Monitoring marketing program performance.   Robinson Enterprises, Inc., shifted to a profit contribution approach to internal profit reporting several years ago. The profit contribution format is used in budgeting and in the company's monthly profit reports for individual product lines and for regional and branch offices.

    The company's Western Division has three groups of products, all manufactured in a large factory located in Valejo, California. Profit contribution reports are issued monthly to the division manager, Ms. Jane Andrews. She reviews these carefully, looking for signs that changes in the marketing mix may be appropriate.

    The profit contribution reports show three groups of expenses:

1. Variable costs.
2. Segment-traceable fixed costs.
3. Allocated costs.

    The variable factory cost of goods sold includes direct materials (standard direct manufacturing cost, adjusted by the ratio of actual purchase prices to standard purchase prices during the month), direct labor (standard direct labor cost, adjusted by the ratio of actual wage rates to standard wage rates during the month), and standard variable factory overhead.

    Nontraceable costs are allocated each month on the basis of that month's sales. They include budgeted fixed factory overhead, materials and labor usage variances, factory overhead spending variances, and divisional selling and administrative expenses not traceable to individual product lines.

    The company's main product line, known as the Premium line, has its own sales force and a substantial product-centered advertising campaign. Four months ago, at the beginning of August, Ms. Andrews put into effect a new marketing plan, calling for substantial increases in the amount of promotional effort devoted to the Premium line. The plan called for an $8 increase in monthly direct selling costs to increase sales to $160 a month, up $60 from the $100 previously planned. Seasonal factors were not important.

    The expenditures were made, and results for this product were as follows:

	July	August	September	October	November
Sales revenues	$100	$100	$120	$120	$140
Variable expenses:					
Variable cost of goods sold	55	57	67	69	77
Sales commissions	3	3	3.6	3.6	4.2
Shipping and handling	2	2	2.4	2.4	2.8
Total variable expenses	60	62	73	75	84
Contribution margin	40	38	47	45	56
Direct product selling costs	10	14	14	16	18
Profit Contribution	30	24	33	29	38
Nontraceable costs (allocated)	20	18	24	26	28
Income before taxes	$ 10	$ 6	$ 9	$ 3	$ 10
Order backlog (at selling prices) ..	$200	$220	$215	$240	$270

Noting that "Income before taxes" has just recovered to the level prevailing just before the new plan went into effect, despite a 40 percent increase in sales volume, Ms. Andrews has asked you to analyze these figures and report back to her.

Required:

a. Prepare a brief report in response to this request, including some comment on the apparent results of the new promotional effort. You need not make a complete analysis of the numerical data, but incorporation of some numerical calculations in your report will be desirable.

b. Suggest ways of improving the profit report.

14. **Monitoring marketing program performance.** "I don't understand it. My sales were 10 percent higher than the budget, but I still didn't make the budgeted profit!" lamented Cathy Goldman, manager of the housewares department in a large California department store.

The report from the store's accounting department which prompted Ms. Goldman's comments is reproduced below.

	Actual	Budget	Variance
Sales	$132,000	$120,000	$12,000
Cost of goods sold	92,400	84,000	8,400
Salaries	2,420	2,400	20
Employee benefits and taxes	1,210	960	250
Billing and accounting	5,445	3,600	1,845
Warehousing and receiving	3,045	2,000	1,045
Occupancy charge	13,875	13,750	125
General overhead	6,400	5,800	600
Departmental income	$ 7,205	$ 7,490	$ (285)

The department managers have considerable responsibility, including staffing the department, selecting and ordering merchandise, setting prices, and deciding how much floor space they will use for merchandise display. Hence, the store's management believes that department managers should be responsible for the profit generated by their departments.

A number of the items in the profit statement deserve some explanation. Salaries includes the salaries of all full-time personnel in the department, including the manager. Employee benefits and taxes were budgeted as a percentage of salaries. After the budget was prepared, however, there was a change in the employee benefit plan which resulted in an increase in the percentage charge from 40 percent to 50 percent.

Billing and accounting costs are charged to the department as its share of the customer credit office's expenses. The budgeted amount was based on the assumption that 75 percent of the department's sales would be credit sales, and that the costs of running the customer credit office would be 4 percent of total credit sales. Housewares' credit sales for August were 75 percent of its total sales.

The warehousing and receiving charge is based on the average number of cubic feet of storage space in the store's warehouse used by the department. Housewares was budgeted to use 8,000 cubic feet but actually used 8,700.

The occupancy charge includes building rental, heat, light, maintenance, and property taxes. This charge is based on the square feet of floor space used by the department for merchandise display during the month. Housewares was budgeted to use 11,000 square feet during August, but actually used 11,100.

General overhead is an allocation of the costs of general store management. Costs are allocated to departments on the basis of their gross sales revenues.

Required:

a. Comment on the likely cause (or causes) of each of the variances shown in the August profit statement.
b. Do you believe that the $285 unfavorable profit variance adequately reflects Ms. Goldman's department's performance during August? Briefly defend your position.
c. How would you restructure the profit statement to provide more useful information for evaluating Ms. Goldman's efforts to control costs in her department? (You need not calculate all the numbers in this statement; just lay out its structure and explain briefly your reasons for selecting the structure.)

(Prepared by Michael Ginzberg)

15. **Profit contribution statements: Market withdrawal decision.** Stream and Fall, Inc. has two products, known by the trade names Slip and Slide. Slide was introduced several years ago to compete on a price basis in a mass market, leaving Slip to serve customers interested in a product of high quality and willing to pay for it. The two products are manufactured in the same factory building, but on separate production lines.

The original forecasts called for Slide's sales to reach 300,000 units a month this year. This year's budget established a more modest objective of 250,000 units a month. Actual volume was only 200,000 units last month, while sales of Slip were at their budgeted level of 50,000 units.

Management has asked you to study the desirability of dropping Slide. If this is done, Stream and Fall, Inc. will become a one-product company again. You have decided to begin by drawing up a profit contribution statement for each product. Because top management is not used to profit contribution statements, you want to draw them up with a section below the line for noncontrollable fixed costs.

At the budgeted volumes for this year, the two products were expected to have the following results:

	Slip	Slide
Volume (units per month)	50,000	250,000
Selling price (per unit)	$ 5.00	$ 2.00
Manufacturing cost:		
Direct materials	0.50	0.30
Direct labor	1.00	0.50
Overhead:		
Variable	0.75	0.30
Traceable fixed	0.60	0.30
Allocated fixed	0.15	0.15
Total	3.00	1.55
Sales commission (per unit)	0.25	0.05
Direct selling costs (per month) ...	20,000	40,000
Sales discounts and allowances		
(percent of gross sales)	5%	1%

You have the following additional information:

1. Production volume was equal to sales volume last month. There were no variances in direct materials or direct labor costs last month, and no spending variances in factory overhead.
2. Sales discounts and allowances were at their normal rates last month.
3. Advertising and other direct selling costs were at their budgeted levels last month.

4. Depreciation charges account for $5,000 of Slip's monthly traceable fixed factory overhead costs and $25,000 of Slide's. $4,000 of the nontraceable fixed factory overhead costs could be eliminated if either production line were closed down while the production line for the other product remained in operation.

5. Costs of sales promotion, general company administration, and so forth not otherwise specified above are regarded as fixed and are not traceable to either product. They amount to $78,000 a month and are allocated between the two products each month on the basis of relative gross sales dollars that month. Elimination of either product while the other product remained in the company's line would permit a reduction in these costs of $10,000 a month.

6. Product-related capital expenditures this year are expected to average $7,000 a month for Slip and $10,000 a month for Slide.

7. Each month the company's present costing system allocates nontraceable fixed manufacturing overhead costs between the two products in two stages: (*a*) by applying the predetermined overhead rates listed in the table above to the actual production volume that month; and (*b*) by allocating any over- or underabsorbed amount in proportion to the direct labor costs of production in that month.

Required:

a. Prepare a monthly profit contribution budget for each product for the current year, calculated on a variable costing basis. Include an "allocated charges" section at the bottom to bring each product down to a fully allocated income before taxes, using the company's absorption and allocation formulas.

b. Calculate last month's profit contribution and income before taxes, using the company's allocation and absorption formulas, and show the variances from the budgeted amounts for each product.

c. Judging solely on the basis of the figures you developed for (*b*), how effective was the company's marketing program for Slide last month? Explain, citing figures from the problem.

d. How useful is the variance in income before taxes, as calculated in (*b*), as a measure of the success of the company's product marketing program for each product? What changes in the measurement system would improve the usefulness of the product income figures for this purpose?

e. How would withdrawing Slide from the market affect the company's income and cash flows? What additional information would management reasonably expect to have before deciding what to do about Slide?

Case 12–1: The Federal Company (Identifying response functions)

The Federal Company was a medium-sized manufacturer of consumer soft goods. The headquarters marketing staff in Cleveland was responsible for overall planning and direction of all marketing activities, while responsibility for field selling activities was assigned to the managers of the company's six regional branch offices.

David Halsey, Federal's marketing vice president, was experimenting with a new financial reporting format that he hoped would help him make better promotional expenditure decisions. "Our move to profit contribution reporting several years ago was a step in the right direction," he said, "but it didn't go far enough. For one thing, sales are still reported several months after the promotional activity takes place. This makes for some pretty funny profit contribution figures sometimes.

"For another, they still don't tell me whether I'm spending the right amount in each market area. For example, I was pretty sure that we were spending too much in the Atlanta branch, but I couldn't prove it. I couldn't put the squeeze on the branch manager, either, because he was turning in a larger profit contribution than any of the other branches. I want the system to help me answer this kind of question."

The new reporting system had been worked out by Jack McClendon, Federal's controller. "We made a special study," he said, "trying to find out how long it takes before promotional effort pays off. Frankly, the results aren't very clear, but they have given us something to think about. For instance, we found that calling on a customer more frequently seemed to increase the average order size as well as the total sales volume. I don't know how far we can carry that, but we're certainly going to follow up on it.

"We did find that the orders received in a month correlate pretty well with the current month's field selling and local advertising expenses. I've talked this over with Dave (Halsey) and we've agreed to report sales and cost of goods sold internally on the basis of orders received. That will mean a little more bookkeeping—the company's financial statements will still show revenues from shipments—but I think the benefits are worth it."

Mr. Halsey explained his experimental report structure to the case writer. "The main feature of these reports is that they focus on month-to-month changes rather than on departures from the budget. We still get monthly reports of variances from the profit plan for control purposes, but they don't help us much in decision making.

"Let me show you what I mean. Here is last month's report for the Atlanta branch [Table 1]. The figures in the right-hand column show the changes from the same month a year ago. I'm not sure that that's the right way to go, but we felt that it would be better than a comparison of two successive months.

"Our real emphasis is on the ratios at the bottom of the report. The ratios in the left-hand column are conventional percentage figures. Every company uses these. Our big interest is in the ratio to the right, and I don't know of anyone else who calculates this one. It shows the relationship of the *change* in profit to the change that has taken place in marketing costs. We call this our *response function.* At Atlanta, for example, we got 79 cents for every extra dollar that we spent on field selling and advertising. This is the $107,000 change in branch profit divided by the $136,000 change in field selling and advertising costs."

"That means that you didn't get your money back, doesn't it?"

"No, it's a net figure. We've already deducted the $136,000 from the profit figure, so that we're okay as long as the ratio is positive."

Table 1 Profit performance report, Atlanta branch ($000)

	This Month	Change from Same Month Last Year
Sales (net orders received)	$5,000	+$450
Standard variable manufacturing cost	2,010	+ 181
Standard variable distribution cost	253	+ 22
Contribution margin	2,737	+ 247
Field selling expenses	669	+ 71
Local advertising	523	+ 65
Administration	128	+ 4
Total branch expenses	1,320	+ 140
Branch profit	$1,417	+$107
Effectiveness Ratios:		
Gross margin to sales	0.55	—
Field selling and advertising to sales	0.24	—
Branch profit to sales	0.28	—
Branch profit to field selling and advertising	1.19	0.79

"I'm not sure how much good that ratio will do you," said the case writer. "A lot of other things could have happened, and you can't assume that the increase in sales was all due to the added marketing costs."

"I can't argue with you on that, but we don't take the ratios one by one. What we really want to do is compare the branches, as we do here [in Table 2]. This shows that we were wrong about Atlanta. With a profit ratio of 0.79, it is now giving us more for our added promotional dollar than we get in any other branch. In fact, we're considering spending more money in Atlanta rather than less. Seattle and Denver are at the other extreme. Both of them have negative ratios, and we may decide to cut back on our efforts there."

"I don't understand what the negative ratios mean. Why should they lead you to reduce your promotional outlays in those branches?"

"Well, look at Seattle, for instance. We put an extra $70,000 in there, but our branch profit went down by $7,000. That's a negative response to our effort. The extra $70,000 wasn't a very good investment, in my opinion."

"I can understand the minus figures for Seattle, but what about Denver? There your profit actually went up."

"That's right. We spent less than last year, and we lost some business as a result—sales were down by $67,000. Fortunately, the gross margin on the lost sales was less than the amount we saved in marketing expense. That's what a negative ratio means. Whenever I see a minus sign, it tells me that I can make money by spending less on marketing. With a plus sign, I figure that the market isn't saturated yet, so I should put in a little more money. It doesn't tell me how much more or less to spend, but it gives me the direction."

"How do you allow for changes in general economic conditions? It seems to me that these could have such huge effects on the changes that your ratios would lose all their validity."

"We haven't figured out how to grapple with that one yet. One way is to deal with quarterly data instead of monthly data and compare each quarter with the one before instead of the one a year earlier. The drawback there is that seasonal influences are important in our business, and I don't think the figures would be very useful. Another possibility is to adjust the figures in some way for changes in the gross national product or some other index of the volume of business generally. Even without these changes, though, I think we can use the ratios productively. Don't forget that a change

Table 2 Branch profit comparison ($000)

	Atlanta	Cleveland	Houston	Boston	Denver	Seattle
Sales:						
This year	$5,000	$4,560	$3,076	$3,249	$1,865	$2,722
Change from last year	+ 450	+ 333	+ 243	+ 390	− 67	+ 132
Promotional expense:						
This year	1,192	684	369	520	375	599
Change from last year	+ 136	+ 107	+ 90	+ 135	− 44	+ 70
Branch profit:						
This year	1,417	1,280	831	1,007	634	517
Change from last year	+ 107	+ 76	+ 40	+ 72	+ 5	− 7
Effectiveness ratios:						
Gross margin to sales	0.55	0.52	0.42	0.49	0.58	0.46
Promotional expenses to sales	0.24	0.18	0.12	0.16	0.20	0.22
Branch profit to sales	0.28	0.28	0.27	0.31	0.34	0.19
Response function (change in branch profit to change in promotional expenses)	+0.79	+0.71	+0.44	−0.54	−0.11	−0.10

in business conditions is likely to affect all of our markets. Other things being equal, a change of this kind would produce either minus signs in all branches or plus signs in all branches. We're looking for differences, knowing that the ratios aren't precise and that all they can do is suggest directions we might want to move."

a. Do you agree that Federal should spend more money in Atlanta and less in Denver and Seattle?

b. Do you think that the new reporting system will provide Mr. Halsey with better information for decision making? What changes, if any, would you make in the system to make it more useful?

13 Cost variances in external reporting

When standard costs or predetermined overhead rates are used, variances accumulate in the accounts. Our task in this brief chapter is to try to answer two questions:

1. How the variances should be classified for annual financial reporting.
2. How differences between the standard costs of the inventories and the amounts reported on the balance sheet can be reconciled.

Classifying variances for annual reporting

Three methods of reflecting variances in the annual financial statements need to be considered:

1. Take the entire variance to the income statement for the current year.
2. Assign the entire variance to the balance sheet, to be offset in later periods by variances in the opposite direction.
3. Divide the variance between the balance sheet and the income statement so that the inventory figures will approximate average historical cost.

Taking all variances to income

The argument for taking a variance immediately to the income statement is that standard cost represents the commitment implicit in management's decision to manufacture the product. If cost is greater than this, the excess represents waste. Waste should not be inventoried. Unfavorable volume variances, for example, represent the costs of idle capacity. They are attributable not to the products that were manufactured but to those that weren't produced.

The argument for clearing favorable volume variances to the income statement as they occur is harder to articulate. The argument is that each product should be assigned its full share of the costs of providing capacity. Overutilization of capacity is due to currently favorable conditions which change the profitability of the company's products rather than their costs. Just as the costs of idle capacity are assignable to products not produced, so the benefits from supernormal output accrue to the extra products rather than to the normal output.

Two main arguments can be advanced in opposition to the all-variances-to-income approach to variance disposal. First, the standards or overhead rates may be inaccurate or systematically biased. Any such biases can be revealed on audit, however, so this argument loses much of its sting.

The second argument is more troubling. Some variances are affected by the rate of purchase or by the rate of production. For example, taking price variances to income immediately would entail the recognition of income or loss at the time of purchase, a violation of generally accepted accounting principles. This won't be a major problem if price standards are up to date; if they are out of date, however, a portion of the price variance presumably should be inventoried.

Factory overhead volume variances are more difficult to deal with. The volume variance increases or decreases in inverse proportion to the level of production. Management can increase or decrease reported income by increasing or decreasing its inventories of finished goods. The main control over this is managerial prudence. The carrying costs of excess inventories, including product obsolescence, and the lost sales that are likely to accompany understocking of goods are effective brakes against any long-term manipulation of income by variations in the rate of production. In any given short period, however, variations in inventory levels can have significant effects on the size of the volume variance.

Assigning all variances to the balance sheet

The second possible approach also accepts normal cost as the best measure of product cost but maintains that departures from normal are temporary and will cancel themselves out if a long enough time period is permitted. Therefore, all variances should remain on the balance sheet until offset in later periods by variances in the opposite direction.

This viewpoint would be valid if variances could all be regarded as the result of random forces. Random fluctuations affect totals during short periods, but the longer the reporting period the greater is the likelihood that residual variances are nonrandom. The presumption that 12 months is a long enough time for random variances other than volume variances to cancel each other, together with uncertainty as to the length and average level of business fluctuations, has generally ruled out any extensive support for this second alternative in annual reporting.

Approximating average historical cost

A third possible point of view is that inventory cost should approximate the average historical cost of production. In this view, the variances should be allocated pro rata to the inventories and to the cost of goods sold. If labor variances, for example, average 10 percent of the standard labor cost of the work done, then 10 percent should be added to the standard labor costs placed in inventory during the period; the rest would go to the income statement.

This approach has the disadvantage of inventorying the effects of inefficiencies in operating performance or in the percentage of plant utilization. Furthermore, most of the overhead volume variance will still go to the income statement under this approach, giving management the chance to affect reported income by varying the rate of production. The safeguard here is the same as the one we articulated in our discussion of the all-variances-to-income approach, that commercial considerations limit management's ability to manipulate income by this means except in relatively short periods. (A shift to variable costing would also do the job, but general acceptance of that solution still seems a long way off.)

Current practice in the United States

The Financial Accounting Standards Board has taken no position on the disposition of variances, nor has the International Accounting Standards Committee. The United States Internal Revenue Service is quite specific, however. It requires variances to be prorated for federal income tax purposes if they are significant in amount, except that unfavorable overhead volume variances may be expensed immediately if the overhead rate is based on operations at normal volume. Favorable volume variances must be prorated unless they are immaterial.[1]

Despite the lack of recent statistical data, it is reasonable to assume that practice in the United States is generally consistent with the tax requirement. Favorable variances large enough to be classified as material in amount probably will be divided between the income statement and the balance sheet. Large unfavorable variances also may be prorated, but some of them are likely to be taken to the income statement in their entirety. It is generally accepted, for example, that unrecoverable costs shouldn't be assigned to the inventories. Unfavorable volume variances and large unfavorable spending variances arising during the start-up phase of new facilities are examples of variances that may be placed in this category. If so, they will be deducted from revenues in the year they take place. Unfavorable price variances and other unfavorable variances classified as material in amount but not classified as unrecoverable will be split between the balance sheet and the income statement. If the amounts are regarded as immaterial, of course, most companies are likely to clear all variances to the income statement as they arise.

In this connection we should mention that the use of LIFO is likely to reduce the variance amounts assigned to the inventory. The only inventory to receive a share of the variances under LIFO is the current year's physical inventory increment. This will be a much smaller percentage of the current year's total production than the FIFO inventory percentage. In most cases the LIFO increment will be so small that a full write-off of all variances will be easily justifiable.

Reconciling standard costs with the financial statements

Under most procedures, up-to-date inventory account balances represent the standard costs of the items on hand. These totals may differ from the inventory

---

[1] U.S. Internal Revenue Service, *Regulations,* 1.471–11(d).

figures shown on the company's balance sheet, in three different situations:

1. Newly adopted standards measure anticipated costs and differ substantially from historical cost.
2. Variances are so large that generally accepted accounting principles require them to be reflected pro rata in the reported inventory totals.
3. Inventories are reported on a LIFO basis.

In all three situations, the accountant uses an inventory adjustment account or accounts to bridge the gap between the inventories at standard costs and the amounts reported in the outside financial statements.

Newly adopted standards

The balance in the Inventory Adjustment account on any balance sheet date is simply the difference between total standard cost of the inventory on hand and its average historical cost. It can be either a debit or a credit balance.

For example, a company adopted a standard costing system, effective January 1, 19x1. The inventories on hand at that time had the following standard direct labor costs:

Standard labor cost of the work in process	$ 300,000
Standard labor cost of the finished goods inventory	1,000,000
Total	$1,300,000

The FIFO historical cost of these inventories, as shown on the December 31, 19x0 balance sheet, was $1,378,000.

When the standard costing system was introduced, on January 1, 19x1, two new inventory accounts were set up, one to receive the standard labor costs of all the inventories (both in-process and finished goods), the other to reflect the difference between standard labor cost and the FIFO historical labor cost of the inventories. Similar accounts were set up for the materials and factory overhead costs of the inventories.

The labor cost accounts had the following balances at the beginning of 19x1:

Standard Labor Costs in Inventories	Inventory Adjustment—Labor
Bal. 1/1 1,300,000	Bal. 78,000

Together the balances in these two accounts accounted for the FIFO historical cost of the opening inventory. If the standards had been set at $1,400,000, then the Inventory Adjustment account would have had a credit balance of $22,000. The adoption of standard costing didn't affect the historical cost figures used for financial reporting.

Prorated variances

Reported inventories also depart from standard cost if variances are large enough to be assigned, in part, to the ending inventory.

Exhibit 13–1 Labor cost accounts, 19x1

Standard Labor Costs in Inventories		Inventory Adjustment—Labor	

Bal. 1/1 1,300,000
Standard
  labor
  cost of
  work
  done   5,000,000
	Standard
	labor
	cost of
	goods
	sold 4,750,000
		Bal. 1/1 78,000	

Bal. 12/31 1,550,000			

Labor Cost of Goods Sold		Labor Cost Variances	

Standard
  labor
  cost of
  goods
  sold   4,750,000
		Unfavor-
		  able 500,000
		
		Bal. 400,000
			Favorable 100,000

For example, Exhibit 13–1 summarizes the data in the labor cost accounts at the end of 19x1. All entries in the inventory account during the year were at standard cost, the amounts charged to the cost of goods sold were at standard, and no entries were made in the Inventory Adjustment account. Inventories were to be reported to investors on a FIFO historical cost basis.

Labor cost variances for the year averaged 8 percent of the standard labor cost of the work done ($400,000/$5,000,000). This was classified as material in amount—that is, large enough to be spread on a pro rata basis. Of the $5,000,000 standard labor cost of the work done during the year, $1,550,000 remained in the FIFO inventory at the end of the year; the remaining $3,450,000 went to the cost of goods sold. The variance was split proportionally:[2]

	Standard Labor Cost	Labor Cost Variance (8%)	Adjusted Labor Cost
To ending inventory	$1,550,000	$124,000	$1,674,000
To cost of goods sold	3,450,000	276,000	3,726,000
Total	$5,000,000	$400,000	$5,400,000

---

[2] The ending inventories amounted to $1,550,000/$5,000,000 = 31 percent of the work done during the year. The amount assigned to the inventories therefore should have been the variances arising during the final 31 percent of the year's production. If the variances were not spread evenly throughout the year, the approximation in the illustration would not have been appropriate.

The FIFO labor cost of goods sold therefore was as follows:

	Standard Labor Cost	Variance	Adjusted Labor Cost
From opening inventory	$1,300,000	$ 78,000	$1,378,000
From current production	3,450,000	276,000	3,726,000
Total	$4,750,000	$354,000	$5,104,000

Two adjusting entries were appropriate. The first of these was to transfer the opening balance in the inventory adjustment account to the cost of goods sold:

| Labor Cost of Goods Sold .... | 78,000 | |
| Inventory Adjustment—Labor .... | | 78,000 |

The second entry was to close the variance account:

Labor Cost of Goods Sold	276,000	
Inventory Adjustment—Labor	124,000	
Labor Cost Variances		400,000

As a result, the ending balance in the inventory adjustment account was $124,000, the amount necessary to bridge the gap between the standard labor cost of the ending inventory and the FIFO inventory figure.

To make this procedure work, the variances and the inventory accounts have to be grouped in similar ways. For example, since labor variances must be assigned to the labor content of inventories and of the cost of goods sold, the accountants have to have some way of measuring or approximating the percentage of inventory cost that is accounted for by labor. If we were to carry this notion to the extreme limit, each department's labor and overhead in the finished goods inventory would have to be identified separately. In general, however, much broader groupings ordinarily will be accurate enough to serve the purposes of external reporting.

LIFO inventory adjustment

The use of LIFO is the third reason for the standard cost of the inventory to depart from the amount reported to the public. LIFO inventory costing requires (1) the separate identification of the layer of inventory coming from each year's increment; (2) the measurement of the physical inventory increment or decrement for the current year; and (3) the estimation of the unit cost applicable to the increments or decrements.

For example, suppose our company adopted LIFO on January 1, 19x1, when its inventory had an historical cost of $1,378,000. This was the *LIFO base quantity,* the LIFO cost of the initial inventory layer. The accounts at that time had the following balances (from Exhibit 13–1):

Standard Labor Costs in Inventories	Inventory Adjustment—Labor
Bal. 1/1 1,300,000	Bal. 1/1 78,000

The second step is to calculate the physical inventory increment for 19x1. We can do this by comparing the standard costs of the beginning and ending inventories:

Ending inventory $1,550,000	−	Beginning inventory $1,300,000	=	Inventory increment $250,000

Since each inventory figure represented a set of physical quantities multiplied by the same set of standard prices, the difference between the two can be interpreted as an increase in the physical quantity of goods on hand.

The third step is to estimate the actual cost of the 19x1 increment. Again we might use the 8 percent average variance for the year:

$$\text{Increment} = \$250,000 \times 1.08 = \$270,000$$

The year-end LIFO inventory therefore would be as follows:

Base quantity	$1,378,000
19x1 layer	270,000
Total LIFO cost	$1,648,000

The $250,000 standard cost was already in the inventory account. (Referring back to Exhibit 13–1, we can see that the standard cost of the inventories increased from $1.3 million at the beginning of the year to $1,550,000 at the end, an increase of $250,000.) This leaves just $20,000 of the variance for 19x1 to add to the inventory adjustment account. The entry was:

Inventory Adjustment—Labor	20,000	
Labor Cost of Goods Sold	380,000	
Labor Cost Variances		400,000

This produced the flow of costs illustrated in Exhibit 13–2.

LIFO inventory liquidation. The calculations for an inventory liquidation or decrement are more complicated, but tie right back to the average variances arising in the years in which the various layers were added to the inventory. For example, suppose the standard labor cost of the inventory at the end of 19x2 was $1.4 million, just $150,000 less than the opening balance. This $150,000 came from the 19x1 layer, the last layer added to the inventory. As we just saw, the actual cost of the 19x1 layer was 108 percent of standard cost. The 19x2 LIFO decrement therefore was $150,000 × 1.08 = $162,000. This was $12,000 greater than the standard labor cost of the decrement, and the entry to adjust the accounts was:

Labor Cost of Goods Sold	12,000	
Inventory Adjustment—Labor		12,000

Exhibit 13–2 Distribution of current year's cost variances

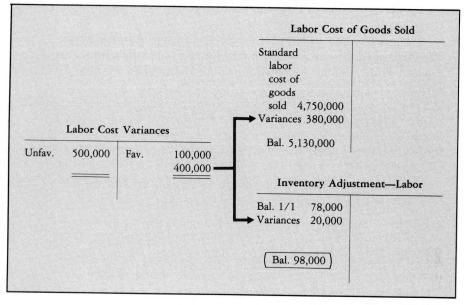

The ending balances in the inventory accounts were as follows:

Standard Labor Costs in Inventories			Inventory Adjustment—Labor		
Bal. 1/1 1,550,000			Bal. 1/1 98,000		
	To cost of goods sold	150,000		To cost of goods sold	12,000
Bal. 1,400,000			Bal. 86,000		

The LIFO cost of the inventory was $1.4 million + $86,000 = $1,486,000, covering the base quantity ($1,378,000) and the remaining two fifths of the 19x1 layer ($108,000).

Prorating materials cost variances

Variances from standard materials and standard overhead costs also must be prorated if they are material in amount. The method is essentially the same as for labor cost variances and an extended illustration is therefore unnecessary. Materials variances do pose one additional problem which needs to be discussed, however—the price variances relate to the quantity *purchased*, while the usage variances relate to the standard materials cost of the *work done*.

For example, suppose a company's inventories had the following standard materials costs on January 1, 19x1:

Raw materials .... $ 80,000
Work in process 10,000
Finished goods 30,000
　　Total $120,000

The FIFO historical cost of these inventories was equal to their standard costs—in other words, the inventory adjustment account started the year with a zero balance.

We have the following information on the company's transactions in 19x1:

Standard cost of materials purchased $200,000
Materials price variance .... 20,000 U.
Standard materials cost of the work done 220,000
Materials usage variance .... 33,000 U.

The standard materials costs of the inventories on hand at the end of 19x1 were as follows:

Raw materials .... $ 27,000
Work in process 25,000
Finished goods 60,000
　　Total standard materials cost in inventory .. $112,000

The flow of materials cost is summarized in Exhibit 13–3.

Exhibit 13–3 Schedule of materials costs, at standard prices

Standard cost of materials issued:		
Materials inventory, January 1, 19x1		$ 80,000
Purchases (at standard prices)		200,000
Total		280,000
Materials inventory, December 31, 19x1		27,000
Standard cost of materials issued		253,000
Less: materials usage variance		33,000
Standard materials cost of work done		220,000
Add: Standard materials cost of work in process,		
January 1, 19x1	10,000	
Less: Standard materials cost of work in process,		
December 31, 19x1	25,000	15,000
Standard materials cost of products finished		205,000
Add: Standard materials cost of finished goods		
inventory, January 1, 19x1	30,000	
Less: Standard materials cost of finished goods		
inventory, December 31, 19x1	60,000	30,000
Standard materials cost of goods sold		$175,000

To divide the variances between the inventories and the cost of goods sold, we need to calculate the average variance percentages:

Average price variance = $20,000/$200,000 = 10%

Average usage variance = $33,000/$220,000 = 15%

Under FIFO, the first costs to be assigned to the goods sold are the costs of the opening inventories. In this case the standard cost of goods sold was greater than the standard cost of the beginning inventory. This means that all of the beginning inventory costs flowed to the income statement for the year; the year-end inventory was measured at the average historical cost of the current year (or, if greater refinement is desired, at the prices paid during the final weeks or months of the year).

Adjusting standard raw materials costs. The usage variance applies only to the work done, not to the materials still in inventory in an unprocessed state. For this reason we can ignore the usage variance in calculating the historical cost of raw materials. The FIFO historical cost of the raw materials inventory was derived by multiplying the standard cost of ending inventory by a factor reflecting the average price variance alone:

	Standard Cost		Adjustment Ratio		Approximate FIFO Historical Cost
Raw materials	$27,000	×	110%	=	$29,700

The $29,700 is only an approximation of historical cost because it was calculated from average relationships. The actual inventories on hand at the end of the year may have been made up of items subject to price movements either greater or less than the 10 percent average annual rate of price increase.

Adjusting standard materials costs of work in process and finished goods. The adjustment ratio for work in process and finished goods is more complicated, because it includes both price and usage variances.[3] Since the actual quantity used was $33,000/$220,000 = 15 percent greater than the standard quantity, standard cost must be multiplied by 1.15. This yields the standard cost of the actual quantities used. To restate this latter figure at actual historical prices, we need to multiply it by 1.10. These two calculations are combined in the adjustments summarized in the following table:

	Standard Cost	Adjustment Ratio (percent)	Approximate FIFO Historical Cost
Raw materials	$ 27,000	110	$ 29,700
Work in process	25,000	110 × 1.15	31,625
Finished goods	60,000	110 × 1.15	75,900
Total	$112,000		$137,225

Closing the variance accounts. The difference between the standard cost and the approximate FIFO historical cost was $137,225 − $112,000 = $25,225. This was the portion of the variances for the year to be assigned to the inventory. The remainder ($20,000 + $33,000 − $25,225 = $27,775)

---

[3] A case can be made for expensing unfavorable usage variances, on the grounds that they represent unrecoverable costs due to production inefficiencies. If this approach is followed, only price variances and favorable usage variances will be reflected in the adjustment ratios.

was classified as part of the cost of goods sold. The variance accounts were closed out by the following journal entry at the end of the year:

Materials Cost of Goods Sold	27,775	
Inventory Adjustment—Materials	25,225	
Materials Price Variance		20,000
Materials Usage Variance		33,000

Adjusting for changes in standard costs

Changes in standard costs require changes in the balances in the inventory accounts, but they don't change the amounts to be reported to the public as the historical cost of the inventories. Suppose our FIFO company from the last example recalculated its standard materials costs for 19x2, bringing the total up from $112,000 at 19x1 standards to $150,000 at 19x2 standards. This means that $38,000 had to be added to the Standard Materials Costs in Inventories account, to bring it up to its proper level at the beginning of 19x2. The accompanying credit had to be to the Inventory Adjustment—Materials account, so that the net book value of the inventories didn't change:

Standard Materials Cost in Inventories		Inventory Adjustment—Materials	
Bal. 12/31 112,000		Bal. 12/31 25,225	
Adjustment 38,000			Adjustment 38,000
Bal. 1/1 150,000			Bal. 1/1 12,775

The book value of the inventory remained unchanged, $137,225.

Summary

It can be argued that all variances should be taken to the income statement in the year in which they arise. The argument is that variances reflect departures from the conditions on which current plans were based. Unfavorable variances reflect unrecoverable costs; favorable variances reflect unanticipated gains.

This treatment is widely used for variances classified as immaterial. If variances are material in amount, however, they generally must be spread pro rata over the goods sold and the goods on hand. Large unfavorable variances due to idle capacity or gross inefficiency are the exceptions, to be reported as part of the current expenses, on the grounds that they represent unrecoverable waste.

In any case, when the inventory figures reported on the published financial statements differ from current standard costs, a reconciling account or accounts must be set up to keep track of the differences. The final section of this chapter showed how this can be done without maintaining dual records of actual and standard costs on a product-by-product basis.

Independent study problems (Solutions in Appendix B)

1. **Prorating materials variances.** The Weston Company's inventory accounts show the standard costs of the items on hand. For public financial reporting the

year's variances are spread proportionately between the cost of goods sold and balance sheet amounts. You are given the following data:

1. Inventories (at standard cost):

	January 1	December 31
Raw materials....................	$10,000	$15,000
Materials in process	6,100	5,000
Materials in finished goods	8,000	7,000

2. Materials issued, at standard cost, $30,000.
3. Materials usage variance for the year, $5,000, unfavorable.
4. January 1 balance in the Materials Usage Variance in Inventory account, $900 Cr. No entries were made in this account during the year.
5. No materials price variances were applicable to the January 1 inventories and no materials price variances arose during the year.

Required:

a. Compute the FIFO cost of goods sold for the year.
b. Prepare an end-of-period entry to close out the Materials Usage Variance account and adjust the Materials Usage Variance Inventory account to its appropriate year-end balance.

2. **Disposing of factory overhead variances.** Factory overhead was applied to products last year by means of a predetermined overhead rate of $3 a direct labor hour. The amount of factory overhead absorbed by production last year was $1.5 million. The overhead volume variance for the year was $300,000, unfavorable; favorable overhead spending variances of $75,000 were accumulated during the year.

The standard overhead costs of the goods in inventory at the beginning and end of last year were as follows:

Beginning of year $400,000
End of year 440,000

The company used an Inventory Adjustment—Overhead account in 19x1. This account had a credit balance of $180,000 at the beginning of the year. Overhead volume variances were not included in the calculation of inventory cost for external reporting; inventory cost otherwise was to approximate LIFO actual historical cost.

Required:

a. Calculate the overhead cost of the inventory on a LIFO basis at the end of last year.
b. Calculate the amount of factory overhead cost to be treated as expense on the company's published income statement for last year.
c. Calculate the appropriate year-end balance in the Inventory Adjustment—Overhead account.

Exercises and problems

3. **Discussion question; variance disposal with partial data.** A company has only one cost of goods sold account and one account for the standard cost of its finished goods inventories. Each department has its own work in process accounts, and the fully accumulated standard cost of the semiprocessed goods a department receives is classified as materials cost in that department.

Required:

Outline a procedure for assigning a pro rata share of the overhead spending variances to the ending inventory. Your procedure should require the collection of no data not already recorded in the company's cost accounts.

4. **Adjustment ratios; overhead costs.** Dandridge Company incurred $1,560,000 in factory overhead costs in 19x1. The overhead spending variance was $240,000, unfavorable; the overhead volume variance was $120,000, unfavorable. Inventories were reported to the public on a FIFO basis.

Required:

a. Calculate the ratio that could be used to adjust the standard overhead cost of the ending inventory to its approximate FIFO historical cost.

b. What ratio would you use if both overhead variances were favorable and actual overhead costs were as reported above? Does your answer reflect a difference in concept or merely an arithmetic difference? Explain.

5. **Adjustment ratios; materials costs.** Ashton Company bought materials for $462,000 in 19x1. These materials had a standard cost of $420,000. In 19x1 the company used materials with a standard cost of $399,000. The materials usage variance was $19,000, unfavorable.

The inventory at the end of 19x1 consisted of items with standard materials costs as follows:

	Ending Balance	Change from Beginning Balance
Materials	$101,000	to be calculated
Materials in process	30,000	+$ 4,000
Materials cost of finished goods	120,000	+ 20,000

Required:

a. Calculate the ratio or ratios to be used to translate the standard costs of materials purchased and used in 19x1 into their approximate historical cost equivalents.

b. Calculate the approximate FIFO cost of the materials content of the ending inventory. How much of the current year's materials cost variances are included in the ending inventory?

c. Calculate the amount that would be added to the materials cost of the historical cost inventory in 19x1 if inventory were accounted for on a LIFO basis. How much of the current year's materials cost variances would be included in the ending inventory?

6. **Prorating overhead variances: Effect on income.** The predetermined overhead rate in the Marston Company was $2 a machine-hour in 19x1. Product costs for this year included the following factory overhead costs, based on this rate:

Inventory, January 1	$ 30,000
Goods manufactured this year	100,000
Inventory, December 31	30,000

Unabsorbed factory overhead for 19x1 amounted to $20,000. This entire amount was deducted from revenues on the company's income statement for the year 19x1.

Required:

a. What effect did the use of a predetermined overhead rate for product costing in 19x1 instead of actual overhead cost for the year have on income before taxes for 19x1 and 19x2, assuming that inventory cost flows followed the FIFO principle?

b.   How would your answer differ if LIFO were in use, assuming that physical inventories were the same at the end of 19x1 as at the beginning?

7.   **Effects of production volume variations.**   The Hotchkiss Company measures inventories and the cost of goods sold at their standard costs for routine record-keeping purposes. All unfavorable overhead cost variances are charged against revenues at year-end.

Standard fixed overhead costs are calculated at a rate of $2 a standard direct labor hour. Budgeted fixed overhead costs amount to $42,000 a month. Production in the first three quarters of the year amounted to 150,000 standard direct labor hours; actual fixed overhead cost in that period totaled $370,000.

Production in the fourth quarter was originally scheduled to require 45,000 standard direct labor hours, but before the quarter began management decided to increase production to 60,000 standard direct labor hours in the fourth quarter, even though the original sales forecast still seemed valid. Actual sales in the fourth quarter equalled the forecasted amounts, and the ending inventory consisted of products with 55,000 standard direct labor hours.

Required:

a.   What effects did management's fourth-quarter decision have on reported income before taxes and on the reported fixed overhead cost of the year-end inventory? Quantify these effects.

b.   How would your answer to (a) have differed if the overhead volume variance had been prorated over the actual production for the year?

c.   What other effects is the decision likely to have produced? Specify these effects but don't attempt to quantify them.

8.   **Disposing of factory cost variances.**   The trial balances of the Andrews Company included the following figures at the beginning and end of the year 19x1:

	January 1	December 31
Sales revenue		$1,500,000
Direct labor cost of goods sold		200,000
Direct materials cost of goods sold		600,000
Overhead cost of goods sold		400,000
Overhead in process	$ 50,000	80,000
Overhead in finished goods	100,000	120,000
Factory overhead (debit)		594,000
Factory overhead absorbed (credit)		450,000
Selling and administrative expenses		250,000

You have the following additional information:

1.   The company's inventories were costed on a FIFO basis.
2.   Standard costs were not used, but a predetermined rate of 200 percent of direct labor cost was used to absorb factory overhead costs.
3.   The factory overhead variance in 19x0 was very small and was deducted in full on the 19x0 income statement.
4.   Factory overhead costs in 19x1 were expected to conform to the following estimated relationship:
     Annual overhead = $360,000 + 80% of direct labor cost of goods produced

Required:

a.   Compute reported income before taxes for the year, on the assumption that the cost of inventories to be reported on the year-end balance sheet is to approximate actual cost rather than normal cost.

b.   Recalculate income before taxes on the assumption that unfavorable overhead volume variances are to be taken to the current income statement in their entirety, but other variances are to be prorated.

c. Compare the effects of these two methods on income before taxes for 19x1 and 19x2. Which of these methods would you choose, or would you recommend writing off the entire overhead variance against income in 19x1? Give your reasons.

9. **Prorating materials variances.** Artemis Publications publishes books. Unlike most publishers, it has its own printing plant. Its inventories of materials (paper stock, ink, and bookbinding supplies) and unsold books were costed on a FIFO basis, including a pro rata share of applicable variances. You have the following data for the year 19x1:

1. Inventory balances:

	January 1	December 31
Materials inventory (at standard)	$390	$500
Materials in process	0	0
Materials in finished goods (at standard)	300	400

2. Materials purchased: actual cost $2,200, standard cost, $2,000.
3. Materials usage variances: $90 (unfavorable).
4. The Materials Variances in Inventories account had a $20 debit balance on January 1. No entries were made in the account during 19x1.

Required:

a. Calculate the standard cost of materials issued during the year.
b. Calculate the standard materials cost of goods finished during the year.
c. Calculate the standard materials cost of goods sold during the year.
d. Calculate the correct end-of-year balance in the Materials Variances in Inventories account.
e. Calculate the FIFO historical materials cost of goods sold during the year, including a prorated share of price and usage variances.
f. What entry should be made to bring the Materials Variances in Inventories account to its correct balance at the end of the year? You may assume that separate accounts were used to accumulate the materials price and materials usage variances during the year.

10. **Prorating labor cost variances: FIFO and LIFO.** A company maintains three separate accounts for the materials, labor, and overhead content of inventories, plus accompanying accounts for the inventoried portion of cost variances. A standard costing system is in use, and inventories for public financial reporting are costed on a FIFO basis. Data for 19x1 are:

1. The standard labor costs of the inventories:

	January 1	December 31
Labor in process	$ 8,000	$14,000
Labor in finished goods...............	17,000	21,000
Total	$25,000	$35,000

2. Direct labor, 8,050 hours (standard wage rate, $6 an hour; actual wages, $50,232).
3. Labor usage variance for the year at standard wage rates, $6,300 (unfavorable).
4. The Labor Variances in Inventory account had a $1,000 debit balance on January 1. No entries were made in this account during the year.

Required:

a. Compute the standard labor cost of goods sold.

b. Compute the labor cost of goods sold on a FIFO historical cost basis, dividing the variances among labor in process, labor in finished goods, and the labor cost of goods sold. (Suggestion: deal with the usage variance first. Labor rate and usage variances were accumulated in two separate accounts during the year.)

c. Prepare a journal entry to close out the year's variances and adjust the inventory accounts to their appropriate year-end balances.

6. Recompute the labor cost of goods sold for the year assuming a LIFO basis of inventory costing and inventorying only the appropriate portion of the labor rate variance.

11. **Approximating FIFO cost; new standards; journal entries.** The Schouten Corporation has a basic plan standard costing system in its factory. The factory accounts reflect the following data in 19x1:

	Trial Balance January 1 Dr.	Cr.	Transactions during 19x1	Dr.		Cr.	Trial Balance December 31 Dr.	Cr.
Materials	43,000		(1)	120,000	(2)	110,400	52,600	
Work-in-process:								
Materials	12,000		(2)	110,400	(5)	110,000	17,000	
			(6)	4,600				
Labor	3,000		(3)	31,500	(5)	27,000	6,000	
					(7)	1,500		
Overhead	6,000		(8)	60,000	(5)	54,000	12,000	
Finished goods:								
Materials	16,000		(5)	110,000	(9)	106,000	20,000	
Labor	4,000		(5)	27,000	(9)	27,000	4,000	
Overhead	8,000		(5)	54,000	(9)	54,000	8,000	
Inventory adjustment		2,000						2,000
Head office		90,000			(1)	132,000		324,390
					(3)	33,390		
					(4)	69,000		
Cost of goods sold ..			(9)	187,000			187,000	
Overhead summary .			(4)	69,000			69,000	
Overhead absorbed .					(8)	60,000		60,000
Materials price								
variance.........			(1)	12,000			12,000	
Materials usage								
variance.........					(6)	4,600		4,600
Labor rate variance .			(3)	1,890			1,890	
Labor usage variance			(7)	1,500			1,500	

The inventory account balances in the December 31, 19x1 trial balance measure the standard costs of the inventories on that date. The Schouten Corporation measures its inventories on an approximate FIFO basis for public financial reporting, however. Variances are prorated for this purpose once a year, at their average for the year.

New standard costs were developed for 19x2 and the standard costs of the inventories on hand on December 31, 19x1 were recalculated, using these new standards. The results were as follows:

Raw materials	$ 57,000
Materials in process	19,000
Labor in process	7,000
Overhead in process	13,300
Materials in finished goods..............	23,000
Labor in finished goods	5,000
Overhead in finished goods	9,500
Total	$133,800

Required:

a. Identify the standard cost of the materials purchased and the standard cost of the factory's output for the year, cost-element-by-cost-element.

b. Calculate separate average variance ratios for materials, labor, and overhead. Remember to calculate separate ratios for price and usage variances.

c. Prorate all variances, using these ratios, and determine the FIFO cost of goods sold and the year-end FIFO historical cost of the raw materials, work in process, and finished goods inventories.

d. Prepare an entry or entries to close all temporary accounts. (The Head Office account is a permanent account; its balance measures the amount the head office has invested in the factory's inventories.)

e. Prepare an entry to reflect the adoption of new standards for 19x2 and draw up a new trial balance as of January 1, 19x2.

12. **Conversion to LIFO; journal entries.** Before closing its books for 19x1, the Schouten Corporation (problem 11) decided to put the materials content of its inventories (including raw materials, work in process, and finished goods) on LIFO as of January 1, 19x1. All other inventories were to remain on FIFO. None of the January 1, 19x1 balance in the Inventory Adjustment account was to be assigned to the materials components of the opening inventory.

Required:

a. Calculate the cost of goods sold with materials on a LIFO basis and labor and overhead on FIFO.

b. Determine the correct December 31, 19x1 balance for the Inventory Adjustment account, after the adjustment to the new standards.

part **2** Further topics in activity costing and decisions

14 Process costing

The method used to measure the cost of a product or service (product cost) depends on the methods used to produce that product or service. Job order costing, as we saw in Chapter 2, is appropriate when individual production centers work on a number of different jobs. Process costing, on the other hand, is called for when a particular product or service is needed in large enough volumes to require the full-time use of production or service facilities for considerable periods of time.

Our objective in this chapter is to explain what process costing is and how process costing information can be used. We'll cover five topics:

1. How to decide whether process costing can be used.
2. Using process costing to calculate the costs of individual products or services.
3. Integrating process costing calculations into the financial statements.
4. Using process costing information for control reporting.
5. Using variable costing in process production.

Feasibility of process costing

Process costing is a method of assigning costs to individual units of product by dividing all the costs in a given category in a production center (e.g., processing labor in the heat treating department) by the number of units of some denominator common to all product units in the center's output for a period (e.g., the number, weight, or surface area of the products processed during the period). We refer to this common denominator as the *output* or the amount of *work done* during the period.

In most cases, both costs and output are departmentalized—that is, separate unit cost figures are calculated for each of the cost centers in which production takes place. Exhibit 14–1, for example, shows a factory with three production centers (departments) producing a single product. The physical flows move steadily from left to right, and separate unit costs are calculated for each department.

Process costing can be used to apportion a production center's costs only if the center's output is homogeneous. Output is clearly homogeneous if the

Exhibit 14–1 Product flows in straight sequential processing

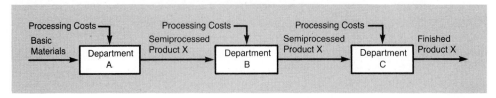

production center always processes identical units of a single product, as in Exhibit 14–1. Output is also homogeneous from a process costing standpoint if the production center performs the same operation or operations on each unit of product, even if these units aren't homogeneous in themselves. For example, the output of an inspection department may be the number of units inspected, or the number of seams checked, or some similar denominator common to all products, even if the inspections are performed on a wide variety of different products.

Exhibit 14–2 diagrams two more situations in which process costing can be used. In the upper panel, the output of one production center (department A) is split between two subsequent production centers for separate processing into two different products. All units of product within each department are identical to each other.

Exhibit 14–2 Product flows in parallel processing

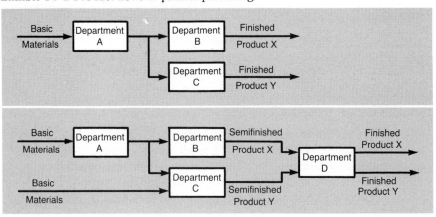

In the lower panel, the outputs of both department B and department C go through department D. Although the products are different, each unit of each product is processed in an identical way (e.g., inspection). The essential point is that each unit in the denominator of the unit cost fraction must have the same relationship to the costs in the numerator as every other unit. When this is the case, we say the output is homogeneous and process costing can be used.

Calculating product cost

Process costing can be used either in cost estimation before production takes place or in cost measurement after the fact. In either case, the procedure for calculating or estimating product cost consists of six steps:

1. Identify the production centers.
2. Accumulate or estimate each production center's operating costs for a specified period of time.
3. Measure or estimate each production center's output for this same time period.
4. Divide cost by output to obtain average unit cost.
5. Add the unit costs of various production centers to obtain the unit costs of individual products.

Identifying the production centers

A production process may be subdivided into subprocesses, each the province of a separate production center, for any of three reasons:

1. Management needs control information in finer detail so that it can identify problem spots more precisely.
2. Output is homogeneous for individual subprocesses but not for the process as a whole.
3. Different subprocesses are likely to process different numbers of units in a given time period.

Management has to decide in each case whether these advantages are great enough to justify the additional clerical costs further subdivision would entail.

Measuring costs

A production center's costs consists of those traceable to it and those that are allocated to it by the methods we described in Chapter 7. A separate unit cost is usually calculated for each cost element. To keep our illustrations simple, however, we'll recognize only three classes of costs: (1) the costs of materials placed in process in their entirety when the production center begins its work on a unit of output; (2) conversion costs, incurred at relatively steady rates as the work progresses; and (3) the costs of finishing materials, applied in their entirety at the end of processing, just before the unit of product leaves the production center.

Measuring output

The output in any period is the sum of the number of units completed, plus or minus the change in the amount of work in process. We made a similar set of calculations in our explanation of standard costing in Chapter 9.

For example, suppose department B receives partly processed goods from department A and transfers its finished output to the finished goods warehouse.

It began the month of June with an inventory of 10,000 units of product, half-processed in this department. It completed work on 89,000 units of product during the month and transferred this amount to the finished goods warehouse. It also had 6,000 units of half-completed product in process at the end of the month.

Our first problem is to calculate the number of units of product department B was able to obtain from the semifinished units it received during June. These are department B's raw materials. They are put into process in their entirety when department B starts its production operations; each unit of work in process therefore contains all of these materials it will ever have.

The first element in the output calculation is the number of units of product completed during the month. Department B received the materials inputs for some of these units (the units in the June 1 inventory in process) in May. These units therefore should be subtracted from the number of units completed:

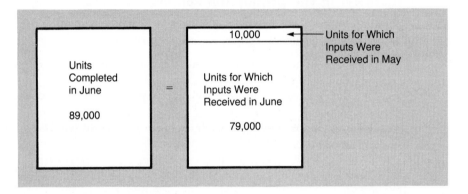

Department B also started work in June on 6,000 units which were still unfinished at the end of the month. These, too, were part of the output department B was able to derive from the semifinished inputs it received from department A in June. The full calculation of the output therefore is as follows:

Units completed in June	89,000
Units in process, June 30	6,000
	95,000
Less: Units in process, June 1	10,000
Output in June (units)	85,000

This 85,000-unit figure is also known as *equivalent production* in department B with respect to the costs of its basic materials (the semifinished units it receives from department A).

This output figure can't be used to calculate department B's average cost of converting or processing the inputs it receives from department A. The reason is that the units in process on any given date aren't fully equivalent to completed units because some costs will still have to be incurred to complete them. Incomplete units, in other words, should be counted only in proportion to the percentage of the required inputs that have already been expended on them.

For example, suppose the conversion costs are incurred at a steady rate as the work passes through the department. The units in process at the beginning and end of June were half-processed in department B. We can translate the units in process into an equivalent number of fully completed units by multiplying them by this completion percentage:

	Number of Units	Percent of Work Done	Equivalent Units
June 1	10,000	50%	5,000
June 30	6,000	50	3,000

To determine the output figure to use in calculating the conversion cost per unit, we need only insert the amounts in the right-hand column in our output formula:

```
Units completed ....................   89,000
Equivalent units in June 30 inventory
    (½ of 6,000) .....................    3,000
                                         92,000
Less: Equivalent of work done in
        prior periods on June 1
        inventory (½ of 10,000) ........    5,000
    Output (equivalent units) ...........   87,000
```

This output figure is also known as *equivalent production* with respect to the costs department B incurred in processing the semifinished units it received from department A.

The rationale for this calculation is diagrammed in Exhibit 14–3. Of the 89,000 units completed during the month (upper block in the diagram), the equivalent of 5,000 units was actually produced during the previous month, and thus must be subtracted (unshaded area at the left of the block). This indicates that the work actually done during June on the units completed during the month was the equivalent of complete processing of 84,000 units

Exhibit 14–3 Calculation of equivalent production with respect to conversion costs

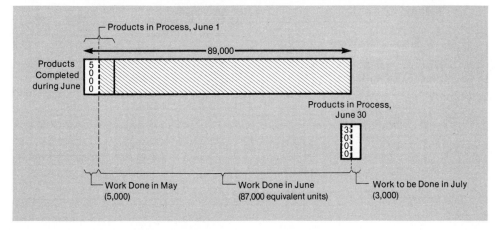

of finished product (shaded area in the upper block). To this we must add the 3,000-unit equivalent of the inventory still in process at the end of the month, represented by the shaded area in the lower block of the exhibit. The total of these figures is equivalent production. Equivalent production in June was smaller than the number of units completed because the amount of work in process decreased between the beginning and the end of the month.

Department B uses one final kind of input, finishing materials, applied to the units completed as they are transferred out of the department. The output calculation for the costs of these materials is very simple: output is equal to the number of units completed.

In summary, then, our output or equivalent production figures in this illustration have been based on the following assumptions:

1. With respect to the costs of *basic materials* (in this case, semifinished products received from department A), each unit of work in process is fully equivalent to a unit of finished product.
2. With respect to the costs of *finishing materials,* units in process count for nothing because the finishing materials are applied only to the units completed and transferred to the finished goods warehouse.
3. With respect to *conversion costs,* each unit of work in process is equivalent to half a unit of finished product because half of the work necessary to complete it has already been performed.

If these assumptions don't fit a particular case, the accountant must substitute other assumptions that do fit.

Calculating unit cost

Calculating the unit costs of departmental operations is a simple matter once the cost divisors have been calculated. For example, department A's costs in June amounted to 60 cents a unit for the materials it used and 40 cents for conversion, a total of $1 a unit. Department B was charged $1 for each semifinished unit it received from department A (department A's average full cost), plus the other costs listed in the first column of Exhibit 14–4. Unit costs for

Exhibit 14–4 Calculation of unit costs of current month's production

	Total Cost	Equivalent Units	Unit Cost
Materials from department A	$ 85,000	85,000	$1.00
Finishing materials	17,800	89,000	0.20
Conversion costs:			
Productive labor....................	8,700	87,000	0.10
Idle time	870	87,000	0.01
Overtime premiums	870	87,000	0.01
Supplies..........................	3,480	87,000	0.04
Other costs	7,830	87,000	0.09
Total conversion cost	21,750		0.25
Total cost of June production	$124,550		$1.45

June were calculated by dividing these costs by the equivalent-unit divisors in the second column of the exhibit.

Notice that materials, labor, and other costs of department A are merged in a single figure in department B. To department B's manager, these are just like the costs of any other materials. If a unit is spoiled, the entire cost of that unit is lost. It doesn't matter whether prior departments' labor costs amounted to 10 percent or 90 percent of the total. We'll study the effects of spoilage later in this chapter.

Calculating product cost: The final step

The unit cost of a product is the sum of the unit costs of the processes it passes through. This means that process costing can be used if different products pass through a process—the only requirement is that the production center performs the same *operation* on all the products that pass through it.

For example, suppose department C processes 50,000 units of product X and 40,000 units of product Y at a total processing cost of $180,000. It performs identical operations on each unit of each product, so that a single divisor of 90,000 units can be used to unitize the processing costs. The department's costs can be summarized as follows:

	Total Cost	Equivalent Production	Unit Cost Product X	Unit Cost Product Y
Costs from prior departments:				
Product X	$ 80,000	50,000	$1.60	—
Product Y	96,000	40,000	—	$2.40
Labor	72,000	90,000	0.80	0.80
Other conversion costs	108,000	90,000	1.20	1.20
Total	$356,000		$3.60	$4.40

Conversion cost is the same for each product, but total unit cost differs because the unit costs of prior departments' work were different.

Integrating process costing into financial statements

The unit costing procedures described above can be applied either to historical costs or to estimates of future costs. Slightly different procedures may be used for financial accounting, however, to assign costs to units transferred from department to department, to finished goods inventory, and to the cost of goods sold. In this section we'll study four questions:

1. Why special calculations are needed for this purpose.
2. What happens when first-in, first-out inventory costing is used.
3. What effect the use of the moving average method has on process costing.
4. The accounting entries needed to implement process costing.

Why special calculations are needed for financial accounting purposes

Suppose department B's 10,000-unit opening inventory had a total materials cost of $10,500, based on the department's experience with materials costs during May. The total materials cost this department was responsible for in June therefore was as follows:

Cost of opening inventory of materials in process $10,500
Costs of materials transferred from department A 85,000

    Total materials cost to be accounted for $95,500

If the $1 unit cost we calculated for the month of June were to be applied both to the ending inventory and to the units finished during the month, only $95,000 would be accounted for:

Units finished (at $1 each) $89,000
Units in ending inventory (at $1 each) 6,000

    Total cost accounted for $95,000

The $500 discrepancy between the two totals arises because the cost of the opening inventory was ignored in the unit cost calculation for June; yet these costs entered into the cost pool that had to be distributed.

One way of dealing with this problem is to measure all inventories and transfers at standard cost and take all variances to the income statement. Predetermining the unit price of transfers in this way would be the best way to keep uncontrollable materials cost variances out of the control reports of subsequent departments. If these variances are large enough in the aggregate to be classified as material in amount, however, the company is likely to have to use some method of inventory costing that takes the beginning inventory cost into consideration. We'll look at two of these methods—the FIFO and moving-average methods.

First-in, first-out method

Under first-in, first-out (FIFO) inventory costing, beginning-of-period inventory cost balances are transferred from a department with the first transferred units equivalent in number to the equivalent units in the opening inventory. All other costs are assigned to the work done during the current period. In our example, we had 10,000 units in process at the beginning of the month. The costs of this opening inventory and the costs incurred during June were as follows:

	Materials from Department A	Finishing Materials	Conversion Costs	Total Cost
Work in process, June 1	$10,500	—	$ 1,100	$ 11,600
Current month's costs (Exhibit 14–4)	85,000	$17,800	21,750	124,550
Total cost to be distributed	$95,500	$17,800	$22,850	$136,150

Completion of work on the opening inventory during the month of June added another $1,250 in conversion costs (the 10,000 units were half-processed at June's average conversion cost of 25 cents a unit), plus $2,000 in finishing materials (10,000 units at 20 cents a unit). Thus under FIFO the first 10,000 units completed would be transferred at $11,600 plus $1,250 plus $2,000, a total of $14,850, to an appropriate Finished Goods Inventory account.

The other 79,000 units completed in June would be costed at the average cost for the month, which we calculated in Exhibit 14–4 ($1 for basic materials, 20 cents for finishing materials, and 25 cents for department B's conversion costs). The total cost of output transferred to finished goods therefore would be:

	First 10,000 Units Finished		Next 79,000 Units Finished		Total Cost of Goods Finished
	Per Unit	Total	Per Unit	Total	
Materials from Department A ..	$1.05	$10,500	$1.00	$ 79,000	$ 89,500
Finishing materials	0.20	2,000	0.20	15,800	17,800
Conversion	0.235	2,350	0.25	19,750	22,100
Total		$14,850		$114,550	$129,400

For convenience, no distinction would be made in finished goods inventories between the first 10,000 and the next 79,000 units of product. They would all be entered at an average cost of approximately $1.454 a pound ($129,400 divided by 89,000). This simplification would also be made if the work were transferred to another department rather than to finished inventories.

The inventory remaining in department B on June 30 would be FIFO-costed at average cost for the current month:

Materials:	6,000 units × $1	$6,000
Conversion:	6,000 units, half-processed, × $0.125	750
	Total cost of ending inventory in process..............	$6,750

The Fifo distribution of department B's costs for the month of June is summarized in Exhibit 14–5.

Moving average method

The calculation procedure can be simplified slightly by using a single average cost (referred to as a moving average) to apply to all product units in a department during a particular period of time.

For example, the total cost of materials in process in department B during June was $95,500 (opening balance plus $85,000 for materials received from department A during the month). The only units available to absorb these costs were the 89,000 units finished and transferred out of the department during the month and the 6,000 units still in process at the end of the month, a total of 95,000 units.

The average materials cost for these 95,000 units was $95,500 ÷ 95,000 = $1.00526 a unit. (Carrying the answer to this many decimal places is both

Exhibit 14-5 Distribution of department B's costs: FIFO method

	Total Amount	Per Equivalent Unit
Costs in department:		
Materials (from department A):		
In process, 6/1	$ 10,500	$1.050
Received	85,000	1.000
Total	95,500	xxx
Finishing materials	17,800	0.200
Conversion costs:		
In process, 6/1	1,100	0.220
Productive labor	8,700	0.100
Other	13,050	0.150
Total	22,850	xxx
Total departmental cost	$136,150	xxx
Cost distribution:		
To finished products:		
Materials (from department A)	$ 89,500	$1.006
Finishing materials	17,800	0.200
Conversion	22,100	0.248
Total finished products	129,400	1.454
In process, 6/30:		
Materials (from department A)	6,000	1.000
Conversion	750	0.125
Total in process, 6/30	6,750	1.125
Total cost distributed	$136,150	xxx

meaningless and unnecessary; we have done it here simply to remove the rounding errors from the illustration.) This average would be used to measure the materials cost of the units in process at the end of the month as well as the materials cost of the units finished during the month.

This cost distribution is illustrated in the following diagram:

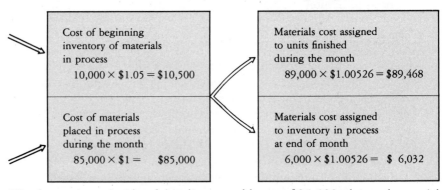

The figures in each side of this diagram add up to $95,500, the total materials cost within the department's responsibility during the month.

A similar calculation can be made to distribute the $22,850 in departmental conversion costs ($1,100 from the beginning work in process, $8,700 in labor cost for the month, and $13,050 in other conversion costs). The unit cost divisor in this case would be 92,000 units, because the ending inventory was only half processed (89,000 units of fully completed products plus the equivalent of 3,000 units in the ending inventory). Average cost would be $22,850 ÷ 92,000 = $0.24837 a unit.

The conversion cost to be transferred therefore would be $22,105 (89,000 units × $0.24837), leaving $745 (3,000 equivalent units × $0.24837) as the cost of the ending inventory in process. These calculations are summarized in Exhibit 14–6. (Unit costs in the right hand column have been rounded to the nearest tenth of a cent.)

Exhibit 14–6 Distribution of department B's costs: Moving-average method

	Total	Per Unit
Costs in department:		
Materials:		
In process, 6/1	$ 10,500	$1.050
Received	85,000	1.000
Total	95,500	1.005
Finishing materials	17,800	0.200
Conversion costs:		
In process, 6/1	1,100	0.220
Productive labor	8,700	0.100
Other	13,050	0.150
Total	22,850	0.248
Total departmental cost	$136,150	$1.453
Cost distribution:		
To finished products:		
Materials	$ 89,468	$1.005
Finishing materials	17,800	0.200
Conversion	22,105	0.248
Total finished products	129,373	1.453
In process, 6/30:		
Materials	6,032	1.005
Conversion	745	0.124
Total in process, 6/30	6,777	1.129
Total cost distributed	$136,150	xxx

The unit cost divisor under the moving-average approach differs from equivalent production by the number of equivalent units in the opening inventory:

	Materials	Conversion
Units completed during period	89,000	89,000
Plus: In process, end of period	6,000	3,000
Cost divisor, moving average	95,000	92,000
Less: In process, start of period	10,000	5,000
Equivalent production	85,000	87,000

The peculiarity of the average cost calculation is that the sum of the number of units finished and the number of those still in process at the *end* of the period is divided into the sum of the costs incurred during the period and the costs at the *beginning* of the period. The reason for this is that the latter sum reflects all of the *costs* while the former sum represents all of the *units* available to absorb these costs. Equivalent production, on the other hand, is used as a divisor for the current month's costs only, and this requires the subtraction of the opening inventory.

The differences between the moving-average and FIFO methods should not be overstressed. The resultant unit costs will not depart materially from each other unless the production cycle is particularly long and monthly cost per unit of equivalent production changes rapidly. For this reason, the choice between the two ordinarily can be made on the basis of convenience. *In any case, equivalent production is the only legitimate divisor in calculating current unit cost because it is the only one that measures the amount of work done, the amount for which the current period's costs were incurred.*

Recording costs in process costing

Operating costs in process production will be departmentalized for control reporting. The question is how these costs will flow through the inventory accounts for public financial reporting.

One possibility is to use a single work-in-process account for an entire factory. Under this system, operating costs would be charged to the work-in-process account as they arose, to be transferred to a finished goods inventory account when products emerged from the final processing stage. Transfers of the costs of semiprocessed work from department to department would be recorded on worksheets only, as part of the calculation of unit costs.

Another possibility is to use departmental work-in-process accounts, with interdepartmental transfers of semiprocessed work recorded in journals and ledger accounts. Let's illustrate this system as it might be applied to department B's transactions in June, using the moving-average method.

Before we can prepare journal entries to record the costs and the transfers, we have to know the structure of the company's accounts and the details of its accounting procedures. To describe an actual system would require far more pages than we can spare here, so let's assume that department B has eight object-of-expenditure accounts, two work-in-process accounts, and two distributional accounts:

Object of Expenditure	*Work in Process*
Materials Transferred In	Materials in Process
Finishing Materials	Conversion Costs in Process
Productive Labor	
Idle Time	*Distribution*
Overtime Premiums	Materials Costs Distributed
Supplies	Conversion Costs Distributed
Other Costs	
Scrap Recovery	

With this structure we might have the following series of entries to record department B's transactions in June under the moving average method (all figures come from Exhibits 14–4 and 14–6):

(1)

Materials Transferred In—Department B	85,000	
Materials Costs Distributed—Department A		51,000
Conversion Costs Distributed—Department A		34,000

To record transfers of semiprocessed work from department A to department B.

(2)

Finishing Materials—Department B	17,800	
Materials Inventory		17,800

To record materials issued to Department B from stockroom.

(3)

Supplies—Department B	3,480	
Materials Inventory		3,480

To record costs of supplies issued to Department B from stockroom.

(4)

Productive Labor—Department B	8,700	
Idle Time—Department B	870	
Overtime Premiums—Department B	870	
Wages Payable		10,440

To record labor costs in Department B.

(5)

Other Costs—Department B	7,830	
Accounts Payable (etc.)		7,830

To record other conversion costs in Department B.

(6)

Finished Goods Inventory	129,373	
Materials Costs Distributed—Department B		107,268
Conversion Costs Distributed—Department B		22,105

To record transfer of finished products to the finished goods inventory.

(7)

Materials Costs Distributed—Department B	107,268	
Materials Transferred In—Department B		85,000
Finishing Materials—Department B		17,800
Materials in Process—Department B		4,468

To record the decrease of the cost of materials in process from $10,500 to $6,032 and to close the current operating accounts.

(8)

Conversion Costs Distributed—Department B	22,105	
Productive Labor—Department B		8,700
Idle Time—Department B		870
Overtime Premiums—Department B		870
Supplies—Department B		3,480
Other Costs—Department B		7,830
Conversion Costs in Process—Department B		355

To record the decrease of conversion costs in process from $1,100 to $745 and to close the current operating accounts.

After these entries are posted, the work in process accounts show the following:

Materials in Process—Department B				Conversion Costs in Process—Department B			
Bal. 6/1	10,500			Bal. 6/1	1,100		
		(6)	4,468			(7)	355
Bal. 7/1	6,032			Bal. 7/1	745		

The only one of department B's accounts we didn't use in our illustration was the Scrap Recovery account. Since department B recovered no scrap in June, we had no entry to make. The entry to record scrap recovery in this system would take the following form:

Scrap Inventory (at market value)	xxx	
Scrap Recovery—Department B		xxx

We must emphasize that these entries are purely illustrative of the flows of costs in a system of this sort. The actual entries will differ from company to company, even if the work in process accounts are departmentalized. The crucial tasks are to calculate unit costs and to determine the costs of the inventories; the procdures to reflect these key figures in the accounts are distinctly secondary.

Using process costing information in control reporting

Management has the same need for control information in process production as in job order production. In this section we'll see how both historical process costing and standard process costing might be used for this purpose.

Historical costing

Product cost in process costing is also departmental cost. For this reason, unit product cost is often used to provide departmental control information. An example of a production center control report is shown in Exhibit 14–7.

In this exhibit, departmental costs are classified into several descriptive categories and a unit cost is computed for each. Extra columns are provided to show last-month, year-to-date, and prior-year figures. Space is usually added for explanations of important changes in the figures.

Reports of this kind are attention-getting devices. They may lead immediately to corrective action or eventually to decisions on changes in methods, equipment used, and so forth. They have a number of shortcomings, however:

1. Comparison is with the past, not with what was expected or what should have happened.
2. Average fixed cost varies with volume, and the manager doesn't control volume.
3. Input prices vary, and the manager doesn't control prices.

Standard costs and flexible budgets can be used to eliminate all three of these objections, as we shall see in a moment. Historical comparisons can be

Exhibit 14–7   Departmental cost report: Process production

Cost Center: 5116—Coke Batteries					Month: <u>October</u>
			Last Month, 40,000 Tons	Year Ago, 43,000 Tons	Year to Date	
	Current Month, 44,000 Tons				This Year	Last Year
Cost Item	Cost	Per Unit	Per Unit	Per Unit	Per Unit	Per Unit
Direct materials	$981,200	$22.30	$22.38	$21.98	$22.54	$21.65
Less: Recoveries	(230,121)	(5.23)	(5.22)	(5.26)	(5.58)	(5.41)
Net direct materials	751,079	17.07	17.16	16.72	16.96	16.24
Indirect materials	1,463	0.03	0.03	0.03	0.03	0.03
Fuels	79,538	1.81	1.77	1.75	1.76	1.68
Labor	13,251	0.30	0.31	0.26	0.31	0.27
Utilities	2,604	0.06	0.06	0.07	0.06	0.06
Services	41,623	0.95	1.05	0.88	1.03	0.85
Maintenance	5,190	0.12	0.13	0.16	0.11	0.12
Administrative	8,095	0.18	0.22	0.17	0.19	0.17
Total	$902,843	$20.52	$20.73	$20.04	$20.45	$19.42

made cheaply, however, and may be good enough if volume and input prices remain relatively constant.

Standard costing

Standard costing is much easier to apply to process production than to job order production. In fact, the parallels between historical process costing and basic plan standard costing (Chapter 9) are startling (see Exhibit 14–8). A

Exhibit 14–8 Historical process costing versus basic plan standard costing

Historical Process Costing	Basic Plan Standard Costing
Control figures are departmental unit costs.	Control figures are departmental cost variances.
Unit costs are calculated at the end of the period.	Cost variances are calculated at the end of the period.
Departmental output is equal to the work completed ± the change in work in process, measured in physical units.	Departmental output is equal to the work completed ± the change in work in process, measured at standard cost.

historical process costing system can be converted to a standard costing system simply by using standard prices to measure departmental inputs and standard costs to measure departmental outputs.

In our earlier illustration, we assumed that none of the materials department B received from department A were lost in the conversion process. We'll have to change this assumption if we want to illustrate the use of standard costing. Furthermore, we'll have to subdivide department B's conversion costs and develop a cost standard for each element.

Suppose we have the following standards for the costs of materials and labor in department B:

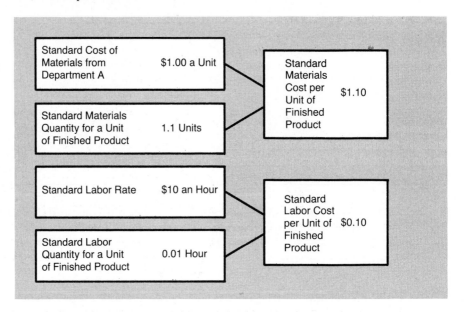

The inventory in process on June 1 consisted of the materials required for 10,000 units of finished product. Half of department B's conversion operations had already been performed on these units. The standard materials and labor costs of the June 1 inventory therefore were as follows:

Materials from department A ..... 10,000 × $1.10 $11,000
Departmental labor .... 5,000 × $0.10   500

Department B received 85,000 units of input from department A during the month of June, at a standard price of $1 a unit. It used 870 hours of productive labor, at a standard labor rate of $10 an hour. The materials and labor costs it was responsible for therefore were as follows:

Materials from Department A (at standard price)		Productive Labor (at standard labor rate)	
Beginning inventory	$11,000	Beginning inventory	$ 500
Received during June:		June departmental labor:	
85,000 × $1.00	85,000	870 × $10.00	8,700
Total responsibility	$95,000	Total responsibility	$9,200

Department B completed work on 72,000 units of finished product in June with a standard materials cost of 72,000 × $1.10 = $79,200 and standard labor costs of 72,000 × $0.10 = $7,200. Department B also had 6,000 half-processed units in process at the end of the month. With these figures we can calculate the standard cost of the month's output and determine the variances in these two cost elements:

	Materials from Department A	Productive Labor
Standard cost of output:		
Units completed	$79,200	$7,200
Ending inventory	6,600	300
	85,800	7,500
Beginning inventory	11,000	500
Standard cost of output	74,800	7,000
Standard cost of input	85,000	8,700
Usage variance	$10,200 unfavorable	$1,700 unfavorable

The large variances in this case reflected a higher than standard rate of unit spoilage during the month of June.

The elements in the calculation of the standard cost of the output are exactly the same as those we used to calcualte equivalent production earlier in this chapter:

Units completed + Equivalent units in ending inventory − equivalent units in beginning inventory = Equivalent production.

The only difference is that we are now measuring equivalent production in dollars of standard cost rather than in physical units.

Flexible budgets

Calculations like those in preceding paragraphs can be made for every cost element expected to vary proportionally with volume. Standard costs don't provide control information for fixed and semivariable cost elements, however. Just as in job order production, cost standards for these elements must be provided by flexible budgets. Overtime premium, for example, may average 1 cent a unit when volume is 90,000 units, but may rise to 2 cents when volume goes up to 100,000 units a month.

Shrinkage, accretion, and spoilage

Products often change in size, form, or quantity as they move through a production process. The main changes are:

1. *Changes of form:* The finished product may be measured one way (by weight or unit count, for example), in-process inventory another (by volume or length).
2. *Accretion:* A unit of work in process will yield more than a unit of finished product (for example, through the addition of water).
3. *Shrinkage:* A unit of work in process will yield less than a unit of finished product.
4. *Spoilage:* Units in process are lost or damaged in the processing operation and must be discarded, repaired, or sold as "seconds."

All of these affect the calculation of the output equivalents of the work in process; shrinkage and spoilage also may affect the methods of reporting costs.

Adjusting the number of units in process

If units in process on an inventory date are expected to shrink, grow, or change their form before emerging as finished units, the in-process inventories must be translated to their normal equivalent in finished units. For example, suppose a production center finishes work on 120,000 gallons of product during the month and has 40,000 gallons of semiprocessed product in process at the end of the month. Under normal circumstances, inventory at this stage is expected to shrink by 25 percent before conversion is completed. The appropriate figure to enter into the output calculation is thus 75 percent of 40,000 gallons—that is, 30,000 finished gallons. If the company figures that half of the department's work has been done on these in-process inventories, only 15,000 equivalent gallons should enter into the divisor for conversion costs.

In summary, assuming no beginning inventory, the equivalent production cost divisors would be:

	Actual Gallons	Equivalent Materials	Equivalent Conversion
Units completed	120,000	120,000	120,000
Units in process (end)	40,000	30,000	15,000
Total	160,000	150,000	135,000

Accounting for the costs of spoilage

Few processes are so tightly conceived that all productive inputs emerge as good products ready for sale or further processing. Leakages occur through spoilage, evaporation, on-premises consumption, and other factors. Much of this leakage is unavoidable, a necessary part of the cost of producing units of good product. In standard costing systems, the standards typically allow for normal spoilage; deviations from normal show up as variances. In the absence of standard costing, one of the following two methods is usually used:

1. Adjust unit cost by spreading the costs of spoiled units over all good production.
2. Identify the costs of spoiled units and report them separately.

Method 1. Adjusting unit cost for spoiled units. The easiest solution is to average the cost of lost or spoiled units into the cost of the remaining units of good product. For example, suppose department B had 10,000 units of product in process on June 1 and 6,000 units in process on June 30, half processed in each case. It received 85,000 units of product during June, just as in our earlier illustration. Instead of finishing 89,000 units, however, department B finished only 72,000 units and spoiled the other 17,000. The spoilage occurred in each case just before processing in department B was half completed. In other words, the units in process at the beginning and end of the month were subject to no further spoilage. These quantities are diagrammed in Exhibit 14–9.

Exhibit 14–9 Product flows, including spoilage

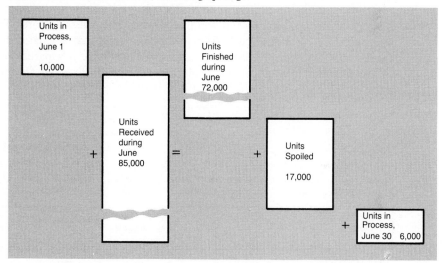

In this situation, the number of equivalent units of good product can be calculated as follows:

	Outputs from		
	Prior Dept. Costs	Finishing Materials	Conversion Inputs
Units finished during June	72,000	72,000	72,000
Work in process, June 30	6,000	—	3,000
Moving average divisors	78,000	72,000	75,000
Work in process, June 1	10,000	—	5,000
Equivalent production	68,000	72,000	70,000

The number of units spoiled didn't enter this calculation; we looked only at outputs (units finished plus the change in work in process), not at the inputs.

The costs of the materials received from department A in June were $85,000 and conversion costs totaled $21,750, as in our previous illustration, but finishing materials costs were only $14,400 because only 72,000 units were finished. The average cost calculation is as follows:

	Prior Dept. Costs	Finishing Materials	Conversion Costs	Total Costs
Total cost	$85,000	$14,400	$21,750	$121,150
Equivalent production	68,000	72,000	70,000	
Average unit cost	$1.250	$0.200	$0.311	$1.761

Any scrap recovery under this method is taken as a reduction of unit cost. For example, suppose the 17,000 spoiled units had an immediate scrap value of 10 cents each, or $1,700 in total. This amount could be deducted either from prior department costs or from departmental conversion costs. Treating scrap recovery as a deduction from prior department costs (materials costs) can be supported on the assumption that salvage value is a partial recovery of the materials content of the semifinished products received from department A. This gives us the following unit costs:

	Prior Dept. Costs	Finishing Materials	Conversion Costs	Total Costs
Total cost....................	$85,000	$14,400	$21,750	$121,150
Less: Salvage	1,700	—	—	1,700
Net cost	$83,300	$14,400	$21,750	$119,450
Equivalent production	68,000	72,000	70,000	
Average unit cost	$1.225	$0.200	$0.311	$1.736

Method 2. Separating the costs of spoiled units. The second method of accounting for the costs of spoiled units is to transfer their costs to a separate overhead or expense category. To do this, we need to recalculate the cost divisors to include spoiled units as well as good units. The procedure is simple:

1. Calculate the number of equivalent units spoiled, element by element.
2. Add these figures to the equivalent production figures.[1]
3. Divide total cost by the revised cost divisors to get average cost.
4. Multiply these average costs by the number of equivalent units spoiled.

In this case spoiled units are half-processed in the department but complete as to prior department costs. The revised cost divisors are:

---

[1] If unit costs are calculated by the moving-average method for financial accounting purposes, equivalent spoiled units should be added to the moving-average divisors calculated by method 1.

	Prior Dept. Costs	Finishing Materials	Conversion Costs
Equivalent production	68,000	72,000	70,000
Equivalent units spoiled	17,000	—	8,500
Cost divisors, including spoiled units	85,000	72,000	78,500

Using these divisors, we get the following average unit costs:

Prior department costs	$85,000/85,000 = $1.000
Finishing materials costs	$14,400/72,000 = 0.200
Conversion costs	$21,750/78,500 = 0.277
Total	$1.477

The total cost of the spoiled units is:

Materials: 17,000 × $1.00	$17,000
Conversion: 17,000 × ½ × $0.277	2,355
Total	$19,355

These costs are not averaged into the costs of the good units. The average materials cost of the good units, for example, remains at $1.

Under this approach, the salvage value of the spoiled units should be deducted from their cost to determine the net cost of spoilage. Since the spoiled units in our example were sold for 10 cents each, the net cost of spoilage was reduced to $19,355 − $1,700 = $17,655 (see Exhibit 14–10).

Exhibit 14–10 Calculating the net cost of spoilage

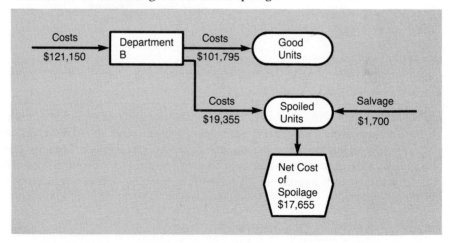

The entry to record the costs assigned to the spoiled units might be as follows:

Spoilage—Department B	19,355	
Materials Costs Distributed—Department B		17,000
Conversion Costs Distributed—Department B		2,355

The entry to record the scrap recovery would be:

```
Cash ...............................................  1,700
    Scrap Recovery—Department B .........................            1,700
```

The net loss is the difference between the balances in the Spoilage and Scrap Recovery accounts.

Advantage of Method 2. The main advantage of Method 2 is that it places a dollar amount on the spoiled quantities and thereby calls attention to the dollar effect of spoilage. This amount shouldn't be treated as a loss, however. Some spoilage is normal, and product cost should include a provision for this normal experience. For control, too, what we want is the deviation from normal rather than the actual cost, taken by itself.

To accomplish these objectives, the spoilage loss can be reported as a departmental overhead cost and the flexible budget can reflect normal spoilage relationships. The monthly overhead report then will show the actual spoilage, the flexible budget, and the spending variance for the month. The spending variance should be excluded from product cost.

Effect of spoilage on unit cost. Method 1 has one advantage over Method 2—it is considerably simpler. If management chooses Method 1, it can still get control information on spoilage costs by calculating the effect of spoilage on average unit cost each period. It can do this by comparing the unit costs derived by the two methods:

	Prior Dept. Costs	Finishing Materials	Conversion Costs	Total Costs
Unit cost, including spoilage effect (Method 1)	$1.225	$0.200	$0.311	$1.736
Unit cost, excluding spoilage effect (Method 2)	1.000	0.200	0.277	1.477
Effect of spoilage on unit cost	$0.225	$ —	$0.034	$0.259

We have performed this calculation on the costs of equivalent production. Similar calculations can be performed on unit costs derived by the moving average method. Since the calculation of spoilage effects is made primarily to provide control information, however, we prefer to perform it on the costs for the current month, which relate only to equivalent production.

Variable costing in process production

All of our illustrations so far have been based on full absorption costing. Process costing can also be based on variable costing. Two situations need to be distinguished:

1. All of the production center's costs can be classified as either wholly fixed or wholly and proportionately variable.
2. Some of the production center's costs are semivariable.

Process costing for wholly variable costs

Variable costing is simple if each of a production center's cost elements can be classified as wholly fixed or wholly variable. In such cases each variable cost element can be divided by an appropriate cost divisor; the fixed costs do not enter the unit cost calculation.

Exhibit 14–11 shows the calculation of unit cost in the mixing and grinding department of a cement mill. Eight cost elements are classified as variable, and an average unit cost is computed for each element each month. The fixed costs, however, are not averaged over the units produced.

Exhibit 14–11 Mixing and grinding department—Variable costing, month of November

	Total Cost	Unit Cost
Variable costs:		
Operating labor	$ 6,541	$0.0327
Auxiliary labor	303	0.0015
Payroll charges	1,298	0.0065
Fuel and water	2,527	0.0126
Light and power	9,806	0.0490
Grinding supplies	953	0.0048
Dust collector	427	0.0021
Total variable	$21,855	$0.1090
Fixed costs:		
Supervision	712	
Maintenance labor	2,299	
Maintenance materials	1,956	
Total fixed	$ 4,967	

The output figures used in this kind of calculation are measured in the way described in the last section. The only difference is that the cost divisors are applied solely to the variable cost elements.

Variable costing with semivariable costs

The main defect with the method just described is that it doesn't provide for semivariable costs. When these are material in amount, the correct approach is to use a predetermined overhead rate, at least for those components of cost that cannot reasonably be assumed to be completely and proportionately variable.

Exhibit 14–12 illustrates how this change might affect unit costing in the cement mill's mixing and grinding department. One item previously classified as variable has now been reclassified as semivariable on the ground that it includes a fixed cost component, while two items not previously included in product cost have been moved from the fixed to the semivariable category. For each element, actual costs for the month are shown for the information

Exhibit 14–12 Mixing and grinding department—Variable costing
using predetermined rates for semivariable cost elements

	Total Cost	Unit Cost
Variable costs:		
Operating labor	$ 6,541	$0.0327
Auxiliary labor	303	0.0015
Payroll charges	1,298	0.0065
Fuel and water	2,527	0.0126
Grinding supplies	953	0.0048
Dust collector	427	0.0021
Total variable	12,049	0.0602
Semivariable costs:		
Light and power	9,806	0.042*
Maintenance labor	2,299	0.005*
Maintenance materials	1,956	0.009*
Total semivariable	14,061	0.056*
Total product cost	xxx	$0.1162
Fixed costs:		
Supervision	712	

* Predetermined rates for variable cost component only.

of the department head, but the unit cost figures shown in the semivariable
cost section of the exhibit are predetermined and represent the variable component only. They do not reflect the current month's cost experience in any
way.

The unit cost figure of $0.1162 a barrel is a hybrid: partly predetermined
and partly based on cost performance for the month. This makes it very similar
to unit cost under job order costing, in which actual direct labor and materials
costs are mingled with overhead applied on the basis of predetermined overhead rates.

Summary

Whenever the output of a production center is sufficiently homogeneous to
be measured in physical units, unit cost can be determined by the process
costing method. In process costing, unit cost is determined by dividing each
production center's costs by its output for a specified period of time.

The only difficult question is how to calculate output for this purpose. The
solution is to group resource inputs into classes selected so that inputs in
each class are applied at approximately the same stage of the production process.
For each class, output is equal to the number of units finished by the production
center during the period plus or minus the change in the number of equivalent
finished units in process. If in-process inventories increase, then output is
greater than the number of units finished, and vice versa.

Unit costs calculated in this way are sometimes used for control reporting. Care needs to be taken, however, to analyze the effects of changing volume and to use standard cost benchmarks rather than the average cost in some previous period. Process costing can also be used to generate unit costs on a variable costing basis.

Finally, process costing figures can be integrated quite easily into the financial accounting records. The illustration in this chapter showed how this could be done, using both first-in, first-out and moving-average inventory cost bookkeeping.

Independent study problems (solutions in Appendix B)

1. **Unit costs, two departments, no spoilage.** The Butts Company has a two-process factory in which all materials are placed in process in department A at the start of processing and semifinished products are transferred to department B for completion. No additional materials are introduced in department B. The following data relate to the month of June:

Department A:
   Beginning inventory (50 units, 30 percent completed): materials, $45, conversion costs, $41.
   Raw materials received during month (100 units), $105.
   Conversion costs incurred during month, $399.
   Ending inventory: 60 units, one-third completed.

Department B:
   Beginning inventory (40 units, one-half completed): materials, $213; conversion costs, $150.
   Conversion costs incurred during month, $570.
   Ending inventory: 45 units, two-thirds completed.

No product units were lost in either department during the month.

Required:

a. For department A, calculate unit costs for the unit, then calculate the cost of the work in process on June 30 and the cost of goods transferred to department B during the month, using the moving average basis for the transfer calculation.

b. Repeat these calculations for department B, using the FIFO basis to calculate the cost of the work in process on June 30 and the cost of goods transferred out of the department during the month.

2. **Unit costs, one department, spoilage.** The Stanley Chemical Company uses a process costing system of unit cost determination. The company's factory consists of two departments: raw materials are first mixed in the mixing department and then transferred to the refining department for completion. Units of product still in process in a department at the end of a month are assumed to be 100 percent complete as to materials and 50 percent complete as to conversion costs in that department.

You are given the following data for the refining department for the month of January:

Quantities:	
In process, January 1	4,000
Transferred in	93,000
Transferred out	82,000
In process, January 31	10,000
Costs:	
In process, January 1:	
Materials (from mixing)	$ 2,800
Conversion	2,346
Materials received from mixing	81,840
Labor	61,200
Other variable conversion costs	15,300
Fixed conversion costs	30,600
Total cost	$194,086

Units of product lost in production are assumed to be fully processed; their cost is to be spread evenly over the equivalent good production.

Required:

a. Calculate the cost divisors for the month.
b. Calculate a separate unit cost for each cost element in the month of January.
c. Calculate the effect of the lost units on unit costs.
d. Calculate the costs assigned to the goods finished and the costs of the ending in-process inventory, using the moving average method.

3. **Calculating variances.** The Stanley Chemical Company (problem 2) is considering the adoption of standard costing. Tentative cost standards for the refining department are as follows (per unit of refining output):

Materials from mixing, 1.05 pounds × $0.90	$0.945 a pound
Variable conversion costs:	
Labor, 0.07 hours × $10	0.70 a pound
Other variable costs	0.15 a pound
Fixed conversion costs (stated as $0.30 a unit	
for product costing purposes)	30,000 a month

The department's costs for the month of January were recalculated at the new standard input prices with the following results:

In process, January 1:	
Materials from mixing	$ 3,780
Conversion	2,300
Costs incurred in January:	
Materials received from mixing	83,700
Labor	59,000
Other variable conversion costs	13,900
Fixed conversion costs	31,300
Total	$193,980

Required:

a. Calculate a cost variance for each of the refining department's four cost elements for the month of January. This variance should reflect the department's success in controlling its costs during the month.
b. What is the explanation of the difference between the costs of the January 1 inventory and the costs charged to refining in this problem and the amounts charged to refining in problem 2?

Exercises and problems

4. **Equivalent units: Multiple choice.**   Select the best answer to each of the following questions:

1. The Ace company had computed the number of physical units completed by Department A in the month of April, 19x1, as follows:

   From work in process on April 1, 19x1 10,000
   From April production 30,000
      Total 40,000

   Materials are added at the beginning of the process. Units of work in process at April 30, 19x1, were 8,000. The work in process at April 1, 19x1, was 80 percent complete as to conversion costs and the work in process at April 30, 19x1, was 60 percent complete as to conversion costs. The equivalent units of production in the month of April, 19x1, appropriate for calculations required by the FIFO method were:

   a. For materials, 38,000; for conversion costs, 36,800.
   b. For materials, 38,000; for conversion costs, 38,000.
   c. For materials, 48,000; for conversion costs, 44,800.
   d. For materials, 48,000; for conversion costs, 48,000.

2. The Wiring Department is the second stage of Flem Company's production cycle. On May 1, the beginning work in process contained 25,000 units which were 60 percent complete as to conversion costs. During May, 100,000 units were transferred to the Wiring Department from the first stage of Flem's production cycle. No units were lost in production in May, and on May 31, the ending work in process contained 20,000 units which were 80 percent complete as to conversion costs. Materials costs are added at the end of the process. Using the moving average method, the equivalent units were:

	For Costs Transferred In	For Materials	For Costs of Conversion
a.	100,000	125,000	100,000
b.	125,000	105,000	105,000
c.	125,000	105,000	121,000
d.	125,000	125,000	121,000

3. Walton, Incorporated, had 8,000 units of work in process in department A on October 1, 19x1. These units were 60 percent complete as to conversion costs. Materials are added in the beginning of the process. During the month of October, 34,000 units were started and 36,000 units were completed. Walton had 6,000 units of work in process on October 31, 19x1. These units were 80 percent complete as to conversion costs. By how much did the equivalent units for the month of October using the moving-average method exceed the equivalent units for the month of October used in the application of the FIFO method?

   a. For materials, 0; for conversion costs, 3,200.
   b. For materials, 0; for conversion costs, 4,800.
   c. For materials, 8,000; for conversion costs, 3,200.
   d. For materials, 8,000; for conversion costs, 4,800.

   (CPA)

5. **Cost calculations: Multiple choice.**   Select the best answer to each of the following questions:

1. The cutting department is the first stage of Mark Company's production cycle. Conversion costs for this department were 80 percent complete as to the beginning work in process and 50 percent complete as to the ending work in process. Information as to conversion costs in the cutting department for January, 19x0, is as follows:

	Units	Conversion Costs
Work in process at January 1, 19x0	25,000	$ 22,000
Units started and costs incurred in January	135,000	143,000
Units completed and transferred to next department in January	100,000	

No units were lost in production during the month.

Using the FIFO method, what was the conversion cost of the work in process in the cutting department at January 31, 19x0?

a. $33,000; b. $38,100; c. $39,000; d. $45,000.

2. Maurice Company adds materials at the beginning of the process in the forming department, which is the first of two stages of its production cycle. Information concerning the materials used in the forming department in April, 19x1, is as follows:

	Units	Costs
Work in process at April 1, 19x1	12,000	$ 6,000
Units started during April	100,000	51,120
Units completed and transferred to next department during April	88,000	

No units were lost in production during the month.

Using the moving average method, what was the materials cost of the work in process at April 30, 19x1?

a. $6,120; b. $11,040; c. $12,000; d. $12,240.

3. Roy Company manufactures product X in a two-stage production cycle in departments A and B. Materials are added at the beginning of the process in department B. An analysis of the costs relating to work in process and production activity in department B for February, 19x0, is as follows:

	Costs Transferred in	Costs of Materials	Conversion Costs
Work in process, February 1	$12,000	$2,500	$1,000
February activity: costs added	29,000	5,500	5,000

Conversion costs for department B were 50 percent complete as to the 6,000 units in the beginning work in process and 75 percent complete as to the 8,000 units in the ending work in process. 12,000 units were completed and transferred out of department B during February, 19x0. Roy Company uses the moving average method of cost distribution.

The total cost per unit of product transferred out of department B in February, 19x0, rounded to the nearest cent, was:

a. $2.75; b. $2.78; c. $2.82; d. $2.85.

(CPA)

6. **Cost distribution: Multiple choice.**   Information for the month of May concerning department A, the first stage of Wit Corporation's production cycle is as follows:

	Materials	Conversion
Work in process, beginning	$ 4,000	$ 3,000
Current costs	20,000	16,000
Total costs	$ 24,000	$19,000
Equivalent units, based on moving average	100,000	95,000

Goods completed during May, 90,000 units; ending work in process, 10,000 units.

How would the total costs accounted for be distributed, using the moving-average method?

	To Goods Completed	To Ending Work in Process
a.	$39,600	$3,400
b.	39,600	4,400
c.	43,000	0
d.	44,000	3,400

(CPA, adapted)

7. **Supplying missing information.**   Two processes are independent of each other. Work in process inventories in each process are complete as to materials and half complete as to conversion costs. Operations in process A are accounted for by the moving average method; FIFO is used for process B. Make the necessary calculations to supply the missing figures in the following table:

	Process A	Process B
Units:		
In process, beginning of month	10,000	20,000
Received during month	50,000	100,000
Transferred out during month	40,000	106,000
In process, end of month	14,000	14,000
Materials costs:		
a. In process, beginning of month	$ 21,900	$?
b. Received during month	?	?
c. Transferred out during month	?	422,000
d. In process, end of month	32,200	?
Conversion costs:		
e. In process, beginning of month	?	16,000
f. Operations, current month	127,050	?
g. Transferred out during month	120,000	?
h. In process, end of month	?	?
Unit cost, moving average method:		
i. Materials	2.30	n.a.
j. Conversion	?	n.a.
Average cost of current month's production:		
k. Materials	?	4.00
l. Conversion	3.025	1.50

8. **Cost divisor exercise.**   Department Alpha takes raw materials from the stockroom and shapes them into blanks for widgets. On January 1, it had 20,000 partly processed widget blanks on hand, half processed in the department. During

January, it received 40 tons of materials and delivered 200,000 widget blanks to department Beta. On January 31, it had 50,000 widget blanks on hand, half processed in the department.

Required:

    a. Calculate two cost divisors, one for materials and one for conversion costs, to measure equivalent production during the month.

    b. Explain why the 40-ton figure was irrelevant to your calculations.

9. **Cost divisor exercise.** Department Gamma polishes discs, coats them with plastic, and transfers them to department Delta. The plastic coating is placed on the polished discs by opening a pipeline valve just before the polished discs are transferred to department Delta.

    Department Gamma received 200,000 unpolished discs from the storeroom during January and delivered 210,000 coated discs to department Delta. It had 60,000 discs in process on January 1 and 50,000 discs in process on January 31. Work in process inventories are always regarded as complete as to prior department costs and half processed in the department.

Required:

    a. Calculate three cost divisors, one for discs, one for plastic coating material, and one for conversion costs, to measure the department's equivalent production during January.

    b. Calculate the moving average cost divisors for each of these three cost elements.

    c. Explain the rationale behind the assumption that the inventories were half processed in the department.

10. **Cost divisor exercise.** The finishing department receives assembled products from the assembly department, performs a number of operations on them, and transfers the finished units to the shipping platform. A certain amount of spoilage is expected, and spoilage can take place at any point in the finishing process. Spoiled units have no value.

    The finishing department had 18,000 units of product in process on January 1, received 300,000 units of product from the assembly department during January, spoiled 73,000 units during the month, transferred 200,000 units to the shipping platform, and had 45,000 units in process on January 31.

    Units in process at any time are assumed to be complete as to prior department costs and half processed by the finishing department; half of the eventual spoilage is assumed to have taken place. In calculating the number of equivalent units in the work-in-process inventory, management makes the assumption that 20 percent of the units entering the department will be spoiled between the time they enter and the time the units are finished.

Required:

    a. Calculate two divisors, one for prior department costs and one for finishing department conversion costs, to measure the month's equivalent production.

    b. Recalculate the divisors on the assumption that costs are to be assigned to the spoiled units. Assume that the spoilage took place when the spoiled units were half processed.

11. **Unit cost exercise.** Department Able produces doodads. It started the month of May with no doodads in process, completed 16,000 doodads during the month, and ended the month with 4,000 doodads in process, complete as to materials and half-processed on the average.

    The department's costs for the month consisted of 15,000 pounds of materials at $3 a pound, and $29,700 in conversion costs.

Required:

    a. Calculate unit costs for the month.

b. Calculate the total cost of the ending work-in-process inventory.
c. Calculate the total cost of the goods finished during May.

12. **Cost distribution exercise: Moving average.** Ardway Corporation manufactures containers. Department Able makes container blanks; department Baker shapes the blanks into finished containers. The average cost of the work done in department Able is used to measure the unit cost of the blanks received by department Baker.

On June 1, department Baker had 5,000 containers in process. It received 20,000 blanks during the month, 2,000 of which were unsuitable for processing and had to be sold to a scrap dealer for $100. It completed work on 22,000 containers during the month and had 1,000 containers in process on June 30. Inventory costs are determined on a moving-average basis. Containers in process on any date are assumed to be half-processed.

The beginning inventory had a materials cost (blanks) of $4,800 and conversion costs of $3,000. Department Baker was charged $21,000 for the 20,000 container blanks received in the department during the month. The month's conversion costs amounted to $14,640.

Required:

a. Calculate the average cost of the work done in department Baker during the month, with separate calculations for materials and for conversion costs. Explain how you handled the 2,000 scrapped container blanks and your reasons for choosing this method.
b. Does the average cost this month appear to have been higher or lower or the same as in May? Explain how you figured this out.
c. Calculate the cost of the ending inventory.

13. **Unit costs; effects of spoilage.** Department Charlie processes flanges. It started the month of July with no flanges in process. It received 2,400 unprocessed flanges at a cost of $7.92 each, used 1,470 hours of processing labor at a labor rate of $10 an hour, and spent $13,860 on other conversion inputs. Processing labor is regarded as completely variable with the equivalent number of flanges processed; $6,300 of the other conversion costs in July were fixed, while the other $7,560 were variable with production.

Department Charlie completed work on 1,800 flanges during the month and ruined 200 half-processed flanges due to a severe malfunctioning of a major piece of equipment. The ruined flanges were sold immediately for scrap at a price of $1 each. This amount was credited to department Charlie as a deduction from its conversion costs. The department had 400 semiprocessed flanges in process at the end of the month.

Required:

a. Assuming that the cost of the spoiled units is to be averaged into the cost of the good units produced, and that product costing is on a full-costing basis, calculate the unit cost of the equivalent units produced during the month.
b. Perform the same calculations, but assuming that the cost of spoiled units is to be reported separately, as a loss occurring during the period.
c. Use figures from your answer to (b) to calculate the net loss from spoilage during July.
d. Assuming that costs are accounted for by the method described in (a), calculate the effect of spoilage on the unit costs of good units.
e. Calculate the incremental cost, element by element, of the units spoiled during the month.
f. Does the figure you calculated in answer to (e) provide a more accurate measure of the net spoilage loss than the figure you calculated in answer to (c)? Explain your answer.

14. **Standard costs.** Standard materials costs in department Charlie (problem 13) are $8 per finished flange. Standard labor cost is $7 a flange, at a standard wage rate of $10 an hour. Other variable conversion costs have a standard cost of $4 a flange, before deducting scrap credits. The standard scrap credit (classified as a deduction from variable conversion costs) is 10 cents an equivalent unit, based on a scrap price of $1 per unit scrapped. Fixed conversion costs are budgeted at $6,250 a month. Standard costs are calculated on the basis of a normal volume of 2,500 flanges a month.

   Required:

   a. Calculate the standard cost of the work performed in July.
   b. Calculate the variance from standard cost for each cost element.
   c. Provide a brief comment on the apparent reason or reasons for each of these variances.

15. **Unit cost, FIFO cost, and moving-average cost.** The following costs were charged to process 2 of the H Company during July:

Costs transferred from process 1	$184,000
Materials added in process 2	34,000
Conversion costs	104,000

   Production figures for the month for process 2 were:

Work in process, July 1	2,000 pounds, 60% completed
Finished during July	20,000 pounds
Work in process, July 31	5,000 pounds, 40% completed

   Process 2 materials are not added to the semifinished product received from process 1 until the very end of processing in process 2. The work in process in process 2 on July 1 had a cost of $22,500. Of this, $17,050 was the cost of materials transferred from process 1, and $5,450 was conversion cost in process 2.

   Required:

   a. Calculate the cost divisors.
   b. Calculate unit costs for the month.
   c. Calculate the July 31 cost of the work in process and the cost of units transferred out of the process during July, using the FIFO method.
   d. Calculate the July 31 cost of the work in process and the cost of units transferred out of the process during July, using the moving-average method.
   e. Explain why you did or did not use the figures you calculated in (*b*) to answer parts (*c*) and (*d*).

16. **Journal entries.** Department A started the month of June with work in process costing $3,480 for materials and $1,260 for conversion costs. The department received materials costing $53,520 from the storeroom during June and incurred $34,740 in conversion costs. It transferred 85,000 units of semiprocessed product to department B, at a materials cost of $51,000 and conversion costs of $34,000. The materials cost of the work in process on June 30 was $6,000; the conversion costs in process on that date amounted to $2,000.

   Required:

   Using an account structure similar to the one described in this chapter, prepare a set of journal entries to record the month's transactions. A single account, Accounts and Wages Payable, may be used for the credit side of the entry recording conversion costs.

17. **Unit costs, by element.** Thermal Products, Inc., uses a process costing system to account for manufacturing costs in one of its plants. The Pical department in this plant is devoted to the manufacture of a product known as Pical. Two materials

are used in the manufacture of this product: Corex, brought from outside suppliers and issued to the Pical department from materials inventory, and Formula 42X, supplied by another department in the plant, the forming department. Completed units of Pical are transferred to finished goods inventory.

The following labor and materials costs were incurred by the Pical department during the month of October:

1. Materials used: Corex, 10,000 pounds at 55 cents a pound; Formula 42X, 2,000 gallons at $1.32 a gallon. (Costs in the forming department in October averaged 80 cents a gallon for materials, 25 cents for labor, and 27 cents for other conversion costs, a total of $1.32.)
2. Labor costs: leader, 168 hours at $10 an hour; operators, 350 hours at $9 an hour; and lifters, 840 hours at $7 an hour.

The Pical department had 1,000 pounds of Pical in process on October 1. All of the necessary materials had been provided for these units at a total cost of $1,750; half of the necessary labor operations had been performed, at a total labor cost of $500. The department completed work on 10,000 pounds of Pical during the month of October, and transferred this quantity to finished goods. Two thousand pounds of semiprocessed product remained in inventory in the Pical department at the end of the month, complete as to materials but only half-processed in the department.

Required:

a. Calculate the unit cost of each class of materials in the Pical department and each class of labor, on an equivalent production basis.
b. Calculate the materials and labor cost of goods finished by the Pical department in October and the cost of the work in process in the department at the end of October. Use the FIFO method for this purpose.

18. **Standard costing: Variances.**   Thermal Products (problem 17) decided to adopt a standard costing system in the Pical department and elsewhere in the factory. Standard materials and labor costs of a pound of Pical were:

Materials:	
Corex—0.95 pounds × $0.52	$0.494
Formula 42X—0.18 gallons × $1.25	0.225
Total materials	$0.719
Labor:	
Leader—0.018 hours × $9.50	$0.171
Operators—0.036 hours × $9.00	0.324
Lifters—0.09 hours × $6.50	0.585
Total labor	$1.080

The standard labor and materials costs of the October 1 inventory in process in the Pical department were: materials, $719; Pical department labor, $540.

Required:

a. Using these data and the data supplied in problem 17, calculate the standard cost of the work done in the Pical department in October.
b. Calculate the usage variances for materials and labor.
c. Do the variances you calculated in (b) provide management with better control information than the unit cost data called for by problem 17(a)? Explain what is gained and what is lost, if anything, by the shift to standard costs.

19. **Unit cost: Anticipated shrinkage.**   Materials are received in department A, converted, and then transferred to department B, where final conversion takes place. The following data relate to the operations of department A for December:

	Quantity	Cost
Inventory in process, December 1:		
Materials	95	$ 228
Conversion costs		72
Materials added from stockroom	520	1,242
Conversion costs	—	528
Units completed and transferred to department B	310	?
Inventory in process, December 31:		
Materials	190	?
Conversion costs		?

All materials are placed in process at the start of conversion—thus all work in process is complete as to materials. A total shrinkage of 10 percent is regarded as normal in department A, however, and it is assumed that half of the expected shrinkage has already taken place in the inventory in process at any time.

Inventory in process is assumed to be half-processed in the department, and the costs of lost units are to be spread over all equivalent good units produced.

Required:

a. Calculate the percentage of shrinkage in this department. Is this large enough to be regarded as important?

b. Should unit cost be based on the number of units available or on the number of units remaining after shrinkage has taken place?

c. What is equivalent production for the month with respect to (1) materials and (2) conversion costs?

d. Compute the unit costs that you would report to management to reflect the efficiency of the department's operations for the month.

e. Using the moving-average method, compute the costs to be transferred to department B and the costs of work still in process in department A at the end of December.

20. **Cost distribution schedule, two departments.** The Tawny Company's Albany factory has two departments, mixing and curing. Costs are accumulated in departmental accounts, and at the end of each month the goods transferred from mixing to curing and from curing to finished goods are costed on a moving-average basis. The following information is available for the month of July:

	Mixing	Curing
Pounds of product in process, July 1	1,000	10,000
Pounds of materials received:		
From storeroom (at 50 cents a pound)	40,000	—
From mixing department	—	35,000
Pounds of product transferred out	35,000	25,000
Pounds of product in process, July 31	6,000	20,000
Cost of work in process, July 1:		
Materials	$ 582	$ 9,400
Departmental conversion	279	1,705
Departmental conversion costs, July	15,600	8,970

The beginning inventory in each department was half-processed. The ending inventory in the mixing department was three-quarters processed; the ending inventory in curing was half-processed.

Required:

a. Calculate materials costs and conversion costs per equivalent pound in each department: (1) on the basis of equivalent production for the month; and (2) on a moving-average basis.

b. Prepare a table showing the costs to be accounted for in each department and how you would distribute these costs between the work completed and the work still in process at the end of the month.

21. **Journal entries.** Using the account structure described in this chapter, prepare journal entries to record the July transactions of the mixing and curing departments in problem 20.

22. **Standard costs: Spoilage.** The molding department delivers molded products to the coating department, where they are coated and moved to the heat treating department for further processing. Coating is charged for the standard materials, labor, and variable overhead costs of the molded units: $8.10 for material, $3.60 for molding labor, and $1.80 for variable overhead costs. Fixed overhead costs are not included in product costs.

Standard costs in the coating department are based on the assumptions that (1) 10 percent of the molded units will be spoiled in coating; and (2) the recovery value of the spoiled units will be $1 each. Standard labor cost is 0.9 labor hours for each unit of good product at a standard labor rate of $8 an hour. Conversion costs amount to $1 a labor hour plus $40,950 a month. Spoilage is identified when the products are inspected at the end of the coating process. The value of scrap recovered is credited to the department as a separate item at the time the spoiled units are sold.

You have the following information on the coating department for the month of March.

1. Work in process, March 1: 4,000 units, half-processed in the coating department.
2. Molded products received from the molding department: 18,600 units.
3. Products finished and transferred to heat treating: 19,800 units.
4. Labor cost: 15,750 hours at $8.10.
5. Scrap recovered and sold for cash: 1,980 units at $2 each.
6. Other conversion, costs: $59,535.
7. Work in process, March 31: 2,000 units, half-processed.

Required:

a. Calculate the standard variable cost of a unit of coated product.
b. Calculate the necessary cost divisors, calculate unit costs for each cost element in the coating department for the month of March, and determine the differences between actual unit costs and standard unit costs. (For this purpose, standard unit costs for "other conversion costs" should be defined as the average flexible budget at the actual labor volume.)
c. Calculate the materials usage variance, the labor usage variance, the spending variance in "other conversion costs," and the scrap recovery variance for the month. What interpretation do you make of the scrap recovery variance?

23. **Control comparisons: Anticipated shrinkage.** The Andrews Metals Company operates two refining units of equal size, with identical equipment, paying identical wage rates. The following data relate to the operations of these two units during the month of September:

	Selby Mill	Franklin Mill
Quantities:		
Pounds in process, Sept. 1 (half-completed)	9,800	8,400
Pounds received	78,000	52,000
Pounds refined, completed	60,000	37,500
Pounds in process, Sept. 30 (half-completed)	7,700	9,800
Costs:		
Materials in process, Sept. 1	$ 8,000	$ 6,400
Conversion costs in process, Sept. 1	7,000	5,600
Materials	75,311	49,536
Supervision	5,965	5,805
Operating labor	60,843	36,765
Depreciation	31,018	30,960
Scrap credit	(1,779)	(1,161)

A certain amount of shrinkage is expected in the refining process, inasmuch as the refined metal weighs less than the ore concentrate from which it is refined. This weight loss takes place continuously during processing and is assumed to be proportionate to the percentage of completion. For the purpose of costing materials in process, it is assumed that the refined metal constitutes 75 percent of the ore concentrate, by weight.

Required:

Prepare an analysis that will assist management in comparing the relative efficiency of the two plant managers in controlling operating costs. Indicate what additional information you would like to have, if any.

24. **Cost distribution sheet: Usefulness of unit costs.** Dashing Dachshund Dippers are made in two sequential processes, bristle toning and assembly. The bristle toning department manufacturers bristle sets, while the assembly department assembles the final product. The data are:

Bristle toning department:
Opening inventory: 400 units, 100 percent complete as to materials ($1,900) and 50 percent complete as to conversion costs ($1,860).
Units started during month: 3,150.
Bristle sets completed and transferred to assembly: 3,000.
Units spoiled: 50. This is considered normal; scrap recovery of $75 is credited against current period materials cost.
Closing inventory: 100 percent complete as to materials, 40 percent complete as to conversion costs.
Costs for the current period: materials, $9,375 (before credit for scrap recovery); labor, $6,000; other conversion costs (variable), $4,500; other conversion costs (fixed), $3,000.
Unit costs are determined by the moving average method.

Assembly department:
Opening inventory: 200 units, 100 percent complete as to materials ($5,300) and 25 percent complete as to conversion costs ($975).
Materials required in this process (per finished unit): two bristle sets from bristle toning; one bristle holder, at $3 (required at start of process).
Units started: 1,500.
Units transferred to finished goods: 1,500.
Units spoiled: none.
Closing inventory: 100 percent complete as to materials, 75 percent complete as to conversion costs.
Costs for the current period: materials, to be computed from data given above; labor, $8,000; other conversion costs (variable), $6,400; other conversion costs (fixed), $4,800.

Ending inventories and transfers to finished goods are costed on a FIFO basis.

Required:

a. Prepare a production cost summary and distribution sheet, distributing the full costs of each department by the method specified.

b. What unit costs should be reported to management as the costs of operations for the month? Should any distinction be made between fixed and variable costs in such calculations?

c. What are the shortcomings of these unit cost figures for managerial decision making?

(Adapted from a problem by John C. Burton.)

15 Costing joint products

The illustrations of job order and process costing in previous chapters all dealt with manufacturing operations in which processing a given set of materials yields only one kind of product. Job order and process costing can also be used when the processing of a single input or set of inputs yields two or more products simultaneously. These are known as joint products. Examples are gasoline and heating oil, cowhides and beef carcasses.

Unfortunately, job order or process costing can only measure the cost of the joint products as a group. If costs are to be assigned to individual joint products, an additional set of calculations must be made. This chapter is concerned with four aspects of this process:

1. Recognizing joint products and the joint costs of producing them.
2. Analyzing the joint costs of fixed-yield processes to identify the costs relevant to managerial decisions.
3. Distributing joint costs among the various joint products for financial accounting purposes.
4. Analyzing joint costs when management can influence the relative yields of the various joint products.

Recognizing joint products and joint costs

The point in a production process at which a distinctly identifiable product or material is separated for sale, use, or further independent processing is known as a *split-off point.* The separated product and the other products or materials from which it is separated are the joint products of the stage or stages in the production process preceding the split-off point.

Exhibit 15–1 shows a process with two split-off points. Raw materials are first cooked, after which three separate products are split off: grease, a glue and water mixture, and a residue. Both the glue-water mixture and the residue are subjected to separate processing. Processing the mixture yields one product only: glue. Processing the residue, on the other hand, yields two products: grease and tankage stock. The latter is then cooked once again to yield fertilizer tankage.

Notice that all three outputs of the first production process are joint products,

Exhibit 15–1 Split-off points in joint production

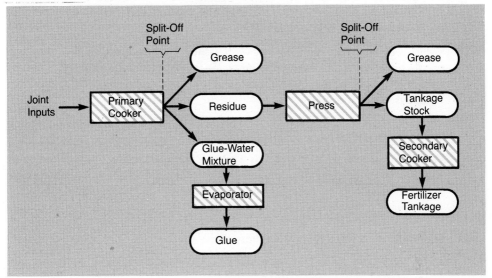

even though only one of them is in final salable condition. Joint production ends at the split-off point; therefore, the joint products are the products that emerge at this point. We may seem to be splitting hairs to say so, but the third joint product of this first process is the glue-water mixture, not the glue. The glue is the output of a separate process.

This distinction has a strong bearing on the classification of costs. *Joint costs* are the costs of those input factors that are necessary for the manufacture of all the joint products as a group. They are not traceable to any one of the various joint products. The costs of operating the primary cooker are joint costs of all the outputs of that process.

Separable costs, on the other hand, are the costs that are traceable to the processing of a single joint product after the split-off point. The costs of operating the evaporator are separable costs of glue manufacture. These are also referred to as *specific costs.*

In some cases, the classification of a cost as either joint or separable depends on which product or products are being discussed. The costs of operating the press, for example, are separable costs of processing the residue, but they are joint costs of the grease and tankage stock emerging from that process.

Joint costs in decision making

Joint costs need to be handled carefully in analyses designed to help management make decisions. To emphasize this point, we need to consider two kinds of decisions:

1. Decisions relating to the joint products as a group—e.g., discontinue total production or expand total production.

2. Decisions relating to the depth of additional processing to be applied to individual joint products—e.g., sell the product as it stands or process it further before sale.

To keep the discussion simple, we'll assume for the moment that the joint production process is a fixed-yield process—that is, each joint product's percentage of the total physical output is fixed by formula, as in certain chemical reactions.

Joint products as a group

For the group of joint products as a whole, the question is whether the total revenue to be derived from the sale of all joint products, less any processing and distribution costs necessary to place these products in marketable form, is adequate to cover the incremental costs of the joint inputs. For example, the decision to work a mine which produces ore containing gold, zinc, and lead must be based on consideration of the market prices of all three metals.

Individual joint products

Once it has been determined that joint production is profitable, the next question is how far to process each of the joint products. For example, should cowhides be tanned or should they be sold on the market untanned? For this kind of decision, the question is whether the sale value of the product can be increased by more than the incremental separable costs. In other words, in deciding whether to tan the hides management should measure the cost of the untanned hides at their opportunity cost. If hides can be sold untanned for 40 cents a pound, then 40 cents a pound is the opportunity cost of any hides that are retained for further processing. (Not selling the hides at 40 cents requires the same economic sacrifice as buying hides at 40 cents; this is the meaning of opportunity cost.) The relevant comparison is:

Market value of tanned hides		$0.50
Less: Market value of untanned hides	$0.40	
Incremental separate processing cost	0.08	0.48
Incremental processing profit		$0.02

This kind of comparison is valid even if the joint product in question is totally valueless and unmarketable at the split-off point. The absence of a market for one of the joint products merely means that opportunity cost for that product is zero. The desirability of processing this product further, therefore, can be determined by comparing the costs of further processing with the net market proceeds from the product after processing. Since the joint costs will be unaffected by the decision on further processing, management should ignore them in making this decision.

Separable costs and joint production decisions

The separable costs of further processing and distribution of individual products may in some cases have a bearing on the decision whether to manufacture the joint products as a group. In making this decision, the incremental profit from further processing should be considered but processing losses from further processing should be ignored.

For example, suppose processing 2,500 tons of material X will yield 2,000 tons of product A and 500 tons of product B at a total incremental joint cost of $78,000. Product A can be sold for $40 a ton, but product B is unsalable without further processing. After further processing, product B can be sold for $15 a ton, but incremental separable processing costs total $4,000. The decision to continue joint production should be based on the following calculations:

	A	B	Total
Sales revenues	$80,000	$7,500	$87,500
Incremental separable processing cost	—	4,000	4,000
Product profit contribution	80,000	3,500	83,500
Incremental joint processing cost			78,000
Total incremental profit from production			$ 5,500

Since the incremental profit is positive, production should take place.[1]

But suppose product B can be sold for only $1.50 a ton, or total revenues of only $750. Suppose further that unprocessed units of product B must be trucked away at a cost of $1 a ton. Under these circumstances, management can't justify processing product B:

	If Process Further	If Don't Process	Difference
Sales revenues (500 tons)	$ 750	—	$ 750
Incremental costs	4,000	$500	3,500
Incremental profit/(loss)	$(3,250)	$(500)	$(2,750)

Since management is under no compulsion to subject product B to further processing, and since processing it would be undesirable, management can ignore the $2,750 processing loss in calculating the desirability of joint processing. The calculation of the profit from joint processing therefore is as follows:

Sales revenues, product A		$80,000
Less: Joint processing costs	$78,000	
Removal costs, product B	500	78,500
Total incremental profit from production		$ 1,500

This calculation shows that operation of the joint process is marginally profitable.

Costing co-products for financial reporting

Inventories of joint products must be measured at historical cost in financial statements prepared in accordance with generally accepted accounting princi-

---

[1] Production may also require incremental investments in inventories and receivables which may be large enough to make production undesirable. We'll study the effects of investment increments in Chapter 18.

ples. The historical cost of an individual joint product is not a measurable quantity, however—historical costs can be measured only for the group of joint products as a whole. As a result, the accountant has to use a formula of some sort to allocate the joint costs to the various joint products. In this section we'll discuss four formulas that might be used when each of the joint products is a *co-product,* contributing a significant percentage of the total market value of the joint products as a group:

1. Physical unit basis.
2. Net realization basis.
3. Uniform percentage contribution basis.
4. Relative sale value at spit-off basis.

Physical unit basis of allocation

The simplest method of allocation is to count the number of units of each of the joint products, add these figures together, and then divide the total number of units into the total joint cost to get an average unit cost. Under this method, all products have the same unit cost.

For example, suppose producing 100,000 board feet of lumber costs a lumber mill $10,000. This lumber is inspected and divided into five different quality grades, in the following proportions:

Grade	Thousand Board Feet
Clear	10
Industrial	20
No. 1	40
No. 2	20
No. 3	10
Total	100

In this case the average cost of $10,000 divided by 100, or $100 per thousand board feet, would be used to measure the cost of each of the five grades of lumber.

If this method is used, the various joint products will have different apparent profit rates. Suppose, for instance, the various grades of lumber can be sold at the following prices per thousand feet:

Grade	Price
Clear	$240
Industrial	180
No. 1	150
No. 2	120
No. 3	60

If each grade is assigned a cost of $100 per thousand feet, some grades will appear to be very profitable and one grade will even show a loss, as illustrated in Exhibit 15–2.

The main defect of this method is that it ignores the cost-value relationship

Exhibit 15–2 Profit margins reflecting the physical unit basis of allocation

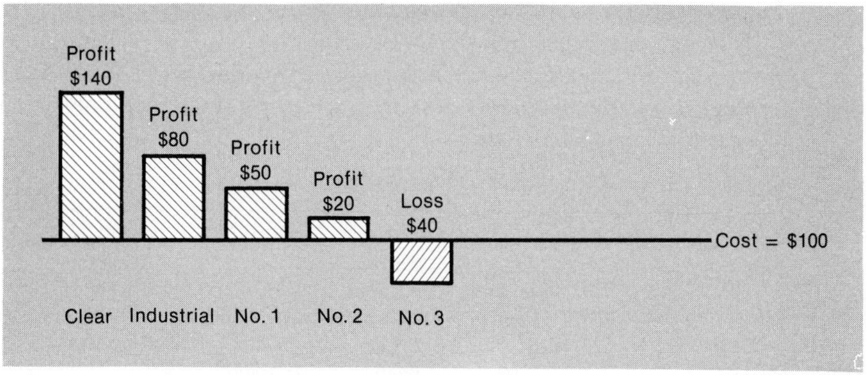

implicit in accounting measurements of nonmonetary assets. The purpose of costs is to create values. The use of cost to measure assets is based on the assumption that a prudent manager will not incur costs unless the value created is likely to exceed the costs. If the value of the group is greater than the cost of producing it, then no portion of the joint cost can be said to be unproductive. Use of the $100 figure for all grades implies that some of the joint costs are more productive than others, an economic impossibility. When applied to the poorest grade of lumber, it produces an even more absurd result—an apparent loss on production. If this were true, the company could avoid the loss by not producing No. 3 lumber; since this can't be done without sacrificing the other grades as well, the cost figure must be wrong.

Support for this conclusion can be found in another quarter as well. Clear evidence that outputs are not equally costly is provided by the premiums that ordinarily must be paid for higher quality inputs. For example, if a given stand of timber is expected to yield a high proportion of the higher valued grades of lumber, the timber rights will command a higher price than if the lower grades predominate. Therefore, since output value affects input cost, it would seem reasonable to reflect value differences in the cost allocation.

Net realization basis of allocation

The net realization basis of joint cost allocation avoids the defects of the physical basis. When the net realization basis is selected, the joint costs are allocated to the co-products in proportion to their respective percentages of the total net realization from all of the co-products combined. Net realization is defined as the selling price of the end product less any costs necessary to process it after the split-off point, sell it, and distribute it.

For example, suppose our lumber company markets its output of clear and industrial grades without further processing, but sells the other three grades only after processing each of them separately. Clear lumber can be sold without any additional marketing costs, and industrial grade lumber requires very little marketing effort. The products made from the other three grades are costly to produce and distribute, but the net realization is greater than the unprocessed lumber would generate if sold without processing.

The necessary data are shown in Exhibit 15–3. The selling prices of the finished products are shown in column (2). Column (4) shows the separate costs of processing and marketing the various products, and column (5) shows the net realization from each.

Exhibit 15–3 Calculation of net realization

Grade	(1) Thousand Feet Produced	(2) End-Product Selling Price	(3) End-Product Sales Value (1) × (2)	(4) Separate Processing and Marketing Costs	(5) Net Realization (3) − (4)
Clear	10	$240	$ 2,400	—	$ 2,400
Industrial	20	180	3,600	$ 80	3,520
No. 1	40	190	7,600	1,200	6,400
No. 2	20	160	3,200	640	2,560
No. 3	10	150	1,500	380	1,120
Total	100		$18,300	$2,300	$16,000

Cost allocations can now be based on these net realization figures, as in Exhibit 15–4. Each product's percentage of the total net realization of all five products combined, from column (3), is applied to the total joint cost of $10,000 to determine the amount to be allocated to each, shown in column (4). These amounts are then divided by the outputs of the various joint products to derive the unit cost figures in column (5). Thus clear lumber provides 15 percent of the net realization and is allocated 15 percent of the joint cost, or $1,500. This amounts to $150 for each thousand board feet.

Exhibit 15–4 Cost allocation on a net realization basis

Grade	(1) Thousand Feet Produced	(2) Net Realization	(3) Percent of Total Net Realization	(4) Joint Cost Allocated (3) × $10,000	(5) Allocated Unit Cost (4) ÷ (1)
Clear	10	$ 2,400	15%	$ 1,500	$150
Industrial	20	3,520	22	2,200	110
No. 1	40	6,400	40	4,000	100
No. 2	20	2,560	16	1,600	80
No. 3	10	1,120	7	700	70
Total	100	$16,000	100%	$10,000	

Uniform percentage contribution basis of allocation

A peculiarity of the net realization method is to assign all of the profits to the joint process, none to the separate processes. The result is that the ratio of profit contribution to sales revenues is greater for co-products with little processing than for those requiring a great deal. These ratios are shown in Exhibit 15–5.

Exhibit 15–5 Effect of net realization method on profit contribution ratios

Grade	(1) End-Product Sales Value	(2) Separate Costs	(3) Share of Joint Costs	(4) Profit Contribution (1) − (2) − (3)	(5) Profit Contribution Ratio (4) ÷ (1)
Clear	$ 2,400	—	$ 1,500	$ 900	37.5%
Industrial	3,600	$ 80	2,200	1,320	36.7
No. 1	7,600	1,200	4,000	2,400	31.6
No. 2	3,200	640	1,600	960	30.0
No. 3	1,500	380	700	420	28.0
Total	$18,300	$2,300	$10,000	$6,000	32.8%

The net realization method can be modified to eliminate these apparent variations in profitability. The solution is to calculate the overall profit contribution ratio, use this to calculate the profit contribution for each product, and then subtract the system-wide profit contribution and the separate costs from sales revenue figures. We call this the *uniform percentage contribution method.*

The average profit contribution ratio in our example is approximately 32.8 percent, the figure in the lower right corner of Exhibit 15–5. The revised calculations based on this figure are shown in Exhibit 15–6. The effect of the change is to shift costs to the products with relatively little separate processing or marketing.

Exhibit 15–6 Cost allocation on a uniform percentage contribution basis

Grade	(1) Thousand Feet Produced	(2) End-Product Sales Value	(3) Profit Contribution (2) × 32.8%	(4) Separable Costs	(5) Share of Joint Costs (2) − (3) − (4)	(6) Joint Cost per Unit (5) ÷ (1)
Industrial	10	$ 2,400	$ 787	—	$ 1,613	$161.30
Clear	20	3,600	1,180	$ 80	2,340	117.00
No. 1	40	7,600	2,492	1,200	3,908	97.70
No. 2	20	3,200	1,049	640	1,511	75.55
No. 3	10	1,500	492	380	628	62.80
Total	100	$18,300	$6,000	$2,300	$10,000	

Relative sale value at split-off point method

A fourth method of joint cost allocation is sometimes suggested: the relative sale value at split-off point method. Under this approach, processing operations and market values arising after the split-off point are ignored. For example, suppose our five grades of lumber could be sold without separate completion costs, at the following prices:

Clear	$240
Industrial	170
No. 1	120
No. 2	80
No. 3	30

Allocating the $10,000 in joint costs in proportion to the sale values of the five grades at the split-off would produce the figures shown in Exhibit 15–7.

Exhibit 15–7 The relative sale value at split-off point method

Grade	(1) Thousand Board Feet	(2) Selling Price, Unprocessed	(3) Sale Value, Unprocessed (1) × (2)	(4) Percent of Total Sale Value	(5) Allocated Joint Cost (4) × $10,000	(6) Allocated Unit Cost (5) ÷ (1)
Clear	10	$240	$ 2,400	19.2%	$ 1,920	$192
Industrial	20	170	3,400	27.2	2,720	136
No. 1	40	120	4,800	38.4	3,840	96
No. 2	20	80	1,600	12.8	1,280	64
No. 3	10	30	300	2.4	240	24
Total	100		$12,500	100.0%	$10,000	

The main drawback of this method is that it ignores the economics of the production process. Many products are either not salable at all as they emerge at the split-off point or would never be sold in that form because the margin from further processing is very large. Products with the smallest value at the split-off point may even be the most valuable when processed and sold.

In extreme cases the total sale value at the split-off point will be less than total joint cost. Since the logic underlying value-based allocation methods is that costs are incurred to create values, this third allocation method implies in these cases that the excess of cost over sale value at the split-off point is wasted. In fact, the entire operation, including further processing, may be very profitable indeed.

The relative sale value at split-off point method may not even have the advantage of simplicity. Since further processing is extremely profitable, the company won't be active in the markets for unprocessed products and won't have sale value information at its fingertips, nor is it likely to find an active market in the unprocessed products. Deriving meaningful sale value estimates in these circumstances is likely to be difficult and expensive. Adding this defect to the conceptual shortcomings of this method, we'll give it short shrift.

Relevance of the unit cost figures

Either the net realization or the uniform percentage contribution method will provide unit costs for inventory measurement that are smaller than the net realizable value of the units in inventory, unless all products are being sold at a loss. Neither of these methods provides unit costs with any managerial significance, however. The decision maker needs measures of the sacrifices the company must make to secure units of the individual products. No method designed to allocate all of the joint costs to the various joint products will provide this information.

For example, suppose the clear lumber can be converted into cabinets at an incremental cost of $100 per thousand square feet. The cabinets can be sold at a price of $300. If the lumber is charged against this proposal at the $150 unit cost derived in Exhibit 15–4, the proposal will look quite profitable:

Revenue		$300
Less: Joint processing cost	$150	
Separable processing cost	100	250
Operating margin		$ 50

In view of the opportunity costs, however, the proposal is clearly unprofitable:

Incremental revenue from sale of cabinets	$300
Less: Potential revenue from sale of unprocessed lumber	240
Incremental revenue	60
Incremental separable costs	100
Incremental processing gain/(loss)	$(40)

Since the total joint cost will be $10,000 whether the lumber is processed or sold "as is," the accountant's unit cost is a sunk cost and irrelevant to this decision.

The costing of by-products

In principle, either the relative net realization method or the uniform percentage contribution method can be used in any joint cost situation to derive cost figures for financial accounting purposes. These methods are modified in practice, however, when one or more of the joint products is classified as a by-product.

Defining by-products

Although the distinction between by-products and co-products or main products is inevitably imprecise, a reasonable working definition is that a by-product is a joint product with a net realization that is an immaterial proportion of the total net realization of all the joint products combined.

Any distinction between co-products and by-products must be regarded as strictly temporary, to be reconsidered as conditions change. Gasoline, for example, was originally thought of as a by-product in the manufacture of kerosene. With the growth of the automobile and electric lighting, kerosene became the by-product; but the jet airliner brought kerosene back into the picture as a major product once more.

Illustration of by-product costing

The costing method known as the by-product method consists of subtracting the net realizable value of the by-products from the total of the joint costs. The residual is then divided among the co-products.

For example, suppose a process yields three products, A, B, and C. Product C is to be treated as a by-product, A and B as co-products. The total cost of processing a 1,000-pound batch of products is $934. Yield and market value data are as follows:

Product	Yield (pounds)	Market Value per Pound	Total Market Value
A	200	$1.90	$ 380
B	500	1.50	750
C	300	0.10	30
Total	1,000		$1,160

The first step in the by-product method is to subtract the net realizable value of the by-product from the total joint cost. If product C is sold without further processing or marketing effort, its net realization will be equal to its market value. The calculation of the amount of cost to be assigned to the co-products is as follows:

Joint cost	$934
Less: Value of by-product	30
Cost assigned to co-products	$904

The remainder of the joint cost is then apportioned between the co-products by one of the methods described earlier. If neither of the co-products requires further processing, the net realization method will produce the following allocations:

Product	Percent of Total Net Realization	Total Cost Allocated	Allocated Cost per Pound
A	33.6	$304	$1.52
B	66.4	600	1.20
Total	100.0	$904	

This method assigns to the by-product a cost equal to its anticipated value. In the example, joint cost amounts to $934, but only $904 of this is assigned to the co-products. The remaining $30 goes to product C, which then shows neither a profit nor a loss.

Extending the by-product method to main products

The by-product method focuses decisions on the co-products as a group—that is, it identifies the portion of the total joint cost that the net realization from the co-products must cover if the operation is to be profitable. The method may also be extended to provide this same information for individual co-products—in other words, a given co-product can be treated as the focus of costing, with the net realization from *each* of the other joint products deducted from total joint cost.

In our simple three-product illustration, for example, the total joint cost was $934. The net realization was $750 from product B and $30 from product C. The net joint cost to be assigned to product A therefore is as follows:

Total joint cost $934
Net realization:
  Product B $750
  Product C   30   780
Net cost of product A .... $154 = $0.77 a pound

The same calculation can be performed to get the net cost of product B:

Total joint cost $934
Net realization:
  Product A $380
  Product C   30   410
Net cost of product B .... $524 = $1.048 a pound

If the net realization of each of the other products is reasonably certain, the unit cost figures emerging from these calculations can be regarded as the full costs of producing the individual products. And if the net realization figures are subtracted from the incremental cost of expanding the rate of production, the unit cost figure will be a usable measure of a product's incremental cost.

The approach, in other words, might be a way of solving the unsolvable—that is, determining the costs attributable to individual joint products. It is valid, however, only if the net realization of the other joint products is linearly proportional to volume. If increasing the rate of production reduces the marginal net realization of one or more joint products, the by-product approach to co-product costing must be abandoned or modified to reflect the departure from proportionality.

Joint costs of variable-yield processes

When management can change the individual products' percentages of the total physical output by changing the input mix in some way, we can determine each product's incremental cost. The technique is to compare the total cost of joint production with a given set of inputs to the total cost of another set of inputs that will yield the same quantities of all of the joint products except one. The difference in the total cost of the two sets of inputs is the incremental cost of the incremental quantity of the joint product which has varied in total output.

To illustrate, suppose materials costing $100 can be processed for $50 to yield 20 units of X and 50 units of Y. If higher quality materials costing $120 are used instead, the output of X will go up to 25 units; the output of Y will remain at 50 units. The increments are calculated in Exhibit 15–8, showing that the incremental cost of a unit of product X is $4 a unit.

The same data can be used to calculate the incremental cost of product Y. The trick is to find two input combinations yielding identical quantities of product X but different quantities of product Y. For example, if the more expensive materials are used but only four fifths as many units of materials are processed, the outputs will be reduced by 20 percent. Materials costs will also be reduced by 20 percent, but processing costs are likely to include

Exhibit 15–8 Calculating incremental product cost when proportions are variable

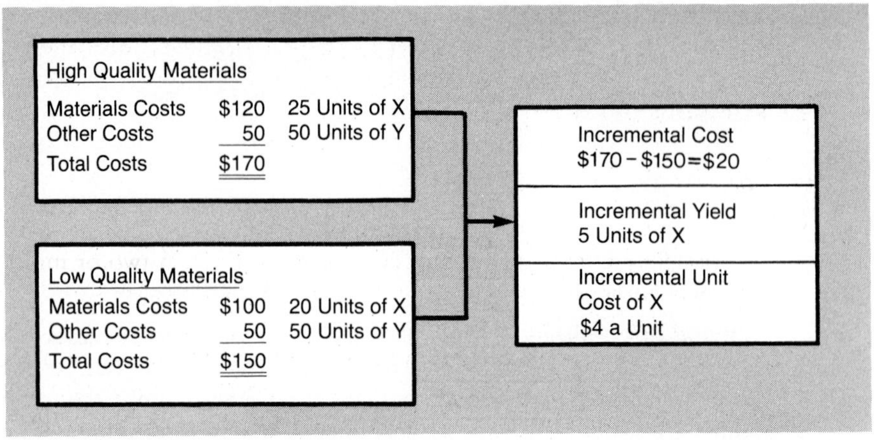

at least some fixed costs which won't be reduced proportionally. Suppose processing costs go down by only 16 percent, from $50 to $42. In this case, we get the comparison shown in Exhibit 15–9. By increasing total cost from $138 to $150 we can increase the output of product Y by 10 units, while keeping the output of product X constant at 20 units. The average incremental cost of a unit of product Y therefore is ($150 − $138)/10 = $1.20 a unit.

Exhibit 15–9 Calculating the incremental cost of product Y

	(1)	(2)	(3)	(4)	(5)
	High-Quality Materials			Low-Quality	
	Full Batch	Conversion Factor	80% Batch	Materials (full batch)	Increment (3) − (4)
Materials costs	$120	0.80	$ 96	$100	$ 4
Processing costs	50	0.84	42	50	8
Total cost	$170		$138	$150	$12
Output (units):					
Product X	25	0.80	20	20	—
Product Y	50	0.80	40	50	10

Measurement difficulties

Few situations are likely to be as simple as the one we have just illustrated, and more complex mathematical techniques must be used. (In mathematical terms, the objective is to determine the partial derivative of cost in response to a marginal change in the rate of output of an individual product.) Even in simple situations, however, the approach we have described is likely to yield not one cost figure for each product but a schedule of costs, the amount increasing as the product's proportion of total output increases. For example, the cost of increasing the gasoline yield from a run of crude oil from 35 to 36 percent is likely to be a good deal less than the cost of increasing it from 40 to 41 percent.

Calculations of this sort are made routinely in industries such as oil refining in which production operations are highly automated and technically advanced. The usefulness of the results, however, depends on the quality of the estimates of the relationships between costs and yields. If the quality of these estimates is low, the estimates of incremental costs will be unreliable.

Summary

When products are manufactured independently, a large number of costs can be attributed clearly to one product or another. When two or more products are produced jointly from a single set of inputs, however, the joint costs cannot be attributed clearly to individual products.

Either of two methods can be used to develop unit costs that will be adequate for public financial reporting of inventory costs: the relative net realization method or the uniform percentage contribution method. No method that routinely allocates all the joint costs to one joint product or another produces costs that are relevant to managerial decisions, however. Products that emerge from fixed-yield processes should be measured for decision purposes by their opportunity costs; those emerging from variable-yield processes should be measured either at opportunity cost or at the incremental cost of increasing the relative yield of each individual joint product, the choice depending on the decision to be made.

Opportunity cost is used routinely only for joint products classified as by-products; incremental cost is calculated only in highly sophisticated systems which are able to deal with changes in incremental cost as the relative product mix varies.

Independent study problems (solutions in Appendix B)

1. **Unit cost for inventory measurement.** The Zandrum Company processes a group of raw materials in a single processing operation. The output of this operation consists of three products destined for further processing in the company's factory and one by-product that is sold "as is" to fertilizer manufacturers. None of the three products that are processed further is salable in the form in which it emerges from joint production.

   The company's policy is to treat by-product values as reductions of joint cost and to allocate net joint cost among the co-products by the net realization method. During July, the costs of raw materials and joint processing amounted to $21,500. Other data were as follows:

Product	Quantity Produced (units)	Final Selling Price	Estimated Cost per Unit to Complete
A	1,000	$ 6.20	$0.90
B	2,000	3.80	0.80
C	2,500	10.00	2.52
D	10,000	0.05	—

   Required:

   a. Calculate the unit costs of the three co-products by the net realization method. How much cost is assigned to each unit of the by-product?

b. Recalculate unit costs by the physical unit method. Is this method likely to be acceptable for financial reporting? Explain your reasoning.

2. **Uniform percentage contribution method.** Recalculate the unit costs of the three co-products from the data supplied in problem 1, using the uniform percentage contribution method. Are these unit costs likely to be more useful to management than those you calculated in answering problem 1(*a*)? Explain your reasoning.

3. **Calculating net realization.** A process with joint costs of $10,000 yields 1,000 pounds of product alpha and 800 pounds of product omega. Omega is sold for $10 a pound without further processing.

   Alpha is processed further at a cost of $5,000 to yield 600 pounds of product beta and 500 pounds of product gamma. Gamma is sold for $12 a pound without additional processing. Beta is processed again, at a cost of $3,200, to yield 400 gallons of product delta and a residue. Delta is sold at a price of $15 a gallon. The residue from the delta process is sold for $200.

   Required:
   Calculate the net realization from joint product alpha.

4. **Joint costs in decision making.** A factory processes 300,000 pounds of material X each month to produce 100,000 pounds of Y and 200,000 pounds of Z. Product Y sells for 60 cents a pound; product Z sells for 45 cents. The costs of this process are as follows:

Materials: 300,000 × $0.20	$ 60,000
Variable processing	30,000
Fixed processing	10,000
Total	$100,000

   These costs are divided between the two products in proportion to their relative market values. The unit cost of Y is 40 cents; Z has a unit cost of 30 cents.

   A proposal has just been made to subject product Y to further processing by mixing it with other purchased materials. This would take the entire current output of product Y. The new product, known as Y-Plus, would sell at a price of $1.30 a package. Each package of Y-Plus would require one pound of product Y as raw material. Additional costs of other materials, labor, and overhead to process Y into Y-Plus would total $80,000 a month. The effects of the changeover on selling and administrative costs and on revenues from the sale of product Z would be negligible.

   Required:
   a. Should the proposal be accepted? Show your calculations. How useful was the 40-cent unit cost figure in this calculation?
   b. Assume that the Y-Plus proposal has been rejected. An opportunity has arisen to sell an additional 20,000 pounds of Z at a price of 35 cents a pound. The existing market for Z would not be affected by acceptance of this proposal. All units of Y would be sold at a uniform price. What is the minimum price of Y that would make this a profitable proposal?
   c. Assume that both the Y-Plus and Z proposals have been rejected. A new material has just become available. Processing costs would remain the same, but the process would yield two pounds of Y for every three pounds of Z. Total volume would be limited to 300,000 pounds of material, as at present. What is the maximum price the company could afford to pay for the new material?

Exercises and problems

5. **Supplying missing figure: Multiple choice.** O'Connor Company manufactures product J and product K from a joint process. For product J, 4,000 units were

produced having a sale value at split-off of $15,000. If product J were processed further, the additional costs would be $3,000 and the sale value would be $20,000. For product K, 2,000 units were produced having a sale value at split-off of $10,000. If product K were processed further, the additional costs would be $1,000 and the sale value would be $12,000.

Required:

1. Using the relative sale value at split-off approach, the portion of the total joint product cost allocated to product J was $9,000. What was the total joint product cost?

   a. $14,400;   *b.* $15,000;   *c.* $18,400;   *d.* $19,000.

2. You have been asked to decide whether the relative sale value approach should be used in this situation. Which one of the following statements would you use to support the use of this approach?
   a. It produces results very similar to those yielded by other value-based approaches.
   b. Other approaches would be valid because further processing of both products would be unprofitable.
   c. It gives all products identical profit contribution ratios.
   d. It gives management a better set of unit cost figures for use in further-processing decisions.

                                                              (CPA, extended)

6. **Allocating joint costs: Multiple choice.** Helen Corporation manufactures products W, X, Y, and Z from a joint process. Additional information is as follows:

Product	Units Produced	Sale Value at Split-off	If Processed Further Additional Costs	Sale Value
W	6,000	$ 80,000	$ 7,500	$ 90,000
X	5,000	60,000	6,000	70,000
Y	4,000	40,000	4,000	50,000
Z	3,000	20,000	2,500	30,000
Total	18,000	$200,000	$20,000	$240,000

Required:

1. Assuming that total joint costs of $160,000 were allocated using the relative sale value at split-off approach, what joint costs were allocated to each product?

	W	X	Y	Z
a.	$40,000	$40,000	$40,000	$40,000
b.	$53,333	$44,444	$35,556	$26,667
c.	$60,000	$46,667	$33,333	$20,000
d.	$64,000	$48,000	$32,000	$16,000

2. Assuming that total joint costs of $160,000 were allocated using the net realization method, what were the joint costs allocated to each product?

	W	X	Y	Z
a.	$53,333	$44,444	$35,556	$26,667
b.	$60,000	$46,667	$33,333	$20,000
c.	$60,000	$46,545	$33,455	$20,000
d.	$64,000	$48,000	$32,000	$16,000

3. Assuming that total joint costs of $160,000 were allocated using the uniform percentage contribution method, what were the joint costs allocated to each product?

	W	X	Y	Z
a.	$40,000	$40,000	$40,000	$40,000
b.	$60,000	$46,500	$33,500	$20,000
c.	$64,000	$48,000	$32,000	$16,000
d.	$67,500	$49,000	$31,000	$12,500

(CPA, extended)

7. **Find the missing figure: Multiple choice.** Stowe, Inc., produces two joint products, PEL and VEL. During March, 19x1, further processing costs beyond the split-off point, needed to convert the products into salable form, were $8,000 and $12,000 for 800 units of PEL and 400 units of VEL, respectively. PEL sells for $25 a unit and VEL sells for $50 a unit. $9,000 of the joint costs were allocated to product PEL, based on the net realization method. What were the total joint costs in March, 19x1?

a. $15,000; b. $22,500; c. $27,000; d. $36,000.

(CPA, adapted)

8. **Relative sale value basis; interpretation.** A process with joint costs of $1,500 yields 100 units of product A and 50 units of product B. Product A is sold for $10 a unit without further processing. Product B would be sold for $4 a unit; instead, management uses all 50 units of B to make 50 units of product C at a separate processing cost of $2 a unit. Product C is sold at a price of $15 a unit.

Required:

a. Calculate unit costs of products A and B on a relative sale value at split-off basis.
b. What inferences as to the profitability of the two products would you draw if you were to interpret the unit cost figures literally? Are these reasonable inferences to draw? Explain your position.

9. **Costing inventories: Separate processing.** During the past year the Atom Chemical Company converted raw materials into 500,000 pounds of material A and 1 million gallons of liquid B. The total joint cost of production was $388,000. Material A was not marketable without further processing. After the joint products were separated, the company converted material A into material C at an additional cost of 3 cents a pound. The sale price of material C was 40 cents a pound and that of liquid B 30 cents a gallon.

Required:

a. Prepare a physical flow diagram of these processes. Enter cost, quantity, and price data on this diagram.
b. Compute the unit cost that you would use to measure each of these products for public financial reporting. State the basis on which your calculations were made and give your reasons for choosing it.

10. **Supplying missing information.** Jonathan Company manufactures products N, P, and R in a joint process. Make the necessary calculations to supply the data missing from the following table:

	Product N	Product P	Product R	Total
a. Units produced	6,000	?	?	12,100
b. Sale value at split-off	$?	$?	$25,000	$100,000
c. Sale value if processed further	?	45,000	30,000	?
d. Additional cost of further processing	5,500	?	?	20,000
e. Net realization after further processing	49,500	?	?	?
f. Allocated joint costs, relative sale value at split-off basis	24,000	?	?	60,000
g. Allocated joint costs, net realization basis	27,000	?	13,800	?
h. Average joint cost per unit, net realization basis	?	12.80	?	xxx

(CPA, extended)

11. **Separate processing decision: Relevance of unit cost.** A company processes soybeans. The initial process separates soybean oil and leaves a cakelike residue. The cake is then ground and moisturized to form soybean meal.

Last week the company processed 10,000 bushels of soybeans to yield 45 tons of soybean oil and 225 tons of cake. Further processing of the cake yielded 250 tons of meal, the increase in weight resulting from added moisture.

The cost of the beans was $6 a bushel, the costs of joint processing were $14,400 and the costs of processing the cake into meal amounted to $2,500. The market price of meal was $150 a ton, and the market price of oil was $1,000 a ton. Cake ordinarily isn't sold without further processing.

Required:

a. Compute unit costs for the week using the net realization method of cost allocation.

b. Compute unit costs allocating joint costs on a physical unit basis.

c. The company has an opportunity to sell 25 tons of cake. What figure would you use as the cost of cake for the purpose of deciding whether to take advantage of this opportunity?

12. **Classifying a product as a by-product.** The Jensen Chemical Company has a plant which produces two chemicals, borine and selinate, in a single joint process. The total cost incurred to the split-off point is $864,000 a month. Monthly production is 2 million gallons of borine and 300,000 pounds of selinate.

Borine is processed further to make one of the company's branded products, Tri-Bor. The net realization from sales of Tri-Bor, after deducting separate processing costs, is equivalent to 45 cents a gallon of borine. The average selling price of selinate is 20 cents a pound.

Required:

a. Compute the total cost and unit cost of borine on the assumption that selinate is a co-product.

b. Compute the total cost and unit cost of borine on the assumption that selinate is a by-product.

c. Would you classify selinate as a by-product or as a co-product? Defend your recommendation.

13. **Costing a by-product.** Products A, B, and C are joint products. Products A and B are treated as co-products; product C is treated as a by-product, its market value of $20 a pound being subtracted from joint costs at the time of split-off. The remaining joint costs are allocated between the co-products on a relative net realization basis.

During July, joint product costs amounted to $85,000 and costs of separate processing of product B totaled $10,000. The month's production was as follows:

Product A .... 30,000 lbs.
Product B .... 10,000 lbs.
Product C .... 200 lbs.

Product A sells at a net price of $2 a pound; product B is sold at a price of $4 a pound.

Required:

a. How much of the joint cost is assigned to each unit of product C?
b. How much of the joint cost is assigned to each unit of product A?
c. In view of its high price per pound, do you agree with the company's decision to treat product C as a by-product? Explain briefly.
d. A proposal has been made to cost inventories of product A at $2 a pound and unprocessed product B at zero, on the ground that these figures represent their opportunity costs. Comment briefly on this proposal.

14. **Profitability of a processed joint product.** Product X and material Y are produced at a joint cost of $105,000 a month. Material Y is then processed further at a cost of $20,000 a month to become product Z.

Both X and Z are sold outright to a chain of grocery stores and the company incurs no selling expenses on these products. Material Y cannot be sold without further processing and cannot be obtained from other sources outside the company.

In a normal month, output consists of the following quantities and prices:

Joint process:
  Product X, 10,000 units, sold at $10 each.
  Material Y, 5,000 pounds.
Separate process:
  Product Z, 3,000 units, sold at $20 each.

Required:

a. How much profit does the company earn on sales of product Z?
b. This company has 100 units of product X in its inventory. Given only the information above, at what amount would you expect the company to report this inventory on its balance sheet? Explain your calculations and your reasons for selecting the method you used.

15. **Maximum purchase price.** A company processes a raw material to yield two products, Dip and Nod. A unit of Dip sells for 50 cents, a Nod brings in 40 cents.

The process is now operating at full capacity, processing 10,000 pounds of raw materials each week to yield 20,000 units of Dip and 10,000 units of Nod. The company could sell more at these prices, but the existing equipment can't be used to process more than 10,000 pounds a month.

Weekly processing cost (excluding the costs of the raw materials) are as follows:

Fixed $3,000
Variable 5,000

The fixed costs include $1,000 of depreciation, salaries of security guards, taxes, insurance, and other costs that would continue even if the process were to shut down entirely for a time; the remaining fixed costs are necessary to support any level of production up to full capacity. The variable costs vary in proportion to the number of pounds of materials processed.

Required:

a. What is the maximum price the company could pay for its raw materials without reporting a loss on this operation?
b. What is the maximum price the company could pay for its raw materials without finding it more profitable to shut the process down temporarily?

c. How would you change your answer to (b) if you found that the output of Nod could be converted into Snooze at a cost of $1,500? Snooze sells for 60 cents a unit.

d. How would you change your answer to (b) if you found that Dip could be converted into Plunge at a cost of $3,500? Plunge sells for 65 cents a unit.

16. **Expanding production of joint products.** A department processes 10,000 pounds of materials a month to manufacture two products, alpha and beta. Materials cost 40 cents a pound, and processing 10,000 pounds costs $2,300. The yield is 6,000 pounds of alpha and 4,000 pounds of beta. Alpha sells for $1 a pound; beta sells for 25 cents. The allocation of joint costs, based on the net realization method, produces unit costs of 90 cents a pound for alpha and 22.5 cents a pound for beta.

The market for alpha is very strong and the company could sell an additional 3,000 units of this product each month at the current price. The present facilities are inadequate to process more than 10,000 pounds of materials, but the company can rent additional equipment for $500 a month to process an additional 5,000 pounds of materials. Other additional processing costs would be $1,000 a month.

Required:

a. How can the company afford to sell beta for 25 cents when the materials alone cost 40 cents a pound?

b. What is the company's profit or loss from beta?

c. Under what conditions would you recommend renting the additional equipment?

17. **Effect of materials quality on product cost.** A substitute material for the raw material described in problem 16 costs 48.4 cents a pound. Processing 10,000 pounds of this material would yield 8,000 pounds of alpha and 2,000 pounds of beta. Processing costs would not be affected by the substitution.

Required:

a. Recalculate product cost by the net realization method.

b. Calculate the cost of alpha on an incremental basis.

c. Should the substitution be made? Show your calculations.

18. **Inclusion of separable costs in costing joint products.** The Stendahl Company has used the net realization method to allocate joint costs between two products, A and B. Product A has a sale value of $10 a unit, while product B has no sale value without further processing. After separate processing, product B is sold for $6 a pound.

The company has just hired a new chief accountant, who feels that the net realization method assigns too much cost to product B. "We need both of these products to make the process pay," he said recently. "This means that every dollar we spend processing product B makes just as great a contribution to earnings as a dollar spent on the main process."

Production in a typical month amounts to 5,000 units of product A and 10,000 units of product B. The costs of the joint process amount to $67,000 and separate processing of product B costs $10,000. The chief accountant's proposal is to place all costs in a single pool and allocate them on the basis of the relative sale value of the two products. The ratio is:

$$\frac{\text{Cost}}{\text{Sales value}} = \frac{\$67,000 + \$10,000}{5,000 \times \$10 + 10,000 \times \$6} = 70 \text{ percent}$$

Required:

a. What unit costs would emerge if the chief accountant's proposal were adopted?

b. What unit costs would be derived from the net realization method?

c. Which allocation method would you support? Give the reasons for your choice.

(Based on a suggestion by Lawrence Benninger)

19. **Production continuation decisions.** Colonial Company makes three products in a joint process. Each of these products can be sold as it emerges from the joint process or processed further for eventual sale at a higher price. All three products are now being sold after further processing. The prices of all products have been depressed for some time and seem likely to remain low for some time to come. The estimated average cost of a batch of joint inputs at current operating volumes is $90. The sale values and further processing costs of the three products emerging from a $90 batch of joint inputs are as follows:

Product	Sale Value at Split-off	Further Processing Cost	Sale Value After Further Processing
A	$40	$ 4	$ 50
B	20	12	30
C	10	18	25
Total	$70	$34	$105

Management is very concerned by the losses these products are experiencing and is trying to decide whether to sell them without further processing, sell them in their fully processed form, discontinue production until market conditions improve, or take some other action. It has collected the following additional cost information for the outputs associated with a $90 batch of joint inputs:

	Variable with Volume	Fixed but Avoidable with Shutdown of Process	Fixed, Not Avoidable with Shutdown of Process	Total
Cost of joint process	$50	$22	$18	$90
Cost of separate process A	2	1	1	4
Cost of separate process B	6	5	1	12
Cost of separate process C	10	7	1	18

Required:

a. What action do you recommend? Present the calculations necessary to support your position.
b. Management has an opportunity to modify the units that emerge from separate process C at an incremental cost of $9. The modified products would be sold at a price of $35. Should this opportunity be grasped? Show the calculations necessary to support your position.

20. **Joint costs and decisions.** The ABC Company uses raw materials A and B in a process which yields two products, X and Y, in fixed proportions. The company has no other operations. The following figures are forecasted for an average month during the coming year:

1. Materials used: A, 5,000 pounds, $29,800; B, 500 gallons, $11,000.
2. Product output: X, 4,000 pounds; Y, 2,000 pounds; waste, 1,000 pounds.
3. Processing costs: variable, $8,000; fixed, $9,600. Fixed costs include the salary of the department head, straight-line depreciation on building and equipment, and amortization of the costs of developing the process some years ago.

4. Product selling prices: X, $15 a pound; Y, $40 a pound.
5. Direct product selling expenses: X, $16,000; Y, $44,000.
6. General selling and administrative expenses (not allocated to individual products), $14,000.
7. The company pays Ace Disposal Company a flat fee of $3,200 a month to remove and dispose of all waste produced by this process.
8. All selling and administrative expenses are fixed, and are paid in cash.

Required:

a. On the basis of this information, prepare an estimate of average factory cost per unit for each product.
b. Explain and defend the method you used in (*a*) to allocate joint costs.
c. By treating the waste, the ABC Company can convert it into a product selling for $4 a pound. Unfortunately, the incremental cost of processing the waste in this manner would be $5 a pound. Should the company process the waste? What is the highest cost per pound the company could afford to pay for processing the waste?
d. The sales manager says that increasing direct selling cost by $2,000 a month would increase sales of product X by 10 percent, without reducing the price. Assuming that the cost figures are correct, make calculations to determine the conditions necessary to justify accepting this proposal. What contribution did the unit cost figure you developed in answering (a) make to your analysis of this question?

21. **Measuring departmental average cost.**   The Wilde Corporation operates a factory with two production departments. Materials first pass through department I, where a substantial loss in weight takes place at the start of processing. The semiprocessed materials pass on to department II, where they are processed further to form two separate products, Elong and Ulong, together with a waste material known as "tailings." The following data refer to the month of April.

	Department I	Department II
Quantities (pounds)		
Materials received	100,000	80,000 (from dept. I)
Work in process, April 1 (materials 100% complete, one half processed in department)	20,000	None
Work completed	80,000	20,000 Elong / 50,000 Ulong / 8,000 tailings
Work in process, April 30 (materials 100% complete, one third processed in department)	15,000	None
Costs:		
Costs in process, April 1:		
Materials	$ 8,100	None
Processing costs	6,000	None
Materials received	28,000	?
Processing costs incurred	46,700	$31,050

Sales and selling costs during April were as follows:

	Elong	Ulong	Tailings
Selling price per pound	$ 3.00	$ 2.00	$0.10
Units sold (pounds)	18,000	70,000	8,000
Traceable costs of packing and delivery ...	$2,700	$14,000	0

The traceable costs of packing and delivery were wholly variable with the number of pounds sold. In addition, fixed selling and administrative costs, not traceable to any product, amounted to $40,000 for the month.

The company uses the moving-average method of inventory costing. Joint cost is allocated on the basis of the net realization method. Tailings are to be treated as a by-product.

Required:

a. Compute the total cost and cost per unit of department I inventory in process on April 30.

b. Compute the unit costs that would be used in recording the transfer to finished goods inventory of Elong, Ulong, and tailings, respectively.

c. Prepare unit cost figures for department I, based on equivalent production for the month. Suggest and describe at least one way to derive analogous figures for department II.

22. **Accepting a special order; usefulness of standard joint cost.** The management of Lincoln Products Company is considering a customer's request for a monthly shipment of 10,000 pounds of Awlcon, an industrial chemical, at a selling price of 70 cents a pound. This is considerably less than its current list price of 90 cents, but higher than its standard manufacturing cost (66 cents). Management would like to accept this contract, but only if it will increase the company's profits.

Awlcon is a specialty product, not available from other manufacturers. It is used as a processing chemical in several industries; the largest present user buys about 5,000 pounds a month. The proposed contract would be the company's first breakthrough into the rubber products industry. Because the end uses are so different, management has little fear that lower prices to the rubber manufacturers would spread to its other customers. In any case, management is convinced that it will never penetrate this industry without some price concessions.

Awlcon is manufactured in two stages. In the first stage, raw materials are processed to produce two intermediates, in fixed proportions. One of these intermediates is then processed further to yield a product called Tincon; the other intermediate is converted into Awlcon in a separate finishing operation.

The Awlcon finishing process yields both finished Awlcon and a waste material. This waste material has no market value, but the company is able to convert it into a salable product called Griscon. The company can sell as much Griscon as it can produce, at a price of 30 cents a pound.

The company has a standard costing system which yields the following total standard cost per pound for each product, based on the net realization method:

Tincon $0.38
Awlcon 0.66
Griscon 0.30

Volume, costs, and prices are expected to be at normal levels for the next year. Production quantity, market price per pound, and sales volume are as follows in a normal month:

	Quantity (pounds)	Market Price	Market Value
Tincon	400,000	variable	$194,000
Awlcon	100,000	$0.90	90,000
Griscon	10,000	0.30	3,000
Total			$287,000

At these normal volumes, materials and processing costs are expected to total as follows:

	Basic Process	Separate Finishing Processes		
		Tincon	Awlcon	Griscon
Materials	$64,000	$22,000	$ 3,000	$ 200
Labor	30,000	45,000	18,000	1,100
Variable overhead	6,000	10,000	5,000	100
Fixed overhead	10,000	5,000	1,000	600
Total	$110,000	$82,000	$27,000	$2,000

Output can be increased or decreased fairly easily by as much as 25 percent of normal volume. Any larger increase would require an expansion of plant capacity. Within these limits, materials, labor, and variable overhead costs tend to vary directly and proportionately with volume, while fixed costs remain fairly stable. Selling and administrative costs are entirely fixed and none of them can be traced to any of the three products.

Required:

a. Prepare a diagram showing the flow of products through the various processes.
b. Verify the calculation of the standard cost figures. Griscon is treated as a by-product.
c. Under what conditions, if any, would you recommend acceptance of this order? Quantify your answer insofar as you are able.
d. For what purpose or purposes, if any, would you find the company's standard unit cost figures useful?

Case 15–1: The Williamson Chocolate Co., Ltd.*

The Williamson Chocolate Co., Ltd., which has its headquarters and principal factory in Leicester, England, has been engaged in the production of chocolate and cocoa products since the beginning of this century. Subsidiary companies have been established in Canada, Australia, and South Africa, and each of the subsidiaries manufactures the more important of the company's products and markets them in its home market.

The Australian company is located in Melbourne, where all of its manufacturing activities take place. Warehouses for local distribution are also maintained in Sydney, Adelaide, and Perth. The main output at the factory is chocolate in bars. Cocoa beans, the principal raw material for the manufacture of chocolate, are imported from abroad. As a rule, the beans are cleaned, roasted, ground, and then passed through a press. In the press, cocoa butter is separated from cocoa powder, which comes out of the press in the form of cocoa cake. The cocoa butter leaves the press in liquid form because of the heat that is generated during the press operation. The cocoa butter is then stored in large tanks, ready for use in the current production of chocolate.

The Melbourne factory was a net user of cocoa butter, i.e., its chocolate production called for more cocoa butter than could be obtained from the pressing of cocoa beans adequate to supply its need for cocoa powder. This extra cocoa butter could have been imported but it was subject to a heavy import duty, and the local management believed that it was cheaper to import beans and extract the cocoa butter from them. As a result of implementing this policy the factory found itself with a steadily mounting stock of cocoa powder.

The following figures show how the stock of cocoa powder (in pounds) increased during the period 1978–80:

* This case was written by David Solomons. Copyright 1981 by l'Institut pour l'Etude des Méthodes de Direction de l'Entreprise (IMEDE), Lausanne, Switzerland. Reproduced by permission. Places and dates have been disguised.

1978:		
Stock at January 1, 1978		30,500
Output of press		416,975
		447,475
Less: Usage in 1978		324,500
Stock at December 31, 1978		122,975
1979:		
Output of press		638,750
		761,725
Less: Usage in 1979	506,420	
Sales in 1979	35,500	541,920
Stock at December 31, 1979		219,805
1980:		
Output of press		792,125
		1,011,930
Less: Usage in 1980	641,600	
Sales in 1980	43,385	684,985
Stock of cocoa powder, December 31, 1980 ...		326,945

These large stocks of cocoa powder held at the factory caused a serious storage problem, and the local management made continuous efforts to find profitable outlets for the excess cocoa powder. However, the sale of this powder on the Australian market raised a question as to the costs to be assigned to it. In accordance with accounting instructions issued by the head office in London 10 years earlier, the cost of the cocoa beans purchased, together with the labor and overhead costs of the pressing process had to be allocated between the cocoa butter and the cocoa cake on the basis of the fat content remaining in these two products after the pressing operations. This gave a cost for cocoa powder of about $1.50 a pound or about 50 percent above its current market price at the end of 1980. The company was therefore unable to dispose of its excess stock of cocoa cake without incurring a considerable loss. No write-down to market value had been made for financial reporting purposes because the powder was pooled with other inventories for the application of the lower-of-cost-or-market test.

During 1981, cocoa prices fell further and the subsidiary was unable to sell any large quantities of its excess stocks, because its costs were too high. There was practically no market in Australia for cocoa cake. Williamson Chocolate did succeed, however, in exchanging 13,000 pounds of cake against 2,000 pounds of cocoa butter with another manufacturer.

In the middle of 1981, John Cannon, the marketing manager, brought forward a scheme to market a new cocoa preparation for making a hot chocolate drink. The marketing prospects seemed good so long as the selling price could be kept low enough. This new product offered a promising means of disposing of the excess stocks of cocoa powder but only if they were costed out at substantially less than the cost allocated to them in the books.

The production manager, David Parker, supported this proposal with enthusiasm. He had repeatedly drawn the attention of the subsidiary's managing director, T. D. Woodstock, to the storage problem created by the cocoa stocks, and he welcomed the possibility which now opened up of dealing with this problem once for all. Besides, he said, he had never been able to see the logic of basing the cost of cocoa powder on its fat content. It was its flavor which was important, and fat content had little to do with flavor.

Both Mr. Cannon and Mr. Parker were surprised to find that Mr. Woodstock was not unreservedly enthusiastic about Mr. Cannon's proposal. He pointed out that if cocoa powder were charged to the new product at present cost levels, the product would never show a profit; and without a drop in the price of cocoa beans greater than anyone could at present foresee, the only way to reduce the cost of cocoa powder would be to change the basis of cost allocation between cocoa powder and cocoa butter. This could not be done without permission from London and he was by no means certain that such permission would be given unless some basis of cost allocation which was clearly better than the present one could be proposed. It was all very well to attack the present basis of allocation, as Mr. Parker had done. But unless he or somebody else could suggest a better one, why should London agree to a change?

Mr. Woodstock went on to point out that there was another aspect of the matter which made him reluctant to approach London. If the allocation of costs to cocoa powder were reduced, with a consequent increase in the cost of cocoa butter, the calculation which had been supplied to London in 1977 to support the expenditure of $200,000 on a new cocoa press would be completely undermined. Only on the basis of the present cost of producing cocoa butter as compared with the cost of importing it could investment in the press have been justified. If more cost were to be allocated to cocoa butter, it might be shown that it ought to be imported after all, and the investment in the press would be shown to have been misguided.

a. What alternative methods of eliminating the surplus cocoa powder were available to Mr. Woodstock in 1981?

b. Prepare a rough format for a worksheet suitable for use in organizing the data relevant to the choice among these alternatives. (*Suggestion:* A column should be established for each alternative you identified in answer to *a.*)

c. What should Mr. Woodstock tell London? Should he recommend a change in the allocation method?

d. If the method isn't changed, in what circumstances would you recommend that the new product be introduced?

16 Costing marketing and service activities

Job order costing can be used to cost some of the services an organization provides to itself. The services of company print shops and research and development departments are good examples. Neither job order costing nor process costing techniques can be used in most cases, however, to assign internal service, support, and marketing costs to individual product lines or other revenue segments. The purpose of this chapter is to show how cost accounting can be used to estimate and analyze the costs of these kinds of activities. The discussion is in four parts:

1. *Functional cost analysis*—measuring the costs of individual marketing and administrative service functions.
2. *Segment cost analysis*—assigning functional costs to individual marketing segments.
3. Using segment cost analysis to measure the costs of servicing individual *product lines.*
4. Using segment cost analysis to measure the costs of filling customer *orders of different sizes.*

Functional cost analysis

The first stage in costing marketing and administrative service activities is to measure or estimate the costs of individual *functions.* A function is any activity of one or more marketing or administrative service centers.

Reasons for functional cost analysis

Management may wish to measure or estimate the costs of performing individual functions to help answer five questions:

1. *Does the function cost more than it's worth?* Benefits may be hard to measure, but cost/benefit analysis is impossible without estimates of costs.
2. *Can the function be performed more cheaply by outside contractors?* This question doesn't arise for all functions, but it needs to be asked from time to time.
3. *How many people and how much equipment are needed to perform the function?* This can be especially important at budget time.

4. *Is the cost center performing efficiently?* This is a continuing concern, in the office no less than in the factory.
5. *How much functional cost does a marketing segment require?* Functional cost centers serve or contribute to programs. Program evaluation requires knowledge of functional cost.

Approaches to functional cost analysis

Functional cost analysis is very simple when a cost center is devoted exclusively to a single function, such as payroll preparation. The techniques of process costing are directly applicable.

Many functions, however, share one or more cost centers. For example, a study of the operations of a billing and order processing department might reveal the following separate processes:

1. Order recording.
2. Credit reviewing.
3. Invoicing—headings.
4. Invoicing—line items.
5. Order file maintenance.
6. Correspondence.

Process costing is impractical in this situation because the output of the cost center is not homogeneous. Job order costing is out of the question because the typical task is so small that task-oriented timekeeping and requisitioning procedures would be uneconomical and counterproductive. Furthermore, even when work is done in batches, data on the costs of individual batches have little meaning. Unlike work in a factory job shop, every batch is much like every other batch, except perhaps for its length. The function, in other words, comprises many repetitions of the same operation, not a unique combination of different operations.

As a result, the costs of marketing and administrative service functions are measured, if they are measured at all, in the ways described in Exhibit 16–1.

Exhibit 16–1 Usual approaches to functional costing

1. If employees or equipment are assigned exclusively to one function for significant, clearly measurable time periods	Time records are used to allocate labor and equipment costs to individual functions, but not to specific batches or work orders.
2. If these conditions are not present	Labor and equipment costs are either assigned to functions by statistical or engineering techniques or left unassigned.
3. In most situations	The costs of materials (office supplies, for the most part) are classified as cost center overheads and are allocated to functions, if at all, as part of some broadly conceived average of all overhead costs.

Time recording

Time records can be kept for people or for equipment. Computer use, for example, is usually very closely monitored. If computer jobs can be traced to specific functions, then equipment time and cost also can be identified with those functions.

Labor time recording is more spotty. Time clocks are seldom used because at least one of the following three conditions is present:

1. Employees don't work on one function long enough at a stretch—a payroll clerk, for example, may be engaged in information retrieval 20 times a day, but never spend more than a few minutes on this activity at any one time.
2. Work done off-premises is beyond the reach of the company's time clocks—sales functions, for example.
3. Office workers lack a timekeeping tradition—this has been one way they have differentiated themselves from factory workers, a differentiation they like to retain.

Whatever the reason, the most common method of timekeeping off the factory floor is the honor system. The employees fill in their own time cards at the end of each day, basing their entries on whatever record-keeping systems seem appropriate. Most employees keep no records at all, but estimate at the end of each day how they have spent their time. An example of a weekly time card for a clerk in credit and collections is shown in Exhibit 16–2.

Exhibit 16–2 Weekly time card

Name: P. Jones Dept.: Credit					Week: June 5	
	M	T	W	T	F	Total
Credit check	1	2	4	S	3	10
Collection	4	4	3	I	2	13
Inquiries	2	1	—	C	2	5
				K		
Total	7	7	7		7	28

Honor system time records are obviously inaccurate, but their main weakness has nothing to do with the method used to collect the data. The weakness is that certain kinds of time are not traceable to specific production functions. For example, suppose management decides that all sales force activities are either direct selling or market research functions. At each call the sales representatives perform both functions—and they are also likely to have to wait. The waiting time is seldom traceable to one function or the other. The same is true of time spent traveling from one prospective buyer's office to another.

This brings us back to our concept of *attributable cost*. As applied here, it has the following definition:

> *Attributable cost:* the amount of cost that could be eliminated if the company were to discontinue a specific function, given enough time to reduce functional capacity to zero.

Any allocation of such elements as travel and waiting time should reflect this concept. Once such allocations are made, however, a certain amount of cost will remain unallocated, attributable to no one function but common to them all. Allocation of these costs would have no analytical significance.

Engineering techniques

The second major approach to functional cost measurement is an industrial engineering approach. Two kinds of engineering techniques are used:

1. *Engineered standards.* To establish how much time each activity *ought* to take—applicable only to standardized, repetitive activities.
2. *Work sampling.* To establish how much time each activity *has taken*—applicable only to on-premises activities.

Engineered standards call for careful investigation of the input requirements of each function. The engineering method most commonly used today is some variant of the Methods Time Measurement (MTM) technique. Under this approach, the operations are first studied to identify the major tasks to be performed. Standard time allowances for each task are then obtained from commercially available tables.

Work sampling consists largely of recording what people are doing at particular instants of time, selected at random, during some longer time period. For example, the sampling plan may require the recording of the activities being performed by each clerk in the office at 9:12, 10:34, and so on. From a number of such samples taken at various times, a percentage time distribution can be obtained, and the estimated times to perform the various repetitive service activities can be derived from this.

The work sampling and engineering methods of deriving cost standards are applicable primarily or exclusively to labor costs. Work sampling has both the advantage and the disadvantage of indicating what the costs are rather than what they should be. The disadvantage in this approach is that it gives management little assurance that its costs are reasonable. The advantage is that it provides management with information as to what its money is buying. Furthermore, these studies can indicate trends in functional cost if they are carried out periodically.

These methods are expensive and they ordinarily cannot be justified except as a by-product of a program of work simplification and methods improvement. In other words, the added accuracy of the data derived from engineered standards is ordinarily insufficient by itself to justify the cost and disruption entailed in developing the standards.

Control of functional activities

One of our five reasons for studying functional cost is to estimate functional efficiency. For example, a control report prepared for a cost center preparing invoices and payrolls might show the following:

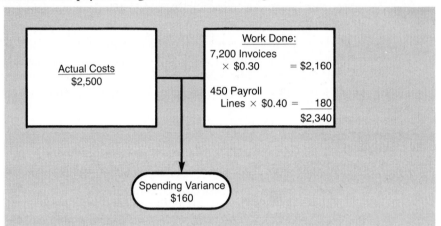

This kind of comparison is useful, but its benefits should not be overstressed. It doesn't measure short-term cost control performance. Most marketing and administrative costs are fixed in the short run, as we explained in Chapter 12. For this reason, variances of this sort are more likely to reflect variations in the overall demand for functional services than functional efficiency or inefficiency.

Segment cost analysis

One reason for identifying the costs of individual functions is to provide a basis for segment cost analysis—that is, for estimating the amount of cost attributable to individual marketing segments. This section sets forth the methods used for this purpose in a general way; the remainder of the chapter will then show how these methods can be used to estimate the costs of several kinds of marketing segments.

The relationship between functional costs and segments is illustrated in Exhibit 16–3. Assigning costs to functions is the first phase; reassigning them to segments is the second. This second phase consists of four stages:

1. Identify the marketing segments to be studied.
2. Identify any functional costs traceable to individual segments.
3. Identify any other costs of responsive functions that are attributable to individual segments.
4. Identify any costs of programmed functions that are attributable to individual segments.

Exhibit 16–3 Relationship between functional costs and segment costs

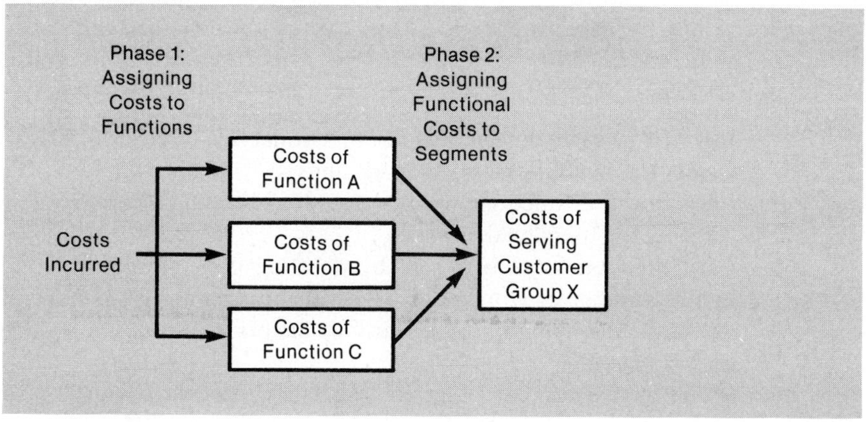

Stage 1.   Identifying marketing segments

The first stage in the analysis is to identify the marketing segments to be studied. Typical bases for marketing segmentation are the product line, the region, the customer group, the order size, and the channel of distribution.

The choice of the revenue segments to be studied depends on the purpose of the analysis. Product-line segments will be selected if the question is whether a given product line is pulling its own weight. Geographical segments will be used if the problem is whether a specific region is profitable enough to justify the time and effort the company is devoting to it.

Stage 2.   Identifying segment-traceable costs

As always, the primary basis for cost assignment is traceability. Some costs can be classified directly by segment as well as by function. These should be treated as direct costs of the segments unless doing so would add substantially to the cost of data processing.

Most segment-traceable costs are the costs of programmed activities—advertising, direct selling, and so forth—but they may include some responsive activities as well. The costs of a fleet of delivery trucks, for example, can often be traced entirely to retail sales or wholesale sales, or to one region or another, if those are the revenue segments management is interested in.

Terminology reminder

Responsive activities: undertaken by a cost center to provide necessary service or support to activities centered elsewhere in the organization.

Programmed activities: undertaken at management's initiative to meet objectives other than meeting demands for service imposed on the organization unit from outside.

Stage 3. Assigning the costs of responsive functions

When the traceability criterion fails, some other method must be used to assign functional costs to segments. For responsive functions, this is a five-step process:

1. Identify the main determinants of functional cost—referred to as governing factors or, in some cases, as work units.
2. Identify those functional costs that are divisible enough to vary with the demand for functional services.
3. Calculate functional unit cost by dividing divisible costs (from step 2) by the number of work units or governing factors (from step 1).
4. Calculate the number of governing factors or work units required by each segment.
5. Multiply the number of governing factors or work units by functional unit costs.

Only the first two of these require discussion; the three final steps are routine.

Step 1. Selecting governing factors and work units. The criteria for selecting an allocation base for a given function are simple:

1. Does it correlate well with variations in the total cost of the function?
2. Can it be measured easily for each segment?

The measure that best meets the first of these criteria is a measure of the influences that determine how much cost will be incurred to perform the function. We shall refer to these cost determinants as *governing factors*. The governing factors for functional costs are those aspects of segment activity that determine the need for functional services. Examples are the number of customer orders obtained and the number of deliveries to be made.

These governing factors determine the need for services, but the services themselves may have other names. The demand for payroll services, for example, may depend on the total number of employee-hours, but the output of the payroll department is measured by the number of payroll lines written. These output units are known as *work units:*

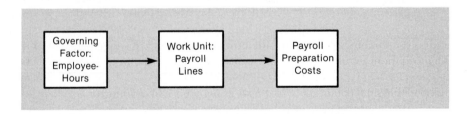

Whether the analysis is based on governing factors or on work units depends to some extent on the nature of the activity. For this purpose we recognize two kinds of functions:

1. Repetitive service functions.
2. Diversified service functions.

Repetitive service functions are those for which output is relatively homogeneous—for example, one payroll line is very much like another payroll line. Work units usually can be established for these. For an order processing department, the work units might be:

Task	Work Unit
Order recording	Total orders received
Credit reviewing	Charge orders received
Invoicing—headings	Invoices }or line items
Invoicing—line items	Line items }
Order file maintenance	Total orders received
Correspondence	Letters written

Different work units might be appropriate for different cost elements if they have different variability patterns. For example, in the delivery department:

Element	Work Unit
Loading labor	Total pounds loaded
Gas, oil, and maintenance	Miles
Bulk delivery labor	Miles
Route delivery labor	Deliveries
Bulk unloading labor	Deliveries

Even here, the work unit is not entirely homogeneous—for example, bulk delivery labor costs will vary with traffic conditions as well as with miles traveled—but the unit selected is a fairly reliable index of the output requirement.

The work unit is not always a good basis for assigning functional costs to segments. For example, the payroll line is generally a good measure of the output of payroll preparation. It may be a very poor assignment base, however, because payroll lines can't be traced to segments. In other words, payroll lines do not meet the second of our two selection criteria. In this situation, the accountant must either fall back on the governing factor as the allocation base, or, as a last resort, find a substitute measure of the volume of segment activity that can be identified easily with the segments and also correlates well in total with the total demand for functional service. If no such measure can be found, then the functional cost should not be allocated to the segment.

Diversified service functions differ from repetitive service functions only in that the units of output are many, nonstandardized, and constantly changing. Examples include the duties of a good part of the executive force, office management, secretarial work, telephone switchboard operation, and similar tasks. Secretarial output could possibly be measured in terms of the number of telephone calls made, number of letters typed, number of visitors received, and so forth, but there is so little homogeneity within any one of these measures that they offer very little promise for standardization.

Service volume for diversified service activities has to be measured indirectly, in units of some governing factor or factors. For example, the governing factor for an employee recreation function might well be the number of company employees. Selection of such units is ordinarily not very difficult, the only practical problem being that so many different factors may be selected for the various functions that obtaining statistics would become a massive job. The typical solution is to try to reduce the number of measuring rods so that one index will serve a number of functions.

Step 2. Identifying attributable cost. The second step in assigning the costs of responsive functions to segments is to decide how much of the cost of the function is assignable. Short-run variable cost is a poor concept for this purpose. First, short-run variability is likely to be insignificant. Second, the decisions for which this kind of costing is relevant are not short-run decisions. They attempt to resolve questions such as:

1. Should we abandon product line A?
2. Should we accept small orders and, if so, should we impose a surcharge on orders smaller than a certain size?
3. Should we distribute our products directly to retail outlets or channel them through wholesalers?

In each case the choice affects a substantial volume of business, enough to have a significant impact on the amount of functional service capacity needed.

The fixed costs of responsive functions are often highly divisible, and this provides the basis for estimates of attributable cost. The usefulness of segment cost analysis, therefore, depends on the ability of attributable cost to approximate incremental cost for the alternatives being evaluated. The rule throughout this chapter will be to include in functional unit cost only those cost elements that seem sufficiently divisible to justify the assumption of proportionate changes in response to substantial changes in the total volume of functional activity.

Notice that the attributable cost concept has been applied twice, first to measure the amount of cost attributable to the performance of individual functions, and then to measure how much of this is attributable to individual marketing segments. As this suggests, not all costs attributable to specific functions can be attributed to specific marketing segments; some functional costs therefore should not be redistributed to segments in any managerially-oriented analysis. Our objective is to find out how much cost the segment makes necessary, not to find a segment for every cost.

Stage 4. Nontraceable, attributable programmed costs

The final stage in the analysis is to estimate the amount of nontraceable programmed costs, if any, that can be attributed to individual marketing segments. Probably the best estimates will be judgmental estimates by marketing management, supported by such data as the time records in sales representatives' call reports. The accountant should resist the temptation, however, to make sure that these allocations distribute nontraceable costs in full. To repeat, it is highly unlikely that the total of the attributable costs for the various segments will equal total functional cost.

Product-line analysis

The most obvious illustration of segment cost analysis is in the analysis of the profitability of individual product lines. Suppose, for example, that a company wishes to decide which of its three product lines deserves the most short-run promotional effort, as well as which of them appear to have weaknesses that if not corrected will endanger their long-run survival. Estimated sales volume and factory costs for the coming year are as follows:

	Line A	Line B	Line C
Sales revenues	$1,200,000	$900,000	$950,000
Variable factory cost	500,000	450,000	350,000
Variable factory margin	700,000	450,000	600,000
Attributable fixed factory cost	50,000	30,000	—
Attributable factory margin	$ 650,000	$420,000	$600,000

Choosing the three segments constituted stage 1 of our analytical routine. The other three stages are:

1. Identify traceable costs.
2. Identify other attributable costs of product-related service activities.
3. Identify other attributable costs of programmed activities.

Traceable costs

Three groups of cost elements—sales commissions, product management costs, and the costs of samples and product sales brochures—are completely traceable to individual product lines in our illustration. Sales commissions are calculated at a rate of 1 percent of gross sales. The other two cost elements are expected to be as follows:

	Line A	Line B	Line C
Product management	$23,000	$21,000	$22,000
Samples and brochures	8,000	7,000	10,500

Product-related service costs

Our second task is to identify any other product-related nonmanufacturing functions and assign appropriate portions of their costs to the segments we're interested in. To simplify the presentation, we'll assume that our illustrative company has found only four product-related functions: product handling, storage value, storage space, and inspection.

Product handling. Management has identified the number of pounds of product handled as an appropriate governing factor for product handling costs. Average costs per pound are:

Average variable costs .... $0.05 a pound
Average attributable (divisible) fixed cost .... 0.015 a pound

Estimates of the number of pounds of materials handled in a year are shown in the first column of the following table, while the second and third columns reflect the multiplication of these numbers by the average cost figures:

	Number of Pounds	Variable Costs	Attributable Fixed Costs
Line A	2,000,000	$100,000	$30,000
Line B	400,000	20,000	6,000
Line C	300,000	15,000	4,500

Because our estimates are based on the concept of attributable cost and because supervisory costs identifiable with the product handling function are not divisible, these assignments of costs to segments include no supervisory costs. Remember once again that our purpose is to estimate the consequences of serving a segment, not to distribute functional costs.

Storage value. Our illustrative company divides the costs of carrying inventories into two groups: those determined by the value of the inventory and those determined by the amount of warehouse space set aside for it. Although amounts in both of these categories will change with volume, variations are more likely to relate to changes in planned volume than to changes in actual volume. For this reason, we are classifying the costs of both functions as fixed rather than as variable in the short run.

Management estimates that inventory carrying costs based on the dollar costs of the inventories (*product value*) are now averaging 20 percent of the average current cost of the inventory. Average inventories and cost allocations at this rate are as follows:

	Average Inventory (at current cost)	Attributable Storage Costs at 20 Percent of Inventory Cost
Line A	$300,000	$60,000
Line B	180,000	36,000
Line C	160,000	32,000

This portion of storage costs includes the costs of insuring the inventories and of inventory taxes, as well as the costs of inventory-related spoilage. The largest single component, however, consists of a cost that is unlikely to appear in the factory's cost accounts: this is the cost of interest on the capital required to finance the company's inventories. Since we'll be discussing interest costs in some detail in the next two chapters, we'll do no more here than point out that if a revenue segment requires inventories, these inventories require capital funds that can be obtained only at a cost. This cost should be assigned to the revenue segment in any managerially oriented analysis.

Storage space. The other component of inventory storage cost is the cost of providing space to store the inventories the segment requires. In any short period the amount of storage space is likely to be fixed, but given time the company ordinarily can expand or contract its space commitments. This responsiveness of space commitments to segment requirements should be reflected in attributable cost.

In our illustration, management uses the number of square feet of space required as the governing factor for space costs; the cost of space is $4 a square foot. The three product lines' space requirements and the resulting cost allocations are as follows:

	Warehouse Space Requirements (square feet)	Space Costs Allocated
Line A	50,000	$200,000
Line B	6,500	26,000
Line C	5,000	20,000

Once again we have costs that tie into the factory accounts only imperfectly. The $4 figure represents opportunity cost, not the average internal cost of the company's warehouses. Average internal cost is highly unlikely to measure the opportunity cost of space occupied and almost never should be used for decision purposes.

The figure we use to measure opportunity cost depends on the time horizon of the analysis. For short-run analysis, opportunity cost may even be close to zero. In most cases, however, the analyses we're describing in this chapter have a long-term focus and a current or projected market rate is appropriate.

An alternative to the use of opportunity cost rates is to estimate the cost to the company of providing space on a continuing basis in the future. This will include depreciation, property taxes, and insurance calculated on the basis of the replacement cost of storage facilities rather than their historical cost. Annual depreciation isn't a cash flow, of course, but an ongoing operation requires periodic expenditures to maintain capacity. Depreciation calculated on a replacement cost basis is likely to be an adequate approximation of the average annual cash flow requirement unless the problem calls for the techniques of capital expenditure analysis we'll describe in Chapter 18.

Inspection.   The fourth product-related function is inspection. A sample of each batch of products is inspected upon arrival in the warehouse and upon withdrawal for shipment to customers. Product inspection is performed partly by full-time salaried inspectors and partly by other company personnel assigned part-time to this function. The part-timers provide the flexibility to vary the size of the work force as the work load varies. As a result, management classifies inspection as a variable cost, averaging $10 an inspection hour. Estimated inspection times and the cost allocations are as follows:

	Number of Inspection Hours	Allocated Inspection Cost
Line A	10,000	$100,000
Line B	1,000	10,000
Line C	1,250	12,500

Customer-related service costs

Before completing our illustration, we should point out that we haven't included the costs of any customer-related service functions, such as order processing, billing, and customer bookkeeping. The amount of these costs is determined by such customer characteristics as the number of orders per year. These costs should be included in product-line analysis only if clear relationships between functional activities and product-related governing factors can be found.

For example, do buyers of line A place fewer orders per year than buyers of line B or line C? If so, then differences in order-processing costs should be reflected in the analysis.

Nontraceable programmed costs

Our final set of costs are the costs of programmed activities that can't be traced explicitly to individual segments. The major nontraceable programmed costs in most situations are the costs of the field sales force, $200,000 for our illustrative company. The simplest way to allocate these costs is in proportion to some segment-related variable, such as the number of sales orders received or the amount of time the sales force devotes to each segment. Unfortunately, as we have said before, allocations of this kind are extremely unlikely to measure the costs the company could avoid if it withdrew from the segment. Even if time records were perfect, we'd still have to face the fact that the sales force ordinarily spends much of its time on activities that are common

Exhibit 16–4 Product-line profit forecasts

	Product Line A		Product Line B		Product Line C	
	Amount	Percent	Amount	Percent	Amount	Percent
Sales revenues	$1,200,000	100.0	$900,000	100.0	$950,000	100.0
Variable product costs:						
Factory	500,000	41.7	450,000	50.0	350,000	36.8
Product handling	100,000	8.3	20,000	2.2	15,000	1.6
Inspection	100,000	8.3	10,000	1.1	12,500	1.3
Sales commissions	12,000	1.0	9,000	1.0	9,500	1.0
Total variable product cost	712,000	59.3	489,000	54.3	387,000	40.7
Contribution margin	488,000	40.7	411,000	45.7	563,000	59.3
Attributable fixed costs:						
Factory	50,000		30,000		—	
Product management	23,000		21,000		22,000	
Samples and brochures	8,000		7,000		10,500	
Product handling	30,000		6,000		4,500	
Storage value	60,000		36,000		32,000	
Storage space	200,000		26,000		20,000	
Total attributable fixed cost	371,000	30.9	126,000	14.0	89,000	9.4
Product contribution	$ 117,000	9.8	$285,000	31.7	$474,000	49.9

to two or more product lines—e.g., traveling, waiting to see customers, and collecting market data. Even the time spent talking to individual customers may not be product-traceable if the sales people are able to discuss two or more products in the same sales presentation.

Meaningful allocations of programmed costs can be made if management is willing and able to get away from the historical averages and use its judgment to approximate attributable cost. Failing that, the best solution is to leave the costs of field selling unallocated for decision purposes, measuring product-line profit on a profit contribution basis.

The profitability estimates in Exhibit 16–4 reflect this latter approach. This exhibit, incidentally, maintains the distinction between variable costs and attributable fixed costs. Since segment profitability analysis usually has a long-term focus, this distinction is relatively unimportant, but we have included it here for consistency with our presentations in earlier chapters.

Consistency with incremental approach

If carried out as described here, product cost analysis is in no sense inconsistent with the incremental approach to decision making advocated in preceding chapters. The methods outlined in this chapter are designed to get better data on cost increments. The introduction of attributable cost figures is intended to serve the purposes for which many accountants have computed full cost in the past, but for which full cost figures are inappropriate.

No one should pretend that this approach contains the magic formula that will automatically produce the right cost for every situation. Routine cost analysis of this sort is always a substitute for a detailed item-by-item estimate of incremental cost, and is almost inevitably inferior to the latter.

The advantage of the attributable cost figures is that they can be prepared in advance and at less cost than custom-tailored estimates. In a medium-sized office with 20 cost centers and 10 cost elements, in each, for example, 200 separate estimates would have to be made for each decision, and this would be prohibitively expensive. What routine cost analysis does is provide a reasonable approximation to incremental cost. As long as the analyst avoids the full cost fallacy, this can be accurate enough for the purpose.

Cost analysis by size of order

A product-line classification was chosen as the first illustration of cost analysis of nonmanufacturing activities because product-line analysis was already familiar from earlier chapters. In a sense, it was a poor starting point, however, because most problems calling for distribution cost analysis relate to some dimension of the customer mix.

One important form of customer-related analysis is the estimation of the costs of handling orders of different sizes. This "unit of sale" analysis can be used by management in such matters as setting minimum order sizes, establishing a quantity discount structure, or altering methods of promoting and distributing products to small-order customers.

Basic method

Estimates of the costs of handling orders of different sizes can be obtained from the functional cost totals, derived by the methods described earlier. Every functional cost element which has a governing factor that depends on the number, size, or other dimension of customer orders is germane to the analysis. Other items should be rigorously excluded. The cost of writing a customer invoice, for example, is clearly an order-related cost; the salary of the marketing vice president just as clearly is not.

A thorough example would have so many cost elements that a whole chapter would be required to discuss it. To illustrate the method, however, let us assume that functional cost analyses have revealed the following unit cost totals:

Governing Factor	Unit Cost
Number of orders	$1.00 per order
Value of orders	0.001 per dollar
Number of product units ordered	0.03 per unit
Number of order lines	0.01 per line

This table, of course, represents the summation of all of the functional cost elements governed by each of the factors listed; a full example would have to list each function separately.

The next step is to find out how many units of each of these governing factors are associated with orders of various sizes. For example, a sample of orders might yield the following statistics:

Order Size	Number of Governing Factor Units			
	Orders	Order Value	Product Units	Order Lines
$ 1–$ 99	50,000	$ 1,000,000	200,000	100,000
100– 199	20,000	2,600,000	500,000	60,000
200– 499	20,000	5,600,000	1,100,000	80,000
500 and up	10,000	6,000,000	1,200,000	50,000
Total	100,000	$15,200,000	3,000,000	290,000

Because the question in this case is how much it costs to obtain and service an order, these statistics next should be restated as averages, as follows:

Order Size	Average Number of Governing Factor Units per Order			
	Orders	Order Value	Product Units	Order lines
$ 1–$ 99	1	$ 20	4	2.0
100– 199	1	130	25	3.0
200– 499	1	280	55	4.0
500 and up	1	600	120	5.0
Average	1	$152	30	2.9

The final step is to multiply these statistics by the unit cost figures cited earlier. The end result is the unit cost of an order, as summarized below:

Order Size	Each Order	Costs Attributed to Value of the Order	Number of Units in Order	Number of Order Lines	Total Cost per Order
$ 1–$ 99	$1.00	$0.02	$0.12	$0.02	$1.16
100– 199	1.00	0.13	0.75	0.03	1.91
200– 499	1.00	0.28	1.65	0.04	2.97
500 and up	1.00	0.60	3.60	0.05	5.25
Average........	$1.00	$0.152	$0.90	$0.029	$2.08

Orders that contribute less product contribution margin or attributable profit than the amounts shown in the right-hand column are not covering their costs.

In practice, this analysis could be further simplified by consolidating two or more governing factors that are highly correlated. In this example, for instance, the number of units in each order correlated very closely with the value of the order. This can be checked by computing average value per unit, which in this case is virtually constant. Another simplification would be to omit insignificant variables, in this case the number of order lines.

The quantity discount problem

The preceding analysis could serve as a basis for the establishment of a quantity discount schedule. From an economic point of view, the quantity discount structure is a means of discriminating among different segments of the market to obtain a greater total revenue from a given physical sales volume than could be derived from a one-price policy.

Public policy in the United States has been to discourage systematic discrimination of this sort in manufacturing industries, principally through the provisions of the Robinson-Patman Act. The Robinson-Patman Act was enacted by the U.S. Congress in 1936 and is enforced by the Federal Trade Commission. It prohibits quoting different prices to different customers who compete with each other, if interstate commerce is affected. A seller accused of violating the Robinson-Patman Act has five possible defenses:

1. Interstate commerce is not affected.
2. Competition is not affected.
3. Quoting a lower price to one customer than to another is necessary to meet an equally low price quoted by a competitor.
4. The products sold at different prices are very different from each other.
5. The price difference is fully justified by differences in the cost of serving the different customers.

The fifth of these is known as the cost justification defense. Although it can be applied to any kind of price differential, it has been used most often in attempts to defend published discount schedules for purchases in quantities larger than some minimum amount. To illustrate briefly how cost data might be used in justifying quantity discounts, suppose that the company in the previous illustration has offered quantity discounts as follows:

Size of Order	Discount
$ 1–$ 99	None
100– 199	3%
200– 499	5
500 and up	7

If this structure is to be justified, the cost differential per dollar of order value must be at least as great as the percentages indicated. In other words, if it costs 10 percent less per order dollar to process a $600 order than to process a $20 order, then any discount of 10 percent or less is justifiable on a cost basis. The computed cost differentials in this example are:

	(1)	(2)	(3)	(4)
			Average Cost	Cost Differen-
	Average	Average	per Order	tial from
	Order	Cost per	Dollar	Base Class
Order Size	Value	Order	(2) ÷ (1)	$0.0580 − (3)
$ 1–$ 99	$ 20	$1.16	$0.0580	—
100– 199	130	1.91	0.0147	$0.0433
200– 499	280	2.97	0.0106	0.0474
500 and up	600	5.25	0.0088	0.0492

This table shows that the 3 percent discount offered to customers purchasing in $100–$199 quantities is more than justified by the cost savings attributable to these orders ($0.0580 − $0.0147 = $0.0433, or 4.33 percent of the amount of the order at list prices). The discounts offered to customers buying in larger quantities cannot be justified in this way, however. The 5 percent discount offered to the third class of invoices is 0.26 of a percentage point greater than the cost differential ($0.0580 − $0.0106 = $0.0474, or 4.74 percent), and the gap is even wider in the case of the top discount category.

A moment's reflection will indicate that these cost differentials per order dollar are not created by those functional cost elements that vary directly with order dollars. These average 60 cents for a $600 order and 2 cents for a $20 order, or 0.1 cent per order dollar in both cases. In more general terms, *the costs that are relevant to the quantity discount structure are those that are order-related but do not vary proportionately with the size of the order.* When order size is measured in dollars, the relevant costs are those that do not vary in proportion to the dollar value of the individual order but do vary with the number of orders or order elements.

Calculations of the costs of processing orders should measure the attributable costs of orders of different sizes if the figures are to be used by management in making order size decisions. The Federal Trade Commission, however, accepts only full-cost calculations for Robinson-Patman purposes. If $1 is the attributable cost of processing an order, full cost might be $1.05 or $1.25. Full-cost order-size differentials are likely to be slightly greater than attributable cost differentials.

Exclusion of manufacturing cost differentials

No mention has been made thus far of possible differentials in manufacturing costs for orders of different sizes. The reason is that in most cases manufacturing cost per unit is a function of the total volume of production rather than of the volume generated by any one order.

For example, suppose a company usually sells its products in batches of 50 units each. It is considering offering a discount to anyone ordering the product in batches of 100 units. It has the following estimates of manufacturing costs:

Size of Batch	Total Cost	Unit Cost
50	$ 6,000	$120
100	10,000	100

These figures seem to support a discount of up to $20 for the larger order, because a batch of 100 units can be manufactured for an average of $20 a unit less than a batch of 50 units.

This analysis would be valid if each customer's order were always produced separately. If this is not the case, then two customer orders for 50 units each could be combined; they, too, would then enjoy the $100 average cost.

Manufacturing cost differentials can be relevant to the quantity discount question, if the Robinson-Patman Act doesn't apply. The question is a different one, however. The question is whether the incremental costs of serving a larger *total* volume are smaller than the price differential that must be granted to large customers to get their business.

Suppose the total business of customers buying in batches larger than 50 units amounts to 400 units a month. Without a $10 discount these customers won't buy. The total business of the company's smaller customers amounts to 600 units a month. The relevant cost figures are:

	(1) Monthly Volume	(2) Monthly Cost	(3) Unit Cost (2) ÷ (1)
Without discounts	600	$48,000	$80.00
With quantity discounts	1,000	75,000	75.00
Difference	400	$27,000	$67.50

This shows that the differential manufacturing cost of selling the large orders is only $67.50; this is $12.50 less than the average manufacturing cost of filling the small orders. On commerical grounds, therefore, it can be argued that a $10 discount is justified.

This is a correct analysis, but *it has nothing to do with order size.* The real question is what has to be done to keep enough price-sensitive orders coming in to keep the order level at 1,000 units a month. The analysis so far has treated the larger orders as the marginal orders, the ones to which the lower

Exhibit 16–5 Effect of order-ranking on attribution of incremental costs

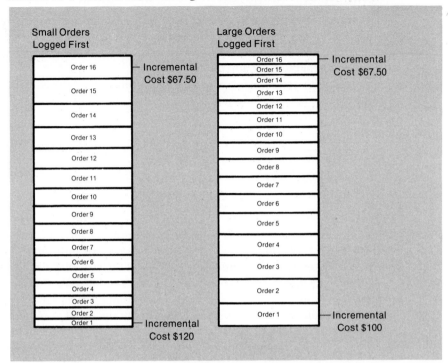

incremental costs should be assigned, as in the left-hand diagram in Exhibit 16–5. We could just as well array the orders with the little orders on top, as in the right-hand diagram, or in any other sequence. In other words, the $67.50 cost figure really applies to *each* order in the house because each can be considered the marginal order. Robinson-Patman considerations aside, any customers who have to be given a $10 discount to keep their orders coming in should get it. For any order that will come in without a discount, management has no reason to give one.

Applications in service businesses

Many service businesses carry out their end-product activities much as the manufacturing business carries out its internal service activities: each cost center provides more than one kind of service; individual service batches are either too small to make job order costing feasible or too similar to make it worthwhile. It shouldn't be surprising to find, therefore, that the methods we have been describing in this chapter have also been found useful in service businesses. Two brief illustrations should demonstrate the similarities.[1]

---

[1] For other examples, see John Dearden, "Cost Accounting Comes to Service Industries," *Harvard Business Review,* September–October 1978, pp. 132–40.

Commercial banking

One of the most familiar service businesses is the commercial bank. The costs of servicing a checking account depend on the number of deposits, the number of checks written, and the complexity of the statements issued to the depositor. The bank usually asks the depositor to pay for these services, either directly or by maintaining a large balance in the account at all times.

The functions related to depositors' accounts can be classified into two groups:

1. One-time functions—opening and closing accounts, handling stop-payment orders, etc.
2. Continuing functions—accepting deposits, cashing checks, transferring funds, insuring deposits, issuing statements, etc.

The costs of each function can be related to one or more governing factors or work units. By identifying the amount of each governing factor arising from a given class of depositors, the bank's management can identify cost-price relationships that are out of line. It can then take whatever action it deems appropriate.

Intercity trucking

Transportation businesses often have highly complex cost structures. The most extreme example is the U.S. Postal Service, with hundreds of thousands of employees, millions of shipping and destination points, tens of thousands of processing and transfer points. The costing problem is staggering.

The problems faced by a typical intercity trucking company are similar, but somewhat simpler. Exhibit 16–6 is a simplified diagram of the flow of

Exhibit 16–6 Flows of shipments in intercity trucking

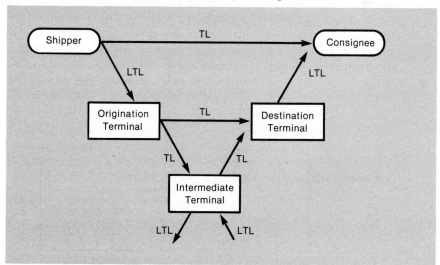

TL = truckload shipments.
LTL = less-than-truckload shipments.

trucking services in one such firm. In this firm shipments big enough to preempt a truck's full capacity are loaded at the shipper's premises and delivered directly to the consignee. Other shipments are consolidated in the origination terminal into truckload lots. Some of these are trucked directly to a destination terminal; others are taken to an intermediate terminal for reloading and reshipment.

Management's main interest in costing centers on questions such as the profitability of individual traffic lanes (e.g., New York to Cleveland, Houston to Denver), the profitability of shipments of different sizes, the profitability of shipments going different distances, and the productivity of different responsibility centers within the organization. The main functional groupings are pickup and delivery, platform operations, line-haul, and billing and collecting. The costs of the various functions can be assigned to revenue segments by the techniques described in this chapter or by statistical regression analysis, described in Chapter 20.

Summary

Job order and process costing are often too expensive to use in costing marketing and service activities. When this is true, the accountant can use another technique, functional and segment cost analysis. This is still not cheap, even with the computer, but it can be used to develop cost estimates at lower cost than would otherwise be possible.

The costs of a marketing or service function are measured in two stages. The first stage is to identify any costs traceable to the function; the second is to use engineering techniques or managerial judgment to identify any other costs attributable to the function.

Although functional costs are useful in themselves, they also enter into the calculation of the costs attributable to individual marketing segments. To make these calculations, the accountant has to relate functional costs to measures of the forces leading to functional costs. These measures are referred to as governing factors. The costs of service functions assignable to a marketing segment are then obtained by multiplying the unit costs of service functions by estimates of the number of each governing factor associated with that segment.

The governing factors for programmed activities in marketing cannot be used to assign the costs of these activities to segments, however. Marketing costs, in particular, are difficult to assign to segments unless they can be traced directly to them. All allocations should reflect the concept of attributable cost, and this provides for leaving some costs in a common, unallocated pool. Only in this way will segment cost have the meaning attributed to it.

Independent study problems (solutions in Appendix B)

1. **Assigning functional costs to order-size segments.** The Angel Meat Company has studied its selling and administrative expenses to determine the costs attributable to individual functions. A study of the costs attributable to individual responsive functions shows that most of them are likely to vary, in time, with one of the

following three indicators of sales volume: (1) number of orders; (2) number of items; and (3) number of hundredweights. Classification of expenses on these bases yields the following monthly totals:

	Packing	Delivery	Administrative	Total
Fixed and indivisible	$ 3,000	$ 6,000	$30,000	$ 39,000
Variable according to:				
Number of orders	4,000	23,400	1,200	28,600
Number of items	5,000	11,600	1,400	18,000
Number of hundredweight	6,800	10,000	2,400	19,200
Total	$18,800	$51,000	$35,000	$104,800

Selling costs amount to $92,000 a month. Selling effort is directed toward customer groups in proportion to their perceived sales potentials, but the correlation between actual and potential sales is far from perfect.

Analysis of orders received during the analysis period shows the following data:

Size of Order (pounds)	Orders	Items	Total Cwt.	Sales
Less than 50	56,000	81,800	14,000	$160,000
50–199	58,000	168,200	52,200	340,000
200–499	12,000	45,600	37,200	100,000
500–999	8,000	48,000	56,000	90,000
1,000 and over	2,000	16,400	20,600	40,000
All orders	136,000	360,000	180,000	$730,000

Required:

a. Calculate the amount of selling and administrative expense attributable to orders in each size class, expressed as an average per hundredweight. (Round to the nearest tenth of a cent.)

b. Which factors account for the class-to-class differences in unit costs? What is their common characteristic?

2. **Segment cost analysis: Sales regions.**   Blandish Mills, Inc., manufactures and sells three products. Its market is divided into three sales regions for which the following monthly data are typical:

Orders:	Region A	Region B	Region C
Number of orders	800	900	1,500
Number of units:			
Product X	2,000	1,000	10,000
Product Y	8,000	14,000	7,000
Product Z	5,000	5,000	10,000
Shipments (pounds)	25,000	30,000	55,000
Number of customers	2,000	2,200	3,000
Number of new customers	50	55	100
Number of employees	15	16	20
Sales discounts and allowances	$ 1,000	$ 2,000	$ 4,000
Sales salaries	5,000	6,000	8,000
Sales travel expense	3,000	3,000	2,000
Regional office expenses	4,000	4,500	5,000

Factory cost, selling price, and sales commissions on each of the three products are:

	Selling Price	Standard Factory Cost	Sales Commissions
Product X	$ 5	$4	$0.25
Product Y	10	6	0.50
Product Z	2	1	0.10

Customer defaults ("bad debts") are expected to average one half of 1 percent of gross sales.

Variable factory costs represent 75 percent of total factory cost at normal volume. Sixty percent of the fixed factory costs are reasonably divisible.

Unit costs have been developed for a number of the activities performed in the head office, as follows:

Payroll	$12.00 per employee per month
Order processing	2.40 per order
Packing and shipping	0.06 per pound
Credit review	24.00 per new customer
Cashier	0.50 per customer
General accounting	0.70 per customer

These unit costs represent cost elements that are almost entirely fixed in the short run but are divisible and thus variable in response to large changes in volume. They do not include highly indivisible costs such as space rental.

Divisional and corporate expenses, other than those already listed, are as follows in a typical month:

Marketing division management salaries	$10,000
Freight and delivery	6,050
Advertising.................................	8,000
Other marketing division expenses	12,000
Corporate management expenses	20,000

Marketing division management consists of the division manager ($3,000 a month), a director of market research ($2,000), a staff assistant ($1,400), and three secretaries. The division manager and staff assistant spend about half of their time in general analytical and policy work, one quarter in region C, and the remainder divided equally between the other two regions. The director of market research does no work on a regional basis.

Freight and delivery costs amount to 8 cents a pound in regions A and B and 3 cents a pound in region C.

Advertising costs consist of $5,000 in national media and $1,000 in local media in each of the sales regions.

Other marketing division expenses consist of office rent, executive travel expense, office supplies, utilities, computer rentals, and so forth.

Corporate management expenses consist of salaries and expenses of the company's president and corporate staffs, depreciation, taxes and insurance on the headquarters building, and similar charges.

Required:

Prepare a statement that will best indicate the relative profitability of the three sales regions. Think carefully about how you want to handle fixed factory costs and the costs of marketing and corporate management.

Exercises and problems

3. **Order-size segments.** Investigation in Carswell Company has identified the following cost relationships:

Order processing . . . . $5.00 per order
Picking and packing . . . .   0.50 per order
Delivery . . . . $\begin{cases} 8.00 \text{ per order} \\ 0.60 \text{ per item} \end{cases}$

An analysis of customer orders during the past year has revealed the following distribution:

Size of Order	Orders	Items	Sales Revenues	Cost of Goods Sold
Less than $25	35,000	75,000	$ 400,000	$ 240,000
$ 25–$ 99	25,000	100,000	540,000	320,000
$100–$199	15,000	130,000	680,000	430,000
$200–$499	10,000	250,000	1,400,000	800,000
$500 and more	5,000	200,000	1,200,000	700,000
Total	90,000	755,000	$4,220,000	$2,490,000

Required:

a. Calculate the amount of order processing, picking and packing, and delivery costs assignable to individual order-size segments.
b. Calculate the average profitability of an order in each order-size segment. What conclusions might you draw from this analysis?
c. Cost of goods sold is assigned to order-size segments in this problem on the basis of the items actually shipped on orders in each segment. What assumption underlies this practice? What is the main alternative and when would you adopt it?

4. **Manufacturing and selling cost differentials.** Saddle Company manufactures a narrow line of products which it sells through a network of wholesale distributors. All products are sold to customers in all size groups and an effort is made to keep all items in stock, to enable the company to fill orders promptly. As order volume picks up, the average length of production run is increased; as volume falls, production runs are shortened.

The company estimates the costs of serving its customers are distributed as follows:

Size of Order (standard direct labor hours required)	Manufacturing Set-up Cost per Standard Direct Labor Hour	Order Processing Cost per Standard Direct Labor Hour	Selling Cost per Standard Direct Labor Hour	Total Cost per Standard Direct Labor Hour
1–100	$12	$0.68	$1.00	$13.68
101–200	4	0.56	0.25	4.81
200 and more . .	2	0.53	0.09	2.62

Manufacturing set-up costs amount to about $600 for each equipment change-over. Order processing costs amount to $9 an order plus variable costs which vary with various factors but which have an overall rate of variability of about 50 cents a standard direct labor hour. Selling costs average $25 a call; the amounts allocated to individual order-size segments are based on the average number of calls made to customers in each order-size group.

Management has proposed developing a quantity discount schedule based on these figures.

Required:

a. To what extent are the unit cost differentials likely to be useful in justifying the discount schedule to interested outsiders? Explain your reasoning.
b. To what extent are these unit cost figures likely to be useful to management in evaluating the profitability of its efforts to serve customers in different

size classes? Explain any differences between your answer here and your answer to (a).

5. **Assigning functional costs to sales territories.** The Montgomery Company sells its products in three territories. Management has established the following standard administrative expenses to be used in preparing profit and loss statements for each territory:

Credit .... $ 5.00 per new account
Collection .... 10.00 per overdue account
Bookkeeping .... 0.35 per transaction
Stenographic....................... 0.60 per letter
Other clerical .... 1.00 per customer account
Executive salaries .... 0.03 per sales dollar
Other administrative expense .... 0.02 per sales dollar

The following data were recorded for the month of October:

	Territory A	Territory B	Territory C
New accounts	80	140	100
Overdue accounts	50	60	60
Transactions.................	10,000	18,000	16,000
Letters	400	500	600
Customer accounts	500	1,000	800
Sales......................	$200,000	$300,000	$250,000

Required:

a. Compute the amount of head office administration cost per dollar of sales in each territory for the month of October.

b. Comment on the usefulness of the comparison of these costs among territories.

6. **Segment profitability analysis.** Raymond Distributors, Inc., is a major distributor of medical and laboratory equipment and technical supplies to industrial and institutional customers. It does no manufacturing. Its operating costs, other than the cost of goods sold, are classified into five main functional categories: marketing, warehousing, delivery, order processing, and general administrative expenses.

Raymond's management is evaluating the company's programs for marketing its products to its institutional customers—hospitals, nursing homes, universities, and other institutions—accounting for about 35 percent of sales revenue and 40 percent of the cost of goods sold. The purpose of this evaluation is to decide whether changes should be made to increase the profitability of sales to these customers. Management has collected the following data:

	Traceable to		Not Traceable to Any Specific Customer Group
	Institutional Customers	All Other Customers	
Dollar statistics:			
Sales revenues	$6,000,000	$10,000,000	
Cost of goods sold	4,200,000	6,000,000	
Delivery and administrative expenses	600,000	800,000	$ 840,000
Order processing costs			1,100,000
Marketing administration	100,000	200,000	
Sales salaries and travel			810,000
Unit statistics:			
Number of orders	50,000	60,000	
Hours spent by sales force ...	8,000	10,000	18,000

The estimated attributable cost of processing an order is $10. The company's treasurer has suggested allocating the administrative expenses between customer groups on the basis of sales revenues and sales salaries and travel expenses in proportion to sales force hours, but regression analysis has failed to identify clear cost relationships with these variables.

Required:

Prepare an analysis of the profitability of institutional sales for management's use. Explain and justify the basis on which you have assigned costs to the institutional sales segment.

7. **Order-size analysis; engineering approach.** As part of the preparation for its defense in a Robinson-Patman case, C. E. Niehoff & Company conducted a series of time and motion studies of order-processing operations. Seventeen orders of varying sizes were selected for study, and the processing times were obtained for each of these by a time-study engineer. The engineer then added 25 percent to these observed times to allow for personal needs and fatigue. The total processing times, priced at standard wage rates for individual operations, are listed in the table below:

Order Number	Number of Items	Number of Packages	Net Billing	Processing Cost	Cost per Dollar
44524	1	2	$ 12.00	$ 1.1909	9.92¢
44525	6	23	37.66	1.3141	3.49
44576	20	29	45.14	1.9457	4.31
44575	8	49	56.51	2.0506	3.66
45968	33	69	125.20	2.6529	2.11
44572	25	116	134.47	3.2335	2.33
46162	37	171	206.79	3.6094	1.74
44577	36	86	208.64	3.3236	1.59
44573	63	163	223.76	4.7155	2.11
45969	49	110	259.80	3.8108	1.47
45945	56	163	305.01	5.4135	1.77
46161	49	236	341.79	4.4516	1.30
44991	68	391	496.98	7.1486	1.44
45078	81	334	523.22	8.6659	1.66
45301	101	623	785.80	10.7736	1.36
45079	94	598	811.57	11.4696	1.41
44993	89	469	846.66	10.3696	1.23

Source: Herbert F. Taggart, *Cost Justification* (Ann Arbor: University of Michigan, Graduate School of Business Administration, Bureau of Business Research, 1959), p. 408.

Required:

a. On a sheet of graph paper, plot processing costs per dollar of net billing against size of order (measured by net billing) and draw a line of relationship freehand, as accurately as you can.

b. Assuming that these are the best data available, indicate how you would use these figures in: (1) setting a minimum order size; (2) estimating the profitability of different customer groups.

c. Comment on the methods used to obtain the data and their adequacy for the purposes outlined in (b).

8. **Determining functional cost.** The personnel department of Mansdowne Manufacturing Company has the following costs:

Salaries............................	$17,000
Advertising	1,200
Rent..............................	1,000
Postage and supplies	400
Telephone	200
Depreciation	100
Computer services	300
Total	$20,200

Five personnel functions have been identified:

Personnel records.
Recruiting.
Management development.
Labor relations.
Wage and salary administration.

You have the following additional information:

1. The salaries of the Department's 10 employees are classified as follows:

	Number	Total Salaries
Director	1	$ 2,800
Assistant director	1	2,200
Recruiting......................	2	3,600
Labor relations	1	2,400
Personnel records	2	2,000
General clerical	3	4,000
Total	10	$17,000

2. The director has made the following estimates for five employees who work on more than one function:

	Director	Assistant	Clerical
Personnel records....................	—	10%	20%
Recruiting.........................	10%	40	30
Management development.............	50	30	20
Labor relations	10	10	10
Wage and salary administration	30	10	20

3. The director and assistant director have similar skills; they divide the total work of administering the department in the proportions shown in the time distribution.
4. All advertising costs relate to the recruiting function.
5. The department is charged rent for the space it occupies in the company's headquarters building. The rental charge is based on the average cost of owning and operating the building. If the company didn't own the building but had to buy it at today's real estate prices, the annual costs of owning and operating the building would be about 10 percent higher.
6. Comparable space in the building is now being rented to other tenants at $1,500 a month, but a considerable amount of rentable space is now vacant. The amount of work space occupied by individual employees varies only slightly from employee to employee.
7. The director estimates that half of the postage and supplies and half of the telephone charges relate to recruiting; another 20 percent relates to management development; the rest is unidentified.

8. Computer services are 90 percent for personnel records, 10 percent for wage and salary administration.
9. Depreciation is for office furniture and equipment. Average annual replacement expenditures are approximately 20 percent higher than the annual depreciation charge.

Required:

a. Using the time distribution provided and basing your estimates on historical costs, prepare estimates of the costs of each of the five personnel functions. All costs of the personnel department should be distributed to one function or another for this purpose.
b. How would you modify your answer to (*a*) if you were instructed to prepare cost estimates to be used in deciding whether to have individual functions performed by outside contractors on a continuing basis? Explain your treatment of each item.
c. Which of these functions should be allocated to segments for purposes of product-line analysis?

9. **Interpreting service department variances.** A company charges the managers of its three product divisions for head office services, using the following charging rates:

Head Office Department	Charging Rate
Credit department	$ 0.30 per order
Billing department	0.95 per order
Payroll department	2.50 per employee
Accounts receivable department	0.40 per order
General accounting department	0.30 per entry
Treasurer	0.35 per customer remittance
General sales manager	2,000.00 per month to each division
Legal department	3,000.00 per month to each division
Executive management	10,000.00 per month to each division

Statistics for the month of February were as follows:

No. of orders received	3,900
No. of employees	860
No. of entries	9,300
No. of customer remittances	4,600

Head office expenses and volume-adjusted budget allowances for February were:

Department	Actual	Budget
Credit	$ 1,350	$ 1,400
Billing	4,150	4,000
Payroll	2,400	2,200
Accounts receivable	1,730	1,800
General accounting	2,910	2,850
Treasurer	1,680	1,700
General sales manager	5,630	6,000
Legal	6,200	9,000
Executive management	30,400	30,000

Required:

a. Compute the undistributed cost for each head office department for the month of February, and divide it into volume and spending variance components.
b. How would you expect management to respond to large variances in the

head office departments? How, if at all, do they differ from factory overhead variances?

10. **Functional cost analysis; service department.** The print shop in the head office of David Metrics, Inc. was a busy place. David Metrics was a large management consulting firm with headquarters in New York and branch offices in 14 other cities in various parts of the United States. Using several high-speed mimeograph machines, a high-speed copying machine, and a small copier, the print shop staff reproduced a large volume of internal memoranda, working drafts, and reports to the company's clients, and did a significant amount of work for other tenants of the office building in which the company's headquarters were located. No typing was done in the print shop; all mimeograph stencils and master copies for the copying machines were prepared by the departments or outside customers from whom the work orders were received.

Jonathan David, the firm's administrative vice president and brother of the president, felt that the print shop's costs were getting out of hand. "This doesn't tell me much," he said, pointing to the department's cost summary for the preceding month. "I know we've been doing a lot more copying work since we put in the high-speed copier, but I can't believe that one new machine has been responsible for the big cost increases we have had in this department."

Jane Rogers, the office manager in the New York headquarters, agreed to pull together some better figures for Mr. David. With the help of one of the firm's consulting engineers, Ms. Rogers carried out a quick work sampling study of the print shop's machine operators. This study showed that the operators' time was divided in the following proportions:

Operating mimeograph machines	20 percent
Operating copying machines	29
Out of room	10
Telephoning	5
Writing	2
Collating mimeograph work	17
Collating copying work	8
Waiting	6
Wrapping	3

The routine cost report for the print shop during this same period showed the following breakdown:

Supervisor's salary	$ 2,000
Clerical salaries	8,400
Paper and supplies	4,928
Maintenance, mimeograph machines	160
Rentals, copying machines	5,800
Depreciation, mimeograph machines	120
Space charge	480
Total	$21,888

The work load during this period was:

	Mimeograph	Copying
Number of work orders	5,000	20,000
Number of stencils processed	25,000	n.a.
Number of copies made	500,000	58,000

Ms. Rogers pointed out that most writing and telephoning was in connection with inquiries about the status of individual work orders. Virtually all wrapping time was spent on mimeographing work. Wrapping time is a function of the number of copies in the order.

After observing a number of representative operations, Ms. Rogers estimated that paper and supplies for copying work cost about twice as much per copy as the paper and supplies for mimeograph work. Copying machine rentals are based on the number of copies made.

Required:

a. Assuming that these data are typical, prepare costs estimates for each of the two classes of work done in this department, for use in decisions on how much mimeographing and copying work will be given to this department. You should distribute all costs that appear likely to vary in response to major variations in the department's work load.

b. Stencils cost approximately 30 cents each. Adding these costs to those of the print shop itself, calculate the cost of a 50-copy run of a 40-page report (1) by mimeograph machine, and (2) by copier. In either case the finished copies would be wrapped for delivery.

c. How else might Mr. David use the figures derived in (a)?

11. **Product-line analysis.** The Lucky Products Company manufactures and sells a line of electronics components to government contractors, telephone companies, and manufacturers of radio and television receivers and transmitters. Sales for the current year are expected to total $5 million, distributed as follows:

	Government	Telephone	Radio-TV
Sales	$1,200,000	$3,000,000	$800,000
Standard cost of goods sold	1,000,000	2,400,000	500,000
Gross margin	$ 200,000	$ 600,000	$300,000

Concerned by the low margin on its government business, management has initiated a study of the profitability of the three classes of its business. The following information has been collected.

Standard cost is based on the full costing principle. Supplementary variable cost figures indicate the following ratios of variable cost to full cost at standard volume:

Government .... 70 percent
Telephone 75
Radio-television 80

No factory department is devoted solely to any one class of business.

The following amounts of out-of-pocket fixed factory costs could be eliminated each year if one class of business were to be dropped, the others remaining in service:

Government $100,000
Telephone 500,000
Radio-television 200,000

Bookkeeping costs—that is, the costs of inventory record keeping, order receiving and filling, invoicing, accounts receivable bookkeeping, and collecting—total $150,000 a year. These are regarded as fixed, but have increased from year to year in parallel with the increase in the number of invoice lines. A sample of the invoices prepared this year indicates the following numbers of invoice lines for the three classes of business:

Government	4,000
Telephone	6,000
Radio-television	20,000

Warehousing costs amount to $58,000 a year, almost entirely in wages and salaries of warehouse and storeroom personnel. Warehouse costs tend to vary from year to year, roughly in proportion to the standard cost of goods sold to telephone companies and radio-television manufacturers. Government products are transferred immediately to government supply depots and do not enter the Lucky Products warehouse space.

The costs of central administration, including executive salaries, amount to $240,000 a year. These are almost completely unaffected by the volume of business done.

The company's research and development department has operating costs of $100,000 a year. The department consists of two research engineers, three technicians, and a variety of test equipment. The two engineers specialize in different fields, and both provide essential support for all three classes of business.

The costs of field selling total $250,000 a year. None of this is accepted by the government as a cost of the government products, but it includes $50,000 a year to cover the salary and expenses of a sales engineer to work full-time on identifying sales opportunities and preparing bids and proposals in this market. The only other information on these costs is the number of calls made by the other salespeople in the course of a year: 500 on telephone companies and 2,500 on radio-television manufacturers. The sales manager estimates that a call at a telephone company is likely to take about three times as long as a call on a radio-television manufacturer. All the salespeople are paid on a straight salary basis, with no commissions.

Advertising accounts for $100,000 a year. Of this, $70,000 is directed specifically to manufacturers of radio-television equipment and $30,000 is for advertisements in engineering journals read by engineers in all industries.

All of the company's operations are contained in a single building. Fixed costs of providing this space amount to $120,000 a year. These costs are included in factory overhead cost—that is, no space costs are allocated to other company divisions. Space occupancy is as follows:

Executive offices	10 percent
Factory	68
Sales	5
Warehouse	10
Bookkeeping	5
Research and development	2

The location and layout of the building make it virtually impossible to sublet any space that might become idle.

Required:

a. Prepare a revised estimate of profitability for each class of business and explain the methods and assumptions that you used in the process. (Suggestion: start by listing the total cost in each category; then decide how much to allocate to each class of business.)

b. What course(s) of action or further investigation would you suggest on the basis of this information?

12. **District profitability analysis.** The Western Appliances, Ltd. income statement for the year ended December 31, 19x1 appears below:

Sales (1.9 million units)		$3,800,000
Cost of goods sold	$2,280,000	
Bad debts	11,500	2,291,500
Gross profit		1,508,500
Packing and shipping:		
Shipping containers	$ 91,750	
Packing and shipping labor expenses	221,250	
Freight-out	375,750	688,750
Selling expenses (excluding advertising):		
Sales manager's salary	15,200	
Sales representatives' salaries	32,000	
Sales representatives' commissions	24,000	
Agency commissions	30,000	101,200
Advertising:		
Local newspapers	43,500	
National magazines	57,000	100,500
Administrative expenses (fixed)		64,750	966,700
Net operating profit		$ 533,300

The company distributes a single product in a variety of colors. The selling price is $2 a unit.

The product is distributed in four market areas—A, B, C, and D.

District A is the district in which the company's distribution center and offices are located. No salespeople are employed. Orders are received through the mail and by telephone, and customers send their trucks to the distribution center to pick up their orders when ready.

District B is located 100 miles from the distribution center. The company employs four sales representatives in this area, each on a commission basis. The company also places a quarter-page advertisement once each week in the local newspaper.

District C is located 200 miles from the distribution center. The company employs eight sales representatives in the area, each on a salary basis. The company takes one quarter of a page of advertising three times a week in the local paper in district C; the cost per insertion is twice as much as that in district B.

District D is an agency. It is 400 miles distant from the distribution center. The company shares with the agency the cost of a quarter-page weekly advertisement in the local paper on a 1:3 ratio, the space cost being the same as in district B.

The product is packaged in containers of three different sizes: namely, 16s (small), 32s (medium), and 48s (large), and shipments are made in case lots only. It is assumed that each order calls for one case.

Sales and agency commissions are paid on a flat percentage of sales basis.

The following unit costs per case have been determined:

	Small	Medium	Large
Container	$1	$1.50	$2
Packing and shipping labor expenses	3	3.50	4
Freight-out (cost per 100 miles)	2	3.50	5

A statistical analysis of the marketing operation during 19x1 shows the following, in total and by districts:

	Total	A	B	C	D
Number of orders					
Small cases	22,500	2,500	—	20,000	—
Medium cases	30,500	5,000	7,500	15,000	3,000
Large cases	11,750	—	7,500	—	4,250
Estimated bad debts—					
percent of sales		¼ of 1%	⅛ of 1%	⅜ of 1%	½ of 1%

Required:

a. Prepare a set of statements showing the profitability of each sales district. Describe and defend the basis on which costs were assigned to each district.
b. Calculate the total profit attributable to each case size, and from these figures calculate profit per case and per unit in each case size. Describe and defend the basis on which costs were assigned to each size group.
c. It has been proposed that an additional $50,000 a year be spent on local advertising in district C. By how much must the sales volume of the district increase to warrant such an expenditure?

(SMAC, adapted)

13. **Regional profitability analysis.** The Scent Company sells men's toiletries to retail stores throughout the United States. For planning and control purposes the Scent Company is organized into 12 geographic regions with two to six territories within each region. One salesperson is assigned to each territory and has exclusive rights to all sales made in that territory. Merchandise is shipped from the manufacturing plant to the 12 regional warehouses, and the sales in each territory are shipped from the regional warehouse. National headquarters allocates a specific amount at the beginning of the year for regional advertising.

The net sales of the Scent Company for the current year total $10 million. Costs incurred by national headquarters for national administration, advertising and warehousing are summarized as follows:

National administration	$250,000
National advertising	125,000
National warehousing	175,000
	$550,000

The results of operations for the South Atlantic Region for the current year are presented below:

Net sales		$900,000
Deductions:		
Advertising	$ 54,700	
Bad debts	3,600	
Cost of goods sold	460,000	
Freight out	22,600	
Insurance	10,000	
Salaries and employee benefits ...	81,600	
Sales commissions	36,000	
Supplies	12,000	
Travel and entertainment	14,100	
Wages and employee benefits	36,000	
Warehouse depreciation	8,000	
Warehouse operating costs	15,000	
Total deductions		753,600
Regional contribution		$146,400

The South Atlantic Region consists of two territories—Green and Purple. The following cost analyses and statistics for the current year are representative of past experience and are representative of expected future operations:

	Green	Purple	Total
Sales	$300,000	$600,000	$900,000
Cost of goods sold	184,000	276,000	460,000
Advertising	21,800	32,900	54,700
Travel and entertainment	6,300	7,800	14,100
Freight out	9,000	13,600	22,600
Units sold	150,000	350,000	500,000
Pounds shipped	210,000	390,000	600,000
Sales force miles traveled	21,600	38,400	60,000

Other information on the items in the statement of operations:

1. Bad debts have averaged 0.4 percent of net sales in the past.
2. 30 percent of the insurance is for protection of the inventory while it is in the regional warehouse; the remainder is on the warehouse itself.
3. Salaries and employee benefits consist of the following items:

Regional vice president	$24,000
Regional marketing manager	15,000
Regional warehouse manager	13,400
Salespeople (one for each territory with each receiving the same base salary)	15,600
Employee benefits (20 percent)	13,600
	$81,600

4. Each sales representative receives a base salary [item (3) above] plus a 4 percent commission on all items sold in the territory. No employee benefit costs arise in connection with sales commissions.
5. Supplies are used in the warehouse for packing the merchandise that is shipped.
6. Travel and entertainment costs are incurred by the salespeople calling on their customers.
7. Wages and employee benefits relate to the hourly paid employees who fill orders in the warehouse.
8. The warehouse operating costs cover heat, light, maintenance, and so forth.

Required:

a. Prepare a cost schedule for the South Atlantic Region, separating the operating costs into the fixed and variable components of order-getting, order-filling, and administration, using the following format:

	Territory Costs		Regional	Total
	Green	Purple	Costs	Costs
Order-getting				
Order-filling				
Administration ...				

b. Suppose top management is considering splitting the Purple territory into two separate territories (Red and Blue). Which of the data supplied would be relevant to this decision? What other data would you collect to aid top management in this decision?
c. If Scent Company keeps its records in accordance with the classifications required in (a), can standards and flexible budgets be used in planning and controlling marketing costs?

(CMA, adapted)

Case 16–1: Robson, Ltd.* (profitability of small orders)

"Sorry to be late, John," Alan Thurston said. "I had a customer in my office and I just couldn't get rid of him."

"That's okay, Alan. I just got here myself. I hope you made a big sale."

"No such luck. I'll bet this customer has never done more than $100 worth of business with us and yet he sat in my office asking questions for an hour. We have too many customers like him."

Mr. Thurston was the sales manager of Robson, Ltd., a small Australian manufacturer of industrial supplies. He made the statement quoted above as he sat down to lunch with Mr. John Axelson, the company's controller. After they had ordered their lunch, Mr. Thurston returned to the subject. "I know how my sales stack up," he said, "but I have no idea how much money we make on the big customers or how much we lose on the little ones. Could you put some figures together for me on this?"

"I can't get at it myself right now," said Mr. Axelson, "but why don't we put Peter on it? It would be good experience for him and I don't have anything else important for him to do at the moment." Peter Halford was Mr. Thurston's nephew and was working at Robson, Ltd. during his summer holidays from the university. This was his second summer with Robson, and Mr. Axelson felt that he knew enough about the company to be able to get the figures Mr. Thurston wanted.

Mr. Halford first collected the statistics shown in Table 1. He started by classifying all the company's customers and active prospects on the basis of the total amount of business they had done with Robson in the last complete fiscal year. At one extreme, he found that 46 customers had bought more than $10,000 each during the previous year, while 1,872 customers and prospects (all referred to by the company as "customers") had bought absolutely nothing.

Table 1 Customer statistics

	Group					
	A	**B**	**C**	**D**	**E**	**F**
Annual sales to each customer	$ 10,000 or more	$ 2,000– $ 9,999	$ 1,000– $ 1,999	$ 200– $ 999	$1–$199	$0
Total annual sales	$800,000	$500,000	$300,000	$200,000	$200,000	—
Total gross margin	160,000	110,000	75,000	48,000	49,000	—
Total variable manufac- turing profit	280,000	190,000	120,000	79,000	81,000	—
Number of customers	46	117	234	420	2,521	1,872
Sales calls per year	230	585	940	1,680	4,575	3,740
Customer orders per year	700	800	1,000	2,000	5,000	—
Average sales per customer	$ 17,391	$ 4,274	$ 1,282	$ 476	$ 79	—
Average sales per order	1,143	625	300	100	40	—

Fortunately for Mr. Halford, the company's sales records were quite complete, and he was able to identify the gross margin (sales minus the cost of goods sold) for each customer. As a result of some work he had been doing that summer, he was also able to make an estimate of the variable component of the cost of goods sold, and this permitted him to assemble the set of figures identified in Table 1 as "total variable manufacturing profit" (sales minus variable manufacturing cost of goods sold). The profit-sales ratios varied slightly from group to group, mainly because of differences in the discounts granted to different customers.

The statistics on sales calls and customer orders were readily available in the files, although Mr. Halford had to work fairly hard to dig them out.

Next Mr. Halford turned to the task of identifying the cost of serving individual customers. At his request, Mr. Thurston got all of his salespeople to keep a record of their time for one week. This showed the following breakdown:

Call time (waiting for and talking to customers)	50%
Travel time	30
Office time (preparing reports, following up on orders, etc.) . .	20
Total	100%

The 10-person sales force was organized regionally, the individual representatives having their own sales territories. Some territories were relatively compact, while others required a good deal of traveling. Each representative was responsible for promoting all of the company's products.

Mr. Halford summarized the annual costs of the sales department and computed the average cost per sales call, as follows:

	Amount	Per Call
Sales supervision	$ 18,800	$ 1.60
Sales salaries and benefits	122,200	10.40
Clerical salaries	8,460	0.72
Sales travel	79,900	6.80
Customer entertainment	14,100	1.20
Samples	7,050	0.60
Rent	2,350	0.20
Other	2,820	0.24
Total	$255,680	$21.76

This was the estimated cost of the sales department for the current year. The only omission was $4,230 of clerical salaries which Mr. Halford excluded from the total above on the basis of Mr. Thurston's estimate that the office staff devoted only two thirds of its time to matters related to the sales force (typing expense accounts, preparing payrolls, etc.). The remaining one third of office clerical time was spent processing customer orders and thus should not be included in the cost per call figures. Instead, Mr. Halford included this amount in a rough estimate of the clerical cost of processing an order. Orders came both through the sales force and directly from the customers, by mail or telephone. The office procedure was the same in either case and Mr. Halford estimated that the total cost of clerical salaries and benefits averaged about $2.40 an order. He thought that he could get a more accurate figure if he tried, but he didn't

Table 2 Statement of customer profitability

	Groups					
	A	**B**	**C**	**D**	**E**	**F**
Selling costs (number of calls × $21.76)	$ 5,005	$ 12,730	$20,454	$36,557	$ 99,552	$ 81,382
Order-filling costs (number of orders × $2.40)	1,680	1,920	2,400	4,800	12,000	—
Total expense	6,685	14,650	22,854	41,357	111,552	81,382
Excess of gross margin over expense	153,315	95,350	52,146	6,643	(62,552)	(81,382)
Excess of variable manufac-turing profit over expense	273,315	175,350	97,146	37,643	(30,552)	(81,382)

have enough time to study the costs of other items such as depreciation on office equipment, office supplies, and office rent.

On the basis of these figures, Mr. Halford prepared the analysis of customer profitability shown in Table 2. "This will really make Uncle Alan sit up and take notice," he said. "Even on the most favorable calculation, we still lose $30,000 a year on our small customers and pour more than $80,000 down the drain on customers who don't buy anything at all. I'll bet he changes his sales policy now." He walked confidently toward Mr. Axelson's office to show him the results of the analysis.

Do these data mean that Robson, Ltd. would be able to increase its profits by discontinuing sales calls on the customers in groups E and F? Indicate how you would interpret the data. Also describe any changes in analytical method that you would recommend. Remember that this is a small company and that Mr. Halford had only a few weeks, at most, to study this problem.

17 Short-run optimization models

In deciding how to use the resources available to it, management generally uses *decision models,* either explicitly or implicitly. A decision model is a description of the relationships presumed to exist between the possible courses of action and the other variables in the real situation the model represents, together with a set of rules and procedures to be used in comparing alternatives and developing a recommended course of action.

We used very simple decision models in earlier chapters to illustrate management's uses of accounting information. The purpose of this chapter is to explain two slightly more complicated models and describe the data they call for. The two models are:

1. Linear programming, for rationing capacity when two or more resources are scarce.
2. An inventory decision model, for setting the inventory level and the size of production or purchase orders.

We'll begin by demonstrating the logic of linear programming in the context of a trial-and-error procedure for allocating scarce resources.

Rationing capacity: A trial-and-error solution

The question in linear programming is how to allocate two or more scarce resources among various possible uses. We'll assume in this section that the decision rule is to adopt the pattern of resource uses that promises to generate the greatest profit contribution. We'll use a three-step procedure:

1. Estimate the relationships among the various variables.
2. Estimate the results to be achieved by one possible resource allocation pattern.
3. Try other possible patterns until no further improvement of results can be found.

Estimating the relationships

Three sets of relationships must be estimated in a capacity-rationing situation:

1. The profitability of each of the competing uses of capacity.

2. The amount of capacity each competing use requires.
3. The total amount of capacity available.

For example, a company manufactures two products, each of which is processed in the same two production departments. The company has received more orders than it can fill with its existing facilities and needs to decide how much of each product to produce. Capacity in each department is measured by the number of machine-hours available for production—4,500 hours in department X and 7,500 hours in department Y.

Since the total capacity will remain constant, no matter which solution is chosen, capacity costs will be unaffected by the decision and can be ignored. This means that the profitability of each product can be measured by its contribution margin. The estimated contribution margins and the capacity required per unit are shown in Exhibit 17–1.

Exhibit 17–1 Contribution margin and capacity required

	Product A	Product B
Contribution margin per unit:		
Selling price	$45	$15
Variable costs	35	9
Contribution margin	$10	$ 6
Machine-hours required per unit:		
In department X	4	1
In department Y	2	3
Sales orders (units)	1,000	2,500

The first trial solution

The first step in the analysis is to relate the contribution margin to the amount of capacity required. If one product has a higher contribution margin per unit of capacity in *each* department, then it is clearly preferable to the other. This isn't the case here:

	Product A	Product B
Contribution per hour:		
In department X	$2.50	$6
In department Y	5.00	2

In other words, product A is a more profitable use of department Y's resources than product B, while product B uses department X's resources more profitably than product A does.

These contribution margin figures don't give us much help in deciding which possible solution to try first. One is as logical as another. Fortunately, it doesn't matter—we'll come to the same conclusion no matter where we start. So let's be arbitrary and start by seeing what would happen if the company were to produce as many units of product A as department X is capable of manufacturing. From Exhibit 17–1 we find that one unit of product A requires four hours of machine time in department X. Since department X's capacity is 4,500 hours, it could produce as many as 1,125 units of product A. With each unit of product A requiring 2 hours of time in department Y, this level of production would absorb 2,250 hours of department Y's capacity. The results under this solution would be as follows:

	Units of Output	Capacity Utilized		Contribution Margin
		Dept. X	Dept. Y	
Product A	1,125	4,500	2,250	$11,250
Product B	0	0	0	0
Total		4,500	2,250	$11,250
Capacity available		4,500	7,500	
Idle capacity		0	5,250	

The second trial solution

The first trial solution would leave 5,250 hours of department Y's capacity unused. Product B uses department Y more intensively than product A does. This suggests that the company might find it profitable to shift at least some resources from A to B.

To implement this idea, we might try a second solution in which the company would produce as much of product B as department Y could handle. Since one unit of B requires three hours in department Y (from Exhibit 17–1), this department's capacity would be completely absorbed by 2,500 units of product B:

	Units of Output	Capacity Utilized		Contribution Margin
		Dept. X	Dept. Y	
Product A	0	0	0	0
Product B	2,500	2,500	7,500	$15,000
Total		2,500	7,500	$15,000
Capacity available		4,500	7,500	
Idle capacity		2,000	0	

Product B's contribution margin is $6 a unit, and the total contribution would be $15,000. This is better than the results under the first solution, but this time some of department X's capacity would be idle.

The optimal solution

To see whether any other solution would improve the anticipated results still further, we need to calculate the net gain or loss from reducing the output of product B by one unit, while increasing the output of product A. In this case, reducing product B's output by one unit would release enough capacity in department Y (three hours) to make one and a half units of product A (at two hours a unit). In other words, the company would lose the profit on one unit of B and gain the profit on one and a half units of A:

Gain: $1.5 \times \$10$ $15
Loss: $1.0 \times \$6$ 6
    Net gain .... $ 9

Notice what we have just discovered. When department X is underutilized, management can increase its profits by substituting product A for product B. Similarly, when department Y is underutilized, profit can be increased by substituting product B for product A. This suggests that the optimal solution will be reached when both departments are fully utilized, with capacity allocations somewhere between those in our own trial solutions.

To move from the second solution to the optimal solution, we need to substitute production of product A for production of product B until department X's idle capacity is fully utilized. As we just saw, the company can substitute one and a half units of A for one unit of B without changing the total number of hours used in department Y. Each such substitution uses up five hours of department X's idle capacity:

Added production of A: $1\frac{1}{2} \times 4$ .... 6 hours
Less: Reduced production of B: 1×1 ...... 1 hour
    Net increase in use of department X ..... 5 hours

Because department X had an idle capacity of 2,000 hours in the second trial solution, both departments will be operating at capacity if $2,000/5 = 400$ units of B are subtracted from that solution and product A is manufactured in their place. This will bring production of B down from 2,500 units to 2,100 and will release enough capacity to produce 600 units of A:

	Units Produced	Hours Required		Contribution Margin
		Dept. X	Dept. Y	
Product A	600	2,400	1,200	$ 6,000
Product B	2,100	2,100	6,300	12,600
Total		4,500	7,500	$18,600

Capacity is fully utilized in each department under this solution. Furthermore, the $18,600 total profit contribution is $3,600 greater than in the better of the two trial solutions. The amount of the improvement could have been predicted: The benefit from substituting one and a half units of A for one unit of B was $9, and we made 400 of these substitutions.

Rationing capacity by linear programming

The technique we have just described is a special case of a widely used technique known as linear programming. Linear programming consists of a set of mathematical procedures by which management finds the capacity-occupancy pattern that will maximize or minimize a performance measure that management has selected. In this section we shall see how a formal linear programming technique can be applied to an illustrative capacity-rationing problem. The discussion has five parts:

1. Constructing the program.
2. Solving the problem graphically.

3. Calculating the value of changes in the amount of productive capacity (shadow prices).
4. Using the program in sensitivity analysis.
5. Specifying the accounting data to be used.

Constructing the program

The first step in linear programming is to identify the decision variables, the ones management can influence directly. We have two decision variables in our simple illustration:

A = Number of units of product A to be manufactured and sold.
B = Number of units of product B to be manufactured and sold.

The next step is to identify the relationship between these variables and the measure to be maximized or minimized. This relationship is known as the *objective function,* because it shows the relationship (function, in mathematical terms) between the decision variables and the measuring units in which management expresses its objective. In this case the objective is profit maximization and the objective function is:

$$\text{Total contribution margin} = \$10 \times A + \$6 \times B$$

We can insert fixed costs in this equation or leave them out without affecting the analysis. Since the decision will affect only the number of units of A and B produced, total fixed costs will be the same no matter which solution is chosen. Only the contribution margin will be affected.

The third step in linear programming is to identify the conditions that an acceptable solution must meet. These are referred to as the *constraints.* The constraints in the illustration are:

1. The capacity of department X is 4,500 hours.
2. The capacity of department Y is 7,500 hours.
3. Output of product A cannot be negative.
4. Output of product B cannot be negative.

The first constraint can be expressed mathematically as an inequality—that is, production of the two products must use no more than 4,500 hours in total. Mathematically:

$$\text{Hours used for } A + \text{hours used for } B \leq 4,500$$

Since we know that each unit of product A requires four hours of department X time and each unit of product B requires one hour, we can restate the inequality as follows:

$$4A + 1B \leq 4,500 \tag{1}$$

A similar translation of the capacity constraint for department Y yields the following inequality:

$$2A + 3B \leq 7,500 \tag{2}$$

518

The third and fourth constraints may seem superfluous, but they must be introduced to rule out nonsensical solutions that might otherwise emerge from a mechanistic application of the mathematical problem-solving technique. The mathematical expression of the constraints is as follows:

$$A \geq 0 \qquad (3)$$
$$B \geq 0 \qquad (4)$$

Graphic solution

This problem can be solved by a number of different linear programming techniques. One of these, the graphic method, is the clearest way to show the logic underlying them all. This form of analysis takes place in three stages:

1. Diagramming the constraints.
2. Diagramming the objective function.
3. Identifying the profit-maximizing output combination.

Diagramming the constraints. The first task is to prepare a sheet of graph paper and draw in the constraints. Exhibit 17–2 shows a graph with a line representing the first constraint drawn in. Drawing this line is a three-step process:

1. Find what value of B just satisfies the first constraint when the output of A is zero:

$$4 \times 0 + 1 \times B \leq 4,500 \qquad (1)$$

That is, when $A = 0$, B must be less than or equal to 4,500 units. The point labeled P identifies the $A = 0$, $B = 4,500$ output combination.

2. Find what value of A just satisfies the first constraint when the output of B is zero:

$$4 \times A + 1 \times 0 \leq 4,500 \qquad (1)$$

Exhibit 17–2 Graph showing first constraint

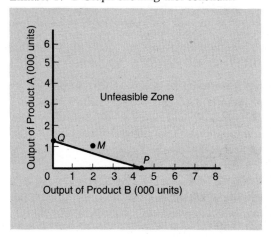

This shows that the output of A can't be greater than $4,500/4 = 1,125$ units when B's output is zero. This output combination is labeled point Q.

3. Draw a straight line through these two points.

None of the output combinations in the shaded area in the diagram is feasible because department X's capacity is too small to handle any combination in this area. Suppose we tried to schedule 1,000 units of A and 2,000 units of B, for example—point M in the diagram. This would require the following amounts of time in department X:

Product A 1,000 × 4 .... 4,000 hours
Product B 2,000 × 1 .... 2,000 hours
Total .... 6,000 hours

This is clearly impossible because department X has only 4,500 hours available.

A line representing the second constraint can be located by the same method, by solving inequality (2) for two different pairs of values:

1. When $A = 0$:

$$2 \times 0 + 3 \times B \leq 7,500 \tag{2}$$
$$B \leq 2,500$$

2. When $B = 0$:

$$2 \times A + 3 \times 0 \leq 7,500 \tag{2}$$
$$A \leq 3,750$$

These two combinations are identified as points R and S in Exhibit 17–3. The line connecting these two points establishes the maximum output of department Y. Every output combination in the unshaded area to the right of the SR line calls for more time than department Y has available.

The third and fourth constraints are also shown in Exhibit 17–3. The shading to the left of the vertical axis indicates that negative outputs of product B

Exhibit 17–3 Graph showing all constraints

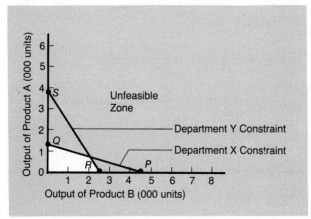

are impossible. Similarly, the shading below the base line shows that negative outputs of product A are impossible.

Diagramming the objective function. Once all the constraints have been drawn in, we can see that only a few possible output combinations are feasible. These are the combinations in the unshaded area of Exhibit 17–3. These combinations are not all equally profitable. To find the best one, we have to find some way of putting the objective function into the diagram.

This is the most difficult step to visualize, but the procedure is basically very simple. We start by picking any output combination and computing the anticipated profit from that combination. An easy combination to plot is the combination of no units of A and 1,000 units of B. The contribution margin for this combination is:

$$\text{Contribution margin} = 0 + 1{,}000 \times \$6 = \$6{,}000$$

The next step is to find another output combination that provides this same $6,000 contribution margin. This time the easiest solution is to let B equal zero, so that the output of A can be calculated from the following equation:

$$\$6{,}000 = \$10 \times A + 0$$

From this it is easy to see that it takes 600 units of A to generate a $6,000 contribution margin.

These two points, labeled T and V, have been plotted in Exhibit 17–4 and a straight line has been drawn between them. (Ignore the other dashed lines for the moment and concentrate on the one joining points T and V.)

Exhibit 17–4 Linear programming: Graphic solution

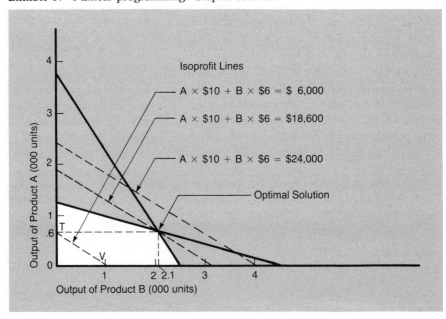

Because the profit relationship in the objective function is linear, every point on this line represents an output combination that will produce a $6,000 contribution margin. We call this an *isoprofit* line.

Even more important, all points to the "northeast" of this line represent output combinations that will yield more than $6,000. Since many of the points to the northeast of the $6,000 line are in the feasible region of the chart, it is clear that the company can find a combination with a contribution margin greater than $6,000.

Identifying the profit-maximizing solution.   The third step is to draw other isoprofit lines parallel to the first, moving progressively outward. Each line stands for a higher profit total than the one before, as shown in the exhibit. The maximum profit solution is found when an isoprofit line crosses the last outer edge of the feasible output zone, the unshaded area in the diagram.

In this case, the maximum possible contribution margin is $18,600, obtainable when the output of A is 600 units and the output of B is 2,100 units:

	Output (units)	Department X Hours	Department Y Hours	Contribution Margin
Product A	600	2,400	1,200	$ 6,000
Product B	2,100	2,100	6,300	12,600
Total		4,500	7,500	$18,600

This solution just uses up all the available time in both departments. We can also see from Exhibit 17–4 that the $18,600 isoprofit line is the highest one to touch the feasible zone. Any other feasible output combination is on a lower isoprofit line, and all other output combinations producing $18,600 or more fall in the unfeasible zone.

The solution to a linear program is always located at the point of an angle at the edge of the feasible zone, unless the maximum isoprofit line coincides with one of the constraint boundaries. In that limiting case, any combination along that boundary will be equally desirable.

In summary: (1) the capacity constraints define the feasible region; (2) the best combination of outputs is found by moving the isoprofit line out until it reaches the farthest limit of the feasible region; and (3) this combination normally will be at the intersection of two of the constraint lines or on one of the axes.

Developing shadow prices

The constraints in linear programs are ordinarily less rigid than the mathematical formulation would imply. If the payoff is great enough, management often can find a way to alter the constraint. The linear program can be used to identify the constraints that are most worth changing.

For example, suppose department X's capacity could be increased by one hour, to 4,501 hours. Suppose also that fractional outputs are feasible. The question is how much the company would be willing to pay to get an additional hour of capacity in department X. Department Y's capacity is to remain un-changed.

The best way to calculate the value of the additional capacity is to solve the set of linear equations with constraint (1) located at 4,501 hours instead of 4,500:

$$4A + 1B \leq 4,501 \tag{1a}$$

Since the graphic solution doesn't deal very accurately with differences as small as single units, we won't try to use it here. The logic is simple, however. We saw earlier that if the company has five hours of idle time in department X and no idle time in department Y, the best way to use this is to reduce production of product B by one unit and increase output of product A by one and a half units. If only one hour of time is idle, each of these figures should be reduced to one fifth. This means that one additional hour of time in department X would permit the following adjustment:

Product A: $+0.2 \times 1.5 = +0.3$ unit
Product B: $-0.2 \times 1.0 = -0.2$ unit

The profit contribution of a unit of product A is $10; that of product B is $6. The extra hour of capacity therefore would increase total company profit by $0.3 \times \$10 - 0.2 \times \$6 = \$1.80$. In other words, an hour of department X capacity is worth $1.80. This is referred to as department X's *shadow price.*

A similar calculation can be made for department Y. Additional capacity in department Y, unaccompanied by an increase in the capacity of department X, can be used only by substituting some units of product B for product A. Since a unit of A requires four hours in department X and a unit of B takes only one hour, the substitution would be in a four-to-one ratio. Adding four units of B would increase usage of department Y by 12 hours, less the 2 hours saved by the cutback in production of A there, a net increase of 10 hours. Since we are only adding one hour of capacity, we can handle only one tenth of this substitution, permitting the following adjustment:

Product A: $-0.1 \times 1 = -0.1$ unit
Product B: $+0.1 \times 4 = +0.4$ unit

The addition of an hour of department Y capacity therefore would be worth $0.4 \times \$6 - 0.1 \times \$10 = \$1.40$.

Sensitivity analysis

The calculation of shadow prices is a simple example of sensitivity analysis. Sensitivity analysis is any procedure designed to test the responsiveness of the action recommendation or of the amount of any variable to changes or errors in any of the other variables in a decision model.

Since the action recommendations are the main reason for applying decision models, we shall focus on this aspect of sensitivity analysis. Some recommendations are relatively sensitive to changes in decision variables, as in the left-hand diagram of Exhibit 17–5. This shows that recommendation Y is valid

Exhibit 17–5 Sensitivity of action recommendation to variations in a decision variable

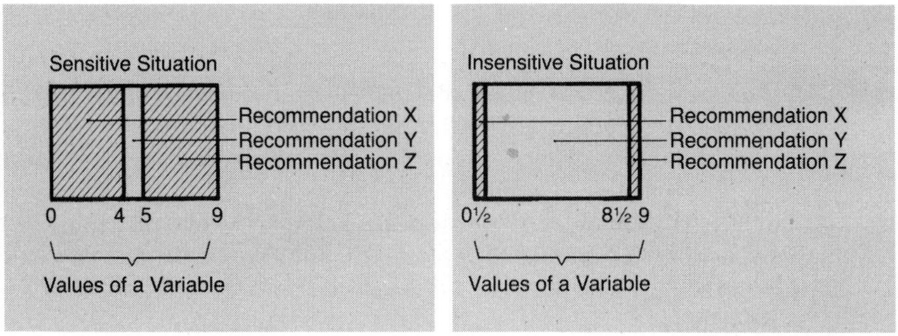

only if the variable has a value between four and five. The right-hand diagram, in contrast, shows a highly insensitive situation in which recommendation Y is valid for any value of the variable from one half to eight and a half.

In our illustration, the action recommendation (how much of A and how much of B to produce) is highly sensitive to changes in the constraints. We saw this in our analysis of shadow prices. The action recommendation is highly insensitive, however, to changes in the relative contribution margins of the two products. The action recommendation will not change at all unless the ratio of one contribution margin to the other changes substantially.

For example, remember that each unit of product A requires as much of department X's capacity as four units of product B. Suppose product A's contribution margin is $30, while product B's contribution margin remains at $6. The objective function is now:

$$\text{Contribution margin} = \$30\ A + \$6\ B.$$

If all of department X's capacity is used to produce product A, the company will be able to manufacture 1,125 units:

$$\frac{\text{Total department X capacity}}{\text{Hours in department X for a unit of product A}} = \frac{4,500 \text{ hours}}{4 \text{ hours}}$$
$$= 1,125 \text{ units}.$$

If this is done, the situation will be as follows:

Total contribution margin	$1,125 \times \$30$	$= \$33,750$
Department Y hours required	$1,125 \times 2$	$= 2,250$ hours
Idle capacity in department Y	$7,500 - 2,250$	$= 5,250$ hours

In these circumstances, the total contribution margin can't be increased by substituting product B for product A, even though that substitution would use some of department Y's idle capacity. Remember that product B requires one hour in department X, while product A needs 4 hours. This means that reducing production of A by one unit would provide enough capacity to produce four units of B. The effect on profit would be:

Add four units of B at $6	$24
Subtract one unit of A at $30	30
Loss from substitution	$ 6

This new objective function is shown in the new isoprofit line in Exhibit 17–6. The slope of the isoprofit line is now flatter than the slope of the constraint for department X. The company can reach the highest feasible isoprofit line ($33,750) only by devoting all of department X's capacity to product A. This is the solution indicated by the point at which the $33,750 isoprofit line touches the left-hand edge of the diagram. This is the only output combination in the feasible zone that will produce a total contribution margin as large as $33,750.

What does this have to do with sensitivity analysis? It shows that the output combination decision will not be shifted toward product A unless the contribution margin of product A is more than four times the contribution margin of product B. (With contribution margins of $24 for A and $6 for B, each product would return the same contribution margin per department X hour.)

This analysis revealed department X's capacity as the more important scarce resource. If product B is much more profitable than product A, however, the company may be able to justify using all of department Y's capacity to produce product B, leaving product A out in the cold. Again the point at which this change would be made is determined by the ratio of the contribution margin of a unit of product B to the contribution margin of a unit of product A. Since department Y needs three hours to produce a unit of B and two hours to produce a unit of A, the contribution margin of B would have to be at least 3/2 of the contribution margin of A to justify the extreme solution of producing all B and no A.

In other words, the action recommendation will be the same for any ratio of the two contribution margin figures falling between the following limits:

$$\left(\frac{P_A}{P_B}=\frac{4}{1}\right) \geq \text{Actual ratio} \geq \left(\frac{P_A}{P_B}=\frac{2}{3}\right)$$

Exhibit 17–6 Effect of change in relative profit ratio

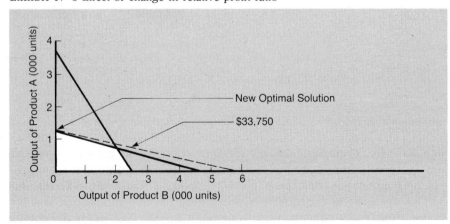

(P_A is the contribution margin of product A; P_B is the contribution margin of product B.) The estimated ratio in our illustration was $10/$6 = 5/3$, far from either end of the range.

The reason for this application of sensitivity analysis is uncertainty. Management probably doesn't know the contribution margin figures with certainty, and this analysis indicates how serious this lack of knowledge is likely to be. In our example, it wasn't serious at all because the error would have had to be very great to affect management's decision.

Accounting data required

Accountants need to be able to construct and solve linear programs because they may have to recommend actions in decision situations. For this purpose they should study linear programming in far greater depth than we have room for here.

Our main reason for introducing linear programming in this text is to examine a question that most descriptions of the method overlook or pass over very lightly—how to measure the costs of different uses of the organization's capacity. We start with the requirement that the cost figures used in the contribution margin multipliers in the objective function should measure the response of cost to changes in volume within the range affected by the decision. Three cost questions remain to be resolved:

1. Steps in the cost function.
2. Changes in rates of variability.
3. Variable costs that are unaffected by the operations mix at full capacity.

Steps in the cost function.   The easiest of these to deal with is the question of how to handle steps in the cost-volume relationship. We have given this question enough attention in previous chapters to make any lengthy discussion unnecessary. Since linear programming can deal only with linear relationships, increments or steps in fixed costs must be either excluded or averaged. If the steps are relatively close together, they should be averaged into the variable costing figure. Otherwise they should be excluded.

Changes in rates of variability.   A second question is how to deal with changes in rates of variability. For example, capacity operations may require the use of high-cost suppliers for 10 percent of total materials. In this situation, the full penalty price—that is, the price paid to high-cost suppliers—should be used to cost all the materials used, on the grounds that this approximates marginal cost. This will give products with low materials requirements a larger share of the optimal product mix.

The only flaw in this approach is that if the cost penalty is big enough, it may increase the production of products with low materials requirements so far that the need for high-cost purchases disappears. If the adjustment is this large, then models of greater complexity must be developed.

Variable costs unaffected by product mix. The final question is how to deal with costs that vary with the degree of utilization of capacity but are not affected by the product mix once capacity is reached. For example, suppose that capacity in department X is measured in labor hours and that when the department is operating at capacity, it has 16 employees, no more and no less. This means that total labor cost will be the same no matter which products are manufactured, as long as all of the capacity is used.

Although this would seem to describe a typical sunk cost situation, department X's labor cost should not be left out of the objective function. The reason is that linear programming does not preclude solutions that do not use all of the available capacity. Consider, for example, the following set of figures:

	Product A	Product B
Labor hours in department X	4	1
Labor cost in department X at $8 an hour	$32	$ 8
Other variable costs	23	6
Total variable cost	55	14
Selling price	45	15
Contribution margin	−$10	$ 1

The objective function, in other words, is:

$$\text{Contribution margin} = -\$10 \times A + \$1 \times B.$$

Since production of even one unit of product A would be unprofitable, it is clear that the best decision in this case would be to produce no product A at all. Department Y's capacity would limit output of product B to 2,500 units and these would use only 2,500 hours of department X time, leaving 2,000 hours of idle capacity. The labor cost of these 2,000 hours is a variable cost and is incremental to any decision between full utilization and less than full utilization. Only those costs that will be the same whether capacity is used or not should be excluded from the objective function.

Solutions by the simplex method

The graphic method of solving linear programs has two major limitations: (1) it can't be used if management has more than two decision variables to manipulate; and (2) it is time consuming because each program has to be solved manually in its entirety. To get around either or both of these limitations, the analyst is likely to use a method that works directly from the mathematical relationships to a solution. The most popular of these methods is the simplex method.

We don't have enough room here to describe and illustrate the simplex method.[1] In essence, however, it is a trial-and-error method in which the successive trials are rigidly prescribed and mechanistically applied. This makes

---

[1] For a description of the simplex method, consult a good textbook in quantitative analysis, linear mathematics, or operations research. A specialized work is by Saul I. Gass, *Linear Programming: Methods and Applications,* 4th ed. (New York: McGraw-Hill, 1975).

it ideally suited for solution by computer, and most problems in linear programming can be solved quickly with the help of readily available computer programs.

Inventory decision models

One of the most frequent routine actions is the placing of production or purchase orders. Management must decide what to produce or buy, when, and in what quantity. A number of decision models have been developed to take the judgment out of many of these decisions so that management can delegate the authority to lower-level managers or clerical personnel. In this section we'll study three aspects of one of these models:

1. Calculating the economic order quantity.
2. Calculating desired safety stocks and reorder points.
3. Identifying the data needed.

The economic order quantity

The key relationship in our inventory model is between the size of the order and the average amount of the inventory during a period of time. At a given usage rate, the average inventory quantity will vary directly with the size of the order.

For example, a company needs 10 units of a certain item each week. It now buys a week's requirements at a time—that is, each order is for 10 units. The inventory on hand varies from 10 units (just after the receipt of the latest order quantity) to zero (just before the receipt of the next order quantity). If the consumption rate is steady during the week, the average inventory will be halfway between 10 and zero, or 5 units.

This behavior pattern is illustrated in the left-hand panel of Exhibit 17–7. Inventory quantity starts at 10, falls gradually to zero, and then bounces back to 10 when the new shipment is received. The inventory level in the right-hand panel shows the same pattern, but the purchase quantity is doubled, to 20 units. This means that orders have to be placed only every other week, but the average inventory goes up to 10 units.

Exhibit 17–7 Effect of order quantity on average inventory

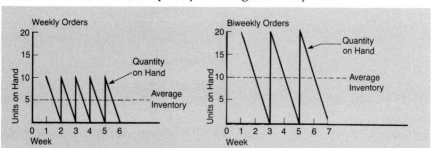

This relationship is significant because costs are ordinarily affected by the number of orders placed in a given time period and by the average inventory quantity. Weekly purchases, for example, require 50 times as many orders as annual purchases, and therefore approximately 50 times as much clerical time, 50 times as many forms, and 50 times as much postage. The average inventory is only one 50th as large, however, which means that less storage space will have to be provided, less insurance will be carried, less capital will be tied up, and fewer units will deteriorate or become obsolete.

The other major variable that is common to all inventory models is the rate at which the item is used, usually referred to as the *demand rate* or *demand*. Other things being equal, both order size and average inventory will be large if the demand is great and small if it is small.

The decision rule in the simplest inventory decision models is to minimize total inventory cost, given a stable level of demand that is known with absolute certainty. The objective function is:

$$TC = N \times C_o + I \times C_c$$

in which

TC = The annual inventory cost.
N = The number of orders per year.
I = The average inventory quantity.
C_o = The cost of processing an average order.
C_c = The cost of carrying a unit of inventory for a year.

Since inventory carrying costs at a given demand level vary directly with order size and purchase costs vary inversely, cost minimization is a matter of increasing the order quantity until the marginal carrying cost of further increases in inventory would exceed the marginal reduction in ordering cost. The simplest formula used to calculate this point is:[2]

$$EOQ = \sqrt{\frac{2\,DC_o}{C_c}}$$

where EOQ is the economic order quantity and D is the number of units used per year.

For example, suppose the annual demand (D) is 10,000 units and the order processing cost (C_o) is $16. The purchase price is $5 and the annual carrying cost per dollar of inventory is 40 cents. Carrying cost per unit (C_c) therefore is $5 × 0.40 = $2. The economic order quantity is:

$$EOQ = \sqrt{\frac{2 \times 10,000 \times \$16}{\$2}} = 400 \text{ units}$$

The purchasing and inventory costs associated with this purchase quantity can be summarized as shown in Exhibit 17–8.

---

[2] This is derived by differentiating the total cost equation with respect to order quantity, setting the derivative equal to zero, and solving for EOQ. For a simple derivation of this formula, see Martin K. Starr, *Production Management: Systems and Synthesis,* 2d ed. (Englewood Cliffs, N.J.: Prentice-Hall, 1972), pp. 280–81.

Exhibit 17–8 Components of the annual cost of inventoried merchandise

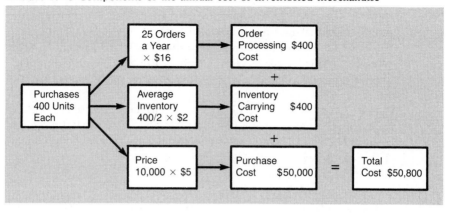

No other purchase quantity would produce a total cost as low as $50,800.

Safety stocks and reorder points

Orders typically must be given to suppliers many days or weeks before delivery is desired. This interval is known as the *lead time,* and an essential element of any inventory decision model is the *reorder point,* identified by the model as the signal to place a new purchase order.

Lead time would pose no problem if an order placed when the quantity on hand was just equal to the quantity that would be used during the lead time would arrive just as the existing stock was exhausted. The real world is not this simple. Both the rate of use and the length of the lead time are uncertain. This means that *stock-outs* can occur. A stock-out is a failure to fill a customer's order or a materials requisition on the desired delivery date because the goods ordered are not available.

Management can reduce the number of stock-outs by providing a *safety stock,* that is, extra inventory to allow for the possibility that demand will increase or replenishment will be delayed. The problem is to adjust the size of the safety stock so that the carrying cost of the last unit in the inventory is just equal to the stock-out cost avoided by having that unit in stock. The solution can be reached in four steps:

1. Formulating the basic model.
2. Calculating the stock-out costs.
3. Calculating the costs of the safety stock.
4. Calculating the optimal safety stock.

The basic model.   Suppose the economic order quantity for a part used in the factory is 200 units, with an average usage of 20 units a week. The lead time is four weeks. This means that if no safety stock is carried, a reorder will be placed when the inventory reaches 80 units (four weeks' supply). Since both the lead time and the demand are uncertain quantities, the company will be out of stock some of the time if it carries no safety stock. This will happen whenever more than 80 units are demanded between the time of reorder and the time the goods are received.

To avoid overcomplicating the arithmetic, let us assume that lead time is certain but that demand varies between 10 and 30 units a week, with the various demands occurring at the following frequencies:

Four-Week Demand (units)	Percentage Probability
40	5
60	10
80	70
100	10
120	5

In other words, demand is expected to exceed the 80-unit reorder date inventory during 15 percent of the reorder intervals, when weekly demand is more than 20 units.

Management has several options here. One is to carry a zero safety stock and accept the likelihood of being out of stock 15 percent of the time. Another is to reduce the stock-out frequency to 5 percent by carrying a 20-unit safety stock—that is, by placing the order while five weeks' supply is on hand instead of four. Finally, the stock-out probability can be reduced to zero by increasing the safety stock to 40 units, a two-week normal supply, reordering when 120 units are in inventory.

To choose among these alternatives, management needs two sets of estimates: (1) the stock-out costs associated with each safety stock level, and (2) the inventory level corresponding to each safety stock level.

Stock-out costs. Stock-outs can be costly. If the result is the loss of a customer order, at least part of the cost is the opportunity cost of the lost order. If the result is an outside purchase to fill the customer's order, the cost is the penalty paid for prompt delivery. If the result is deferred delivery to the customer, the cost is the value of repeat orders that will be lost because of failure to deliver on time this time. In all three cases, the stock-out may increase the amount of idle time and disrupt production flows, thereby increasing factory costs for the volume of work done.

The calculation of the stock-out costs associated with different safety-stock levels requires a merging of the stock-out probabilities with the costs of individual stock-outs. This calculation is illustrated in Exhibit 17–9. Starting on the first line, we see that with a zero safety stock the company will be 20 units short 10 percent of the time. Since orders are placed every 10 weeks, on the average, and the factory operates 50 weeks a year, five orders will be placed in an average year. This means that 10 units will be out of stock on an annual basis (20 × 10% × 5 times a year).

The next line in the exhibit shows that the zero safety stock will lead to a few 40-unit stock-outs as well as the 20-unit stock-outs covered on the first

Exhibit 17–9 Calculation of stock-out costs

(1) Safety Stock (units)	(2) Units Short per Order Period	(3) Order Periods per Year	(4) Prob- ability	(5) Expected Units Short per Year $(2) \times (3) \times (4)$	(6) Expected Annual Stock-Out Cost $(5) \times \$18$
0	20	5	0.10	10	
	40	5	0.05	$\underline{10}$	
				20	\$360
20	20	5	0.05	5	90
40	0	5	0.00	0	0

line. This will happen 5 percent of the time, or 10 units a year. If stock-out costs amount to \$18 a unit, annual stock-out costs of a zero safety stock will be \$360. Similar calculations for two other safety stock levels are summarized on the final two lines.

Safety-stock costs.   Safety stocks are also costly. By increasing the average inventory quantity, they increase inventory carrying costs. The next step in the analysis, therefore, is to calculate the carrying costs of different levels of safety stocks.

The carrying cost of the safety stocks is determined by multiplying the increase in the average inventory by the carrying cost per unit. If the safety stock is 20 units and the carrying cost is \$6 a unit, the carrying cost of the safety stock will be \$120 a year. If the safety stock is 40 units, the carrying cost will be \$240.

The optimal safety stock.   With these figures, calculating the optimal safety stock is simple:

Safety Stock	Carrying Cost	Stock-Out Cost	Total Cost
0	\$ 0	\$360	\$360
20	120	90	210
40	240	0	240

In other words, the company can minimize the cost of its safety stock by providing a safety stock of 20 units and a reorder level of 100 units (the safety stock plus the normal consumption during the four-week lead time).

Data requirements

Many other inventory decision models have been developed, most of them more complex than the one described above. Most of them require the same kinds of data, however, and discussion of the data requirements of one will serve them all.

Order quantity models call for three kinds of physical unit data: demand, out-of-stock, and inventory quantities. Although many companies fail to record out-of-stock data, measurement of these quantities poses no conceptual problems. The main task is to make sure that information is available in usable form.

Cost data are more difficult to prescribe. Three cost factors must be estimated:

1. Order cost.
2. Carrying cost.
3. Stock-out cost.

Order costs. Order processing costs consist mainly of clerical salaries and equipment rentals. Although these are fixed costs, most of them should be included in the order cost function. The reason is that total order cost depends on the joint outcome of thousands of order quantity decisions. Although a single extra order will cost little more than a few cents for paper and postage, a 10 percent increase is likely to require an additional order clerk and a 20 percent increase may call for another purchasing officer.

The fixed costs to be included in the estimated cost of placing an order should be those that vary in steps as anticipated volume goes up or down. We have referred to these earlier as attributable fixed costs.

Carrying costs. Carrying costs are of two different kinds: those that vary with the cost or value of the average inventory, and those that vary with the physical quantity of the average inventory. Insurance, financing, and spoilage costs are in the former category; the cost of warehouse space may vary with the latter.

Once again, and for the same reason as for order costs, carrying costs should be based on the attributable-cost concept. If the company can adjust the amount of storage space it occupies and if the amount of space and the number of storage personnel are sensitive to changes in the inventory level, their costs should be included in the carrying cost multiplier.

The largest component of the carrying cost figure is likely to be one that doesn't appear in the historical accounting records at all. This is a charge for the amount of capital needed to finance the inventory. This charge is necessary whether the capital is supplied by the owners of the company or by lenders—both of them provide capital only if they can reasonably expect to be paid for doing so. The lenders receive interest, the owners get dividends and appreciation in the market value of their investments.

The figure used to charge for the use of capital is known as the cost of capital. It is a key figure in decision models designed to help management decide whether to spend money in one period to obtain benefits in others. This will be our topic in the next chapter.

Stock-out costs. Stock-out costs are the most difficult to measure and estimate. As we noted earlier, the cost depends on the consequences of the stock-out—loss of current sales, premium payments for rush delivery, loss of future sales, extra factory costs, or some combination of these.

If the result of the stock-out is lost sales, the cost ordinarily can be measured by the product's contribution margin. In most cases standard variable manufacturing cost will be a reasonable approximation of the marginal cost of production. Variable sales commissions and other short-run variable selling and administrative costs should also be entered at average variable cost. Step-function increments in fixed costs should be excluded, because the aggregate volume of stock-outs is likely to be insufficient to permit significant reductions in divisible fixed costs.

If stock-outs lead to rush orders and subcontracting rather than lost sales, the stock-out cost is the difference between the internal variable cost of manufacture and the costs of dealing outside. The latter should include such hidden penalties as the costs of extra telephone calls, the costs of preparing specifications and choosing among suppliers, and the costs of expediting delivery.

The costs of idle labor time, including allowances for fringe benefits and other related costs, must also be included in the stock-out cost. This refers to idleness of wage-related employees, not salaried personnel; again on the grounds that the volume differential seldom will be large enough and last long enough to permit any significant adjustment of salary costs to lower aggregate volume. For this reason, idle time costs are likely to be considerably smaller in connection with models governing reorder points of purchased merchandise than for goods purchased for processing or internal consumption.

Summary

Management now has an almost bewildering number of quantitative decision models to choose among. Each of these has its own data requirements. This chapter has attempted to throw some light on these requirements by discussing two different kinds of optimization models.

The first section of the chapter dealt with a linear programming model, designed to help management decide how to ration available capacity among various potential uses of that capacity. For linear programming, incremental costs must fit a linear formula—that is, a single unit cost figure must be used for each product or other potential use of capacity. This usually means average short-run variable costs. If steps in fixed costs are small enough to be affected by the outcome of the program, however, they should be averaged into the variable cost figures.

One short section was also devoted to an introduction to sensitivity analysis. Although linear programming lends itself very easily to sensitivity analysis, any decision model can be examined for sensitivity, both to examine the impact of uncertainty on the quality of the decision and to explore the desirability of altering, adding, or eliminating constraints.

The final section introduced a simple inventory decision model, by which economic order quantities and reorder points can be determined if management is willing to make certain simplifying assumptions about the behavior of product demand. For these models the appropriate cost concept is attributable cost, because the aggregate effect of the decisions to be based on the model is likely to introduce changes in fixed costs.

Independent study problems (solutions in Appendix B)

1. **Linear programming; Graphic solution.** Product A has a contribution margin of $5 a unit, while product B's margin is $8. The company can sell as many as 2,000 units of each product without reducing the unit contribution margin.

   A unit of product A requires two hours in department X and two hours in department Y. A unit of product B requires one hour in department X and four hours in department Y.

   Department X has 3,000 hours available for these two products, while department Y has 6,000 hours available.

   Required:

   a. Construct the objective function and formulate the constraints.
   b. What is the optimal production schedule? What is the anticipated total contribution margin at this level of production?
   c. How sensitive is the scheduling decision to variations in the contribution margin of product A?

2. **Economic order quantity.** The cost of processing a purchase order is $36. Carrying costs average 20 percent of average inventory cost. The company expects to use 10,000 units of material X during the next year. The purchase price is expected to be $2.50 a unit.

   Required:

   a. Determine the economic order quantity, using the formula supplied in this chapter.
   b. Calculate the total annual cost of processing purchase orders and carrying inventories, assuming a zero safety stock.
   c. Assuming a certain lead time of three weeks and a constant rate of usage, calculate the inventory reorder point. (For convenience, the year is assumed to consist of 50 weeks.)

3. **Safety stocks.** Stock-out costs for material X (problem 2) are measured by the cost of idle labor time plus penalty costs for emergency deliveries. Management estimates that these amount to $1 for each unit not on hand when it is needed. The usage of this material during the three-week reorder period is expected to correspond to the following pattern:

Usage during Three-Week Period	Probability of This Usage
400	.10
500	.20
600	.40
700	.20
800	.10

   Required:

   a. What safety stock should be carried? (You should consider only multiples of 100 units.) Show your calculations.
   b. How would your answer change if the stock-out cost were $0.75 a unit instead of $1? $0.50? $0.10?

Exercises and problems

4. **Linear programming: Multiple choice.** The Random Company manufactures two products, Zeta and Beta. Each product must pass through two processing operations. All materials are introduced at the start of process 1. There are no

work-in-process inventories. Random may produce either one product exclusively or various combinations of both products subject to the following:

	Process 1	Process 2	Contribution Margin per Unit
Hours required to produce one unit of:			
Zeta	1	1	$4.00
Beta	2	3	5.25
Total capacity in hours per day	1,000	1,275	

A shortage of technical labor has limited Beta production to 400 units per day. Assume that all relationships between capacity and production are linear, and that all of the above data and relationships are deterministic rather than probabilistic.

Required:

1. Given the objective to maximize total contribution margin, what is the production constraint for process 1?

   a. Zeta + Beta ≤ 1,000;   *b.* Zeta + 2 Beta ≤ 1,000;
   c. Zeta + Beta ≥ 1,000;   *d.* Zeta + 2 Beta ≥ 1,000.

2. Given the objective to maximize total contribution margin, what is the labor constraint for production of Beta?

   a. Beta ≤ 400;   *b.* Beta ≥ 400;   *c.* Beta ≤ 425;   *d.* Beta ≥ 425.

3. What is the objective function of the data presented?

   a.   Zeta + 2 Beta = $9.25.
   b. $4.00 Zeta + 3($5.25) Beta = Total contribution margin.
   c. $4.00 Zeta + $5.25 Beta = Total contribution margin.
   d.   2($4.00) Zeta + 3($5.25) Beta = Total contribution margin.

                                                                      (CPA)

5. **Linear programming: Multiple choice.**   Patsy, Inc., manufactures two products, X and Y. Each product must be processed in each of three departments: machining, assembling, and finishing. The hours needed to produce one unit of product per department and the maximum possible hours per department follow:

Department	Production Hours per Unit		Maximum Capacity in Hours
	X	Y	
Machining	2	1	420
Assembling	2	2	500
Finishing	2	3	600

Other restrictions are: X ≥ 50; Y ≥ 50.
   The objective function is to maximize profits where profit = $4X + $2Y.

Required:

Given the objective function and constraints, what is the most profitable number of units of X and Y, respectively, to manufacture?

   a. 150 and 100;   *b.* 165 and 90;   *c.* 170 and 80;   *d.* 200 and 50.

                                                                      (CPA)

6. **Linear programming: Multiple choice.**   A company markets two products, Alpha and Gamma. The marginal contributions per gallon are $5 for Alpha and $4 for Gamma. Both products consist of two ingredients, D and K. Alpha contains

80 percent D and 20 percent K, while the proportions of the same ingredients in Gamma are 40 percent and 60 percent, respectively. The current inventory is 16,000 gallons of D and 6,000 gallons of K. The only company producing D and K is on strike and will neither deliver nor produce them in the foreseeable future.

The company wishes to know the numbers of gallons of Alpha and Gamma it should produce with its present stock of raw materials to maximize its total contribution.

1. The objective function for this problem could be expressed as
   a. $f \max = 0X_1 + 0X_2 + 5X_3 + 5X_4$
   b. $f \min = 5X_1 + 4X_2 + 0X_3 + 0X_4$
   c. $f \max = 5X_1 + 4X_2 + 0X_3 + 0X_4$
   d. $f \max = X_1 + X_2 + 5X_3 + 4X_4$
   e. $f \max = 4X_1 + 5X_2 + X_3 + X_4$

2. The constraint imposed by the quantity of D on hand could be expressed as:
   a. $X_1 + X_2 \geq 16,000$
   b. $X_1 + X_2 \leq 16,000$
   c. $.4X_1 + .6X_2 \leq 16,000$
   d. $.8X_1 + .4X_2 \geq 16,000$
   e. $.8X_1 + .4X_2 \leq 16,000$

3. The constraint imposed by the quantity of K on hand could be expressed as
   a. $X_1 + X_2 \geq 6,000$
   b. $X_1 + X_2 \leq 6,000$
   c. $.8X_1 + .2X_2 \leq 6,000$
   d. $.8X_1 + .2X_2 \geq 6,000$
   e. $.2X_1 + .6X_2 \leq 6,000$

4. To maximize total contribution the company should produce and market
   a. 106,000 gallons of Alpha only.
   b. 90,000 gallons of Alpha and 16,000 gallons of Gamma.
   c. 16,000 gallons of Alpha and 90,000 gallons of Gamma.
   d. 18,000 gallons of Alpha and 4,000 gallons of Gamma.
   e. 4,000 gallons of Alpha and 18,000 gallons of Gamma.

5. Assuming that the marginal contributions per gallon are $7 for Alpha and $9 for Gamma, the company should produce and market
   a. 106,000 gallons of Alpha only.
   b. 90,000 gallons of Alpha and 16,000 gallons of Gamma.
   c. 16,000 gallons of Alpha and 90,000 gallons of Gamma.
   d. 18,000 gallons of Alpha and 4,000 gallons of Gamma.
   e. 4,000 gallons of Alpha and 18,000 gallons of Gamma.

(CPA)

7. **Economic order quantity: Multiple choice.** A company places orders for inventory with its suppliers for a certain item for which the order size is determined in advance as

$$\text{Order size} = \sqrt{\frac{2 \times \frac{\text{Cost to place}}{\text{one order}} \times \frac{\text{Demand per}}{\text{period}}}{\frac{\text{Cost to hold one unit}}{\text{for one period}}}}$$

All orders are the same size. When the policy is implemented, demand per period is only one-half what was expected when order size was computed. Consequently, actual total inventory cost will be

a. Larger than if the expected demand per period had occurred and larger than if the actual demand per period had been used to calculate order size.

   b. Larger than if the expected demand per period had occurred and smaller than if the actual demand per period had been used to calculate order size.

   c. Smaller than if the expected demand per period had occurred and larger than if the actual demand per period had been used to calculate order size.

   d. Smaller than if the expected demand per period had occurred and smaller than if the actual demand per period had been used to calculate order size.

                     (CPA)

8. **Inventory decision model: Multiple choice.** A manufacturer expects to produce 200,000 widgets during the year to supply a demand which is uniform throughout the year. The setup cost for each production run of widgets is $144 and the variable cost of producing each widget is $5. The cost of carrying one widget in inventory is $0.20 a year. After a batch of widgets is produced and placed in inventory, it is sold at a uniform rate, and inventory is exhausted when the next batch of widgets is completed.

  Management wishes an equation to describe the above situation and determine the optimal quantity of widgets to produce in each run so as to minimize total production and inventory carrying costs.

  X = Number of widgets to be produced in each production run.

1. The number of production runs to be made during the year should be expressed as:

  a. 200,000 + 144X;   *b.* 200,000 + X;   *c.* 200,000;   *d.* 200,000/X;   *e.* X/200,000.

2. Total setup costs for the year can be expressed as:

  a. $144(200,000/X)$;   *b.* $\$200,000/X$;   *c.* $\$144X$;   *d.* $\$144X/200,000$;   *e.* $\$144/200,000 + \$X$.

3. Total cost of carrying inventory during the fiscal year can be expressed as:

  a. $\$0.20(\$144X)$;   *b.* $\$.20X$;   *c.* $\$0.20(200,000/X)$;   *d.* $\$0.20(X/2)$;   *e.* $\$0.20(\$144X/200,000)$.

4. The quantity of widgets which should be produced in each run to minimize total costs is:

  a. 19,060;   *b.* 16,970;   *c.* 16,000;   *d.* 12,480;   *e.* 12,000.

                 (CPA, adapted)

9. **Objective function and constraints.** The Witchell Corporation manufactures and sells three grades, A, B, and C, of a single wood product. Each grade must be processed through three phases—cutting, fitting, and finishing—before it is sold.

  The following unit information is provided:

	A	B	C
Selling price	$10.00	$15.00	$20.00
Direct labor	5.00	6.00	9.00
Direct materials	.70	.70	1.00
Variable overhead	1.00	1.20	1.80
Fixed overhead	.60	.72	1.08
Materials requirements in board feet	7	7	10
Labor requirements in hours:			
Cutting	$\frac{3}{6}$	$\frac{3}{6}$	$\frac{4}{6}$
Fitting	$\frac{1}{6}$	$\frac{1}{6}$	$\frac{2}{6}$
Finishing	$\frac{1}{6}$	$\frac{2}{6}$	$\frac{3}{6}$

Only 5,000 board feet per week can be obtained.

The cutting department has 180 hours of labor available each week. The fitting and finishing departments each have 120 hours of labor available each week. No overtime is allowed.

Contract commitments require the company to make 50 units of A per week. In addition, company policy is to produce at least 50 additional units of A and 50 units of B and 50 units of C each week to remain active in each of the three markets. Because of competition only 130 units of C can be sold each week.

Required:

Formulate and label the linear objective function and the constraint functions necessary to maximize the contribution margin.

(CMA, adapted)

10. **Production schedule: Graphic solution.** Graph A presents the constraint functions for a chair manufacturing company whose production problem can be solved by linear programming. The company earns $8 for each kitchen chair and $5 for each office chair sold.

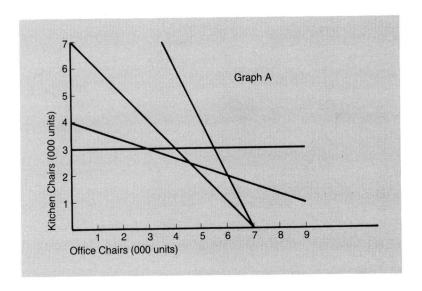

Required:

a. What is the profit-maximizing production schedule?
b. How did you select this production schedule?
c. Would your answer to (*a*) have been different if the office chairs had earned $1 each instead of $5? Explain.

(CMA, adapted)

11. **Payoff table; safety stock and reorder point.** The Starr Company manufactures several products. One of its main products requires an electric motor. The management of Starr Company uses the economic order quantity formula (EOQ) to determine the optimum number of motors to order. Management now wants to determine how much safety stock to order.

Starr Company uses 30,000 electric motors annually (300 working days). Using the EOQ formula, the company orders 3,000 motors at a time. The lead time for an order is five days. The annual cost of carrying one motor in safety stock is $10. Management has also estimated that the cost of being out of stock is $20 for each motor the company is short.

Starr Company has analyzed the usage during past reorder periods by examining the inventory records. The records indicate the following usage patterns during the past reorder periods.

Usage during Lead Time	Times Quantity Was Used
440	6
460	12
480	16
500	130
520	20
540	10
560	6
	200

Required:

a. Construct a payoff table (see Chapter 5) and determine the level of safety stock Starr Company should maintain if it wishes to minimize the expected value of its costs.
b. Calculate the reorder point on this basis.

(CMA, adapted)

12. **Setup costs; inventory decision model.** A single large machine is the only equipment used in Beaman Company's department P. Many different products are processed on the machine, and management is interested in finding the most economical lot size in which each product should be manufactured. The following information has been obtained for use in calculating the setup cost for product A:

1. Two workers from the maintenance department have to spend four hours each to set up the equipment, working as a team. It is the company's policy to provide its maintenance force with a 40-hour week, adjusting the size of the maintenance staff only if changes in the size of the work load are substantial and likely to persist.
2. Department P's machine is operated by a crew of six, each with a basic wage rate of $10 an hour. While the machine is being set up, the members of the crew perform minor finishing operations and carry out other productive tasks to the extent that such work is available. Experience indicates that they are idle approximately 60 percent of the time required for machine setup.
3. A typical month has 20 producing days of eight hours each. The department's operating crew is expected to be idle about 12 hours in an average month, given the present production lot sizes.
4. Department P's costs other than direct materials, the wages of the operating crew, and setup labor are expected to average the following monthly amounts, given the present lot sizes:

Supervision	$2,200
Idle time	720
Payroll taxes and insurance	2,360
Maintenance labor	711
Supplies	600
Power	560
Depreciation	760
Space	120
Total	$8,031

5. All payroll taxes and insurance costs on operating labor, idle time, and supervision are classified as overhead. They average approximately 20 percent of the gross payroll.

6. The cost of idle time is classified as a variable departmental overhead cost. Sixty percent of the amount budgeted is due to machine changeovers; the other 40 percent is due to other production delays. Payroll taxes and insurance on idle time wages in the department are included in the monthly budget for payroll taxes and insurance. If the average lot size is changed, total idle time will also change.

7. Maintenance labor is charged to department P at $18 an hour. No separate charge for payroll taxes and insurance on maintenance labor is made; these costs are included in the $18 rate. Maintenance labor charges (other than setup labor) are classified as departmental overhead and are expected to be roughly proportional to the number of productive hours of the operating crew. Setup labor is charged to individual job orders as an element of direct labor cost.

8. The costs of operating supplies are expected to be roughly proportional to the number of productive hours of the operating crew.

9. The costs of operating the maintenance department, other than maintenance labor, payroll taxes and insurance, are completely fixed and indivisible.

10. Department P's depreciation, power, space, and supervisory costs are regarded as fixed costs.

Required:

Estimate the cost of setting up the machine, for use in establishing economic order quantities. Explain how you derived each of the components of your estimate.

13. **Linear programming: Estimating unit costs.** Department 17 is now fully utilized, producing several products. It is operating two shifts a day; third-shift and overtime operations are not feasible.

Labor costs of the second shift are recorded separately from those of the first shift. Output statistics are also recorded separately. Materials, supplies, utilities, and all other nonlabor costs are not assignable to individual shifts.

Output in department 17 is measured by the number of standard direct labor hours for the work done. Costs and output in the current month are expected to be as follows:

	First Shift	Second Shift	Total
Output (standard direct labor hours) ...	4,000	3,000	7,000
Actual direct labor hours	3,850	3,150	7,000
Direct labor	$38,500	$31,500	$70,000
Indirect labor	6,160	5,040	11,200
Supervision	4,900	3,500	8,400
Shift differential (on direct labor, indirect labor, and supervision)	—	4,004	4,004
Labor benefits and payroll taxes	12,390	11,011	23,401
Supplies			3,500
Power			4,200
Other costs			14,000

Materials yields are the same on both shifts; materials usage in the current month is expected to total 28,000 pounds. Direct labor performance is poorer on the second shift than on the first shift because (1) the best workers are assigned to the first shift, and (2) the crews are more affected by fatigue during the evening hours. The union contract provides that fluctuations in work loads be handled insofar as possible by varying the production schedule for the second shift; first-shift operations are seldom affected.

Analysis of historical data indicates that cost variability in this department is as follows:

Item	Variability Pattern
Direct labor	100% variable with direct labor hours
Indirect labor	70% variable with direct labor hours, 30% fixed and indivisible
Supervision	100% fixed and indivisible for each shift
Shift differential	Proportional to second-shift direct labor, indirect labor and supervision
Labor benefits and payroll taxes	Proportional to total gross wages and salaries
Supplies	100% variable with weight of materials used
Power	100% variable with weight of materials used
Other costs	10% variable with direct labor hours, 90% fixed and indivisible

Required:

a. In preparing the objective function for use in a linear programming solution to the problem of allocating department 17's capacity, should product costs be based on experience in the first shift, experience in the second shift, or average experience? Explain your position.

b. Prepare an estimate, consistent with your answer to (*a*), of the amount of department 17's costs that should be inserted in the objective function as part of the unit cost of a product requiring 4 pounds of materials costing $2 a pound and 2 standard direct labor hours in department 17.

14. **Inventory decision model.** The Robney Company is a restaurant supplier. One of its products is a special meatcutter with a disposable blade. The blades are sold in packages of 12 blades for $20 a package.

After a number of years, it has been determined that the demand for replacement blades is at a constant rate of 2,000 packages a month. The Robney Company buys the packages from a manufacturer for $10 each. The manufacturer requires a three-day lead time from date of order to date of delivery. The ordering cost is $2.40 per order and the carrying cost is at an annual rate of 20 percent. Robney has adopted the order quantity formula described in this chapter.

Required:

a. Calculate:
    (1) The economic order quantity.
    (2) The number of orders needed per year.
    (3) The total cost of buying and carrying blades for a year.

b. Assuming there is no safety stock and that the present inventory level is 200 packages, when should the next order be placed? (Use 360 days equals one year.)

c. Suppose the number of units sold in a three-day period is uncertain. It shows the following pattern:

Usage	Probability
170	.04
180	.10
190	.20
200	.32
210	.20
220	.10
230	.04

What level of safety stock (in a multiple of 10 units) would you recommend if the stock-out cost is 20 cents for each unit out of stock when it is needed?

d. Discuss the problems most companies would have in attempting to apply these formulas to their inventory problems.

(CMA, adapted)

15. **Objective function and constraints.** A company manufactures three products, A, B, and C. These three products have been well received in the market, and at current selling prices the company can sell all it can produce. Data for these three products are as follows:

	A	B	C
Selling price	$15	$19	$24
Materials cost	5	10	13
Other variable costs (paid when incurred)	6	4	7
Portion of selling price collected in month of sale	1/3	0	0

Each product requires one unit of its own special raw material. These materials are not interchangeable—that is, A's material may not be used for B or C, B's may not be used for A or C, and so on. The raw materials inventories will be as follows on January 1:

200 units of material for A at $5 . . . . $1,000
120 units of material for B at $10   1,200
50 units of material for C at $13   650

Additional quantities of these materials can be acquired from nearby suppliers on a few hours' notice. Materials are always paid for in cash when they are received.

The products pass through two departments. The maximum machine time available during January is 400 hours in department 1 and 800 hours in department 2. Machine time for processing a unit in each department is:

	Hours Required by Unit of		
	A	B	C
Department 1	1/2	1	1/4
Department 2	1	1	4 1/2

Departmental fixed costs (for both departments) will be $900 in January. This includes $200 in depreciation charges; the other fixed costs will be paid for as they are incurred.

The January 1 cash balance is expected to be $6,660. The ending cash balance cannot be less than $3,000. Due to a seasonal shutdown, the company will have no outstanding accounts receivable on January 1.

Required:

Formulate an objective function to maximize profits and specify the constraints this function is subject to. (Note: Since the use of existing materials has a different effect on cash from that of newly purchased materials, let A_1, B_1 and C_1 be the amount of existing materials, A_2, B_2, and C_2 the amount of newly purchased materials.)

(Written by the author and adapted for use in an SMAC examination)

16. **Production decision: Sensitivity analysis.** The management of Danielson, Inc. is preparing its production schedule for the next three months. The company

sells two products, A and B, which it manufactures in two departments, X and Y. Department X has a total capacity of 2,700 labor hours a month, while department Y has a monthly capacity of 3,000 machine-hours.

Danielson is now entering its busy season. Orders are flowing in at a record rate, and management knows that it will not be able to fill all of them. Fortunately, the two products are bought by different customers, so that refusal of orders for one product will not lead to cancellation of orders for the other.

The company's accountants have gathered the following information on unit costs, prices, and input requirements for the two products:

	A	B
Materials used (pounds)	2	1
Labor hours, department X	1	3
Machine-hours, department Y	2	3
Selling price	$47	$53
Sales commissions	2	1
Direct labor cost:		
Department X	5	15
Department Y	6	12

The Danielson company has 5,400 pounds of materials in inventory. More materials are on order, but will not be delivered in time for use during the next quarter. The materials now on hand cost $7 a pound; the units on order will cost $8 a pound when delivered.

Overhead costs in department X vary with the number of direct labor hours used, at a rate of $1 per direct labor hour. Variable overhead costs in department Y amount to one third of departmental direct labor cost.

Required:

a. Develop the objective function and express the constraints in a form suitable for the use of linear programming.

b. Prepare a recommended production schedule for each of the next three months. The production level will be the same each month.

c. How, if at all, would your recommendation change if you found that two former company employees, now in retirement, would be willing to return to work in department X for a few months on a part-time basis at regular wage rates? These employees would be willing to put in a total of 200 hours a month during the next three months.

d. Danielson, Inc., could increase the price of product A by $7 a unit without losing a significant number of orders. How, if at all, would such a change affect your recommendation?

17. **Inventory decision: Calculating the parameters.** The Acme Belt Company is a wholesale distributor. Management has decided to determine purchase order quantities on the basis of a formula designed to minimize total cost. The cost parameters are to reflect the following elements:

Purchase Price:	Storage Cost:
Invoice price	Insurance
Freight and carting	Taxes
	Interest
Purchase Order Cost:	Breakage and spoilage
Forms and supplies	Space rental
Order preparation	Warehouse operation
Processing payments	
Receiving and inspection	

You have the following information:

The invoice price of product X is $10 a unit, with a 5 percent discount on purchase orders of 1,000 units or more. Annual consumption of product X averages 10,000 units.

Freight charges on product X amount to $2.50 a unit.

The purchasing department is responsible for preparing all purchase orders. It processes approximately 2,000 purchase orders a month. Its costs consist of the salaries of the purchasing agent and assistant ($2,500 a month, including fringe benefits); salaries of six order clerks ($4,000 a month, including fringe benefits); and the costs of forms, supplies, and other variable inputs ($200 a month).

Payments are processed in the accounting department. Work sampling studies indicate that the labor cost of processing an order, including fringe benefits, averages $4 an order. The rental cost of the data processing equipment for the time used to process an average order amounts to $1. Electricity and other variable costs of data processing amount to 20 cents an order.

All purchased items are inspected in the shipping and receiving department. Wages in this department amount to $6,000 a month, plus $1,200 for the supervisor. Approximately one third of the workers' time is devoted to receiving and inspecting incoming goods, with the remainder being devoted to shipping finished products. The supervisor's time is not included in this percentage. Workers' total time tends to vary with the total number of orders received and shipped.

Annual insurance and personal property taxes amount to 7 percent of the cost of the average amount of inventory on hand.

The company has a small amount of short-term, seasonal bank debt at an interest rate of 18 percent a year. Capital expenditure proposals are expected to produce a return on investment of at least 20 percent before taxes.

Breakage and spoilage each month amount to 0.0833 percent of the items in storage.

The company rents one warehouse on a 20-year lease at an average annual cost of $2 a square foot. Comparable warehouse space in the area now rents for $3 a square foot. The company's warehouse can be sublet at current commercial rental rates, but only in its entirety. A unit of product X requires one fifth of a square foot of space, but space must be available for twice the anticipated average inventory quantity. One fifth of the total floor space must be reserved for aisles, etc.

All warehouse labor costs are incurred to move goods into and out of the warehouse. They average 10 percent of the average inventory cost in an average year.

Required:

a. Calculate purchasing cost per order and carrying cost per inventory dollar. Explain your treatment of each item.

b. Should the company take advantage of the discount? What order size should it establish?

c. To what extent would historical records help you provide the data from which these cost parameters could be derived? What information sources would you use to supplement or replace historical records for this purpose? What analytical methods would you apply to your basic data?

18. **Profit planning; Minimum sales requirements.** In November 19x4, the Springfield Manufacturing Company was preparing its budget for 19x5. As the first step it prepared the following pro forma income statement for 19x4 based on the first 10 months' operations and revised plans for the last two months.

Sales		$3,000,000
Materials..........................	$1,105,000	
Labor	310,000	
Factory overhead	775,000	
Selling and administrative	450,000	2,640,000
Income before income taxes		$ 360,000

These results were better than had been expected and operations were close to capacity, but Springfield's management was not convinced that demand would remain at present levels and hence had not planned any increase in plant capacity. Its equipment was specialized and made to its order; a lead time in excess of one year was necessary on all plant additions.

Springfield produced three products with the following annual sales volumes:

100,000 units of product A at $20.................	$2,000,000
40,000 units of product B at $10.................	400,000
20,000 units of product C at $30.................	600,000
Total sales	$3,000,000

Management had ordered a profit analysis for each product and had the following information, based on operations at normal volume:

	A	B	C
Material	$ 6	$ 4.00	$17.25
Labor	2	1.00	3.50
Factory overhead	5	2.50	8.75
Selling and administrative	3	1.50	4.50
Total costs	16	9.00	34.00
Selling price	20	10.00	30.00
Profit/(Loss)	$ 4	$ 1.00	$ (4.00)

Factory overhead was applied on the basis of direct labor cost at a rate of 250 percent; approximately 20 percent of the overhead was variable and did vary with labor costs. Selling and administrative costs were allocated on the basis of sales at the rate of 15 percent; approximately one half of this was variable and did vary with sales in dollars.

As the next step in the planning process, the sales department was asked to make estimates of what it could sell. These estimates were reviewed and accepted by the firm's consulting economist and by top management. They were as follows:

Product A	130,000 units
Product B	50,000
Product C	50,000

Production of these quantities was immediately recognized as being impossible. Practical capacity was 66,000 machine-hours in department 1 and 63,000 machine-hours in department 2. The industrial engineering department reported that these limits could not be increased without the purchase of additional equipment. Anticipated sales for 19x5 would require operating department 1 at 136 percent of capacity and department 2 at 121 percent. Standard costs for the three products, each of which required activity in both departments, were based on the following production rates:

	Rates per Hour		
	A	B	C
Department 1	2	4	4
Department 2	4	8	1⅓

Four solutions to the problem of limited capacity were rejected. First, subcontracting the production out to other firms was considered to be unprofitable because of problems of maintaining quality. Second, operating a second shift was impossible because of shortage of labor. Third, operating overtime would have created problems because a large number of employees were moonlighting and would therefore have refused to work more than the normal 40-hour week. Finally, price increases were ruled out. Although they would result in higher profits in 19x5, the long-run competitive position of the firm would be weakened, resulting in lower profits in the future.

The treasurer, Max Pitcher, then suggested that product C had been carried at a loss too long and that it was time to eliminate it from the product line. He argued that if all facilities were used to produce A and B, profits would be increased.

Paul Jones, the sales manager, objected to this solution because of the need to carry a full line. In addition he maintained that the firm's regular customers had provided and would continue to provide a solid base for the firm's activities and that these customers' needs must be met. He provided a list of these customers and their estimated purchases (in units) which totaled as follows:

Product A 80,000
Product B 32,000
Product C 12,000

It was impossible to verify these contentions, but they appeared to be reasonable, and therefore the president concurred.

Mr. Pitcher acquiesced reluctantly, but he maintained that the remaining capacity should be used to produce A and B. Because A produced four times as much profit as B, he suggested that the production of A (that is, the amount in excess of the 80,000 minimum set by the sales manager) be four times that of B (that is, the amount in excess of the 32,000 minimum set by the sales manager).

David Farragut, the production manager, made some quick calculations and said that this would result in budgeted production and sales of:

Product A .... 106,666 units
Product B 38,667
Product C 12,000

On this basis Mr. Pitcher made the following profit forecast:

Product A: 106,666 at $4 .... $426,664
Product B: 38,667 at $1 38,667
Product C: 12,000 at −$4 .... (48,000)
Total $417,331

As this would represent an increase of more than 15 percent over the current year, there was a general feeling of self-satisfaction. Before final approval was given, however, the president, Alice LeGrand, said she would like to have her new assistant check over the figures. Somewhat piqued, Mr. Pitcher agreed and at that point the group adjourned.

Required:

The president has just asked you to review the above information and report to her tomorrow. Prepare this report, using nontechnical language and indicating how much of each product should be produced and what the income before taxes is likely to be.

(Prepared by Carl L. Nelson)

19. **Shadow prices; effect of constraints.**   The president of Springfield Manufacturing Company (problem 18) is impressed with your report but believes that a more formal structuring of the relationships would be useful.

Required:

a.   Formulate this as a linear programming problem.
b.   Calculate the shadow prices by finding the optimal product mix and addition to profit if one hour is added to the capacity of each department, the capacity of the other being held constant.
c.   How much profit, if any, is lost in the short run as a result of the imposition of the minimum sales constraints? Show your calculations.

18 Capital expenditure decisions

The capacity rationing and economic order quantity models we described in Chapter 17 are single-period models—that is, costs and benefits are so close to each other in time that they can be assumed to occur simultaneously. The purpose of this chapter is to study the data requirements of a decision model designed to help management choose between alternatives which differ in the timing of the cash flows they will generate.

In choices of this sort, management must compare the incremental cash outflows in one or more time periods with the incremental cash inflows in another time period or periods. We refer to these choices as *investment problems.* In particular, we'll see how a multiperiod model can be applied to proposals to acquire land, buildings, and equipment—that is, *capital expenditure proposals*—in which most of the incremental cash outflows take place before most of the incremental cash inflows are received.

Decisions based on net present value

The basic idea in capital expenditure analysis is to see whether the value of the future cash flows a proposed action will generate exceeds the amount of cash the company has to spend or forgo to get them. For example, suppose an entrepreneur offers to pay $1,000 one year from today to any investor who will give the entrepreneur $925 today. In deciding whether to accept this offer, the investor has to have some way of figuring whether the $1,000 future amount is worth more or less than the $925 present sum.

Future value

Future sums can't be compared directly with present amounts because decision makers place lower values on future cash flows than on present cash. Money, in other words, has a time value. Other things being equal, dollars expected to be available in the future are worth less than the same number of dollars now.

One reason for placing a premium on present money is that the future is uncertain. The longer the wait, the greater the probability that conditions will change and the less likely that the promise of future money will be made good. The second reason is that the dollar received today can be invested to grow to more than a dollar in the future. This future amount is known as the *future value* of today's dollar.

For example, if a bank will pay $1,100 one year from now in return for a $1,000 deposit today, it is paying interest at the rate of 10 percent a year. This relationship can be expressed mathematically in the following expression:

$$F_1 = P(1 + r) \tag{1}$$

in which P = The present outlay or deposit in the bank, r = The rate of interest, and F_1 = Future value one year hence. If P = $1,000 and r = 0.1, then F_1 = $1,100.

Continuing the example, if the $1,100 is left in the bank for a second year, it will build up by the end of the two years to $1,100 + ($1,100 × 0.1) = $1,210. Interest in this second year amounts to $110 and is greater than the first year's interest because the bank is now paying interest not only on the original investment but also on the interest earned during the first year. The mathematical formula for computing the future value of a present sum two years later is:

$$F_2 = F_1(1 + r) = P(1 + r)(1 + r) = P(1 + r)^2 \tag{2}$$

If r = 0.1, $(1 + r)^2$ will be 1.21 and the future value of $1,000 now will be $1,210.

Extending these calculations beyond two years reveals the relationships shown graphically in Exhibit 18–1. Starting with $1,000, the depositor's account will build at 10 percent to $1,100 in one year, $1,210 in two years, and so on, up to $6,727.50 at the end of 20 years.

This form of interest calculation, in which interest is earned on previously earned interest, is known as *compounding*. In this case interest has been compounded annually, meaning that interest is added to the bank balance only

Exhibit 18–1 Future values equivalent to a present value of $1,000 (annual compounding at 10 percent a year)

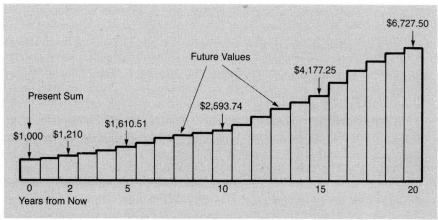

once a year. In general, it can be shown that if an amount P is put out at interest of r percent a year, compounded annually, at the end of n years it will have grown to a future value (F_n) of the following amount:

$$F_n = P(1 + r)^n \tag{3}$$

Present value

The relationship in equation (3) can be inverted to focus attention on the *present value* of a future amount. The present value of a future sum is the amount which, if invested now at compound interest at the specified rate, will grow to an amount equal to the future sum at the specified future date. Present value and future value, in other words, are just two ends of the same relationship. Since all of the bars in Exhibit 18–1 are future values of $1,000, it follows that each of them has the same present value, $1,000. An investor who considers 10 percent annual compound interest as a satisfactory return on money should regard each of these amounts as fully equivalent to each of the others.

The formula for computing present value from known or estimated future values can be found by turning equation (3) around. Since $F_n = P(1 + r)^n$, then

$$P = F_n(1 + r)^{-n} \tag{4}$$

This shows that the present value of any future sum can be determined by multiplying the latter by $(1 + r)^{-n}$ or by dividing it by $(1 + r)^n$. If n is two years, r is 10 percent, and an asset is expected to yield a cash inflow of $1,000 two years from now, then the present value of this asset today is:

$$P = \$1,000/(1.1)^2 = \$1,000 \times 0.82645 = \$826.45.$$

In other words, $826.45 will grow to $1,000 in two years if it is invested now at 10 percent interest, compounded annually; it is therefore the present value of that future amount.

The process of multiplying a future sum by a present value multiplier is known as *discounting*. For this reason, present values are also known as *discounted cash flows;* the multipliers are known as *discount factors*.

Present value of a series of cash flows

Present value can be calculated not only for a single future amount but for a series of future cash flows, each coming at a different time. For example, suppose management expects a proposed $2,000 outlay now will generate cash receipts of $1,000 a year for three years, starting a year from now. If 10 percent is the discount rate, the first $1,000 receipt is worth $1,000/1.1 = \$909.09. The second receipt is worth $826.45, as we saw in the preceding section. The third receipt is worth $1,000/(1.1)^3 = \$751.31. The present value of the series is the sum of these three present values, $2,486.85.

This series of equal annual cash flows is an example of an *annuity*. We can calculate its present value by adding the present values of the individual cash flows, as in the preceding paragraph. A much simpler method is to add the annual discount factors and multiply this sum by the amount of the annual cash flow.

Interest tables

The calculation of discount factors (for example, $1/(1.1)^3 = .75131$) is time consuming. Fortunately, we don't have to make these calculations by hand. We can use a computer or a calculator containing a present-value program. If we don't have ready access to either of these, we can consult published tables of discount factors. We've provided an abbreviated set of these *interest tables* in Appendix A at the end of this book, together with instructions for using them.

Net present value

Our purpose in introducing the present value concept is to use it in evaluating capital expenditure proposals. Capital expenditures lead to both cash outlays and cash receipts. The difference between the total present value of the cash outlays and the total present value of the cash receipts is known as *net present value.*

For example, suppose the business is deciding whether to invest $925 now to receive $1,000 a year from now. The discount rate is 10 percent, based on annual compounding. These estimates are reflected in the following table:

Date	Cash Inflow (+) or Outflow (−)	Present Value at 10 Percent Multiplier	Amount
Immediately	−$ 925	1.000*	−$925
One year from now	+ 1,000	0.909	+ 909
Net present value			−$ 16

* The present value multiplier for an immediate payment or receipt is always 1.000. A dollar tomorrow is worth less than a dollar today, but a dollar today is a dollar. (Mathematically, if $n = 0$, then $(1 + r)^n = 1$.)

The array in the first two columns is known as a *timetable* of cash flows. Inflows are identified by plus signs; outflows are listed as minuses. The present values of the cash flows and their net present value are shown in the right-hand column.

The meaning of the discount rate

The discount rate we apply to future cash flows should be the minimum rate of return that will persuade owners and lenders to allow the organization to use their money. The percentage yield investors demand as a minimum reward for investing money in a company is the company's *cost of capital.* Risky companies have high capital costs; low-risk companies have low capital costs. If the expected reward is lower than the cost of capital, management won't find enough investors willing to invest their money in the company.

7.   If we set the discount rate equal to the cost of capital and the net present value of a capital expenditure proposal is positive, then the benefits from the expenditure will exceed its costs. For example, if the cost of capital is 10 percent, the company will find the proposal we described in the preceding section unattractive. The present value of the cash it would receive from this investment is $16 less than the $925 it would have to pay now to get this benefit. Another way of saying this is that if the firm requires a 10 percent return on investment, the future cash receipt of $1,000 is not big enough to repay the original investment ($925) plus a return on investment at an annual rate of 10 percent ($925 × 0.10 = $92.50).

Putting this still a different way, we can see that the company has to make two sacrifices to obtain the $1,000 a year from now: an outlay of $925 and $92.50 as the cost of obtaining $925 from its investors for a full year, a total of $1,017.50. From this viewpoint it appears that cost exceeds value by $17.50, again leading to rejection of the proposal. (Except for a rounding error, $17.50 is the future value of the $16 net present value we calculated in the table above.)

The argument for net present value

The advantage of the present value model is that it is the only one sensitive both to the timing of the anticipated cash flows and to the cost of capital. For example, a company can invest in any or all of the following proposals:

Years from Now	Net Cash Receipts (+) or Cash Outlays (−)		
	Proposal X	Proposal Y	Proposal Z
0	−$13,000	−$13,000	−$13,000
1	+ 1,000	+ 5,000	+ 9,000
2	+ 5,000	+ 5,000	+ 5,000
3	+ 9,000	+ 5,000	+ 1,000
Total cash flow	+$ 2,000	+$ 2,000	+$ 2,000

These three proposals have identical lifetime total cash flows, but they are far from equally desirable. Proposal Z is the best proposal because cash is received earlier under this proposal than under either of the others. Proposal X is the worst of the three.

These differences appear clearly in present value calculations. Assuming a 10 percent cost of capital, the present values of these proposals are:

Years from Now	Present Value Multipliers*	Proposal X	Proposal Y	Proposal Z
0	1.000	−$13,000	−$13,000	−$13,000
1	0.909	+ 909	+ 4,545	+ 8,181
2	0.826	+ 4,130	+ 4,130	+ 4,130
3	0.751	+ 6,759	+ 3,755	+ 750
Net present value		−$ 1,202	−$ 570	+$ 61

* From Table 1, Appendix A.

In this case, proposals X and Y promise a return on investment of less than 10 percent; only proposal Z promises a return in excess of 10 percent. Only proposal Z should be accepted. The present value measure, in other words, permits management to compare proposals that differ in the timing of their cash flows. Present value is the means by which all cash flows of all proposals can be restated at their equivalent values at a common point in time. These three proposals, therefore, can be compared directly with each other.

Calculating net present value: The procedure

The objective of the net present value model is to find out whether a given proposal promises a rate of return on investment at least equal to the minimum acceptable rate. If the rate of return is greater than the minimum rate, net present value will be positive. If the rate of return is too low, net present value will be negative. The procedure for determining which of these states exists is as follows:

1. Identify the proposal and at least one alternative to accepting it.
2. Estimate the cash flows, year by year, that would result if the proposal were accepted; make a similar set of estimates for each alternative being considered.
3. Discount the cash flows for each alternative to determine their present values and add these together to derive the *net present value* of this alternative.
4. Choose the alternative with the greatest present value.

Step 1:   Identify the alternatives.   A company is considering a proposal to invest $34,000 (proposal A). To evaluate this proposal, management has to identify at least one alternative to accepting it. If it has no alternative, it has no decision to make. In this case management has decided to introduce only one alternative: *reject proposal A.*

Step 2:   Estimate the cash flows.   One way to proceed would be to estimate the cash flows for the entire company under each alternative. This might be necessary for truly major capital expenditure proposals that would affect the basic nature and structure of the company's operations. A simpler approach, adequate for most capital-expenditure decisions, is to select one alternative as a benchmark and measure the cash flows of each other alternative as differences from that benchmark.

The reasons for identifying a benchmark alternative are described more fully in Chapter 4. In this case management has selected "reject proposal A" as the benchmark alternative. The cash flows relative to this benchmark are as follows:

Years from Now	Cash Flow
0..............	−$34,000
1..............	+ 10,000
2..............	+ 10,000
3..............	+ 10,000
4..............	+ 10,000
5..............	+ 10,000
Total.........	+$16,000

As usual, cash receipts are identified by (+) signs; the cash outlay is identified by a (−) sign.

Step 3: Discount the cash flows. This company regards 10 percent as the minimum acceptable rate of return on investment. Present-value multipliers can be taken from the 10 percent column of Table 1 in Appendix A. These multipliers and the present values of the incremental cash flows from proposal A are shown in Exhibit 18–2.

Exhibit 18–2 Calculating the net present value of proposal A

Years from Now	(1) Cash Flow	(2) Present Value at 10 Percent Multiplier (Table 1)	(3) Present Value at 10 Percent Amount (1) × (2)
0..............	−$34,000	1.000	−$34,000
1..............	+ 10,000	0.909	+ 9,090
2..............	+ 10,000	0.826	+ 8,260
3..............	+ 10,000	0.751	+ 7,510
4..............	+ 10,000	0.683	+ 6,830
5..............	+ 10,000	0.621	+ 6,210
Net present value........................			+$ 3,900

Step 4: Choose the best alternative. The decision rule implicit in the net present value model is to choose the alternative with the greatest net present value. Exhibit 18–2 shows that proposal A has a greater net present value than the only available alternative (the benchmark). This means that the cash flows it is expected to generate will be more than enough to recover the $34,000 initial outlay and to provide a 10 percent rate of return on the company's investment for five years. Since the company finds 10 percent an acceptable rate of return, it should be happy to accept proposal A.

Effect of varying the discount rate

Present value is extremely sensitive to the choice of the discount rate. The greater the rate at which future cash flows are discounted, the smaller the present value of a given stream of cash flows. Take proposal A, for example. In the preceding section we found that it has a net present value of $3,900 if the cash flows are discounted at 10 percent. If we use a discount rate of 15 percent, however, net present value becomes negative:

Years from Now	Cash Flow	Present Value at 15 Percent Multiplier*	Amount
0	−$34,000	1.000	−$34,000
1–5..............	+ 10,000 a year	3.352	+ 33,520
Net present value			−$ 480

* From Table 2, Appendix A.

The present value of the cash receipts at a 15 percent discount rate is only $33,520, producing a negative net present value. This means that the cash flows are not big enough to produce a rate of return as high as 15 percent.

The reason for this difference is that as the discount rate increases, more of each cash flow will go to pay the cost of capital on the amount invested, leaving less to repay the investment itself. This being the case, the company will be willing to invest less to obtain a given set of future cash receipts.

For example, if the discount rate is 10 percent and the company spends $34,000 on proposal A, the first year's interest (cost of capital) is $3,400. This can be met from the $10,000 cash receipt in the first year, leaving $6,600 as a partial recovery of the original investment. The unrecovered portion of the investment thus falls from $34,000 to $27,400 at the end of the first year. Interest on that in the second year is $2,740, leaving $7,260 of the second year's cash receipts to be treated as a recovery of another portion of the initial outlay. Continuing these calculations for three more years produces the following table:

Year	(1) Unrecovered Investment, Beginning of Year	(2) Interest at 10 Percent	(3) Amortization of Investment [$10,000 − (2)]	(4) Unrecovered Investment, End of Year (1) − (3)
1	$34,000	$3,400	$6,600	$27,400
2	27,400	2,740	7,260	20,140
3	20,140	2,014	7,986	12,154
4	12,154	1,215	8,785	3,369
5	3,369	337	9,663	(6,294)

By the end of the fifth year, the entire investment has been recovered, despite annual interest payments at a 10 percent rate, and the firm still has $6,294 left over (see Exhibit 18–3). In other words, the company could have paid more than 10 percent interest from the cash flows from this investment.[1]

---

[1] The $6,294 residual is the future value of $3,900 five years later, compounded annually at 10 percent.

Exhibit 18–3 The investment recovery pattern

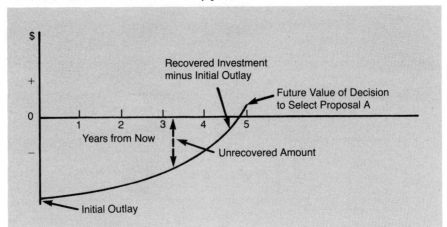

If we repeat this calculation using a 15 percent cost of capital, we get an entirely different result:

Year	(1) Unrecovered Investment, Beginning of Year	(2) Interest at 15 Percent	(3) Amortization of Investment [$10,000 − (2)]	(4) Unrecovered Investment, End of Year (1) − (3)
1	$34,000	$5,100	$4,900	$29,100
2	29,100	4,365	5,635	23,465
3	23,465	3,520	6,480	16,985
4	16,985	2,548	7,452	9,533
5	9,533	1,430	8,570	963

As this shows, $963 of the $34,000 initial cash outlay will remain unrecovered at the end of the five years if the company has a 15 percent cost of capital. (Except for a minor rounding error, $963 is the future value in five years of $480 now, the amount we calculated earlier as the negative net present value of proposal A at 15 percent.)

The internal rate of return

Net present value is sometimes an awkward figure to use in discussing the merits of individual capital expenditure proposals. For this reason some companies prefer to use the *internal rate of return,* defined as that rate of discount at which the net present value is zero. Calculating the internal rate of return is a three-step, trial-and-error process:

Step 1. Discount all cash flows at a trial rate. We have already performed this step. The net present value of the cash flows at 10 percent is

$3,900. This indicates that the rate of return is greater than 10 percent, but it doesn't show how much greater.

Step 2.   Discount all cash flows at a second trial rate.   Since we know that the internal rate of return is higher than 10 percent, a reasonable second trial rate is 15 percent. Again, we have already performed this step. The net present value of the cash flows at 15 percent is −$480. We now know the internal rate of return is less than 15 percent because the proposal won't earn enough to cover a 15 percent cost of capital.

Step 3.   Interpolate.   The true rate of return is somewhere between 10 percent and 15 percent. It is the rate of return at which net present value equals zero. We can approximate this by interpolating between two points on a graph, as shown in Exhibit 18–4. We can do the same thing algebraically, again rounding the answer to the nearest 10th of a percent:

Exhibit 18–4 Interpolating to approximate the internal rate of return

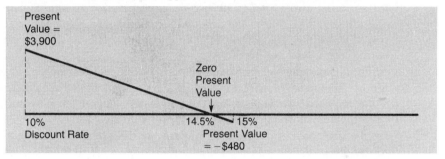

$$\text{Approximate rate} = 10\% + \frac{\$3,900}{\$3,900 + \$480} \times (15\% - 10\%) = 14.5\%$$

($3,900 + $480 = $4,380 is the total distance between +$3,900 and −$480.)

The compounding interval

Present value is affected to some extent by the length of the compounding interval. Interest may be compounded once a year, once every six months, quarterly, monthly, daily, or even instantaneously. The more frequently interest must be compounded, the less a given stream of future cash flows is worth today.

For example, suppose we have a proposal which is expected to generate a single cash receipt of $10,000 two years from now. If the interest rate is 10 percent a year and interest is compounded once a year, the present value of this cash receipt will be $10,000/(1.10)² = $8,264. If the compounding interval is cut in half, to six months, and an interest rate of 5 percent a period is used, the present value of this cash receipt will be $10,000/(1.05)⁴ = $8,227.

(1.05 is raised to the fourth power because there are four six-month periods in two years.) The present value is $37 smaller now because the company demands that interest be compounded twice a year—therefore $37 more of the future cash flow must be used to cover the cost of capital.

We'll use annual compounding—a one-year compounding interval—throughout this chapter. This is generally accurate enough, given the error ranges in the estimates of future cash flows. When precision is important, however, the compounding interval ordinarily should be reduced. In most money market operations today, daily compounding is commonplace because money can be invested or borrowed for a period as short as a single day.

Other measures of the acceptability of proposals

Two measures of the desirability of capital expenditure proposals are often used to supplement or substitute for present value calculations. The first of these is the *payback period,* the time that will elapse before cumulative cash receipts will equal cumulative cash outlays. For example, proposal D, calling for an initial outlay of $10,000, with an expectation of annual cash receipts of $4,000 and $6,000 in the first two years of its life, has a two-year payback period ($4,000 + $6,000 = $10,000). Presumably, the shorter the payback period, the better the proposal.

The main defect of payback period is that it ignores the estimated useful life of the proposed expenditures. If the facilities to be acquired will have to be replaced two years from now, or if the market for the product dries up at the end of that time, the expenditure will have achieved no net earnings for the company. Alternatively, if a large portion of the investment outlay is for working capital with a high end-of-life recovery value, the proposal may be more desirable than another with a shorter payback period but no end-of-life value.

The second supplemental measure of the value of an individual proposal is the so-called *average return on investment.* This is calculated by dividing the average incremental lifetime earnings (net cash flow less incremental depreciation) either by the initial investment outlay or by an average of the initial outlay and end-of-life residual value. Suppose proposal D is expected to be productive for three years, with cash receipts of $8,000 in the third year and no end-of-life residual value. Incremental annual earnings, assuming straight-line depreciation, are calculated as follows:

Year	Incremental Cash Flow	Incremental Depreciation	Incremental Earnings
1	$ 4,000	$ 3,333	$ 667
2	6,000	3,333	2,667
3	8,000	3,334	4,666
Total	$18,000	$10,000	$8,000
Average	$ 6,000	$ 3,333	$2,667

The average return on investment, using the initial outlay as the denominator, is $2,667/$10,000 = 26.7 percent. If we take the $5,000 average investment as the denominator, the average rate of return is 53.3 percent. In contrast, the internal rate of return, calculated by the discounted cash flow method we described earlier, is about 32 percent.

This method does consider the expected life of the facilities, and it does consider the amount of end-of-life salvage. It fails, however, to allow for differences in timing of outlays and receipts. By this method a project in which no receipts appear until the 10th year will appear to be just as profitable as a project in which most of the cash is received in the first few years of the project's life, as long as the average is the same.

Estimating the cash flows: Initial outlays

Any subdivision of the cash flows associated with a capital expenditure proposal is partly arbitrary. All that matters is the amount and timing of the cash flows; whether some are called investment outlays while others are called maintenance expenses is relevant only insofar as the classification coincides with the classification scheme used by the taxing authorities to determine the tax effects of the outlays. We find it convenient, however, to distinguish four components of the cash flow stream:

1. The initial outlay.
2. Secondary investment outlays.
3. Operating cash flows.
4. End-of-life residual values.

The initial outlay consists of all the cash flows that must take place before significant operating receipts or cost savings begin to flow in. It contains some or all of the following:

1. Cash outlays for plant and equipment.
2. Opportunity costs of existing facilities to be incorporated in the proposal.
3. Outlays for working capital.
4. Disposal values of facilities to be displaced by the proposal.
5. Immediate income tax effects.

Outlays for plant and equipment

For most proposals, the major outlays are for the acquisition and installation of physical facilities. For example, a proposal to modernize a factory is expected to require the following outlays before the investment begins to bring in cash receipts:

Equipment	$80,000
Installation	10,000
Training and test runs	7,000
Total	$97,000

If these outlays are spread over a period longer than six months, they should be divided and dated at the nearest year-end. In most cases it is accurate enough to assume that all these cash flows take place at one time. In this case we'll assume they all take place within a very short period, which we'll refer to as the *zero date.*

Existing facilities used

One of the company's present machines, now idle, will be put back in service only if the modernization proposal is approved. No cash needs to be paid for this machine—the company already owns it. Even so, it belongs in the timetable. By accepting the proposal, management will make this machine unavailable for any other use. This proposal therefore should be charged for the machine's value in its best other use—that is, its opportunity cost.

In this case, management agrees that the machine will be sold if it is not needed for the modernization proposal. The estimated sale price is $12,000. This is part of the investment outlay because in accepting the proposal the company is depriving itself of $12,000 in cash:

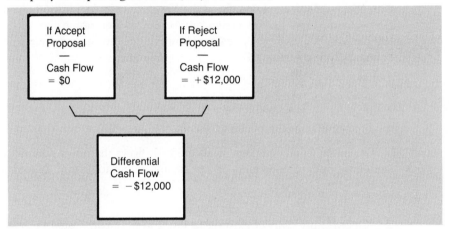

A cash receipt forgone is always equivalent to a cash outlay. The book value of the equipment doesn't measure either current or future cash flows, and therefore should be ignored.

Working capital

Capital expenditure proposals often require outlays for resources other than land, buildings, and equipment. Cash outlays for product development, working capital, or market research are just as much part of the investment required by a capital expenditure proposal as outlays for fixed assets.

The only additional outlays required by our illustrative modernization proposal are outlays for working capital. To use the new equipment effectively, management will have to increase inventories by $5,000, of which suppliers will provide only $3,000. In addition, management will have to immobilize $1,000 of cash to support the additional volume of activity the proposal will generate. Putting these together, we get a working capital requirement of $5,000 + $1,000 − $3,000 = $3,000, all to be provided at the same time the equipment is put in place.

The proposal also calls for a further increase in working capital, as receivables arise from the first year's operations. It is often convenient to include this increase as part of the initial outlay. It actually arises, however, because sales revenues exceed collections from customers in the course of operations. For this reason we'll handle it as part of the operating cash flow.

Displaced facilities

The cash flows we have mentioned overstate the amount of investment that will be necessary. If the proposal is accepted, a machine now serving a standby purpose can be disposed of. This machine has a tax basis (book value) of only $1,000, but once again opportunity cost, not book value, is the right measure of the cash flow. Opportunity cost is measured by the machine's scrap value, $6,000. The displaced machine, in other words, can finance $6,000 of the gross pretax outlays the proposal will require.

This may become clearer if we point out once again that we are really comparing two alternatives in our cash flow estimates:

A Accept the Proposal and Dispose of Existing Standby Equipment +$6,000	B Reject the Proposal and Keep the Standby Equipment +$0

The only way to get the $6,000 cash inflow is to accept this proposal. It therefore becomes a cash inflow attributable to the proposal and must be included in the timetable.

Tax effects of the initial outlay

Income taxes are cash flows. Like other cash flows, their amount and timing can affect the present value of capital expenditure proposals.

Each country provides its own taxing rules, and individual states, provinces, and local governmental bodies may also tax the organization's income. These rules are often extremely complex; they also change frequently. For these reasons we can only illustrate how some kinds of tax provisions can affect the cash flows.

Tax rates also vary and different tax rates are likely to apply to different portions of the taxable income stream. To simplify the presentation, we'll assume that a tax rate of 40 percent is applied to all items affecting taxable income. We'll also assume that the company has taxable income from other sources to offset any losses the proposal would otherwise generate for tax purposes. Losses therefore are also subject to the 40 percent tax rate.

Our initial outlay has four separate kinds of tax effects: a tax credit, a tax deduction, a tax-deductible loss, and a taxable gain. (A tax credit is a direct reduction in the amount of tax due; a tax deduction is a reduction in the amount of taxable income.)

Tax credit.   Many governments offer tax credits to induce business firms to invest in facilities or to increase their inventories, thereby providing jobs and stimulating the economy. In our illustration, the $80,000 outlay for new equipment is eligible for a 10 percent tax credit. This will reduce the tax by $8,000, and this amount should be deducted in calculating the initial outlay.

Tax deduction.   Some portions of the initial outlay may be deducted from taxable income immediately; others must be capitalized for tax purposes. In our illustration, both the purchase price and the installation cost of the new equipment will be capitalized and depreciated for tax purposes over a period of years. The $7,000 in training and test-run costs, however, will be fully deductible from taxable revenues right away. At a 40 percent tax rate, this will reduce current taxes by $2,800. The after-tax outlay for these items therefore is $7,000 − $2,800 = $4,200.

Tax-deductible loss.   We have already seen that accepting the proposal will deprive the company of the $12,000 cash flow from selling an idle machine. It will also deprive the company of the right to enter the loss from the sale of the machine on the current income tax return. The loss for tax purposes is the difference between the proceeds from the sale and book value for tax purposes (the "tax basis"), which in this case happens to be $20,000:

Sale value	$12,000
Tax basis	20,000
Tax-deductible loss	$ 8,000

Since this would reduce taxable income, it would also reduce taxes. Using the machine will deprive the company of this tax reduction. It thus becomes another cash outflow arising from the proposed investment. At a tax rate of 40 percent, the tax effect is $3,200. The aftertax cash flow is:

Sale value	$12,000
Tax reduction due to loss	3,200
Aftertax cash flow	$15,200

Taxable gain.   The final element in the initial outlay calculation, the sale of the displaced machine, also has a tax effect. The market value of this machine is $6,000, and the tax basis is $1,000, so the taxable gain is $5,000. The cash flows are:

Market value	$6,000
Tax on the gain: 40% × $5,000	2,000
Aftertax cash flow	$4,000

The aftertax investment outlay.   All these figures are summarized in Exhibit 18–5. In this case the net difference between the pretax and aftertax amounts is relatively small, less than 6 percent; in other cases it will be much higher.

Exhibit 18–5 Calculation of incremental aftertax initial outlay

Item	Incremental Outlay before Tax	Tax Effect	Incremental Outlay after Tax
Equipment, installed	$ 90,000	$(8,000)	$ 82,000
Working capital	3,000	0	3,000
Training and test runs	7,000	(2,800)	4,200
Surplus equipment used	12,000	3,200	15,200
Equipment displaced	(6,000)	2,000	(4,000)
Total	$106,000	$(5,600)	$100,400

We might also display the aftertax cash flows in another way:

	If Accept Proposal	If Reject Proposal	Incremental Cash Flow
Equipment, installed	−$82,000	—	−$ 82,000
Working capital	− 3,000	—	− 3,000
Training and test runs	− 4,200	—	− 4,200
Surplus equipment	—	+$15,200	− 15,200
Displaced equipment	+ 4,000	—	+ 4,000
Net outlay	−$85,200	+$15,200	−$100,400

Minus signs identify cash outlays; plus signs identify cash receipts. This form of display has the advantage of showing the alternatives clearly; the net increment is the same, however.

Estimating cash flows: Secondary outlays

Management can often predict special outlays that will have to be made in later time periods to keep the investment alive. These, too, may be for equipment or for additional working capital. Each has to be examined for its tax implications.

Secondary investment outlays of this sort are no different in concept from the initial outlay, and need no further discussion here. The only secondary investment outlay management anticipates for the plant modernization proposal is $20,000 to replace equipment at the end of the fifth year. This will have no immediate impact on taxes, and $20,000 is the after-tax cash flow.

Estimating operating cash flows

The incremental pretax operating cash flow in our illustrative modernization proposal is expected to come partly from increased sales volume, partly from reduced operating costs. Once again we could present the cash flows under our two alternatives in two columns, with an incremental column at the right:

Years from Zero Date	If Accept Proposal	If Reject Proposal	Incremental Cash Flow
1	X	Y	X − Y

In this case, however, management has much less confidence in its ability to forecast the absolute results under each alternative than in its ability to forecast the differences between them. Both costs and expenses are expected to increase from year to year, but the gap between the two alternatives is expected to remain roughly constant at $9,000 a year in increased revenues and $16,000 in reduced operating expenses (other than depreciation and income taxes), a total of $25,000.

Translating income into cash flow

The $25,000 increment we just described is an increase in operating income before depreciation and income taxes. What we want, of course, is the increment in cash flow. In this illustration, we have only one adjustment to make to convert the former into the latter, to reflect a $2,000, one-time increase in accounts receivable during the first year of operations. In other words, the first year's net incremental cash flow will be $2,000 smaller than incremental operating income because the incremental collections from customers will be $2,000 smaller than the increment in sales revenues in that year. The first year's pretax operating cash flows therefore are expected to be as follows:

Increase in collections: $9,000 − $2,000	$ 7,000
Decrease in disbursements	16,000
Incremental pretax operating cash flow, first year	$23,000

An alternative approach is to record the operating cash flow as $25,000, with the $2,000 increase in receivables shown as part of the initial investment outlay. The approach described here is essentially the same, but it may be slightly clearer and the cash flow may be timed more accurately.

Adjusting for income taxes

The next step in the analysis is to calculate the effect of the estimated increments in operating income on the company's income taxes. In this calculation we usually start with the pretax cash flows, but the spread between the revenues and expenses shown on the company's income tax returns is likely to differ significantly from the pretax cash flow figures. One source of difference between these two amounts is the effect of accrual accounting on taxable income, as described in the preceding paragraphs. Another source is governmental attempts to influence taxpayer behavior by disallowing certain kinds of cash outflows as deductions from taxable income (e.g., court fines and penalties in some taxing jurisdictions) or by accelerating or decelerating the recognition of certain kinds of revenues or expenses.

The only significant differences between pretax cash flow and incremental taxable income in our illustration are the first-year increase in receivables we just described and incremental tax depreciation. Depreciation charges aren't cash flows, but they do enter into the calculation of taxable income, which does affect cash flow. Incremental depreciation in this case is the difference between the quantities described in the two right-hand boxes below:

Depreciation on property required by the project		

	Tax Basis	Tax Depreciation
New equipment	$90,000 ⎫	
Existing machine	20,000 ⎬ 20% of declining balance
Secondary investment	20,000 ⎭	

Depreciation on property displaced by the project		

	Tax Basis	Tax Depreciation
Displaced machine	$1,000	$500 a year for two years

Depreciation calculated on these bases is summarized in Exhibit 18–6. Following tax practice in the United States, our illustrative company doesn't have to deduct the $8,000 initial tax credit from the cost of the equipment in determining its initial tax basis. The $110,000 tax basis shown at the top of

Exhibit 18–6 Calculation of incremental tax depreciation

	(1)	(2)	(3)	(4)	(5)	(6)
Year	Tax Basis, Start of Year	Additions	Tax Depreciation 20% × [(1) + (2)]	Tax Basis, End of Year (1) + (2) − (3)	Tax Depreciation, Replaced Equipment	Incremental Tax Depreciation (3) − (5)
1	$110,000	—	$22,000	$88,000	$500	$21,500
2	88,000	—	17,600	$70,400	500	17,100
3	70,400	—	14,080	56,320	—	14,080
4	56,320	—	11,264	45,056	—	11,264
5	45,056	—	9,012	36,044	—	9,012
6	36,044	$20,000	11,209	44,835	—	11,209
7	44,835	—	8,967	35,868	—	8,967
8	35,868	—	7,174	28,694	—	7,174
9	28,694	—	5,739	22,955	—	5,739
10	22,955	—	4,591	18,364	—	4,591

column (1) therefore is the full capitalized cost of the new equipment ($90,000) plus the $20,000 remaining basis (initial basis minus tax depreciation to date) of the existing equipment the company is incorporating into the proposal. Tax depreciation on the equipment required by the proposal is determined in this illustration by multiplying the tax basis by 20 percent.[2] It amounts to

---

[2] Tax depreciation in the United States for depreciable assets acquired in 1981 and later is based on the *accelerated cost recovery system* rather than on the double-rate, declining-balance method illustrated here. This method, which was adopted after this chapter was set in type, generally leads to shorter tax lives and more rapid amortization for tax purposes than the methods in use for assets acquired before 1981.

$22,000 in the first year, which reduces the tax basis to $88,000, which then becomes the basis for the calculation in the second year.

The tax depreciation figures in column (3) of Exhibit 18–6 don't measure *incremental* tax depreciation. If the proposal is rejected, the equipment it would displace will be kept. Tax depreciation of $500 a year will be recorded for the first two years, until the equipment is fully depreciated. This means that incremental tax depreciation for each of the first two years is $500 less than the figures shown in column (3). The incremental depreciation schedule is shown in column (6).

Our reason for deducting tax depreciation on the displaced equipment may be easier to understand if it is recognized as a simple time shift. If the proposal is accepted, the equipment will be replaced and $1,000 will be deducted immediately from taxable income. We incorporated this $1,000 deduction in our calculation of the tax effect of the initial outlay. If the proposal is rejected, on the other hand, the equipment will be retained and the $1,000 will be deducted from taxable income during the next two years.

Aftertax operating cash flows

Given the before-tax cash flows and the tax depreciation figures, we can calculate taxable income, income tax effects, and aftertax cash flows. Exhibit 18–7 summarizes the operating cash flow calculations. The figures in column (1) show the estimated effect of the proposal on the company's tax return, except for tax depreciation. The next three columns are used to calculate the income tax effect. Column (5) shows the estimated pretax cash flows, in this case identical to the figures in column (1) except for the $2,000 increment in accounts receivable in the first year. The incremental cash flow is then found by subtracting the incremental tax in column (4) from the pretax cash flow.

Exhibit 18–7 Calculation of aftertax operating cash flows

Year	(1) Incremental Income before Depreciation and Income Tax	(2) Incremental Tax Depreciation	(3) Incremental Taxable Income (1) − (2)	(4) Incremental Income Tax 40% × (3)	(5) Incremental Cash Flow before Income Tax	(6) Incremental Cash Flow (5) − (4)
1	$ 25,000	$ 21,500	$ 3,500	$ 1,400	$ 23,000	$ 21,600
2	25,000	17,100	7,900	3,160	25,000	21,840
3	25,000	14,080	10,920	4,368	25,000	20,632
4	25,000	11,264	13,736	5,494	25,000	19,506
5	25,000	9,012	15,988	6,395	25,000	18,605
6	25,000	11,209	13,791	5,516	25,000	19,484
7	25,000	8,967	16,033	6,413	25,000	18,587
8	25,000	7,174	17,826	7,130	25,000	17,870
9	25,000	5,739	19,261	7,704	25,000	17,296
10	25,000	4,591	20,409	8,164	25,000	16,836
Total ..	$250,000	$110,636	$139,364	$55,744	$248,000	$192,256

Notice how the declining-charge depreciation has changed the constant annual before-tax cash flow into a stream of gradually declining amounts. This makes this proposal more valuable than if only the straight-line method were available.

End-of-life residual value

The final cash flow associated with a capital expenditure proposal is the cash value of the facilities and working capital remaining when the project's life comes to an end. This value is usually referred to as the residual value or, less elegantly, as salvage value. Residual values are quite important for short-lived investments, less so for projects with long lives. To find out whether residual values are important, we should always prepare rough estimates except for extremely long-lived projects.

Pretax residual values

Management expects the plant modernization expenditures to be productive for about 10 years, for the reasons we'll describe later, in the section headed "Economic life." At the end of that time the company can renovate the facilities once more or liquidate them. If it liquidates, it can reasonably expect to recover most of its investment in working capital, together with the salvage value of the remaining equipment.

The pretax incremental residual value relevant to today's capital expenditure decision is shown in Exhibit 18–8. This shows that the company expects to be able to recover $10,000 from the sale of equipment and $5,000 from the liquidation of the incremental working capital required by today's proposal. The incremental residual value is $1,500 less than $15,000, however. If the proposal is rejected, the company will keep its standby machine instead of

Exhibit 18–8 Calculation of incremental pretax residual value

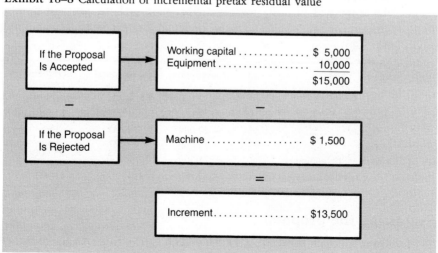

selling it now. The estimated sale value of that machine 10 years from now is $1,500, and this must be deducted in calculating the pretax incremental residual value from today's proposal.

Notice that what we have done is insert this old machine in the timetable twice, once as part of the initial investment and once as part of the residual value. The current salvage value of this machine, $6,000, was entered into the timetable through Exhibit 18–5 as a cash receipt (deduction from the initial cash outlay); its value 10 years from now should be classified as an outlay (deduction from the end-of-life salvage value), as in the following table:

Years from Now	If Proposal Is Accepted	If Proposal Is Rejected	Incremental Cash Flows
0	+$6,000		+$6,000
10	—	+$1,500	− 1,500

Taxes on the residual values

The $5,000 estimated liquidation value of the incremental working capital is just equal to its tax basis ($1,000 in cash, $2,000 in receivables, $5,000 in inventories, less $3,000 in trade payables) and no taxable gain or loss will arise.

The equipment required by the proposal will have a tax basis of $18,364 at the end of 10 years, as we saw in the bottom line of Exhibit 18–6. This is $8,364 greater than the anticipated salvage value. If we assume that losses on the sale of equipment are deductible from revenues in the calculation of taxable income, then a tax credit will arise 10 years from now as a result of the sale of this equipment. If the 40 percent tax rate is applicable to this loss, the tax credit will be 0.4 × $8,364 = $3,345. The cash flow from the sale of the equipment therefore will be $3,345 *larger* than its sale value.

The standby machine the company will still have if the proposal is rejected will be fully depreciated 10 years from now. The $1,500 liquidation value therefore will be fully taxable at that time and the tax will be $600 if the 40 percent rate applies. The incremental aftertax residual value therefore is $17,445:

	Incremental Pretax Cash Flow	Incremental Income Tax	Incremental Aftertax Cash Flow
Working capital	$ 5,000	—	$ 5,000
Equipment....................	10,000	$(3,345)	13,345
Total	15,000	(3,345)	18,345
Less: Standby equipment	1,500	600	900
Net residual value	$13,500	$(3,945)	$17,445

Evaluating the proposal

Once the cash flow estimates have been made, three stages of the evaluation process remain:

1. Calculating the net present value of the proposal.
2. Verifying the benchmark and revising the analysis, if appropriate.
3. Adjusting for uncertainty.

Calculating present value

Once the cash flows have been estimated, calculating present value is a simple matter. The first step is to enter the cash flows in a timetable, as in the first three columns of Exhibit 18–9. The first column shows the initial outlay, the renovation outlay five years later, and the end-of-life residual value. These are added to the operating cash flows to get the total cash flow figures in column (3). The minimum acceptable rate of return in our illustrative company is 10 percent after taxes. Using present value factors for a 10 percent discount rate, we get the figures shown in the right-hand column of the exhibit.

These calculations show that the present value of the modernization proposal is $14,661, the total of the figures in the right-hand column. This means that, if the estimates are correct, the future operating cash receipts will be big enough to pay back the amounts invested ($100,400 and $20,000) and pay interest on these amounts at an annual rate of 10 percent after taxes, with enough left over to increase the company's value now by $14,661. Other things being equal, the proposal should be accepted.

In practice, we might wish to shift some of the cash flows to different points in the timetable. Operating cash flows take place throughout the year, for example, not at the end of the year, tax payments may lag the tax accrual by a number of months, and residual values may flow in after the end of the 10th year. In most cases, however, the impact of these refinements on the calculated present value will be too small to have a significant impact on the capital expenditure decision.

Exhibit 18–9 Calculation of present value

	(1)	(2)	(3)	(4)	(5)
			Total	Present Value at 10%	
Years from Now	Investment Cash Flow after Taxes	Operating Cash Flow after Taxes	Cash Flow after Taxes (1) + (2)	Multiplier*	Amount (3) × (4)
0..........	−$100,400	—	−$100,400	1.000	−$100,400
1..........	—	$ 21,600	+ 21,600	0.909	+ 19,634
2..........	—	+ 21,840	21,840	0.826	+ 18,040
3..........	—	+ 20,632	+ 20,632	0.751	+ 15,495
4..........	—	+ 19,506	+ 19,506	0.683	+ 13,323
5..........	− 20,000	+ 18,605	− 1,395	0.621	− 866
6..........	—	+ 19,484	+ 19,484	0.564	+ 10,989
7..........	—	+ 18,587	+ 18,587	0.513	+ 9,535
8..........	—	+ 17,870	+ 17,870	0.467	+ 8,345
9..........	—	+ 17,296	+ 17,296	0.424	+ 7,334
10..........	+ 17,445	+ 16,836	+ 34,281	0.386	+ 13,232
Total					+$ 14,661

* From Table 1, Appendix A.

Verifying the benchmark

The second stage in the evaluation process is making sure the proposal has been compared with the right benchmark. Two possibilities are worth noting:

1. The benefits sought can be achieved with a smaller investment outlay.
2. The benefits sought are inadequate to cover both the new investment and the continuing investment in existing facilities and working capital.

Same benefit; smaller investment. Many investment proposals are designed to provide capacity to handle new products or move into new markets. The cash flow estimates assign all the benefits from the new product or market to the proposed investment outlay. This may be a mistake.

A proposal to build a new warehouse, for example, may show a high net present value because warehouse space is necessary to support the sales of a new product. It may be, however, that some of the present warehouse space used to store low-margin items would be just as suitable for the new product as the new warehouse. Recognizing this can put the proposal in an entirely different light because it redefines the benchmark.

Suppose the products with the lowest profit contributions provide total cash flows of $100,000, before deducting warehouse costs. The new product, requiring the same amount of space, would have total cash flows of $500,000. The company can improve its cash position by $400,000 without one penny of additional invesement in warehouse space. This means that the new warehouse is really being built to enable the company to continue to sell its present low-margin products. The question is whether the investment in the new warehouse can be justified by annual cash flows of $100,000, not $500,000.

The disinvestment benchmark. Investments that appear worth making if the analysis is based on an invest/don't invest comparison may be totally unjustified if they are in support of unprofitable activities. The company might be better off to discontinue the activity entirely than to continue on its present course. If this is so, then the cash inflows from the new investment proposal must be large enough to support both the new investment and the liquidation value of the present investment as well.

For example, suppose the company facing our plant modernization proposal could liquidate the present plant, equipment, and working capital now for $500,000 after taxes. If the plant were kept open but not modernized, its annual operating cash flow after taxes would be about $60,000, but routine replacement expenditures would run about $40,000 a year. At the end of 10 years the plant, equipment, and working capital would bring in about $400,000, again after taxes.

These figures are summarized in Exhibit 18–10. It is clear that unless something drastic can be done to improve the cash flows, the plant should be closed. This being the case, continued operation is no longer the relevant benchmark. The question now is whether the proposed modernization is good enough to restore this operation to health. If not, the additional expenditure would be wasted. The comparison, in other words, should be between the

Exhibit 18–10 Present value of continuing the present operation

Years from Now	Cash Flow after Taxes			Present Value at 10 Percent	
	If Sell Now	If Keep	Difference	Multiplier	Amount
0..........	+$500,000	—	−$500,000	1.000	−$500,000
1 to 10	—	+$ 20,000 a year	+ 20,000 a year	6.145*	+ 122,900
10	—	+ 400,000	+ 400,000	0.386†	+ 154,400
Total					−$222,700

* From Table 2, Appendix A.
† From Table 1, Appendix A.

proposal and the best available alternative, in this case to close down. The calculation is:

Present value if operated in present condition (Exhibit 18–10) .... −$222,700
Present value of contribution from renovation (Exhibit 18–9) .... + 14,661
   Net present value .... −$208,039

The renovation proposal is not good enough. Instead of pouring good money after bad, the company should close the plant and reinvest the proceeds elsewhere.

Adjusting for uncertainty

The decision model we have been describing so far is deterministic—that is, each value is assumed to be known with certainty. In fact, each of the determinants of net present value—market size, wage rates, economic life, selling prices, and so on—is better described by a probability distribution than by a single value. The number of combinations of possible values is enormous, completely beyond our ability to calculate or digest.

One way out of this is to calculate limit values, by bracketing anticipated cash flows with pessimistic and optimistic estimates. A project with an anticipated net present value of $250,000, for example, might actually have a negative present value if events turn out to be worse than anticipated, or have a net present value of $1 million if the situation proves better than management now anticipates. This can be very useful information. Decision making is a judgmental process and these bracketing calculations can give management a better feel for the variability of the end result.

The weakness of this approach is that it ignores the probabilities. Should the pessimistic estimates reflect the worst conceivable values of the variables or values somewhere in the lowest quartile of the probability distribution? The apparent variability of the net present value or rate of return will depend on how this question is answered.

An alternative approach is to *simulate* the results, using a five-step process known as the Monte Carlo method:

1. Estimate the probability distribution for each important variable.
2. Select combinations of these values at random, giving each possible value a chance of being selected proportional to its probability.
3. Calculate net present value or rate of return for each of these combinations.
4. List the results of all the combinations tested, showing how many indicated a net present value of, say, −$10,000, how many had a net present value of −$5,000, and so on. This is known as a frequency distribution.
5. Plot this frequency distribution on a chart or charts.[3]

The two charts in Exhibit 18–11 show the frequency distributions associated with two competing proposals. Management can accept only one of these. The probabilities of different payoffs are symmetrically distributed for each proposal. Proposal A has a lower expected value than proposal B—50 percent of the simulations had a net present value of less than $10,000, as opposed to $15,000 for proposal B. Proposal A is much more certain, however. Almost all the simulated combinations for this proposal had present values between $5,000 and $15,000, while proposal B had quite a few with negative net present values and some with net present values in excess of $30,000.

Exhibit 18–11 Simulation charts for two competing proposals

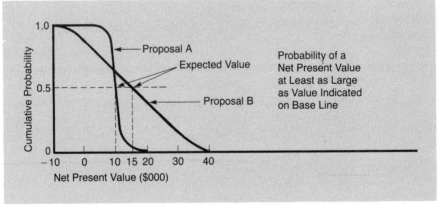

If the decision makers' utility function is linear, they will take proposal B because it offers the higher net present value. The decision makers may weight a possible loss more heavily than a possible gain, however. If so, they may favor proposal A because it has a much smaller probability of producing a loss. The capital expenditure simulation chart will help them make this kind of comparison.

---

[3] An explanation of this approach published some years ago but still the clearest explanation around is by David B. Hertz, "Risk Analysis in Capital Investment" *Harvard Business Review,* January–February 1964, pp. 95–106. See also his "Investment Policies that Pay Off," *Harvard Business Review,* January–February 1968, pp. 96–108.

The impact of inflation

Inflation affects both the cost of capital and the cash flows emanating from capital expenditures. The aftertax cost of debt capital in the United States, for example, rose from less than 3 percent in the mid-1950s to 9 percent and more in the early 1980s, as investors sought to compensate themselves for the declining purchasing power of the money they would be receiving in return for the use of their funds. Inflation also affected the cash flows during this period. Equipment that was originally expected to produce labor savings at labor costs of $5 an hour turned out to yield savings of $10 an hour as wage rates and employee benefits rose.

Management should build its expectations of future prices and wage rates into its cash flow forecasts. As the cost of capital goes up, with its built-in adjustment for inflation, the apparent desirability of capital expenditure proposals will fall unless the cash flow estimates are adjusted accordingly. Some proposals will benefit, as their cash flow rates advance more rapidly than the rate of inflation; others will suffer, as the markets in which they operate fail to provide benefits matching the rate of inflationary change. This means that multiplying currently anticipated cash flows by some general-purpose index of the overall inflation rate won't work. Management has to be able to distinguish between proposals that will benefit from inflation or resist its inroads and others that will suffer.

Economic life

In principle, cash flows should be estimated for the period known as the economic life of the investment. The economic life of any asset is the time elapsing between the time of acquisition and the time at which the combined forces ✳ of obsolescence and deterioration justify replacing it or withdrawing it from service. The economic life of any tangible asset is the *shortest* of the following three figures:

1. Physical life.
2. Technological life.
3. Market life of the asset's output.

Although many assets can be repaired and kept in service almost indefinitely, physical life generally comes to an end when replacing an asset is cheaper than continuing to repair it. Physical life is seldom the measure of economic life in a rapidly changing economy, however. New processes and new equipment often make existing equipment obsolete long before physical life comes to an end—that is, the spread between the cash flows from operating the asset and the cash flows from operating a new asset may become wide enough to justify replacement even if the old asset's operating costs have not risen at all.

Finally, the product market may change even before this happens, so that the company can no longer sell the asset's output at a profitable price. When this happens, life comes to an end even though technological obsolescence has not yet taken its toll.

The economic life of an investment project may be very different from the life of any one of the assets required by the project. It may include buildings with a life of 50 years, production equipment with a life of 15 years, test equipment with a 3-year life, and working capital with an infinite life. The estimated life of such a project is determined not so much by the lives of the physical facilities as by the expected duration of the stream of cash flows generated by the project. The life of the investment, in other words, will end when the present value of the remaining cash flows has fallen below the recovery value of the facilities and working capital.

Multiple alternatives

So far we have assumed that the decision maker has only two alternatives: accept the proposal or reject it. This is not always true. For major capital expenditure proposals, management should insist that a real effort be made to identify one or more substitute proposals that might fill the same needs in different ways. Once this has been done, management should select the proposal with the greatest positive net present value; if none of the proposals has a positive net present value, all should be rejected.

For example, we saw earlier that proposal A has an estimated present value of $3,900. Instead of accepting this proposal, however, management can accept either proposal B or proposal C. The cash flows and multipliers for proposals B and C are as follows:

	(1)	(2)	(3)	(4)	(5)
			Proposal B		Proposal C
	Present				
Years	Value		Present		Present
from	Multiplier	Cash	Value	Cash	Value
Now	at 10 Percent	Flow	(1) × (2)	Flow	(1) × (4)
0............	1.000	−$56,000	−$56,000	−$45,000	−$45,000
1............	0.909	+ 16,000	+ 14,544	+ 15,000	+ 13,635
2............	0.826	+ 16,000	+ 13,216	+ 15,000	+ 12,390
3............	0.751	+ 16,000	+ 12,016	+ 15,000	+ 11,265
4............	0.683	+ 16,000	+ 10,928	+ 10,000	+ 6,830
5............	0.621	+ 16,000	+ 9,936	+ 5,000	+ 3,105
Net present value.................			+$ 4,640		+$ 2,225

Proposal B offers a higher net present value than proposal A; the net present value of proposal C is lower than that of either of the other two. Proposal B therefore should be chosen.

Incremental rate of return. The same conclusion can be reached by internal rate of return calculations, but the path is slightly more difficult. To begin with, we know that the internal rate of return for proposal B is better than 10 percent because it has a positive net present value at that rate. If we try 15 percent, we get a negative net present value:

Years from Now	Cash Flow	Multiplier at 15 Percent	Present Value
0	−$56,000	1.000	−$56,000
1–5	+ 16,000 a year	3.352	+ 53,632
Net present value			−$ 2,368

Interpolating, we find that the internal rate of return for proposal B is 13.3 percent. Earlier we found that the internal rate of return for proposal A is approximately 14.5 percent. Here is the paradox: proposal B has a lower internal rate of return than proposal A, but proposal B has a greater net present value at 10 percent than proposal A (+$4,640 instead of +$3,900).

The way out of this dilemma is to calculate the *incremental* internal rate of return. What is the additional return from the additional investment proposal B requires? The increments are as follows:

[handwritten note: cremental IRR]

Years from Now	Proposal A	Proposal B	Increment (B − A)
0	−$34,000	−$56,000	−$22,000
1–5	+ 10,000 a year	+ 16,000 a year	+ 6,000 a year

At a discount rate of 10 percent, the increments have a net present value of $6,000 × 3.791 − $22,000 = +$746. At a 15 percent rate, net present value is −$1,888. The approximate rate of return is 11.4 percent.

Now we can see that the additional $22,000, while not producing a rate of return as high as that of the first $34,000, still does better than 10 percent. What is important is not the average but the contribution each incremental outlay can make.

This illustration explains why we prefer the net present value approach. Net present value provides a clearer basis for comparing mutually exclusive proposals as long as the company has enough money to finance all the proposals that produce rates of return greater than the minimum acceptable rate. The rate of return can still be calculated to reassure those who are uneasy with net present value figures that the overall rate of return is higher than the cost of capital.

Some recurring questions

The measures of costs or of revenues and expenses prepared for financial reporting are sometimes allowed to affect investment decisions even though they don't measure current cash flows and therefore are irrelevant to the decisions. Similarly, some cash flows, though not project related, are sometimes incorrectly included in cash flow timetables.

Our analysis of the plant modernization proposal has dealt with four of these situations:

1. The unamortized costs of existing facilities or programs have been ignored.
2. No deductions have been made for depreciation on new equipment.
3. Internal cost allocations and absorptions have been ignored unless they approximate the differential cash flows.
4. No provision has been made for cash flows arising from borrowing or debt repayment transactions.

A brief review of each of these should help avoid misunderstandings later on.

Unamortized costs

Management often finds it difficult to ignore amounts spent in the past to provide equipment or to develop new products. Suppose, for example, an automobile company has spent $400 million to design, test, tool, and market a new automobile model. Sales have been disappointing and management is considering discontinuing the model. Only $220 million of the development and marketing costs have been amortized, however, leaving $180 million in tooling costs to be written off now if the company decides to drop the model from the line.

The $180 million in unamortized costs is irrelevant to the decision to discontinue the model—it is not a cash flow. Even so, managers may allow it to cloud their thinking in either of the following ways:

1. Money is always spent to create value. Belief that a value has been created is slow to die, and managers are often reluctant to terminate an old project. ("It's a shame to write off all that money. If we just put in another $100 million, the model is sure to take hold.")
2. Managers often think of costs as amounts to be recovered. If not recovered as originally intended they have to be charged against something else. ("We can't accept that proposal. It won't cover amortization of the costs of tooling we already have.") Result: proposals that don't bring in enough cash to cover depreciation of past outlays as well as future cash outlays may be turned down.

These are two examples of the _sunk cost fallacy,_ the notion that costs not yet amortized are somehow relevant to decision making. One of these makes it harder to get rid of old projects; the other makes it harder to adopt new ones. The relevant concept in both cases is opportunity cost: What is the present salvage value of the investment, and by how much will that salvage value decline if the investment is not liquidated now? The amounts invested in the past are sunk costs; neither they nor amortization of them are relevant to today's decisions.

Depreciation on new facilities

Annual depreciation charges on the equipment required by the plant modernization proposal were not reflected in the $25,000 annual cash flow. Depreciation charges don't measure cash flows. This doesn't mean that present value calculations overlook depreciation, however. Depreciation is real and can't be ignored. It is the difference between the initial outlay and the end-of-life salvage value:

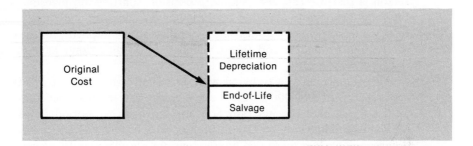

Accountants recognize depreciation for financial reporting by spreading it in some fashion over the assets' estimated lives. They reflect it in present value analysis by entering two amounts in the cash flow timetable—the initial outlay and the end-of-life salvage value—at the times these cash flows take place.

For example, on an investment proposal calling for an outlay of $60,000 now and a residual value of $3,000 in three years, the lifetime depreciation amounts to $57,000. This enters the timetable in the following way:

Time	Cash Flow
0	−$60,000
3	+ 3,000
Total	−$57,000

Entering depreciation again in the form of annual deductions from cash receipts would be double counting.

Allocations and cost absorption

A third source of difficulty is the practice of reassigning overhead costs by means of overhead rates and interdepartmental cost allocations. One company, for instance, applies factory overhead to products by means of a predetermined overhead rate of $2 a direct labor dollar. It is very unlikely, however, that the company will save $2 in overhead for every dollar of direct labor it saves. In fact, most laborsaving investments actually increase total company overhead rather than the other way around.

Interdepartmental cost allocations can be misleading in a very similar way. In our example, plant modernization will decrease the amount of floor space required by the operations affected by the proposal. This will reduce the amount of building occupancy costs allocated to these operations. The opportunity cost of the space saved is zero, however, because the company has no way of using it or renting it out. The cash flow estimates must ignore this apparent difference in costs.

The treatment of interest

Timetables for capital expenditure proposals don't show borrowings as cash inflows; they don't show interest and debt retirements as cash outflows. The reason is that the capital-expenditure decision controls the investment of *all* the long-term funds available to the company, not just the funds available from the shareowners. The discounting process allows implicitly for the rewards the long-term lenders and shareowners require—they don't have to be deducted a second time.

For example, take a proposal with an initial cash outlay of $34,000 and cash receipts of $10,000 a year for five years. The left-hand block in Exhibit 18–12 shows that the net cash flow for the five-year period is +$16,000; the right-hand block shows that the present value is only +$3,910. The $12,090 difference between these two figures represents interest at 10 percent on the investment for the full life of the project.

Exhibit 18–12 Calculation of implicit interest

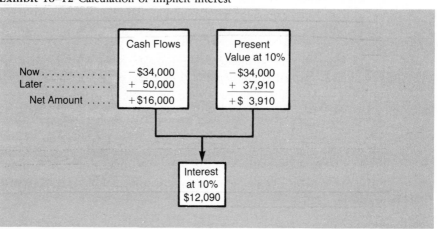

The explanation is that the figures in the left-hand block represent the present values of the cash flows at a *zero* rate of interest. The figures in the right-hand column are smaller because interest at 10 percent has been subtracted. This being the case, charging interest explicitly against the cash flows generated by a proposal would be double counting. Interest on seasonal short-term debt, on the other hand, is an explicit cash outlay that is not provided for by the discounting process. It should be deducted in computing annual cash flows. Similarly, interest on any seasonal investments of project funds can be regarded as a cash inflow for the project.

Summary

Many of management's resource allocation problems can be classified as investment problems. Decision models for investment problems must provide a mechanism for comparing incremental cash outflows in one or more time periods with the incremental cash inflows in another time period or periods.

The model that does this most satisfactorily is the present value model, in which all anticipated incremental cash flows are discounted to their present equivalents at a discount rate based on the cost of capital. Other things being equal, the alternative with the greatest positive net present value should be selected; proposals with negative net present values should be rejected. A related technique is the calculation of each project's internal rate of return, which can then be compared directly with the cost of capital.

In calculating net present value or the internal rate of return, the analyst has to estimate the economic life of the investment, the amount and timing of the investment outlays, the amount and timing of the operating cash flows, and the end-of-life salvage value attributable to the proposal.

All of these estimates should reflect differential or incremental cash flows, not accounting allocations made for other purposes. Sunk costs should be ignored. Finally, all cash flows should be adjusted for the impact of income taxes.

Once the analysis has been completed, management still has to evaluate the proposal. For one thing, the sponsors of the proposal may have based their analysis on the wrong benchmark—the company may be better off to discontinue an activity completely than to pour more money into it. Another problem is that the cash flows are uncertain.

Appendix: The cost of capital

For any given company at any given time, the price that the company must pay to obtain funds through the issuance of a given type of security is determined by market forces. Generally speaking, this price can be expressed as the percentage expected yield that investors in that type of security demand as a reward for investing their money. From these data on demanded yields, the company can estimate its cost of capital, the cost of attracting funds into the company. This cost has two components: (1) the cost of debt capital; and (2) the cost of equity capital.

Cost of debt capital. The cost of debt capital is the rate of interest that equates the present value of the future stream of interest payments (after allowing for income tax effects) and maturity date repayment of face value to the current net proceeds from sale of the debt instruments. For example, assume that bonds with a coupon rate of 12.5 percent and a 20-year maturity can be sold at their face value. After providing for the tax deductibility of interest at a tax rate of 40 percent, the aftertax cost of this debt offering is 7.5 percent.

Cost of equity capital. The concept of the cost of equity capital is an unfamiliar one. Traditional terminology refers to the *cost* of debt and the *return* on equity. In financial accounting, interest is deducted as an expense in computing net income, but dividends are regarded as distributions of previously retained earnings. These distinctions, however, result from the nature of the legal relationships between the firm and the suppliers of capital, not from any inherent differences in the basic objectives of those who provide capital funds. Stockholders are just as interested in reward as bondholders or other lenders; only the form and legal status of the rewards are different.

The cost of equity capital is far more difficult to estimate because funds obtained from stockholders require no firm contractual commitment to future payments. Stockholders do have expectations, however, and the cost of equity capital can be defined as the rate of discount that stockholders apply to the expected future receipts from stock ownership to determine the price they are willing to pay. To determine this rate, we need data on the market price of the stock and the stockholders' future expectations. The latter information being unavailable, the analyst typically falls back on a study of past relationships between market prices, dividends, and capital appreciation.

As a simple illustration of the concept, if a stock is selling for $20 a share and the company's earnings are stable at $3 a share, this is some evidence that the marginal stockholders in the company are willing to pay $6.67 for each dollar of earnings. To attract additional funds into the business, therefore, the company must be able to communicate an expectation that these funds will also earn a return of at least 15 percent on investment, and perhaps more.

The cost of equity capital for any company includes a risk premium in addition to the cost of risk-free capital. The size of this premium depends on the perceived risks of investing in that company relative to the risks of investing in the market generally. The so-called capital asset pricing model links the size of the risk premium to the contribution the stock makes to the variability of a diversified portfolio. Companies whose stock prices are very sensitive to movements in the stock market will have high-risk premiums, and vice versa.[4]

Weighted average cost of capital. Most companies use both debt and equity capital. Utility companies have a high proportion of debt, mining companies relatively little. A company's average cost of capital will depend not only on the costs of the two kinds of capital but also on the proportions in which they are to be used.

What this means is that the minimum acceptable rate of return should be based on a weighted average of the costs of debt and equity capital. The weights should represent the relative place each has in the company's financing plans:

---

[4] James H. Lorie and Mary T. Hamilton, *The Stock Market: Theories and Evidence* (Homewood, Ill.: Richard D. Irwin, 1973).

	Aftertax Capital Cost	Weight	Weighted Capital Cost
Debt	7.5%	40%	3.0%
Equity	15.0	60	9.0
Combined			12.0%

Independent study problems (solutions in Appendix B)

1. **Calculating present value and internal rate of return.** Calculate net present value at 10 percent, compounded annually, and the internal rate of return for each of the following capital expenditure proposals. You should assume that the initial outlay is made at the reference date and each subsequent cash flow takes place at the end of the year in which it arises.

   a. Initial outlay $10,000
   Annual cash receipts .... $ 1,750
   Estimated life .... 10 years
   End-of-life residual value .... None

   b. Initial outlay $10,000
   Annual cash receipts:
      First five years .... $ 2,000
      Second five years .... $ 1,500
   Estimated life .... 10 years
   End-of-life residual value .... None

   c. Initial outlay $10,000
   Annual cash receipts:
      First five years .... $ 1,500
      Second five years .... $ 2,000
   Estimated life .... 10 years
   End-of-life residual value .... None

   d. Initial outlay $10,000
   Annual cash receipts .... $ 1,350
   Estimated life .... 10 years
   End-of-life residual value .... $ 4,000

   e. Initial outlay $10,000
   Annual cash receipts .... $ 1,750
   Estimated life .... 15 years
   End-of-life residual value .... None

2. **Calculating payback period and average return on investment.** For each of the capital expenditure proposals described in problem 1, calculate the payback period and the average return on investment, using average lifetime investment as the denominator.

3. **Equivalent annuity.** Alpha Company has just signed a contract with its research manager. The contract provides for the manager to receive a regular monthly salary until the manager retires five years from today. In addition, Alpha Company has agreed to make annual payments to a trustee to enable the trustee to make a series of five annual payments of $20,000 each to the research manager. The trustee will make the first payment to the manager exactly one year after the retirement date.

   The annual payments to the trustee will be identical in amount. The first of these payments is to be made immediately; the last payment is to be made the day the manager retires.

Required:

Calculate the amount of each annual payment to the trustee if the trustee compounds interest annually at 8 percent.

4. **Estimating cash flows.** The expected life of a proposed new facility is 10 years, the installed cost will be $50,000, and the expected end-of-life salvage value is zero. The equipment will replace facilities now in use that have a tax basis of $30,000 and a market value of $10,000. The remaining tax life of the old facilities is eight years. The investment outlay and all the initial tax effects they will produce will be realized on the zero date.

Double-rate, declining-balance depreciation will be used on the new facilities. The undepreciated balance remaining at the end of five years will be depreciated on a straight-line basis over the next five years. The present facilities are being depreciated by the straight-line method down to an end-of-life salvage value of zero.

Estimated before-tax, before-depreciation cash savings amount to $20,000 a year. The tax rate is 50 percent, and all savings and taxes are assumed to take place at the end of the year.

Required:

a. Compute the incremental aftertax present value of this proposal at 10 percent.
b. Compute the incremental aftertax internal rate of return on this proposal.

Exercises and problems

5. **Present value exercises.** Prepare a timetable of cash flows for each of the following independent proposals, calculate the net present value, and indicate whether the outlay should be made. You may decide to accept some, all, or none of these proposals. The minumum acceptable rate of return is 10 percent.

a. Immediate outlay, $100; cash to be received at one year intervals for 10 years, the first to be received exactly 1 year after the immediate outlay, $15 a year.
b. Immediate outlay, $67; cash receipts, $20 a year for five years, starting one year after the immediate outlay.
c. Immediate outlay, $100; cash receipts $15 a year for 5 years, starting 1 year after the immediate outlay, plus one additional receipt of $75 10 years after the immediate outlay.
d. Immediate outlay, $67; cash receipts: $35 one year later, $30 two years later, $20 three years later, $10 four years later, and $5 five years later.
e. Immediate outlay, $67; cash receipts: $5 one year later, $10 two years later, $20 three years later, $30 four years later, and $35 five years later.

6. **Mutually exclusive proposals.** The company can accept only one of the proposals described in problem 5. Which one would you recommend? Why would you recommend it?

7. **Internal rate of return.** Calculate the internal rate of return for each of the exercises in problem 5. Do these calculations point to the same recommendations you made in answer in problems 5 and 6? Does this seem reasonable?

8. **Payback period and average return on investment.** Calculate the payback period and the average return on average investment for each of the situations described in problem 5. Assume straight-line depreciation. How satisfactory is each of these measures as a device for ranking investment proposals? In your analysis of this question, you should use net present value and the internal rate of return as comparison standards.

9. **Amortization schedule.** A machine costs $29,910 payable immediately in cash. Use of this machine is expected to reduce cash outflows by $10,000 a year for five years. The controller has calculated that the internal rate of return from the purchase of this machine would be 20 percent. Cash flows take place at one year intervals and interest is compounded annually.

Required:

Without using the interest tables, prepare a schedule showing the amount of each annual cash flow that can be regarded as a recovery of part of the $29,910 investment in the machine, and the amount to be regarded as a return on investment (to the nearest dollar).

10. **Maximum purchase price.** Frank Destry has been offered the opportunity to submit a bid for the right to provide catering services in a private club. The contract would run for eight years, and Mr. Destry estimates that his net cash receipts from the catering business would amount to approximately $12,000 a year. If he accepts the contract, he will have to make an initial investment of $2,000 in equipment.

Required:

What is the maximum price that Mr. Destry can afford to bid for the catering privilege, assuming that he requires a 14 percent return on his investment? (Ignore income taxes.)

11. **Payback period and average return: Multiple choice.** Plastics, Inc., is considering the purchase of a $40,000 machine which will be depreciated for tax purposes on a straight-line basis over an eight-year period with no salvage value. The machine is expected to generate net cash flows of $12,000 a year, before income taxes. The income tax rate is 50 percent.

1. What is the payback period?

  a. 2.4 years; *b.* 2.6 years; *c.* 3.3 years; *d.* 4.7 years.

2. What is the average (book value) rate of return, using the initial investment as the denominator?

  a. 8.75%; *b.* 17.50%; *c.* 23.75%; *d.* 30.00%.   (CPA)

12. **Missing figures: Multiple choice.** Choose the answer that will supply the missing figure in each of the following.

1. Cause Company is planning to invest in a machine with a useful life of five years and no salvage value. The machine is expected to produce cash flow from operations, net of income taxes, of $20,000 in each of the five years. Each cash flow will come in at year-end and the expected internal rate of return is 10 percent. How much will the machine cost?

  a. $32,220; *b.* $62,100; *c.* $75,820; *d.* $122,100.

2. Virginia Company invested in a four-year project. The company's minimum acceptable rate of return is 10 percent. The project is expected to yield the following cash inflows, net of income taxes:

Year 1	$4,000
Year 2	4,400
Year 3	4,800
Year 4	5,200

  Assuming that each cash inflow comes in at the end of the year and that the project promises a positive net present value of $1,000, what was the amount of the original investment?

  a. $2,552; *b.* $4,552; *c.* $13,427; *d.* $17,400.

3. Polar Company is planning to purchase a new machine for $30,000. The payback period is expected to be five years. The new machine is expected to produce cash flows from operations, net of income taxes, of $7,000 a year in each of the first three years and $5,500 in the fourth year. Depreciation of $5,000 a year will be charged to income for each of the five years of the payback period. What is the amount of cash flow from operations, net of taxes, that the new machine is expected to produce in the last (fifth) year of the payback period?

   a. $1,000;　*b.* $3,500;　*c.* $5,000;　*d.* $8,500.

4. Scott, Inc., is planning to invest $120,000 in a 10-year project. Scott estimates that the annual cash inflow, net of income taxes, from this project will be $20,000. Scott's desired rate of return on investments of this type is 10 percent. Scott's expected internal rate of return on its investment in this project is:

   a. Less than 10 percent, but more than 0 percent.
   b. 10 percent.
   c. Less than 12 percent, but more than 10 percent.
   d. 12 percent.

   (CPA, adapted)

13. **Indifference point.** Ander Company can invest $4,980 in a piece of equipment with a three-year life. The minimum desired rate of return is 10 percent after taxes and the annual expected cash savings amount to $2,500 (net of taxes) and will be received at year-end. The amount (rounded to the nearest dollar) by which the annual cash flows could change before the company would be indifferent to acquiring the equipment is a

   a. Decrease of $418.
   b. Decrease of $2,480.
   c. Decrease of $1,237.
   d. Decrease of $498.
   e. Decrease of $2,520.

   (CMA, adapted)

14. **Present value calculations: Multiple choice.** Rockyford Company must replace some machinery. This machinery has zero book value but its current market value is $1,800. One possible alternative is to invest in new machinery which has a cost of $40,000. This new machinery would produce estimated annual pretax operating cash savings of $12,500. The estimated useful life of the new machinery is four years.

   Rockyford uses straight-line depreciation for book purposes and the double-rate, declining-balance method for tax purposes for the entire four-year period. The new machinery would have an estimated salvage value of $2,000 at the end of four years, but this can be ignored in calculating annual tax depreciation charges. Any end-of-life book value will be deducted from end-of-life salvage value for tax purposes at the end of four years. The investment in this new machinery would require an additional investment in working capital of $3,000, recoverable at the end of four years.

   If Rockyford accepts this investment proposal, the disposal of the old machinery and the investment in the new equipment will take place on December 31, 19x0. The cash flows from the investment will occur during the calendar years 19x1–19x4. Rockyford is subject to a 40 percent income tax rate for all ordinary income and capital gains and has a 10 percent aftertax cost of capital. All operating and tax cash flows are assumed to occur at year-end. (All calculations should be rounded to the nearest dollar.)

1. The present value of the after-tax cash flow arising from the disposal of the old machinery in 19x0 is:

    a. $6,638;   b. $720;   c. $1,800;   d. $1,080;   e. Some other amount.

2. The present value of the tax effect of depreciation at the end of 19x1 is:

    a. $7,272;   b. $10,908;   c. $6,908;   d. $3,636;   e. Some other amount.

3. The present value of the net effect of the project on the company's income tax payments in 19x2 (year 2) is:

    a. +$3,304;   b. −$4,130;   c. −$826;   d. +$826;   e. Some other amount.

4. The present value of the aftertax cash flows from operating savings for all four years combined (19x1–19x4) is:

    a. $23,775;   b. $39,625;   c. $36,528;   d. $15,850;   e. Some other amount.

5. The present value of the aftertax cash flow arising from the disposal of the new machinery at its salvage value at the end of 19x4 is:

    a. $1,366;   b. $1,229;   c. $1,571;   d. $1,503;   e. Some other amount.

                                                             (CMA adapted)

15. **Present value; internal rate of return.** A capital expenditure proposal is expected to produce the following cash flows:

Outlays:	
Two years before operations commence	$10,000
One year before operations commence	30,000
One day before operations commence	20,000
Ten years after operations begin	20,000
Receipts:	
Each year for the first three years of operations	5,000
Each year for the next ten years	10,000
Each year for the next five years	8,000
18 years after operations begin	12,000

Required:

a. Prepare a timetable of cash flows. Each year's receipts can be assumed to come in at the end of the year.
b. Compute the net present value of this proposal at a discount rate of 15 percent.
c. Calculate the internal rate of return.

16. **Equivalent annuity: Financing college fees.** Barbara and Daniel Porges both work. Barbara is an account executive with an advertising agency, Daniel is an assistant vice president of a bank. They have three children. The oldest child will begin her high school sophomore year next month, the second child is two years behind the first, and the third child is one year behind the second.

All three children have done well in school and Mr. and Mrs. Porges expect all three to attend four-year colleges after graduation from high school. Annual college expenses will average $10,000 for each child, payable at the beginning of the college year.

Mr. and Mrs. Porges have decided to put aside a fixed amount of money each year to provide a college fund for their children. The first payment into the fund will be made a year from now; the last will be made a year before the payment is made for the youngest child's senior college year. No provision will be made for graduate school.

The fund will be placed with a trustee who expects to be able to credit the fund with income at a rate of 14 percent, compounded annually.

Required:

a. Set up a timetable showing the deposits in the fund and the amounts to be withdrawn for college expenses, year by year. The zero date should be the date of the first deposit in the fund. (The amount of the annual deposit is unknown and should be represented by a symbol.)

b. Calculate the amount Mr. and Mrs. Porges should deposit in the fund each year.

c. Verify your answer to (b) by preparing a schedule of deposits, interest, and fee payments, year by year.

17. **Calculating residual future amount.** Learning of the Porges family's plan to build up a college fund (problem 16), Dvorak Investment Advisory Services, Inc., has offered to manage the fund, crediting it with income at a rate of 15 percent, compounded annually. Assuming annual deposits with Dvorak in the amounts you calculated in answering problem 16, how much will the Porges family have left in the fund immediately after Dvorak makes the final college expense payment?

18. **Cost-reducing investment.** An investment in equipment would reduce factory labor costs by $20,000 a year for five years. Factory overhead costs are assigned to products by means of a predetermined overhead rate of 75 percent of direct labor cost. Forty percent of factory overhead costs at normal volume are proportionally variable with volume. Maintenance and energy requirements of the new machine would increase fixed factory overhead costs by $2,000 a year.

The equipment would cost $72,000 and would be depreciated for tax purposes on a sum-of-the-years'-digits basis over a five-year period, with zero salvage anticipated. The company has a minimum acceptable aftertax return on investment of 10 percent. The tax rate is 40 percent. All operating and tax cash flows are assumed to occur at year-end.

Required:

a. Prepare a table of cash flows for this proposal.

b. Calculate net present value. Should the investment be made?

19. **Estimating necessary cash receipts.** Orville Iron Nerves has been offered the opportunity to provide catering services at a private golf club. The contract would run for eight years and would require a payment of $7,000 a year at the end of each year.

Mr. Iron Nerves estimates that $8,000 would have to be paid in cash immediately to buy the necessary equipment. The equipment would have an eight-year life, zero salvage value, and would be depreciated on a straight-line basis for tax purposes. He also estimates a 40 percent contribution margin from sales resulting from the catering service.

Required:

If Mr. Iron Nerves wants to earn a 14 percent return after taxes on his investment, if the income tax rate is 50 percent, and if receipts from sales are the same for each of the eight years, how many dollars of sales receipts must the catering services provide each year? You should assume that cash flows always take place at the end of the year.

(Prepared by Philip Meyers)

20. **Pretax versus aftertax analysis.** You have the following figures relating to a proposal to purchase and install new factory equipment:

1. The company's cost of capital is 10 percent after taxes; this is assumed to be equivalent to 20 percent before taxes.

2. Initial investment outlays amount to $80,000, of which $30,000 can be expensed immediately for tax purposes.

3. The capitalized portion of the initial outlay is subject to special tax treatment. Fifty percent of the capitalized cost can be written off in equal annual installments during the first five years. The remainder is subject to depreciation at the normal straight-line rate of 6 percent per year, including the first five years.

4. The investment is expected to produce net cash receipts (before taxes) of $16,500 a year for the first five years, $11,500 a year for the next five years, and $6,500 a year for the third five years.

5. It is expected that the facilities will be retired at the end of 15 years and that salvage value will be $5,000.

6. All taxes are to be computed on the basis of a 50 percent tax rate.

Required:

Analyze this proposal on both a before-tax and an aftertax basis. How, if at all, would your recommendation to management be different if you used the before-tax basis instead of the aftertax basis?

21. **Tax shield.** It is sometimes useful to separate the aftertax cash flows into two parts: (1) the pretax cash flows, less the taxes that would accrue to these cash flows in the absence of depreciation charges and other items on the tax return not representing current cash flows; and (2) the effects of these other items on taxes. This second component is known as the tax shield.

Required:

Make this separation for the proposal described in problem 20 and calculate the present value of each of these two components.

22. **Investment in new facilities: Relevant benchmark.** The Artling Corporation manufactures four products in four identical processing operations. The only differences among the four products are in the raw materials used. The facilities are completely interchangeable, although they differ slightly, with newer machines having higher depreciation and generally lower operating costs than older machines. Processing costs (that is, all costs other than material costs) are determined by the machines used, not by the product being manufactured.

The company is now considering a proposal to acquire a fifth set of processing facilities to manufacture a new, higher grade of product, using a more expensive raw material that has just come on the market. All machines, new as well as old, would still be completely interchangeable but the new machine would probably be used to make the new product.

The following table shows the selling prices of the five products and all of the costs per pound that would be incurred in the factory to operate the machines:

Product	Machine Used	Selling Price	Materials Cost	Depreciation Cost	Other Factory Costs	Gross Margin
A	1	$0.60	$0.15	$0.08	$0.31	$0.06
B	2	0.66	0.20	0.08	0.30	0.08
C	3	0.73	0.25	0.09	0.28	0.11
D	4	0.81	0.30	0.09	0.29	0.13
E*	5*	0.90	0.35	0.10	0.29	0.16

*Proposed.

Depreciation cost per pound is based on estimated annual production of 200,000 pounds of each product and an estimated life of 10 years. Estimated salvage value of the production equipment is zero; in fact, once the facilities are installed, their only market value is their scrap value.

In support of the proposal to add the fifth product and corresponding facilities, the sales manager of the Artling Company has pointed out that this would increase the company's gross margin by $32,000 ($0.16 a pound on an added sales volume of 200,000 pounds annually). Variable selling and administrative costs amount to 5 percent of sales.

Required:

Compute the incremental annual cash flow that you would use in deciding whether the proposed investment is adequately profitable. State your reasoning. Ignore income taxes.

23. **Capital expenditure simulation chart.** Kendall Enterprises regards 10 percent as the minimum acceptable rate of return on investment for new capital expenditure proposals. Kendall's management is now considering two alternative investment proposals. Each of these calls for an initial investment outlay of $1 million. Probabilities were assigned to various values of the determinants of the rate of return, 20 sets of values were selected at random for each proposal, and the internal rate of return was calculated for each set. These calculated rates of return were as follows:

Proposal A				Proposal B			
15.0	18.6	14.9	11.4	14.4	14.9	15.0	15.8
14.7	13.5	17.1	15.6	15.6	13.5	15.0	15.1
14.0	15.3	19.5	15.0	15.0	14.6	15.4	15.2
16.0	16.5	12.2	17.8	13.9	15.0	15.1	16.1
10.5	15.1	14.4	12.9	14.8	14.2	16.5	14.9

Required:

a. Prepare a capital expenditure simulation chart.

b. Which of these two proposals would you recommend to management? Indicate the criterion or criteria you based your recommendation on. If you are unable to make a recommendation, explain why.

24. **Benchmark alternative; unprofitable operations.** National Corporation bought Summit Corporation five years ago. Summit is a franchiser of restaurants operating under the name Omar's Tent and serving items with a middle eastern flavor. The franchise business has been depressed for the past two years, so depressed that Summit has had a $10,000 operating cash deficit each year. This seems likely to continue unless something is done.

Gerald Avakian, Summit's founder and former owner, has offered to buy the company back for $125,000 any time National wants to sell in the next 10 years. National paid him $3 million for Summit's stock five years ago, however, and none of this has been amortized. Unfortunately, National's tax position is such that if it sells Summit back to Mr. Avakian it will receive no tax credit on the loss incurred in the sale.

National's management is now considering three proposals it has received from Summit. The three proposals are mutually exclusive—acceptance of one means rejection of the others. In each case Summit's management expects the proposed new facilities to be economically productive for 10 years and to have no salvage value at the end of that time. Operating cash flows may be assumed to occur at the end of the year.

1. *Proposal A.* Invest $100,000 in a new dough-making facility to supply the franchisees with bread dough to be baked on the premises. Management estimates this would bring an additional cash inflow of $40,000 a year, after taxes.

2. *Proposal B.* Invest $400,000 in a new baking and packaging facility to supply franchisees with frozen bread to be served in the restaurants and also sold there in packages under the brand name Omar's Loaf. This would bring in

additional aftertax cash flows, rising from $50,000 in the first year to $75,000 in the second and $100,000 in each year after the second.

3. *Proposal C.* Invest $300,000 in a new baking facility to supply suitably located franchisees with freshly baked bread daily. This would produce additional annual cash inflows of $70,000, after taxes.

Required:

National Corporation has a minimum acceptable rate of return on investment of 12 percent, after taxes. Assuming that all the cash flow estimates are valid, what action should National's management take? As part of your answer, calculate the incremental rate of return of your recommended alternative over the next best alternative.

25. **Adjusting for inflation.** Nelson Company plans to introduce a new product, requiring immediate outlays of $200,000 for equipment and $100,000 for working capital. The product will sell at a price of $18 a unit the first two years, increasing to $20 in the third year, and then increasing $1 a year for each of the next five years after that to reach a final plateau at $25 a unit. Operating cash outlays for manufacturing costs will be as follows:

	First Year	Annual Rate of Increase
Direct materials	$5 a unit	10%
Direct labor	2 a unit	5
Variable overhead	1 a unit	8
Fixed overhead	$40,000	4

Equipment depreciation for tax purposes will be by the straight-line method for a 10-year life, with zero anticipated salvage value for the equipment at the end of that time. No tax credits are available for this equipment purchase now. Working capital investments will be fully recoverable at book value at the end of the product's life cycle, which management expects will be at the end of 10 years.

Sales and production volume are expected to reach 10,000 units the 1st year, 20,000 the 2nd year, and 25,000 in the 3rd year, continuing at that level through the 8th year, then decline to 20,000 in the 9th year and 15,000 units in the 10th year as substitute products take over.

To achieve these volumes, marketing expenditures will be $90,000 the 1st year and $60,000 the 2nd year, rising each year thereafter by 5 percent of the previous year's expenditure until the 10th year. Marketing outlays in the 10th year will be cut to half the level they would otherwise reach in that year, as the product is gradually phased out.

The income tax rate will be 45 percent for the entire period and the cost of capital is 15 percent, after taxes. It should be assumed that each year's operating cash flows are received at year-end and that income taxes on the year's taxable income are also paid at year-end. Annual compounding is appropriate.

Required:

a. Prepare a timetable of cash flows for this proposal. Should Nelson Company's management accept it and introduce the new product?

b. If inflation is generally expected to amount to about 6 percent a year, does this proposal appear likely to help the company protect itself from the effects of inflation? Your answer should be largely qualitative; no detailed calculations should be undertaken.

26. **Closing a branch office.** The Barnstable Company manufactures and distributes through retail outlets a line of electrical products and appliances. Distribution of the company's products is accomplished through 12 regional branch offices,

each of which has responsibility for maintaining adequate inventories, granting customer credit, and for collecting accounts receivable. List prices are established in the head office of the Barnstable Company, but each branch manager has authority to set the policy on discounts, returns, and allowances to meet competitive conditions in the region served by that branch.

For a number of years the company has followed the practice of preparing income statements for each branch. The San Francisco branch profit has declined from approximately $50,000 a year five years ago to a loss of $38,000 last year. Last year's income statements for this branch and a somewhat larger branch at Los Angeles were as follows ($000):

	San Francisco	Los Angeles
Gross sales (at list prices)	$488	$675
Discounts, freight, returns, and allowances	72	58
Net sales	416	617
Manufacturing cost of goods sold (at standard)	293	367
Gross margin	123	250
Branch expenses:		
Salaries and commissions..........................	73	104
Travel and entertainment	15	16
Office expense	12	13
Bad debt losses	5	3
Miscellaneous....................................	6	5
Total branch expenses	111	141
Branch margin....................................	12	109
Home office charges	50	74
Branch net profit (Loss)	$(38)	$ 35

Capital invested at the branch consists of $90,000 in receivables (after deducting a provision for uncollectible accounts) and $50,000 in inventories. Because the branch has no depreciable assets, no depreciation charges are included in the branch expenses.

The controller of the Barnstable Company has undertaken an analysis to determine whether it would be profitable to close the San Francisco branch and serve the region from Los Angeles. Analysis of costs and expenses has produced the following estimates:

1. If the San Francisco branch remains in operation, branch margins at both the San Francisco and Los Angeles branches are likely to remain at last year's levels for the foreseeable future.
2. If the San Francisco branch were closed, approximately $400,000 in gross sales could be retained by sales people working out of Los Angeles. Discounts, freight, returns, and allowances on these sales would total $60,000 a year. The product mix in the San Francisco area would be the same at this lower volume as at the current sales volume.
3. An analysis of the company's factory costs indicates that manufacturing costs are approximately 70 percent variable and 30 percent fixed at standard volumes.
4. The San Francisco branch has five sales representatives on its payroll. Each sales representative is paid a salary of $2,000 a year plus a sales commission. Sales commissions are computed at 12 percent of net sales. If the San Francisco office were closed, two of its sales people would be added to the Los Angeles sales force at the same salary and commission rates. The other three San Francisco sales people would be transferred to other positions in the company, as replacements for other employees who are retiring or leaving the company.
5. Closing of the San Francisco office would eliminate completely all other San

Francisco branch expenses, but it is estimated that expenses of the Los Angeles office would be increased by $36,000 a year in addition to the specific items mentioned above.

6. Home office administrative expense is distributed to the branches at 12 percent of net sales. Past experience has indicated, however, that the variable portion of these expenses is only 4 percent of net sales.

7. The Los Angeles investment in inventory and receivables would increase by $20,000 and $80,000, respectively, if the San Francisco branch were closed and the San Francisco area were served from Los Angeles.

8. After taxes at 50 percent, the company's minimum acceptable return on investment is 8 percent.

Required:

a. If you had to choose between operating the San Francisco branch and abandoning the territory entirely, what would you do? Show your calculations.

b. Given the added choice of serving the territory from Los Angeles, which of the three alternatives would you recommend? Show your calculations.

27. **Introduce a new product: Rent or buy equipment.**   Edwards Corporation is a manufacturing concern that produces and sells a wide range of products. The company not only mass produces a number of products and equipment components but also is capable of producing special-purpose manufacturing equipment to customer specifications.

The firm is considering adding a new stapler to one of its product lines. More equipment will be required to produce the new stapler. There are three alternative ways to acquire the needed equipment: (1) purchase general-purpose equipment, (2) lease general-purpose equipment, (3) build special-purpose equipment. A fourth alternative, purchase of the special-purpose equipment, has been ruled out because it would be prohibitively expensive.

The general-purpose equipment can be purchased for $125,000. The equipment has an estimated salvage of $15,000 at the end of its useful life of 10 years. At the end of five years the equipment can be used elsewhere in the plant or be sold for $40,000.

Alternatively, the general-purpose equipment can be acquired by a five-year lease for $40,000 annual rent. The lessor will assume all responsibility for taxes, insurance, and maintenance.

Finally, special-purpose equipment can be constructed by the contract equipment department of the Edwards Corporation. While the department is operating at a level which is normal for the time of year, it is below full capacity. The department could produce the equipment without interfering with its regular revenue-producing activities.

The estimated departmental costs for the construction of the special-purpose equipment are

Materials and parts	$ 75,000
Direct labor	60,000
Variable overhead (50 percent of direct labor dollars)	30,000
Fixed overhead (25 percent of direct labor dollars)	15,000
Total	$180,000

Corporation general and administrative costs are fixed, averaging 20 percent of the direct labor dollar content of factory production.

Additional working capital of $60,000 will have to be provided if any of these three alternatives is selected. Half the increase in working capital will be required immediately, the other half by the end of the first year. This working capital can be recovered at any time if the company decides to discontinue manufacture and sale of the new stapler.

Engineering and management studies provide the following revenue and cost estimates (excluding lease payments and depreciation) for producing the new stapler depending upon the equipment used:

	General-purpose Equipment		Self Constructed Equipment
	Leased	Purchased	
Unit selling price	$ 5.00	$ 5.00	$ 5.00
Unit production costs:			
Materials	1.80	1.80	1.70
Conversion costs	1.60	1.60	1.40
Total unit production costs	3.40	3.40	3.10
Unit contribution margin	1.60	1.60	1.90
Estimated unit volume	40,000	40,000	40,000
Estimated total contribution margin	$64,000	$64,000	$76,000
Other costs:			
Supervision	16,000	16,000	18,000
Taxes and insurance	—	3,000	5,000
Maintenance	—	3,000	2,000
Total	16,000	22,000	25,000

The company will depreciate the general-purpose machine over 10 years on the sum-of-the-years-digits (SYD) method for tax purposes. At the end of five years the accumulated depreciation will total $80,000. The special-purpose machine will be depreciated over five years on the SYD method. Its salvage value at the end of that time is estimated to be $30,000.

The company uses an after-tax cost of capital of 10 percent. Its marginal tax rate is 40 percent.

Required:

a. Calculate the net present value for each of the three alternatives that Edwards Corporation has at its disposal.

b. Should Edwards Corporation select any of the three options, and if so, which one? Explain your answer.

(CMA, adapted)

Case 18–1: Sovad, S.A.* (expansion proposal)

Mr. Walter Weber, general manager of Sovad, S.A., looked across his desk at Mr. Karl Huber, the company's sales manager. Mr. Huber had just suggested that Sovad increase its capacity to manufacture automatic timing devices.

"All right," said Mr. Weber, "let's see if the profits from the increased sales will give us a big enough return on investment. As soon as you're ready, give Mr. Berner (the company's controller) your estimates of sales and what you'll need for advertising and sales promotion. He can work with purchasing and manufacturing to get the rest of the data he needs. I'll ask him to give me a recommendation on your proposal sometime next week."

Sovad, S.A. was a manufacturer of industrial controls and precision instruments, with headquarters and manufacturing facilities in Winterthur, Switzerland. Its manufac-

* Copyright by l'Institut pour l'Etude des Méthodes de Direction de l'Entreprise (IMEDE), Lausanne, Switzerland. Reprinted by permission. Amounts have been restated in dollars.

turing operations in 1981 were conducted entirely in Winterthur, but more than half of its 1981 sales were made in other countries.

First introduced in 1978, the company's automatic timers had been well received by Sovad's customers both at home and abroad. By 1981 Sovad was selling all that it could manufacture. Mr. Huber was convinced that he could expand his sales in Switzerland by large amounts if adequate factory capacity could be provided.

Before coming to Mr. Weber with his suggestion, Mr. Huber had discussed the idea of expansion with Mr. Gluck, the company's director of manufacturing. "Our Winterthur factory is already crowded," Mr. Gluck told him. "The authorities won't give us a building permit to expand it, but I know of some vacant space that we can rent in Zurich for $50,000 a year. We could put all the timer operations in there." Zurich is only 15 miles from Winterthur and Mr. Gluck was confident that he could supervise manufacturing operations in both places without difficulty.

Working with Mr. Gluck, Mr. Huber prepared the preliminary estimates shown in Table 1. As he gave this exhibit to Mr. Berner, Mr. Huber remarked that an eight-month payback period was hard to beat. He hoped that Mr. Berner wouldn't take too long to pass the proposal on to Mr. Weber for approval.

Table 1
ZURICH TIMER FACTORY Preliminary profitability estimate

Sales (300,000 units at $5)		$1,500,000
Out of pocket expenses:		
Factory labor and materials (300,000 units at $2.84)	$852,000	
Rent	50,000	
Other factory costs (not including depreciation)	70,000	
Marketing expenses	160,000	
Total expenses		1,132,000
Profit contribution		$ 368,000
Equipment required:		
New equipment to be purchased	$250,000	
Old equipment, to be moved from Winterthur	0	
Cost of moving old equipment from Winterthur		
and installing it at Zurich	5,000	
Total		$ 255,000

$$\text{Payback period} = \frac{\$255,000}{\$368,000} = 0.69 \text{ years} = 8.3 \text{ months.}$$

In the course of his examination of these figures, Mr. Berner discovered two things. First, the sales and expense figures given in Table 1 were not expected to be achieved until the third year of the new factory's operation. Second, they represented the *total* sales and expenses of the timers. Since the company was already selling 100,000 timers a year, Mr. Berner did not believe that the profit on these units should be used to justify the opening of the new factory. As he put it, "The data that we need are differential or incremental figures, the differences between having the new factory and not having it." Mr. Huber estimated that he would be able to sell 300,000 timers a year after a two-year introductory period. His detailed estimates of annual sales and marketing expenses are summarized in Table 2.

Mr. Berner knew that these volumes of sales would require sizable investments in working capital which Mr. Huber had omitted from Table 1. On the basis of the company's past experience, he estimated that the cumulative balance of working capital required at the beginning of each year would be as follows:

If timers are manufactured in Zurich:

Year 1	$700,000
Year 2	750,000
Year 3	800,000
If timers are not manufactured in Zurich	$300,000

Table 2

ZURICH TIMER FACTORY Estimated annual timer sales and marketing expenses

	Annual Sales		Annual Marketing Costs
	Units	Value	
If all timers are manufactured in Zurich:			
Year 1	200,000	$1,000,000	$260,000
Year 2	250,000	1,250,000	260,000
Year 3 and after	300,000	1,500,000	160,000
If timers are not manufactured in Zurich	100,000	$ 500,000	$ 60,000

When questioned about the manufacturing cost estimates in Table 1, Mr. Gluck gave Mr. Berner the figures shown in Table 3. Mr. Gluck explained that if the Zurich factory were opened, all automatic timer production would be shifted to Zurich. If the expansion proposal were to be rejected, however, the cost of producing 100,000 timers a year at Winterthur would be $3.10 a unit plus $20,000 a year. All of these costs could be eliminated if operations were transferred to Zurich.

Table 3

ZURICH TIMER FACTORY Estimated factory costs

	Variable Costs per Unit	Fixed Costs per Year		
		Rental	Depreciation	Other
Year 1	$2.96	$50,000	$25,000	$70,000
Year 2	2.88	50,000	25,000	70,000
Year 3 and after	2.84	50,000	25,000	70,000

Mr. Berner also questioned Mr. Gluck about the equipment that would be moved from Winterthur to Zurich. "That is the old test equipment that we are now replacing here in Winterthur," he replied. "It's perfectly adequate for the timers, and it saves us from buying new equipment for the new location. It's fully depreciated on our books, but it's in perfect condition and I see no reason why it wouldn't last for years.

"If we don't open up in Zurich, we'll sell this old equipment locally for about $10,000. If we keep it, our only cost will be about $5,000 to get it from Winterthur to Zurich. We can subtract this $5,000 from the taxable income from our other operations right away, even before we start operating at Zurich."

For purposes of analysis, Mr. Berner and Mr. Huber agreed that the new Zurich plant should be able to operate for at least 10 years and that the company's investment in working capital would be a reasonable measure of the value of the Zurich assets at the end of that time.

In evaluating capital expenditure proposals, Mr. Berner used an income tax rate of 30 percent of ordinary taxable income. Gains on the sale of equipment were also taxed at a 30 percent rate. Depreciation for tax purposes on the new equipment to be purchased for the Zurich plant would be $50,000 a year for five years.

a. Prepare a timetable of the before-tax cash flows attributable to this expansion proposal.

b. Restate the cash flows on an aftertax basis. If Sovad's minimum acceptable aftertax rate of return was 14 percent, should the company have opened the Zurich factory? Show your calculations.

19 Costs for pricing decisions

Deciding how much to charge customers for products or services calls for several kinds of decision models. We'll use the space available here to discuss four topics that relate most closely to the use of cost accounting data in pricing:

1. Pricing strategy.
2. A short-run profit-maximizing model.
3. Cost-based pricing formulas.
4. Price differentiation.

Pricing strategies

The pricing strategy establishes the role price is expected to play in the marketing mix and what it is expected to accomplish. Two basic strategies are available:

SR π max insensitive to P ▸ 1. *Skimming pricing* is a short-run profit-maximizing strategy. It calls for relatively high prices, reflecting a decision that marketing effort should be directed toward exploiting those portions of the market that are relatively insensitive to price.

mass marketing price sensitive 2. *Penetration pricing* is a strategy for mass marketing. It calls for relatively low prices as a means of gaining rapid acceptance of the product in the price-sensitive sections of the market.

Choosing an initial pricing strategy

1) elasticity 2) competition The initial pricing strategy for a new product depends on two factors: (1) the sensitivity of sales to variations in price; and (2) the ability of other companies to introduce satisfactory competing products.

The price charged for a product or service will affect the number of units sold. Other things being equal, the lower the price the bigger the volume of sales. The economist refers to one of these price-quantity relationships as a *demand schedule.* When diagrammed, it becomes a *demand curve,* as in Exhibit 19–1. Points A and B are only two of the many possible price combinations. They indicate that at a price of P_A, the quantity sold will be Q_A, while a price of P_B will increase the number of units sold to Q_B.

Exhibit 19–1 Demand curve

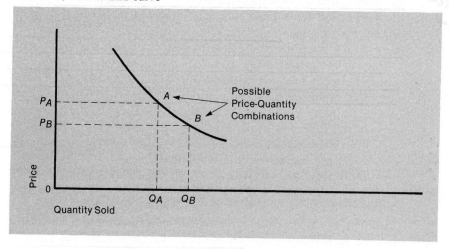

The sensitivity of sales to price, referred to by economists as the *price-elasticity of demand,* depends on the value customers place on the product and on their ability to meet their needs by using other products already on the market or by manufacturing the product themselves. Demand will be highly elastic if the price is close to the costs customers would incur if they were to meet their needs in other ways or if it is high relative to the values most customers place on the product. Under the opposite conditions, elasticity will be low—that is, it will be *inelastic.*

A skimming price attempts to take advantage of the relatively inelastic portion of the demand schedule. For example, a high initial price may be a profitable way to capitalize on the novelty appeal of a new product when the responsiveness of sales to lower prices would be slight. Automobiles, television sets, ball-point pens, and pocket calculators all went through a skimming pricing stage when they were first placed on the market.

Skimming pricing may also provide a form of insurance against unexpected costs of manufacturing or distribution. It is easier to lower prices than it is to raise them, and manufacturing or engineering difficulties may raise product cost substantially above the estimates during the early shakedown period.

Penetration pricing is the appropriate strategy if the product has to compete with close substitutes already familiar and acceptable to the potential customer. In this situation the demand curve for the new product is likely to be highly elastic at prices in the competitive range, meaning that small price premiums over the prices of competing products will reduce sales enormously. A new dishwashing product, for example, will be difficult to market if its price is significantly higher than the prices of the many competing products already on the market.

Penetration pricing is also advisable if the market is large and competitors can enter it quickly and cheaply. Profitable skimming pricing requires one

skimming:
need barriers
to entry

or more significant barriers to the entry of competing products—patent protection, the need for massive amounts of capital investment, or strong brand loyalty, for example. High barriers to entry make profitable skimming feasible by reducing the price elasticity of the company's product at higher prices.

Penetration pricing may even create its own barriers to entry. A penetration price denies potential competitors a price advantage and makes it more difficult and more expensive for them to acquire a large share of the market. Furthermore, the more experience the company has in producing the product or service, the lower its production costs are likely to be. These lower costs give it another competitive advantage over the would-be challenger. We'll discuss this experience effect in the next chapter.

Changing from skimming to penetration pricing

Deciding when to reduce a skimming price is more difficult than deciding to skim in the first place. By keeping the price high, the innovator offers potential competitors a tempting opportunity, a chance to enter the market with the competitive advantage of a low selling price. Whether they can take advantage of this opportunity depends on the strength of the barriers to the entry of competitors.

One pattern prices are likely to follow if entry barriers are weak is shown in the left-hand diagram in Exhibit 19–2. The price remains high for a short time as the innovator exploits the product's initial advantage. As the market expands, others see its potential and prepare to enter. To anticipate this, the innovator reduces the price. This leads to even greater volume and lower production costs. Knowing that competitors can also achieve low costs through mass production, the innovator continues to reduce the price until the economies of scale, experience, and technological advance have been largely exploited. At this point the product can be said to have reached maturity and further price declines will be relatively modest.

Exhibit 19–2 Effect of entry barriers on pricing patterns

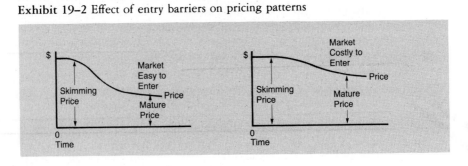

The picture is very different when entry barriers are high, as in the right-hand diagram of Exhibit 19–2. Price is likely to stay at the skimming level for some time, until the innovator concludes that the upper portions of the market are becoming saturated, making it attractive to reduce the price to tap a part of the market that is more sensitive than the first. This may take a good deal of time. Another stimulus to price reductions is the emergence of new partial substitutes for the innovator's product. Management can keep the entry barriers high by reducing prices gradually, taking advantage of the continuing experience effect on its production costs to maintain the profit margin at a high level.

Management's job, in other words, is to judge the strength of the entry barriers and to estimate when they will be breached. Reducing price too soon reduces profits needlessly; reducing them too late leads to losses of market share which are likely to be accompanied by reductions in profit.

A short-run economic pricing model

Whether management skims or tries to penetrate the market on a mass basis, it must estimate the effect of price on volume. The only difference is that in setting a skimming price management is interested in short-run elasticity; for penetration pricing its focus is on the longer term.

Estimated or assumed price-volume relationships are central features of the models economists have developed to explain how prices and output are likely to behave. In this section we shall describe one of these models, discuss the methods management might use to estimate price-volume relationships, and examine some of the factors that often make it difficult to use the model directly in pricing.

The basic model

The central feature of this economic model is the assumption that the firm will try to set the price that will maximize its profits, the difference between total revenue and total cost. Using this model is a three-step process:

1. Estimate total quantity sold and total revenue at each of several possible prices.
2. Estimate total cost at each of these quantities.
3. Subtract total cost from total revenue at each price and select the price that maximizes the profit.

Estimating total revenue. If the demand curve has the shape of the one in Exhibit 19–1, price must be reduced to increase the quantity sold. If a large increase in volume results from a small decrease in price, total revenue will increase as volume increases. If a large price cut is necessary to increase total volume, total revenue may even fall as total volume goes up.

For example, suppose management estimates that 10 units can be sold if the price is $20, for a total revenue of $200, as shown in the first line of the following table:

Price	Units Sold	Total Revenue	Effect of Added Volume on Total Revenue
$20	10	$200	xx
19	11	209	+$9
18	12	216	+ 7
17	13	221	+ 5
16	14	224	+ 3
15	15	225	+ 1
14	16	224	− 1

Reducing the price from $20 to $19 increases total revenue by $9, as shown in the second line. Each successive price reduction is less effective in increasing total revenue than the one before. Reducing the price from $15 to $14 actually reduces total revenue.

Estimating total cost. Total cost is also different for different volumes. Suppose costs are as follows in our example:

Units Sold	Total Cost	Effect of Added Volume on Total Cost
10	$180	xx
11	182	+$2
12	185	+ 3
13	189	+ 4
14	194	+ 5
15	200	+ 6
16	207	+ 7

In this version of the model, programmed costs are the same at all volumes. If increases in volume are to be achieved by increases in the costs of programmed activities, these cost increases must be included in the model.

Finding the profit-maximizing price. The final step in this model is to calculate the profit at each volume and select the most profitable price-volume combination. This step is diagrammed in Exhibit 19–3. As this shows, the spread between total revenue (TR) and total cost (TC) increases as long as total revenue is climbing more rapidly than total cost. When total cost is climbing more rapidly than total revenue, actions that increase the number of units sold actually narrow the profit spread.

As this suggests, profit is at its maximum when the two rates of increase are equal—that is, when the two lines are parallel. This occurs in this case at a volume slightly in excess of 13 units.

Marginal cost and marginal revenue. These relationships can also be expressed in terms of marginal revenue and marginal cost. Marginal cost was defined in Chapter 4 as the increment in total cost as the result of increasing volume by one unit. Marginal revenue is the increase in total revenue that results from the sale of one additional unit of product.

Marginal revenue (MR) and marginal cost (MC) at any volume are deter-

Exhibit 19-3 The profit-maximizing volume

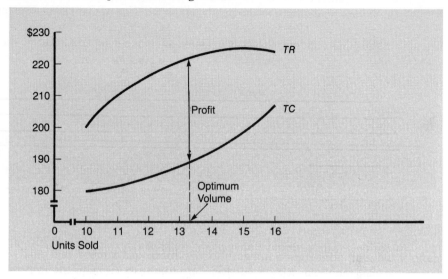

mined by measuring the rates of climb or slopes of the total revenue and total cost curves at that volume.

These curves are shown in Exhibit 19-4. To move from sales of 10 units to sales of 11, management would have to reduce the price from $20 to $19, as we have already seen. This would increase total revenue from $200

Exhibit 19-4 Equating marginal cost and marginal revenue

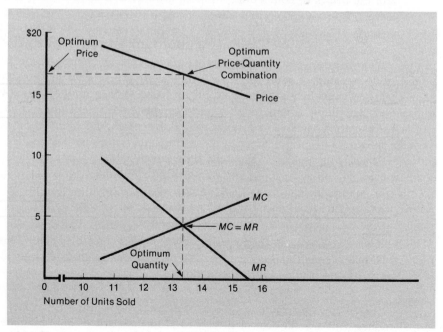

602

to $209, an increase of $9. This is the marginal revenue of the 11th unit, shown on the diagram as the height of the *MR* line at that point. The marginal revenue of the 12th unit is $7, of the 13th is $5, and so on.

Marginal cost can also be calculated by comparing total cost at successive volume levels. The marginal cost of the 11th unit is $2, of the 12th unit is $3, and so on.

The optimal price-quantity combination is determined by the intersection of the marginal revenue and marginal cost curves. Lowering the price below this level would increase revenues by less than it would increase costs. Raising the price above the optimum would decrease revenues by more than it would decrease costs. In this case the two lines intersect just to the right of the 13-unit point. Since fractional units can't be sold, the optimal volume is the whole-unit output closest to the intersection point, 13 units, to be sold at a price of $17 each.

Estimating price-volume relationships

Management can use any of four techniques to estimate the impact of price on sales volume:

1. Informed judgment.
2. Statistical analysis of historical data.
3. Price experimentation.
4. Product value analysis.

Informed judgment. Marketing personnel, familiar with their customers and the prices of competing products, are likely to have a good idea of the price range within which a new product will be competitive. For products already on the market, they may also be able to estimate the impact of modest increases or decreases in product price.

Management can get these estimates quickly and cheaply, and in many cases the analysis goes no farther. This approach is difficult to extend very far, however. Few managers are likely to be able to estimate sales at prices outside a limited range; and for new products the forecasting errors are apt to be extremely high.

Statistical analysis. Economists have had some success in applying statistical tests to historical data to identify apparent price-volume relationships in some industries. The technique is worth considering, but it is unlikely to prove very useful in forecasting the demand curve for specific products in specific firms. Too many factors other than price affect sales. For new products the situation is no better because historical data are not available. This means that management's best means of getting data on which to base its judgment must be one of the other two methods.

Pricing experiments. Some companies have used experimental techniques with a great deal of success to produce more reliable estimates of the

best for low-priced consumer prods. of short life + little technical complexity effect of price on sales. For example, one company recently placed a new product on sale in three representative regional markets before launching it nationally.

1. Every attempt was made to ensure the comparability of the three regions.
2. Three prices were selected for testing, one in each market.

Analysis of the sales responses in the three markets indicated that although profit per unit was highest at the highest of the three prices, total profit was the greatest at the medium price. These figures are shown in Exhibit 19–5.

Exhibit 19–5 Estimated profit-price relationship

Retail price	$1.95	$2.45	$2.95
Estimated unit sales	800,000	600,000	300,000
Price to dealers	$1.17	$1.47	$1.77
Estimated revenues....................	$936,000	$882,000	$531,000
Variable costs:			
Variable manufacturing costs	504,000	378,000	189,000
Variable selling costs	80,160	70,920	40,860
Traceable fixed costs	135,000	135,000	120,000
Total product costs	719,160	583,920	349,860
Product profit	$216,840	$298,080	$181,140

At a retail price of $2.45, the product was expected to return $54,000 less in sales revenues than at a $1.95 retail price, but the contribution toward fixed costs and profits was expected to be the greatest at the $2.45 price.

Pricing experiments are not always feasible or reliable. For one thing, comparable test markets for some products are hard to find. Second, even if the markets are comparable, something may happen in one or more of them during the test to make the results less useful. For example, the distributors of a substitute product may launch a major promotional campaign in one of the test markets, cutting substantially into the company's sales.

Third, markets for industrial products are difficult to keep separate. Purchasing agents in the high-priced areas are bound to find out and demand equal treatment. Fourth, price-sensitive customers take longer to reach, and management may be unwilling to delay the pricing decision until the results are in.

For all these reasons, price experimentation is usually limited to low-priced consumer products of short life and little technical complexity. One or more of the other methods has to be used for products not meeting these specifications.

Product value analysis. People buy a product or a service because it has value to them. If management can figure out how many people are likely to value the product highly and how many will place a low value on it, costly and time-consuming experiments will be unnecessary.

For example, a machinery manufacturer has a file of detailed estimates of the costs of operations in its customers' factories. When a new product is developed, experienced engineers estimate the potential cost savings for large and small customers. A rough estimate of the demand schedule is prepared from these data—sales of 100 machines if the price is $20,000, sales of 250 machines if the price is $15,000, and so on. Matching this against cost estimates points toward the optimum price.

Product value analysis ordinarily enters into pricing implicitly rather than explicitly. Although few companies have the kinds of value estimates described above, they are seldom completely in the dark. Experienced executives may be able to tailor prices to customer values without even realizing that they are doing anything so systematic.

implicit

Limitations of the model *(SR-π-max model)*

Although this model illustrates the general nature of the economic approach to product pricing, it is seldom used in practice. This can be explained by one or more of the following:

1. Adequate data are not available.
2. Other aspects of the marketing mix are more important than price.
3. The market is oligopolistic.
4. Short-run profit maximization may have harmful long-run consequences.

Lack of data. Usable estimates of the relationship between volume and cost are usually available. Data on price-quantity relationships are much harder to get, however, as we indicated a moment ago. If management is unwilling to rely on the data it has from informed judgment, price experiments, or product value analysis, the model can't be used.

Nonprice competition. A second explanation of management's failure to use the short-run profit-maximization model is that price is only one element in the marketing mix. The marketing mix consists of all the devices the company uses to market its products more effectively and efficiently—the amounts and kinds of selling effort, the design of the product and its packaging, the price charged, the credit terms offered, and the channels of distribution used. What management does with one of these has an impact on the effectiveness of the others. Low prices will bring in big volume, for example, only if the company uses the right tools to let customers know about them.

optimal mix vs optimal price

As a result, management looks for an optimal marketing mix rather than an optimal price. This adds a third dimension to the analysis, ruling out any simplistic application of the two-dimensional model.

Oligopolistic markets. Revenues depend on many factors other than the company's own price. For example, a company can seldom assume that management's decisions as to price will not induce retaliatory pricing decisions by competing sellers. The circumstances under which this assumption is largely valid are those of *monopoly* (no directly competing product in the market) or *monopolistic competition* (many sellers of similar but not necessarily identical products, with no single seller having a large enough share of the market to permit competitors to identify the effects of other individual sellers' pricing decisions on their sales).

In the intermediate situation, known as _oligopoly_ (a market in which a few large sellers occupy a large share of the market), the marginal revenue curve of the individual seller depends on the reactions of competitors to changes in the seller's prices. If the oligopolistic seller finds that competitors will raise their prices in response to a price increase and lower their prices in response to a price cut, then the seller's demand curve takes the same general shape as the demand curve for the market as a whole, except insofar as product differentiation affects the price sensitivity of sales.

A different situation arises if competitors will match price reductions but will not follow price increases. Sellers who try to raise their prices will find that their sales will fall off sharply as customers shift their purchases to other firms whose prices have not risen. If they lower their prices, on the other hand, their competitors will follow suit and the only source of increased revenue will be a share of any general expansion of total industry sales.

This effect is shown in Exhibit 19–6. Both the demand curve and the marginal revenue curve are interrupted or "kinked" at the sales volume (V_a) expected at the existing price (P_a). Although marginal revenue at this volume may be greater than marginal cost (as in Exhibit 19–6), any attempt to expand volume by price reductions will produce a substantial drop in marginal revenue. In this illustration the reduced marginal revenue is less than marginal cost, and thus the price reduction will be unprofitable.

A kink of this sort is likely to appear immediately only if most other firms in the industry are not operating at the limits of practical capacity. If capacity is fully utilized, competitors might find it profitable to meet any price rises, which would eliminate the kink. If they do not raise their prices but cannot absorb any additional volume immediately, the kink effect will not be felt

Exhibit 19–6 Oligopolistic kinked demand curve

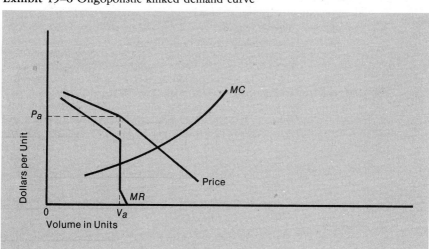

by the high-priced seller until outside capacity has grown sufficiently to permit competitors to take advantage of all the orders that are forthcoming at existing prices. If most sellers suspect the existence of a kink of the kind illustrated here, and if they also assume that total industry sales are inelastic (relatively insensitive to price reductions), this is enough to explain why prices in many oligopolistic industries do not decline significantly during periods of idle capacity.

Long-run consequences. The fourth reason why management may not set prices on the basis of a short-run profit-maximization model is that today's prices may have consequences extending far beyond the present period. Charging a high price today may bar the company from the market tomorrow.

This objection really applies only to skimming pricing; if the model is applied to a product for which a penetration pricing strategy has been adopted, the cost and demand curves presumably reflect longer term relationships. If the skimming price appears likely to have unfavorable long-term consequences, then the decision to adopt skimming pricing should be reversed.

Cost-based pricing formulas

The difficulties inherent in pricing models based directly on profit-maximizing decision rules may lead management to seek simpler approaches. Many of these approaches tie price to estimates of the cost of the product or service to be sold (*cost-plus pricing*) or on cost plus the investment necessary to support the product or service (*return on investment pricing*). In some situations, the customer may even agree to prices based explicitly on the seller's costs. We'll discuss these latter arrangements, known as reimbursement pricing, in Chapter 21. In this section we'll discuss four aspects of the cost-based pricing formulas management may use in nonreimbursement situations:

1. Reasons for cost-based formula pricing.
2. The structure of the cost base.
3. The markup percentage.
4. Departures from formula-based prices.

Reasons for cost-based formula pricing

We know that average cost depends on volume and volume is affected by price. Cost-based pricing therefore appears to require circular reasoning. Despite this, we see four main reasons for the popularity of cost-based formulas:

1. Cost-based pricing is a method of uncertainty absorption.
2. Cost-based pricing may be the only apparent path to survival.
3. Cost estimates may help management predict competitors' long-term pricing goals.
4. Cost-based formulas permit management to delegate pricing authority to their subordinates.

Uncertainty absorption.   One valid explanation of the popularity of cost-plus pricing is that the decision makers must make decisions in the face of a host of uncertainties. They can't possibly cope with all of these uncertainties. To keep their sanity, they have to find some way of ignoring some of them or of getting others to accept responsibility for dealing with them. This is known as uncertainty absorption. One such device is to accept a pricing formula that seems reasonable on the surface. By accepting this, the manager feels free to ignore this source of uncertainty.

Survival pricing.   The second explanation is closely related to the first. In some situations, the alternative to product success is liquidation of all or part of the organization. Rather than liquidate, management may set a price that will assure a profit if a specified volume can be achieved. If the volume materializes, the organization survives; if not, liquidation may be the only way out. Private schools' tuition decisions very often fall in this category.

Competitive costing.   The third explanation of the popularity of cost-based pricing is that estimates of the company's own costs may help the decision makers predict either their competitors' costs or a competitive price. For example, if the company has been operating for some time in a market in which markups over cost average 50 percent, management may be able to assume that the same relationships will hold on new products.

This kind of thinking is particularly valid in oligopolistic industries. Recognizing that price competition is likely to be self-defeating, price-setting executives may set a price that they feel will not attract competitors unduly and then focus their competitive efforts on other factors such as delivery, credit terms, and so forth. If every company uses cost as a basis for pricing standard products, a substantial measure of price stability can be achieved even under conditions of idle capacity.

Routinizing the pricing decision.   The fourth reason for formula pricing is that many firms have so many products they can't afford to analyze the price-volume relationships for them all. Department stores, supermarkets, and discount houses can't hope to apply a profit-maximization model to each of their thousands of pricing decisions.

Once again, by using a pricing rule that seems to work reasonably well, management can devote more time to other dimensions of the marketing mix. Management is not unaware that price affects volume and volume affects average cost—it merely has to cope with this phenomenon in other ways.

The structure of the cost base

In its simplest form, the cost-based pricing formula consists of an estimate of product cost and a percentage markup:

$$\text{Cost} + \text{Markup} = \text{Price} \quad Or \quad \text{Cost} \times (1 + \text{Markup fraction}) = \text{Price}$$

The cost component of this formula sometimes can be constructed very simply. In retailing, for example, product cost is likely to be the purchase price of the merchandise. In a service organization, such as a consulting firm, the cost base is likely to consist of the amounts of various kinds of direct time and the costs of other direct inputs, such as photographic services and printing.

In manufacturing organizations, and in some nonmanufacturing companies as well, the cost base is likely to include various components of overhead cost. Exhibit 19–7 shows one such estimate. Estimates of the direct factory inputs required by the product are entered in the upper portion of the form. Factory overhead costs are then applied, using predetermined departmental overhead rates. To provide a flexible data base, fixed overheads are separated from the variable costs. The final section, at the bottom of the form, summarizes the various cost elements and shows the average unit cost.

Exhibit 19–7 Product cost estimate sheet

COST ESTIMATE SUMMARY

Product No.: 172-41-B
Quantity: 1,000

Prepared by: JD
Date: 5/15/x4

Direct materials		
Tooling		$ 907
Fixtures		—
Process		1,728
Total		$2,635

Direct labor			
Dept.		Set-up	Operating
11		$22	$ 950
14		12	380
17		5	260
22		18	1,400
24		14	190
Total		$71	$3,180

Factory overhead			Hourly Rates		Amounts	
Dept.	Hours		Variable	Fixed	Variable	Fixed
11	200 mach. hrs.		$0.30	$3.00	$ 60	$ 600
14	110 mach. hrs.		0.80	2.80	88	308
17	25 dir. lab. hrs.		1.00	2.00	25	50
22	100 dir. lab. hrs.		0.60	0.90	60	90
24	20 dir. lab. hrs.		0.70	1.10	14	22
Total					$247	$1,070

Cost summary		
Direct materials		$2,635
Set-up labor		71
Operating labor		3,180
Variable overhead		247
Total variable cost		6,133
Fixed factory overhead		1,070
Total factory cost		$7,203 $7.203 a unit

Exhibit 19–7 makes no provision for selling and administrative costs or for the costs of the company's research and development program. Many pricing formulas do include provisions for some or all of these costs. From a managerial point of view, the least helpful of these provisions reflects a broad average of all selling and administrative costs, applied as a percentage of direct cost or some other product-related base. These allocations add nothing to management's understanding of the product's economic position, however. In our opinion, any such broadly based provisions should be included as a component of the markup percentage, where they show up as amounts that need to be covered by an average product but aren't costs of the specific product being priced.

Some selling and administrative costs are product-specific, of course—product advertising, samples, and product management, for example. An average of these costs can be calculated at the sales volume management believes is a normal commerical volume for the specific product. This makes the pricing formula more sensitive to differences in marketing strategy.

Exhibit 19–7 also omits another element of cost that is included in many cost-based formulas, the cost of capital. For example, suppose $1 million in investment is required to support a particular product at an intended sales volume of 100,000 units a year. The cost of capital, adjusted to its pretax equivalent, is 30 percent. The estimated capital cost component of this product's cost is:

$$\text{Capital cost} = \frac{30\% \times \$1,000,000}{100,000} = \$3 \text{ a unit.}$$

The introduction of capital cost into the cost base adapts the pricing formula to return-on-investment pricing. Some managers may prefer to classify the cost of capital as an element of the markup. We think of investment capital as a productive input, however, much like labor and materials. If the amount of the investment is determined by the characteristics of each individual product, the cost base should reflect the effects of these characteristics.

Most cost-based pricing formulas in the United States appear to reflect a full-cost concept.[1] If the formula includes only manufacturing costs, it will include a provision for *all* factory costs; if it includes selling and administrative costs, it is likely to provide for all such costs at some target volume.

We prefer the concept of attributable cost, the cost that could be avoided, in time, if the product were not in the line and capacity were reduced accordingly. The main argument for this approach is that the purpose of the cost element in the pricing formula is to supply guidance to what a competitive price is likely to be. Empirical evidence is lacking on the relationship between average cost and competitive or "normal" prices, but it might be presumed that long-run normal prices will bear some relation to attributable cost. If a

---

[1] A study by the National Association of Accountants found a relatively small percentage of the companies in its sample using variable costing information. *Current Usage of Fixed and Variable Expense Analysis* (New York: National Association of Accountants, 1980).

company is unlikely to cover the costs attributable to a product, then it ordinarily will not introduce it. If the product is already on the market, it will be withdrawn as soon as other uses of capacity become available or as capacity wears out and needs replacement.

The markup percentage

The second component of the cost-based pricing formula is the markup percentage. The company's long-term survival depends on its ability to obtain prices for its products that will cover not only the costs assigned to those products but also the total of all its other costs, including the cost of capital invested for general business purposes, not specifically assignable to individual products. These costs are the basis for the formula markup percentage.

This doesn't mean that the markup percentage has to be the same on every product. Different products face different competitive conditions, and management must adapt its pricing policy to fit each market. Sometimes the markups correspond to well-established differences in custom or competitive position. Department stores, for example, typically vary the markup from department to department. Cosmetics may carry an 80 percent markup on cost, while the markup on major appliances may be only 30 percent.

The use of customary markups is not a permanent guarantee of success in pricing. Feasible markups don't remain constant forever. The markups that have been normal for the past 20 years may suddenly turn out to be unobtainable. The neighborhood grocer found this out in the 30s, when the supermarket established a new pattern in food retailing by reducing costs and increasing turnover, thereby building an adequate profit margin at lower prices than the neighborhood grocer's. The same fate befell the full-service department store with the growth of discount retailing in the 50s. Managers who spot these possibilities early can grab a big share of the market; those who wait until the change takes place may be sorry.

Departures from formula-based prices

Except in highly structured market situations, prices calculated from cost-based formulas are *target prices.* Actual prices may be either higher or lower, depending on market conditions. Remember that managers are paid to exercise their judgment, not solve equations. If the target price is much lower than the prouduct ought to be worth to its intended customers, the manager may add something to the target. If competing products are selling at prices well below the target, the company may have to accept a lower than normal markup unless the product offers valuable features the competitors don't have. In other words, it is reasonable to expect some prices to be higher than the target and some to be lower. In fact, negative markups are not unknown—that is, some products may sell at prices lower than the costs assigned to them. Even at these low prices these products yield incremental cash inflows—the company is better off to sell them than to drop them from the line.

We should emphasize here that pricing each and every product at or above full cost is no guarantee that a profit will ensue. The reason is that many costs are fixed, so that unit cost depends on volume. If prices have been set on the basis of estimated cost at normal volume, as shown in the right-hand portion of Exhibit 19–8, but if volume turns out to be much smaller than normal—that is, at some point in the left-hand side of the diagram—actual average cost will be greater than price and a loss will ensue. Furthermore, unless demand is highly inelastic, pricing products on the basis of estimated actual average cost at estimated actual volume is likely to defeat its own purpose, as the higher price drives additional customers away and reduces volume still further.

Exhibit 19–8 Effect of volume on success of cost-based prices

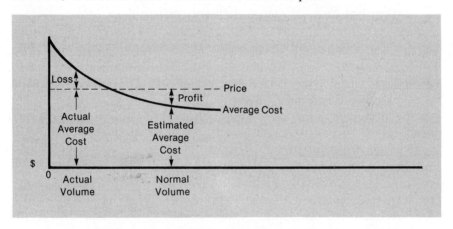

Prices of custom products or unique services are likely to be even more sensitive to economic conditions than the prices of catalog items. For these, pricing is largely a matter of bidding or negotiating with individual customers, order by order. In other words, a separate pricing decision has to be made for each sale.

The bid price is likely to depend on the number of orders already accepted and on the company's recent bidding experience. If the company is already using most of its capacity, the pricer will not do much price shading except possibly on orders that appear likely to lead to repeat business when greater available capacity exists. If recent bids at normal levels have found ready acceptance, the company will feel justified in increasing the provision for profit on bids for new work. If substantial idle capacity exists, however, and full cost bidding has been failing to secure orders, the pricing executive faced with the choice of losing the order or quoting a price that is lower than the normal level is likely to accept the latter course and bid at some point intermediate between the estimated specific cost of the order and the normal price.

Price differentiation

So far we haven't admitted that the same product might be sold to different customers at different prices, but some price differentiation has crept in nevertheless. For one thing, some skimming price strategies result in price differentiation based on the time of purchase—those buying early pay more than those buying late. Also, some pricing of custom products may be a subtle form of price differentiation—the products or services may be virtually the same, but their prices may be very different. Finally, the quantity discounts we discussed in Chapter 16 certainly produce price differentials.

Price differentiation may go beyond these examples. In this final section we shall explain why price differentiation may be desirable, see what the seller has to do to make it work, and look at the forces that limit the firm's ability to differentiate its prices.

The benefits of price differentiation

Price differentiation can have both private and public benefits. The private benefit is probably obvious. Suppose an appliance dealer has two potential customers for television sets. One customer will buy a set if the price is no higher than $200; the other will buy only if the price is $110 or lower. The cost of each set is $80.

In this situation, the dealer can make $90 more if it can sell the two sets at each buyer's maximum price than if it has to adhere to a one-price policy, as we can see in Exhibit 19–9.

Exhibit 19–9 Private benefits of price discrimination

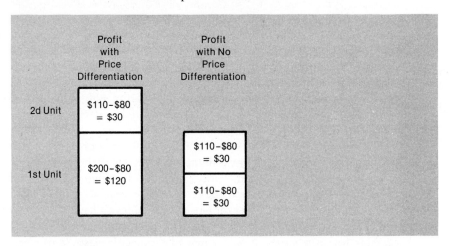

The seller, of course, needs to consider the likelihood that a price concession now will spoil the market for future sales. Fortunately, this danger is often more imagined than real. If excess capacity exists in the future, the company will probably be happy to grant the same kind of price concessions it finds profitable now. If, on the other hand, the excess capacity disappears in the future, the company won't be willing to grant price concessions to obtain added sales, and therefore the possibility of spoiling future markets may not be a serious objection.

The public benefit from price differentiation is less obvious. It arises when a one-price policy would fail to cover total costs, resulting in the product's withdrawal from the market. For example, suppose it costs $60 to buy each television set, plus $150 in fixed costs to run the store. Again only two customers are in the market, one willing to pay $200, the other willing to pay only $110. By differentiating the price, the dealer can sell two sets and make a profit:

Revenues: $200 + $110 .... $310
Costs: $150 + 2 × $60   270
    Profit .... $ 40

If the dealer has to quote the same price to both customers ($110), the store will lose money, no matter what price is quoted. The result: The store will close and neither customer will have a chance to buy the product.

A more complicated situation is reflected in Exhibit 19–10. The diagram at the left shows a conventional downward-sloping demand curve and a downward-sloping average cost curve. Average cost is greater than price at every possible volume; if price is set at the level P_D, volume will be Q_D and the total loss will be the lightly shaded area between average cost and price. Without price differentiation, in other words, this product won't be offered on the market.

Suppose the market can be divided into four segments, however, with a separate price in each, the maximum price the customers in that market are willing to pay. This possibility is shown in the right-hand diagram in Exhibit 19–10. The price in segment A is P_A, and the quantity sold in A is ($Q_A - Q_O$). The total revenue from segment A is $P_A \times (Q_A - Q_O)$, the area of the first block at the left of the diagram. The price in segment B is P_B, the quantity sold is $Q_B - Q_A$, and the revenue is $P_B \times (Q_B - Q_A)$. If the total area of the four revenue blocks is greater than the total cost (the area of the rectangle

Exhibit 19–10 Price differentiation to make production possible

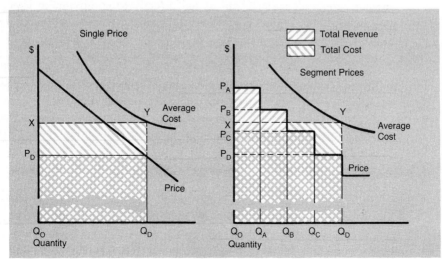

$Q_0 Q_D YX$), the company will cover its costs and consumers will be able to satisfy their wants. (The lower fare quoted by a transit agency for off-peak travel is one familiar application of this idea.)

Bases for price differentiation

The markets for personal services (medicine or law, for example) are relatively easy to segment because customers in one segment can't resell the services to potential customers in another segment. Segmenting the market for tangible goods requires something more, however. We have already mentioned two methods of market segmentation—by time of purchase (skimming) and by order quantity (quantity discounts). Three other possible segmentation bases are worth mentioning: location, function, and product content.

Location. Sellers of products subject to high transportation costs may charge different prices to customers located in different regions. Products sold at low prices to customers on the West Coast, for example, can't filter back to the East Coast unless the price differential is greater than the cost of shipping and handling.

Locational differences also permit price differentiation between urban and suburban stores, between uptown and downtown, between slum and vacation resort. Here the barrier is not the cost of reshipping merchandise from one location to another but the unlikelihood of individual customers' seeking out the lower priced outlets.

Function. Segmentation can also be based on differences in the functions performed by different groups of customers. Wholesalers, retailers, and final customers usually pay different prices, presumably because wholesalers and retailers perform different functions. If these price differences depart materially from the costs of performing functional services, however, the company's prices in the high-priced segments (e.g., final customers) are likely to be eroded. Putative wholesalers can begin to sell directly to consumers at lower prices than retailers can quote. When this happens, the whole structure is likely to collapse.

Product content. A final way of segmenting the market is to offer different products to different groups of customers. The product difference can be physical—a better finish, a better fabric, more chrome and tinsel. Or it might be a difference in service—carpeted showroom floors, attentive salesclerks, faster delivery, and so forth. The only requirement is that enough customers value the differences highly enough to buy the higher priced product.

Limitations on price differentiation

The main limitation on the seller's ability to differentiate prices is the customer's ability to cross segment lines. If enough purchasers decide that a product sold under a discount label is just as good as a nationally advertised product, this form of price differentiation will no longer be workable. The easier it is to move from one segment to another, the narrower the feasible price spread. And the narrower the spread, the less likely that price differentiation will be profitable.

A second limitation is the ability of competitors to underprice the seller in the high-priced segments. Successful price differentiation implies some weakness in the strength of competition. In fact, price differentiation is probably most widespread in regulated industries in which competition is restricted by law and by high investment barriers to the entry of competing sellers.

Laws of one kind or another may also prevent or limit price differentiation. We have already mentioned the Robinson-Patman Act (see Chapter 16, above). Other examples are state regulation of milk and liquor prices, and so-called fair trade laws. Public consumer agencies and private consumer groups may also have an impact. The main restriction, however, is the force of competition. When this is strong, price differentiation will be very limited.

Summary

Product prices should reflect consciously selected pricing strategies. Skimming pricing is a short-run, profit-maximizing strategy; penetration pricing may also maximize short-run profit, but its main focus is on the longer term. The ability to skim the market depends on the strength of the barriers to the entry of competing products—the weaker the barrier, the greater the argument for penetration pricing.

Some pricing models require data on price-volume and cost-volume relationships. These models are difficult to apply, for several reasons. As a result, management often resorts to pricing formulas, mostly based on estimates of product cost. These cost estimates are most logically based on the attributable cost concept, although the real question is which formula provides the best indication of the normal price. If attributable cost or its conceptually weaker cousin, full cost, is used, it should be supplemented by data on variable cost for use in decisions with shorter time horizons.

The main variable in a cost-based pricing formula is the markup over cost. These markups will differ from product to product and from time to time. Management may use standard markups to calculate target prices or even to quote actual prices in some circumstances. It must be alert, however, to differences in competitive conditions which make departures from target prices desirable.

Management may even be able to increase its profits by quoting different prices to different buyers of the same product. To do this, it must be able to divide its market into segments, each separate from the others and each with its own degree of price sensitivity. Price differentiation may also be the only feasible method of covering costs and therefore the only way of assuring that the market will be served.

Independent study problems (solutions in Appendix B)

1. **The short-run economic pricing model.** The Magellan Company has been selling its product at a price of $0.80 and has decided to investigate the profitability of increasing the price to compensate the company for recent increases in operating cost. The controller of the company has analyzed the company's costs, and has derived the following cost estimates:

Monthly Output (units)	Operating Costs Fixed Cost	Marginal Cost per Unit
50,000 and less	$10,000	$0.60
50,001–60,000	10,000	0.61
60,001–70,000	10,000	0.62
70,001–80,000	11,000	0.64
80,001–90,000	11,000	0.67
90,001–100,000	11,000	0.71
100,001–110,000	12,000	0.75
110,001–120,000	12,000	0.79
120,001–130,000	13,000	0.85

The market research department has recently studied prices and performance of competitive products and has derived an estimate of the effect of price on sales volume. The manager of market research has presented the following figures to the controller hesitantly, saying that she doesn't know how reliable they are but that they are the best she can do. She adds that in good years sales would exceed these figures, but on the average she thinks her estimate would be borne out.

Price per Unit	Monthly Unit Sales
$0.75	100,000
0.80	90,000
0.85	80,000
0.90	70,000
0.95	60,000
1.00	50,000

Required:

Prepare a statement that will indicate the most profitable price at which the product might be sold.

2. **Price differentiation.** The Hammer Company manufactures a product that it distributes through its own sales branches in the midwestern United States. The company's president, John Martin, was recently approached by a West Coast distributor who was interested in obtaining a franchise for distribution of the product in seven western states not now served by the company. The distributor offered to pay Hammer $32.50 a unit and offer it for sale to retailers at a price of $42.50. The distributor would pay freight charges to the West Coast, averaging $3.50 a unit. No sales commissions would have to be paid on these sales. Mr. Martin promised that he would consider the offer.

The product is now sold to retailers in Hammer's present market area at a price of $44 delivered. Sales commissions are computed at 5 percent of sales. Freight averages $1.50 a unit. Other selling and administrative costs are regarded as fixed and amount to $4.50 a unit. Manufacturing cost amounts to $29.50 a unit, as follows:

Materials	$18.70
Labor	3.00
Variable overhead	3.30
Fixed overhead	4.50
Total	$29.50

Manufacturing capacity is adequate to handle the increased volume, which Mr. Martin estimates would amount to 10,000 units a month, but fixed factory overhead would probably increase by $15,000 a month.

Required:

a. Would you advise Mr. Martin to accept the arrangement suggested by the West Coast distributor?

b. What factors other than those mentioned above should be considered in making this decision?

Exercises and problems

3. **Economic pricing model.** Daniel Seder Associates is a market research firm, specializing in testing consumer reactions to new products. Its methods are slightly different from its competitors, and it has built a good reputation.

Prices in this industry are ordinarily quoted on the basis of a flat fee, the amount depending on the size of the job. In preparing his bids, Mr. Seder has been using a flat price of $20 an hour, and has gotten all the work he could handle at that price.

Mr. Seder decided a few months ago to experiment with different bidding formulas to see whether he could increase his earnings by putting in higher bids on new work. The results were interesting; at various prices per hour, the percentage of bids accepted was:

$30.00	32%
27.50	42
25.00	50
22.50	56
20.00	60

The total volume of work available for bidding calls for about 5,000 professional hours in an average month. Mr. Seder figures that he can handle up to 2,800 hours of work a month, which would give him about half of the local market. In fact, this is the level at which he has been operating for many months.

The costs of the professional staff are approximately constant from month to month. The bulk of the field work is done by a regular staff of part-time employees, but a few smaller firms are available to fill in (at higher prices) when the Seder load gets too heavy. Based on his past experience, Mr. Seder estimates that his monthly costs will be as follows:

Volume (hours)	Total Cost
1,500	$33,500
1,700	34,900
1,900	36,300
2,100	38,700
2,300	40,300
2,500	41,900
2,700	43,900
2,800	45,100

Required:

What hourly price should Mr. Seder use in bidding? Present an analysis to back up your recommendations.

4. **Effect of market structure on pricing.** The wholesale meat industry in the western region of the United States is characterized by a very large number of firms with no one firm dominating the market. The Perry Wholesale Meat Company specializes in the preparation and distribution of ground beef to restaurants and institutions. Perry is interested in expanding its production of ground beef because of available capacity and the rapid growth of franchise hamburger outlets in its market area. The regional trade association has estimated the ground beef demand function for the region to be $P = \$2.00 - \$0.02Q$ (in which $P =$ Price per pound and $Q =$ Number of truckload lots of 30,000 pounds each).

Perry's management has found that it can sell all of the ground beef it can produce at 99 cents a pound. The controller's office has estimated the total costs, including a normal return on investment, for various levels of production, as shown below:

Company's Total Ground Beef Production (pounds)	Company's Total Estimated Production Costs Including a Normal Return on Investment
120,000	$120,000
150,000	149,000
180,000	178,200
210,000	207,900
240,000	238,000

Each production level requires a slightly larger investment than the next smaller production level.

Required:

a. What selling price should the Perry Wholesale Meat Company charge for the ground beef? Explain your answer.

b. What level of production will maximize total return on investment for the Perry Wholesale Meat Company? Explain your answer.

c. What pricing and output strategy would the Perry Wholesale Meat Company find most profitable if it were the exclusive distributor of ground beef in the western region of the United States? Explain your answer.

(CMA)

5. **Pricing formula.** Duvall Company manufactures product X in departments A and B, which also manufacture other products, using the same equipment. One unit of product X requires the following:

Material M:	8 pounds at $3 a pound, used in department A
Material P:	4 units at $5 each, attached in department B
Labor:	2 hours at $12 an hour in department A
	3 hours at $10 an hour in department B

You have the following information about overhead rates in the two factory departments:

	Department A	Department B
Denominator of the overhead rate	Pounds of direct materials	Direct labor hours
Overhead rate at 80 percent of practical capacity:		
Variable overhead costs	$ .80	$ 2.00
Fixed overhead costs	2.20	3.00
Depreciation component of fixed overhead rate (included above)...................	0.80	0.10
Net plant and equipment	7,000,000	120,000
Total depreciation (per month)	80,000	1,000

Marketing costs traceable to product X amount to $20,000 a month. The product requires a working capital of $120,000 to support a target volume of 1,000 units a month.

Required:

a. Assuming that management uses a return-on-investment pricing formula with a pretax profit contribution large enough to provide a 30 percent rate of return on investment, what is the formula price for product X?

b. If product X is well established in its market, how might Duvall Company use the formula price?

c. If product X is a new product, about to be introduced on the market, how might management use the formula price?

6. **Bidding with idle capacity.**   The Aybec Foundry Company is feeling the effects of a general overexpansion of the foundry industry in the Boston area. Its monthly production cost budget for the next six months is based on an output of only 500 tons of castings a month, which is less than half of practical capacity. The prices of castings vary with the composition of the metal and the shape of the mold, but they average $250 a ton. The condensed monthly production cost budget at the 500-ton level is as follows:

	Core Making	Melting and Pouring	Molding	Cleaning and Grinding
Labor	$18,000	$28,000	$10,500	$7,500
Variable overhead	3,000	1,000	1,000	1,000
Fixed overhead	5,000	9,000	2,000	1,000
Total labor and overhead	$26,000	$38,000	$13,500	$9,500
Labor and overhead per direct labor hour	$13.00	$9.50	$9.00	$7.60

Operation at this level has brought the company very close to the break-even point. The lack of work also means that some of the most highly skilled workers will probably have to be laid off, and if this happens they may not be available when volume picks up later on. Accordingly, when a customer asked for bids on a large casting order, the plant manager asked the plant accountant to prepare a bid "at cost."

The order is for 90,000 castings, each weighing about 30 pounds, to be delivered on a regular schedule during the next six months. Materials required would cost $1 per casting after deducting scrap credits. The direct labor hours per casting required for each department would be:

Core making	0.09
Melting and pouring	0.15
Molding	0.06
Cleaning and grinding	0.06

Variable overhead would bear a normal relationship to labor cost in the melting and pouring department and in the molding department. In core making and cleaning and grinding, however, the extra labor requirements would not be accompanied by proportionate increases in variable overhead. Total variable overhead would increase by $1.20 for every additional labor hour in core making and by 30 cents for every additional labor hour in cleaning and grinding. Standard wage rates are in effect in each department, and no labor variances are anticipated.

To handle an order as large as this, certain increases in fixed factory overhead would be necessary, amounting to $1,000 a month for all departments combined. No increases in selling and administrative expense are anticipated, but the company uses a standard selling and administrative expense rate of $12 per ton of castings in its pricing work. Production for this order would be spread evenly over the six-month period.

Required:

a. Prepare a revised monthly factory cost budget, reflecting the addition of this order.

b. What is the lowest price that the plant manager could quote without selling at a loss? Show your calculations.

7. **Full-cost formula pricing.** Aberdeen Appliances, Inc., is bringing out its 19x1 line of household appliances. Sales during 19x0 were at record levels and an equally good year is forecast for 19x1. Disposable consumer income is expected to be at all-time record levels, and the entire appliance industry is booming.

The appliance business has always been highly competitive, and Aberdeen feels that at least part of its success has lain in its ability to keep its costs at competitive levels. The contract that has just been negotiated with the labor union representing the company's factory employees has raised wage rates by 10 percent for next year, however, and management is worried about the effects on the profit margin.

The old and new standard costs for Aberdeen's electric buffet grill–deep fryer combination are shown in the table below. The new standard costs reflect the new wage rates, changes in model design, and changes in manufacturing methods.

	19x0	19x1
Standard costs:		
Materials and parts	$ 8.50	$ 9.10
Labor	4.00	4.30
Factory overhead	6.00	6.50
Total	$18.50	$19.90

The 19x0 model was sold to dealers at $25. In view of the higher costs of the new model, management is considering setting the price on the 19x1 model at $27. This would keep the percentage markup over standard cost at 35 percent, the level prevailing for the 19x0 model.

Standard overhead costs are based on estimated costs at normal volume. Factory cost variances on this product in 19x0 amounted to about 10 cents, mostly unfavorable materials price variances. The introduction of new production equipment has created difficulties with the local labor union, however, and Aberdeen Appliances is now budgeting an unfavorable labor usage variance of 50 cents a unit on the grill-fryer combination. Other variances are expected to be minimal.

No estimates of the sensitivity of sales volume to changes in price have been made, and none can be made before management must reach a decision on the price for the new model.

Required:

To the extent that you can judge from the data given, should the price on the new model be set at $27, lower than this, or higher than this? Give reasons for your answer.

8. **Contribution margin figures in pricing.**   E. Berg and Sons build custom-made pleasure boats ranging in price from $10,000 to $250,000. For the past 30 years, Mr. Berg, Sr., has determined the selling price of each boat by estimating the costs of material, labor, and a prorated portion of overhead, then adding 20 percent to these estimated costs to provide a profit margin.

For example, a recent price quotation was determined as follows:

Direct materials	$ 5,000
Direct labor	8,000
Overhead	2,000
Estimated cost	15,000
Plus 20 percent	3,000
Selling price	$18,000

The overhead figure was determined by estimating average overhead costs per direct labor dollar during the year ahead, including selling and administrative costs as well as boatyard overheads.

The customer in this case rejected the $18,000 quotation. Since the work was to be done during a slack period, Mr. Berg reduced the markup to 5 percent and submitted a second bid of $15,750. Mr. Berg often does this during slack periods, and as a result the average markup for the year is expected to be about 15 percent. Even so, the customer in this case rejected the second offer and countered with a $15,000 offer of his own.

Mr. Ed Berg, Jr., has just completed a course on pricing and believes the firm could use some of the techniques discussed in the course. The course emphasized using contribution margin figures in pricing, and Mr. Berg, Jr., feels such an approach would be helpful in determining the selling prices of the company's boats. He has estimated that $90,000 of the $150,000 estimated overhead cost for the year is fixed; the remainder is variable in direct proportion to direct labor.

Required:

a.   What is the difference in net income for the year between accepting or rejecting the customer's offer? Are fixed costs likely to be affected?

b.   What is the minimum selling price Mr. Berg could have quoted without reducing net income?

c.   What advantages does the contribution margin approach to pricing have over the approach used by Mr. Berg, Sr.?

d.   What pitfalls are there, if any, in contribution margin pricing?

(CMA, adapted)

9. **Price increase: Role of cost data.**   Mandel Company has been a major manufacturer of industrial pulleys for many years, manufacturing all of its requirements in a pulley mill located in Buffalo, New York. Technical change has been gradual and most competing products are virtually identical to the Mandel models. Mandel has some slight advantage due to its long record of product reliability and prompt delivery, but management hasn't presumed on this advantage to try to obtain premium prices.

Mandel has been known as the price leader in the market for industrial pulleys for many years. When Mandel increased its prices in 19x1 and 19x2 while the market appeared strong, for example, all major competitors raised their prices almost immediately; when Mandel reduced its prices in 19x5 in the face of substantial idle capacity, all competitors followed suit within a few weeks. List prices have remained at the 19x5 levels for the last two years, although management believes some of its competitors have given discounts on large orders from time to time. Mandel's manufacturing capacity has remained relatively constant for the past 10 years, and total industry capacity has shrunk only slightly in response to low industry demand.

It is now early in 19x7. Operating costs have been rising every year and Mandel's profit margin on pulleys is very slim. The market began to improve in the latter half of last year (19x6) and management is trying to decide whether to raise its prices. The company's analysts have collected the following information on costs, prices, and market shares (prices and unit costs refer to Mandel's standard model; prices of other models were raised and lowered at the same time):

| Year | Selling Price | Variable Cost per Unit | Traceable Fixed Costs | | Mandel's Unit Sales | Market Share |
			Manufacturing	Marketing		
19x0 ...	$8.00	$3.90	$1,000,000	$500,000	500,000	40%
19x1 ...	8.50	3.85	1,040,000	550,000	520,000	41
19x2 ...	9.00	3.85	1,100,000	570,000	450,000	39
19x3 ...	9.00	3.88	1,120,000	540,000	550,000	42
19x4 ...	9.00	3.90	1,150,000	530,000	480,000	38
19x5 ...	8.50	4.00	1,100,000	550,000	400,000	40
19x6 ...	8.50	4.15	1,200,000	600,000	450,000	38
19x7* ...	?	4.50	1,300,000	650,000	?	?

* Estimate.

Industry sales in 19x7 are expected to jump to 1,400,000 units. Given the anticipated increase in costs, Mandel's controller is urging a price increase to at least $9 a unit. Marketing management is hesitant. Other companies in the market are subject to the same cost increases, but most of them still have some capacity to expand their sales volume without incurring heavy cost penalties. Total industry capacity probably amounts to about 1,800,000 units, and Mandel has about 40 percent of that.

Marketing management believes Mandel will capture 40 percent of the market in 19x7 if it holds the price at $8.50, the increase in share coming from a decline in the amount of secret price cutting by some competitors. If the price goes up to $9.00 and competitors go along, Mandel's share will probably hold at 38 percent; if competitors keep their prices at $8.50, however, Mandel's share is likely to drop to 30 percent. Since industry demand appears to be highly price inelastic, a loss of 8 percent of market share would defeat the purpose of the price increase.

Required:

a. Did Mandel make a mistake in lowering its prices in 19x5? Did it hurt its cash position as a result?

b. Should Mandel raise its price to $9 in 19x7? Will it increase its cash position as a result? Show calculations and present arguments to support your position.

10. **Formula pricing; product value analysis.** "We price to achieve a target return on investment," Al Doherty said. "First, we estimate the amount of facilities and working capital necessary to support each product. Eighteen percent is our target return on investment, before taxes, and this gives us the amount of profit we have to achieve. Then we figure out what it will cost us to operate at normal volume. Adding this to the target return gives us the price to set."

"Don't you consider the effect of price on volume?"

"Not directly. We figure that if we can't reach normal volume at a price that gives us our target return, then we don't want the product."

Mr. Doherty is the marketing vice president of Usher Enterprises, Inc., a medium-sized manufacturer of adhesives, abrasives, and industrial chemicals. He is responsible for the entire marketing program, including the establishment of product selling prices. For major pricing decisions he has a price advisory committee made up of the controller, the production manager, the industrial engineer, and himself, but the final decision is his because his performance is judged on the basis of return on investment.

At the moment Mr. Doherty is wrestling with the problem of setting a price on a new product for use in the paper processing industries. Usher's major competitor, Hinden Products, Inc., has a product with characteristics that have given it an enormous competitive advantage in paper processing industries. It sells for $3, and at this price has forced all competing products out of this market.

The only problem with the Hinden product is that it is costly to use. Users have to spend between 50 cents and $2 for auxiliary materials for every pound of the Hinden product they use. Mr. Doherty estimates that the cost penalties for using Hinden's product are as follows:

Cost Penalty	Pounds Sold (monthly)
$0.50	40,000
1.00	80,000
1.50	120,000
2.00	160,000
Total	400,000

Usher's new product would eliminate these cost penalties.

Paper industries' consumption of the Hinden product has been growing at a rate of about 100,000 pounds a year, or 8,300 pounds a month. Hinden sells the same product to other industries in which it does not have a cost penalty, but Usher's sales organization is inadequate to cover these other industries. The decision on Usher's new product will be based solely on its performance in the paper processing industries.

Introduction of the new product would be fairly easy. Investment in plant and equipment and working capital would amount to $5 million plus $10 for each pound of product sold in an average month. Introductory promotional costs would be negligible because Usher's sales force is already in regular contact with customers in the paper processing industries, and no large initial burst of media advertising would be required.

All cost estimates have been prepared on the basis of a normal volume of 200,000 pounds a month. Factory costs for the new product would amount to $200,000 a month plus $2 a pound, up to a volume ceiling of about 250,000 pounds a month. Beyond that, cost penalties would begin to increase rather rapidly and would quickly become prohibitive. Rather than go above 250,000 pounds a month, management would either limit sales or begin the construction of additional facilities.

Selling and product management costs for the new product would average $60,000 a month. These costs would be classified as fixed.

The company's central administration costs average 6 percent of factory cost at normal volume. These are fixed costs and would not change immediately if the new product were introduced. They would probably creep up gradually, however, for an eventual increase of about $20,000 a month.

Engineering and research and development costs to date have totaled $600,000. This amount has been expensed for external financial reporting, but it has been capitalized for internal reporting of product profitability. If Usher introduces the new product, the $600,000 will be charged against operations on a straight-line basis over the next 60 months. If Usher decides not to introduce the product, the entire amount will be expensed immediately.

Required:

a. What price would be set if the company's pricing formula were used? Show your calculations.

b. Do the data indicate that the price should be set at the target level? Make calculations that you think would help management decide what price to set and indicate how they might be used.

11. **Pricing strategy: New product.** The Oppenheim Company is just completing the construction of a new facility to manufacture a new product. This product is intended for sale to manufacturers of a wide variety of products in which it would be used as a component part, ordinarily hidden from the view of the ultimate consumer.

Competing products sell at prices ranging from $3.80 to $4.80, but differences in product specifications and design make direct comparisons difficult. Furthermore, the company believes that there is some price shading for large volume customers, but has thus far been unable to determine its extent.

Sales in this market are quite difficult to forecast, at least in part because individual orders tend to be fairly large and the loss of one order can make the difference between a good forecast and a highly inaccurate one.

In making the decision to enter this market, the Oppenheim management believed that it would be able to sell 150,000 units a month within three years after commencing operations if its prices were competitive. Market conditions have changed materially since the initial decision was made, and even with heavy promotional outlays at the outset, the company is not confident that it can meet the original sales target.

The company's reputation for product quality and delivery performance is such, however, that the sales manager has suggested setting a premium price of $5 a unit. The sales force is quite confident that it can sell 80,000 units a month in the first year at that price. Management thinks it unlikely, however, that the company could sell more than 80,000 units a month in the first year no matter how low a price was set. Buyers in this market try out new components in their less popular lines, often waiting two or three years before incorporating components of improved design into their major products, and this latter portion of the market tends to be highly price-sensitive.

It is estimated that materials will cost 80 cents a unit at monthly volumes of 100,000 units or less and 70 cents a unit if monthly volume is in excess of that figure. Labor costs will amount to $1.40 a unit. Factory overhead is to be budgeted at $90,000 per month plus 42 cents a unit. By-products from the process are expected to yield 24 cents for each unit of the main product manufactured. The plant's output can be increased to 250,000 units a month, but for all output in excess of 200,000 units a month labor cost will increase to $1.70 a unit and variable overhead will rise to 65 cents a unit.

An intensive sales promotion campaign is now being prepared to launch the new product. Advertising and special promotion activities costing $750,000 will be spread over the first year of the new product in addition to sales commissions of 5 percent of sales. Thereafter it is expected that selling costs attributable to the new product will be $20,000 a month plus commissions. No change in administrative or other nonmanufacturing expenses is expected to accompany the introduction of the new product.

The company's selling and administrative expenses (including advertising and sales representatives' commissions), together with its reported net income before taxes, have in the past averaged about 40 percent of manufacturing cost. This comes very close to a pricing formula that the company has used on many occasions: 145 percent of budgeted manufacturing cost at normal volume.

Required:

a. Compute unit cost on whatever basis you feel would be most helpful to management in setting an initial price on this product. Prepare a summary report to present this figure and any others that you would want management to see, including any charts or diagrams that you would find useful in getting your analysis across.

b. Would you recommend skimming pricing or penetration pricing in this situation? You should interpret a skimming price as a price in excess of the target price based on average cost at normal volume. State the arguments for and against your recommendation, and suggest a price for management to consider.

12. **Defining product cost for pricing purposes: New product.** Lundstrom Company's factory consists of three production departments and two service departments, with the following normal monthly overhead costs:

	Production Departments			Service Departments	
	A	B	C	M	N
Direct overhead:					
Variable	$ 5,200	$16,000	$10,500	$ 7,500	—
Fixed—divisible	6,000	4,500	2,000	—	—
Fixed—indivisible	800	1,500	3,000	2,000	$10,000
Allocated (full cost basis):					
General factory	2,000	2,000	2,000	—	—
Department M	1,000	4,000	5,000	—	—
Department N	5,000	2,000	2,500	500	—
Total	$20,000	$30,000	$25,000	$10,000	$10,000
Normal volume	20,000 dir. lab. hours	10,000 dir. lab. hours	12,500 machine- hours	2,000 service- hours	100,000 sq. ft.

Consumption of service department M's services is regarded as a divisible fixed cost in department A and as proportionately variable with volume in departments B and C. General factory overheads are entirely fixed and largely indivisible.

Product X has just been developed by the Lundstrom Company and is now ready for commercialization. It will be listed in the company's next product catalog, and orders will be taken for immediate or deferred delivery at list price. Lundstrom has already spent about $1 million to bring product X to the commercialization stage, but these costs have already been expensed both for financial reporting and for income tax purposes.

Product X will compete with more than 100 products offered by 36 competing companies in the Lundstrom market area. Its biggest competition will come from the Deane Company's product P, which now sells 5,000 units a month, about 35 percent of the potential market for product X, at a unit price of $89. Lundstrom's market share in other product lines in its own region ranges from 5 to 35 percent, with most products between 10 and 15 percent. Prices in this market have been relatively stable for several years, with productivity gains offsetting inflationary pressures.

Product X has a number of significant advantages over product P and other competing products already on the market, and competitors will not be able to match these distinctive features for at least a year. The Lundstrom sales department is enthusiastic about the new product and feels that at a competitive price product X could achieve a good share of the market, probably about 15 percent, during the first year. Whether it could keep or increase its market share in subsequent years would depend in part on customers' experience with the product and in part on competitors' responses to product X. Lundstrom's factory has ample capacity to fill orders at this level and can expand production easily next year if the product is successful in its first year.

The company's development engineers estimate that after an initial six-month learning period, production inputs for a unit of product X will be: direct materials, $15; direct labor, $35; department A, three direct labor hours; department B, one and a half direct labor hours; and department C, two machine-hours. Errors in the engineers' estimates at this stage of product development have generally been within 10 percent of actual costs in the past, and underestimates have been just as frequent as overestimates.

Markups over factory cost on the company's other regular products average about 40 percent of full factory cost and generally range between 25 and 45 percent.

Most selling and administrative expenses will be the same no matter what price is set on product X. Selling costs attributable to this product are expected to amount to about $25,000 a month, not counting any special price deals that might be made to stimulate sales during the introductory period.

Required:

a. What kind of pricing strategy appears to be appropriate for product X? Explain why you favor this strategy.

b. For what purpose or purposes would management probably want to use estimates of the cost of a unit of product X? Would average full cost, average attributable cost, or average variable cost be the most appropriate costing basis for these purposes? Explain.

c. Prepare an estimate or estimates of the costs of product X, consistent with your answer to (*b*).

d. Recommend a selling price for product X. Support your recommendation, using figures from the problem to whatever extent you deem appropriate.

Case 19–1: Sanders Company (contract bidding)

Pierre Malin was adamant. "I know the competition is rough, he said, "but if we can't get enough out of this to cover our costs then we have no business going in."

"I couldn't agree more," George Riley replied, "but you're measuring costs the wrong way."

Pierre was the general manager and George was the controller of the Sanders Company, a small manufacturer of molded plastics products. At issue was the price to be quoted in a sealed bid the company was submitting for a large order of drinking cups to be supplied to a local school board.

The company's molding department consists of a group of injection molding machines with interchangeable dies. Each die has a number of openings or "cavities" in the shape of the product to be molded. The molding operation consists of closing the machine, whereupon melted polystyrene is forced under pressure into the die. There it is cooled into solid form by the circulation of cold water until it reaches a predetermined temperature, at which point the die opens and the molded products are ejected. The operator then closes the machine, and the process is repeated.

The drinking cups were a relatively new product for the Sanders Company, but orders for this product had been coming in at a fairly steady rate. The reason for Mr. Riley's enthusiasm was that this was the first opportunity to penetrate the large institutional market in the area. The initial contract was for 500 gross (6,000 dozen), but the potential market was many times that amount every year.

Standard product cost was based on engineering studies of physical input requirements and cost estimates prepared by the accounting department. Standard cost was as follows:

	Cents per Dozen Cups
Materials	12.0
Labor	5.5
Overhead	2.2
Total standard cost ...	19.7

The standard cost of the plastic powder used as raw material is $9 per thousand cups, reflecting normal wastage. Standard materials cost also includes $1 a thousand to amortize the cost of the dies used.

The labor cost of the molding operation is a function of (1) the number of cavities per die, (2) the length of the molding cycle (interval between closings), and (3) the number and compensation of operators tending each machine. The number of cavities per die is determined largely by the size and shape of the molded product, although the number of cavities actually in use may be reduced by blocking off one or more cavities that have developed defects that would lead to the rejection of finished products. Because of the high costs of die removal and setup, a die may be kept in operation with a fairly substantial number of its cavities blocked off.

The length of the molding cycle depends on how quickly the operator responds to the opening of the die. While the die is closed, the operator inspects the molded products and separates them from the plastic framework to which they are attached when ejected. An operator may delay clearing and closing the machine if these tasks haven't been finished when the machine opens.

The Sanders Company typically assigns one worker to a machine, with a reliever for each 10 machines. This reliever also keeps the machines supplied with raw material. The machine operators and relievers are paid at the rate of $7.25 an hour, with time and a half for overtime. Each worker is entitled to a 15-minute rest period each morning and afternoon and a half-hour lunch period, as part of a normal eight-hour shift. The machine is operated by the reliever during the smoking period, but it remains idle during the lunch period. A study of recent experience revealed that each operator was idle for an average of 15 minutes a day while minor repairs or adjustments were being made to the machine. This idle time is not recorded separately on a routine basis. If a machine is to be out of operation for a half-hour or more, the operator is assigned to other tasks, such as correcting minor defects in rejected products.

The standard labor cost of an hour of machine time is $8.80, computed as follows:

Machine-hours per day: 10 machines at 7.25 hours each	
(total time less lunch and normal waiting time)	72.5
Daily labor cost for 10 machines:	
10 operators, 8 hours at $7.25 an hour	$580.00
1 reliever, 8 hours at $7.25 an hour	58.00
Total	638.00
Labor cost per machine-hour	$ 8.80

If the operator acts immediately, the complete cycle time is 25 seconds, but standards reflect an average cycle time of 30 seconds. The dies for the cups contain 20 cavities, but standard cost reflects the assumption that 20 percent of the cavities will be blocked. This would indicate a standard production rate of 1,920 cups an hour, and a standard labor cost of 5.5 cents a dozen.

Overhead cost is based on full absorption costing at normal volume. Variable costs account for approximately 30 percent of overhead cost at normal volume. The variation is in proportion to changes in labor cost.

Mr. Malin felt that standard cost was a poor basis for cost estimation in this case. "Our work force is very green," he said, "and I expect that cycle time will be 20

628

percent longer than standard. Overall volume is down, too, and this means that we can't take advantage of quantity discounts on our purchases. This will add 11 percent to the purchase prices of plastic powder. Besides, the lower volume means that we'll probably have to add 10 percent to our standard overhead cost to carry the cost of idle capacity. All of these things bring our costs up close to 22 cents a dozen, without any allowance for profit. I don't think we can win the contract on that basis."

"You're probably right on that score," George answered. "My guess is that we'll have to put in a bid of 21 cents a dozen if we really want this order. With standard cost at 19.7 cents a dozen, this shaves the margin pretty thin, but I think we ought to go ahead. This is a big market, and I think that standard cost gives us a better guideline than your expected actual cost figure. We can't expect our customers to pay for our inefficiencies."

   a. Would a bid of 21 cents give Sanders an incremental profit contribution on the school contract? Show your calculations.

   b. Which of the following should be included in the cost estimate for pricing purposes: (1) lack of quantity discounts on materials; (2) inexperienced labor force; (3) idle capacity; (4) blocked cavities; and (5) amortization of the cost of dies?

   c. Should Sanders Company enter a bid on this contract? If so, what price should it bid? Summarize your reasoning.

Case 19–2: Clovis, S.A.* (price differentiation)

Clovis, S.A. manufactures a line of roller skates which it sells in France and other European countries. The company has just received a proposal from Empire Importing Company of New York to introduce Clovis skates into the U.S. market, but at lower net prices than the company now receives on its European sales.

Clovis has no foreign subsidiaries, all foreign sales being made through independent wholesale distributors in the various countries. The company sells seven different models, all manufactured in the company's plant at Lyon, France.

Annual sales volume is now approximately 3.5 million pairs. Sales of the most expensive models have remained approximately constant for the past several years, but unit sales of the moderately priced models have declined about 25 percent from the levels of a few years ago, despite successive price reductions in most European markets, as competitors have increased their shares of the market at Clovis's expense. The overall European market is about the same size as it was a few years ago.

Empire Importing is convinced that it can market three of the Clovis models in the United States as high-quality items. Typical cost and price data for one of these, Model TM-5, are shown in Table 1. The other two models have similar cost-price relationships. Markups over manufacturing cost in other European countries are less than in Switzerland but greater than in Italy.

The proposal is to offer the products for sale through department stores and discount houses in the eastern part of the United States. Empire Importing would sell Model TM-5 to retailers at a price of $17.15 a pair plus freight from New York. Empire would pay Clovis $9.20 a pair, plus all shipping charges and U.S. import duties, estimated at $4.50 a pair for the TM-5. It would be responsible for all advertising and sales promotion in the United States, would bear all U.S. credit risks, and would have exclusive rights to market Clovis skates east of the Mississippi River for a period of five years.

Mr. J. R. Martell, Clovis's sales manager, is strongly attracted by this proposal. Empire executives are convinced that they can sell 100,000 pairs of skates this year

---

Table 1 Selected price and cost data (dollars per pair)

	France	Switzerland	Italy
Price data			
Retail price	$24.00	$30.08	$24.30
Wholesale price	18.00	22.00	18.10
Factory price	13.80	15.12	10.35
Cost data			
Manufacturing cost:			
Variable cost	6.70	6.70	6.70
Fixed cost	2.10	2.10	2.10
Selling and administrative expense—fixed	1.50	1.50	1.50
Average shipping costs*	1.50	1.80	2.10
Import tariff*	—	1.51	1.65
Approximate retail price range:			
Competing products	20.50–34.00	22.13–42.56	9.41–23.52
All Clovis models	20.50–30.50	26.67–36.89	18.82–24.30†

* Paid by wholesale distributor; factory prices do not cover shipping costs or import duties.
†Model TM-6, Clovis's most expensive model, is not marketed in Italy.

and that within three years they will be able to increase their U.S. volume to 300,000 pairs a year. Manufacturing overhead is now underabsorbed, and capacity exists in the Lyon factory to manufacture more than the 300,000 pairs per year required to supply Empire Importing. The overhead rates from which the unit cost figures in Table 1 were derived were based on an annual volume of about 4,100,000 pairs of skates. Most fixed overheads are not traceable to any one product, but represent capacity costs for the combined production of skates and skate parts.

The present level of fixed costs could probably be maintained if sales were to increase by 100,000 pairs a year, but additional supervisory and clerical personnel would be required to handle a larger increase. Clovis's accounting department has assembled estimates that the accompanying increases in total fixed costs would average approximately $180,000 a year from the second year onward. Variable manufacturing cost per pair would be approximately as shown in Table 1.

Mr. Pepincourt, Clovis's president, is not entirely convinced of the wisdom of entering the U.S. market on this basis. The company's policy has been to market no product at less than full cost, although in some countries such as Italy the profit margin above full cost has been very thin. Furthermore, expansion into the U.S. market would mean that Clovis would have to spend approximately $150,000 three or four years from now to replace certain items of factory equipment now in use. If the company does not accept the Empire Importing proposal or find other ways to increase volume, production lines can be reorganized at negligible cost, thereby making it possible to dispose of this equipment now. Thus the Empire proposal would commit Clovis to an investment which Mr. Pepincourt is reluctant to make. On the other hand, the working capital necessary to support the company's entry into the United States would be negligible.

The equipment referred to in the previous paragraph has no salvage value at the present time, but depreciation on it is included in factory fixed costs at $15,000 a year. Other fixed costs associated with this equipment amount to approximately $60,000 a year.

Shipping charges and European tarrifs are high enough so that reexportation of Clovis skates from New York to Europe would not be feasible, but Mr. Pepincourt is worried nevertheless that if he agrees to this proposal his sales manager will begin to propose major price concessions in other markets as well.

a. Calculate the contribution United States shipments would make to Clovis's profits at volumes of 100,000, 200,000, and 300,000 units a year.

b. Given your calculations in (*a*), should Clovis introduce its skates in the United States at the price proposed by Empire Importing Company? Be sure to consider possible arguments for rejecting the conclusions based on your calculations and explain either why you find these arguments convincing or why you are willing to base your decision on the calculations.

20 Statistical cost estimation

Estimates of the relationships between costs and other variables are needed both in flexible budgeting and in most managerial decision models. Management uses many different techniques to identify these relationships. This chapter will examine some of the methods used in this kind of analysis. It consists of three parts:

1. A review of nonmathematical methods of estimating relationships between costs and other variables.
2. A study of mathematical methods of estimating these relationships.
3. An examination of a particular kind of cost relationship, the effect of experience on cost, referred to as the learning curve.

Nonmathematical methods

Some estimates are based on engineers' analyses of technological relationships. Methods study and work sampling are two engineering techniques we have already mentioned. Two other techniques—the judgment method and graphic curve fitting—are often used by themselves, often in conjunction with mathematical techniques, and need to be discussed. We'll also say a few words about a third method, the high-low points method.

Judgment method

In the final analysis, all cost estimation is judgmental. No matter how rigorous the mathematical technique, it cannot capture all the influences on cost, many of them operating in subtle ways. Nor can it capture the future, which is usually what the analyst is interested in. In the judgment method, also known as the *inspection of accounts* method, the manager and the accountant classify the costs in each object-of-expenditure account as wholly fixed, wholly variable, or a mixture of the two. For wholly variable cost elements, a single average cost figure is selected; for wholly fixed elements, a total cost for the time period is called for; and for mixed cost elements, the manager provides any cost formula that seems to describe the relationship best.

This approach seldom appeals to the technician, but it has several advantages:

1. It permits managers to specify relationships that are difficult to establish statistically—e.g., step functions.
2. It requires managers to participate actively in cost analysis, increasing their understanding of the ways costs behave.
3. It isn't restricted to historical data, but can be used directly to identify estimated future relationships.

The main disadvantage of the judgment method is that it may fail to use relevant data that are readily available. As a result, most managers will use some historical data in preparing judgmental estimates—the more data they use, the more technical analysis they are likely to need to support their judgment.

Graphic method

The judgment method relies mainly on historical experience, supplemented in most cases by at least some historical data. Engineering methods also draw heavily from the past. The graphic method goes even further, relying exclusively on past data. Before describing this method, however, we need to define a few terms. A *regression equation* identifies an estimated relationship between a dependent variable (cost) and one or more independent variables (production volume, air temperature, and so on), based on historical or experimental observations. If the equation includes only one independent variable, it is referred to as a *simple regression*, and the regression equation can be traced on an ordinary sheet of graph paper as a *regression line.*

If the dependent variable is cost, the independent variable is volume, and the relationship is assumed to be linear, the regression line can be described by the equation for a straight line:

$$y = a + bx$$

in which

x = Volume per period.
y = Total cost per period at that volume.
a = Total fixed cost per period.
b = Average variable cost per unit of volume.

If fixed costs amount to $3,000 a month and variable costs average 50 cents a direct labor hour, the equation for the regression line is:

$$\text{Cost} = \$3,000 + \$0.50 \times \text{Direct labor hours}$$

The constant, a, may not be a good estimate of costs at zero volume. It is simply a residual, determined by extending the regression line from the experienced volume range in a straight line back to the zero-volume level. To simplify the terminology, however, we refer to this amount as total fixed cost.

Regression analysis is the process by which a regression equation is derived. In the graphic method, the analyst draws a line ("fits a curve") on a sheet of graph paper to approximate the relationship revealed by a series of past

Exhibit 20–1 A regression line fitted by the graphic method

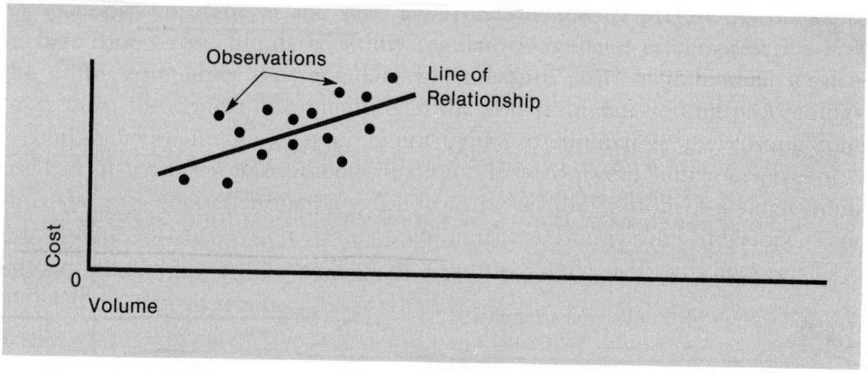

cost-volume observations plotted on the same graph.[1] One of these is shown in Exhibit 20–1.

This may seem a haphazard way of drawing a regression line, but it often produces results very close to those emerging from more rigorous mathematical techniques. Two skilled statisticians, looking independently at the observations plotted in Exhibit 20–1, are likely to come up with very similar estimates of relationship.

Computer programs for regression analysis are now so widely available and so easy to use that the advantage the graphic method once had—it was cheaper to use—has evaporated. Drawing the scatter diagram—that is, plotting the observations on graph paper—is often useful, however, even if a mathematical curve-fitting technique is used. It provides a visual impression of the relationship and of the dispersion of the estimates.

High-low points method

An even simpler method of estimating cost-volume relationships from historical data is the high-low points method. This consists of selecting the periods of highest and lowest volumes in the past and relating the difference in volume to the difference in cost between these two volumes. For example:

	Volume (direct labor hours)	Indirect Labor Cost
High volume	9,500	$3,400
Low volume	5,000	2,500
Difference	4,500	$ 900

$$\frac{\$900}{4,500} = \$0.20 \text{ a direct labor hour.}$$

---

[1] The graphic method may also be used in *multiple regression analysis* (two or more independent variables). See William A. Spurr and Charles P. Bonini, *Statistical Analysis for Business Decisions,* rev. ed. (Homewood, Ill.: Richard D. Irwin, 1973), pp. 499–503.

The $0.20 is interpreted as the average variable cost within this range.

The high-low points method uses a two-step calculation to derive an estimate of total fixed cost:

est. total FC

1. Multiply the average variable cost by the low volume ($0.20 × 5,000 direct labor hours = $1,000).
2. Subtract this figure from the observed total cost at the low volume ($2,500 − $1,500).

This method is extremely vulnerable to random variations in cost. Even if the highs and the lows are based on averages of several high points and several low points, the fact remains that the relationship is estimated solely from data at the extremes, ignoring all the observations in between. For this reason it should be used seldom, if at all.

est. solely from extremes

The least squares method: Simple linear regression

Most technical analysis of cost relationships is done mathematically, for two reasons:

1. It can be done quickly and routinely on the computer.
2. It permits numerical measures of the reliability of the estimated relationship.

The mathematical method most commonly used for this purpose is least squares regression analysis. In this section we'll see how this method can be used to develop linear estimates of relationships between two variables.[2]

Preparing the data

The first step in a regression analysis is to collect the necessary observations. Six guidelines should be noted:

1. Each observation should cover a time period long enough to smooth out major random fluctuations in cost, but not so long that the output rate varies substantially within the period.
2. Enough observations should be provided to produce a substantial number of degrees of freedom. (This term is explained later in this section.)
3. The period within which the observations are made shouldn't be so long that major changes in cost structure have taken place within it, affecting some of the observations but not all of them. (Installation of major new equipment after half the observations have been made, for example, would destroy the relevance of the preinstallation observations.)
4. Observations should cover all portions of the likely output range; the

---

[2] We can do no more than review the fundamentals of mathematical regression analysis in the few pages available here. Anyone needing to apply this method independently should study a standard statistics text such as the one by Spurr and Bonini, *Statistical Analysis for Business Decisions,* chaps. 16–17; for a more advanced treatment, see Edmond Malinvaud, *Statistical Methods of Econometrics,* 2d rev. ed. (New York: American Elsevier, 1970), chaps. 3–10.

regression equation should be regarded as valid only for the covered portion of the range.

5.   Data collection routines should ensure that costs are recorded as resources are used or committed; volume should be recorded as it occurs. (Unofficial inventorying of issued supplies on the shop floor and failure to consider changes in work in process are two common collection errors.)

6.   Each observation must provide a value of each of the variables.

Meeting these specifications is often difficult. To get enough observations (the second guideline) we may be tempted to shorten each observation period (violating the first guideline) or to accept observations made during very early time periods (violating the third guideline). We must be careful, therefore, to inspect the data to detect extreme items, changes in input prices, changes in operating methods, and spurious cost relationships. These can be handled as follows:

1.   Observations should be corrected for changes in input prices—e.g., labor costs recorded before a 5 percent wage increase should be multiplied by 1.05.

2.   If operating methods have changed, observations made prior to the change should be dropped from the analysis. If the effect of the methods change can be estimated reliably, the data may be adjusted to allow for it, but this is a risky step.

3.   Observations affected by extraordinary events (strikes, floods, and so on) should be excluded from the analysis. These often show up in a scatter diagram as extreme items, far outside the pattern traced by the other observations.

4.   Cost variations produced by accounting allocation and absorption techniques should be ignored; accounting allocations in some cases should be based on regression equations rather than the other way around. (Cost distributions based on time or usage records should not be excluded on these grounds if they measure the attributable cost of the resources used.)

Calculating the regression equation

The least squares method is based on a mathematical idea that the line that fits a set of data best has the following property:

✳   The sum of the squares of the vertical deviations of the actual observations from this line is less than the sum of the squares of the vertical deviations from any other line that might be drawn on the chart.

This is illustrated in Exhibit 20–2. Each of the observed values of y is labeled y_o; the corresponding point on the regression line is y_c. The difference between the two is the vertical distance between y_o and y_c at the observed volume. Σ is the mathematical symbol for a sum.

The regression equation for a straight line with this property and representing the relationship between y and x can be found by calculating the sums

Exhibit 20–2 Property of a least squares regression line

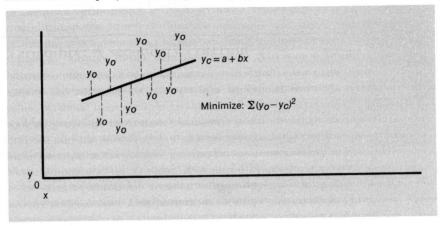

required by the following two equations, known as the _normal equations_, and solving for *a* and *b:*

$$\Sigma y = an + b\Sigma x$$
$$\Sigma xy = a\Sigma x + b\Sigma x^2$$

in which n = the number of observations of cost and volume.

To make these normal equations easier to work with, we can translate them into the following form:

$$a = \frac{\Sigma y}{n} - \frac{b\Sigma x}{n} \qquad (1)$$

$$b = \frac{n\Sigma xy - \Sigma x\Sigma y}{n\Sigma x^2 - (\Sigma x)^2} \qquad (2)$$

To illustrate the method without unnecessary arithmetic, let us suppose we have six cost/volume observations from which we wish to estimate the relationship between cost and volume. The observations and the computational quantities required by the two normal equations are as follows:

Volume	Cost		
x	y	xy	x^2
3	5	15	9
4	6	24	16
5	6	30	25
6	9	54	36
7	9	63	49
8	10	80	64
$\Sigma = 33$	45	266	199

n, of course, is 6 because we have six observations.

Substituting these amounts in the normal equations, we get the following:

$$a = 45/6 - (33/6)b \tag{1}$$
$$b = (6 \times 266 - 33 \times 45)/(6 \times 199 - (33)^2) \tag{2}$$

Solving equation (2), we find that b equals $111/105 = 1.057$. Putting this in equation (1) yields a value of $a = 7.500 - 5.814 = 1.686$. The regression line therefore is described by the following equation:

$$y = \$1.686 + \$1.057\ x.$$

The value for b is known as a _regression coefficient_. It indicates the estimated change in y that will accompany a unit change in x if there is no change in any of the influences on y other than x (see Exhibit 20–3).

Exhibit 20–3 Diagram of a regression coefficient

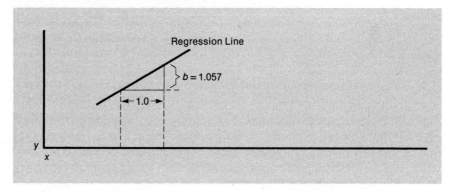

We can use this formula to predict the cost that will be incurred at any volume in the customary range. At a volume of 3, for example, cost should be $\$1.686 + 3 \times \$1.057 = \$4.857$. This is $\$0.143$ less than the amount observed at that volume. Repeating this calculation for each of the other observed volumes, we get the following comparison:

Volume	Observed Cost	Calculated Cost	Deviation	Deviation²
x	y_o	y_c	$(y_o - y_c)$	$(y_o - y_c)^2$
3	$ 5	$ 4.857	+$0.143	0.0204
4	6	5.914	+ 0.086	0.0074
5	6	6.971	− 0.971	0.9428
6	9	8.028	+ 0.972	0.9448
7	9	9.085	− 0.085	0.0072
8	10	10.142	− 0.142	0.0202
$\Sigma =$				1.9428

These observations, predictions, and deviations are diagrammed in Exhibit 20–4. Because we had no observations at volumes less than 3, this part of the regression line is shown as a dashed line. This regression line has the property required by the least squares method: it minimizes the sum of the squares of the cost deviations from the line. If we were to alter either a or b, the sum of the squared deviations would be greater than 1.9428.

Exhibit 20–4 Mathematically fitted regression line

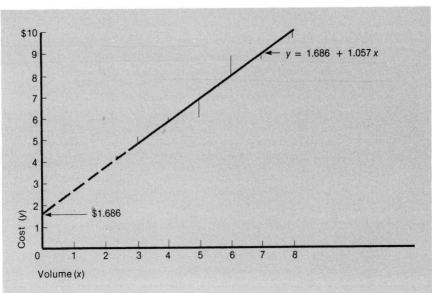

Tests of reliability

Before a regression equation can be used, the manager needs to know how closely it has fit the observed facts in the past. We'll look at three measures of reliability:

1. The coefficient of determination.
2. The standard error of the estimate.
3. The standard error of the coefficient.

The coefficient of determination. If the regression line were to fit the actual observations perfectly, all of the observed points would lie on the line. This suggests that reliability is related to the size of the deviations of the actual observations (y_o) from the calculated values (y_c). These figures are captured in the *residual variation,* defined as the average of the sum of the squared deviations. Its symbol is $s_e{}^2$:

$$s_e{}^2 = \Sigma(y_o - y_c)^2/n = 1.9428/6 = 0.324$$

The smaller this figure, the better the fit.

residual variation ✳

The next question, however, is how much better a fit the regression equation is than something simpler. It may be that we could predict costs almost as well by assuming they will be equal to the average of all the observations. In other words, how much predictive ability did we gain by introducing volume (x) as an independent variable?

We can answer this by calculating the deviations of the individual cost observations (y_0) from the average of the six figures ($\bar{y}$):

Observed Cost (y)	Average Cost ($\bar{y}$)	Deviation ($\bar{y}_0 - \bar{y}$)	Deviation² ($\bar{y}_0 - \bar{y}$)²
5	7.5	−2.5	6.25
6	7.5	−1.5	2.25
6	7.5	−1.5	2.25
9	7.5	+1.5	2.25
9	7.5	+1.5	2.25
10	7.5	+2.5	6.25
Σ =			21.50

The statistician's measure of the size of the dispersion of a set of figures around their mean is known as the *variance*. Its symbol is s^2. To try to reduce the danger of confusing this with our term for deviations from standard cost, we shall refer to the statistical variance as the *variation.* It is defined as the average of the sum of the squared deviations from the mean:

$$s^2 = \Sigma(y_0 - \bar{y})^2/n.$$

In this case the total variation is $21.50/6 = 3.583$.

Now we can see the significance of the residual variation we calculated earlier. By introducing variations in volume as a possible way of predicting variations in cost, we accounted for all but 0.324 of the total variation of 3.583. In other words, volume variations accounted for more than 90 percent of the variation of cost around its mean. This relationship is summarized in the *coefficient of determination* (r^2):

$$r^2 = 1 - \frac{\Sigma(y_0 - y_c)^2}{\Sigma(y_0 - \bar{y})^2}$$

$$= 1 - 1.9428/21.5 = 1 - 0.09 = 0.91$$

The general term for the degree of association between variables is *correlation*. In fact, the symbol, r, stands for a quantity known as the *coefficient of correlation*, the square root of the coefficient of determination. If all the observations fall on the regression line, $\Sigma(y_0 - y_c)^2$ will be zero, and both r and r^2 will be equal to 1. This is known as *perfect correlation.* On the other hand, if the deviations from the predicted values are as great as the deviations from the mean, then $\Sigma(y_0 - y_c)^2/\Sigma(y_0 - \bar{y})^2$ will equal 1, and r^2 will equal zero. This is known as no correlation of *zero correlation.*

Standard error of the estimate.   Although the coefficient of determination says something about the reliability of estimates of the dependent variable based on the regression equation, it doesn't measure the absolute size of the probable deviations from the line. This is the role of the standard error of the estimate (s_e). For any set of observations, the standard error of the estimate can be calculated from the following formula:

$$s_e = \sqrt{\Sigma(y_o - y_c)^2 / n}$$

In this case, the calculation is:

$$s_e = \sqrt{1.9428/6} = 0.569$$

This is not the only set of observations that might be collected, however. It is usually a sample from some larger "population." The population in this case consists of all combinations of cost and volume that might occur in the present operation. Our six observations may reflect the characteristics of the population perfectly—or they may be very unusual, not representative of the population at all.

If our objective is to calculate the expected amount of variation around the true line of relationship—the one that would emerge if the entire population were included—then we have to allow for the possibility that the standard error of the line drawn from the sample may not be the same as the standard error of a line drawn from the population as a whole.

The way to do this is to adjust the formula to conform to the number of *degrees of freedom* allowed by the observations. The revised formula is:

$$s_e = \sqrt{\Sigma(y_o - y_c)^2 / (n - m)}$$

in which $m =$ the number of constants and regression coefficients, and $(n - m)$ is the number of degrees of freedom. In our example, $m = 2$, leaving four degrees of freedom.[3] The standard error of the estimate therefore is:

$$s_e = \sqrt{1.9428/4} = 0.697$$

We don't have the space to explain this adjustment in full, but a few words about degrees of freedom may help. Each observation in a sample is free to take any value in the possible range. Once a coefficient has been calculated from a set of observations, however, at least one of them is no longer free to vary. With six observations, five can vary but the sixth must take whatever value is necessary to keep the coefficient at its calculated value. If two coefficients are calculated, two restrictions are imposed on the set of observations.

The number of degrees of freedom is important because it is one determinant of the reliability of a sample. The larger the number of degrees of freedom, the more likely the coefficients from the sample will be close to the coefficients in the population as a whole.

---

[3] To avoid calculating all the values of y_c, we can use the following formula to calculate the standard error of the estimate for a linear regression equation with one independent variable:

$$s_e = \sqrt{\frac{\Sigma y^2 - a\Sigma y - b\Sigma xy}{n - 2}}$$

Confidence intervals. Our main reason for calculating the standard error of the estimate is to use it to establish _confidence intervals._ A confidence interval is a range of values of the dependent variable within which we may have a specified degree of confidence the true value lies. Different confidence intervals can be calculated for different degrees of confidence.

Statisticians can demonstrate, for example, that there are two chances out of three that the interval specified by ($y_c \pm s_e$) will include the true value of y if the observations are distributed normally about the line.[4] For $x = 5$, the calculated value of y is $1.686 + 1.057 \times 5 = 6.971$. Since $s_e = 0.697$, we can state that the chances are two out of three that cost will be between 6.274 and 7.668 (6.971 ± 0.697).

If the interval is widened to ($y_c \pm 1.96\ s_e$), the confidence level goes up to 95 percent. A 95 percent confidence interval for our illustrative relationship is diagrammed in Exhibit 20–5.

Exhibit 20–5 A 95 percent confidence interval

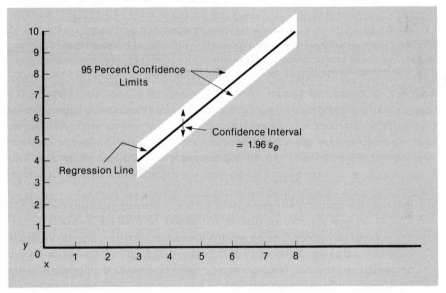

Standard error of the coefficient. The standard error of the estimate measures the reliability of the estimates of total cost. Another important question is how reliable the regression coefficient is, because the analysis often focuses on the _rate of variability_ rather than on the absolute level of the prediction. The formula for the standard error of the b coefficient (s_b) can be expressed as follows:

$$s_b = \frac{s_e}{\sqrt{\Sigma(x_0 - \bar{x})^2}}$$

---

[4] The observations in our illustration were not distributed normally. To eliminate this objection we would have had to use a larger, more complex set of numbers. Since our only purpose was to illustrate the method, we chose numerical simplicity over technical precision.

This measures the relationship of the standard error of the estimate to the variation in x around its mean. If the xs cover a wide range, s_b will be small; if the values of x cover only a narrow portion of the range, s_b will be large. (In the extreme case, if all the values of x are equal to their mean, $(x_0 - \bar{x})^2$ will be zero and s_b will be infinitely large. Putting this another way, you can't measure a regression coefficient if your sample doesn't cover the range.)

To simplify the calculation of s_b, we can restate the denominator in quantities we have already calculated:

$$s_b = \frac{s_e}{\sqrt{\Sigma x_0^2 - \bar{x}\,\Sigma x_0}}$$

In this case:

$$s_b = 0.697/\sqrt{199 - 5.5 \times 33} = 0.697/4.1833 = 0.167$$

This says that the b value of 1.057 has a standard error of 0.167. The question is whether this is big enough to cast doubt on the proposition that the b in the population as a whole is something other than zero.

To answer this question, we can calculate the ratio of the coefficient to its standard error. This is called its *t-value*. The calculation in this case is:

$$t\text{-value} = b/s_b = 1.057/0.167 = 6.329$$

t-value *

This says that the b in the sample is 6.329 standard errors from zero. Intuitively, we can say that it doesn't seem likely that b would be this far from zero even if the sample wasn't representative. Statisticians don't like intuition, however. Instead, they use a table showing how many multiples of the standard error of the regression coefficient are reasonable, given a specified number of degrees of freedom and a given probability level.

A partial set of these values of t is given in Exhibit 20–6. To interpret this, let's pick one figure from the table, the figure for 4 degrees of freedom in the column headed 0.95. This says that there are only five chances in 100 that a sample would turn up a b coefficient greater than 2.776 s_b if the b coefficient for the population as a whole were zero. The 2.776 s_b is known as the confidence interval—if the value of the coefficient is larger than this, we can be 95 percent confident that it reflects a real relationship in the population.

The 95 percent confidence interval for the b coefficient in our illustration is

$$1.057 \pm 2.776 \times 0.167 = 1.057 \pm 0.464.$$

In other words, we can be 95 percent confident that the true value of the variable cost coefficient is somewhere between 0.593 and 1.521. From a similar set of calculations, we can also be 90 percent confident that the true value is within ± 0.356 of 1.057.

These ranges are quite large, despite the high r^2 we derived earlier. The reason is that we used an example with few observations, leaving few degrees of freedom. The greater the number of degrees of freedom, the more confident

Exhibit 20–6 Partial table of *t*-values*

Degrees of Freedom	Maximum Values of *t* Consistent with Confidence Interval with Probability of		
	0.90	0.95	0.99
1	6.314	12.706	63.657
2	2.920	4.303	9.925
3	2.353	3.182	5.841
4	2.132	2.776	4.604
5	2.015	2.571	4.032
6	1.943	2.447	3.707
7	1.895	2.365	3.499
8	1.860	2.306	3.355
9	1.833	2.262	3.250
10	1.812	2.228	3.169
11	1.796	2.201	3.106
12	1.782	2.179	3.055
13	1.771	2.160	3.012
14	1.761	2.145	2.977
15	1.753	2.131	2.947
25	1.708	2.060	2.787
Infinite	1.645	1.960	2.576

* The headings of *t*-tables usually identify the probabilities of values falling in one tail of a bell-shaped distribution. We have reversed the legend for greater clarity, emphasizing the probabilities of the value falling in the main body of the distribution, not in the tail. The probability 0.95, for example, is the ratio of the unshaded area in the diagram at the right to half the area under the curve. This column in a typical *t*-table is headed $t_{.025}$, indicating that 2.5 percent of the area under the whole curve lies in the shaded area under the curve at the extreme right. This is 5 percent of the area under the right-hand side of the bell; the unshaded area thus occupies 95 percent of that total.

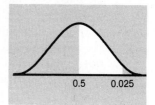

we can be that the sample is representative. The farther down in Exhibit 20–6 we go, the smaller the *t*-values are.

Technical assumptions

So far we have assumed that if enough usable observations can be found, management can rely on the regression equations within the stated confidence intervals. This is true only if a number of technical assumptions are valid. The main technical assumptions underlying simple linear regression analysis can be summarized in two sentences:

1. The relationship between the variables in the population is linear.
2. The values of the "disturbance term" ($y_o - y_c$) are normally distributed, independent of each other, and with constant variance.

The significance of these assumptions and what to do when they are violated are questions that must be left to books on statistical methods.[5] We mention them here merely to sound a note of caution. Although the standard errors may produce relatively narrow confidence intervals, they may not mean much if the analytical assumptions are invalid.

Evaluating the equation

Once the equation has been calculated, management has to decide what to do with it. This is not just a matter of testing the statistical reliability of the equation and the validity of the technical assumptions. Management may find the estimates adequate for some purposes even if their statistical reliability is low. In other cases, management may decide to repeat the analysis, perhaps with a different combination of variables, perhaps with a revised set of data, in the hope of improving the reliability of the results.

Even if management decides the results are good enough, the analysis isn't necessarily finished. The least squares method is designed to estimate the relationships that *have existed* between cost and other variables in the past. To use these estimated relationships to predict the future or to establish performance standards, the manager must decide how closely the future is likely to reproduce the conditions that prevailed in the past. At a minimum, price increases and methods changes have to be allowed for specifically, both in the fixed cost and in the b coefficient.

Management always has the option of rejecting the findings out of hand, of course. Sometimes the results of a regression analysis just don't ring true. We are not saying that management's accumulated knowledge is always superior to mathematically derived estimates. Far from it. Figures can be wrong, however, and management should not shrink from using its judgment if it has good reason to doubt the figures. Regression analysis is a tool to help management, not replace it.

Other least squares regressions

A regression analysis based on simple pairings of observations of two variables may not be good enough. In this section we shall look briefly at three possible extensions of the method:

1. Multiple regression analysis.
2. Nonlinear regression analysis.
3. Lagged regression analysis.

Multiple regression analysis

Cost is seldom determined by one variable only. For example, in a plant which generates its own steam and uses this steam both for heating and for

---

[5] For example, Malinvaud, *Statistical Methods of Econometrics;* a brief explanation of these assumptions in nontechnical language can be found in George J. Benston, "Multiple Regression Analysis of Cost Behavior," *Accounting Review,* October 1966, pp. 657–72, and in Spurr and Bonini, *Statistical Analysis for Business Decisions,* pp. 469–70.

motive power, two of the important determinants of cost are likely to be the number of "degree-days" (65°F. minus average outside temperature for each day) and the number of machine-hours.

A simple regression of cost on machine-hours is likely to have a relatively low coefficient of determination because the b coefficient will not capture the effects of variations in outside temperature. This suggests that one way to account for more of the total variation is to add one or more additional independent variables. Each additional variable should add a little more to our ability to understand how costs behave.

An analysis with two or more independent variables is known as multiple regression analysis. If there are two independent variables and the relationship is assumed to be linear, the regression equation will take the following form:

$$y = a + b_1 x_1 + b_2 x_2$$

in which

$y = $ Total cost.
$a = $ Total fixed cost.
$x_1 = $ The number of machine-hours.
$b_1 = $ The regression coefficient for machine-hours.
$x_2 = $ The number of degree-days.
$b_2 = $ The regression coefficient for degree-days.

Once again, the constant, a, doesn't necessarily measure the amount of cost that will be incurred at zero volume; it is a synthetic figure, derived by extending the relationships within the customary range of the independent variables, for which we have data, down to the zero level, for which we have no data. The important figures are b_1 and b_2: b_1 is supposed to show how y will change with a unit change in x_1, assuming that x_2 and all unidentified variables remain constant; similarly, b_2 measures the estimated change in y for a unit change in x_2, if x_1 remains constant.

To illustrate, suppose we have the following observations:[6]

x_1	x_2	y
1	3	11
2	5	23
3	1	5
4	2	12
5	3	19
6	5	31
7	8	48
8	6	40
$\Sigma = 36$	33	189

---

[6] This illustration has been borrowed from Clifford H. Springer, Robert E. Herlihy, and Robert I. Beggs, *Advanced Methods and Models* (Homewood, Ill.: Richard D. Irwin, 1965), pp. 249–50.

The normal equations for a regression equation with two independent variables are as follows:[7]

$$\Sigma y = an + b_1\Sigma x_1 + b_2\Sigma x_2$$
$$\Sigma x_1 y = a\Sigma x_1 + b_1\Sigma(x_1^2) + b_2\Sigma x_1 x_2$$
$$\Sigma x_2 y = a\Sigma x_2 + b_1\Sigma x_1 x_2 + b_2\Sigma(x_2^2)$$

The required sums are:

$$\Sigma x_2^2 = 204$$
$$\Sigma x_2^2 = 173$$
$$\Sigma x_1 x_2 = 173$$
$$\Sigma x_1 y = 1{,}057$$
$$\Sigma x_2 y = 1{,}013$$

The solution, for those who want to try a hand at it, is as follows:

$$y = -6 + 2x_1 + 5x_2$$

This indicates that y will go up \$2 for every additional unit of x_1 and \$5 for each additional unit of x_2. The -6 value for a seems to indicate that costs would be negative at $x_1 = x_2 = 0$, but as we have said before this merely indicates that the relationship summarized in the equation doesn't go as far as the origin.

The coefficient of multiple determination and the standard errors of the individual regression coefficients can be calculated with the aid of formulas similar to those we used in our discussion of simple regression, but a good deal more complicated.[8] Many multiple regression analyses go even farther, including the calculation of the so-called beta coefficients (β). These are the b coefficients, adjusted to units of comparable size. (b_1, for example, might be stated in hours and b_2 in pounds.) The betas show the *relative* impact on y of variations in each of the xs. In this way they can help management see which variables are the most important and which are the least.

Even for a set of data as simple as those in our illustration, hand calculation of the coefficients and standard errors is tedious and costly. Fortunately, standard computer programs are available to do this more efficiently and more quickly. These programs generate most of the important quantities automatically, and include them routinely in the printed results.

Multiple regression analysis rests on the same technical assumptions that underlie simple regression analysis, plus one more. It assumes that the independent variations are not related to each other. Any such relationship is known as *colinearity*. If two independent variables move up and down together, the regression coefficients won't measure what happens when one moves up or

colinearity

---

[7] Springer, Herlihy, and Beggs, pp. 246–48, offer a simple but extremely clear explanation of the logic behind these equations.

[8] The formulas and an explanation of their meaning can be found in statistics texts such as Spurr and Bonini, *Statistical Analysis for Business Decisions,* chap. 17; for a discussion of the problems of using this method in cost analysis, see Benston, "Multiple Regression Analysis of Cost Behavior," and Robert Jensen, "Multiple Regression Models for Cost Control—Assumptions and Limitations," *Accounting Review,* April 1967, pp. 265–72.

down while the other stays constant. The introduction of additional variables may produce a higher coefficient of determination, and this is likely to be desirable, but if colinearity is high it will reduce the reliability of the individual regression coefficients.

Nonlinear regression

Regression analysis can also be used to develop nonlinear cost equations. This is seldom done, partly because nonlinearities are not large enough to show up clearly, partly because cost behavior in the usual volume range is likely to be fairly linear, and partly because nonlinear analysis is more complicated.

One way to deal with the complexity problem is to try to fit a nonlinear expression that can be translated into a linear format. For example, Sidney Davidson and Robert Roy found that a line based on the logarithms of a set of observations described a newspaper's composing room costs much better than a line based on the raw data.[9] The relationship took the following form:

$$\log C = a + b \log X + c \log Z$$

in which

C = Composing room time.
X = The number of "assembly units" (a measure of the difficulty of the job).
Z = The amount of newspaper space used.

In other words, the analysts identified linear relationships between the logarithm of cost and the logarithms of the other variables. This represents a nonlinear relationship in terms of the raw data, but because the relationship was linear in terms of the logarithms the statistical problems were no greater than those the investigators would have encountered in fitting a linear equation to the raw data.

Lagged regression

In some processes, cost may relate to variables identified with earlier or later periods. This can be dealt with, to some extent, by more effective data collection procedures. In other cases, the regression equation should relate the cost in one period to an independent variable one or more periods earlier or later.

For example, inspection costs and the costs of rework (repairing defective units) are likely to vary with the amount of production in a previous period or periods. The analyst might try a one-month lag, regressing cost in period t on production in period $t - 1$, or a two-month lag, regressing cost on production in period $t - 2$. Improvement in the coefficient of determination when this is done is evidence of a lagged relationship.

---

[9] Sidney Davidson and Robert H. Roy, "A Case Study in Newspaper Operations," in Robert H. Roy (ed.), *Operations Research and Systems Engineering* (Baltimore, Md.: Johns Hopkins University Press, 1960).

648

Learning curve analysis

serial correlation [handwritten margin note]

One of the problems encountered in regression analysis is <u>serial correlation—</u>that is, <u>the quantities observed in one period depend in part on the quantities experienced in a previous period.</u> When this happens, the statistician has an additional task—to try to identify systematic patterns in period-to-period movements in cost.

Analysis of seasonal patterns, cyclical movements, and long-term trends, for example, has long been part of the statistician's stock in trade. In more recent years another pattern of relationship has been discovered—<u>a reduction in cost resulting from repetitive performance of the same task.</u> Patterns of this kind are referred to as learning curves. In this section we shall explain what they are and how they relate to accounting.

Nature of the learning curve

The first time a new operation is performed, both the personnel and the operating procedures are untried. As the operation is repeated, the work goes more smoothly and labor costs go down. This is likely to continue for some time. In fact, the pattern is so regular that the rate of decline established at the outset can be used in predicting operating labor costs well in advance.

learning ratio [handwritten margin note]

The effect of experience on cost is summarized in the *learning ratio* or improvement ratio. This is usually defined by the following equation:

$$\text{Learning ratio} = \frac{\text{Average labor cost for the first } 2X \text{ units}}{\text{Average labor cost for the first } X \text{ units}}$$

If the average labor cost for the first 500 units is $12.50 and the average labor cost for the first 1,000 units is $10, the learning ratio is 80 percent:

$$\text{Learning ratio} = \$10/\$12.50 = 80 \text{ percent}$$

 In other words, <u>every time cumulative output doubles, average cost declines to 80 percent of the previous amount.</u> Since the average cost of the first 1,000 units was $10, the average cost of the first 2,000 units will be expected to be 20 percent less, or $8 a unit.

Learning curve diagrams. The effect of learning shows up clearly in a diagram known as a learning curve. An 80 percent learning ratio is translated into an 80 percent learning curve in Exhibit 20–7. The diagram at the left is plotted on ordinary graph paper. It shows costs declining rapidly at first, then more slowly. If the curve were extended, further reductions would eventually become small enough to be ignored. The right-hand diagram shows the same relationship on logarithmic paper. <u>It is a straight line because the *rate* of decrease is constant.</u>

Learning curve equations. Mathematicians have been able to express the learning relationship in equations. The basic equation is:

$$Y = KX^s \qquad (1)$$

Exhibit 20–7 An 80 percent learning curve

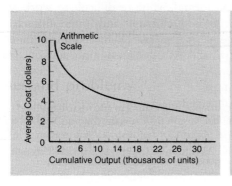 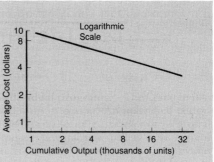

in which Y is the cumulative average labor cost, K the labor cost of the first unit, X the cumulative production, and S the improvement exponent. The improvement exponent is calculated as follows:

$$S = \frac{\text{Logarithm of the learning ratio}}{\text{Logarithm of 2}}$$

The improvement exponent can take any value between -1 and zero. The exponent for an 80 percent learning curve, for example, is -0.322.

Equation (1) can be restated in logarithmic form:

$$\log Y = \log K + S \log X \tag{2}$$

This is identical in form to the general formula for a straight line, which is why the relationship shows up as a straight line on logarithmic paper.

Cumulative total cost. Each of the first two equations defines cumulative _average cost._ Either of them can be converted easily to a formula for the total labor cost of all units produced up to a given point. Total cost can always be calculated from a known average cost by multiplying the average by the total number of units. When we do this to equation (1), we get the following formula:

$$\text{Total cost} = XY = X(KX^S) = KX^{S+1} \tag{3}$$

Incremental cost. If producing a second 1,000 units is to reduce cumulative average cost from \$10 to \$8, the cost of the second 1,000 units will have to be only \$6,000, or \$6 each:

	Total Cost	Units	Average Cost
First 1,000 units	\$10,000	1,000	\$10
Second 1,000 units	6,000	1,000	6
Total	\$16,000	2,000	\$ 8

Defining the learning curve in terms of this incremental relationship would be useful, but the mathematical formula is more difficult to work with. As a result, learning curve improvement ratios are usually stated as percentage reductions in cumulative average labor cost. Incremental cost can be calculated by solving equation (3) for two different cumulative production totals, then subtracting one from the other.

Although most processes improve as the company gains experience with them, learning curves can be observed mainly in processes that can be thought of as new. Most of them are based on companies' experiences with new products or new models, but the same pattern can be found in new factories as well. All that is necessary is repetitive production over an extended period of time.

Learning curve applications

Knowledge of the learning curve can be useful both in planning and in control. Standard costs for new operations, for example, should be revised frequently to reflect the anticipated learning pattern. For well-established operations, of course, the learning effect is likely to be negligible and can be ignored.

The main impact of learning curve analysis is likely to be on the data collected for use in decision making, particularly in connection with product pricing and marketing strategy decisions. Take the following simplified illustration, for example, A company has been asked to bid on an order for 4,000 units of a product which has already had a run of 4,000 units at an average labor cost of $64 and an 80 percent improvement curve. The incremental labor cost of the next 4,000 units can then be computed as follows:

New average cost:	80 percent of $64 ...		$51.20
New total cost:	8,000 × $51.20	$409,600	
Old total cost:	4,000 × $64	256,000	
Total incremental cost:	....	$153,600	
Average incremental cost:	$153,600/4,000		$38.40

An ability to forecast this cost reduction may make the difference between landing and losing a profitable order.

The importance of the learning curve extends far beyond the individual pricing decision. The potential learning effect makes market penetration and share of the market more valuable and therefore worth spending more to obtain.[10] The reason is that a large market share gives the firm more experience than a firm with a smaller share. This experience translates into lower operating costs and these enable the firm to compete more effectively either by reducing prices or by spending more on marketing than competitors can afford to spend.

Locating the learning curve

Learning curves are not theoretical abstractions. They are based on observations of actual events. When a historical record exists, the relationship between

---

[10] The Boston Consulting Group has done much to publicize this idea. See *Perspectives on Experience* (Boston: Boston Consulting Group, 1970).

cost and experience can be estimated by applying regression analysis to the first differences of the historical observations—that is, the *changes* in cumulative average cost as volume increases.

In new situations, for which historical data are few or nonexistent, the curves for previous products or processes with known improvement factors can be used if management can identify similarities with the new situations. Estimates prepared in this way are subject to error, but they are likely to be better than estimates predicated on a zero improvement factor. Ironically, the shape of the improvement function may be much more accurately predictable than the cost of the initial units, and it is these that most cost estimation techniques focus on.

Summary

Cost accounting is concerned not only with identifying costs with activities but also with estimating how costs will respond to changes in volume or other variables. Some of these estimates are based on the judgment of experienced managers and accountants; some are prepared by engineers on the basis of past experience, theoretical calculations, or experimental observations; and still others are based on statistical analyses of historical data.

This chapter has focused for the most part on a statistical technique known as regression analysis, in which a line or plane of relationship is fitted to observed values of cost and one or more independent variables. Simple linear regression analysis is used to estimate a straight-line relationship between cost and one independent variable; multiple regression analysis is used when two or more independent variables are considered simultaneously.

These analyses can be performed graphically for either one or two independent variables. It is generally more convenient, however, to fit the regression line by solving a set of regression equations, using what is known as the method of least squares. These analyses can be performed quickly and cheaply on the computer. Computer programs include tests of the statistical reliability of the calculated relationships, and the results of any such tests are printed automatically with the regression equation. The main caution to be observed is that least squares regression analysis is based on a number of technical assumptions; if these are invalid, some or all of the tests of reliability will also be invalid.

Another statistical technique is the derivation and use of learning curves, reflecting the improvement in labor performance in successive iterations of a new task. These are generally identified through regression analysis, and their main importance is in predicting future costs for decision purposes.

Independent study problems (solutions in Appendix B)

1.   **Least squares regression analysis.**   Monthly power cost and machine-hour data for the Shelby Company for the 12 months of 19x0 were as follows:

Month	Machine-Hours	Cost
January	3,500	$1,000
February	4,200	1,100
March	4,900	1,300
April	4,400	1,200
May	4,300	1,200
June	3,800	1,100
July	3,300	1,090
August	4,100	1,280
September	4,700	1,400
October	3,800	1,210
November	3,000	1,080
December	4,000	1,230

Power costs during 19x0 were affected by a 10 percent increase in power rates (prices paid for power). This rate increase was effective on July 1, 19x0. No further increase is expected during 19x1.

Required:

a. Prepare the data and develop a line of relationship between power cost and machine-hours, using the least squares method.
b. Calculate the coefficient of determination and the standard error of the estimate.
c. Use the relationship you derived in (*a*) to estimate costs at 2,500, 4,000, and 5,500 machine-hours.
d. How much confidence would you have in these cost estimates?

2. **Preparing a bid: Learning curve analysis.** A customer has asked your company to prepare a bid on supplying 800 units of a new product. Production will be in batches of 100 units. You estimate that costs for the first batch of 100 units will average $100 a unit. You also expect that a 90 percent learning curve will apply to the cumulative labor costs on this contract.

Required:

a. Prepare an estimate of the labor costs of fulfilling this contract.
b. Estimate the incremental labor cost of extending the production run to produce an additional 800 units.
c. Estimate the incremental labor cost of extending the production run from 800 to 900 units. (*Note:* you may use either the formula or a graph to derive this estimate.)

Exercises and problems

3. **Regression exercises.** MacKenzie Park manufactures and sells trivets. Labor hours and production costs for the last four months of last year, when conditions were similar to those prevailing this year, were as follows:

Month	Labor Hours	Production Costs
September	2,500	$ 20,000
October	3,500	25,000
November	4,500	30,000
December	3,500	25,000
	14,000	$100,000

Let

$a =$ Fixed production costs per month.
$b =$ Variable production costs per labor hour.
$n =$ Number of months.
$x =$ Labor hours per month.
$y =$ Total monthly production costs.

Based on the above information, select the best answer to each of the following questions:

1. Monthly production costs could be expressed by

   a. $y = ax + b$;   b. $y = a + bx$;   c. $y = b + ax$;   d. $y = x + ab$.

2. According to the least squares method of computation, the fixed monthly production cost of trivets is approximately

   a. $10,000;   b. $9,500;   c. $7,500;   d. $5,000.

3. The variable production cost per labor hour based on the least squares method of computation, is

   a. $6.00;   b. $5.00;   c. $3.00;   d. $2.00.

4. The usefulness of the estimating equation based on these observations is very limited because it has

   a.   A high covariance.
   b.   Few degrees of freedom.
   c.   A high beta coefficient.
   d.   A low coefficient of determination.

                                                          (CPA, adapted)

4. **Learning curve exercise.**   The average number of minutes required to assemble trivets is predictable based on an 80 percent learning curve. The trivets are produced in lots of 300 units and 60 minutes of labor are required to assemble each first lot.

   Let

   $MT =$ Marginal time for the xth lot.
   $M =$ Marginal time for the first lot.
   $X =$ Lots produced.
   $b =$ Exponent expressing the improvement; b has the range $-1 \le b \le 0$.

   1. A normal graph, i.e., not a log or log-log graph, of average minutes per lot of production where cumulative lots are represented by the x-axis and average minutes per lot are represented by the y-axis, would produce a

      a.   Linear function sloping downward to the right.
      b.   Linear function sloping upward to the right.
      c.   Curvilinear function sloping upward to the right at an increasing rate.
      d.   Curvilinear function sloping downward to the right at a decreasing rate.

   2. A log-log graph of average minutes per lot of production, where cumulative lots are represented by the x-axis and average minutes per lot are represented by the y-axis, would produce a

      a.   Linear function sloping downward to the right.
      b.   Linear function sloping upward to the right.
      c.   Curvilinear function sloping upward to the right at a decreasing rate.
      d.   Curvilinear function sloping downward to the right at a decreasing rate.

3. The average number of minutes required per lot to complete four lots is approximately

   a. 60.0;   b. 48.5;   c. 38.4;   d. 30.7.

4. Average time to produce X lots of trivets could be expressed

   a. MX^{b+1};   b. MX^b;   c. MT^{b+1};   d. MX^{b-1}.

5. Assuming that $b = -0.322$, the average number of minutes required to produce X lots of trivets could be expressed

   a. $40.08X^{.678}$;   b. $40.08X$;   c. $60X^{-.322}$;   d. $60X^{1.322}$.   (CPA)

5. **Flexible budget allowance.** Carbo Electronics Company is installing a flexible budgeting system in its factory. As part of this effort, the controller has prepared least squares regression equations for each of the major cost elements for each factory department. The estimating equation for indirect labor in the assembly department is:

   Indirect labor cost = $2,000 a month + $1 an assembly labor hour

   The coefficient of correlation is .62.

   The assembly department manager has refused to accept this equation, saying the amount of indirect labor is determined by the number of people on the payroll, not by any formula.

   Required:
   How would you respond? What should the manager be asked to do?

6. **Simple regression exercise.** Lotus Corporation makes aluminum windows and doors. Prices are calculated on the basis of the size of the window or door, in square feet. You have the following data for 10 different orders, each for 100 windows:

Window Size (sq. ft.)	Materials Cost
3	$210
8	450
4	260
6	340
4	240
7	380
5	300
7	410
5	320
6	370

Required:
a. Calculate a linear regression equation by the method of least squares.
b. Calculate the coefficient of determination and the standard error of the estimate.
c. What conclusions might management draw from this analysis?

7. **Determining variable costs.** The management of Johnson Brothers has an opportunity to sign a contract with a customer for all of the customer's requirements

for plastic caps for the next year. The customer would pay $2,000 a month plus $4 for each thousand caps delivered.

A least squares analysis of historical data has produced an estimated average variable cost of $3.50 a unit. The process is well established and no noticeable learning effect is likely, but management is concerned that the $3.50 figure may be too low. The quantity ordered could be very large, as many as 1 million caps a month, and Johnson Brothers is not in a position to absorb substantial losses.

The regression equation was based on an analysis of cost-volume data for 15 two-week periods when operating conditions were not affected by major identifiable events. These data were adjusted for changes in materials prices and wage rates. A staff assistant has made the following calculations:

1. Sum of the squared deviations of costs from the regression line: 187,200.
2. Sum of the squared deviations of costs from their mean: 748,800.
3. Sum of the squared deviations of volume from mean volume: 90,000.

Required:

Prepare an analysis that will help management assess the reliability of the variable cost estimate.

8. **Regression analysis.** The manager of department X is developing a flexible budget for the next year. In the past, indirect materials costs have been budgeted as proportionally variable costs, but the factory controller wants to test this assumption.

The following are the hourly volume and the indirect materials cost totals:

Hours	Cost	Hours	Cost
3,000	$3,300	2,820	$2,820
2,130	2,070	2,640	2,070
2,700	2,730	2,850	2,400
2,610	2,550	2,730	2,340
2,880	2,760	2,670	2,430
2,670	2,400	2,700	2,370

The factory controller derived the following regression equation from these observations:

$$\text{Indirect materials cost} = -\$604 + \$1.157 \times \text{labor hours}$$

Required:

a. Plot the observations on a scatter chart.
b. Calculate the coefficient of determination and the standard error of the estimate. (For this calculation you should round the y_c values to the nearest dollar.)
c. How would you interpret the negative constant in the regression equation? What figures would you establish for the coming year's flexible budget?

9. **Effect of lot size on cost.** The management of the Portage Corporation has found that labor cost variances in the factory are more likely to be favorable when overall production volume is high and unfavorable when overall production volume is low. (Volume is measured by the amount of standard labor cost.) To check this, labor time was recorded in a recent period, job by job and department by department. Data for jobs of an unusual nature were discarded, leaving the following job totals:

Job	Standard Labor Cost	Actual Labor Cost
426	$1,050	$ 990
428	440	460
433	610	600
434	420	440
437	770	740
445	780	760
446	870	850
447	310	330
450	1,030	1,000
454	840	810
461	530	540
465	400	430
467	560	560
469	370	390
472	690	670
473	930	890

Required:

a. Calculate the regression equation.
b. How reliable is this equation? Calculate the coefficient of determination and the standard error of the estimate.
c. What is the meaning of the constant term in this equation?
d. How would you use the findings of this analysis?

10. **Interpreting regression data.** The controller of the Connecticut Electronics Company believes that the identification of the variable and fixed components of the firm's costs will enable management to make better planning and control decisions. Among the costs the controller is concerned about is the cost of indirect supplies.

A member of the controller's staff has suggested that a simple linear regression model be used to determine the cost behavior of the indirect supplies. The regression equation shown below was developed from 40 pairs of observations using the least squares method of regression analysis. The regression equation and related measures are as follows:

$$S = \$200 + \$4H$$

in which

S = Total monthly costs of indirect supplies
H = Number of machine-hours per month
Standard error of estimate: $S_e = 100$
Coefficient of correlation: $r = .87$

Required:

a. When a simple linear regression model is used to draw inferences about a population relationship from sample data, what assumptions must be made before the inferences can be accepted as valid?
b. Assuming the assumptions identified in (a) are satisfied here:
   (1) Explain the meaning of "200" and "4" in the regression equation.
   (2) Calculate the estimated cost of indirect supplies in a month in which 900 machine-hours are to be used.
   (3) Calculate, for 900 machine-hours, the range of the estimate for the cost of indirect supplies with a 95 percent confidence interval; this calculation will be used to judge whether the cost estimate is good enough for planning purposes.

c. Explain the meaning of the .87 value of *r* in the context of management's interest in predicting the total cost of indirect supplies.

(CMA, adapted)

11. **Using regression data.** McMaster Manufacturing Company is planning production for the 19x0 calendar year. Management has reliable estimates of direct labor and materials costs, but is uncertain about overhead costs which seem to fluctuate in response to both direct labor hours and machine-hours. The controller has run three linear regression analyses, with the following results:

Detail	Regression 1	Regression 2	Regression 3
Independent variable (X)	Labor hours	Machine-hours	Machine-hours
Dependent variable (Y)	Overhead cost	Overhead cost	Labor hours
a	40,200	47,300	1,200
b	4.90	8.30	1.70
r^2	0.84	0.72	0.89
S_e	3,060	4,350	1,710
S_b	2.31	6.11	2.41

These figures were derived from 12 monthly observations.

Required:

a. What overhead budget formula should McMaster use? Explain how you arrived at your conclusion, including an explanation of the tests of significance you used.
b. Should the controller run a multiple regression on *both* direct labor and machine hours? Why or why not?

(SMAC, adapted)

12. **Using regression data.** A company which manufactures a special electrical gauge wishes to determine the relationship(s) between overhead costs and the number of gauges produced. The accountant has collected data from the last five months of operations, covering monthly operating volumes of zero, 150, 125, 110, and 175 gauges. By considering number of gauges as the independent variable *x,* and overhead cost as the dependent variable *y,* the accountant has presumed a linear relationship of the form $y = a + bx$ and has produced the following statistics:

$a = 115$
$b = 1.9$
$r^2 = .9727$
$S_e = 11.21$
$S_b = 0.1835$

Required:

a. Give two reasons for supporting the accountant's assumption that the cost relationship is linear.
b. Assuming that the accountant is correct in making the linearity assumption, calculate a 95 percent confidence interval for the variable overhead cost per gauge.
c. Predict the value of variable overhead costs if 180 gauges are produced.

(SMAC, adapted)

13. **Regression analysis: Production decision.** The Johnstar Company makes a very expensive chemical product. The costs average about $1,000 a pound and the material sells for $2,500 a pound. The material is very dangerous; therefore, it is made each day to fill the customer orders for the day. Failure to deliver the quantity required results in a shutdown for the customers and high cost penalty for Johnstar (plus customer ill will).

Predicting the final weight of a batch of the chemical being processed has been a serious problem. This is critical because of the serious cost of failure to meet customer needs.

The company's consultants recommended that the batches be weighed one-half way through the six-hour processing period. They proposed that linear regression be used to predict the final weight from the midpoint weight. If the prediction indicated that too little of the chemical would be available, then a new batch could be started and still delivered in time to satisfy customers' needs for the day.

Included in the report of a study made by the consultants during a one-week period were the following items:

Observation	Weight (3 hrs.)	Final Weight	Observation	Weight (3 hrs.)	Final Weight
1	55	90	11	60	80
2	45	75	12	35	60
3	40	80	13	35	80
4	60	80	14	55	60
5	40	45	15	35	75
6	60	80	16	50	90
7	50	80	17	30	60
8	55	95	18	60	105
9	50	100	19	50	60
10	35	75	20	20	30

Data from the regression analysis:

Coefficient of determination	0.4126
Coefficient of correlation	0.6424
Coefficients of the regression equation	
Constant	+28.6
Independent variable	+ 1.008
Standard error of the estimate	14.2
Standard error of the regression coefficient for the independent variable	.2796
The t-statistic for a 95 percent confidence interval (18 degrees of freedom)	2.101

Required:

a. Using the results of the regression analysis by the consultants, estimate the final weight of today's first batch which weighs 42 pounds at the end of three hours processing time.

b. Customer orders for today total 68 pounds. The nature of the process is such that the smallest batch that can be started will weigh at least 20 pounds at the end of six hours. Using only the data from the regression analysis, would you start another batch? (Remember that today's first batch weighed 42 pounds at the end of three hours.)

c. Is the relationship between the variables such that this regression analysis provides an adequate prediction model for the Johnstar Co.? Explain your answer.

(CMA)

14. **Regression analysis: Choice of methods.** The Ramon Company manufactures a wide range of products at several different plant locations. The Franklin plant, which manufactures electrical components, has been experiencing difficulties with fluctuating monthly overhead costs. The fluctuations have made it difficult to estimate the level of overhead that will be incurred for any one month.

Management wants to be able to estimate overhead costs accurately in order to plan its operation and financial needs better. A trade association publication to which Ramon Co. subscribes indicates that, for companies manufacturing electrical components, overhead tends to vary with direct labor hours.

One member of the accounting staff has proposed that the cost behavior pattern of the overhead costs be determined. Then overhead costs could be predicted from the budgeted direct labor hours.

Another member of the accounting staff suggested that a good starting place for determining the cost behavior pattern of overhead costs would be an analysis of historical data. The historical cost behavior pattern would provide a basis for estimating future overhead costs. The methods proposed for determining the cost behavior pattern included the high-low method, the scattergraph method, simple linear regression, multiple regression, and exponential smoothing. Of these methods Ramon Co. decided to employ the high-low method, the scattergraph method, and simple linear regression. Data on direct labor hours and the respective overhead costs incurred were collected for the past two years. The raw data are as follows:

	19x3		19x4	
Month	Direct Labor Hours	Overhead Costs	Direct Labor Hours	Overhead Costs
January	20,000	$84,000	21,000	$86,000
February	25,000	99,000	24,000	93,000
March	22,000	89,500	23,000	93,000
April	23,000	90,000	22,000	87,000
May	20,000	81,500	20,000	80,000
June	19,000	75,500	18,000	76,500
July	14,000	70,500	12,000	67,500
August	10,000	64,500	13,000	71,000
September	12,000	69,000	15,000	73,500
October	17,000	75,000	17,000	72,500
November	16,000	71,500	15,000	71,000
December	19,000	78,000	18,000	75,000

Using linear regression, the following data were obtained:

1. Coefficient of determination .... .9109
2. Coefficient of correlation .... .9544
3. Coefficients of regression equation:
   Constant 39,859
   Independent variable 2.1549
4. Standard error of the estimate 2,840
5. Standard error of the regression coefficient
   for the independent variable .... .1437
6. True t-statistic for a 95 percent confidence
   interval (22 degrees of freedom) 2.074

Required:

a. Plot the observations on a scatter diagram and draw a line of relationship freehand.
b. Using the high-low points method, determine the cost behavior pattern of the overhead costs for the Franklin plant.
c. Using the results of the regression analysis, estimate the overhead costs for 22,500 direct labor hours. Do the same for the other two methods.
d. Of the three proposed methods, which one should Ramon Company use to determine the historical cost behavior pattern of Franklin plant's overhead

costs? Explain your answer completely, indicating the reasons why the other methods are less desirable.

(CMA, adapted)

15. **Regression analysis: Preparing the data.** The Wyman Company has been working for several months on the development of cost estimates for its Rutherford factory. One department's principal labor cost is the cost of processing labor. All other labor costs are classified as "indirect" labor.

Operating volume in this department is measured by the number of processing labor hours. Processing labor hours and indirect labor costs for the past two years were:

| | 19x1 | | 19x2 | |
| | Processing Labor Hours | Indirect Labor Costs | Processing Labor Hours | Indirect Labor Costs |
Month				
January	9,000	$12,820	12,000	$18,800
February	8,000	11,290	10,000	14,730
March	6,000	12,400	11,000	17,050
April	7,000	13,100	10,000	15,220
May	8,000	11,540	11,000	16,350
June	7,000	10,600	12,000	17,900
July	8,000	11,580	12,000	15,700
August	9,000	12,600	9,000	11,860
September	7,000	9,820	10,000	13,050
October	6,000	8,800	8,000	10,120
November	7,000	9,680	6,000	7,960
December	9,000	12,430	7,000	9,180

Additional information:

1. Rearrangement of the department's machines on July 1, 19x2, made it possible to reduce materials handling time. The factory's industrial engineer estimates that this reduction has led to a saving in indirect labor costs of approximately 20 cents a processing labor hour every month since that time. The rearrangement has had no effect on the amount of overtime worked.

2. Employees are paid a premium of 50 percent of their regular hourly wage rate for each hour of overtime work. Overtime premiums are classified as overhead costs, but management doesn't segregate them in separate accounts. As a result, the overtime premiums paid on processing labor and indirect labor time in this department have been included in the indirect labor cost figures given above. Analysis of payroll documents shows that overtime premiums were as follows during the two years:

Month	19x1	19x2
January	$520	$2,400
February	290	930
March	0	1,750
April	0	920
May	340	1,250
June	100	1,800
July	280	1,500
August	600	560
September	120	1,150
October	0	320
November	80	0
December	630	80

3. Wage rates were 5 percent higher in 19x2 than in 19x1. Wage rates will remain at their 19x2 level throughout the current year.
4. A fire destroyed a machine in March 19x1. Employees whose wages would otherwise have been identified as processing labor costs were assigned to other tasks classified as indirect labor until the replacement machine was ready for operation on April 10, 19x1.

Required:

Separate overtime premiums from other components of indirect labor costs, make any other adjustments that seem appropriate, and prepare separate estimating equations for overtime premiums and for the other components of indirect labor cost.

16. **Learning curve: Annual model changeover.**   Serkin Corporation is in an industry with an annual model changeover. Standard labor costs in the assembly department for this year were based on a 90 percent learning curve and production of 640,000 units during the model year. The labor costs of the first 10,000 units assembled this year were expected to average $2 a unit.

Production in the first three months of the model year totaled 160,000 units. Production in the fourth month totaled 80,000 units and required $94,000 in assembly labor, at standard wage rates.

Required:

a. Calculate the labor usage variance for the fourth month, to the nearest 10th of a cent.
b. Was assembly labor performance at an acceptable level in the fourth month? Show your calculations.
c. If production for the year is to total 640,000 units, and if the costs of units produced after the fourth month are at the levels specified by the original learning curve, would you expect production of the final 320,000 units to lead to favorable or unfavorable labor usage variances? Show calculations to support your conclusions.

17. **Learning curve: Contract bidding.**   Technologics, Inc., manufactures products that incorporate advanced technological features. Each new product is virtually unique, and the effect of learning on cost is very pronounced.

A customer has asked for a price quotation on an order for 512 sensometers. They would be produced in series, one at a time. Technologics' engineers estimate that the initial setup costs would total $10,000, production labor costs of the first unit would amount to $4,000, and an 80 percent cumulative learning curve would apply to production labor costs. Production would be spread over an eight-month period.

Required:

a. Using the formula provided in the chapter, estimate the labor cost of the entire order.
b. The customer feels that the bid based on your estimate in (a) is too high. You are unwilling to reduce your bid for this quantity, but the customer has suggested that you rebid on the basis of a total production run of 750 units, spread over 12 months. Prepare a new cost estimate.
c. The customer changed his mind and accepted your original bid for the 512-unit contract. Midway through that contract he asks you to bid on extending the contract to cover an additional 238 units. Prepare an estimate of labor costs that would be useful to management in the evaluation of this possibility.

18. **Learning curve: Cost forecasting.**   The Amdur Company recently completed development work on a new product and commenced production on a limited scale. The product has found favor with the company's customers, and the company intends to expand production to a rate of 1,000 units a week.

Labor costs for the first 2,000 units have totaled $20,000. Judging from past experience, the company's industrial engineers have estimated that a 90 percent learning curve will be applicable to this product.

Required:

a. Compute cumulative total labor cost and cumulative average labor cost for the first 128,000 units.

b. On a sheet of graph paper, prepare a diagram showing cumulative total cost for various cumulative volumes between 2,000 and 128,000 units.

c. From the diagram in (b), prepare a schedule showing the additional labor costs of producing each additional 4,000 units of product from zero to 128,000 cumulative units.

d. Much of the company's business consists of providing customers with specially selected combinations of the company's products. Each customer's package is different from the others, and competition is very keen. Cost estimates for each package are prepared by combining the product cost figures shown in the standard cost file. What labor cost standard would you establish for the first year for use in this way?

19. **Learning curve: Preparing bids: Effect on cash flow.** Famous Aircraft Company has developed a new short-hop jet airplane which is scheduled to go into production in about six months. Management is now reviewing its tentative pricing decision, and will seek firm purchase commitments from the airlines as soon as a final decision is reached.

The plane will be manufactured in the company's San Fernando factory. The first production run of 10 planes will take about 12 months to complete, at a variable cost of $700,000 a plane, and the company's controller estimates that the cumulative average variable cost will follow an 80 percent learning curve thereafter.

The out-of-pocket fixed costs of operating the factory are expected to amount to $200,000 a month, regardless of the number of planes manufactured. Without the new plane, Famous Aircraft would have no need for this factory.

If the plane gains acceptance, orders will come in quickly for delivery one, two, and three years later. On the basis of the interest expressed by various commercial airlines, Famous Aircraft's management believes that it can sell about 250 of these planes, with deliveries spread over a six-year period on the following schedule:

Year	Planes
1	10
2	30
3	60
4	60
5	60
6	30
Total	250

Competition with British and French aircraft manufacturers is intense, however, and Famous Aircraft is worried that it will lose its foreign markets if it sets too high a price on the new plane.

The company's market research department estimates that the total world market for this type of plane will amount to about 450 planes during the next six years. Both Boeing and British Aircraft are known to have somewhat similar planes in development, but the Famous management believes that it is at least six months closer to actual production than either of these competitors. In each past generation of airplanes, the manufacturer to get a plane in production first has been able to capture more than half of the market.

Required:

a. Construct a curve for use in cost forecasting.

b. Prepare production cost estimates for total production runs of 160 planes and 250 planes.

c. What pricing strategy would you follow in this situation? Indicate how you might use cost figures in arriving at a price.

d. Useful information on the demand schedule seldom can be obtained by asking potential customers how much they would be likely to buy at different prices. Market experimentation is also impractical in capital goods markets of this type. Suggest an alternative way of trying to obtain this kind of information for Famous Aircraft's management. (Suggestion: Examine the motives that lead airline companies to buy new planes.)

e. It is now two years after the new plane went into production. A price of $450,000 was set, and a total of 40 planes was produced during the first two years at the costs estimated in advance. A temporary decline in the volume of air travel has led to a stretch-out in delivery schedules, so that only 40 additional planes are to be produced and delivered this year instead of the 60 originally planned. Compute the effect of the stretch-out on the company's income for the year.

21 Reimbursement costing: Cost accounting standards

Costs assigned to manufactured products for inventory measurement purposes generally include only the costs of purchased parts and materials, plus the manufacturing costs of converting these parts and materials into finished goods. The costs of administering the company and of marketing the products to customers are not included in inventory cost.

The costs assigned to individual activities, projects, or programs for purposes of managerial decision making may include some marketing costs and some administrative costs, depending on the nature of the activity and the scope of the decisions to be made. Here, too, however, some costs will not be included, on the grounds that these costs will not be affected by the decisions to be made. The cost of the president's salary is the most obvious example of these costs.

In some situations, the accountants may be called upon to develop product costs on an all-inclusive basis, in which all of the company's costs are distributed in some fashion among all of the company's end-product activities. Cost figures prepared on this basis are generally required in situations in which the prices paid for goods or services by a customer or by a funding agency are determined on the basis of cost analyses accepted by the customers or their representatives— that is, *reimbursement costing.*

Reimbursement costing situations fall generally into three categories:

1. Cost-based contract pricing, in which the cost formulas apply directly to the contracted work.
2. Regulated pricing, in which prices are determined on the basis of quasi-judicial proceedings between the company and a regulatory body.
3. Program support, in which not-for-profit organizations seek full or partial reimbursement for the costs of their various services or activities.

It is extremely important in reimbursement costing for the parties to agree on the concepts governing the measurement of cost. Negotiating the definition of cost for each contract or by each pair of spending/reimbursing organizations would be chaotic and prohibitively time-consuming, however. For this reason, rules are generally established by some higher authority to govern all costing of a given kind of activity or in a given industry. Costing rules have been established for various parts of the health care industry in the United States, for example—by federal and state governments and by private organizations such as Blue Cross. Similarly, utility regulatory agencies either prescribe how the utility companies they regulate will measure costs of individual services or rule on the companies' methods in the course of rate-setting proceedings.

Our purpose in this chapter is not to try to summarize the costing rules used in all cost reimbursement situations. Instead, we'll limit ourselves to a discussion of general principles, followed by an illustration of a single reimbursement costing system, embodied in the costing rules developed and adopted by the United States Cost Accounting Standards Board between 1972 and 1980.

Basic criteria for reimbursement costing[1]

If they are to be internally consistent, reimbursement costing standards should be based on a set of clearly enunciated costing criteria. Criteria reflecting the following concepts are likely to be at the center of any such set:

1. Inclusiveness.
2. Causality.
3. Traceability.
4. Variability.
5. Capacity provided.
6. Beneficiality.

In discussing these criteria we'll ignore the complexities of a multitiered costing structure, in which some costs are identified first with intermediate activities before being reassigned to end-product activities. Instead, we'll focus on the end-product activities—individual contracts, services, or programs.

Inclusiveness: The full-costing criterion

Reimbursement costing generally calls for the measurement of the costs of individual activities on an all-inclusive basis—that is, the cost of an activity should include a share of all of the costs necessary to carry out that activity and to provide general administrative support and continuity for the organization carrying out the activity. We prefer to describe this as an *all-inclusive* cost, to distinguish this cost criterion from the criterion governing the measurement of the cost of manufactured products for external financial reporting and taxation. Common practice is to refer to both kinds of calculations as *full-cost* calculations, however, and we'll adopt that practice here.

Full costing can be justified on two grounds. First, the costs of overall corporate administration and similar activities are necessary to the completion of the individual contracts or other activities being costed. The question there-

---

[1] Much of the discussion in this section is derived in part from the author's paper, "Cost Accounting Principles for External Reporting: A Conceptual Framework," in Stephen A. Zeff, Joel Demski, and Nicholas Dopuch, eds., *Essays in Honor of William A. Paton, Pioneer Accounting Theorist* (Ann Arbor: Division of Research, Graduate School of Business Administration, University of Michigan, 1979), pp. 157–83.

fore is not whether these are costs of end-product activities but how much of these costs should be assigned to each activity.

Second, if the costs incurred to provide general administrative support and organizational continuity aren't assigned to individual activities, the amounts received from reimbursement agencies are less likely to cover them. Some reimbursement arrangements provide only for the reimbursement of costs, with no allowance for profit; the organization won't be compensated for any costs that are unassigned to reimbursable activities.

Other reimbursement arrangements, such as government contracts with privately owned, profit-seeking businesses, do provide for the reimbursement to include an allowance for profit. For these, it would be possible to provide for the costs of general administrative support and organizational continuity by increasing the allowed profit percentage, as we suggested in our discussion of target pricing markups in Chapter 19. We need to remember, however, that most reimbursements are made from public or quasi-public funds. Payments from these funds are often subject to scrutiny by politically-oriented observers, legitimately concerned with the reasonableness of payments from the public purse. An allowed profit margin of, say, 30 percent is unlikely to appear reasonable to these observers, even if most of it is designed to compensate the organization for a proportionate share of its ongoing expenditures for administrative support and organizational continuity. This problem can be minimized by assigning a share of these costs to each activity.

Causality: The primary implementation criterion

The inclusiveness criterion merely specifies the cost elements to be included in the cost of individual end-product activities. The main problem is to find criteria to guide the choice of the methods used to distribute these cost elements to the activities.

The primary criterion used for this purpose is the criterion of causality. Causality is a relationship between a cost and an activity such that the activity cannot be carried out effectively if the cost is not incurred. If such a relationship exists, we can say that the activity causes the cost.

Our constant objective in earlier chapters was to find out how much cost was caused by individual job orders, services, or other activities. To be consistent, therefore, we should start with this criterion as we begin to carry out the mandate of developing full-cost data for reimbursement purposes. Furthermore, reimbursement presumably is designed to compensate the contractor or other performing organization for using resources to meet the needs of the reimbursing agency or of those it represents (e.g., insured hospital patients). It is reasonable to assume, therefore, that causality is no less a governing criterion in reimbursement costing than in activity costing for managerial decision purposes.

Traceability: Presumptive evidence of causality

Although causality is the underlying costing criterion, some means must be found for making it operational. The concept of traceability is the basis for the first operational criterion. Traceability is the attribute of a cost that permits the resources represented by the cost to be identified in their entirety with a specific activity or other costing entity.

The traceability criterion provides that any cost traceable to an activity at reasonable cost should be included in the costs of that activity. The argument for this criterion is that traceability is prima facie evidence that a causal relationship exists between the activity and the cost. If the activity hadn't been initiated, the costs traceable to that activity wouldn't have been incurred.

The traceability criterion must be applied carefully when only part of a set of interchangeable resources is used in a given activity. For example, building space is often at least partially interchangeable. One space may have been leased recently at an annual rental approximating current market rates, another space may be in a building the company has owned for several decades. If the two spaces are interchangeable, then the causality criterion would suggest measuring *each* at the *same* cost.

A strict interpretation of historical causality would require *each* space to be measured at the cost of the one most recently acquired. After all, the relevant question is, what costs would not have been incurred if the company hadn't provided the capacity to carry out the specific end-product activity in question. The implication is that the newly leased space was acquired because management anticipated the need to perform not only the activities made possible by using the older space but additional activities as well. Since each of a group of activities being conducted simultaneously can be regarded as the "additional" cost objective, each can be assigned the cost of the space it takes to carry out additional activities. (The amount of capacity required in any given period is a function of the total production load, regardless of the sequence in which orders were received.)

Although this argument is virtually irrefutable, it violates the full-costing criterion, since this approach will either overdistribute or underdistribute the costs clearly attributable to the need to provide space for achieving all of the cost objectives combined. That being the case, the traceability criterion has to be modified; if similar interchangeable resources are available for carrying out an activity, and if these resources have different unit prices, the unit price used in calculating the cost to be assigned to individual activities should be the average unit price of the entire group of interchangeable resources.

The implementation of this idea will depend on how clear the interchangeability is and how much verification is required. In a relatively easy case, two different workers who have identical skills and identical job classifications but different seniority probably should have identical charging rates. Little disagreement about seniority is likely to arise, and the recorded job ratings would probably be acceptable as verification of the interchangeability.

At the other extreme, the interchangeability of 100,000 square feet of space in a downtown office building with the same amount of space in a manufacturing plant in the country is not obvious on the surface. If the purpose of costing is to help management decide whether to discontinue an activity in one of these locations, a judgmental estimate with little verification is likely to be acceptable. If the purpose is to measure cost for reimbursement purposes, however, judgmental estimates of this sort are likely to be rejected for lack of adequate verification.

Variability: A secondary criterion

Not all of the resources consumed in carrying out a particular end-product activity are traceable to it, even in a superficial way. The consumption of some of these nontraceable resources in individual periods is likely to be roughly proportional to some characteristic of individual end-product activities in these periods, however. For example, the amount of labor used in moving materials from stockrooms to production locations is likely to be closely related to the amounts of direct material required by production.

In cases of this sort, a causal relationship can be assumed between the activity and the cost. This permits us to adopt the variability criterion: When costs not traceable to individual end-product activities vary in total with variations in some characteristic of those activities, they should be assigned to activities on the basis of the estimated rate of variability.

The only conceptual problem likely to be encountered in applying this criterion arises whenever variability is demonstrably nonlinear. The clearest example of this is the variability of overtime premiums. Budgeted overtime premiums may be virtually zero through the lower reaches of the possible volume range but rise steadily after volume exceeds a certain threshhold level, the pattern of behavior represented by the solid line in Exhibit 21–1.

A strict application of the variability criterion would require the use of an incremental costing rate, represented by the slope of the solid line in Exhibit 21–1. This solution would create the same problem that arose when we tried

Exhibit 21–1 Average versus incremental cost distribution rates

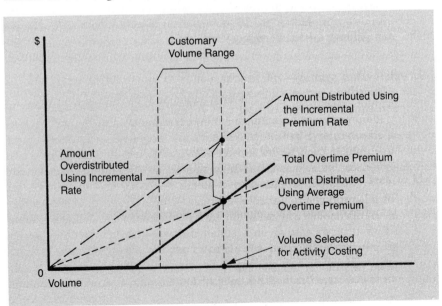

to use the incremental rate for interchangeable resources. The total amount assigned to activities using this incremental rate will be proportional to total volume, represented by the dotted line in the exhibit (parallel to the solid line but starting at the origin). Use of the incremental rate, in other words, would overdistribute overtime premiums at all volumes. This would violate the full-costing criterion and would be unacceptable to the reimbursing agencies. As a result, costs of this sort should be distributed on the basis of an *average* rate of variability spanning the range of volume from zero to some point in the customary volume range, usually the volume actually achieved. The amount distributed on this basis is represented by the dashed line in the diagram. The argument to support this approach is that during an extended period, overtime premiums will vary in this proportion rather than in the nonlinear fashion included in the short-term budget.

Notice that the rate of variability is to be expressed as a rate per unit of some common characteristic of the end-product activity. This characteristic can be either an input measure (the total number of input units used to carry out the activity) or an output measure, indicating the amount of production arising from the activity itself.

Capacity provided: Another secondary criterion

Many of the costs necessary to carry out end-product activities but not traceable to them are capacity costs. The causal relationship between the activity and such costs is more indirect than in the case of the variable costs. The key phrase, however, is that they are necessary to the performance of the activity. If they weren't incurred, the activity couldn't be carried out. The various activities supported by the costs of providing capacity are therefore the causes of those costs. The only question is what proportion of total capacity cost can be attributed to each of the supported activities.

The answer to this question is embodied in the capacity-provided criterion: The costs of providing capacity should be assigned to the activities relying on that capacity in proportion to their relative occupancy of the capacity when it is used fully. In other words, if an activity uses capacity only at off-peak periods, it should not be charged a portion of capacity costs because it plays no role in causing the organization to incur any of these capacity costs.

The capacity-provided criterion is applicable mainly to fixed costs, the costs of making capacity available, whether it is used or not. The question is how much volume a given set of fixed costs is to be spread over. The principal candidates are estimated normal volume, planned current volume, and actual current volume. From a theoretical point of view, normal volume is the preferred denominator of the allocation ratio, in that it provides cost figures that most closely approximate the designed average cost of the facilities. Long-term anticipated volume determines the amount of designed capacity; this, in turn, affects the amount of fixed cost. In the absence of economies or diseconomies of scale, average cost at designed capacity is an accurate measure of the cost of providing goods or services.

If either normal volume or planned current volume is chosen as the denominator volume, however, costs inevitably will be either under- or overdistributed, as the now-familiar diagram in Exhibit 21–2 indicates. Reimbursing agencies are often reluctant to allow overabsorption; managers of the performing organizations are equally reluctant to have their organizations pay for unabsorbed costs. The usual result is that average cost is calculated on the basis of actual volume. Actual average costs are used instead of standard costs for the same reason.

The capacity-provided criterion, in other words, can lead us to violate the causality criterion in either of two ways. First, by using actual volume to measure the unit cost of capacity, we under- or overstate the long-run average cost of providing capacity. Second, if expansion or contraction of capacity will lead to a change in total capacity cost that is either greater or less than the proportionate change in capacity, then the average cost of a unit of capacity will be an inaccurate measure of the causal relationship between capacity costs and the activity. The full-costing criterion forces us to accept this inaccuracy, however, just as it forces us to modify the variability criterion.

Beneficiality: A criterion of last resort

Clear causal relationships between cost and activity can't always be determined. An additional criterion or criteria therefore must be found if the full-costing criterion is to be implemented. The most widely used criterion for this purpose is based on the concept of beneficiality, or benefit received. An activity is said to benefit from a cost if that cost is necessary to carry out the activity.

The key words in this definition are the words, *necessary to.* We don't need

Exhibit 21–2 Under- or overdistribution from the use of a nonactual volume denominator

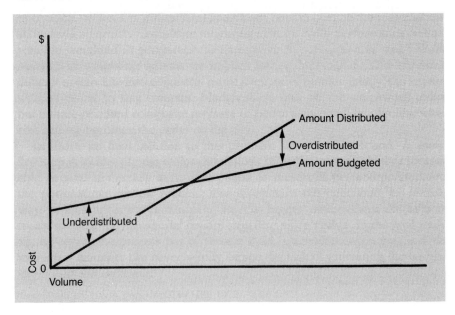

to be able to measure direct benefits such as cost reductions or a greater ability to meet delivery deadlines; we merely need to show that the costs are necessary to carry out the activity and others like it on a continuing basis.

The assignment of general administrative costs and the costs of independent research and development to individual end-product activities is ordinarily justified by the beneficiality criterion. These costs are incurred either because they are necessary to support current end-product activities or because they are necessary to maintain the continuity of the organization. The main problem is to find some common characteristic of the end-product activities that can be measured and used as the denominator of a cost-distribution ratio.

Standards issued by the Cost Accounting Standards Board[2]

The United States Cost Accounting Standards Board (CASB) was established by the Congress in 1971 to develop and promulgate uniform cost accounting standards primarily for use in connection with negotiated defense contracts with the United States government. The board defined a cost accounting standard in the following terms:

> A Cost Accounting Standard is a statment formally issued by the Cost Accounting Standards Board that (1) enunciates a principle or principles to be followed, (2) establishes practices to be applied, or (3) specifies criteria to be employed in selecting from alternative principles and practices in estimating, accumulating, and reporting costs of contracts subject to the rules of the Board.[3]

In contract costing, the end-product activity is the individual contract, which the CAS Board referred to as a *final cost objective.* The board's definitions of this and other key terms are reproduced in Exhibit 21–3. Notice that the definitions of *allocate* and *direct cost* differ from the definitions of those terms in earlier chapters; the board's definitions will be used throughout this chapter.

The board issued 19 standards between 1972 and 1980 and ceased operation on September 30, 1980. Its standards remain in effect until revised or repealed in ways to be prescribed by the U.S. Congress. The remainder of this chapter will describe the board's standards, classified in three groups:

1. Constraining standards.
2. Standards for assigning costs to periods.
3. Standards for assigning costs to cost objectives.

Constraining standards

The CASB issued four standards serving as constraints on the contractor's measurement system:[4]

---

[2] This section draws heavily on Gordon Shillinglaw and Nelson H. Shapiro, "The Cost Accounting Standards Board," in John C. Burton, Russell E. Palmer, and Robert S. Kay, *Handbook of Accounting and Auditing* (Boston: Warren, Gorham & Lamont, 1981), chap. 42.

[3] U.S. Cost Accounting Standards Board, *Restatement of Objectives, Policies and Concepts* (Washington, D.C.: 1977), p. 1.

[4] The standards, rules and regulations of the CAS Board are contained in Title 4, Chapter III, Code of Federal Regulations. Each standard constitutes a part of Title 4, identified by a three-digit number, starting with 401. Part 400 contains definitions of technical terms.

Exhibit 21-3 Official definitions of key CASB terms

Allocate. To assign an item of cost, or a group of items of cost, to one or more cost objectives. This term includes both direct assignment of cost and the reassignment of a share from an indirect cost pool.

Business unit. Any segment of an organization, or an entire business organization which is not divided into segments.

Cost objective. A function, organizational subdivision, contract or other work unit for which cost data are desired and for which provision is made to accumulate and measure the cost of processes, products, jobs, capitalized projects, etc.

Direct cost. Any cost which is identified specifically with a particular final cost objective.

Final cost objective. A cost objective which has allocated to it both direct and indirect costs, and, in the contractor's accumulation system, is one of the final accumulation points.

Home office. An office responsible for directing or managing two or more, but not necessarily all, segments of an organization. . . . An organization which has intermediate levels, such as groups, may have several home offices which report to a common home office.

Indirect cost pool. A grouping of incurred costs identified with two or more objectives but not identified specifically with any final cost objective.

Segment. One of two or more divisions, product departments, plants, or other subdivisions of an organization reporting directly to a home office, usually identified with responsibility for profit and/or producing a product or service. . . .

CAS 401. Consistency in estimating, accumulating, and reporting costs.

CAS 402. Consistency in allocating costs incurred for the same purpose.

CAS 405. Accounting for unallowable costs.

CAS 406. Cost accounting period.

Consistency. The first two standards to be issued, 401 and 402, set forth the fundamental criteria for consistency. They were designed to meet some of the strongest criticisms of the cost accounting practices that had been followed by some contractors prior to the formation of the CASB.

CAS 401 requires the contractor to accumulate and report costs on the same basis it uses in preparing cost estimates for contract bidding purposes. In flexibly priced contracts (e.g., cost-plus-fixed-fee), this prevents the contractor from bidding low on the basis of one cost accounting practice and then charging higher amounts to the government on the basis of some other practice. *CAS 401* also requires the contractor to prepare cost estimates on the same basis it expects to use in accumulating costs. For fixed price contracts, this prevents the contractor from preparing a cost estimate based on one practice when it expects to account for its costs through some other practice that would allocate fewer costs to that contract. An example of a cost accounting practice that is inconsistent with *CAS 401* is the estimation of labor costs by function—

assembly, machining, etc.—when such costs will be accumulated for contract costing in a single account encompassing all functions.

CAS 402 forbids double counting: ". . . each type of cost is [to be] allocated only once and on only one basis to any contract or other cost objective. . . . All costs incurred for the same purpose, in like circumstances, are either direct costs only or indirect costs only with respect to final cost objectives." An example of double counting is the charging of any kind of cost such as travel, supervision, or quality control directly to a contract when other travel, supervision, or quality control costs incurred in like circumstances are treated as indirect costs.

Unallowable costs.   Some costs allocable to individual contracts aren't allowable in calculating the contract price—that is, the government won't reimburse the contractor for these costs. CAS 405 deals with the identification of costs that aren't allowable. The board described its position on allowability as follows:

> Allowability is a procurement concept affecting contract price and in most cases is established in regulatory or contractual provisions. . . . The use of Cost Accounting Standards has no direct bearing on the allowability of those individual items of cost which are subject to limitations or exclusions set forth in the contract or which are otherwise specified as unallowable by the government.[5]

CAS 405 provides that unallowable costs should be subject to the same measurement principles as allowable costs. If one of the costs in a denominator used to calculate an overhead rate is unallowable, for example, it remains in the denominator. This means that the overhead costs that would have been allocated to the contract as a percentage of the unallowable cost also must be classified as unallowable.

Cost accounting period.   CAS 406 requires the contractor to use the same cost accounting period for accumulating costs in indirect cost pools as it uses in establishing the allocation bases for those pools. In general, the cost accounting period must be the fiscal year, but the standard recognizes a number of situations in which some other period may be used. The standard also requires that appropriate annual deferrals, accruals, and other adjustments be made in determining the cost-accounting period to which costs should be assigned.

Standards for assigning costs to periods

The standards for assigning costs to periods are generally similar to those the contractor would use for external financial reporting. The following standards fall in this category:

CAS 404.   Capitalization of tangible assets.
CAS 408.   Costs of compensated personal absence.
CAS 409.   Depreciation of tangible capital assets.

---

[5] Restatement of Objectives, Policies and Concepts, 1977, pp. 2–3.

CAS 411. Acquisition costs of material.

CAS 412. Composition and measurement of pension cost.

CAS 413. Adjustment and allocation of pension cost.

CAS 415. The costs of deferred personal compensation.

CAS 416. Insurance costs.

CAS 417. Cost of money as an element of the cost of capital assets under construction.

Capitalization of tangible assets. *CAS 404* requires the contractor to capitalize the costs of tangible capital assets, with a written capitalization policy specifying the economic and physical characteristics associated with the assets to be capitalized, including a minimum service life and a minimum acquisition cost. *CAS 417* requires the capitalization of interest accrued during the period of construction as part of the cost of a tangible asset. Interest is to be capitalized on the total cost of the asset, not just the part financed by specific borrowing.

CAS 411 requires that inventory cost be defined as net delivered cost and that an inventory costing method be chosen and used consistently for each type of materials. It permits the contractor to charge individual contracts directly only for materials purchased specifically for those individual contracts.

Depreciation. *CAS 409* provides for the assignment of depreciation to cost accounting periods and provides a set of broad criteria to be applied in calculating annual depreciation charges. Boiled down to their essentials, the main provisions are:

1. The depreciable amount is original cost minus estimated residual value.
2. The depreciable amount is to be spread over the asset(s)' useful life.
3. The depreciation pattern must reflect the pattern of asset service consumption (e.g., straight line if the services are likely to be consumed in equal annual amounts).
4. Gains or losses on disposal are to be assigned to the periods in which disposals take place.

CAS 409 also provides instructions for assigning depreciation costs to cost objectives within the period. The main provisions are:

1. Direct charges to cost objectives can be made only if depreciation charges are calculated on a usage basis.
2. Depreciation within an organization unit providing chargeable services to other cost objectives is to be included as part of the chargeable costs of that organization unit.
3. Other depreciation charges are to be included in appropriate indirect cost pools.

Many industry representatives objected to this standard's provision requiring the use of estimated useful life as the amortization period. They generally preferred the use of tax life or the life estimate used for company financial statements; these life estimates are often shorter than the actual lives of depreciable assets. They expressed concern that longer life estimates would delay cash receipts, reduce incentives for modernization, increase administrative record-keeping costs, and create differences between the depreciation amounts determined for contract costing and those used in financial statements. The CASB took the position, however, that cost for contract costing purposes should be based on cost accounting concepts and not on tax lives, which may be artificially shortened to achieve various nonaccounting goals.

Fringe benefits. *CAS 408* has two main requirements: "(*a*) The costs of compensated personal absence [vacation, holiday, and sick pay] shall be assigned to the cost accounting period or periods in which the entitlement was earned. (*b*) The costs of compensated personal absence for an entire cost accounting period shall be allocated pro rata on an annual basis among the final cost objectives of that period."

CAS 412 provides that pension costs can be accrued only to the extent they are accompanied by current payments or by binding commitments to make future payments. These costs include the normal cost of the current period, determined actuarially, together with an appropriate part of any unfunded actuarial liability, interest on the unfunded portion, and an adjustment for any actuarial gains or losses. *CAS 413* describes how actuarial gains and losses are to be calculated and how pension costs are to be allocated to segments.

CAS 415 requires the use of accrual accounting to assign the costs of deferred compensation to cost accounting periods. (Deferred compensation includes future payments of cash, other assets, or shares of the contractor's stock during some limited period of time.) The cost is to be recognized in the period in which the contractor incurs an obligation to compensate an employee at a later time. Cost is to be measured by the present value of the future amounts to be paid by the contractor.

Insurance costs. *CAS 416* provides that the amount of insurance cost to be assigned to a cost accounting period is the projected average loss for that period plus insurance administration expenses. The allocation of insurance costs to cost objectives is based on the factors that determine the cost, except that insurance costs may be allocated along with other indirect costs if the resulting allocation to cost objectives is substantially the same.

Standards for assigning costs to cost objectives

Although the standards in the second group include a few provisions governing the assignment of costs to cost objectives within a period, only the six standards in the third group are concerned primarily with intraperiod cost allocation:

CAS 403.	Allocation of home office expenses to segments.
CAS 407.	Use of standard costs for direct materials and direct labor.
CAS 410.	Allocation of business unit general and administrative expenses to final cost objectives.
CAS 414.	Cost of money as an element of the cost of facilities capital.
CAS 418.	Allocation of direct and indirect costs.
CAS 420.	Independent research and development and bid and proposal costs.

General structure. The CAS Board never published a statement explaining the overall structure of the standards it was issuing. The diagram in Exhibit 21–4 illustrates the cost distribution patterns that are either spelled out in these six standards or can be inferred from them. This diagram shows three basic levels of cost accumulation: the home office, the segment, and the final cost objectives. The costs of the home office are divided among the segments it serves and administers. The costs of the segments are then divided among the final cost objectives. Home office costs fall into three categories; segment costs are of five different types. Each of these may be subdivided further.

Allocation of home office expenses to segments. *CAS 403* deals with home office expenses, which consist mainly of (1) the costs of centralized service functions, including staff management functions, (2) central payments and accruals, and (3) residual expenses.

Centralized service functions are functions that, but for the existence of a home office, would be performed or acquired by some or all of the segments individually. Examples include centrally performed personnel administration and cen-

Exhibit 21–4 Implicit structure of cost flows in cost accounting standards

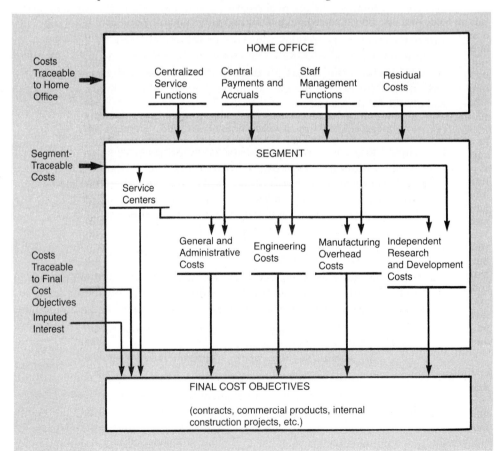

tralized data processing. If these costs can be traced directly to a specific segment, they must be charged to that segment. If they are not traceable to a segment, the standard prescribes the use of a hierarchy of allocation bases. This hierarchy applies to all allocations of costs from intermediate cost objectives (e.g., the activities of a home office computer center) to other cost objectives (e.g., the activities of individual segments or individual contracts or other final cost objectives). The allocations of the costs of intermediate cost objectives, including centralized service functions in a home office, are to be allocated by methods chosen on the basis of the following hierarchy of criteria:

1. If the intermediate cost objective provides services or operating capacity to other cost objectives and if the *inputs* used in the intermediate cost objective can be identified with those other cost objectives, the costs should be allocated on the basis of the average cost per input unit in the intermediate cost objective. For example, the costs of a computer programming department might be distributed in proportion to the number of programming hours identified with individual segments. (It may be convenient to think of this as a form of job order costing for the activities in the intermediate cost objective.)

2. If the intermediate cost objective provides service or operating capacity to other cost objectives but the inputs used in the intermediate cost objective can't be identified readily with those other cost objectives, the contractor should look for a measure of the *output* of the intermediate cost objective and allocate its costs in proportion to the number of units of output provided to other cost objectives. For example, the costs of a print shop might be allocated on the basis of the number of printed pages prepared for other cost objectives. (This is similar to a process costing calculation.)

3. When neither the inputs nor the outputs of an intermediate cost objective can be identified with other specific cost objectives, a *surrogate* should be sought that seems likely to vary in the long run with the cost of services provided by the intermediate cost objective. This surrogate is usually some measure of the activity in the cost objectives receiving service or support from the intermediate cost objective. For example, the number of employees in the departments served by a personnel department may be a useful basis for assigning the costs of maintaining personnel records to the cost objectives identified with those departments.

4. Any costs for which no homogeneous measure of input or output or a surrogate can be identified with the cost objectives they serve or support should be allocated among those cost objectives in proportion to their shares of the *total activity* of all the cost objectives as a group. For example, the costs of a plant manager's office might be allocated to final cost objectives in proportion to the total of all other factory costs assigned to those final cost objectives.

Central payments and accruals are those that, but for the existence of the home office, would be accrued or paid by the individual segments. Common examples are group insurance costs, local property taxes, and payrolls paid by a home office on behalf of its segments. The standard provides that these payments and accruals are to be assigned directly to individual segments if they can be traced to the segments. Otherwise, they are to be assigned to segments "using an allocation base representative of the factors on which the total payment is based."

Residual expenses are all those not falling in either of the first two categories. A typical example is the salary of the chief executive officer. It is to be allocated to the segments on a base representing the segments' total activity. The standard prescribes a formula to be used for this purpose if the amount exceeds a specified limit.

Standard costs for direct materials and direct labor. *CAS 407* provides a basis on which standard costing systems for direct labor and direct material can be used in determining the cost of covered contracts. Separate labor rate standards, for example, must be set for each homogeneous group of workers or for each crew working as an integral team. Materials price variances must be accumulated separately for each homogeneous group of materials. When the price variances are segregated at the time of purchase, they must be spread pro rata at least once a year between materials inventory and the production units to which the materials were issued. Labor cost variances must also be accumulated by production unit.

The effect of these requirements is to make contract cost approximate the historical cost of the labor and materials inputs. The homogeneity requirement means that variances will be matched fairly closely with the standard inputs they relate to. Large variance pools are allocated in proportion to standard costs.

Allocation of general and administrative overheads. *CAS 410* contains two main provisions:

1. Each business unit is to have a pool of general and administrative (G&A) costs, and this is to be allocated directly to final cost objectives.
2. General and administrative costs of any business unit are to be allocated by means of a cost input base.

Cost input may mean all the operating costs of the business unit other than general and administrative costs and independent research and development and bid and proposal costs ("total cost input"), or it may mean total cost input less the costs of materials and purchased services ("value added"), or it may mean a single cost element, such as direct labor. General and administrative costs can't be allocated as a percentage of sales or cost of sales, however, because these are output measures. Instead, they must be assigned to contract work in process before it is ready for delivery to the government. In the prefatory comments to *CAS 410,* the board explained its reason for precluding the use of an output base:

> The Board's position is that the measurement of a cost of sales base is representative, in part, of the productive activities of prior periods and is subject to fluctuations which can distort the allocation of G&A expenses to activities of the current

period. Although the measurement of cost of sales is based on a recorded date of sale, that is not necessarily an index of the activities of the period.

CAS 410 has given rise to a good deal of controversy, centering on whether the standard established a hierarchy of cost input measures starting with total cost input and working down to a single input index applicable in specified circumstances. The conceptual issue is which of these measures best reflects the causality criterion. If different measures are appropriate in different circumstances, then alternatives should be allowed, but the standard should specify the circumstances under which each method is appropriate. Without this guidance each contractor would be free to choose the measure that appeared most likely to maximize the contractor's profits, and this was a result the legislation creating the CAS Board was intended to prevent.

Imputed interest on facilities capital.   *CAS 414* plowed new ground. For the first time, imputed interest was recognized as an element of contract cost. The amount of imputed interest is computed by applying a long-term commercial borrowing rate to the individual contractor's investment in facilities. Neither actual interest incurred nor the contractor's actual borrowing rate is a consideration in determining the amount of imputed interest. The standard requires the following:

1. Interest must be imputed to individual contracts.
2. The amount to be imputed is to be based on the amount of *facilities* used to support work on individual contracts. (Investments in working capital are specifically excluded from the provisions of this standard.)
3. The interest rate is to be based on an average of long-term commercial borrowing rates calculated periodically by the secretary of the treasury.
4. Imputed interest assignable to an indirect cost pool must be allocated to final cost objectives in proportion to the number of "allocation base units" (direct labor hours, and so on) identified with the contract.

To implement this standard, the contractor must assign the costs of facilities to individual business units. The standard provides a form to be used to make this calculation. The main criterion, as usual, is traceability of the investment to the business unit and to the specific overhead cost pools within this business unit. For facilities not traceable to individual overhead cost pools, the costs are to be allocated "on any reasonable basis that approximates the actual absorption of depreciation or amortization of such facilities." In other words, imputed interest is to parallel the depreciation allocation.

Allocation of indirect costs to final cost objectives.   One of the board's most difficult tasks was the development of *CAS 418,* covering the allocation of the costs of a business unit to final cost objectives. The problem was to develop a structure that would promote uniformity in the contracting community without requiring individual contractors to establish more costing pools than would be economically feasible.

CAS 418 provides guidance in general terms for handling indirect costs of a business unit other than those covered by *CAS 410* or *CAS 420.* It requires that each business unit have a written statement of accounting policies and practices for classifying costs as direct or indirect. It also requires that the pools of indirect costs should be homogeneous.

This standard distinguishes between (1) indirect cost pools containing a material amount of the costs of management or supervision of activities involving direct labor or direct materials costs, and (2) other indirect cost pools. Costs in pools of the former type are to be allocated on bases that are representative of the activity being managed. For example, direct labor might be used as a base for allocating manufacturing overhead costs. Costs in indirect cost pools of the second type, mostly the costs of service centers, are to be assigned to the cost objectives served (*a*) on the basis of inputs in the pool whose use can also be traced to specific cost objectives, (*b*) on the basis of the amount of service provided by the activities in the pool (the output of the pool), or (*c*) on the basis of a surrogate for service inputs. In other words, the same allocation hierarchy is to be used here as in the allocation of the home office's costs of centralized service functions, as prescribed in *CAS 403*.

Independent research and development and bid and proposal costs. *CAS 420* requires the costs of independent research and development (IR&D) and bid and proposal (B&P) activities to be accumulated by individual projects. IR&D is defined as effort in basic and applied research, development, systems, and other concept formulation activities that aren't performed under contract or grant. B&P is defined as effort in preparing and submitting any bid or proposal that is not required under the terms of an existing contract or grant.

The costs of IR&D and B&P projects must include the direct costs incurred solely for the particular projects plus an appropriate share of all indirect costs except general and administrative costs. The costs of these projects are assigned to final cost objectives on the basis of an index of activity, in most cases the same index used to allocate general and administrative costs to final cost objectives.

Summary

Organizations sometimes measure the costs of individual end-product activities or programs for reimbursement purposes: contract costing, regulatory pricing, or not-for-profit program support. Cost measurements for these purposes are likely to be on an all-inclusive or full-costing basis, and the measurement rules will be specified in advance by some measurement authority.

The primary criterion or principle governing these measurements should be the causality criterion: Costs should be assigned to the activities which cause them to be incurred. The traceability, variability, and facilities provided criteria are designed to implement the causality criterion; the criterion of beneficiality or benefit provided is introduced to permit the development of all-inclusive cost figures when direct causation can't be determined.

From 1972 to 1980 the United States Cost Accounting Standards Board issued a set of 19 cost accounting standards applicable primarily to U.S. defense contracts. The summary of these standards in the latter part of this chapter is designed to illustrate the application of basic reimbursement costing criteria in a specific context. Reimbursement costing rules in other jurisdictions will take different forms, depending on the circumstances and the context in which reimbursement takes place.

Exercises and problems

1. **Not-for-profit organization: Costing individual programs.** The Crabtree Ballet Company stages 30 different ballets during its season. An individual performance may be devoted to a single, full-length ballet (e.g., *Giselle*) or to several shorter ballets. Each year Crabtree introduces several new ballets in its current repertoire, but the bulk of the repertoire consists of ballets presented in previous seasons. Costumes and sets for individual ballets are placed in storage between presentations.

   Crabtree's board of trustees is planning to approach several potential new donors to seek funds to support next season's new ballets. Your job is to develop a set of cost estimates to be presented to these donors. The donors are generous, but they are also realistic. They will be very quick to spot any attempt on your part to manipulate the distribution of costs to substantiate large requests for funds.

   You have decided to treat each ballet, whether new or old, as a separate cost objective. Choreographers', performers', directors', and musicians' time, and the costs of sets and costumes will be identified with individual ballets. Theater maintenance and back-of-the-house costs (e.g., the costs of ticket sellers and ushers) will be treated as a single cost objective. The other two cost objectives will be development (fund raising) and general administrative support (e.g., the salary of the director of the company and the costs of the administrative and general clerical staffs). Every cost will be traced to one of these cost objectives or, if it isn't readily traceable, will be classified as a cost of general administrative support.

   Required:

   a. Should any portion of the costs classified as theater, development, or administrative support be allocated to individual ballets? Justify your position.

   b. While waiting for your answer to (*a*), the board of trustees has decided to obtain estimates of the all-inclusive (full) cost of the new ballets scheduled for introduction during the coming year. What denominator or denominators should be used to assign theater, development, and general administrative support costs to individual ballets? Explain your choices.

2. **Regulatory accounting standards.** Many regulated utility companies (e.g., gas, electricity, telephone service) in the United States now provide services that compete directly with services provided by unregulated companies. Partly as a result of this development, utility regulatory commissions in the United States are increasingly concerned that utility service prices or rates be reasonably proportional to the costs of providing individual utility services.

   Required:

   a. Why might the utility commissions be worried that the utility companies might assign "too small" a proportion of total cost to the services which face competition from unregulated companies? Why should the commissions worry that "too large" a percentage of total cost will be assigned to these services?

   b. What criterion or criteria would you apply to try to insure that the allocations developed are neither too large nor too small?

3. **Indirect cost pools.** Carter Company operates a hardware factory and a boatyard, with the following statistics:

		Boatyard		
	Hardware Factory	Boat Repair	Boat Building	Total
Number of employees	300	210	490	1,000
Number of job orders per year . . .	500	25	5	530
Number of direct labor hours	200,000	250,000	550,000	1,000,000
Direct labor cost	$2,100,000	$3,100,000	$6,800,000	$12,000,000
Direct materials cost	4,000,000	1,000,000	5,000,000	10,000,000
Overhead cost	6,300,000	2,200,000	5,000,000	13,500,000

Management has decided to accumulate the manufacturing overhead costs of the hardware factory and the boatyard in a single cost pool for product costing purposes, with an overhead rate based on direct labor hours. A government contracting officer (a government employee) has recommended that three manufacturing overhead pools be established, one for the hardware factory, one for the boat repair section of the boatyard, and one for the boatbuilding section. One of the job orders in the boatbuilding section is on a cost-based negotiated government contract, and 15 of the boat repair jobs are on government contracts of this type. All of the output of the hardware factory is destined for civilian markets.

Required:

What position would you take in the dispute between Carter Company's management and the government contracting officer? Justify your position with respect to costing criteria and cost accounting standards.

4. **Allocating central payments and accruals.** A company pays franchise taxes to the state of California. The franchise tax is calculated by multiplying California's "share" of the company's net income by the franchise tax rate. The state's share is determined by calculating the percentage of the company's employees, assets, and sales located in California. The state's right to levy taxes on this basis has been confirmed in numerous court cases.

The company has two segments for contract costing purposes: a military products (MP) division, located in Texas, and a civilian products (CP) division, located in California. Last year the CP division's share of company employees, assets, and sales was 60 percent of the total, and therefore 60 percent of the company's $10,000,000 pretax income for the year was determined to be California's share subject to the franchise tax. On this basis, the California franchise tax for this company was $1 million. Statistics for the year were:

	MP Division	CP Division
Pretax income (after headquarters allocation but before California tax)	$9,000,000	$1,000,000
Percent of employees, assets and sales	40%	60%
Percent of employees	60	40

Required:

a. Which standard of the Cost Accounting Standards Board governs the allocation of the California franchise tax between divisions? Given the description of that standard in this chapter, how much would you allocate to each division? Explain.

b. If you were in a position to issue a cost accounting standard governing the allocation of franchise taxes of this sort, would your standard lead to the same allocations you made in answer to (a)? Explain.

5. **Contract costing: Allocating property taxes.** Blaze Company has two operating divisions and a home office. Property taxes levied by local governments and property insurance premiums are paid by the home office; plant and equipment depreciation records are also kept in the home office and depreciation calculations are made by home office personnel.

The home office charges property insurance and depreciation costs to the two divisions on the basis of insured values and the costs of depreciable property located in each division. The controller wants to distribute the costs of local property taxes to the divisions on the same basis—that is, at the amounts levied on the properties in each division. This is called the assessment basis of cost distribution. The president argues for allocations in proportion to the number of employees in each division (headcount basis), on the grounds that taxes go to taxing jurisdictions which use them to provide benefits to the people living and working in those jurisdictions. The treasurer claims that the allocations should be in proportion to floor space (space basis), on the grounds that floor space is interchangeable. You have the following data:

	Division A	Division B	Total
Property taxes levied	$3,000,000	$1,000,000	$4,000,000
Property insurance costs	750,000	500,000	1,250,000
Depreciation	4,200,000	1,800,000	6,000,000
Number of employees	15,000	15,000	30,000
Number of square feet of floor space ..	1,000,000	3,000,000	4,000,000

Required:

a. How much property tax should be assigned to each division for contract costing purposes? State the criterion governing your choice and your reasons for selecting it and for applying it as you are recommending. You may refer to CAS for guidance but your choice should rest on your analysis of the arguments rather than on the authority of the standards.

b. Explain your reasons for rejecting views expressed by any Blaze Company executive whose recommendation doesn't coincide with yours.

6. **Discussion question: Allocations of common costs.** Random Fund, Inc., is an investment company which invests funds provided by its shareholders in a diversified portfolio of corporate securities. Decisions to buy or sell securities are made by employees of Waite & Watchem (W&W), an investment counselling firm, under the terms of an investment advisory agreement between Waite & Watchem and Random Fund. This agreement also specifies the fees Random Fund will pay to Waite and Watchem.

Each year Random Fund's board of directors must approve (or disapprove) the renewal of the investment advisory agreement. One factor the board usually considers in this context is the ratio of profit to fees Waite & Watchem has earned from its Random Fund work during the past period. Presumably, if Waite & Watchem has earned an extremely high rate of profit, the fee is higher than it ought to be and the board should negotiate a reduction for the following year.

Waite & Watchem manages several funds as well as Random Fund. It allocates its operating costs among these funds in various ways. Two of its costs are as follows:

1. Waite & Watchem has purchased a fidelity bond to insure each fund it manages against embezzlement by Waite & Watchem personnel. The insurance coverage amounts to $10 million and the annual premium is $15,000.

2. Frank Warner is Waite & Watchem's president. His salary is $150,000 a year. He spends 5 percent of his time specifically on Random Fund business, 30 percent of his time specifically on the business of other funds managed

by the firm, and 65 percent of his time on general administrative and promotional work.

Random Fund's assets amount to 20 percent of the assets of all of Waite & Watchem's funds combined, and the fees Random Fund has paid Waite & Watchem this year are 18 percent of the total fees Waite & Watchem has received this year from all of the funds it manages. Waite & Watchem's personnel (including Frank Warner) spend 12 percent of their time on Random Fund affairs, 68 percent of their time on other funds, and 20 percent of their time on other activities.

Required:

a. How much of the fidelity bond premium should be assigned to Random Fund in connection with the preparation of the profitability figures to be presented to Random Fund's directors? Explain your reasoning and specify the criterion or criteria you have applied.

b. How much of Frank Warner's salary should be assigned to Random Fund in this connection? Explain and specify the criterion or criteria.

7. **Contract costing: Effect of cost input base.** Tronics Corporation's business consists entirely of CAS-covered contracts with government agencies. Revenues are recognized as portions of the work are completed and delivered to the government. Payments from the government are received shortly after the work is delivered. The company's general and administrative costs (G&A) this year amount to $1,000,000. The cost of goods sold this year, excluding G&A costs, amounts to $10,000,000. Total cost input to contracts this year, again excluding G&A costs, also amounts to $10,000,000. Sixty percent of each of these latter two totals represents the costs of materials and purchased parts.

Studies by Tronics staff members have shown that the costs of the activities classified by Tronics as general and administrative activities can be broken down roughly as follows:

Purchasing materials and component parts	12%
Inventory accounting and storekeeping	5
Payroll accounting	25
Customer billing and accounts receivable accounting . . .	15
Wage and salary administration	10
Accounts payable accounting	3
General administration	30
Total	100%

Required:

a. What effect, if any, would the use of a total cost input base instead of a cost of goods sold base for assigning G&A costs to contracts have on the company's income and cash flows?

b. Management wishes to apply G&A costs to contracts on a direct labor hour base rather than a total cost input base, claiming that the use of a direct labor base will reflect the underlying causal and beneficial relationships more clearly. If your choice weren't constrained by *CAS 410,* would you favor management's proposal, oppose it, or be indifferent to it on the grounds that it would have no effect on total contract cost? Explain your position.

8. **Contract costing: Separate facilities.** Thorelli Corporation accumulates its manufacturing overhead costs in a single pool for product costing purposes. Costs are assigned to contracts and other final cost objectives on a direct labor hour base. Most of the company's products flow through several factory departments; until this year no department was devoted exclusively to a single product or contract.

This year Thorelli began work on contract NVT64U for the U.S. Navy. This contract is of the cost-plus-fixed-fee type. Work on the contract is performed entirely in a new department that was set up in a previously unused loft in the factory. This department works exclusively on contract NVT64U. Other departments have continued to work this year both on other government contracts and on products for civilian markets.

Because the new department is working exclusively on contract NVT64U this year, Thorelli's management has decided to classify the costs of supervision, materials handling labor, and equipment depreciation in this department as direct costs of this contract. Costs in these categories are treated as indirect costs in other departments. You have the following data on these costs:

	New Department	Other Departments
Supervision	$ 40,000	$250,000
Materials handling	60,000	346,000
Equipment depreciation	50,000	160,000
Total	$150,000	$756,000

All other indirect manufacturing costs in this company total $1,050,000 this year. Supervisory and materials handling time in the new department amounts to 10,000 hours this year. The time of other workers classified as direct labor in this department amounts to 20,000 hours. Direct labor time in all other departments combined adds up to 180,000 hours this year.

Required:

a. By how much will management's decision to classify the supervisory, materials handling, and equipment depreciation costs in the new department as direct costs of contract NVT64U increase or decrease the amount of cost assigned to this contract?

b. Do you agree with management's decision to classify these costs as direct costs of this contract? Would you agree if the contract weren't covered by cost accounting standards? Explain.

9. **Designing a new cost accounting standard: Seldom-used facilities.**   Aeronautical Systems, Inc. (ASI), has a wind tunnel with fixed costs of $1 million a year and variable costs of $5,000 for each hour the tunnel is in operation. The current annual budget calls for the use of the wind tunnel a total of 200 hours; 150 of these hours are budgeted for use in connection with cost-based negotiated contracts with the U.S. government.

Actual usage of the wind tunnel in the first 11 months of this year has amounted to 220 hours, including 150 hours on cost-based negotiated government contracts subject to the standards of the Cost Accounting Standards Board. In all of these contracts, the government will reimburse ASI for its actual costs plus a fixed fee. No more use of the wind tunnel is scheduled in the final month of the year, but a major automobile manufacturer has asked to be allowed to use it for 12 hours this month, at a price of $8,000 an hour.

If the automobile manufacturer's proposal is rejected, manufacturing overhead costs other than wind tunnel costs will total $12 million on a volume of 500,000 direct labor hours, including 325,000 hours on cost-based negotiated government contracts. Use of the wind tunnel by the automobile manufacturer would cause ASI to use 120 additional manufacturing direct labor hours; manufacturing overhead costs other than wind tunnel costs would not be affected. Manufacturing overhead costs other than wind tunnel costs are applied to final cost objectives on a direct labor hour base.

ASI's established accounting practice, which has been accepted by the government's auditors, is to treat the wind tunnel as a service center, distributing its costs to final cost objectives and to the company's independent research and development projects in proportion to actual usage. If the automobile manufacturer's proposal is accepted, the government's auditor wants ASI to treat this use of the wind tunnel as a final cost objective. ASI wants to classify it as an "incidental use" of the facilities, with the $96,000 price treated as miscellaneous revenues.

Required:

a. Assuming the automobile manufacturer's proposal is rejected, calculate the amount of wind tunnel costs to be assigned to cost-based negotiated government contracts this year if the company's established accounting practice is followed.

b. Assuming the automobile manufacturer's proposal is accepted and the auditor's recommendation is followed, how much of the wind tunnel's costs will be assigned to government contracts? How much of these costs will be assigned to these contracts if ASI's recommendation is followed?

c. Suppose you are in a position to design and promulgate a cost accounting standard to govern the allocation of wind tunnel costs to final cost objectives. What method of allocation would most clearly reflect the criteria of causality and beneficiality? You may recommend methods not previously described in this problem as well as those mentioned above. In your answer you should explain how the allocations under your recommended method would differ from those you made in answer to the previous parts of this problem and why your allocations are superior. Your recommendation should provide a satisfactory solution to the problems raised by the automobile manufacturer's proposal.

10. **Program costing: Not-for-profit organization.** Local Community Services, Inc. (LCS), operates a day-care center, a prenatal-care and information program, and supplementary teaching programs for students in local schools. It recognizes six programs:

> Day care.
> Prenatal.
> Elementary teaching.
> High school enrichment.
> Development (fund raising).
> Administration.

You have the following information on expenses, income, and support for the current year:

Income and support:	
Fees and charges	$ 40,000
Income from special activities	30,000
Contributions and grants	270,000
Investment income	10,000
Total income and support	350,000
Expenses:	
Salaries and wages	257,000
Supplies	20,000
Rent	70,000
Utilities	5,000
Special activities costs	8,000
Miscellaneous	7,000
Total expenses	367,000
Difference between income and support and expenses	$(17,000)

The board of trustees are concerned by the size of the current deficit and have asked for program-based financial statements and a plan to eliminate the deficit next year. You have the following additional information:

1. Of the fees and charges, $38,000 was received from the parents of day care children, either directly or through the parents' employers. The remaining $2,000 came from a small group of adults enrolled on an experimental basis in the high school enrichment program.
2. Income from special activities consists of amounts received from charity balls, fund-raising dinners, and other activities organized by the board of trustees in cooperation with the director.
3. Salaries and wages (including fringe benefits) were as follows:

Director	$ 38,000
Development officer	25,000
Business manager	22,000
Secretaries and typists	20,000*
Janitors	32,000
Day-care staff	25,000
Prenatal staff	15,000
Elementary teaching faculty	30,000
High school enrichment faculty	50,000
Total	$257,000

* Management estimates that 40 percent of secretarial time was devoted to fund raising; the remainder was spent in support of the director and business manager.

4. LCS rents space in two adjacent buildings, for which you have the following information:

	Main Building	Annex Building
Annual rental	$45,000	$25,000
Janitorial service salaries	20,000	12,000
Utilities	3,500	1,500
Total floor space (sq. ft.)	6,850	5,000
Percent of floor space:		
Day care		80%
Prenatal		20
Elementary teaching	30%	
High school enrichment	40	
Development	10	
Administration	20	

5. Most miscellaneous expenses were for postage in connection with fund raising activities, but no precise data are available.
6. Supplies costs included the costs of teaching materials, cleaning supplies, stationery, and office supplies.

Required:

a. Prepare a columnar summary of income, support, and expenses, with a separate column for each program, *for use by LCS's management.*
b. Explain and justify the basis on which you assigned each element of income, support, and expense to individual programs. Explain and justify your treatment of the costs of development and administration programs (i.e., explain why you did or did not reallocate them to the other four programs).

c. A volunteer consultant has pointed out that various governmental agencies and private foundations might be able to fund portions of the costs of some of LCS's programs, thereby enabling LCS to serve a larger segment of the community and eliminate its deficit at the same time. Would the figures you developed in answer to (a) be suitable for submitting reimbursement claims to these organizations? If so, explain how they would be used. if not, outline and justify the approach you would take to convert the system to this purpose. (*Note:* Do not recommend any changes that would add materially to the clerical cost of operating the system.)

part 3 Further topics in periodic planning and control

22 Behavioral aspects of responsibility accounting

This final group of chapters takes us back to responsibility accounting, accounting's contribution to managerial control processes. Some of this discussion will focus on technical matters, some will deal with the interpretations management should place on the accounting figures. A planning and control system is useful, however, only if it affects the actions taken by the people who make up the organization. Before going farther, therefore, we need to look at the behavioral side of systems design—how do behavioral factors enter into the design of a system and how do they affect the likelihood the system will be successful?

For convenience, we have divided the chapter into two parts. The first part deals with the interactions between the accounting system and other aspects of management's systems for planning and controlling the organization's activities. The second part focuses on some of the behavioral problems encountered in the administration of managerial accounting systems, particularly those parts we have referred to as responsibility accounting—that is, the preparation of performance standards and the reporting of results.

Behavioral factors in system design

A responsibility accounting system is part of the larger system designed by management to help it achieve the organization's goals. Most responsibility accounting systems have the following implicit behavioral assumptions:

1. Other elements of the managerial system will be effective in inducing managers to strive to reach or surpass budgeted performance levels—the budgeted standards by themselves are not motivational.
2. The participation of subordinate managers in setting standards is necessary to the success of the managerial system.
3. Performance standards should be set at levels described as "tight but attainable."
4. The system is to facilitate *management by exception*—that is, management relies on the reporting of variances to ration its time effectively.
5. Management will apply the *controllability criterion*—that is, managers are expected to respond only to variances arising within their own jurisdictions.

6. When the organization has two or more explicit goals, conflicts between these goals must be resolved outside the accounting system.

Other elements as motivating forces

The first assumption underlying managerial reporting systems is that other elements, not the budgets or standards themselves, will be effective in motivating managers to strive to reach or surpass budgeted performance levels. This doesn't come automatically. Individual motivation is determined by the needs of the individuals themselves and their perception that performance (e.g., achieving budgeted performance) will lead to the satisfaction of these needs.[1] It is management's task to bring the goals of the individual and those of the organization together. If management is successful, then we say that *goal congruence* has been achieved. Achieving goal congruence is the way to validate this first assumption of responsibility accounting.

Goals of the organization and of the individuals in it are said to be congruent if the individuals have accepted the organization's goals as their own. This is known as *internalizing* the organization's goals. For individuals to internalize a goal, they must believe that achieving it will satisfy their needs better than not achieving it. Goals that individuals have internalized are known as *aspiration levels*, the performance levels they undertake to reach.

Several factors affect the probability that individuals will internalize budgeted goals as their aspiration levels. One of these is past experience—success or failure in reaching budgeted goals in previous periods. Another is the priority they assign to their own needs for personal achievement. A third is the likelihood that meeting the budget will provide this sense of achievement. Still another is what they expect to be able to achieve under expected conditions.[2] The relationships among these factors are diagrammed in Exhibit 22–1.

Participation

What goes on in the box in the middle of Exhibit 22–1 isn't always clear, but it does depend on the social environment in which the aspiration levels are being formed. One way of structuring the social environment to try to develop goal congruence is to have subordinate managers participate in the process of setting performance standards. We need to discuss five aspects of the role of participation in this process:

1. What participation means.
2. What contribution it can make.
3. How it can be affected by group dynamics.

---

[1] Edward E. Lawler III, *Motivation in Work Organizations* (Monterey, Calif.: Brooks/Cole, 1973). The relationships between control systems and individual needs are summarized in an excellent book by Edward E. Lawler III and John Grant Rhode, *Information and Control in Organizations* (Pacific Palisades, Calif.: Goodyear Publishing, 1976), esp. chap. 2.

[2] For a more extended discussion of the factors that influence performance, see L. W. Porter, E. E. Lawler III, and J. R. Hackman, *Behavior in Organizations* (New York: McGraw-Hill, 1975).

Exhibit 22-1 Influences on personal aspiration levels

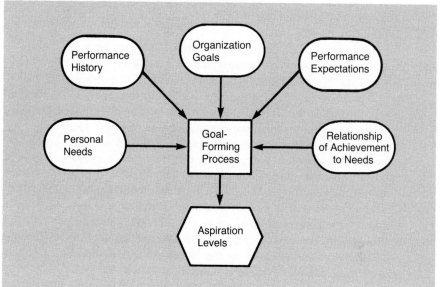

4. The impact of managerial style and cultural background.
5. The necessary conditions for successful participation.

The nature of participation.   Participation was an integral part of the periodic planning process described in Chapter 8. That description emphasized the subordinate's responsibility to originate proposals and the superior's responsibility to evaluate, question, and suggest changes.

These roles can also be reversed, at least in part. Superiors can propose, while their subordinates respond. If the system is to be participative, however, both parties must understand that proposals made by higher management provide a basis for discussion, not instructions. Participation means that decisions affecting individual managers' operations are to some extent joint decisions of the managers and their superiors. It is thus more than mere consultation, by which superiors inform themselves of their subordinates' views but make the decisions themselves.

Participation doesn't mean that both subordinate and superior must be in full agreement on every decision. In some cases the superior will try to influence the decision but will not go as far as using the veto, even though convinced that the subordinate is taking the wrong tack. More often, the superior's view will prevail and the subordinate will have to approve a plan regarded as less than optimal. When this happens, something else must be present if goal congruence is not to be lost.

The contribution of participation.   The main advantage of participation is to help managers perceive that the objectives or performance standards are reasonable. This in turn will help them internalize the standards, which is important to what is known as *intrinsic* motivation. (Intrinsic motivation is motivation arising from within the individual, rather than from the need for praise or tangible reward.)[3]

Participation accomplishes this result in part because it requires a great deal of communication between superior and subordinates. This helps everyone get a clearer picture of the requirements of the job and of how difficult it will be to achieve different objectives. Subordinates are more likely to internalize objectives that they perceive to be reasonable, and participation may be a good way to establish the reasonableness of the objectives.

These same results sometimes can be achieved without participation. Lawler and Rhode, for example, conclude that the main problem is to get subordinates to perceive standards as reasonable. This can be done without participation, if the subordinates can be led to trust those who set the standards.[4] The main argument for participation, however, is that it is a necessary mechanism to create this feeling of trust. If this is so, then subordinate managers will be more likely to strive to achieve the planned results if they have participated actively and influentially in the development of the plan and have agreed with their superiors that it is feasible.

Group dynamics.　Participation may be a useful way of using the individual's membership in groups to increase the acceptability of the organization's goals. Every individual belongs to many groups—the family, the neighborhood, the work group, and so on. The effectiveness of participation in securing goal congruence depends to a large extent on the values and attitudes held by the various groups the individual manager belongs to and on the strength of the manager's commitment to each group. The forces operating within the group and affecting the positions taken by individuals in the group are known as *group dynamics.*

Group dynamics in work-related groups can have a significant effect on job-related aspiration levels and group member behavior.[5] Individual managers belong to at least four intersecting groups in connection with their work, as illustrated in Exhibit 22–2.[6] Here the organization is viewed as a network, with the manager at the center. The manager shares one group with a superior (labeled as group *a*), another with subordinates (*d*), another with managers in similar positions elsewhere in the organization (*b*), and still another with the organization's staff (*c*). The dynamics of each of these groups will influence the manager's own goals, although not all to the same extent.

The amount of influence group membership will have on the individuals'

---

[3] Lawler and Rhode, *Information and Control in Organizations,* p. 69.

[4] For a discussion of the situations in which participation is most appropriate, see V. H. Vroom and P. W. Yetton, *Leadership and Decision Making* (Pittsburgh: University of Pittsburgh Press, 1973).

[5] J. R. Hackman, "Group Influences on Individuals," in *Handbook of Industrial and Organizational Psychology,* edited by M. D. Dunnette, (Chicago: Rand McNally, 1976).

[6] This diagram is from G. H. Hofstede, *The Game of Budget Control* (Assen, The Netherlands: Koninklijke Van Gorcum & Comp., 1967), p. 57. Two groups are said to intersect if some but not all members belong to both groups.

Exhibit 22–2 Position of the manager in the social network of the organization

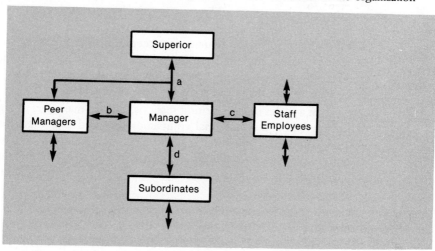

aspiration levels depends on how strongly they are attracted to the group. The strength of the attraction determines the *cohesiveness* of the group, the degree to which individual members value their group membership.

Individuals join or remain in a group mainly because they believe that it will help them attain their own individual goals. The greater the value placed on membership, the greater will be the likelihood that different members will have similar goals. In fact, conforming to the goals of the other members is a way of ensuring continued membership in the group. ("Membership" here means social acceptance rather than nominal affiliation in a formally constituted group). Valuing their own membership and anxious to keep it, individuals will tend to accept goals which seen to be consistent with those of others in the group. The more strongly the available information seems to indicate acceptance by others in a cohesive group, the greater the likelihood that individuals will adopt the goal as their own.

Group dynamics may also work against acceptance of the organization's objectives, of course. If the group is strong and the group leaders have rejected the organization's goals, they will be able to reduce the likelihood that others will accept them.

Managerial style and cultural influences. The patterns and effects of group dynamics are not the same at all times and in all situations. Different managers, for example, find that different managerial styles are suited to their different personalities. Similarly, different styles may be appropriate for different kinds of tasks or in different cultural environments. A democratic style may be completely inappropriate, at least in the short run, if subordinates have never experienced it in situations they regard as comparable.

Example. The introduction of participative budgeting in a large electrical equipment factory some years ago was received very coldly by most of the first-level supervisors, despite enthusiastic support from their superiors and the presence of a highly sensitive, multifunctional installation team in the factory for a period of many months. The reason seemed to be that the supervisors were reluctant to accept the risk of censure for failure to achieve targets they had set themselves. Without participation, blame could always be assigned elsewhere, at least in the supervisors' minds. It took many months to rid most to them of this fear.

Example. In a series of case-writing sessions, the top managers of a number of Europe-based multinational companies reported that their managers in some countries, even at fairly high levels, were reluctant to participate in budgetary planning. Those in other countries, given the same top management environment, were both ready and eager for greater autonomy.

Conditions for successful participation. Several conditions are likely to be necessary to allow participation to achieve its objective, managerial motivation. One is that the initial gap between the individual's goals and those of the organization shouldn't be so large that it can't be bridged. Another is that the managers' cultural background and environment permit them to participate in substance as well as in form.

Perhaps most important of all, higher managers participating in the decisions should play an active, constructive leadership role. Group cohesiveness can be a constructive force; it can also be destructive. Strong individuals may use their groups to mobilize support for their personal grievances or as springboards to political power. If managerial leadership is weak, the participation process can be turned against the organization's goals.

Reasonably attainable standards

The third behavioral assumption underlying most responsibility accounting systems is that performance standards should be set at levels described as "tight but attainable" or "reasonably attainable." The argument for this assumption is that as long as performance standards do not exceed amounts that are reasonably attainable, managers will internalize them. Managers and their subordinates will react to standards set below this level ("loose standards") by exerting a less than optimal amount of effort; they will regard standards set tighter than the reasonably attainable level as unrealistic and will cease striving to achieve them. Edward Lawler and John Rhode cite a number of empirical studies to conclude that "intrinsic motivation is most likely to be present when standards or budgets . . . have *somewhat less* than a 50/50 chance of being attained."[7]

Unfortunately, our definition of a reasonably attainable standard is far from precise. For example, the chart in Exhibit 22–3 shows the results of an analysis of a sample of 100 time tickets. None of these time tickets showed a time less than 4 or more than 12 minutes per piece. The time of 8 minutes was

---

[7] Lawler and Rhode, *Information and Control in Organizations*, p. 71 (italics added).

Exhibit 22–3 Setting tight but attainable standards by historical analysis

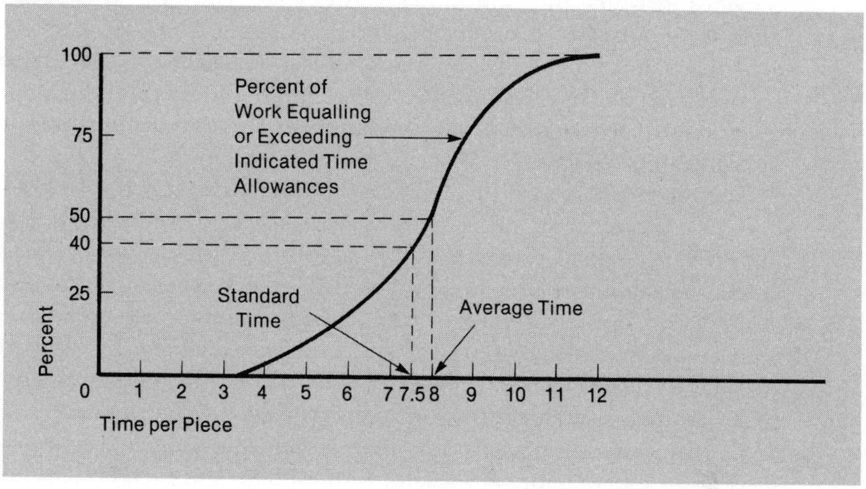

met or bettered 50 percent of the time, the midpoint on the curve. The company might choose to set the standard at 7.5 minutes, arguing that 40 percent of the workers in the sample were able to reach that performance level or better. The workers might claim, however, that 45 percent or 48 percent would be a better measure of the level that is reasonably attainable. In other words, accepting the concept of reasonable attainability merely alters the focus of the discussion; it doesn't remove the reason for discussion.

Workers and managers often have a good idea of the performance level that is tight but attainable. The main problem is to design a package of techniques to motivate the affected personnel to perform better than they would in the absence of the standards. In a pioneering work done some time ago, Andrew Stedry suggested that one way to do this might be to manipulate standards to influence aspiration levels without worrying whether the standards themselves were internalized.[8] He suggested that standards be adapted to reflect each individual's aspiration level. The standard would be raised in an attempt to pull the aspiration level upward; this, in turn would improve performance. If actual performance still remained so far short of the aspiration level that the aspiration level would be reduced, the standard would be reduced, too. Later, when the performance gap had been narrowed, the standard would be raised again.

It can be argued that Stedry's suggestion was mainly an effort to establish the tight but attainable level of performance, because he recognized that the gap between the standard and the level individuals perceive to be attainable can't be allowed to get too wide. The main objections to his suggestion, however, are that it calls for a separate standard for each individual and that it ignores deferred effects of manipulative activities.

---

[8] Andrew Stedry, *Budget Control and Cost Behavior* (Englewood Cliffs, N.J.: Prentice-Hall, 1960); and Andrew Stedry and E. Kay, *The Effects of Goal Difficulty on Performance: A Field Experiment* (Cambridge, Mass.: Sloan School of Management, Massachusetts Institute of Technology, 1964).

The first of these objections rules out applying this approach to repetitive activities in which different individuals can see that they have been assigned different standards. This objection shouldn't apply, however, to programmed activities that are likely to be unique to each manager. Managers can't really compare standards if their activities are very different. Therefore they are less likely than workers doing similar tasks on a production line to spot a discriminatory application of standards.

The second objection to an approach that deliberately rejects goal congruence as a means to an end is that it may lead to counterproductive behavior. Supervisors react to pressure in various but predictable ways. One response is to internalize the pressure by working harder, checking on subordinates more often—in effect, trying to transmit the pressure to the next level. Tensions tend to mount under these circumstances, as management has to work harder to keep the gains that have already been made. Grievances mount and the relationships between supervisors and subordinates deteriorate.

The supervisor's capacity for internalization is limited, particularly when it ceases to lead to improved results. At this point, and even before, supervisors are likely to seek ways of relieving the pressure. One way is to unite with their subordinates against "the boss." That is, pressure may lead them to identify more with the manager-subordinate group (group d in Exhibit 22–2) and less with the manager-superior group. By doing this, they can create problems for the superior and thereby transmit the pressure back up the line where it came from.

Another way of relieving pressure is to seek ways of beating the system. To avoid a subsequent tightening of standards, methods improvements will not be disclosed to staff or higher management. Materials will be hoarded for use when variances are unfavorable. Records will be falsified by misclassifying costs or misrepresenting output.

This brings us back to our earlier discussion of participation and motivation. Our conclusions are presented in an integrated format in Exhibit 22–4. This is in the form of a decision tree, and identifies a managerial control strategy appropriate to various combinations of factors.

Management by exception

The fourth behavioral assumption of responsibility accounting is that reports emphasizing significantly large variances will induce managers to devote their time to those aspects of their operations that depart from the norm. We have referred to this before as the principle of management by exception.

The alternatives to exception reporting are so unsatisfactory that the exception reporting assumption is very difficult to deny. Omitting reports altogether, for example, isn't a realistic alternative. The importance of feedback information to reinforce individuals' commitments to their goals is too well documented to allow us to doubt the desirability of a reporting mechanism of some kind.[9]

A more serious alternative might be to report absolute results only, with

[9] A. Zander, *Motives and Goals in Groups* (New York: Academic Press, 1971).

Exhibit 22–4 Style, climate, and cultural influences on control behavior

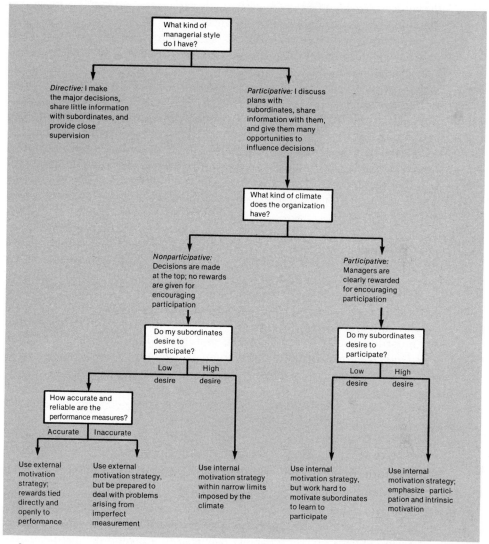

Source: Derived from Cortlandt Cammann and David A. Nadler, "Fit Control Systems to Your Managerial Style," *Harvard Business Review*, January–February 1976, pp. 65–72, with an assist from Lawler and Rhode, p. 185.

no explicit performance standards. This will be satisfactory if management can supply its own implicit standards. This becomes more and more difficult, however, as the organization becomes larger and more complex. For this reason it has to be ruled out as a general solution.

In short, the exception reporting assumption seems solidly grounded. One danger should be recognized, however. The reporting system may seem to emphasize failure, with only failures and extraordinary successes coming to the attention of higher management. Meeting the performance standard is successful performance, after all, but it ordinarily gets little recognition. Furthermore, the recognition given to favorable variances often seems to be weaker than the response to unfavorable variances.

Seeing these evidences of apparent bias, subordinates are led to view the system as punitive rather than informative. A common result is that people become defensive. They may question the fairness of the standard or use various devices to cover up variances as they arise and prevent them from being reported.

The focus on failures can also place a premium on cautious behavior. This may be consistent with the organization's goals, of course. For example, a food manufacturer cannot allow a supervisor to try to reduce cost by departing from the standard procedures used to kill bacteria, no matter how big the potential cost saving. The penalty to the company for failure of this experiment could be catastrophic, and any such experiment must take place in a formal research context.

In a research organization, in contrast, management may want to encourage the research staff to try new approaches that raise immediate costs but offer the possibility of completing projects ahead of time. Since these approaches may not work, however, the result may be unfavorable cost variances. If these are emphasized unduly, the research staff is likely to play it safe. This may have serious effects on the company's competitive position.[10]

This suggests that care should be taken to minimize the punitive role of the reporting system and emphasize its usefulness to the subordinate. Furthermore, major efforts should be made to emphasize positive as well as negative aspects of performance, to provide "positive reinforcement."

The controllability criterion

The fifth behavioral assumption of responsibility accounting is that managers are expected to respond only to variances arising within their own jurisdiction. Again the assumption itself seems inescapable, but two possible side effects should be guarded against:

1. Managers may attempt to shift responsibility—getting unfavorable variances assigned to others is one way of getting a better performance rating.
2. Overemphasis on controllability may lead to a greater compartmentalization of the organization.

The second of these is the more subtle of the two. By failing to recognize organizational interdependence, the responsibility accounting structure may add fuel to interdepartmental conflicts as the various managers seek to keep evidences of failure out of their own reports.

For example, sales and production ordinarily take place in different depart-

---

[10] In their study of large research organizations, Sayles and Chandler found a good deal of evidence of these tendencies. Leonard R. Sayles and Margaret K. Chandler, *Managing Large Systems: Organizations for the Future* (New York: Harper & Row, 1971), p. 299.

ments in a manufacturing firm. One department gets the orders; the other fills them. The sales force wants to be able to offer its customers the widest possible choice of products and features, all for prompt delivery. The task of the production manager, on the other hand, is a lot easier with long production runs and a steady delivery schedule. This requires fewer products, long lead times, and few or no special modifications to meet individual customer's needs. The production manager complains that the sales manager accepts orders that are very expensive to fill; the sales manager objects to the production manager's inflexibility and insensitivity to marketing problems. Both are right; the problem is how to get each manager to consider the other's point of view.

Many companies have attempted to obtain the necessary coordination among production, sales, and other functions by appointing product managers, one for each product. The product manager sees the interrelationships and attempts to reconcile the needs of the various parties. The project manager in a research organization has the same job, although usually with more authority than most product managers have.

Accountants haven't tried to attack this problem to any significant extent. One possibility is to issue reports on a project, product, or program basis rather than for individual departments. Thus a factory manager might get several reports, one for each product manufactured. Each of these reports would include sales figures as well as engineering and production costs. The implication would be that responsibility is shared rather than divided. Similarly, each department supervisor might get a report or reports showing total performance in a group of departments as well as a separate report for the supervisor's own department.

It may even be that the positive benefits of interdepartmental conflict make it undesirable to try to eliminate it entirely, even if that were possible. Interdepartmental conflict may be better than intradepartmental conflict, for example, and may be a relatively harmless way of letting the manager let off steam. It may also be a way of getting problems out in the open where they can at least be attacked, and maybe even solved.

Management's problem is to decide how much conflict is desirable. The accountant's problem is to design the reporting system so that it doesn't produce more conflict than management wants.

Harmonization of conflicting goals

Our final assumption is that when a responsibility segment has more than one goal, any conflicts between goals must be resolved outside the accounting system. Pollution abatement and current profit, for example, may be conflicting goals. Delivery speed and cost minimization may be another. The accounting system can report progress toward each of these goals, and may help management analyze the trade-offs between them, but the eventual resolution of any such conflicts is left outside the routine responsibility accounting system.

To reconcile conflicting organizational goals, the accounting system would have to measure all of them in monetary terms. Penalties for late delivery could be built into the responsibility reporting structure, for example; so could the cost of continuing pollution. If this were done, then both costs and benefits would be reflected in the responsible manager's control reports. Any conflict could be resolved by a simple comparison process.

Efforts to make major movements in this direction have generally foundered on measurement difficulties. One reaction to these difficulties has been to avoid measuring certain aspects of performance at all:

> *Example.* When asked what his company was doing to present its side of the argument to the public by demonstrating its progress toward pollution abatement, the financial officer of a large electric utility admitted that the only figures he had were summaries of expenditures. Further attempts at measurement were made only under pressure from governmental bodies.

The danger in this is that managers may be moved to emphasize those variables that are measured to the neglect of variables that are not. For example, the managers of staff departments may be led to concentrate exclusively on minimizing the current cost of performing their current functions. By ignoring the development of personnel in their departments, however, they may be depleting human capital. This may not show up in the accounting reports for several years.

Many control systems do measure variables that aren't reflected immediately in reports on financial performance. Variables such as market share, emission of pollutants, product reliability, absenteeism, and community activity are included—both in budgetary planning and in periodic feedback reporting. Nonmonetary measures are used because monetary equivalents are essentially unmeasurable.

Even as further progress is made in this direction, however, the resolution of conflicts between organizational goals must remain outside the responsibility accounting structure. Composite weighting systems, with performance on each variable weighted in proportion to its relative importance, just won't work. Managerial weighting systems are implicit rather than explicit, and extremely difficult to translate into numerical form. Even more fundamentally, the implicit weights refuse to stay constant. Market share may be the watchword today, but a share-oriented composite measure of performance will be obsolete when cost-cutting becomes the order of the day.

In short, no final solution to this problem has yet been found. A useful first step is to identify the major dimensions of performance, whether measurable or not. If this has been done, each of these can be incorporated into the performance review process. The accountant can contribute by seeking ways of measuring the nonfinancial aspects; higher management can help by trying to make the managerial reward structure more visible. In the final analysis, however, the process has to remain fluid, somewhat subjective, and the individual manager can never wholly escape the task of estimating the weights implicit in the structure.

Behavioral problems in system administration

Undesired behavioral responses to budgetary control systems sometimes arise from the methods of implementation rather than from any inherent defects. Two possible sources of such responses are:

1. Insensitivity on the part of the budgeting staff.
2. Irresponsibility of operating managers.

Insensitivity of the budgeting staff

A frequent complaint is that accountants and people on the budget director's staff are insensitive to operating problems and to the needs of operating managers. In many of their contacts with operating managers, the accountants appear as adversaries. Their job is to *criticize* budget proposals, to *investigate* variances, to *enforce* compliance with prescribed procedures, and to *keep higher management informed.* In short, they are paid to find fault with the operating manager—the more fault they find, the more successful they are apt to be.

Furthermore, accountants are likely to report their findings in the first instance to their boss or to higher levels of operating management rather than to the executives immediately concerned. These executives are likely to resent this and react by obstructing the accountants' work if they can.

As a consequence, accountants sometimes encounter defensiveness, hostility, and conflict. Accountants who are aware of these problems can avoid them or at least minimize their impact. One way is by changing their attitudes toward the job and toward the operating executives. By reporting their findings in the first place to the managers who have the responsibility to act, for example, the accountants can help these managers do their job. Doing this should help the accountants build more effective relationships.

A closely related possibility is to change most accountants' formal role to that of facilitators. In this way, most of the accounting people would spend their time providing feedback and working with the line managers on their problems and decisions. For example, the accountants can try to make sure that the operating managers have enough technical help before budgetary plans are submitted, thereby reducing the number of defects to be uncovered during the review process. Similarly, if they are engaged in postmortem investigations, they can incorporate in their reports the steps the managers are taking to respond to variances that have arisen.[11]

Irresponsibility of operating managers

Budgeting and performance review are stressful activities. Operating managers needing to relieve pressure at such times may be inclined to strike out at

---

[11] The results of a pioneering study of the relationships between accountants and operating personnel were summarized in a perceptive research report by Herbert A. Simon, George Kozmetsky, Harold Guetzkow, and Gordon Tyndall, *Centralization vs. Decentralization in Organizing the Controller's Department* (New York: Controllership Foundation, 1954).

the accountants, both because they are visible participants in these activities and because manager-accountant groups are less crucial than the other groupings in Exhibit 22–2. Fighting with the boss or with subordinates is dangerous business; fighting with accountants may seem safer.

Another result of this same problem is a tendency for managers to improve their relationships with their subordinates by citing the accountant or the budgeting system as the sources of burdensome requirements. For example, rather than ask a subordinate to do something because it is worth doing, the manager may justify the request on the grounds that the accountants insist on it. By making the accountants, the budget director, or even the system itself as the villain of the piece, the manager hopes to avoid unpleasant conflicts with subordinates. This also cuts down the amount of time spent explaining why something must be done.

This kind of behavior can make it difficult for the controller's staff to get their work done. The easiest solution to these difficulties is to play the same game—"I don't like this any better than you do, but top management says it has to be done." A better approach in the long run is to keep explaining the process and, even better, keep producing useful results. Managers who find the responsibility accounting system helpful are likely to cooperate with the accountants much more readily than those who don't.[12]

Summary

The responsibility accounting structure is based on a number of implicit assumptions about the behavior of individuals and groups making up the organization. The most fundamental of these is that individuals will strive to achieve the performance levels represented in the current operating budget. The mechanism that is relied upon to accomplish this is participation in managerial decision making by managers at all operating levels. Participation is designed to get the managers to internalize the budgetary standards, thereby converting them into personal aspiration levels. Participation works best when the superior's personal style is open, when the organizational climate is favorable to participation, and when the subordinates have a strong desire to participate. Participation in these situations can harness the forces leading to intrinsic motivation.

Participation is unlikely to have much effect when the superior manager's style is autocratic, the climate is restrictive, and the subordinate manager would rather receive orders than participate. In intermediate situations, management may try to use the positive aspects of group dynamics to secure some of the motivational benefits of participation. If a group can be induced to accept performance standards, each member of the group will find it easier to accept them as well.

The accounting structure also contains potentially destructive elements. Management by exception and the concept of controllability, for example, can lead to excessive departmentalization of effort and counterproductive efforts

---

[12] David A. Nadler, Philip H. Mirvis, and Cortlandt Cammann, "The Ongoing Feedback System: Experimenting with a New Managerial Tool," *Organizational Dynamics,* Spring 1976, pp. 63–80.

to shift blame or the chance of being blamed. Furthermore, the very nature of the accountant's job creates opportunities for conflict with operating personnel. If senior management tries to use the budget as a pressure device, these opportunities multiply and lead eventually to counterproductive behavior.

Solutions to most of the behavioral problems that arise in connection with the budgetary control system lie outside the accounting area. The accountant can contribute to these solutions, however: first, by being more sensitive to the needs and attitudes of operating personnel; and second, by devising methods of measurement and reporting that will further the control objectives of operating management.

Exercises and problems

1.   **Setting the standard performance level.**   Alpha Company is installing a standard costing system in its factory for the first time. You have been asked to choose among four possible bases for setting standards. To help you choose, management has given the following data on container costs for one of the company's products:

1.   Each unit of product requires one container.
2.   Average performance last year: 1,050 containers used per 1,000 units of product.
3.   Average performance of engineering department test run using average experienced workers: 1,030 containers used per 1,000 units of product.
4.   Best performance found by engineering department: 1,015 containers used per 1,000 units of product.

Required:

a.   Taking each of these four standards in turn, indicate what the materials usage variance would mean and whether it is more likely to be favorable or unfavorable.

b.   Taking behavioral factors into account, which of these standards would you choose? How would you introduce it? Give the reasons for your choice.

2.   **Setting a standard performance level.**   The Alton Company is expanding its punch press department. It is about to purchase three new punch presses from Equipment Manufacturers, Inc. Equipment Manufacturers' engineers report that their mechanical studies indicate that for Alton's intended use, the output rate for one press should be 1,000 pieces an hour.

Alton has similar presses now in operation. Production from these presses averaged 600 pieces an hour last month, based on the following record of performance:

Worker	Hourly Output
L. Jones	750
J. Green	750
R. Smith	600
H. Brown	500
R. Alters	550
G. Hoag	450
Total	3,600
Average	600

Alton's management also plans to institute a standard cost accounting system in the near future. The company's engineers are supporting a standard based on 1,000 pieces an hour, the accounting department is arguing for 750 pieces an hour, and the production department supervisor is arguing for 600 pieces an hour.

Required:

a. What arguments would the various proponents be likely to use to support their recommendations?
b. Which alternative best reconciles the needs of cost control and the motivation of improved performance? Explain why you made that choice.

(CMA, adapted)

3. **Group dynamics.** Bert Jackson got a summer job. He worked in an office with three other people, all of whom has been on the job for about a month when Bert was hired. Bert had just finished his freshman year in college; Carl Martin, the team leader and the oldest member of the team, had just graduated from college and planned to enroll as a part-time law student in the fall.

Carl reported to Janet Davis, the office manager. Janet was a woman in her late 30s and had been with the company for more than 15 years. She supervised a staff of six full-time employees in addition to Carl's team of temporary workers. She also used part-time employees for peak clerical loads.

The team's assignment was to convert the office's master customer file into a form suitable for computerization. The worker first took the customer's folder from the file and copied data from it onto a special form. He or she obtained additional data from one or more directories; occasionally a subsidiary file was consulted, and on rare occasions Janet was asked to supply some missing information.

The completed forms were assembled in batches of 50. Each week the team was expected to deliver seven batches to the keypunch operators in the computer center. Once a month the forms and a computer printout were returned to the office for verification. The team had been complimented several times on the accuracy of its work.

Each member of the team, including Carl and Bert, did the same work; none of them specialized in any one phase of it. Once or twice a day Janet asked Carl to send someone on an errand. These assignments usually went to Bert, who welcomed the change of pace.

Bert learned the job quickly and by the second day was completing as many forms as each of the others. His first Friday on the job he reported to his family that the team had completed 430 forms that week but had turned in only seven batches of 50 forms each. The reason was to have a reserve for next week, in case the team didn't meet the 350 unit quota then. "After all," Bert said, "we don't want them to raise our quota. If we turned in eight batches this week, they'd expect us to do that every week."

At the end of the second week Carl reported to Janet that Bert was working out very well and should be moved from probationary status with a raise of 10 cents an hour. Seven batches of forms were turned in, with 60 forms held back for the next week.

Required:

a. Comment on the group processes observed here.
b. What action, if any, should Janet take after accidentally discovering that the team occasionally holds back part of its production. What alternatives did you consider and why did you reject them?

4. **Multiple performance criteria.** Berton, Inc., is a large, decentralized electronics firm. Berton uses a multiple criteria performance evaluation system in measuring the achievements of its divisions. The criteria used are:

1. Profitability.
2. Market position.

3. Productivity.
4. Product leadership.
5. Personnel development.
6. Strengthening of employee attitudes.
7. Public responsibility.
8. Balance between short-range and long-range goals.

Management is now considering a proposal to combine these eight criteria in a single index which would be used to measure the overall performance of each division's management.

Required:

a. Identify and discuss briefly the advantages of a multiple criteria performance system over a single criterion performance system.
b. Is the use of multiple criteria in this situation likely to lead toward goal congruence? Explain.
c. Assuming management has been able to develop some kind of rating scale for each of the eight listed criteria, what would management have to do to enable the controller's staff to consolidate the eight ratings and combine them into a single index of managerial performance? What difficulties would management encounter in developing and administering a system of this sort?
d. Suppose management has been able to surmount the difficulties you identified in your answer to (c). What impact would it have on you if you were a division manager?

(CMA, adapted)

5. **Plant controller's role.**   When he retired in 19x2, Ted Osborn had been controller at Massena Company's Saratoga plant for 20 years. His replacement in the plant controller's job, Ray Tibbs, was 33 years old and had been with the company for six years, first as a staff assistant to Massena's corporate controller and then for three years as assistant plant controller at the company's largest plant. At Saratoga, Mr. Tibbs reported directly to Phil Haymes, the plant manager.

After a month on his new job, Mr. Tibbs told Mr. Haymes that the plant's procedures for recording the purchase and receipt of materials didn't conform to the procedures spelled out in the corporate controller's manual. He also said he'd found out that reports on the plant's inventory position the plant had to send to Massena's headquarters each month had been based for many years on informal guesses because the plant's record-keeping system didn't provide the required data soon enough. He told Mr. Haymes he expected to be able to make the necessary changes in about six months to correct both of those problems.

Mr. Tibbs also mentioned that the Saratoga plant didn't have as good a cost and production reporting system as Mr. Tibbs had worked with in his previous plant. He asked Mr. Haymes for approval to develop procedures that would allow him to give plant management at all levels the kinds of information management at his former plant had found useful. He thought he could make these changes, as well as the procedural changes now underway, without adding any new personnel. He would need some help from the computer systems analyst and one of the computer programmers in the plant, however, and two or three of the plant accounting staff would have to receive some outside training so they could operate the new system.

These changes seemed quite sweeping to Mr. Haymes, and that evening he called Mr. Osborn for advice. Mr. Osborn said he knew the procedures didn't "follow the book," as he put it, but he'd always managed to get his reports out on time. Nobody had ever complained about his work, either. "Sure, we guessed the inventory figures," he said, "but nobody ever used them anyway. We always picked up any errors in the annual inventory count."

Mr. Osborn sighed when told that Mr. Tibbs wanted to revise the internal reporting system. "You have to watch these young people. They're always wanting to change things. He hasn't talked to me about these changes, but my old staff lets me know what's going on. I tell them to be patient—he'll calm down after a while. Anyway, I always gave you what I thought you needed and you never objected."

Required:

a. What organizational and behavioral problems did Mr. Tibbs face as he moved into his new job?

b. How much leeway should Mr. Haymes have in determining the scope of Mr. Tibb's work and the way he carries it out?

c. Were Mr. Tibb's actions appropriate in the circumstances? In what ways, if any, could he have proceeded more effectively? Were Mr. Osborn's criticisms well founded?

6. **Production standards; interdepartmental conflict.** Campo Motor Parts, Inc. manufactures a wide variety of automotive parts and supplies. A basic plan standard costing system is in use in each of its factories.

One of the company's lines is a line of windshield wipers for trucks and passenger vehicles. The windshield wiper consists of four principal mechanical parts: the blade, the blade holder, the wiper arm, and a mounting bracket. The blade holders and wiper arms are made in the metal shop, the mounting brackets are made in the casting department, and the blades are purchased from a rubber manufacturer.

Holders, arms, brackets and blades are assembled in the assembly department. The blades, blade holders, and arms are brought together in a subassembly. This is then fitted on a mounting bracket. If the subassembly fits, the assembled mechanism is placed in a box and readied for transfer to the shipping room, where it is mated with an electrical actuating mechanism that is produced elsewhere in the factory.

Each batch of parts is inspected before delivery to the assembly department. Slight flaws are difficult to detect, however, and often show up only as the units are being assembled. A particularly common problem is a poor fit between the arm and blade assembly and the mounting bracket. This can be corrected by the assembler, but the correction takes from 10 to 60 seconds.

The standard assembly time includes provision for a normal percentage of defective parts and subassemblies. Whenever a sizable unfavorable labor usage variance arises, however, the chief of assembly is inclined to claim that defective parts were the cause. The head of the castings department says that process control in that department is so tight that the mounting brackets cannot be at fault. The metal shop supervisor believes that the chief of assembly is merely trying to pass the buck. If excessive defects do occur, however, they must come from the casting process.

The plant manager has learned to live with this kind of bickering, but lately the problem has become much worse. Several months ago the company introduced a new type of wiper, requiring much tighter fitting parts. Engineered standard times were established for the new model on the basis of time studies. Labor variances in the castings department and the metal shop have been negligible; in the assembly department they have been large and unfavorable. The product manager insists that if these cost problems cannot be licked the work will be subcontracted to an outside firm. The plant manager doesn't want this to happen and has asked your advice.

Required:

a. Is it likely that the standard costing system is partly responsible for the high costs of the new model? Give reasons to support your point of view.

b. What changes, if any, would you make in the measurement and reporting system to alleviate the problems that have arisen? Give reasons for the position you have taken.

7. **Performance standards for motivation.**   Ray Carlson, president of Scientific Equipment Manufacturing Company, wants to introduce standard costing into his company's factory. As a result of his participation in a two-week management development course at a nearby university, Mr. Carlson is convinced that some kind of standard costing system is just what he needs to strengthen his control over factory cost. The factory now has a simple job order costing system, and no one has ever attempted to establish standard costs.

Scientific Equipment makes and sells a line of highly technical equipment for industrial users. The company is located in a small midwestern city with a population of 80,000 people. Quality, or the supplier's ability to meet exacting technical specifications, is a major consideration for most of the company's customers when deciding where to place an order.

Production is organized on a job order basis, and orders are typically manufactured to customer specifications. Most of the orders can be filled by producing items of standard design and specifications, or items which require only minor modifications of the standard designs. Jobs requiring major redesign and the use of nonstandardized production techniques amount to 30 percent of the total. The cost estimates that Mr. Carlson uses in developing price bids for this kind of nonstandardized business have been close to the actual costs of filling the orders in most cases, or at least close enough to satisfy Mr. Carlson.

Scientific Equipment is a small company, with about 75 employees. The two largest segments of the work force are 30 machine operators and 20 assemblers. The machine operators are all men. Their jobs require a considerable degree of skill and experience. The assemblers, on the other hand, are all women. Their jobs are relatively routine but require a good deal of concentration to avoid costly assembly defects. The employees generally lunch together in a nearby cafeteria. Many of the men socialize off the job, and so do several of the women.

Mr. Carlson is considering engaging a consulting firm to develop and install a standard costing system. A letter from the managing partner of the consulting firm contained the following key paragraphs:

> In order to motivate people to their maximum productivity, standards must be based upon the company's best workers and what they can achieve. If the standard were lower, the high performers could meet it too easily and it wouldn't offer sufficient motivation for the low performers. I'd set the standard at the level of performance of the top 10 to 15 percent of your employees. This would establish a high aspiration level for your people and, therefore, motivate their best efforts.
>
> I also suggest that superior performance be well rewarded. This means that employees who exceed standard should receive a substantial bonus, while those who do not exceed standard should receive no bonus.

Since Mr. Carlson doesn't feel qualified to evaluate this kind of statement, he has contacted the faculty member who conducted the sessions on standard costing at the local university (you), asking what you think of the philosophy underlying the proposed system.

Required:

a. Prepare a reply to Mr. Carlson. Should he engage the consultant?

b. If you agree with the consultant's basic approach, outline how you would implement it at Scientific Equipment Manufacturing Company. If you disagree with the consultant, state the basic principles underlying an alternative system and outline how you would go about developing a standard costing system for this company.

(Prepared by Eric Flamholtz)

8. **Separate standards for motivation and for control.**   Harden Company was experiencing increased production costs. The primary area of concern identified

by management was direct labor. The company was considering adopting a standard cost system to help control labor and other costs. Useful historical data were not available because detailed production records had not been maintained.

Harden Company retained Finch & Associates, an engineering consulting firm, to establish labor standards. After a complete study of the work process, the engineers recommended a labor standard of 1 unit of production every 30 minutes or 16 units a day for each worker. Finch further advised that Harden's wage rates were below the prevailing rate of $12 an hour.

Harden's production vice president thought this labor standard was too tight and the employees would be unable to attain it. From his experience with the labor force, he believed a labor standard of 40 minutes a unit or 12 units a day for each worker would be more reasonable.

Dan Jones, Harden's president, believed the standard should be set at a high level to motivate the workers, but he also recognized the standard should be set at a level to provide adequate information for control and reasonable cost comparisons. After much discussion, the management decided to use a dual standard. The labor standard recommended by the engineering firm of one unit every 30 minutes would be employed in the plant as a motivation device, and a cost standard of 40 minutes a unit would be used in reporting. Management also concluded that the workers would not be informed of the cost standard used for reporting purposes. The production vice president conducted several sessions prior to implementation in the plant informing the workers of the new standard cost system and answering questions. The new standards were not related to incentive pay but were introduced at the time wages were increased to $12 an hour.

The new standard cost system was implemented on January 1. At the end of six months of operation, the following statistics on labor performance were presented to top management:

	Jan.	Feb.	Mar.	Apr.	May	June
Production (units) ...	5,100	5,000	4,700	4,500	4,300	4,400
Direct labor hours ...	3,000	2,900	2,900	3,000	3,000	3,100
Variance from labor standard	$5,400U	$4,800U	$6,600U	$9,000U	$10,200U	$10,800U
Variance from cost standard	$4,800F	$5,200F	$2,800F	$ 0	$ 1,600U	$2,000U

Raw material quality, labor mix, and plant facilities and conditions did not change to any great extent during the six-month period.

Required:

a. Discuss the impact of different types of standards on motivation, and specifically discuss the effect on motivation in Harden Company's plant of adopting the labor standard recommended by the engineering firm.

b. Evaluate Harden Company's decision to employ dual standards in its standard cost system.

(CMA)

9. **Staff-line relationships.*** Sussex Products, Ltd., is a British manufacturer of a diversified line of industrial cleaning compounds, disinfectants, and pesticides. Its production division consists of six manufacturing plants and a small divisional headquarters staff. On September 3, 1973, P. J. Evans, manager of the production

---

* Abridged version of a case, Sussex Products, Ltd. (A), copyright by l'Institut pour l'Etude des Méthodes de Direction de l'Entreprise (IMEDE), Lausanne, Switzerland. Reproduced by permission.

division, sent the following memorandum to T. P. E. Brown, the manager of the Leatherslade plant:

> We draw your attention to the following section of our regulations for internal control (ACC/17—6/6/69):
>
> "The allocation of duties and responsibilities within a plant shall be designed in such a way that there will be a system of checks and balances whereby the work of one employee shall always be checked by the work of another employee, working independently."
>
> We are, of course, of the opinion that plant managers should do their utmost to avoid loss to the company from fraud by employees. On the other hand, we are also particularly anxious to keep paperwork in our productive units to a strict minimum. We therefore point out that there should be no duplication of work merely for the sake of control, and that control systems should be devised in such a way that the work of one clerk can be checked with the work that another clerk would have done anyway.

On January 13, 1974, F. G. Marples, a member of the company's internal audit staff, arrived at the Leatherslade plant, carrying the following letter from Mr. Evans to Mr. Brown:

> This letter serves to introduce the bearer, Mr. F. G. Marples, who has been charged by management to undertake an internal audit of your plant.
>
> The scope of his audit is determined by accepted auditing practice and will include in particular an examination of control procedures in the light of the company's regulations for internal control (ACC/17—6/6/69).
>
> Mr. Marples is to have access to all the books of account and records necessary to complete his audit and we are sure we can rely on you to see that he is provided with all the explanations of which he stands in need.
>
> He will discuss with you the findings of his audit before he leaves your plant.

A week later Mr. Brown telephoned Mr. Evans to complain about the behavior of Mr. Marples and his assistant, and followed his call with the following memorandum:

> As I explained on the phone, I find it difficult to hold myself responsible for the reactions of my people to the internal auditors' attitude to their task. Quite apart from the auditors' inability to observe the common forms of politeness and business etiquette with supervisory staff and their attempt to browbeat employees with many years' service with the company, matters were brought to a head this week when Mr. Marples' assistant was discovered after the normal closing hours hiding behind the stocks in the finished goods warehouse. I can only assume that the purpose of this subterfuge was to spy on warehouse staff who were having to work overtime as a result of the delay occasioned in their work by the lengthy checking and rechecking of finished goods stocks insisted on by the auditors.
>
> As you know, our union is becoming particularly militant in preparation for our negotiations with them which are due this spring. I therefore requested that the audit at present be discontinued and resumed later in the year. You, however, stated that for head office reasons the audit must go on.

That same day Mr. Marples wrote B. W. Smith, the company's chief auditor, as follows:

> As this is a first audit, one naturally expects some difficulties to arise, but I very much regret to report that in this instance there seems to be some definite ill will in the reaction of plant management.
>
> I had the usual discussion with the plant manager on the second day we

were here and explained to him the purpose and scope of our audit, but unfortunately was unable to elicit any positive reaction from him. In the following days the atmosphere rapidly degenerated to the point where both Mr. Walker and I were followed whenever we left the office to check anything in the plant.

The day before yesterday Mr. Walker returned to the finished goods warehouse to recover some notes which he had inadvertently left there, whereupon he was grasped by both arms by one of the factory foremen who had followed him there and was taken by force to the manager's office.

I would not normally bother you with the details of such rather childish behavior were it not for veiled threats subsequently issued by Mr. Brown that this incident, which I consider to have been rigged, was to be used for political purposes at head office.

Required:

a. Assuming Mr. Marples' statement of the facts is accurate, what is your explanation of Mr. Brown's hostility and lack of cooperation?

b. What, if anything, could Messrs. Evans, Smith, and Marples have done to avoid the difficulties which arose?

23 Classification and analysis of variances from standard cost

Unit standard costs and flexible budgets can be used to develop spending variances for direct labor, direct materials, and departmental overhead costs, in the ways we described in Chapters 9–11. The spending variances can be subdivided into input price and usage components by applying standard prices to the input quantities actually used in operations. These breakdowns may not be fine enough to meet management's needs, however. The main purpose of this chapter is to show why and how additional detail may be provided and used.

Usage variances in standard costing on the comprehensive plan

Labor and materials variances can be subdivided as part of the regular cost-recording routine. We use the term *comprehensive plan* to refer to systems which derive detailed variance information in this way. Management is most likely to adopt the comprehensive plan when the first level managers need steering control information—that is, when they must rely on detailed usage variance information in deciding how to respond to usage variances. To see why this is so, we need to examine five questions:

1. What the comprehensive plan is and how it differs from the basic plan.
2. What kinds of reports can be generated from data derived under the comprehensive plan.
3. How the causes of individual variances are likely to be identified and reported.
4. How a set of accounts might be constructed and used to implement the comprehensive plan.
5. What benefits and costs are likely to appear under the comprehensive plan.

Characteristics of the comprehensive plan

The comprehensive plan has three main characteristics that distinguish it from the basic plan:[1]

1. Direct labor and materials usage variances are identified as the work is performed. (In basic plan systems these variances are identified at the end of the reporting period.)
2. Direct labor and materials usage variances are available in great detail and can be classified on many different bases. (In basic plan systems these variances are available only as production center totals for the reporting period as a whole.)
3. Work-in-Process account balances are stated at standard cost at all times. (In the basic plan the Work-in-Process account balances are stated at standard cost only at the end of each period.)

All of these differences hinge on the ability of the system to identify the usage variances as they occur. This is done by putting more data on the labor time tickets and materials requisitions than they carry in a basic plan.

Labor time tickets. For the comprehensive plan, a separate time ticket must be prepared for each separate labor operation. A sample time ticket is shown in Exhibit 23–1. Each ticket is a record of the work done and of the variance arising from it. Time is recorded in this case in 10ths of hours. All the data on this form can be written or punched in advance except the actual time and the variance time. Data from the file of standard wage rates can then be used to restate these figures in dollars and cents.

Exhibit 23–1 Comprehensive plan labor time ticket

Item: Base plate No. 423	Date 4/7/x1
Batch quantity: 1,000 pieces	
	Actual hours:
Operation: 472—Press	Finish _____ 11.1
Department: A	Start _____ 8.1
Operator: P. Jones	Difference _____ 3.0
Job No.: X4474	Standard hours _2.5_
	Variance hours _0.5_

Materials requisitions. When materials usage is recorded by flow meters, as in some chemical operations, the usage variances can be identified on materials usage forms similar to labor time tickets. When a requisition system is used, however, the usage variances and the standard costs of the work done may be recorded separately. At the time a production order is prepared, a

---

[1] *Comprehensive plan* and *basic plan* are terms used here to describe the main features of two different kinds of standard costing systems. Specific details of these systems will vary widely from company to company, but their main characteristics can be recognized quite easily. The basic plan is described in Chapter 9.

Exhibit 23–2 Use of materials requisitions in the comprehensive plan

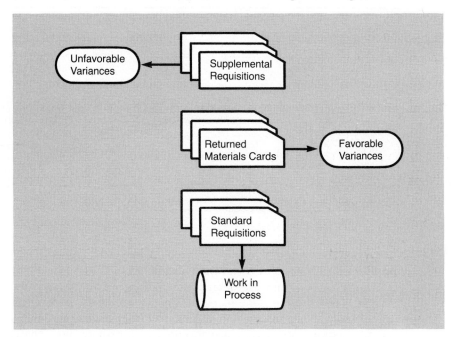

standard requisition card is prepared for the standard quantity of each material shown on the standard cost sheet. When a department begins work on the job, the department head exchanges the cards for the standard quantities shown on them.

Whenever additional materials are issued to cover excessive spoilage as the job progresses, a supplemental requisition card of a different color and with a distinctive code number is prepared, showing the quantity and code number of each of the supplemental materials. Similarly, if a job is completed without consuming all of the materials issued, the excess materials are returned to the stockroom, where a returned materials card is filled out with the quantity of each material returned.

The supplemental requisitions in this system measure the unfavorable materials usage variances; the returned materials cards measure the favorable variances, as we can see in Exhibit 23–2. Each standard requisition measures the amount of work done, the amount to be added to the work in process. The file of standard materials prices can be used to restate all these figures in monetary terms.

Comprehensive plan reporting to management

The comprehensive plan allows the accountant to prepare variance reports in great detail. In many factories, for example, a printout of the previous day's labor performance is placed on each supervisor's desk at the start of

Exhibit 23–3 Daily labor variance report

			Variance	
Operator	Standard Hours	Actual Direct Hours (Including Personal Time)	Hours	Percent of Standard
Brown, P.	8.2	8.0	0.2	2.4
Conrad, T. T.	8.6	8.0	0.6	7.0
Ennis, J.	3.3	4.0	(0.7)	(21.2)
Gordon, L.	8.4	9.5	(1.1)	(13.1)
King, M.	7.9	8.0	(0.1)	(1.3)

Department: Machining
Supervisor: P. B. Naum
Date: 3/6

each workday, with a separate line or lines for each operator. A truncated example of such a report is shown in Exhibit 23–3.

Reports of this kind are appropriate if they are to be used as steering controls. They may help the manager identify problems, trace them to their source, and do something about them before they have done much damage. Too frequent reporting may actually defeat its own purpose, however, by not making sufficient allowance for normal fluctuations in productive efficiency. Additional detail also makes reports difficult to read and obscures significant relationships. It also increases system cost. It is especially inappropriate when the manager's main need is for scorecard information rather than for steering control information.

For all these reasons, selective reporting is probably a better solution. At one extreme, the detailed variance data can be placed in a file, available to anyone who may need a special analysis for a specific purpose, but not reported routinely to anyone. Alternatively, only variances larger than specified amounts or percentages might be reported, all others remaining on file for later summarization and analysis.

Recording the causes of usage variances

Even though the department head may be able to identify the causes of variances as they occur, higher management cannot. The system may be designed, therefore, to keep track of the most important causes of variances, not for steering controls, but to provide scorecard information on the control efforts of the production center managers. To make this possible, someone close to the operation has to identify the cause of each usage variance larger than some threshold amount and enter this explanation on the time ticket. The amounts in each category are then summarized and reported to management each month.

Comprehensive causal identification systems are costly and therefore rare. Management usually does ask, however, that variances due to certain specific causes be identified routinely and reported periodically. These are causes that are likely to occur frequently if they are not kept under control. When this is done, the usage variances will be reported in two sections—those due to the specified causes, one by one, and those due to all other causes combined.

Factorywide Work-in-Process accounts

One way to implement the comprehensive plan is to use the familiar sequential inventory account structure, with separate accounts for materials and parts, work in process, and finished goods inventories. The procedure can be described as a series of six steps:

1. Set up a single, plantwide Work-in-Process account.
2. Set up departmental usage variance accounts.
3. Charge standard costs to the Work-in-Process account.
4. Charge or credit usage variances to the variance accounts as they occur.
5. Record interdepartmental transfers in physical quantities only.
6. Transfer the standard cost of work completed from the Work-in-Process account to finished goods inventory accounts.

Step 1. Set up a single Work-in-Process account for the entire factory and enter the standard cost of the inventory in process at the beginning of the period. The Colson Company's work in process in its two factory departments at the beginning of September had a standard materials cost of $4,290, a standard labor cost of $2,110, and standard overhead cost of $3,900, for a total of $10,300. The Work-in-Process account therefore showed the following:

Work-in-Process

Bal. 9/1 10,300	

The components of standard cost—three cost elements in each department— aren't segregated in separate inventory accounts because the balance in a single Work-in-Process account can serve as a control total for the entire factory.

Step 2. Set up a usage variance account for each direct materials and each direct labor cost element in each production center. The Colson Company uses two such accounts for each department, one for labor and one for materials. Additional usage variance accounts may be provided if the causes of portions of the variance are to be identified as part of the normal cost recording routine.

Step 3. Charge the Work-in-Process account for the standard labor and materials costs of the operations performed during the period. During September the machining department used standard requisitions to draw materials with a total standard materials cost of $31,800. The entry summarizing these requisitions was:

(1)

Work-in-Process	31,800	
Materials and Parts		31,800

This traced the movement of the materials from the storeroom to the factory floor.

Step 4. Charge or credit the departmental usage variance accounts for all differences between actual and standard quantities used, measured at standard prices or wage rates. Separate materials requisitions are prepared for materials required in excess of the standard quantities. The entry summarizing the standard cost of the materials issued on these supplemental requisitions to the machining department during the month of September was:

(2)

Materials Usage Variance—Machining	2,350	
Materials and Parts		2,350

Conversely, returned materials cards are evidence of less than standard usage and lead to credits to the variance account. The standard cost of the returned materials in this case was $450, summarized in the following entry:

(3)

Materials and Parts	450	
Materials Usage Variance—Machining		450

Because the amounts shown on the supplemental requisitions exceeded the total amounts shown on the returned materials cards, the net materials usage variance for the period was unfavorable. It was shown directly by the balance in the usage variance account at the end of the period:

Materials Usage Variance—Machining

(2) Supplemental requisitions	2,350	(3) Returned materials	450
Bal. 1,900			

The individual supplemental requisitions and returned materials cards then provided a basis for detailed analysis of the overall variance by job or product or type of materials.

The Colson Company's procedures for recording labor time are similar, except that both the standard time and the variance from standard are recorded on the time ticket, not on separate documents. The standard costs shown on the time tickets are debited to the Work-in-Process account, while the differences between these amounts and the actual times recorded on the tickets are either debited or credited to the variance accounts.

In this case, the standard labor cost of the work done in the machining department during the month totaled $17,000. This amount was charged to work-in-process. An additional $930 in direct labor costs, again at the standard wage rates, was charged directly to the usage variance account because actual time on some of the time tickets was greater than the standard time. This was partially offset by favorable variances on other jobs, however, and these totaled $430. These figures can all be summarized in a single entry:

(4)

Work-in-Process	17,000	
Labor Usage Variance—Machining	930	
Labor Usage Variance—Machining		430
Payroll Cost Summary		17,500

The Labor Usage Variance—Machining account now has a debit balance of $500, reflecting labor performance slightly poorer than standard:

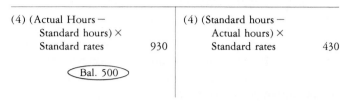

Labor Usage Variance—Machining

(4) (Actual Hours − Standard hours) × Standard rates	930	(4) (Standard hours − Actual hours) × Standard rates	430
Bal. 500			

Another variance was detected in this case after the machining department performed its work. Several castings in one job lot were spoiled in the machining operation and had to be scrapped. The standard costs of these spoiled casting were: standard materials, labor, and overhead costs in other departments (regarded by the machining department as the cost of the materials it receives), $80; standard labor cost of the operations performed in the machining department, $5. The $5 standard direct labor cost in machining was included in the $17,000 entered in Work-in-Process by entry (4).

The full $85 could be treated as an addition to the machining department's variances in September—$80 for materials and $5 for labor—but since both components came from the same cause, management preferred to see the entire amount as a single figure, the cost of spoilage. The required entry therefore was a credit to Work-in-Process, to show that the work represented by these costs was no longer in process, and a debit to an overhead account:

(5)

Spoilage Cost—Machining	85	
Work-in-Process		85

The balance in the spoilage cost account would be reported to management at the end of the month, in comparison with the flexible budget for spoilage at the month's actual production level.

Step 5. Make no entry to record the transfer of semiprocessed work from production center to production center; records of departmental inventories in process are maintained in physical quantities only. Once the decision has been made to use a single work-in-process account for the entire factory, transfers of partially processed goods from one department to another neither increase nor decrease the amounts covered by this account.

Step 6. Credit the Work-in-Process account and charge the Finished Goods Inventory account for the actual quantities of goods finished during the period. The final transfer of products to the finished goods warehouse is the signal to the accounting department to transfer the standard cost of the completed products from Work-in-Process to the Finished Goods Inventory account. As each job was finished, a copy of the job order was detached and sent to the accounting office. The accountants consulted the standard cost file to find the standard cost of the units completed in each job. Adding these together for the entire month, the accountants found that the standard cost of all jobs completed in September was $118,000. Since these jobs were no longer in process at the end of September, their costs had to be removed from the Work-in-Process account. The entry was:

(6)

Finished Goods Inventory	118,000	
Work-in-Process		118,000

This included the standard costs of all operations performed and all materials required in all departments, not just the department in which final processing took place. (If the completed units are component parts, delivered to the parts storeroom for later use in production, the charge will be to a materials and parts inventory account.)

The factory started the month with a Work-in-Process balance of only $10,300. Entry (1) recorded $31,800 in standard materials issued to the machining department, while entry (4) recorded $17,000 in standard labor cost in that department, and entry (5) took $85 out of Work-in-Process as a result of spoilage. The Work-in-Process account was also debited for other standard costs during the month:

Standard overhead cost—machining	$34,000
Standard direct materials cost—casting	27,000
Standard direct labor cost—casting	15,200
Standard overhead cost—casting	18,500
Total	$94,700

After entry (6) and all other entries were posted, the Work-in-Process account showed the following:

Work-in-Process

Bal.	10,300	(5)	85
(1)	31,800	(6)	118,000
(4)	17,000		
(x)	94,700		
Bal. 35,715			

If all entries were made correctly, the work in process on September 30 had a standard cost of $35,715.

Costs and benefits of the comprehensive plan

Many factors enter into the design of a standard costing system, such as the availability of competent people, the strength of management's commitment to standard costing, and the amount of time the accountants have to get the system installed. The two most important considerations are the benefits management hopes to gain from the system and the costs of installing and operating it. Comprehensive plan systems are likely to be more costly than the basic plan systems we described in Chapter 9. System costs depend largely on the number of documents to be processed, the amount of data to be extracted from them, the amount of processing to be done, the size and accessibility of the files, and the number and complexity of the reports to be issued. All of these factors relate to the amount of detail to be provided and the frequency of the control reports. The greater the detail and the more frequent the reports, the higher the cost. Since these are characteristics of the comprehensive plan, it is likely to be more costly than a basic plan system.

The benefits of comprehensive plan systems, if any, arise mainly from their usefulness as steering controls, to alert first-level supervisors to situations needing immediate attention. When this is important, then the accounting reports need to come out quickly, frequently, and in great detail. This is what the comprehensive plan does.

The second benefit from the comprehensive plan is that it provides a file of data management can draw on for more detailed scorecard information than is available under the basic plan. Variances can be summarized by equipment, by operator, by product, and so forth. A manager, for example, may be fully aware of the difficulties of maintaining standards on a particular machine; the variance file provides a cumulative record of how costly these difficulties are. This record may even provide the necessary support for a proposal to replace the machine.

The final decision must reflect management's comparison of the added costs of the comprehensive plan with the benefits to be gained. The important thing is to pose the question in this form, to avoid elaborating the system when a simpler system would do the job management has in mind.

Statistical approaches to variance investigation

Routine recording of the causes of the usage variances generated by a comprehensive plan system is cumbersome and costly. An alternative approach is to use statistical techniques to decide when a variance is big enough and important enough to warrant investigation. This section deals with two related techniques: (1) the development and use of statistical control limits; and (2) a cost/benefit investigation decision model.

Statistical control limits

No process is likely to be so rigidly programmed that no deviation is possible as long as the process is in control. A certain amount of random variation around the standard is expected.

This notion is embodied in *statistical control charts,* like the one illustrated in Exhibit 23–4. The solid line running horizontally across the middle of this chart represents the expected average time required for a specific operation on a specific machine. The horizontal dashed lines above and below it represent the limits within which actual operating times would normally be expected to fall. If actual performance remains within these limits, the variance is presumed to result from noncontrollable, random forces; if an observation falls outside the limits it is presumed to be the result of some event or condition out of the ordinary.

The control chart in Exhibit 23–4 was used by the managers of a machine shop to monitor the operating performance of a hand-operated polishing machine. Five time tickets were chosen at random each day and the average

Exhibit 23–4 Statistical control chart

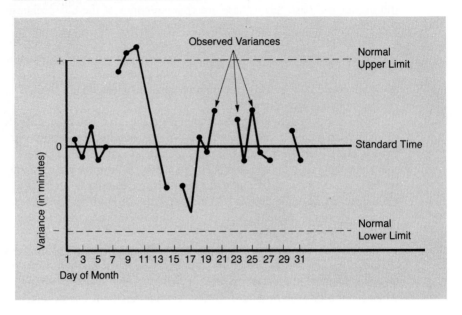

variance percentage was plotted on the chart. When the upper limit was breached on the 10th of the month, an investigation was made. By the 12th of the month, performance was well down in the normal range again.

Whether an observation outside the limits is significant depends on how the limits were chosen and how stable the process is. Ideally, the limits should be based on the variation found in a set of historical observations, made when the operation presumably was in a state of control. If these observations distributed themselves normally around their mean, then statistical confidence intervals can be calculated from the standard deviation(s) of the observations. The standard deviation is calculated from the following formula:

$$s = \sqrt{\frac{\Sigma(y - \bar{y})^2}{n - 1}}$$

in which

$y =$ Observed value.
$\bar{y} =$ Mean of the observed values.
$n =$ Number of observations.

As long as operating conditions remain unchanged, we can be confident (for reasons explained in the appendix to this chapter) that there is only 1 chance in 100 that an observation falling more than 2.58 standard deviations from the mean resulted from a random fluctuation in the process.[2] The other 99 percent of the time it will be the result of some nonrandom event or condition.

---

[2] If the standard is not equal to the mean of these observations, the standard will not fall in the middle of the control range.

The calculation and application of statistical control limits by this method is illustrated in the appendix to this chapter. The applicability of this technique to cost control is highly limited, however, for several reasons:

1. Few operations are duplicated frequently enough to make it possible to develop and apply the statistical limits.
2. Historical observations reflect a variety of conditions. If the operation was not in control when an observation was made, that observation should not be used in the calculation of the distribution of the normal range of observations. Deciding which observations represented experience under controlled conditions is very difficult.
3. Each observation is a statistical sample which should include more than one measurement so that the range of variability in the sample can be tested. This further restricts the technique to operations in which this kind of sampling is feasible.

In short, statistical control charts are likely to be highly useful in evaluating the purity of successive batches of aspirin, turned out by the millions in a repetitive operation. They are less likely to be useful in controlling the costs of direct materials and direct labor whenever production methods and output are not homogeneous.

An investigation decision model

Even if all the conditions necessary for the development of statistical control limits are present, investigation of a large observed variance may not be worthwhile:

1. Investigations cost money, and the penalty for not correcting the problem may not be big enough to warrant spending this money.
2. There is a very small chance (1 in 100 with ±2.58 standard deviation limits) that the extreme observation may have been the result of a random fluctuation. Paying for an investigation here is completely fruitless.
3. The investigation may reveal that the cause of the variance is uncorrectable and that the company's best action is to continue to operate at the higher cost. Again, the costs of investigation are unproductive.

A number of decision models have been developed to deal with these variables.[3] For example, suppose an investigation will cost $100. The penalty for not finding a correctable cause is $300, the present value of the cost saving to be achieved by removing the cause of the variance. If the $100 is spent and nothing is found, the company is $100 worse off. This is represented by the "maximum loss" bar at the left of Exhibit 23–5. If the money is spent and the cause is found and corrected, the company is $300 − $100 = $200 better off. This is the meaning of the "maximum benefit" bar at the right. If

---

[3] For example, see Thomas R. Dyckman, "The Investigation of Cost Variances," *Journal of Accounting Research,* Fall 1969, pp. 215–44.

Exhibit 23–5 Costs and benefits of variance investigation

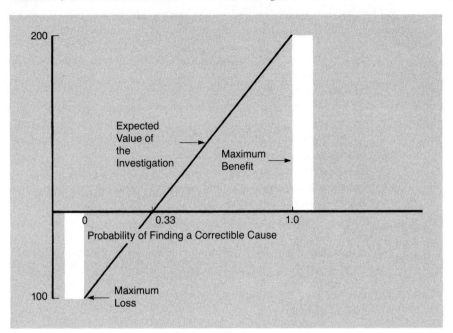

the probability of finding a correctable cause is, say, .25, then the expected value of the investigation is as follows:

Expected benefit: .25 × $200 .... $50
Expected loss: .75 × $100 .... <u>75</u>
  Expected value of investigation .... −$25

In other words, if the company made 100 of these investigations it would spend 100 × $100 = $10,000 and would benefit 25 × $300 = $7,500. It would lose $2,500 by investigating, or $25 per investigation.

In this case it should spend the money to investigate only if the probability of finding a correctable cause is greater than .33.

Analytical examination of cost variances

The effects of some variance causes are too difficult or expensive to measure by the classification techniques we mentioned earlier. Some of these can be measured analytically, however, on the basis of estimated relationships between cost and factors other than output. We isolated the (labor) input efficiency variance in factory overhead cost by this method in Chapter 11; in this section we'll provide five other examples:

1. Effect of materials usage variance on labor usage variance.
2. Labor or equipment substitution variances.
3. Labor mix variances.
4. Materials mix and yield variances.
5. Seasonal variances in production volume.

Our task in each case is to estimate the amount of the total variance resulting from this particular cause. When this is removed, the residual indicates the amount to be attributed to other causes.

The analyses illustrated in this section are not the only possibilities. If management can identify a factor whose influence it wants to measure, the accountant can measure it by holding everything constant except that one factor, as we have done throughout.

Materials yield component of labor usage variance

In process production and other materials-paced operations, the amount of labor used depends on three variables: the volume of output, the quantity of direct materials used, and labor efficiency. Labor usage will change if the quantity of direct materials used changes, even if output and labor efficiency remain unchanged. In these cases we say that the amount of labor required is a function of materials usage. A portion of the labor usage variance therefore can be said to result from the materials usage variance, rather than from the control of labor costs themselves.

For example, suppose three pounds of direct materials and two hours of direct labor are the standard inputs for a unit of product X. The standard wage rate is $10 an hour. The standard direct labor cost of product X therefore is $2 \times \$10 = \$20$. We have the following data for the month of June:

Direct materials processed .... 3,000 pounds
Direct labor .... 1,950 hours
Product output .... 900 units

The labor usage variance for the month is $1,500, unfavorable:

| Actual Usage $1,950 \times \$10$ = $19,500 | − | Standard Usage $900 \times 2 \times \$10$ = $18,000 | = | Usage Variance $150 \times \$10$ = $1,500 Unfavorable |

The question is how much of this was due to the materials usage variance. To answer this, we must first find out how big the materials usage variance was. In this case, the calculation is simple:

Standard Materials Quantity = 900 Units × 3 Pounds = 2,700 Pounds

Since 3,000 pounds of materials were processed, the materials usage variance was 300 pounds, unfavorable.

This is a materials-paced operation, and two hours of labor are necessary to process three pounds of materials. Processing an extra 300 pounds of materials therefore required an extra 200 hours of direct labor. Other things being equal, the labor usage variance should have been $200 \times \$10 = \$2,000$, and unfavorable. It was actually only $1,500. This means that the labor usage variance also had a favorable component of some kind, amounting to 50 hours

× \$10 = \$500. This we call the *labor performance variance,* the portion of the usage variance due to all causes other than the ones we have been able to account for.

In other words, whenever labor costs are governed by materials input flows as well as by output quantities, two components of the labor usage variance can be identified:

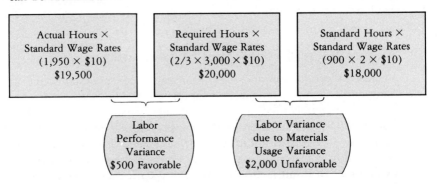

The term *required hours* refers to the standard hours required by the given quantity of materials inputs.

Labor or equipment substitution variances

Direct labor or materials usage variances may arise because the work has been performed on substitute equipment or by individuals with skills other than those specified in standard costs. The difference between actual and standard usage in one of these substituted operations may not be due entirely to the substitution, however. If management wants to separate the substitution effect, it has to (*a*) identify the substitutions when they take place, and (*b*) prepare alternative cost standards applicable to each substitute production arrangement it appears likely to adopt.

For example, a drilling operation on a certain piece part is normally assigned to a new drill press with a standard time of 21 hours for a standard lot size. It can also be performed on a slower machine in 25 hours. The actual operating time last week was 27 hours, 6 hours more than the standard time. With this information, the breakdown of the variance is simple:

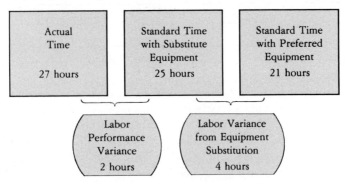

At a standard wage rate of $10 an hour, a $40 equipment substitution variance would be reported. The labor performance variance, the portion of the labor usage variance due to causes other than equipment substitution, would be 2 × $10 = $20.

Identifying substitution variances in this way is expensive. The methods staff must estimate not one standard cost for each operation, but two or even more. This effort ordinarily can't be justified by the value of the control information it provides; alternative standards typically will be available only if they are developed to help the scheduling staff decide which operations to put on each machine.

Labor mix variances

Although calculation of labor substitution variances may not be feasible, management may be able to estimate the effects of labor substitution analytically, from statistics for the period as a whole. Suppose a department performed work on three products during July, with standard direct labor costs as shown in Exhibit 23–6. The department's actual direct labor cost was $32,600, as shown in the second column of the table in Exhibit 23–7. The standard direct labor costs from Exhibit 23–6 appear in the third column, and the direct labor spending variance (the total direct labor cost variance in July) shows up in the column at the right.

Exhibit 23–6 Derivation of standard direct labor cost

	Product A	Product B	Product C	Total Standard Direct Labor hours	Standard Labor Rate per Hour	Standard Direct Labor Cost
Output in July (units)	500	300	100			
Standard direct labor hours per unit:						
Grade 1	2	2	2			
Grade 2	1	3	4			
Total standard direct labor hours:						
Grade 1	1,000	600	200	1,800	$10	$18,000
Grade 2	500	900	400	1,800	8	14,400
Total				3,600		$32,400

Exhibit 23–7 Calculation of labor spending variance

	Actual Direct Labor		Standard Direct Labor Cost	Labor Spending Variance
	Hours	Cost		
Pay grade 1	1,900	$19,500	$18,000	$1,500 unfav.
Pay grade 2	1,600	13,100	14,400	1,300 fav.
Total	3,500	$32,600	$32,400	$ 200 unfav.

To subdivide the direct labor spending variance, we need to make two additional calculations. First, we need to recalculate actual labor usage at standard hourly rates:

Pay grade 1	1,900 hours × $10	$19,000
Pay grade 2	1,600 hours × $8	12,800
Total		$31,800

Next, we need to estimate what the same number of direct labor hours (3,500) should have cost if the two pay grades had remained in their standard proportions, or standard mix. We get the standard mix from the hourly figures in the fourth column of Exhibit 23–6. The cost standards for the three products manufactured this month called for a labor mix of 1,800 grade 1 employees and 1,800 grade 2 employees. If actual labor quantities had been in these proportions, the average standard wage rate would have been $9, just halfway between $10 and $8. If the 3,500 hours of actual direct labor time had been at a standard mix, therefore, direct labor cost should have been 3,500 × $9 = $31,500. The difference between this total and the total standard cost at the actual labor mix ($31,800), is the *labor mix variance.*

We're now in a position to subdivide the direct labor spending variance into three component parts, as follows:

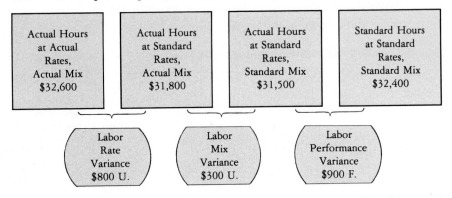

Again the labor performance variance measures the portion of the labor variance we haven't been able to attribute to specific influences. It reflects the use of 100 hours less than the standard labor quantity, at an average standard wage rate of $9 an hour.

The calculation of the mix and performance variances is based on the assumption that workers in the two grades can substitute for each other with no gain or loss in efficiency. In fact, some of the $900 favorable labor performance variance may have been the result of grade 1 employees substituting for grade 2 workers (the unfavorable mix) and working more efficiently than the grade 2 people ordinarily performing the work. All this kind of analysis can do is call management's attention to the variations in mix; management still has to decide what this means and what to do about it.

The remaining question is where the variances are likely to be located. This will depend on the design of the costing system. If labor time is charged to departments at the standard wage rate for each individual pay grade, the labor mix variance will be part of the departmental labor usage variance. We can show this schematically in T-accounts:

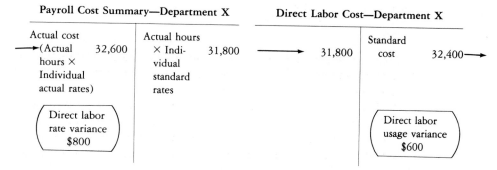

The $600 direct labor usage variance in the right-hand account is the sum of the $900 favorable labor performance variance and the $300 unfavorable labor rate variance.

A second possibility is to charge labor to departments at a single standard wage rate for all pay grades combined. If this is done, the labor mix variance will be part of the labor rate variance. Our simplified T-accounts will show the following:

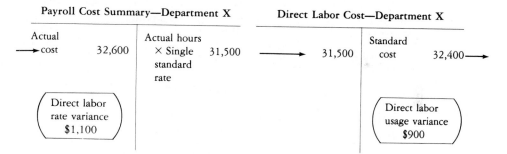

Now the usage variance includes only the labor performance component; the other two components are intermingled in the payroll summary account.

Materials mix and yield variances

Materials inputs also may be partially interchangeable. For example, suppose a process combines two materials into a finished product. The production standard calls for these two materials to be used in equal proportions, but the proportions are difficult to control precisely. In these circumstances, management may wish to subdivide the materials variance, using the same method we just applied to labor inputs.

Suppose the product has a standard materials cost of $3.30 a unit, calculated as follows:

Material	Standard Quantity (pounds)	Standard Price	Standard Cost
A	0.55	$2	$1.10
B	0.55	4	2.20
Total	1.10		$3.30

In May, the process used 600 pounds of A and 500 pounds of B to produce 900 units of product. The total usage variance can be calculated very simply:

Input		Output	
A 600 × $2	$1,200	900 × $3.30	$2,970
B 500 × $4	2,000		
	$3,200		

Materials usage
variance
$230 unfavorable

This can be subdivided into materials mix and materials yield components by the following procedure:

1. Calculate the average standard cost per unit of *input* at the standard input mix:

$$\frac{\$3.30}{1.1 \text{ pounds}} = \$3 \text{ a pound}$$

2. Multiply this average standard cost by the actual quantity of materials used:

$$1,100 \times \$3 = \$3,300$$

3. Calculate the *materials mix variance* by comparing this quantity with the standard cost of the materials actually used:

$$\$3,300 - \$3,200 = \$100 \text{ favorable}$$

4. Calculate the *materials yield variance* by comparing the quantity calculated in (2) with the standard cost of the actual output:

$$\$2,970 - \$3,300 = \$330 \text{ unfavorable}$$

(The yield variance can also be calculated by comparing the amount of product 1,100 pounds of materials ought to have yielded [1,100/1.1 = 1,000 units] with the actual yield [900 units], each measured at standard cost [$3.30].)

This analysis assumes that materials mix is a controllable variable and that the different kinds of materials are interchangeable within limits. In other words, management's task is to use no more of the more expensive materials than is absolutely necessary. If these assumptions are true, isolation of the mix variance will give management some useful information.

Seasonal variations in the overhead volume variance

Volume variances in overhead costs can also be subdivided analytically. In Chapter 11 we learned that the volume variance in the overhead costs of production departments is measured by the difference between the amount of overhead cost absorbed by the actual production volume and the amount of overhead budgeted for that volume. In general, it is equal to the fixed-cost component of the overhead rate multiplied by the difference between actual volume and the volume level at which the overhead rate was calculated.

Suppose fixed costs are budgeted at $20,000 a month and are absorbed in product cost at $2 a standard direct labor hour, reflecting a normal volume of 10,000 standard direct labor hours a month. Actual production in February 19x1 was 7,000 standard hours, and the production volume variance in overhead cost was:

Budgeted fixed cost	10,000 × $2 =	$20,000
Standard fixed cost	7,000 × $2 =	14,000
Overhead volume variance	3,000 × $2 =	$ 6,000 unfavorable

Production volume is highly seasonal, however, and February production is normally budgeted at only 6,000 standard direct labor hours. This means that actual volume in February 19x1 exceeded the company's normal expectations by 1,000 hours. We can subdivide the volume variance as follows:

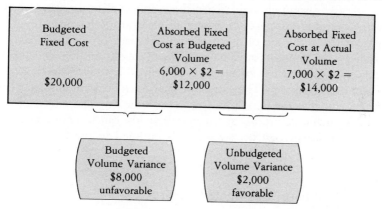

The month profit performance report should call attention to this:

	Actual	Budget	Variance
Sales revenues	xxx	xxx	xxx
:	:	:	:
Factory overhead volume variance	(6,000)	(8,000)	2,000
:	:	:	:

We might also argue that management should include the results of this sort of analysis in its interim financial reports to outsiders. A comment such as the following might be appropriate:

Production volume in the first quarter of this year was X percent greater than the amount budgeted for this period. We anticipated a $Y million charge against revenues in the first quarter, the costs of sustaining idle facilities during the quarter. The actual cost of carrying idle facilities was $Z million during this quarter.

Summary

Basic plan standard costing systems are inadequate if management relies on standard costing to generate steering control information. Comprehensive plan systems are designed to meet this need. In comprehensive plan systems, usage variances are identified as they occur and are reported promptly to the first-level supervisor, usually in considerable detail.

Scorecard variance summaries can be prepared on several bases if the comprehensive plan is used—by operator, by operation, by machine, and by product are all possibilities. These reports can't show the causes of the variances, however, unless someone identifies the cause as each variance arises. Systems don't oridinarily go this far, but they may provide for identifying the variances due to a few major causes, such as equipment substitution or waiting for materials. Variances identified in this way are often reclassified as overhead costs.

The first-level supervisors can usually explain each variance as it occurs, if they are asked soon enough. When they can't explain the variance, statistical control charts or variance investigation decision models may be useful. The main barrier to the use of these techniques is lack of adequate data, but they do indicate the thought patterns management should adopt in deciding whether to investigate the causes of any large variances that may arise.

All this costs money. The extra costs may even be great enough to persuade management that the basic plan is a better solution. The effects of important variables, such as labor mix and materials yields, can be approximated analytically and at lower cost by the methods outlined in the final section of this chapter.

Appendix: Calculation of control limits

Statistical control charts are based on the assumption that the number of times any given value of a variable will arise in a controlled system can be predicted from the so-called *normal curve*. The normal curve describes the number of times a given value will be observed if the mean value is known and all departures from the mean are due to purely random forces.

If we know the mean and the standard deviation of any normal distribution, we can predict the number of times the observed value will be a certain distance from the mean—say, two standard deviations away. If we observe a value outside that limit, we can calculate the probability that the difference between the observed value and the mean was due to random causes. The farther from the mean, the greater the probability that the cause was something other than random.

Calculating control limits for any process, based on the assumption that departures from the mean can be predicted from the normal curve, is a seven-step procedure:

Step 1.   Select a number of samples of actual experience under controlled conditions. The Aurora Company took 20 samples of five observations each of the operation of its No. 2 machine. Each observation recorded the time spent processing a single batch of products. Although the product varied from batch to batch, all batches were of the same size (100 units) and the operation was identical for each batch. The machine was in perfect adjustment for each batch and the supervisor was present and active. The observed values are shown in Exhibit 23–8.

Exhibit 23–8 Sample observations of machine operation

	Labor Time (minutes)						
Sample	Batch 1	Batch 2	Batch 3	Batch 4	Batch 5	Mean (X)	Range (R)
1	42	50	48	54	51	49.0	12
2	50	49	56	51	50	51.2	7
3	45	51	50	46	49	48.2	6
4	50	49	52	48	49	49.6	4
5	43	51	47	51	50	48.4	8
6	47	54	48	52	52	50.6	7
7	50	49	53	52	44	49.6	9
8	46	53	60	55	48	52.4	14
9	46	51	49	53	52	50.2	7
10	52	47	48	47	51	49.0	5
11	49	51	50	52	49	50.2	3
12	50	48	53	49	53	50.6	5
13	54	51	56	48	52	52.2	8
14	49	50	45	49	51	48.8	6
15	46	55	50	47	53	50.2	9
16	50	47	54	48	55	50.8	8
17	49	51	50	54	53	51.4	5
18	52	48	47	45	46	47.6	7
19	47	51	49	52	50	49.8	5
20	52	53	51	47	48	50.2	6

Step 2.   For each sample, calculate the mean (X) and the range (R) of the observed values. The observations in the first sample had values of 42, 50, 48, 54, and 51 minutes. The mean was 49 minutes and the range (the distance between the highest and lowest values) was 12 minutes. These figures are shown in the two right-hand columns of Exhibit 23–8.

Step 3.   Calculate the mean ($\overline{X}$) of the sample means. For the Aurora Company's machine, this was 50 minutes.

Step 4. Calculate the mean ($\overline{R}$) of the ranges in the various samples. The mean range here was 7.05 minutes.

Step 5. With the aid of statistical tables, calculate upper and lower control limits for the sample mean. The formula for these limits is:

$$\text{Control limit } (CL)_X = \overline{X} \pm A_2 \overline{R},$$

in which, A_2 is taken from a statistical table. The size of A_2 depends on the desired width of the control interval and the number of observations in the sample. For a control interval of ± 3 standard deviations and five observations in each sample, $A_2 = 0.58.$[4] The control limits are:

Upper control limit $(UCL_X) = 50.0 + 0.58 \times 7.05 = 54.1$ minutes
Lower control limit $(LCL_X) = 50.0 - 0.58 \times 7.05 = 45.9$ minutes

Step 6. With the aid of statistical tables, calculate upper and lower control limits for the range of values in the sample. The formulas are:

$$UCL_R = D_4 \overline{R}$$
$$LCL_R = D_3 \overline{R}$$

D_4 and D_3 are statistical values, taken from a table. For a control interval of ± 3 standard deviations and five observations in each sample, $D_4 = 2.11$ and $D_3 = 0$. For the Aurora Company's machine, the limits are:

$$UCL_R = 2.11 \times 7.05 = 14.9 \text{ minutes}$$
$$LCL_R = 0 \text{ minutes}$$

Step 7. Plot the means and control limits on two control charts, one for the sample mean and one for the range. The means and ranges in subsequent samples can be plotted on these charts to see whether the operation is still in control.

Independent study problems (solutions in Appendix B)

1. **Accounts for the comprehensive plan.** The Irwin Seating Company manufactures a line of metal and wooden chairs for sale to large industrial buyers. Its standard costing system follows the comprehensive plan, with separate accounts for raw materials, materials in process, labor in process, and finished goods inventories. (Overhead costs are ignored in this problem.)

   The following events took place in the wooden chair department last September:

---

[4] These factors are taken from Eugene L. Grant and Richard S. Leavenworth, *Statistical Quality Control*, 4th ed. (New York: McGraw-Hill, 1972), table C.

Materials purchased and placed in inventory:	
Standard prices	$123,000
Actual prices..................................	131,000
Direct materials (at standard prices):	
Standard requisitions...........................	140,000
Supplemental requisitions	12,000
Returned to storeroom	8,000
Direct labor:	
Standard hours at standard wage rates	80,000
Actual hours at standard wage rates	85,600
Direct labor payrolls:	
Accrued wages payable, September 1	8,200
September payrolls, covering period of August 30–	
September 24, inclusive (paid entirely in cash)	79,500
Accrued wages payable, September 30	16,300
Standard cost of chairs finished:	
Direct materials	122,400
Direct labor	76,500
Standard cost of chairs sold:	
Direct materials	115,200
Direct labor	68,300

Required:

a. Account for the month's transactions, using journal entries and T-accounts, with a separate account for each cost variance you are able to identify.

b. What could be done to trace the major causes of the materials usage variances?

2. **Statistical control limits.** Yesterday the Aurora Company's No. 2 machine was used to manufacture five batches of products. The labor times were 57, 62, 49, 68, and 59 minutes.

Required:

a. Using the control limits developed in the Appendix to this chapter, determine whether the operation was in control yesterday.

b. Does the illustration in the Appendix seem realistic? What conditions must be present to make this approach feasible?

3. **Variance investigation decision.** The Youngblood Company uses a basic plan standard costing system in its factory. Unfavorable variances in a process have been about $2,000 a month. If the cause of the variance can be found, and if that cause is correctible, it will take two months to correct it. The correction, if made, would be effective for two months.

Investigation of the variance will cost $500. Correcting the cause, if a correctible cause is found, will cost $1,000. Management believes the probability of finding a correctible cause is .6.

Required:

a. Would you recommend launching an investigation?

b. What is the minimum probability of finding a correctible cause that would justify an investigation?

4. **Labor mix variance.** A department's employees are grouped into three pay grades, with standard hourly wage rates as follows:

Grade	Rate
1	$5.50
2	6.00
3	7.00

A single department-wide standard wage rate of $6.50 an hour is used for product costing. Data for October are: (1) actual department wages, $57,000; (2) standard labor cost of the month's output, $59,000; (3) actual labor hours: grade 1—2,000; grade 2—4,000; grade 3—3,000.

Required:

Analyze the department's labor variances for the month.

5. **Materials usage component of labor usage variance.** A factory department produces only one product. At standard, this product uses two pounds of direct materials at a standard price of $4 a pound, or $8 a unit. Each pound of direct materials requires one and a half direct labor hours of processing time. The standard wage rate is $10 an hour, so the standard labor cost in this department is $30 for each unit of product.

The department produced 1,000 units of this product in December, with the following direct materials and direct labor costs:

	Standard Cost per Unit	Actual Input Quantities	Actual Cost, December
Direct materials	$ 8	2,300 lbs.	$ 9,200
Direct labor	30	3,200 hrs.	33,600

Required:

Calculate the total direct labor variance for the month and break it down into as many component parts as you are able to identify.

Exercises and problems

6. **Comprehensive plan: Journal entries.** Colson Enterprises has a comprehensive plan standard costing system in its one-department factory. The factory records showed the following data for the month of August:

1. Standard cost of inventory in process, August 1: direct materials, $40,000; direct labor, $32,000; factory overhead, $48,000.
2. Standard cost of materials received from storeroom: standard requisitions, $82,000; supplemental requisitions, $11,000.
3. Standard cost of materials returned to storeroom: $3,000.
4. Direct labor, $97,000 (at standard wage rates); standard labor cost of work done, $99,000.
5. Standard cost of goods completed and transferred to finished goods inventory: direct materials, $76,000; direct labor, $95,000; factory overhead, $145,000.
6. Standard cost of the work done on goods spoiled in production: direct materials, $4,000; direct labor, $8,000. No overhead costs are assigned to spoiled units. The spoiled units are junked, with no salvage value.
7. Standard cost of inventory in process, August 31: direct materials, $42,000; direct labor, $28,000; factory overhead, $44,000.

Required:

a. List the differences between standard costs and the amounts charged to production for direct materials and direct labor.

b. Prepare journal entries to record the transactions listed above. Colson Enterprises uses one Materials Inventory account, one Work-in-Process account, and one Finished Goods Inventory account.

7. **Labor variance analysis: Effect of materials usage.** A department processes two products at the following standard costs:

	Materials (pounds)	Labor	
		Hours	Cost
Product A	10	5	$30
Product B	20	10	60

The amount of labor actually used depends on the weight of material processed rather than the number of units of product completed.

During January the following data were registered in this department:

Materials used:	25,000 pounds
Labor used:	12,000 hours, $74,000
Products produced:	Product A, 1,000 units
	Product B, 600 units

Required:

a. Calculate the total labor spending variance for this department for the month of January.

b. Analyze this variance, labeling each component clearly. Does it appear that the manager exercised adequate control over departmental labor costs during the month?

8. **Labor mix variance.**   Actual wages total $30,000. The standard wage rate used for product costing is $8 an hour. Actual labor time totals 2,500 hours of grade A labor, with a standard wage rate of $10 an hour, and 1,500 hours of grade B labor, with a standard wage rate of $7 an hour. The month's output has a standard labor cost of $31,600.

Required:

a. Calculate and analyze the labor spending variance.

b. Do the company's procedures record the labor mix variance as a portion of the labor rate variance or as part of the labor usage variance?

c. Calculate the standard proportions of grade A and grade B labor implicit in the $8 standard wage rate used for product costing. Under what circumstances would you regard the use of a single composite rate an acceptable means of product costing and responsibility accounting?

9. **Materials mix variance.**   The Rushby Chemical Company manufactures a certain product by mixing three kinds of materials in large batches. The blendmaster has the responsibility for maintaining the quality of the product, and this often requires altering the proportions of the various ingredients. Standard costs are used to provide materials control information. The standard materials inputs per batch are:

	Quantity (pounds)	Price (per pound)	Standard Cost of Materials
Bulk material	420	$0.06	$25.20
Coloring material	70	0.12	8.40
Setting material	10	0.25	2.50
Total batch	500		$36.10

The finished product is packed in 50-pound boxes; the standard materials cost of each box is therefore $3.61.

During January, the following materials were put in process:

Bulk material	181,000 lbs.
Coloring material	33,000
Setting material	6,000
Total	220,000 lbs

Inventories in process totaled 5,000 pounds at the beginning of the month and 8,000 pounds at the end of the month. It is assumed that these inventories consisted of materials in their standard proportions. Finished output during January amounted to 4,100 boxes.

Required:

a. Compute the total materials usage variance for the month and break it down into mix and yield components.

b. Who, if anyone, in the management of the company would be interested in seeing this breakdown of the usage variance?

10. **Statistical control limits.** Control charts used to evaluate the quality of batches of manufactured products generally describe the normal distributions of the means and ranges of the observations in individual samples. To test the quality of a batch, several samples are drawn from the batch and the mean and range are calculated for the attribute being tested.

When applied to cost control, the procedure is sometimes modified to test individual observations against control charts based on the variability of individual observations.

Required:

a. Calculate control limits within ±3 standard deviations of the mean, based on the individual observations in Exhibit 23–8 in the Appendix to this chapter.

b. Are these control limits wider or narrower than the control limits for the sample means calculated in the Appendix? What explanation can you offer for this?

c. Why is it difficult to develop control limits for costs based on the distribution of sample means and ranges? Would it be easier to do this for overhead costs than for direct labor costs? Explain.

11. **Investigation decision.** Management is concerned by persistent labor usage variances in one department. The methods department has proposed spending $1,000 to investigate the causes of these variances. If the process proves to be out of control and a cause is found, management estimates the cost of corrective action will be $2,000, regardless of the cause of the variances. The present value of the future costs that can be eliminated by the corrective action, if one can be taken, is $4,000.

Required:

a. If the probability of finding a correctable cause is .4, should the investigation be undertaken? Show your calculations.

b. Which of the estimates required by this analysis are likely to be readily available? Explain.

12. **Labor variance analysis.** The Dade Corporation operates a single plant, manufacturing molded plastic products. Production in the molding department is performed by crews of workers in three separate wage rate classifications. A "standard crew hour" consists of 10 labor hours, distributed among the pay grades as follows:

Pay Grade	Hours	Standard Rate	Standard Cost
FA–1	2	$7.00	$14.00
FA–2	3	5.60	16.80
FA–3	5	4.80	24.00
Total	10	xxx	$54.80

Standard output is 1,000 pounds of finished product per standard crew hour, and on this basis standard labor cost per 1,000 pounds of product is $54.80.

During February charges to the molding department included 650 hours of

FA–1 labor, 1,000 hours of FA–2 labor, and 1,600 hours of FA–3 labor. Output of the molding department totaled 330,000 pounds of finished product. There were no in-process inventories either at the beginning or at the end of the month. The department operated 160 hours during February, using two production crews throughout the period. All of this was classified as productive time except for five hours of idle time recorded by one crew while machinery was being repaired. The departmental payroll for the month totaled $18,000.

Required:

a. Calculate the total labor spending variance for the month.
b. Subdivide the variance into five component parts, in the following sequence: labor rate variance, labor mix variance, crew size variance, idle time variance, labor performance variance.
c. Which of these components are likely to be controllable in the molding department?

13. **Reporting detailed variances. Comprehensive plan versus basic plan.** Department A had six direct production workers on July 26.

The time tickets for work in this department on July 26 showed the following details:

Name	Job No.	Indirect Acct. No.	Machine No.	Actual Hours	Standard Hours
Cooley	7762		X12	3.2	3.0
Cooley	7915		X12	1.4	0.9
Cooley		A14		0.6	—
Cooley	7915		X12	2.2	2.2
Cooley	7185		T44	0.8	0.6
Donaldson	8044		T44	1.4	1.8
Donaldson		A12		2.8	—
Donaldson	7918		L95	4.8	4.3
George		A16		0.8	—
George		A14		0.4	—
George	7511		X16	2.0	1.2
George	7716		X16	1.1	0.5
George		A14		0.2	—
George		A17		3.5	—
Sugarman	8345		X22	6.0	5.6
Sugarman		A15		0.3	—
Sugarman	7996		X16	2.2	2.3
Taussig	8212		L95	1.5	1.3
Taussig	7694		T44	2.3	2.5
Taussig		A14		0.6	—
Taussig	7694		T44	1.6	1.7
Taussig	7819		X22	3.0	2.8
Young		A12		1.0	—
Young	8076		X45	4.4	4.7
Young		A12		0.8	—
Young	8015		X45	1.1	1.3
Young	7995		X45	1.4	1.6

The standard wage rate for all workers in this department is $8 an hour. All have identical job descriptions; wage rates differ because of differences in seniority. The six workers on July 26 had the following hourly wage rates:

J. Cooley $8.00
R. Donaldson 8.20
F. George 7.80
T. Sugarman 8.40
S. Taussig 8.00
L. Young 8.40

Required:

a. Calculate the amount of labor cost that should be charged to department A for work done on July 26 for inclusion in responsibility accounting reports on the department head's performance in controlling labor costs that day. Ignore overtime premiums.
b. Using figures you developed in answer to (*a*), together with any other data you choose to use, prepare a summary of the day's variances from standard direct labor cost in a form useful to the department head.
c. Prepare a summary of the departmental direct labor cost variances, showing only the amount of detail that would be available in a basic plan system with a daily reporting interval. For this purpose you may assume that all the jobs referred to in the table were started and finished on July 26, leaving no work in process at the end of the day.

14. **Investigation decision.** Joan Able has just joined Hilson, Ltd., as comptroller. The company manufactures precision instruments. Ms. Able has determined from historical production records that there is a 55 percent chance that the quality will not be up to company standards, and some form of adjustment will be necessary to bring the instruments up to normal specifications. The cost of investigation is $13,500. If adjustments are required, the incremental cost savings (net of adjustment costs, but excluding the cost of investigation) are estimated to be as follows:

Anticipated Incremental Cost Savings	Probability
$10,000	.10
25,000	.25
28,000	.35
30,000	.20
32,000	.10

Required:

Should Ms. Able investigate? Show your calculations.

(SMAC)

15. **Statistical control limits.** Robert Johnson has just been appointed chief cost accountant for a medium size manufacturing firm. His first assignment is to investigate whether material usage in the plant is under control. He recalled studying

statistical quality control techniques in one of his management accounting courses and decided to apply these techniques in his investigation. Searching the data files for the past six months, he found materials usage data for individual items of product A in department X. He took samples of four units each, one sample for each hour, from the data for each of a number of days in this period, selected at random. The following three samples are representative of the samples he took:

Sample	Cost of Each Item			
1	$94	$87	$85	$94
2	82	94	94	78
3	94	90	94	86

The control limits specified for the arithmetic mean are $88 ± $6. After preparing a control chart for the sample means, and one for the individual observations, Johnson detected some interesting results.

Required:

a. Prepare the two control charts, using the designated control limits.
b. Comment on any differences between the two charts as to whether the process is in control.
c. What explanation can you suggest for the differences between the patterns shown in the two charts?

(SMAC, adapted)

16. **Materials variances.** The Scent Makers Company, Ltd., produces a kind of perfume for men. To make this perfume, three different types of fluids are used. The standard proportions of these three fluids—Dycone, Cycone, and Bycone— are 2/5, 3/10, and 3/10; their standard costs are $6, $3.50, and $2.50 per gallon, respectively. The standard yield is 80 gallons of perfume from 100 gallons of mix, and yield has been close to standard in each of the past few months.

The company maintains a policy of not carrying any raw materials in inventory, as storage space is costly. Budgeted production is 4,160,000 gallons of perfume this year. Last week the company produced 75,000 gallons of perfume at a total raw materials cost of $449,500. The actual numbers of gallons used and the purchase cost per gallon for each of the three fluids were as follows:

	Gallons	Cost per Gallon
Dycone	45,000	$5.50
Cycone	35,000	4.20
Bycone	20,000	2.75

Required:

a. Calculate the price, yield, and mix variances for each of the three fluids. Reconcile these variances with the total materials spending variance.
b. Explain the managerial significance of the price, yield, and mix variances in this situation.

(SMAC)

17. **Comprehensive plan: Effect of machine substitution.** The Cottrell Company uses a comprehensive plan standard costing system in its factory. Some variances are identified with their causes at the time they arise; others are merely identified with the department, machine, operator, and job order number.

One department has two kinds of machines, model X and model Y. These machines are interchangeable but not equally efficient. Standard labor hours per unit of product on each type of machine are:

Product	Model X	Model Y
A	1.0	1.2
B	2.0	2.6
C	3.0	2.8
D	4.0	5.0

Standard product cost is based, in each case, on the more efficient machine model for that product—that is, C's standard cost is based on model Y machine time, while standard cost for the other three products presumes the use of model X machines. The data for March are:

1. Actual labor hours, including items (4) and (5) below, 2,200.
2. Standard wage rate, $7 an hour.
3. Actual wages, $16,000.
4. Labor hours waiting for machine repair, 40 hours.
5. Labor hours correcting defects in products rejected in inspection; product B, 50 hours; product C, 30 hours.
6. Production (units of product) on each type of machine:

Product	Model X	Model Y
A	500	—
B	200	100
C	—	150
D	140	50

Required:

a. Compute and analyze the labor variance for the month in as much detail as the data permit. Explain the meaning of each variance component that you identify.

b. Assuming that a maximum of 1,460 hours on model X machines and 1,200 hours on model Y machines was available for production during the month, after subtracting waiting and rework time and allowing an adequate margin for variations in efficiency, did the department achieve the most efficient scheduling of its equipment? How is any scheduling inefficiency reflected in the labor variance? Explain and quantify if possible.

18. **Labor variance analysis.** Joe is concerned about the large unfavorable labor usage variance that arose in his department last month. He has had a small favorable variance for several months, and he thinks his crew worked just as effectively last month as in previous months. This makes him believe that something must be wrong with the calculations, but he admits he doesn't understand them. The variance was reported as follows:

Standard labor cost of output (120,000 pounds at 12.9 cents) ...	$15,480
Actual labor hours at standard wage rate	17,170
Labor usage variance	($ 1,690)

The product is made in batches which start with 1,200 pounds of material. The standard calls for the following labor quantities for each batch:

Labor Class	Standard Labor Rate	Standard Labor Hours	Standard Labor Cost
Class 6	$9	3	$ 27
Class 5	8	6	48
Class 3	6	9	54
Total		18	$129

The raw material is of uneven quality, and the product yield from a batch varies with the quality of the raw materials used. The standard output is 1,000 pounds, resulting in a standard labor cost of 12.9 cents a pound.

Joe's work force is a crew of 12 workers. The standard crew consists of two class 6 workers, four class 5 workers, and six class 3 workers. Lower rated employees cannot do the work of the higher rated employees, but the reverse is possible with some slight loss in efficiency and a resulting increase in labor hours.

The standard work day is nine hours. Last month had 23 working days, for a total of 207 standard working hours. Premiums for overtime hours are charged to overhead accounts and do not enter this problem.

Last month, 165,000 pounds of material were used to produce 120,000 pounds of product. The actual amounts of labor used were as follows:

Labor Class	Labor Hours	Labor Rate	Labor Cost
Class 6	390	$9	$ 3,510
Class 5	980	8	7,840
Class 3	970	6	5,820
Total	2,340		$17,170

Joe's work force last month, assigned to him by the personnel department, consisted of two class 6 workers, five class 5 workers, and five class 3 workers.

Required:

What would you tell Joe? Can you get him "off the hook" with the plant manager? (*Suggestion:* Try to separate the effects of crew mix, labor performance, and materials yield.)

(Prepared by Carl L. Nelson)

19. **Seasonal variations: Interim reporting.** The controller of Navar Corporation wants to issue to stockholders quarterly income statements that will be predictive of expected annual results. All fixed costs for the year would be allocated among quarters in proportion to the number of units expected to be sold in each quarter, stating that the annual income can then be predicted through use of the following equation:

$$\text{Annual income} = \text{Quarterly income} \times \frac{100 \text{ percent}}{\text{Percent of unit sales applicable to quarter}}$$

Navar expects the following activity for the year (in $000):

	Units	Average per Unit	Total (000s)
Sales revenue:			
First quarter	500,000	$2.00	$1,000
Second quarter	100,000	1.50	150
Third quarter	200,000	2.00	400
Fourth quarter	200,000	2.00	400
Total	1,000,000		1,950
Costs to be incurred:			
Variable:			
Manufacturing		0.70	700
Selling and administrative		0.25	250
Total variable		0.95	950
Fixed:			
Manufacturing			380
Selling and administrative			220
Total fixed			600
Income before taxes			$ 400

Required:

a. Ignoring income taxes and assuming that Navar's activities do not vary from expectations, will the controller's plan reach the desired objective? If not, how can it be modified to do so? Explain, using illustrative computations.

b. How should the effect of variations of actual activity from expected activity be treated in Navar's quarterly income statements?

c. What assumptions has the controller made in regard to inventories? Discuss.

(CPA)

20. **Reporting variances to management.** Consolidated Industries operates several large factories in various parts of the world. Its factory in Rapperswil, Switzerland manufactures industrial machinery and parts for customers in several countries. Most of the products are custom-designed, and all production is on a job order basis. Standard labor costs have been established for the most frequently performed operations in the factory, however.

Hans Hassenpfeffer is a department foreman in the Rapperswil factory. Each morning he receives a labor report listing the previous day's performance of each worker in his department. This report contains one line for each task performed by each worker during the day. Below is an excerpt from the report for January 23 listing all tasks performed on that day by Anna Buri and Jorg Staub, two workers in Mr. Hasenpfeffer's department:

Employee Name	Job or Acct. No.	Rated Work			Other Actual Hours	
		Operation No.	Actual Hours	Standard Hours	Gain (Loss)	Nonrated Work	Nonpro- ductive
Buri, Anna	J75008	179–32	8.0	7.8	(0.2)		
Staub, Jorg	J75006	176–40	2.2	1.4	(0.8)		
Staub, Jorg	A1406						0.5
Staub, Jorg	J75012					2.4	
Staub, Jorg	J75023	179–32	2.9	2.0	(0.9)		

Nonrated work consists of all productive tasks for which no standards have been prepared. Nonproductive time is time spent waiting for materials, waiting for machine repair, etc. The twice-daily coffee breaks are not recorded as nonproductive time, however. Instead, standard labor hours include a provision for this factor.

Mr. Hasenpfeffer has 12 workers in his department, and the typical daily report consists of approximately 40 lines. All workers in this department are paid a fixed hourly wage, which varies considerably from worker to worker.

Required:

a. This report is part of a much broader standard costing system that has been used in this factory for a number of years. Would you guess that this system is a basic plan system or a comprehensive plan system? Why do you think so?

b. Would you recommend that this report be prepared and given to Mr. Hasenpfeffer each morning? State the assumptions or reasons behind your recommendation.

c. Assume that the company's management has answered (b) in the negative. Would you recommend that the information necessary to prepare the daily report should continue to be collected and stored for possible future use? Give your reasons or, if you are not ready to make a recommendation without further data, describe how you would analyze this question.

d. Assume that the company's management has answered (b) in the affirmative, but that it wants a departmental labor performance summary report prepared each month. What information now likely to be available in this system would you recommend presenting on this monthly report? Give your reasons.

e. If you were Mr. Hasenpfeffer, what action, if any, would you probably take on the basis of the portion of the report dealing with Ms. Buri and Mr. Staub? Is Ms. Buri a better worker than Mr. Staub?

24 Project control

Research and development (R&D) and similar activities that we classify as independent programs or projects have three distinctive characteristics: each project or program is undertaken at management's initiative to meet objectives other than the objective of satisfying demands for service imposed on the organization unit from outside, each is unique, and each is large enough to call for a separate managerial control effort. This chapter will examine the control tools available at each of the three stages—project approval, scheduling, and progress review—diagrammed in Exhibit 24-1. In discussing these, we'll focus primarily on R&D projects, but construction projects, feasibility studies, and other independent programs have the same characteristics.

Exhibit 24-1 Stages in project control.

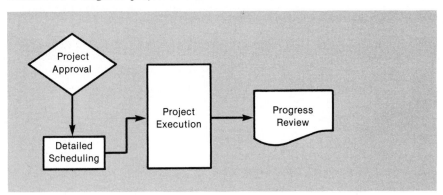

Project approval

The approval of research and development proposals is the most crucial phase in the control process. We need to look at two questions:

1. What criteria should be used to evaluate individual proposals?
2. When should these criteria be applied?

Approval criteria

In principle, the test to be applied to R&D proposals is the same test we applied to capital expenditure proposals: Is the present value of the expected cash flows positive or negative? The main trouble with this test is the difficulty of quantifying it. Both costs and benefits are highly uncertain quantities in most cases. Confronted with this uncertainty, management is often tempted to abandon the profitability approach. Instead, research and development budgets are set as total spending limits, tied to some general index of company activity or profitability. Some typical indexes are:

1. Percent of sales.
2. Percent of the pretax profit contribution.
3. Dollars per employee.

The target ratio may be based on the company's own past expenditures or on the activities of its competitors. The base (sales, profit contribution, or employees) may be a current figure or an average covering a number of years.

The main weakness of budgeting research and development from the top down is that it is likely to lead to neglected opportunities or wasted resources. If research management comes up with more good projects than it can handle within the budget limits, some will have to be deferred or rejected. If promising proposals are scarce, on the other hand, some of the available money will go to projects of dubious merit. In either case, the company loses. Competitive ratios or past experience should serve as reference points, not as guides to decisions.

Even if the overall budget is based on an aggregate ratio, management must still develop preference or priority ratings for individual projects. These will depend to some extent on individual estimates of costs and benefits and in part on the relationships of individual proposals to the company's overall strategic plan. Since top management is responsible for strategic planning, and since project ranking will affect its ability to carry out these plans, top management can't afford to abdicate its responsibility for major project ranking decisions.

Review of proposals

R&D proposals typically are evaluated not once but several times. The first of these reviews is likely to take place at budget time, leading to preliminary rejection or approval of individual proposals. The second review is conducted just before expenditures are to begin, and leads to formal authorization to commence work. Each stage has its own characteristics which need to be explored briefly.

Budget review.   Once each year, as part of the annual budgetary planning, research management prepares a tentative list of projects and expenditures for the coming year. These budgeted expenditures are usually listed two ways, by project and by object of expenditure.

	Project A	Project B	⁓	Research Administration
Professional salaries			⁓	
Clerical salaries			⁓	
Supplies			⁓	
Travel			⁓	
Total			⁓	

If the research organization is departmentalized, the budget will also contain an organizational dimension, just as it does for manufacturing and marketing activities.

Some projects in the tentative budget are continuing projects, already approved and under way at the beginning of the year. These are reviewed to see whether they should be continued without change, modified, or discontinued. Others are specific proposals, not yet under way but under study and nearly ready for final decisions.

Most research and development budgets also contain a third element, a forecast of the total expenditures required by projects to be conceived and presented for approval later in the year. Budgeted expenditures in this third category should be relatively small, however. Most research and development projects take months to conceive and plan. Management is generally aware of most of the projects that will mature in time to affect expenditures during the budget period.

Even at this preliminary stage, rough estimates of costs and benefits should be made. This approach has several advantages:

1. It requires management to examine the economic basis for research decisions long before these decisions must be made.
2. It identifies the key variables and assumptions so that they can be analyzed and discussed.
3. It provides a record of management's expectations to serve as a point of reference for future estimates as the project matures.
4. It gives higher management a rough basis for comparing marginal research and development projects with other kinds of expenditure proposals—for plant and equipment, community service, dividends, methods analysis, and so on.

Project approval. Inclusion of a project in the annual budget is not necessarily the same as project approval. The decision to initiate a project should not be made until management is ready to make the first expenditures. One reason is that the final project review is management's last chance to avoid spending money. The decision to intitate a project is also a decision to hire staff or to keep staff on the payroll who would otherwise be released. Once the commitment is made, the money flows out almost automatically.

The second reason is that by delaying approval until this stage, management can use later information. Later information is at least as good as earlier information, and probably better. Management has no reason to deny itself the right to use this better, later information.

Exhibit 24–2 illustrates one kind of project estimate form, in this case covering a small project for the development of a new product. In this exhibit, project labor costs are subdivided by task and the tasks are grouped into phases, each phase ending at some readily recognizable point in the development process. The estimated time to complete each phase is shown at the bottom of the sheet, and project totals, including a rough estimate of profit potential, are shown in the summary section at the top of the form. Additional supporting sheets, not shown here, present further detail on the nature of the project and on the derivation of the estimates.

Exhibit 24–2 Research project estimate

RESEARCH DIVISION
PROJECT ESTIMATE SHEET

Project No.: 16321
Project Title: Sandfly Attachment
Project Supervisor: G. Hill

Date: 10/15/x0
Type: New Product

Completion Estimate 9 Months

Estimated Annual Profit $30,000

Cost Estimate:
Labor and Services $ 8,000
Materials 7,200
Equipment 4,800
Total $20,000

Task	Phase 1, Specifications		Phase 2, Drawings		Phase 3, Prototype	
	Hours	Cost	Hours	Cost	Hours	Cost
Synthesis and analysis	150	$2,400				
Design specifications	25	400				
Breadboarding	50	700				
Layout	25	350				
Parts list			40	$ 400		
Schematics			75	750		
Test specifications			40	400		
Fabrication					150	$1,200
Assembly					50	300
Wiring					25	300
Test					50	800
Total labor and services	250	$3,850	155	$1,550	275	$2,600
Materials and purchased parts		$2,000		$ 500		$4,700
Equipment		$3,000		—		$1,800
Completion time	4 months		2 months		3 months	

Detailed scheduling

Timing is crucial to the success of research and development projects. Great emphasis therefore is placed on time scheduling and time control. In this section we'll look at four time scheduling aids:

1. Network diagrams.
2. Float diagrams.
3. Departmental resource commitment charts.
4. Uncertainty and the PERT diagram.

Network diagrams

Every construction project, every research and development project, every consulting assignment can be described as a set of interdependent activities. These activities sometimes can be linked together in a single sequential chain. In other projects some activities can be performed simultaneously with others. Still other projects have conditional sequences, in which the outcome of one activity determines the activity to be carried out next.

Interdependencies between activities are usually represented in network diagrams. A network diagram is a chart showing the sequential relationships between the constituent tasks required to carry out a project or program, beginning with a single starting point and ending at a single completion point. Exhibit 24–3 is a typical, though very simple, network. The rectangles represent

Exhibit 24–3 Project network with time estimates

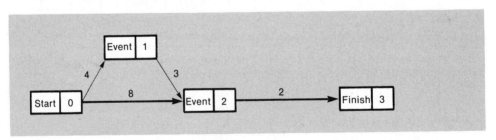

events that occur at specific moments during the course of the project; the connecting lines stand for *activities,* the means of getting from one event to another. Several features of this diagram deserve comment:

1. The direction of progress toward completion of the project is indicated by the arrowheads on the activity lines.
2. The numbers in the event blanks are used to identify the events for computer programming.
3. The numbers on the arrows are the amounts of time required to complete individual activities. (For example, the arrow from start to event 1 indicates that this activity is expected to take four weeks.)
4. The activities are not numbered, but it is convenient to identify them by the numbers of the events they link together. (For example, the activity linking events 2 and 3 can be referred to as activity 23.)

Some of the relationships in the network are concurrent; others are sequential. For example, two separate sets of activities must be completed independently in order to reach event 2—these are concurrent sets of activities. The activities linking events 0 and 1 and events 1 and 2, on the other hand, are sequential—the second one can't be started until the first one is completed.

Most networks for research and development projects are very large and require high-capacity electronic computers. The networking technique can be applied to simpler tasks without the use of computers, however, both inside and outside the research division.

Critical path.   Once the network has been completed, management can estimate the amount of time it will take to complete the project. Each activity sequence is known as a *path*. The network in Exhibit 24–3 has two paths:

Path	Time Required
0–1–2–3	$4 + 3 + 2 = 9$
0–2–3	$8 + 2 \quad = 10$

The 0–2–3 path is the *critical path,* the sequence of activities requiring the longest total elapsed time from start to finish. The arrows on this path are heavier than the others.

Calculating slack time.   The event blocks in the network diagram can be expanded to show how much slack time any one path contains. This is a two-step process:

Step 1. Enter the *earliest possible start time* for each activity in the lower left corner of the event block, starting at time zero and following the arrows to the right. For block 0, zero is the appropriate number; for block 2, the earliest start time is eight weeks (subpath 0-1-2 can be completed in seven weeks, but we can't get to block 2 until *all* of the first three activities have been completed—this means until after the eight weeks required by activity 02. Event blocks with this information appear as shown in Exhibit 24–4.

Exhibit 24–4 Project network diagram with earliest start times

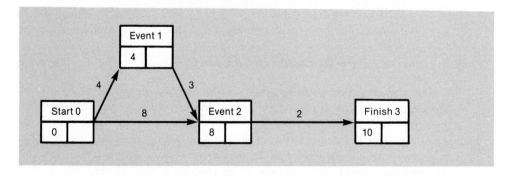

Step 2. In the lower right corner of each block enter the *latest possible start time* consistent with a scheduled completion date. These figures are calculated

by counting backward from the final block. If 10 weeks is the desired completion date, then activity 23 must be started no later than 2 weeks earlier—that is, 8 weeks after the zero date. Event blocks with this information are shown in Exhibit 24–5.

Exhibit 24–5 Project network diagram with latest start times

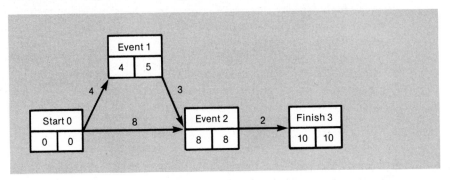

Notice that the two numbers in the block for event 1 are not identical. The difference is known as *slack time,* or slack. Although activity 12 can be started as late as five weeks after the zero date, event 1 is expected to be reached a week earlier. Any path containing an activity that can be started earlier than the latest start date is known as a *slack path.* Slack gives management flexibility. Either activity 01 or activity 12 can be completed a week late without delaying the project's completion date.

Cost slopes.   If the critical path is too long to meet a desired completion date, it may be possible to devote more resources to one or more of the activities on the critical path and thus shorten the total time requirement. Shortening the time required for an activity on one of the slack paths, on the other hand, would not advance the completion date at all.

Management needs to decide whether to shorten the critical path and, if so, which activity or activities to accelerate. These decisions have two variables:

1.   The penalty for late completion or premium for early completion of the project.
2.   The cost of accelerating the project timetable.

The cost of acceleration depends on the activity management chooses to accelerate. The cost of saving one time unit by adding resources to speed up work on an activity is referred to as a *cost slope.* By the same token, the amount that would be saved by stretching an activity out is also a cost slope. Both of these are illustrated in Exhibit 24–6. If management shortens this activity by one week, total cost will go up from $5,000 to $6,000. The $1,000 increase is the slope of the total cost line as it moves upward to the left. By spreading the activity over five weeks instead of four, on the other hand, management could save $200. This is the slope of the cost curve in this segment.

Exhibit 24–6 Cost slopes

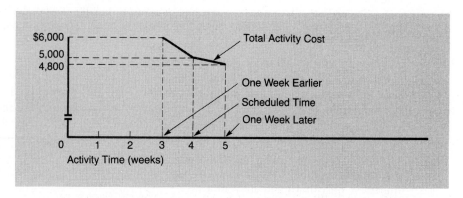

To illustrate this idea more fully, we need a slightly more complex network than the one we have been using. The network in Exhibit 24–7 has 10 activities instead of 4, and three subpaths containing slack. The dollar figures on the activity arrows are the estimated costs of those activities. The critical path is 17 weeks long.

Suppose this is a development project being carried out for an outside customer. The customer insists that the project be completed in 16 weeks. Otherwise the contract will go to a competitor and the company will lose a $10,000 profit contribution. Management needs to cut a week off the scheduled time if this project is to be undertaken.

The one-week cost slopes for increasing or decreasing estimated time for all activities on the critical path are:

Activity	Cost Penalty to Decrease	Cost Saving If Increased
01	$2,000	$ 0
12	1,000	200
24	1,500	800
45	500	500
56	800	700
67	1,500	100

Exhibit 24–7 Project network with time and cost estimates

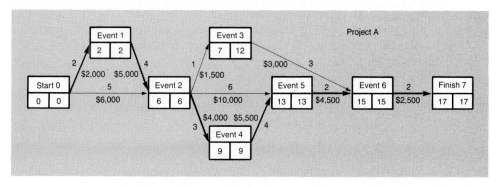

The cheapest way to gain a week's time is to speed up activity 45 at a penalty cost of $500. Every other activity has a greater penalty. Since the cost of losing the contract is $10,000, the $500 penalty is well worth absorbing.

Dummy activities.   All of the activities in Exhibit 24–7 were time-consuming activities. Most network diagrams also include one or more activities that take no time at all. These are called dummy activities. Activity 01 at the left-hand side of the diagram in Exhibit 24–8 is a dummy activity, showing that activity 12 may be started just as soon as activity 02, if management chooses to do this. (Dummy activities are represented by dashed lines between events.) We could show the same relationships by drawing two arrows from event 0 to event 2, but using the dummy activity makes it easier to identify the latest start times and slack times.

Exhibit 24–8 Network with dummy activities

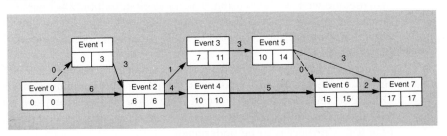

Activity 56 is also a dummy activity, showing that activity 35 must be completed before activity 67 can be started. Events 5 and 6 can't be drawn as a single event because activity 57 can be started even if activity 46 hasn't been completed.

Float diagrams

Network diagrams like those in the two preceding exhibits make the interdependencies clearly visible and identify the critical path. They have two shortcomings, however: (1) by focusing on events rather than on activities, they don't show the latest possible starting time for the first activity on a slack path; and (2) they aren't keyed to a calendar—that is, they show times, not dates.

Both of these additional bits of information could be added to the network diagram, but we prefer to use a float diagram instead. A float diagram is simply a network in which activities are shown as horizontal bars, proportional to the expected elapsed time, and linkages between activities are shown as dated vertical lines.

The float diagram corresponding to the network diagram in Exhibit 24–7 is shown in Exhibit 24–9. We can easily see that activity 01 must be completed before activity 12, and both 02 and 12 must be completed before 23, 24, or 25 can be started. Activity 24 must be started at the end of week 6 if the project is to be completed at the end of the 17th week.

Exhibit 24–9 Float diagram

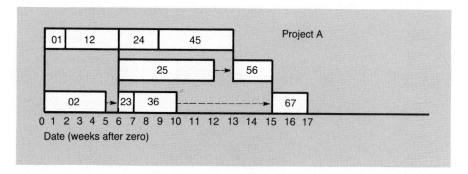

The horizontal dashed lines represent the amount of *float* in the noncritical paths. The amount of float for any activity is calculated from the following formula:

$$\text{Float} = (\text{Latest finish time} - \text{Earliest start time}) - \text{Activity time}$$

Activity 25, for example, must be finished by the end of 13 weeks if activity 56 is to be started on schedule. It can be started as early as the end of six weeks, when activity 12 is scheduled for completion. Since the time required for activity 25 is six weeks, the total amount of float in this activity is one week:

$$\text{Float} = (13 - 6) - 6 = 1 \text{ week}$$

The length of each of the dashed lines in Exhibit 24–9 identifies the amount of float for *each* of the activities in the bar segment in which it appears. For example, both activity 23 and activity 36 have a five-week float. Our convention is to show the float at the right of each segment, but it could just as well be drawn at the left or even between activities in the segment (between 23 and 36, for example). It shows how much flexibility management has in scheduling the activities in that segment.

Resource commitment tables and charts

The float diagram can be used for scheduling resources if calendar dates are inserted on the horizontal scale. It won't reveal whether the resources the project requires will be available on schedule, however. To find this out, management can construct either resource commitment tables or resource commitment charts. Tables are more convenient to work with and more readily placed on the computer. Charts have more visual impact, however, and we'll use one here.

For example, the customer insists that project A, the project we diagrammed in Exhibits 24–7 and 24–9, must be completed in 17 weeks. Management has constructed the resource commitment chart shown in Exhibit 24–10 to see what problems project A will create. The crucial resource in this case is

Exhibit 24–10 Resource commitment chart: Professional staff hours

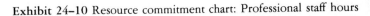
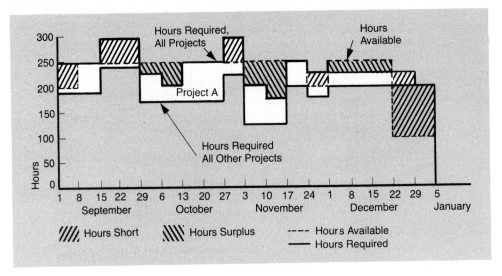

professional staff time, shown on the vertical scale. The height of the lower solid line in the exhibit shows the number of professional staff hours required by all other projects in each of the next 18 weeks. The unshaded areas show project A's requirements, week by week, and the upper solid line shows the total requirement, including project A. The height of the dashed line shows the amount of professional time expected to be available each week, and the number of hours over or short in any week is represented by the vertical distance in the diagonally striped area.

This chart shows that professional staff time will be slightly out of balance for most of the next 16 weeks, with some weeks of shortage and some of surplus. The shortages and surpluses just about cancel each other. The chart also shows that because of the year-end holidays, professional time will be totally inadequate to meet the tentative project schedule for the final two weeks of the year, including the final week of project A.

The first of these can be handled in most cases by trying different schedule combinations to see which one will minimize the cost of schedule adjustments. By starting activity 02 a week late and spreading activities 01 and 12 over a slightly longer period, management could balance the resource requirements for the first four weeks. The cost saving from this stretch-out is $200, but one week on the critical path will be lost. Management can make that up by accelerating activity 45 during the first part of November, when professional time is in surplus. The estimated cost penalty for a one-week speedup in this activity is $500. The net effect of this shift is $300. The question is whether this is a smaller penalty than the penalties from adjustments in other projects.

The second problem is more difficult. No amount of rescheduling within the 18-week period will eliminate the end-of-year time shortage. Management has four alternatives:

1. Add overtime during the first 16 weeks.
2. Add someone to the professional staff.
3. Stretch one of the projects into the next year and accept the penalty for late completion.
4. Discontinue one of the projects.

The resource commitment chart won't help management make this choice, but it does make the need for a choice apparent.

Uncertainty and PERT time estimates

All the estimates we have used so far have been single valued—that is, we have assumed that time and cost can be predicted with absolute certainty. Unfortunately, project time and cost estimates are likely to be very uncertain. Management makes firm commitments based on single-valued estimates at its peril.

For example, suppose management is considering a simple, two-phase research project which it expects to complete in 11 months. The time estimates (in months) are:

	Minimum	Most Likely	Maximum
Stage 1	6	8	12
Stage 2	2	3	5
Total	8	11	17

If management's estimates are correct, the program could be completed as early as 8 months or not until 17 months.

Decision trees of the kind we introduced in Chapter 5 can be very useful in displaying the uncertainties inherent in individual research and development

Exhibit 24–11 Components of PERT time estimates

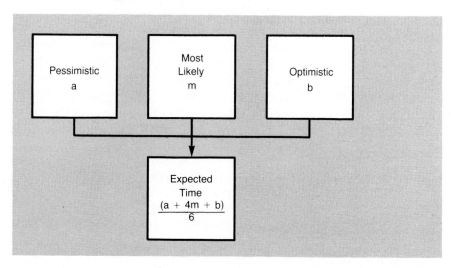

projects. For projects with many activities, however, they quickly become unwieldy and confusing. One approach is to place the entire analysis on a computer. The distribution of possible outcomes then can be approximated by running the computer program many times, using a different combination of estimates each time. This is another example of the technique known as simulation.

The most widely known network technique recognizing uncertainty is PERT (program evaluation and review technique). PERT networks are identical to those we illustrated earlier, with one important exception—four time estimates are provided for each activity instead of one, as shown in Exhibit 24–11.

The formula for expected time (t_e) in Exhibit 24–11 is a substitute for explicit probability estimates. For example, the expected time estimate for stage 1 of the two-stage project we mentioned earlier would be calculated as follows:

	Estimated Time	Weight	Expected Time
Optimistic	6	⅙	1
Most likely	8	⅘	5⅓
Pessimistic	12	⅙	2
Expected time			8⅓

This is slightly longer than the most likely time (8 months) because the pessimistic estimate (12 months) is farther from the most likely time than the optimistic estimate (6 months).

These expected time estimates are used in the same way as single time estimates—to identify the critical path and calculate such figures as earliest possible start time, latest possible start time, slack and float. They also allow management to estimate the probability of meeting a target date.

The expected time estimates are based on the notion that if similar activities are repeated many times, the average activity time will converge on the PERT time estimate rather than on the most likely time estimate. This isn't the place to examine PERT in any detail or to evaluate its limitations. We bring it up mainly as a warning against taking simple network time estimates too literally. The probability of completing a project in the time indicated by single-valued estimates is generally far less than the probability that it will be completed either sooner or later. If precise timing is crucial, management will need to do much more than prepare a single set of time estimates and resource schedules.

Progress review

The third stage in the control of research and development projects and other unique programmed activities is feedback reporting. Whereas feedback reporting in the factory is most likely to be department oriented, the focus in the research and development organization is on the individual project, for two reasons:

1. The projects are relatively few in number and each one accounts for a substantial share of total activity (the typical job order factory has many jobs, few of them accounting for a major fraction of total activity).
2. First-level control responsibility is assigned to the project manager (no one person has responsibility for a particular job order in the typical factory).

We'll concentrate in this final section on project-oriented progress reporting, leaving department reporting for a few final comments at the end.

Project reporting

Project costs can be compared with either or both of two benchmarks:

1. The initial project budget.
2. A progress-adjusted budget.

Comparisons with initial budget estimates.   One kind of project cost report compares project costs with the amounts originally budgeted for the time period covered by the report. Exhibit 24–12 is a simple example of this type of report. This shows that spending on project 16321 in April was $1,540 greater than the amount budgeted and was more than double the budget estimate for the month. On a cumulative basis, actual spending exceeded the budget by $1,480, almost a third of the budgeted amount.

Exhibit 24–12 Project spending report

RESEARCH DIVISION
MONTHLY PROJECT SPENDING REPORT

Project No.:   16321   Month: April
Project Title: Sandfly Attachment   Supervisor: G. Hill

Start Date: 3/6/x1
Scheduled Completion: 11/30/x1

	This Month			To Date		
	Actual	Budget	Variance	Actual	Budget	Variance
Salaries, professional	$ 800	$ 550	$ (250)	$1,550	$1,000	$ (550)
Salaries, technical	300	220	(80)	900	450	(450)
Laboratory services	15	—	(15)	15	—	(15)
Drafting supplies	25	30	5	95	100	5
Outside services	—	—	—	20	—	(20)
Purchased parts	350	—	(350)	350	—	(350)
Equipment	1,350	500	(850)	3,100	3,000	(100)
Total	$2,840	$1,300	$(1,540)	$6,030	$4,550	$(1,480)

Reports of this kind identify projects on which rates of expenditure are out of line with preestablished schedules, but they ignore one vital element— progress. Project costs have no meaning except in comparison with the progress achieved toward project objectives. Thus Exhibit 24–12 would seem to indicate that project 16321 is running far in excess of its budget, but it may be that resources were available much sooner than had been anticipated and that more progress was made than had been scheduled originally.

Progress-oriented reporting. The cost control comparisons in factory cost reporting contrast two sets of quantities: the standard costs of the resources actually used and budgeted resource usage for the amount of work actually done during the period. With activity-based cost and time estimates, we can make the same kinds of comparisons for independent programs such as R&D projects. All we need to do is compare actual project cost with planned cost for the amount of project progress actually achieved during the period. These comparisons tell us whether the project has been exceeding the cost perfor-

Exhibit 24–13 Progress-adjusted cost comparison report

RESEARCH DIVISION
MONTHLY PROJECT COST REPORT

Project No.: 16321
Project Title: Sandfly Attachment
Month: April
Supervisor: G. Hill

Start Date: 3/6/x1
Current Status: Phase 1
Scheduled Completion: 11/30/x1
Estimated Completion: 10/31/x1

		This Month			To Date		
Activity	Percent Complete	Budgeted for Work Done	Actual Cost	(Over-) Under-run	Budgeted for Work Done	Actual Cost	(Over-) Under-run
Synthesis and analysis	100	$1,200	$1,050	$ 150	$2,400	$2,490	$(90)
Design specifications	20	80	90	(10)	80	90	(10)
Breadboarding		not yet started					
Layout		not yet started					
Total labor and services		1,280	1,140	140	2,480	2,580	(100)
Materials and purchased parts		500	350	150	500	350	150
Equipment		1,300	1,350	(50)	3,000	3,100	(100)
Total		$3,080	$2,840	$ 240	$5,980	$6,030	$(50)

mance standards management has set up. Any such excess is known as an *overrun*.

Some of the same data can be used to compare actual progress with planned progress on the project. These comparisons tell management whether the project is on schedule, whether one or more slack path activities have been delayed or have run so far over the time estimates that they are now on the critical path, and so on.

A report in this form for project 16321 is presented in Exhibit 24–13. This shows all the activities in phase 1 of this project, but includes budget estimates only for the two activities on which resources were expended during March and April. The first activity, synthesis and analysis, was completed during April. The entire budget allowance for this activity, therefore, appears in the first line of the cumulative budget column at the right. The second activity, preparation of design specifications, wasn't originally scheduled to begin until May, but early completion of the synthesis and analysis stage allowed the design staff to begin work on this activity in April. Some 20 percent of the design work was done in April, and the budget for this portion of the design budget is entered in the second line of the report.

As this report shows, total project costs in April were $240 less than the budget provided for. This offset unfavorable variances in March, leaving a cumulative overrun of only $50 for the two months as a whole.

Future-oriented reports.   The report in Exhibit 24–13 lists a revised expected completion date, but it says little else about what the future is likely to hold in store for this project. The diagram in Exhibit 24–14 provides this

Exhibit 24–14 Integrated project progress chart

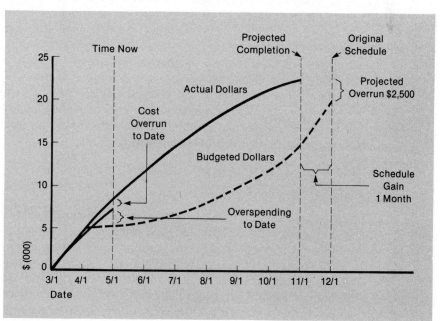

additional information in pictorial form. It directs attention to four aspects of project performance:

1. Cost overrun or underrun to date: total spending minus budgeted spending for the work performed.
2. Expenditure lag or overexpenditure to date: total spending minus budgeted spending.
3. Schedule gain or slippage: expected completion date minus originally scheduled date.
4. Anticipated cost overrun or underrun: expected project cost minus budgeted project cost.

The third and fourth of these aspects focus on the future rather than on the past. Both costs and completion dates are reestimated and compared with the original estimates. In this way the chart can serve as a form of steering control.

Charts like the one in Exhibit 24–14 can be constructed for project segments as well as for the project as a whole, as long as the chart of accounts is subdivided to permit recording of actual costs by segments. In the typical case, the clerical cost of recording project costs by individual activities in prohibitive, and so larger groups of activities known as *work packages* are treated as costing units for this purpose.

Using the progress report. The periodic progress reports serve to alert management to actual and anticipated departures from plans so that appropriate adjustments can be made. They can also signal the need to consider discontinuing the project or changing its scope or direction. Reaching a key point in the project network, sometimes referred to as a *milestone,* is one occasion for reviewing a project's rationale; a serious overrun or schedule slippage is another. A large schedule slippage or cost overrun isn't necessarily fatal, but it can't be ignored.

The question, of course, is not whether the project has overrun its budget or is behind schedule. The question is how much more money will have to be spent and what is the expected value of the payoff. Both of these factors reflect the future, not the past, and the future appears to be changing constantly. For this reason every project should be reviewed periodically even if the progress reports indicate it is progressing satisfactorily.

Departmental performance review

Departmental cost reports emphasizing differences between departmental budget allowances and total costs are of little value in the control of research and development costs. Most costs are either salaries or are closely related to salaries. Total expenditures for these inputs are controlled by decisions to hire and retain personnel; these, in turn, are the outcome of project approvals. Once the budget is approved, expenditures are likely to conform very closely to the amount budgeted, with few variances of any importance.

Departmental cost reporting can be made more meaningful if it can be integrated with the project performance reports. One approach is to assign to each department the costs and progress of the projects headed by project managers in that department. (Each project is typically the direct responsibility of a project manager.) Progress made by each department is measured by the estimated costs of the work done on its projects' activities during that period. Costs include the department's own costs plus the costs of work done in other departments on the department's projects. The department is credited for the costs of the work it does on other departments' projects. A departmental performance report prepared on this basis would contain the following elements:

Budgeted cost of work done on projects
    headed by departmental personnel $14,000
Transfers to other departments   1,500
    Total credits..........................   15,500
Departmental costs $9,900
Transfers from other departments 4,800   14,700
    Departmental variance .... $ 800

The flaw in this is that it may transfer some cost variances from the departments in which they arise to the departments for which the work was done. Management has no summary information, classifying the variances by their department of origin. To meet this objection, the system might provide for a departmental classification of progress achieved on each project. If this is done, the hours or costs accumulated on all projects in each department can be compared with the hours or costs budgeted for the tasks actually performed on those projects in that department.

This second alternative is likely to provide better information, but it may be more expensive, if progress is difficult to identify by department. We repeat the point we made at the beginning, however. Research and development work is project oriented, and performance reporting must have the same focus. Departmental reporting plays a strictly secondary role.

Summary

Research and development activities are project centered, programmed activities. Control is a three-stage process—initial approval, detailed scheduling, and progress review, including implicit or explicit project reapproval.

Research budgets are often set in the aggregate, on the basis of an overall rule of thumb. Budgets set in this way can neglect opportunities or waste funds on low-yield projects. A preferable approach is to regard research and development proposals as a particular kind of capital expenditure proposals with highly uncertain costs and benefits.

The main devices for detailed scheduling are network diagrams and float diagrams, showing the relationships among the various phases of individual projects. These can be used to identify the critical path and the amount of slack or float in the noncritical paths. Adjustments can be made in the critical

764

path to fit the project into a desired time limit. Departmental resource commitment charts can then be used to adapt the overall schedule to the quantities of resources available. A computer is usually necessary to handle networking and scheduling problems of any magnitude, however.

The project networks or activity lists can be used to organize the data for control reporting. Performance reports need to match costs with the amount of progress actually achieved, not the amounts originally budgeted for the calendar period. These reports should be project centered and should include revised estimates of future costs and progress. Serious overruns or schedule slippages on certain projects may even signal difficulties that make it unlikely that further expenditures will have big enough payoffs to justify keeping these projects alive. There is no need to wait for the next budget review date to decide to drop an unpromising project.

Independent study problems (solutions in Appendix B)

1. **Project planning.** The market research manager is preparing to submit a market survey proposal to the marketing vice president. The project will cost $105,000. In the following table of time estimates, each activity is identified by a two-digit number, the first digit denoting the preceding event and the second digit indicating the event that signals the end of the activity:

Activity	Estimated Time (weeks)
01	1
02	3
03	5
14	2
25	4
35	3
46	6
56	2
57	1
69	4
78	2
89	2

Required:

a. Draw a network and trace the critical path.
b. Draw a float diagram.
c. The marketing vice president agrees to the time schedule embodied in the project network, but is not sure the project is worth undertaking. What quantitative estimates would you try to submit to throw light on this decision?

2. **Performance report.** The management services division of a large public accounting firm would like to be able to offer its clients a new service. A team chosen from the consulting staff has been trying to develop the capability to provide this service. The following network was drawn up when this development project was approved (the numbers on the arrows are estimates of time required, in weeks):

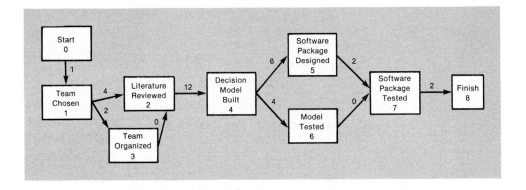

The estimated cost of the project was $200,000, and time and funds for the first eight weeks were budgeted as follows:

Week	Activity	Cost	Milestone to Be Reached
1	01	$ 5,000	Team selected.
2	12	6,000	—
	13	1,000	
3	12	4,000	
	13	1,000	Team organized.
4	12	5,000	—
5	12	5,000	Literature summary distributed.
6	24	8,000	—
7	24	10,000	Preliminary model conference.
8	24	7,000	Model type selected.

The total budgeted cost of activity 24 (model construction) was $70,000.

The literature search was completed and the literature summary was distributed at the end of the fourth week. The total cost to that point was $22,000. At that time the project leader saw no reason to revise the estimates of the time and costs of the remaining activities.

Work on the construction of the model was begun immediately. It is now the end of the eighth week, and you have the following information:

1. Cost incurred to date: $51,000.
2. Milestone reached, end of eighth week: preliminary model conference.
3. Estimated additional time to complete construction of model: 12 weeks.
4. Estimated future costs to complete construction of model: $65,000.
5. No changes have been made in estimates of time or costs for activities scheduled to take place after the model has been built.

Required:

a. Prepare a project performance report covering the first eight weeks.
b. What questions should management ask in reviewing this report? What actions might be taken?

Exercises and problems

3. **Network diagram: Multiple choice.** A construction company has contracted to erect a new building and has asked for assistance in analyzing the project. Using the program evaluation review technique (PERT), the following network has been developed:

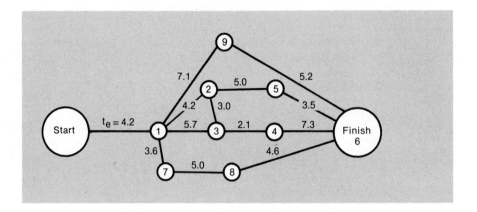

All paths from the start point to the finish point, event 6, represent activities or processes that must be completed before the entire project, the building, will be completed. The numbers above the paths or line segments represent expected completion times for the activities or processes. The expected time is based upon the commonly used, 1–4–1, three-estimate method. For example, the three-estimate method gives an estimated time of 4.2 weeks to complete event 1.

1. The critical path is:
   a. 1–2–5–6.
   b. 1–2–3–4–6.
   c. 1–3–4–6.
   d. 1–7–8–6.
   e. 1–9–6.
2. Slack time on path 1–9–6 equals
   a. 4.3.
   b. 2.8.
   c. 0.9.
   d. 0.4.
   e. 0.0.
3. The latest time for reaching event 6 via path 1–2–5–6 is
   a. 20.8.
   b. 19.3.
   c. 17.4.
   d. 16.5.
   e. 12.7.
4. The earliest time for reaching event 6 via path 1–2–5–6 is
   a. 20.8.
   b. 16.9.
   c. 16.5.
   d. 12.7.
   e. 3.5.
5. If all other paths are operating on schedule but path segment 7–8 has an unfavorable time variance of 1.9,
   a. The critical path will be shortened.
   b. The critical path will be eliminated.
   c. The critical path will be unaffected.
   d. Another path will become the critical path.
   e. The critical path will have an increased time of 1.9.

(CPA)

4. **Float diagram.** The management of the construction company (problem 3) finds it difficult to interpret the network and has asked your help.

Required:

a. Prepare a float diagram for this project.

b. Calculate the amount of float on each of the noncritical paths.

c. The company will have only enough personnel in the fifth, sixth, and seventh weeks to engage in two activities simultaneously. Which two would you select, and why? What problems would this shortage of personnel create and how might these problems be solved?

5. **Project network.** The Villard Company recently initiated a new product development project estimated to cost $31,500. The list of activities constituting this project, together with estimates of the number of weeks each activity would take and the cost to carry it out, is shown in the table below. In this table each activity is identified by a two-digit number, the first digit denoting the preceding event and the second digit indicating the event that signals the end of the activity:

Activity	Estimated Time (weeks)	Estimated Cost
01	2	$ 1,100
12	1	500
23	3	2,500
24	7	3,500
25	2	2,200
34	3	3,300
35	1	400
45	5	4,000
49	3	1,600
56	2	900
67	1	1,200
68	6	4,200
78	2	700
79	4	4,100
89	3	1,300
Total		$31,500

Required:

a. Draw a network to represent this project.

b. List the events the critical path passes through and indicate the number of weeks the project was expected to take.

6. **Performance reporting.** Eight weeks after the Villard Company started its product development project (problem 5), activities 01, 12, 24, and 25 had been completed and activity 23 was approximately half finished. It was estimated that an additional two weeks and $1,500 would be necessary to finish activity 23. No other estimates had to be revised. As originally approved, the schedule called for completion of activities 01, 12, 23, and 25 in the first eight weeks, with activity 24 to be five-sevenths finished and activity 34 to be two-thirds finished. Costs incurred during the first eight weeks were:

Activity	Amount
01	$1,150
12	250
23	2,400
24	3,000
25	2,500
Total	$9,300

Required:

  a. Prepare a report summarizing the performance and status of this project at the end of the first eight weeks.

  b. What additional information would you find particularly useful at this point?

7. **PERT time; critical path.** The Dryfus Company specializes in large construction projects. The company's management regularly employs PERT in planning and coordinating its construction projects. The following schedule of separable activities and their expected completion times have been developed for an office building which is to be constructed by Dryfus Company:

Activity Description	Predecessor Activity	Expected Activity Completion Time (in weeks)
a. Excavation	—	2
b. Foundation	*a*	3
c. Underground utilities	*a*	7
d. Rough plumbing	*b*	4
e. Framing	*b*	5
f. Roofing	*e*	3
g. Electrical work	*f*	3
h. Interior walls	*d,g*	4
i. Finish plumbing	*h*	2
j. Exterior finishing	*f*	6
k. Landscaping	*c,i,j*	2

Required:

  a. Identify the critical path for this project and determine the expected project completion time in weeks.

  b. Explain the meaning of the "expected activity completion time," as it is calculated in the PERT method.

(CMA, adapted)

8. **Project network: Supplying missing data.** Sangemi, Inc. manufactures industrial parts. It has a sizeable methods engineering department, responsible for finding ways to increase operating efficiency.

  One of the company's manufacturing processes suddenly became very unreliable and management halted production. The chief methods engineer has proposed solving this problem by beginning work immediately on the project described in the following network:

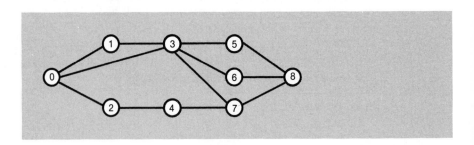

Required:

  a. Supply the data necessary to fill in the blanks marked by dashes in the accompanying table:

Activity	t_o	t_m	t_p	t_e	LFT	EST	LST	Slack
—	6	8	10	8.0	14.5	0	6.5	6.5
02	3	3	6	3.5	3.5	0	—	—
03	4	5	—	—	15.5	0	10.0	10.0
13	1	1	1	1.0	—	8.0	—	6.5
24	—	6	11	6.5	10.0	3.5	3.5	—
35	5	6	10	6.5	22.0	9.0	—	6.5
36	2	—	4	3.0	24.0	9.0	21.0	12.0
37	0	0	0	0.0	19.5	9.0	19.5	—
47	7	9	14	9.5	19.5	10.0	10.0	0.0
58	4	4	7	—	26.5	15.5	22.0	6.5
68	1	2	6	2.5	—	12.0	24.0	12.0
78	4	7	10	7.0	26.5	—	19.5	0.0

t_o, t_m, t_p = Optimistic, most likely, pessimistic time.
$\quad t_e$ = PERT expected time.
EST = Earliest start time.
LST = Latest start time.
LFT = Latest finish time.

b. Identify the critical path. What is the project's scheduled completion date?
c. Suppose the required completion date is two time periods earlier than the figure you derived in (*b*). Which column(s) would be affected by this change?

9. **Project performance report: Follow-up decisions.** Broadway Contractors, Inc., has a contract to remodel one of the university laboratories. The contract price is $160,000, based on an estimated cost of $130,000. The contract calls for completion of the job in 12 weeks, with a penalty of $10,000 for each week of delay beyond that period. The original network for this project showed the following sequences of activities:

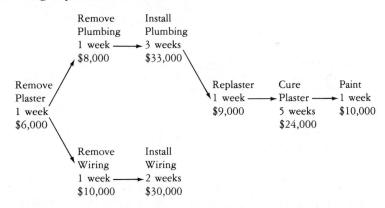

Removal of the old plumbing and removal of the old wiring were scheduled to take place simultaneously, to be followed immediately by the installation of the new plumbing and the new wiring. The job was started on the scheduled date and the following work was done during the first three weeks:

Activity	Cost
Remove plaster	$ 6,200
Remove plumbing	16,000
Remove wiring	9,200
Install wiring (half completed)	15,000

Management now estimates that installation of the new plumbing will take four weeks and will cost $40,000. All other cost and time estimates are unchanged.

The project can be speeded up, but only at a cost. The estimated costs of such a speed-up are:

	Additional Expenditures That Must Be Made to Save	
	One Week	Two Weeks
Install plumbing	$ 8,000	$19,000
Cure plaster	10,500	18,500

Required:

a. Prepare a summary report that will show management the past performance and present status of this contract.

b. Should the company spend additional money to speed up one or more activities? If so, which one(s) and by how many weeks? State your reasons.

10. **Resource commitment table.** The manager of the methods department of Acme Gear Company is scheduled to begin a new project (project C) next week. It has two projects (A and B) already under way and a straight-time capacity of 200 labor hours a week. Up to 20 hours of overtime are available each week, at a premium of $6 an hour.

When completed, project A is expected to save the company $200 a week in labor costs, project B is expected to save $300 a week, and project C is expected to save $400 a week.

Each activity in one of these projects is assigned a two-digit number. The first digit designates the event immediately preceding this activity; the second digit identifies the following event. The final event in each project is event 9. Only project A is to be completed during the next 13 weeks.

You have the following data about the activities in these three projects to be scheduled for work in this 13-week period:

Project and Activity	Scheduled Start Date, Beginning of Week	Slack (weeks)	Weeks to Complete	Hours Required per Week
A–67	1	0	4	40
A–69	1	5	5	20
A–78	5	0	3	30
A–89	8	0	3	60
B–36	1	4	7	40
B–45	1	0	6	20
B–46	1	8	3	60
B–56	7	0	5	40
B–67	12	0	4	80
C–01	1	0	2	80
C–12	3	0	3	40
C–13	3	3	5	20
C–14	3	7	2	40
C–24	6	2	4	30
C–25	6	0	8	60
C–36	8	3	3	40

Work on any activity can be interrupted for a week or more without affecting the total number of hours required for that activity. If an activity has to be scheduled in any week for less than the number of hours normally required for that activity, the lost time must be rescheduled during a week in which that activity is not already scheduled—in no week can any activity be scheduled for more than the number of hours listed in the table.

Required:

a. Prepare diagrams showing the portions of the networks for these three projects represented by the activities listed in the table. Indicate which activities are on the critical path in each case.

b. Prepare a resource commitment table for the next 13 weeks.

c. Recommend a set of adjustments that will make it feasible to undertake all three projects. Indicate the criteria you used in making these adjustments.

11. **Project network: Cost slopes.**   Cheerful Calorie Contributors, Inc. operates a chain of ice cream stores. The company has expanded steadily for several years, opening a new store every month, on the average. As a result of this experience, management has been able to develop a fairly precise standard operating procedure for opening a new store. The chief operating officer has drawn up the following description of this procedure:

> The first step in opening a store is finding a desirable location in the general area we wish to enter. This generally takes about four days. As soon as we find our location, our engineering department begins drawing plans for the store, including layouts for furniture and for built-in freezers. Plan preparation takes six days.
>
> During this time our real estate department is negotiating rental terms. Since we pay premium rates and obtain virtually every location that we choose, we do not delay the drawing up of the plans for the two days that these negotiations consume.
>
> After terms are negotiated, the lease must be drawn up by our legal department and approved by outside counsel. This process takes six days. We do not actually start installing furniture or freezers until the lease is approved.
>
> When the engineering department completes its plans, they are submitted to the city for approval. This takes seven days. Neither the furniture nor the freezers can be installed before plans are approved by the city.
>
> Furniture can be ordered as soon as plans are completed, since if the city rejects the location, the furniture can be used elsewhere. It takes eight days for furniture to be ordered and delivered. (The ordering process takes one day and delivery is made seven days later.) Installation in the store requires four days.
>
> No ordering time is involved in the case of freezers, since CCC keeps a supply on hand, but building them in and installing and testing the necessary electrical and plumbing facilities takes nine days.
>
> Once the plans have been drawn, the personnel department can identify a manager and hire a staff, a process requiring five days. Then the manager and staff must be trained for six days at CCC's large modern training facility. Once trained, they can begin planning the operation of the store and order the necessary inventory of ice cream and supplies. This process takes four days. The order for the initial inventory can't be placed before the end of the second day; the remaining two days are devoted to drawing up work schedules, arranging for trash collection, and so forth. The staff aren't prepared to take delivery of the inventory until the end of the fourth day of operations planning or the beginning of the day after the last of the freezers and furniture have been installed, whichever comes later. The order for the inventory must be placed at least two days before the desired delivery date. If the facilities aren't ready to receive the inventory at the end of this two-day period, the suppliers will store it on their premises until the

CCC premises are ready. It takes one full day to shelve the inventory once it has been delivered.

After freezers, furniture, and inventory are all in place a final preopening cleanup is required. This takes two days.

This is the normal procedure, but the company has found it can reduce the time to complete some of these activities by spending more money on them. The following actions are the only possibilities:

Additions	Time Saving
$200	One day in installing freezers
$100 (in addition to the $200 above)	A second day in installing freezers
$150	One day in hiring staff
$ 50	One day in installing furniture
$120	One day in training staff
$175	One day in drawing plans
$210 (in addition to the $175 above)	A second day in drawing plans
$300	One day in preopening cleanup

Required:

a. Construct a network describing the process, enter the time requirements under the normal procedure, and identify the critical path.

b. How long does the entire process normally take?

c. Which of the time-saving options would you recommend if the company wants to reduce total project time by one day? By two days? By three days? Show your calculations.

d. Management is in a great hurry to open its next store. What is the shortest possible time in which the project can be completed? What is the incremental cost of shortening the timetable in this way?

(Adapted from a problem written by John C. Burton)

12. **Departmental performance report.** The Argus Company's research division has approximately 80 employees, organized as shown in the accompanying table:

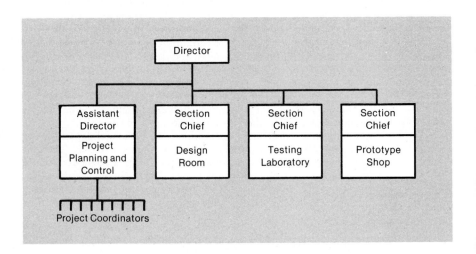

Research proposals are prepared initially in the project planning and control section (PPC). Once a project is approved, an engineer on the PPC staff is appointed project coordinator, with authority to direct that project, evaluate progress, and attempt to keep it on schedule. Line authority over the research staff is vested in the three section chiefs, however.

The project coordinators receive cost and progress reports on their projects every month. In addition, each section chief receives a summary report on cost performance in that section. This is a two-page report, with an overall departmental summary on the first page and an element-by-element comparison on the second. The first-page summary for the testing laboratory for last October showed the following information:

	Budget	Actual	Variance
Project 246	$ 4,700	$ 4,650	$ 50
Project 289	1,300	3,300	(2,000)
Project 294	5,200	3,530	1,670
Total	$11,200	$11,480	$ (280)

Required:

a. What useful information, if any, would this report give to the section chief in charge of the testing laboratory?

b. What changes would you make in this report to make it more useful to management?

13. **Cost slopes: PERT time.**   Speedy Scientific, Inc., has a government contract to design and develop an air pollution control device. The contract calls for a fee equal to the estimated cost for the most likely estimated time plus a fixed amount of $3 million. The contract provides for completion in 36 months with a penalty of $200,000 for each month or part of a month in excess of 36 months.

A study of the design problems likely to be encountered has given rise to the following schedule of times and costs:

Activity	Estimated Time (months)			Estimated Cost for Most Likely Time	Marginal Cost per Month
	Earliest	Most Likely	Latest		
01	6	8	12	$ 1,000,000	$ 50,000
02	3	5	8	2,000,000	20,000
04	6	10	15	4,000,000	10,000
13	10	12	14	1,500,000	30,000
14	12	16	20	5,000,000	100,000
24	6	7	10	1,800,000	25,000
25	6	9	10	3,000,000	40,000
36	2	2	5	3,500,000	15,000
46	3	4	8	2,500,000	10,000
47	6	8	10	2,000,000	30,000
57	2	3	5	500,000	35,000
68	7	9	12	1,500,000	20,000
78	10	11	14	4,500,000	50,000
Total				$32,800,000	

Each figure listed as marginal cost per month is the estimated change in costs for a one-month increase or decrease in the most likely estimated time. The earliest and latest time estimates would not be changed by a change in the most likely estimated time. Each activity's most likely time can be reduced to the earliest possible time by incurring marginal costs for the required number of weeks. Each activity's most likely time can be increased, but no further cost saving from further delay is possible once the most likely time has been extended to the latest possible time.

Required:

a. Present a schedule showing eight different paths leading to completion and the time in months taken for each path. Calculate the length of each path both on a most likely time basis and on a PERT time basis. Identify the critical path. (*Hint:* A network diagram may help.)

b. If the most likely activity times are all realized, what will be the net fee earned by the corporation?

c. How much can the corporation save by diverting resources from those activities which are not critical but neither increasing nor decreasing the length of the critical path you determined in answer to (*a*)?

d. Assuming management wishes to maximize the probable profit on this contract, by how many weeks would you recommend shortening the critical path? List the actions necessary to accomplish this reduction and their effects on costs, revenues, and activity times.

(SMAC, adapted)

Case 24–1: Space Constructors, Inc. (B)* (project reporting)

After restudying other elements of the overall construction program, Mr. Alison and Mr. Phillips decided that a 10-week schedule for the construction of a remote control building would be acceptable. They were able to draw the critical path diagram shown in Exhibit 1.

Exhibit 1 Revised critical path diagram for remote control building project

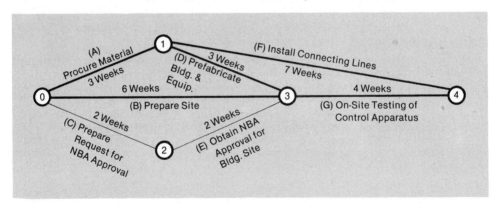

Mr. Alison was field construction supervisor for Space Constructors, Inc. Mr. Phillips was project engineer in charge of the job of constructing a remote control building. This project was an integral part of the work covered by a large construction contract that had been awarded to Space Constructors some months earlier.

Using this information, Mr. Alison and Mr. Phillips agreed on the cost and production schedule summarized in Table 1. "I think that we can meet the 10-week deadline with this schedule," Mr. Phillips said, "but we'll have to watch our progress very closely as we go along. We'll take our first reading at the end of three weeks and see where we stand. If we have to make adjustments, we can make them then."

* This case was prepared as a follow-up to "Space Constructors, Inc.," Case No. EA-P380 (copyright 1965 by the President and Fellows of Harvard College). Copyright by l'Institut pour l'Étude des Méthodes de Direction de l'Entreprise (IMEDE), Lausanne, Switzerland, Reproduced by permission.

Table 1 Construction schedule for remote control building project

					Cost to Be Incurred during Week						
Activity	1	2	3	4	5	6	7	8	9	10	Total
A ······	$1,667	$1,667	$1,666	—	—	—	—	—	—	—	$ 5,000
B ······	2,333	2,333	2,334	$ 2,334	$ 2,333	$2,333	—	—	—	—	14,000
C ······	1,250	1,250	—	—	—	—	—	—	—	—	2,500
D* ······	—	—	—	6,000	6,000	6,000	—	—	—	—	18,000
E ······	—	—	—	4,000	4,000	—	—	—	—	—	8,000
F ······	—	—	—	1,643	1,643	1,643	$1,643	$1,643	$1,643	$1,642	11,500
G ······	—	—	—	—	—	—	2,500	2,500	2,500	2,500	10,000
Total ··	$5,250	$5,250	$4,000	$13,977	$13,976	$9,976	$4,143	$4,143	$4,143	$4,142	$69,000

* Crash schedule, providing for maximum permissible amount of overtime work.

Table 2 Weekly cost report for remote control building project (week of October 15–19)

	This Week			Cumulative		
Activity	Budgeted Costs*	Actual Costs	(Over) Under	Budgeted Costs*	Actual Costs	(Over) Under
A ········	$1,666	$ 500	$ 1,166	5,000	$ 4,900	$ 100
B ········	2,334	2,300	34	7,000	6,800	200
C ········	—	350	(350)	2,500	2,350	150
D ········	—	1,500	(1,500)	—	1,500	(1,500)
Total ·····	$4,000	$4,650	$ (650)	$14,500	$15,550	$(1,050)

* From Table 1.

"I guess that's soon enough," Mr. Alison replied, "but we can't lose sight of the costs on this project. We've gone way over our estimates on those underground installations, and we have to be particularly careful to keep our costs under control on the remaining parts of the contract."

On Monday, October 1, work began on activities A, B, and C. All personnel were scheduled to work a regular five-day week during each of the first three weeks, with no overtime.

At the end of the third week, Mr. Phillips asked each of his project supervisors to report the amount of progress they had made on the activities under their supervision. The following information reached Mr. Phillips's desk late Monday afternoon, October 22:

Activity	Date Started	Completed as of Oct. 19	Weeks Needed to Complete
A	10–1	100%	—
B	10–1	33	4
C	10–1	100	—
D	10–18	10	3

Activity starts and completions were reported routinely to Mr. Phillips, so he already knew that activity A had been completed three days ahead of schedule and that as a result the project supervisor had been able to start activity D two days ahead of schedule. Because of this head start, the amount of overtime work scheduled for activity D had been reduced. No overtime work was performed on any activity during the first three weeks.

Activity F, on the other hand, had not been started early. The necessary personnel had been fully assigned to other projects and the project supervisor had not been able to get them rescheduled. They had reported for work on the remote control building site on Monday, October 22, however, and Mr. Phillips saw no reason why activity F should not be completed on time.

Mr. Phillips also received two reports from his cost accountant. The first of these was the regular weekly cost report for the project, shown in Table 2. The second was a revised set of cost estimates, prepared during the early afternoon by the cost accountant in cooperation with the project supervisors. Expected future costs per week for each activity were:

B .... $2,500 (four weeks)
D .... $5,500 (three weeks)
E .... $4,000 (two weeks)
F .... $1,643 (seven weeks)
G .... $2,500 (four weeks)

a. A program of the kind illustrated in Exhibit 1 cannot be implemented unless enough resources of the required kinds can be made available at the dates indicated. How would you use the data summarized in Table 1 to test the feasibility of the proposed construction schedule?

b. Why did Mr. Phillips want a performance report at the end of three weeks? What kinds of decisions did he have to make at that time?

c. In the light of your answer to question (*b*), what was wrong with the weekly cost report (Table 2)?

d. Prepare a report or reports that would have told Mr. Phillips what he needed to know about his performance during the first three weeks of the remote control building project.

e. What should Mr. Phillips have done on the basis of the information provided by your report?

25 Divisional profit reporting

Profit is the main private objective of business enterprises. Management therefore is held accountable for the amount of profit it generates. We discussed profit contribution reporting to marketing management in Chapter 12. Now it is time to see how profits can be reported to top management. In this chapter we'll examine four related topics:

1. The organizational setting in which divisional profit reporting to management takes place.
2. The purposes internal profit reporting is intended to serve, and the appropriate performance standard for each of these purposes.
3. The form the divisional profit measure should take.
4. Significant measurement problems the accountant will encounter.

The organizational setting

Profit performance reports can be issued for any segment of the company's business. A business segment is any portion of the company's business for which both revenues and expenses can be identified. Our attention in this chapter will focus on reports covering business segments that are the particular responsibility of a single manager or group of managers below the chief executive officer level. The organization units responsible for these business segments may be called divisions, or groups, or subsidiary companies, or departments. We'll use the term *division* to identify them all.

Organizations in which the managers reporting to the chief executive officer are responsible for generating profits in specific business segments are generally referred to as *decentralized* companies. Their major operating divisions are known as *profit centers* or *investment centers*. Other units have characteristics that lead us to classify them as *administered centers*. In this section we'll see how these and other kinds of organization units fit into the decentralized organization.

Profit centers

The profit center is intended to be very much like an independent business enterprise. It has four main characteristics:

Main charac̄s. of π ctr.

1. It has a profit objective.
2. Its management has authority to make decisions affecting the major determinants of profit, including the power to choose its markets and sources of supply.
3. Its management is expected to use profit-based decision rules.
4. Its management is accountable to higher management for the amount of profit generated.

The second of these is the only one that gives us any trouble. Top management always reserves certain kinds of authority, particularly over financing and capital expenditures. Divisional autonomy is also limited by the need to have the divisions conform to overall company policies and to coordinate their activities with those of other divisions.

What this says is that decentralization is really a matter of degree rather than a question of either/or, but no division can be a profit center, as we use that term, unless the following two kinds of authority are delegated to the division manager:

distinguishes π ctr. from division

1. The division is free to sell most of its output to outside customers.
2. The division is free to choose the sources of supply for most of the materials and other goods and services it buys.

The first of these means that manufacturing divisions can't be classified as profit centers. The sales volume of a manufacturing division is entirely dependent on the number of orders obtained by the marketing division or divisions. Volume isn't within the manufacturing manager's sphere of control. A manufacturing division can be a profit center only if it has an adequate marketing staff of its own, products salable on the outside market, and freedom to sell these products outside the company. Any manufacturing division with these characteristics is not a manufacturing division as that term is usually understood.

The second condition means that marketing divisions can't be classified as profit centers, either. The marketing division exists to market the output of the manufacturing division. The marketing manager can't refuse to promote the manufacturing division's products or services just because better or cheaper substitutes are available from other sources. Any such decision must be made by higher management, with responsibility for both manufacturing and marketing.

＊ The result is that the typical profit center is a division selling a limited number of product lines or serving a specific geographical area. It encompasses both the means of providing goods or services and the means of marketing them. In manufacturing companies factories are the means of providing the goods; in merchandising companies this role is played by the people who buy the merchandise; and in service organizations the role is played by those who perform the services the customers buy.

Investment centers

is a π ctr.

Most profit center managers have some control over the amount of funds invested in the activities of their profit centers. Accounts receivable, inventories, and trade accounts payable are often largely or entirely within the profit center manager's jurisdiction.

To emphasize the manager's responsibility to control the amount invested, these profit centers are sometimes called investment centers. An investment center is a profit center in which the manager has authority to make decisions affecting a significant amount of invested capital.

In practice, almost all profit centers are investment centers. Most profit center managers can influence the amount of inventories and at least some other elements of working capital. Furthermore, both profit center managers and investment center managers can make some expenditures for plant and equipment without referring the proposals to higher management, but this authority is always limited—major proposals have to be approved higher up. The larger the unit, or the closer the manager is to the top of the hierarchy, the higher the authorization limit is likely to be, but it will never be infinite.

Administered centers

Many organization units aren't allowed to choose their sources of supply but otherwise have all of the characteristics of profit centers. Their managers can set prices, plot marketing strategy, decide how many employees to have, and establish desired inventory levels. Sometimes they even have the power to decide which of the company's products to carry.

We call units with these characteristics *administered centers*. Given the features administered centers share with profit centers, they should receive the same treatment except in the establishment of the prices they pay for goods they receive from other divisions, a topic we'll return to in the next chapter.

Why companies decentralize

Companies decentralize because they want their division managers to act like well-financed entrepreneurs. They expect this behavior to yield benefits such as the following:

1. Decisions will be made more quickly, with less red tape.
2. Decisions will be better, because the decentralized manager can bring more time and closer knowledge to individual decisions than top management could provide.
3. Division managers will base their decisions on profits rather than on narrower functional measures such as unit cost or total sales.
4. Top management will have more time to concentrate on strategic planning and other higher-level activities.
5. Division managers will recognize specific parts of the company's income as the result of their own efforts, and this will reinforce their motivation to strive for greater profits.
6. The company will be more dynamic, because division managers will be freer to use initiative and imagination in planning and carrying out their activities.

7. More people will have a chance to make profit-based decisions. This will increase the size and experience level of the pool of qualified candidates for senior managerial positions.[1]

Decentralization isn't always the right way to go, of course. For one thing, subordinate managers will make mistakes managers with more experience might be able to avoid. Second, some actions that increase a profit center's profits may hurt other divisions and the entire company as well. This is called *suboptimization*. Third, decentralized companies are likely to have more staff personnel, both because more managers need staff assistance and because top management needs staff to help in the task of providing central guidance and control of decentralized operations. Finally, the quest for short-term profits may cause the division to underemphasize nonfinancial objectives or to short-change the future.

If management decides to decentralize, it must be assuming that the advantages outweigh the dangers, so that overall profit performance will be better than if all profit-oriented decisions were to be reserved for top management. Other arrangements will have to be made to insure that nonfinancial objectives and long-term considerations will receive enough attention. We'll discuss some of these arrangements later in this chapter.

Service centers

Many organization units in decentralized companies are classified as service centers. A service center is a unit providing services or support to other units in the organization within the limits set by its capacity. Some production departments may even be organized as service centers, outside the boundaries of individual profit centers.

The relationships between service centers and profit centers are illustrated in Exhibit 25–1. These service centers have three common characteristics:

1. The volume of production, service, or support they provide is determined elsewhere in the organization.
2. Their managers are evaluated on the basis of cost, quality, and other internal performance criteria, not on a profit basis.
3. The activities they perform are evaluated either jointly with other activities or on the basis of benefit criteria other than the amount of profit they generate currently (e.g., amount of cost saved, amount of public goodwill created).

The most important service centers are located in corporate headquarters. Corporate staff groups—for legal matters, construction or maintenance of facilities, market research, financial record-keeping and analysis, and so on—play four main roles in connection with decentralization. First, they help top management analyze the strategic plans and implementation proposals submitted by

[1] Robert N. Anthony and John Dearden, *Management Control Systems: Text and Cases,* 4th ed. (Homewood, Ill.: Richard D. Irwin, 1981), p. 212. Copyright © 1981 by Richard D. Irwin, Inc.

Exhibit 25–1 Relationships between service centers and profit centers

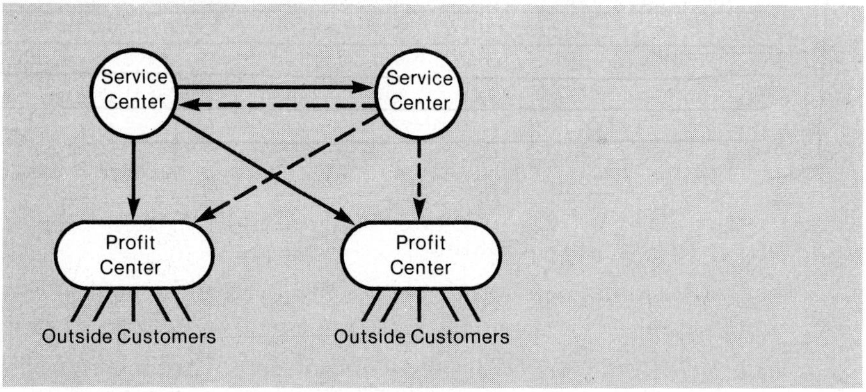

the division managers. Second, they advise and assist the division managers on technical matters, supplementing the divisional staffs. Third, they administer the controls that are designed to set the limits within which the division managers are free to exercise their authority. Minimum expenditure levels in some functional activities (e.g., maintenance or quality control) and the achievement of nonfinancial objectives fall in this category. Finally, they help top management review and evaluate the performance of individual divisions and their managers. In a sense, dealing with central staff is the price the division managers pay for the authority they've been given.

Quasi-profit centers and pseudo-profit centers

Some service centers provide a limited range of measurable services which can also be bought from outside suppliers. Computer services, printing, art work, and technical advice are typical examples. Management may choose to require some of these to operate as quasi-profit centers, competing with outside suppliers for business within the organization. The objective is to motivate the managers to reduce costs or provide better service.

One company, for example, has a reproduction shop, performing a wide variety of photographic and printing services for other units within the company. Its "customers" have free access to outside organizations offering the same kinds of services. The shop manager isn't free to solicit business from outside customers. The shop is expected to compete with outside suppliers by offering better or faster service internally at or below the market price.

The quasi-profit center isn't exactly the mirror image of the administered center. In theory, it can price itself out of the market, or turn down the opportunity to bid on jobs it doesn't like. This seldom happens in practice, however. The main result is to establish a sort of market-based transfer price for the services provided. We'll examine this possibility in detail in Chapter 26.

Quasi-profit centers shouldn't be confused with the service centers (including production centers) we refer to as *pseudo-profit centers*. These are service centers

service ctrs

pseudo vs. quasi!

which aren't in competition with outside suppliers, but are the sole suppliers of specified goods or services to other parts of the organization, charging prices that are designed to cover their costs and provide a profit margin as well. While the prices charged by quasi-profit centers are expected to influence division managers' decisions on where to acquire goods or services, the prices charged by pseudo-profit centers have no such purpose. They provide the illusion of a profit measure, but not the substance.

Evaluating profit performance

Divisional profit performance reports are likely to be used in any or all of three ways:

1. To help division managers improve the profitability of their divisions' operations (*operations evaluation*).
2. To help higher management evaluate the desirability of continuing the divisions' activities (*economic evaluation*).
3. To help higher management evaluate the performance of profit-responsible division managers (*managerial evaluation*).

Operations evaluation

Division managers can use divisional profit reports to help them find ways to improve the profitability of the activities they are responsible for. The primary question is whether better operating methods can be found. To answer this question, management may wish to compare operating results with evaluation standards derived from any of a number of sources:

1. The current profit plan.
2. Historical results.
3. Competitors' performance.
4. Managerial experience.
5. Engineering studies.

Operations evaluation is largely a process of looking for clues. These clues usually emerge from comparisons of detailed operating ratios rather than figures summarizing overall results. Are we using more materials than the standards call for? Has our volume gone up as fast as competitors' volume? Are competitors getting better responses from incremental marketing dollars than we are?

Unfortunately, we can't do justice to these and similar questions here. As a result, we'll concentrate in this chapter on questions of overall profit performance, and return in Chapter 27 to the detailed analysis of performance operations evaluation requires.

Economic evaluation

Economic evaluation is the process by which higher management decides whether a division's activities produce benefits commensurate with their costs.

cost vs. benefit

quate ROI

For revenue-generating divisions (profit centers, investment centers, and administered centers), the question is whether the division's activities are generating enough income to support the capital invested in it. In other words, is the division generating an adequate rate of return on investment (ROI)?

To answer this question, we should compare the return we are getting with a standard based on the cost of capital, applied uniformly to all divisions in a given risk category. Differences in market environment don't justify the use of different standards for different divisions—our only concern is whether invested capital produces more than it costs. Adequate economic performance in a hostile environment justifies continuation; poor economic performance in a favorable environment calls for discontinuation unless the situation can be turned around.

future cash flows vs net liquidation value

True economic evaluation is forward-looking, designed to help management decide whether to liquidate the division or continue its activities. This decision requires a comparison of the present value of the future cash flows from continued operation of the division's activities with the present value of the aftertax net liquidation value of the facilities and working capital they require. In other words, both the return and the investment in the return on investment calculation for economic evaluation are future cash flows.

In the situation diagrammed in Exhibit 25–2, the future return isn't big enough to provide a rate of return high enough to justify a decision to forgo receiving the cash flow that would be generated if the division's net assets were liquidated—the present value of the future cash flows is smaller than the present liquidation value. The difference in present value is the amount we have labeled the *discontinuation profit.*

discontinuation profit

Exhibit 25–2 Elements in economic evaluation

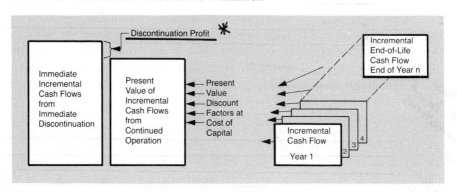

Unfortunately, routine periodic divisional profit reports don't provide these cash flow estimates. Estimation of cash flows takes too much time and costs too much to justify doing it very often. Besides, most divisions most of the time aren't serious candidates for discontinuation and even a small amount of effort wouldn't be worth while. As a result, routine periodic divisional profit performance reports are always retrospective, based on observations of actual results. Even so, they can be very useful in two ways in connection with economic evaluation:

1. To direct top management's attention to divisions, or activities within divisions, that persistently earn less than the target return on investment.
2. To show how viable the division's activities are likely to be on a continuing basis—i.e., are the division's revenues covering all the costs attributable to them; if not, the future is bleak, no matter how favorable the current cash flow relationships.

Managerial evaluation

The certainty that managerial profit performance will be evaluated is an essential feature of profit decentralization. Top management can't afford to delegate decision authority without providing some way of finding out how well that authority has been used.

The basis of evaluation. The manager plays many roles—coordinator, motivator, troubleshooter, teacher, adviser, regulator, and perhaps even therapist. Managers are likely to be evaluated on how well they play several of these roles. Profit reporting, however, is mainly used to judge how well the manager has controlled revenues, costs, and the amount invested in the division.

Criteria for selecting standards. Standards to be used in evaluating division managers' profit performance need to meet two major requirements:

1. Current attainability by competent division managers.
2. Consistency with the degree of profit controllability.

Both of these are necessary if the managers are to internalize the standards as their own and accept responsibility for achieving them.

Attainability. Each division is to some extent unique. Profit differences can be created by variations in the age or condition of production facilities; by differences in local wage structures, transportation costs, and raw material prices; by differences in the types of products handled or customers served; or by differences in the degree of competition faced in the marketplace. Each manager's performance should be evaluated in the light of the situation facing the division. This means that the standard must be different from division to division and must be changed from period to period as conditions change.

Controllability. Profit performance should be defined to exclude any variances that are not to some significant extent within the control of the division manager. We shouldn't define the problem away, however, by adopting a profit definition that eliminates so many of the possible sources of variances that the manager is relieved of most profit control responsibilities. No variable is ever completely controllable; controllability always means the ability to influence a cost or revenue within limits.

Variations in divisional sales, for example, are an important aspect of managerial performance even though they may result in large part from changes in general business conditions. Changes in the business environment can and should be considered in evaluating profit performance, but not in calculating the profit figures on which the evaluation is to be based.

Developing the standard.   The performance standard that comes closest to satisfying the attainability and controllability criteria is *budgeted performance.* A carefully conceived budget is by definition attainable with good management under expected conditions. By adopting the budget, the division manager accepts it as reasonable and attainable, even if difficult. For its part, top management, in accepting and approving the budget, signifies agreement that better than planned performance is not reasonably attainable under current conditions. The standard then needs to be adjusted only for the effects of unforeseen changes in the economic environment in which the division has operated during the period. Barring such changes, meeting the budget is good performance.

One result of setting standards in this way is that the managers of some of the company's divisions will be judged on the basis of ROI standards that are much higher than those applied to other division managers. No longer do we have a single standard for all divisions in a given risk category, as we did in economic evaluation. For example, suppose a company uses a 12 percent rate of return as a cutoff rate in its acquisition and capital expenditure decisions. This standard is shown by the dashed horizontal line in Exhibit 25–3. The company's transit division, represented by the small blocks at the left of the diagram, is now earning a 6 percent return on investment and management is delighted. The manager has increased the operating cash flow, has developed bus charter business to reduce idle time, and has far exceeded top management's expectations for this division.

The educational division, in contrast, is earning 16 percent, but its growth is far slower than management had hoped for and slower than other companies in the field have actually achieved. Turnover of personnel is very high, despite high salaries, and most of the cash flow comes from operations that were

Exhibit 25–3 Differential profit standards for managerial evaluation

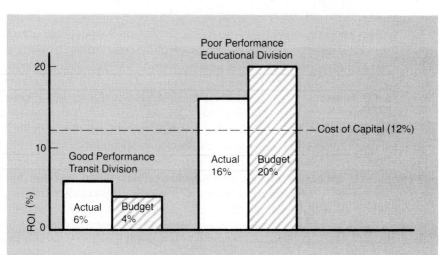

well established before the present division manager was appointed two years ago. Top management is seriously considering removing the division manager for poor profit performance.

This differential approach permits the division managers to influence the standards they will be judged by. As we pointed out in Chapter 22, this offers the possibility of greater goal congruence. It also offers the division managers an opportunity to make their jobs easier by setting unnecessarily low budgets. Two safeguards are therefore essential:

1. Active top management participation in budgeting setting.
2. Inclusion of improvement targets in the budgeting process.

A 6 percent return on investment may be good performance for the transit division this year, but no management would be happy maintaining that percentage indefinitely. Recognizing this, top management should judge division managers' performance at least as much by the quality of their budget proposals as by their success in carrying them out.

Control over divisional investment. Control over divisional investment isn't achieved primarily through historical comparisons:

1. Most of the division's plant and equipment investment remains substantially unchanged for long periods and is thus not currently controllable.
2. Control over current capital expenditures is achieved by project review and justification procedures that emphasize future expectations rather than past performance; most of these decisions are made at the top management level rather than by the division managers.

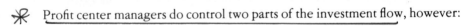 Profit center managers do control two parts of the investment flow, however:

1. Capital expenditures on small projects within the managers' authorization limits.
2. Investments in working capital.

Auditing the results of even a sample of the small capital expenditure projects would be difficult, probably inconclusive, and prohibitively expensive. Instead, top management ordinarily exercises control by having the division manager build estimates of the total effect of these expenditures into the annual profit plan. These are merged with the many other assumptions and forecasts built into the plan. Profit reporting then indicates how successful management has been in achieving the anticipated results.

Profit center managers generally have greater freedom to invest in working capital than to make new capital expenditures on plant and equipment. They may be able to affect the amount of receivables, for example, by deciding how many slow-paying customers to sell to and by regulating their efforts to collect overdue accounts. They can influence inventory levels by changing reorder points and production quantities. And they can affect the amount of accounts payable to some extent by taking full advantage of suppliers' credit terms. The profit plan therefore should include budgeted levels of working capital; these can then be compared with the levels actually achieved, in ways we'll describe in the next section.

Choosing the measure of profit performance

For managerial evaluation, the divisional profit measure should include all elements the division manager can influence or control. By the same token, the divisional performance measure should exclude variances arising from factors the division managers can't influence. For economic evaluation, on the other hand, the divisional profit measure should reflect all the revenues, expenses, gains, and losses attributable to the division's activities, together with an estimate of the resources committed to the support of those activities. We refer to these amounts as *attributable profit* and *attributable investment.*

Four possible measures of profit performance should be evaluated on the basis of the two criteria we described in the preceding paragraph:

1. Profit contribution.
2. Net income.
3. Return on investment.
4. Residual income.

Profit contribution

Profit contribution is often used to measure performance in marketing, as we saw in Chapter 12. Divisional profit contribution—divisional revenues less the cost of goods sold and other expenses traceable to the division—may be usable for the same purpose in divisional performance evaluation.

Profit contribution is relatively simple to measure and contains no allocations of headquarters expenses for the managers to argue about. It clearly meets neither of the criteria we've established, however. It is of limited usefulness in economic evaluation because it overlooks centrally administered costs attributable to the division and doesn't reflect divisional investment at all.

Profit contribution comes closer to meeting the managerial evaluation criterion because it is likely to encompass most of the income statement elements controllable by the division manager and only those elements. Its main shortcoming is that it ignores the investments under the division manager's control. A division may be able to increase its profit contribution by increasing its investments in inventories and receivables. Unless the profit performance measure reflects these investments, it will provide a misleading impression of managerial performance. The manager will get the benefits of the investment with none of the costs.

Net income

Divisional net income is determined by subtracting allocated service and support center expenses and corporate income tax expense from divisional profit contribution. Exhibit 25–4, for example, shows one month's income statement for the food division of Ormsby, Inc. Both profit contribution and net income

Exhibit 25–4
FOOD DIVISION Divisional income statement, March 19x1

	Actual	Planned	
Net sales	$3,495,000	$3,600,000	$(105,000)
Divisional expenses:			
Cost of goods sold	$2,169,000	$2,205,000	(36,000)
Marketing	538,000	535,000	3,000
Division administration	73,000	75,000	(2,000)
Income taxes	372,000	408,000	(36,000)
Total division expense	3,152,000	3,223,000	(71,000)
Profit contribution	343,000	377,000	(34,000)
Head office charges (after taxes)	173,000	173,000	—
Net income	$ 170,000	$ 204,000	$ (34,000)

are identified on this report. Income taxes are deducted to make the profit figures comparable with the cost of capital.

Divisional net income will be better than profit contribution for economic evaluation if the allocations of headquarters expenses approximate the amount of headquarters expenses attributable to the division's activities. It still doesn't reflect attributable investment, however, and it fails the managerial evaluation test because it reflects allocations of headquarters expenses the manager can't control and also fails to reflect controllable investments.

Return on investment (ROI)

We've already said that the standard for economic evaluation is expressed as a rate of return on investment. We shouldn't be surprised, therefore, to find that ROI is the most widely used measure of divisional profit performance.[2] The ratio is:

$$\text{Return on investment} = \frac{\text{Net income}}{\text{Investment}}$$

We already know from Exhibit 25–4 that the food division's net income in March was $170,000. Assuming no seasonal influences, this is equivalent to $170,000 × 12 = $2,040,000 a year. The company's net investment in the division totaled $11,330,000, as shown in Exhibit 25–5. The return on investment in March therefore was 18 percent:

$$\text{ROI} = \$2,040,000/\$11,330,000 = 18 \text{ percent}$$

most widely used measure of divisional performance

[2] James S. Reece and William R. Cool, "Measuring Investment Center Performance," *Harvard Business Review,* June 1978, p. 29.

Exhibit 25–5
FOOD DIVISION Net investment, March 31, 19x1

Traceable assets:		
Accounts receivable		$ 4,192,000
Inventories		3,748,000
Prepayments		59,000
Property, plant and equipment, net		5,558,000
Total traceable assets		13,557,000
Traceable current liabilities:		
Accounts payable	$2,618,000	
Accruals	274,000	
Total traceable current liabilities		2,892,000
Net traceable investment		10,665,000
Centrally administered assets:		
Cash.............................		419,000
Other (net)		246,000
Divisional net investment		$11,330,000

Return on investment has a number of advantages over any profit measure that fails to reflect divisional investment:

1. Both the earnings and investment components of the ROI ratio are essential to economic evaluation.
2. The impact of capital expenditures can't be audited on a project-by-project basis but does show up in the ROI ratio.
3. Emphasis on the ROI ratio keeps management aware of the need to use assets economically.
4. Similar ratios can be calculated for other parts of the company and other companies in the industry.

ROI measurements have serious shortcomings, however, that suggest they should be used only with caution:

1. Either profit or investment or both may be measured in ways that bias the return on investment figure, leading to faulty investment/disinvestment decisions.
2. Some determinants of return on investment are not controllable by division management, and this reduces the usefulness of ROI-based reports in managerial evaluation.
3. Division management can manipulate the ROI figure by shifting programmed expenditures and even some expenditures on responsive activities from one period to another.
4. Decisions that maximize divisional ROI may be suboptimal.

The first two of these stem from the measurement difficulties we'll study in the next section. The third shortcoming applies to all four performance measures, and we'll deal with it at the end of the chapter. This leaves the suboptimization problem to be covered here. For example, suppose the manager of the food division is authorized to spend up to $500,000 on small projects within the division's authorization limits. The manager is now considering a group of proposals with the following characteristics:

Investment outlay $500,000
Increment in divisional income,
   first year .... $ 70,000
Internal rate of return 13%

Each of the projects has an internal rate of return at least equal to 12 percent, the company's cutoff rate for capital investment proposals.

The usual project review analysis would point to accepting these proposals:

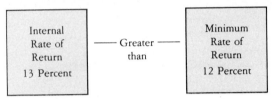

But how will they affect the divisional return on investment?

Before	After
$\dfrac{\$2,040,000}{\$11,330,000} = 18 \text{ percent}$	$\dfrac{\$2,110,000}{\$11,830,000} = 17.8 \text{ percent}$

The effect is small, but the direction is clearly downward. If the manager is attempting to maximize the divisional return on investment, the investments won't be made. Clearly, some means must be found to convince the manager to make these investments. One possibility is to measure performance by residual income other than by ROI.

Residual income

Residual income is defined as divisional income less an investment carrying charge, determined by multiplying divisional investment by an interest rate based on the cost of capital. The interest rate should be an aftertax rate if

Exhibit 25–6
FOOD DIVISION Statement of residual income, March 19x1

	Actual	Planned	Over/(Under)
Net sales	$3,495,000	$3,600,000	$(105,000)
Expenses:			
Cost of goods sold	2,169,000	2,205,000	(36,000)
Marketing	538,000	535,000	3,000
Division administration	73,000	75,000	(2,000)
Income taxes	372,000	408,000	(36,000)
Head office charges	173,000	173,000	—
Total expense	3,325,000	3,396,000	(71,000)
Net income	170,000	204,000	(34,000)
Investment charges	113,300	107,000	(6,300)
Residual income	$ 56,700	$ 97,000	$ (40,300)

income taxes have been deducted in calculating divisional income; for monthly reporting it should be divided by 12.

For example, the food division's profit report for March would show the figures summarized in Exhibit 25–6. The investment carrying charge on the next to the last line was calculated as follows:

$$\text{Annual rate}/12 \times \text{Investment} = \text{Monthly charge}$$
$$12\%/12 \times \$11,330,000 = \$113,300$$

The variance in this item was $6,300 because the division exceeded its budgeted investment, a fact Exhibit 25–4 ignored.

Advantages of residual income.   Residual income is like return on investment in that it incorporates both income and investment in a single measure. It has two main advantages over ROI:

1. It states both earnings and investment on the same scale so that a variance in one is comparable to a variance in the other.
2. It is more consistent with decision rules embodying the maximization of present value.

A common scale.   Income statement amounts represent flows of economic quantities during a period of time. Balance sheet amounts, however, represent static quantities, at a specific date. Multiplying these static quantities by an interest rate places them on a flow scale. This allows management to make a direct comparison between an investment variance and a variance in a determinant of income. A $1 million unfavorable inventory variance, for example, would be justified at Ormsby, Inc., if it were the means of achieving a monthly saving of $10,000 or more in materials costs. The calculation is:

Increase in investment charge = $12\%/12 \times \$1,000,000 = \$10,000$ a month

Consistency with managerial decision rules.   We saw earlier that the use of ROI may lead to suboptimization in divisions already achieving high ROI ratios. Use of residual income can reduce this danger. In our illustration we had a $500,000 investment bring in $70,000 in new earnings the first year. The investment charges in this situation would be:

Before	After
$11,330,000 × 12% = $1,359,600	$11,830,000 × 12% = $1,419,600

We saw in previous exhibits that the food division's net income was $170,000 in March, representing an annual rate of $2,040,000. Putting the new investments in this division presumably would increase the year's divisional income by $70,000, to $2,110,000. Residual income therefore would increase by $10,000:

	Before	After	Increase
Divisional income	$2,040,000	$2,110,000	$70,000
Investment charge	1,359,600	1,419,600	60,000
Residual income	$ 680,400	$ 690,400	$10,000

Although the investment will reduce ROI, it will increase residual income. Since the investment is clearly profitable (an internal rate of return of 13 percent), residual income must be a superior performance measure in this case because it produces a signal that is consistent with the managerial decision rule.

Limitations of residual income. Aside from the two advantages we just discussed, residual income shares most of the limitations of ROI:

1. It doesn't provide a direct decision criterion for capital expenditure decisions, which must be based on increments in cash flows, not increments in income. A sound investment with a deferred payoff will depress both ROI and residual income.
2. Division management can manipulate it by altering the timing of some revenues and expenses.
3. It reflects a mixture of controllable and noncontrollable elements.

We'll take up these issues in the sections that follow.

Income measurement problems

Some of the defects of ROI and residual income as measures of divisional profit performance arise from difficult measurement problems, including the following:

1. Some costs incurred to support the division's activities are incurred in service and support centers outside the division—the question is how many of these *common costs* should be charged to the division.
2. Most interest costs arising from corporate borrowing are not traceable to individual divisions. The question is whether *corporate interest expense* should be allocated among the divisions.
3. *Revenues* of one division may be related, either positively or negatively, to the revenues of other divisions.
4. The *depreciation method* used can affect the apparent effects of investment decisions.
5. *Income taxes* are levied on the basis of corporate income; their allocation to divisions depends in part on how the other measurement problems are resolved.
6. Some of the resources used to produce current revenues are measured at the *unit costs of previous periods* rather than those of the current period.
7. Some of the division's output may be transferred to other divisions; some of the materials, component parts, and services it uses may be transferred from other divisions. The question is what *transfer prices* should be used.

We'll discuss the first six of these here, leaving transfer pricing to Chapter 26.

Common costs

The allocations of common costs to individual divisions for managerial purposes should be based on the concepts of attributability (for economic evaluation) and controllability (for managerial evaluation).

If the company uses the attributability concept in the allocation of headquarters costs, some of these costs will remain unallocated because satisfactory measures of attributability can't be found. Many companies allocate nonattributable common costs among their divisions, however, using simple allocation formulas such as average cost per sales dollar. In any serious effort to evaluate economic performance, these allocations should be removed.

If the objective of divisional reporting is managerial evaluation, the only common costs to be allocated should be the costs of central services which are provided at least partly at the division manager's discretion. Only if division management can influence the quantity of service or support provided can it be said to have any current responsibility for the cost of that service or support.

If noncontrollable costs are allocated to the divisions, either because they are attributable to those divisions' activities or because management insists on a full distribution of all costs, the accountants have four options. First, they can segment the income statement, with an intermediate figure labeled *controllable profit,* followed "below the line" by a list of noncontrollable expenses. Second, regardless of whether they construct a noncontrollable section in the income statement, they can adjust the budget for all noncontrollable items to equal the amounts charged to the division, thereby removing spending variances from the divisional profit report.

A third possibility is to leave the budget untouched but set the allocations each month equal to the amounts budgeted. Like the second method, this will remove noncontrollable variances from the divisional performance reports entirely.

None of these solutions is adequate if headquarters costs respond to variables division management can control. For example, suppose studies have indicated that headquarters personnel department costs increase and decrease in proportion to long-term changes in the number of employees on the company's payroll. A division has a budgeted work force of 10,000 employees; the budgeted charge for headquarters personnel department activities is $40,000 a month. If management wants to motivate the division manager to consider headquarters personnel department costs in decisions affecting the number of employees, it can calculate its allocations at a *predetermined rate* of $40,000/10,000 = $4 an employee.

Since this formula will be known in advance, the division managers will be able to predict the impact of their decisions on the amounts allocated. A division's flexible budget will adjust each month to the current volume level; variances from the flexible budget for allocated personnel department costs will reflect the division's success in handling its current volume with the number of employees appropriate to that volume.

Interest expense

In general, corporate interest expense should not be allocated to divisions. The issue in economic evaluation is whether the division's earnings are adequate to cover the cost of the company's funds invested in it. Interest is the cost of the debt portion of these funds only; allocations of interest on debt probably understate the full cost of all the funds the company has provided. Residual income calculations, requiring allocations at the cost of capital rate, are a better way to show the economic effects of divisional investments.

Two exceptions to this general rule are appropriate. First, interest expense arising from short-term divisional borrowing to meet seasonal needs at the division manager's discretion is clearly relevant to both economic evaluation and managerial evaluation and should be deducted from divisional revenues.

Second, when a division's activities are so different from those of the rest of the company that it is set up as a subsidiary corporation with its own financial structure, interest on its own long-term debt should be deducted from divisional revenues for economic evaluation. The economic question in these cases is whether the *parent* company's investment is earning an adequate rate of return. Finance company subsidiaries of manufacturing companies are good examples; foreign subsidiaries usually fall into this category as well. Whether interest on divisional borrowings is deducted in reports for use in managerial evaluation depends on whether borrowing is a divisional responsibility.

Revenue interdependence

An increase in the revenues of one division may cause the revenues of another division to increase (complementarity) or decrease (substitutability). These effects are virtually impossible to measure routinely because specific revenue transactions can't be traced to other specific transactions or to specific aborted transactions. Revenue interdependence usually must be identified by statistical analysis, not tied to the routine periodic reporting structure. If interdependencies are extremely strong, management probably should reconsider its decision to recognize both divisions as profit centers.

Depreciation

Most companies deduct depreciation from divisional revenues, just as they deduct other divisional expenses. Both straight-line and accelerated depreciation methods are likely to depress the rate of return on investment when depreciable assets are young, however, because depreciation calculated on these bases is likely to overstate the decline in the assets' present value. The only depreciation formulas that avoid this problem are those that consider the investment charge, otherwise known as *implicit interest,* in calculating the depreciation schedule. Take the following five-year investment, for example:

Year	Cash Flow after Taxes	Present Value at 14%
0	−$10,000	−$10,000
1	− 1,000	− 877
2	+ 1,000	+ 769
3	+ 4,000	+ 2,700
4	+ 9,000	+ 5,328
5	+ 4,000	+ 2,076
Net present value		−$ 4

[margin note: IRR = rate at which NPV = 0]

The net present value of this project at 14 percent is very close to zero, indicating an internal rate of return of almost exactly 14 percent. If we use this rate in connection with what is known as the *annuity method* of depreciation, the depreciation schedule will take the following pattern:

[margin note: annuity method of depr.]

(1) Investment, Beginning of year	(2) Implicit Interest at 14% [(1) × 14%]	(3) Cash Flow (from previous table)	(4) Annuity Method Depreciation [(3) − (2)]	(5) Investment, End of Year [(1) − (4)]	(6) Reported Rate of Return [(2) ÷ (1)]
$10,000	$1,400	−$1,000	−$2,400	$12,400	14%
12,400	1,736	1,000	− 736	13,136	14
13,136	1,839	4,000	2,161	10,975	14
10,975	1,537	9,000	7,463	3,512	14
3,512	492	4,000	3,508	4*	14

* Rounding error.

[margin note: negative depr.]

The depreciation charges in column (4) are designed to permit the company to report a 14 percent return on investment each year, as in column (6). To do this, however, management would have to be willing to report *negative depreciation* in the first two years in this case. Perhaps for this reason, or perhaps because management believes most investments produce most of their cash inflows in the early years, management has continued to favor straight-line and accelerated depreciation methods for financial reporting purposes.

[margin note: depr. relevant to econ. 1°4 to eval.]

We should remember, of course, that depreciation is relevant primarily to economic evaluation. Annual depreciation is governed primarily by capital expenditure decisions, most of which are made by higher management. In the wake of major capital expenditure programs, however, top management is likely to judge progress by examining movements in ROI or residual income. If it chooses to live with straight-line or accelerated depreciation schedules, despite their tendency to shift earnings to the later years of investment life, management needs to make an effort to build the estimated effects of capital expenditures into the annual profit plan and focus its attention on variances from the plan rather than on absolute levels of ROI or residual income.

Income taxes

Although income taxes are clearly relevant to economic evaluation, they have no independent bearing on managerial evaluation unless the division manager is in a position to affect the taxability of the division's income. Given the relevance of income taxes to economic evaluation, however, it is generally advisable to allocate them to divisions in reports prepared for this purpose. Once again, the criterion should be attributability—by how much would the corporation's income taxes be reduced (or increased) if the division's activities were separated out.

Adjusting for changing resource prices

The depreciation and cost of goods sold figures in Exhibit 25–4 were based on historical cost, reflecting the dominant practice in the United States. Most depreciable assets in use today were acquired when acquisition prices were lower than they are now, however. A similar time lag affects some cost of goods sold figures, particularly when inventories are measured on a FIFO basis. As a result, the expense figures are likely to understate the current cost of the resources that have to be used to obtain current revenues. They may serve to cover up a deteriorating profit situation until price levels stabilize and asset replacement at higher prices begins to make itself felt in lower return on investment figures.

The solution to this problem is to base depreciation and the cost of goods sold on replacement cost. Most companies in the United States have shied away from doing this, perceiving the benefits to be less than the costs of measuring replacement cost. With high rates of inflation apparently a continuing fact of life, and with the required development of replacement cost figures for external financial reporting, the internal use of these figures is likely to increase.

Investment measurement problems

Every company has some assets that are administered centrally, either because they are necessary to perform central office or service functions or because central administration represents a more efficient use of resources. The question is to what extent centrally administered assets and liabilities should be allocated to divisions for the purposes of economic evaluation and managerial evaluation.

Defining the investment base

Divisional investment may be defined in many ways. Five possibilities should be listed:

1. *Traceable assets.* All assets identifiable specifically with the division, regardless of their physical location.
2. *Controllable investment.* All assets controllable by division management, less any current liabilities within its jurisdiction.
3. *Total assets.* All assets of the division, including a share of corporate cash and other centrally administered assets.

econ. eval. ⇐ 4. *Net investment.* The division's share of total assets less noninterest bearing
current liabilities—i.e., the division's share of the total investment of stockholders and lender creditors.

5. *Stockholders' equity.* The owners' share of the investment in divisional assets.

We used *net investment* figures in our discussion of return on investment
and residual income because net investment is more comparable than the others
to the cost of capital. It includes all the funds provided to the firm for an
interestlike return—i.e., owners' equity, long-term debt, and short-term, inter-
est-bearing debt. It is therefore more suitable for economic evaluation, in
which the cost of capital is the relevant performance standard.

Controllable investment would be more suitable for managerial evaluation,
but would be totally unsuitable for economic evaluation. It omits investments
attributable to the division but not controllable by division management. Since
a single set of reports usually serves both purposes, and since noncontrollable
variances can be dealt with in other ways, we decided not to use this.

Traceable assets is easier to measure than either of the first two, but is relevant
neither to economic evaluation nor to managerial evaluation. It excludes attributable assets that are not directly traceable to the division, includes assets
that are traceable but not controllable, and excludes short-term liabilities entirely. Furthermore, if the reports are to be used in operations evaluation,
figures based on traceable assets are likely to be noncomparable from division
to division and from company to company. For example, one division may
handle all its own inventories and receivables, while another uses central billing
and warehousing services, thereby burying some of its investment in the common pool.

Total assets is not very different in concept from net investment and is often
used in its place. It may distort economic evaluation comparisons, however,
because it includes in the investment base varying amounts of assets financed
by suppliers and employees, not by investors.

The *equity of the parent company's stockholders* in any division is not measurable.
The funds provided to a division can't be identified specifically as debt funds
or equity funds. The financing mix is a characteristic of the corporation and
is the same for all divisions. Allocating 40 percent debt to one division and
60 percent to another would be arbitrary and meaningless.

In the preceding section we did suggest using what may appear to be a
variant of the stockholders' equity method in measuring the profit performance
of subsidiaries in foreign countries or in ventures very dissimilar to the activities
of the parent. To be consistent, the investment base in these divisions should
be the parent company's investment. Notice that this is a broader base than
a stockholders' equity base would be, however. The parent company's investment includes parent company equity and parent company debt; the subsidiary
company's financing is separate and doesn't affect the parent company's borrowing capacity. Thus the parent company's cost of capital remains a comparable
benchmark for tracking the performance of the parent's investments in these
divisions. In other words, parent equity is simply a special way of measuring
net investment in these special situations.

Allocating centrally administered assets

The most accurate way to attribute assets to divisions is to trace them directly as they are incurred. Receivables, for example, often can be coded by division even though billing and accounts receivable operations are performed centrally. If routine coding is too expensive, the divisional distribution can be approximated by sampling

Statistical analysis can be used to allocate some assets for which adequate measures of traceability can't be found. Cash, for example, can seldom be traced satisfactorily to the operations of individual divisions. To find out how much cash is needed to support a division's activities, the staff might perform a Monte Carlo simulation or carry out statistical regression analyses to estimate the relationships between cash and such independent variables as sales volume and employment.

If allocations are limited to assets for which measures of attributability can be found, some centrally administered assets will remain unallocated. Most of the assets of a central research laboratory are likely to fall in this category, for example. Allocations of these assets have no bearing on economic evaluation, but most companies allocating centrally administered assets to divisions allocate these nonattributable assets, using plausible but arbitrary allocation rules.

If the profit measure is to be used in managerial evaluation, the only relevant allocations are of assets that are controllable by the division managers. In general, the only centrally administered assets that are likely to be at least partially controllable are those that can be traced to individual divisions. If allocations of noncontrollable assets are made, variances in these allocations should be suppressed or ignored in managerial evaluation, by one of the following methods:

1. Allocate predetermined amount, equal to budget.
2. Allocate at a predetermined rate, equal to budgeted rate.
3. Allocate by any method, but adjust budget to eliminate variance.
4. Allocate by any method, but report variance as noncontrollable.

Allocating centrally administered liabilities

Centrally administered trade payables and other noninterest-bearing short-term obligations attributable to the division should be deducted from divisional assets if investment is defined as net investment. The same methods of attribution are appropriate for these as for centrally administered current assets. Long-term liabilities shouldn't be allocated, however, because the debt-equity mix is a characteristic of the company as a whole. This was our reason for rejecting the stockholders' equity as the investment base.

Accumulated depreciation

A few companies don't deduct accumulated depreciation in calculating divisional investment. They argue that deducting depreciation reduces the investment figure as assets age, thereby increasing the apparent ROI or residual income. This, they say, reduces the division managers' incentive to make or recommend new investments or to dispose of old, inefficient equipment.

This argument has its opposite side. As assets age, revenues may decrease and operating costs may rise, reducing the ratio of earnings to asset cost. Managers will be anxious to get rid of older assets, thereby increasing their earnings without major increases in gross assets, even though the incremental cash flows may not be high enough to justify the additional expenditures.

Most companies have concluded that net book value is a better measure of effective investment than gross cost. The undesirable effects of any overstatement of divisional profitability resulting from this can be avoided by recognizing that asset acquisition and disposal decisions should be based on the present value of incremental cash flows, not on reported ROI or residual income.

Adjusting investment figures for changes in resource prices

In the preceding section we argued that depreciation and the cost of goods sold should be measured at current replacement costs. The same treatment should be extended to inventories and net plant and equipment, and for the same reasons. With income overstating the margin over current cost and with the investment base understating current investment requirements, the division's ROI or residual income can be very misleading.

Achieving long-term goals

Earlier in this chapter we mentioned that one of the dangers of profit-based decentralization is that the managers of profit centers, investment centers, or administered centers will sacrifice the company's long-term interests to increase short-term profits. Two ways of counteracting this tendency can be tried: (1) establishing additional criteria for evaluating the performance of division managers; and (2) establishing centrally-administered constraints and guidelines.

Multiple performance criteria

Current income figures can never capture the full effect of current actions. Decisions made now may pay off or have disastrous consequences a generation hence, when the present managerial force has long since departed from the scene. The effects of some of the actions affecting future profitability affect nonfinancial variables today, however—examples include the rate of growth, market share, community attitudes, employee safety, and productivity. One way to insure that managers let these variables affect their decisions is to build them explicitly into the planning process. When top management wants the division managers to work toward these goals, it will require them to set specific nonprofit objectives and include these in their proposed operating plans. These proposed objectives will be reviewed by top management or by the headquarters staff; after revision, they will become standards against which future performance can be measured.

We pointed out in Chapter 22 that the development of multiple performance criteria may help achieve goal congruence because more dimensions of the managers' activities can be encompassed in the performance measure. Management faces two problems in using this technique, however. First, some goals are difficult to quantify. For example, a company may decide that each of its divisions is to strive to be a "good citizen" of the communities in which it operates. This generally means that divisional personnel should be active in local civic activities, that the division will contribute funds or other resources to community-sponsored projects, that divisional facilities will be attractive, and so on. The results of a division's efforts to contribute to a community in these ways are very difficult to quantify. As a result, management is likely to measure performance more by comparing actual inputs with planned inputs than by measuring divisional outputs.

The second problem management faces when it attempts to recognize two or more divisional goals is that these goals may be inconsistent with each other. Expenditures designed to meet citizenship objectives may reduce current income, for example; expansion of management development activities may reduce the current rate of growth.

The presence of inconsistent goals forces the division managers to determine the amount of effort to devote to the pursuit of each goal. In formal weighting systems, overall performance is measured by adding the points assigned to a division's progress toward each of several objectives. These systems are unlikely to succeed, however, because division management can achieve good overall scores while neglecting low-point objectives entirely.

Even if no formal weighting system has been adopted, division managers are likely to learn to identify top management's implicit priorities by watching the responses to their successes or failures in meeting the various objectives. If top management wants the divisions to pursue nonprofit objectives, therefore, it must be prepared to react both when they are met and when they are missed.

Centrally administered constraints and guidelines

In addition to or as a partial substitute for multiple performance criteria, management may choose to rely on centrally administered constraints and guidelines. These may take the form of minimum performance objectives, one in each performance dimension. These objectives limit the manager's freedom to sacrifice progress toward one objective to achieve greater progress toward another. Each objective may be set by top management before divisional planning begins, or it may be set in negotiation between divisional and top management in just the same way as the division's profit objectives are set.

Another possibility is to give central staff groups authority to review and reject portions of proposed divisional plans, and to audit compliance with centrally established standards. Internal control systems are subjected to this kind of review, for example. Similarly, a central maintenance staff might have the authority to make sure that divisional maintenance expenditures will be adequate to keep plant and equipment from accumulating "deferred maintenance" obligations. Provisions for employee safety and recreation programs, management development, research and development, and many other kinds of activities may be subject to scrutiny by central staff groups.

These arrangements reduce the autonomy of the division managers, leading to some violation of the profit center concept. The profit center structure is only a means to an end, however, and top management is free to modify it if the benefits of these modifications seem likely to exceed the costs. The main requirement is that the objectives, constraints, and guidelines be clearly understood in advance and adhered to throughout.

Summary

Business organizations with more than one clearly identifiable product line or market segment are likely to find it desirable to measure the profit performance of each of these segments. These measurements have some or all of four purposes: (1) to analyze the effectiveness of the methods used to manufacture and market the company's products (operations evaluation); (2) to see whether each segment is earning enough to provide an adequate return on the amount of funds invested in the segment (economic evaluation); (3) to analyze the performance of the managers in charge of this segment (managerial evaluation); and (4) to reinforce the managers' commitment to work toward overall company profit goals (motivational reinforcement).

The third and fourth of these purposes are applicable mainly when the segment is a profit center or investment center in a decentralized company. Decentralization attempts to combine the advantages of large-scale organization with the advantages of flexibility and specialization the small firm has. To implement this idea, top management has to delegate a good deal of authority; internal profit reporting provides the means by which division managers can he held accountable for the exercise of this authority.

Divisional profit performance reports generally encompass both profit and the investment committed to the division's activities, expressed either as a return on investment ratio or as residual income, defined as divisional income less implicit interest on divisional investment. These measures are designed primarily for use in economic evaluation, in which the performance standard is the company's cost of capital. The appropriate measurement concepts are attributable profit and attributable investment.

For managerial evaluation, controllability is the key concept, and the standard must be adapted to fit each division's particular circumstances—budgeted performance is the appropriate standard here, with special effort required to make sure the budget itself reflects strong managerial commitments to company goals. A return on investment standard, applied uniformly to all divisions in all circumstances, is inappropriate for use in managerial evaluation.

None of these measures is perfect. All can be manipulated to some extent; all can lead to some suboptimization. Management has to be aware of these possibilities and to build controls into the system to insure that achievement of short-term profit maximization doesn't have excessive countervailing long-term penalties. Multiple performance objectives and centrally administered constraints are possible means of exerting these controls.

Independent study problems (solutions in Appendix B)

1. **Foreign subsidiary as a profit center.** Jacques Dalmas is the managing director of Alifrance, S.A., the French subsidiary of Allen Brands, Inc. Allen Brands owns 100 percent of the voting stock in Alifrance, which sells only products manufactured and distributed by Allen Brands. It has no manufacturing facilities of its own and makes no sales outside France.

   Allen Brands bills Alifrance at the regular wholesale prices of the articles shipped. Alifrance pays all taxes, customs duties, and transportation charges on the merchandise it buys from Allen Brands. Mr. Dalmas and his staff decide what prices to charge, which products to offer for sale, how to market them, and how much inventory to carry, all subject to head office approval of the annual profit plan.

   Required:
   a. Is Alifrance a profit center?
   b. Should top management consider Alifrance's profit performance in evaluating Mr. Dalmas's managerial performance?

2. **Return on investment versus residual income.** The investment in division A consists of $200,000 in traceable working capital, $400,000 in traceable plant and equipment, and $100,000 in centrally administered assets, allocated to the division at a rate of one sixth of traceable investment. The budgeted amounts for these three totals were $150,000, $420,000, and $95,000.

   Division A's net income for the year is $63,000, after deducting $30,000 in traceable depreciation, $40,000 in head office charges (allocated to the division at the rate of 5 percent of sales) and income taxes at 50 percent. The budgeted amounts were $70,000, $32,000, $45,000, and 50 percent.

   The company estimates that its cost of capital is 12 percent, after taxes.

   Required:
   a. Calculate budgeted and actual return on investment.
   b. Calculate budgeted and actual residual income.
   c. Discuss the division manager's performance.
   d. What action should management take in response to your evaluation of this division's activities, based on the figures supplied here?

Exercises and problems

3. **Legal department as a profit center.** Goldsachs and Merrill is an investment banking firm. It has three divisions organized as profit centers: underwriting, brokerage, and portfolio management. Its legal department, with direct costs of $1 million a year, provides legal services to all three divisions and to corporate management, recommends the use of outside counsel in certain cases, and provides liaison between company personnel and outside counsel working on specific cases or issues.

   The costs of outside counsel are assigned to the divisions for which their services are provided. The legal department itself is treated as a service center, its costs being allocated among the three operating divisions in proportion to their revenues, as follows:

Underwriting	....	$ 300,000
Brokerage	....	600,000
Portfolio management	....	100,000
Total	....	$1,000,000

The controller of Goldsachs and Merrill has proposed treating the legal department as a profit center. The department would charge the divisions on the basis of a fee schedule similar to those being charged by independent law firms for comparable services. Individual division managers would be free to use outside law firms, set up their own legal staffs, or dispense with legal services entirely.

The controller summed up the arguments for the proposal in the following way: "In the final analysis, it is management that decides whether to initiate lawsuits, whether to defend lawsuits or settle out of court, and how much to spend for legal advice. The functions of the legal department are clearly subsidiary to these responsibilities of management. If this is true at the corporate level, I see no reason why it shouldn't be true at the divisional level as well. I suggest leaving the amount and source of legal services up to the good business judgment of the division managers."

The controller estimates that application of this proposal to this year's legal department activities would have led to the following internal charges:

Underwriting	....	$ 800,000
Brokerage	....	400,000
Portfolio management	....	100,000
Corporate management	....	700,000
Total	....	$2,000,000

Required:

Should the legal division be established as a profit center? Prepare a brief report to support your recommendation.

4. **Retrospective reporting versus decision analysis.**   Acto Division of Collins Company can be sold to Zero Corporation for $5 million, after taxes. Collins' net investment in Acto Division is $12 million, on an historical cost basis. Restating inventories and plant and equipment at current replacement cost would increase net investment to $15 million.

Acto Division last year had traceable income (after taxes) of $240,000 and net income (also after taxes) of $120,000. If Collins continues to operate Acto Division, it will generate an annual cash flow of $850,000, after taxes. The prospects for improving either income or cash flow in the next five years are extremely dim.

If Collins decides not to accept Zero Corporation's offer, it can count on selling the division to someone else for $4 million (after taxes) any time in the next five years.

Collins Company is willing to make capital expenditures in operations with Acto's risk characteristics if the anticipated internal rate of return is at least 12 percent, after taxes.

Required:

a.   Calculate ROI for last year on an historical cost basis.
b.   Calculate residual income for last year.
c.   Should Collins Company accept Zero Corporation's offer? Show your calculations. How do the replacement cost figures affect the decision?

5. **Allocations of head office expenses.**   The Ray Manufacturing Company is decentralized in several divisions, including the textile products division. The following statistical information relates to the company as a whole and the textile products division for the month of June:

	Entire Company		Textile Products	
	Budget	Actual	Budget	Actual
Number of employees	5,000	4,600	800	780
Total payrolls	$ 3,500,000	$3,175,000	$ 480,000	$ 485,000
Factory payrolls	$ 2,400,000	$2,200,000	$ 375,000	$ 365,000
Net sales	$10,000,000	$9,000,000	$1,500,000	$1,600,000

All budget data in this table have been taken from the planning budget for the month.

Actual head office selling and administrative expenses are fully distributed among the divisions each month. All head office expenses are assumed to be fixed with respect to volume. Budgeted and actual head office expenses, together with the relevant allocation bases, were as follows during the month of June:

	Basis	Budget	Actual
Accounting department	Employees	$120,000	$115,000
Manufacturing department	Factory payrolls	60,000	62,000
Marketing department	Net sales	50,000	51,000
Advertising	Net sales	200,000	280,000
Executive offices	Total payrolls	70,000	68,000

Required:

a. Prepare a budgeted allocation of head office expenses for the textile products division, based on budget data only.

b. Compute the amount of head office expenses to be charged to the division for the month.

c. Compute the variances in the charges for these five items that will appear in the textile products division profit report for the month. What effect do they have on divisional return on investment? What relevance do they have to economic evaluation?

6. **Calculating net investment.** The asset and liability records of the Deutsch Instruments Company show the following account balances (in $000):

	Centrally Administered	Traceable to		
		Division A	Division B	Division C
Cash	$360	$ 10	$ 20	$ 15
Receivables	400	—	—	—
Inventories	—	300	450	400
Plant and equipment	100	500	1,500	1,000
Allowance for depreciation	(40)	(200)	(700)	(300)
Total assets	$820	$ 610	$1,270	$1,115
Accounts payable	30	80	140	100
Accrued liabilities	30	20	30	25
Bonds payable	200	—	—	—
Total liabilities	$260	$ 100	$ 170	$ 125

No further divisional identification of undistributed asset balances is possible, but the president of the company has insisted that divisional net income be expressed as a percentage of divisional net investment, including a share of centrally administered net investment. Further information on company activities for the most recent year follows (in $000):

	Division A	Division B	Division C
Net sales	$1,500	$2,400	$2,100
Division payroll	400	600	500
Materials received	500	800	800
Head office expense distributed	80	120	100
Division net income	150	300	380

Required:

a. Allocate centrally administered net investment in proportion to divisional net income and calculate a rate of return on investment on that basis.

b. The president has objected to the calculation you made in answer to (a) and has asked you to develop an allocation scheme that will more closely approximate the amount of centrally administered net investment attributable to each division's activities. The president still insists, however, that you leave no centrally administered net investment undistributed. Select an allocation basis for each centrally administered amount to be distributed in compliance with the president's instructions. State the assumptions underlying your choices.

c. Distribute centrally administered net investment on the bases you selected in answer to (b) and calculate the ROI for each division. Comment on the meaning, if any, of any differences between these ROI figures and those you calculated, in answer to (a).

7. **Comparison of two divisions.**   BIG Industries, Inc. is a decentralized, multidivision company engaged in a variety of businesses. The following data summarize the operations of two of BIG's divisions (Able and Baker) during 19x1:

	Able Division		Baker Division	
	Budget	Actual	Budget	Actual
Net sales	$100	$110	$300	$280
Cost of goods sold*	40	44	150	150
Selling and administrative expense	30	30	80	80
Income before taxes	30	36	70	50
* Including depreciation	10	10	12	12

The following figures were taken from the two divisions' statements of financial position at December 31, 19x1:

	Able Division		Baker Division	
	Budget	Actual	Budget	Actual
Current assets	$140	$150	$105	$100
Fixed assets (cost)	218	220	275	275
Accumulated depreciation	177	176	25	25
Current liabilities	45	50	55	50

During 19x1 the market conditions facing each division were about what had been expected when the 19x1 budgets were drawn up. The company estimated that its pretax cost of capital in 19x1 was about 20 percent.

Required:

a. Which division is in the more profitable business? Cite figures to support your conclusions and defend the measures you have chosen.
b. Which division manager is doing the better job of running the division? Again cite figures to support your conclusions and defend the measures you have chosen.

(Prepared by Michael Ginzberg)

8. **Performance evaluation; effect of new investment.**   Two years ago Dopple Corporation's top management approved a proposal to make a substantial capital investment in division X. The investment was made and the facilities came into operation early this year. Last year's results, this year's budget reflecting the new investment, and this year's actual results are as follows:

	Last Year	Budget This Year	Actual This Year
Sales revenues	$10,000,000	$14,000,000	$14,300,000
Expenses (including income taxes)	8,950,000	13,500,000	13,670,000
Net income	1,050,000	500,000	630,000
Working capital	$ 1,000,000	$ 1,300,000	$ 1,400,000
Plant and equipment	5,000,000	11,200,000	11,200,000
Total investment	6,000,000	12,500,000	12,600,000

Allocations and internal transfer prices had insignificant effects on the figures in this table.

Dopple Corporation insists that all major capital expenditures be expected to earn a rate of return on investment of at least 15 percent, after income taxes. Division X's investment proposal met that test. The budget figures in the table above were based on the estimates used to justify the investment decision.

Required:

a. Calculate the return on investment and residual income for division X last year, as budgeted for this year, and this year's actual.
b. Why did budgeted income decrease even though the new capital expenditures were expected to produce an incremental rate of return on investment in excess of 15 percent?
c. Does the management of division X appear to have been effective in managing the division this year? As part of your answer, identify the performance standard you have used to make this judgment.
d. Do division X's activities appear to be profitable? As part of your answer identify the performance standard you have used to make this judgment.

9. **Gross versus net assets.**   Divisional investment in plant and equipment in the Torrid Tomato Company is measured by the depreciated historical cost of the division's plant and equipment. The manager of the tomato paste division has complained that this is discriminatory because the paste division is a young division, with relatively new assets. Depreciation charges are high and so is the depreciated cost; both of these depress the division's annual ROI. The catsup division, in contrast, has many old facilities, some of them completely amortized. Both depreciated cost and annual depreciation are low. This helps the catsup division maintain a high ROI. The summary figures are:

	Catsup	Paste
Plant and equipment	$1,000	$500
Less: Accumulated depreciation	800	100
Net plant and equipment	200	400
Working capital	900	300
Net investment..................	1,100	700
Revenues	$1,000	$600
Expenses:		
Depreciation......................	50	80
Other (including taxes)	800	436
Net income	150	84
Return on investment	13.6%	12%

The paste division manager suggests measuring plant and equipment at its original cost, with no deduction for accumulated depreciation. No depreciation charges would be deducted from divisional revenues. The division manager believes this would deprive the managers of the older divisions of the unfair advantages of having older, more fully depreciated facilities.

Required:

a. Recalculate the rate of return on investment for each division on the basis recommended by the manager of the paste division.

b. Which division is more profitable than the other? Explain how you reached this conclusion.

c. What explanation can you give for the concern expressed by the manager of the paste division about the division's low rate of return on investment? Is this a legitimate worry?

d. Would division managers be more likely, less likely, or neither more nor less likely to submit major capital expenditure proposals than they are now? State the reason(s) supporting your conclusions on this point.

e. What action would you recommend on the proposed measurement change? Why would you recommend this?

10. **Department as profit center; relevance of expense variances.** The Val-U-Rite Department Store has a number of merchandise departments—cosmetics, jewelry, housewares, and so on—plus a number of service departments—personnel, credit, cashier, accounting, and so forth.

Each merchandise department manager is responsible for the amount of profit generated in his or her department. Each department selects the merchandise that it wishes to stock and sell; the amount of selling space allotted to each merchandise department is determined by the store's top management and varies to some extent from season to season. Selling prices are set by the individual department managers.

The profit report for the housewares department for the month of January showed the following (to narrow the list of issues to be considered, some figures have been omitted):

	Actual	Budget	Variance
Sales revenues	$415,000	$400,000	$15,000
Cost of merchandise sold	249,000	240,000	(9,000)
Gross margin	166,000	160,000	6,000
Operating expenses:			
Direct salaries	59,800	60,000	200
Floor space occupied	5,800	5,000	(800)
Receiving and warehousing	9,200	8,000	(1,200)
.	.	.	.
.	.	.	.
.	.	.	.
Total operating expense	143,000	138,000	(5,000)
Departmental margin	$ 23,000	$ 22,000	$ 1,000

The $5,800 in floor space charges was computed by multiplying the number of square feet of floor space in the housewares department by the average cost of owning and operating the store building during January (depreciation, insurance, taxes, heat, light, and so forth).

The $9,200 in receiving and warehousing costs was the sum of two figures: (1) the number of labor hours spent handling housewares merchandise in the receiving and warehousing department during January, multiplied by the average hourly cost of labor and supervision in this department during the month; and (2) the number of cubic feet of storage space occupied by housewares inventories, multiplied by the average cost of operating the warehouse in January (excluding labor and supervision) per cubic foot of warehouse space.

The amount of floor space occupied by the housewares department and the amount of warehouse space occupied by housewares inventories in January were equal to the amounts budgeted for these purposes.

The figures shown in the "budget" column are the amounts included in the budget for January, prepared when the budget for the entire year was drawn up.

Required:

a. Is the housewares department a profit center? List the elements in this situation that support your answer to this question. List the elements that would support an opposite answer. Should profit performance reports be prepared for this department for managerial evaluation purposes?

b. Indicate how the January variances in the charges for floor space occupied by the housewares department and for receiving and warehousing are likely to have arisen. Should these variances appear in the housewares division's profit performance report, if one is prepared?

c. Would it be feasible to calculate return on investment or residual income for the housewares department? Give reasons to support your answer.

11. **Depreciation method; replacement costing.** The top management of the Global Girdle Company is worried that the managers of the more profitable divisions will be reluctant to submit capital expenditure proposals that will depress near-term earnings and ROI. It has adopted two procedures it hopes will reduce the depressing effect of new investment on reported divisional performance:

1. Assets are measured on the basis of replacement cost, less depreciation, and depreciation is calculated on a replacement cost basis.
2. Divisional performance is measured by residual income, not ROI, with an investment charge calculated at 10 percent of average net investment.

Management regards these as partial solutions. It points to the Dandy Dirndl Division, the company's newest. It was formed two years ago to be in a position to capitalize on an opportunity associated with next year's Olympic Games. The initial investment was $120, of which $100 was in assets being depreciated on a straight-line basis over a five-year period and $20 was an investment in working capital. The anticipated cash flows were:

Time	Aftertax Cash Flow
0	−$120
1	+ 10
2	+ 20
3	+ 60
4	+ 40
5	+ 36

The final cash flow includes $20, representing the anticipated liquidation value of the working capital needed to support this division's activities and $16 representing the cash flow from the fifth year's operations. The internal rate of return was expected to be 10 percent, a satisfactory rate for this company.

Dandy Dirndl's income for the second year was reported as follows:

Revenues		$84.0
Expenses:		
Depreciation	$22.0	
Other expenses (including taxes)	60.0	
Investment charge at 10%	7.7	89.7
Residual income (loss)		$(5.7)

The estimated facilities replacement cost in the second year was $110. Replacement cost depreciation was 20 percent of this, or $22. Undepreciated replacement cost was 80 percent of replacement cost (new) at the beginning of the year and 60 percent of this at the end of the year, an average of $77 for the year. The investment charge in the income statement was based on this figure.

Top management noted that the negative residual income was not a serious problem in this case because the division was set up as a special venture by top management. The managers of ongoing divisions might hesitate before recommending such investments in their own divisions, however, because they wouldn't like to have their residual income figures depressed.

Required:

a. Why did management expect the two devices it had already adopted to encourage the division managers to submit capital expenditure proposals?

b. Identify a depreciation method that would not depress residual income in this case, and calculate depreciation for each of the five years using this method on an historical-cost basis.

c. Restate the historical-cost depreciation for Dandy Dirndl's second year (from your answer to [b]) to a replacement-cost basis and use this figure to make a revised calculation of residual income.

d. Other than changing the depreciation schedule as proposed in (b) and (c), what could top management do to encourage division managers to submit sound capital expenditure proposals with deferred payoffs? Explain how your suggestion or suggestions would achieve this result.

12. **Managerial performance evaluation.** George Johnson was hired on July 1, 19x1 as assistant general manager of the Botel Division of Staple, Inc. It was understood that he would be elevated to general manager of the division on January 1, 19x3, when the then current general manager retired. This was done on the scheduled date. In addition to becoming acquainted with the division and the general manager's duties in his first year and a half with the company,

Mr. Johnson was specifically charged with the responsibility for development of the 19x2 and 19x3 budgets. As general manager in 19x3, he was, obviously, responsible for the 19x4 budget.

The Staple Company is a multiproduct company which is highly decentralized. Each division is quite autonomous. Corporate top management approves division prepared operating budgets but seldom makes major changes in them. Corporate top management participates actively in decisions requiring capital investment (for expansion or replacement) and makes the final decisions. The division management is responsible for implementing the capital program. The major device used by the Staple Corporation to measure division performance is Contribution Return on Division Net Investment. The Botel Division budgets presented in the following table were approved by top management. (The budget is approved in December each year and is not revised, no matter how large the observed departures from the planned results.)

	Actual			Budget	
	19x1	19x2	19x3	19x2	19x3
Sales	$1,000	$1,500	$1,800	$2,000	$2,400
Less division variable costs:					
Material and Labor	250	375	450	500	600
Repairs	50	75	50	100	120
Supplies........................	20	30	36	40	48
Less division managed costs:					
Employee Training	30	35	25	40	45
Maintenance	50	55	40	60	70
Less division committed costs:					
Depreciation.....................	120	160	160	200	200
Rent	80	100	110	140	140
Total	600	830	871	1,080	1,223
Division net contribution	400	670	929	920	1,177
Division investment:					
Accounts receivable	100	150	180	200	240
Inventory	200	300	270	400	480
Fixed assets......................	1,590	2,565	2,800	3,380	4,000
Less: accounts and wages payable	(150)	(225)	(350)	(300)	(360)
Net investment	1,740	2,790	2,900	3,680	4,360
Contribution return on net investment ...	23%	24%	32%	25%	27%

Required:

a. Identify Mr. Johnson's responsibilities under the management and measurement program described above.

b. Appraise the performance of Mr. Johnson in 19x3.

c. Recommend to the president any changes in the responsibilities assigned to managers or in the measurement methods used to evaluate division management based upon your analysis.

(CMA)

13. **Statement preparation: Managerial evaluation.** Dorsey Company is a medium-sized, diversified manufacturing company. Each of its divisions is classified as an investment center, with its own manufacturing facilities and its own sales force.

The profit plan and operating results of Dorsey's Germicide Division last year were as follows (in $000):

	Actual	Planned
Sales	$22,000	$20,000
Expenses:		
Standard cost of goods sold	15,000	14,000
Factory cost variances	1,100	800
Selling expenses	2,900	3,000
Administrative expenses	1,600	1,500
Income taxes (at 40 percent)	560	280
Total expenses	21,160	19,580
Net income	$ 840	$ 420

The following are the averages of the monthly balance sheet amounts planned and recorded last year (in $000):

	Actual	Planned
Current assets	$ 6,800	$ 6,000
Fixed assets	8,100	8,000
Total assets	14,900	14,000
Current liabilities.................	3,800	4,000
Net investment	$11,100	$10,000

You have the following additional information:

1. All goods sold by this division are manufactured in the division's own factory. Selling expenses are all traceable to the division. They do not vary significantly with variations in actual sales.

2. Budgeted administrative expenses included a charge for the costs of the Dorsey Corporation's central administrative offices. This charge was computed at 4 percent of sales. Central administration costs do not vary in response to changes in sales volume within the year. As the company expands, however, these costs tend to rise and the 4 percent average has been relatively constant for many years.

3. The budgeted net investment in current assets included $1.5 million in cash. Cash balances are administered by the corporate treasurer's office and are allocated among the divisions on the basis of divisional sales.

4. Budgeted fixed assets included $500,000 as the Germicide Division's share of the company's investments in its headquarters offices and laboratories.

5. Average accounts receivable, inventories, and other current assets traceable to the Germicide Division last year totaled $5,000,000; average current liabilities amounted to $3,800,000. Average fixed assets traceable to the division amounted to $7,600,000.

6. Production volume equalled sales volume last year; inventories of manufactured and semiprocessed products were the same at the end of the year as at the beginning.

7. The company's minimum rate of return on investment for capital expenditure analysis purposes is 10 percent, after taxes.

Required:

a. Prepare a profit report for use in appraising managerial performance in the Germicide Products Division during the year.

b. Prepare a brief description of the principle or principles you followed in (*a*), referring to items in the report to show how you applied the principle(s) you selected.

c. What additional information would you want to have before evaluating division management's profit performance last year? Why would you find this information useful?

Case 25–1: Dundee Products, Inc.

George Dickson would like to take on a new customer, but is worried about his rate of return on investment (ROI). Mr. Dickson is in charge of the Cleveland branch of the Esco division of Dundee Products, Inc., a large conglomerate. Esco is a national distributor of industrial supplies, purchased from a number of manufacturers and sold through a network of 17 regional branches. Most of Dundee's other divisions deal in consumer goods; none of them sells any of its products through the Esco division.

Like the managers of the other branches, Mr. Dickson reports to Frank Corbett, Esco's executive vice president. Each branch is treated as a small profit center and each branch manager has virtually complete discretion over the methods of sales promotion to be used, the products to stock, and the customers to be served within the branch's geographical area. All products are selected from a list supplied by Esco's central purchasing office.

Selling prices are set at Esco's headquarters, but each branch manager can alter the terms of sale to reflect differences in risk and profitability of doing business with different customers. Each branch does its own billing and collection work. The profit performance of the branches and their managers is judged each year on the basis of the rate of return achieved on the investment in the branch, mainly the investment in storage space, the inventories on hand, and the receivables outstanding.

The profit plan

Each September, every branch manager submits a tentative profit plan to Mr. Corbett. This plan is a complete summary of the manager's marketing plans, including estimates of the amounts to be spent for field selling, the sales level to be achieved, the costs of warehousing, and the levels of the proposed investments in inventories and receivables. The anticipated first-year effects of proposed investments in physical facilities and equipment are also reflected in this tentative plan.

The proposed profit plans are reviewed critically by Mr. Corbett and his staff, who question the assumptions on which the projections have been based, make sure that alternative plans have been studied carefully, see whether the proposals are within the company's capacity, offer suggestions for improvement, and provide technical help in revising the proposals.

Once Mr. Corbett and the branch managers have come to an agreement, the plans are consolidated into an overall profit plan for the Esco division as a whole. Last-minute adjustments are sometimes made at this stage, but most of the inconsistencies ordinarily have been removed during the staff review.

The profit plans from all of the Dundee divisions are reviewed by corporate staff. Divisional plans are discussed informally as they are being formulated, and as a result relatively few changes are made in the plans after formal submission. The main reason for change at this point is a refusal by top management to fund facilities and equipment proposals at the levels anticipated by the division managers. This requires a reworking of the budgetary proposals in the light of the revised guidelines.

The current profit plan for the Cleveland branch is summarized in the first column of Table 1. Cleveland has been one of the division's most profitable outlets in the past, with rates of return ranging from 17 to 21 percent, but a major expenditure of funds on a new warehouse building and new materials handling equipment has brought the budgeted rate of return down to the 13.6 percent figure shown in Table 1. Even so, this is substantially greater than the 9 percent after-tax figure adopted by Dundee's top management as a minimum profit standard for investments in warehouses and sales offices.

Measurement methods

For internal reporting, Dundee measures investments in physical facilities at original cost less straight-line depreciation. Inventories in the Esco division are costed on a first-in, first-out (FIFO) basis. Receivables are shown at full face value, less an allowance

Table 1 Esco Division, Cleveland Branch pro forma profit plan ($000)

	Current Plan	Adjusted for Cut-Rate Line*
Net sales	$2,728	$3,740
Cost of goods sold†	1,982	2,792
Gross margin	746	948
Branch expenses‡	264	334
Income before tax	482	614
Income tax	265	338
Net income	217	276
Current assets:		
Cash§	$ 35	$ 50
Accounts receivable	253	398
Inventories	702	1,132
Total current assets	990	1,580
Less accounts payable§	346	431
Net working capital	644	1,149
Land	91	91
Buildings (net of depreciation)	704	704
Equipment (net of depreciation)	185	215
Net investment, end of year	1,624	2,159
Net investment, beginning of year	1,572	2,111
Average net investment	$1,598	$2,135
Rate of return (ROI)	13.6%	12.9%

* Based on 12 months' operations for comparative purposes.

† Purchase price plus estimated headquarters purchasing department cost.

‡ Including charges for head office services.

§ Based on head office estimates of amounts attributable to this branch.

for uncollectible amounts that is adjusted once a year on the basis of a headquarters staff review of the outstanding account balances.

All payrolls and payments to vendors are processed at Esco's divisional headquarters; the branch managers control only small petty cash accounts and have no direct liabilities of their own. The branch profit plans include a provision for cash and accounts payable, however, based on head office staff estimates of the amounts attributable to each branch's operations. These provisions are calculated from standard formulas, which are also used to compute the amounts shown in the monthly performance reports for each branch.

Investments in facilities and working capital at divisional and corporate headquarters are very small, and none of this investment is allocated to the individual branches.

Each branch is charged at predetermined unit prices for head office services such as payroll preparation and vendor payment. In addition, a flat charge of 2 percent of sales is made to cover the average cost of head office administration. Division headquarters charges each branch with the net invoice price of all goods consigned to the branch, plus 1 percent of this amount to cover the cost of the divisional purchasing department, which does all the purchasing for the branches.

The new opportunity

The operations at the Cleveland branch are proceeding more or less according to plan, and Mr. Dickson expects that when all the results are in at the end of the year he'll be very close to the planned levels of revenue and expense.

His new warehouse was built to meet the company's anticipated growth in the Cleveland area in the next 10 years, however, and a good deal of space is currently unused. Reasoning that his method of operation would enable him to offer better warehousing service to local companies with large inventories of nonperishable merchandise than local storage warehouses could provide, Mr. Dickson has spent a considerable amount of time during the past few months looking for one or two such customers.

Preliminary contracts with Cut-Rate Drugs, Inc., a St. Louis-based supplier of cosmetics, proprietary medicines, and other articles typically sold in drug stores, have progressed to such a point that Mr. Dickson has to make up his mind whether to expand into this line of business. Under the proposed arrangement, Cut-Rate would ship its products to the Cleveland warehouse, billing the Esco division on terms of net 30 days. This merchandise would be stored in a separate section of the warehouse.

In accordance with the Cut-Rate method of operation, all store deliveries would be in full case lots. Sales and deliveries would be made by four drivers who would be transferred from the Cut-Rate payroll. Cut-Rate would also lease its local fleet of four delivery vehicles to Mr. Dickson for the duration of the agreement. Mr. Dickson would become responsible for billing the drug stores and collecting the amounts due from them for the merchandise.

"This looks like a natural for us," Mr. Dickson said last week. "Only the sales force would be separate. Otherwise, the operation would be just like what we're doing now with our regular lines. We carry stock, sell, deliver, and collect, and we're pretty good at our job. I see no reason why we shouldn't do just as well with the Cut-Rate line. Our branches in Denver and Atlanta are doing the same sort of thing and seem to be making a go of it.

"The figures seem to bear me out, too. We'd get an extra $59,000 in profit on a $535,000 increase in investment, a rate of return of about 11 percent. The return to the company would be even greater, because our figures reflect the 2 percent surcharge that headquarters skims off the top of all our operations. I can't see how headquarters costs would go up by a penny as a result of this operation.

"The only problem is that our overall rate of return would go down from 13.6 percent to about 12.9 percent on an annual basis. You can see this in the right-hand column of the pro forma budget I gave you this morning [Table 1]. We've already come down from 17 percent as a result of the new warehouse and I don't think I'm going to look very good if I ring in with an even lower rate this year. I think I have a crack at the division manager's job when Frank Corbett retires in a couple of years and I don't want to do anything to rock the boat now. Frank tells me that he'll okay the increase in my inventories and receivables if I want to go ahead, but I'm afraid of that drop in the ROI."

"What kind of commitment would you have to make with Cut-Rate?" the case writer asked. "Could you get out of this easily if it didn't work out the way you expected?"

"Oh, we'd have no problem there. The deal is that either party could cancel the arrangement on six months' notice, and it would take us six months to clean things up anyway. They'd buy back the unsold inventory at book value. The drivers would go back to Cut-Rate, too, unless they wanted to stay with us and we had room for them."

"What's in it for Cut-Rate? What's wrong with the way they've been operating? I've been taught to be suspicious of people who want to give up part of their business."

"Well, anything's possible, of course, but I think this is on the level. They've been supervising the local sales force from St. Louis, using a local storage warehouse as a transhipment depot. The sales force is okay, but they've had a lot of trouble with the warehouse. Those people are good at dead storage, but they don't know the first thing about field warehousing. That's our business, and the people at Cut-Rate are pretty sure that we can increase their volume and cut their costs, too. Besides, they have a lot of money tied up in inventories and receivables. We figure that with our controls we can handle the higher volume with a smaller investment. It's unprofitable for them and very profitable for us, and you can't find a better basis for a deal than that.''

    a. Should Mr. Dickson go ahead with the Cut-Rate venture? Prepare a summary of the calculations and arguments on both sides of these questions.

    b. How would you decide whether the Cleveland branch's reported profit or return on investment is satisfactory or unsatisfactory? What profit standards would you adopt in this connection, and where would you get them?

    c. Should the measurement system be changed in any way to make it more consistent with the company's objectives? Give reasons to support your suggestions.

26 Interdivisional transfer pricing

Profit centers and other organization units for which profit performance measures must be prepared often buy from and sell to each other, sometimes in substantial quantities. Goods transferred from one division or subsidiary to another are *intermediate products*. The division the intermediate product is transferred from is the *supplying division;* the division receiving the intermediate product is the *buying division.* The product sold by the buying division is known as the *final product.* The prices used to record transfers of intermediate products from supplying divisions to buying divisions are known as transfer prices. The purpose of this chapter is to study the factors that shape the setting of transfer prices in various situations.

Purposes of transfer prices

The prices at which intermediate products are transferred have four immediate purposes:

1. To establish the amounts for which the manager of the buying division has assumed responsibility and for which the manager of the supplying division has been relieved of responsibility.
2. To determine for each division manager the profitability of individual transactions and classes of transactions in which the intermediate products figure.
3. To measure, for internal accountability and reporting, inventories of intermediate products or other products manufactured from them.
4. To measure the flow of resources from one jurisdiction to another, for use in calculations to be made by individuals or organizations outside the company in connection with income taxation, regulated pricing, and so on.

Criteria for transfer pricing

Any transfer price can serve each of the purposes listed in the preceding paragraph if the interested parties agree. A high price will establish the amount of responsibility, the profit margin, the inventory amount, and the flow of resources; a low price does the same. Some transfer prices meet system objectives better than others, however. In this section we'll develop a set of system design criteria based on the impact of the transfer price on the division managers' decisions, managerial evaluation, and economic evaluation of the division's activities, with a brief reference to the impact of transfer pricing on the company's taxes and interjurisdictional transfers of funds.

Divisional resource allocation decisions

In a decentralized company, the manager of the buying division sees the transfer price as the incremental cost of the intermediate product. This leads to the first criterion for selecting a transfer pricing policy: *the transfer price should lead division management to make the same decisions headquarters management would make if it had the time to study the problem and apply all the data available to the managers of both divisions.* If the transfer price leads to departures from this ideal, it is said to cause suboptimization.

For example, suppose a division can produce only 100 units of product X each month. It can either transfer these units to another division for conversion into product Z or sell them to an outside customer. For some reason a transfer price of $1,100 a unit has been set for product X. The costs and revenues associated with these alternatives are diagrammed in Exhibit 26–1.

Exhibit 26–1 A processing decision

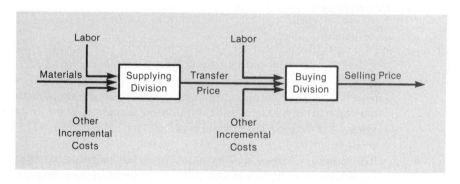

Given all this information, a manager responsible for *both* divisions would decide that the interdivisional transfer would be in the company's interests:

	Sell Product X	Manufacture and Sell Product Z	Difference
Revenues	$1,000	$1,800	$800
Costs:			
Processing	—	650	650
Marketing	180	200	20
Profit contribution	$ 820	$ 950	$130

If decision authority were delegated to the divisions, the manager of the supplying division would be happy to make the transfer. Product X would then bring in $1,100 in revenues, $100 more than the price charged the outside customer, and without spending $180 to sell it. The manager of the buying division, however, wouldn't buy the product at this price:

Estimated revenues		$1,800
Estimated costs:		
Materials (product X)	$1,100	
Processing and selling	850	1,950
Estimated processing profit (loss)		$ (150)

This would force the supplying division to take the next best alternative, sale of product X to the outside customer.

A transfer price of $1,100 would lead to suboptimization because it would deny the buying division the opportunity to make an outside sale that would benefit the company as a whole. This kind of suboptimization could be avoided by reducing the transfer price to the supplying division's opportunity cost, measured in this case by the net market value of the outside sale ($1,000 − $180 = $820). At this price the manager of the buying division would reach the profit maximizing solution:

Estimated revenues		$1,800
Estimated costs:		
Materials (product X)	$820	
Processing and selling	850	1,670
Estimated processing profit		$ 130

An $820 price here will satisfy our resource allocation objective if the supplying division's incremental costs of manufacturing the intermediate product are less than $820. Suppose we find, however, that the supplying division's incremental costs of manufacturing this product amount to $900. If the transfer price is set at $820, we'll see the following:

1. The buying division will have too great an incentive to buy, because the cost to the company will be understated by $80 (the difference between $900 and $820).
2. The supplying division will be unwilling to sell to anyone, because its incremental revenues will be $80 less than its incremental costs.

In this case the $820 market value of the intermediate product isn't a valid measure of the sacrifice necessary to provide intermediate products to the buying division. The supplying division would rather not produce at all than take advantage of this opportunity.

We can now restate our first transfer pricing criterion in operational terms:

For managerial guidance in decision making, the transfer price charged the buying division should be the incremental cost to the supplying division or the net market value of the intermediate product, whichever is higher.

Evaluating managerial performance

Transfer prices have a second impact, this time on the image of the division that will be transmitted to top management. For example, suppose a division has budgeted residual income of $210,000 but reports only $116,000, as shown in the following table:

	Actual	Budget	Over/(Under)
Sales	$1,600,000	$1,650,000	$(50,000)
Cost of goods sold	1,150,000	1,100,000	50,000
Divisional overhead	235,000	240,000	(5,000)
Investment carrying charge	99,000	100,000	(1,000)
Total charges	1,484,000	1,440,000	44,000
Residual income	$ 116,000	$ 210,000	$(94,000)

If internal transfers are important, the variance in residual income could be due mainly to low transfer prices on the products the division sells to sister divisions or high transfer prices on the products it buys internally.

The danger is that the division managers will think the transfer price is affecting their performance ratings unfairly. This can lead to dissension and can even defeat the main purpose of profit decentralization by impairing the managers' motivations to produce profits. This leads to the second transfer pricing criterion:

The transfer pricing system should be designed so that the division managers will regard the transfer prices as fair.

This second criterion is a statement of a goal rather than an absolute, quantifiable measure. Fairness is a subjective quality, and what one manager regards as fair may seem totally unfair to another.

A corollary of this criterion is that the transfer price, or at least the formula for arriving at the transfer price, should be set before the transfer is made rather than afterward. This permits division managers to know in advance what prices they will receive or what prices they will pay for transferred goods. This eliminates one source of uncertainty and permits the division managers to predict more accurately the effects of their decisions on their reported profits.

Economic evaluation of the division's activities

From the company's point of view, a supplying division's contribution to the joint profit emerging from sale of the final product is measured by the difference between its costs of supplying the intermediate product on a continuing basis and the amount it would have to pay outsiders for an equivalent product. The buying division's contribution, on the other hand, is the difference between the net revenue from the final product and the buying division's costs of obtaining those revenues, including as a cost the amount of net revenue the company forgoes by not selling the intermediate product to an outside customer.

Both the outside purchase price and the potential net selling price of the intermediate product are measures of the intermediate product's market value. This allows us to state the third criterion for a transfer pricing system:

> *For economic evaluation, the transfer price should approximate the market value of the intermediate product.*

In general, market value and outside purchase cost are assumed to be close enough to each other so that one figure can serve in the economic evaluation of both divisions. If the intermediate product is neither offered for sale nor available on the open market, market price can be approximated for economic evaluation purposes by estimating the cost to the buying division of manufacturing it, including imputed interest on the investment necessary to support this production.

Conflicts between the third criterion and either or both of the first two can be resolved in either of two ways:

1. Use two sets of transfer prices, one for each purpose.
2. Select a transfer pricing system to meet one purpose, making necessary adjustments whenever divisional profit performance is to be evaluated for the other purpose.

We tend to favor the second of these, subordinating the third criterion to the first two. Economic evaluation takes place relatively infrequently, whereas division managers make resource allocation decisions every day. The first criterion, therefore, is likely to be more important than the third. The infrequency of economic evaluation decisions also leads us to doubt that the creation of a parallel set of transfer prices would be worth its cost. Separate estimates can be prepared for economic evaluation when they are needed rather than all the time.

Fiscal management

Transfer prices between division or subsidiaries in different tax jurisdictions may affect the amount of taxes the company must pay. Furthermore, when the two parties to a transfer are in different countries, and one of those countries restricts the amount of funds the company can transfer out of the country, the transfer price may affect the amount of cash available for investment and other purposes.

We'll ignore these fiscal variables, and concentrate exclusively on the managerial aspects of transfer pricing. We'll do this for three reasons. First, the rules governing the selection of transfer prices for governmental use are established by governments. The company ordinarily has some leeway in applying these rules, but the range of choice is relatively limited.

Second, the rules vary from country to country, and this limits our ability to generalize.

Third, and most important, transfer prices meeting governmental requirements are unlikely to satisfy the three criteria we have just established. Taxation and foreign exchange controls are designed to achieve governmental objectives—fewer imports, more taxes, more jobs, and so on. The authorities aren't interested in helping management make decisions or evaluate divisional performance. If the governmental rules preclude transfer prices consistent with managerially oriented criteria, then management should try to find economical and legal ways to maintain two parallel transfer pricing systems.

Managerially oriented transfer pricing between profit centers

Transfer prices can be established in either of two ways: by dictation or by negotiation. They can be based on cost, on market price, or on some combination of the two. In this section we'll examine four possibilities:

1. Dictated prices based on full cost.
2. Dictated prices based on marginal cost.
3. Dictated prices based on market price quotations.
4. Market-based negotiated prices.

Dictated prices based on full cost

Price dictation can take either of two forms. In the simpler case, the pricing authority (higher management or one of the two divisions) establishes a price, which is then used to record transfers of the intermediate product. In other situations, the price dictator prescribes a pricing formula, such as the following:

Price = 110 percent of standard manufacturing cost.

The most popular basis for dictated prices is full cost.[1] The price may be set equal to average actual manufacturing cost, standard manufacturing cost, average total cost of the supplying division (including administrative overheads), or any of the above plus a markup to provide a profit margin to the supplying division. The implicit assumption is that a transfer price set in this way measures the supplying division's long-run incremental cost of supplying the intermediate product on a continuing basis.

Every measure of full cost reflects specific levels of operating volume and efficiency. If the long-run cost justification has any meaning, full cost should be measured at standard efficiency at normal volume. For example, suppose a supplying division has a cost budget of $75,000 in fixed costs plus variable costs of $9 for each unit of intermediate product. The normal volume is 25,000 units. Actual volume, however, is only 15,000 units and average variable cost is $9.50. If the transfer price is set equal to actual average full cost, it will be $75,000/15,000 + $9.50 = $14.50. At standard cost, the transfer price will be $75,000/25,000 + $9 = $12. The $2.50 difference between

---

[1] Richard F. Vancil, *Decentralization: Ambiguity by Design* (Homewood, Ill.: Richard D. Irwin, 1979), p. 180.

these two possible prices is the effect of the inefficient use of resources; it isn't part of the long run cost function.

Even if a particular set of full-cost based prices approximates long run incremental cost, it will fail to provide a sound guide to current resource utilization decisions, as required by our first design criterion. As long as a supplying division is operating below capacity—that is, on the relatively flat portion of the average variable cost curve—transfer prices based on full cost will overstate the supplying division's economic sacrifice and suboptimization may result.

subopt. ✗

For example, suppose a division manager is faced with the problem of choosing between an outside vendor and an internal supplying division for all or part of the buying division's requirements of a certain intermediate product. The full cost transfer price is $12, but the product can be obtained from an outside vendor at a delivered price of $10 a unit. Given these conditions, the division manager has a $2 incentive to buy the product outside, other things such as reliability and quality being equal.

But now suppose the internal supplying division is operating at 60 percent of capacity. The opportunity cost of internal transfers is the average variable cost, $9, not the $12 full cost. This means that if the product is bought outside, the supplying division will lose a $3 contribution toward its fixed costs; the loss in total company profit will be $1 a unit.

The situation will be just the reverse if the supplying division is pressing its capacity limits. At full capacity, the market value of the intermediate product is likely to be higher than average full cost. If the transfer price is based on full cost, the buying division will receive a signal that understates the sacrifice the company makes in making the intermediate product available to the buying division. A forced transfer at this price may be suboptimal and will be perceived as unfair by the supplying division manager.

Top management can prevent these kinds of suboptimization in either of two ways: (1) by changing the transfer price unilaterally; or (2) by ordering the parties to effect the transfer at the full cost price, if analysis indicates this would benefit the company. Each of these actions is incompatible with decentralization, as it reduces the profit responsibility of one division or the other.

Dictated prices based on marginal cost *unsuitable in decentralized environ.*

The shortcomings of full-cost transfer pricing have led to suggestions that marginal costs be used instead.[2] The underlying assumption is that marginal cost measures the supplying division's short-run incremental cost of supplying the intermediate product. The following three-step procedure is suggested:

= incremental cost

1. Each buying division manager is provided with a schedule representing the marginal costs of each supplying division at various volumes of operations. These are the prices the division must pay for additional quantities of the intermediate products.

---

[2] Jack Hirshleifer, "On the Economics of Transfer Pricing," *The Journal of Business of the University of Chicago,* July 1956, pp. 172–84; David Solomons, *Divisional Performance: Measurement and Control* (New York: Financial Executives Research Foundation, 1965).

2.   The buying division manager combines this schedule with the division's own schedule of marginal processing costs to determine a composite marginal cost schedule for the final products.

3.   The buying division manager calculates the volume at which the marginal revenue from the sale of an additional unit of the final product is just adequate to cover total marginal cost, and places an order for this quantity of the intermediate product.

Most models reflecting this concept assume that marginal cost increases and marginal revenue decreases as volume increases within existing capacity limits, giving us the diagram in Exhibit 26–2. The optimum production and transfer quantity is identified by the intersection of the marginal revenue and marginal cost lines (point M). At any higher volume, the benefit from increasing production (marginal revenue) will be less than the cost of obtaining it (marginal cost).

Exhibit 26–2 Deciding volume with marginal cost transfer pricing

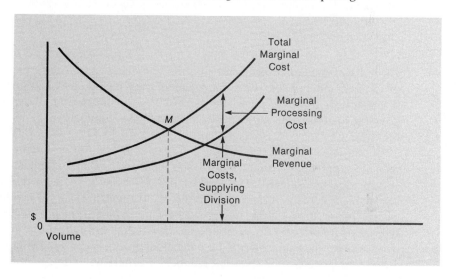

Although marginal cost transfer prices may in some cases give the division managers the proper guidance for decision making, three problems make it an unsuitable solution in a decentralized environment:

1.   Marginal cost is *indeterminate* when two or more divisions use or sell the same intermediate product.
2.   Marginal cost may be *less than market value* when operations are at capacity.
3.   Marginal cost prices may seem *unfair.*

Indeterminacy of marginal cost.   If the supplying division supplies more than one buying division or markets some of its output outside, and if marginal cost increases with volume, marginal cost won't be known until all buying divisions and outside customers place their orders. For example, suppose a supplying division has the marginal cost (MC) schedule diagrammed in Exhibit

824

Exhibit 26–3 Indeterminacy of marginal cost

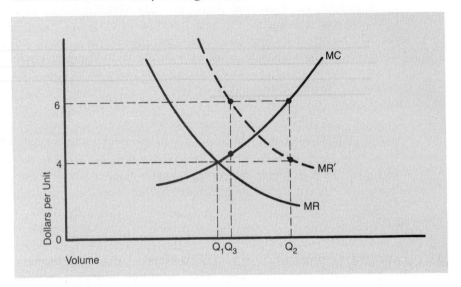

26–3. Its management estimates that the combined marginal revenue curve of its own independent operations and of two buying divisions it supplies would follow the path traced by the MR line in the exhibit. Based on this estimate, management quotes a transfer price of $4 a unit, and plans to produce Q₁ units.

But suppose one of the buying divisions is in a stronger market position than the supplying division believed, and the true combined marginal revenue ·curve is located at MR'. The total of the orders at a $4 price will be Q₂, but at this volume marginal cost will be $6. If the supplying division doesn't change its price, it will be selling some of its output at an incremental loss. If it raises its price to $6, total volume demanded will fall to Q₃, and when that happens marginal cost will be only about $4.50. If the supplying division reduces its price to this level the number of orders will rise again to exceed Q₃, marginal cost will rise, and so on.

All of the proposed solutions to this problem require the intervention of a central planner who will be able by one means or another to consolidate the schedules and determine the equilibrium point. This would abrogate the authority of the division managers and weaken the profit center structure. Only if the supplying division's marginal cost remains constant throughout the applicable range can be problem of indeterminacy be resolved within a decentralized environment, and other problems arise when that occurs, as we'll see in a moment.

Marginal cost may be less than market value. The second barrier to marginal cost transfer pricing is that it is inapplicable when the market value of the intermediate product is or appears to be greater than its marginal cost. In theory, this would not happen, because the supplying division would increase its rate of output until marginal cost equaled net marginal revenue. In fact, the company's knowledge of its marginal costs is almost never good enough to extend the cost schedule to this point; or else the company is unwilling or unable to engage in subcontracting or other high-cost devices to expand its short-run capacity to deliver products.

As a result, when the supplying division is operating at capacity, top management may have to permit it to get a transfer price greater than the previously calculated marginal cost; alternatively, top management may direct the supplying division to divert some of its output from external to internal customers, at a sacrifice of divisional income. Under the former solution, the marginal cost basis for transfer pricing is acknowledged to be inadequate; under the latter, divisional authority is abrogated.

Marginal cost prices may seem unfair.   Three factors may reduce the appearance of fairness in marginal cost transfer pricing. First, as we have already pointed out, the methods available to cope with inequalities between marginal cost and the market value of the intermediate product require departures from marginal cost or an abrogation of managerial autonomy. Any abrogation of authority weakens the perception of fairness.

Second, even if the transfer price is equal to marginal cost and no sacrifice of market value takes place, the transfer price is likely to be less than average full cost or the net prices charged the supplying division's outside customers. Transfers will appear to be less desirable than outside sales, exerting a downward pull on the supplying division's income. Forcing transfers at these low prices is likely to have a further impact on the perceived fairness of the system.

Third, marginal cost transfer pricing is likely to make the supplying division seem less profitable, particularly during periods of partial idle capacity. If the marginal cost curve is relatively flat, most of the profit contribution of internally transferred goods will be lodged in the internal buying division. The supplying division manager therefore may find it more difficult to justify capital expenditure proposals. If the system is seen to discriminate against the supplying division in this way, this may reduce the manager's commitment to the system's objectives.

Dictated prices based on market price quotations

If the profit centers were, in fact, independent businesses, any transfer of intermediate products would require a market transaction for which a market price would be recorded. This suggests that market prices could also be used to price transfers between divisions. Market price information might be obtained by consulting price catalogs, by soliciting bids from outside firms, or by examining published data on completed market transactions.

The notion behind this proposal is that if the market price is an accurate measure of the sacrifice the supplying division makes when it transfers goods to the buying division, it will provide appropriate guidance to the two division managers in their resource allocation decisions. It will also serve as a valid basis for the economic evaluation of each division's activities and should be accepted as fair by both parties.

Unfortunately, market price isn't necessarily an accurate measure of the supplying division's sacrifice. One problem is that market price quotations for some products and some commodities refer to a small number of unrepresentative transactions. Another problem is that the supplying division itself may set the market price, sell many units at that price, but be unable to sell additional units at that price, even though it has ample capacity to supply them. This is evidence that the *value* of these products in the market is lower than the *price* at which they are offered. The company therefore sacrifices less than the market price when the supplying division transfers the intermediate product internally.

The consequences of this kind of disparity can be serious. If the buying division is required to pay the quoted price for any units it obtains from the supplying division, it may process or market a smaller quantity of the intermediate product or it may seek an outside source at a lower price. If this lower price exceeds the supplying division's marginal cost, then the outside purchase will constitute suboptimization. If top management intervenes, however, forcing the use of transferred product rather than outside purchases, divisional autonomy will be reduced and the fairness concept will be violated.

Market price should be used only when it clearly represents the sacrifice the company must make to make the intermediate product available to the buying division.

Market-based negotiated prices

A strict market price system is a dictated price system. The rigidity of dictated market prices can be removed by allowing or requiring the division managers to deal with each other as they deal with outside customers and suppliers. We call this negotiated transfer pricing.

The nature of negotiated prices.   Negotiation usually begins with a price quotation from the supplying division. From this point any of four routes can be taken: (1) the buying division may accept the price; (2) the buying division may bluff and bargain to get a lower price; (3) the buying division may obtain competing bids and negotiate with each possible supplier to get the best price/service combination; or (4) the buying division may reject the bid and either buy outside or not buy at all, without further discussion of the price. The same sequence can be initiated by a price offer from the buying division.

No matter which of these outcomes takes place, the price can be classified as a negotiated price. The essence of negotiation is in the managers' freedom to accept or reject a price or to initiate a change from the initial bid or offer price. Whether such a change actually takes place is irrelevant.

The case for negotiated transfer prices.   Negotiation systems are based on the notion that the individual division managers, with intimate knowledge of their own markets and opportunities, are in the best position to decide whether internal transfers will take place. Part of the division manager's job is to be aware of market conditions affecting the division's operations. Each division manager is expected to make many decisions in which estimates of opportunity cost are crucial. The internal transfer decision is simply one of many.

A simple situation of this kind is illustrated in Exhibit 26–4. This shows a supplying division with average total costs of $17 and some outside customers paying enough to yield $18 a unit after marketing costs are deducted. The shaded area in the block representing the supplying division is the amount of capacity now devoted to filling outside customers' orders—the rest is idle.

Exhibit 26–4 Market influences on transfer pricing negotiations

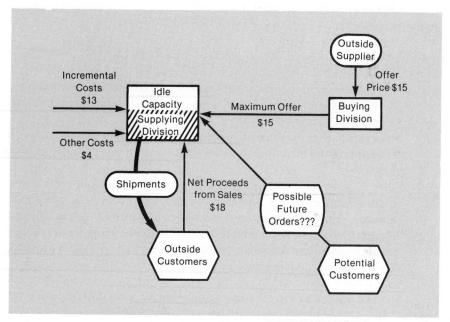

The buying division has an opportunity to buy the intermediate product from an outside supplier for $15, and has offered to pay this amount to the supplying division. The situation can be summarized quickly:

1. The buying division won't buy at a higher price.
2. It appears that the company will be better off if the transfer takes place (cost will be $13, not $15).
3. The supplying division will be $2 better off ($15 − $13) if it fills the order than if it lets the capacity stand idle.

In these circumstances it would seem that the two division managers have a mutual interest in reaching agreement on a transfer price. They should fail to agree only if the supplying division's manager estimates that the potential customers in the lower right-hand corner of the diagram are likely to come in with higher priced orders that will fill the division's capacity.

Division managers are paid to exercise their judgment in situations like this. They are expected to be right often enough to justify giving them the authority to make these decisions. The presumption is that the managers will negotiate an agreement if interdivisional transfers seem to be in the company's best interests because both managers will benefit if this is the case.

Negotiation should also contribute to the participants' sense of the fairness of the system, if the conditions necessary to negotiation are present. Without negotiation, internal transfers are either take-it-or-leave-it decisions or command decisions made by higher management. In either case the division managers' freedom of action is reduced, and this reduces their accountability for profit. Negotiation restores the managers' freedom of action and thereby increases their accountability for profits.

Necessary conditions for negotiated transfer pricing. These arguments are valid only if four conditions are met:

1. There must be some form of outside market for the intermediate product.
2. Any available market information should be communicated to both parties to the negotiation.
3. Both parties must have freedom to deal outside.
4. Top management must indicate its support of the principle of negotiation.

1. Existence of outside markets. The existence of an outside market for the intermediate product is important in negotiation because it provides both parties with an alternative. In the absence of an outside market, the bargaining range is likely to be considerably wider because the buying and selling divisions are in the position known to economists as bilateral monopoly—that is, the market for the intermediate product consists of two firms, one buying and one selling, and neither has an outside alternative. Under these conditions the market price is likely to be indeterminate within a fairly wide range.

2. Access to information. Both parties to the negotiation need access to market price information. Dissemination of information relating to the outside market should reduce the bargaining range and permit negotiation to take place in an atmosphere conducive to producing transfer prices that are fair approximations to opportunity cost. Some would even say they need access to internal cost information as well, and for the same reason.

3. Freedom to buy and sell outside. The lack of real freedom to buy or sell outside weakens the effectiveness of negotiation as a means of promoting sound resource allocation. Opportunity costs can't be determined reliably enough unless management has some way to test the market. Freedom to enter the market provides the necessary mechanism. Without buying freedom, transfer prices are less likely to feel the pressure of competitive forces and will remain higher than they should be to guide the managers of the buying divisions in their pricing and output decisions. With their costs kept at artificially high levels, the buying divisions will be unable to accept orders that would prove profitable to the company as a whole.

It should be remembered that freedom to deal outside does not necessarily mean that a substantial volume of purchases will actually be made from outside suppliers when idle internal capacity exists. Freedom must be accompanied by an obligation to negotiate internally. The buying division manager will normally prefer to buy from another unit of the company if the intermediate products are available at competitive prices. On the other side, the supplying division faced with idle capacity should be willing to reduce transfer prices to retain the business as long as some margin remains over the incremental costs of serving the internal customer.

4. *Top management support.* Strong top management support is essential to reduce the amount of umpiring top management is called upon to do. A system of negotiation can be undermined quickly if top management is ready to step in and arbitrate disputes whenever they arise. Appealing to the umpire is a form of dodging responsibility. Unless top management makes it clear that appeals for arbitration will reflect unfavorably on the executive ability of the negotiators, umpiring is likely to become frequent.

Weaknesses of price negotiation.   One weakness of interdivisional transfer price negotiation is that *negotiation is time consuming.* Although a five minute telephone call will do the job on occasion, major negotiations can extend over several weeks, backed by extensive staff work.   *time consuming*

A related problem is that, if the bargaining range is wide and the volume of transfers is large, *divisional profit will be very sensitive to the division manager's ability as a bargainer.* Wide bargaining ranges and massive transfers are generally found when the conditions required for effective negotiation are poorly met. In such cases the process will be perceived as a charade by at least one of the parties and this will throw the entire profit decentralization concept into disrepute. Even if negotiation is the standard procedure, therefore, top management should provide in advance for the use of other procedures when negotiation is unfeasible and would be destructive.

The third weakness is that *negotiation is a divisive process.* It emphasizes the conflicting interests of the various division managers rather than their mutual interest in the company's prosperity. Although we have said that agreement to transfer internally is in the interest of both parties if the supplying division's opportunity costs are low and the opportunity costs of the buying division are high, the process of reaching this agreement works in the opposite direction.

Pricing transfers when negotiation is inappropriate

Many transfers take place when some or all of the conditions necessary to negotiation are absent. All transfers to administered centers fall into this category. Lacking freedom to buy outside, the administered center has little bargaining power. Negotiation would be a meaningless ritual. In these circumstances

830

management should consider three possible transfer pricing methods we haven't discussed previously:

1. Variable cost plus lump-sum retainer.
2. Market in/cost out.
3. Mathematical programming.

Reminder: Characteristics of an administered center

1. It sells goods mainly to <u>outside customers.</u>
2. It has a profit objective, profit-oriented decision rules, and profit accountability.
3. It obtains a large percentage of its raw materials (or salable merchandise) from other parts of the company and is denied access to other sources of these items.

None of these methods is fully consistent with profit decentralization because each of them requires intervention by a central planning authority either in pricing or in decisions on where to acquire and where to use intermediate products. When negotiation is impossible, however, some weakening of the decentralization concept is inevitable—the question is which method is likely to be the most effective in these circumstances.

Variable cost plus retainer

When supplying divisions are the only reliable source of certain intermediate products, a few companies have turned to a <u>variant of marginal cost transfer pricing,</u> diagrammed in Exhibit 26–5. <u>Transferred units are priced at standard</u> <u>average variable cost per unit;</u> the buying division is also charged a lump sum retainer to cover a portion of the supplying division's fixed costs and perhaps a profit allowance as well. This is a <u>dictated price system,</u> in which standard cost and the size of the retainer are set or approved by top manage-

[handwritten margin note: Std. avg. var. cost/unit + retainer to cover some fixed costs]

Exhibit 26–5 Variable cost plus retainer

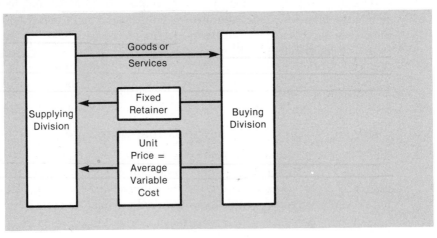

ment, depending on the amount of capacity reserved for the buying division.

The purpose of the variable cost charge is to guide the buying division's management in short-run capacity utilization decisions. The purposes of the retainer are to provide some guidance in economic evaluation and to promote a sense of fairness in both divisions.

This system will work as long as the supplying division is operating below capacity and the assumption of constant average variable cost remains valid. Once the division begins to press the limits of its capacity, however, something else must be done. For example, suppose a supplying division manufactures a certain intermediate product that is neither sold on the market nor available from outside suppliers. There is no market price. The division has been selling 10 percent of its total output of all products internally and 90 percent to outside customers; the retainer has been established on the assumption that this allocation will continue. During the year the buying division finds that its sales are running ahead of budget, and the manager requests additional quantities of the intermediate product.

If the supplying division has idle capacity, this additional demand can and should be met at standard variable cost. No distortion of the supplying division's profit should result. But if the supplying division is operating at or near capacity, the additional volume for the final product division can be obtained only by diverting capacity from outside sales of other products of the supplying division or by incurring costs in excess of standard variable cost, perhaps by increased subcontracting, increased use of overtime, or use of less productive standby equipment. In this hybrid situation, who makes the decisions and how are these decisions reflected in the transfer prices?

The answers to these questions are not entirely clear, but one solution is worth exploring—require the division managers to negotiate to see if they can agree on a price for the incremental transfers:

1. If the increased volume can be reached only by curtailing production of products now being sold outside the company, the supplying division will demand the same dollar markup over variable cost from its internal customer that it would lose by reducing its sales to outside customers.
2. If the supplying division can expand its total output by using resources which cost more than standards call for, then its management must demand a price that is at least adequate to cover the incremental cost of production by the more costly methods.

The buying division will be willing to pay these higher prices only if the sale value of these additional units is adequate to cover the transfer prices plus any additional costs of further processing and distribution.

This transfer pricing method may seem inconsistent with the profit center concept. In fact, it is the transfer requirement, not the transfer pricing method, that is the inconsistent element. Since the supplying division is the only source of supply, and the buying division is the only customer, the negotiating range is extremely wide. To avoid the dysfunctional effects of negotiation, higher management will have to get into the transfer pricing process. The variable cost plus retainer approach is a method of meeting the three transfer pricing criteria in this situation.

The variable cost plus retainer system has two defects. First, it may not always achieve its objective of promoting a sense of fairness. The supplying division neither participates in the buying division's successes nor shares in its failures. In a sense, the retainer guarantees the supplying division's profit, while the buying division is exposed to the risks and rewards of volume fluctuations. The manager of the buying division may regard this as less than fair.

The other objection is that it may bias the economic evaluation process. The problem is that the total profit contribution of the final product is the result of the efforts of the two divisions combined. In the absence of information on the market value of the intermediate product, management has no way of splitting this profit contribution between the two divisions that will measure the profit attributable to each. In fact, the total profit contribution may even be applicable to *each* division if eliminating either would lead to the loss of the whole profit.

This flaw can't be ignored, but we return to the point we made at the beginning of the chapter, in discussing transfer pricing criteria: the requirements of economic evaluation are often so difficult to satisfy that we must select transfer pricing methods that don't meet them all. Since we have elected to give primary emphasis to the divisional decision-making and fairness criteria, we can't rule out the variable cost plus retainer method just because it doesn't meet the economic evaluation criterion.

Market in/cost out (dual pricing $)

A second alternative when the intermediate product has no immediate market value is one we have labeled the *market in/cost out* method.[3] In a market in/cost out system, sometimes referred to as a *dual pricing* system, the buying division is charged a price equal to marginal cost (usually assumed to be equal to average variable cost), while the supplying division receives a price equal to the selling price of the buying division's finished product, less the average incremental cost of processing and marketing it. When this method is used, *each* division is credited with the full profit margin arising from the buying division's sales of its finished product.

For example, suppose the supplying division has an average variable cost of $3. The buying division sells the product for $6 after paying $2 to process and market it. The total incremental profit from this series of transactions is $1. The transfer prices in a market in/cost out system are $4 to the supplying division and $3 to the buying division, as shown in Exhibit 26–6. Each division reports the full $1 incremental profit on the transfer.

The purpose of a market in/cost out transfer pricing system is to emphasize the mutuality of interest of the two divisions. To the extent that the buying division uses transferred products, it is essentially an extension of the supplying

---

[3] A somewhat similar method is supported by Joshua Ronen and George McKinney III, "Transfer Pricing for Divisional Autonomy," *Journal of Accounting Research* (Spring 1970), pp. 99–112.

Exhibit 26–6 Market in/cost out transfer pricing

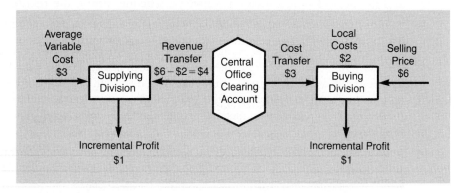

division. Crediting the supplying division with the buying division's profit contribution emphasizes this and gives the supplying division an incentive to make the transfers. Charging the buying division at variable cost gives it the same incentive.

This mutuality of interest breaks down when the supplying division reaches the limits of its capacity. At this point transfers to the buying division force the supplying division to deny products to its own outside customers. The solution here is not to negotiate, because the buying division has no alternative sources of supply.

Probably the best solution is to maintain the variable cost transfer price for the budgeted transfer volume, with a higher price for any additional quantities, reflecting the current opportunity cost of the supplying division. In this way the buying division's decisions will have to reflect opportunity cost, but its overall profit performance won't be undermined. As long as the higher prices are published in advance, this should maintain the impression of fairness which is an essential requirement of any transfer pricing system.

The market in/cost out method may be better for economic evaluation than the variable cost plus retainer method. The presumption is that the total profit contribution of the final product would be lost if *either* division were to discontinue its activities relating to the intermediate product. If this presumption is untrue, then we're back where we were with the variable cost plus retainer method. No routine formula will be able to reflect the attributability of profit to individual divisions without doing serious damage to the other two criteria.

Mathematically programmed prices

A third method management might consider when conditions aren't ripe for negotiated transfer pricing is some form of mathematical programming. This method combines marginal cost and market price information in a single model.

For example, an oil company controls the output of one of its large refineries with the help of a linear programming model. Part of the output of one of the refinery's products is transferred to a nearby petrochemical plant. The linear programming model is solved every quarter for various transfer volumes, and the petrochemical division is given a schedule listing the transfer prices for various quantities. The division manager then decides how much to buy during the quarter.

When the refinery is operating below capacity, the transfer prices represent the marginal cost of serving the petrochemical plant. At full capacity, the transfer price is the sale value of the transferred output. Since this is considerably higher than marginal cost, the petrochemical manager will often find it profitable to buy substitute materials from outside sources when the refinery is at capacity.

Prices derived from the application of linear programs or other mathematical resource allocation models are superior to marginal cost prices whenever elements of production capacity are fully utilized. The programmed price under these conditions is an approximation to opportunity cost, thereby reducing the danger of suboptimization.

Unfortunately, mathematically programmed transfer prices are much less consistent with profit decentralization than prices determined by either of the other two methods we have just discussed. The reason is that decisions on the allocation of the intermediate product are made entirely by central management, whereas these decisions remain entirely with the division managers in a market in/cost out system and at least partly with the division managers in a variable cost plus retainer system. It has even been suggested that if mathematical programming accounts for a major portion of the input or output of any division, that division perhaps should be reabsorbed into the division which is its major supplier or customer.[4]

To maintain the appearance of decentralized decision making without suboptimization, several writers have advocated an iterative procedure rather than a firm set of predetermined transfer prices.[5] Under this plan the division managers would supply a central analytical staff with preliminary estimates of their output plan and input needs. The central staff would enter these plans into a large-scale linear program and transmit the resulting quantities and transfer prices to the division managers.

Upon receipt of the results of this first run, the division managers would review their initial plans and submit revised estimates to headquarters. The linear program would be run again with these data and the results would once again be sent to the division managers. By the end of the third or fourth iteration, the divisional plans would approximate the optimal solution and further iteration would become unnecessary.

Whether this procedure would preserve the decentralization pattern or un-

---

[4] A. Rashad Abdel-khalik and Edward J. Lusk, "Transfer Pricing—A Synthesis," *The Accounting Review,* January, 1974, pp. 8–23, at p. 16.

[5] William J. Baumol and Tibor Fabian, "Decomposition, Pricing for Decentralization and External Economies," *Management Science,* September 1964, pp. 1–32; Andrew Whinston, "Price Guides in Decentralized Organizations," in *New Perspectives in Organization Research,* edited by W. W. Cooper, H. J. Leavitt, and M. W. Shelly II (New York: John Wiley, 1964), pp. 405–48; Nicholas Dopuch and David F. Drake, "Accounting Implications of a Mathematical Programming Approach to the Transfer Price Problem," *Journal of Accounting Research,* Spring 1964, pp. 10–24.

dermine it is a behavioral question for which no data are available. The method would seem to have a positive benefit if the quality of the data considered by the division managers in later iterations were higher than the quality of the data they supplied initially to a central decision staff.

It must be remembered, however, that real decision authority in these situations rests in the supplying division, where the computer program is run. The other division managers may come to regard the iterative process as an unproductive game, taking a good deal of time and energy but played for someone else's benefit. This could reduce the credibility of the entire profit measurement system, and thereby reduce its motivational impact. If central programming is necessary and the division managers have enough autonomy in other respects to justify retaining the profit center/administered center structure, the programming probably should remain in the open, without the transparent disguise the decomposition approach provides.

Summary

Transfer prices on goods or services transferred between profit centers should guide the profit center managers toward decisions that will lead to an economic allocation of resources. They should also be perceived as fair by the profit center managers, so as not to weaken their motivation. Finally, if possible, they should help top management evaluate the profitability of the division's activities. This last criterion may be difficult to implement, however, and in general can be subordinated to the other two.

Transfer prices might be based on cost, or market value, or some combination of the two. They can be dictated by central management or derived by negotiation between the parties. Market-based negotiated prices are the only ones fully consistent with the profit center concept. Other methods should be used only for transfers to administered centers or for transfers between profit centers when the conditions necessary for successful negotiation are absent.

The methods most likely to be consistent with the managerially oriented system design criteria in these latter situations are market in/cost out transfer pricing and transfers at variable cost plus lump sum retainers. Mathematically programmed transfer prices may also be used, but these require such a substantial abrogation of divisional authority that management may even wish to reconsider its decision to decentralize any units for which mathematically programmed prices are appropriate.

Independent study problems (solutions in Appendix B)

1. **Meeting a competitor's bid.** Ballou Corporation, a diversified manufacturing company, has seven main product divisions, each with its own manufacturing facilities and selling most of its output to outside customers. One of these divisions, the Hull Division, manufactures and sells a broad range of industrial chemicals.

   Hull Division supplies product X to outside customers and also to the Hingham Division, another of Ballou's seven product divisions. Hingham Division uses product X as a raw material in the manufacture of several products. Hull charges

Hingham $1.80 a pound for product X, 10 percent less than it charges its outside customers.

Hingham has been happy with this arrangement for several years, but an outside supplier has just offered to supply a perfectly satisfactory substitute for product X at a firm contract price of $1.60 a pound, delivered at the Hingham factory. The Hingham Division manager has proposed that the interdivisional transfer price of product X be reduced to $1.60 to meet the competing offer; otherwise, the contract will go outside.

You are the assistant controller in the Hingham Division. Your division manager has just given you a copy of Hull division's estimated monthly income statement for product X (in $000):

Sales—outside (100,000 lbs. at $2)		$200
Sales—Hingham (50,000 lbs. at $1.80)		90
Total sales		290
Product-traceable costs:		
Variable manufacturing costs ($0.90 per lb.)	$135	
Sales commissions—outside sales	10	
Depreciation	20	
Other traceable fixed costs	40	205
Product profit contribution		85
Share of divisional fixed costs		60
Income before taxes		$ 25

The fixed costs traceable to product X wouldn't be reduced if production volume were reduced by a third. The divisional fixed costs, allocated among the division's products at a flat 40 cents a pound, are even stickier. These costs would continue even if Hull Division stopped making product X entirely.

Required:

a. Draft a short memorandum, outlining the points Hingham's manager should make in trying to convince Hull's manager to reduce the transfer price.
b. Is negotiation the right way to determine a transfer price in this situation?

2. **Transfers to foreign subsidiary.** Elsa Corporation is a wholly owned subsidiary of Ballou Corporation, established to market the company's products in other countries in the Western Hemisphere. It handles only Ballou products, including many products manufactured in the Hull Division (see problem 1). It does no manufacturing of its own.

Elsa has never introduced product X into its markets because in its ordinary uses product X requires support facilities Elsa is in no position to provide. Elsa's manager has found a new use for this product, however, and is convinced the division could sell 20,000 pounds a month at a price of $1.80 a pound. Transportation costs to these markets would amount to 5 cents a pound and incremental local marketing costs would amount to $2,000 a month. Elsa will start marketing product X only if the transfer price is cut to $1.50 a pound.

Required:

a. As manager of the Hull Division, would you reduce the transfer price?
b. Is negotiation a good way to reach transfer prices in situations like this? (Ignore any effects the transfer price might have on taxes and customs duties.)

Exercises and problems

3. **Profit sharing transfer prices.** A proposal has been made to set the transfer price for goods transferred between two profit centers midway between standard manufacturing cost and market price. The argument is that this will eliminate

the need for negotiation, avoid suboptimization, and foster the perception of fairness.

Required:

Prepare an analysis of this proposal. Is it likely to achieve the results claimed for it?

4. **Pricing different volumes.** Caplow Company is a multidivisional company, and its division managers have been delegated full profit responsibility and complete autonomy to accept or reject transfers to or from other divisions. Division A produces a subassembly with a ready competitive market. This subassembly is currently used by division B for a final product which is sold outside at $1,200 a unit. Division A charges division B $700 a unit for the subassembly, the price division A charges its outside customers. Variable costs are $520 in division A and $600 in division B; fixed costs are unaffected by the volume of business represented by this subassembly or the final product made from it. The subassembly isn't available from any outside supplier.

The manager of division B feels that division A should transfer the subassembly at a price lower than market because division B is unable to make a profit if it has to pay the market price.

Required:

a. Compute division B's contribution margin if transfers are made at the $700 price, and also the total contribution margin for the company.
b. Assume division A can sell all its production in the open market at a price of $700 a unit. Should division A transfer goods to division B? If so, at what price?
c. Assume division A can produce 1,000 units a month, but can sell only 500 units in the open market at $700 each. A 20 percent price reduction would be necessary to sell full capacity. Division B could sell as many as 1,000 units of the final product at the $1,200 price. Should transfers be made? If so, how many units should be transferred and at what price? Submit a schedule showing comparisons of contribution margins under three different alternatives to support your decision.

(SMAC, adapted)

5. **Selecting a source of supply.** The Barnaby Corporation was formed two years ago as a merger of two previously independent companies, Dover and Elmsford. These two companies, now Barnaby divisions, have been operated since the merger just as they were before the merger, as if they were still independent businesses. Each has its own sales force and its own production facilities. Interdivisional transactions are rare and the company has never established a transfer pricing policy.

The Dover division now buys 10,000 metal handles a month from the Fowler Company for use on one of its products, a canister-type vacuum cleaner. The Elmsford division recently offered to supply these handles to Dover at a price of 90 cents apiece. The Dover division manager was interested, but not at a 90-cent price. The current purchase price was 82 cents and the Fowler Company had already offered a firm contract for the next year's requirements at this price.

The Elmsford division has a modern, well-equipped factory. Although its equipment is not ideally suited to the production of small items like the Dover handles, labor and materials costs on such items are only a few cents higher than in more suitably equipped plants.

Because of his high costs, Dick Baker, the manager of the Elmsford division, doesn't see how he can cut the price much below 90 cents. According to his own calculations, cost would be 85 cents, as follows:

Materials	$0.55
Labor	0.10
Factory overhead	0.20
Total	$0.85

Because this would be an internal sale, no selling expense would be incurred.

Mr. Baker knows that many of his factory overhead costs are fixed and that he has more than enough idle capacity to take on this business without difficulty. Only about 30 percent of the factory overhead cost of making the handles represents incremental cost. Furthermore, he would have no difficulty in expanding his work force by the small amounts necessary to take on the production of these handles. Mr. Baker feels, however, that any business that does not cover at least its share of fixed factory overhead offers no long-term promise and is better left alone. It reduces the average rate of profitability and ties down part of the division's productive capacity.

The Dover division manager has just decided to continue buying the handles from the Fowler Company at the 82-cent price.

Required:

a. On the basis of the data available to you, and ignoring the transfer price, do you believe that the Dover division should buy its handles from the Elmsford division?

b. If you had the power to set the transfer price in this situation, what price would you set?

c. Assuming that the calculations in (*a*) indicated that Elmsford should supply the handles, should the top management of the Barnaby Corporation step in and order the Dover division to buy them from Elmsford at the transfer price you selected in (*b*)? Explain.

6. **Selecting a source of supply.** Company B has several product divisions. Each of these has its own manufacturing facilities and sells all or most of its output to outside customers. The company's policy is to allow division managers to choose their sources of supply and, when buying from or selling to sister divisions, to negotiate the prices just as they would for outside purchases or sales.

One of the company's divisions, division X, buys all of its requirements of its main raw material, fleuron, from division Y. Fleuron is one of several products manufactured in division Y, and its full manufacturing cost in division Y is 88 cents a pound at normal volume.

Until recently, division Y was willing to supply fleuron to division X at a transfer price of 80 cents a pound, just 4 cents more than division Y's estimated incremental cost. Division Y is now operating at capacity, however, and is unable to meet all of its outside customers' demands for fleuron at its selling price of $1 a pound. Division Y has threatened to cut off supplies to division X unless division X will agree to pay the market price.

Division X is resisting this pressure. The division's budget for the current year was based on an estimated consumption of 1 million pounds of fleuron each month at a price of 80 cents. Since the division's budgeted income before taxes is only $250,000 a month, a price increase to $1 would bring the division very close to the break-even point.

Division X's purchasing office has found an outside source of a substitute material at a price of 95 cents. This material is slightly different from fleuron and therefore division Y couldn't buy it and resell it to its outside customers at the $1 price it gets for fleuron. The substitute material would meet division X's needs just as well as fleuron, but division X's manager sees no reason to go outside when a sister division can supply its requirements at a lower cost. Even if cost were measured at division Y's full manufacturing cost of 88 cents a pound, division X would still be giving division Y a 12-cent profit on every pound and would fall $80,000 a month short of its budgeted profit.

Required:

a. If you were to make this decision without regard for the views of the individual division managers, where should division X obtain its materials? Support your answer with figures from the problem.

b. Again assuming you are in a position to dictate the transfer price in this situation, should division X be quoted a price of 80 cents, 88 cents, 95 cents, or some other amount for each pound of fleuron it needs? Explain your reasoning.

c. Given the company's transfer pricing system, is division X likely to obtain its materials from the source you recommended in (*a*)? Is the transfer price likely to be set at the level you recommended in answer to (*b*)? Explain.

d. How, if at all, would you change your answers to (*a*) and (*b*) if you learned that division Y had agreed at the beginning of the year to supply up to 1 million pounds a month for 12 months at a fixed price of 80 cents a pound? Explain.

e. Should the company's transfer pricing system be changed so that disputes of this sort won't arise, or should the present system be continued? Explain your reasoning, including the arguments favoring any changes you believe should be made.

7. **Selecting a source of supply.** The Gunnco Corporation has several divisions operating as profit centers. Two of these are the Ajax and Defco divisions. Each of these divisions sells most of its output to customers outside the Gunnco group.

Divisional residual income is used in the periodic evaluations of the performance of the divisions and of the division managers. Residual income for each division is calculated by deducting interest at a pretax annual rate of 18 percent on Gunnco's net investment in the division.

The Ajax division is now operating at capacity, meaning that it could expand its total production and sales volume in the near term only at a very high cost. Defco, on the other hand, is now operating at only 50 percent of its capacity, with many of its production employees either on unpaid furlough or on a short workweek. The division's administrative and clerical staffs have not been cut, with the result that a good deal of administrative capacity is idle.

Defco's manager is actively seeking profitable ways to utilize the division's idle capacity. A commercial airplane manufacturer has offered to buy 1,000 brake units from Defco, to be delivered during the next 12 months at a price of $52.50 each. Defco could meet this delivery schedule without difficulty. Defco's management sees this order as an opportunity to penetrate a new market which holds promise of substantial future growth, and is anxious to meet the price, if at all possible. Defco's estimated cost of the brake unit is as follows:

Purchased parts—outside vendors	$22.50
Ajax electrical fitting No. 1726	5.00
Other variable costs	14.00
Fixed overhead and administration	8.00
Total cost per unit	$49.50

Defco's total fixed overhead and administrative costs are unlikely to increase as a result of the brake unit order, but Defco's management believes any business it takes on should cover its fair share of the division's costs.

Defco's management estimates that $5,000 in additional working capital would be required to support the brake unit business.

The Ajax fitting required for this brake unit would be supplied by the Ajax division. This fitting is now being produced and sold to Ajax's outside customers at a price of $7.50 each, and approximately 10,000 of these fittings are likely to be sold this year at that price. Ajax's variable cost of producing fitting No. 1726 is $4.25 each. Standard fixed cost is $1.25 a unit, Ajax is now running a favorable overhead volume variance of 20 percent of standard fixed cost, but none of this is distributed to individual products.

Other transfers to Defco now account for about 5 percent of Ajax's total volume; the transfer prices negotiated for these are generally the prices Ajax charges its outside customers for the same products. These prices aren't in dispute.

Defco could obtain roughly similar fittings from outside suppliers for about $7.50, the same price Ajax charges. If it had to pay this much, however, Defco's profit margin on the brake unit would virtually disappear. Since Defco's marketing people see no possibility of getting a higher price for the brake units, Defco's manager has asked the Ajax manager to supply these fittings at a price of $5 each.

Required:

a. As the Ajax division controller, would you recommend that Ajax supply fitting No. 1726 to Defco at the $5 price? Cite figures and explain your reasoning in two or three well-chosen sentences. (Ignore income taxes.)

b. Suppose Ajax refuses to sell at any price less than $7.50. As the Defco division controller, would you recommend paying this price? Again cite figures and explain your reasoning.

c. As the Gunnco corporate controller, would you recommend that top management classify this item as one for which the transfer price should be set by top management? Give a brief explanation of your reasoning.

(CMA, adapted)

8. **Market price transfers: Manufacturing division.** A. R. Oma, Inc. manufactures a line of men's perfumes and after-shaving lotions. The manufacturing process is basically a series of mixing operations with the addition of certain aromatic and coloring ingredients; the finished product is packaged in a company-produced glass bottle and packed in cases containing six bottles.

A. R. Oma feels that the sale of its product is heavily influenced by the appearance and appeal of the bottle and has, therefore, devoted considerable managerial effort to the bottle production process. This has resulted in the development of certain unique bottle production processes in which management takes considerable pride.

The two areas (i.e., perfume production and bottle manufacture) have evolved over the years in an almost independent manner; in fact, a rivalry has developed between management personnel as to "which division is the more important" to A. R. Oma. This attitude is probably intensified because the bottle manufacturing plant was purchased intact 10 years ago and no real interchange of management personnel or ideas (except at the top corporate level) has taken place.

Since the acquisition, all bottle production has been absorbed by the perfume manufacturing plant. The perfume production division buys all its bottles from the bottle production division. Each division is considered a separate profit center and is evaluated as such. As the new corporate controller, you are responsible for defining the proper transfer prices to use in crediting the bottle production profit center and in debiting the perfume production profit center.

At your request, the bottle division general manager has asked certain other bottle manufacturers to quote prices for the quantities and sizes demanded by the perfume division. These competitive prices are:

Volume (equivalent cases*)	Total Price	Price per Case
2,000,000	$ 4,000,000	$2.00
4,000,000	7,000,000	1.75
6,000,000	10,000,000	1.67

* An "equivalent case" represents six bottles each.

A cost analysis of the internal bottle plant indicates that it can produce bottles at these costs:

Volume (equivalent cases)	Total Cost	Cost per Case
2,000,000	$3,200,000	$1.60
4,000,000	5,200,000	1.30
6,000,000	7,200,000	1.20

(Your cost analysts point out that these costs represent fixed costs of $1.2 million and variable costs of $1 per equivalent case.)

These figures have given rise to considerable corporate discussion as to the proper value to use in the transfer of bottles to the perfume division. This interest is heightened because a significant portion of a division manager's income is an incentive bonus based on profit center results.

The perfume production division has the following costs in addition to the bottle costs:

Volume (cases)	Total Cost	Cost per Case
2,000,000	$16,400,000	$8.20
4,000,000	32,400,000	8.10
6,000,000	48,400,000	8.07

After considerable analysis, the marketing research department has furnished you with the following price-demand relationship for the finished product:

Sales Volume (cases)	Total Sales Revenue	Sales Price per Case
2,000,000	$25,000,000	$12.50
4,000,000	45,600,000	11.40
6,000,000	63,900,000	10.65

Required:

a. The A. R. Oma Company has used market price transfer prices in the past. Using the current market prices and costs, and assuming a volume of 6 million cases, calculate income before taxes for:
   (1) The bottle division.
   (2) The perfume division.
   (3) The corporation.
b. Is this production and sales level the most profitable volume for
   (1) The bottle division?
   (2) The perfume division?
   (3) The corporation?
   Explain your answer.
c. Should the bottle and perfume divisions be treated as separate profit centers? Explain why or why not.
d. In view of your answer to (c), how should the transfer price be set, and what price(s) would you recommend? Explain your reasoning.

                                                                    (CMA, adapted)

9. **Manufacturing division: Umpiring a dispute.**   Cliffside Enterprises has three divisions. Division A has its own marketing and manufacturing facilities, and so does division B. Division C is strictly a manufacturing division, sending approximately 40 percent of its output to division A and 60 percent to division B. These transfers account for about one third of the goods and materials purchased

by division A and by division B and for about 10 percent of each division's total operating cost. Division C's total operating cost amounts to about $4 million a year.

Each division has a profit target, established by agreement with top management at the beginning of this year. Division C's profit reflected the budgeted volume of transfers to the other two divisions, multiplied by transfer prices equal to standard full factory cost plus 15 percent to cover administrative costs and profit. These transfer prices are referred to by division C as "standard prices."

Top management has just decided to replace the existing transfer pricing system with a system of negotiated transfer prices. The new transfer prices will apply to all new orders placed by division A or division B with either of the other divisions. The following information has been placed on the table to aid the negotiators of the first proposed contract under the new system, a transfer of 2,000 polished disks from division C to division A:

Data provided by division C:	
Standard price per unit	$23
Standard variable cost per unit	15
Data provided by division A:	
Purchase price available from outside vendor	19
Maximum value to division A	18

Division A would incorporate the disks in one of its products. It calculated the "maximum value" by subtracting from the list price of that product ($130) division A's own standard manufacturing costs other than the cost of the disks ($75), average selling and administrative costs ($25), and profit markup ($12).

Division C is now producing less than its budgeted volume overall, but its deliveries to division A so far this year have exceeded the amounts budgeted at the beginning of the year.

The manager of division A has demanded a price of $15, saying that this is the only cost the company would incur to produce the disks, but is willing to pay a price of $16.50, which is halfway between $15 and the disks' maximum value. The manager of division C has agreed that the division's total fixed costs would be unaffected by acceptance of the offer, but is insisting on a $23 transfer price, pointing out that the division's profit plan calls for transfers at standard prices.

The two managers have been unable to agree and have asked you, the company's executive vice president, to settle the dispute.

Required:

a. Division A has three options. It can buy disks from division C; it can buy disks externally; or it can stop making the product in which it uses these disks. Regardless of the transfer price, which of these three options would you, as executive vice president, like division A to pick? State your reasoning.

b. Assuming that you, acting as executive vice president, have agreed to set the transfer price on this occasion, choose a transfer price from the following list and explain clearly why you have chosen it: $23; $21; $19; $18; $17; $16.50; $15; $15 + an $8,000 retainer (to contribute to division C's fixed costs and profit); or $15 cost to division A and $30 revenue ($12 + $18 "maximum value") to division C.

c. Should division C be classified as a profit center? If so, what causes you to classify it as such? If not, what is it? What difference does it make?

d. Given your answer to (c), either recommend retaining the present transfer pricing system or identify changes you would like to see made. Give your reasons.

10. **Marketing division: Request for umpiring.** Venezia Glass, Ltd., has three operating divisions: bottles, fine glass, and mail order. Venezia's top management expects each of these divisions to operate as a profit center; their managers' ability to generate profits is a key factor in promotion and compensation decisions.

The mail order division sells glass figurines and other "tabletop" products to customers on its mail lists. Originally conceived as a means of increasing the fine glass division's sales, the mail order business was run by the fine glass division's marketing department until 10 years ago, when it was set up as a separate profit center to handle anticipated future growth. The new division was allowed to buy some of its items from sources outside the company, but the company's executive vice president had to approve any major outside purchases of items the fine glass division was equipped and qualified to supply.

The bottle and fine glass divisions have their own manufacturing facilities and their own sales forces. The mail order division has no manufacturing facilities of its own. Eighty percent of mail order's products are manufactured by the fine glass division. The remaining 20 percent is bought from Sandringham Glass Company or Wallace Corporation, the only other major manufacturers of fine glass products in the country. The fine glass division markets 75 percent of its output through department and specialty stores; the remaining 25 percent goes to the mail order division.

Joan Roberts, president of the mail order division, is unhappy with the transfer prices charged by the fine glass division, claiming they don't allow her to make a profit; they also keep her from making offerings to her mail lists, because the profit margin is too narrow to justify the expenses of the mailings.

When the mail order division was formed 10 years ago, the two division managers at the time agreed on a price schedule and agreed to renegotiate the prices as costs and market conditions changed. Both division managers were content with this arrangement for the first three years, and price changes were very small. Seven years ago the fine glass division had the first of a series of major cost increases and announced a substantial increase in its dealer prices. Sam Peterson, then president of the mail order division, objected to a comparable increase in the transfer prices, but agreed to accept them after a lengthy and sometimes bitter series of arguments.

The fine glass division has posted four other price increases in the last seven years, each one bitterly fought by the mail order division. Ms. Roberts succeeded Mr. Peterson two years ago, when Mr. Peterson was appointed executive vice president of Venezia Glass, Ltd.

Last month the fine glass division announced another 10 percent increase in the transfer prices. Ms. Roberts was so infuriated she dictated a memorandum to Mr. Peterson, protesting the change. She pointed out that mail order volume had fallen off, as had the entire fine glass market. "I don't want to go outside," she said. "I know they need volume in fine glass, but raising prices is a funny way to go about it."

Sandringham Glass Company hasn't raised its prices and has even offered to manufacture a substantial portion of the mail order division's requirements at the same prices it is already quoting on other work for the mail order division. Ms. Roberts has also received favorable price quotations from two small glass companies, each of which claims to be able to handle 10 percent of the division's total volume. In her memorandum she asked Mr. Peterson to set the transfer prices equal to the outside price quotations she had received from Sandringham and the others.

Tom Young, president of the fine glass division, was just as angry as Ms. Roberts. "You can't compare our work with Sandringham's or anybody else's," he said. "These small outfits simply can't meet our quality standards, and Sandringham isn't much better. Besides, we just built a new plant and we have to have that volume. If we meet Sandringham's prices we'll just about break even."

Required:

Prepare a report for Mr. Peterson, analyzing the problem and suggesting a course of action he might take.

Case 26–1: The Wolsey Corporation (freedom to buy outside)

The Wolsey Corporation established an industrial products division about 15 years ago. Its purpose was to find applications in industrial markets for products and technology that other company divisions had developed successfully for the company's commercial and consumer markets.

In its first 14 years, the industrial products division was required to buy from other company divisions any component part or product that it required and that was manufactured by those divisions for sale to outside customers. For special parts not manufactured by other divisions for sale to outside customers, the industrial products division was required to use internal sources if other divisions had adequate capacity and facilities. As a result, approximately 85 percent of the materials cost in industrial products plants represented parts and processed materials transferred from other divisions. These transfers were made at standard product cost.

Early last year the president of the Wolsey Corporation issued the following directive:

Memorandum to: Division Managers
Subject: Interdivisional Transfers

1. To place all divisions on a more competitive footing, each division manager is hereby authorized to negotiate with outside vendors for the purchase of all processed materials, component parts, and products now purchased from other divisions of the company, except (*a*) products sold directly under the company's brand name without further processing, and (*b*) components and processed material on Schedule T-146, for which specifications and drawings are classified company confidential.
2. Before any order is placed with an outside vendor for an item currently being supplied from another division, that division must be given a chance to meet the outside price and promised delivery schedule. No such procedure need be followed on orders in amounts of less than $500.
3. Before any order is placed with an outside vendor for a new item, all divisions should be notified and given a chance to bid on the item. This procedure need not be followed for orders amounting to less than $500.
4. Transfers between divisions will continue to be made at standard cost for all items that have not been covered by the negotiations referred to in paragraphs 2 and 3 above. These standard costs are to be approved in all cases by the corporate methods department. Negotiated prices that are less than standard cost will be reported to the accounting department on Form PR-12-60, and do not require review by the corporate staff.
5. The cooperation of all personnel is requested to make this system effective. Each division will keep a record of outside purchases and the savings accomplished thereby.

Shortly after this memorandum was circulated, the president called a meeting of division managers to explain the new procedure and to answer questions that had arisen. The manager of the small machinery division was skeptical. He said, "Does this mean that if I have idle capacity I can be forced to transfer at less than standard cost? It seems to me that that is just the time when I need transfers at standard cost more than ever to help me absorb my overhead." Most of the other division managers were more sympathetic to the new system, although they were not certain exactly how it would work.

Upon his return from this meeting, the manager of the industrial products division instructed the divisional controller to obtain outside quotations on a metal housing used in one of the division's products. This housing was then being cast in the small machinery division's foundry at a standard cost of $22.17 per casting. The castings were then machined to required tolerances in the industrial products division, and the standard cost of this operation was $6.18. Inquiries at local foundries produced a bid from the Gray Foundry Company of $23.75 per casting, plus $175 for the cost of an aluminum pattern. These castings would be produced by a more modern process and would not require any machining in the industrial products division. Annual requirements were expected to average 500 castings.

The manager of industrial products then prepared the following cost estimate and submitted it to the small machinery manager, noting that unless the indicated price could be met, the order would be placed with Gray Foundry:

Cost of outside purchase:		
Pattern....................................	$ 175	
Castings—500 at $23.75	11,875	
Total purchase cost...........................	12,050	
Less: Cost of machining, 500 at $6.18	3,090	
Maximum transfer price	$ 8,960 = $17.92 per casting	

The manager of the small machinery division exploded when he received this estimate. "This is just what I was afraid of. You don't even know whether these people can live up to their promises and you want me to accept an order at less than cost. How do you expect me to cover my overhead? They are only quoting you this price to get your business, and once you are on the hook, they will raise their prices. As long as I have idle capacity, it is foolish to go outside—the whole company will suffer if you do very much of this. Against my better judgment, however, I'll quote you a price of $19.62. This doesn't cover depreciation on foundry equipment, and it's as low as I can go."

The industrial products manager rejected this offer and placed an initial order for 200 castings with the Gray Foundry Company, whereupon the small machinery manager appealed to the president, claiming that the new system was unworkable and unreasonable.

The president had hoped to avoid participation in disputes of this kind, but since this was the first case he felt that it warranted his attention. A staff assistant was assigned to study the problem and he made the following breakdown of standard costs:

	Variable Cost	Fixed Cost	Total Standard Cost
Casting	$17.95	$4.22	$22.17
Machining	4.15	2.03	6.18

He also found that materials price variances in the foundry were likely to be unfavorable amounting to 12 cents per casting.

a. Assuming you are in a position to dictate a solution to both divisions, prepare an analysis that will indicate whether future castings should be acquired from the Gray Foundry Company or from the small machinery division. List any assumptions you had to make in order to reach a conclusion on this question.

b. Would it be possible for the two divisions to find a mutually acceptable transfer price? If so, within what range would this transfer price fall? Show your calculations.

c. Is negotiation appropriate for these castings? Give your reasons.

d. Which features of the company's transfer pricing policy would you change and which ones would you retain? Give your reasons.

Case 26–2: Hoppit Chemical Company (programmed prices)

The Moorhouse division of the Hoppit Chemical Company has 14 chemical plants located in various parts of the United States. Its profit contribution after deducting all divisional overheads runs about $50 million a year, and in exceptionally good years may even reach $75 million.

The company's Allworth division is much smaller, with only two plants and an annual profit contribution of about $2.5 million. Four years ago, the Allworth division constructed a new plant on a site adjacent to one of the main plants of the Moorhouse division. The idea was to take advantage of a plentiful supply of a chemical known as amalite, a product of the Moorhouse plant. Amalite was made in the Moorhouse plant from the waste residue thrown off by the plant's primary production process.

Before the Allworth plant was built, amalite had been manufactured only intermittently, whenever its market price was high enough to justify the conversion expenditures. The market for amalite had been weak for some time, however, and the Hoppit market research department forecasted that this condition would continue to prevail for many years to come as amalite was gradually displaced by petroleum derivatives in one of its main uses. Under these circumstances, it seemed a good move to build the new plant to convert amalite into another chemical product with a considerably higher market value.

A transfer price system was devised and accepted by the managers of both divisions when the new plant went into production. Under this system, Allworth's management initiated the process each quarter by telling Moorhouse how much amalite it expected to need during the next quarter. The Moorhouse division then quoted a set of prices for different quantites of amalite to be delivered during that quarter. These prices were based primarily on the estimated incremental costs of processing different quantities of Moorhouse waste into amalite. For example, during the first two years the plant was in operation, a typical transfer price schedule was as follows:

Transfers (pounds)	Total Transfer Price
1,000,000 or less	$0.40 per lb. (minimum 500,000 lbs.)
1,000,000–2,500,000	$400,000 + $0.30 per lb. in excess of 1,000,000
More than 2,500,000	$850,000 + $0.40 per lb. in excess of 2,500,000

With this schedule in hand, Allworth's management could then decide how much amalite to order from Moorhouse during the next quarter.

The transfer pricing system also provided that transfers would be made at anticipated net market price whenever the Moorhouse plant's capacity for producing amalite was expected to be inadequate to serve all of its outside customers and Allworth too.

The Allworth plant was not completely dependent on Moorhouse amalite for raw materials. It could also use a commercially available product known as flemite. The purchase cost of flemite was considerably higher than the transfer prices prevailing during the first two years of the new plant's operations, however, and flemite was not used. Outside purchases of amalite were impractical for the same reason.

Each year each division manager in the Hoppit Chemical Company is required to prepare a profit plan. In drawing up their plans, the Allworth and Moorhouse managers get together and agree on a forecast of the transfer prices expected to prevail during the coming year. This price schedule is then built into the divisional profit plans for the year.

Shortly after the beginning of the current year, the market price of amalite took a sudden jump to 50 cents a pound, and Moorhouse could sell all it could produce at this price. Moorhouse therefore set 50 cents as the transfer price for the second quarter. Because flemite was available at a price of 45 cents, however, Moorhouse sold most of its amalite on the market and bought flemite to meet its supply commitment to the Allworth plant. Both division managers agreed that this was in the best interest of the Hoppit Chemical Company.

At the same time, however, Mr. C. P. Jones, the Allworth division manager, refused to approve the transfer charge at 45 cents on the ground that this would create a substantial profit variance, amounting to approximately $250,000 a quarter, through no fault of anyone in the Allworth division. As Mr. Jones pointed out, when the plant was constructed he could have signed a long-term contract with outside suppliers of amalite at a price of 40 cents a pound, but he was not allowed by Hoppit's top management to do so. Mr. Jones felt that Moorhouse was under an obligation to continue to supply amalite or a substitute at a price within the range that was forecasted when the plant was built.

Mr. John England, Moorhouse's chief cost analyst and the man responsible for the transfer price calculations, did not agree. "Even if they had signed a contract like that," he said, "we would still have to make our decisions on the basis of current market conditions. If Allworth can't make an incremental profit on the basis of current market prices, then the plant should be shut down until materials prices go back down or selling prices of the Allworth products go up. If we let them have this stuff at 40 cents, the company could be losing as much as 5 cents on every pound they use."

  a. Do you feel that Mr. Jones is justified in asking for a long-term price commitment from Moorhouse, or is Mr. England right in saying that the transfer price should reflect current market conditions?

  b. Should the transfer pricing system be changed, and if so in what way? Can you identify any other defects in the system? Explain your reasoning.

Case 26–3: AB Thorsten (D)* (transfers to foreign subsidiary)

Anders Ekstrom, managing director of Sweden's AB Thorsten, is apprehensive about the profit position of XL–4, an industrial adhesive product.[1] He is now selling XL–4 at a price of Skr. 1,850 a ton, which is Skr. 300 less than its delivered cost. At the same time, Mr. Gillot, senior vice president of Roget S.A., and Ekstrom's immediate superior in Belgium, is wondering what decision he should take regarding Ekstrom's request that he lower the price at which the Belgian company sells XL–4 to the Swedish company.

AB Thorsten is a wholly owned subsidiary of Roget S.A., one of the largest chemical companies in Belgium. Thorsten buys XL–4 from Roget's Industrial Chemical Products Division, at a transfer price of Skr. 1,700 a ton (Skr. 2,150 with transport costs and import duties). This case describes the problems faced by management as it tries to resolve a conflict arising from this transfer price. It covers a 14-month period, during which the following events took place:

1. Fourteen months ago, Ekstrom introduced XL–4 to Swedish customers at a price of Skr. 2,500.
2. Six months ago, after his request for a lower transfer price was turned down, he lowered the price to a more competitive Skr. 2,200.
3. Two months ago, his request for a lower transfer price again denied, he reduced his selling price a second time, to Skr. 1,850.

Ekstrom now says that he may withdraw XL–4 from the Swedish market if he can't find a way to make it show a profit.

---

  * Source: Copyright © 1969, 1981 by l'Institut pour l'Etude des Méthodes de Direction de l'Entreprise (IMEDE), Lausanne, Switzerland. Published by permission.

  [1] The letters "AB" and "S.A." are the equivalent designations in Sweden and Belgium of "Corp." or "Inc." in the United States and "Ltd." in the United Kingdom. The title of "managing director" in Sweden and in Britain is approximately the same as that of "chief executive officer" in the United States. The letters "Skr," identify the Swedish monetary unit, the krone.

Organization structure: Roget S.A.

Roget S.A. began operations 40 years ago, manufacturing and selling chemicals in the domestic Belgian market. It has grown steadily, partly through growth and partly through purchase of companies such as Thorsten, so that it now produces 208 products in 21 factories. Its organization structure is shown in Exhibit 1.

Exhibit 1
ROGET S.A. Organization chart

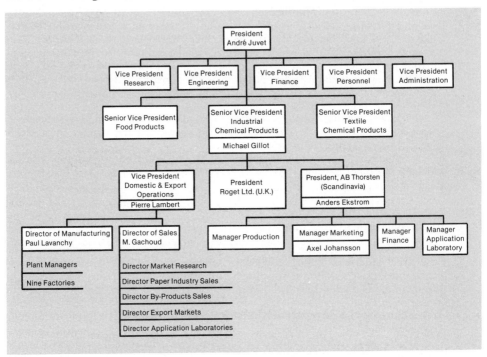

According to Mr. Juvet, Roget's managing director, "we are organized on a divisional basis. For example, take the Industrial Chemical Products Division, headed by Mr. Gillot. This is set up as a separate company, and Gillot is responsible for profits. This concept of decentralization is extended down to the departments under him—except that they are responsible for profits on a geographic basis instead of a product basis.

"One of these is the Domestic Department, under Mr. Lambert. This department sells industrial chemicals throughout Belgium and exports its products to countries in which we do not manufacture. It has its own factories to supply both of these markets, and its own sales force in Belgium. The Domestic Department, like our other Brussels-based departments, markets most of its export volume through our foreign subsidiaries and uses independent selling agents only in countries where we don't have our own personnel.

"Mr. Lambert runs this department on his own. He is responsible for its profits just as he would be if it were an independent company. In much the same way, Ekstrom is responsible for the profits made by AB Thorsten.

"A big company like Roget benefits from this kind of organization. We must divide the work of management. No man can do it all. Placing responsibility for profits enables us to measure the result of operations, and is an important means of attracting and motivating top quality executives. Each head of a product division will have more initiative and will work harder if he is in effect head of his own company. Our bonus system, based on division profits, adds to this kind of motivation."

Company background: AB Thorsten

AB Thorsten was purchased by Roget eight years ago. After a period of low profits and shrinking sales in Sweden, Roget employed Mr. Anders Ekstrom as managing director. A 38-year-old graduate of the Royal Institute of Technology, with 16 years' experience in production and marketing, Ekstrom appears to be an executive with a good deal of ambition and a wide acquaintance with modern financial and planning techniques.

When he joined the company, Ekstrom decided that the best way to restore Thorsten's profitability was to introduce new products, promote them aggressively, and back them up with a first-class technical services staff. In the four years since he became managing director, Thorsten's sales have increased from Skr. 7 million to Skr. 20 million, and profits have increased in an even higher ratio.

Early history of the XL–4 project

XL–4 is an adhesive product used in the paper-converting industry, and one which Ekstrom and his management are sure will enjoy a large market in Sweden. XL–4 is a proprietary product. No competitor has a product exactly like it, and patent protection prevents other suppliers from manufacturing it.

Although total production in Roget's Belgian plant for all other markets is 600 tons a year, Ekstrom's market studies have convinced him that 400 tons a year can be sold to paper companies in Sweden, provided that his customer engineering staff helps customers to modify their own equipment, and that the price can be lowered. He has conclusive evidence that large paper companies can reap significant cost savings due to lower materials handling costs and faster drying times.

Ekstrom and his top manufacturing and sales executives spent six months preparing a feasibility study which proposed building a plant in Sweden to manufacture XL–4, and presented this at a Thorsten board meeting one month later. He states, "we did a complete market study, engineering study, and financial study, using discounted cash flows, which showed that we should build a factory in Sweden with a payback period of four years and a rate of return of 15 percent on invested capital. This was presented at a Thorsten board meeting in Stockholm and approved unanimously.[2]

"In our proposal, we suggested an initial selling price of Skr. 2,000 a ton, to be cut to Skr. 1,850 a ton at the end of the first year. We didn't make specific estimates of demand elasticity, but 400 tons represented 50 percent of the market and our cost calculations indicated that a price greater than Skr. 1,850 would keep us from reaching this goal.

"During the next two months, several things happened. First Mr. Gillot informed me that there were objections from Lambert [vice president, Domestic and Export Department], Lavanchy [director of manufacturing in Lambert's department] and Gachoud [director of sales in the same department]. I convinced him that we should hold a meeting with all these men in Brussels, but that meeting ended in chaos, with me arguing over and over for the plant in Sweden and the others saying over and over that we would have too many problems in manufacturing, and that we did not have the capabilities and experience in the adhesives industry that they possessed in Belgium. They also had no confidence in my market projection, saying that they didn't think we could sell 400 tons a year. Finally, Mr. Gillot asked the Belgian executives to study the matter further and give him a formal report on whether the plant should be built."

---

[2] Swedish law requires that all corporations have two Swedish directors for every foreign director. Thorsten's board is composed of a Swedish banker, a Stockholm industrialist, Mr. Ekstrom, and M. Gillot, a senior vice president of Roget S.A.

Rejection of the Swedish proposal

After studying all of the reports on the XL–4 project, Gillot decided not to approve the proposal for a Swedish plant. "I am sorry to inform you," he wrote to Ekstrom, "that your proposal to manufacture XL–4 in Sweden has been rejected. I know that you and your management have done an outstanding job of market research, engineering planning, and profit estimation, and we agree that the plant would be profitable if you had a market of 400 tons and we couldn't supply it from here. This is no time to make this investment, however. First, it seems more profitable for our Belgian plant to make XL–4 and export it to Sweden. We have ample excess capacity to supply 400 tons to Sweden for the next few years. The savings obtainable from using this idle capacity more than offset the disadvantage of paying Swedish import duties. Second, executives in our Domestic Division here are convinced that the product should be made in Belgium where we have the experience and know-how. They are also not sure that you can sell 400 tons a year in Sweden.

"I want you to know, however, that we in Headquarters are most appreciative of the kind of work you are doing in Sweden. This adverse decision in no way reflects a lack of confidence in you or a failure on our part to recognize your outstanding performance as the managing director of one of our most important daughter companies."

Introduction of XL–4 into Sweden

Immediately after this decision, Ekstrom decided to order XL–4 from Roget's Domestic and Export Department. "At this point, I decided to prove to them that the market is here. They quoted me a delivered price of Skr. 2,150 a ton (head office billing price of Skr. 1,700, plus Skr. 50 transportation and Skr. 400 import duty).[3] Because of heavy promotion and customer engineering costs (my engineers helping paper companies adapt their machinery), I had to have a gross margin of Skr. 350 a ton. This meant I had to sell it for Skr. 2,500." He penciled the following table:

Head office billing price	Skr. 1,700
Shipping cost	50
Import duty	400
Delivered cost	Skr. 2,150
Allowance for promotion and engineering costs	350
Swedish selling price	Skr. 2,500

"I knew I could never achieve sales of 400 tons a year at this price. It was higher than the prices of other adhesives suitable for this market, and Swedish paper companies are very cost-conscious. I knew we could do some business at this price, however, and this would give our engineers some practical experience in converting customers' equipment to take XL–4. Later on, we could reduce the price and try for the main market.

"I wrote to Mr. Gachoud, director of sales for the domestic and export department in Brussels, showing him the figures, saying that we could eventually reach 400 tons a year in sales, and asking him to reduce the head office billing price. He declined.

"For the next eight months sales were disappointing. At the end of this period, still having faith in our research over the last two years, I decided to lower the price to Skr. 2,200. I hoped that this would induce paper companies to try XL–4 and prove to themselves that it would lower their costs significantly. Of course, this was only Skr. 50 more than my cost, and I could hardly continue permanently on that basis.

---

[3] Some of these figures are actually expressed in Belgian francs. To avoid possible confusion, all figures have been expressed at their Swedish kroner equivalents.

With me and my company being judged on profits, it is not worth our while to spend all of this time and resources on XL–4 for such a small markup.

"Sales did increase during the next four months, to 150 tons, and I knew I could sell about 200 tons regularly at this price. But I was still intent on proving the market at 400 tons.

"This time I went personally to see Mr. Gachoud in Brussels, and practically demanded that he lower the price of XL–4 exported from Belgium to Sweden. He explained that with a sales volume of 150–200 tons a year in Sweden, sold at an export transfer price of Skr. 1,700, and with strong doubts in his mind that we could ever reach 400 tons a year, he couldn't agree to the reduction.

"At this point I decided to prove that I was right by executing a bold move, backed up by the use of modern financial planning methods. I lowered the price to Skr. 1,850 a ton. I figured that someone in Brussels had to understand my reasoning, if I explained it well enough and backed it up with forceful direct action.

"Please don't get the idea that this was simply a political trick. I wouldn't have done it if I hadn't believed that it would bring in added profits for the group as a whole. I felt sure that volume would go up to 400 tons, and at that rate we would produce a profit contribution of at least Skr. 113,000 a year for the Roget group. This is Skr. 24,000 more than I could hope for at the old price and a volume of 200 tons.

"I showed my calculations to Mr. Gillot after I had decided to go ahead. Here is a little table of figures that I sent to him then [all figures are in Swedish kroner]:

	At 200 tons		At 400 tons	
	Per Ton	Total	Per Ton	Total
Selling price	2,200	440,000	1,850	740,000
Variable costs:				
Manufacturing (Belgium)	930		930	
Shipping (Belgium–Sweden)	50		50	
Import duty (Sweden)	400		400	
Total variable costs	1,380	276,000	1,380	552,000
Factory margin		164,000		188,000
Promotional costs		75,000		75,000
Profit contribution to Roget group		89,000		113,000

"Let me explain this table. I knew that the Belgian cost accountants used a figure equivalent to Skr. 1,250 a ton as the full cost of manufacturing XL–4. The production people told me, however, that the Belgian plant had enough capacity to supply me with 400 tons of XL–4 a year without additional investment for expansion, and that they could manufacture the additional 400 tons at a variable cost of Skr. 930 a ton. This meant that the fixed costs were sunk costs and I could ignore them. This is why the manufacturing cost figure in the table is Skr. 930.

"Adding in the transportation costs and import duties brings the total variable costs to Skr. 1,380 a ton. My own promotional and engineering costs amounted to about Skr. 130,000 during the first year, but we were already over that hump. They are budgeted for this year at Skr. 75,000 and will go down to Skr. 50,000 a year from now on, mostly for technical services to customers. To avoid an argument, though, I used Skr. 75,000 in the table I sent to Mr. Gillot.

"This gives me the profit contribution of Skr. 113,000 a year that you see at the bottom of the table. This is Skr. 24,000 more than I could have expected at the old price. To me that's conclusive.

"I tell you all this to emphasize that my main motive was to improve our group's profit performance. Even so, I must admit that I still hope to persuade Mr. Gillot to let me build an XL–4 factory in Sweden. That plant will be profitable at a volume of

400 tons and a price of Skr. 1,850, and I suppose that this may have been at the back of my mind, too. If I can show him that the 400 tons is not a Swedish dream, I think he'll go along. It's ridiculous to pay import duties that amount to more than 20 percent of the selling price if you don't have to, and if I could have convinced him on the size of the market 14 months ago, I think I would have had my plant."

In the two months since this last price reduction, sales of XL–4 have increased to a rate of 270 tons a year. Ekstrom feels certain that within another 12 months he will reach the 400-ton level. He also says, however, that he finds himself in a quandary. "The Swedish company is losing Skr. 300 on every ton we sell, plus a great deal of selling and engineering time that could be switched to other products. This is bound to affect the profits of my company when I give my annual report to Mr. Gillot. This is why I quit trying to deal with Gachoud. Last week I wrote to Mr. Gillot, asking him to direct Gachoud to sell me the product at Skr. 1,100. I'm hoping for a reply this week."

The parent company's transfer pricing policy

Mr. Gillot has not yet decided what to do with this request. As he says, "Transfer pricing in this company is pretty unsystematic. Each of us division managers is expected to price his own products, and the top management executive committee doesn't interfere. I have the same kind of authority over transfer prices as I have over the prices we charge our independent agents. We've never thought of them as separate problems. I've never been in a situation like this, though, and I want to think it through carefully before I act.

"Our attitude toward transfer pricing is probably the result of the way we operated in foreign markets in the beginning. We developed our export trade for many years by selling our products to independent agents around the world. We still do a lot of business that way. These agents estimated the prices at which they could sell the product and then negotiated with the export sales manager in Brussels for the best price they could get.

"When we began setting up our own daughter companies in our bigger markets, we just continued the same practice. Of course, daughter companies like Thorsten cannot shift to a competing supplier, but they have great freedom otherwise. For example, they can try to negotiate prices with us here at headquarters. This healthy competition within the company keeps us all alert. If they think Belgium is too rigid, they can refuse to market that particular product in their home country. Or, if they can justify building their own manufacturing plants, they can make the product themselves and not deal with the Belgian export department at all."

A Norwegian example

Head office practices have resulted in head office billing prices that vary widely from market to market. In some cases, outside agents are able to obtain products at lower prices than Roget charges to its own subsidiaries. Ekstrom particularly wanted to tell the case writers about a Norwegian example. XL–4 is sold in Norway through an independent agent. This agent sells XL–4 to his customers at the equivalent of Skr. 1,290 plus Norwegian import duty. He persuaded Gachoud to sell him XL–4 at a price of Skr. 1,225, thus in effect giving him an agent's commission of Skr. 65 a ton. Roget also agreed to pay the shipping costs to Norway, amounting to Skr. 52 a ton. This meant that Roget received only Skr. 1,173 a ton to cover manufacturing and administrative costs and provide a profit margin. This was less than the average full cost of production in Belgium (Skr. 1,250) and Skr. 527 less than the Skr. 1,700 price at which Roget billed AB Thorsten.

"At one point," Ekstrom says, "I even thought of buying my XL–4 through the Norwegian agent. But then I realized this would be destructive warfare against Belgium. The total profits of the Roget group of companies would be less by the amount of the Norwegian agent's commission. I would be blamed for this when Lambert or Gillot reported it to the Executive Committee."

Other factors to consider

Division managers' performance in Roget S.A. was judged largely on the basis of the amount of profit they were able to generate on product sales, including both sales to agents and sales to subsidiary companies. The managing board relied on this to induce the division managers to work for greater company profits.

The performance of the daughter company managers was appraised in much the same way. Ekstrom, for example, knew that group management in Brussels judged his performance on the basis of the amount of profit reported on AB Thorsten's income statement. Because of his success in the past four years, Roget's managing board gave him a good deal more freedom than the managers of any of the other subsidiaries enjoyed, but this happy state of affairs would come to an end if Thorsten's reported profits began to slide.

Gillot says that he must also consider three other factors before reaching a decision. First, Ekstrom's profit analysis must be evaluated. Second, Ekstrom's feelings of responsibility as head of the Swedish company must not be destroyed. Finally, he must review the points made by Lambert and Gachoud. Gillot says that Lambert told him, "If Ekstrom decides to take advantage of company rules and discontinues selling XL–4 in Sweden, we can certainly find an independent agent in Sweden to handle it. That's one bridge we'll never have to cross, though. Ekstrom will never push it that far. He believes in introducing new products as the key to his success. If we stand fast, he will simply raise the price back to a level that is profitable for both of us."

Taxes and foreign exchange regulations had no bearing on M. Gillot's decision. Income tax rates in Belgium were about the same as in Sweden, and no restrictions were placed on Thorsten's ability to obtain foreign exchange to pay for imported goods or pay dividends. In fact, Roget's top management insisted that each daughter company play the role of good citizen in its own country, by measuring taxable income on the same basis as that used by management in the evaluation of the subsidiary's pretax profit performance. No attempt was to be made to divert taxable income from one country to another.

*   *   *   *

At the present time, both Ekstrom on the one hand, and Lambert and Gachoud on the other, are waiting for Mr. Gillot to settle the transfer pricing question and let them know his decision.

    a. Should Mr. Ekstrom have introduced XL–4 into Sweden? (This question should be examined both from Mr. Ekstrom's viewpoint and from the Roget point of view.)

    b. Should Mr. Gachoud have lowered the price?

    c. Why did Mr. Gachoud and Mr. Ekstrom fail to agree?

    d. Is negotiation the best means of arriving at a transfer price in this situation? Can you suggest a better way?

27 Profit analysis

Deviations from profit plans measure the effects of changes in conditions, poor forecasting, or variations in managerial effectiveness. Since the reasons for these deviations are not always clear, further analysis and explanation are usually necessary.

The main purpose of this chapter is to outline a method the accountant can use to break the total profit variance into a set of interrelated components. This will be followed by a brief discussion of an alternative approach, focusing on ratios and trends.

Sales volume, price, and spending variances

The profit variance for any business or any business segment is the difference between the amount of profit actually reported and the profit embodied in the operating plan for the period. For example, Exhibit 27–1 shows the reported profit performance of Bounty Oil Company, a local fuel oil dealer, in a recent period. The profit variance was $11,000, unfavorable, as shown by the figure at the bottom of the right-hand column.

Exhibit 27–1
BOUNTY OIL COMPANY Profit variance

	Actual	Budget	Over/(Under)
Gallons sold	1,100,000	1,000,000	100,000
Sales revenues	$1,400,000	$1,250,000	$150,000
Cost of goods sold	1,150,000	1,000,000	150,000
Gross profit	250,000	250,000	—
Variable selling and administrative expense	56,000	50,000	6,000
Contribution margin	194,000	200,000	(6,000)
Fixed selling and administrative expense	125,000	120,000	(5,000)
Income before taxes	$ 69,000	$ 80,000	$ (11,000)

The profit variance in this case can be subdivided analytically into four major components:

1. Sales volume variance.
2. Selling price variance.
3. Merchandise cost variance.
4. Selling and administrative spending variance.

This breakdown won't identify the *causes* of the profit variance, but is designed to help management understand how those causes have manifested themselves.

Sales volume variance

The sales volume variance is the portion of the total profit variance that can be attributed to the difference between budgeted and actual physical sales volume. It is measured by multiplying the difference in physical unit sales by the budgeted volume-responsive margin per unit. In a nonmanufacturing business the volume-responsive margin is the contribution margin.

For example, Bounty Oil's budgeted contribution margin was as follows:

	Total	Per Gallon
Sales revenue	$1,250,000	$1.25
Cost of goods sold	1,000,000	1.00
Gross profit	250,000	0.25
Variable selling and administrative expense	50,000	0.05
Contribution margin	$ 200,000	$0.20

The unit contribution margin figure indicates that the company expected to gain or lose 20 cents for each gallon of fuel oil sales over or under the budgeted volume, if all other factors remained unchanged. Since volume exceeded the budgeted volume by 100,000 gallons, income before taxes should have gone up by 100,000 × $0.20 = $20,000. This is the figure we call the sales volume variance, and in this case it was *favorable,* contributing to an increase in income before taxes.

The sales volume variance can also be calculated in a line-by-line analysis. If no changes other than volume had taken place, a 100,000-gallon (10 percent) increase in volume should have produced the figures shown in the middle column in the following table:

	Original Budget	Volume-Adjusted Budget	Effect of Variance in Sales Volume
Sales revenues	$1,250,000	$1,375,000	$125,000
Cost of goods sold	1,000,000	1,100,000	100,000
Gross profit	250,000	275,000	25,000
Variable selling and administrative expense	50,000	55,000	5,000
Contribution margin	200,000	220,000	20,000
Fixed selling and administrative expense	120,000	120,000	—
Income before taxes	$ 80,000	$ 100,000	$ 20,000

The differences between the adjusted budget figures and the original budget determine the size of the sales volume variance.

Selling price variance

The selling price variance is the impact on profit of differences between budgeted and actual selling prices. It is measured by comparing the adjusted profit budget (at actual sales volume) with a restated budget (also at actual sales volume) based on actual selling prices.

To illustrate, suppose the variable selling and administrative expenses at Bounty Oil consist of sales commissions at 4 percent of sales revenues. At actual sales volume and actual selling prices, sales revenues amounted to $1.4 million (from Exhibit 27–1); sales commissions should have been 0.04 × $1.4 million = $56,000. The effect of increased prices can be determined by making the following comparison:

	Restated Budget at Actual Volume		Effect of Selling Price Variance
	Budgeted Selling Prices	At Actual Selling Price	
Sales revenues	$1,375,000	$1,400,000	$25,000
Cost of goods sold	1,100,000	1,100,000	—
Gross profit	275,000	300,000	25,000
Variable selling and administrative expenses	55,000	56,000	1,000
Contribution margin	220,000	244,000	24,000
Fixed selling and administrative expenses	120,000	120,000	—
Income before taxes	$ 100,000	$ 124,000	$24,000

In other words, the price per gallon was slightly higher than the budgeted price, giving Bounty Oil an extra $25,000 at actual sales volume; this, in turn, increased the sales commissions by $1,000, leaving a net selling price variance of $24,000, favorable.

Notice that the selling price variance is really the result of two influences: the change in price and the change in volume. With the actual selling prices, the selling price variance would have been only 1,000,000/1,100,000 × $24,000 = $21,818 if physical volume had remained at the 1 million gallon level. We could recognize the $2,182 difference between these two measures of the price variance as a joint price/volume variance, but this probably wouldn't give management much additional information. The accepted convention is to attribute the entire amount to the price variance.

Input price and spending variance

The rest of the profit variance in this illustration is due to factors familiar to us from our earlier study of cost variances: variances in input prices and in input usage.

First, if the cost of the fuel oil sold had remained at its budgeted price of $1 a gallon, the cost of goods sold would have been $1.1 million at the actual volume for this period. Instead, it amounted to $1,150,000 (from Exhibit 27–1), reflecting an average cost of about $1.045 a gallon. The $50,000 increase in the cost of goods sold due to these higher prices is simply an *input price variance,* much like the materials price variance we discussed in Chapter 9.

The final component of the profit variance in our illustration comes from spending variances in fixed selling and administrative expenses. These were budgeted at $120,000, and none of our previous adjustments has changed that figure. From Exhibit 27–1 we find that actual spending amounted to $125,000, reflecting a $5,000 unfavorable spending variance. Without further information we don't know how much of this spending variance was due to increased usage (e.g., more lines of advertising space) and how much was due to increased input prices (e.g., higher rates per line). This variance is identical in concept to the manufacturing overhead spending variances we introduced for the first time in Chapter 10.

Variance summary

Our analysis of Bounty Oil's profit variance is now complete and is summarized in Exhibit 27–2. From the summary at the bottom of the exhibit management can see easily that the major factor in the unfavorable profit performance this period was the sharp overrun in the unit cost of goods sold. The analysis doesn't show what caused this increase, or what management ought to do about it, but it does make the issues a good deal sharper than they were when we had only Exhibit 27–1.

Notice how we analyzed the variance, starting with the original budget and *changing one factor at a time,* keeping all other factors constant. Our usual presentation in earlier chapters was to show actual results at the left, a performance standard in the middle, and the variances at the right. We used that same format in Exhibit 27–1. For analytical purposes, however, it is more convenient to start with the budget figures and work toward the actual results. The reason is that we have adopted the common convention of isolating the sale volume variance first, measuring it at budgeted prices and budgeted spending patterns.

Effect of the analytical sequence

We should point out here that we could have developed different figures for all but he spending variance in selling and administrative expenses if we had chosen to measure the variances in a different sequence. For example, suppose we had chosen to start with the selling price variance, followed by the oil cost price variance and the sales volume variance, in that order. The average selling price for the period was $1,400,000/1,100,000 \cong $1.28 a gallon, with an average sales commission of $0.04 \times $1.28 \cong $0.05 a gallon. The average oil cost price was $1,150,000/1,100,000 \cong $1.045. Using these

Exhibit 27–2
BOUNTY OIL COMPANY Variance summary

	Original Budget	Budgeted Prices and Spending	Budgeted Input Prices and Spending	Actual Oil Cost Prices, Budgeted Selling and Administrative Spending	Actual Results
			Adjusted Budget, Actual Volume		
			Actual Selling Prices		
Sales revenues	$1,250,000	$1,375,000	$1,400,000	$1,400,000	$1,400,000
Cost of goods sold	1,000,000	1,100,000	1,100,000	1,150,000	1,150,000
Gross profit	250,000	275,000	300,000	250,000	250,000
Variable selling and administrative expenses . .	50,000	55,000	56,000	56,000	56,000
Contribution margin	200,000	220,000	244,000	194,000	194,000
Fixed selling and administrative expenses . .	120,000	120,000	120,000	120,000	125,000
Income before taxes	$ 80,000	$ 100,000	$ 124,000	$ 74,000	$ 69,000

Sales volume variance	Selling price variance	Oil cost price variance	Selling and administrative spending variance
$20,000 F.	$24,000 F.	$50,000 U.	$5,000 U.

actual prices, the volume variance would be $100,000 \times ($1.28 - $1.045 - $0.05) = $18,500$, instead of the $20,000 we calculated earlier.

The $18,500 figure would be a better measure of the effect of the volume deviations in the current period. We usually calculate the volume variance at standard prices, however, so we can make direct comparisons of the sales volume variances of different periods. If volume is always measured at the same prices, then any change in the volume variance is the result of a change in volume, not a mixture of price and volume effects.

Sales mix variance

Management is interested not only in variations in the sales volumes of individual products but in variations in sales mix as well, the relative proportions in which the company's various products are sold. Some products are more profitable than others and management must be alert to detect shifts in demand that enrich or dilute the profitability of the company's sales.

To show how this kind of analysis can be made, we'll have to expand our illustration. Suppose Bounty Oil Company has a second line of business, buying and selling spot-market gasoline to independent retailers. The original budget and the volume-adjusted budget for Bounty's gasoline business are shown in the central pair of columns in Exhibit 27–3. With a budgeted contribution

Exhibit 27–3
BOUNTY OIL COMPANY Combined sales volume variances

	(1) Fuel Oil	(2) Fuel Oil	(3) Gasoline	(4) Gasoline	(5) Total	(6) Total
	Original Budget	Volume-Adjusted Budget	Original Budget	Volume-Adjusted Budget	Original Budget	Volume-Adjusted Budget
Gallons sold	1,000,000	1,100,000	800,000	840,000	1,800,000	1,940,000
Sales revenues	$1,250,000	$1,375,000	$880,000	$924,000	$2,130,000	$2,299,000
Cost of goods sold	1,000,000	1,100,000	640,000	672,000	1,640,000	1,772,000
Gross profit	250,000	275,000	240,000	252,000	490,000	527,000
Variable selling and administrative expenses	50,000	55,000	—	—	50,000	55,000
Contribution margin	200,000	220,000	240,000	252,000	440,000	472,000
Fixed selling and administrative expenses	120,000	120,000	80,000	80,000	200,000	200,000
Income before taxes	$ 80,000	$ 100,000	$160,000	$172,000	$ 240,000	$ 272,000
Sales Volume Variance	$20,000 F.		$12,000 F.		$32,000 F.	

margin of $240,000/800,000 = $0.30 (from column (3)), the 40,000-gallon favorable variance in gasoline sales translates into a $12,000 favorable sales volume variance. The total sales volume variance of the two products combined therefore was $32,000, the figure at the lower right-hand corner of the exhibit.

The question we're interested in is whether the combined sales volume variance would have been larger or smaller if the increase in gallonage had been proportional to the budgeted mix. To answer this question, we need two figures:

1. A figure representing the variation in overall physical volume.
2. A measure of the average profitability of one unit of overall volume.

Volume can be measured by (1) the number of units sold; (2) sales revenues at standard prices; or (3) standard product costs. Suppose we use the number of gallons sold, for example. The original budget called for total sales of 1.8 million gallons of product, while actual volume amounted to 1,940,000 gallons (from the first line of columns (5) and (6) in the exhibit).

We can calculate average profitability from column (5). The budgeted average contribution margin was $440,000/1,800,000 = $0.24444 a gallon. If the 140,000-gallon increase in volume had been at the budgeted mix, therefore, the total of the volume variances would have been 140,000 × $0.24444 = $34,222. Since the volume variances actually totaled only $32,000, an unfavorable mix variance of $2,222 must have taken place.

The mix variance can also be separated from the combined volume variance in a line by line format, as in Exhibit 27–4. Columns (2) and (4) come from columns (5) and (6) in Exhibit 27–3. The revenue and variable cost figures

Exhibit 27–4
BOUNTY OIL COMPANY Calculation of sales mix variance

	(1) Per Gallon	(2) Total	(3) At Budgeted Mix*	(4) At Actual Mix
	Original Budget		Volume-Adjusted Budget	
Sales revenues	$1.183333	$2,130,000	$2,295,666	$2,299,000
Cost of goods sold	0.911111	1,640,000	1,767,555	1,772,000
Gross profit	0.272222	490,000	528,111	527,000
Variable selling and administrative expenses	0.027778	50,000	53,889	55,000
Contribution margin	0.244444	440,000	474,222	472,000
Fixed selling and administrative expenses		200,000	200,000	200,000
Income before taxes		$ 240,000	$ 274,222	$ 272,000
			Sales volume variance $34,222 F.	Sales mix variance $2,222 U.

* Col. (1) × 1,940,000 gallons.

in column (3) were developed by multiplying the actual volume (1,940,000 gallons) by the budgeted figures per gallon in column (1). For example, the budgeted average price was $2,130,000/1,800,000 = $1.18333 a gallon. (We carry this to five decimal places to avoid rounding errors in the illustration.) If actual volume had been at the budgeted mix, total revenue would have been 1,940,000 × $1.18333 = $2,295,666.

A similar ratio was calculated and used to adjust the variable selling and administrative expense budget to the 1,940,000-gallon level. No ratio calculation was made for the fixed selling and administrative expenses because these aren't expected to change in response to changes in volume or changes in mix. The column-to-column differences in the income before tax figures then split the combined volume variance into volume and mix components. In this case we can see that although the effect of the change in mix was unfavorable, its impact on the profit figure was very slight.

Composite index of volume

Before leaving the discussion of the sales mix variance, we need to add one more complication to our illustration. In most practical situations, the company has too many products and too many measures of unit volume to permit calculating an average profit per physical unit. For example, suppose Bounty Oil has a repair business as well as the fuel oil and gasoline lines. No single physical measure—gallons or labor hours—can be applied to each of these products.

In these circumstances, physical volume must be represented by some dollar-weighted quantity. Each product's sales may be weighted either by its budgeted selling price or by its budgeted unit cost. For instance, suppose we have the following figures:

	Budgeted Volume in Units	Budgeted Selling Price per Unit	Budgeted Sales Revenues
Fuel oil	1,000,000 gallons	$ 1.25/gallon	$1,250,000
Gasoline	800,000 gallons	1.10/gallon	880,000
Repairs	40,000 hours	20.00/hour	800,000
Total			$2,930,000

Weighting the actual physical units of volume by the same set of budgeted selling prices then will give us a measure of overall physical volume, untainted by variances in unit prices. Actual sales dollars don't come into the calculation of the mix and volume variances; they don't enter the analysis until we move on to the calculation of the selling price variance.

To illustrate the separation of the mix variance in these circumstances, let's go back to our familiar two-product illustration. Instead of measuring overall volume in gallons, we'll measure it by multiplying each product's gallonage by budgeted selling prices. Each variable item on the income statement then can be expressed as a ratio to this figure. Going back to Exhibit 27–3, we find in column (5) that the budgeted cost of goods sold was $1,640,000 on budgeted sales of $2,130,000, an average of 76.9953 percent of budgeted

Exhibit 27–5
BOUNTY OIL COMPANY Calculation of sales mix variances (volume measured in sales dollars at budgeted prices)

	(1) Original Budget		(3) Volume-Adjusted Budget	(4)
	Percent of Sales	Total	At Budgeted Mix*	At Actual Mix
Sales revenues	100.0000	$2,130,000	$2,299,000	$2,299,000
Cost of goods sold	76.9953	1,640,000	1,770,122	1,772,000
Gross profit	23.0047	490,000	528,878	527,000
Variable selling and administrative expenses	2.3474	50,000	53,967	55,000
Contribution margin	20.6573	440,000	474,911	472,000
Fixed selling and administrative expenses		200,000	200,000	200,000
Income before taxes		$ 240,000	$ 274,911	$ 272,000

Sales volume variance $34,911 F.   Sales mix variance $2,911 U.

* Col. (1) × $2,299,000.

sales. Variable selling and administrative expenses were $50,000/$2,130,000 = 2.3474 percent of budgeted sales, and the budgeted contribution margin was 20.6573 percent of budgeted sales.

These percentages have been used to calculate the volume-adjusted budget figures in the middle column of Exhibit 27–5. The variance calculations in this exhibit are identical in form to those in Exhibit 27–4; the only difference is in the way we have calculated overall physical volume. The volume/mix split is only slightly different in this case from the split we calculated using gallonage as our measure of physical volume.

Profit variance analysis in manufacturing companies

Analysis of the profit variances of manufacturing companies is identical to the analysis we have been describing, with the addition of a set of factory cost variances.

Sales volume variance

The Holbeach Company manufactures a number of industrial products. Budget and actual profit data for the month of May are summarized in Exhibit 27–6. To simplify the analysis, we'll assume that all selling and administrative expenses were fixed and gave rise to no variances in May.

Our first task is to identify the sales volume variance. Because the company

Exhibit 27–6
HOLBEACH COMPANY Profit variance, month of May

	Actual	Budget	Over/(Under)
Gross sales (at list prices)	$470,000	$500,000	$(30,000)
Discounts and allowances	30,000	25,000	5,000
Net sales (at actual prices)	440,000	475,000	(35,000)
Standard cost of goods sold	345,000	375,000	(30,000)
Gross margin	95,000	100,000	(5,000)
Factory cost variances	14,000 U.	2,000 U.	12,000
Selling and administrative expenses	45,000	45,000	0
Income before taxes	$ 36,000	$ 53,000	$(17,000)

has a variety of different products, no single measure of overall physical volume is available. All sales are recorded at list price, however, with price reductions recorded as sales discounts and allowances. Gross revenues at list prices therefore can serve as the common measure of physical volume. (An equally acceptable alternative would be to use the standard cost of goods sold, which also is unaffected by variations in prices from period to period.)

Actual gross sales in May amounted to only $470,000, just $30,000 less than the amount budgeted. To estimate the effect of this $30,000 variance in physical volume, we need first to calculate the budgeted cost/volume ratios for all items that are expected to vary proportionally with sales:

	Budgeted Amount	Budgeted Percent of Gross Sales
Gross sales	$500,000	100%
Discounts and allowances	25,000	5
Net sales	475,000	95
Standard cost of goods sold	375,000	75
Gross margin	$100,000	20%

Since in this case we're assuming that selling and administrative expenses are fixed, they won't be affected by variations in sales volume, mix, or price and can be ignored at this stage of the analysis. We can also ignore factory cost variances because they too are unaffected by fluctuations in sales volume. They are affected by *production* volume fluctuations, however, and we'll examine those effects in the next section.

Net sales were budgeted in this instance at 95 percent of list prices, reflecting an assumption that actual prices would be 5 percent below list prices during the month.

Our classification of the standard cost of goods sold as proportionally variable may come as a surprise, in view of the emphasis we placed in earlier chapters on the distinction between fixed and variable production costs. The explanation is that profit variance analysis focuses on the income statement, and full manufacturing cost of the goods sold is an income statement item under absorption costing. If sales volume increases by 10 percent, then the standard cost of goods sold ought to go up by 10 percent, too. With selling and administrative expenses entirely fixed and the full cost of goods sold completely variable, the gross margin figure will serve the same role as the contribution margin in our Bounty Oil Company illustration.

Once we've calculated the budgeted income statement percentages, it's a simple matter to calculate the sales volume variance. The calculations are shown in Exhibit 27–7. For emphasis, we've shown the sales volume variance in two places, first as the difference between the gross margin figures in columns (2) and (3) and second as the net result of the variance calculations in column (4).

Sales mix variance

The calculations in Exhibit 27–7 reflected the assumption that the company's various products were sold in their budgeted proportions in May. To test this assumption, we need to recalculate the profit budget at actual volume and actual mix, while still using budgeted selling prices to weight the various products. In this case we start with $470,000 actual gross sales, deduct the budgeted 5 percent discounts and allowances, and then deduct the standard costs of the goods the company actually sold during the month, $345,000 (from Exhibit 27–6). The calculation of the sales mix variance is as follows:

	Volume-Adjusted Budget at Budgeted Prices	
	At Actual Mix	At Budgeted Mix [Exhibit 27–7, Col. (2)]
Gross sales	$470,000	$470,000
Discounts and allowances	23,500	23,500
Net sales	446,500	446,500
Standard cost of goods sold	345,000	352,500
Gross margin	101,000	94,000
Sales Mix Variance	$7,000 F.	

As this shows, sales in May included a higher-than-budgeted percentage of products with high gross margin percentages.

Notice what we've gained by calculating the sales mix variance. We could have simply compared the original budget with a budget adjusted to the actual volume and mix of products sold. The difference between these two quantities, $1,500 and favorable in this case, is the sum of the sales volume variances of the company's many products, and we could logically classify it as an aggregate sales volume variance if we wished. Our contribution in calculating the sales mix variance was to point out that this $1,500 variance was the result of two offsetting movements—a decrease in overall volume and an enrichment of the mix. This information should help management understand the effects of the forces affecting the company's profits.

Exhibit 27–7
HOLBEACH COMPANY Sales volume variance

	(1)	(2)	(3)	(4)
	Original Budget Percentages	Volume-Adjusted Budget [(1) × $470,000]	Original Budget	Over/ (Under)
Gross sales	100%	$470,000	$500,000	$(30,000)
Discounts and allowances ..	5	23,500	25,000	(1,500)
Net sales	95	446,500	475,000	(28,500)
Standard cost of goods sold	75	352,500	375,000	(22,500)
Gross margin	20	$ 94,000	$100,000	$ (6,000)
Sales Volume Variance		$6,000 U.		

Selling price variances

The final component of the total variance in reported gross margin in this instance is the selling price variance. We just estimated that discounts and allowances on gross sales of $470,000 should have been $23,500 if budgeted relationships had held true. Actual discounts and allowances (from Exhibit 27–6) amounted to $30,000. Since these discounts and allowances in this case had no impact on selling and administrative expenses, the selling price variance in May was $30,000 − $23,500 = $6,500 and was unfavorable.

This figure is shown in the lower right-hand corner of Exhibit 27–8, which summarizes our analysis so far. Once again, notice how we changed one factor at a time as we moved from column to column. This is an essential feature of this kind of variance analysis.

Exhibit 27–8
HOLBEACH COMPANY Analysis of variance in gross margin

	Original Budget	Volume-Adjusted Budget At Budgeted Mix	Volume-Adjusted Budget At Actual Mix	Actual Sales at Actual Selling Prices
Gross sales	$500,000	$470,000	$470,000	$470,000
Discounts and allowances	25,000	23,500	23,500	30,000
Net sales	475,000	446,500	446,500	440,000
Standard cost of goods sold ...	375,000	352,500	345,000	345,000
Gross margin	100,000	94,000	101,500	95,000
		Sales volume variance $6,000 U.	Sales mix variance $7,500 F.	Selling price variance $6,500 U.

A word of caution is appropriate here. These variances may not be independent, as we have been implying. The enrichment of the mix, for example, may have been achieved either by cutting prices on the high-margin products or by shifting selling effort from easy-to-sell, low-margin products, thereby reducing overall volume. Our analysis tells management what the symptoms are; diagnosis and cure must start from there.

Production cost variances

The analysis of production cost variances differs in only two respects from the analysis we learned in earlier chapters. First, we are interested only in the variances that appear on the income statement. Since all variances are usually taken immediately to the income statement, at least for internal reporting, we'll assume that Holbeach Company follows that practice, too.

Second, we are interested in the *differences* between the variances that were budgeted for the period and the variances that actually arose during the period. It sometimes comes as a surprise to find that companies actually budget cost variances. They may do this for many reasons. Seasonal variation is one of these; the impact of a severe depression is another (for example, automobile manufacturing in the United States in 1980–81). Others include the temporary use of inexperienced workers or off-standard equipment, and the learning effect as it relates to the introduction of new production equipment or new product models.

Whatever the reason, management is less interested in the absolute size of the variance than in the size of the departure from the budgeted level. The budgeted variance is no surprise; the variance in that variance is what concerns management.

Referring back to Exhibit 27–6, we find that Holbeach Company budgeted an unfavorable manufacturing cost variance of $2,000 in May; the actual variance was $14,000, also unfavorable. Our problem is to account for the $12,000 difference between these two figures.

Factory cost variances fall generally into the following major categories:

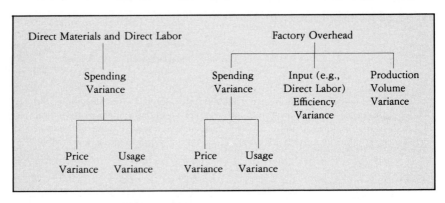

We spent a good deal of time on these variances in earlier chapters, so we'll keep the illustration as simple as possible by assuming that Holbeach Company budgeted no variances in direct materials or in direct labor costs for the month of May. The unfavorable budgeted manufacturing cost variance was an overhead volume variance, reflecting a lower level of production than the normal level on which standard overhead cost was based.

Holbeach measured manufacturing volume by the number of standard direct labor hours and assigned overhead to products at a rate of $14 a standard direct labor hour: $10 for average fixed costs at a normal volume of 5,000 standard direct labor hours, and $4 for standard variable overhead cost per hour. The budget for May called for a production volume of 4,800 standard direct labor hours, which was 200 hours lower than the normal volume. A zero spending variance was budgeted for factory overhead costs.

Given this information, and using the analytical techniques we first introduced in Chapter 11, we get the following breakdown of the budgeted factory overhead variance:

Budgeted Overhead Costs, Current Period	Flexible Budget at Actual Volume $50,000 + $4 × 4,800 Std.DLHrs.	Overhead Costs Absorbed at Actual Volume $14 × 4,800 Std.DLHrs.
$69,200	$69,200	$67,200
	Overhead Spending Variance $0	Overhead Volume Variance $2,000 U.

Production during the month of May amounted to only 4,000 standard direct labor hours, but there were no spending variances in either direct materials or direct labor. Actual overhead costs amounted to $70,000, the amount absorbed (at $14 a standard direct labor hour) was $56,000, and the analysis of the overhead cost variance was as follows:

Actual Overhead Costs	Flexible Budget at Actual Volume $50,000 + $4 × 4,000 Std.DLHrs.	Overhead Costs Absorbed at Actual Volume $14 × 4,000 Std.DLHrs.
$70,000	$66,000	$56,000
	Overhead Spending Variance $4,000 U.	Overhead Volume Variance $10,000 U.

We can now subdivide the $12,000 income statement variance in factory cost variances as follows:

	Actual	Budgeted	Variance
Overhead spending variance	$ 4,000 U.	$ —	$ 4,000 U.
Overhead volume variance	10,000 U.	2,000 U.	8,000 U.
Total	$14,000 U.	$2,000 U.	$12,000 U.

These figures are incorporated in the final variance summary in Exhibit 27–9.

Impact of production volume on income

Holbeach Company probably could have increased its income before taxes in May without increasing sales volume. By increasing production by an additional 800 standard direct labor hours—that is, up to the originally budgeted volume—Holbeach could have added $8,000 to income before taxes. (The standard overhead rate included $10 for fixed overhead costs.)

We first called attention to this phenomenon of recognizing income at the time of production in Chapter 13. By increasing its production, however, Holbeach would have increased its investment in inventory, too. The carrying costs on this additional inventory may have been great enough to reduce any possible temptation to maintain or increase production levels merely as a way of increasing reported income. Management may also have feared the penalty costs of overtime premiums and other means of maintaining or increasing production levels.

Except for growth factors, which ordinarily will be relatively small, the level of production must balance the level of sales during any extended period. If we wish, therefore, we can divide the volume variance into two components: (1) the amount associated with a variance in production volume equal to the current variance in sales volume; and (2) the amount due to unbudgeted increases or decreases of the inventory.

Holbeach, for example, saw the standard cost of goods sold fall $30,000 short of its $375,000 budgeted level in May, a variance of 8 percent. To maintain the inventory at a constant level, management would have had to reduce the rate of production by 8 percent, or $0.08 \times 4,800 = 384$ standard direct labor hours. At a fixed overhead rate of $10 a standard direct labor hour, $3,840 of the unbudgeted overhead volume variance can be regarded as an addition to the unfavorable sales volume variance. The other $4,160 was the result of decreasing the production level even more sharply, to 4,000 standard direct labor hours. In other words, it was the result of an unbudgeted reduction in inventory.

Profit variance analysis: Variable costing basis

This split of the overhead volume variance will seem desirable to those who wish to see income reporting converted to a variable costing basis. A variance analysis on a variable costing basis is summarized in Exhibit 27–10. We calculated budgeted standard variable cost of goods sold in the first column by

Exhibit 27–9
HOLBEACH COMPANY Variance analysis summary, full-costing basis

	Original Budget	Volume-Adjusted Budget At Budgeted Mix	Volume-Adjusted Budget At Actual Mix	Actual Sales at Actual Selling Prices	Actual Production Volume	Actual Results
Gross sales	$500,000	$470,000	$470,000	$470,000	$470,000	$470,000
Discounts and allowances ...	25,000	23,500	23,500	30,000	30,000	30,000
Net sales	475,000	446,500	446,500	440,000	440,000	440,000
Standard cost of goods sold	375,000	352,500	345,000	345,000	345,000	345,000
Gross margin	100,000	94,000	101,500	95,000	95,000	95,000
Factory cost variances	2,000	2,000	2,000	2,000	10,000	14,000
S&A expenses	45,000	45,000	45,000	45,000	45,000	45,000
Income before tax	$ 53,000	$ 47,000	$ 54,500	$ 48,000	$ 40,000	$ 36,000
	Sales Volume Variance $6,000 U.	Sales Mix Variance $7,500 F.	Selling Price Variance $6,500 U.	Production Volume Variance $8,000 U.	Overhead Spending Variance $4,000 U.	

Exhibit 27–10
HOLBEACH COMPANY Variance analysis summary, variable costing basis

	Original Budget	Volume-Adjusted Budget At Budgeted Mix	Volume-Adjusted Budget At Actual Mix	Actual Sales at Actual Selling Prices	Actual Results
Gross sales	$500,000	$470,000	$470,000	$470,000	$470,000
Discounts and allowances	25,000	23,500	23,500	30,000	30,000
Net sales	475,000	446,500	446,500	440,000	440,000
Standard variable cost of goods sold	327,000	307,380	300,840	300,840	300,840
Contribution margin	148,000	139,120	145,660	139,160	139,160
Fixed factory overhead	50,000	50,000	50,000	50,000	50,000
Factory overhead spending variances	—	—	—	—	4,000
Selling and administrative expenses	45,000	45,000	45,000	45,000	45,000
Income before taxes	$ 53,000	$ 44,120	$ 50,660	$ 44,160	$ 40,160
		Sales Volume Variance $8,880 U.	Sales Mix Variance $6,540 F.	Selling Price Variance $6,500 U.	Factory Overhead Spending Variance $4,000 U.

subtracting the fixed factory overhead cost of 4,800 hours × $10 = $48,000 from the $375,000 budgeted standard full cost of goods sold shown in Exhibit 27–9. (We assumed that budgeted production and sales volumes were identical.) The $48,000 was added to the $2,000 budgeted unfavorable overhead volume variance to give us the $50,000 budgeted fixed factory overhead. Factory overhead cost spending variances were placed on a separate line because we don't know whether they originated in elements of fixed costs or in elements of variable costs. This classification would come out in a detailed listing of the spending variances.

We calculated the standard variable cost of goods sold figures in the other columns by multiplying the full cost of goods sold figures in Exhibit 27–9 by the ratio of budgeted standard variable cost of goods sold to budgeted full cost of goods sold ($327,000/$375,000 = 87.2 percent.)

The sales volume and sales mix variances are bigger on a variable costing basis than they were under full costing because the contribution margin per unit is bigger than the figure we used in lieu of contribution margin in full costing—that figure treated the fixed overhead component of the cost of goods sold as a variable cost of producing current income. The net result of this difference in measurement basis is that the total of the sales mix and sales volume variances in Exhibit 27–10 ($2,340, unfavorable) differs from the total of these two variances on a full-costing basis ($1,500, favorable) by

$3,840. This is the portion of the full-costing production volume variance we attributed earlier to the unbudgeted reduction in sales volume.

The total variance in income before taxes on a variable costing basis (from Exhibit 27–10) is $53,000 − $40,160 = $12,840, unfavorable. This is $4,160 less than the $17,000 variance we studied in our full-costing analysis. This $4,160 is the figure we identified in our analysis of the full-costing figures as the result of the unbudgeted inventory reduction. Since Holbeach Company reduced its inventories in May, it transferred $4,160 in fixed factory overhead from its full-cost inventory balances to the cost of goods sold; no such transfer took place in variable costing.

Limitations of the analysis

Useful though it is, this analytical technique suffers from three defects. One of these has already been mentioned. The relative sizes of the variances depend on the sequence in which they are computed. That is, the size of the sales volume variance will depend on whether it reflects actual or standard prices, and so on. Confusion can be minimized by adopting a standardized sequence, but the resulting variances give only orders of magnitude and cannot be interpreted literally.

Second, the profit plan does not necessarily represent what the manager should have been able to accomplish during the period, given the conditions that actually prevailed. In an attempt to deal with this, Joel Demski has provided a model by which the total variance can be divided into two parts, one representing the difference between the original plan and the correct plan in the prevailing circumstances, and the other measuring the difference between the adjusted plan and the actual results.[1] This latter component can then be subjected to the kind of analysis described in this chapter. Although application of this model requires more data than are generally available, the approach represents an improvement over existing practice and deserves efforts to implement it.

The third defect is even more fundamental. Even if the first two defects could be overcome, the analysis illustrated in this chapter doesn't indicate *why* the price variance is as large or as small as it is or why volume failed to meet the budgeted amounts. In fact, the variances may even be interdependent. Volume may be down because price is too high, the mix may be good because the more profitable product is underpriced, and so on.

All that technical variance analysis can do is provide a convenient summary of symptoms. Identification of the underlying causes then becomes a matter for managerial detective work. The technical breakdown can be very useful, however, in pointing the finger at areas that should be investigated. If the analysis shows that the main problem seems to be the sales mix, management

---

[1] For descriptions of this model, see Joel Demski, "An Accounting System Structured on a Linear Programming Model," *Accounting Review,* October 1967, pp. 701–12, and "Predictive Ability of Alternative Performance Measurement Models," *Journal of Accounting Research,* Spring 1969, pp. 96–115.

is likely to be much closer to finding a solution than if this information isn't available.

Profit ratio and trend analysis

A second approach to profit performance reporting is through ratio and trend analysis. At its simplest, this takes the form of a single chart showing the progress of earnings or return on investment from period to period. This kind of chart can have a strong visual impact, and is widely used. It throws little light on the forces that affect reported performance, however. Recognizing this, some companies supplement the return on investment chart with a series of backup charts, each one dealing with some dimension of performance.

One such chart system is diagrammed in Exhibit 27–11. Each block in this exhibit represents a separate chart or table. The words appearing in the spaces between vertically adjacent blocks describe the relationship between these blocks and the block they are joined to at the left. The basic return on investment (ROI) ratio, for example, can be broken into two component ratios:

$$\text{ROI} = \frac{\text{Profit}}{\text{Investment}} = \frac{\text{Profit}}{\text{Sales}} \times \frac{\text{Sales}}{\text{Investment}}$$

A drop in the return on investment ratio that is accompanied by a decline in the earnings percentage has a different meaning from a drop that is accompanied by a reduction in turnover.

A low turnover ratio, for example, may have arisen because total investment increased more rapidly than sales. The increment in investment, in turn, may have been located entirely in the finished goods inventories. Management knows, therefore, that the explanation for the decline in turnover must be sought in the reason for the inventory buildup. By moving farther and farther to the right on this diagram, management can get deeper and deeper into the details of the company's operations. In the process, the major causes of the problem may come to light.

The ratios and other figures used in this system are used by top management to identify favorable and unfavorable trends. While a declining sales margin percentage means nothing in itself, it may be a very bad sign if asset turnover is not increasing at the same time. Unexpected movements revealed in this way initiate a search for explanations, which in turn can trigger management action.

Summary

Comparisons of actual results with the amounts budgeted provide only the crudest of signals to management. The techniques described in this chapter have been developed to provide signals that are more finely tuned.

The most significant of these techniques is profit variance analysis, by which the overall profit variance for a given product line or division is subdivided

Exhibit 27-11 Relationship of factors affecting return on net investment

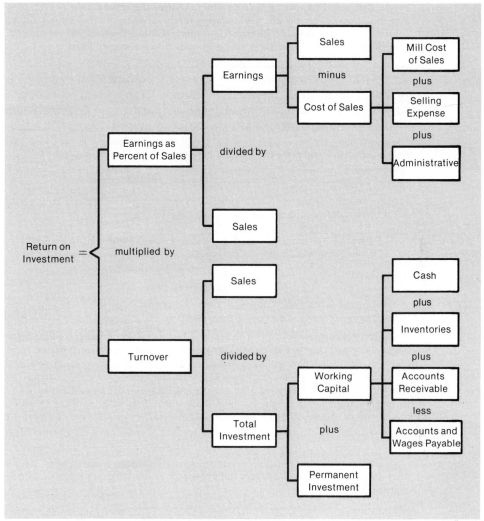

Source: Adapted from E. I. duPont de Nemours & Co., *Executive Committee Control Charts: A Description of the duPont System for Appraising Operating Performance.*

into portions attributed to departures from budgeted sales volume, sales mix, selling price, production volume, factory spending, and selling and administrative spending.

Another technique is interperiod ratio comparison. Although these comparisons ordinarily ignore planned ratios, and although the various ratios are not independent of each other, this kind of analysis does identify trends that seem to be developing and may help management decide to take action before the need for action otherwise would have become apparent.

Independent study problems (solutions in Appendix B)

1. **Profit variance analysis: Single product.** From the information below, compute the amount of the profit variance due to variations in (*a*) selling prices, (*b*) sales volume, and (*c*) other factors, in as much detail as you deem appropriate. Selling and administrative expenses are assumed to be wholly fixed.

	Budget	Actual
Units sold	10,000	11,000
Sales	$60,000	$60,500
Cost of goods sold	36,000	40,000
Gross margin	24,000	20,500
Selling and administrative expenses	18,000	18,500
Income before income taxes	$ 6,000	$ 2,000

2. **Profit variance analysis: Manufacturing company.** The cost of goods sold in problem 1 equaled total manufacturing cost. The details were:

	Budget	Actual
Direct materials	$10,000	$11,200
Direct labor	13,000	14,700
Factory overhead	13,000	14,100
Total cost of goods sold	$36,000	$40,000

Additional information: (1) All materials prices, wage rates, and other input prices were at budgeted levels. (2) Production volume and sales volume were identical. (3) Factory overhead is budgeted at $7,800 plus 40 percent of actual direct labor cost. (4) The company has a standard costing system; no factory cost variances were budgeted this period. All factory cost variances are taken to the income statement for the period in which they arise and are included this period in the amounts in the "Actual" column.

Required:
Prepare a revised analysis of the variances.

3. **Sales mix variance.** A company sells three products. Sales and cost of goods sold last month were as follows:

	Units Sold	Revenue	Unit Cost
Budget:			
Product X	10,000	$20,000	$1.20
Product Y	5,000	30,000	4.20
Product Z	4,000	20,000	4.00
Total	19,000	$70,000	
Actual:			
Product X	10,800	$23,100	$1.20
Product Y	4,000	23,600	4.20
Product Z	5,200	25,500	4.00
Total	20,000	$72,200	

Required:
a. Calculate the reported gross margin and the total variance in gross margin.

b.   Divide this total variance into price, volume, and mix components, using revenues at budgeted selling prices to measure aggregate volume.
c.   How would your answer to b) have differed if you had used the number of units sold to measure aggregate volume? Which measure is the correct one?

Exercises and problems

4.   **Profit variance exercises: Nonmanufacturing firms.**   The exercises in this set are designed to demonstrate different aspects of profit variance analysis. Each one has a lesson that should be noted; they should be solved in the sequence in which they are presented.

Exercise A

Company Alpha buys a single commodity at wholesale and sells it at retail. Selling and administrative expenses are entirely fixed. You have the following financial information:

	Budget	Actual
Units sold	1,000,000	900,000
Revenues	$5,000,000	$4,750,000
Cost of goods sold	3,000,000	2,810,000
Gross margin	2,000,000	1,940,000
Selling and administrative expenses	1,000,000	1,045,000
Income before taxes	$1,000,000	$ 895,000

Required:

Analyze the variance between budgeted and actual results for the period.

Exercise B

Company Beta buys a commodity at wholesale and sells it at retail. Selling and administrative expenses are expected to vary according to the following formula:

$$\text{Total expenses} = \$800,000 + \$0.20 \times \text{Number of units sold}$$

You have the following financial information:

	Budget	Actual
Units sold	900,000	950,000
Revenues	$4,500,000	$5,000,000
Cost of goods sold	2,700,000	2,850,000
Gross margin	1,800,000	2,150,000
Selling and administrative expenses	980,000	1,000,000
Income before taxes	$ 820,000	$1,150,000

Required:

Analyze the variance between budgeted and actual results for the period.

Exercise C

Company Gamma buys two commodities at wholesale and sells them at retail. Product X was budgeted to cost $4 this period and sell for $7 a pound, while product Y was budgeted to cost $3 and to sell for $4 a gallon. Selling and administrative expenses were budgeted at $1,500,000 and are entirely fixed.

The income statement for the period showed the following budgeted and actual results:

	Budgeted	Actual
Units sold:		
Product X	600,000 lbs.	550,000 lbs.
Product Y	200,000 gal.	300,000 gal.
Sales revenues	$5,000,000	$4,950,000
Cost of goods sold	3,000,000	3,100,000
Gross margin	2,000,000	1,850,000
Selling and administrative expenses	1,500,000	1,510,000
Income before taxes	$ 500,000	$ 340,000

Required:

Analyze the variance between budgeted and actual results for this period.

5. **Exercises: Nonmanufacturing company.** Company Delta buys a large number of items at wholesale and sells them at retail. These items are grouped into two major product lines, X and Y. Selling and administrative expenses are entirely fixed. The following information is taken from the original budget for the period:

	Line X	Line Y	Total
Sales revenues	$3,600,000	$2,400,000	$6,000,000
Cost of goods sold	2,400,000	1,800,000	4,200,000
Gross margin	1,200,000	600,000	1,800,000
Selling and administrative expenses			1,000,000
Income before taxes			$ 800,000

Actual results for the period were as follows:

	Line X	Line Y	Total
Sales revenues	$3,370,000	$2,790,000	$6,160,000
Cost of goods sold	2,340,000	2,070,000	4,410,000
Gross margin	1,030,000	720,000	1,750,000
Selling and administrative expenses			1,040,000
Income before taxes			$ 710,000

Exercise D

Management has asked you to prepare an analysis of the variance in Delta Company's income before taxes.

Required:

a. Calculate the following three variances: (1) gross margin variance, line X; (2) gross margin variance, line Y; and spending variance, selling and administrative expenses.

b. Assuming that sales revenue is a satisfactory measure of physical volume, prepare an analysis of Company Delta's variance in income before taxes.

c. What condition must sales revenue satisfy to make it suitable for use as a measure of physical sales volume? Why must it satisfy this condition?

Exercise E

The facts are the same as in Exercise D, except that you have the additional information that actual sales, measured at budgeted prices, were as follows:

Line X	....	$3,450,000
Line Y	....	2,800,000
Total	....	$6,250,000

Required:

Analyze the variance between budgeted and actual results for the period.

Exercise F

The facts are the same as in Exercise E, but in addition you find that industry sales for line X were at the level forecasted when the budget for this period was adopted, whereas industry sales for line Y were 15 percent greater than their budgeted level. Spot checks of competitors' prices during the year indicated that most of these prices held firm during the year.

Required:

Using this information, comment on the company's profit performance for the period.

Exercise G

The facts are the same as in Exercise E, except that selling and administrative expenses are expected to be described by the following formula:

Selling and administrative expense = $700,000 + 5% × sales revenue

Required:

Prepare a revised analysis of the profit variance, using this additional information.

6. **Profit variance analysis: Nonmanufacturing firm.**   The ABC Sales Company operates a wholesale outlet. It buys merchandise from two or three manufacturers and sells these goods to retailers. Its planned and actual results for a recent period were as follows:

	Planned	Actual
Selling price per unit	$10	$9.50
Sales volume, units	50,000	52,000
Cost of goods sold	$300,000	$318,000
Selling and administrative cost	$100,000	$115,000
	+$0.20 a unit	

Required:

a. Calculate planned income before taxes for the period.
b. Calculate actual income before taxes for the period.
c. Analyze the difference between (*a*) and *b*) to measure the effects on net income of deviations in sales volume, selling price, and merchandise purchase prices, and the effect of departures from budgeted selling and administrative expense. Ignore income taxes.

7. **Exercises: Manufacturing company.**   Company Theta is a manufacturing firm, making and selling a single product. It has no selling and administrative expenses. All sales are at a price of $5 and manufacturing costs are expected to approximate the following budget formula:

Total cost = $1,000,000 + $2 × Number of units produced

You have the following volume data:

	Units Sold	Units Produced
Normal	1,000,000	1,000,000
Budgeted, this period	1,000,000	1,000,000
Actual, this period	900,000	900,000

Company Theta assigns factory cost to products at standard cost on a variable costing basis. All production cost variances are classified as expenses of the periods in which they arise.

Exercise J

Company Theta produces and sells 900,000 units this period. Actual production costs total $2,800,000.

Required:

a. How much of the period's production cost would be assigned to products and how much would be classified directly as expense (1) in the budget drawn up at the beginning of the period, and (2) in the actual records for the period?
b. Prepare a budgeted income statement for the period, the actual income statement, and an analysis of the differences between the two.

Exercise K

The facts are the same as in Exercise J, except that the actual production volume is 1 million units and actual production cost is $3 million.

Required:

a. Calculate and analyze the profit variance for the period.
b. Prepare an annotated comparison of the results of this analysis with the results of the analysis in Exercise J.

Exercise L

Company Omicron is identical to Company Theta in all respects except that it assigns factory costs to production at standard cost on a full-costing basis. All other facts are the same as in Exercise J.

Required:

a. How much of the period's production cost would be assigned to products and how much would be classified directly as expense (1) in the budget drawn up at the beginning of the period, and (2) in the actual records for the period?
b. Prepare a budgeted income statement for the period, the actual income statement, and an analysis of the differences between the two.

Exercise M

The facts are the same as in Exercise L except that the company manufactures 1 million units and actual production cost is $3 million.

Required:

a. Prepare a budgeted income statement for the period, the actual income statement, and an analysis of the differences between the two.
b. Compare the results of this analysis with the results of your analyses of Exercises K and L.

Exercise N

Company Omega is a manufacturing company, making and selling a single product. It has no selling and administrative expenses. All sales are at a price of $5 and manufacturing costs are expected to approximate the following budget formula:

$$\text{Total cost} = \$1,000,000 + \$2 \times \text{Number of units produced}$$

You have the following volume data:

	No. of Units Sold	No. of Units Produced
Normal	1,000,000	1,000,000
Budgeted, this period	1,000,000	940,000
Actual, this period	850,000	900,000

Company Omega assigns factory costs to products at standard cost on a full-costing basis. Actual production costs this period total $2,875,000. All production cost variances are classified as expenses of the periods in which they arise.

Required:

a. How much of the period's production cost would be assigned to products and how much would be classified directly as expense (1) in the budget drawn up at the beginning of the period, and (2) in the actual records for the period?

b. Prepare a budgeted income statement for the period, the actual income statement, and an analysis of the differences between the two.

8. **Exercise: Selling and administrative expenses.** Selling and administrative expenses in Rowe Company can be estimated from the following formula:

$$\text{Total expense} = \$10,000 + 0.05 \times \text{Sales revenues}$$

The company budgeted $500,000 in sales revenues in July on a budgeted sales volume of 100,000 units of product. Actual volume in July amounted to 105,000 units, at an average selling price of $4.70. Actual selling and administrative expenses amounted to $36,000.

Required:

Calculate and analyze the amount of the variance in income before taxes attributable to variances in selling and administrative expenses.

9. **Exercise: Factory overhead cost variances.** David Company uses full costing for the products it manufactures. It uses an overhead rate of $4 a standard direct labor hour. All cost variances are taken to the income statement for the period in which they arise. The flexible budget for factory overhead costs is expressed in the following formula:

$$\text{Overhead cost} = \$15,000 + \$1.50 \times \text{Standard direct labor hours}$$

Budgeted production volume in June totaled 5,800 standard direct labor hours; actual production in June amounted to 6,500 standard direct labor hours. When the profit plan was prepared, management expected factory overhead costs in June to total $23,000; actual factory overhead costs that month amounted to $24,500.

Required:

a. Calculate the amount of the factory overhead cost variance included in the profit plan for June and the actual variance for the month.

b. Analyze the portion of the variance in income before taxes for the month that was attributable to factory overhead cost variances.

10. **Supplying missing information.** Selling and administrative expenses in Parker Company are entirely fixed. Make the necessary calculations and fill in the blanks in the following table:

a.	Budgeted sales in units	100,000
b.	Budgeted sales in dollars	?
c.	Budgeted average selling price	$10
d.	Budgeted contribution margin per unit	?
e.	Budgeted total contribution margin	?
f.	Budgeted cost of goods sold	?
g.	Actual sales in units	90,000
h.	Actual sales in dollars	?
i.	Actual average selling price	$10.30
j.	Actual total contribution margin	?
k.	Actual cost of goods sold	$545,000
l.	Sales volume variance	$ 40,000 U.
m.	Selling price variance	?
n.	Merchandise cost price variance	?
o.	Total variance in contribution margin	$ 18,000 U.

11. **Change in sales; change in production.** A firm has made the following estimates of the percentage of expenses to sales revenue, based on a normal sales volume of $10 million:

Variable manufacturing	30%
Fixed manufacturing	40
Variable selling and administrative	15
Fixed selling and administrative	5
Total expense	90%

Inventory is measured at full absorption cost, based on normal volume. Anticipated sales volume for the current period is $8 million. All production cost variances are taken directly to the income statement as they arise.

Required:
   d. What would be the effect on net income of increasing sales by $1 million without an increase in production?
   b. What would be the effect on net income of increasing production by a quantity of goods that has a sales value of $1 million without an increase in sales?

12. **Deviation from expected loss.** Woodbridge, Inc., after several years of profitable operation, showed a loss of $2 million in 19x3, accompanied by a severe cash shortage. Woodbridge seethed with activity as a result: New financial controls were installed, and a new sales manager was hired. By the end of 19x4, the new organization was fully operating and Mr. James Woodbridge, the company's president, was optimistic about the future despite the 19x4 loss of $1.3 million on sales of $5 million.

Looking ahead, Mr. Woodbridge was convinced that the firm could attain a volume of $10 million in a few years, with the following profit results (in $000):

Sales........................		$10,000
Variable production costs.......	$5,000	
Fixed production costs	2,000	
Variable selling costs	1,000	
Fixed selling costs	1,000	9,000
Net income before taxes		$ 1,000

Variable costs were expected to vary in proportion to changes in physical volume. Standard product costs in the factory were established on the basis of the physical volume required for an annual sales volume of $10 million. All production cost variances were to be taken directly to the income statement for the period in which they arose.

The initial profit budget for 19x5 called for sales of $6.5 million (at standard prices) and a net loss (before taxes) of $400,000. Actual volume for 19x5 was $7 million, also at standard prices. At this volume a loss of $200,000 was budgeted, but the company's cash position had improved so much by the end of 19x5 that Mr. Woodbridge thought the company might have broken even. Therefore, he was aghast when he received the following income statement (in $000):

Sales (at actual prices)		$6,860
Standard cost of goods sold	$4,900	
Selling expenses	1,720	
Factory overhead volume variance	900	
Other factory cost variances	30	7,550
Net loss		$ (690)

"What happened?" he gasped. Tell him, in as much detail as possible.

(Prepared by Carl L. Nelson)

13. **Ratio decomposition.**   Pinshaw Enterprises, Inc. is a large manufacturing corporation with operations throughout the United States and in many other countries. It is organized on a product line basis in the United States and on a regional basis abroad. Each of the domestic divisions in the United States is relatively autonomous, with its own manufacturing facilities and its own marketing organization. Profits are reported monthly to management and quarterly to shareholders.

In reviewing the profit performance of each of the company's divisions, management uses a ratio analysis scheme similar to the one described in the final section of this chapter. You have been told that the return on investment in the Able Division fell from 20 percent in the first quarter to 14.7 percent in the second quarter. You are given the following data (in $000):

	First Quarter	Second Quarter
Sales	$100	$105
Cost of goods sold	60	66
Operating expenses	20	24
Income taxes.....................	8	6
Total expenses	88	96
Net income	12	9
Traceable investment:		
Receivables	$ 50	$ 54
Inventories	60	62
Plant and equipment	120	122
Total traceable assets	230	238
Accounts payable	20	25
Net traceable investment............	210	213
Centrally administered assets	30	32
Net investment....................	$240	$245

Required:

a. Verify the computation of the return on investment ratios given above.

b. Break the return on investment ratios down into component ratios. Try to explain what has happened, using ratios only.

14. **Adequacy of product markup.**   Van Dyk Corporation distributes cigars, cigarettes, and pipe tobacco to retail outlets. Cigars have the biggest percentage of profit markups, and cigarettes have the smallest. The markups also vary to some

extent from brand to brand within each product class, but these variations are relatively small.

Johann van Dyk, the company's president and chief stockholder, is worried. The warehouse seems as busy as ever, the delivery trucks seem to be as heavily loaded, but profits have been close to zero for several months.

Last month was very much like earlier months. Budgeted and actual data for the month were as follows:

	Budget		Actual	
	Cases	Amount	Cases	Amount
Sales:				
Cigars	500	$ 60,000	300	$ 35,000
Cigarettes...........	2,125	204,000	2,300	220,000
Pipe tobacco	800	24,000	700	22,000
Total		$288,000		$277,000
Cost of goods sold:				
Cigars		$ 36,000		$ 22,000
Cigarettes...........		163,200		180,000
Pipe tobacco		16,800		15,000
Total		$216,000		$217,000

Operating expenses are almost entirely fixed within the customary operating range and have been running very close to budget.

Required:

Mr. van Dyk thinks that he may have to press the manufacturers for an increase in the spread between the prices he pays and the prices charged the retail dealers. Before doing this, however, he has decided to ask you to analyze last month's figures. Analyze the profit variance for the month and prepare a table summarizing the results of that analysis. What advice would you give Mr. van Dyk?

15. **Effect of market factors.** The Arsco Company makes three grades of indoor-outdoor carpets. The sales volume for the annual budget is determined by estimating the total market volume for indoor-outdoor carpet, and then applying the company's prior year market share, adjusted for planned changes due to company programs for the coming year. The volume is apportioned among the three grades based upon the prior year's product mix, again adjusted for planned changes due to company programs for the coming year.

Given below are the company budget for 19x3 and the results of operations for 19x3.

	Budget			
	Grade 1	Grade 2	Grade 3	Total
Sales—Units	1,000 rolls	1,000 rolls	2,000 rolls	4,000 rolls
Sales dollars (000 omitted)	$1,000	$2,000	$3,000	$6,000
Variable expense	700	1,600	2,300	4,600
Contribution margin	300	400	700	1,400
Traceable fixed expense	200	200	300	700
Traceable margin	$ 100	$ 200	$ 400	700
Selling and administrative expense ...				250
Net income				$ 450

	Actual			
	Grade 1	Grade 2	Grade 3	Total
Sales—Units	800 rolls	1,000 rolls	2,100 rolls	3,900 rolls
Sales—dollars (000 omitted)........	$810	$2,000	$3,000	$5,810
Variable expenses	560	1,610	2,320	4,490
Contribution margin	250	390	680	1,320
Traceable fixed expense............	210	220	315	745
Traceable margin	$ 40	$ 170	$ 365	575
Selling and administrative expense ...				275
Net income				$ 300

Industry volume was estimated at 40,000 rolls for budgeting purposes. Actual industry volume for 19x3 was 38,000 rolls.

Required:

a.   Calculate the profit impact of the unit sales volume variance for 19x3 using budgeted contribution margins.

b.   What portion of the variance, if any, can be attributed to the state of the carpet market?

c.   What is the dollar impact on profits (using budgeted contribution margins) of the shift in product mix from the budgeted mix?

(CMA)

16. **Supplying missing data.** Your superior in the financial analysis department of the Dexter Division of National Brands, Inc. had just started a report to management explaining the division's failure to meet its budget for the third quarter of the current fiscal year when she was called to San Francisco on a more pressing problem. Giving you her partially finished report and the underlying data, she asked you to have it finished upon her return.

She had jotted down the following partial set of conclusions when she was called away:

Increase (or decrease) in sales volume	?	F or U?
Increase in selling prices	?	F
Increase (or decrease) in production volume (can I tell how much was to adjust production to sales and how much was to change the inventory by an amount different from the budgeted change?)	?	F or U?
Increase in manufacturing costs as a result of cost increases or decreased efficiency (can I tell how much for each?)	9,000 U	
Increase in selling and administrative costs as a result of cost increases or decreased efficiency (can I tell how much for each?)	4,800 U	
Difference between budgeted income and actual income	$ 800 U	

Attached to this were the following:

1.   Budgeted income statement:

Sales		$500,000
Cost of goods sold—at standard		310,000
Gross margin		190,000
Factory overhead volume variance.......	$ 57,000	
Factory overhead spending variance	0	
Other factory variances	(8,000)	
Selling and administrative expenses	125,000	174,000
Income before income taxes		$ 16,000

2. Notes on costs and the budget:

   a. We produced more than 200 products, but there is a close relationship among them. As a result, the following percentages of selling price are very representative of the products' standard factory costs:

Material	20%
Labor	10
Overhead	32
Total standard cost	62%

   b. The budget was based on an increase in the finished goods inventory of $6,200 and no change in the work-in-process inventory.

   c. Factory overhead was budgeted at $210,000 plus 20 percent of direct labor costs.

   d. Standard output required a direct labor cost of $70,000. Because of the expansion program, we were operating far below standard output; hence the large volume variance.

   e. Selling and administrative expenses were budgeted at $100,000 plus 5 percent of sales at actual prices.

3. The actual income statement was:

Sales		$504,000
Cost of goods sold—at standard		303,800
Gross margin		200,200
Overhead volume variance	54,000	
Overhead spending variance	4,000	
Other manufacturing cost variances	(3,000)	
Selling and administrative expenses	130,000	185,000
Income before income taxes		$ 15,200

4. Costs continued their upward climb. In response, we increased our prices by 4 percent in late January. The best guess is that $140,000 in sales were at the old prices; no really hard figures are available because we're still making some shipments at the old prices.

(Prepared by Carl L. Nelson)

17. **Comprehensive analysis: Two products.** The Moontide Company's Crescent Division manufactures and sells two products. Both products are manufactured in the division's only factory. A full-cost standard costing system is in use in this factory.

The Crescent Division operates under an annual profit plan. Each month the division manager receives a report comparing the division's income for the month with that month's share of the annual profit plan. The report for June showed a budgeted income before taxes of $10,000, and actual income of $12,800.

In preparing to analyze the difference between these two figures, you have collected the following information:

1. Standard product cost per unit (full cost basis):

	A	B
Direct materials	$1	$1
Direct labor	1	2
Factory overhead	2	4
Total	$4	$7

2. Profit plan for the month of June:

	Product A	Product B	Total
Units sold	30,000	10,000	
Net sales	$150,000	$100,000	$250,000
Standard cost of goods sold	120,000	70,000	190,000
Gross margin	30,000	30,000	60,000
Less deductions:			
Selling and administrative expenses			32,000
Variances in factory direct			
labor and materials costs			2,500
Underabsorbed factory			
overhead costs			15,500
Total deductions			50,000
Income before taxes			$ 10,000

3. Budgeted factory overhead cost for both products combined: $90,000 + (0.5 × Standard direct labor cost).
4. Budgeted production volume: product A, 30,000 units; product B, 10,000 units.
5. Total budgeted selling and administrative expenses for both products combined: $27,000 + 2 percent of net sales.
6. Actual production volume during June: product A, 34,000 units; product B, 9,200 units.
7. Actual factory overhead cost during June: $114,800.
8. Actual profit reported for the month of June:

	A	B	Total
Units sold	36,000	9,000	
Net sales	$181,000	$84,000	$265,000
Standard cost of goods sold	144,000	63,000	207,000
Gross margin	37,000	21,000	58,000
Less deductions:			
Selling and administrative expenses			33,000
Variances in factory direct labor			
and materials costs			2,200
Underabsorbed factory overhead costs ...			10,000
Total deductions			45,200
Income before taxes			$ 12,800

Required:

a. Prepare an analysis of the month's operations, indicating insofar as possible the sources of the $2,800 departure from budgeted income before taxes.
b. Without actually making any calculations, explain how the results of your analysis would differ if a variable costing system were in use. Would the total variance be the same or different? Which of the component variances would change in amount?

Appendix A
Compound interest tables
for present value calculations

The tables in this appendix contain the multipliers or conversion factors necessary to convert cash flows of one or more periods into their equivalent values at some other point in time. The basic explanation of the reasons for conversion is given in Chapter 18; only the mechanical details of how the numbers in the tables should be used are explained here. If more extensive tables or specialized tables are needed, they can be found in readily available financial handbooks or can be derived from fairly simple computer programs.

Table 1. Present value of $1

Each figure in Table 1 is the present value on a given reference date of $1 to be paid or received n periods later. To obtain the present value of any sum:

1. Select a date to serve as a reference date.
2. Determine the number of periods (n) between the reference date and the date on which the cash is to be paid or received.
3. Determine the interest rate (r) at which amounts are to be discounted.
4. Find the figure from Table 1 corresponding to these values of n and r.
5. Multiply the cash sum by this figure.

For example, to find the present value of $10,000 to be received five years from now, discounted at a compound annual rate of 8 percent, multiply $10,000 by the number 0.681 from the 8 percent column of Table 1. This says that $6,810 invested now at 8 percent will grow to $10,000 in five years if the interest is left on deposit and reinvested each year at 8 percent interest.

Extending Table 1

Table 1 can be extended easily to provide multipliers for any number of periods. The procedure is simple:

1. Select the column for the desired interest rate.
2. From this column select any two or more multipliers for which the number

of periods adds up to the number of periods (n) for which a multiplier is needed.

3. Multiply these multipliers.

For example, the present value of $1 twenty years after the reference date at 8 percent compounded annually can be calculated in many ways. Three of these, identical except for a rounding error, are:

Multiplier for ($n=10$) × Multiplier for ($n=10$) = 0.463 × 0.463 = 0.214
Multiplier for ($n=\ \ 5$) × Multiplier for ($n=15$) = 0.681 × 0.315 = 0.215
Multiplier for ($n=\ \ 1$) × Multiplier for ($n=19$) = 0.926 × 0.232 = 0.215

Why does this work? Suppose the company expects to receive $1 20 years from now. Multiplying it by the discount factor for $n = 10$ brings it to its present value *at a point 10 years from now,* $0.463. That amount is not the present value today, however. It is the future value 10 years from now. The present value today of any sum 10 years in the future can be calculated by discounting it for 10 years—in other words, by multiplying $0.463 by 0.463.

Using table 1 with shorter compounding intervals

If interest at a given nominal annual rate is compounded semiannually, then the discount factor should be taken from the column in Table 1 corresponding to one half the annual rate and from the row corresponding to twice the number of years. With quarterly compounding, the discount factor should be taken from the column corresponding to one fourth of the annual interest rate and from the row corresponding to four times the number of years. For example, for a cash flow 5 years after the reference date and a nominal interest rate of 20 percent, the factors from Table 1 are as follows:

Compounding Interval	Column	Row	Factor
12 months..........	20%	5	0.402
6 months..........	10	10	0.386
3 months..........	5	20	0.377

Discount factors appropriate to short compounding intervals ordinarily must be used if great accuracy is desired, but annual compounding is usually accurate enough for use in capital expenditure analysis.

Table 2. Present value of an annuity of $1 per period

The present value of a series of cash flows can always be determined by using the multipliers in Table 1. For example, a series of three payments of $10,000 each, the first one a year from now, the second a year later, and the third a year after that, has a present value at 8 percent, compounded annually, as follows:

Years after Reference Date	Cash Flow	Multiplier at 8 Percent (Table 1)	Present Value at 8 Percent
1	$10,000	0.926	$ 9,260
2	10,000	0.857	8,570
3	10,000	0.794	7,940
Total			$25,770

Doing this for a large number of periods would be time consuming. Table 2 has been developed for use whenever the cash flows in a series are identical each period (an *annuity*). The multipliers in Table 2 for a three-year annuity at 8 percent is 2.577. Multiplying this by the $10,000 annual cash flow produces a present value of $25,770, identical to the figure we derived above. *Each multiplier in Table 2 is merely the sum of the multipliers in Table 1* for periods 1 through *n*.

Converting Table 2 to earlier equivalents

The multipliers in Table 2 are used to calculate the present value of a series of cash payments or receipts on a date exactly one period prior to the date of the first payment or receipt. To find the present value at a still earlier date, the present value of the annuity can be multiplied by the multiplier from Table 1 for the number of additional years desired.

For example, the present value at 8 percent of a 10-year, $10,000 annuity is:

$$\$10,000 \times 6.710 = \$67,100$$

Suppose, however, that the first payment in this annuity is five years from now and that we want to know its present value as of today. The $67,100 figure is the present value *one year before the first payment is made,* or four years from now:

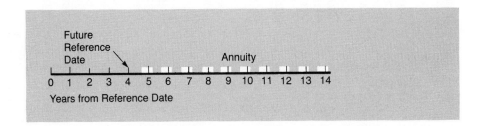

The present value today, therefore, can be obtained by multiplying $67,100 by the four-year multiplier from Table 1:

$$\$67,100 \times 0.735 = \$49,318$$

Table 1 Present value of $1 received or paid in a lump sum n periods after the reference date (discounted once each period for n periods)

n	5%	6%	7%	8%	9%	10%	11%	12%	13%	14%	15%	20%	25%	30%	40%
1	0.952	0.943	0.935	0.926	0.917	0.909	0.901	0.893	0.885	0.877	0.870	0.833	0.800	0.769	0.714
2	0.907	0.890	0.873	0.857	0.842	0.826	0.812	0.797	0.783	0.769	0.756	0.694	0.640	0.592	0.510
3	0.864	0.840	0.816	0.794	0.772	0.751	0.731	0.712	0.693	0.675	0.658	0.579	0.512	0.455	0.364
4	0.823	0.792	0.763	0.735	0.708	0.683	0.659	0.636	0.613	0.592	0.572	0.482	0.410	0.350	0.260
5	0.784	0.747	0.713	0.681	0.650	0.621	0.593	0.567	0.543	0.519	0.497	0.402	0.328	0.269	0.186
6	0.746	0.705	0.666	0.630	0.596	0.564	0.535	0.507	0.480	0.456	0.432	0.335	0.262	0.207	0.133
7	0.711	0.665	0.623	0.583	0.547	0.513	0.482	0.452	0.425	0.400	0.376	0.279	0.210	0.159	0.095
8	0.677	0.627	0.582	0.540	0.502	0.467	0.434	0.404	0.376	0.351	0.327	0.233	0.168	0.123	0.068
9	0.645	0.592	0.543	0.500	0.460	0.424	0.391	0.361	0.333	0.308	0.284	0.194	0.134	0.094	0.048
10	0.614	0.558	0.508	0.463	0.422	0.386	0.352	0.322	0.295	0.270	0.247	0.162	0.107	0.073	0.035
11	0.585	0.527	0.475	0.429	0.388	0.350	0.317	0.287	0.261	0.237	0.215	0.135	0.086	0.056	0.025
12	0.557	0.497	0.444	0.397	0.356	0.319	0.286	0.257	0.231	0.208	0.187	0.112	0.069	0.043	0.018
13	0.530	0.469	0.415	0.368	0.326	0.290	0.258	0.229	0.204	0.182	0.163	0.093	0.055	0.033	0.013
14	0.505	0.442	0.388	0.340	0.299	0.263	0.232	0.205	0.181	0.160	0.141	0.078	0.044	0.025	0.009
15	0.481	0.417	0.362	0.315	0.275	0.239	0.209	0.183	0.160	0.140	0.123	0.065	0.035	0.020	0.006
16	0.458	0.394	0.339	0.292	0.252	0.218	0.188	0.163	0.142	0.123	0.107	0.054	0.028	0.015	0.005
17	0.436	0.371	0.317	0.270	0.231	0.198	0.170	0.146	0.125	0.108	0.093	0.045	0.023	0.012	0.003
18	0.416	0.350	0.296	0.250	0.212	0.180	0.153	0.130	0.111	0.095	0.081	0.038	0.018	0.009	0.002
19	0.396	0.331	0.277	0.232	0.194	0.164	0.138	0.116	0.098	0.083	0.070	0.031	0.014	0.007	0.002
20	0.377	0.312	0.258	0.215	0.178	0.149	0.124	0.104	0.087	0.073	0.061	0.026	0.012	0.005	0.001
21	0.359	0.294	0.242	0.199	0.164	0.135	0.112	0.093	0.077	0.064	0.053	0.022	0.009	0.004	0.001
22	0.342	0.278	0.226	0.184	0.150	0.123	0.101	0.083	0.068	0.056	0.046	0.018	0.007	0.003	0.001
23	0.326	0.262	0.211	0.170	0.138	0.112	0.091	0.074	0.060	0.049	0.040	0.015	0.006	0.002	—
24	0.310	0.247	0.197	0.158	0.126	0.102	0.082	0.066	0.053	0.043	0.035	0.013	0.005	0.002	—
25	0.295	0.233	0.184	0.146	0.116	0.092	0.074	0.059	0.047	0.038	0.030	0.010	0.004	0.001	—
30	0.231	0.174	0.131	0.099	0.075	0.057	0.044	0.033	0.026	0.020	0.015	0.004	0.001	—	—
35	0.181	0.130	0.094	0.068	0.049	0.036	0.026	0.019	0.014	0.010	0.008	0.002	—	—	—
40	0.142	0.097	0.067	0.046	0.032	0.022	0.015	0.011	0.008	0.005	0.004	0.001	—	—	—
45	0.111	0.073	0.048	0.031	0.021	0.014	0.009	0.006	0.004	0.003	0.002	—	—	—	—
50	0.087	0.054	0.034	0.021	0.013	0.009	0.005	0.003	0.002	0.001	0.001	—	—	—	—

$$P = F_n(1 + r)^{-n}$$

Table 2 Present value of an annuity of $1 a period for n periods, received or paid as a series of lump sums at the end of individual periods (discounted once each period for n periods)

n	5%	6%	7%	8%	9%	10%	11%	12%	13%	14%	15%	20%	25%	30%	40%
1	0.952	0.943	0.935	0.926	0.917	0.909	0.901	0.893	0.885	0.877	0.870	0.833	0.800	0.769	0.714
2	1.859	1.833	1.808	1.783	1.759	1.736	1.713	1.690	1.668	1.647	1.626	1.528	1.440	1.361	1.224
3	2.723	2.673	2.624	2.577	2.531	2.487	2.444	2.402	2.361	2.322	2.283	2.106	1.952	1.816	1.589
4	3.546	3.465	3.387	3.312	3.240	3.170	3.102	3.037	2.974	2.914	2.855	2.589	2.362	2.166	1.849
5	4.329	4.212	4.100	3.993	3.890	3.791	3.696	3.605	3.517	3.433	3.352	2.991	2.689	2.436	2.035
6	5.076	4.917	4.767	4.623	4.486	4.355	4.231	4.111	3.998	3.889	3.784	3.326	2.951	2.643	2.168
7	5.786	5.582	5.389	5.206	5.033	4.868	4.712	4.564	4.423	4.288	4.160	3.605	3.161	2.802	2.263
8	6.463	6.210	5.971	5.747	5.535	5.335	5.146	4.968	4.799	4.639	4.487	3.837	3.329	2.925	2.331
9	7.108	6.802	6.515	6.247	5.995	5.759	5.537	5.328	5.132	4.946	4.772	4.031	3.463	3.019	2.379
10	7.722	7.360	7.024	6.710	6.418	6.145	5.889	5.650	5.426	5.216	5.019	4.192	3.571	3.092	2.414
11	8.306	7.887	7.499	7.139	6.805	6.495	6.207	5.938	5.687	5.453	5.234	4.327	3.656	3.147	2.438
12	8.863	8.384	7.943	7.536	7.161	6.814	6.492	6.194	5.918	5.660	5.421	4.439	3.725	3.190	2.456
13	9.394	8.853	8.358	7.904	7.487	7.103	6.750	6.424	6.122	5.842	5.583	4.533	3.780	3.223	2.468
14	9.899	9.295	8.745	8.244	7.786	7.367	6.982	6.628	6.302	6.002	5.724	4.611	3.824	3.249	2.477
15	10.380	9.712	9.108	8.559	8.061	7.606	7.191	6.811	6.462	6.142	5.847	4.675	3.859	3.268	2.484
16	10.838	10.106	9.447	8.851	8.313	7.824	7.379	6.974	6.604	6.265	5.954	4.730	3.887	3.283	2.489
17	11.274	10.477	9.763	9.122	8.544	8.022	7.549	7.120	6.729	6.373	6.047	4.775	3.910	3.295	2.492
18	11.690	10.828	10.059	9.372	8.756	8.201	7.702	7.250	6.840	6.467	6.128	4.812	3.928	3.304	2.494
19	12.085	11.158	10.336	9.604	8.950	8.365	7.839	7.366	6.938	6.550	6.198	4.844	3.942	3.311	2.496
20	12.462	11.470	10.594	9.818	9.129	8.514	7.963	7.469	7.025	6.623	6.259	4.870	3.954	3.316	2.497
21	12.821	11.764	10.836	10.017	9.292	8.649	8.075	7.562	7.102	6.687	6.312	4.891	3.963	3.320	2.498
22	13.163	12.042	11.061	10.201	9.442	8.772	8.176	7.645	7.170	6.743	6.359	4.909	3.970	3.323	2.498
23	13.489	12.303	11.272	10.371	9.580	8.883	8.266	7.718	7.230	6.792	6.399	4.925	3.976	3.325	2.499
24	13.799	12.550	11.469	10.529	9.707	8.985	8.348	7.784	7.283	6.835	6.434	4.937	3.981	3.327	2.499
25	14.094	12.783	11.654	10.675	9.823	9.077	8.422	7.843	7.330	6.873	6.464	4.948	3.985	3.329	2.499
30	15.372	13.765	12.409	11.258	10.274	9.427	8.694	8.055	7.496	7.003	6.566	4.979	3.995	3.332	2.500
35	16.374	14.498	12.948	11.655	10.567	9.644	8.855	8.176	7.586	7.070	6.617	4.992	3.998	3.333	2.500
40	17.159	15.046	13.332	11.925	10.757	9.779	8.951	8.244	7.634	7.105	6.642	4.997	3.999	3.333	2.500
45	17.774	15.456	13.606	12.108	10.881	9.863	9.008	8.283	7.661	7.123	6.654	4.999	4.000	3.333	2.500
50	18.256	15.762	13.801	12.233	10.962	9.915	9.042	8.305	7.675	7.133	6.661	4.999	4.000	3.333	2.500

$$P = A\left[\frac{1-(1+r)^{-n}}{r}\right]$$

The same figure can be derived in a different way. A 10-year annuity starting 5 years from now is the same as a 14-year annuity minus the first four payments. The multiplier in Table 2 for 14 years at 8 percent is 8.244 and the multiplier for 4 years is 3.312. The appropriate multiplier, therefore, is:

$$8.244 - 3.312 = 4.932$$

Multiplying this by the $10,000 annuity produces a present value of $49,320, which differs only by an insignificant rounding error from the answer we derived earlier.

Finding equivalent annuities

It is sometimes useful to find an annuity that is equivalent to a given present sum. This is a simple arithmetic operation, once the present sum, the number of future annual cash payments or receipts, and the interest rate are known. The formula for the present value of an annuity can be expressed as:

Present value = Table 2 multiplier × Annual cash flow

Turning this equation around, we find:

Annual cash flow = Present value ÷ Table 2 multiplier

The 10-year annuity that is equivalent at 8 percent interest to a present sum of $100,000 is:

Annual cash flow = $100,000/6.710 = $14,903

In other words, anyone who wants to buy a 10-year annuity of $14,903 a year in an 8 percent market will have to pay $100,000 for it.

Using table 2 with shorter compounding intervals

Table 2 can be used in conjunction with compounding intervals shorter than one year, but only if the cash flows are received or paid in equal amounts at the end of each compounding interval. For example, if the compounding interval is a quarter year and if cash is to be received or paid in equal quarterly amounts at the end of each quarter, the discount factor should be taken from the column of Table 2 representing one fourth of the nominal interest rate and the row for four times the number of years in the annuity. The multiplier to be used to determine the present value of an annuity of $1,000 a quarter for 40 quarters ($4,000 a year for 10 years, received in quarterly installments) at a nominal rate of 20 percent a year (5 percent a quarter) is 17.159 (from the 40-period row of the 5 percent column in Table 2). The present value of this annuity therefore is $1,000 × 17.159 = $17,159.

If the cash flows occur once a year but interest is to be compounded more frequently than once a year, Table 2 can't be used.

Appendix B
Solutions to independent study problems

Chapter 1

1–1. One effect of closing the Atlanta branch might be to lose some clients or some client assignments. Another effect might be to increase (or decrease) the costs of serving individual client accounts.

In the first case, the decision presumably hinges on the profitability of the work done for the client assignments which would be lost; the decision therefore would in effect be a decision whether to perform this work. In the second case, the problem is essentially one of choosing a method of service delivery: Management must take into consideration the effects on costs in New York and Chicago as well as those in Atlanta. In each case the focus is on the activities being performed rather than on the organization unit performing them.

The relevant data would include data on revenues from the branch and from each client, the specific costs of serving each client, the costs of operating the branch itself, and estimates of the effects of closing the branch on revenues and costs of the other two offices.

1–2. For external financial reporting, Marquard Associates need only follow generally accepted accounting principles, thereby making appropriate classifications of assets, liabilities, and owners' equities on a firm-wide basis. For managerial planning and control, however, the firm will need to develop estimates of costs and profitability by client or by responsibility. These kinds of segmentation are seldom called for in external financial reports.

The new controller, if one is hired, presumably would redesign the firm's system of recording costs and revenues so that they could be segmented and reported on activity and responsibility bases, would provide advice and technical assistance to the partners on questions of financial planning, and would prepare periodic performance reports for review by the partners.

The data classified by activity (client and assignment) would be used in future bidding and job acceptance decisions; they might also be used in some cases to renegotiate fees on particularly costly assignments. The data classified by responsibility would be compared with the budgetary plan or with other performance standards.

1–3. Steering control information might consist of advance booking data on individual flights and on individual origin/destination pairs. These data, combined with similar historical information might be used to signal the need to expand or curtail individual portions of the service, to discontinue service at some airports altogether, or to expand the size of ground crews in some locations.

Other information that might serve steering control purposes would be data on the costs and revenues of individual flights, individual origin/destination pairs, and individual origin or destination points; data on operating statistics such as fuel consumption, maintenance cost, on-ground costs in comparison to plan, and maintenance turn-around time in Chicago.

Scorecard information would consist largely of comparisons, by responsibility, of actual costs and revenues with the amounts budgeted, perhaps adjusted for variations in external conditions.

Chapter 2

2–1. The new ventures make the enterprise more complex. Management will need control information by department (president's office, sales and controller's office), by product line (glue and findings), and by customer group (shoe trade and furniture manufacturers). Which of these segments deserves more emphasis? Which of them deserves less, or even deserves to be dropped? Which of the department heads is performing well? Which one is performing poorly?

One student provided the following additional account codes to accumulate data management might use to try to answer these questions:

President's office	100
Sales department	200
Sales manager	210
Shoe trades—general	220
Shoe trades—glue	221
Shoe trades—findings	222
Furniture trades—general	230
Furniture trades—glue	231
Controller's office	300

The object-of-expenditure accounts should also be reviewed to see whether they will provide the amount of detail management will need.

2–2. *a.* Overhead rate = $900,000/100,000 = $9 a direct labor hour.
  b. Cost of job No. 423:

Materials	$ 800
Labor	400
Overhead: 60 × $9	540
Total	$1,740

2–3. The amount to be charged to the job is 41 hours at $8 an hour, or $328. The overtime premium is a function of the total load on the production facilities. It is not specifically related to job M227.

An economist might suggest that the entire 41 hours should be imputed a cost of $12 an hour, on the grounds that the company could have avoided 41 hours of overtime premium by not doing this job. In other words, doing job M227 caused the company to spend 41 × $12 = $492. This is not the kind of cost calculation that is made to support routine entries in the job cost sheets, however.

Chapter 3

3–1. *a.*

Materials (21,000 × $0.66)	$13,860
Materials returned (800 × $0.66)	(528)
Labor (2,000 × $6.68)	13,360
Overhead	8,000
Total	$34,692

$$\text{Unit cost} = \frac{\$34,692}{9,800} = \$3.54$$

b. Work-in-Process   35,220
    Materials Inventory   13,860
    Wages Payable   13,360
    Factory Overhead Absorbed   8,000

    Materials Inventory   528
    Work-in-Process   528

    Finished Goods   34,692
    Work-in-Process   34,692

3–2. a.

Material and Supplies		
Bal. 12,650	(2)	7,250
(1) 4,500		
Bal. 9,900		

Work-in-Process		
Bal. 8,320	(6)	12,650
(2) 6,320		
(3) 3,300		
(5) 4,950		
Bal. 10,240		

Accrued Payroll		
	(3)	7,780

Finished Goods		
Bal. 11,100	(8)	14,500
(6) 12,650		
Bal. 9,250		

Accounts Payable		
	(1)	4,500
	(4a)	2,700
	(4b)	1,835

Cost of Goods Sold		
(8) 14,500		

Indirect Materials		
(2) 930		

Indirect Labor		
(3) 1,880		

Other Factory Overhead		
(4a) 2,700		

Sell. and Admin. Salaries		
(3) 2,600		

Other Sell. and Adm. Exp.		
(4b) 1,835		

Factory Overhead Absorbed		
	(5)	4,950

Accounts Receivable		
(7) 19,350		

Sales Revenue		
	(7)	19,350

b. Inventory balances: see T-accounts in solution to (a).

    Overhead over- or underabsorbed:
      Actual overhead:
        Indirect materials . . . . $ 930
        Indirect labor   1,880
        Other factory overhead   2,700
          Total factory overhead   5,510
        Overhead absorbed   4,950
          Overhead underabsorbed . . . . $ 560

c.

ACE APPLIANCE COMPANY
Statement of Income
For the Month Ended October 31

Sales		$19,350
Cost of goods sold (Schedule A)		15,060
Gross margin		4,290
Selling and administrative expense		4,435
Net income (loss)		$ (145)

Schedule A: Cost of Goods Sold

Direct materials		$ 6,320
Direct labor		3,300
Factory overhead absorbed		4,950
Total factory costs charged to production		14,570
Less: Increase in work in process:		
Work in process, October 31	$10,240	
Work in process, October 1	8,320	(1,920)
Cost of goods finished		12,650
Add: Decrease in finished goods:		
Finished goods, October 1	11,100	
Finished goods, October 31	9,250	1,850
Cost of goods sold		14,500
Add: Underabsorbed overhead		560
Cost of goods sold (adjusted)		$15,060

Chapter 4

4-1.

Output Rate	Average Total Cost	Average Fixed Cost	Average Variable Cost	Marginal Cost
1	$11.00	$10.00	$1.00	$1.00
2	6.00	5.00	1.00	1.00
3	4.33	3.33	1.00	1.00
4	3.50	2.50	1.00	1.00
5	3.00	2.00	1.00	1.00
6	2.67	1.67	1.00	1.00
7	2.43	1.43	1.00	1.00
8	2.25	1.25	1.00	1.00
9	2.22	1.11	1.11	2.00
10	2.30	1.00	1.30	3.00

4-2. Differential cost is the effect of the decision on total cost:

Total cost if the service is provided: 25 × $14,000	$350,000
Total cost if the service is not provided: 10 × $15,500	155,000
Differential cost	$195,000

The proposal should be approved.

4-3. The only relevant figure is opportunity cost, reflecting the cash flows Ms. Smith will receive in the future. None of the past prices is relevant to this decision because Ms. Smith can do nothing now to change them. The $6 figure was an opportunity cost in

19x5. Her decision not to sell then was the same as a decision to buy 200 shares at that price at that time. It no longer has any more relevance, however, than the $15 and $20 historical purchase prices. Even the $8 figure has no relevance because the $10 tender offer makes that the effective floor under the market price—it can't go lower as long as the tender offer is in effect, and it will go higher only if enough shareholders believe that the stock is worth more than $10.

4–4.

	Make No Change	Emphasize Product A	Emphasize Product B
Contribution margin:			
Product A @ $3	$ 60,000	$ 72,000	$ 45,000
Product B @ $5	50,000	45,000	70,000
Total	110,000	117,000	115,000
Selling and administrative costs	20,000	18,000	24,000
Fixed manufacturing overhead	60,000	60,000	60,000
Income before taxes	$ 30,000	$ 39,000	$ 31,000

The emphasis on product A should be increased, despite its lower unit contribution margin.

4–5.

	Part 104	Part 173	Part 221
Incremental manufacturing costs:			
Direct materials	$216	$ 460	$110
Direct labor	240	780	240
Factory overhead:			
Indirect labor (20%)*	48	156	48
Indirect materials (5%)*	12	39	12
Service charges (5%)*	12	39	12
Total	528	1,474	422
Incremental purchasing costs:			
Purchase price	480	1,400	400
Purchasing and handling	100	100	100
Total	580	1,500	500
Advantage of manufacturing	$ 52	$ 26	$ 78

* These are the rates of increase as direct labor cost goes from $10,000 to $11,500 and from $11,500 to $13,000. For example, indirect labor goes up by $300 for a $1,500 increase in direct labor cost, an average of 20 percent.

In each case, manufacturing is cheaper than purchasing. The company should continue to manufacture all three of these parts, at least for the time being.

Chapter 5

5-1.   *a.*

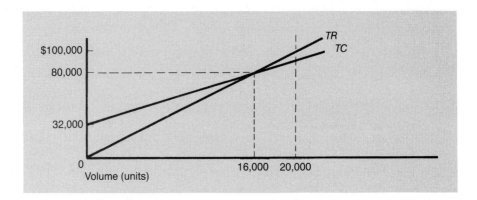

b.   Break-even point: $32,000/($5 − $3) = 16,000 units
Margin of safety: 20,000 − 16,000 = 4,000 units

Anticipated income before taxes:

Revenues at $5	$100,000
Variable costs at $3	60,000
Fixed costs	32,000
Income before taxes	$ 8,000

c.   (1)   Break-even point: $32,000/($5.50 − $3) = 12,800 units
Margin of safety: 18,000 − 12,800 = 5,200 units

Anticipated income before taxes:

Revenues at $5.50	$99,000
Variable costs at $3	54,000
Fixed costs	32,000
Income before taxes	$13,000

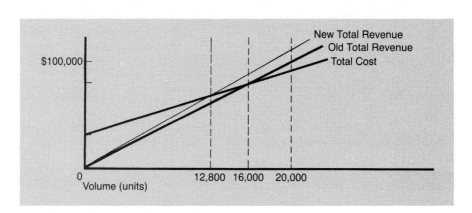

(2)   The effect of the price increase is to increase the spread between total cost
and total revenue at any given volume. When volume is measured in physical

units, as it is in this case, this increased spread is reflected in the profit-volume chart as a steeper slope for the total revenue line.

(3) Profit target: 1.1 × $8,000 .... $ 8,800
     Total fixed costs 32,000
           Needed contribution margin $40,800

           Crossover volume = $40,800/$2.50 = 16,320 units

(4) The increase in unit contribution margin decreases risk, while the decrease in volume increases it. Since the margin of safety increases, presumably overall risk is decreased.

d. (1) Break-even point: $36,000/($4.60 − $3) = 22,500 units

    (2) Profit target: 1.1 × $8,000 .... $ 8,800
         Total fixed cost 36,000
               Needed contribution margin $44,800

               Crossover point = $44,800/$1.60 = 28,000 units

    (3) Both the decrease in unit contribution margin and the increase in fixed costs serve to increase risk; with no information on anticipated volume we can't judge the effect on the margin of safety. The crossover point requires a 40 percent increase in unit sales, however, and this would require a very high price elasticity. Risk therefore would probably increase substantially if the proposal were adopted.

5–2.   a.

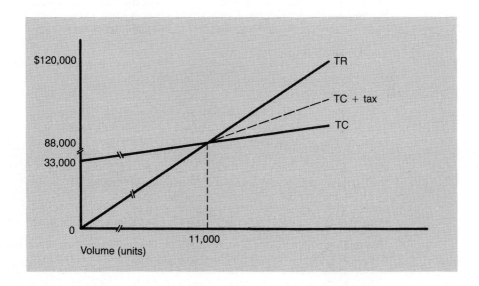

b. $6,300 = (1 − 0.4)($8 − $5)V − (1 − 0.4)($33,000)

                V = $26,100/$1.80 = 14,500 units

c. $10,800/3 = (1 − 0.4)($8 − $5)V − (1 − 0.4)($33,000)

                V = $23,400/$1.80 = 13,000 units

5-3. *a.* The first step is to calculate the average contribution margin at the assumed mix:

	Units	Revenue	Contribution Margin	Average
Product A	30,000	$150,000	$60,000	
Product B	40,000	100,000	30,000	
Total		$250,000	$90,000	90/250 = 36 percent

The *break-even sales volume* is obtained by dividing this average into the fixed costs:

$$\$72,000/0.36 = \$200,000$$

Margin of safety:
Actual sales:
Product A: 30,000 × $5	$150,000
Product B: 40,000 × $2.50	100,000
Total sales	$250,000
Break-even volume	200,000
Margin of safety	$ 50,000

b.

	Break-even Dollars	Break-even Units
Product A	$36,000/0.4 = $ 90,000	18,000
Product B	36,000/0.3 = 120,000	48,000
Total	$210,000	66,000

The total of these break-even volumes differs from the break-even volume calculated in *a* because the product mix if each product is at its break-even volume is different from the present mix, which was used to calculate the break-even volume in *a*. The average contribution margin at this mix is 32.7 percent, rather than the 36 percent we calculated in *a*.

c.

	Sales Revenue	Contribution Margin
Product A	40,000 × $5 = $200,000	× 0.4 = $ 80,000
Product B	32,000 × $2.50 = 80,000	× 0.3 = 24,000
Total	$280,000	$104,000

Average contribution margin ratio = $104,000/$280,000 = 37.14%
Total fixed cost = $72,000 + $9,700 = $81,700
Break-even volume = $81,700/0.3714 = $219,962
Margin of safety = $280,000 − $219,962 = $60,038

The increase in fixed costs increases risk, but the mix has gotten richer and the margin of safety has increased. Presumably overall risk has decreased:

	Now	Proposed
Contribution margin	$90,000	$104,000
Fixed costs	72,000	81,700
Income before tax	$18,000	$ 22,300

Both the change in income before taxes and the change in riskiness point toward the acceptance of this proposal.

5-4.   *a.*

Probability	.1	.2	.3	.2	.15	.05	
No. Demanded	10	11	12	13	14	15	
No. Produced							Expected Value
10	10	10	10	10	10	10	10.0
11	8	11	11	11	11	11	10.7
12	6	9	12	12	12	12	10.8
13	4	7	10	13	13	13	10.0
14	2	5	8	11	14	14	8.6
15	0	3	6	9	12	15	6.75

b. Expected value is maximized at a volume of 12 units.

c. The maximum possible gain is associated with production of 15 units. The minimum possible loss is associated with production of 10 units. Although no actual loss takes place, this is the best solution in the worst possible state of nature, and this is what this decision rule means.

5-5.   *a.*

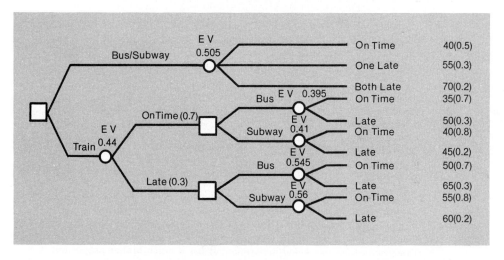

b. The expected values have been entered above the event nodes in the decision tree. Ms. Green can minimize her travel time by taking the train and then the bus. The bus is better than the subway whether the train is late or on time.

c. To answer this, tabulate the possible times on the train/bus combination, one for each possible branch:

Time (minutes)	Probability	Cumulative Probability
35	.7 × .7 = .49	0.49
50	.7 × .3 = .21	0.70
50	.3 × .7 = .21	0.91
65	.3 × .3 = .09	1.00

If she leaves home just before 8:10, she will reach the office on time 91 percent of the time.

Chapter 6

6–1. *a.* Full costing overhead rates:

Department A: $25,000/5,000 = $5 a direct labor hour
Department B: $60,000/10,000 = $6 a pound

Job order costs:

	Job 1	Job 2
Direct materials	$2,400	$ 4,800
Direct labor:		
Department A	1,620	900
Department B	420	280
Overhead:		
Department A at $5	900	500
Department B at $6	2,880	9,000
Total	8,220	15,480
Unit cost	$13.70	$15.48

b. Variable costing overhead rates:

Department A: $15,000/5,000 = $3 a direct labor hour
Department B: $20,000/10,000 = $2 a pound

Job order costs:

	Job 1	Job 2
Direct materials	$2,400	$4,800
Direct labor:		
Department A	1,620	900
Department B	420	280
Overhead:		
Department A at $3	540	300
Department B at $2	960	3,000
Total	5,940	9,280
Unit cost	$9.90	$9.28

c. Variable unit cost of job 2 is less than that of job 1; full cost was greater for job 2 than for job 1. The main reason is that job 2 used much more of department B's capacity than job 1 and department B has a much higher proportion of fixed costs than department A. Total profit is thus much more sensitive to variations in sales of product Y (job 2) than to variations in sales of product X.

6–2. *a.*

	1st Quarter	2d Quarter
Sales	$300,000	$450,000
Cost of goods sold	220,000	330,000
Gross margin	80,000	120,000
Less:		
Selling and administrative expenses	25,000	27,000
Underabsorbed overhead	—	36,000
Total deductions	25,000	63,000
Income before taxes	55,000	57,000
Ending inventory	$110,000	$ 44,000

b.

	1st Quarter	2d Quarter
Sales	$300,000	$450,000
Cost of goods sold	100,000	150,000
Gross margin	200,000	300,000
Less:		
Selling and administrative expenses	25,000	27,000
Fixed overhead	180,000	180,000
Total deductions	205,000	207,000
Income (loss) before taxes	(5,000)	93,000
Ending inventory	$ 50,000	$ 20,000

c.

	Full Costing	Variable Costing
Sales	$450,000	$450,000
Cost of goods sold	330,000	150,000
Gross margin	120,000	300,000
Less:		
Selling and administrative expenses	27,000	27,000
Fixed costs	—	180,000
Total deductions	27,000	207,000
Income before taxes	93,000	93,000
Ending inventory	$110,000	$ 50,000

Chapter 7

7–1.

a.   Dept. S charging rate $= \dfrac{\$2,000}{20,000} + \$0.20 = \$0.30/\text{Service unit}$

Component of departmental overhead rates:

Dept. 1: $1,000 \times \$0.30/10,000$ .... $0.03/direct labor hour
Dept. 2: $5,000 \times \$0.30/ 8,000$ .... $0.1875/direct labor hour
Dept. 3: $8,000 \times \$0.30/20,000$ $0.12/machine-hour
Dept. 4: $6,000 \times \$0.30/15,000$ .... $0.12/direct labor hour

Cost of S service included in cost of 1,000 units of product A:

Dept. 1: $\$0.03 \times 10$ .... $ 0.30
Dept. 2: $\$0.1875 \times 20$ 3.75
Dept. 3: $\$0.12 \times 100$ 12.00
Dept. 4: $\$0.12 \times 5$ 0.60
    Total $16.65

b.   Cost of S service included in cost of 1,000 units of product A under variable costing:

Dept. 1: No department S cost because departmental
        consumption of S service is fixed .... —
Dept. 2: $\$0.20 \times \frac{5}{8} \times 20$ .... $ 2.50
Dept. 3: $\$0.20 \times \frac{8}{20} \times 100$ 8.00
Dept. 4: $\$0.20 \times \frac{6}{15} \times 5$ 0.40
    Total $10.90

7-2.   *a.*   Step 1:   Allocate building costs ($5,000):

Office	Storeroom	Maintenance	Able	Baker
750	500	250	2,000	1,500

Step 2:   Allocate office costs, including share of building costs ($6,370 + $750). Hours spent in building and office departments should not be included in the allocation base because the building department's costs have already been allocated and the office department can't allocate costs to itself. The allocation base therefore is 8,900 labor hours, and the allocation is:

Storeroom	Maintenance	Able	Baker
240	400	4,480	2,000

Step 3:   Allocate storeroom costs ($2,260 + $500 + $240):

Maintenance	Able	Baker
150	1,050	1,800

Step 4.   Allocate maintenance costs ($6,000 + $250 + $400 + $150). Only 400 maintenance hours enter into the calculation. The 10 hours used in the office must be ignored because that department's costs have already been allocated. The allocation is:

Able	Baker
2,550	4,250

The cost distribution sheet now shows the following:

	Building	Office	Store-room	Mainte-nance	Able	Baker
Direct overhead	$ 5,000	$ 6,370	$ 2,260	$ 6,000	$ 2,770	$ 3,100
Allocations:						
Building	(5,000)	750	500	250	2,000	1,500
Office		(7,120)	240	400	4,480	2,000
Storeroom			(3,000)	150	1,050	1,800
Maintenance				(6,800)	2,550	4,250
Total					$12,850	$12,650
Normal volume (Direct labor hours)					5,000	2,000
Overhead rate					$2.57	$6.325

b.

	Able	Baker	Service
Direct overhead	$2,770	$3,100	$19,630
Direct labor hours	5,000	2,000	7,000
Overhead rate	$0.554	$1.55	$2.804

c.

	Job 123	Job 321
Allocation method:		
Able at $2.57 an hour	$12.85	$ 5.14
Baker at $6.325 an hour	12.65	31.62
Total	$25.50	$36.76

Direct apportionment:

Able at $0.554 an hour	$ 2.77	$ 1.11
Baker at $1.55 an hour	3.10	7.75
Service at $2.804 an hour	19.63	19.63
Total	$25.50	$28.49

7-3.   *a.*   Dept. A: $\dfrac{\$12,000}{6,000 \text{ units}} = \$2/\text{unit}$

Dept. B: $\dfrac{\$18,000}{8,000 \text{ units}} = \$2.25/\text{unit}$

Dept. C: $\dfrac{\$20,000}{12,000 \text{ units}} = \$1.67/\text{unit}$

b.

	Dept. A	Dept. B	Dept. C	Production
Direct charges	$12,000	$18,000	$20,000	xxx
Allocations:				
Service dept. A	(12,000)	1,800	1,200	$ 9,000
Service dept. B		(19,800)	2,949	16,851
Service dept. C			(24,149)	24,149

Charging rates:
   Department A: $12,000/8,000 = $1.50/service unit
   Department B: $19,800/9,400 = $2.1064/service unit
   Department C: $24,149/12,000 = $2.0124/service unit

c.   Dept. A = $2.0788/unit
   Dept. B = $2.2146/unit
   Dept. C = $1.6510/unit

Computations:

$$\text{Rate}_A = \frac{\$12,000 + 600 \times \text{Rate}_B + 2,000 \times \text{Rate}_C}{8,000} \tag{1}$$

$$\text{Rate}_B = \frac{\$18,000 + 1,200 \times \text{Rate}_A + 1,000 \times \text{Rate}_C}{10,000} \tag{2}$$

$$\text{Rate}_C = \frac{\$20,000 + 800 \times \text{Rate}_A + 1,400 \times \text{Rate}_B}{15,000} \tag{3}$$

$$8,000 \ \text{Rate}_A = 12,000 + 600 \times \text{Rate}_B + 2,000 \times \text{Rate}_C \tag{1a}$$
$$\text{Rate}_A = 1.5 + 0.075 \ \text{Rate}_B + 0.25 \ \text{Rate}_C \tag{1b}$$

Substituting (1*b*) in equations (2) and (3):

$$10,000 \ \text{Rate}_B = 18,000 + (1,800 + 90 \ \text{Rate}_B + 300 \ \text{Rate}_C) + 1,000 \ \text{Rate}_C$$
$$9,910 \ \text{Rate}_B = 19,800 + 1,300 \ \text{Rate}_C \tag{2a}$$

$$15,000 \ \text{Rate}_C = 20,000 + (1,200 + 60 \ \text{Rate}_B + 200 \ \text{Rate}_C) + 1,400 \ \text{Rate}_B$$
$$14,800 \ \text{Rate}_C = 21,200 + 1,460 \ \text{Rate}_B \tag{3a}$$

Solving (2*a*) for Rate$_B$:

$$\text{Rate}_B = \frac{19,800}{9,910} + \frac{1,300}{9,910} \ \text{Rate}_C$$

Substituting in (3a):

$$14,800\ \text{Rate}_C = \$21,200 + \frac{1,460 \times 19,800}{9,910} + \frac{1,460 \times 1,300}{9,910}\ \text{Rate}_C$$
$$\text{Rate}_C = \$1.6510/\text{unit}$$

Substituting this in (2a):

$$9,910\ \text{Rate}_B = 19,800 + (1,300 \times \$1.6510)$$
$$\text{Rate}_B = \$2.2146/\text{unit}$$

Substituting in (1b):

$$\text{Rate}_A = \$1.5 + 0.075 \times \$2.2146 + 0.25 \times \$1.6510$$
$$\text{Rate}_A = \$2.0788/\text{unit}$$

Chapter 8

8–1. *a.*

	Division A	Division B	Division C	Total
Profit plan:				
Sales revenues	$1,000	$3,000	$2,100	$6,100
Divisional expenses:				
Cost of goods sold	650	1,650	1,260	3,560
Marketing	150	500	300	950
Administrative	150	300	200	650
Total	950	2,450	1,760	5,160
Divisional profit contribution	50	550	340	940
Headquarters expenses				400
Net income				540
Cash budget:				
Revenues	1,000	3,000	2,100	6,100
Less: Increase in receivables	10	200	50	260
Collections	990	2,800	2,050	5,840
Cost of goods sold	650	1,650	1,260	3,560
Add: Inventory increase	50	100	50	200
Purchases	700	1,750	1,310	3,760
Less: Increase in payables	15	50	80	145
Payments to suppliers	685	1,700	1,230	3,615
Division marketing costs	150	500	300	950
Division administration (expense less depreciation)	145	285	180	610
Total division disbursements	980	2,485	1,710	5,175
Division cash flow	10	315	340	665
Central administration				390
Equipment purchases				130
Dividends				350
Total head office disbursements				870
Net decrease in cash				(205)

b.

Anticipated cash balance: $290 − $205		$ 85
Minimum cash balance: 5% × $6,100		305
Cash shortage		$220

Since the company has only a $100 line of credit, the proposed plan is not financially feasible.

Chapter 9

9–1.   *a.*   Preparing a diagram like this is almost always a good way to begin problems of this sort:

b.   One way is to trace a pound of powder through to the end:

$$
\begin{aligned}
&\left.\begin{array}{ll}
\text{1 lb.} & \text{0.75 gal.}\\
\text{powder} \longrightarrow & \text{concentrate}\\[6pt]
& \text{0.75} \times \text{0.5 lb.}\\
& \text{sugar}
\end{array}\right\}
\begin{array}{l}
\text{0.75 gal.}\\
\text{liquid} = 6 \text{ pints} \times 0.98 = 5.88\\
\qquad\qquad\qquad\text{jars of}\\
\qquad\qquad\qquad\text{product}
\end{array}
\end{aligned}
$$

Powder/jar = 1 lb./5.88 = 0.170/jar
Sugar/jar = 0.375 lb./5.88 = 0.064/jar
Jars/jar = 1,005/1,000 = 1.005 jars/jar

c.   Standard materials cost:

Powder: $0.80/lb. × 0.170 . . . . $0.136
Sugar: $0.25/lb. × 0.064 . . . .   0.016
Jars: $2.40/doz. × 1.005/12 . . . .   0.201
Standard materials cost/jar . . . . $0.353 per pint jar

9–2.

Completed	10,000 × $40	$400,000
End of month inventory	1,000 × ½ × $40	20,000
		420,000
Beginning of month inventory	4,000 × ½ × $40	80,000
Standard labor cost		$340,000

9–3.   *a.*

Actual cost	85,000 × $5.10		$433,500
Standard cost:			
Product X 5,000 × $50		$250,000	
Product Y 6,000 × $25		150,000	
Total standard cost			400,000
Materials spending variance			$(33,500)
Actual quantity at standard price	85,000 × $5	425,000	
Materials price variance	$433,500 − $425,000		(8,500)
Materials usage variance	$425,000 − $400,000		(25,000)

b.   If we assume the price variance is excluded at the time of purchase, we get the following:

Materials price variance	100,000 × ($5.10 − $5.00)	$(10,000)
Materials usage variance		(25,000) as before

The difference in the price variance, of course, arises because of the difference in the amount purchased.

9–4.   *a.*   Labor rate variance:

Actual quantity at actual rate	$760	⎫ Labor rate	
Actual quantity at standard rate	720	⎭ variance	$40 U.
Materials price variance:			
Actual quantity at actual prices	$320	⎫ Materials	
Actual quantity at standard prices	300	⎭ price variance	$20 U.

Labor usage variance:
Input: Actual quantity at standard
prices $720
Output: Standard quantity at
  standard prices—
    Units finished $650
    Ending work in process   20   670

Labor usage variance $50 U.

Materials usage variance:
Input: Actual quantity at standard
prices $500
Output: Standard quantity at
  standard prices—
    Units finished $490
    Ending work in process   40   530

Materials usage variance $30 F.

b. This means that some of the work on completed products was done last month. This means that this month's performance was worse than we thought:

Materials usage variance:	
Input	$500
Output: $490 + $40 − $100	430
Materials usage variance	$ 70 Unfavorable

Labor usage variance:	
Input	$720
Output: $650 + $20 − $10	660
Labor usage variance	$ 60 Unfavorable

9–5.

Materials

Bal.	1,000	(4)	500
(3)	300		

Materials Price Variance

(3)	20		

Materials in Process —Finishing

Bal.	?		
(6)	1,140		

Materials in Process —Shaping

Bal.	100	(6)	490
(7a)	430		
Bal.	40		

Labor in Process —Shaping

Bal.	10	(6)	650
(7b)	660		
Bal.	20		

Accounts Payable

		(3)	320

Direct Materials Used —Shaping

(4)	500		
		(8)	500

Direct Labor Used —Shaping

(5b)	720		
		(9)	720

Wages Payable

		(5a)	760

Standard Direct Materials—Shaping

		(7a)	430
(8)	430		

Standard Direct Labor—Shaping

		(7b)	660
(9)	660		

Payroll Cost Summary

(5a)	760	(5b)	720
		(10)	40

Materials Usage Variance—Shaping		Labor Usage Variance—Shaping		Labor Rate Variance—Shaping	
(8)	70	(9)	60	(10)	40

Chapter 10

10–1. *a.* Actual overhead $21,700
Budgeted overhead: $12,000 + $.80 × 9,000 ...   19,200
Spending variance .... $ 2,500 Unfav.

The number of units of product is ignored in this situation, because overhead costs vary with the amount of materials used rather than with the output of the product. A meaningful performance standard for overhead cost must reflect this relationship.

b. This calls for an adjustment of the actual cost figures:

Fixed overhead: $11,800/1.02 .... $11,569
Variable overhead: $9,900/1.05   9,429
  Total $20,998

The breakdown of the spending variance is as follows:

Actual at actual prices $21,700
Actual at budgeted prices (see above) .. 20,998
  Input price variance.............. $ 702 Unfav.
Budgeted at budgeted prices 19,200
  Input usage variance ....   1,798 Unfav.

c. A fixed cost is not necessarily noncontrollable. The department head has the responsibility to supervise and coordinate the department's activities, even those that are not affected by the volume of business done. In this case, we can see the following:

Cleaning labor: Fixed, but controllable
Depreciation: Fixed, noncontrollable.
Materials handling labor: Variable, controllable.
Royalty: Variable, controllable through control of materials usage; if royalty were based on production output, it would be variable but noncontrollable.

10–2. *a.*

	Month 4			Month 5		
	Actual	Budget	Variance	Actual	Budget	Variance
Controllable:						
Nonproductive time	$ 800	$1,000	$ 200	$1,200	$ 750	$(450)
Other indirect labor	3,700	4,000	300	3,600	3,500	(100)
Operating supplies	650	600	(50)	430	450	20
Total controllable	5,150	5,600	450	5,230	4,700	(530)
Noncontrollable:						
Depreciation	2,100	2,000	(100)	2,150	2,000	(150)
Building service charges ..	770	700	(70)	730	700	(30)
Total	$8,020	$8,300	$ 280	$8,110	$7,400	$(710)

b. Only the first three overhead cost items listed are likely to be of any significance in evaluating the cost control performance of the department supervisor, and of these nonproductive time and other indirect labor have the greatest impact. Depreciation and building service charges are noncontrollable and have no bearing on managerial evaluation in this department.

c. Labor costs did not go down with decreasing volume. There are many possible reasons for this. This may merely be a time lag—management may have decided not to cut the labor force to meet the volume reduction in the hope that volume would recover quickly. This should be examined more critically if volume continues at these newer and lower levels. We cannot ignore any one month's reports, but we need to examine them in the context of a longer period of time. Even two months is likely to be too short a period for random forces to have averaged themselves out.

The other item in which the variance has increased is depreciation, and this should be labeled as noncontrollable.

10–3. *a.* Department M should be charged for department S services because those services are measurable and controllable. The best basis for the charge is actual consumption, multiplied by a predetermined rate. The full cost rate is $45,000/10,000 = $4.50 an hour. The charge for February therefore should be 1,100 × $4.50 = $4,950.

b. The variance on department M's report:

Budget	900 hours	$4,050
Actual	1,100 hours	4,950
Variance	200 hours	$ (900)

c. Budget at 8,000 hours:

8,000 × $2.50 + $20,000	$40,000
Actual	42,000
Spending variance	$(2,000)
Charge out: 8,000 × $4.50	$36,000
Actual	42,000
Total undistributed	$(6,000)

d. The variable overhead rate is $2.50. The variable charge should be 1,100 × $2.50 = $2,750. Department M's share of the fixed costs is $20,000/10 = $2,000 a month. The spending variance is:

	Actual Charge	Budgeted Charge	Variance
Variable component	$2,750	$2,250	$500 Unfavorable
Fixed component	2,000	2,000	—
Total	$4,750	$4,250	$500 Unfavorable

Chapter 11

11–1.

Actual overhead	$19,900	
Budget at actual volume:		
$10,000 + 4,200 × $2.50	20,500	
Overhead spending variance		$ 600 F.
Absorbed overhead: 4,200 × $4.50	18,900	
Overhead volume variance		1,600 U.
Total overhead variance		$1,000 U.

11–2. *a.* Because overhead costs vary with *actual* machine-hours, a three-variance system should be used:

Actual $21,750
Budget at actual hours 21,500
   Spending variance .... $ 250 U.
Budget at standard hours 22,000
   Machine efficiency variance .....   500 F.
Standard 20,000
   Volume variance ....   2,000 U.
      Total variance .... $1,750 U.

b. This now requires a two-variance analysis. The volume variance remains the same, but the spending variance is $250, and favorable:

Actual $21,750
Budget at standard hours   22,000
   Spending variance .... $ 250 F.

11-3 a.

Materials Inventory			
Bal.	11,400	(3)	6,000
(2)	5,400		
Bal.	10,800		

Matls. in Process.—Dept. I			
Bal.	2,400	(6a)	900
(8)	6,300	(6b)	3,000
		(6c)	3,600
Bal.	1,200		

Direct Materials Used—Dept. I			
(3)	6,000		
		(10)	6,000

Standard Direct Materials—Dept. I			
		(8)	6,300
(10)	6,300		

Labor in Process—Dept I			
Bal.	3,200	(6a)	4,800
(9)	31,600	(6b)	6,000
		(6c)	4,000
Bal.	2,800		

Overhead in Process—Dept. I			
Bal.	2,400	(6a)	3,600
(7)	18,300	(6b)	9,000
		(6c)	6,000
Bal.	2,100		

Direct Labor Used—Dept. I			
(4b)	28,000		
		(11)	28,000

Standard Direct Labor—Dept. I			
		(9)	31,600
(11)	31,600		

Overhead Summary—Dept. I			
(5)	25,500	(13)	23,000*
		(14)	2,500

Overhead Absorbed—Dept. II			
(15)	22,100*	(7)	18,300
		(16)	3,800

Matls. in Process—Dept. II	
(6a)	9,300
(6b)	21,000
(6c)	15,600

Payables, etc.	
(2)	5,850
(4a)	28,400
(5)	25,500

Purchase Price Variance			Payroll Cost Summary		
(2)	450		(4a)	28,400	(4b)	28,000
					(12)	400

Materials Usage Variance—Dept. I		Labor Usage Variance—Dept. I	
	(10) 300		(11) 3,600

Overhead Spending Var.—Dept. I		Labor Rate Variance—Dept. I	
(14) 2,500		(12) 400	

Ov. Lab. Eff. Var.—Dept. I		Overhead Volume Var.—Dept. I	
(13) 23,000*	(15) 22,100*	(16) 3,800	
Bal. 900			

* Budget at actual hours: $16,000 + $2 \times 3,500 = $23,000
Budget at standard hours: $16,000 + $2 \times 3,050 = $22,100

Entries (13) and (15) may be omitted, but they facilitate the breakdown of the overhead variance. Entries (4a) and (4b) may be combined as a single entry.

b.

Materials price variance	$ (450)
Labor rate variance	(400)
Materials usage variance	300
Labor usage variance	3,600
Overhead spending variance	(2,500)
Overhead labor efficiency variance	(900)
Overhead volume variance	(3,800)
Total variance	$(4,150)

Chapter 12

12–1. *a.*

ZODIAC ADVISORY SERVICES, INC.
Comparative Statement of Segment Income
For Last Month

	Counselling Services			Instructional Services		
	Actual	Budget	Over/ (Under) Budget	Actual	Budget	Over/ (Under) Budget
Revenues	$25,000	$33,000	$(8,000)	$15,000	$12,000	$3,000
Professional staff salaries	10,400	13,200	(2,800)	7,300	7,200	100
Contribution margin	14,600	19,800	(5,200)	7,700	4,800	2,900
Marketing expenses	2,000	2,100	(100)	3,200	3,100	100
Profit contribution	12,600	17,700	(5,100)	4,500	1,700	2,800
Administrative expenses	2,160	2,880	(720)	1,710	1,620	90
Income before income tax	$10,440	$14,820	$(4,380)	$ 2,790	$ 80	$2,710

ZODIAK ADVISORY SERVICES, INC.
Comparative Statement of Income
For Last Month

	Actual	Budget	Over/ (Under) Budget
Revenues	$40,000	$45,000	$(5,000)
Professional staff salaries	17,700	20,400	(2,700)
Contribution margin	22,300	24,600	(2,300)
Marketing expenses	5,200	5,200	—
Profit contribution	17,100	19,400	(2,300)
Administrative expenses	4,700	4,500	200
Income before income tax . .	$12,400	$14,900	$(2,500)

b. Budgeted for actual volume $4,500
Allocated to segments ($2,160 + $1,710) . . .   3,870
Volume variance . . . . $ 630

The appropriate solution is to treat this as a fixed cost in each segment, because the amount of corporate administrative expense is unaffected by variations in the level of segment activity. This can be accomplished by distributing the volume variance in such a way as to eliminate the variances in the amounts allocated, as in the 3rd line of the following table:

	Counselling	Instruction	Total
Budgeted allocation	$ 2,880	$1,620	$ 4,500
Actual allocation	2,160	1,710	3,870
Required increase/(decrease)	720	(90)	630
Income before tax as previously calculated	10,440	2,790	13,230
Adjusted segment income before tax	9,720	2,880	12,600
Budgeted income	14,820	80	14,900
Adjusted variance in segment income	$(5,100)	$2,800	$(2,300)

c. The total spending variance is $4,700 − $4,500 = $200, unfavorable. Distributing this in proportion to the budgeted allocations would allocate $128 to counselling and $72 to instruction. Such an allocation would serve neither a control purpose nor a decision purpose. Furthermore, it would introduce a noncontrollable element into the segment income statement, thereby weakening the usefulness of this statement as a control device. For these reasons, the allocations should not be made.

12–2. a. The first step is to separate the fixed and variable components of the cost of goods sold. Since the total cost of goods sold went up by 10 percent, the variable portion also must have gone up by 10 percent, from $290 to $319. Knowing this, we can construct the report very easily:

	Actual		Budget		Variance
Sales		$550		$500	$ 50
Variable expenses:					
Cost of goods sold	$319		$290		(29)
Sales commissions	11		10		(1)
Delivery	16	346	14	314	(2)
Contribution margin . . .		204		186	18
Product advertising		11		11	—
Profit contribution		$193		$175	$ 18

None of the fixed costs except product advertising is traceable to individual products, nor is any of the factory spending variance.

b. We start with two facts:

1. Budgeted standard factory cost totaled $350.
2. The variable portion of budgeted standard factory cost was $290.

The fixed overhead costs allocated to product A in the budget therefore must have amounted to $60. Since production of A increased by 10 percent, the amount of fixed overhead absorbed also went up by 10 percent, to $66. Other things being equal, a *favorable* volume variance of $6 should be assigned to product A if profit reporting is to be on a full-cost basis. This means that product B must have been responsible for an unfavorable volume variance amounting to $36 and that's how it should be reported.

The actual spending variance in factory costs amounted to $10. The budgeted spending variance also happened to be $10. Although allocation of these amounts provides no new managerial information, if management insists that the variance be allocated, allocating it in proportion to the budgeted allocation will do little harm—in this case it will do even less harm than usual because the actual amount allocated equals the budgeted allocation. The restructured profit contribution statement shows:

	Actual		Budget		Variance
Sales		$550		$500	$50
Variable expenses:					
Standard cost of goods sold	$385		$350		(35)
Sales commissions	11		10		(1)
Delivery	16	412	14	374	(2)
Contribution margin		138		126	12
Product advertising		11		11	—
Factory cost variances		(2)		4	6
Profit contribution		$129		$111	$18

c. Product A seems to be in good shape. Its sales are up 10 percent and so is its profit contribution. The marketing manager may even see this as evidence of market strength that ought to be exploited even more vigorously than now.

The main problem seems to be with product B. Its production and sales seem to be only 60 percent of their budgeted levels (absorption of $90 of factory overhead instead of $150). As a result, product A is assigned a much bigger share of factory variances and selling and administrative expenses. Management should devote its efforts to product B.

Chapter 13

13–1. a. Our first task is to calculate the standard materials cost of goods sold. The first step in this calculation is to find the standard materials cost of the work done during the year. The materials issued had a standard cost of $30,000, but $5,000 of this was a usage variance. Therefore, the standard materials cost of the work done was $30,000 − $5,000 = $25,000. We can adjust this for the changes in inventories to get the standard materials cost of goods sold:

Standard materials cost of work done..............	$25,000
Decrease in work-in-process	1,100
Decrease in finished goods	1,000
Standard materials cost of goods sold	$27,100

The second task is to prorate the usage variance. Assuming that materials usage variances are proportional to standard costs, the variance ratio is $5,000/$25,000 = 20 percent. Applying this ratio to ending work-in-process and finished goods inventories:

To work-in-process: $5,000 × 20%	$ 1,000
To finished goods: $7,000 × 20%	1,400
Total variance to inventories	2,400
Remainder, to cost of goods sold	$ 2,600

Since this is a FIFO system, the materials cost of goods sold includes the $900 favorable materials usage variance assigned to the January 1 inventory, and the $2,600 unfavorable variance for this year. The full calcualtion is:

Standard materials cost of goods sold	$27,100
Materials usage variance:	
From prior year	(900)
From this year	2,600
FIFO historical materials cost of goods sold	$28,800

b. The inventory variance account now has a $900 credit balance. It should have a $2,400 debit balance. The clearest way to make the adjustment is through the two following entries:

Materials Usage Variance in Inventory	900	
Cost of Goods Sold		900
To transfer the opening balance.		
Materials Usage Variance in Inventory	2,400	
Cost of Goods Sold	2,600	
Materials Usage Variance		5,000
To prorate the materials usage variance for the year.		

13–2. a. The spending variance had to be spread over actual production; none was to be assigned to idle capacity. The spending variance ratio therefore was $75,000/$1,500,000 = 5 percent, favorable. Actual spending, in other words, was 95 percent of standard overhead cost. The ending LIFO inventory was:

Beginning inventory	$220,000
Increment: $40,000 × 0.95	38,000
Ending inventory	$258,000

b. Overhead cost on the income statement:

Standard overhead cost	$1,460,000
Volume variance	300,000
Spending variance	(73,000)
Net expense	$1,687,000

c. Inventory Adjustment account:

Beginning balance	$180,000 cr.
Current increment	2,000 cr.
Ending balance	$182,000 cr.

Chapter 14

14–1.

	Department A		Department B	
	Materials	Conversion	Materials	Conversion
Cost divisors:				
Finished	90	90	85	85
Ending inventory	60	20	45	30
Moving average divisors ...	150	110	130	115
Beginning inventory	50	15	40	20
Equivalent production	100	95	90	95
Total cost	$105	$399	$450*	$570
Unit cost, this month	$1.05	$4.20	$5	$6

* Transferred from department A: 90 units × $5—the $5 is taken from the table below.

Costs to be distributed:				
In process, 6/1	$ 45	$ 41	$213	$150
Charged to department	105	399	450	570
Total	$150	$440	$663	$720
Moving average divisors, department A (from above) ..	150	110		
Moving average costs, department A	$ 1	$ 4		
FIFO unit costs, department B			$ 5	$ 6
Costs distributed:				
In process, 6/30	60	80	225	180
To department B	90	360		
To finished goods			438*	540*
Total	$150	$440	$663	$720

* Determined by subtracting ending inventory from total cost.

14–2. *a.*

	Materials		Conversion	
	With Spoilage	Without Spoilage*	With Spoilage	Without Spoilage*
Finished	82,000	87,000	82,000	87,000
Ending inventory	10,000	10,000	5,000	5,000
Moving average divisors	92,000	97,000	87,000	92,000
Beginning inventory	4,000	4,000	2,000	2,000
Equivalent production	88,000	93,000	85,000	90,000

*Spoilage = Beginning inventory (4,000) + units received (93,000) − units transferred (82,000) − ending inventory (10,000) = 5,000

The second set of divisors is not called for in instruction (*a*), but since we'll need them in (*c*) we have calculated them here for convenience.

b. In calculating current unit costs, the costs of the beginning inventory are irrelevant and the equivalent production divisors should be used.

	Total Cost	Divisor	Unit Cost
Materials	$ 81,840	88,000	$0.93
Labor	61,200	85,000	0.72
Other variable costs	15,300	85,000	0.18
Fixed conversion costs	30,600	85,000	0.36
Total	$188,940		$2.19

c. To calculate the effect of lost units, we need to calculate unit cost as if no units had been lost, and then subtract these from the figures in (b):

	Total Cost	Divisor	Unit Cost	Effect of Lost Units
Materials	$ 81,840	93,000	$0.88	$0.05
Labor	61,200	90,000	0.68	0.04
Other variable costs	15,300	90,000	0.17	0.01
Fixed conversion costs	30,600	90,000	0.34	0.02
Total	$188,940		$2.07	$0.12

d.

	Materials	Conversion	Total
Total cost to be distributed:			
In process, 1/1	$ 2,800	$ 2,346	$ 5,146
Current costs	81,840	107,100	188,940
Total cost to be distributed	$84,640	$109,446	$194,086
Divisors [from (a)]	92,000	87,000	
Moving average unit cost	$0.92	$1.258	
Costs distributed:			
To goods transferred (82,000)	$75,440	$103,156	$178,596
To goods in process, 1/31 (10,000)	9,200	6,290	15,490
Total cost distributed	$84,640	$109,446	$194,086

14–3. a.

	Actual	Performance Standard	Variance
Materials from mixing	$ 83,700	88,000 × $.945 = $ 83,160	$ (540)
Labor	59,000	85,000 × $.70 = 59,500	500
Other variable costs	13,900	85,000 × $.15 = 12,750	(1,150)
Fixed conversion costs	31,300	30,000	(1,300)
Total	$187,900	$185,410	$(2,490)

b. Current charges were based on actual input prices in problem 2 and on standard prices in this problem. The June 1 inventories were stated at actual historical input prices *and quantities* in problem 2 and at standard cost in this problem.

Chapter 15

15–1. a. Step 1. Calculate the value of the output:

Product	Unit Price	Completion Costs	Net Value per Unit	Total Value
A	$ 6.20	$0.90	$5.30	$ 5,300
B	3.80	0.80	3.00	6,000
C	10.00	2.52	7.48	18,700
Total				$30,000

Step 2. Calculate the net cost:

$$\text{Cost } \$21,500 - \text{By-product value } \$500 = \$21,000$$

Step 3. Calculate the cost/value ratio:

$$\$21,000/30,000 = 70 \text{ percent}$$

Step 4. Allocate the joint costs:

Product	Value	70 Percent	Joint Cost per Unit	Completion Cost per Unit	Total Unit Cost
A	$ 5,300	$ 3,710	$3.71	$0.90	$4.61
B	6,000	4,200	2.10	0.80	2.90
C	18,700	13,090	5.236	2.52	7.756

Cost of by-product D is $0.05. Deducting this value from the joint costs is equivalent to assigning 5 cents of the costs to each unit of the by-product.

b. Total number of physical units (excluding by-product): 5,500

$$\text{Unit cost: } \$21,000/5,500 = \$3.82 \text{ a unit.}$$

This would not be acceptable because it would indicate that product B was produced at a loss. Since the production decision is based on total cost and total revenue, it is impossible to lose money on any one without losing money on them all as long as forecasted conditions materialize.

15–2. Overall profit contribution:

Revenues: $6,200 + $7,600 + $25,000 .... $38,800
Expenses: $21,500 + $900 + $1,600 + $6,300 − $200   30,100
    Profit contribution .... $ 8,700

Profit contribution ratio = $8,700/$38,800 = 22.42%.

	(1) Sale Value	(2) Profit Contribution at 22.42 Percent	(3) Completion Costs	(4) Allocated Joint Cost (1) − (2) − (3)	(5) Joint Cost per Unit
Product					
A	$ 6,200	$1,390	$ 900	$ 3,910	$3.910
B	7,600	1,704	1,600	4,296	2.148
C	25,000	5,605	6,300	13,095	5.238
Total ...	$38,800	$8,699	$8,800	$21,301	

These unit cost figures have no more relevance to managerial decision making than those we calculated in answer to (*a*), for the reasons cited in the chapter. Their sole advantage is that they avoid measures of the relative profitability of individual joint products that might be misleading.

15–3.

Net value, alpha = Net value, beta + Net value, gamma − Cost to process alpha
Net value of beta = Net value of delta + Value of residue − Cost to process beta
$$= 400 \times \$15 + \$200 - \$3,200 = \$3,000$$
Net value of gamma = $500 \times \$12 = \$6,000$
Net value of alpha = $\$3,000 + \$6,000 - \$5,000 = \$4,000$

15–4. *a.* The 40-cent figure was irrelevant. If management accepts the proposal, it must give up the sale of product Y—in other words, it must sacrifice the revenues from this source. These revenues measure the opportunity cost of the new product. On these grounds, the Y-Plus proposal should be rejected:

Revenue	$ 1.30
Less: Incremental processing $0.80	
Opportunity cost 0.60	1.40
Processing loss	$(0.10)

b. To get 20,000 pounds of Z, the factory will have to process 30,000 pounds of materials. Materials and variable processing costs amount to 30 cents a pound. The other calculations are:

Additional materials and variable processing	
costs: 30,000 × $0.30	$ 9,000
Additional revenues from Z: 20,000 × $0.35	7,000
Additional revenue needed from Y	2,000
Current revenues from Y	60,000
Minimum revenues needed from Y	$ 62,000
Production of Y: 100,000 + 10,000 lbs.	110,000
Average price of Y: $62,000/110,000	$0.564

If the price of Y falls as far as $0.564 a pound, the company will be no better off than it is now.

c. Since processing costs will be unaffected, the margin for the purchase of materials must come from the revenues:

	New Material	Present Material
Y:	120,000 × $0.60 = $ 72,000	$ 60,000
Z:	180,000 × $0.45 = 81,000	90,000
Total	$153,000	$150,000

This means that the company can afford to pay up to $3,000 more for the new materials, or $63,000.

The maximum price is $63,000/300,000 = $0.21 a pound.

Chapter 16

16–1.   a.

Size of Order (pounds)	Order-Based	Item-Based	Weight-Based	Total	Average per Cwt.
Less than 50	$11,776	$ 4,090	$ 1,493	$17,359	$1.240
50–199	12,197	8,410	5,568	26,175	0.501
200–499	2,524	2,280	3,968	8,772	0.236
500–999	1,682	2,400	5,973	10,055	0.180
1,000 and over	421	820	2,197	3,438	0.167
All orders	$28,600	$18,000	$19,199	$65,799	$0.366

Indivisible fixed costs aren't allocated because they aren't affected significantly by variations in the number of orders, number of items, or weight of products shipped. Selling costs aren't distributed because they relate to sales potential, not to actual order size.

b. All of the differences in unit cost come from costs that are determined by the number of orders or number of items. Weight-based costs average $19,200/180,000 = $0.107 a hundredweight in each size class.

16–2.   *Step 1. Identify all the traceable items.*   These items are sales, cost of sales, sales salaries, sales commissions, sales discounts and allowances, sales travel, regional office expenses, freight and delivery, and local advertising. The cost of goods sold can be stated either at attributable cost or at full cost, since we are concerned only with the relative profitability of the various regions. We prefer the attributable cost calculation because it provides a more complete picture of the region's contribution to the corporate well-being. Attributable factory costs consist of the variable costs (75 percent of the normal amount) and 60 percent of the fixed overhead (60 percent of 25 percent = 15 percent), a total of 90 percent of normal unit cost.

Step 2. Apply formulas for customer defaults and for divisible repetitive service functions. They are payroll, order processing, packing and shipping, credit review, cashier, and general accounting.

Step 3. Ignore the other costs. These cannot be identified clearly with individual sales regions. This is just as true of marketing management expenses as of other common expenses. Managerial time allocations say very little about attributability, particularly when the staffs are this small.

Step 4. Summarize the calculations in a table, as follows:

	Region A	Region B	Region C	Total
Sales:				
Product X	$ 10,000	$ 5,000	$ 50,000	$ 65,000
Product Y	80,000	140,000	70,000	290,000
Product Z	10,000	10,000	20,000	40,000
Total	100,000	155,000	140,000	395,000
Customer defaults	500	775	700	1,975
Discounts and allowances	1,000	2,000	4,000	7,000
Net sales	98,500	152,225	135,300	386,025
Cost of goods sold (90% of full cost):				
Product X at $3.60	7,200	3,600	36,000	46,800
Product Y at $5.40	43,200	75,600	37,800	156,000
Product Z at $ .90	4,500	4,500	9,000	18,000
Total cost of sales	54,900	83,700	82,800	221,400
Gross margin	43,600	68,525	52,500	164,625
Regional expenses:				
Sales commissions	5,000	7,750	7,000	19,750
Sales salaries	5,000	6,000	8,000	19,000
Sales travel	3,000	3,000	2,000	8,000
Regional office	4,000	4,500	5,000	13,500
Freight and delivery	2,000	2,400	1,650	6,050
Advertising	1,000	1,000	1,000	3,000
Allocated charges:				
Payroll	180	192	240	612
Order processing	1,920	2,160	3,600	7,680
Packing and shipping	1,500	1,800	3,300	6,600
Credit review	1,200	1,320	2,400	4,920
Cashier	1,000	1,100	1,500	3,600
General accounting	1,400	1,540	2,100	5,040
Total	27,200	32,762	37,790	97,752
Attributable profit	$ 16,400	$ 35,763	$ 14,710	66,873
Percent of sales	16.4%	23.1%	10.5%	
Nonattributable expenses:				
Manufacturing (10% of full cost) .				24,600
Marketing division salaries				10,000
National advertising				5,000
Other marketing				12,000
Corporate management				20,000
Total				71,600
Income (loss) before taxes				$ (4,727)

Chapter 17

17-1.   *a.*   The company's objective is to make a profit. Ignoring fixed costs, which aren't specified in the problem and would be irrelevant in any case, profit is equal to $5 for each unit of product A sold plus $8 for each unit of product B. Expressed in mathematical form, the objective function is:

$$\text{Profit} = \$5A + \$8B$$

The first constraint is that only 3,000 hours of department X time are available. Each unit of product A requires two hours in this department, and each unit of product B needs one hour. These relationships can be expressed as an inequality:

$$2A + B \leq 3,000$$

The inequality for department Y can be calculated and expressed in the same way:

$$2A + 4B \leq 6,000$$

The other constraints are that sales of neither product can exceed 2,000 units and that negative sales volumes are not admissible. We can express these constraints in two separate inequalities:

$$2,000 \geq A \geq 0$$
$$2,000 \geq B \geq 0$$

b.   Construction of the departmental constraint lines:

$$A = 0, \ B = 3,000 \qquad B = 0, \ A = 1,500 \quad (\text{Dept. X})$$
$$A = 0, \ B = 1,500 \qquad B = 0, \ A = 3,000 \quad (\text{Dept. Y})$$

Slope of the isoprofit lines:

$$A = 0, \ B = 5 \qquad B = 0, \ A = 8$$

Drawing the graph:

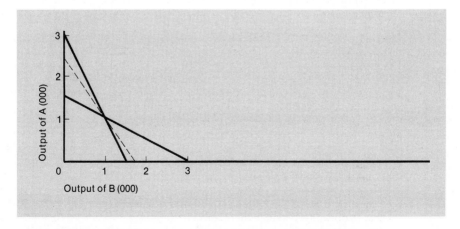

The optimal solution is to produce 1,000 units of each product, for a total contribution margin of $13,000:

Product	No. of Units	Contribution Margin Per Unit	Contribution Margin Total
A	1,000	$5	$ 5,000
B	1,000	8	8,000
Total			$13,000

An alternative approach is to start with a tentative solution (e.g., $B = 0$, $A = 1,500$, using all the capacity of department X), and then see whether profit can be improved by substituting (e.g., one unit of B can be obtained by sacrificing half a unit of A, for a profit gain of $8 - 2.50). This substitution uses up three hours of department Y's idle time, and 1,000 of these substitutions are possible. The optimal solution is as computed above.

c. If the contribution margin of product A rises beyond $16, the optimal solution will be to manufacture no product B. If it falls below $4, the optimal solution will be to manufacture no product A. Between these two values, the optimal decision will be the same.

17-2. a.

$$EOQ = \sqrt{\frac{2 \times 10,000 \times 36}{.2 \times \$2.50}} = 1,200 \text{ units}$$

b. Average inventory $= 1,200/2 = 600$ units

Carrying cost	$= 0.2 \times \$2.50 \times 600 = \$300$	
Number of orders	$= 10,000/1,200 = 8\frac{1}{3}$	
Processing costs	$= 8\frac{1}{3} \times \$36$	$= \underline{\quad 300}$
Total cost		$\$600$

c. Average usage $= 10,000/50 = 200$ units a week

Reorder level $= 3 \times 200 = 600$ units

17-3. a. The maximum usage level is 800 units a week, 200 units above the average usage during the reorder period. Therefore, we need to make calculations only for safety stocks of 200, 100, and zero units.

Carrying costs:
0 units:	$ 0
100 units $\times 0.2 \times \$2.50$	50
200 units $\times 0.2 \times \$2.50$	100

Stock-out costs:

Safety Stock	Units Short per Order Period	Probability Percent	Expected Number of Units Short	Number of Orders per Year	Stock-out Costs at $1
0..........	100	0.20	20		
	200	0.10	$\underline{20}$		
			40	$8\frac{1}{3}$	$333
100..........	100	0.10	$\overline{10}$	$8\frac{1}{3}$	83
200..........	0	—	0	—	0

The total cost is $333 with a zero safety stock, $133 with a 100-unit safety stock, and $100 with a 200-unit safety stock. In this case a 200-unit safety stock is optimal.

b. At 75 cents a unit, a 200-unit stock-out level remains optimal. Total costs at a 100-unit level would be $62.50 + $50 = $112.50, or $12.50 more than at the 200-unit level.

At 50 cents, the optimal solution would be a 100-unit safety stock (total cost $91.67). At $0.10, a zero safety stock would be appropriate (total costs only $33.33 instead of $58.33 with a 100-unit safety stock).

Chapter 18

18–1. Each of these proposals has the same average annual cash flow after the initial outlay is made ($1,750), but present value ranges from a small negative sum to + $3,310 and the internal rate of return varies from 9.7 percent to 15.6 percent:

Time	Cash Flow	10 Percent Factor	Present Value at 10 Percent	Present Value at X Percent	Internal Rate of Return
a.				*12%*	
0	−$10,000	1.000	−$10,000	−$10,000	
1–10	+ 1,750/yr.	6.145	+ 10,754	+ 9,888	
Net pres. value ...			+$ 754	−$ 112	11.7%
b.				*15%*	
0	−$10,000	1.000	−$10,000	−$10,000	
1–10	+ 1,500/yr.	6.145	+ 9,217	+ 7,529	
1–5	+ 500/yr.	3.791	+ 1,896	+ 1,676	
Net pres. value ...			+$ 1,113	−$ 795	12.9%
c.				*11%*	
0	−$10,000	1.000	−$10,000	−$10,000	
1–5	+ 1,500/yr.	3.791	+ 5,686	+ 5,544	
6–10	+ 2,000/yr.	2.354	+ 4,708	+ 4,386	
Net pres. value ...			+$ 394	−$ 70	10.8%
d.				*9%*	
0	−$10,000	1.000	−$10,000	−$10,000	
1–10	+ 1,350/yr.	6.145	+ 8,296	+ 8,665	
10	+ 4,000	0.386	+ 1,544	+ 1,688	
Net pres. value ...			−$ 160	+$ 352	9.7%
e.				*15%*	
0	−$10,000	1.000	−$10,000	−$10,000	
1–15	+ 1,750/yr.	7.606	+ 13,310	+ 10,232	
Net pres. value ...			+$ 3,310	+$ 232	
				20%	
0	−$10,000			−$10,000	
1–15	+ 1,750/yr.			+ 8,181	
Net pres. value ...				−$ 1,819	15.6%

18–2. Payback period:
a. 10,000/1,750 = 5.7 years (6 years if payments come in annually).
b. 10/000/2,000 = 5 years.
c. 6.25 years (7 years with annual payments).
d. 10,000/1,350 = 7.4 years (8 years with annual payments).
e. 10,000/1,750 = 5.7 years (6 years with annual payments).

Average return on investment:

	Average Cash Flow	Average Depreciation	Average Income	Average Investment*	Average Return (percent)
a.	1,750	1,000	750	5,000	15%
b.	1,750	1,000	750	5,000	15
c.	1,750	1,000	750	5,000	15
d.	1,350	600	750	7,000	10.7
e.	1,750	667	1,083	5,000	21.7

* These averages are halfway between the initial investment and the end-of-life salvage value.

18–3. The key to the solution of most investment problems is to locate the cash flows on a time scale. As we pointed out in the chapter, most analysts simplify the analysis by assuming that each cash flow takes place either at the beginning or at the end of a year. In this case no such assumption is necessary—the timing of the cash flows is described in precise terms. If we take the date of the first payment to the trustee as the zero date, we can construct the following diagram:

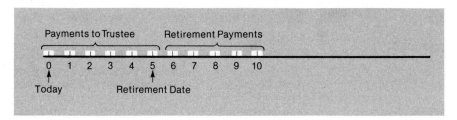

Retirement annuity for years 6 to 10:

This is equivalent to the difference between a 10-year annuity and a five-year annuity. The multipliers from Table 2 in Appendix A are:

$$6.710 - 3.993 = 2.717$$

The present value of the series of five payments of $20,000 each therefore is $2.717 \times \$20,000 = \$54,340$.

Payments to the trustee:

By putting these on a time scale, we can see that six payments are called for, not five. The annuity tables cover series of cash flows in which the first payment comes one period after the zero date. The five-year annuity factor therefore covers all but the first payment. The discount factor for the first payment is 1.000. Therefore the annuity factor is $3.993 + 1.000 = 4.993$.

The series of annual payments (X) has a present value of $4.993X$.

The problem is solved by finding the X with a present value equal to the present value of the retirement payments:

$$4.993X = \$54,340$$
$$X = \$10,883.24$$

18–4. *a.*

Initial outlay:		
Cost of machine		−$50,000
Less: Sale value of old machine	$10,000	
Tax reduction on retirement loss on old machine	10,000	+ 20,000
Net initial outlay		−$30,000

Present value at 10% of after-tax future cash
   savings (see table below) ....   + 68,566
          Net present value ....   +$38,566

Calculation of discounted cash flows:

(1) Years Hence	(2) Net Book Value of New Machine	(3) Tax Depreciation	(4) Depreciation on Old Machine	(5) Increase in Depreciation	(6) Taxable Income	(7) Income Tax	(8) After-tax Cash Flow	(9) Present Value at 10 Percent
1	$50,000	$10,000	$ 3,750	$ 6,250	$ 13,750	$ 6,875	$ 13,125	$11,931
2	40,000	8,000	3,750	4,250	15,750	7,875	12,125	10,015
3	32,000	6,400	3,750	2,650	17,350	8,675	11,325	8,505
4	25,600	5,120	3,750	1,370	18,630	9,315	10,685	7,298
5	20,480	4,096	3,750	346	19,654	9,827	10,173	6,317
6	16,384	3,277	3,750	−473	20,473	10,237	9,763	5,506
7	13,107	3,277	3,750	−473	20,473	10,237	9,763	5,008
8	9,830	3,277	3,750	−473	20,473	10,237	9,763	4,559
9	6,553	3,277	—	3,277	16,723	8,361	11,639	4,935
10	3,276	3,276	—	3,276	16,724	8,362	11,638	4,492
Total ...		$50,000	$30,000	$20,000	$180,000	$90,000	$110,000	$68,566

(3) 20% of (2) through year 6, then straight-line amortization of remaining book value for the last four years.
(4) 12.5% of $30,000 (remaining book value).
(5) Col. 4 − Col. 3.
(6) $20,000 cash flow less increase in depreciation (col. 5).
(7) 50% of col. 6.
(8) $20,000 less col. 7.
(9) Col. 8 × Table 1, Appendix A.

b. The rate lies between 30 and 40 percent and must be approximated by interpolation. The calculations are:

Year	30 Percent Factor	Present Value at 30 Percent	40 Percent Factor	Present Value at 40 Percent
0	1.000	−$30,000	1.000	−$30,000
1	0.769	+ 10,093	0.714	+ 9,371
2	0.592	+ 7,178	0.510	+ 6,184
3	0.455	+ 5,153	0.364	+ 4,122
4	0.350	+ 3,740	0.260	+ 2,778
5	0.269	+ 2,737	0.186	+ 1,892
6	0.207	+ 2,021	0.133	+ 1,298
7	0.159	+ 1,552	0.095	+ 927
8	0.123	+ 1,201	0.068	+ 664
9	0.094	+ 1,094	0.048	+ 559
10	0.073	+ 850	0.035	+ 407
Net present value		+$ 5,619		−$ 1,798

$$\text{Rate of return} = 30\% + \frac{5,619}{5,619 + 1,798} \times 10\% = 37.6\%$$

Chapter 19

19-1.

Price	Sales (units)	Sales Revenues	Fixed Costs	Variable Costs	Total Costs	Profit Margin
$0.75	100,000	$75,000	$11,000	$62,500	$73,500	$ 1,500
0.80	90,000	72,000	11,000	55,400	66,400	5,600
0.85	80,000	68,000	11,000	48,700	59,700	8,300
0.90	70,000	63,000	10,000	42,300	52,300	10,700
0.95	60,000	57,000	10,000	36,100	46,100	10,900
1.00	50,000	50,000	10,000	30,000	40,000	10,000

The most profitable price is $0.95 per unit.

19-2. *a.*

	West Coast	Midwest
Sales	$32.50	$44.00
Variable costs:		
Materials	18.70	18.70
Labor	3.00	3.00
Variable overhead	3.30	3.30
Freight	—	1.50
Commissions	—	2.20
Total variable cost	25.00	28.70
Contribution margin	$ 7.50	$15.30

The indications are that the company could increase its profit by $7.50 × 10,000 = $75,000 − $15,000 a month, or $60,000. All present fixed costs can be charged against existing sales in making this decision.

b. One factor that definitely should be considered is whether the West Coast distributors would reship the products to distributors in the Midwest. The delivered cost in the Midwest would be $39.50. This is substantially less than the price now quoted to Midwest dealers, but whether it is low enough to tempt the West Coast distributors to set up a clandestine distribution outlet in the company's present market areas is not clear. The West Coast distributor would be unlikely to risk the loss of a franchise on which a good deal of promotional effort has been exerted, unless, of course, West Coast operations are unprofitable.

It is fairly certain that reshipment by West Coast dealers is unlikely, nor is it likely that ultimate industrial purchasers who have consuming plants in both areas would find it profitable to buy in the West and reship to the Midwest. There may be some questions on these points in the edges of the company's sales territory, but the issue is probably not serious.

Another problem is how to react to complaints by Midwest retailers when they hear of the lower West Coast retail price. There is probably no Robinson-Patman problem because this is in the nature of a trade discount and the areas are noncompeting, but dealers might exert pressure to get a reduction in the $44 price.

A more fundamental question, of course, is whether the company could go into the West Coast and perform the distribution function more economically—or whether the product would sell as well at $44 as at $42.50 on the West Coast. If either of these questions can be answered affirmatively, the justification for giving the West Coast distributor a special price disappears. This illustrates the point that pricing is not an isolated decision problem. Pricing decisions are intermingled with decisions on a wide range of marketing issues which can't be ignored.

Chapter 20

20-1. a. The first step in this problem is to adjust January–June power costs for the rate increase:

January: $1,000 × 1.1 .... $1,100
February: 1,100 × 1.1   1,210
March: 1,300 × 1.1   1,430
April: 1,200 × 1.1   1,320
May: 1,200 × 1.1   1,320
June: 1,100 × 1.1   1,210

Then, let y = Cost and x = Machine-hours.

x	y_o(adj.)	xy	x^2
3,500	1,100	3,850,000	12,250,000
4,200	1,210	5,082,000	17,640,000
4,900	1,430	7,007,000	24,010,000
4,400	1,320	5,808,000	19,360,000
4,300	1,320	5,676,000	18,490,000
3,800	1,210	4,598,000	14,440,000
3,300	1,090	3,597,000	10,890,000
4,100	1,280	5,248,000	16,810,000
4,700	1,400	6,580,000	22,090,000
3,800	1,210	4,598,000	14,440,000
3,000	1,080	3,240,000	9,000,000
4,000	1,230	4,920,000	16,000,000
Σ = 48,000	14,880	60,204,000	195,420,000

The normal equations can be solved to yield the following estimating equation:

Power costs = $440 + $0.20 x Machine-hours

b. The formula for r^2 is:

$$r^2 = 1 - \frac{\Sigma(y_o - y_c)^2}{\Sigma(y_o - \bar{y})^2}$$

y_c	$y_o - y_c$	$(y_o - y_c)^2$	$y_o - \bar{y}$	$(y_o - \bar{y})^2$
1,140	−40	1,600	−140	19,600
1,280	−70	4,900	− 30	900
1,420	10	100	+190	36,100
1,320	—	—	+ 80	6,400
1,300	20	400	+ 80	6,400
1,200	10	100	− 30	900
1,100	−10	100	−150	22,500
1,260	20	400	+ 40	1,600
1,380	20	400	+160	25,600
1,200	10	100	− 30	900
1,040	40	1,600	−160	25,600
1,240	−10	100	− 10	100
Σ = 14,880	—	9,800	—	146,600

$$r^2 = 1 - \frac{9,800}{146,600} = 0.933$$

The formula for the standard error is:

$$s_e = \sqrt{\frac{\Sigma(y_0 - y_c)^2}{n-2}}$$

$$s_e = \sqrt{9,800/10} = \$31.30$$

c.

Volume	Cost Forecast
2,500	$ 940
4,000	1,240
5,500	1,540

d. This is a highly reliable estimating formula with a high coefficient of determination and very narrow confidence interval. At a volume of 4,000 machine-hours, for example, the 95 percent confidence interval is $\pm 1.96 \times \$31.30 = \pm\$61.35$. We can be 95 percent certain that the true value lies between $1,178.65 and $1,301.35.

This may seem like a wide range, but actual data seldom yield ranges this narrow.

We must be much more cautious about the predicted cost at the extreme volumes, however. None of the actual observations was even close to either of these volumes and we have no assurance that the relationship extends this far.

20–2. a. Average cost decreases by 10 percent every time the cumulative total production doubles. Therefore:

Average cost of first 200 units $= 0.9 \times$ Average cost of first 100 units
Average cost of first 400 units $= 0.9 \times$ Average cost of first 200 units
Average cost of first 800 units $= 0.9 \times$ Average cost of first 400 units

Combining these, we find that the average cost of the first 800 units $= 0.9 \times 0.9 \times 0.9 \times \$100 = \$72.90$

$$\text{Total cost} = 800 \times \$72.90 = \$58,320$$

b. Average cost of the first 1,600 units $= 0.9 \times \$72.90 = \$65.61$
Total cost of 1,600 units $\quad = 1,600 \times \$65.61 = \$104,976$
Additional cost of 2nd 800 units $\quad = \$104,976 - \$58,320$
$\quad\quad = \$46,656$, or \$58.32/unit

c. Because this increase will not increase cumulative production to twice some figure we already have, we need to use the formula given in the chapter:

Average cost $\quad = \$10,000 \times 9^s$ where $s = \dfrac{-0.0458}{0.301} = -0.15216$

Log av. cost $\quad = \log 10,000 - 0.15216 \log 9$
$\quad\quad = 4 - 0.1452 = 3.8548$
Average cost $\quad = \$71.5833$/unit
Total cost $\quad = 900 \times \$71.5833 = \$64,425$
Incremental cost $= \$64,425 - \$58,320 = \$6,105$ or \$61.05/unit

Chapter 23

23–1. a. (1) Materials   123,000
          Materials Price Variance   8,000
              Accounts Payable   131,000

    (2) Materials in Process 140,000*
          Materials   140,000

(3)	Materials Usage Variance	12,000	
	Materials		12,000
(4)	Materials	8,000	
	Materials Usage Variance		8,000
(5)	Labor in Process	80,000*	
	Labor Usage Variance	5,600	
	Payroll Cost Summary		85,600
(6)	Accrued Wages Payable	79,500	
	Cash		79,500
(7)	Payroll Cost Summary	87,600	
	Accrued Wages Payable		87,600†
(8)	Finished Goods	198,900	
	Materials in Process		122,400
	Labor in Process		76,500
(9)	Labor Rate Variance	2,000	
	Payroll Cost Summary		2,000
(10)	Cost of Goods Sold	183,500	
	Finished Goods		183,500

* The initial entry may be to a Materials Used or Direct Labor Cost account, with a subsequent transfer to inventory.
† Amount paid + $8,100 increase in Accrued Wages Payable.

Materials			
(1)	123,000	(2)	140,000
(4)	8,000	(3)	12,000

Materials in Process			
(2)	140,000	(8)	122,400

Labor in Process			
(5)	80,000	(8)	76,500

Materials Price Variance		
(1)	8,000	

Materials Usage Variance			
(3)	12,000	(4)	8,000

Labor Usage Variance		
(5)	5,600	

Payroll Cost Summary			
(7)	87,600	(5)	85,600
		(9)	2,000

Accrued Wages Payable			
(6)	79,500	Bal.	8,200
		(7)	87,600

Finished Goods			
(8)	198,900	(10)	183,500

Labor Rate Variance		
(9)	2,000	

Cost of Goods Sold	
(10)	183,500

b. The supplemental requisitions and the time tickets would have to be coded by cause as the variances occurred. A list of major causes would be given to the supervisor or clerk, who would mark the document whenever one of these causes arose.

23–2.   *a.* The control limits were breached, both by the mean and by the range:

$$\bar{X} = 59$$
$$R = 19$$

The presumption is that the operation was out of control.

     b. Control limits can be developed and used in this way only for highly repetitive activities in which one set of operations is very much like any other. If many products are manufactured, process variability must relate solely to the process, not to the characteristics of individual products. In other words, the variance must not be influenced by the product mix.

       It is also unlikely that many operations will be so homogeneous that the individual observations in a sample will be comparable to each other. In the Appendix to this chapter, all batches were of identical size and required the same operation. This condition is rare in multiproduct operations.

23–3.   *a.* Benefit = \$2,000 × 2 − \$1,000 = \$3,000

Expected value of the benefit = 0.6 × \$3,000	\$1,800
Cost	500
Net value of the benefit	\$1,300

The investigation should be launched.

     b. The break-even formula is:

$$\text{Benefit} \times \text{Probability} - \text{Cost} = \text{Zero}$$
$$\$3,000 \times p - \$500 = 0$$
$$p = \$500/\$3,000 = 0.17$$

23–4.

Actual labor cost	\$57,000	
Actual labor hours at standard rates	56,000	
Labor rate variance		\$1,000 U.
Actual labor hours at standard rates, standard mix		
(9,000 hours × \$6.50)	58,500	
Labor mix variance		2,500 F.
Standard labor cost	59,000	
Labor performance variance		500 F.
Total labor variance		\$2,000 F.

23–5.

Actual hours × Actual rates: 3,200 × ?	\$33,600	
Actual hours × Standard rates: 3,200 × \$10	32,000	
Labor rate variance		\$1,600 U.
Required hours × Standard rates: 2,300 × 1½ × \$10 ...	34,500	
Labor performance variance		2,500 U.
Standard hours × Standard rates: 1,000 × 3 × \$10	30,000	
Effect of materials usage variance		4,500 U.
Total labor spending variance		\$3,600 U.

Check figure:
Materials quantity variance = 2,300 − 2,000 = 300 pounds
Effect = 300 × 1½ × \$10 = \$4,500

Chapter 24

24–1.   *a.*

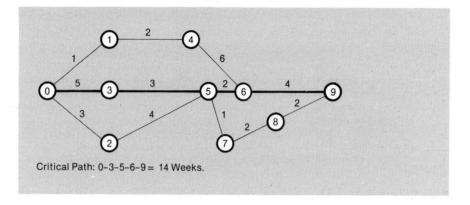

Critical Path: 0–3–5–6–9 = 14 Weeks.

b.

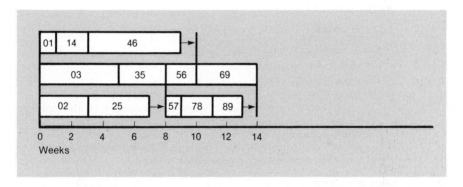

c. What management wants is an estimate or estimates of the cash flows emerging as a result of the market survey. The survey may be in preparation for the introduction of a new product, or for a change in some element of the marketing mix, or to identify a market opportunity. The project will be successful if it provides data that change management's plans and thereby improve the company's cash flows. The question is how probable this is, and what the cash costs and payoffs will be. This is an excellent place to draw a decision tree with this information.

24–2.   *a.* We have less detail than we would usually expect to find. Our report therefore has to be very condensed. We can start with some calculations:

	First 4 Weeks	Second 4 Weeks	Total
Budgeted cost of work done:			
Activity 01	$ 5,000	—	$ 5,000
Activity 12	20,000	—	20,000
Activity 13	2,000	—	2,000
Activity 24	—	$18,000	18,000
Total	27,000	18,000	45,000
Budgeted expenditures	22,000	30,000	52,000

Report on cost performance:

Actual cost	$22,000	$29,000	$51,000
Budgeted cost of work done	27,000	18,000	45,000
Budgeted expenditures	22,000	30,000	52,000
Spending variance	5,000 F.	11,000 U.	6,000 U.
(Over)/underexpenditure	—	1,000	1,000

Report on schedule slippage to date:

Preliminary model conference held one week late—one week behind schedule on the critical path.

Revision of forecasts:

Cost of activity 24:	
Incurred to date	$29,000
Future spending	65,000
Total	94,000
Original estimate	70,000
Estimated overrun	$24,000
Schedule in weeks, activity 24:	
Early start	− 1
Elapsed time to date	4
Estimated time to complete	12
Revised schedule from originally scheduled start	15
Original time estimate	12
Estimated schedule slippage	3

We have to find ways to present these figures effectively. Revised float diagrams or cumulative expenditure/progress charts are often useful.

b. The crucial questions are the same as those management must have posed when it approved the project in the first place: (1) what are the potential payoffs; and (2) what are the probabilities associated with each?

The costs incurred to date are sunk costs, but the difficulties encountered in constructing the model may lead management to question the validity of the revised estimates of incremental time and costs. It is also possible, though unlikely, that management now has a better estimate of the market potential of the new service. If so, the cost/benefit comparison will have to be based on revised estimates of both costs and benefits.

The main possible actions here are to continue the project, replace the project leader, or discontinue the project. The choice will depend on the estimated future cash flows and probabilities and on management's appraisal of the reasons for the difficulties encountered to date.

Chapter 25

25–1. a. Alifrance is not a profit center because it controls neither the source of its merchandise nor the prices paid for it. It controls almost every determinant of profit other than source and purchase price, however, and therefore is quite far along the continuum between a centrally controlled unit and a completely autonomous unit. It falls into the category we have described as administered centers.

b. Because Mr. Dalmas has control over many of the determinants of profit, profit performance should be one of the key indicators of his managerial ability. The question of what price to set on the merchandise transferred should not affect this evaluation, however. We shall take up this question in Chapter 26.

25-2.   *a.*

	Budgeted	Actual
Income	$ 70,000	$ 63,000
Investment	665,000	700,000
Return on investment	10.5%	9.0%

b.

Income	$70,000	$ 63,000
Investment charge at 12%	79,800	84,000
Residual income (loss)	$(9,800)	$(21,000)

c.   Neither the ROI figures nor the residual income figures are relevant to managerial evaluation because of the changes in the allocated amounts and the changes in traceable investments and depreciation, none of which is controllable in any meaningful sense of the word. Using budgeted amounts to replace the actual amounts reported for these elements, we can calculate a revised residual income figure as follows:

Working capital (actual)		$200,000
Traceable plant and equipment (budgeted)		420,000
Allocated investments (budgeted)		95,000
Adjusted investment		715,000
Income as reported		63,000
Less: Change in depreciation	$2,000	
Change in allocations	5,000	(7,000)
Add: Tax on the changes		3,500
Adjusted income		59,500
Carrying charge (12% × $715,000)		(85,800)
Adjusted residual income (loss)		$ (26,300)

This indicates that the division manager's performance was actually a good deal worse than the initial comparisons indicated. One problem is that investment in working capital exceeded the plan by $50,000. Sales volume was $100,000 less than the budgeted amount (evidenced by the decrease in the allocation of head office costs), so this factor can't account for the increase in working capital. Furthermore, the decrease in sales volume was accompanied by a $10,500 aftertax decrease in divisional income (from $70,000 to $59,500). The sources of this decrease should be investigated to see how much of it was within the division manager's control.

d.   The figures don't permit the calculation of residual income or ROI on an attributable basis because the formulas don't measure attributability. The ratio of profit contribution to traceable investment is 13.8 percent ($63,000 income plus 50 percent of $40,000 in head office charges, divided by $600,000 traceable investment). This indicates that the division may be paying its way. If a study finds that attributable costs and investments in the head office are large enough to push the division's attributable return on investment substantially below 12 percent, then top management should analyze the division's incremental cash flows, both now and in the future when major capital investments are being considered. The purpose: to find out whether withdrawal would be desirable.

Chapter 26

26-1.   *a.*   The memorandum should stress the following points:

(1)   If the alternative is idleness, the only incremental costs may be the variable costs of 90 cents a pound, and this is far less than the proposed transfer

price. Hull's profit will be 70 cents greater for every pound of X it processes for the Hingham division. Without these 50,000 pounds, product X would show a loss of $20,000 after deducting its share of division fixed costs; with this production, the net profit figure would be $15,000. This can be summarized in the following schedules for the Hull division:

	If Hingham Buys from Hull @ $1.60	If Hingham Buys Outside
Sales—outside (100,000 lbs.)	$200,000	$200,000
Sales—Hingham (50,000 lbs.)	80,000	—
Total sales	280,000	200,000
Product-traceable costs:		
Variable manufacturing costs	135,000	90,000
Sales commissions	10,000	10,000
Depreciation	20,000	20,000
Other traceable costs	40,000	40,000
Total traceable costs	205,000	160,000
Product profit contribution	75,000	40,000
Share of division fixed costs	60,000	60,000
Income before taxes	$ 15,000	$(20,000)

(2) If the Hull division will retain idle workers on the payroll to avoid losing a skilled work force, the incremental cost could be even less than 90 cents a pound because some labor costs would be sunk.

(3) Even if the traceable fixed costs increase in steps, it is unlikely that these could be high enough to make an incremental loss. At the present volume they average only 27 cents a pound.

(4) The Hull division manager should recognize a longer-term problem—if cheaper substitutes are available, this may indicate a serious competitive weakness for the long run.

b. Some economists establish such a strict set of necessary conditions for the use of negotiation that they are almost never met. If you are willing to use the criteria established in this chapter, however, negotiation should be appropriate here. Hull has access to outside customer markets; Hingham has access to outside suppliers. If Hull were busy, the company might even be better off to have Hingham buy outside. If profit decentralization is to mean anything, we must rely on the division managers to identify situations of this type.

26–2. a. The same arguments favoring a $1.60 transfer price for the Hingham division (problem 1) support granting the $1.50 transfer price, unless Hull division is operating so close to capacity it would incur substantial cost penalties or opportunity costs to meet Elsa's demands.

b. Elsa division is an administered center, responsible for profits but with no choice of supplier. In these circumstances, the manager has little bargaining power, and the market value of the intermediate product is unknown to either party. Average variable cost plus retainer or market in/cost out—each of these would be established by top management decree—would be more appropriate than negotiation.

Chapter 27

27–1.

	Original Budget	Actual Volume	Actual Selling Prices	Actual Cost of Goods Sold	Actual Results
Sales revenues	$60,000	$66,000	$60,500	$60,500	$60,500
Cost of goods sold	36,000	39,600	39,600	40,000	40,000
Gross margin	24,000	26,400	20,900	20,500	20,500
Selling and administrative expenses	18,000	18,000	18,000	18,000	18,500
Income before taxes	6,000	8,400	2,900	2,500	2,000

	Sales Volume Variance $2,400 F.	Selling Price Variance $5,500 U.	Merchandise Cost Price Variance $400 U.	Selling and Administrative Spending Variance $500 U.

27–2. The sales volume, selling price, and selling and administrative expense spending variances are unaffected by this additional information. We can break the $400 merchandise cost price variance down as follows:

	Original Budget	Volume-Adjusted Cost of Goods Sold	Flexible Budget at Actual Volume	Actual Expense
Direct materials	$10,000	$11,000	$11,000	$11,200
Direct labor	13,000	14,300	14,300	14,700
Factory overhead	13,000	14,300	13,520	14,100
Total	36,000	39,600	38,820	40,000

	Included in Calculation of Sales Volume Variance $3,600	Production Volume Variance $780 F.	Input Usage Variances: Direct materials Direct labor Overhead Total	
			Direct materials	$ 200 U.
			Direct labor	400 U.
			Overhead	580 U.
			Total	$1,180 U.

The spending variances in this case are all usage variances because the problem states that all input prices were at budgeted levels. Using the three-variance method of overhead variance analysis, the overhead usage variance can be further subdivided, as follows:

Flexible Budget at $14,300 Direct Labor Cost	Flexible Budget at $14,700 Direct Labor Cost	Actual Factory Overhead Cost
$13,520	$13,680	$14,100

Labor
Efficiency
Variance
$160 U.

Overhead
Input Usage
Variance
$420 U.

27–3. a.

	(1)	(2)	(3)	(4)	(5)	(6)	(7)
	Budgeted Results			Actual Results			Profit Variance
Product	Reve-nues	Cost of Goods Sold	Gross Margin	Reve-nues	Cost of Goods Sold	Gross Margin	(6) − (3)
X ..	$20,000	$12,000	$ 8,000	$23,100	$12,960	$10,140	$2,140 F.
Y ..	30,000	21,000	9,000	23,600	16,800	6,800	2,200 U
Z ..	20,000	16,000	4,000	25,500	20,800	4,700	700 F.
Total ..	$70,000	$49,000	$21,000	$72,200	$50,560	$21,640	$ 640 F.

b. *Step 1:* Derive a composite measure of actual volume by multiplying actual unit sales by budgeted prices. The selling price variances emerge as a by-product of this calculation:

Product	Units Sold	Budgeted Price	Calculated Revenue	Actual Revenue	Selling Price Variance
X	10,800	$2	$21,600	$23,100	$1,500 F.
Y	4,000	6	24,000	23,600	400 U.
Z	5,200	5	26,000	25,500	500 U.
Total	20,000		$71,600	$72,200	$ 600 F.

Step 2: Calculate the budgeted margins for the actual sales volumes and compare these figures with the budgeted margins for the budgeted sales volumes—to determine the sales volume variance for each product:

Product	Calculated Revenue	Cost of Goods Sold at Budgeted Unit Costs	Calculated Gross Margin	Budgeted Gross Margin	Sales Volume Variance
X	$21,600	$12,960	$ 8,640	$ 8,000	$ 640 F.
Y	24,000	16,800	7,200	9,000	1,800 U.
Z	26,000	20,800	5,200	4,000	1,200 F.
Total	$71,600	$50,560	$21,040	$21,000	$ 40 F.

Step 3: Because the $40 total of the three sales volume figures results from a combination of sales volume and sales mix variations, calculate the budgeted average gross margin per sales dollar and use this to calculate the sales mix variance:

$$\frac{\text{Budgeted gross margin}}{\text{Budgeted revenues}} = \frac{\$21,000}{\$70,000} = 30\%$$

Budgeted gross margin $21,000
Calculated revenues × budgeted
    percent ($71,600 × 0.3) 21,480
    Sales volume variance . . . . $480 F.
Sum of calculated gross margins for
    individual products 21,040
    Sales mix variance . . . .   440 U.

Step 4: Prepare the variance summary:

Selling price . . . . $600 F.
Sales volume . . . .   480 F.
Sales mix . . . .   440 U.
    Total . . . . $640 F.

c. The budgeted gross margin per unit was $21,000/19,000 units = $1.105. Using this instead of the 30 percent contribution margin ratio produces the following analysis:

Budgeted gross margin $21,000
Actual units sold × Budgeted margin
    per unit (20,000 × $1.105)   22,100
    Sales volume variance . . . . $1,100 F.
Sum of actual calculated gross margins for
    individual products   21,040
    Sales mix variance . . . .   1,060 U.

This isn't necessarily more correct than the analysis in (b). This method simply weights low-priced units more heavily than the method used in (b). Since the number of units increased more sharply than revenues, the volume variance appears larger here than in (b). If management measures its market penetration by the number of units sold rather than by sales dollars, then this method will meet management's needs better than the method used in (b).

Index

A

Abdel-khalik, A. Rashad, 834 n
Absorption costing, 150
  income, 160
Accounting; *see also* Cost accounting
  aspects and types, 11–16
  behavioral aspects, 691–702
  financial, 11–12
  generally accepted principles, 12
  limitations, 15–16
  organization of function, 13–14
  reimbursement; *see* Reimbursement accounting
  tax, and Tax accounting
Activities
  defined, 6
  level of, 78–79
  programmed, 81–82
  responsive, 78–79
Activity charges
  allocations for, 315
  defined, 189
  in profit reporting, 365
Activity denominators, 183
Adaptive response, to steering controls, 8
Administered centers, 779
  defined, 830
Aftertax investment outlay, 562–63
All-inclusive cost, 665
Allocate, defined, 672
Allocation(s)
  activity outlays, 315
  basic data, 185–87
  building services costs, 187–88
  capacity charges, 315
  clerical costs, 188–89
  for control reporting, 311–17
  of costs, 177–95
  cross, 196–97
  departmental overhead rates, 191
  factory management costs, 190–91
  flexible budget, 312–13
  management costs, 189–90
  net realization basis, 455–56

Allocation(s)—*Cont.*
  one-step, 178–79
  overhead rates in variable costing, 191–93
  peak-based methods, 183–84
  physical unit basis of, 454–55
  of profit reporting, 364–65
  purpose of periodic, 311
  of residual costs, 185
  stepped costs, 193–94
  two-part, 184–85
  under attributable costing, 195
  under or overdistribution, 316
  uniform percentage contribution basis, 456–57
  use of two-part tariff, 316–17
  wage charges, 313–15
Allocation denominators
  activity, 183
  capacity, 183–84
  usage, 183
Annuity, 550–51
Annuity method of depreciation, 795
Anthony, Robert N., 780 n
Apportionment, 176–77
  rates, 176–77
Armed Services Defense Acquisition Regulations, 13
Assets
  centrally administered, 798
  total, 796–97
  traceable, 796–97
Attributable costing
  allocations, 195
  concept of, 160–62
  defined, 479
  segment cost analysis, 484
  weakness, 162
Attributable profit, 364–65
Average cost distribution, 421–24
Average costs, 161
Average historical costs, 395–96
Average return on investment, 558–59

B

Banking, 495
Basic plan system of costing, 264–73, 714 n

Bates, Donald L., 211 n
Baumol, William J., 834 n
Beggs, Robert I., 645 n, 646 n
Behavioral problems, system administration, 703–4
Benchmark alternative, 74–75
Benninger, Lawrence, 470
Benston, George J., 644 n, 646 n
Bonini, Charles P., 633 n, 634 n, 644 n, 646 n
Boston Consulting Group, 650 n
Branch sales/expenses, 214–15
Break-even charts, 112–13
Break-even point, tax effects, 114
Break-even volume, multi-volume business, 119
Britain, accounting organizations, 15
Budget
  defined, 5
  flexible; see Flexible budget
  operating and financial, 209
Budgeting
  allocating manufacturing costs, 221–22
  branch office proposals, 215–16
  constraint, 216
  control of marketing costs, 361–79
  control of overhead costs, 300–317
  defined, 5
  direct labor requirement, 219
  direct materials requirement, 218
  estimating branch sales/expenses, 214–15
  estimating contribution margin, 214
  estimating production cost, 212–14
  factory cost data, 219–20
  factory overhead costs, 219
  final marketing proposal, 217–18
  fixed/variable costs, 221–22
  iterative process, 229
  management participation, 310–11
  marketing plan, 212–18
  overhead cost variances, 333–47
  physical resource plans and production schedules, 220–21
  production plan and manufacturing cost, 218–21
  profit plan, 221–23
  program/zero base, 231–34
  purposes of, 230–31
  review/revision/approval, 226–29
  seasonal patterns, 229–30
  statement of objectives, 210–12
  tentative profit plan, 222–23
  testing marketing plan, 216–17
Building service costs, 187–88
Burden center, 31
Burton, John C., 449, 671 n
Business unit, defined, 672
Buying division, 816
By-products
  costing, 459–61
  defined, 459
  main product costing, 460–61

C

Cammann, Cortlandt, 704 n
Canada, accounting organizations, 15

Capacity charges
  allocations, 315
  defined, 188
  in profit reporting, 365
Capacity costs, defined, 80
Capacity denominators, 183–84
Capacity, idle, 84–87
Capacity rationing decisions, 89–90
Capital
  cost of, 551, 579–81
  weighted average cost of, 580–81
Capital budget, 223–24
Capital expenditure analysis, 548–79
  adjusting for uncertainty, 571–72
  allocations/cost absorptions, 577–78
  average rate of return, 558–59
  calculating present value, 569
  depreciation on new facilities, 577
  economic life of investment, 573–74
  evaluation, 568–72
  future value, 548–50
  impact of inflation, 573
  initial outlays, 559–63
  internal rate of return, 556–57
  investment proposals, 570–71
  Monte Carlo method, 572
  multiple alternatives, 574–75
  net present value, 548–59
  payback period, 558
  present value, 550–51
  residual value, 567–68
  treatment of interest, 578
  unamortized costs, 576
Capitalization of tangible assets, 674
Carrying costs, types, 532
CASB; see Cost Accounting Standards Board
Cash budget, 224–26
Cash flow(s)
  adjustment for income taxes, 564–67
  after tax, 566–67
  displaced facilities, 561
  end of life residual values, 567–68
  existing facilities use, 560
  and income, 564
  incremental, 73–75
  incremental rate of return, 574–75
  initial outlays, 559–63
  to measure results, 72–73
  measuring, 548–59
  operating, 563–64
  outlays for plant/equipment, 559–60
  secondary outlays, 563–67
  tax depreciation allowance, 564–66
  tax effects of initial outlays, 561–63
  working capital, 560–61
Cash flow diagrams, 115
Central payments and accruals, 677–78
Centralized service functions, 676–77
Centrally-tabulated costs, 182
Certificate in Management Accounting (CMA), 15
Chandler, Margaret K., 700 n

Charging rate, 35, 187, 311
  for interdepartmental allocations, 311–17
Clerical costs, 188–89
Coefficient of determination, 638–39
Commercial banking, 495
Common costs, 28, 792, 793–94
Composite index of volume, 861–62
Compounding, 549–50
Compounding interval, 557–58
Comprehensive plan
  causes of quantity variance, 716–17
  characteristics, 714–15
  costs and benefits, 720–21
  factory work-in-process accounts, 716–20
  labor time tickets, 714
  materials requisitions, 714–15
  reporting to management, 715–16
  usage variances in standard costing, 713–21
Confidence intervals, 651
Constraint, 216
Contract costing, 13
Contribution margin, 214
  defined, 89
Contribution margin ratio,
  defined, 89
  multiproduct business, 120–22
Control, by feedback response, 9
Control account, 52–53
Control limits, calculating, 732–34
Control processes, 10–11
Control reporting
  interdepartmental allocations, 311–17
  process costing, 426–29
Controllability criterion, 260, 691, 700–701
Controllable investment, 796–97
Controllable profit, 365–66, 793
Controller, 13
Conversion costs, 422–24
Cool, William R., 788 n
Cooper, W. W., 834 n
Corporate interest expense, 792
Corrective response, to steering controls, 8
Correlation, 639
Cost(s)
  activity classification, 24
  all-inclusive, 665
  attributable, 160–62
  building services, 187–88
  of capital, 551, 579–81
  centrally tabulated, 182
  classification problems, 34–38
  classifications of, 21–25
  clerical, 188–89
  common, 28, 792–94
  control of direct labor, 255–77
  control of materials, 255–77
  direct/indirect, 21–22, 177
  direct labor, 27–28
  direct materials, 26–27
  employee benefits, 35–36
  estimated average overhead, 30–31
  factory overhead, 28–32

Cost(s)—Cont.
  factory management, 190–91
  fixed, 80–82
  homogeneous, 23
  management, 189–90
  marginal; see Marginal costs
  marketing; see Marketing costs
  noncontrollable, 305
  object of expenditure, 22–24
  opportunity; see Opportunity costs
  organization segment, 21–22
  overtime premiums, 36–37
  prime, 28
  rejected units, 37–38
  residual; see Residual costs
  resource allocation decisions, 72–78
  rework labor, 38
  scrap recovery, 38
  semivariable, 82
  similar purposes, 34–35
  standard; see Standard costs
  step-variable, 81
  sunk; see Sunk costs
  unamortized, 576
  variable, 78–80; see also Cost variances
Cost accounting
  aspects, 11–16
  behavioral aspects, 691–705
  constraining standards, 671–73
  defined, 14–15
  practitioners, 14–15
  purchase and use of materials, 52–53
  service industries, 494–96
Cost accounting cycle, 52–61
  factory overhead costs, 55
  job completion/sales, 57–58
  labor costs, 53–55
  manufacturing costs statement, 60–61
  overhead absorption, 56
  under or overabsorbed factory overhead, 59–60
Cost accounting standards, 671–80
  assigning costs to cost objectives, 675–80
  assigning costs to periods, 673–75
  capitalization of tangible assets, 674
  consistency, 672–73
  cost accounting period, 673
  depreciation, 674–75
  direct materials/direct labor, 678
  fringe benefits, 675
  general/administrative overhead, 678–79
  home office expenses, 676–78
  imputed interest on facilities capital, 679
  indirect cost/final cost objectives, 679–80
  unallowable costs, 673
Cost Accounting Standards Board (CASB), 13, 671–80
Cost analysis
  by size of order, 489–94
  types, 476–96
Cost-based pricing formulas
  departures from, 610–11
  markup percentage, 610

Cost-based pricing formulas—*Cont.*
 reasons for, 606–7
 structure, 607–10
Cost centers, 22
 overhead rates, 31
 service/support, 175
Cost control standards
 departmental overhead spending variances,
  303–4
 flexible budgets, 302–3
Cost flows, summary, 58–59
Cost of goods sold account, 58
Cost indivisibility, 161
Cost information, 25
Cost input, 678
Cost justification defense, 491–92
Cost objective, 672
Cost-plus pricing, 606
Cost reassignment methods, 176–82
 apportionment, 176–77
 cross allocations, 179–80
 interdepartmental allocation, 177
 one-step allocation, 178–79
 sequential allocation, 180–82
Cost reduction, 161–62
Cost-reimbursement contracts, 12–13
Cost sheet, 32
Cost slopes, 752–54
Cost variances
 accounting in U.S., 397
 analyses of, 713–32
 analytical examination, 724–32
 in annual reporting, 394–96
 balance sheet, 395
 changes in standard costs, 404
 closing accounts, 403–4
 control limits, 732–34
 decision model, 723–24
 favorable/unfavorable, 265
 in financial statements, 396–404
 inventory account balances, 396–404
 labor/equipment substitution variances, 726–27
 labor mix, 727–29
 LIFO inventory adjustment, 399–401
 marketing, 361–79
 materials, 401–4
 materials mix and yield, 729–30
 materials/labor usage, 725–26
 newly adopted standards, 397
 prorated, 397–99
 seasonal variations in volume overhead, 731–32
 standard raw materials, 403
 statistical control limits, 721–23
Costing
 of byproducts, 459–61
 co-products, 453–59
 full; *see* Full costing
 graphic method, 632–33
 high-low points method, 633–34
 historical, 426–27
 of individual activities, 25–34
 judgment method, 631–32

Costing—*Cont.*
 learning curve analysis, 648–51
 least squares method, 634–44
 least squares regression, 644–47
 marketing and service activities, 476–96
 mathematical methods, 634–51
 multiple regression analysis, 644–47
 nonlinear regression, 647
 nonmathematical methods, 631–34
 process; *see* Process costing
 project control, 746–63
 reimbursement; *see* Reimbursement costing
 simple linear regression, 634–44
 transportation industries, 495–96
 variable, 150–63; *see also* Cost variances
Costing entity
 size, 24–25
 types, 24
Creep of fixed costs, 123
Critical path, 751
Cross allocation, 179–80
 procedures, 196–97
Customary volume range, 117
Customer-related service costs, 488

D

Davidson, Sidney, 647 n
Dearden, John, 494 n, 780 n
Debt capital, 579
Decision analysis, 72–94
Decision branches, 130
Decision making
 devices, 111–35
 and joint costs, 451–53
 payoff tables, 123–29
 profit-volume charts, 111–23
 types, 451–52
Decision models
 capital expenditure, 548–79
 cost-based pricing formulas, 606–11
 linear programming, 513–27
 price differentiation, 611–15
 pricing, 596–615
 pricing strategies, 596–99
 short-run economic pricing, 599–606
Decision rules, 127–28
Decision tables, inventory model, 527–33
Decision tree analysis, 129–33
Decisions
 capacity rationing, 89–90
 product emphasis, 90–93
 resource allocation, 72–78
Demand, price elasticity of, 597
Demand curve, 596
 kinked, 605–6
Demand schedule, 596
Demski, Joel, 665 n, 871
Departmental cost reporting, 762–63
Depreciation, 674–75
 accumulated, 798–99
 negative, 795
Depreciation charges, 564–66, 577

Depreciation method, 792, 794–95
  annuity, 795
  implicit interest, 794–95
Differential cash flow, 73–74
Differential cost, 76
Differential principle, 72
Direct cost, 177
  defined, 672
Direct costing systems, 151 n
Direct labor
  controlling costs, 255–77
  costs, 27–28
Direct materials costs, 26–27
Direct production activities, 24
Discontinuation profit, 783
Discount rate, 551–52
Disinvestment, 570–71
  effect of variance in, 554–56
Diversified service functions, 483–84
Dollar variances, 263–64
Dopuch, Nicholas, 665 n, 834 n
Down time, 55
Drake, David F., 834 n
Dual pricing system, 832
Dual rate system, 184
Dummy activities, 754
Dunnette, M. D., 694 n
Dyckman, Thomas R., 723 n

                    E

Earnings gap, 115
Economic evaluation, 9
Economic life of investment, 573–74
Economies of scale, 161
Effectiveness, defined, 8
Efficiency, defined, 8
Eldredge, David L., 211 n
Employee benefits, 35–36
End-of-period adjustments, 158–59
Engineered standards, 479
Engineering techniques, 479
Equity capital, cost of, 580
Equity stockholders, 797
Equivalent production
  in average costing, 424
  defined, 417–18
Event branches, 130
Event node, 130
Expected value, 126–29
  decision rules, 127–28
  defined, 123
  maximizing, 127–28
  utility, 128–29
Expenses, 57, 112

                    F

Fabian, Tibor, 834 n
Factory management costs, 190–91
Factory overhead absorbed account, 56
Factory overhead cost variances, 333–37
Factory overhead costs, 28–32
Factory-wide work-in-process accounts, 716–20

Federal Trade Commission, 491
Feedback, 9
FIFO; see First-in, first-out
Final cost objective, 671, 672
Final product, 816
Financial accounting, 11–12
Financial Accounting Standards Board, 12, 397
Financial budget, 223–27
  capital budget, 223–24
  cash budget, 224–26
  defined, 209
  review, 227–29
Financial Executives Institute (FEI), 14–15
Financial reporting
  classification of cost variances, 394–404
  costing co-products, 453–59
Financial statements
  FIFO method, 420–21
  moving average method, 421–24
  process costing, 419–26
  special calculations, 420
Finished Goods Inventory, 57–58
First-in, first-out (FIFO), 397, 404
  historical cost, 402–3
  in process costing, 420–21
Fiscal management, 820–21
Fixed charge, 115
Fixed costs, 221–22
  creep of, 123
  product traceable, 118
  programmed activities, 81–82
  responsive activities, 80–81
Fixed Overhead Costs in Inventory account, 159
Flamholtz, Eric, 709
Flexible budgets
  activity charges, 315
  behavioral problems, 310–11
  capacity charges, 315
  cost-volume relationships, 308–9
  defined, 320–23
  development, 308–11
  inspection of accounts method, 309
  interdepartmental allocations, 311–17
  judgment method, 309
  measuring volume, 309–10
  process costing, 429
  two-part tariff, 316–17
  under/overdistribution of service and support
    costs, 316
  usage charges, 313–15
Float diagrams, 754–55
Floor space, costs of, 187–88
Fringe benefits, 675
Full-cost overhead rates
  allocation denominators, 182–85
  sequential allocation, 182–91
Full costing, 150, 665–66
  profit contribution reporting, 376–79
Functional cost analysis, 477
  control of function activities, 480
  engineering techniques, 479–80

944

Functional cost analysis—*Cont.*
  reasons for, 476–77
  time recording, 478–79
Funds flow diagrams, 115
Future value, 549

G

Gass, Saul I., 526 n
General sales manager, 371
Ginzberg, Michael, 806
Goal congruance, 692
Goal internalizing, 692
Goals
  harmonization of, 701–2
  long-term profit, 799–801
Gordon, Myron J., 160 n
Government, program budgeting, 232
Grant, Eugene L., 734 n
Graphic method of costing, 632–33
Grass-roots approach to sales, 215
Group dynamics, 694–95
Guetzkow, Harold, 703 n

H

Hackman, J. R., 692 n, 694 n
Hamilton, Mary T., 580 n
Herlihy, Robert E., 645 n, 646 n
Hertz, David B., 572 n
High-low points method of costing, 633–34
Hirschleifer, Jack, 822 n
Historical costing, 426–27
Hofstede, G. H., 694 n
Home office, 672
Honor system time recording, 478–79

I

Idle capacity, 84–87
Income
  defined, 112
  reported, 153–59
Income measurement problems, 792–96
  changing resource prices, 796
  common costs, 793–94
  depreciation method, 794–95
  income taxes, 795–96
  interest expense, 794
  investment, 796
  revenue interdependence, 794
Income taxes, 792, 795–96
  effects, 113–14
  effect on cash flows, 561–63
  and secondary outlays, 564–67
Incremental cash flow, 73–74
Incremental cost, 76
Incremental principle, 72
Incremental profit, 73–74
Incremental rate of return, 574–75
Indirect cost, 177
  pool, 672
Indirect labor, 29
Indirect materials, 29
  inventory, 53

Indivisibilities, 161
Inflation, 573
Initial outlays, 559–63
Implicit interest, 794–95
Input, 30, 256
  costs, 260
  efficiency variance, 343
Inspection, of inventory, 487
Inspection of accounts method, 309, 631–32
Institute of Management Accountants, 15
Institute of Management Accounting, 15
Insurance costs, 675
Interdepartmental allocation, 177
Interest, 578
  compounding, 549–50
  of expense, 794
  tables, 551
Intermediate product, 816
Internal rate of return, 556–57
International Accounting Standards Committee, 397
Inventory
  inspection, 487
  product handling, 485–86
  storage space, 486–87
  storage value, 486
  using materials from, 87–88
Inventory account balances, adjusting, 396–404
Inventory adjustment account, 397
  FIFO, 402–4
  LIFO, 399–401
Inventory Adjustment to Income, 158
Inventory decision models
  data requirements, 531–33
  economic order quantity, 527–29
  safety stocks and reorder points, 529–31
Inventory liquidation, LIFO, 400–401
Investment
  controllable, 796–97
  economic life of, 573–74
  net, 797
Investment centers, 778–79
Investment measurement problems, 796–99
  accumulated depreciation, 798–99
  allocating centrally administered assets, 798
  allocating centrally administered liabilities, 798
  changing resource prices, 799
  defining investment base, 796–97
Investment outlay, after taxes, 562–63
Investment problems, 548–79

J-K

Jensen, Robert, 646 n
Job completion, 57
Job costing, 151
Job cost sheet, 27
Job order costing, 25–34
  factory overhead component, 32
  use, 52
Joint costing
  of byproducts, 459–61
  in decision making, 451–53
  defined, 451

Joint costing—*Cont.*
  and joint products, 450–51
  net realization basis of allocation, 455–56
  physical unit basis of allocation, 454–55
  relative sale value at split-off point, 457–58
  relevance of unit cost figures, 458–59
  uniform percentage contribution basis, 456–57
  variable-yield processes, 461–63
Joint products
  costing, 450–63
  defined, 450
  for financial reporting, 453–59
  groups, 452
  individual, 452
  separable costs, 452–53
Judgment method of costing, 309, 631–32
Kay, E., 697 n
Kay, Robert S., 671 n
Kozmetsky, George, 703 n

L

Labor costs, 53–55
  distribution, 54–55
  liability payment aspects, 53–54
  payroll accrual, 54
  standard, 262–63
Labor efficiency variance, 342–43
Labor/equipment substitution variance, 726–27
Labor, indirect, 29
Labor mix variances, 727–29
Labor quantity standards, 275–77
Labor rate variances, 270–71
  defined, 259
Labor time tickets, 714
Labor usage variance, 725–26
Lagged regression, 647
Last-in, first-out (LIFO), 397
  base quantity, 349
  inventory adjustment, 399–401
  inventory liquidation, 400–401
Lawler, Edward E., III, 692 n, 694, 696
Lead time, 529
Learning curve
  analysis, 648–51
  applications, 650
  diagrams, 648
  equations, 648–49
  locating, 650–51
  nature of, 648–50
Least squares method of costing, 634–44
Least squares regression, 644–47
Leavenworth, Richard S., 734 n
Leavitt, H. J., 834 n
Level of activity, 78–79
Liabilities, centrally administered, 798
Liability-payment aspect of labor costs, 53–54
LIFO; *see* Last-in, first-out
Linear programming
  accounting data required, 525–26
  developing shadow prices, 521–22
  graphic solution, 518–21
  rationing capacity, 516–27

Linear programming—*Cont.*
  resource allocation, 513–16
  sensitivity analysis, 522–25
  simplex method, 526–27
Linear regression analysis, 634–44
Linear utility function, 129
Long-range periodic planning, 4
Lorie, James H., 580 n
Lusk, Edward J., 834 n

M

McCullough, Patrick J., 293 n
McKinney, George, III, 832 n
Malinvaud, Edmond, 634 n, 644 n
Management
  decision-making devices, 111–35
  decision-oriented cost figures, 72–94
  divisional profit reporting, 777–801
  organizational control, 255–77
  participation in budgeting, 310–11
  project reporting standards, 366–67
  role of variable costing, 150–63
  transfer pricing, 816–35
Management costs, 189–90
Management by exception, 691, 698–700
  defined, 255
Managerial accounting, 6
Managerial control, 6–11
Managerial evaluation, 9
Managerial planning
  characteristics, 3–6
  cost accounting for, 6
Manufacturing companies, profit variance analysis,
  862–71
Manufacturing cost budget, 218–21
Manufacturing cost differentials, 493–94
Manufacturing cost statement, 60–61
Manufacturing expense, defined, 57 n
Margin of safety, 113
Marginal cost
  defined, 82–84
  indeterminacy, 823–24
  less than market value, 824–25
  transfer prices based on, 822–25
  unfair prices, 825
Market-based negotiated prices, 826–29
Market in/cost out, 832–33
Market price, and transfer price, 825–26
Marketing
  pricing models, 596–616
  profit contribution reporting, 363–66
  profit reporting standards, 366–67
  profit reporting system, 367–74
  profit reports in analysis of, 374–76
  single/multisegment operation, 377–79
  time lags, 376
Marketing costs, control of, 361–79
Marketing function, 362–63
Marketing plan, 212–18
Marketing response functions, 374–76
Markets, monopoly and oligopoly, 604–6
Markup percentage, 610

Materials
  controlling costs, 255–77
  purchase and use of, 52–53
Materials costs, 88–89
  prorating variances, 401–4
  standard, 262
Materials inventory account, 52–53
Materials mixed yield variances, 728–30
Materials quantity standards, 274–75
Materials requisition, 26, 714–15
Materials spending variance, 272
Methods time measurement, 479
Meyers, Philip, 586
Mirvis, Philip H., 704 n
Money
  annuity value, 888–92
  present value, 887–88
Monopolistic competition, 604–5
Monopoly, 604
Monte Carlo method of analysis, 572
Moving average method, in process costing, 421–24
Multiple regression analysis, 644–47
Multiproduct business, profit charting, 118–19
Multiproduct profit functions, 120–22

N

Nadler, David A., 704 n
National Association of Accountants (NAA), 14–15, 609 n
Negative depreciation, 795
Nelson, Carl L., 546, 881
Net cash flow, 73
Net income, 787–88
Net investments, 797
Net present value, 552–53
  calculating, 553–54
  defined, 551
  compounding rate of return, 557–58
  varying discount rate, 554–56
Network diagrams, 750–54
Nonlinear cost relationships, 151–53
Nonlinear regression, 647
Nonlinear utility function, 128–29
Nonprice competition, 604
Normal curve, 732
Normal volume, 32–34
Novick, David, 232 n

O

Object of expenditure, 23
Objective probabilities, 125–26
Oligopolistic markets, 604–6
Oligopoly, defined, 605
One-step allocations, 178–79
Open to buy allowance, 7
Operating budget, 210–23
  defined, 209
  review, 227
Operating costs, 12–38
Operating volume, 30

Opportunity costs, 77–78
Order costs, 532
Order-filling activities, 24, 363
Order-getting activities, 24, 362–63
Organizational budgeting, 231
Organizational units
  administered centers, 779
  investment centers, 778–79
  profit centers, 777–78
  pseudo-profit centers, 781–82
  quasi-profit centers, 781–82
  reasons for decentralization, 779–80
  service centers, 780–81
Outcome, 123
Output, 30
  defined, 256
  measuring, 261–63
  measuring costs, 415–18
Overhead
  absorption, 56
  center, 31
  over or underabsorbed, 31
Overhead cost variance
  defined, 59
  factory, 333–47
  labor efficiency, 342–43
  origins, 333–38
  reconciling, 340–41, 344–47
  spending variance, 338–39, 342, 345–46
  three variance approach, 341–45
  total, 335–38, 345
  two-variance approach, 338–41
  volume variance, 339–40, 343, 346
  without standard costing, 345–47
Overhead costs
  controlling, 300–317
  factory, 28–32
  standard; see Standard overhead costs
  supportive; see Supportive overhead costs
Overhead in process account, 337–38
Overhead rates
  after-the-fact, 30
  cost center, 31
  normal volume, 32–34
  predetermined, 30–31
  purpose, 340
  service costs, 175–95
  under variable costing, 153
Overhead spending variance(s)
  allocations for control reporting, 311–17
  departmental, 303–4
  flexible budgets, 302–3, 308–11
  monthly reporting, 306
  noncontrollable costs, 305
  price and usage components, 304–5
  transitory influences, 307–8
Overhead summary account, 336–38
Overhead volume variance, seasonal aberrations, 731–32
Over or underabsorbed overhead, 31
Overtime premiums, 36–37

P-Q

Palmer, Russell E., 671 n
Participation
  in contribution, 693–94
  cultural differences, 695–96
  group dynamics, 694–95
  managerial style, 695–96
  nature of, 693
  role in system design, 692–96
  successful, 696
Path, defined, 751
Payback period, 558
Payoff, defined, 123
Payoff tables, 123–29
  expected value, 126–29
  outcomes and payoffs, 123–25
  probabilities, 125–26
Payroll accounting, 53–55
Payroll accrual, 54
Payroll cost summary, 271
Penetration pricing, 596–99
  defined, 596
Perfect correlation, 639
Performance standard(s)
  defined, 255–56
  historical, 256
PERT (program evaluation and review technique)
  time estimates, 757–58
Physical resources plans, 220–21
Planning
  focus, 5–6
  long-range periodic, 4
  managerial; see Managerial planning
  project and situation, 4–5
  short-range periodic, 5
  strategic, 4
Porter, L. W., 692 n
Present value, 550–51
  calculating, 569
  cash flows, 550–51
Price differentiation, 611–15
  bases for, 614
  benefits, 612–14
  limitations, 614–15
Price-elasticity of demand, 597
Price-quantity combination, 602
Price variances, 255–77
Prices
  regulation, 615
  resource, 305
  transfer; see Transfer prices
Pricing
  markup percentage, 610
  uncertainties, 610–11
Pricing experiments, 602–3
Pricing strategies
  initial, 596–98
  skimming/penetration pricing, 596–99
  types, 596
Pricing system, dual, 832
Prime costs, 28

Probabilities
  defined, 125
  objective/subjective, 125–26
Probability adjusted profit charts, 133–35
Process costing
  control reporting, 426–29
  costs of spoilage, 430–34
  feasibility, 413–14
  FIFO method, 420–21
  in financial statements, 419–26
  flexible budgets, 429
  historical costing, 426–27
  measuring costs, 415
  measuring output, 415–18
  moving average method, 421–24
  product change, 429–34
  product cost, 415–19
  production centers, 415
  recording costs, 424–26
  standard costing, 427–29
  unit cost, 418–19
  units in process, 430
  wholly variable costs, 435
Process production, 434–36
Product
  final, 816
  intermediate, 816
Product change
  costs of spoilage, 430–34
  units in process, 430
Product costing
  calculation, 415–19
  defined, 24
  direct labor costs, 213
  direct materials cost, 213
  standard, 277
  variable overhead costs, 213–14
Product emphasis decisions, 90–93
Product handling, 485–86
Production center, 26
Production cost variance, 866–69
Production order, 26
Production plan, 218–21
Production, process costing, 413–36
Production schedules, 220–21
Product-line analysis
  consistency with incremental approach, 489
  customer-related service costs, 488
  nontraceable programmed costs, 488–89
  product-related service costs, 485–87
  traceable costs, 485
Product-line reports, 370–71
Product managers, 371–74
Product mix
  changes in marketing expenditures, 91–92
  complementarity and substitutability, 92–93
  defined, 90–91
  effort/result ratios, 91
  substitution effects, 93
Product pricing, 596–615
Product-related service costs, 485–87

Products
  profit charting, 118–22
  shrinkage/accretion/spoilage, 429–34
  value analysis, 603–4
Profit(s)
  attributable, 364–65
  controllable, 365–66, 793
  discontinuation, 783
Profit analysis
  composite index of volume, 861–62
  impact of production volume on income, 869
  input price and spending variance, 856–57
  limitations, 871–72
  in manufacturing companies, 862–71
  production cost variances, 866–69
  sales mix variances, 858–61, 864–65
  sales volume variance, 855–56, 862–64
  selling price variance, 856, 865–66
  variable costing basis, 869–71
Profit centers, 777–78
  managers, 784–87
  transfer prices between, 821–29
Profit contribution, 787
  defined, 118
Profit contribution reporting, 363–66
  under full costing, 376–79
  multisegment operation, 377–79
  single segment operation, 377
Profit functions, 120–22
Profit maximization, 599–606
Profit performance
  centrally administered constraints/guidelines,
    800–801
  economic evaluation, 782–84
  income measurement problems, 792–96
  investment measurement problems, 796–99
  long-term goals, 799–801
  managerial evaluation, 784–87
  multiple criteria, 799–800
  net income, 787–88
  operations evaluation, 782
  profit contribution, 787
  reports, 777–801
  residual income, 790–92
  return on investment, 788–90
Profit ratio, and trend analysis, 872
Profit reporting, 367–74
  base level reports, 368–71
  divisional, 777–801
  general sales manager, 371
  market response functions, 374–76
  for marketing analysis, 374–76
  organizational setting, 777–82
  product-line reports, 70–71
  product manager, 371–74
  sales force performance, 369–70
  standards, 366–67
  time lags, 376
Profit responsiveness, 118
Profit variances, 854–72
Profit-volume charts, 111–23
  break-even point/margin of safety, 112–13

Profit-volume charts—*Cont.*
  cash flow and funds flow programs, 115
  customary volume range, 117
  dynamic effects, 122–23
  fixed charge coverage, 115–17
  income tax effects, 113–14
  minimum profit level, 115–17
  multiproduct business, 118–19
  multiproduct profit functions, 120–22
  persistent shifts in demand, 123
  probability adjusted, 133–35
  profit responsiveness, 118
  temporary volume shifts, 122
  transitional effects, 122
Program budgeting, 231–34
Program evaluation and review technique; *see* PERT
Programmed activities, 81–82, 481
Project and situation planning, 4–5
Project control
  approval criteria, 747
  budget review, 747–48
  calculating slack time, 751–52
  cost slopes, 752–54
  critical path, 751
  departmental performance review, 762–63
  detailed scheduling, 750–58
  dummy activities, 754
  float diagrams, 654–55
  future budget reporting, 761–62
  initial budget comparisons, 759–60
  network diagrams, 750–54
  PERT time estimates, 757–78
  progress budget reporting, 760–61
  progress review, 758–59
  reporting, 759–62
  resource commitment tables/charts, 755–57
  review of proposals, 747–49
  time estimates, 757–58
  work packages, 762
Pseudo-profit centers, 781–82
Pyhrr, Peter A., 233 n
Quantity discounts, 491–92
Quantity variances, 716–17
Quasi-profit centers, 781–82

R

Rate of variability, 641
Raw materials costs, 403
Reasonably attainable standards, 696–98
Redistributions, 182
Reece, James S., 788 n
Registered Industrial Accountant, 15
Regression
  lagged, 647
  nonlinear, 647
Regression analysis, 632–33
Regression equation, 632, 634–44
Regression line, 632
Reimbursement accounting, 12–13
Reimbursement costing
  basic criteria, 665–71
  beneficiality criteria, 670–71

Reimbursement costing—*Cont.*
  capacity-provided criterion, 669–70
  characteristics, 664–65
  full costing criterion, 665–66
  primary implementation criterion, 666
  traceability, 666–68
  variability criterion, 668–69
Relative sale value at split-off point method, 457–58
Reorder point, 529
Repetitive service functions, 483
Replanning, 8
Reported income, 153–59
Research and development proposals, 747–49
Residual costs, 185
Residual expenses, 678
Residual income, 790–92
  advantages, 791
  limitations, 792
Residual values, 567–68
Residual variation, 638–39
Resource allocation decisions
  capacity rationing decisions, 89–90
  impact of cost variability, 84–93
  incremental cash flows, 73–75
  incremental costs, 75–77
  marginal costs, 82–84
  net cash flows, 72–73
  opportunity costs, 77–78
  product emphasis decisions, 90–93
  semivariable costs, 82
  sunk costs, 77
  use of idle capacity, 84–87
  using materials from inventory, 88–89
  variable costs, 78–80
Resource commitment, tables and charts, 755–57
Resources
  changing prices, 796, 799
  controllable prices, 305
Responsibility accounting, 691–705
Responsibility centers, 10
  organizational, 21–22
  traceability criterion, 21
Responsive activities
  costing, 482–84
  defined, 78–79, 481
Return on investment, 788–90, 791–92
  pricing, 606
Returned materials card, 27
Revenue, 112
  interdependence, 794
Rework labor, 38
Rhode, John Grant, 692 n, 694, 696
Robinson-Patman Act of 1936; 491, 493, 615
ROI; *see* Return on investment
Ronen, Joshua, 160 n, 832 n
Roy, Robert H., 647 n

S

Safety-stock costs, 531
  defined, 529
  optimal, 531

Sales, 57
  budgeting, 214–15
Sales force performance, 369–70
Sales mix variance, 858–61, 864–65
Sales volume variance, 855–56, 862–64
Sayles, Leonard R., 700 n
Scoreboard controls, 8–10
Scrap recovery, 38
Segment cost analysis
  attributable costs, 484
  marketing, 481
  nontraceable programmed costs, 484–85
  responsive functions, 482–84
  segment-traceable costs, 481
  stages of, 480–85
Segment, defined, 672
Selling price variance, 856, 865–66
Semivariable costs, 82
Sensitivity analysis, 522–25
Separable costs, 451
  joint production, 452–53
Sequential allocation, 180–91
Service businesses, 494–96
Service centers, 175, 780–81
  allocating stepped costs, 193–94
Service costs, in overhead rates, 175–85
Service functions, 482–83
Service inputs
  and outputs, 183
  usage measure, 190
Service and support activities, 24
Service usage, 194
Shadow prices, 521–22
Shapiro, Nelson H., 671 n
Shelly, M. W., II, 834 n
Shillinglaw, Gordon, 160 n, 671 n
Short-range periodic planning, 5
Short-run economic pricing
  estimating total cost, 600
  estimating total revenue, 599–600
  finding profit-maximizing price, 600
  limitations, 604–6
  marginal cost/marginal revenue, 600–602
  price-volume relationships, 602–4
Short-term cost-volume relationship, 78–84
Simon, Herbert A., 703 n
Simple linear regression, 634–44
Simple regression, 632
Skimming price, 596–99
Slack path, 752
Slack time, 751–52
Smith, Theodore A., 211 n
Society of Management Accountants of Canada, 15
Solomons, David, 473 n, 822 n
Special orders, evaluating, 84–87
Specific costs, 451
Spending variance(s)
  analysis, 255–77
  defined, 256–57
  mathematical notations, 278–81
  overhead costs, 300–317, 338–39, 342, 345–46
  reconciling, 259–60

Split-off point, 450
Spoilage, costs of, 430–34
Springer, Clifford H., 645 n, 646 n
Spurr, William A., 633 n, 634 n, 644 n, 646 n
Standard cost files, 273–77
Standard costing, 427–29
  adjustments, 404
  basic plan system, 264–73
  characteristics, 272–73
  controlling overhead costs, 300–317
  defined, 256, 264
  financial statements, 396–404
  labor rate variance, 270–71
  omission in overhead cost variances, 345–47
  reconciling variances, 271–72
  recording materials purchases, 264–66
  usage variance, 266–70, 713–21
  variances, 256–60
Standard error of the coefficient, 641–43
Standard error of the estimate, 639–40
Standard labor costs, 262–63, 274
Standard labor quantities, 275–77
Standard materials cost, 262, 274
Standard materials quantities, 274–75
Standard operations cost, 256
Standard overhead account, 337–38
Standard overhead costs
  defined, 300, 333
  determination, 333–35
Standard price, 256
Standard product costs, 277
  defined, 256
Standard raw materials costs, 403
Statistical control charts, 721, 732–34
Stedry, Andrew, 697
Steering controls, 7–8
Steiner, George A., 211 n
Stepped costs, allocating, 193–94
Step-variable capacity costs, 81
Stockholders' equity, 797
Stock-out costs, 530–31, 533–34
Stock-outs, 529
Storage space, 486–87
Storage value, 486
Strategic planning, 4
Subjective probabilities, 125–26
Subsidiary ledger, defined, 53
Substitution effects, 93
Sunk cost fallacy, 576
Sunk costs, defined, 77
Supplying division, 816
Support centers, 175
Supportive overhead costs
  controlling, 300–317
  defined, 301
Sweden, corporation law, 849 n
System administration
  behavioral aspects, 703–4
  budgeting staff insensitivity, 703
  irresponsibility of operating managers, 703–4
System design
  behavioral aspects, 691–702

System design—Cont.
  controllability criterion, 700–701
  harmonization of conflicting goals, 701–2
  management by exception, 698–700
  participation, 692–96
  reasonably attainable goals, 696–98

T

T-accounts, 729
Target prices, 610
Tax accounting, 12
Tax credits, 562
Tax-deductible loss, 562
Tax deductions, 562
Tax depreciation allowance, 564–66
Tax depreciation charges, 577
Taxable gain, 562
Time lags, sales, 376
Time recording, 478–79
Total assets, 796–97
Total cost, 161
Traceability criterion, 21
Traceable assets, 796–97
Transfer prices, 792
  based on full cost, 821–22
  based on marginal cost, 822–25
  based on market price quotations, 825–26
  between profit centers, 821–29
  criteria, 816–21
  divisional activities, 819–20
  divisional resource allocation decisions, 817–18
  fiscal management, 820–21
  inappropriate negotiation, 829–35
  interdivisional, 816–35
  managerial performance, 819
  market-base negotiated prices, 826–29
  market in/market out, 832–33
  mathematically programmed, 833–35
  negotiated, 826–29
  purpose, 816
  variable cost plus retainer, 830–32
Trucking, intercity, 495–96
Two-part tariff system, 184
  in monthly applications, 316–17
Tyndall, Gordon, 703 n

U

Under or overabsorbed factory overhead, 59–60
Uniform percentage contribution method, 457
Unit cost
  calculation, 418–19
  effect of spoilage, 434
  of previous periods, 792
  relevance of figures, 458–59
Unit of sale analysis, 489–94
  basic method, 490–91
  manufacturing cost differentials, 493–94
  quantity discount problem, 491–92
United States
  accounting for cost variances, 397
  Cost Accounting Standards Board, 665, 671–80

United States—*Cont.*
  Internal Revenue Service, 397
  Securities and Exchange Commission, 11–12
Usage charges, 190
  determination of, 313–15
  in profit reporting, 365
Usage denominators, 183
Usage variances
  calculating, 263
  defined, 257
  dollar value, 258
  input costs, 260
  isolating, 266–70
  output, 261–63
  physical measures of, 257–58
  standard costing/comprehensive plan, 713–21
Utility, 128–29

V

Value-added index, 185
Vancil, Richard F., 821 n
Variable cost plus retainer, 830–32
Variable costing, 78–80, 150–63, 221
  basis, 150–51
  concept of attributable cost, 160–62
  data for managerial decisions, 159
  end-of-period adjustments, 158–59
  measuring income, 159–60
  nonlinear cost relationships, 151–53
  overhead rate, 153
  predetermined overhead rates, 191–93
  preliminary appraisal, 159–62
  process production, 434–36
  production equals sales, 154–56
  production/sales at normal volume, 153–54
  production/sales at subnormal volume, 156–57
  reported income effect, 153–59

Variable costing—*Cont.*
  sales exceed production, 157–58
  semivariable costs, 435–36
Variable-yield processes, 461–63
Variance investigation
  decision model, 723–24
  statistical control limits, 721–23
Variances, 639
  analysis of, 713–32
  in annual reporting, 394–96
  dollar, 263–64
  factory overhead costs, 333–47
  favorable/unfavorable, 258
  fundamental rule, 272
  marketing cost, 361–79
  mathematical notations, 278–81
  prorated, 397–99
  reconciling, 259–60
Volume, level of output measure, 310
Volume variance
  interpretation, 340
  of overhead cost, 339–40, 343, 346
  seasonal variations, 731–32

W-Y-Z

Whinston, Andrew, 834 n
Working capital, 560–61
Work-in-process accounts, 716–20
Work-in-process inventory, 53
Work packages, 762
Work sampling, 479
Yes/no controls, 7
Yetton, P. W., 694 n
Zander, A., 698 n
Zeff, Stephen A., 665 n
Zero-base budgeting, 231–34
Zero correlation, 639

This book has been set VideoComp in 10 and 9 point Garamond. Part titles are 24 point Garamond. Part numbers and chapter titles are 18 point Garamond. The size of the type page is 31 by 49 picas.